Crime in the United States

2001

Uniform Crime Reports

Printed Annually
Federal Bureau of Investigation
U.S. Department of Justice
Washington, D.C. 20535

Advisory:
Criminal Justice Information Systems Committee,
International Association of Chiefs of Police;
Criminal Justice Information Services Committee,
National Sheriffs' Association;
Criminal Justice Information Services Advisory Policy Board

For sale by Superintendent of Documents
U.S. Government Printing Office, Mail Stop: SSOP, Washington, D.C. 20402-9328
ISBN 0-16-051211-5

Foreword

Like every other organization and individual in the United States, the FBI has struggled to comprehend the events of September 11, 2001. Apart from investigating the crime scenes in New York City; Somerset County, Pennsylvania; and Arlington County, Virginia (the Pentagon); following leads, and addressing a myriad of concerns resulting from these attacks, the FBI through its Uniform Crime Reporting (UCR) Program has struggled with how to report the data to the public. Begun in 1929, the UCR Program captures criminal offenses, which include murder and nonnegligent manslaughter, forcible rape, aggravated assault, robbery, burglary, larceny-theft, and motor vehicle theft, reported to local or state law enforcement agencies. In its original design, the creators of the Program probably could not conceive of heinous attacks of domestic or international terrorism being committed within the confines of this Nation. Theirs was a national crime data collection system based on the cooperation of city, county, and state law enforcement agencies voluntarily reporting crimes that were a product of the society of the time. However, that society has evolved into a more complex, global society of the twenty-first century that is faced with fighting crimes that previously had been unimaginable. The FBI recognizes that the UCR Program must evolve to be able to capture the crimes of this modern era. As it currently exists, the UCR Program is limited in its ability to report the offenses committed at the World Trade Center, in the airways above Pennsylvania, and at the Pentagon. Recognizing the limitations of the Program, yet also recognizing that many agencies and researchers will have a specific, nontraditional application for the statistical data associated with these offenses, the FBI has compiled a special report, which can be found in Section V of this publication. For the most part, the data associated with the events of September 11, 2001, are not included in the standard tables found in *Crime in the United States*. The number of deaths is so great that combining it with the traditional crime statistics will have an outlier effect that falsely skews all types of measurements in the Program's analyses.

September 11 will always be remembered as a tragic day in the history of this Nation. However, the attacks did serve as a wake-up call to law enforcement and the American public with regard to the shortcomings in the measures we take to protect our country from harm. It has reminded us that we must transform these measures to meet new realities. The UCR Program recognizes that it, too, must transform and equip itself to contend with ever-changing realities. In the coming years, the Program will address these issues and recommit itself to the task of serving, in the best way possible, this Nation and its law enforcement agencies.

Crime Factors

Each year when *Crime in the United States* is published, many entities—news media, tourism agencies, and other groups with an interest in crime in our Nation—use reported Crime Index figures to compile rankings of cities and counties. These rankings, however, are merely a quick choice made by the data user, and they provide no insight into the many variables that mold the crime in a particular town, city, county, state, or region. Consequently, these rankings lead to simplistic and/or incomplete analyses which often create misleading perceptions adversely affecting cities and counties, along with their residents. To assess criminality and law enforcement's response from jurisdiction to jurisdiction, one must consider many variables, some of which, while having significant impact on crime, are not readily measurable nor applicable pervasively among all locales. Geographic and demographic factors specific to each jurisdiction must be considered and applied if one is going to make an accurate and complete assessment of crime in that jurisdiction. Several sources of information are available that may assist the responsible researcher in exploring the many variables that affect crime in a particular locale. The U.S. Bureau of the Census data, for example, can be utilized to better understand the makeup of a locale's population. The transience of the population, its racial and ethnic makeup, its composition by age and gender, education levels, and prevalent family structures are all key factors in assessing and comprehending the crime issue.

Local chambers of commerce, planning offices, or similar entities provide information regarding the economic and cultural makeup of cities and counties. Understanding a jurisdiction's industrial/ economic base, its dependence upon neighboring jurisdictions, its transportation system, its economic dependence on nonresidents (such as tourists and convention attendees), its proximity to military installations, correctional facilities, state penitentiaries, prisons, jails, etc., all contribute to accurately gauging and interpreting the crime known to and reported by law enforcement.

The strength (personnel and other resources) and the aggressiveness of a jurisdiction's law enforcement agency are also key factors. Although information pertaining to the number of sworn and civilian law enforcement employees can be found in this publication, it cannot alone be used as an assessment of the emphasis that a community places on enforcing the law. For example, one city may report more crime than a comparable one, not because there is more crime, but rather because its law enforcement agency through proactive efforts identifies more offenses. Attitudes of the citizens toward crime and their crime reporting practices, especially concerning more minor offenses, have an impact on the volume of crimes known to police.

It is incumbent upon all data users to become as well educated as possible about how to understand and quantify the nature and extent of crime in the United States and in any of the nearly 17,000 jurisdictions represented by law enforcement contributors to this Program. Valid assessments are possible only with careful study and analysis of the various unique conditions affecting each local law enforcement jurisdiction.

Historically, the causes and origins of crime have been the subjects of investigation by many disciplines. Some factors that are known to affect the volume and type of crime occurring from place to place are:

> Population density and degree of urbanization.
> Variations in composition of the population, particularly youth concentration.
> Stability of population with respect to residents' mobility, commuting patterns, and transient factors.
> Modes of transportation and highway system.
> Economic conditions, including median income, poverty level, and job availability.

Cultural factors and educational, recreational, and religious characteristics.

Family conditions with respect to divorce and family cohesiveness.

Climate.

Effective strength of law enforcement agencies.

Administrative and investigative emphases of law enforcement.

Policies of other components of the criminal justice system (i.e., prosecutorial, judicial, correctional, and probational).

Citizens' attitudes toward crime.

Crime reporting practices of the citizenry.

The Uniform Crime Reports give a nationwide view of crime based on statistics contributed by state and local law enforcement agencies. Population size is the only correlate of crime utilized in this publication. Although many of the listed factors equally affect the crime of a particular area, the UCR Program makes no attempt to relate them to the data presented. *The reader is, therefore, cautioned against comparing statistical data of individual reporting units from cities, counties, metropolitan areas, states, or colleges and universities solely on the basis of their population coverage or student enrollment.* Until data users examine all the variables that affect crime in a town, city, county, state, region, or college or university, they can make no meaningful comparisons.

Data users are cautioned against comparing crime trends presented in this report and those estimated by the National Crime Victimization Survey (NCVS), administered by the Bureau of Justice Statistics. Because of differences in methodology and crime coverage, the two programs examine the Nation's crime problem from somewhat different perspectives, and their results are not strictly comparable. The definitional and procedural differences can account for many of the apparent discrepancies in results from the two programs.

The national Uniform Crime Reporting (UCR) Program would like to hear from you.

The staff at the national UCR Program are continually striving to improve their publications. We would appreciate it if the primary user of this publication would complete the evaluation form at the end of this book and either mail it to us at the indicated address or fax it: 304-625-5394.

Contents

Section I—Summary of the Uniform Crime Reporting(UCR) Program   1

Section II—Crime Index Offenses Reported   9
Narrative comments:

   Crime Index Total   10
   Violent Crime: 14
      Murder and nonnegligent manslaughter   19
      Forcible rape   29
      Robbery   32
      Aggravated assault   37
   Property Crime: 40
      Burglary   44
      Larceny-theft   48
      Motor vehicle theft   53
      Arson   56
   Hate Crime   59
   Crime Index Tabulations   64

Figures:
   (2.1) Crime clock, 2001   7
   (2.2) Crime Index total, 1997-2001   15
   (2.3) Crime Index offenses, percent distribution, 2001   16
   (2.4) Regional violent and property crime rates, 2001   17
   (2.5) Violent crime, 1997-2001   18
   (2.6) Murder, 1997-2001   20
   (2.7) Murder by relationship, 2001   25
   (2.8) Forcible rape, 1997-2001   30
   (2.9) Robbery, 1997-2001   34
   (2.10) Robbery categories, 1997-2001   36
   (2.11) Aggravated assault, 1997-2001   39
   (2.12) Property crime, 1997-2001   41
   (2.13) Burglary, 1997-2001   45
   (2.14) Burglary residential/nonresidential, 1997-2001   46
   (2.15) Larceny-theft, 1997-2001   49
   (2.16) Larceny-theft categories, 1997-2001   50
   (2.17) Larceny-theft analysis, 2001   52
   (2.18) Motor vehicle theft, 1997-2001   55
   (2.19) Bias-motivated offenses, 2001   61

Tables:
   (2.1) Crime Index total by month, percent distribution, 1997-2001   10
   (2.2) Violent crime total by month, percent distribution, 1997-2001   14
   Murder:
   (2.3) Month, percent distribution, 1997-2001   19
   (2.4) Victims, by race and sex, 2001   20
   (2.5) Victims, by age, sex, and race, 2001   21
   (2.6) Offenders, by age, sex, and race, 2001   21
   (2.7) Victim/offender relationship, by age, 2001   22

Tables—Continued

(2.8) Victim/offender relationship, by race and sex, 2001	22
(2.9) Types of weapons used, percent distribution by region, 2001	23
(2.10) Victims, by weapon, 1997-2001	23
(2.11) Victims by age, by weapon, 2001	23
(2.12) Circumstances, by relationship, 2001	24
(2.13) Circumstances, by weapon, 2001	26
(2.14) Circumstances, 1997-2001	27
(2.15) Circumstances, by victim's sex, 2001	27

Justifiable homicide by weapon, 1997-2001:

(2.16) Law enforcement	28
(2.17) Private citizen	28

Forcible rape:

(2.18) Month, percent distribution, 1997-2001	29

Robbery:

(2.19) Month, percent distribution, 1997-2001	32
(2.20) Region, percent distribution, 2001	33
(2.21) Population group, percent distribution, 2001	34
(2.22) Types of weapons used, by region, percent distribution, 2001	35

Aggravated assault:

(2.23) Month, percent distribution, 1997-2001	37
(2.24) Types of weapons used, by region, percent distribution, 2001	38
(2.25) Property crime total by month, percent distribution, 1997-2001	40

Burglary:

(2.26) Month, percent distribution, 1997-2001	44

Larceny-theft:

(2.27) Month, percent distribution, 1997-2001	48
(2.28) Percent distribution by region, 2001	49

Motor vehicle theft:

(2.29) Month, percent distribution, 1997-2001	53
(2.30) Region, percent distribution, 2001	54

Arson:

(2.31) Rate, by population group, 2001	56
(2.32) Type of property, 2001	57

Hate Crime:

(2.33) Number of incidents, offenses, victims, and known offenders, by bias motivation, 2001	60
(2.34) Number of offenses, victims, and known offenders, by offense, 2001	60
(2.35) Number of known offenders, by race, 2001	61
(2.36) Agency hate crime reporting, by state, 2001	62

Index of crime:

(1) United States, 1982-2001	64
(2) United States, 2001	65
(3) Offense and population distribution by region, 2001	65
(4) Region, geographic division, and state, 2000-2001	66
(5) State, 2001	76
(6) Metropolitan Statistical Area, 2001	87
(7) Offense analysis, United States, 1997-2001	117

Offenses known to law enforcement:

(8) City 10,000 and over in population, 2001	118

(9) University and college by state, 2001   165

(10) Suburban county by state, 2001   177

(11) Rural county 25,000 and over in population, 2001   192

Crime trends:

(12) Population group, 2000-2001   201

(13) Suburban and nonsuburban cities, by population group, 2000-2001   203

(14) Suburban and nonsuburban counties, by population group, 2000-2001   205

(15) Breakdown of offenses known, by population group, 2000-2001   206

Rate: number of crimes per 100,000 inhabitants:

(16) Population group, 2001   209

(17) Suburban and nonsuburban cities, by population group, 2001   211

(18) Suburban and nonsuburban counties, by population group, 2001   212

(19) Breakdown of offenses known, by population group, 2001   213

(20) Murder, by state, 2001, type of weapon   215

(21) Robbery, by state, 2001, type of weapon   216

(22) Aggravated assault, by state, 2001, type of weapon   217

(23) Offense analysis, number and percent change, 2000-2001   218

(24) Property stolen and recovered, by type and value, 2001   218

Section III—Crime Index Offenses Cleared   **219**

Narrative comments

Figure:

(3.1) Crimes cleared by arrest, 2001   221

Tables:

Percent of offenses cleared by arrest or Exceptional Means:

(25) Population group, 2001   222

(26) Geographic region and division, 2001   224

(27) Breakdown of offenses known, by population group, 2001   226

(28) Number of offenses cleared by arrest, of persons under 18 years of age, by population group, 2001   228

Section IV—Persons Arrested   **231**

Narrative comments

(4.1) Arrests for drug abuse violations, by region, 2001   232

Tables:

(29) Estimated arrests, United States, 2001   233

Number and rate of arrests:

(30) Geographic region, 2001   235

(31) Population group, 2001   236

Ten-year arrest trends:

(32) Totals, 1992-2001   238

(33) Sex, 1992-2001   239

Five-year arrest trends:

(34) Totals, 1997-2001   240

(35) Sex, 1997-2001   241

Tables—Continued

Current year over previous year arrest trends:

    (36) Totals, 2000-2001 242

    (37) Sex, 2000-2001 243

Arrests:

    (38) Age, 2001 244

    (39) Males, by age, 2001 246

    (40) Females, by age, 2001 248

    (41) Persons under 15, 18, 21, and 25 years of age, 2001 250

    (42) Sex, 2001 251

    (43) Race, 2001 252

City arrest trends:

    (44) 2000-2001 255

    (45) Sex, 2000-2001 256

City arrests:

    (46) Age, 2001 257

    (47) Persons under 15, 18, 21, and 25 years of age, 2001 259

    (48) Sex, 2001 260

    (49) Race, 2001 261

Suburban county arrest trends:

    (50) 2000-2001 264

    (51) Sex, 2000-2001 265

Suburban county arrests:

    (52) Age, 2001 266

    (53) Persons under 15, 18, 21, and 25 years of age, 2001 268

    (54) Sex, 2001 269

    (55) Race, 2001 270

Rural county arrest trends:

    (56) 2000-2001 273

    (57) Sex, 2000-2001 274

Rural county arrests:

    (58) Age, 2001 275

    (59) Persons under 15, 18, 21, and 25 years of age, 2001 277

    (60) Sex, 2001 278

    (61) Race, 2001 279

Suburban area arrest trends:

    (62) 2000-2001 282

    (63) Sex, 2000-2001 283

Suburban area arrests:

    (64) Age, 2001 284

    (65) Persons under 15, 18, 21, and 25 years of age, 2001 286

    (66) Sex, 2001 287

    (67) Race, 2001 288

    (68) Police disposition of juvenile offenders taken into custody, 2001 ... 291

    (69) Arrests, by state, 2001 292

Section V—Special Report **301**

Narrative comments

Tables—Continued

Tables:
  Murder Victims of 9/11/2001 Terrorist Attacks
    (5.1) Race, Sex, and Location, 2001 302
    (5.2) Total All Locations by Age, Sex, and Race, 2001 304
    (5.3) New York City World Trade Center by Age, Sex, and Race, 2001 304
    (5.4) Pentagon by Age, Sex, and Race, 2001 305
    (5.5) Somerset County, Pennsylvania by Age, Sex, and Race, 2001 305
  Murder Offenders of 9/11/2001 Terrorist Attacks
    (5.6) by Age, 2001 306
  Injuries from Violent Crime, 2000, Number of Victims
    (5.7) by Selected Offense and Injury Type, 2000 308
    (5.8) by Location and Injury Type, 2000 309
    (5.9) by Weapon and Injury Type, 2000 310
    (5.10) by Victim Age, Sex, and Race and Injury Type, 2000 311
    (5.11) Percent Distribution of Victims by Relationship of the Victim to the Offender
         and Injury Type, 2000 312
    (5.12) by Offender Age, Sex, and Race and Injury Type, 2000 313

Section VI—Law Enforcement Personnel **315**
Narrative comments

Tables:
  Full-time law enforcement employees as of October 31, 2001:
    (70) Employees, number and rate per 1,000 inhabitants, geographic region and
        division by population group 318
    (71) Officers, number and rate per 1,000 inhabitants, geographic region and
        division by population group 319
    (72) Employees, range in rate per 1,000 inhabitants by population group 320
    (73) Officers, range in rate per 1,000 inhabitants by population group 321
    (74) Employees, percent male and female by population group 322
    (75) Civilian employees, percent of total by population group 323
    (76) State law enforcement employees 324
    (77) Law enforcement employees by state 326
    (78) City by state 327
    (79) University and college by state 399
    (80) Suburban county by state 405
    (81) Rural county by state 412
    (82) Other agencies by state 430

Section VII—Appendices **433**
Appendix I—Methodology 434
Appendix II—Offenses in Uniform Crime Reporting 446
Appendix III—Uniform Crime Reporting Area Definitions 448
Appendix IV—The Nation's Two Crime Measures 451
Appendix V—Directory of State Uniform Crime Reporting Programs 454
Appendix VI—National Uniform Crime Reporting Program Directory 461
Appendix VII—Uniform Crime Reporting Publications List 462

SECTION I

Summary of the Uniform Crime Reporting (UCR) Program

The Uniform Crime Reporting Program is a nationwide, cooperative statistical effort of nearly 17,000 city, county, and state law enforcement agencies voluntarily reporting data on crimes brought to their attention. During 2001, law enforcement agencies active in the UCR Program represented 92 percent of the total population as established by the Bureau of the Census. The coverage amounted to 93 percent of the United States population in Metropolitan Statistical Areas (MSAs), 87 percent of the population in cities outside metropolitan areas, and 88 percent in rural counties.

Since 1930, the FBI has administered the Uniform Crime Reporting Program and issued periodic assessments of the nature and type of crime in the Nation. The Program's primary objective is to generate a reliable set of criminal statistics for use in law enforcement administration, operation, and management; however, its data have over the years become one of the country's leading social indicators. The American public looks to Uniform Crime Reports for information on fluctuations in the level of crime, and criminologists, sociologists, legislators, municipal planners, the media, and other students of criminal justice use the statistics for varied research and planning purposes.

Historical Background

Recognizing a need for national crime statistics, the International Association of Chiefs of Police (IACP) formed the Committee on Uniform Crime Records in the 1920s to develop a system of uniform police statistics. Establishing offenses known to law enforcement as the appropriate measure, the Committee evaluated various crimes on the basis of their seriousness, frequency of occurrence, pervasiveness in all geographic areas of the country, and likelihood of being reported to law enforcement. After studying state criminal codes and making an evaluation of the recordkeeping practices in use, the Committee completed a plan for crime reporting that became the foundation of the UCR Program in 1929.

Seven main classifications of crime were chosen to gauge fluctuations in the overall volume and rate of crime. These seven classifications that eventually became known as the Crime Index included the violent crimes of murder and nonnegligent manslaughter, forcible rape, robbery, and aggravated assault and the property crimes of burglary, larceny-theft, and motor vehicle theft. By congressional mandate, arson was added as the eighth Index offense in 1979.

During the early planning of the Program, it was recognized that the differences among criminal codes precluded a mere aggregation of state statistics to arrive at a national total. Further, because of the variances in punishment for the same offenses in different state codes, no distinction between felony and misdemeanor crimes was possible. To avoid these problems and provide nationwide uniformity in crime reporting, standardized offense definitions by which law enforcement agencies were to submit data without regard for local statutes were formulated. The definitions used by the Program are set forth in Appendix II of this publication.

In January 1930, 400 cities representing 20 million inhabitants in 43 states began participating in the UCR Program. Congress enacted Title 28, Section 534, of the United States Code authorizing the Attorney General to gather crime information that same year. The Attorney General, in turn, designated the FBI to serve as the national clearinghouse for the data collected. Since that time, data based on uniform classifications and procedures for reporting have been obtained from the Nation's law enforcement agencies.

Advisory Groups

Providing vital links between local law enforcement and the FBI in the conduct of the UCR Program are the Criminal Justice Information Systems Committees of the IACP and the National Sheriffs' Association (NSA). The IACP, as it has since the Program began, represents the thousands of police departments nationwide. The NSA encourages sheriffs throughout the country to participate fully in the Program. Both committees serve in advisory capacities concerning the UCR Program's operation.

To function in an advisory capacity concerning UCR policy and to provide suggestions on UCR data usage, a Data Providers' Advisory Policy Board (APB) was established in August 1988. The Board operated until 1993 when a new Board, designed to address all FBI criminal justice information services, was approved. The Board functions in an advisory capacity concerning UCR policy and data collection and use. The UCR Subcommittee of the Board ensures continuing emphasis on UCR-related issues.

The Association of State Uniform Crime Reporting Programs and committees focus on UCR within individual state law enforcement associations and are also active in promoting interest in the UCR Program. These organizations foster widespread and more intelligent use of uniform crime statistics and lend assistance to contributors when needed.

Redesign of UCR

Although the UCR Program remained virtually unchanged throughout the years in terms of the data collected and disseminated, a broad utility had evolved for UCR by the 1980s. Recognizing the need for improved statistics, law enforcement called for a thorough evaluative study that would modernize the UCR Program. The FBI fully concurred with the need for an updated Program and lent its complete support, formulating a comprehensive three-phase redesign effort. The Bureau of Justice Statistics (BJS), the Department of Justice agency responsible for funding criminal justice information projects, agreed to underwrite the first two phases. Conducted by an independent contractor, these phases were structured to determine what, if any, changes should be made to the current Program. The third phase would involve implementation of the changes identified. Abt Associates Inc. of Cambridge, Massachusetts, overseen by the FBI, BJS, and a Steering Committee comprised of prestigious individuals representing a myriad of disciplines, commenced the first phase in 1982.

During the first phase, the historical evolution of the UCR Program was examined. All aspects of the Program, including the objectives and intended user audience, data items, reporting mechanisms, quality control issues, publications and user services, and relationships with other criminal justice data systems, were studied.

Early in 1984, a conference on the future of UCR, held in Elkridge, Maryland, launched the second phase of the study that examined the potential of UCR and concluded with a set of recommended changes. Attendees at this conference reviewed work conducted during the first phase and discussed the recommendations that should be considered during phase two.

Findings from the evaluation's first phase and input on alternatives for the future were also major topics of discussion at the seventh National UCR Conference in July 1984. A survey of law enforcement agencies overlapped phases one and two.

Phase two ended in early 1985 with the production of a draft, *Blueprint for the Future of the Uniform Crime Reporting Program*. The study's Steering Committee reviewed the draft report at a March 1985 meeting and made various recommendations for revision. The Committee members, however, endorsed the report's concepts.

In April 1985, the phase two recommendations were presented at the eighth National UCR Conference. Various considerations for the final report were set forth, and the overall concept for the revised Program was unanimously approved. The joint IACP/NSA Committee on UCR also issued a resolution endorsing the *Blueprint*.

The final report, the *Blueprint for the Future of the Uniform Crime Reporting Program*, was released in the summer of 1985. It specifically outlined recommendations for an expanded, improved UCR Program to meet future informational needs. There were three recommended areas of enhancement to the UCR Program. First, offenses and arrests would be reported using an incident-based system. Second, data would be collected on two levels. Agencies in level one would report important details about those offenses comprising the current Crime Index, their victims, and arrestees. Law enforcement agencies covering populations of over 100,000 and a sampling of smaller agencies that would collect expanded detail on all significant offenses would be included in level two. The third proposal involved introducing a quality assurance program.

To begin implementation, the FBI awarded a contract to develop new offense definitions and data elements for the redesigned system. The work involved (a) revising the definitions of certain Index offenses, (b) identifying additional significant offenses to be reported, (c) refining definitions for both, and (d) developing data elements (incident details) for all UCR offenses in order to fulfill the requirements of incident-based reporting versus the current summary reporting.

Concurrent with the preparation of the data elements, the FBI studied the various state systems to select an experimental site for implementing the redesigned Program. In view of its long-standing incident-based Program and well-established staff dedicated solely to UCR, the South Carolina Law Enforcement Division (SLED) was chosen. The SLED agreed to adapt its existing system to meet the requirements of the redesigned Program and collect data on both offenses and arrests relating to the newly defined offenses.

To assist SLED with the pilot project, offense definitions and data elements developed under the private contract were put at the staff's disposal. Also, FBI automated data processing personnel developed Automated Data Capture Specifications for use in adapting the state's data processing procedures to incorporate the revised system. The BJS supplied funding to facilitate software revisions needed by the state. SLED completed its testing of the new Program in late 1987.

Following the completion of the pilot project conducted by SLED, the FBI produced a draft of guidelines for an enhanced UCR Program. Law enforcement executives from around the country were then invited to a conference in Orange Beach, Alabama, where the guidelines were presented for final review.

During the conference, three overall recommendations were passed without dissent:

first, that there be established a new, incident-based national crime reporting system; second, that the FBI manage this Program; and third, that an Advisory Policy Board composed of law enforcement executives be formed to assist in directing and implementing the new Program.

Information about the redesigned UCR Program, called the National Incident-Based Reporting System, or NIBRS, is contained in three documents. *Data Collection Guidelines* contains a system overview and descriptions of the offenses, offense codes, reports, data elements, and data values used in the system. *Data Submission Specifications* is for the use of state and local systems personnel who are responsible for preparing magnetic media for submission to the FBI. *Error Message Manual* contains designations of mandatory and optional data elements, data element edits, and error messages.

A NIBRS edition of the *UCR Handbook* was published to assist law enforcement agency data contributors implementing NIBRS within their departments. This document is geared toward familiarizing local and state law enforcement personnel with the definitions, policies, and procedures of NIBRS. It does not contain the technical coding and data transmission requirements presented in the other three NIBRS publications.

NIBRS collects data on each single incident and arrest within 22 crime categories. For each offense known to police within these categories, incident, victim, property, offender, and arrestee information are gathered when available. The goal of the redesign is to modernize crime information by collecting data presently maintained in law enforcement records; the enhanced UCR Program is, therefore, a by-product of current records systems. The integrity of UCR's long-running statistical series will, of course, be maintained.

It became apparent during the development of the prototype system that the level one and level two reporting proposed in the *Blueprint* might not be the most practical approach. Many state and local law enforcement administrators indicated that the collection of data on all pertinent offenses could be handled with more ease than could the extraction of selected ones. Although "Limited" participation, equivalent to the *Blueprint's* level one, remains an option, most reporting jurisdictions, upon implementation, go immediately to "Full" participation, meeting all NIBRS' data submission requirements.

Implementation of NIBRS is occurring at a pace commensurate with the resources, abilities, and limitations of the contributing law enforcement agencies. The FBI was able to accept NIBRS data as of January 1989, and to date, the following 22 state programs have been certified for NIBRS participation: Arkansas, Colorado, Connecticut, Delaware, Idaho, Iowa, Kansas, Kentucky, Massachusetts, Michigan, Nebraska, North Dakota, Ohio, South Carolina, South Dakota, Tennessee, Texas, Utah, Vermont, Virginia, West Virginia, and Wisconsin. In addition, the Metro Transit Police Department in Washington, D.C. was certified to submit NIBRS data to the national Program in 2001.

Twelve state programs and several local law enforcement agencies in two nonprogram states are in various stages of testing NIBRS. Eight other state agencies, as well as agencies in the District of Columbia and Guam, are in various stages of planning and development.

Recent Developments

QUALITY ASSURANCE REVIEW— Initially implemented in June 1997 as a pilot program designed to augment the current national UCR Program, the Quality Assurance Review (QAR) conducted by the CJIS Audit Unit (CAU) became a permanent function in January 2000. The purpose of the QAR is to ensure that each state UCR Program adheres to summary and incident-based reporting methods that are consistent with UCR standards in order to achieve uniform crime reporting nationwide. In 2001, the QAR incorporated a statistical sampling methodology to select records for data quality review and to project the number of discrepant crime reports a state UCR Program submits to the national UCR Program. Agencies are encouraged to avail themselves of the opportunity to assess the integrity of their data and to receive assistance in complying with Program requirements. The CAU in 2001 performed audits of agencies in 11 states:

Alabama, Arizona, Connecticut, Florida, Kansas, Maryland, Missouri, New Mexico, Oklahoma, South Carolina, and Wyoming.

NIBRS—The detailed, accurate, and meaningful data produced by NIBRS benefit local agencies. Armed with comprehensive crime data, local agencies can better make their case to acquire and effectively allocate the resources needed to fight crime. Currently, 4,192 law enforcement agencies contribute NIBRS data to the national UCR Program. The data submitted by these agencies represent 17 percent of the U.S. population and 15 percent of the crime statistics collected by the UCR Program.

Recently, the *Handbook For Acquiring A Records Management System (RMS) That Is Compatible With The National Incident-Based Reporting System (NIBRS)* was developed under the sponsorship of the FBI's Criminal Justice Information Services (CJIS) Division and the BJS. This handbook provides comprehensive, step-by-step guidance to local law enforcement agencies that are, or are considering, implementing an automated incident-based records management system that is compatible and compliant with NIBRS. The handbook provides instructions on planning for and conducting a system acquisition and preparing the agency for conversion to the new system and to NIBRS. It includes implementation tips from other agencies and vendors and presents relevant examples. The handbook is a companion document to a cost model that helps law enforcement agencies estimate the costs of implementing and operating such a system. The handbook is available on the FBI Internet site at www.fbi.gov/ucr/ucr.htm.

The CJIS Division's Programs Support Section is currently working on the conceptual design of a new set of publications to exhibit NIBRS data. Each component of the NIBRS Publication Series will demonstrate that the NIBRS data set provides richer and more detailed information about crime across a variety of geographic units than has been previously available. Recognizing that there is a responsibility on the part of the national Program to demonstrate the utility of NIBRS, each component of the NIBRS Publication Series will:

• Demonstrate the potential uses of NIBRS.

• Convey a change in philosophical approach to crime analysis and publication.

• Provide for the development of tools to assist others in using and analyzing NIBRS data.

The Measurement of White-Collar Crime Using Uniform Crime Reporting (UCR) Data, a report in the series, is available on the FBI's Internet site at www.fbi.gov/ucr/ucr.htm and is just one example of the analysis possible with NIBRS data.

CRIME CLOCK

Every 2.7 seconds   One Crime Index Offense

Every 3.0 seconds   One Property Crime

Every 4.5 seconds   One Larceny-theft

Every 14.9 seconds   One Burglary

Every 25.7 seconds   One Motor Vehicle Theft

Every 22.0 seconds   One Violent Crime

Every 34.8 seconds   One Aggravated Assault

Every 1.2 minutes   One Robbery

Every 5.8 minutes   One Forcible Rape

Every 32.9 minutes One Murder

The Crime Clock should be viewed with care. The most aggregate representation
of UCR data, it conveys the annual reported crime experience by showing a rela-
tive frequency of occurrence of Index offenses. It should not be taken to imply a
regularity in the commission of crime. The Crime Clock represents the annual
ratio of crime to fixed time intervals.

SECTION II
Crime Index Offenses Reported

Crime Index Total

Definition

The Uniform Crime Reporting (UCR) Program's Crime Index is composed of selected offenses used to gauge fluctuations in the volume and rate of crime reported to law enforcement. These selected offenses include the violent crimes of murder and nonnegligent manslaughter, forcible rape, robbery, and aggravated assault, and the property crimes of burglary, larceny-theft, and motor vehicle theft. The crime classifications were selected at the inception of the UCR Program in 1929 because they were considered by law enforcement and criminologists of the time to be the most serious and the most commonly reported crimes occurring in all areas of the Nation. Arson was added to the Index in 1979 by congressional mandate, and the UCR Program established the Modified Crime Index to include arson. More information regarding the Crime Index can be found in Appendix II of this report.

Trend

Year	Number of offenses	Rate per 100,000 inhabitants
2000	11,608,070	4,124.8
2001	11,849,006	4,160.5
Percent change	+2.1	+0.9

Special Note Regarding the Events of September 11, 2001

Due to the unique nature and the statistical implications inherent in the events of September 11, 2001, the crimes committed in those attacks are not included in the UCR Program's offense rate, trend, or clearance data. Information regarding the September attacks are provided in a special report in this publication. (See Section V.)

National Offenses, Trends, and Rates

The estimated number of Crime Index offenses for 2001 was 11,849,006. This number reflects an increase of 2.1 percent from the 2000 estimate, the first increase since 1991. However, when looking at 5- and 10-year trends, the 2001 figure represents a 10.2-percent decrease from the 1997 figure and also a 17.9-percent decline from the 1992 level. (See Table 1.)

In 2001, violent crime comprised 12.1 percent and property crime accounted for 87.9 percent of the Crime Index total. The property crime of larceny-theft, which comprised 59.7 percent of the Crime Index, was the most frequently occurring of all Index crimes, with an estimated 7,076,171 offenses. The violent crime of murder, which accounted for 0.1 percent of the Crime Index, occurred least frequently with an estimated total of 15,980 offenses. (See Table 1.)

An estimated monetary value of $17.1 billion in stolen property was reported in 2001. Thefts of motor vehicles accounted for the greatest monetary loss, followed by thefts of jewelry and precious metals; currency, notes, etc.; and televisions, radios, stereos, etc.

Table 2.1

Crime Index Total by Month
Percent Distribution, 1997-2001

Month	1997	1998	1999	2000	2001
January	8.2	8.5	8.0	7.7	7.7
February	7.3	7.5	7.2	7.3	6.8
March	8.0	8.2	8.0	8.2	7.9
April	8.0	8.0	7.9	8.0	8.1
May	8.4	8.4	8.4	8.7	8.6
June	8.5	8.5	8.6	8.6	8.5
July	9.1	9.0	9.1	9.1	9.0
August	9.0	9.0	9.2	9.1	8.9
September	8.6	8.4	8.5	8.5	8.5
October	8.7	8.5	8.7	8.8	9.1
November	7.9	7.8	8.2	8.0	8.3
December	8.3	8.2	8.4	7.9	8.5

An estimated 32.4 percent of property reported stolen in 2001 was recovered. Property types with the greatest percentage of recoveries were motor vehicles, clothing and furs, livestock, and consumable goods. (See Table 24.)

The Crime Index rate per 100,000 inhabitants in 2001 was 4,160.5, a 0.9-percent increase from the 2000 rate. In addition, this number reflected a 15.6-percent decrease from the 1997 rate and a 26.5-percent decline from the 1992 rate. (See Table 1.)

Regional Offense Distributions and Rates

The United States is divided into four regions: the Northeast, the Midwest, the South, and the West. (See Appendix III.) In 2001, data collected regarding the Nation's four regions reflect the following:

The Northeast

The Northeast comprised 18.9 percent of the Nation's population in 2001 and posted 13.7 percent of the Crime Index offenses reported to the UCR Program. (See Table 3.) The Northeast was the only region to experience decreases in the number of offenses and the rate per 100,000 inhabitants in 2001. This region showed a 1.5-percent decrease in Crime Index offenses from 2000 and a 1.9-percent decline in the rate per 100,000 inhabitants. (See Table 4.)

The Midwest

The Midwest, which accounted for 22.7 percent of the U.S. population, recorded 21.7 percent of the Nation's Crime Index offenses in 2001. (See Table 3.) This region experienced an increase in both the volume (1.6 percent) and the rate of Crime Index offenses per 100,000 persons (1.1 percent) over the prior year's volume and rate. (See Table 4.)

The South

The South, the Nation's most populous region in 2001, comprised 35.8 percent of the total population and experienced 40.9 percent of the total Crime Index offenses. (See Table 3.) The number of offenses reported in this region increased 1.9 percent from the 2000 level. The Crime Index rate per 100,000 inhabitants increased 0.3 percent. (See Table 4.)

The West

The West, which constituted 22.6 percent of the population, accounted for 23.7 percent of the Nation's Crime Index offenses. (See Table 3.) In 2001, this region had a 5.1-percent increase in the number of offenses compared to 2000 levels and a 3.0-percent increase in rate. (See Table 4.)

Community Types

The UCR Program's data are often presented in aggregations representing three types of communities: Metropolitan Statistical Areas (MSAs) which made up approximately 80 percent of the total U.S. population in 2001, cities outside MSAs which comprised approximately 8 percent of the Nation's population, and rural counties which accounted for approximately 12 percent of the U.S. population during 2001. (See Appendix III and Table 2.)

In 2001, the Nation's MSAs experienced an Index crime rate of 4,474.9 per 100,000 persons. Cities outside of MSAs had a crime rate of 4,450.4 per 100,000 inhabitants, and rural counties had a crime rate of 1,892.4 per 100,000 persons. (See Table 2.)

Population Groups Trends and Rates

The population group classifications used by the UCR Program comprise six city and two county designations. (See Appendix III for more information on population groups.) In 2001, the Nation's cities collectively experienced an increase of 2.0 percent in the total number of crimes reported and had a rate of 5,124.8 Index crimes per 100,000 inhabitants. Additionally, suburban counties and rural counties experienced increases in total crimes reported—2.4 percent and 1.9 percent, respectively—with rates of 3,038.9 and 1,979.2 Crime Index offenses per 100,000 persons, respectively. (See Tables 12 and 16.)

Within city groupings, the largest increase of reported crime, 4.1 percent, was in cities with populations of 250,000 to 499,999. The smallest change in volume from 2000, a 0.5 percent increase, occurred in cities with populations of 1 million and over. In 2001, cities with populations spanning 500,000 to 999,999 had a rate of 7,328.0 Crime Index offenses per 100,000 inhabitants, the highest among the Nation's cities. Cities with populations of 10,000 to 24,999 had the lowest rate of offenses per 100,000 inhabitants—3,875.4. (See Tables 12 and 16.)

Clearances

Clearances occur either by arrest or by exceptional means, i.e. when circumstances beyond the control of law enforcement prevent the placing of formal charges against the offender. (More information regarding clearances can be found in Section III of this report.) In 2001, 19.6 percent of Crime Index offenses were cleared overall. Law enforcement nationwide cleared 16.2 percent of property crimes and 46.2 percent of violent crimes. (See Table 25.)

Among the Crime Index offenses in 2001, murder was the offense cleared most often— 62.4 percent. Burglary offenses experienced the lowest percentage of clearances—12.7 percent. (See Table 25.)

Clearances and Juveniles

When an offender under the age of 18 is cited to appear in juvenile court or before other juvenile authorities, the UCR Program records that incident as clearance by arrest, even though a physical arrest may not have occurred. In addition, according to Program definitions, clearances involving both adult and juvenile offenders are classified as adult clearances.

Nationally, 18.6 percent of the total clearances for 2001 involved only persons under the age of 18. The Crime Index offense with the highest percentage of juvenile clearances was larceny-theft (21.9 percent). The offense with the lowest percentage of juvenile clearances (5.0 percent) was murder and nonnegligent manslaughter. Arson is typically an offense with a large involvement of juvenile offenders; of arson offenses cleared, 45.5 percent involved only juvenile offenders. (See Table 28.)

Arrests

Total Arrests

The estimated total of Crime Index offense arrests for 2001 was 2,245,597, approxi-

mately 16.4 percent of the U.S. total estimated arrests. Of that total, approximately 27.9 percent were arrests made for violent crimes and 72.1 percent were arrests for property crimes. Larceny-theft arrests accounted for 71.7 percent of all property crime arrests. Aggravated assaults made up the greatest portion, 76.2 percent, of violent crime arrests. (See Table 29.)

Arrest Trends

The total Crime Index arrests for all ages for 2001 declined slightly—0.7 percent—from 2000 levels. In viewing the data by age, the total number of adults arrested increased 1.0 percent from the 2000 figure, and the total number of juvenile arrests declined 5.0 percent when compared to the previous year's number.

Arrests for arson offenses increased more than arrests for any other Index crime category in 2001. The number of arson arrests was up 14.7 percent from the prior year's figure as arson arrests of adults increased 22.8 percent and arson arrests for juveniles increased 8.1 percent from 2000 to 2001. (See Table 36.)

Looking at a 5-year trend, overall, the number of Crime Index arrests in 2001 decreased 17.7 percent from 1997 arrests. Violent crime arrests decreased 11.4 percent, and property crime arrests fell 20.0 percent in that 5-year period. In 2001, juvenile and adult arrests for Crime Index offenses also decreased (28.1 percent and 13.2 percent, respectively) when compared to 1997 arrest data. (See Table 34.)

Ten-year trends in Crime Index offense arrests showed an overall 22.5-percent decrease. Juvenile arrests in that time frame fell 30.7 percent, and adult arrests declined 19.1 percent. (See Table 32.)

The number of males arrested for Crime Index offenses in 2001 decreased 1.0 percent from the number arrested in 2000. The number of females arrested in 2001 rose slightly (0.2 percent) from the 2000 level. Additionally, the number of juvenile males arrested in 2001 dropped 6.6 percent, and the percentage of juvenile females declined 1.3 percent when compared to the prior year's number. (See Table 37.)

When comparing 1997 to 2001 arrest data, the 5-year trend indicated that the number of males arrested decreased 19.1 percent, and the number of females arrested declined 13.6 percent. The number of juvenile males arrested decreased 31.2 percent in 2001 from the 1997 total, and the number of juvenile females arrested dropped 19.3 percent. (See Table 35.)

The number of males arrested in 2001 fell 26.8 percent when compared to the number arrested in 1992. The number of females arrested decreased 7.9 percent in that same 10-year period. Additionally, the number of juvenile males arrested dropped 37.7 percent, and the number of juvenile females arrested declined 5.5 percent. (See Table 33.)

Distribution

In 2001, statistics showed that 73.8 percent of all persons arrested for Crime Index offenses were over the age of 18, and 26.2 percent were under age 18. Of the total number of juveniles arrested, 36.9 percent were under age 15. (See Table 38.) Additionally, 73.3 percent of all persons arrested for Crime Index offenses in 2001 were males, and 26.7 percent were females. (See Table 42.) Of the persons arrested, 64.4 percent were white, 33.1 percent were black. The remainder were of other races. (See Table 43.)

Violent Crime Total

Definition

According to the Uniform Crime Reporting definitions, violent crime is composed of four offenses: murder and nonnegligent manslaughter, forcible rape, robbery, and aggravated assault. All violent crimes involve force or threat of force.

Trend

Year	Number of offenses	Rate per 100,000 inhabitants
2000	1,425,486	506.5
2001	1,436,611	504.4
Percent change	+0.8	- 0.4

National Trends, Distributions, and Rates

For the first time since 1992, data reported to the UCR Program indicated a slight increase in the violent crime estimate for the Nation. A comparison of the 2001 violent crime estimate of 1,436,611 with the 2000 estimate demonstrated a 0.8-percent rise. However, the 2001 number was substantially lower than the violent crime volumes of both 5 and 10 years ago. Violent crime estimates in 2001 were 12.2 percent lower than the figure in 1997 and 25.7 percent below the 1992 estimate. Within the violent crime category, robbery volume rose 3.7 percent, and murder volume increased 2.5 percent. Forcible rape recorded the smallest increase of all violent crimes at 0.3 percent. The estimated number of aggravated assaults represented a slight decrease for the year, 0.5 percent.

Proportionally, aggravated assault accounted for the largest share of violent crimes, 63.1 percent. Robbery constituted 29.4 percent of total violent crimes, forcible rape comprised 6.3 percent, and murder made up 1.1 percent of the total.

Computing the violent crime rate per 100,000 persons for 2001 resulted in an overall estimate of 504.4 offenses per 100,000 individuals; this figure marked a 0.4-percent decrease from the 2000 rate. Aggravated assault occurrences registered a rate of 318.5 per 100,000 inhabitants, a decrease of 1.7 percent from the 2000 rate. Robbery posted a rate of 148.5, an increase of 2.4 percent over the previous year's rate. Forcible rape was measured at a rate of 31.8 offenses per 100,000 persons, indicating a decrease of 0.8 percent in the forcible rape rate since 2000. Murder and nonnegligent manslaughter had a rate of 5.6 per 100,000 population, a 1.3-percent increase from the previous year's rate.

A comparison of the 2001 violent crime rate with those recorded 5 and 10 years ago indicated a 17.4-percent decrease since 1997 and a 33.4-percent drop since 1992. National crime estimates and rates for the past 20 years are documented in Table 1.

Table 2.2

Violent Crime Total by Month
Percent Distribution, 1997-2001

Month	1997	1998	1999	2000	2001
January	8.1	8.4	8.2	7.7	7.6
February	7.2	7.2	7.1	7.4	7.0
March	8.2	8.1	7.9	8.4	8.3
April	8.0	8.0	8.1	8.3	8.5
May	8.9	8.7	8.8	9.1	9.0
June	8.7	8.5	8.5	8.6	8.6
July	9.2	9.1	9.3	9.0	9.0
August	9.2	9.2	9.1	8.9	8.7
September	8.7	8.6	8.4	8.6	8.8
October	8.5	8.5	8.6	8.7	8.9
November	7.8	7.7	8.0	7.6	7.9
December	7.6	7.8	8.0	7.7	7.9

Regional Offense Distributions and Rates

The United States is divided into four regions: the Northeast, the Midwest, the South, and the West. A map of the United States delineating the regions is included in Appendix III. Estimated crime volume, rates, and percent changes by region are published in Table 4.

The Northeast

During 2001, 16.1 percent of violent crime occurred in the Northeastern States, which claimed 18.9 percent of the population. (See Table 3.) The region registered a 2.7-percent decrease in the estimated volume of violent crime. The Northeast experienced 429.7 violent offenses per 100,000 people, a decrease of 3.1 percent since 2000. However, the number of murders within the region increased 5.6 percent, and the murder rate per 100,000 increased 4.4 percent over the previous year's rate. (See Table 4.)

The Midwest

The Midwest, which contained 22.7 percent of the U.S. population, reported 19.5 percent of the total violent crime that occurred in 2001. The region had a 1.6-percent rise in violent crime volume over the prior year's estimated volume. The region recorded a violent crime rate of 432.0 per 100,000 persons, an increase of 1.1 percent over the 2000 rate. The number of murders within the region increased 3.4 percent, and the murder rate per 100,000 persons increased 2.9 percent. (See Tables 3 and 4.)

The South

During 2001, 41.1 percent of all violent crimes occurred in the South, which was the Nation's most heavily populated region with 35.8 percent of the U.S. population. (See Table 3.) The Southern States recorded a rate of 579.9 violent crime offenses per 100,000 persons—a drop of 0.3 percent from the 2000 figure. Regarding the volume of violent crime occurrences, the South experienced an overall 1.3-percent rise. However, this region was the only one to report a decrease in the number of murders (-1.5 percent) and a decline in the murder rate (-3.0 percent). (See Table 4.)

The West

Approximately 22.6 percent of the population resided in the West, which reported 23.3 percent of total violent crimes in 2001. (See Table 3.) The Western Region registered 520.3 violent crimes per 100,000 persons, a decline from the prior year's figure of 0.3 percent. However, the West reported a small increase in the volume of violent crimes (1.7 percent) including an 8.0-percent increase in the number of murders and a 5.9-percent increase in the murder rate. (See Table 4.)

Community Types

Metropolitan Statistical Areas, or MSAs, are those community types made up of a central city or urbanized area of at least 50,000 inhabitants, the county containing that city or area, and any other adjacent suburban counties with close cultural and economic ties to the area. In 2001, approximately 80 percent of the U.S. population

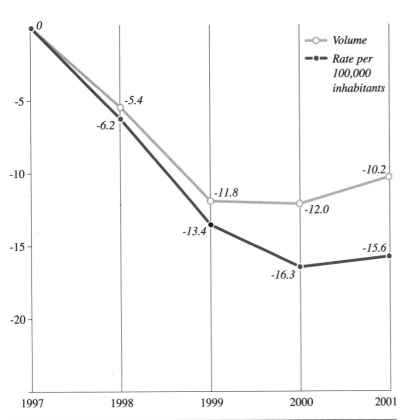

Figure 2.2

Crime Index
Percent change from 1997

resided in an MSA, and this community type accounted for 88.7 percent of the Nation's total violent crime. Within MSAs, violent crime was measured at a rate of 560.0 offenses per 100,000 persons in 2001. Cities outside metropolitan statistical areas, which accounted for 8 percent of the population of the Nation, recorded a rate of 392.8 violent crimes per 100,000 people. Collectively, these cities experienced 6.2 percent of the country's violent crime volume. The Nation's rural counties, accounting for 12 percent of the Nation's population, registered a violent crime rate of 211.0 offenses per 100,000 inhabitants, and they accounted for the remaining 5.1 percent of violent crime. (Based on Table 2.)

Population Groups Trends and Rates

Cities in the United States, when viewed as a collective group, reported an increase of 0.4 percent in the volume of violent crime when compared to the previous year's data. The Nation's cities with populations of 100,000 to 499,999 experienced the greatest rise in violent crime, 1.8 percent. Those communities with populations under 10,000 reported a minimal increase of 0.1 percent. Cities of 25,000 to 49,999 in population recorded a decrease of 0.7 percent in violent crime, and cities within the 500,000 to 999,999 population range reported a 0.3-percent decline. Rural and suburban counties both showed increases in violent crime volume, 0.6 and 0.5 percent, respectively. Crime trends for cities and counties can be found in Table 12.

Weapons Distribution

Data concerning weapons usage are collected for the crimes of murder, robbery, and aggravated assault. Personal weapons such as hands, fists, feet, etc. were used in 31.1 percent of those crimes. Firearms were involved in 26.2 percent of incidents. Knives or cutting instruments were used in 14.9 percent of violent crimes. Other dangerous weapons were employed in the remaining 27.8 percent of offenses. (See Tables 19 and 2.10.) Weapon information is not collected for forcible rape.

Clearances

For UCR purposes, a clearance is counted when a crime is solved either by arrest or by exceptional means, i.e., when some reason outside the control of law enforcement precludes making an arrest. In the United States in 2001, 46.2 percent of all violent crimes were cleared. Within this category, 62.4 percent of murders were cleared, 56.1 percent of aggravated assaults, 44.3 percent of forcible rapes, and 24.9 percent of robberies were cleared. (See Table 25.)

Clearances and Juveniles

When an offender under the age of 18 is cited to appear in juvenile court or before other juvenile authorities, the UCR Program records that incident as cleared by arrest, even though a physical arrest may not have occurred. In

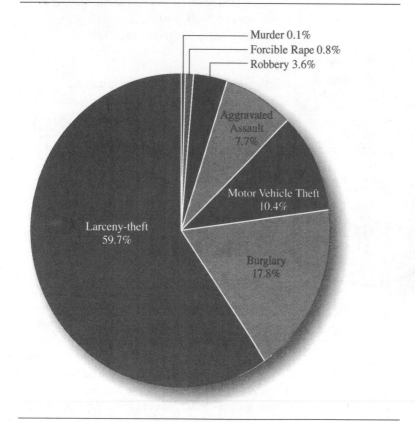

Figure 2.3

Crime Index Offenses
Percent distribution [1]2001

Murder 0.1%
Forcible Rape 0.8%
Robbery 3.6%
Aggravated Assault 7.7%
Motor Vehicle Theft 10.4%
Larceny-theft 59.7%
Burglary 17.8%

[1] Due to rounding, the percentages do not add to 100.0 percent.

Figure 2.4

Regional Crime Rates 2001
Violent and property crimes, per 100,000 inhabitants

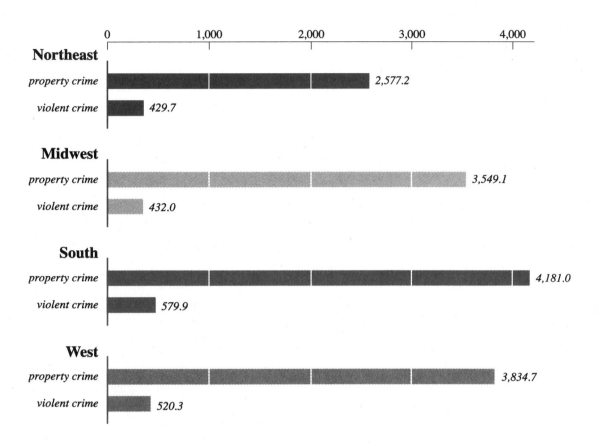

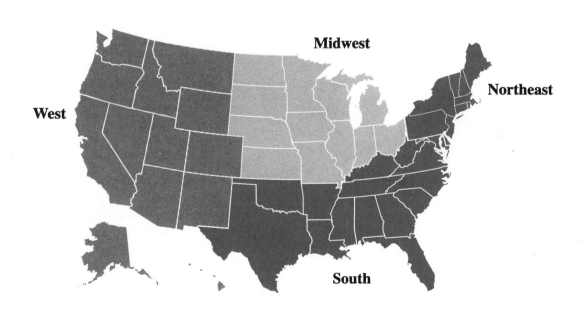

addition, as defined by the Program, clearances involving both adult and juvenile offenders are classified as adult clearances. Therefore, juveniles who accompany an adult in the commission of an offense were not included in these figures.

Nationally, 12.1 percent of violent crime clearances involved persons under 18 years of age. Among violent crimes, robbery had the highest juvenile clearances, 14.4 percent. Clearances for the offense of forcible rape involved only juveniles in 12.4 percent of cases. Juveniles were the perpetrators in 11.8 percent of aggravated assault cases cleared. The crime of murder posted the lowest juvenile clearances, 5.0 percent. (See Table 28.) The topic of clearances is discussed further in Section III.

Arrests

In 2001, there were an estimated 627,132 arrests for violent crimes. Approximately

4.6 percent of total estimated arrests for that year involved a crime of violence. Aggravated assault accounted for 76.2 percent of estimated violent crime arrests; robbery, 17.3 percent; forcible rape, 4.3 percent; and murder, 2.2 percent. (See Table 29.)

Violent crime arrests in 2001 increased 0.1 percent from the previous year's figure. However, three of the four violent crime offenses showed decreases in arrests for 2001. Murder arrests were down 2.6 percent, forcible rape arrests declined 2.3 percent, aggravated assault arrests fell 0.1 percent. Robbery alone showed an increase in arrests, 2.1 percent. Five- and 10-year comparisons of total violent crime arrests indicated an 11.4-percent decrease from the number of arrests in 1997, and a 10.7-percent decline from the 1992 number. (See Tables 32, 34, and 36.)

The Nation recorded a violent crime arrest rate of 225.6 per 100,000 inhabitants in 2001. The Western Region had the highest violent crime arrest rate at 289.1 per 100,000 persons. The South followed with 202.1, the Northeast with 198.7, and the Midwest with 187.2 arrests per 100,000 inhabitants. (See Table 30.)

Collectively, the Nation's cities registered a rate of 255.9 violent crime arrests per 100,000 people. Within this group, cities with more than 250,000 in population reported an arrest rate of 359.0. The lowest rate was recorded by law enforcement agencies in cities of 10,000 to 24,999 inhabitants, 167.9 arrests per 100,000 persons. Suburban counties reported a violent crime arrest rate of 167.6 per 100,000 people, and rural counties registered a rate of 137.1. (See Table 31.) The topic of arrests is discussed in greater detail in Section IV.

Arrestees

The number of persons under 18 years of age arrested for violent crime decreased 1.9 percent, and arrests of adults increased 0.5 percent in 2001. When considering gender, males accounted for 82.7 percent of total arrests. Arrestees were most often adults (84.6 percent) and most often white (60.2 percent). Blacks made up 37.6 percent, and other races accounted for the remainder of violent crime arrests. (See Tables 36, 38, 42, and 43.)

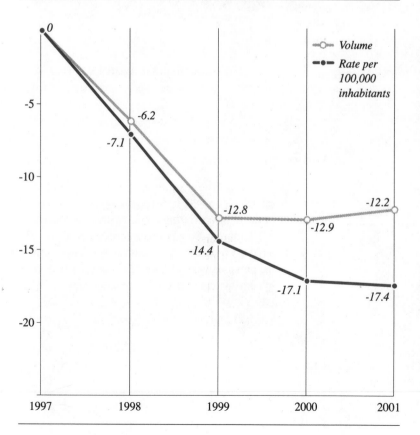

Figure 2.5

Violent Crime
Percent change from 1997

Murder

Definition

Murder and nonnegligent manslaughter, as defined in the Uniform Crime Reporting Program, is the willful (nonnegligent) killing of one human being by another.

The classification of this offense, as for all other Crime Index offenses, is based solely on police investigation as opposed to the determination of a court, medical examiner, coroner, jury, or other judicial body. Not included in the count for this offense classification are deaths caused by negligence, suicide, or accident; justifiable homicides; and attempts to murder or assaults to murder, which are scored as aggravated assaults.

Trend

Year	Number of offenses	Rate per 100,000 inhabitants
2000	15,586	5.5
2001	15,980	5.6
Percent change	+2.5	+1.3

National Offenses and Trends

Approximately 15,980 persons were murder victims in 2001. This estimate indicated a 2.5-percent increase over the 2000 approximation, and it was the second consecutive annual increase in the number of murders occurring nationwide. However, the 2001 estimate represented a 12.2-percent decrease from the 1997 estimate and a 32.7-percent drop from the

estimate recorded for 1992. The 2001 estimate yielded a rate of 5.6 murders for every 100,000 U.S. inhabitants. That rate is 1.3 percent higher than the rate estimated for 2000. (See Table 1.)

Regional Offense Distributions and Rates

The United States is divided into four regions: the Northeast, the Midwest, the South, and the West. (See Appendix III.) In 2001, data collected from the Nation's four regions reflect the following:

The Northeast

The Northeast, with 18.9 percent of the Nation's population, accounted for 14.3 percent of the murders during 2001. With an estimated 2,278 murders, the Northeastern States registered a 5.6-percent rise in murder volume from the previous year's figure. The rate per 100,000 inhabitants showed a 4.4-percent increase in the murder rate for the region— 4.2 murders per 100,000 persons. (See Tables 3 and 4.)

Table 2.3

Murder by Month[1]
Percent Distribution, 1997-2001

Month	1997	1998	1999	2000	2001
January	8.7	9.1	8.8	8.4	8.0
February	7.3	7.2	7.1	7.3	6.1
March	8.5	8.3	7.6	7.6	7.2
April	7.6	7.7	7.7	7.7	8.0
May	7.9	8.4	8.3	8.5	8.2
June	8.7	8.4	8.1	8.5	8.4
July	9.0	8.7	9.1	9.3	9.5
August	8.7	9.2	9.1	9.4	9.1
September	8.2	8.3	8.7	8.3	8.7
October	8.6	8.3	8.4	8.7	9.3
November	8.2	7.6	8.2	7.7	8.4
December	8.6	8.8	8.8	8.7	9.2

[1] The murder and nonnegligent homicides that occurred as a result of the events of September 11, 2001, were not included in any murder tables (Tables 2.3-2.15). See special report, Section V.

The Midwest

The Midwest, which represented 22.7 percent of the U.S. population in 2001, accounted for 21.3 percent of the Nation's murders. The region had an estimated 3,405 murders, an increase of 3.4 percent from the 2000 number. The Midwestern States experienced 5.3 murders per 100,000 inhabitants, an increase of 2.9 percent over the murder rate recorded for 2000. (See Tables 3 and 4.)

The South

The Southern Region of the Nation accounted for 35.8 percent of the population and 42.4 percent of the murders committed in 2001. The Southern States experienced an estimated 6,780 murders, which represented a 1.5-percent drop for this region from the previous year's volume. The region posted a murder rate of 6.7 per 100,000 inhabitants, a 3.0-percent decline from the 2000 rate. The South was the only

			Sex		
Race	Total	Male	Female	Unknown
White	6,750	4,785	1,962	3
Black	6,446	5,350	1,095	1
Other race	368	245	123	0
Unknown race	188	123	34	31
Total[2]	13,752	10,503	3,214	35

Table 2.4

Murder Victims[1]
by Race and Sex, 2001

[1] The murder and nonnegligent homicides that occurred as a result of the events of September 11, 2001, were not included in any murder tables (Tables 2.3-2.15). See special report, Section V.
[2] Total number of murder victims for whom supplemental homicide data were received.

region to report a decline in both murder volume and rate. (See Tables 3 and 4.)

The West

This region accounted for 22.6 percent of the population and 22.0 percent of murders in 2001. An estimated 3,517 murders occurred in the Western States during 2001, representing an 8.0-percent increase in murder from the 2000 volume. The West experienced a 5.9-percent rise in the murder rate from the previous year's figure, with 5.5 murders per 100,000 people. (See Tables 3 and 4.)

Community Types

Metropolitan Statistical Areas, or MSAs, are those community types made up of a central city of at least 50,000 inhabitants, the county containing that city, and adjacent areas with strong economic or cultural ties to the central city. MSAs accounted for approximately 80 percent of the U.S. population in 2001, and they experienced 87.0 percent of total estimated murders. Murder occurred at a rate of 6.1 per 100,000 inhabitants of MSAs for 2001. Those cities outside of metropolitan areas, which accounted for 8 percent of the Nation's population, reported an estimated 3.5 murders per 100,000 people and 5.0 percent of the murder volume. The Nation's rural counties, with 12 percent of the population, reported 8.0 percent of the total murders and 3.7 murders per 100,000 people. (See Table 2.)

Figure 2.6

Murder
Percent change from 1997

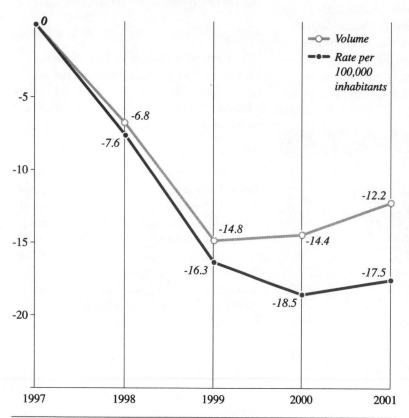

Table 2.5

Murder Victims[1]
by Age, Sex, and Race, 2001

Age	Total	Sex			Race			
		Male	Female	Unknown	White	Black	Other	Unknown
Total	13,752	10,503	3,214	35	6,750	6,446	368	188
Percent distribution[2]	100.0	76.4	23.4	0.3	49.1	46.9	2.7	1.4
Under 18[3]	1,402	934	464	4	724	615	46	17
Under 22[3]	3,499	2,760	735	4	1,608	1,763	100	28
18 and over[3]	12,054	9,371	2,678	5	5,902	5,732	317	103
Infant (under 1)	220	126	93	1	123	83	8	6
1 to 4	320	171	148	1	174	135	6	5
5 to 8	99	55	44	0	69	28	2	0
9 to 12	86	44	42	0	50	30	4	2
13 to 16	390	291	99	0	190	182	16	2
17 to 19	1,227	1,061	164	2	517	668	34	8
20 to 24	2,651	2,299	352	0	1,104	1,474	56	17
25 to 29	2,024	1,682	342	0	853	1,115	32	24
30 to 34	1,516	1,177	339	0	696	761	49	10
35 to 39	1,341	947	394	0	684	615	33	9
40 to 44	1,084	746	336	2	572	471	33	8
45 to 49	778	564	211	3	444	292	32	10
50 to 54	544	409	135	0	324	192	21	7
55 to 59	330	230	100	0	216	98	13	3
60 to 64	247	168	79	0	168	64	9	6
65 to 69	184	123	61	0	131	42	9	2
70 to 74	146	84	62	0	106	37	3	0
75 and over	269	128	141	0	205	60	3	1
Unknown	296	198	72	26	124	99	5	68

[1] The murder and nonnegligent homicides that occurred as a result of the events of September 11, 2001, were not included in any murder tables (Tables 2.3-2.15). See special report, Section V.
[2] Because of rounding, the percentages may not add to total.
[3] Does not include unknown ages.

Table 2.6

Murder Offenders[1]
by Age, Sex, and Race, 2001

Age	Total	Sex			Race			
		Male	Female	Unknown	White	Black	Other	Unknown
Total	15,488	10,126	1,086	4,276	5,174	5,521	273	4,520
Percent distribution[2]	100.0	65.4	7.0	27.6	33.4	35.6	1.8	29.2
Under 18[3]	835	743	89	3	368	426	35	6
Under 22[3]	3,515	3,241	269	5	1,500	1,884	102	29
18 and over[3]	9,278	8,316	953	9	4,578	4,395	230	75
Infant (under 1)	0	0	0	0	0	0	0	0
1 to 4	0	0	0	0	0	0	0	0
5 to 8	0	0	0	0	0	0	0	0
9 to 12	14	13	1	0	7	6	0	1
13 to 16	454	388	63	3	196	234	20	4
17 to 19	1,695	1,570	123	2	732	894	55	14
20 to 24	2,767	2,565	202	0	1,172	1,521	54	20
25 to 29	1,571	1,413	157	1	746	771	39	15
30 to 34	992	874	118	0	520	439	27	6
35 to 39	855	725	130	0	476	356	19	4
40 to 44	645	536	109	0	367	253	22	3
45 to 49	455	405	49	1	282	158	10	5
50 to 54	272	233	34	5	165	93	8	6
55 to 59	158	130	28	0	120	33	3	2
60 to 64	85	72	13	0	56	25	4	0
65 to 69	59	51	8	0	36	19	3	1
70 to 74	37	34	3	0	26	11	0	0
75 and over	54	50	4	0	45	8	1	0
Unknown	5,375	1,067	44	4,264	228	700	8	4,439

[1] The murder and nonnegligent homicides that occurred as a result of the events of September 11, 2001, were not included in any murder tables (Tables 2.3-2.15). See special report, Section V.
[2] Because of rounding, the percentages may not add to total.
[3] Does not include unknown ages.

Population Groups Trends and Rates

Collectively, the Nation's cities experienced a 3.5-percent increase in the number of murders over the previous year's estimate. Cities with populations of 250,000–499,999 recorded the largest increase in murder, 10.2 percent. Cities with 25,000–49,999 inhabitants experienced the only decrease in the number of murders, down 5.5 percent from the 2000 estimate. (See Table 12.)

Considering murder rates per 100,000 individuals, cities with 500,000–999,999 in population reported the highest murder rate at 14.3. Those cities with populations of 10,000–24,999 posted the lowest rate at 2.8 per 100,000 people. Suburban counties recorded a murder rate of 3.8; rural counties registered a rate of 3.6 murders per 100,000 inhabitants. (See Table 16.)

Supplementary Homicide Reports

During 2001, UCR contributing agencies submitted supplemental information concerning 13,752 homicides. The Supplementary Homicide Report (SHR) supplies data on the age, sex, and race of both the victim and the offender, the type of weapon used, the relationship of the victim to the offender, and the circumstance surrounding the incident.

Victims

Based upon the 2001 SHR data, the victims of homicide were most often male (76.6 percent) and adult (89.6 percent). By race, 49.8 percent of murder victims were white, and 47.5 percent were black. The remaining victims, 2.7 percent, were of other races (Asian or Pacific Islander and American Indian or Alaskan Native). Of the total murder victims where age and sex were known, 9.1 percent of males and 14.8 percent of females were under 18 years of age. (See Table 2.5.)

Of the homicides for which supplemental data were received, the victim-offender relationship was unknown for 44.6 percent of the victims. Approximately 42.3 percent of the victims knew their assailants (29.2 percent were acquainted with their killers and 13.1 percent were related to them). Another 13.1 percent of murder victims were known to have been murdered by a stranger. The 2001 SHR data indicated that nearly a third of female victims were slain by a husband or boyfriend, 32.2 percent. Male homicide victims were killed by

---

Table 2.7

Murder Victim/Offender Relationship
by Age, 2001
[Single victim/single offender]

| Age of victim | Total | Age of offender | | |
		Under 18	18 and over	Unknown
Total	6,987	369	5,974	644
Under 18	767	113	610	44
18 and over	6,085	252	5,265	568
Unknown	135	4	99	32

Table 2.8

Murder Victim/Offender Relationship
by Race and Sex, 2001
[Single victim/single offender]

| Race of victim | Total | Race of offender | | | | Sex of offender | | |
		White	Black	Other	Unknown	Male	Female	Unknown
White victims	3,644	3,059	475	48	62	3,249	333	62
Black victims	3,087	180	2,802	10	95	2,656	336	95
Other race victims	179	52	24	98	5	156	18	5
Unknown race	77	31	20	2	24	46	5	26

| Sex of victim | Total | Race of offender | | | | Sex of offender | | |
		White	Black	Other	Unknown	Male	Female	Unknown
Male victims	4,910	2,161	2,525	97	127	4,269	512	129
Female victims	1,996	1,129	775	59	33	1,788	175	33
Unknown sex	81	32	21	2	26	50	5	26

Table 2.9

Murder, Types of Weapons Used[1]
Percent Distribution by Region, 2001

Region	Total all weapons[2]	Firearms	Knives or cutting instruments	Unknown or other dangerous weapons	Personal weapons (hands, fists, feet, etc.)[3]
Total	100.0	63.4	13.1	16.8	6.7
Northeastern States	100.0	60.2	17.4	14.1	8.3
Midwestern States	100.0	57.4	9.5	26.9	6.2
Southern States	100.0	65.8	12.6	14.9	6.7
Western States	100.0	66.8	14.0	13.0	6.2

[1] The murder and nonnegligent homicides that occurred as a result of the events of September 11, 2001, were not included in any murder tables (Tables 2.3-2.15). See special report, Section V.
[2] Because of rounding, the percentages may not add to total.
[3] Pushed is included in personal weapons.

Table 2.10

Murder Victims[1]
by Weapon, 1997-2001

Weapons	1997	1998	1999	2000	2001
Total	15,837	14,276	13,011	13,230	13,752
Total firearms:	10,729	9,257	8,480	8,661	8,719
Handguns	8,441	7,430	6,658	6,778	6,790
Rifles	638	548	400	411	389
Shotguns	643	633	531	485	497
Other guns	35	16	92	53	58
Firearms, type not stated	972	630	799	934	985
Knives or cutting instruments	2,055	1,899	1,712	1,782	1,796
Blunt objects (clubs, hammers, etc.)	724	755	756	617	661
Personal weapons (hands, fists, feet, etc.)[2]	1,010	964	885	927	925
Poison	6	6	11	8	10
Explosives	8	10	0	9	4
Fire	140	132	133	134	104
Narcotics	37	35	26	20	34
Drowning	34	28	28	15	23
Strangulation	224	213	190	166	152
Asphyxiation	88	101	106	92	112
Other weapons or weapons not stated	782	876	684	799	1,212

[1] The murder and nonnegligent homicides that occurred as a result of the events of September 11, 2001, were not included in any murder tables (Tables 2.3-2.15). See special report, Section V.
[2] Pushed is included in personal weapons.

Table 2.11

Murder Victims by Age[1]
by Weapon, 2001

Age	Total	Firearms	Knives or cutting instruments	Blunt objects (clubs, hammers, etc.)	Personal weapons (hands, fists, feet, etc.)[2]	Poison	Explosives	Fire	Narcotics	Strangulation	Asphyxiation	Other weapon or weapon not stated[3]
Total	13,752	8,719	1,796	661	925	10	4	104	34	152	112	1,235
Percent distribution[4]	100.0	63.4	13.1	4.8	6.7	0.1	[5]	0.8	0.2	1.1	0.8	9.0
Under 18[6]	1,402	612	102	58	322	3	1	36	4	16	45	203
Under 22[6]	3,499	2,249	294	98	358	3	3	44	12	31	49	358
18 and over[6]	12,054	7,955	1,667	592	576	7	3	64	29	135	65	961
Infant (under 1)	220	14	3	16	105	0	0	2	1	2	24	53
1 to 4	320	38	11	14	173	1	0	16	0	2	10	55
5 to 8	99	36	9	7	13	1	1	9	0	1	5	17
9 to 12	86	36	13	2	10	0	0	7	1	2	2	13
13 to 16	390	269	37	11	16	1	0	1	1	7	3	44
17 to 19	1,227	956	113	23	23	0	1	7	5	7	3	89
20 to 24	2,651	2,050	272	49	53	0	2	3	7	19	8	188
25 to 29	2,024	1,511	231	41	57	2	0	6	2	15	9	150
30 to 34	1,516	1,070	196	64	58	0	0	4	1	20	6	97
35 to 39	1,341	871	219	55	69	1	0	7	3	13	4	99
40 to 44	1,084	599	197	76	91	0	0	3	4	14	5	95
45 to 49	778	370	147	82	66	1	0	7	1	13	6	85
50 to 54	544	283	102	56	44	0	0	5	2	12	2	38
55 to 59	330	150	61	43	35	1	0	3	1	3	2	31
60 to 64	247	114	35	27	22	0	0	7	1	7	4	30
65 to 69	184	68	46	16	21	0	0	4	0	4	3	22
70 to 74	146	55	29	26	8	1	0	4	2	3	4	14
75 and over	269	77	48	42	34	1	0	5	1	7	10	44
Unknown	296	152	27	11	27	0	0	4	1	1	2	71

[1] The murder and nonnegligent homicides that occurred as a result of the events of September 11, 2001, were not included in any murder tables (Tables 2.3-2.15). See special report, Section V.
[2] Pushed is included in personal weapons.
[3] Includes drowning.
[4] Because of rounding, the percentages may not add to total.
[5] Less than one-tenth of 1 percent.
[6] Does not include unknown ages.

Table 2.12

Murder Circumstances[1]
by Relationship.[2] 2001

Circumstances	Total	Husband	Wife	Mother	Father	Son	Daughter	Brother	Sister	Other family	Acquaintance	Friend	Boyfriend	Girlfriend	Neighbor	Employee	Employer	Stranger	Unknown
Total[3]	13,752	142	600	94	110	253	218	73	26	284	2,979	342	153	434	88	5	12	1,803	6,136
Felony type total:	2,279	3	19	9	7	18	17	3	4	39	497	43	1	14	15	1	4	531	1,054
Rape	59	0	0	0	0	0	0	0	0	3	13	4	0	0	2	0	0	14	23
Robbery	1,042	0	0	1	3	0	0	0	0	14	182	16	0	0	6	1	3	353	463
Burglary	73	0	3	0	0	2	0	0	0	4	12	2	0	3	1	0	0	16	30
Larceny-theft	16	0	0	0	0	0	0	0	0	0	4	0	1	2	0	0	1	6	2
Motor vehicle theft	20	0	0	1	0	0	0	0	0	0	7	0	0	2	1	0	0	5	4
Arson	70	0	3	0	1	0	4	1	3	3	8	0	0	0	2	0	0	9	36
Prostitution and commercialized vice	5	0	0	0	0	0	0	0	0	0	1	0	0	0	0	0	0	3	1
Other sex offenses	7	0	0	0	0	0	0	0	0	0	4	0	0	0	0	0	0	2	1
Narcotic drug laws	558	1	0	0	0	1	0	1	0	3	199	15	0	2	2	0	0	61	273
Gambling	3	0	0	0	0	0	0	0	0	0	2	0	0	0	0	0	0	0	1
Other - not specified	426	2	13	7	3	15	13	1	1	12	65	6	0	5	1	0	0	62	220
Suspected felony type	72	0	0	0	0	1	0	0	0	0	8	2	0	0	0	0	0	1	60
Other than felony type total:	6,948	118	511	71	86	208	179	60	19	198	2,007	263	139	363	66	4	4	909	1,743
Romantic triangle	118	2	10	0	0	0	0	0	1	8	52	5	3	8	1	0	0	18	10
Child killed by babysitter	37	0	0	0	0	2	4	0	0	2	26	1	0	0	0	0	0	0	2
Brawl due to influence of alcohol	151	1	4	0	0	0	1	3	1	4	59	14	1	3	5	0	0	31	24
Brawl due to influence of narcotics	118	1	2	0	1	1	0	1	0	0	54	5	0	0	1	0	0	16	36
Argument over money or property	194	1	5	2	2	1	0	5	2	6	101	15	0	1	5	0	0	8	40
Other arguments	3,544	91	354	38	62	40	30	40	8	116	1,065	164	113	288	42	3	3	490	597
Gangland killings	74	1	0	0	0	0	0	0	0	0	20	1	0	0	0	0	0	9	44
Juvenile gang killings	865	0	0	0	0	0	0	0	0	1	209	0	0	0	0	0	0	140	514
Institutional killings	8	0	0	0	0	0	0	0	0	0	8	0	0	0	0	0	0	0	0
Sniper attack	7	0	0	0	1	0	0	0	0	0	1	0	0	0	0	0	0	3	2
Other - not specified	1,832	21	136	31	20	164	144	11	7	61	412	58	22	63	12	1	1	194	474
Unknown	4,453	21	70	14	17	26	22	10	3	47	467	34	13	57	7	0	4	362	3,279

[1] The murder and nonnegligent homicides that occurred as a result of the events of September 11, 2001, were not included in any murder tables (Tables 2.3-2.15). See special report, Section V.
[2] Relationship is that of victim to offender.
[3] Total murder victims for whom supplemental homicide data were received.

Figure 2.7

Murder by relationship[1]

Percent distribution, Volume by known relationship

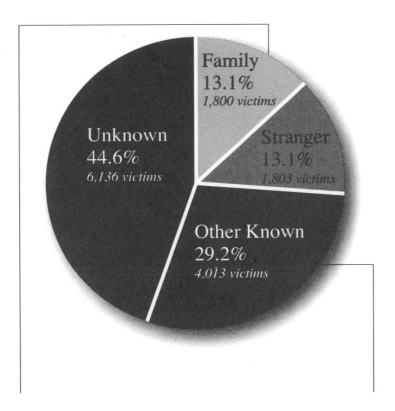

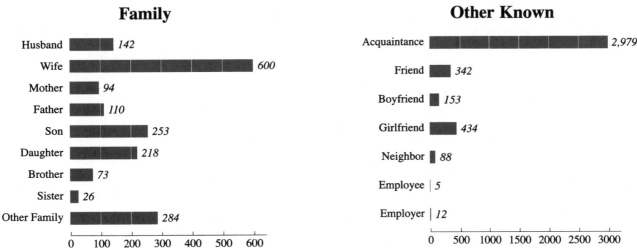

[1] Relationship is that of victim to offender.
Figures are based on 13,752 murder victims for whom Supplementary Homicide Report data were received.

Table 2.13

Murder Circumstances[1]
by Weapon, 2001

Circumstances	Total murder victims	Total firearms	Handguns	Rifles	Shotguns	Other guns or type not stated	Knives or cutting instruments	Blunt objects (clubs, hammers, etc.)	Personal weapons (hands, fists, feet, etc.)	Poison	Pushed or thrown out window	Explosives	Fire	Narcotics	Drowning	Strangulation	Asphyxiation	Other
Total[2]	13,752	8,719	6,790	389	497	1,043	1,796	661	924	10	1	4	104	34	23	152	112	1,212
Felony type total:	2,279	1,473	1,187	68	75	143	182	115	106	1	0	0	50	8	3	25	27	289
Rape	59	7	7	0	0	0	10	4	15	0	0	0	1	1	0	9	2	10
Robbery	1,042	752	632	28	36	56	95	64	45	0	0	0	2	0	2	6	11	65
Burglary	73	39	28	4	5	2	10	12	5	0	0	0	0	0	0	1	3	3
Larceny-theft	16	9	8	1	0	0	2	4	0	0	0	0	0	0	0	0	0	1
Motor vehicle theft	20	10	4	2	0	4	4	4	1	0	0	0	0	0	0	0	0	3
Arson	70	3	3	0	0	0	4	0	2	0	0	0	43	0	0	1	1	16
Prostitution and commercialized vice	5	1	1	0	0	0	3	0	0	0	0	0	0	0	0	0	0	1
Other sex offenses	7	1	1	0	0	0	3	1	0	0	0	0	0	0	0	1	0	1
Narcotic drug laws	558	431	357	19	15	40	21	14	11	0	0	0	2	6	0	1	2	70
Gambling	3	3	2	0	1	0	0	0	0	0	0	0	0	0	0	0	0	0
Other - not specified	426	217	144	14	18	41	30	14	27	1	0	0	2	1	1	6	8	119
Suspected felony type	72	58	41	2	5	10	7	5	0	0	0	0	1	0	1	0	0	0
Other than felony type total:	6,948	4,109	3,259	225	291	334	1,146	334	619	5	1	4	34	16	15	73	62	530
Romantic triangle	118	81	64	8	6	3	23	5	1	0	0	0	0	0	0	2	0	6
Child killed by babysitter	37	0	0	0	0	0	0	3	22	0	0	0	0	0	0	1	2	9
Brawl due to influence of alcohol	151	67	57	4	4	2	40	9	20	0	0	0	2	0	0	1	0	12
Brawl due to influence of narcotics	118	79	68	1	2	8	15	14	3	0	0	0	1	1	0	1	0	4
Argument over money or property	194	129	97	9	14	9	27	13	14	0	0	0	0	0	0	0	0	11
Other arguments	3,544	2,074	1,634	113	161	166	812	196	250	2	1	2	10	3	1	46	12	135
Gangland killings	74	62	49	6	2	5	5	4	1	0	0	0	0	0	1	0	0	6
Juvenile gang killings	865	735	644	26	24	41	27	0	3	0	0	0	0	0	0	1	0	95
Institutional killings	8	0	0	0	0	0	5	0	2	0	0	0	0	0	0	0	0	0
Sniper attack	7	6	1	3	0	2	0	0	0	0	0	0	1	0	0	0	1	1
Other - not specified	1,832	876	645	55	78	98	192	90	303	3	0	2	21	12	14	21	47	251
Unknown	4,453	3,079	2,303	94	126	556	461	207	199	4	0	0	19	10	4	54	23	393

[1] The murder and nonnegligent homicides that occurred as a result of the events of September 11, 2001, were not included in any murder tables (Tables 2.3-2.15). See special report, Section V.
[2] Total murder victims for whom supplemental homicide data were received.

Table 2.14

Murder Circumstances, 1997-2001[1]

Circumstances	1997	1998	1999	2000	2001
Total[2]	15,837	14,276	13,011	13,230	13,752
Felony type total:	2,968	2,514	2,215	2,229	2,279
Rape	67	62	47	58	59
Robbery	1,509	1,244	1,057	1,077	1,042
Burglary	101	92	81	76	73
Larceny-theft	16	17	14	23	16
Motor vehicle theft	18	17	12	25	20
Arson	92	83	66	81	70
Prostitution and commercialized vice	7	15	8	6	5
Other sex offenses	23	20	19	10	7
Narcotic drug laws	802	682	581	589	558
Gambling	19	12	17	12	3
Other - not specified	314	270	313	272	426
Suspected felony type	153	104	65	60	72
Other than felony type total:	7,666	7,232	6,880	6,871	6,948
Romantic triangle	176	187	137	122	118
Child killed by babysitter	24	23	34	30	37
Brawl due to influence of alcohol	239	213	203	188	151
Brawl due to influence of narcotics	106	117	127	99	118
Argument over money or property	287	241	213	206	194
Other arguments	4,476	4,129	3,471	3,589	3,544
Gangland killings	86	73	122	65	74
Juvenile gang killings	783	628	580	653	865
Institutional killings	19	15	13	10	8
Sniper attack	8	16	5	8	7
Other - not specified	1,462	1,590	1,975	1,901	1,832
Unknown	5,050	4,426	3,851	4,070	4,453

[1] The murder and nonnegligent homicides that occurred as a result of the events of September 11, 2001, were not included in any murder tables (Tables 2.3-2.15). See special report, Section V.

[2] Total number of murder victims for whom supplemental homicide data were received.

a wife or girlfriend in 2.8 percent of the incidents. (Based on Table 2.12.)

Offenders

Reviewing the supplemental data for which age, sex, and race of offenders were known revealed that 90.3 percent of murder offenders were male, and 91.7 percent were over the age of 18. Considering those offenders for which race was known, 50.3 percent of murder offenders were black and 47.2 percent were white. Persons of other races comprised 2.5 percent of offenders. (Based Table 2.6.)

Supplemental data for 2001 indicated that of those incidents with one victim and one offender, 93.6 percent of black homicide victims were killed by a black offender, and 85.4 percent of white victims were slain by white offenders. (See Table 2.8.)

Table 2.15

Murder Circumstances[1]
by Victim Sex, 2001

Circumstances	Total murder victims[2]	Male	Female	Unknown
Total[2]	13,752	10,503	3,214	35
Felony type total:	2,279	1,813	464	2
Rape	59	4	55	0
Robbery	1,042	879	163	0
Burglary	73	49	24	0
Larceny-theft	16	13	3	0
Motor vehicle theft	20	13	7	0
Arson	70	38	31	1
Prostitution and commercialized vice	5	2	3	0
Other sex offenses	7	1	6	0
Narcotic drug laws	558	515	43	0
Gambling	3	3	0	0
Other - not specified	426	296	129	1
Suspected felony type	72	60	12	0
Other than felony type total:	6,948	5,088	1,854	6
Romantic triangle	118	87	31	0
Child killed by babysitter	37	19	18	0
Brawl due to influence of alcohol	151	136	15	0
Brawl due to influence of narcotics	118	99	18	1
Argument over money or property	194	172	22	0
Other arguments	3,544	2,519	1,023	2
Gangland killings	74	71	3	0
Juvenile gang killings	865	813	52	0
Institutional killings	8	8	0	0
Sniper attack	7	6	1	0
Other - not specified	1,832	1,158	671	3
Unknown	4,453	3,542	884	27

[1] The murder and nonnegligent homicides that occurred as a result of the events of September 11, 2001, were not included in any murder tables (Tables 2.3-2.15). See special report, Section V.

[2] Total number of murder victims for whom supplemental homicide data were received.

Weapons

Reviewing those incidents in which the murder weapon was known demonstrated that 69.5 percent involved the use of a firearm. Within the firearm category, handguns were used in 77.9 percent of homicides, shotguns were used in 5.7 percent, and rifles in 4.5 percent. Other or unknown firearms accounted for 12.0 percent. Knives or cutting instruments were employed in 14.3 percent of homicides for which the weapon was known. Personal weapons such as hands, fists, or feet, etc. were used in 7.4 percent of murders. Blunt objects were the weapon used in 5.3 percent of murders. Other dangerous weapons (such as poison, explosives, etc.) accounted for the remainder. (See Table

2.10.) Table 20 contains a breakdown by state of weapons used in homicides.

Circumstances

Supplemental information concerning the circumstance of homicides showed that the victims were involved in an argument with the offender in 28.0 percent of the incidents. A homicide occurred in connection with another felony (e.g., robbery, arson, narcotic drug laws) in 16.6 percent of incidents. In 0.5 percent of homicide cases, investigators suspected that a felony had been in progress. The circumstance was unknown in 32.4 percent of homicides. (See Table 2.12.)

Clearances

For UCR purposes, a crime is cleared when it is solved either by arrest or by exceptional means. An exceptional clearance is counted when circumstances outside the control of law enforcement (such as the death of the offender) preclude making an arrest.

Murder, the most serious offense, was cleared more often than any other Index offense, 62.4 percent.

Murder was also the offense that had the lowest percentage of clearances involving only juveniles, 5.0 percent. (See Table 28.)

By population groups, cities with 25,000–49,999 inhabitants recorded the highest percentage of murders cleared at 77.9 percent. Cities with 250,000 inhabitants or more cleared 56.5 percent of murders, the lowest percentage among population groups. Law enforcement agencies cleared 66.9 percent of murders in suburban counties; 77.5 percent of murders were cleared in rural counties. (See Table 25.)

Arrests

Nationally, there were an estimated 13,653 arrests for murder during 2001. Of those arrested, 51.3 percent were under the age of 25, 41.2 percent fell into the 18–24 age group, and 10.2 percent were under the age of 18. (See Tables 29, 38, and 41.)

In 2001, total arrests for murder decreased 2.6 percent when compared with the previous year's data. (See Table 36.) Five- and 10-year trends in murder arrests showed a drop of 21.2 percent from the 1997 arrest total and a decrease of 34.2 percent from the 1992 figure. (See Tables 32 and 34.)

Male arrests for murder fell 2.0 percent in 2001 when compared to the previous year's figure; however, male arrests declined 23.3 percent from 1997 and 37.2 percent from 1992. Female arrests in 2001 fell 6.8 percent from the prior year, 1.7 percent from 1997 data, and 6.3 percent from 1992 figures. (See Tables 33, 35, and 37.)

Arrests of juveniles for murder fell 2.2 percent during 2001, and arrests of adults decreased 2.6 percent from the 2000 report. Juvenile murder arrests for 2001 represented a 47.3-percent decrease from the total juvenile murder arrests in 1997, and a 62.0-percent decrease from the 1992 total. (See Tables 32, 34, and 36.)

Murder arrestees were most often male (87.5 percent) and adult (89.8 percent). By race, the number of arrestees was nearly evenly split between black arrestees and white arrestees at 48.7 percent and 48.4 percent, respectively. The remaining arrestees were Asian or Pacific Island-

Table 2.16

Justifiable Homicide
by Weapon, Law Enforcement,[1] 1997-2001

Year	Total	Total fire-arms	Hand-guns	Rifles	Shot-guns	Fire-arms, type not stated	Knives or cutting instru-ments	Other danger-ous weapons	Personal weapons
1997	366	363	315	14	20	14	0	1	2
1998	369	367	322	15	18	12	0	0	2
1999	308	305	274	11	15	5	0	1	2
2000	309	308	274	14	13	7	0	1	0
2001	370	368	311	25	11	21	0	2	0

[1] The killing of a felon by a law enforcement officer in the line of duty.

Table 2.17

Justifiable Homicide
by Weapon, Private Citizen,[1] 1997-2001

Year	Total	Total fire-arms	Hand-guns	Rifles	Shot-guns	Fire-arms, type not stated	Knives or cutting instru-ments	Other danger-ous weapons	Personal weapons
1997	280	238	197	16	14	11	28	6	8
1998	196	170	150	6	14	0	17	5	4
1999	192	158	137	5	10	6	18	9	7
2000	164	138	123	4	7	4	15	8	3
2001	215	176	136	10	13	17	25	6	8

[1] The killing of a felon, during the commission of a felony, by a private citizen.

Forcible Rape

Definition

Forcible rape, as defined in the Uniform Crime Reporting Program, is the carnal knowledge of a female forcibly and against her will. Assaults or attempts to commit rape by force or threat of force are also included; however, statutory rape (without force) and other sex offenses are excluded.

Trend

Year	Number of offenses	Rate per 100,000 inhabitants
2000	90,178	32.0
2001	90,491	31.8
Percent change	+0.3	-0.8

National Rates and Trends

The UCR Program has traditionally defined rape victims as females. Approximately 90,491 forcible rapes of females were recorded during 2001. Based on that volume, 62.2 of every 100,000 females were victims of forcible rape in 2001 compared to 62.7 in the previous year. These figures indicated a slight percentage increase in the number of rapes (0.3 percent), but a decrease in the rate of female rapes (0.8 percent).

The 2001 female forcible rape rate of 62.2 continued a downward trend. In 1999, there were an estimated 64.1 rapes for every 100,000 females in the Nation; in 1997, there were 70.3 victims for each 100,000 females; for 1992, the estimate was 83.7.

Regional Offense Distributions and Rates

The United States is divided into four regions: the Northeast, the Midwest, the South, and the West. (See Appendix III.) In 2001, data collected regarding the Nation's four regions reflect the following:

The Northeast

The Northeast Region reported the lowest percentage of the Nation's female rapes at 13.4 percent and the lowest forcible rape rate at 44.0 per 100,000 females. The Northeastern figures showed increases of 1.6 percent in the number of rapes and 1.2 percent in the rate of rapes over the prior year's numbers.

The Midwest

The Midwestern States reported 25.1 percent of the forcible rapes occurring in the Nation in 2001, an increase for the region of 1.5 percent from the prior year's report. A regional rate of 68.6 rape incidents for 100,000 females showed a 1.0-percent increase from the 2000 rate.

The South

Regionally, the highest percentage of female rapes, 37.8 percent, occurred in the South. The

Table 2.18

Forcible Rape by Month
Percent Distribution, 1997-2001

Month	1997	1998	1999	2000	2001
January	7.9	7.9	8.1	8.0	7.6
February	7.0	7.4	7.3	7.5	7.2
March	8.0	8.6	8.2	8.5	8.4
April	8.2	8.2	8.2	8.0	8.3
May	9.1	8.8	8.6	9.0	8.8
June	9.5	8.7	8.8	9.1	8.7
July	9.7	9.6	9.6	9.5	9.7
August	9.4	9.3	9.5	9.3	9.4
September	8.8	8.8	8.3	8.4	8.5
October	8.2	7.9	8.3	8.3	8.4
November	7.4	7.6	7.9	7.5	7.6
December	6.7	7.1	7.2	6.9	7.4

data indicated a modest decline of 0.6 percent in the number of forcible rape occurrences from the 2000 figure. The estimated rate of 65.8 rapes per 100,000 females calculated to a 2.2-percent decline in the South's female rape rate from the 2000 rate.

The West

The West experienced 23.7 percent of the Nation's rape offenses. The incidence of female forcible rape in the Western States showed a slight decline of 0.1 percent from the 2000 estimate, and the rape rate of 65.2 per 100,000 females indicated a decrease of 2.1 percent when compared to the prior year's rate. (See Tables 3 and 4.)

Community Types

In estimating the data by community types, cities outside metropolitan areas reported the highest rate of female rapes in 2001, 67.7

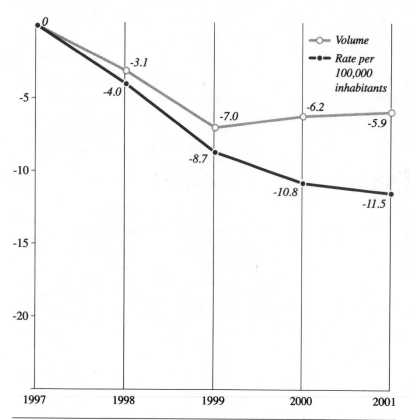

Figure 2.8

Forcible Rape
Percent change from 1997

incidents per 100,000 female inhabitants. This estimate was a decrease from the 69.0 rate recorded in 2000. The Nation's Metropolitan Statistical Areas reported a nominal decrease in the female rape rate, down to 64.4 from the 65.0 recorded the prior year. Rural counties reported the lowest rate of forcible rapes of females in the Nation; however, the rate of 43.8 did indicate a minimal increase from the 2000 rate of 43.4 per 100,000 females. (See Table 2.)

Clearances

For UCR purposes, an offense is cleared when at least one person is arrested and charged or when circumstances beyond the control of law enforcement preclude an arrest for a crime that has been solved, e.g., the victim refuses to cooperate with the prosecution.

Nationally, 44.3 percent of rapes were cleared during 2001 versus 46.1 percent cleared in 2000. Regionally, law enforcement in the Northeast cleared 50.1 percent; in the Midwest, 39.3 percent; in the South, 46.0 percent; and in the West, 43.5 percent of female rapes during 2001. (See Table 26.)

Clearances and Juveniles

When an offender under the age of 18 is cited to appear in juvenile court or before other juvenile authorities, the UCR Program records that incident as a clearance by arrest even though a physical arrest may not have occurred. In addition, according to Program definitions, clearances involving both adult and juvenile offenders are classified as adult clearances.

Nationally, incidents involving only juveniles accounted for 12.4 percent of the overall number of clearances for forcible rape in 2001. The highest percentage of juvenile clearances, 15.7 percent, occurred in cities with populations of 10,000 to 24,999. The lowest percentage of juvenile clearances for forcible rape, 8.8 percent, was recorded in the Nation's eight cities of 1 million and over in population. (See Table 28.)

Arrests

In 2001, law enforcement arrested an estimated 27,270 persons for forcible rape. (See Table 29.) Forcible rape arrests for 2001 were

2.3 percent below the 2000 number, 12.1 percent lower than the 1997 figure, and 28.2 percent lower than the 1992 number. (See Tables 32, 34, and 36.) Two-, 5-, and 10-year trend analyses showed juvenile arrests for forcible rape were down 1.4 percent from the 2000 figure. They were 14.1 percent lower than the 1997 report and 24.5 percent below the 1992 figure. (See Tables 32, 34, and 36.)

Approximately 45.4 percent of persons arrested for forcible rape in 2001 were under the age of 25, 62.7 percent of arrestees were white, and 98.8 percent were males. (See Tables 41, 42, and 43.)

UCR Classifications

The UCR Program counts each offense in which a female of any age is forcibly raped or upon whom an assault to rape or attempt to rape is made. Of the total rapes reported for 2001, 90.0 percent were classified as rapes, and the remainder were attempts. (See Table 19.) Statutory rapes of female victims where no force is used and the victim is under the age of consent are categorized as *other sex offenses*. Sexual attacks on males are classified as assaults or other sex offenses depending on the nature of the crime and the extent of injury. The UCR Program classifies sex offenses (except forcible rape) as Part II offenses and, as such, collects only an aggregate total on these crimes. (See Appendix II.)

Robbery

Definition

The Uniform Crime Reporting Program defines robbery as the taking or attempting to take anything of value from the care, custody, or control of a person or persons by force or threat of force or violence and/or by putting the victim in fear.

Trend

Year	Number of offenses	Rate per 100,000 inhabitants
2000	408,016	145.0
2001	422,921	148.5
Percent change	+3.7	+2.4

Since the underlying motive for robbery is to obtain money or property from a person, every instance of this offense involves at least one victim who has suffered physical and/or psychological trauma. Despite the actual or threatened violence inherent in this very personal crime, for UCR purposes robbery is considered to be a crime against property. Accordingly, law enforcement officials report one offense for each separate robbery occurrence.

National Trends, Rates, and Distributions

The 422,921 robberies estimated for 2001 marked the first increase in this offense nationwide since 1991. This estimate indicated a 3.7-percent increase from the 2000 figure. However, the number of robberies recorded for 2001 was 37.1 percent below the 1992 number.

The 2001 robbery rate for the Nation was 148.5 offenses per 100,000 inhabitants, an increase of 2.4 percent over the previous year's rate. A 10-year comparison, however, revealed that the 2001 rate was 43.7 percent lower than the 1992 rate. (See Table 1.)

Robbery accounted for 29.4 percent of all violent crimes occurring in the United States, and 3.6 percent of all Crime Index offenses. (Based on Table 1.)

Robbery by Weapon

In 2001, robbers used firearms in 42.0 percent of the reported offenses. Thirty-nine percent of robberies involved strong-arming the victim. Offenders used knives or cutting instruments in 8.7 percent of the offenses, and the remaining 10.4 percent of offenses involved other weapons. (See Tables 2.22 and 15.) A state-by-state breakdown of weapons used in robberies is provided in Table 21.

Dollar Loss

Robbers stole more than $532 million from their victims in 2001. The average loss for each instance of robbery nationwide was $1,258. The number of banks robbed during 2001 increased 19.4 percent over the number reported for 2000; those institutions incurred an

Table 2.19

Robbery by Month
Percent Distribution, 1997-2001

Month	1997	1998	1999	2000	2001
January	9.2	9.5	8.9	8.6	8.2
February	7.6	7.5	7.3	7.1	6.5
March	7.9	8.0	7.7	7.7	7.6
April	7.6	7.6	7.6	7.5	7.4
May	8.2	7.9	8.1	8.1	8.1
June	8.0	7.7	8.1	7.9	8.1
July	8.6	8.5	8.7	8.7	8.7
August	8.8	8.7	8.8	9.0	8.7
September	8.5	8.5	8.3	8.5	8.5
October	8.8	9.0	8.8	9.1	9.7
November	8.2	8.3	8.6	8.7	9.1
December	8.6	8.8	9.2	9.0	9.5

average loss of $4,587 per incident. Commercial houses—a classification that includes supermarkets, department stores, restaurants, taverns, finance companies, hotels, motels, etc.—lost an average of $1,881 to robbers per incident. The estimated average loss per incident resulting from robberies at residences was $1,364, followed by streets/highways at $957, and gas or service stations at $686. Losses resulting from convenience store robberies averaged $618. (See Table 23.)

Robbery by Type

Robberies of persons on streets and highways accounted for 44.3 percent of robberies during 2001. Together, robberies of commercial establishments, gas stations, convenience stores, and banks accounted for 26.3 percent of the total robbery offenses reported. Robberies of residences comprised 12.6 percent of the total. The remainder were classified as miscellaneous. (See Table 2.20.)

Regional Offense Distributions and Rates

The U.S. is divided into four regions: the Northeast, the Midwest, the South, and the West. (See Appendix III.) In 2001, data collected regarding the Nation's four regions reflect the following:

The Northeast

The Northeast, which contained 18.9 percent of the population, experienced 19.1 percent of the Nation's robberies during 2001.

The number of robberies declined in the region by 3.6 percent, and the rate per 100,000 inhabitants declined 4.0 percent from the previous year's rate. That region reported the greatest percentage of strong-arm robberies, 46.9 percent, in 2001. (See Tables 2.22, 3, and 4.)

The Midwest

Claiming 22.7 percent of the population in 2001, the Midwest accounted for 19.6 percent of total robberies. The number of robberies occurring in the region increased 1.8 percent from the 2000 number, and the rate per 100,000 inhabitants increased 1.3 percent. (See Tables 3, and 4.)

The South

With 35.8 percent of the population, the Southern States reported 38.4 percent of total robberies. The volume of robbery offenses within the region increased 6.3 percent from the prior year's volume, and the rate per 100,000 inhabitants increased 4.6 percent over the 2000 rate. That region also reported the highest percentage of robberies involving firearms, 46.9 percent. (See Tables 2.22, 3, and 4.)

The West

In 2001, approximately 22.6 percent of the U.S. population resided in the Western States. That region reported 22.9 percent of all robbery offenses. From 2000, the number of robbery offenses increased 7.6 percent in 2001, and the rate per 100,000 in population rose 5.5 percent. (See Tables 3, and 4.)

Population Groups Trends and Rates

All population groups registered increases for the offense in 2001. Cities with fewer than 10,000 inhabitants reported the largest increase in robbery offenses, 8.2 percent. The Nation's 10 cities with more than 1 million residents reported the smallest increase at 0.1 percent. Additional data for population groups can be found in Table 12.

Considering the robbery rate per 100,000 inhabitants, the highest rate was recorded by cities with 1 million and over in population, 426.7. The lowest rate, 16.7 robberies per 100,000 people, was recorded for rural counties. Rates for population groups can be found in Table 16.

Table 2.20

Robbery
Percent Distribution by Region, 2001

Type	United States total	North-eastern states	Mid-western states	Southern states	Western states
Total[1]	100.0	100.0	100.0	100.0	100.0
Street/highway	44.3	59.0	48.8	39.2	42.2
Commercial house	14.4	9.1	10.7	14.7	18.7
Gas or service station	2.9	3.5	3.4	2.5	2.8
Convenience store	6.6	5.9	4.7	7.8	5.9
Residence	12.6	8.9	10.1	16.6	9.6
Bank	2.4	2.1	2.6	2.0	3.1
Miscellaneous	16.9	11.6	19.7	17.2	17.7

[1] Because of rounding, the percentages may not add to total.

Table 2.21

Robbery
Percent Distribution by Population Group, 2001

Type	Group I (63 cities, 250,000 and over; population 39,225,132)	Group II (147 cities, 100,000 to 249,999; population 21,966,729)	Group III (371 cities, 50,000 to 99,999; population 25,559,262)	Group IV (687 cities, 25,000 to 49,999; population 23,999,772)	Group V (1,518 cities, 10,000 to 24,999; population 24,106,371)	Group VI (5,591 cities, under 10,000; population 18,850,852)	County agencies (3,322 agencies; population 77,504,451)
Total[1]	100.0	100.0	100.0	100.0	100.0	100.0	100.0
Street/highway	52.6	43.8	41.3	35.0	29.4	24.6	30.8
Commercial house	12.3	16.4	15.7	16.3	18.1	15.7	16.5
Gas or service station	1.9	3.0	3.5	4.2	4.8	4.5	3.9
Convenience store	4.7	6.6	7.2	8.1	9.3	10.5	10.3
Residence	11.8	12.3	10.8	12.6	13.2	13.2	17.7
Bank	1.6	2.7	3.0	3.4	3.6	4.0	3.2
Miscellaneous	15.1	15.2	18.6	20.3	21.6	27.4	17.5

[1] Because of rounding, the percentages may not add to total.

Clearances

Law enforcement agencies cleared 24.9 percent of all robberies nationwide through arrest or exceptional means in 2001. Clearance rates ranged from the 41.0 percent reported by law enforcement agencies in rural counties to 18.5 percent recorded by those in cities from 500,000 to 999,999 in population. (See Table 25.)

Regionally, the Northeast had the highest clearance rate for robbery at 30.2 percent. The South registered a clearance rate of 24.7 percent. The clearance rate for the Western States was 24.4 percent, followed by the Midwest at 21.2 percent. (See Table 26.)

Clearances and Juveniles

Juvenile offenders, those under 18 years of age, comprised 14.4 percent of robbery clearances in 2001. Juveniles accounted for 16.6 percent of clearances in cities with populations of 25,000 to 49,999 inhabitants and 9.1 percent of clearances in rural counties. Table 28 provides juvenile clearance data.

Arrests

Total Arrests

Law enforcement officers arrested an estimated 108,400 persons for robbery in 2001. Robbery arrests accounted for 4.8 percent of all arrests for Index crimes and 17.3 percent of violent crime arrests. (See Table 29.)

Arrest Trends

Robbery arrests for 2001 increased 2.1 percent nationwide over those for 2000. Arrests of adults (18 years and older) rose 3.9 percent. However, arrests for juveniles (under age 18)

Figure 2.9

Robbery
Percent change from 1997

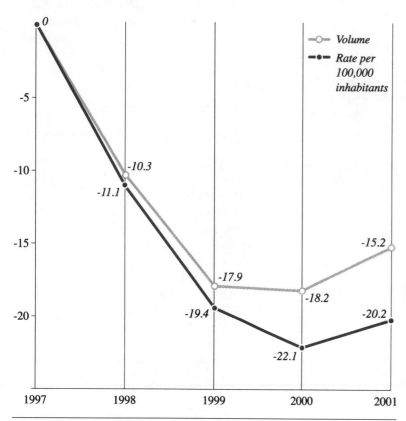

Table 2.22

Robbery, Types of Weapons Used
Percent Distribution by Region, 2001

| Region | Total all weapons[1] | Armed | | | Strong-arm |
		Firearms	Knives or cutting instruments	Other weapons	
Total	100.0	42.0	8.7	10.4	39.0
Northeastern States	100.0	34.6	10.6	7.9	46.9
Midwestern States	100.0	45.1	6.1	9.9	38.9
Southern States	100.0	46.9	7.8	11.8	33.6
Western States	100.0	36.7	10.4	9.7	43.1

[1] Because of rounding, the percentages may not add to total.

decreased 3.5 percent, with arrests of those under 15 years of age falling 11.0 percent. (See Table 36.)

When one looks at arrest data by gender, arrests of males rose 2.0 percent over 2000 data and those of females increased 2.9 percent. Juvenile arrests declined for youths of both sexes, decreasing 3.5 percent for males and 4.0 percent for females. (See Table 37.)

The 5-year trend showed an overall 18.0-percent decrease in the number of persons arrested for robbery: male and female arrests decreased 18.1 percent and 17.4 percent, respectively since 1997. Juvenile arrests also declined for both sexes from 1997 to 2001, male arrests dropping 34.0 percent and female arrests falling 39.8 percent. (See Tables 34 and 35.)

Ten-year trend data showed that when comparing robbery arrests of 2001 with those of 1992, overall arrests were down 25.6 percent, with arrests of males declining 26.8 percent and arrests of females dipping 14.0 percent. Arrests of male juveniles fell 32.5 percent from 1992, and arrests of female juveniles dropped 28.9 percent. (See Tables 32 and 33.)

Distribution

In 2001, a total of 62.0 percent of the persons arrested for robbery were under 25 years of age. The majority of the arrestees, 89.9 percent, were males. By race, 53.8 percent of arrestees were black, 44.5 percent were white, and 1.7 percent were other races. (See Tables 41, 42, and 43.) Breakdowns of male and female arrestees by age are presented in Tables 39 and 40.

Figure 2.10

Robbery Categories
Percent change from 1997

Street

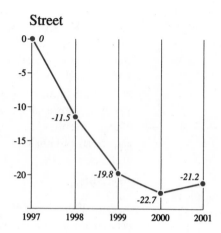

Commercial house

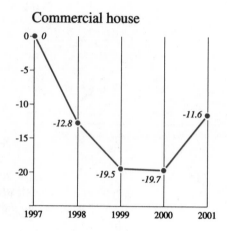

Gas station

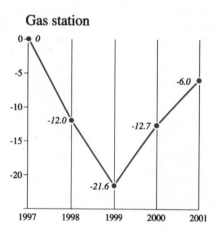

Convenience store

Residence

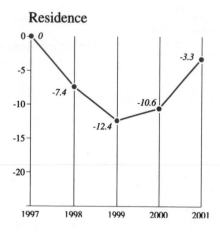

Bank

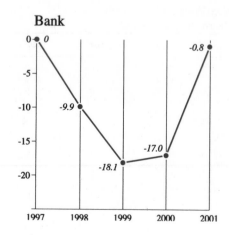

Aggravated Assault

Definition

According to the Uniform Crime Reporting Program, an aggravated assault is an unlawful attack by one person upon another for the purpose of inflicting severe or aggravated bodily injury. This type of assault is usually accompanied by the use of a weapon or by means likely to produce death or great bodily harm. Attempts are included since it is not necessary that an injury result when a gun, knife, or other weapon is used which could and probably would result in serious personal injury if the crime were successfully completed.

Trend

Year	Number of offenses	Rate per 100,000 inhabitants
2000	911,706	324.0
2001	907,219	318.5
Percent change	-0.5	-1.7

National Trends, Rates, and Distributions

With an estimated 907,219 offenses nationally, aggravated assaults accounted for 63.1 percent of the violent crimes in 2001. The number of aggravated assault offenses in 2001 was the lowest since 1987. A 2-, 5-, and 10-year trend analysis showed that the estimated total represented a 0.5-percent decline from 2000 data, an 11.3-percent decrease from the 1997 level, and a 19.5-percent decline from the 1992 total. (See Table 1.)

There were 318.5 reported victims of aggravated assault per 100,000 inhabitants in 2001. Two-, 5-, and 10-year trend data showed that the rate was 1.7 percent lower than in 2000, 16.6 percent lower than it was in 1997, and 27.9 percent lower than in 1992. (See Table 1.)

In 2001, personal weapons such as hands, fists, and feet were used in 27.9 percent of the aggravated assaults; firearms in 18.3 percent; and knives or cutting instruments in 17.8 percent. Blunt objects or other dangerous weapons were used in the remaining 36.0 percent. (See Table 2.24.)

Three of the four weapon categories showed increases in usage when comparing 2001 figures to those from 2000, with personal weapons (hands, fists, feet, etc.) showing the only decrease, 2.3 percent. The increases included firearms, 1.4 percent; other weapons, 0.6 percent; and knives or other cutting instruments, 0.1 percent. (See Table 15.)

Regional Offense Distributions and Rates

The United States is divided into four regions: the Northeast, the Midwest, the South, and the West. (See Appendix III.) In 2001, 42.7 percent of the aggravated assault volume occurred in the South, the Nation's most populous region. The Western Region followed with 23.6 percent, the Midwest Region with 18.8 percent, and the Northeast Region with 15.0 percent. (See Table 3.)

Table 2.23

Aggravated Assault by Month
Percent Distribution, 1997-2001

Month	1997	1998	1999	2000	2001
January	7.5	7.9	7.9	7.6	7.5
February	7.0	7.0	7.0	7.4	7.0
March	8.3	8.1	8.0	8.5	8.4
April	8.2	8.3	8.3	8.4	8.6
May	9.3	9.1	9.1	9.3	9.1
June	9.0	8.9	8.8	8.6	8.6
July	9.5	9.4	9.5	9.0	9.0
August	9.4	9.4	9.2	8.9	8.7
September	8.8	8.7	8.5	8.6	8.8
October	8.4	8.3	8.6	8.7	8.8
November	7.5	7.4	7.7	7.5	7.8
December	7.2	7.4	7.5	7.5	7.7

Regionally, the aggravated assault rates ranged from 253.2 per 100,000 inhabitants in the Northeast to 380.0 per 100,000 in the South. The rates were down in all but one region. The Northeast, West, and South recorded rate decreases of 3.0, 2.7, and 2.0, respectively; however, the rate in the Midwest increased 1.0 percent. (See Table 4.)

Community Types

In 2001, the Nation's Metropolitan Statistical Areas (MSAs) experienced a rate of 343.6 aggravated assaults per 100,000 inhabitants. Cities outside MSAs had a rate of 295.0 aggravated assaults per 100,000 inhabitants, and rural counties had a rate of 168.4 aggravated assaults. (See Table 2.)

Population Groups Trends

By population group, the largest decrease in aggravated assaults, 2.9 percent, was reported in cities with 25,000 to 49,999 inhabitants, followed by cities of under 10,000 in population with a 1.4-percent decline from 2000 data. Cities with 50,000 to 99,999 inhabitants showed a 1.1-percent drop, cities with populations of 250,000 and over had a 0.8-percent decline, and cities with a population of 10,000 to 24,999 experienced a 0.4-percent fall. An increase of 0.2 percent occurred in cities with populations of 100,000 to 249,999 in 2001. Rural counties showed an increase of less than one percent (0.5), and suburban

counties experienced a 1.1-percent decline in aggravated assaults. (See Table 12.)

Clearances

Overall, law enforcement agencies nationwide cleared 56.1 percent of reported aggravated assaults in 2001. Law enforcement in cities with less than 10,000 in population reported the highest percentage of clearances for aggravated assaults, 65.7 percent. Those in rural and suburban counties recorded clearance percentages of 64.9 and 61.7, respectively. (See Table 25.)

Aggravated assaults involving personal weapons such as hands, fists, or feet were cleared 63.8 percent of the time. Aggravated assaults using a knife or cutting instrument were cleared 61.9 percent of the time. Incidents that involved firearms were cleared 41.1 percent of the time. Aggravated assaults using other weapons were cleared 55.3 percent of the time. (See Table 27.)

Geographically, the Northeastern States had the highest percentage of aggravated assaults cleared by arrest—64.4 percent. The Western States followed with 57.8 percent, the Southern States with 53.7 percent, and the Midwestern States with 52.2 percent of aggravated assaults cleared by arrest. (See Table 26.)

Clearances and Juveniles

When an offender under the age of 18 is cited to appear in juvenile court or before other juvenile authorities, the UCR Program records that incident as a clearance by arrest even though a physical arrest may not have occurred. In addition, according to Program definitions, clearances involving both adult and juvenile offenders are classified as adult clearances.

Of the aggravated assault clearances reported both nationally and collectively in the Nation's cities, 11.8 percent involved only persons under the age of 18. In suburban counties, 12.4 percent of aggravated assault clearances involved only juveniles; in rural counties, 10.1 percent of aggravated assault clearances were of persons under the age of 18. (See Table 28.)

Table 2.24

Aggravated Assault, Types of Weapons Used
Percent Distribution by Region, 2001

Region	Total all weapons[1]	Firearms	Knives or cutting instruments	Other weapons (clubs, blunt objects, etc.)	Personal weapons
Total	100.0	18.3	17.8	36.0	27.9
Northeastern States	100.0	13.9	18.4	33.7	34.0
Midwestern States	100.0	19.4	17.2	35.3	28.1
Southern States	100.0	20.0	19.5	38.7	21.9
Western States	100.0	16.8	15.2	32.7	35.3

[1] Because of rounding, the percentages may not add to total.

Figure 2.11

Aggravated Assault
Percent change from 1997

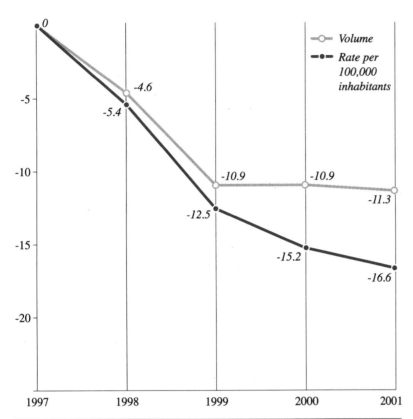

Arrests

Approximately 477,809 persons were arrested for aggravated assault in 2001. Of reported arrests, 79.9 percent were of males and the remaining 20.1 percent were of females. (See Tables 29 and 42.) Sixty-four percent of arrestees for aggravated assault were white, 33.7 percent were black, and the remaining 2.3 percent were of all other races. (See Table 43.)

Total aggravated assault arrests were down 0.1 percent in 2001 from the 2000 figure. (See Table 36.) A comparison of the 5-year figures from 1997 to 2001 showed a 9.4-percent decrease in the total arrests, a 13.2-percent decrease in juvenile arrests, and an 8.8-percent decline in adult arrests. (See Table 34.) Ten-year trend data showed a decline of 4.4 percent in the total arrests, a 13.8-percent decrease in juvenile arrests, and a 2.8-percent drop in adult arrests. (See Table 32.)

Definition

In the UCR Program, property crime includes the offenses of burglary, larceny-theft, motor vehicle theft, and arson. The object of the theft-type offenses is the taking of money or property, but there is no force or threat of force against the victims. Arson is included in the property crime category since it involves the destruction of property, although its victims may be subjected to force. However, because of limited participation and varying collection procedures by local agencies, only limited data are available for arson. Arson statistics are included in trend, clearance, and arrest tables throughout *Crime in the United States*, but they are not included in any estimated volume data. More information on this offense is provided in the arson section in this report.

Trend

Year	Number of offenses[1]	Rate per 100,000 inhabitants[1]
2000	10,182,584	3,618.3
2001	10,412,395	3,656.1
Percent change	+2.3	+1.0

[1]Does not include arson. See Crime Index Tabulations.

National Distributions

Volume

There were an estimated 10,412,395 property crimes reported in 2001. This number reflects an overall increase of 2.3 percent from the offenses reported in 2000, the first year-to-year increase since 1991. In a 5- and 10-year trend analysis, the 2001 volume showed a 9.9-percent decrease when compared to the 1997 volume and a 16.7-percent decrease from the 1992 level.

In 2001, the estimated number of reported motor vehicle thefts represented the largest increase among the property crimes—5.7 percent. Burglary and larceny-theft offenses increased 2.9 percent and 1.5 percent, respectively. (See Table 1.) Although arson is a property crime, it is excluded from the property crime totals.

Rate

The Nation experienced an overall property crime rate of 3,656.1 offenses per 100,000 inhabitants, a 1.0-percent increase from the 2000 rate. The 2001 property crime rate showed a decline of 15.3 percent when compared to the 1997 rate, and a decrease of 25.4 percent when compared to the 1992 rate. The 2001 property crime rate marked the first year-to-year increase since 1991.

Distribution

In 2001, property crimes comprised 87.9 percent of the Crime Index total. Larceny-theft accounted for the highest volume of offenses— 68.0 percent of the Nation's estimated property

Table 2.25					

Property Crime Total by Month
Percent Distribution, 1997-2001

Month	1997	1998	1999	2000	2001
January	8.2	8.6	8.0	7.8	7.8
February	7.3	7.5	7.2	7.3	6.8
March	8.0	8.2	8.0	8.2	7.8
April	8.0	8.0	7.9	7.9	7.9
May	8.4	8.4	8.3	8.6	8.4
June	8.4	8.5	8.6	8.6	8.4
July	9.1	8.9	9.1	9.1	9.0
August	9.0	9.0	9.2	9.2	9.0
September	8.5	8.4	8.5	8.5	8.4
October	8.8	8.5	8.7	8.8	9.2
November	8.0	7.9	8.2	8.1	8.5
December	8.3	8.2	8.4	8.0	8.7

crimes and 59.7 percent of the Crime Index offenses.

In 2001, the estimated dollar loss attributed to property crime losses (excluding arson) was $16.6 billion, an increase of 5.6 percent from the 2000 estimate. Burglary losses were up 9.0 percent from the 2000 level; larceny-theft increased 1.9 percent, and motor vehicle theft rose 6.8 percent from the prior year's estimates.

Arson offenses, which are excluded from estimated property crime tabulations because of limited coverage and law enforcement participation, were estimated at 68,967 in 2001, with an average loss of $11,098. (See Table 2.32.)

Regional Offense Distributions and Rates

The United States is divided into four regions: the Northeast, the Midwest, the South, and the West. (More information on UCR area definitions can be found in Appendix III.) In 2001, data collected regarding the Nation's four regions reflect the following:

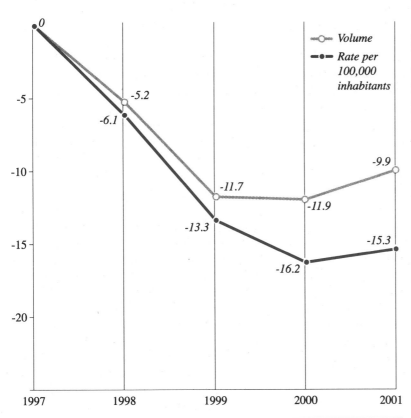

Figure 2.12

Property Crime
Percent change from 1997

The Northeast

The Northeast accounted for 13.3 percent of the total number of property crimes reported in 2001. (See Table 3.) This region was the only region to experience decreases in both the number of property crime offenses and the rate per 100,000 inhabitants. The Northeast had a 1.3-percent decline in offenses when compared to the 2000 total, and a 1.7-percent decline in the property crime rate per 100,000 persons. (See Table 4.)

The Midwest

The Midwest accounted for 22.0 percent of the total property crime offenses reported in 2001. (See Table 3.) This region recorded an increase in both volume (1.6 percent) and the rate per 100,000 inhabitants (1.2 percent) over the prior year's volume and rate. (See Table 4.)

The South

The South accounted for 40.9 percent of the total property crimes reported during 2001. (See Table 3.) This region experienced a 1.9-percent rise in the volume of property crimes and a slight increase (0.3 percent) in the rate per 100,000 inhabitants. (See Table 4.)

The West

The West reported 23.7 percent of the total property crimes during 2001. (See Table 3.) The region reflected a 5.6-percent increase in the volume of property crimes compared to the 2000 volume and a 3.5-percent rise in the property crime rate per 100,000 inhabitants. (See Table 4.)

Community Types

The UCR Program designates three types of communities when presenting crime data: Metropolitan Statistical Areas (MSA), cities outside MSAs, and rural counties. In 2001, MSAs accounted for 85.6 percent of the total estimated property crime offenses and reported an estimated rate of 3,914.9 offenses per 100,000 persons. Cities outside of MSAs accounted for 8.9 percent of the total estimated property crime offenses and had an estimated rate of 4,057.6 offenses per 100,000 inhabitants. Rural counties accounted for 5.6 percent of the total 2001 property crimes and had an estimated rate of 1,681.4 offenses per 100,000 persons. (See Table 2.)

Population Groups Trends and Rates

The Nation's cities collectively, reported an increase of 2.3 percent in the number of property crimes reported in 2001 over the prior year's number. All city groups experienced increases in the number of property crimes reported, the largest increase (4.5 percent) recorded in cities with populations of 250,000 to 499,999. The smallest increase, 0.7 percent, was reported in cities of 1 million or more inhabitants. (See Table 12.)

Clearances

Clearances occur either by arrest or by exceptional means, i.e., when elements beyond the control of law enforcement prevents the placing of formal charges against the offender. (More information regarding clearances can be found in Section III of this report.) In 2001, overall clearances for property crime offenses totaled 16.2 percent. (See Table 25.)

Regionally, clearances of property crimes during 2001 were as follows: the Northeast, 19.8 percent; the Midwest, 15.9 percent; the South, 16.1 percent; and the West, 14.8 percent. In the Nation's cities collectively, 16.2 percent of property crimes were cleared during the year. Among the individual city population groups, the highest property crime clearance percentage in 2001 was reported in cities with 10,000 to 24,999 population—21.2 percent. The lowest percentage of property crimes cleared—10.8 percent—was experienced in cities with populations of 500,000 to 999,999. Additionally, suburban and rural counties each reported property clearance percentages of 15.2 percent and 18.1 percent, respectively. (See Tables 25 and 26.)

Clearances and Juveniles

When an offender under the age of 18 is cited to appear in juvenile court or before other juvenile authorities, the UCR Program records that incident as a clearance by arrest, even though a physical arrest may not have occurred. In addition, according to Program definitions, clearances involving both adult and juvenile offenders are classified as adult clearances.

Nationally, juveniles accounted for 21.1 percent of the overall property crime clearances in 2001. The highest percentage of juvenile clearances—24.0 percent—occurred in cities with populations of 50,000 to 99,999. The lowest percentage of juvenile clearances—17.1 percent—was recorded in the Nation's rural counties. (See Table 28.)

Arrests

Total Arrests

The number of estimated property crime arrests for 2001 was 1,618,465. This figure made up 72.1 percent of the estimated Part I crime (Crime Index offenses) arrests and 11.8 percent of the Nation's total estimated arrests during 2001. The greatest percentage of arrests made for property crimes was for larceny-theft offenses—71.7 percent. The smallest percentage of arrests—1.2 percent—was made for arson offenses. (See Table 29.)

Arrest Rates

The U.S. experienced a rate of 581.8 property crime arrests per 100,000 inhabitants in 2001. The highest property crime arrest rate—608.4 arrests per 100,000 inhabitants—occurred in the Midwest. The lowest property crime arrest rate—481.1 per 100,000 people—was reported in the Northeast. (Table 30 provides breakdowns of arrests for all of the regions.)

The Nation's cities collectively experienced a rate of 691.2 property crime arrests per 100,000 inhabitants. The highest rate—758.8 per 100,000 people—occurred in cities with populations of 250,000 and over. The lowest rate—618.8 per 100,000 people—occurred in cities with populations under 10,000. Suburban and rural counties reported property crime arrest rates of 358.0 and 289.2 per 100,000 inhabitants, respectively. (See Table 31.)

Arrest Trends

Overall, property crime arrests declined slightly—1 percent—from 2000 to 2001. However, among the individual property crimes, arrests increased 0.4 percent for burglaries, 2.7 percent for motor vehicle thefts, and 14.7 percent for arson offenses. The number of arrests for larceny-thefts declined 1.9 percent; however, with its considerable volume, this decrease offset the increases in arson, burglary, and motor vehicle theft arrests and resulted in an overall decline in property crime arrests for 2001. (See Table 36.)

Regarding arrests of juveniles, overall property crime arrests of juveniles decreased 5.6 percent in 2001 when compared to the 2000 figure. Conversely, property crime arrests for adults increased 1.3 percent. (See Table 36.)

Five-year trends in property crime arrest data indicated a 20.0-percent decline in arrests from 1997 to 2001. A 10-year comparison of total property crime arrests between 1992 and 2001 showed a 26.2-percent decrease. Tables 32 and 34 provide more information regarding trend data.

Distribution

In 2001, 69.6 percent of all persons arrested for property crimes were over the age of 18, and 30.4 percent were under age 18. (See Table 38.) Additionally, 69.6 percent of all persons arrested for property crimes in 2001 were males, and 30.4 percent were females. (See Table 42.) Of the persons arrested for property crime offenses, 66.0 percent were white, 31.4 percent were black, and the remainder were other races (Asian or Pacific Islander and American Indian or Alaskan Native). (See Table 43.)

Burglary

Definition

The Uniform Crime Reporting Program defines burglary as the unlawful entry of a structure to commit a felony or theft. The use of force to gain entry is not required to classify an offense as burglary. Burglary in this Program is categorized into three subclassifications: forcible entry, unlawful entry where no force is used, and attempted forcible entry.

Trend

Year	Number of offenses	Rate per 100,000 inhabitants
2000	2,050,992	728.8
2001	2,109,767	740.8
Percent change	+2.9	+1.6

National Offenses, Trends, and Distributions

The number of estimated burglaries for the Nation in 2001 rose 2.9 percent over those reported the previous year. In a 5- and 10-year trend analysis, the estimated 2,109,767 burglaries in 2001 represented a 14.3-percent decline from 1997 totals and a 29.2-percent drop from 1992 estimates. (See Table 1.) When compared to the 1982 estimate, the year with the highest burglary estimate during the last two decades, the 20-year trend showed that the 2001 burglary total was significantly lower, down 38.8 percent. (Based on Table 1.)

The national burglary rate of 740.8 per 100,000 inhabitants for 2001 represented a 1.6-percent increase from the previous year's rate. However, this rate was significantly lower than the totals from 5 and 10 years ago. The 2001 rate was 19.4 percent lower than the 1997 rate and 36.6 percent below the 1992 level. (See Table 1.) In a 20-year comparison, the 2001 rate was 50.2 percent less than the 1982 rate. (Based on Table 1.)

For those agencies that reported statistics for all 12 months of 2001, the data showed that forcible entry accounted for 63.3 percent of burglaries, unlawful entry comprised 30.2 percent, and attempted forcible entry accounted for 6.5 percent. (See Table 19.)

The majority of burglaries, 65.2 percent, were residential. Most residential burglaries, 61.0 percent, occurred during the day, and most nonresidential burglaries, 58.0 percent, occurred at night. Burglaries totaled an estimated $3.3 billion for an average loss per burglary of $1,545. Residential burglaries averaged $1,381, and nonresidential burglaries averaged $1,615 in 2001. (See Table 23.)

The United States is divided into four regions: the Northeast, the Midwest, the South, and the West. A map of the United States delineating the regions is included in Appendix

Table 2.26

Burglary by Month
Percent Distribution, 1997-2001

Month	1997	1998	1999	2000	2001
January	8.4	8.9	8.3	8.1	7.8
February	7.2	7.5	7.2	7.2	6.6
March	7.9	8.2	7.9	8.0	7.6
April	7.8	8.0	7.7	7.8	7.7
May	8.3	8.3	8.2	8.5	8.3
June	8.2	8.2	8.4	8.4	8.2
July	9.1	9.0	9.0	9.2	9.0
August	9.0	9.0	9.1	9.2	9.1
September	8.7	8.4	8.7	8.6	8.6
October	8.8	8.4	8.6	8.7	9.3
November	8.2	7.9	8.4	8.3	8.8
December	8.6	8.2	8.5	8.1	8.9

III. Estimated crime volume, rates, and percent changes by region are published in Table 4.

The Northeast

The fewest burglaries occurred in the Northeastern States, 12.0 percent. (See Table 3.) The Northeast was the only region of the country to experience a decrease in burglary over the previous year's volume with a drop of 1.2 percent. The Northeast was also the only region to report a decrease in the burglary rate, 470.0 per 100,000 in population, down 1.6 percent from the 2000 rate. (See Table 4.)

The Midwest

The Midwestern States accounted for 20.8 percent of burglaries in 2001. (See Table 3.) The burglary total represented a 2.6-percent increase over the previous year's total. The burglary rate of 677.7 per 100,000 persons denoted a 2.1-percent increase in the region's rate since 2000. (See Table 4.)

The South

Proportionately, most burglaries were reported in the Southern States, 44.7 percent. (See Table 3.) The increase in the number of estimated burglaries from 2000 was 4.1 percent in these states collectively. The burglary rate for the region, 926.8 per 100,000 inhabitants, increased by 2.5 percent from the 2000 rate. (See Table 4.)

The West

Western States accounted for 22.5 percent of the estimated burglaries for 2001. (See Table 3.) This total represented a 2.9-percent increase over the 2000 level. States in this region reported a slight upward trend in the burglary rate, 736.4 per 100,000, an increase of 0.9 percent over the rate from the previous year's rate. (See Table 4.)

Community Types

Metropolitan Statistical Areas (MSAs), which made up approximately 80 percent of the total U.S. population in 2001, recorded a rate of 768.8 burglaries per 100,000 persons. For cities outside MSAs, which comprised approximately 8.0 percent of the Nation's population, the rate was 764.3 burglaries per 100,000 inhabitants, and in rural counties, which accounted for approximately 12 percent of the U.S. population during 2001, the rate was 540.1. MSAs comprised 82.9 percent of the estimated burglary volume; other cities made up 8.2 percent; and rural counties, 8.8 percent. (See Table 2.)

Population Groups Trends and Rates

Cities as a whole showed a 2.7-percent increase in burglaries in 2001 over burglaries reported in 2000. Among the population groups, cities with populations of 500,000 to 999,999 saw the largest 1-year increase at 6.3 percent. Cities with populations of 1 million and over in population reported an overall 0.3-percent decrease in burglaries. Both suburban and rural counties showed an increase in reported burglaries, 3.1 percent and 1.9 percent, respectively. (See Table 12.) Collectively, cities recorded a rate of 846.2 burglaries per 100,000 inhabitants. Suburban counties registered a rate of 649.1 per 100,000 persons, and rural counties

---

Figure 2.13

Burglary
Percent change from 1997

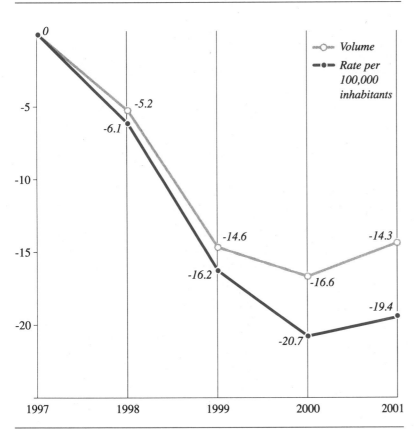

Legend:
- ○ Volume
- ● Rate per 100,000 inhabitants

Data points:
Volume: -5.2 (1998), -14.6 (1999), -16.6 (2000), -14.3 (2001)
Rate: -6.1 (1998), -16.2 (1999), -20.7 (2000), -19.4 (2001)

Figure 2.14

Burglary
Percent change from 1997

Residential

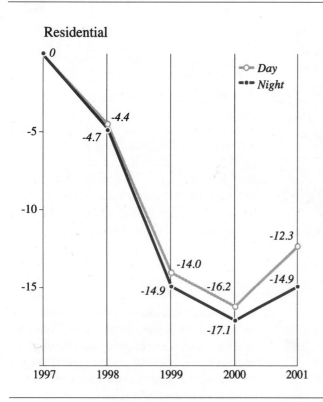

Nonresidential

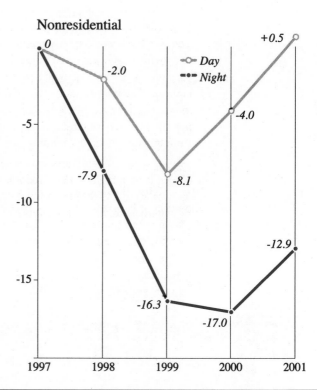

noted a rate of 567.1 per 100,000 inhabitants. (See Table 16.)

Clearances

Clearances occur either by arrest or by exceptional means, i.e., when circumstances beyond the control of law enforcement prevent the placing of formal charges against the offender. (More information regarding clearances can be found in Section III of this report.) In the Nation in 2001, 12.7 percent of burglary offenses were cleared. (See Table 25.) The highest percentage of reported clearances involved unlawful entry, 14.1 percent, followed by forcible entry, 12.3 percent, and attempted forcible entry, 10.7 percent. (See Table 27.)

Law enforcement in the Northeast Region cleared 16.7 percent of burglary offenses. Those in the South cleared 12.7 percent of total burglaries; in the West, 12.1 percent; and in the Midwest, 11.1 percent. (See Table 26.)

Among the Nation's population groups, cities with populations under 10,000 revealed the highest proportion of burglary offenses cleared at 16.4 percent. Those cities with populations of 500,000 to 999,999 cleared the fewest of their burglary offenses, 8.3 percent. Total clearances for all cities was 12.3 percent. (See Table 25.)

When an offender under the age of 18 is cited to appear in juvenile court or before other juvenile authorities, the UCR Program records that incident as cleared by arrest, even though a physical arrest may not have occurred. In addition, according to Program definitions, clearances involving both adult and juvenile offenders are classified as adult clearances. In 2001, 18.5 percent of all burglary clearances involved only juveniles. Communities with populations of fewer than 10,000 had the highest percentage of burglary clearances that involved only juvenile offenders, 21.9 percent. Cities with 500,000 to 999,999 inhabitants had the lowest juvenile clearances for burglary at 14.1 percent. (See Table 28.)

Arrests

The estimated number of arrests nation-wide for burglary for 2001 was 291,444, an arrest rate of 103.3 per 100,000 inhabitants. (See Tables 29 and 30.) Law enforcement agencies in the West recorded the highest rate of burglary arrests, 124.9 per 100,000. Those in the Southern States had an arrest rate of 108.9 per 100,000 persons, followed by the Northeast, 82.2, and the Midwest, 78.0. (See Table 30.) Among the population groups, arrest rates ranged from a high of 131.1 recorded for cities of 100,000 to 249,999 to a low of 84.9 reported by suburban counties. (See Table 31.)

Arrest Trends

Overall, arrests for burglary increased 0.4 percent when compared to the previous year's figure. However, the number of burglary arrests nationwide was considerably lower than the number from 5 and 10 years ago. Burglary arrests were down 18.7 percent from the 1997 figure and 32.7 percent from the 1992 figure. Arrests of juveniles for burglary showed a decrease of 5.6 percent from the 2000 total, 30.3 percent from the 1997 total, and a drop of 40.1 percent from the 1992 total. Arrests of adults in 2001 rose 3.4 percent from the previous year's total; however, the 2001 total is 12.1 percent lower than the 1997 level and 28.7 percent below the 1992 number. (See Tables 32, 34, and 36.)

Distribution

By age of arrestees, 31.0 percent of burglary arrestees were juveniles, and 11.7 percent of the total arrestees were under age 15. (See Table 41.) By gender, males comprised the majority of burglary arrestees, 86.4 percent, in 2001. Of these arrests, 31.6 percent were males under age 18. (Based on Table 39.) For females, 13.6 percent were arrested for burglary and of those, 27.4 percent were juveniles. (Based on Table 40.)

By race, 69.4 percent of burglary arrestees were white, 28.5 percent were black, and other races accounted for the remaining 2.1 percent. Whites made up 68.1 percent, blacks 29.9 percent, and other races comprised 2.0 percent of adult arrestees. For individuals under age 18 arrested for burglary, 72.3 percent were white, 25.2 percent were black, and 2.5 percent were of all other races. (See Table 43.)

Larceny-Theft

Definition

Larceny-theft is the unlawful taking, carrying, leading, or riding away of property from the possession or constructive possession of another. It includes crimes such as shoplifting, pocket-picking, purse-snatching, thefts from motor vehicles, thefts of motor vehicle parts and accessories, bicycle thefts, etc., in which no use of force, violence, or fraud occurs. In the Uniform Crime Reporting Program, this crime category does not include embezzlement, confidence games, forgery, and worthless checks. Motor vehicle theft is also excluded from this category inasmuch as it is a separate Crime Index offense.

Trend

Year	Number of offenses	Rate per 100,000 inhabitants
2000	6,971,590	2,477.3
2001	7,076,171	2,484.6
Percent change	+1.5	+0.3

National Trends, Rates, and Distributions

In 2001, the estimated number of larceny-theft offenses in the Nation exceeded 7 million and cost the Nation an estimated $5.2 billion in losses. Law enforcement agencies reported the estimated 7,076,171 offenses in the following categories:

- Pocket-picking
- Purse-snatching
- Shoplifting
- Thefts from Motor Vehicles (Except theft of motor vehicle parts and accessories)
- Theft of Motor Vehicle Parts and Accessories
- Theft of Bicycles
- Theft from Buildings
- Theft from Coin-Operated Device or Machine
- All Other Larceny-Theft not Specifically Classified.

Examples of thefts in the all other category include thefts from fenced enclosures, boats, and airplanes; and of animals, lawn-mowers, hand tools, and farm and construction equipment, as well as incidents of taking gasoline from a self-service gasoline station without paying.

The estimated 7,076,171 larceny-theft offenses reported to law enforcement in the Nation translated into a larceny every 4.5 seconds and accounted for 59.7 percent of all Crime Index offenses and 68.0 percent of all property crimes. The 2001 estimate was up 1.5 percent from the 2000 estimate of 6,971,590 offenses. However, when looking at the offense over a 5-year and 10-year span, larceny-thefts

Table 2.27

Larceny-theft by Month
Percent Distribution, 1997-2001

Month	1997	1998	1999	2000	2001
January	8.0	8.4	7.8	7.6	7.7
February	7.2	7.5	7.2	7.3	6.8
March	8.0	8.2	8.0	8.2	7.9
April	8.0	8.1	8.0	7.9	8.0
May	8.4	8.4	8.4	8.6	8.6
June	8.6	8.6	8.7	8.8	8.6
July	9.2	9.0	9.1	9.2	9.0
August	9.1	9.0	9.2	9.2	9.1
September	8.5	8.4	8.5	8.5	8.4
October	8.8	8.5	8.7	8.8	9.1
November	7.9	7.8	8.1	8.0	8.3
December	8.3	8.2	8.3	7.9	8.6

Figure 2.15

Larceny-theft
Percent change from 1997

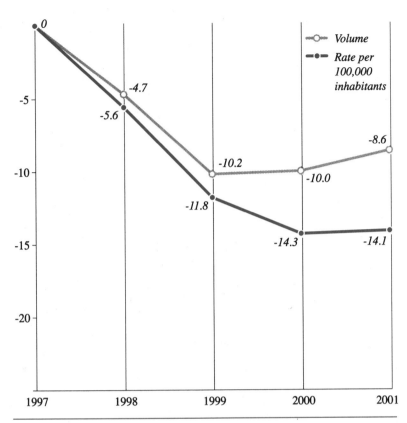

○ Volume
● Rate per 100,000 inhabitants

0
-4.7
-5.6
-10.2
-11.8
-10.0
-8.6
-14.3
-14.1

1997 1998 1999 2000 2001

In 2001, the Nation experienced a rate of larceny-thefts of 2,484.6 per 100,000 population. This figure was a slight increase of 0.3 percent over the 2000 estimated rate but a 14.1-percent decrease in comparison to the 1997 rate and a 19.9-percent decrease when compared to the 1992 rate. (See Table 1.)

Regional Offense Distributions and Rates

The United States is divided into four regions: the Northeast, the Midwest, the South, and the West. (See Appendix III.) In 2001, data collected regarding the Nation's four regions reflect the following: The South, the most populous region, had 40.7 percent of all larceny offenses. The West had 22.9 percent of the total, the Midwest, 22.8 percent, and the Northeast, 13.6 percent of all larcenies. (See Table 3.)

When 2001 regional volumes are compared to the 2000 figures, the lone decrease in volume occurred in the Northeast, with a 1.4-percent drop. Of the regions posting increases, the volume of larceny-thefts in the West rose 4.8 percent. In the Midwest, the volume of larceny-theft offenses increased 1.1 percent, and in the South, the volume was up 0.9 percent. Among the geographic regions in 2001, the South had a rate per 100,000 inhabitants of 2,826.7, and the West had a rate of 2,518.5. The Midwest reported a rate of 2,491.5 per 100,000 inhabitants, and the Northeast, a rate of 1,788.4 per 100,000 population. The larceny-theft rate per 100,000 inhabitants was up 2.7 percent and 0.6 percent in the West and Midwest, respectively; the rate declined 0.6 percent in the South and 1.8 percent in the Northeast. (See Table 4.)

decreased 8.6 percent when compared to the 7,743,760 estimated offenses reported in 1997, and 10.6 percent compared to the 7,915,199 offenses reported in 1992. (See Table 1.)

Community Types

By community types, Metropolitan Statistical Areas had a rate of 2,647.0 larceny offenses per 100,000 inhabitants. Cities outside MSAs had a rate of 3,087.7, and rural counties experienced a rate of 1,014.0 per 100,000 population. (See Table 2.)

Population Groups Trends and Rates

Larceny-thefts increased in all population groups when comparing 2001 and 2000 volume figures. Increases ranged from 3.2 percent in cities with populations of 250,000 to 499,999 to

Table 2.28

Larceny-theft
Percent Distribution by Region, 2001

Type	United States total	North-eastern states	Mid-western states	Southern states	Western states
Total[1]	100.0	100.0	100.0	100.0	100.0
Pocket-picking	0.5	1.1	0.3	0.4	0.4
Purse-snatching	0.5	1.0	0.4	0.4	0.6
Shoplifting	13.8	15.0	12.8	13.3	14.7
From motor vehicles (except accessories)	25.8	21.1	23.9	24.8	31.2
Motor vehicle accessories	10.2	7.9	10.7	10.1	11.2
Bicycles	4.1	5.9	4.5	3.4	4.2
From buildings	13.3	16.8	14.8	11.4	13.7
From coin-operated machines	0.7	0.6	0.6	0.8	0.7
All others	31.0	30.6	31.9	35.4	23.3

[1] Because of rounding, the percentages may not add to total.

Figure 2.16

Larceny-theft categories
Percent change from 1997

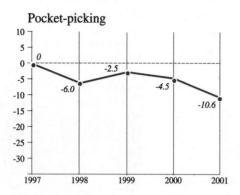

Pocket-picking

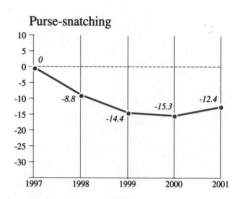

Purse-snatching

Shoplifting

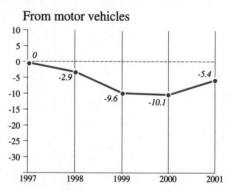

From motor vehicles

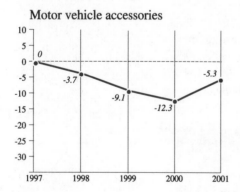

Motor vehicle accessories

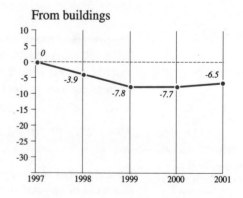

From buildings

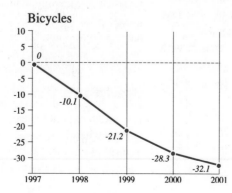

Bicycles

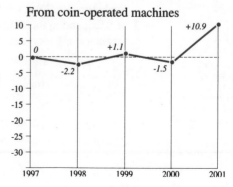

From coin-operated machines

0.5 percent each in cities with 1 million and over inhabitants and cities of 10,000 to 24,999 in population. (See Table 12.) Among cities, those with populations of 500,000 to 999,999 had the highest rate per 100,000 inhabitants at 3,968.8, and cities with a population of 10,000 to 24,999 had the lowest rate at 2,646.9 per 100,000 inhabitants. Suburban counties had a rate of 1,754.8; rural counties had a rate at 1,062.0 per 100,000 inhabitants. (See Table 16.)

Distribution

Nature

Thefts from motor vehicles accounted for 25.8 percent and shoplifting 13.8 percent of all larcenies in 2001. Thefts from buildings made up 13.3 percent of the total; 10.2 percent of larcenies were thefts of motor vehicle accessories. Stolen bicycles comprised 4.1 percent of larcenies. The remainder of larceny-thefts were distributed among coin-operated machines, pocket-pickings, purse-snatchings, and all other larceny-thefts. (See Table 23.)

Loss by Dollar Value

An estimated $5.2 billion in property was lost because of larceny-theft in 2001, an increase from the 2000 estimate of $5.1 billion. The average dollar value per offense was $730, an increase from the $727 in 2000. (See Table 23.)

In 2001, thefts from buildings was the larceny-theft offense with the highest average loss, $1,037. For thefts from motor vehicles, the average value loss was $719, and for thefts of motor vehicle accessories, $451. Purse-snatchings had an average value loss of $331, and thefts of bicycles an average loss of $318. Pocket-picking resulted in an average value loss of $305, and in thefts from coin-operated machines, the loss was $286. The category with the lowest average loss, $182, was shoplifting. For the all other category, the average dollar loss was $1,024. (See Table 23.)

Losses over $200 accounted for 39.4 percent of larceny-thefts, up 3.8 percent from 2000 figures; losses under $50 made up 37.6 percent of larceny-theft offenses, which was up 1.8 percent from 2000; and the remaining 23.0 percent were losses ranging from $50–$200, a 0.5-percent rise from 2000 data. Thefts of items over $200 had an average value of $1,770, thefts of items from $50–$200 had an average value of $115, and thefts of items under $50 had an average value of $18. (See Table 23.)

Trends by Category

Reported thefts from coin-operated machines increased 12.6 percent from 2000 data. Other categories with volume increases from 2000 to 2001 were thefts of motor vehicle accessories, 8.0 percent; thefts from motor vehicles, 5.2 percent; purse-snatchings, 3.4 percent; shoplifting, 2.7 percent; and thefts from buildings, 1.2 percent. However, pocket-picking offenses declined 6.4 percent from the 2000 figure, and thefts of bicycles were down 5.4 percent. (See Table 23.)

Among the larceny types, the sole category with an increase in offenses from 1997 to 2001 was thefts from coin-operated machines, with a 10.9-percent growth. The other larceny-theft categories all posted a reduction in the number of offenses. Thefts of bicycles dropped 32.1 percent when comparing 1997 and 2001 data. Other categories with decreases from 1997 to 2001 were shoplifting, 16.7 percent; purse-snatching, 12.4 percent; and pocket-picking, 10.6 percent. The number of thefts from buildings fell 6.5 percent; thefts from motor vehicles decreased 5.4 percent; and thefts of motor vehicle accessories fell 5.3 percent. (See Figure 2.16.)

Clearances

Of the larceny-thefts reported to law enforcement in 2001, 17.6 percent were cleared by arrest or exceptional means. By population group, cities with 10,000 to 24,999 inhabitants had the highest number of clearances among the Nation's cities, 22.5 percent, and cities with 500,000 to 999,999 inhabitants cleared the least of their larceny-theft offenses, 11.6 percent. Law enforcement in rural counties cleared 17.8 percent of larceny-thefts, and law enforcement in suburban counties cleared 16.0 percent. (See Table 25.)

Figure 2.17

Larceny-theft
Percent distribution[1] 2001

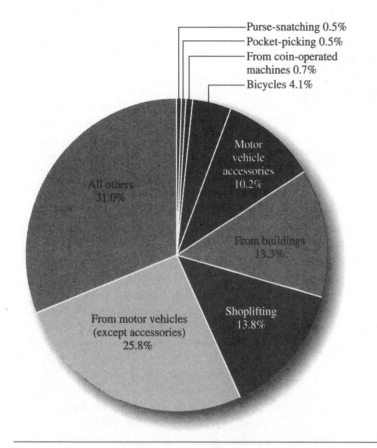

Purse-snatching 0.5%
Pocket-picking 0.5%
From coin-operated machines 0.7%
Bicycles 4.1%
Motor vehicle accessories 10.2%
All others 31.0%
From buildings 13.3%
Shoplifting 13.8%
From motor vehicles (except accessories) 25.8%

[1] Due to rounding, the percentages do not add to 100.0 percent.

Nearly 22 percent (21.9) of all larceny-theft clearances were of juveniles (persons under 18 years of age). By population group, cities with populations of 50,000 to 99,999 inhabitants had the largest percentage of clearances involving only juveniles—25.3. (See Table 28.)

Arrests

The number of estimated arrests for larceny-thefts in the Nation in 2001 was 1,160,821, or 8.5 percent of the 13.7 million total estimated arrests for the United States. Larceny arrests accounted for 71.7 percent of the 1.6 million estimated arrests for all property crimes, and 51.7 percent of the estimated 2.2 million arrests for all Crime Index offenses in 2001. (See Table 29.)

Larceny-theft arrests in 2001 were down 1.9 percent from the 2000 figure. Larceny-theft arrests of juveniles declined 6.3 percent from the 2000 figure. Adult arrests for larceny-thefts showed a slight increase, 0.2 percent, from the 2000 number. (See Table 36.) Arrests of juvenile males went down 9.2 percent, and arrests of juvenile females declined 1.3 percent. (See Table 37.)

In 2001, juvenile arrests accounted for 29.6 percent of all larceny-theft arrests, and adult arrests comprised 70.4 percent. (See Table 38.) Of the juveniles arrested for larceny-theft, 68.9 percent were white, 27.8 percent were black, 2.0 percent were Asian or Pacific Islander, and 1.4 percent were American Indian or Alaskan Native. (See Table 43.)

Males accounted for 63.5 percent of the total arrests for larceny-theft, and females accounted for 36.5 percent of the arrests. (See Table 42.) By race, 66.1 percent of arrestees for larceny-theft in 2001 were white, 31.2 percent were black, 1.5 percent were Asian or Pacific Islander, and the remaining 1.2 percent were American Indian or Alaskan Native. (See Table 43.)

Definition

Defined in the Uniform Crime Reporting Program as the theft or attempted theft of a motor vehicle, this offense category includes the stealing of automobiles, trucks, buses, motorcycles, motorscooters, snowmobiles, etc. The definition excludes the taking of a motor vehicle for temporary use by those persons having lawful access.

Trend

Year	Number of offenses	Rate per 100,000 inhabitants
2000	1,160,002	412.2
2001	1,226,457	430.6
Percent Change	+5.7	+4.5

National Trends, Rates, and Distributions

The estimated 1,226,457 motor vehicle thefts in the Nation in 2001 represent a 5.7-percent increase from the previous year's estimate. When compared to 5 and 10 years ago, the level of motor vehicle theft was down 9.4 percent from the 1997 level and declined 23.9 percent from the 1992 level. For 2001, the Nation's motor vehicle theft rate was 430.6 per 100,000 inhabitants. This rate was up 4.5 percent from the 2000 rate but was 14.8 percent lower than in 1997 and 31.8 percent below the 1992 level. (See Table 1.) By vehicle type, 336.9 automobiles and 86.5 trucks and buses were stolen per 100,000 inhabitants. The theft rate for all other vehicles was 33.4. (See Table 19.)

The average value of motor vehicles reported stolen in 2001 was $6,646. With the estimated total value of all motor vehicles stolen at $8.2 billion, approximately 62.0 percent of that amount was recovered. (See Tables 1, 23, and 24.)

Regional Offense Distributions and Rates

The U.S. is divided into four regions: the Northeast, the Midwest, the South, and the West. (See Appendix III.) In 2001, data collected regarding the Nation's four regions reflect the following:

The Northeast

The Northeastern States accounted for 14.0 percent of all motor vehicle thefts in 2001. (See Table 3.) The region experienced a slight drop, 0.6 percent, in the estimated volume of motor vehicle thefts from the 2000 estimate. The Northeast, with a rate of 318.8 motor vehicle thefts per 100,000 persons, was the only region of the Nation that experienced a decline in the motor vehicle theft rate with a 1.0-percent drop. (See Table 4.)

The Midwest

The Midwestern States reported 20.0 percent of the total estimated motor vehicle

Table 2.29

Motor Vehicle Theft by Month
Percent Distribution, 1997-2001

Month	1997	1998	1999	2000	2001
January	9.0	9.1	8.5	8.1	8.1
February	7.6	7.9	7.3	7.4	6.9
March	8.2	8.5	7.9	8.0	7.7
April	7.9	7.9	7.7	7.6	7.6
May	8.2	8.3	8.0	8.2	8.0
June	8.1	8.1	8.2	8.3	8.2
July	8.7	8.7	8.8	8.9	9.0
August	8.7	8.8	9.0	9.1	8.8
September	8.3	8.3	8.5	8.5	8.5
October	8.6	8.4	8.8	8.7	9.3
November	8.2	7.9	8.5	8.5	8.8
December	8.3	8.1	8.8	8.6	9.2

thefts. (See Table 3.) The total number of vehicle thefts in 2001 was a 3.4-percent increase from the previous year's number. The region had a rate of 379.9 vehicles stolen per 100,000 in population, accounting for a 2.9-percent increase over the 2000 rate. (See Table 4.)

The South

The Southern States reported the highest percentage of motor vehicle thefts among the Nation's four regions with 35.5 percent of the total estimate. (See Table 3.) This region saw a 4.0-percent increase from the 2000 estimate. The rate of 427.6 thefts per 100,000 in population was a 2.4-percent increase over the previous year's rate. (See Table 4.)

The West

The Western States accounted for 30.5 percent of the Nation's motor vehicle thefts. (See Table 3.) This region had the largest rise in the volume of vehicle thefts—12.9 percent—over the 2000 total. The West reported the highest motor vehicle theft rate at 579.7 offenses per 100,000 persons. This rate represents a 10.6-percent rise from the 2000 rate. (See Table 4.)

Community Types

Metropolitan Statistical Areas (MSAs) had a rate of 499.1 motor vehicle thefts per 100,000 persons and accounted for 92.6 percent of all motor vehicle theft offenses; cities outside MSAs, a rate of 205.5 vehicles stolen and 3.8 percent of offenses; and rural counties had a rate of 127.3 motor vehicle thefts per 100,000 persons and accounted for 3.6 percent of all stolen vehicle offenses. (See Table 2.)

Population Groups and Rates

All population groups experienced an increase in reported motor vehicle thefts with those cities 250,000 to 499,999 in population having the greatest increase at 11.3 percent. Cities with 1 million and over inhabitants registered the smallest increase at 2.5 percent. All county groups also saw increases in motor vehicle thefts as suburban counties experienced a 6.0-percent rise and rural counties had a 3.6-percent increase. (See Table 12.)

The highest rate of motor vehicle thefts, 1,072.4 per 100,000 inhabitants, was in cities with populations of 250,000 to 499,999. (See Table 16.) When broken down by vehicle type, cities with populations of 250,000 to 499,999 recorded the highest rate of automobile theft, 834.8 per 100,000 inhabitants. For trucks and buses, cities of 1 million and more in population had the highest theft rate at 279.0 per 100,000 inhabitants. When one examines the other vehicles category, cities of 1 million and over also had the highest theft rate with 58.0 per 100,000 in population. Rural counties had the lowest theft rate of automobiles at 78.5 and also for trucks and buses at 23.9. Cities of 10,000 to 24,999 had the lowest rate of other types of vehicles stolen at 23.9 per 100,000 persons. (See Table 19.)

Clearances

Nationally, clearances of motor vehicle thefts in 2001 totaled 13.6 percent. (See Table 25.) Clearances were highest in the Midwest and South at 15.6 percent. Motor vehicle thefts were cleared at 13.9 percent in the Northeast and 10.8 percent in the West. (See Table 26.)

All cities reporting combined to clear 12.8 percent of motor vehicle thefts. The Nation's smallest cities, those under 10,000 in population, reported the highest clearance percentage at 26.2, and the largest cities, those with 1 million and over in population, had the lowest percentage at 10.0. At the county level, 28.0 percent of motor vehicle thefts were cleared in

Table 2.30

Motor Vehicle Theft
Percent Distribution by Region, 2001

Region	Total[1]	Autos	Trucks and buses	Other vehicles
Total	100.0	73.7	18.9	7.3
Northeastern States	100.0	87.9	6.0	6.1
Midwestern States	100.0	77.7	15.2	7.1
Southern States	100.0	70.9	20.1	8.9
Western States	100.0	70.1	23.8	6.1

[1] Because of rounding, the percentages may not add to total.

Figure 2.18

Motor Vehicle Theft
Percent change from 1997

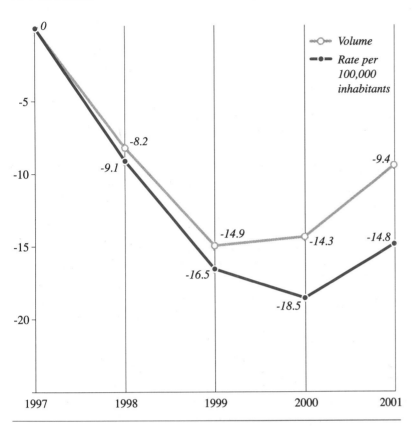

Legend:
- Volume
- Rate per 100,000 inhabitants

Data points:
- 1997: 0
- 1998: Volume -8.2, Rate -9.1
- 1999: Volume -14.9, Rate -16.5
- 2000: Volume -14.3, Rate -18.5
- 2001: Volume -9.4, Rate -14.8

rural counties, and 15.4 percent were cleared in suburban counties. (See Table 25.)

In the Nation, 14.1 percent of automobile thefts were cleared, 11.6 percent of truck and bus thefts were cleared, and 13.1 percent of thefts of other vehicle types were cleared. Law enforcement in rural counties recorded the highest number of clearances for automobiles stolen, 32.1 percent, as well as for stolen trucks and buses, 28.3 percent. Cities 250,000 to 499,999 in population had the highest number of clearances in the other vehicles category at 21.0 percent. (See Table 27.)

Arrests

An estimated 147,451 persons were arrested for motor vehicle theft in the Nation in 2001. (See Tables 29.) The Nation's cities collectively had a rate of 62.1 arrests per 100,000 inhabitants compared to a National rate of 53.3. Among the population groups, those cities with 250,000 and over in population had the highest arrest rate at 113.8 per 100,000 in population, and rural counties had the lowest arrest rate at 28.2. (See Table 31.)

Regionally, the Western States reported the highest rate of arrests per 100,000 persons at 70.2. The Midwestern States had a rate of 64.0, followed by the Southern States at 41.5 and the Northeastern States at 35.3. (See Table 30.)

By gender, males comprised 83.6 percent of all arrestees for motor vehicle theft. (See Table 42.) By race, whites accounted for 57.5 percent of motor vehicle theft arrestees, and blacks made up 39.8 percent. Asian or Pacific Islander, at 1.8 percent, and American Indian or Alaskan Native, at 0.9 percent, accounted for the remainder of arrestees. (See Table 43.)

Arrest Trends

Although the number of arrests were up 2.7 percent over the previous year's figure, motor vehicle theft arrests were down 11.8 percent from the 1997 number and down 30.3 percent from the 1992 number. Nationally, adult arrestees for motor vehicle theft in 2001 increased 5.2 percent from the 2000 total. However, the 2001 total of adult arrestees was 2.9 percent below the 1997 level and 13.1-percent below the 1992 level. Juvenile arrests were down 2.2 percent; they fell significantly over the past decade, with a 25.7-percent decline from the 1997 figure and a 51.3-percent drop from the 1992 figure. (See Tables 32, 34, and 36.)

Arson

Definition

Arson is defined by the Uniform Crime Reporting Program as any willful or malicious burning or attempt to burn, with or without intent to defraud, a dwelling, house, public building, motor vehicle or aircraft, personal property of another, etc.

Only fires determined through investigation to have been willfully or maliciously set are classified as arsons. Fires of suspicious or unknown origins are excluded.

National Coverage

In 2001, 12,242 law enforcement agencies submitted 1–12 months of arson data covering a total of 76,760 arson offenses. Of those agencies, 12,155 contributed supplementary details such as types of structure and estimated value of property damaged. Their reports covered 68,967 arsons. (See Table 2.32.) Reports covering all 12 months in 2001 were submitted to the UCR Program by 8,528 agencies providing law enforcement services to 65.2 percent of the U.S. population.

Collected by the UCR Program since 1979, arson is a unique offense because it is not always investigated by law enforcement. In some communities, arson offenses are investigated by fire marshals within the local fire department. In such cases, the incidents are less likely to be reported to the UCR Program. Because the level of reporting may be lower than for the other Crime Index offenses, arson data should not be regarded as a comprehensive accounting of the national arson problem. Rather, these statistics serve as an indicator of the types of arson incidents occurring in the Nation.

Due to the limited reporting, the UCR Program does not estimate for arson; therefore, arson offenses are not included in tables containing offense estimates. Arson totals reported by individual law enforcement agencies are displayed in Tables 8–11. In these tables, the arson offenses are tallied separately and included in the Modified Crime Index. In addition, arson is not included in the national rate calculations; instead, arson rates are computed separately and presented in Table 2.31. Two-year arson trends are shown in Tables 12–15, and arson clearance data appear in Table 2.32 and Tables 25–28.

Characteristics

Type

Structural arson was the most frequently reported type of arson in 2001, accounting for 42.2 percent of the arson total. Mobile properties (motor vehicles, trailers, etc.) were targeted in 32.5 percent of reported arson offenses, and other types of properties (crops, timber, etc.) comprised the remaining 25.4 percent of offenses. (See Table 2.32.)

Among structural arsons, 60.6 percent were of residential properties of which 42.1 percent were of single-occupancy dwellings. Property that was either uninhabited or abandoned at the time of the arson accounted for 19.3 percent of structure-related arsons. Nationally, structural arsons showed a 2.3-percent decrease from 2000 to 2001. Mobile properties

Table 2.31

Arson Rate
by Population Group, 2001
[8,528 agencies; 2001 estimated population 185,693,054; rate per 100,000 inhabitants]

Population group	Rate
Total	35.5
Total cities	38.8
Group I (cities 250,000 and over)	61.7
(cities 1,000,000 and over)	55.7
(cities 500,000 to 999,999)	57.4
(cities 250,000 to 499,999)	73.2
Group II (cities 100,000 to 249,999)	38.3
Group III (cities 50,000 to 99,999)	31.5
Group IV (cities 25,000 to 49,999)	25.2
Group V (cities 10,000 to 24,999)	20.8
Group VI (cities under 10,000)	26.5
Suburban counties	32.1
Rural counties	19.1
Suburban area[1]	26.7

[1] Includes suburban city and county law enforcement agencies within metropolitan areas. Excludes central cities. Suburban cities and counties are also included in other groups.

Table 2.32

Arson
by Type of Property, 2001
[12,155 agencies; 2001 estimated population 222,587,680]

Property classification	Number of offenses	Percent distribution[1]	Percent not in use	Average damage	Total clearances	Percent cleared[2]	Percent under 18
Total	68,967	100.0		$11,098	11,205	16.2	45.2
Total structure:	29,088	42.2	19.3	20,128	6,435	22.1	45.0
Single occupancy residential	12,243	17.8	22.3	18,392	2,804	22.9	35.6
Other residential	5,370	7.8	15.3	18,531	1,154	21.5	38.5
Storage	2,236	3.2	21.7	20,339	420	18.8	60.7
Industrial/manufacturing	345	0.5	22.9	110,925	172	49.9	37.8
Other commercial	2,871	4.2	14.5	33,622	455	15.8	34.7
Community/public	3,333	4.8	11.3	17,343	950	28.5	76.0
Other structure	2,690	3.9	25.9	8,440	480	17.8	53.3
Total mobile:	22,381	32.5		6,974	1,595	7.1	23.8
Motor vehicles	21,147	30.7		6,813	1,418	6.7	21.7
Other mobile	1,234	1.8		9,724	177	14.3	40.7
Other	17,498	25.4		1,361	3,175	18.1	56.2

[1] Because of rounding, the percentages may not add to total.
[2] Includes offenses cleared by arrest or exceptional means.

and other types of fires, however, showed increases of 12.1 percent and 0.1 percent, respectively. (See Table 15.) The bulk of mobile property arsons, 94.5 percent, involved motor vehicles. (See Table 2.32.)

Dollar Loss

In 2001, the average dollar loss for property damaged or destroyed in reported arsons was $11,098 per incident. Structural losses averaged $20,128, and mobile property losses averaged $6,974 per incident. Average losses for properties categorized as "Other" were estimated at $1,361 per arson. (See Table 2.32.)

Population Groups Trends and Rates

Because population coverage for arson data is lower than for other Crime Index offenses, arson rates per 100,000 inhabitants are tabulated independently. The rates for 2001 presented in Table 2.31 are based on data provided by the 8,528 law enforcement agencies that supplied monthly arson reports for all 12 months of 2001.

For 2001, the rate of arsons was computed at 35.5 offenses per 100,000 population. The Nation's cities registered a collective arson rate of 38.8 per 100,000 inhabitants. The highest rate overall, 73.2, was recorded by cities with 250,000

to 499,999 inhabitants. The lowest rate was posted by rural counties, 19.1. (See Table 2.31.)

Collectively, the Nation's cities reported a 1.0-percent increase in the number of reported arsons in 2001; the largest increase, 7.0 percent, was in cities with populations of 50,000 to 99,999. The greatest decline in arson among cities, 7.8 percent, was seen in cities of 500,000 to 999,999 in population. Both rural and suburban counties showed an increase in volume of 3.3 percent and 4.0 percent, respectively. (See Table 12.)

By arson type, rural counties saw the largest increase in structural arson, up 8.1 percent from 2000. Cities 500,000 to 999,999 in population experienced the greatest decrease, down 14.4 percent. Cities of 250,000 to 499,999 recorded the largest increase in mobile arson, up 22.5 percent from 2000; all population groups experienced an increase in this arson category. Other types of arsons increased in cities of 50,000 to 99,999 by 13.6 percent, whereas cities of 500,000 to 999,999 inhabitants recorded a 14.9-percent decline from the prior year's data. (See Table 15.)

Clearances

In 2001, the Nation's law enforcement agencies cleared 16.0 percent of reported arson offenses. Cities collectively cleared 15.6 percent of all arsons; the highest clearance figure, 25.0 percent, was recorded by agencies in cities under 10,000 in population. Rural counties cleared 24.8 percent, and suburban counties cleared 14.9 percent of arsons reported in their jurisdictions. (See Table 25.)

The Northeastern States cleared 19.9 percent of reported arson offenses in that region, and the Southern States recorded clearances of 17.8 percent. The Midwestern States cleared 14.8 percent of arsons reported in that region, and the Western States cleared 13.7 percent. (See Table 26.)

Among population groups, clearances of structural arson offenses ranged from 30.4 percent for cities with populations under 10,000 in population to 16.0 percent for cities with 250,000 to 499,999 inhabitants. Clearances of mobile vehicle arsons ranged from 16.7 percent for both rural counties and cities under 10,000 in population to 3.8 percent for the Nation's cities with 1 million or more in population. Clearances of arsons of other types of property ranged from 26.0 percent in rural counties to 11.1 percent in cities of 1 million or more inhabitants. (See Table 27.)

Table 2.32 shows clearance data only for those 12,155 agencies that furnished breakdowns by type for the structural and mobile classifications. As can be seen, the highest percentage of arson clearances in 2001 involved incidents of structural fires, 22.1 percent. The lowest percentage of arson clearances involved incidents of mobile vehicle fires at 7.1 percent. Juvenile involvement in arson was higher than for any other Index offense. In 2001, juvenile clearances accounted for 45.2 percent of all arsons cleared.

Arrests

Total Arrests

An estimated 18,749 persons were arrested for arson in 2001. (See Table 29.) Based upon the actual number of arrests reported by the 8,528 agencies submitting 12 months of data, the national arrest rate for arson was calculated at 6.6 per 100,000 persons. The West reported an arrest rate of 8.3 per 100,000 individuals, the

highest regional arrest rate for this offense; the South recorded a rate of 6.0; the Northeast, 5.9; and the Midwest, 5.6. (See Table 30.)

By population group, law enforcement in cities collectively arrested arson offenders at a rate of 7.0 per 100,000 inhabitants; in rural counties, the arrest rate was 5.2; and in suburban counties, 6.1. Law enforcement in cities with 250,000 or more people had the highest rate of arrests for arson, reporting a rate of 8.7 per 100,000 inhabitants. (See Table 31.)

Arrest Trends

Nationwide, 2001 arson arrests increased 14.7 percent over the previous year's figure. Arrests of juveniles (persons under the age of 18) increased 8.1 percent, and adult arrests increased 22.8 percent. (See Table 36.)

In comparing data from 1997 to those of 2001, overall arson arrests declined 3.1 percent for the 5-year period. Though juvenile arrests also dropped 9.3 percent, adult arrests for arson rose 4.1 percent. (See Table 34.) By gender, arrests of females and juvenile females showed increases since 1997 of 12.2 percent and 5.2 percent, respectively. Arson arrests of males decreased for juveniles by 11.0 percent and for males of all ages by 5.5 percent. (See Table 35.)

For the 10-year period 1992–2001, arson arrests declined 6.3 percent, with those for juveniles and adults decreasing 7.4 percent and 5.2 percent, respectively. When analyzing arrest trends by age and gender, arrests of juvenile females and females of all ages showed increases—4.0 percent and 14.6 percent, respectively—as opposed to the declines seen in arrests of juvenile males and males of all ages— 8.7 percent and 9.4 percent, respectively. (See Tables 32 and 33.)

Distribution

In 2001, nearly half of all persons arrested for arson, 49.5 percent, were juveniles. In particular, those under 15 years of age accounted for 31.7 percent of the arson arrest total. Males comprised 84.1 percent of all arson arrestees. By race, 76.9 percent of arson arrestees were white, 20.7 percent were black, and the remaining 2.4 percent were of other races. (See Tables 41–43.)

Hate Crime

Definition

A hate crime, also known as a bias crime, is a criminal offense committed against a person, property, or society which is motivated, in whole or in part, by the offender's bias against a race, religion, disability, sexual orientation, or ethnicity/national origin.

Background

In response to mounting national concern over crimes motivated by bias, Congress enacted the *Hate Crime Statistics Act of 1990* on April 23 of that year. This law required the Attorney General to collect data "about crimes that manifest evidence of prejudice based on race, religion, sexual orientation, or ethnicity." The Attorney General delegated the responsibilities of developing the procedures for and implementing, collecting, and managing hate crime data to the Director of the FBI, who in turn assigned the tasks to the Uniform Crime Reporting (UCR) Program. In September 1994, the Violent Crime Control and Law Enforcement Act amended the Hate Crime Statistics Act to include both physical and mental disabilities as potential bias factors, and the actual collection of disability-bias data began in January 1997. Additionally, the Church Arson Prevention Act of 1996 mandated that hate crime data collection become a permanent part of the UCR Program.

The program developers recognized that hate crimes are not separate, distinct crimes; instead they are traditional offenses motivated by the offender's bias. After much consideration, they decided that hate crime data could be derived by capturing the additional element of bias in those offenses already being reported to the UCR Program. Appending the collection of hate crime statistics to the established UCR data collection procedures would fulfill the directives of the Hate Crime Statistics Act, avoid placing an undue additional reporting burden on law enforcement and, in time, develop a substantial body of data about the nature and frequency of bias crimes occurring throughout the Nation. Accordingly, the program collects details about an offender's bias motivation associated with the following offense types: murder and nonnegligent manslaughter, forcible rape, aggravated assault, simple assault, intimidation, robbery, burglary, larceny-theft, motor vehicle theft, arson, and destruction/damage/vandalism of property. (The national Hate Crime program also collects additional offense types reported by those agencies participating in the National Incident-Based Reporting System and publishes them in tables as "other" or "crimes against society.")

Participation

During 2001, 11,987 law enforcement agencies participated in the Hate Crime program. Of those agencies, approximately 17.6 percent submitted hate crime incident reports to the FBI. These figures indicate a slight increase in the number of agencies submitting data in 2000, when 11,690 agencies participated in the program, and 16.2 percent reported that at least one hate crime had occurred. (See Table 2.36.) During 2001, law enforcement reported 9,726 incidents compared to 8,063[1] incidents reported for the prior year. The following hate crime abstract is based on the data received from those law enforcement agencies that provided 1 to 12 months of hate crime reports during 2001.

Hate Crime Data Collection

The UCR Program data collection guidelines stipulate that a hate crime may have multiple offenses, victims, and offenders within one incident. Thus, in 2001, the 9,726 hate crime incidents reported to the FBI involved 11,447 separate offenses, 12,016 victims, and 9,231 known offenders. Of the total reported single-bias incidents, 44.9 percent were motivated by racial bias, 21.6 percent were driven by prejudice against an ethnicity or national origin, 18.8 percent resulted from a bias against a particular religion, and 14.3 percent involved a sexual-orientation bias. (Based on Table 2.33.)

A *victim*, according to the UCR definition, may be either a person, a business, an institu-

Table 2.33

Incidents, Offenses, Victims, and Known Offenders
by Bias Motivation, 2001

Bias motivation	Incidents	Offenses	Victims[1]	Known offenders[2]
Total	**9,726**	**11,447**	**12,016**	**9,231**
Single-Bias Incidents	**9,717**	**11,426**	**11,994**	**9,218**
Race:	**4,366**	**5,289**	**5,544**	**4,494**
Anti-White	889	1,032	1,063	1,147
Anti-Black	2,900	3,530	3,701	2,819
Anti-American Indian/Alaskan Native	80	95	100	103
Anti-Asian/Pacific Islander	280	349	363	271
Anti-Multiple Races, Group	217	283	317	154
Religion:	**1,828**	**2,004**	**2,118**	**917**
Anti-Jewish	1,043	1,117	1,196	389
Anti-Catholic	38	38	40	12
Anti-Protestant	35	36	36	45
Anti-Islamic	481	546	554	334
Anti-Other Religion	181	211	235	102
Anti-Multiple Religions, Group	45	51	52	28
Anti-Atheism/Agnosticism/etc.	5	5	5	7
Sexual Orientation:	**1,392**	**1,591**	**1,663**	**1,576**
Anti-Male Homosexual	980	1,103	1,152	1,196
Anti-Female Homosexual	205	245	257	170
Anti-Homosexual	173	207	217	179
Anti-Heterosexual	18	20	21	17
Anti-Bisexual	16	16	16	14
Ethnicity/National Origin:	**2,098**	**2,507**	**2,634**	**2,192**
Anti-Hispanic	597	755	812	941
Anti-Other Ethnicity/National Origin	1,501	1,752	1,822	1,251
Disability:	**33**	**35**	**35**	**39**
Anti-Physical	12	12	12	16
Anti-Mental	21	23	23	23
Multiple-Bias Incidents[3]	**9**	**21**	**22**	**13**

[1] The term *victim* may refer to a person, business, institution, or society as a whole.

[2] The term *known offender* does not imply that the identity of the suspect is known, but only that the race of the suspect has been identified, distinguishing him/her from an unknown offender.

[3] A *multiple-bias incident* is a hate crime in which more than one offense type was committed as a result of more than one bias motivations.

tion, or society as a whole. When aggregating the number of hate crime offenses committed against *individuals*, the program counts one offense for each person. The offense types of murder, rape, aggravated assault, simple assault, and intimidation are possible crimes against persons. When counting crimes against *property*, the program allots one offense for each distinct incident regardless of the number of victims. Robbery, burglary, larceny, motor vehicle theft, arson, and destruction/damage/vandalism are the offense types that are possible crimes against property.

Law Enforcement Reports

During 2001, 64.6 percent of reported victims were the targets of crimes against persons, and 34.7 percent of victims were the targets of crimes against property. (Crimes against society comprised 0.6 percent of reports.) Intimidation continued to be the most frequently reported hate crime against individuals and accounted for 55.9 percent of all crimes against persons. Destruction/damage/vandalism of property was the most frequently reported crime against property. Of the 4,175 targets of crimes against property, 83.4 percent were vandalized. (Based on Table 2.34.)

Among all hate crime offenses, intimidation was the most frequently reported offense; it

Table 2.34

Incidents, Offenses, Victims, and Known Offenders
by Offense Type, 2001

Offense type	Incidents[1]	Offenses	Victims[2]	Known offenders[3]
Total	**9,726**	**11,447**	**12,016**	**9,231**
Crimes against persons:	**6,328**	**7,766**	**7,766**	**7,646**
Murder and nonnegligent manslaughter	9	9	9	11
Forcible rape	4	4	4	4
Aggravated assault	942	1,242	1,242	1,715
Simple assault	1,795	2,154	2,154	2,797
Intimidation	3,562	4,338	4,338	3,103
Other[4]	16	19	19	16
Crimes against property:	**3,606**	**3,606**	**4,175**	**1,850**
Robbery	158	158	181	417
Burglary	149	149	179	92
Larceny-theft	149	149	162	111
Motor vehicle theft	15	15	15	9
Arson	90	90	129	86
Destruction/damage/vandalism	3,018	3,018	3,481	1,109
Other[4]	27	27	28	26
Crimes against society[4]	**75**	**75**	**75**	**84**

[1] The actual number of incidents is 9,726. However, the column figures will not add to the total because incidents may include more than one offense type, and these are counted in each appropriate offense type category.

[2] The term *victim* may refer to a person, business, institution, or society as a whole.

[3] The term *known offender* does not imply that the identity of the suspect is known, but only that the race of the suspect has been identified, distinguishing him/her from an unknown offender. The actual number of known offenders is 9,231. However, the column figures will not add to the total because some offenders are responsible for more than one offense, and they are, therefore, counted more than once in this table.

[4] Includes additional offenses collected in NIBRS.

Table 2.35

Race of Known Offenders, 2001[1]

Known offender's race

Total	**9,231**
White	6,049
Black	1,882
American Indian/Alaskan Native	59
Asian/Pacific Islander	84
Multiple Races, Group	403
Unknown Race	754

[1] The term *known offender* does not imply that the identity of the suspect is known, but only that the race of the suspect has been identified, distinguishing him/her from an unknown offender.

Figure 2.19

Bias-motivated Offenses
Percent distribution 2001

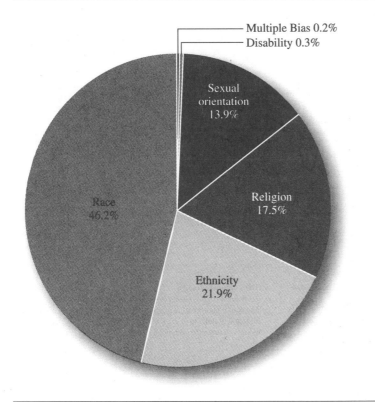

Multiple Bias 0.2%
Disability 0.3%
Sexual orientation 13.9%
Race 46.2%
Ethnicity 21.9%
Religion 17.5%

accounted for 37.9 percent of the total. Damage/destruction/vandalism of property made up 26.4 percent of total offenses; simple assault, 18.8 percent; and aggravated assault, 10.9 percent. (Based on Table 2.34.)

Approximately forty-six percent (46.2) of all single-bias hate crime victims were targets of racial prejudice. Of these victims, 66.8 percent were attacked because of an anti-black bias motivation, and 19.2 percent were attacked due to an anti-white bias motivation. Religious intolerance accounted for 17.7 percent of all victims of reported single-bias hate crimes; of these, 56.5 percent were targeted because of an anti-Jewish motivation, and 26.2 percent were targets due to a prejudice against the Islamic religion. Sexual-orientation bias led to attacks on 13.9 percent of single-bias victims; among these victims, anti-male homosexual bias made up 69.3 percent of the total. Anti-ethnicity or national origin was the underlying motivation for attacks on 22.0 percent of the total single-bias victims; 30.8 percent were victims of anti-Hispanic bias, and 69.2 percent were classified as victims of anti-other ethnicity/national origin. (Based on Table 2.33.)

In 2001, the majority of known hate crime offenders were white, 65.5 percent; 20.4 percent were black, 8.2 percent were of unknown race, and the remainder were of other races or multiple races. (Based on Table 2.35.)

[1] The total number of hate crime incidents for 2000 was updated after the publication of *Crime in the United States 2000*.

Table 2.36

Participating states	Number of participating agencies	Population covered	Agencies submitting incident reports	Total number of incidents reported
Total	**11,987**	**241,799,615**	**2,104**	**9,726**
Alabama	5	268,224	0	0
Alaska	1	263,588	1	20
Arizona	97	4,956,803	26	384
Arkansas	3	81,509	2	3
California	725	34,501,130	273	2,246
Colorado	202	4,330,662	34	126
Connecticut	98	3,362,043	63	166
Delaware	51	794,595	8	17
District of Columbia	2	571,822	2	11
Florida	491	16,360,995	100	302
Georgia	86	1,181,401	11	39
Idaho	114	1,305,535	17	34
Illinois	72	4,812,226	63	282
Indiana	143	3,044,860	28	74
Iowa	223	2,850,263	17	32
Kansas	344	2,299,859	12	71
Kentucky	336	3,475,327	42	82
Louisiana	168	3,881,451	5	10
Maine	182	1,284,775	10	32
Maryland	148	5,375,156	29	231
Massachusetts	338	5,998,889	122	584
Michigan	621	9,887,717	165	442
Minnesota	295	4,951,275	61	210
Mississippi	72	942,337	3	3
Missouri	85	2,336,942	20	65
Montana	102	902,277	7	13
Nebraska	198	1,284,466	15	53
Nevada	36	2,106,074	8	94
New Hampshire	108	654,953	16	27
New Jersey	561	8,484,431	253	767
New Mexico	54	1,153,948	4	20
New York	568	19,008,440	63	712
North Carolina	449	8,109,373	41	85
North Dakota	73	563,213	9	16
Ohio	363	7,602,785	71	363
Oklahoma	298	3,459,483	22	46
Oregon	174	3,460,951	28	222
Pennsylvania	770	10,395,227	42	132
Rhode Island	48	1,058,920	9	63
South Carolina	340	4,058,727	20	41
South Dakota	113	685,419	5	5
Tennessee	445	5,737,946	77	335
Texas	952	21,214,801	89	434
Utah	58	1,730,700	20	65
Vermont	57	562,536	11	17
Virginia	397	7,147,779	69	362
Washington	248	5,913,174	59	278
West Virginia	279	1,756,724	20	39
Wisconsin	359	5,310,699	24	61
Wyoming	35	317,185	8	10

Crime Index Tabulations

The tabular portions of this section organize crime data into various categories based upon population. Data are presented for the Nation as a whole; geographic divisions; individual states; Metropolitan Statistical Areas (MSAs); and cities, towns, and counties. Within these classifications, the statistics on crime volumes are also computed as rates of occurrence per 100,000 U.S. inhabitants.

Although the exact number of crimes occurring within the United States is unknown, criminal activity can be gauged by studying those crimes reported to law enforcement. The reader is cautioned, however, that many factors affect crime volumes and crime types and can cause them to vary from time to time and from place to place. Population, for example, is used in computing crime rates. Since current, permanent population counts are used in their construction, crime rates do not account for transient or seasonal populations. Short-term population variables, such as an influx of day workers, tourists, shoppers, etc. impact all communities to some degree. Other factors contributing to the amount of crime in a given area are discussed in Section I, Crime Factors.

One tool law enforcement administrators can use in analyzing the volume of local crime and the performance of the law enforcement agencies is national data. An analysis, however, should not be based solely on data presented in this publication. A true assessment of a community's crime problem or the effectiveness of law enforcement operations can be made only by including in that assessment all the variables that mold local crime conditions.

Table 1 sets forth national estimates of volume and rate per 100,000 population for all Crime Index offenses covering the past two decades. Table 2 shows estimates of crime volume and rates for 2001 for the Nation as a whole, MSAs, rural counties, and cities and towns outside metropolitan areas. Definitions of these community types can be found in Appendix III.

Data showing the regional distribution of estimated Index crimes along with proportional population estimates are provided in Table 3. A map of the United States illustrating the regions and divisions employed by the UCR Program appears in Appendix III.

Table 4 offers a 2-year trend in the volume and rate estimates by region, geographic division, and state. The incidence and rate of Crime Index offenses for each state and for individual MSAs are shown in Tables 5 and 6. Table 7 offers breakdowns for the offenses of robbery (by location), burglary (by time of day), and larceny-theft (by type) over the past 5 years.

Offenses known to police for cities over 10,000 in population are presented in Table 8, and Table 9 records Index Crimes occurring on college and university campuses, although no population is assigned to educational institutions.

Offenses reported by suburban and rural counties are broken down by state in Tables 10 and 11. Tables 12–19 offer crime trends and rates by population groupings. A description of the population groups defined by the UCR Program can be found in Appendix III.

Data concerning weapons used in the violent crimes of murder, robbery, and aggravated assault are presented in Tables 20–22. Tables 23 and 24 analyze the value of property lost through the crimes of robbery, burglary, and larceny-theft, and offer breakdowns by type and value of property stolen and recovered.

Note

Because the UCR Program does not estimate for arson, arson offenses are not included in the tables containing offense estimates. Arson totals reported by individual law enforcement agencies are displayed in Tables 8–11. Two-year arson trends are shown in Tables 12–15. An in-depth discussion of table construction methodology can be found in Appendix I.

Table 1

Index of Crime[1]
United States, 1982-2001

Population[2]	Crime Index total	Modified Crime Index total[3]	Violent crime[4]	Property crime[4]	Murder and non-negligent man-slaughter	Forcible rape	Robbery	Aggravated assault	Burglary	Larceny-theft	Motor vehicle theft	Arson[3]
				Number of Offenses								
Population by year:												
1982-231,664,458	12,974,400		1,322,390	11,652,000	21,010	78,770	553,130	669,480	3,447,100	7,142,500	1,062,400	
1983-233,791,994	12,108,630		1,258,087	10,850,543	19,308	78,918	506,567	653,294	3,129,851	6,712,759	1,007,933	
1984-235,824,902	11,881,755		1,273,282	10,608,473	18,692	84,233	485,008	685,349	2,984,434	6,591,874	1,032,165	
1985-237,923,795	12,430,357		1,327,767	11,102,590	18,976	87,671	497,874	723,246	3,073,348	6,926,380	1,102,862	
1986-240,132,887	13,211,869		1,489,169	11,722,700	20,613	91,459	542,775	834,322	3,241,410	7,257,153	1,224,137	
1987-242,288,918	13,508,708		1,483,999	12,024,709	20,096	91,111	517,704	855,088	3,236,184	7,499,851	1,288,674	
1988-244,498,982	13,923,086		1,566,221	12,356,865	20,675	92,486	542,968	910,092	3,218,077	7,705,872	1,432,916	
1989-246,819,230	14,251,449		1,646,037	12,605,412	21,500	94,504	578,326	951,707	3,168,170	7,872,442	1,564,800	
1990-249,464,396	14,475,613		1,820,127	12,655,486	23,438	102,555	639,271	1,054,863	3,073,909	7,945,670	1,635,907	
1991-252,153,092	14,872,883		1,911,767	12,961,116	24,703	106,593	687,732	1,092,739	3,157,150	8,142,228	1,661,738	
1992-255,029,699	14,438,191		1,932,274	12,505,917	23,760	109,062	672,478	1,126,974	2,979,884	7,915,199	1,610,834	
1993-257,782,608	14,144,794		1,926,017	12,218,777	24,526	106,014	659,870	1,135,607	2,834,808	7,820,909	1,563,060	
1994-260,327,021	13,989,543		1,857,670	12,131,873	23,326	102,216	618,949	1,113,179	2,712,774	7,879,812	1,539,287	
1995-262,803,276	13,862,727		1,798,792	12,063,935	21,606	97,470	580,509	1,099,207	2,593,784	7,997,710	1,472,441	
1996-265,228,572	13,493,863		1,688,540	11,805,323	19,645	96,252	535,594	1,037,049	2,506,400	7,904,685	1,394,238	
1997-267,783,607	13,194,571		1,636,096	11,558,475	18,208	96,153	498,534	1,023,201	2,460,526	7,743,760	1,354,189	
1998-270,248,003	12,485,714		1,533,887	10,951,827	16,974	93,144	447,186	976,583	2,332,735	7,376,311	1,242,781	
1999-272,690,813	11,634,378		1,426,044	10,208,334	15,522	89,411	409,371	911,740	2,100,739	6,955,520	1,152,075	
2000-281,421,906[5]	11,608,070		1,425,486	10,182,584	15,586	90,178	408,016	911,706	2,050,992	6,971,590	1,160,002	
2001-284,796,887	11,849,006		1,436,611	10,412,395	15,980	90,491	422,921	907,219	2,109,767	7,076,171	1,226,457	
Percent change, number of offenses:												
2001/2000	+2.1		+0.8	+2.3	+2.5	+0.3	+3.7	-0.5	+2.9	+1.5	+5.7	
2001/1997	-10.2		-12.2	-9.9	-12.2	-5.9	-15.2	-11.3	-14.3	-8.6	-9.4	
2001/1992	-17.9		-25.7	-16.7	-32.7	-17.0	-37.1	-19.5	-29.2	-10.6	-23.9	
				Rate per 100,000 Inhabitants								
Year:												
1982	5,600.5		570.8	5,029.7	9.1	34.0	238.8	289.0	1,488.0	3,083.1	458.6	
1983	5,179.2		538.1	4,641.1	8.3	33.8	216.7	279.4	1,338.7	2,871.3	431.1	
1984	5,038.4		539.9	4,498.5	7.9	35.7	205.7	290.6	1,265.5	2,795.2	437.7	
1985	5,224.5		558.1	4,666.4	8.0	36.8	209.3	304.0	1,291.7	2,911.2	463.5	
1986	5,501.9		620.1	4,881.8	8.6	38.1	226.0	347.4	1,349.8	3,022.1	509.8	
1987	5,575.5		612.5	4,963.0	8.3	37.6	213.7	352.9	1,335.7	3,095.4	531.9	
1988	5,694.5		640.6	5,054.0	8.5	37.8	222.1	372.2	1,316.2	3,151.7	586.1	
1989	5,774.0		666.9	5,107.1	8.7	38.3	234.3	385.6	1,283.6	3,189.6	634.0	
1990	5,802.7		729.6	5,073.1	9.4	41.1	256.3	422.9	1,232.2	3,185.1	655.8	
1991	5,898.4		758.2	5,140.2	9.8	42.3	272.7	433.4	1,252.1	3,229.1	659.0	
1992	5,661.4		757.7	4,903.7	9.3	42.8	263.7	441.9	1,168.4	3,103.6	631.6	
1993	5,487.1		747.1	4,740.0	9.5	41.1	256.0	440.5	1,099.7	3,033.9	606.3	
1994	5,373.8		713.6	4,660.2	9.0	39.3	237.8	427.6	1,042.1	3,026.9	591.3	
1995	5,274.9		684.5	4,590.5	8.2	37.1	220.9	418.3	987.0	3,043.2	560.3	
1996	5,087.6		636.6	4,451.0	7.4	36.3	201.9	391.0	945.0	2,980.3	525.7	
1997	4,927.3		611.0	4,316.3	6.8	35.9	186.2	382.1	918.8	2,891.8	505.7	
1998	4,620.1		567.6	4,052.5	6.3	34.5	165.5	361.4	863.2	2,729.5	459.9	
1999	4,266.5		523.0	3,743.6	5.7	32.8	150.1	334.3	770.4	2,550.7	422.5	
2000[5]	4,124.8		506.5	3,618.3	5.5	32.0	145.0	324.0	728.8	2,477.3	412.2	
2001	4,160.5		504.4	3,656.1	5.6	31.8	148.5	318.5	740.8	2,484.6	430.6	
Percent change, rate per 100,000 inhabitants:												
2001/2000	+0.9		-0.4	+1.0	+1.3	-0.8	+2.4	-1.7	+1.6	+0.3	+4.5	
2001/1997	-15.6		-17.4	-15.3	-17.5	-11.5	-20.2	-16.6	-19.4	-14.1	-14.8	
2001/1992	-26.5		-33.4	-25.4	-39.8	-25.7	-43.7	-27.9	-36.6	-19.9	-31.8	

[1] The murder and nonnegligent homicides that occurred as a result of the events of September 11, 2001, were not included in this table. See special report, Section V.
[2] Populations are Bureau of the Census provisional estimates as of July 1 for each year except 1990 and 2000 which are decennial census counts.
[3] Although arson data are included in the trend and clearance tables, sufficient data are not available to estimate totals for this offense.
[4] Violent crimes are offenses of murder, forcible rape, robbery, and aggravated assault. Property crimes are offenses of burglary, larceny-theft, and motor vehicle theft.
[5] The 2000 crime figures have been adjusted. See Crime Trends, Appendix I, for details.

Table 2

Index of Crime[1]
United States, 2001

Area	Population[2]	Crime Index total	Modified Crime Index total[3]	Violent crime[4]	Property crime[4]	Murder and non-negligent man-slaughter	Forcible rape	Robbery	Aggravated assault	Burglary	Larceny-theft	Motor vehicle theft	Arson[3]
United States Total	284,796,887	11,849,006		1,436,611	10,412,395	15,980	90,491	422,921	907,219	2,109,767	7,076,171	1,226,457	
Rate per 100,000 inhabitants		4,160.5		504.4	3,656.1	5.6	31.8	148.5	318.5	740.8	2,484.6	430.6	
Metropolitan Statistical Area	227,597,056												
Area actually reporting[5]	92.2%	9,413,983		1,172,481	8,241,502	12,716	69,435	372,351	717,979	1,626,020	5,549,364	1,066,118	
Estimated totals	100.0%	10,184,729		1,274,565	8,910,164	13,899	74,909	403,651	782,106	1,749,832	6,024,499	1,135,833	
Rate per 100,000 inhabitants		4,474.9		560.0	3,914.9	6.1	32.9	177.4	343.6	768.8	2,647.0	499.1	
Cities Outside Metropolitan Area	22,745,248												
Area actually reporting[5]	79.3%	862,311		77,578	784,733	670	6,599	11,658	58,651	149,136	595,271	40,326	
Estimated totals	100.0%	1,012,260		89,346	922,914	795	7,875	13,569	67,107	173,852	702,314	46,748	
Rate per 100,000 inhabitants		4,450.4		392.8	4,057.6	3.5	34.6	59.7	295.0	764.3	3,087.7	205.5	
Rural Counties	34,454,583												
Area actually reporting[5]	79.3%	573,109		65,139	507,970	1,062	6,440	4,989	52,648	162,780	306,805	38,385	
Estimated totals	100.0%	652,017		72,700	579,317	1,286	7,707	5,701	58,006	186,083	349,358	43,876	
Rate per 100,000 inhabitants		1,892.4		211.0	1,681.4	3.7	22.4	16.5	168.4	540.1	1,014.0	127.3	

[1] The murder and nonnegligent homicides that occurred as a result of the events of September 11, 2001, were not included in this table. See special report, Section V.
[2] Populations are Bureau of the Census 2001 provisional estimates as of July 1, 2001.
[3] Although arson data are included in the trend and clearance tables, sufficient data are not available to estimate totals for this offense.
[4] Violent crimes are offenses of murder, forcible rape, robbery, and aggravated assault. Property crimes are offenses of burglary, larceny-theft, and motor vehicle theft.
[5] The percentage reported under "Area actually reporting" is based upon the population covered by agencies providing 3 months or more of crime reports to the FBI.

Table 3

Index of Crime[1]
Offense and Population Distribution by Region, 2001

Region	Population	Crime Index total	Modified Crime Index total[2]	Violent crime[3]	Property crime[3]	Murder and non-negligent man-slaughter	Forcible rape	Robbery	Aggravated assault	Burglary	Larceny-theft	Motor vehicle theft	Arson[2]
United States Total[4]	**100.0**	**100.0**		**100.0**	**100.0**	**100.0**	**100.0**	**100.0**	**100.0**	**100.0**	**100.0**	**100.0**	
Northeastern States	18.9	13.7		16.1	13.3	14.3	13.4	19.1	15.0	12.0	13.6	14.0	
Midwestern States	22.7	21.7		19.5	22.0	21.3	25.1	19.6	18.8	20.8	22.8	20.0	
Southern States	35.8	40.9		41.1	40.9	42.4	37.8	38.4	42.7	44.7	40.7	35.5	
Western States	22.6	23.7		23.3	23.7	22.0	23.7	22.9	23.6	22.5	22.9	30.5	

[1] The murder and nonnegligent homicides that occurred as a result of the events of September 11, 2001, were not included in this table. See special report, Section V.
[2] Although arson data are included in the trend and clearance tables, sufficient data are not available to estimate totals for this offense.
[3] Violent crimes are offenses of murder, forcible rape, robbery, and aggravated assault. Property crimes are offenses of burglary, larceny-theft, and motor vehicle theft.
[4] Because of rounding, the percentages may not add to total.

Table 4

Index of Crime[1]
by Region, Geographic Division, and State, 2000-2001

Area	Year	Population[2]	Crime Index total		Modified Crime Index total[3]		Violent crime[4]		Property crime[4]		Murder and non-negligent manslaughter	
			Number	Rate per 100,000	Number	Rate per 100,000	Number	Rate per 100,000	Number	Rate per 100,000	Number	Rate per 100,000
United States Total[5,6,7,8]	**2000**	**281,421,906**	**11,608,070**	**4,124.8**			**1,425,486**	**506.5**	**10,182,584**	**3,618.3**	**15,586**	**5.5**
	2001	**284,796,887**	**11,849,006**	**4,160.5**			**1,436,611**	**504.4**	**10,412,395**	**3,656.1**	**15,980**	**5.6**
Percent change			**+2.1**	**+0.9**			**+0.8**	**-0.4**	**+2.3**	**+1.0**	**+2.5**	**+1.3**
Northeast	**2000**	**53,594,378**	**1,642,301**	**3,064.3**			**237,657**	**443.4**	**1,404,644**	**2,620.9**	**2,157**	**4.0**
	2001	**53,805,198**	**1,617,867**	**3,006.9**			**231,208**	**429.7**	**1,386,659**	**2,577.2**	**2,278**	**4.2**
Percent change			**-1.5**	**-1.9**			**-2.7**	**-3.1**	**-1.3**	**-1.7**	**+5.6**	**+4.4**
New England	2000	13,922,517	420,319	3,019.0			48,664	349.5	371,655	2,669.5	314	2.3
	2001	14,022,239	424,276	3,025.7			49,579	353.6	374,697	2,672.2	331	2.4
Percent change			+0.9	+0.2			+1.9	+1.2	+0.8	+0.1	+5.4	+4.7
Connecticut	2000	3,405,565	110,091	3,232.7			11,058	324.7	99,033	2,908.0	98	2.9
	2001	3,425,074	106,791	3,117.9			11,492	335.5	95,299	2,782.4	105	3.1
Percent change			-3.0	-3.6			+3.9	+3.3	-3.8	-4.3	+7.1	+6.5
Maine	2000	1,274,923	33,400	2,619.8			1,397	109.6	32,003	2,510.2	15	1.2
	2001	1,286,670	34,588	2,688.2			1,434	111.5	33,154	2,576.7	18	1.4
Percent change			+3.6	+2.6			+2.6	+1.7	+3.6	+2.7	+20.0	+18.9
Massachusetts	2000	6,349,097	192,131	3,026.1			30,230	476.1	161,901	2,550.0	125	2.0
	2001	6,379,304	197,666	3,098.6			30,587	479.5	167,079	2,619.1	145	2.3
Percent change			+2.9	+2.4			+1.2	+0.7	+3.2	+2.7	+16.0	+15.5
New Hampshire	2000	1,235,786	30,068	2,433.1			2,167	175.4	27,901	2,257.8	22	1.8
	2001	1,259,181	29,233	2,321.6			2,144	170.3	27,089	2,151.3	17	1.4
Percent change			-2.8	-4.6			-1.1	-2.9	-2.9	-4.7	-22.7	-24.2
Rhode Island	2000	1,048,319	36,444	3,476.4			3,121	297.7	33,323	3,178.7	45	4.3
	2001	1,058,920	39,020	3,684.9			3,278	309.6	35,742	3,375.3	39	3.7
Percent change			+7.1	+6.0			+5.0	+4.0	+7.3	+6.2	-13.3	-14.2
Vermont	2000	608,827	18,185	2,986.9			691	113.5	17,494	2,873.4	9	1.5
	2001	613,090	16,978	2,769.3			644	105.0	16,334	2,664.2	7	1.1
Percent change			-6.6	-7.3			-6.8	-7.4	-6.6	-7.3	-22.2	-22.8
Middle Atlantic	2000	39,671,861	1,221,982	3,080.2			188,993	476.4	1,032,989	2,603.8	1,843	4.6
	2001	39,782,959	1,193,591	3,000.3			181,629	456.5	1,011,962	2,543.7	1,947	4.9
Percent change			-2.3	-2.6			-3.9	-4.2	-2.0	-2.3	+5.6	+5.3
New Jersey	2000	8,414,350	265,935	3,160.5			32,298	383.8	233,637	2,776.6	289	3.4
	2001	8,484,431	273,645	3,225.3			33,094	390.1	240,551	2,835.2	336	4.0
Percent change			+2.9	+2.0			+2.5	+1.6	+3.0	+2.1	+16.3	+15.3
New York	2000	18,976,457	588,189	3,099.6			105,111	553.9	483,078	2,545.7	952	5.0
	2001	19,011,378	556,106	2,925.1			98,103	516.0	458,003	2,409.1	960	5.0
Percent change			-5.5	-5.6			-6.7	-6.8	-5.2	-5.4	+0.8	+0.7
Pennsylvania	2000	12,281,054	367,858	2,995.3			51,584	420.0	316,274	2,575.3	602	4.9
	2001	12,287,150	363,840	2,961.1			50,432	410.4	313,408	2,550.7	651	5.3
Percent change			-1.1	-1.1			-2.2	-2.3	-0.9	-1.0	+8.1	+8.1
Midwest[5,6]	**2000**	**64,392,776**	**2,534,459**	**3,935.9**			**275,106**	**427.2**	**2,259,353**	**3,508.7**	**3,293**	**5.1**
	2001	**64,687,414**	**2,575,280**	**3,981.1**			**279,452**	**432.0**	**2,295,828**	**3,549.1**	**3,405**	**5.3**
Percent change			**+1.6**	**+1.1**			**+1.6**	**+1.1**	**+1.6**	**+1.2**	**+3.4**	**+2.9**
East North Central[5,6]	2000	45,155,037	1,794,063	3,973.1			208,220	461.1	1,585,843	3,512.0	2,506	5.5
	2001	45,363,310	1,808,101	3,985.8			210,171	463.3	1,597,930	3,522.5	2,715	6.0
Percent change			+0.8	+0.3			+0.9	+0.5	+0.8	+0.3	+8.3	+7.8
Illinois[5,6]	2000	12,419,293	526,474	4,239.2			81,196	653.8	445,278	3,585.4	898	7.2
	2001	12,482,301	511,494	4,097.8			79,504	636.9	431,990	3,460.8	986	7.9
Percent change			-2.8	-3.3			-2.1	-2.6	-3.0	-3.5	+9.8	+9.2

See footnotes at end of table.

Forcible rape		Robbery		Aggravated assault		Burglary		Larceny-theft		Motor vehicle theft		Arson[3]	
Number	Rate per 100,000	Number	Rate per 100,000	Number	Rate per 100,000	Number	Rate per 100,000	Number	Rate per 100,000	Number	Rate per 100,000	Number	Rate per 100,000
90,178	**32.0**	**408,016**	**145.0**	**911,706**	**324.0**	**2,050,992**	**728.8**	**6,971,590**	**2,477.3**	**1,160,002**	**412.2**		
90,491	**31.8**	**422,921**	**148.5**	**907,219**	**318.5**	**2,109,767**	**740.8**	**7,076,171**	**2,484.6**	**1,226,457**	**430.6**		
+0.3	**-0.8**	**+3.7**	**+2.4**	**-0.5**	**-1.7**	**+2.9**	**+1.6**	**+1.5**	**+0.3**	**+5.7**	**+4.5**		
11,902	**22.2**	**83,633**	**156.0**	**139,965**	**261.2**	**255,874**	**477.4**	**976,144**	**1,821.4**	**172,626**	**322.1**		
12,093	**22.5**	**80,626**	**149.8**	**136,211**	**253.2**	**252,907**	**470.0**	**962,226**	**1,788.4**	**171,526**	**318.8**		
+1.6	**+1.3**	**-3.6**	**-4.0**	**-2.7**	**-3.0**	**-1.2**	**-1.6**	**-1.4**	**-1.8**	**-0.6**	**-1.0**		
3,768	27.1	11,386	81.8	33,196	238.4	69,924	502.2	253,812	1,823.0	47,919	344.2		
3,802	27.1	12,461	88.9	32,985	235.2	71,350	508.8	253,529	1,808.0	49,818	355.3		
+0.9	+0.2	+9.4	+8.7	-0.6	-1.3	+2.0	+1.3	-0.1	-0.8	+4.0	+3.2		
678	19.9	3,832	112.5	6,450	189.4	17,436	512.0	68,498	2,011.4	13,099	384.6		
639	18.7	4,183	122.1	6,565	191.7	17,159	501.0	65,762	1,920.0	12,378	361.4		
-5.8	-6.3	+9.2	+8.5	+1.8	+1.2	-1.6	-2.1	-4.0	-4.5	-5.5	-6.0		
320	25.1	247	19.4	815	63.9	6,775	531.4	23,906	1,875.1	1,322	103.7		
326	25.3	264	20.5	826	64.2	6,898	536.1	24,585	1,910.7	1,671	129.9		
+1.9	+0.9	+6.9	+5.9	+1.3	+0.4	+1.8	+0.9	+2.8	+1.9	+26.4	+25.2		
1,696	26.7	5,815	91.6	22,594	355.9	30,600	482.0	105,425	1,660.5	25,876	407.6		
1,856	29.1	6,476	101.5	22,110	346.6	32,430	508.4	106,821	1,674.5	27,828	436.2		
+9.4	+8.9	+11.4	+10.8	-2.1	-2.6	+6.0	+5.5	+1.3	+0.8	+7.5	+7.0		
522	42.2	453	36.7	1,170	94.7	4,992	404.0	20,761	1,680.0	2,148	173.8		
458	36.4	445	35.3	1,224	97.2	4,889	388.3	20,060	1,593.1	2,140	170.0		
-12.3	-13.9	-1.8	-3.6	+4.6	+2.7	-2.1	-3.9	-3.4	-5.2	-0.4	-2.2		
412	39.3	922	88.0	1,742	166.2	6,620	631.5	22,038	2,102.2	4,665	445.0		
416	39.3	986	93.1	1,837	173.5	6,824	644.4	23,875	2,254.7	5,043	476.2		
+1.0	8	+6.9	+5.9	+5.5	+4.4	+3.1	+2.0	+8.3	+7.3	+8.1	+7.0		
140	23.0	117	19.2	425	69.8	3,501	575.0	13,184	2,165.5	809	132.9		
107	17.5	107	17.5	423	69.0	3,150	513.8	12,426	2,026.8	758	123.6		
-23.6	-24.1	-8.5	-9.2	-0.5	-1.2	-10.0	-10.7	-5.7	-6.4	-6.3	-7.0		
8,134	20.5	72,247	182.1	106,769	269.1	185,950	468.7	722,332	1,820.8	124,707	314.3		
8,291	20.8	68,165	171.3	103,226	259.5	181,557	456.4	708,697	1,781.4	121,708	305.9		
+1.9	+1.6	-5.7	-5.9	-3.3	-3.6	-2.4	-2.6	-1.9	-2.2	-2.4	-2.7		
1,357	16.1	13,553	161.1	17,099	203.2	43,924	522.0	155,562	1,848.8	34,151	405.9		
1,278	15.1	14,110	166.3	17,370	204.7	46,812	551.7	156,031	1,839.0	37,708	444.4		
-5.8	-6.6	+4.1	+3.2	+1.6	+0.7	+6.6	+5.7	+0.3	-0.5	+10.4	+9.5		
3,530	18.6	40,539	213.6	60,090	316.7	87,946	463.4	340,901	1,796.4	54,231	285.8		
3,546	18.7	36,555	192.3	57,042	300.0	80,400	422.9	329,316	1,732.2	48,287	254.0		
+0.5	+0.3	-9.8	-10.0	-5.1	-5.2	-8.6	-8.7	-3.4	-3.6	-11.0	-11.1		
3,247	26.4	18,155	147.8	29,580	240.9	54,080	440.4	225,869	1,839.2	36,325	295.8		
3,467	28.2	17,500	142.4	28,814	234.5	54,345	442.3	223,350	1,817.8	35,713	290.7		
+6.8	+6.7	-3.6	-3.7	-2.6	-2.6	+0.5	+0.4	-1.1	-1.2	-1.7	-1.7		
22,345	**34.7**	**81,546**	**126.6**	**167,922**	**260.8**	**427,314**	**663.6**	**1,594,285**	**2,475.9**	**237,754**	**369.2**		
22,685	**35.1**	**83,015**	**128.3**	**170,347**	**263.3**	**438,361**	**677.7**	**1,611,700**	**2,491.5**	**245,767**	**379.9**		
+1.5	**+1.1**	**+1.8**	**+1.3**	**+1.4**	**+1.0**	**+2.6**	**+2.1**	**+1.1**	**+0.6**	**+3.4**	**+2.9**		
16,146	35.8	65,782	145.7	123,786	274.1	306,567	678.9	1,098,533	2,432.8	180,743	400.3		
16,526	36.4	66,618	146.9	124,312	274.0	317,477	699.9	1,099,612	2,424.0	180,841	398.7		
+2.4	+1.9	+1.3	+0.8	+0.4	8	+3.6	+3.1	+0.1	-0.4	+0.1	-0.4		
3,926	31.6	25,641	206.5	50,731	408.5	81,850	659.1	313,161	2,521.6	50,267	404.7		
3,938	31.5	24,867	199.2	49,713	398.3	78,844	631.6	304,362	2,438.3	48,784	390.8		
+0.3	-0.2	-3.0	-3.5	-2.0	-2.5	-3.7	-4.2	-2.8	-3.3	-3.0	-3.4		

Table 4

Index of Crime[1]
by Region, Geographic Division, and State, 2000-2001—Continued

Area	Year	Population[2]	Crime Index total		Modified Crime Index total[3]		Violent crime[4]		Property crime[4]		Murder and non-negligent manslaughter	
			Number	Rate per 100,000	Number	Rate per 100,000	Number	Rate per 100,000	Number	Rate per 100,000	Number	Rate per 100,000
Indiana	2000	6,080,485	228,135	3,751.9			21,230	349.1	206,905	3,402.8	352	5.8
	2001	6,114,745	234,282	3,831.4			22,734	371.8	211,548	3,459.6	413	6.8
Percent change			+2.7	+2.1			+7.1	+6.5	+2.2	+1.7	+17.3	+16.7
Michigan	2000	9,938,444	408,456	4,109.9			55,159	555.0	353,297	3,554.9	669	6.7
	2001	9,990,817	407,777	4,081.5			55,424	554.7	352,353	3,526.8	672	6.7
Percent change			-0.2	-0.7			+0.5	8	-0.3	-0.8	+0.4	-0.1
Ohio	2000	11,353,140	458,874	4,041.8			37,935	334.1	420,939	3,707.7	418	3.7
	2001	11,373,541	475,138	4,177.6			40,023	351.9	435,115	3,825.7	452	4.0
Percent change			+3.5	+3.4			+5.5	+5.3	+3.4	+3.2	+8.1	+7.9
Wisconsin	2000	5,363,675	172,124	3,209.1			12,700	236.8	159,424	2,972.3	169	3.2
	2001	5,401,906	179,410	3,321.2			12,486	231.1	166,924	3,090.1	192	3.6
Percent change			+4.2	+3.5			-1.7	-2.4	+4.7	+4.0	+13.6	+12.8
West North Central	2000	19,237,739	740,396	3,848.7			66,886	347.7	673,510	3,501.0	787	4.1
	2001	19,324,104	767,179	3,970.1			69,281	358.5	697,898	3,611.5	690	3.6
Percent change			+3.6	+3.2			+3.6	+3.1	+3.6	+3.2	-12.3	-12.7
Iowa	2000	2,926,324	94,630	3,233.7			7,796	266.4	86,834	2,967.3	46	1.6
	2001	2,923,179	96,499	3,301.2			7,865	269.1	88,634	3,032.1	50	1.7
Percent change			+2.0	+2.1			+0.9	+1.0	+2.1	+2.2	+8.7	+8.8
Kansas	2000	2,688,418	118,527	4,408.8			10,470	389.4	108,057	4,019.4	169	6.3
	2001	2,694,641	116,446	4,321.4			10,909	404.8	105,537	3,916.6	92	3.4
Percent change			-1.8	-2.0			+4.2	+4.0	-2.3	-2.6	-45.6	-45.7
Minnesota	2000	4,919,479	171,611	3,488.4			13,813	280.8	157,798	3,207.6	151	3.1
	2001	4,972,294	178,191	3,583.7			13,145	264.4	165,046	3,319.3	119	2.4
Percent change			+3.8	+2.7			-4.8	-5.8	+4.6	+3.5	-21.2	-22.0
Missouri	2000	5,595,211	253,338	4,527.8			27,419	490.0	225,919	4,037.7	347	6.2
	2001	5,629,707	268,883	4,776.1			30,472	541.3	238,411	4,234.9	372	6.6
Percent change			+6.1	+5.5			+11.1	+10.5	+5.5	+4.9	+7.2	+6.5
Nebraska	2000	1,711,263	70,085	4,095.5			5,606	327.6	64,479	3,767.9	63	3.7
	2001	1,713,235	74,177	4,329.6			5,214	304.3	68,963	4,025.3	43	2.5
Percent change			+5.8	+5.7			-7.0	-7.1	+7.0	+6.8	-31.7	-31.8
North Dakota	2000	642,200	14,694	2,288.1			523	81.4	14,171	2,206.6	4	0.6
	2001	634,448	15,339	2,417.7			505	79.6	14,834	2,338.1	7	1.1
Percent change			+4.4	+5.7			-3.4	-2.3	+4.7	+6.0	+75.0	+77.1
South Dakota	2000	754,844	17,511	2,319.8			1,259	166.8	16,252	2,153.0	7	0.9
	2001	756,600	17,644	2,332.0			1,171	154.8	16,473	2,177.2	7	0.9
Percent change			+0.8	+0.5			-7.0	-7.2	+1.4	+1.1	0.0	-0.2
South[5, 6, 7]	2000	100,236,820	4,759,696	4,748.5			582,887	581.5	4,176,809	4,166.9	6,881	6.9
	2001	101,833,099	4,848,185	4,760.9			590,538	579.9	4,257,647	4,181.0	6,780	6.7
Percent change			+1.9	+0.3			+1.3	-0.3	+1.9	+0.3	-1.5	-3.0
South Atlantic[5, 7]	2000	51,769,160	2,502,806	4,834.6			325,690	629.1	2,177,116	4,205.4	3,546	6.8
	2001	52,762,502	2,512,635	4,762.2			324,975	615.9	2,187,660	4,146.2	3,337	6.3
Percent change			+0.4	-1.5			-0.2	-2.1	+0.5	-1.4	-5.9	-7.7
Delaware	2000	783,600	35,090	4,478.1			5,363	684.4	29,727	3,793.6	25	3.2
	2001	796,165	32,267	4,052.8			4,868	611.4	27,399	3,441.4	23	2.9
Percent change			-8.0	-9.5			-9.2	-10.7	-7.8	-9.3	-8.0	-9.5
District of Columbia[7]	2000	572,059	41,626	7,276.5			8,626	1,507.9	33,000	5,768.6	239	41.8
	2001	571,822	44,085	7,709.6			9,931	1,736.7	34,154	5,972.8	232	40.6
Percent change			+5.9	+6.0			+15.1	+15.2	+3.5	+3.5	-2.9	-2.9

See footnotes at end of table.

Forcible rape		Robbery		Aggravated assault		Burglary		Larceny-theft		Motor vehicle theft		Arson[3]	
Number	Rate per 100,000	Number	Rate per 100,000	Number	Rate per 100,000	Number	Rate per 100,000	Number	Rate per 100,000	Number	Rate per 100,000	Number	Rate per 100,000
1,759	28.9	6,282	103.3	12,837	211.1	41,108	676.1	144,707	2,379.9	21,090	346.8		
1,716	28.1	7,171	117.3	13,434	219.7	42,758	699.3	147,291	2,408.8	21,499	351.6		
-2.4	-3.0	+14.2	+13.5	+4.7	+4.1	+4.0	+3.4	+1.8	+1.2	+1.9	+1.4		
5,025	50.6	13,712	138.0	35,753	359.7	69,790	702.2	227,783	2,291.9	55,724	560.7		
5,264	52.7	12,937	129.5	36,551	365.8	72,038	721.0	226,708	2,269.2	53,607	536.6		
+4.8	+4.2	-5.7	-6.1	+2.2	+1.7	+3.2	+2.7	-0.5	-1.0	-3.8	-4.3		
4,271	37.6	15,610	137.5	17,636	155.3	88,636	780.7	293,277	2,583.2	39,026	343.7		
4,466	39.3	17,199	151.2	17,906	157.4	96,910	852.1	295,976	2,602.3	42,229	371.3		
+4.6	+4.4	+10.2	+10.0	+1.5	+1.3	+9.3	+9.1	+0.9	+0.7	+8.2	+8.0		
1,165	21.7	4,537	84.6	6,829	127.3	25,183	469.5	119,605	2,229.9	14,636	272.9		
1,142	21.1	4,444	82.3	6,708	124.2	26,927	498.5	125,275	2,319.1	14,722	272.5		
-2.0	-2.7	-2.0	-2.7	-1.8	-2.5	+6.9	+6.2	+4.7	+4.0	+0.6	-0.1		
6,199	32.2	15,764	81.9	44,136	229.4	120,747	627.7	495,752	2,577.0	57,011	296.3		
6,159	31.9	16,397	84.9	46,035	238.2	120,884	625.6	512,088	2,650.0	64,926	336.0		
-0.6	-1.1	+4.0	+3.6	+4.3	+3.8	+0.1	-0.3	+3.3	+2.8	+13.9	+13.4		
676	23.1	1,071	36.6	6,003	205.1	16,342	558.4	65,118	2,225.2	5,374	183.6		
649	22.2	1,154	39.5	6,012	205.7	16,885	577.6	66,244	2,266.2	5,505	188.3		
-4.0	-3.9	+7.7	+7.9	+0.1	+0.3	+3.3	+3.4	+1.7	+1.8	+2.4	+2.5		
1,022	38.0	2,048	76.2	7,231	269.0	21,484	799.1	80,077	2,978.6	6,496	241.6		
945	35.1	2,423	89.9	7,449	276.4	20,514	761.3	77,038	2,858.9	7,985	296.3		
-7.5	-7.7	+18.3	+18.0	+3.0	+2.8	-4.5	-4.7	-3.8	-4.0	+22.9	+22.6		
2,240	45.5	3,713	75.5	7,709	156.7	26,116	530.9	118,250	2,403.7	13,432	273.0		
2,236	45.0	3,758	75.6	7,032	141.4	25,496	512.8	124,519	2,504.3	15,031	302.3		
-0.2	-1.2	+1.2	+0.1	-8.8	-9.8	-2.4	-3.4	+5.3	+4.2	+11.9	+10.7		
1,351	24.1	7,598	135.8	18,123	323.9	41,685	745.0	159,539	2,851.3	24,695	441.4		
1,383	24.6	7,771	138.0	20,946	372.1	42,977	763.4	167,420	2,973.9	28,014	497.6		
+2.4	+1.7	+2.3	+1.7	+15.6	+14.9	+3.1	+2.5	+4.9	+4.3	+13.4	+12.7		
436	25.5	1,147	67.0	3,960	231.4	10,131	592.0	49,118	2,870.3	5,230	305.6		
431	25.2	1,128	65.8	3,612	210.8	9,760	569.7	52,713	3,076.8	6,490	378.8		
-1.1	-1.3	-1.7	-1.8	-8.8	-8.9	-3.7	-3.8	+7.3	+7.2	+24.1	+23.9		
169	26.3	56	8.7	294	45.8	2,093	325.9	11,092	1,727.2	986	153.5		
164	25.8	60	9.5	274	43.2	2,165	341.2	11,583	1,825.7	1,086	171.2		
-3.0	-1.8	+7.1	+8.5	-6.8	-5.7	+3.4	+4.7	+4.4	+5.7	+10.1	+11.5		
305	40.4	131	17.4	816	108.1	2,896	383.7	12,558	1,663.7	798	105.7		
351	46.4	103	13.6	710	93.8	3,087	408.0	12,571	1,661.5	815	107.7		
+15.1	+14.8	-21.4	-21.6	-13.0	-13.2	+6.6	+6.3	+0.1	-0.1	+2.1	+1.9		
34,432	**34.4**	**152,957**	**152.6**	**388,617**	**387.7**	**906,573**	**904.4**	**2,851,757**	**2,845.0**	**418,479**	**417.5**		
34,225	**33.6**	**162,590**	**159.7**	**386,943**	**380.0**	**943,739**	**926.8**	**2,878,512**	**2,826.7**	**435,396**	**427.6**		
-0.6	**-2.2**	**+6.3**	**+4.6**	**-0.4**	**-2.0**	**+4.1**	**+2.5**	**+0.9**	**-0.6**	**+4.0**	**+2.4**		
17,031	32.9	89,426	172.7	215,687	416.6	469,304	906.5	1,479,625	2,858.1	228,187	440.8		
16,431	31.1	92,074	174.5	213,133	403.9	479,484	908.8	1,476,731	2,798.8	231,445	438.7		
-3.5	-5.3	+3.0	+1.0	-1.2	-3.0	+2.2	+0.2	-0.2	-2.1	+1.4	-0.5		
424	54.1	1,394	177.9	3,520	449.2	5,216	665.6	21,360	2,725.9	3,151	402.1		
420	52.8	1,156	145.2	3,269	410.6	5,144	646.1	19,476	2,446.2	2,779	349.0		
-0.9	-2.5	-17.1	-18.4	-7.1	-8.6	-1.4	-2.9	-8.8	-10.3	-11.8	-13.2		
251	43.9	3,554	621.3	4,582	801.0	4,745	829.5	21,655	3,785.4	6,600	1,153.7		
188	32.9	3,943	689.6	5,568	973.7	5,011	876.3	21,473	3,755.2	7,670	1,341.3		
-25.1	-25.1	+10.9	+11.0	+21.5	+21.6	+5.6	+5.6	-0.8	-0.8	+16.2	+16.3		

Table 4

Index of Crime[1]
by Region, Geographic Division, and State, 2000-2001—Continued

Area	Year	Population[2]	Crime Index total		Modified Crime Index total[3]		Violent crime[4]		Property crime[4]		Murder and non-negligent manslaughter	
			Number	Rate per 100,000	Number	Rate per 100,000	Number	Rate per 100,000	Number	Rate per 100,000	Number	Rate per 100,000
Florida	2000	15,982,378	910,154	5,694.7			129,777	812.0	780,377	4,882.7	903	5.6
	2001	16,396,515	913,230	5,569.7			130,713	797.2	782,517	4,772.5	874	5.3
Percent change			+0.3	-2.2			+0.7	-1.8	+0.3	-2.3	-3.2	-5.7
Georgia	2000	8,186,453	388,949	4,751.1			41,319	504.7	347,630	4,246.4	651	8.0
	2001	8,383,915	389,543	4,646.3			41,671	497.0	347,872	4,149.3	598	7.1
Percent change			+0.2	-2.2			+0.9	-1.5	+0.1	-2.3	-8.1	-10.3
Maryland	2000	5,296,486	255,085	4,816.1			41,663	786.6	213,422	4,029.5	430	8.1
	2001	5,375,156	261,600	4,866.8			42,088	783.0	219,512	4,083.8	446	8.3
Percent change			+2.6	+1.1			+1.0	-0.5	+2.9	+1.3	+3.7	+2.2
North Carolina	2000	8,049,313	395,972	4,919.3			40,051	497.6	355,921	4,421.8	560	7.0
	2001	8,186,268	404,242	4,938.0			40,465	494.3	363,777	4,443.7	505	6.2
Percent change			+2.1	+0.4			+1.0	-0.7	+2.2	+0.5	-9.8	-11.3
South Carolina[5]	2000	4,012,012	214,515	5,346.8			33,225	828.1	181,290	4,518.7	291	7.3
	2001	4,063,011	193,103	4,752.7			29,265	720.3	163,838	4,032.4	255	6.3
Percent change			-10.0	-11.1			-11.9	-13.0	-9.6	-10.8	-12.4	-13.5
Virginia	2000	7,078,515	214,348	3,028.1			19,943	281.7	194,405	2,746.4	401	5.7
	2001	7,187,734	228,445	3,178.3			20,939	291.3	207,506	2,886.9	364	5.1
Percent change			+6.6	+5.0			+5.0	+3.4	+6.7	+5.1	-9.2	-10.6
West Virginia	2000	1,808,344	47,067	2,602.8			5,723	316.5	41,344	2,286.3	46	2.5
	2001	1,801,916	46,120	2,559.5			5,035	279.4	41,085	2,280.1	40	2.2
Percent change			-2.0	-1.7			-12.0	-11.7	-0.6	-0.3	-13.0	-12.7
East South Central[6]	2000	17,022,810	713,914	4,193.9			84,023	493.6	629,891	3,700.3	1,187	7.0
	2001	17,127,962	727,669	4,248.4			82,814	483.5	644,855	3,764.9	1,277	7.5
Percent change			+1.9	+1.3			-1.4	-2.0	+2.4	+1.7	+7.6	+6.9
Alabama	2000	4,447,100	202,159	4,545.9			21,620	486.2	180,539	4,059.7	329	7.4
	2001	4,464,356	192,835	4,319.4			19,582	438.6	173,253	3,880.8	379	8.5
Percent change			-4.6	-5.0			-9.4	-9.8	-4.0	-4.4	+15.2	+14.8
Kentucky[6]	2000	4,041,769	119,626	2,959.7			11,903	294.5	107,723	2,665.2	193	4.8
	2001	4,065,556	119,449	2,938.1			10,448	257.0	109,001	2,681.1	191	4.7
Percent change			-0.1	-0.7			-12.2	-12.7	+1.2	+0.6	-1.0	-1.6
Mississippi	2000	2,844,658	113,911	4,004.4			10,267	360.9	103,644	3,643.5	255	9.0
	2001	2,858,029	119,615	4,185.2			10,006	350.1	109,609	3,835.1	282	9.9
Percent change			+5.0	+4.5			-2.5	-3.0	+5.8	+5.3	+10.6	+10.1
Tennessee	2000	5,689,283	278,218	4,890.2			40,233	707.2	237,985	4,183.0	410	7.2
	2001	5,740,021	295,770	5,152.8			42,778	745.3	252,992	4,407.5	425	7.4
Percent change			+6.3	+5.4			+6.3	+5.4	+6.3	+5.4	+3.7	+2.7
West South Central	2000	31,444,850	1,542,976	4,906.9			173,174	550.7	1,369,802	4,356.2	2,148	6.8
	2001	31,942,635	1,607,881	5,033.7			182,749	572.1	1,425,132	4,461.5	2,166	6.8
Percent change			+4.2	+2.6			+5.5	+3.9	+4.0	+2.4	+0.8	+0.7
Arkansas	2000	2,673,400	110,019	4,115.3			11,904	445.3	98,115	3,670.0	168	6.3
	2001	2,692,090	111,296	4,134.2			12,190	452.8	99,106	3,681.4	148	5.5
Percent change			+1.2	+0.5			+2.4	+1.7	+1.0	+0.3	-11.9	-12.5
Louisiana	2000	4,468,976	242,344	5,422.8			30,440	681.1	211,904	4,741.7	560	12.5
	2001	4,465,430	238,371	5,338.1			30,678	687.0	207,693	4,651.1	501	11.2
Percent change			-1.6	-1.6			+0.8	+0.9	-2.0	-1.9	-10.5	-10.5
Oklahoma	2000	3,450,654	157,302	4,558.6			17,177	497.8	140,125	4,060.8	182	5.3
	2001	3,460,097	159,405	4,607.0			17,726	512.3	141,679	4,094.7	185	5.3
Percent change			+1.3	+1.1			+3.2	+2.9	+1.1	+0.8	+1.6	+1.4

See footnotes at end of table.

Forcible rape		Robbery		Aggravated assault		Burglary		Larceny-theft		Motor vehicle theft		Arson[3]	
Number	Rate per 100,000	Number	Rate per 100,000	Number	Rate per 100,000	Number	Rate per 100,000	Number	Rate per 100,000	Number	Rate per 100,000	Number	Rate per 100,000
7,057	44.2	31,809	199.0	90,008	563.2	172,898	1,081.8	518,298	3,242.9	89,181	558.0		
6,641	40.5	32,867	200.5	90,331	550.9	176,052	1,073.7	516,548	3,150.4	89,917	548.4		
-5.9	-8.3	+3.3	+0.7	+0.4	-2.2	+1.8	-0.7	-0.3	-2.9	+0.8	-1.7		
1,968	24.0	13,250	161.9	25,450	310.9	68,488	836.6	240,440	2,937.0	38,702	472.8		
2,180	26.0	14,402	171.8	24,491	292.1	71,799	856.4	238,484	2,844.5	37,589	448.3		
+10.8	+8.2	+8.7	+6.1	-3.8	-6.0	+4.8	+2.4	-0.8	-3.1	-2.9	-5.2		
1,543	29.1	13,560	256.0	26,130	493.3	39,426	744.4	145,423	2,745.7	28,573	539.5		
1,449	27.0	13,525	251.6	26,668	496.1	41,553	773.1	145,934	2,715.0	32,025	595.8		
-6.1	-7.5	-0.3	-1.7	+2.1	+0.6	+5.4	+3.9	+0.4	-1.1	+12.1	+10.4		
2,181	27.1	12,595	156.5	24,715	307.0	97,888	1,216.1	232,767	2,891.8	25,266	313.9		
2,083	25.4	13,304	162.5	24,573	300.2	101,889	1,244.6	237,241	2,898.0	24,647	301.1		
-4.5	-6.1	+5.6	+3.9	-0.6	-2.2	+4.1	+2.3	+1.9	+0.2	-2.4	-4.1		
1,660	41.4	6,220	155.0	25,054	624.5	40,319	1,005.0	125,385	3,125.2	15,586	388.5		
1,380	34.0	5,310	130.7	22,320	549.3	36,831	906.5	112,247	2,762.7	14,760	363.3		
-16.9	-17.9	-14.6	-15.7	-10.9	-12.0	-8.7	-9.8	-10.5	-11.6	-5.3	-6.5		
1,616	22.8	6,295	88.9	11,631	164.3	30,434	429.9	146,158	2,064.8	17,813	251.6		
1,770	24.6	6,860	95.4	11,945	166.2	31,604	439.7	157,060	2,185.1	18,842	262.1		
+9.5	+7.9	+9.0	+7.3	+2.7	+1.1	+3.8	+2.3	+7.5	+5.8	+5.8	+4.2		
331	18.3	749	41.4	4,597	254.2	9,890	546.9	28,139	1,556.1	3,315	183.3		
320	17.8	707	39.2	3,968	220.2	9,601	532.8	28,268	1,568.8	3,216	178.5		
-3.3	-3.0	-5.6	-5.3	-13.7	-13.4	-2.9	-2.6	+0.5	+0.8	-3.0	-2.6		
5,778	33.9	21,126	124.1	55,932	328.6	148,901	874.7	424,409	2,493.2	56,581	332.4		
5,844	34.1	22,377	130.6	53,316	311.3	156,673	914.7	428,474	2,501.6	59,708	348.6		
+1.1	+0.5	+5.9	+5.3	-4.7	-5.3	+5.2	+4.6	+1.0	+0.3	+5.5	+4.9		
1,482	33.3	5,702	128.2	14,107	317.2	40,331	906.9	127,399	2,864.8	12,809	288.0		
1,369	30.7	5,584	125.1	12,250	274.4	40,642	910.4	119,992	2,687.8	12,619	282.7		
-7.6	-8.0	-2.1	-2.4	-13.2	-13.5	+0.8	+0.4	-5.8	-6.2	-1.5	-1.9		
1,091	27.0	3,256	80.6	7,363	182.2	25,308	626.2	73,141	1,809.6	9,274	229.5		
1,132	27.8	3,280	80.7	5,845	143.8	26,505	651.9	73,152	1,799.3	9,344	229.8		
+3.8	+3.2	+0.7	+0.1	-20.6	-21.1	+4.7	+4.1	[8]	-0.6	+0.8	+0.2		
1,019	35.8	2,703	95.0	6,290	221.1	26,918	946.3	69,758	2,452.2	6,968	245.0		
1,147	40.1	3,294	115.3	5,283	184.8	29,821	1,043.4	70,315	2,460.3	9,473	331.5		
+12.6	+12.0	+21.9	+21.3	-16.0	-16.4	+10.8	+10.3	+0.8	+0.3	+36.0	+35.3		
2,186	38.4	9,465	166.4	28,172	495.2	56,344	990.4	154,111	2,708.8	27,530	483.9		
2,196	38.3	10,219	178.0	29,938	521.6	59,705	1,040.2	165,015	2,874.8	28,272	492.5		
+0.5	-0.4	+8.0	+7.0	+6.3	+5.3	+6.0	+5.0	+7.1	+6.1	+2.7	+1.8		
11,623	37.0	42,405	134.9	116,998	372.1	288,368	917.1	947,723	3,013.9	133,711	425.2		
11,950	37.4	48,139	150.7	120,494	377.2	307,582	962.9	973,307	3,047.0	144,243	451.6		
+2.8	+1.2	+13.5	+11.8	+3.0	+1.4	+6.7	+5.0	+2.7	+1.1	+7.9	+6.2		
848	31.7	2,001	74.8	8,887	332.4	21,443	802.1	69,740	2,608.7	6,932	259.3		
892	33.1	2,181	81.0	8,969	333.2	22,196	824.5	69,590	2,585.0	7,320	271.9		
+5.2	+4.5	+9.0	+8.2	+0.9	+0.2	+3.5	+2.8	-0.2	-0.9	+5.6	+4.9		
1,497	33.5	7,532	168.5	20,851	466.6	46,289	1,035.8	144,345	3,229.9	21,270	475.9		
1,403	31.4	7,864	176.1	20,910	468.3	46,451	1,040.2	139,555	3,125.2	21,687	485.7		
-6.3	-6.2	+4.4	+4.5	+0.3	+0.4	+0.3	+0.4	-3.3	-3.2	+2.0	+2.0		
1,422	41.2	2,615	75.8	12,958	375.5	31,661	917.5	96,116	2,785.4	12,348	357.8		
1,486	42.9	2,746	79.4	13,309	384.6	34,573	999.2	94,537	2,732.2	12,569	363.3		
+4.5	+4.2	+5.0	+4.7	+2.7	+2.4	+9.2	+8.9	-1.6	-1.9	+1.8	+1.5		

Table 4

Index of Crime[1]
by Region, Geographic Division, and State, 2000-2001—Continued

Area	Year	Population[2]	Crime Index total Number	Crime Index total Rate per 100,000	Modified Crime Index total[3] Number	Modified Crime Index total[3] Rate per 100,000	Violent crime[4] Number	Violent crime[4] Rate per 100,000	Property crime[4] Number	Property crime[4] Rate per 100,000	Murder and non-negligent manslaughter Number	Murder and non-negligent manslaughter Rate per 100,000
Texas	2000	20,851,820	1,033,311	4,955.5			113,653	545.1	919,658	4,410.4	1,238	5.9
	2001	21,325,018	1,098,809	5,152.7			122,155	572.8	976,654	4,579.9	1,332	6.2
Percent change			+6.3	+4.0			+7.5	+5.1	+6.2	+3.8	+7.6	+5.2
West[5]	**2000**	**63,197,932**	**2,671,614**	**4,227.4**			**329,836**	**521.9**	**2,341,778**	**3,705.5**	**3,255**	**5.2**
	2001	**64,471,176**	**2,807,674**	**4,354.9**			**335,413**	**520.3**	**2,472,261**	**3,834.7**	**3,517**	**5.5**
Percent change			**+5.1**	**+3.0**			**+1.7**	**-0.3**	**+5.6**	**+3.5**	**+8.0**	**+5.9**
Mountain[5]	2000	18,172,295	848,560	4,669.5			79,009	434.8	769,551	4,234.7	848	4.7
	2001	18,649,916	884,609	4,743.2			83,798	449.3	800,811	4,293.9	977	5.2
Percent change			+4.2	+1.6			+6.1	+3.3	+4.1	+1.4	+15.2	+12.3
Arizona	2000	5,130,632	299,092	5,829.5			27,281	531.7	271,811	5,297.8	359	7.0
	2001	5,307,331	322,549	6,077.4			28,675	540.3	293,874	5,537.1	400	7.5
Percent change			+7.8	+4.3			+5.1	+1.6	+8.1	+4.5	+11.4	+7.7
Colorado	2000	4,301,261	171,304	3,982.6			14,367	334.0	156,937	3,648.6	134	3.1
	2001	4,417,714	186,379	4,218.9			15,492	350.7	170,887	3,868.2	158	3.6
Percent change			+8.8	+5.9			+7.8	+5.0	+8.9	+6.0	+17.9	+14.8
Idaho	2000	1,293,953	41,228	3,186.2			3,267	252.5	37,961	2,933.7	16	1.2
	2001	1,321,006	41,392	3,133.4			3,211	243.1	38,181	2,890.3	30	2.3
Percent change			+0.4	-1.7			-1.7	-3.7	+0.6	-1.5	+87.5	+83.7
Montana[5]	2000	902,195	35,005	3,880.0			2,807	311.1	32,198	3,568.9	20	2.2
	2001	904,433	33,362	3,688.7			3,187	352.4	30,175	3,336.3	34	3.8
Percent change			-4.7	-4.9			+13.5	+13.3	-6.3	-6.5	+70.0	+69.6
Nevada	2000	1,998,257	85,297	4,268.6			10,474	524.2	74,823	3,744.4	129	6.5
	2001	2,106,074	89,845	4,266.0			12,359	586.8	77,486	3,679.2	180	8.5
Percent change			+5.3	-0.1			+18.0	+12.0	+3.6	-1.7	+39.5	+32.4
New Mexico	2000	1,819,046	100,391	5,518.9			13,786	757.9	86,605	4,761.0	135	7.4
	2001	1,829,146	97,383	5,324.0			14,288	781.1	83,095	4,542.8	99	5.4
Percent change			-3.0	-3.5			+3.6	+3.1	-4.1	-4.6	-26.7	-27.1
Utah	2000	2,233,169	99,958	4,476.1			5,711	255.7	94,247	4,220.3	43	1.9
	2001	2,269,789	96,307	4,243.0			5,314	234.1	90,993	4,008.9	67	3.0
Percent change			-3.7	-5.2			-7.0	-8.5	-3.5	-5.0	+55.8	+53.3
Wyoming	2000	493,782	16,285	3,298.0			1,316	266.5	14,969	3,031.5	12	2.4
	2001	494,423	17,392	3,517.6			1,272	257.3	16,120	3,260.4	9	1.8
Percent change			+6.8	+6.7			-3.3	-3.5	+7.7	+7.5	-25.0	-25.1
Pacific	2000	45,025,637·	1,823,054	4,048.9			250,827	557.1	1,572,227	3,491.8	2,407	5.3
	2001	45,821,260	1,923,065	4,196.9			251,615	549.1	1,671,450	3,647.8	2,540	5.5
Percent change			+5.5	+3.7			+0.3	-1.4	+6.3	+4.5	+5.5	+3.7
Alaska	2000	626,932	26,641	4,249.4			3,554	566.9	23,087	3,682.5	27	4.3
	2001	634,892	26,895	4,236.2			3,735	588.3	23,160	3,647.9	39	6.1
Percent change			+1.0	-0.3			+5.1	+3.8	+0.3	-0.9	+44.4	+42.6
California	2000	33,871,648	1,266,714	3,739.7			210,531	621.6	1,056,183	3,118.2	2,079	6.1
	2001	34,501,130	1,346,557	3,902.9			212,855	617.0	1,133,702	3,286.0	2,206	6.4
Percent change			+6.3	+4.4			+1.1	-0.7	+7.3	+5.4	+6.1	+4.2
Hawaii	2000	1,211,537	62,987	5,198.9			2,954	243.8	60,033	4,955.1	35	2.9
	2001	1,224,398	65,947	5,386.1			3,117	254.6	62,830	5,131.5	32	2.6
Percent change			+4.7	+3.6			+5.5	+4.4	+4.7	+3.6	-8.6	-9.5
Oregon	2000	3,421,399	165,780	4,845.4			12,000	350.7	153,780	4,494.7	70	2.0
	2001	3,472,867	175,174	5,044.1			10,650	306.7	164,524	4,737.4	84	2.4
Percent change			+5.7	+4.1			-11.3	-12.6	+7.0	+5.4	+20.0	+18.2

See footnotes at end of table.

Forcible rape		Robbery		Aggravated assault		Burglary		Larceny-theft		Motor vehicle theft		Arson[3]	
Number	Rate per 100,000	Number	Rate per 100,000	Number	Rate per 100,000	Number	Rate per 100,000	Number	Rate per 100,000	Number	Rate per 100,000	Number	Rate per 100,000
7,856	37.7	30,257	145.1	74,302	356.3	188,975	906.3	637,522	3,057.4	93,161	446.8		
8,169	38.3	35,348	165.8	77,306	362.5	204,362	958.3	669,625	3,140.1	102,667	481.4		
+4.0	+1.7	+16.8	+14.2	+4.0	+1.7	+8.1	+5.7	+5.0	+2.7	+10.2	+7.8		
21,499	**34.0**	**89,880**	**142.2**	**215,202**	**340.5**	**461,231**	**729.8**	**1,549,404**	**2,451.7**	**331,143**	**524.0**		
21,488	**33.3**	**96,690**	**150.0**	**213,718**	**331.5**	**474,760**	**736.4**	**1,623,733**	**2,518.5**	**373,768**	**579.7**		
-0.1	**-2.0**	**+7.6**	**+5.5**	**-0.7**	**-2.7**	**+2.9**	**+0.9**	**+4.8**	**+2.7**	**+12.9**	**+10.6**		
6,848	37.7	19,318	106.3	51,995	286.1	145,280	799.5	532,577	2,930.7	91,694	504.6		
6,843	36.7	21,806	116.9	54,172	290.5	148,079	794.0	546,277	2,929.1	106,455	570.8		
-0.1	-2.6	+12.9	+10.0	+4.2	+1.5	+1.9	-0.7	+2.6	-0.1	+16.1	+13.1		
1,577	30.7	7,504	146.3	17,841	347.7	51,902	1,011.6	176,705	3,444.1	43,204	842.1		
1,518	28.6	8,868	167.1	17,889	337.1	54,821	1,032.9	186,850	3,520.6	52,203	983.6		
-3.7	-6.9	+18.2	+14.2	+0.3	-3.1	+5.6	+2.1	+5.7	+2.2	+20.8	+16.8		
1,774	41.2	3,034	70.5	9,425	219.1	27,133	630.8	112,843	2,623.5	16,961	394.3		
1,930	43.7	3,555	80.5	9,849	222.9	28,533	645.9	121,360	2,747.1	20,994	475.2		
+8.8	+5.9	+17.2	+14.1	+4.5	+1.7	+5.2	+2.4	+7.5	+4.7	+23.8	+20.5		
384	29.7	223	17.2	2,644	204.3	7,330	566.5	28,545	2,206.0	2,086	161.2		
425	32.2	245	18.5	2,511	190.1	7,507	568.3	28,285	2,141.2	2,389	180.8		
+10.7	+8.4	+9.9	+7.6	-5.0	-7.0	+2.4	+0.3	-0.9	-2.9	+14.5	+12.2		
308	34.1	203	22.5	2,276	252.3	3,624	401.7	26,678	2,957.0	1,896	210.2		
188	20.8	230	25.4	2,735	302.4	3,670	405.8	24,684	2,729.2	1,821	201.3		
-39.0	-39.1	+13.3	+13.0	+20.2	+19.9	+1.3	+1.0	-7.5	-7.7	-4.0	-4.2		
860	43.0	4,543	227.3	4,942	247.3	17,526	877.1	44,125	2,208.2	13,172	659.2		
883	41.9	4,932	234.2	6,364	302.2	17,711	840.9	45,073	2,140.1	14,702	698.1		
+2.7	-2.6	+8.6	+3.0	+28.8	+22.2	+1.1	-4.1	+2.1	-3.1	+11.6	+5.9		
922	50.7	2,499	137.4	10,230	562.4	21,339	1,173.1	57,925	3,184.4	7,341	403.6		
850	46.5	2,695	147.3	10,644	581.9	19,552	1,068.9	56,406	3,083.7	7,137	390.2		
-7.8	-8.3	+7.8	+7.2	+4.0	+3.5	-8.4	-8.9	-2.6	-3.2	-2.8	-3.3		
863	38.6	1,242	55.6	3,563	159.5	14,348	642.5	73,438	3,288.5	6,461	289.3		
896	39.5	1,197	52.7	3,154	139.0	13,804	608.2	70,676	3,113.8	6,513	286.9		
+3.8	+2.1	-3.6	-5.2	-11.5	-12.9	-3.8	-5.3	-3.8	-5.3	+0.8	-0.8		
160	32.4	70	14.2	1,074	217.5	2,078	420.8	12,318	2,494.6	573	116.0		
153	30.9	84	17.0	1,026	207.5	2,481	501.8	12,943	2,617.8	696	140.8		
-4.4	-4.5	+20.0	+19.8	-4.5	-4.6	+19.4	+19.2	+5.1	+4.9	+21.5	+21.3		
14,651	32.5	70,562	156.7	163,207	362.5	315,951	701.7	1,016,827	2,258.3	239,449	531.8		
14,645	32.0	74,884	163.4	159,546	348.2	326,681	712.9	1,077,456	2,351.4	267,313	583.4		
8	-1.8	+6.1	+4.3	-2.2	-3.9	+3.4	+1.6	+6.0	+4.1	+11.6	+9.7		
497	79.3	490	78.2	2,540	405.1	3,899	621.9	16,838	2,685.8	2,350	374.8		
501	78.9	514	81.0	2,681	422.3	3,847	605.9	16,695	2,629.6	2,618	412.4		
+0.8	-0.5	+4.9	+3.6	+5.6	+4.2	-1.3	-2.6	-0.8	-2.1	+11.4	+10.0		
9,785	28.9	60,249	177.9	138,418	408.7	222,293	656.3	651,855	1,924.5	182,035	537.4		
9,961	28.9	64,545	187.1	136,143	394.6	232,000	672.4	697,669	2,022.2	204,033	591.4		
+1.8	-0.1	+7.1	+5.2	-1.6	-3.4	+4.4	+2.5	+7.0	+5.1	+12.1	+10.0		
346	28.6	1,123	92.7	1,450	119.7	10,665	880.3	43,254	3,570.2	6,114	504.6		
409	33.4	1,142	93.3	1,534	125.3	11,162	911.6	44,925	3,669.2	6,743	550.7		
+18.2	+17.0	+1.7	+0.6	+5.8	+4.7	+4.7	+3.6	+3.9	+2.8	+10.3	+9.1		
1,286	37.6	2,888	84.4	7,756	226.7	25,618	748.8	114,230	3,338.7	13,932	407.2		
1,174	33.8	2,749	79.2	6,643	191.3	26,648	767.3	123,034	3,542.7	14,842	427.4		
-8.7	-10.1	-4.8	-6.2	-14.4	-15.6	+4.0	+2.5	+7.7	+6.1	+6.5	+5.0		

Table 4

Index of Crime[1]

by Region, Geographic Division, and State, 2000-2001—Continued

Area	Year	Population[2]	Crime Index total		Modified Crime Index total[3]		Violent crime[4]		Property crime[4]		Murder and non-negligent manslaughter	
			Number	Rate per 100,000	Number	Rate per 100,000	Number	Rate per 100,000	Number	Rate per 100,000	Number	Rate per 100,000
Washington	2000	5,894,121	300,932	5,105.6			21,788	369.7	279,144	4,736.0	196	3.3
	2001	5,987,973	308,492	5,151.9			21,258	355.0	287,234	4,796.8	179	3.0
Percent change			+2.5	+0.9			-2.4	-4.0	+2.9	+1.3	-8.7	-10.1
Puerto Rico	2000	3,808,610	75,377	1,979.1			12,404	325.7	62,973	1,653.4	693	18.2
	2001	3,839,810	70,117	1,826.1			11,403	297.0	58,714	1,529.1	744	19.4
Percent change			-7.0	-7.7			-8.1	-8.8	-6.8	-7.5	+7.4	+6.5

[1] The murder and nonnegligent homicides that occurred as a result of the events of September 11, 2001, were not included in this table. See special report, Section V.

[2] Populations are Bureau of the Census 2001 provisional estimates as of July 1, 2001, and 2000 decennial counts.

[3] Although arson data are included in the trend and clearance tables, sufficient data are not available to estimate totals for this offense.

[4] Violent crimes are offenses of murder, forcible rape, robbery, and aggravated assault. Property crimes are offenses of burglary, larceny-theft, and motor vehicle theft.

[5] The 2000 crime figures have been adjusted. See Crime Trends, Appendix I, for details.

[6] Limited data for 2001 were available for the states of Illinois and Kentucky; therefore, it was necessary that their crime counts be estimated. See Offense Estimation, Appendix I, for details.

[7] Includes offenses reported by the Zoological Police.

[8] Less than one-tenth of 1 percent.

Offense totals are based on all reporting agencies and estimates for unreported areas.

Forcible rape		Robbery		Aggravated assault		Burglary		Larceny-theft		Motor vehicle theft		Arson[3]	
Number	Rate per 100,000	Number	Rate per 100,000	Number	Rate per 100,000	Number	Rate per 100,000	Number	Rate per 100,000	Number	Rate per 100,000	Number	Rate per 100,000
2,737	46.4	5,812	98.6	13,043	221.3	53,476	907.3	190,650	3,234.6	35,018	594.1		
2,600	43.4	5,934	99.1	12,545	209.5	53,024	885.5	195,133	3,258.7	39,077	652.6		
-5.0	-6.5	+2.1	+0.5	-3.8	-5.3	-0.8	-2.4	+2.4	+0.7	+11.6	+9.8		
228	6.0	8,757	229.9	2,726	71.6	21,057	552.9	28,940	759.9	12,976	340.7		
187	4.9	7,999	208.3	2,473	64.4	19,931	519.1	26,140	680.8	12,643	329.3		
-18.0	-18.6	-8.7	-9.4	-9.3	-10.0	-5.3	-6.1	-9.7	-10.4	-2.6	-3.4		

Table 5

Index of Crime[1]
by State, 2001

Area	Population	Crime Index total	Modified Crime Index total[2]	Violent crime[3]	Property crime[3]	Murder and non-negligent man-slaughter[3]	Forcible rape	Robbery	Aggravated assault	Burglary	Larceny-theft	Motor vehicle theft	Arson[2]
ALABAMA													
Metropolitan Statistical Area	3,121,024												
Area actually reporting	92.8%	145,775		14,422	131,353	271	1,025	4,838	8,288	30,504	90,735	10,114	
Estimated totals	100.0%	154,595		15,181	139,414	282	1,073	5,049	8,777	32,284	96,469	10,661	
Cities outside metropolitan areas	532,212												
Area actually reporting	81.4%	21,521		2,329	19,192	46	125	343	1,815	3,748	14,570	874	
Estimated totals	100.0%	26,454		2,864	23,590	57	154	422	2,231	4,607	17,909	1,074	
Rural	811,120												
Area actually reporting	71.7%	8,456		1,103	7,353	29	102	81	891	2,691	4,028	634	
Estimated totals	100.0%	11,786		1,537	10,249	40	142	113	1,242	3,751	5,614	884	
State Total	**4,464,356**	**192,835**		**19,582**	**173,253**	**379**	**1,369**	**5,584**	**12,250**	**40,642**	**119,992**	**12,619**	
Rate per 100,000 inhabitants		4,319.4		438.6	3,880.8	8.5	30.7	125.1	274.4	910.4	2,687.8	282.7	
ALASKA													
Metropolitan Statistical Area	263,588												
Area actually reporting	100.0%	13,214		1,748	11,466	10	210	384	1,144	1,606	8,648	1,212	
Cities outside metropolitan areas	165,145												
Area actually reporting	76.2%	6,809		983	5,826	12	126	79	766	772	4,405	649	
Estimated totals	100.0%	8,941		1,291	7,650	16	165	104	1,006	1,014	5,784	852	
Rural	206,159												
Area actually reporting	100.0%	4,740		696	4,044	13	126	26	531	1,227	2,263	554	
State Total	**634,892**	**26,895**		**3,735**	**23,160**	**39**	**501**	**514**	**2,681**	**3,847**	**16,695**	**2,618**	
Rate per 100,000 inhabitants		4,236.2		588.3	3,647.9	6.1	78.9	81.0	422.3	605.9	2,629.6	412.4	
ARIZONA													
Metropolitan Statistical Area	4,682,911												
Area actually reporting	99.6%	301,819		26,589	275,230	371	1,416	8,716	16,086	50,802	173,753	50,675	
Estimated totals	100.0%	302,889		26,663	276,226	372	1,421	8,734	16,136	51,021	174,391	50,814	
Cities outside metropolitan areas	297,168												
Area actually reporting	99.1%	12,771		1,002	11,769	8	51	87	856	2,206	8,764	799	
Estimated totals	100.0%	12,887		1,011	11,876	8	51	88	864	2,226	8,844	806	
Rural	327,252												
Area actually reporting	100.0%	6,773		1,001	5,772	20	46	46	889	1,574	3,615	583	
State Total	**5,307,331**	**322,549**		**28,675**	**293,874**	**400**	**1,518**	**8,868**	**17,889**	**54,821**	**186,850**	**52,203**	
Rate per 100,000 inhabitants		6,077.4		540.3	5,537.1	7.5	28.6	167.1	337.1	1,032.9	3,520.6	983.6	
ARKANSAS													
Metropolitan Statistical Area	1,330,256												
Area actually reporting	100.0%	71,929		7,198	64,731	83	580	1,649	4,886	13,319	46,387	5,025	
Cities outside metropolitan areas	498,097												
Area actually reporting	100.0%	26,367		3,338	23,029	31	169	451	2,687	5,157	16,543	1,329	
Rural	863,737												
Area actually reporting	98.7%	12,826		1,632	11,194	34	141	80	1,377	3,670	6,571	953	
Estimated totals	100.0%	13,000		1,654	11,346	34	143	81	1,396	3,720	6,660	966	
State Total	**2,692,090**	**111,296**		**12,190**	**99,106**	**148**	**892**	**2,181**	**8,969**	**22,196**	**69,590**	**7,320**	
Rate per 100,000 inhabitants		4,134.2		452.8	3,681.4	5.5	33.1	81.0	333.2	824.5	2,585.0	271.9	
CALIFORNIA													
Metropolitan Statistical Area	33,359,040												
Area actually reporting	100.0%	1,311,344		208,710	1,102,634	2,166	9,609	64,035	132,900	222,944	678,825	200,865	
Cities outside metropolitan areas	478,856												
Area actually reporting	100.0%	20,583		2,270	18,313	16	158	342	1,754	4,269	12,182	1,862	
Rural	663,234												
Area actually reporting	100.0%	14,630		1,875	12,755	24	194	168	1,489	4,787	6,662	1,306	
State Total	**34,501,130**	**1,346,557**		**212,855**	**1,133,702**	**2,206**	**9,961**	**64,545**	**136,143**	**232,000**	**697,669**	**204,033**	
Rate per 100,000 inhabitants		3,902.9		617.0	3,286.0	6.4	28.9	187.1	394.6	672.4	2,022.2	591.4	

See footnotes at end of table.

Table 5

Index of Crime[1]
by State, 2001—Continued

Area	Population	Crime Index total	Modified Crime Index total[2]	Violent crime[3]	Property crime[3]	Murder and non-negligent man-slaughter	Forcible rape	Robbery	Aggravated assault	Burglary	Larceny-theft	Motor vehicle theft	Arson[2]
COLORADO													
Metropolitan Statistical Area	3,705,331												
Area actually reporting	95.8%	157,191		13,459	143,732	135	1,637	3,336	8,351	24,553	100,180	18,999	
Estimated totals	100.0%	165,481		14,085	151,396	140	1,715	3,484	8,746	25,553	105,814	20,029	
Cities outside metropolitan areas	308,225												
Area actually reporting	76.9%	11,687		707	10,980	4	109	44	550	1,517	8,975	488	
Estimated totals	100.0%	15,205		920	14,285	5	142	57	716	1,974	11,676	635	
Rural	404,158												
Area actually reporting	93.5%	5,325		455	4,870	12	68	13	362	941	3,620	309	
Estimated totals	100.0%	5,693		487	5,206	13	73	14	387	1,006	3,870	330	
State Total	**4,417,714**	**186,379**		**15,492**	**170,887**	**158**	**1,930**	**3,555**	**9,849**	**28,533**	**121,360**	**20,994**	
Rate per 100,000 inhabitants		4,218.9		350.7	3,868.2	3.6	43.7	80.5	222.9	645.9	2,747.1	475.2	
CONNECTICUT													
Metropolitan Statistical Area	2,859,060												
Area actually reporting	100.0%	96,828		10,125	86,703	96	582	4,054	5,393	14,863	60,128	11,712	
Cities outside metropolitan areas	60,372												
Area actually reporting	100.0%	2,334		223	2,111	1	13	30	179	382	1,596	133	
Rural	505,642												
Area actually reporting	100.0%	7,629		1,144	6,485	8	44	99	993	1,914	4,038	533	
State Total	**3,425,074**	**106,791**		**11,492**	**95,299**	**105**	**639**	**4,183**	**6,565**	**17,159**	**65,762**	**12,378**	
Rate per 100,000 inhabitants		3,117.9		335.5	2,782.4	3.1	18.7	122.1	191.7	501.0	1,920.0	361.4	
DELAWARE													
Metropolitan Statistical Area	637,015												
Area actually reporting	99.9%	27,010		3,949	23,061	21	311	1,044	2,573	4,180	16,311	2,570	
Estimated totals	100.0%	27,051		3,954	23,097	21	311	1,045	2,577	4,185	16,340	2,572	
Cities outside metropolitan areas	38,932												
Area actually reporting	100.0%	2,336		318	2,018	0	26	58	234	358	1,586	74	
Rural	120,218												
Area actually reporting	100.0%	2,880		596	2,284	2	83	53	458	601	1,550	133	
State Total	**796,165**	**32,267**		**4,868**	**27,399**	**23**	**420**	**1,156**	**3,269**	**5,144**	**19,476**	**2,779**	
Rate per 100,000 inhabitants		4,052.8		611.4	3,441.4	2.9	52.8	145.2	410.6	646.1	2,446.2	349.0	
DISTRICT OF COLUMBIA[4]													
Metropolitan Statistical Area	571,822												
Area actually reporting	100.0%	44,085		9,931	34,154	232	188	3,943	5,568	5,011	21,473	7,670	
Cities outside metropolitan areas	None												
Rural	None												
Total	**571,822**	**44,085**		**9,931**	**34,154**	**232**	**188**	**3,943**	**5,568**	**5,011**	**21,473**	**7,670**	
Rate per 100,000 inhabitants		7,709.6		1,736.7	5,972.8	40.6	32.9	689.6	973.7	876.3	3,755.2	1,341.3	
FLORIDA													
Metropolitan Statistical Area	15,221,969												
Area actually reporting	99.9%	867,648		124,010	743,638	823	6,157	31,984	85,046	164,687	491,714	87,237	
Estimated totals	100.0%	868,133		124,066	744,067	823	6,159	31,999	85,085	164,774	492,009	87,284	
Cities outside metropolitan areas	236,519												
Area actually reporting	95.5%	15,865		2,103	13,762	13	95	409	1,586	3,134	9,779	849	
Estimated totals	100.0%	16,607		2,201	14,406	14	99	428	1,660	3,281	10,236	889	
Rural	938,027												
Area actually reporting	100.0%	28,490		4,446	24,044	37	383	440	3,586	7,997	14,303	1,744	
State Total	**16,396,515**	**913,230**		**130,713**	**782,517**	**874**	**6,641**	**32,867**	**90,331**	**176,052**	**516,548**	**89,917**	
Rate per 100,000 inhabitants		5,569.7		797.2	4,772.5	5.3	40.5	200.5	550.9	1,073.7	3,150.4	548.4	

See footnotes at end of table.

Table 5

Index of Crime[1]
by State, 2001—Continued

Area	Population	Crime Index total	Modified Crime Index total[2]	Violent crime[3]	Property crime[3]	Murder and non-negligent man-slaughter	Forcible rape	Robbery	Aggravated assault	Burglary	Larceny-theft	Motor vehicle theft	Arson[2]
GEORGIA													
Metropolitan Statistical Area	5,803,341												
Area actually reporting	98.2%	285,094		30,667	254,427	448	1,595	12,602	16,022	51,482	171,787	31,158	
Estimated totals	100.0%	289,868		31,077	258,791	453	1,619	12,759	16,246	52,285	174,872	31,634	
Cities outside metropolitan areas	899,214												
Area actually reporting	91.7%	51,876		5,726	46,150	54	268	1,142	4,262	8,374	35,317	2,459	
Estimated totals	100.0%	56,583		6,246	50,337	59	292	1,246	4,649	9,134	38,521	2,682	
Rural	1,681,360												
Area actually reporting	86.9%	37,447		3,779	33,668	75	234	345	3,125	9,020	21,804	2,844	
Estimated totals	100.0%	43,092		4,348	38,744	86	269	397	3,596	10,380	25,091	3,273	
State Total	**8,383,915**	**389,543**		**41,671**	**347,872**	**598**	**2,180**	**14,402**	**24,491**	**71,799**	**238,484**	**37,589**	
Rate per 100,000 inhabitants		4,646.3		497.0	4,149.3	7.1	26.0	171.8	292.1	856.4	2,844.5	448.3	
HAWAII													
Metropolitan Statistical Area	885,605												
Area actually reporting	100.0%	48,442		2,453	45,989	20	293	999	1,141	7,340	33,052	5,597	
Cities outside metropolitan areas	None												
Rural	338,793												
Area actually reporting	100.0%	17,505		664	16,841	12	116	143	393	3,822	11,873	1,146	
State Total	**1,224,398**	**65,947**		**3,117**	**62,830**	**32**	**409**	**1,142**	**1,534**	**11,162**	**44,925**	**6,743**	
Rate per 100,000 inhabitants		5,386.1		254.6	5,131.5	2.6	33.4	93.3	125.3	911.6	3,669.2	550.7	
IDAHO													
Metropolitan Statistical Area	518,530												
Area actually reporting	100.0%	20,497		1,594	18,903	9	207	135	1,243	3,469	14,165	1,269	
Cities outside metropolitan areas	372,632												
Area actually reporting	97.1%	13,991		878	13,113	8	112	80	678	2,350	10,103	660	
Estimated totals	100.0%	14,402		903	13,499	8	115	82	698	2,419	10,401	679	
Rural	429,844												
Area actually reporting	98.9%	6,422		707	5,715	13	102	28	564	1,601	3,678	436	
Estimated totals	100.0%	6,493		714	5,779	13	103	28	570	1,619	3,719	441	
State Total	**1,321,006**	**41,392**		**3,211**	**38,181**	**30**	**425**	**245**	**2,511**	**7,507**	**28,285**	**2,389**	
Rate per 100,000 inhabitants		3,133.4		243.1	2,890.3	2.3	32.2	18.5	190.1	568.3	2,141.2	180.8	
ILLINOIS[5]													
State Total	**12,482,301**	**511,494**		**79,504**	**431,990**	**986**	**3,938**	**24,867**	**49,713**	**78,844**	**304,362**	**48,784**	
Rate per 100,000 inhabitants		4,097.8		636.9	3,460.8	7.9	31.5	199.2	398.3	631.6	2,438.3	390.8	
INDIANA													
Metropolitan Statistical Area	4,414,639												
Area actually reporting	88.8%	168,472		18,092	150,380	346	1,306	6,338	10,102	30,411	102,938	17,031	
Estimated totals	100.0%	182,738		19,231	163,507	358	1,398	6,598	10,877	32,921	112,304	18,282	
Cities outside metropolitan areas	584,671												
Area actually reporting	79.9%	24,551		1,090	23,461	18	121	276	675	3,581	18,514	1,366	
Estimated totals	100.0%	30,737		1,365	29,372	23	151	346	845	4,483	23,179	1,710	
Rural	1,115,435												
Area actually reporting	50.2%	10,450		1,074	9,376	16	84	114	860	2,689	5,930	757	
Estimated totals	100.0%	20,807		2,138	18,669	32	167	227	1,712	5,354	11,808	1,507	
State Total	**6,114,745**	**234,282**		**22,734**	**211,548**	**413**	**1,716**	**7,171**	**13,434**	**42,758**	**147,291**	**21,499**	
Rate per 100,000 inhabitants		3,831.4		371.8	3,459.6	6.8	28.1	117.3	219.7	699.3	2,408.8	351.6	

See footnotes at end of table.

Table 5

Index of Crime[1]
by State, 2001—Continued

Area	Population	Crime Index total	Modified Crime Index total[2]	Violent crime[3]	Property crime[3]	Murder and non-negligent man-slaughter	Forcible rape	Robbery	Aggravated assault	Burglary	Larceny-theft	Motor vehicle theft	Arson[2]
IOWA													
Metropolitan Statistical Area	1,324,709												
Area actually reporting	98.6%	62,278		5,397	56,881	35	463	979	3,920	10,077	42,887	3,917	
Estimated totals	100.0%	62,862		5,425	57,437	35	465	985	3,940	10,149	43,350	3,938	
Cities outside metropolitan areas	706,401												
Area actually reporting	87.5%	22,951		1,705	21,246	8	130	133	1,434	3,934	16,333	979	
Estimated totals	100.0%	26,231		1,949	24,282	9	149	152	1,639	4,496	18,667	1,119	
Rural	892,069												
Area actually reporting	99.1%	7,341		487	6,854	6	35	17	429	2,220	4,190	444	
Estimated totals	100.0%	7,406		491	6,915	6	35	17	433	2,240	4,227	448	
State Total	**2,923,179**	**96,499**		**7,865**	**88,634**	**50**	**649**	**1,154**	**6,012**	**16,885**	**66,244**	**5,505**	
Rate per 100,000 inhabitants		3,301.2		269.1	3,032.1	1.7	22.2	39.5	205.7	577.6	2,266.2	188.3	
KANSAS													
Metropolitan Statistical Area	1,524,581												
Area actually reporting	92.1%	71,995		7,235	64,760	68	516	2,060	4,591	12,441	46,589	5,730	
Estimated totals	100.0%	75,461		7,562	67,899	71	541	2,119	4,831	13,145	48,767	5,987	
Cities outside metropolitan areas	721,090												
Area actually reporting	82.3%	25,922		1,959	23,963	5	226	224	1,504	4,082	18,643	1,238	
Estimated totals	100.0%	31,497		2,380	29,117	6	275	272	1,827	4,960	22,653	1,504	
Rural	448,970												
Area actually reporting	94.9%	9,003		917	8,086	14	122	30	751	2,286	5,331	469	
Estimated totals	100.0%	9,488		967	8,521	15	129	32	791	2,409	5,618	494	
State Total	**2,694,641**	**116,446**		**10,909**	**105,537**	**92**	**945**	**2,423**	**7,449**	**20,514**	**77,038**	**7,985**	
Rate per 100,000 inhabitants		4,321.4		404.8	3,916.6	3.4	35.1	89.9	276.4	761.3	2,858.9	296.3	
KENTUCKY[5]													
State Total	**4,065,556**	**119,449**		**10,448**	**109,001**	**191**	**1,132**	**3,280**	**5,845**	**26,505**	**73,152**	**9,344**	
Rate per 100,000 inhabitants		2,938.1		257.0	2,681.1	4.7	27.8	80.7	143.8	651.9	1,799.3	229.8	
LOUISIANA													
Metropolitan Statistical Area	3,367,535												
Area actually reporting	98.4%	193,992		23,958	170,034	422	1,111	7,147	15,278	36,441	113,728	19,865	
Estimated totals	100.0%	197,176		24,311	172,865	423	1,130	7,215	15,543	36,992	115,818	20,055	
Cities outside metropolitan areas	366,764												
Area actually reporting	82.9%	20,056		2,733	17,323	21	97	349	2,266	4,225	12,359	739	
Estimated totals	100.0%	24,205		3,298	20,907	25	117	421	2,735	5,099	14,916	892	
Rural	731,131												
Area actually reporting	90.8%	15,420		2,786	12,634	48	142	207	2,389	3,957	8,005	672	
Estimated totals	100.0%	16,990		3,069	13,921	53	156	228	2,632	4,360	8,821	740	
State Total	**4,465,430**	**238,371**		**30,678**	**207,693**	**501**	**1,403**	**7,864**	**20,910**	**46,451**	**139,555**	**21,687**	
Rate per 100,000 inhabitants		5,338.1		687.0	4,651.1	11.2	31.4	176.1	468.3	1,040.2	3,125.2	485.7	
MAINE													
Metropolitan Statistical Area	485,545												
Area actually reporting	99.9%	15,523		669	14,854	6	161	184	318	2,676	11,495	683	
Estimated totals	100.0%	15,536		669	14,867	6	161	184	318	2,678	11,505	684	
Cities outside metropolitan areas	425,744												
Area actually reporting	99.4%	13,320		509	12,811	1	109	69	330	2,291	9,982	538	
Estimated totals	100.0%	13,406		512	12,894	1	110	69	332	2,306	10,047	541	
Rural	375,381												
Area actually reporting	100.0%	5,646		253	5,393	11	55	11	176	1,914	3,033	446	
State Total	**1,286,670**	**34,588**		**1,434**	**33,154**	**18**	**326**	**264**	**826**	**6,898**	**24,585**	**1,671**	
Rate per 100,000 inhabitants		2,688.2		111.5	2,576.7	1.4	25.3	20.5	64.2	536.1	1,910.7	129.9	

See footnotes at end of table.

Table 5

Index of Crime[1]

by State, 2001—Continued

Area	Population	Crime Index total	Modified Crime Index total[2]	Violent crime[3]	Property crime[3]	Murder and non-negligent man-slaughter	Forcible rape	Robbery	Aggravated assault	Burglary	Larceny-theft	Motor vehicle theft	Arson[2]
MARYLAND													
Metropolitan Statistical Area	4,983,985												
Area actually reporting	99.9%	246,892		39,671	207,221	434	1,332	13,196	24,709	38,815	137,057	31,349	
Estimated totals	100.0%	247,234		39,705	207,529	434	1,334	13,209	24,728	38,858	137,274	31,397	
Cities outside metropolitan areas	107,309												
Area actually reporting	100.0%	8,725		1,319	7,406	2	56	248	1,013	1,366	5,675	365	
Rural	283,862												
Area actually reporting	100.0%	5,641		1,064	4,577	10	59	68	927	1,329	2,985	263	
State Total	**5,375,156**	**261,600**		**42,088**	**219,512**	**446**	**1,449**	**13,525**	**26,668**	**41,553**	**145,934**	**32,025**	
Rate per 100,000 inhabitants		4,866.8		783.0	4,083.8	8.3	27.0	251.6	496.1	773.1	2,715.0	595.8	
MASSACHUSETTS													
Metropolitan Statistical Area	6,122,157												
Area actually reporting	96.0%	184,831		28,558	156,273	141	1,739	6,370	20,308	29,995	99,384	26,894	
Estimated totals	100.0%	190,087		29,238	160,849	142	1,786	6,452	20,858	30,917	102,551	27,381	
Cities outside metropolitan areas	247,593												
Area actually reporting	88.9%	6,722		1,190	5,532	3	62	21	1,104	1,343	3,793	396	
Estimated totals	100.0%	7,558		1,338	6,220	3	70	24	1,241	1,510	4,265	445	
Rural	9,554												
Area actually reporting	100.0%	21		11	10	0	0	0	11	3	5	2	
State Total	**6,379,304**	**197,666**		**30,587**	**167,079**	**145**	**1,856**	**6,476**	**22,110**	**32,430**	**106,821**	**27,828**	
Rate per 100,000 inhabitants		3,098.6		479.5	2,619.1	2.3	29.1	101.5	346.6	508.4	1,674.5	436.2	
MICHIGAN													
Metropolitan Statistical Area	8,212,518												
Area actually reporting	99.3%	359,226		51,298	307,928	642	4,114	12,750	33,792	61,428	195,350	51,150	
Estimated totals	100.0%	361,388		51,487	309,901	643	4,134	12,788	33,922	61,748	196,765	51,388	
Cities outside metropolitan areas	586,465												
Area actually reporting	91.8%	18,707		1,201	17,506	7	307	80	807	2,552	14,230	724	
Estimated totals	100.0%	20,371		1,308	19,063	8	334	87	879	2,779	15,496	788	
Rural	1,191,834												
Area actually reporting	98.3%	25,571		2,584	22,987	21	782	61	1,720	7,382	14,199	1,406	
Estimated totals	100.0%	26,018		2,629	23,389	21	796	62	1,750	7,511	14,447	1,431	
State Total	**9,990,817**	**407,777**		**55,424**	**352,353**	**672**	**5,264**	**12,937**	**36,551**	**72,038**	**226,708**	**53,607**	
Rate per 100,000 inhabitants		4,081.5		554.7	3,526.8	6.7	52.7	129.5	365.8	721.0	2,269.2	536.6	
MINNESOTA													
Metropolitan Statistical Area	3,500,541												
Area actually reporting	98.7%	139,026		11,065	127,961	87	1,676	3,608	5,694	18,546	96,753	12,662	
Estimated totals	100.0%	140,653		11,142	129,511	87	1,693	3,625	5,737	18,731	98,012	12,768	
Cities outside metropolitan areas	555,006												
Area actually reporting	94.3%	21,519		1,037	20,482	8	240	100	689	2,634	16,861	987	
Estimated totals	100.0%	22,826		1,100	21,726	8	255	106	731	2,794	17,885	1,047	
Rural	916,747												
Area actually reporting	96.2%	14,159		869	13,290	23	277	26	543	3,822	8,298	1,170	
Estimated totals	100.0%	14,712		903	13,809	24	288	27	564	3,971	8,622	1,216	
State Total	**4,972,294**	**178,191**		**13,145**	**165,046**	**119**	**2,236**	**3,758**	**7,032**	**25,496**	**124,519**	**15,031**	
Rate per 100,000 inhabitants		3,583.7		264.4	3,319.3	2.4	45.0	75.6	141.4	512.8	2,504.3	302.3	
MISSISSIPPI													
Metropolitan Statistical Area	1,028,476												
Area actually reporting	83.5%	52,787		3,971	48,816	103	481	1,734	1,653	11,757	31,707	5,352	
Estimated totals	100.0%	58,352		4,294	54,058	114	531	1,802	1,847	13,171	35,133	5,754	
Cities outside metropolitan areas	654,291												
Area actually reporting	81.8%	33,212		2,732	30,480	56	268	935	1,473	7,738	21,060	1,682	
Estimated totals	100.0%	40,604		3,341	37,263	69	328	1,143	1,801	9,460	25,747	2,056	
Rural	1,175,262												
Area actually reporting	45.6%	9,415		1,080	8,335	45	131	159	745	3,277	4,300	758	
Estimated totals	100.0%	20,659		2,371	18,288	99	288	349	1,635	7,190	9,435	1,663	
State Total	**2,858,029**	**119,615**		**10,006**	**109,609**	**282**	**1,147**	**3,294**	**5,283**	**29,821**	**70,315**	**9,473**	
Rate per 100,000 inhabitants		4,185.2		350.1	3,835.1	9.9	40.1	115.3	184.8	1,043.4	2,460.3	331.5	

See footnotes at end of table.

Table 5

Index of Crime[1]
by State, 2001—Continued

Area	Population	Crime Index total	Modified Crime Index total[2]	Violent crime[3]	Property crime[3]	Murder and non-negligent man-slaughter	Forcible rape	Robbery	Aggravated assault	Burglary	Larceny-theft	Motor vehicle theft	Arson[2]
MISSOURI													
Metropolitan Statistical Area	3,819,525												
Area actually reporting	98.8%	220,713		24,674	196,039	329	1,021	7,375	15,949	33,033	137,289	25,717	
Estimated totals	100.0%	222,774		24,832	197,942	330	1,031	7,409	16,062	33,292	138,771	25,879	
Cities outside metropolitan areas	526,521												
Area actually reporting	97.5%	24,888		2,425	22,463	9	176	258	1,982	3,731	17,803	929	
Estimated totals	100.0%	25,534		2,488	23,046	9	181	265	2,033	3,828	18,265	953	
Rural	1,283,661												
Area actually reporting	95.3%	19,599		3,002	16,597	31	163	92	2,716	5,579	9,892	1,126	
Estimated totals	100.0%	20,575		3,152	17,423	33	171	97	2,851	5,857	10,384	1,182	
State Total	**5,629,707**	**268,883**		**30,472**	**238,411**	**372**	**1,383**	**7,771**	**20,946**	**42,977**	**167,420**	**28,014**	
Rate per 100,000 inhabitants		4,776.1		541.3	4,234.9	6.6	24.6	138.0	372.1	763.4	2,973.9	497.6	
MONTANA													
Metropolitan Statistical Area	306,270												
Area actually reporting	76.2%	12,456		784	11,672	14	49	155	566	1,383	9,609	680	
Estimated totals	100.0%	14,058		993	13,065	14	55	164	760	1,618	10,635	812	
Cities outside metropolitan areas	174,563												
Area actually reporting	49.7%	5,031		404	4,627	3	30	17	354	428	3,967	232	
Estimated totals	100.0%	10,126		813	9,313	6	60	34	713	861	7,985	467	
Rural	423,600												
Area actually reporting	62.0%	5,688		856	4,832	9	45	20	782	738	3,758	336	
Estimated totals	100.0%	9,178		1,381	7,797	14	73	32	1,262	1,191	6,064	542	
State Total	**904,433**	**33,362**		**3,187**	**30,175**	**34**	**188**	**230**	**2,735**	**3,670**	**24,684**	**1,821**	
Rate per 100,000 inhabitants		3,688.7		352.4	3,336.3	3.8	20.8	25.4	302.4	405.8	2,729.2	201.3	
NEBRASKA													
Metropolitan Statistical Area	900,872												
Area actually reporting	100.0%	51,559		4,290	47,269	34	280	1,046	2,930	6,071	35,820	5,378	
Cities outside metropolitan areas	407,707												
Area actually reporting	84.9%	14,245		566	13,679	0	101	60	405	1,946	11,095	638	
Estimated totals	100.0%	16,775		667	16,108	0	119	71	477	2,292	13,065	751	
Rural	404,656												
Area actually reporting	88.9%	5,193		228	4,965	8	28	10	182	1,242	3,402	321	
Estimated totals	100.0%	5,843		257	5,586	9	32	11	205	1,397	3,828	361	
State Total	**1,713,235**	**74,177**		**5,214**	**68,963**	**43**	**431**	**1,128**	**3,612**	**9,760**	**52,713**	**6,490**	
Rate per 100,000 inhabitants		4,329.6		304.3	4,025.3	2.5	25.2	65.8	210.8	569.7	3,076.8	378.8	
NEVADA													
Metropolitan Statistical Area	1,842,036												
Area actually reporting	100.0%	82,852		11,475	71,377	175	782	4,853	5,665	16,284	40,764	14,329	
Cities outside metropolitan areas	45,517												
Area actually reporting	100.0%	1,788		117	1,671	1	14	15	87	326	1,246	99	
Rural	218,521												
Area actually reporting	100.0%	5,205		767	4,438	4	87	64	612	1,101	3,063	274	
State Total	**2,106,074**	**89,845**		**12,359**	**77,486**	**180**	**883**	**4,932**	**6,364**	**17,711**	**45,073**	**14,702**	
Rate per 100,000 inhabitants		4,266.0		586.8	3,679.2	8.5	41.9	234.2	302.2	840.9	2,140.1	698.1	
NEW HAMPSHIRE													
Metropolitan Statistical Area	747,600												
Area actually reporting	71.4%	14,239		1,142	13,097	7	219	317	599	2,335	9,556	1,206	
Estimated totals	100.0%	17,900		1,393	16,507	7	288	355	743	2,968	12,046	1,493	
Cities outside metropolitan areas	430,198												
Area actually reporting	67.5%	6,817		392	6,425	7	115	38	232	1,100	4,946	379	
Estimated totals	100.0%	10,102		580	9,522	10	170	56	344	1,630	7,330	562	
Rural	81,383												
Area actually reporting	5.8%	72		10	62	0	0	2	8	17	40	5	
Estimated totals	100.0%	1,231		171	1,060	0	0	34	137	291	684	85	
State Total	**1,259,181**	**29,233**		**2,144**	**27,089**	**17**	**458**	**445**	**1,224**	**4,889**	**20,060**	**2,140**	
Rate per 100,000 inhabitants		2,321.6		170.3	2,151.3	1.4	36.4	35.3	97.2	388.3	1,593.1	170.0	

See footnotes at end of table.

Table 5

Index of Crime[1]
by State, 2001—Continued

Area	Population	Crime Index total	Modified Crime Index total[2]	Violent crime[3]	Property crime[3]	Murder and non-negligent man-slaughter	Forcible rape	Robbery	Aggravated assault	Burglary	Larceny-theft	Motor vehicle theft	Arson[2]
NEW JERSEY													
Metropolitan Statistical Area	8,484,431												
Area actually reporting	99.9%	272,222		32,984	239,238	336	1,277	14,079	17,292	46,716	154,919	37,603	
Estimated totals	100.0%	273,645		33,094	240,551	336	1,278	14,110	17,370	46,812	156,031	37,708	
Cities outside metropolitan areas	None												
Rural	None												
State Total	**8,484,431**	**273,645**		**33,094**	**240,551**	**336**	**1,278**	**14,110**	**17,370**	**46,812**	**156,031**	**37,708**	
Rate per 100,000 inhabitants		3,225.3		390.1	2,835.2	4.0	15.1	166.3	204.7	551.7	1,839.0	444.4	
NEW MEXICO													
Metropolitan Statistical Area	1,045,351												
Area actually reporting	86.7%	61,426		8,124	53,302	50	434	2,061	5,579	11,820	36,006	5,476	
Estimated totals	100.0%	65,900		9,028	56,872	54	484	2,199	6,291	12,919	38,064	5,889	
Cities outside metropolitan areas	435,707												
Area actually reporting	89.6%	23,151		3,597	19,554	31	234	389	2,943	4,563	14,140	851	
Estimated totals	100.0%	25,844		4,015	21,829	35	261	434	3,285	5,094	15,785	950	
Rural	348,088												
Area actually reporting	86.7%	4,889		1,080	3,809	9	91	54	926	1,334	2,217	258	
Estimated totals	100.0%	5,639		1,245	4,394	10	105	62	1,068	1,539	2,557	298	
State Total	**1,829,146**	**97,383**		**14,288**	**83,095**	**99**	**850**	**2,695**	**10,644**	**19,552**	**56,406**	**7,137**	
Rate per 100,000 inhabitants		5,324.0		781.1	4,542.8	5.4	46.5	147.3	581.9	1,068.9	3,083.7	390.2	
NEW YORK													
Metropolitan Statistical Area	17,505,214												
Area actually reporting	85.7%	474,734		90,627	384,107	897	2,909	35,716	51,105	65,161	273,649	45,297	
Estimated totals	100.0%	523,111		94,801	428,310	937	3,256	36,279	54,329	73,653	307,179	47,478	
Cities outside metropolitan areas	602,372												
Area actually reporting	92.5%	16,682		1,352	15,330	7	135	190	1,020	2,434	12,531	365	
Estimated totals	100.0%	18,041		1,462	16,579	8	146	205	1,103	2,632	13,552	395	
Rural	903,792												
Area actually reporting	95.6%	14,300		1,760	12,540	14	138	68	1,540	3,935	8,209	396	
Estimated totals	100.0%	14,954		1,840	13,114	15	144	71	1,610	4,115	8,585	414	
State Total	**19,011,378**	**556,106**		**98,103**	**458,003**	**960**	**3,546**	**36,555**	**57,042**	**80,400**	**329,316**	**48,287**	
Rate per 100,000 inhabitants		2,925.1		516.0	2,409.1	5.0	18.7	192.3	300.0	422.9	1,732.2	254.0	
NORTH CAROLINA													
Metropolitan Statistical Area	5,529,566												
Area actually reporting	99.6%	293,531		30,046	263,485	346	1,478	10,971	17,251	68,285	176,077	19,123	
Estimated totals	100.0%	295,036		30,149	264,887	346	1,482	11,006	17,315	68,568	177,129	19,190	
Cities outside metropolitan areas	798,564												
Area actually reporting	95.3%	55,301		5,487	49,814	54	253	1,529	3,651	12,635	34,849	2,330	
Estimated totals	100.0%	58,030		5,757	52,273	57	265	1,604	3,831	13,259	36,569	2,445	
Rural	1,858,138												
Area actually reporting	98.4%	50,363		4,487	45,876	100	331	683	3,373	19,743	23,169	2,964	
Estimated totals	100.0%	51,176		4,559	46,617	102	336	694	3,427	20,062	23,543	3,012	
State Total	**8,186,268**	**404,242**		**40,465**	**363,777**	**505**	**2,083**	**13,304**	**24,573**	**101,889**	**237,241**	**24,647**	
Rate per 100,000 inhabitants		4,938.0		494.3	4,443.7	6.2	25.4	162.5	300.2	1,244.6	2,898.0	301.1	
NORTH DAKOTA													
Metropolitan Statistical Area	280,536												
Area actually reporting	99.0%	8,704		313	8,391	4	115	39	155	1,130	6,659	602	
Estimated totals	100.0%	8,805		315	8,490	4	116	39	156	1,141	6,741	608	
Cities outside metropolitan areas	145,318												
Area actually reporting	83.1%	3,727		93	3,634	2	30	13	48	417	2,956	261	
Estimated totals	100.0%	4,485		112	4,373	2	36	16	58	502	3,557	314	
Rural	208,594												
Area actually reporting	75.5%	1,547		59	1,488	1	9	4	45	394	970	124	
Estimated totals	100.0%	2,049		78	1,971	1	12	5	60	522	1,285	164	
State Total	**634,448**	**15,339**		**505**	**14,834**	**7**	**164**	**60**	**274**	**2,165**	**11,583**	**1,086**	
Rate per 100,000 inhabitants		2,417.7		79.6	2,338.1	1.1	25.8	9.5	43.2	341.2	1,825.7	171.2	

See footnotes at end of table.

Table 5

Index of Crime[1]
by State, 2001—Continued

Area	Population	Crime Index total	Modified Crime Index total[2]	Violent crime[3]	Property crime[3]	Murder and non-negligent man-slaughter	Forcible rape	Robbery	Aggravated assault	Burglary	Larceny-theft	Motor vehicle theft	Arson[2]
OHIO													
Metropolitan Statistical Area	9,230,336												
Area actually reporting	83.0%	361,877		34,256	327,621	386	3,546	15,612	14,712	74,997	216,310	36,314	
Estimated totals	100.0%	410,952		36,939	374,013	409	3,929	16,511	16,090	83,290	251,374	39,349	
Cities outside metropolitan areas	783,071												
Area actually reporting	68.0%	27,660		1,345	26,315	14	221	357	753	4,398	20,930	987	
Estimated totals	100.0%	40,679		1,978	38,701	21	325	525	1,107	6,468	30,781	1,452	
Rural	1,360,134												
Area actually reporting	65.5%	15,392		724	14,668	14	139	107	464	4,683	9,050	935	
Estimated totals	100.0%	23,507		1,106	22,401	22	212	163	709	7,152	13,821	1,428	
State Total	11,373,541	475,138		40,023	435,115	452	4,466	17,199	17,906	96,910	295,976	42,229	
Rate per 100,000 inhabitants		4,177.6		351.9	3,825.7	4.0	39.3	151.2	157.4	852.1	2,602.3	371.3	
OKLAHOMA													
Metropolitan Statistical Area	2,103,077												
Area actually reporting	100.0%	117,057		12,761	104,296	115	1,070	2,425	9,151	23,827	70,512	9,957	
Cities outside metropolitan areas	690,391												
Area actually reporting	100.0%	31,843		3,247	28,596	26	297	273	2,651	7,415	19,480	1,701	
Rural	666,629												
Area actually reporting	100.0%	10,505		1,718	8,787	44	119	48	1,507	3,331	4,545	911	
State Total	3,460,097	159,405		17,726	141,679	185	1,486	2,746	13,309	34,573	94,537	12,569	
Rate per 100,000 inhabitants		4,607.0		512.3	4,094.7	5.3	42.9	79.4	384.6	999.2	2,732.2	363.3	
OREGON													
Metropolitan Statistical Area	2,540,011												
Area actually reporting	99.9%	139,004		9,056	129,948	53	969	2,459	5,575	19,684	97,704	12,560	
Estimated totals	100.0%	139,078		9,060	130,018	53	970	2,460	5,577	19,694	97,758	12,566	
Cities outside metropolitan areas	442,064												
Area actually reporting	97.7%	24,901		994	23,907	14	118	232	630	3,938	18,590	1,379	
Estimated totals	100.0%	25,494		1,018	24,476	14	121	238	645	4,032	19,032	1,412	
Rural	490,792												
Area actually reporting	100.0%	10,602		572	10,030	17	83	51	421	2,922	6,244	864	
State Total	3,472,867	175,174		10,650	164,524	84	1,174	2,749	6,643	26,648	123,034	14,842	
Rate per 100,000 inhabitants		5,044.1		306.7	4,737.4	2.4	33.8	79.2	191.3	767.3	3,542.7	427.4	
PENNSYLVANIA													
Metropolitan Statistical Area	10,396,568												
Area actually reporting	88.2%	295,409		43,333	252,076	573	2,758	16,277	23,725	43,006	177,689	31,381	
Estimated totals	100.0%	324,947		46,079	278,868	599	2,948	16,968	25,564	46,693	198,723	33,452	
Cities outside metropolitan areas	798,876												
Area actually reporting	67.6%	14,807		1,799	13,008	15	152	253	1,379	2,004	10,316	688	
Estimated totals	100.0%	21,912		2,662	19,250	22	225	374	2,041	2,966	15,266	1,018	
Rural	1,091,706												
Area actually reporting	100.0%	16,981		1,691	15,290	30	294	158	1,209	4,686	9,361	1,243	
State Total	12,287,150	363,840		50,432	313,408	651	3,467	17,500	28,814	54,345	223,350	35,713	
Rate per 100,000 inhabitants		2,961.1		410.4	2,550.7	5.3	28.2	142.4	234.5	442.3	1,817.8	290.7	
PUERTO RICO													
Metropolitan Statistical Area	3,247,020												
Area actually reporting	100.0%	62,440		10,234	52,206	666	160	7,384	2,024	16,679	23,778	11,749	
Cities outside metropolitan areas	592,790												
Area actually reporting	100.0%	7,677		1,169	6,508	78	27	615	449	3,252	2,362	894	
Total	3,839,810	70,117		11,403	58,714	744	187	7,999	2,473	19,931	26,140	12,643	
Rate per 100,000 inhabitants		1,826.1		297.0	1,529.1	19.4	4.9	208.3	64.4	519.1	680.8	329.3	

See footnotes at end of table.

Table 5

Index of Crime[1]
by State, 2001—Continued

Area	Population	Crime Index total	Modified Crime Index total[2]	Violent crime[3]	Property crime[3]	Murder and non-negligent man-slaughter	Forcible rape	Robbery	Aggravated assault	Burglary	Larceny-theft	Motor vehicle theft	Arson[2]
RHODE ISLAND													
Metropolitan Statistical Area	993,716												
Area actually reporting	100.0%	36,431		3,052	33,379	37	394	943	1,678	6,278	22,193	4,908	
Cities outside metropolitan areas	65,204												
Area actually reporting	100.0%	2,462		210	2,252	0	15	41	154	542	1,604	106	
Rural	None												
Area actually reporting	100.0%	127		16	111	2	7	2	5	4	78	29	
State Total	**1,058,920**	**39,020**		**3,278**	**35,742**	**39**	**416**	**986**	**1,837**	**6,824**	**23,875**	**5,043**	
Rate per 100,000 inhabitants		3,684.9		309.6	3,375.3	3.7	39.3	93.1	173.5	644.4	2,254.7	476.2	
SOUTH CAROLINA													
Metropolitan Statistical Area	2,842,642												
Area actually reporting	99.2%	138,184		19,317	118,867	168	1,017	4,138	13,994	24,981	82,655	11,231	
Estimated totals	100.0%	139,343		19,439	119,904	168	1,021	4,166	14,084	25,144	83,462	11,298	
Cities outside metropolitan areas	307,734												
Area actually reporting	88.1%	19,756		3,665	16,091	28	113	445	3,079	3,268	11,875	948	
Estimated totals	100.0%	22,414		4,158	18,256	32	128	505	3,493	3,708	13,472	1,076	
Rural	912,635												
Area actually reporting	99.6%	31,209		5,643	25,566	55	230	636	4,722	7,944	15,246	2,376	
Estimated totals	100.0%	31,346		5,668	25,678	55	231	639	4,743	7,979	15,313	2,386	
State Total	**4,063,011**	**193,103**		**29,265**	**163,838**	**255**	**1,380**	**5,310**	**22,320**	**36,831**	**112,247**	**14,760**	
Rate per 100,000 inhabitants		4,752.7		720.3	4,032.4	6.3	34.0	130.7	549.3	906.5	2,762.7	363.3	
SOUTH DAKOTA													
Metropolitan Statistical Area	261,585												
Area actually reporting	93.7%	8,936		660	8,276	4	196	71	389	1,419	6,446	411	
Estimated totals	100.0%	9,392		686	8,706	4	209	71	402	1,502	6,777	427	
Cities outside metropolitan areas	208,963												
Area actually reporting	90.8%	5,428		252	5,176	1	89	15	147	866	4,102	208	
Estimated totals	100.0%	5,976		278	5,698	1	98	17	162	953	4,516	229	
Rural	286,052												
Area actually reporting	54.0%	1,229		112	1,117	1	24	8	79	341	690	86	
Estimated totals	100.0%	2,276		207	2,069	2	44	15	146	632	1,278	159	
State Total	**756,600**	**17,644**		**1,171**	**16,473**	**7**	**351**	**103**	**710**	**3,087**	**12,571**	**815**	
Rate per 100,000 inhabitants		2,332.0		154.8	2,177.2	0.9	46.4	13.6	93.8	408.0	1,661.5	107.7	
TENNESSEE													
Metropolitan Statistical Area	3,896,594												
Area actually reporting	99.9%	233,467		34,829	198,638	348	1,791	9,521	23,169	45,336	129,132	24,170	
Estimated totals	100.0%	233,675		34,850	198,825	348	1,792	9,524	23,186	45,364	129,278	24,183	
Cities outside metropolitan areas	651,837												
Area actually reporting	99.9%	36,745		4,319	32,426	27	199	540	3,553	6,570	23,823	2,033	
Estimated totals	100.0%	36,861		4,325	32,536	27	200	542	3,556	6,590	23,909	2,037	
Rural	1,191,590												
Area actually reporting	100.0%	25,234		3,603	21,631	50	204	153	3,196	7,751	11,828	2,052	
State Total	**5,740,021**	**295,770**		**42,778**	**252,992**	**425**	**2,196**	**10,219**	**29,938**	**59,705**	**165,015**	**28,272**	
Rate per 100,000 inhabitants		5,152.8		745.3	4,407.5	7.4	38.3	178.0	521.6	1,040.2	2,874.8	492.5	
TEXAS													
Metropolitan Statistical Area	18,093,364												
Area actually reporting	99.9%	1,007,510		112,536	894,974	1,184	7,211	34,426	69,715	181,724	614,997	98,253	
Estimated totals	100.0%	1,008,215		112,586	895,629	1,184	7,216	34,438	69,748	181,855	615,477	98,297	
Cities outside metropolitan areas	1,442,562												
Area actually reporting	98.4%	60,685		5,869	54,816	57	592	709	4,511	12,231	39,917	2,668	
Estimated totals	100.0%	61,452		5,949	55,503	58	599	717	4,575	12,384	40,417	2,702	
Rural	1,789,092												
Area actually reporting	99.2%	28,908		3,590	25,318	89	351	191	2,959	10,042	13,621	1,655	
Estimated totals	100.0%	29,142		3,620	25,522	90	354	193	2,983	10,123	13,731	1,668	
State Total	**21,325,018**	**1,098,809**		**122,155**	**976,654**	**1,332**	**8,169**	**35,348**	**77,306**	**204,362**	**669,625**	**102,667**	
Rate per 100,000 inhabitants		5,152.7		572.8	4,579.9	6.2	38.3	165.8	362.5	958.3	3,140.1	481.4	

See footnotes at end of table.

Table 5

Index of Crime[1]
by State, 2001—Continued

Area	Population	Crime Index total	Modified Crime Index total[2]	Violent crime[3]	Property crime[3]	Murder and non-negligent man-slaughter	Forcible rape	Robbery	Aggravated assault	Burglary	Larceny-theft	Motor vehicle theft	Arson[2]
UTAH													
Metropolitan Statistical Area	1,736,512												
Area actually reporting	99.8%	82,277		4,570	77,707	55	727	1,158	2,630	11,349	60,481	5,877	
Estimated totals	100.0%	82,391		4,576	77,815	55	728	1,159	2,634	11,365	60,566	5,884	
Cities outside metropolitan areas	286,959												
Area actually reporting	96.3%	8,874		436	8,438	6	111	24	295	1,365	6,722	351	
Estimated totals	100.0%	9,213		452	8,761	6	115	25	306	1,417	6,980	364	
Rural	246,318												
Area actually reporting	96.6%	4,544		277	4,267	6	51	13	207	987	3,024	256	
Estimated totals	100.0%	4,703		286	4,417	6	53	13	214	1,022	3,130	265	
State Total	**2,269,789**	**96,307**		**5,314**	**90,993**	**67**	**896**	**1,197**	**3,154**	**13,804**	**70,676**	**6,513**	
Rate per 100,000 inhabitants		4,243.0		234.1	4,008.9	3.0	39.5	52.7	139.0	608.2	3,113.8	286.9	
VERMONT													
Metropolitan Statistical Area	162,250												
Area actually reporting	100.0%	6,243		252	5,991	5	33	35	179	952	4,793	246	
Cities outside metropolitan areas	204,916												
Area actually reporting	99.4%	7,205		273	6,932	0	48	61	164	1,140	5,523	269	
Estimated totals	100.0%	7,249		274	6,975	0	48	61	165	1,147	5,557	271	
Rural	245,924												
Area actually reporting	100.0%	3,486		118	3,368	2	26	11	79	1,051	2,076	241	
State Total	**613,090**	**16,978**		**644**	**16,334**	**7**	**107**	**107**	**423**	**3,150**	**12,426**	**758**	
Rate per 100,000 inhabitants		2,769.3		105.0	2,664.2	1.1	17.5	17.5	69.0	513.8	2,026.8	123.6	
VIRGINIA													
Metropolitan Statistical Area	5,613,370												
Area actually reporting	96.3%	184,960		16,759	168,201	283	1,294	6,178	9,004	24,663	127,527	16,011	
Estimated totals	100.0%	194,560		17,450	177,110	285	1,357	6,393	9,415	25,528	134,735	16,847	
Cities outside metropolitan areas	442,640												
Area actually reporting	92.4%	14,603		1,309	13,294	22	131	224	932	1,764	10,806	724	
Estimated totals	100.0%	15,806		1,417	14,389	24	142	242	1,009	1,909	11,696	784	
Rural	1,131,724												
Area actually reporting	99.4%	17,972		2,060	15,912	55	269	224	1,512	4,142	10,566	1,204	
Estimated totals	100.0%	18,079		2,072	16,007	55	271	225	1,521	4,167	10,629	1,211	
State Total	**7,187,734**	**228,445**		**20,939**	**207,506**	**364**	**1,770**	**6,860**	**11,945**	**31,604**	**157,060**	**18,842**	
Rate per 100,000 inhabitants		3,178.3		291.3	2,886.9	5.1	24.6	95.4	166.2	439.7	2,185.1	262.1	
WASHINGTON													
Metropolitan Statistical Area	4,977,163												
Area actually reporting	97.8%	256,328		18,559	237,769	155	2,043	5,550	10,811	42,765	159,196	35,808	
Estimated totals	100.0%	261,276		18,853	242,423	158	2,088	5,631	10,976	43,606	162,333	36,484	
Cities outside metropolitan areas	464,069												
Area actually reporting	96.0%	30,054		1,428	28,626	5	293	238	892	4,640	22,578	1,408	
Estimated totals	100.0%	31,302		1,487	29,815	5	305	248	929	4,833	23,516	1,466	
Rural	546,741												
Area actually reporting	100.0%	15,914		918	14,996	16	207	55	640	4,585	9,284	1,127	
State Total	**5,987,973**	**308,492**		**21,258**	**287,234**	**179**	**2,600**	**5,934**	**12,545**	**53,024**	**195,133**	**39,077**	
Rate per 100,000 inhabitants		5,151.9		355.0	4,796.8	3.0	43.4	99.1	209.5	885.5	3,258.7	652.6	

See footnotes at end of table.

Table 5

Index of Crime[1]

by State, 2001—Continued

Area	Population	Crime Index total	Modified Crime Index total[2]	Violent crime[3]	Property crime[3]	Murder and non-negligent man-slaughter	Forcible rape	Robbery	Aggravated assault	Burglary	Larceny-theft	Motor vehicle theft	Arson[2]
WEST VIRGINIA													
Metropolitan Statistical Area	762,844												
Area actually reporting	92.6%	25,060		2,404	22,656	18	180	516	1,690	4,846	16,009	1,801	
Estimated totals	100.0%	26,516		2,551	23,965	19	188	533	1,811	5,126	16,929	1,910	
Cities outside metropolitan areas	278,413												
Area actually reporting	96.6%	7,841		924	6,917	4	49	105	766	1,378	5,204	335	
Estimated totals	100.0%	8,116		957	7,159	4	51	109	793	1,426	5,386	347	
Rural	760,659												
Area actually reporting	97.8%	11,238		1,494	9,744	17	79	64	1,334	2,983	5,823	938	
Estimated totals	100.0%	11,488		1,527	9,961	17	81	65	1,364	3,049	5,953	959	
State Total	**1,801,916**	**46,120**		**5,035**	**41,085**	**40**	**320**	**707**	**3,968**	**9,601**	**28,268**	**3,216**	
Rate per 100,000 inhabitants		2,559.5		279.4	2,280.1	2.2	17.8	39.2	220.2	532.8	1,568.8	178.5	
WISCONSIN													
Metropolitan Statistical Area	3,664,455												
Area actually reporting	98.9%	136,845		10,571	126,274	167	870	4,296	5,238	19,630	93,868	12,776	
Estimated totals	100.0%	138,032		10,609	127,423	167	873	4,309	5,260	19,759	94,833	12,831	
Cities outside metropolitan areas	710,332												
Area actually reporting	98.8%	25,991		980	25,011	11	147	83	739	2,925	21,218	868	
Estimated totals	100.0%	26,303		992	25,311	11	149	84	748	2,960	21,473	878	
Rural	1,027,119												
Area actually reporting	97.1%	14,644		861	13,783	14	117	50	680	4,087	8,712	984	
Estimated totals	100.0%	15,075		885	14,190	14	120	51	700	4,208	8,969	1,013	
State Total	**5,401,906**	**179,410**		**12,486**	**166,924**	**192**	**1,142**	**4,444**	**6,708**	**26,927**	**125,275**	**14,722**	
Rate per 100,000 inhabitants		3,321.2		231.1	3,090.1	3.6	21.1	82.3	124.2	498.5	2,319.1	272.5	
WYOMING													
Metropolitan Statistical Area	148,332												
Area actually reporting	100.0%	6,061		338	5,723	4	63	49	222	998	4,458	267	
Cities outside metropolitan areas	206,928												
Area actually reporting	99.1%	8,776		658	8,118	4	67	29	558	1,040	6,770	308	
Estimated totals	100.0%	8,853		664	8,189	4	68	29	563	1,049	6,829	311	
Rural	139,163												
Area actually reporting	100.0%	2,478		270	2,208	1	22	6	241	434	1,656	118	
State Total	**494,423**	**17,392**		**1,272**	**16,120**	**9**	**153**	**84**	**1,026**	**2,481**	**12,943**	**696**	
Rate per 100,000 inhabitants		3,517.6		257.3	3,260.4	1.8	30.9	17.0	207.5	501.8	2,617.8	140.8	

[1] The murder and nonnegligent homicides that occurred as a result of the events of September 11, 2001, were not included in this table. See special report, Section V.

[2] Although arson data are included in the trend and clearance tables, sufficient data are not available to estimate totals for this offense.

[3] Violent crimes are offenses of murder, forcible rape, robbery, and aggravated assault. Property crimes are offenses of burglary, larceny-theft, and motor vehicle theft.

[4] Includes offenses reported by the Zoological Police.

[5] Limited data for 2001 were available for Illinois and Kentucky; therefore, it was necessary that their crime counts be estimated. See Offense Estimation, Appendix I, for details. Offense totals are based on all reporting agencies and estimates for unreported areas.

Table 6

Index of Crime[1]
by Metropolitan Statistical Area, 2001

Metropolitan Statistical Area	Population	Crime Index total	Modified Crime Index total[2]	Violent crime[3]	Property crime[3]	Murder and non-negligent man-slaughter	Forcible rape	Robbery	Aggravated assault	Burglary	Larceny-theft	Motor vehicle theft	Arson[2]
Abilene, TX M.S.A.	**129,427**												
(Includes Taylor County.)													
City of Abilene	118,561	5,186		383	4,803	2	66	88	227	1,084	3,504	215	
Total area actually reporting	100.0%	5,254		407	4,847	3	66	86	252	1,128	3,498	221	
Rate per 100,000 inhabitants		4,059.4		314.5	3,745.0	2.3	51.0	66.4	194.7	871.5	2,702.7	170.8	
Albany, GA M.S.A.	**123,736**												
(Includes Dougherty and Lee Counties.)													
City of Albany	78,795	5,102		536	4,566	7	37	213	279	1,322	2,909	335	
Total area actually reporting	100.0%	6,284		610	5,674	7	42	229	332	1,601	3,696	377	
Rate per 100,000 inhabitants		5,078.6		493.0	4,585.6	5.7	33.9	185.1	268.3	1,293.9	2,987.0	304.7	
Albuquerque, NM M.S.A.	**716,696**												
(Includes Bernalillo, Sandoval, and Valencia Counties.)													
City of Albuquerque	451,098	39,541		5,259	34,282	34	219	1,610	3,396	6,585	23,535	4,162	
Total area actually reporting	94.1%	48,923		7,049	41,874	43	306	1,865	4,835	8,609	28,299	4,966	
Estimated total	100.0%	50,271		7,325	42,946	44	321	1,908	5,052	8,945	28,908	5,093	
Rate per 100,000 inhabitants		7,014.3		1,022.1	5,992.2	6.1	44.8	266.2	704.9	1,248.1	4,033.5	710.6	
Alexandria, LA M.S.A.[4]	**126,237**												
(Includes Rapides Parish.)													
City of Alexandria[4]	46,305	4,957		648	4,309	5	26	183	434	1,105	3,047	157	
Total area actually reporting	97.4%	7,588		964	6,624	9	45	197	713	2,083	4,228	313	
Estimated total	100.0%	7,783		985	6,798	9	46	201	729	2,117	4,356	325	
Rate per 100,000 inhabitants		6,165.4		780.3	5,385.1	7.1	36.4	159.2	577.5	1,677.0	3,450.7	257.5	
Allentown-Bethlehem-Easton, PA M.S.A.	**638,275**												
(Includes Carbon, Lehigh, and Northampton Counties.)													
City of:													
Allentown	106,685	5,237		618	4,619	8	46	295	269	1,111	3,052	456	
Bethlehem	71,364	2,472		249	2,223	4	14	76	155	427	1,633	163	
Total area actually reporting	82.4%	16,256		1,649	14,607	26	131	503	989	2,620	10,878	1,109	
Estimated total	100.0%	18,969		1,901	17,068	28	148	567	1,158	2,959	12,810	1,299	
Rate per 100,000 inhabitants		2,971.9		297.8	2,674.1	4.4	23.2	88.8	181.4	463.6	2,007.0	203.5	
Altoona, PA M.S.A.	**129,090**												
(Includes Blair County.)													
City of Altoona	49,548	2,057		208	1,849	2	34	72	100	450	1,312	87	
Total area actually reporting	82.1%	3,323		289	3,034	4	44	87	154	671	2,210	153	
Estimated total	100.0%	3,883		342	3,541	5	48	100	189	741	2,608	192	
Rate per 100,000 inhabitants		3,008.0		264.9	2,743.0	3.9	37.2	77.5	146.4	574.0	2,020.3	148.7	
Amarillo, TX M.S.A.	**222,802**												
(Includes Potter and Randall Counties.)													
City of Amarillo	177,567	13,627		1,402	12,225	19	98	277	1,008	2,533	8,747	945	
Total area actually reporting	100.0%	14,698		1,470	13,228	21	100	281	1,068	2,797	9,427	1,004	
Rate per 100,000 inhabitants		6,596.9		659.8	5,937.1	9.4	44.9	126.1	479.3	1,255.4	4,231.1	450.6	
Anchorage, AK M.S.A.	**263,588**												
(Includes Anchorage Borough.)													
Total area actually reporting	100.0%	13,214		1,748	11,466	10	210	384	1,144	1,606	8,648	1,212	
Rate per 100,000 inhabitants		5,013.1		663.2	4,350.0	3.8	79.7	145.7	434.0	609.3	3,280.9	459.8	
Ann Arbor, MI M.S.A.	**581,786**												
(Includes Lenawee, Livingston, and Washtenaw Counties.)													
City of Ann Arbor	114,625	3,880		352	3,528	1	25	125	201	739	2,626	163	
Total area actually reporting	99.4%	17,378		1,557	15,821	25	195	351	986	3,048	11,524	1,249	
Estimated total	100.0%	17,506		1,568	15,938	25	196	353	994	3,067	11,608	1,263	
Rate per 100,000 inhabitants		3,009.0		269.5	2,739.5	4.3	33.7	60.7	170.9	527.2	1,995.2	217.1	
Anniston, AL M.S.A.	**112,685**												
(Includes Calhoun County.)													
City of Anniston	24,370	3,531		538	2,993	8	37	144	349	871	1,920	202	
Total area actually reporting	100.0%	6,591		846	5,745	10	58	205	573	1,467	3,927	351	
Rate per 100,000 inhabitants		5,849.0		750.8	5,098.3	8.9	51.5	181.9	508.5	1,301.9	3,484.9	311.5	
Appleton-Oshkosh-Neenah, WI M.S.A.	**359,119**												
(Includes Calumet, Outagamie, and Winnebago Counties.)													
City of:													
Appleton	70,587	1,912		152	1,760	1	16	8	127	236	1,467	57	
Oshkosh	63,364	2,281		127	2,154	0	13	16	98	251	1,830	73	
Neenah	24,682	528		26	502	0	5	2	19	46	430	26	
Total area actually reporting	99.2%	8,493		410	8,083	1	63	31	315	933	6,869	281	
Estimated total	100.0%	8,582		413	8,169	1	63	32	317	943	6,941	285	
Rate per 100,000 inhabitants		2,389.7		115.0	2,274.7	0.3	17.5	8.9	88.3	262.6	1,932.8	79.4	

See footnotes at end of table.

Table 6

Index of Crime[1]
by Metropolitan Statistical Area, 2001—Continued

Metropolitan Statistical Area	Population	Crime Index total	Modified Crime Index total[2]	Violent crime[3]	Property crime[3]	Murder and non-negligent man-slaughter	Forcible rape	Robbery	Aggravated assault	Burglary	Larceny-theft	Motor vehicle theft	Arson[2]
Asheville, NC M.S.A.	**229,810**												
(Includes Buncombe and Madison Counties.)													
City of Asheville	70,061	4,734		475	4,259	1	42	217	215	905	2,918	436	
Total area actually reporting	99.1%	8,253		743	7,510	1	55	261	426	1,920	4,847	743	
Estimated total	100.0%	8,385		752	7,633	1	55	264	432	1,945	4,939	749	
Rate per 100,000 inhabitants		3,648.7		327.2	3,321.4	0.4	23.9	114.9	188.0	846.4	2,149.2	325.9	
Athens, GA M.S.A.	**157,146**												
(Includes Clarke, Madison, and Oconee Counties.)													
City of Athens-Clarke County	102,843	6,855		451	6,404	8	26	156	261	1,069	4,956	379	
Total area actually reporting	84.2%	7,943		483	7,460	8	29	166	280	1,158	5,862	440	
Estimated total	100.0%	8,790		553	8,237	9	34	196	314	1,329	6,370	538	
Rate per 100,000 inhabitants		5,593.5		351.9	5,241.6	5.7	21.6	124.7	199.8	845.7	4,053.6	342.4	
Atlanta, GA M.S.A.[4]	**4,211,379**												
(Includes Barrow, Bartow, Carroll, Cherokee, Clayton, Cobb, Coweta, DeKalb, Douglas, Fayette, Forsyth, Fulton, Gwinnett, Henry, Newton, Paulding, Pickens, Rockdale, Spalding, and Walton Counties.)													
City of Atlanta	426,511	52,195		10,808	41,387	144	367	4,341	5,956	8,731	25,721	6,935	
Total area actually reporting	98.9%	200,425		23,762	176,663	332	1,133	9,813	12,484	35,909	116,625	24,129	
Estimated total	100.0%	203,230		24,009	179,221	334	1,146	9,900	12,629	36,314	118,529	24,378	
Rate per 100,000 inhabitants		4,825.7		570.1	4,255.6	7.9	27.2	235.1	299.9	862.3	2,814.5	578.9	
Atlantic-Cape May, NJ M.S.A.	**357,833**												
(Includes Atlantic and Cape May Counties.)													
City of Atlantic City	40,854	6,777		743	6,034	5	33	255	450	688	5,168	178	
Total area actually reporting	100.0%	18,769		1,721	17,048	17	106	512	1,086	2,719	13,669	660	
Rate per 100,000 inhabitants		5,245.2		481.0	4,764.2	4.8	29.6	143.1	303.5	759.9	3,819.9	184.4	
Augusta-Aiken, GA-SC M.S.A.	**487,051**												
(Includes Columbia, McDuffie, and Richmond Counties, GA and Aiken and Edgefield Counties, SC.)													
City of Aiken, SC	25,659	1,259		101	1,158	1	7	23	70	170	925	63	
Total area actually reporting	99.0%	20,489		1,644	18,845	33	218	568	825	3,853	13,337	1,655	
Estimated total	100.0%	20,731		1,670	19,061	33	219	574	844	3,887	13,505	1,669	
Rate per 100,000 inhabitants		4,256.4		342.9	3,913.6	6.8	45.0	117.9	173.3	798.1	2,772.8	342.7	
Austin-San Marcos, TX M.S.A.	**1,278,125**												
(Includes Bastrop, Caldwell, Hays, Travis, and Williamson Counties.)													
City of:													
Austin	671,462	43,210		3,129	40,081	26	262	1,171	1,670	7,439	29,276	3,366	
San Marcos	35,521	1,466		125	1,341	0	39	21	65	241	1,040	60	
Total area actually reporting	100.0%	61,894		4,658	57,236	41	458	1,368	2,791	11,255	41,740	4,241	
Rate per 100,000 inhabitants		4,842.6		364.4	4,478.1	3.2	35.8	107.0	218.4	880.6	3,265.7	331.8	
Bakersfield, CA M.S.A.	**673,941**												
(Includes Kern County.)													
City of Bakersfield	251,648	10,255		840	9,415	22	34	324	460	2,035	6,226	1,154	
Total area actually reporting	100.0%	27,195		3,275	23,920	39	191	741	2,304	5,926	15,221	2,773	
Rate per 100,000 inhabitants		4,035.2		485.9	3,549.3	5.8	28.3	110.0	341.9	879.3	2,258.5	411.5	
Baltimore, MD M.S.A.	**2,590,914**												
(Includes Baltimore City, Anne Arundel, Baltimore, Carroll, Harford, Howard, and Queen Anne's Counties.)													
City of:													
Baltimore	660,826	63,488		14,799	48,689	256	296	5,747	8,500	10,899	29,615	8,175	
Annapolis	36,370	2,404		484	1,920	4	11	154	315	333	1,456	131	
Total area actually reporting	100.0%	141,588		26,584	115,004	303	765	8,450	17,066	23,326	77,418	14,260	
Rate per 100,000 inhabitants		5,464.8		1,026.0	4,438.7	11.7	29.5	326.1	658.7	900.3	2,988.1	550.4	
Bangor, ME M.S.A.	**69,017**												
(Includes part of Penobscot and Waldo Counties.)													
City of Bangor	31,763	2,010		58	1,952	1	15	20	22	245	1,642	65	
Total area actually reporting	99.2%	3,052		72	2,980	1	18	25	28	376	2,501	103	
Estimated total	100.0%	3,065		72	2,993	1	18	25	28	378	2,511	104	
Rate per 100,000 inhabitants		4,440.9		104.3	4,336.6	1.4	26.1	36.2	40.6	547.7	3,638.2	150.7	

See footnotes at end of table.

Table 6

Index of Crime[1]

by Metropolitan Statistical Area, 2001—Continued

Metropolitan Statistical Area	Population	Crime Index total	Modified Crime Index total[2]	Violent crime[3]	Property crime[3]	Murder and non-negligent man-slaughter	Forcible rape	Robbery	Aggravated assault	Burglary	Larceny-theft	Motor vehicle theft	Arson[2]
Barnstable-Yarmouth, MA M.S.A.[5]	**163,356**												
(Includes part of Barnstable County.)													
City of:													
Barnstable	48,048	1,726		275	1,451	0	18	34	223	407	919	125	
Yarmouth	24,925	635		59	576	0	2	4	53	143	406	27	
Total area actually reporting	96.6%				3,624	2	34	41		891	2,527	206	
Estimated total	100.0%				3,725	2	35	43		911	2,597	217	
Rate per 100,000 inhabitants					2,280.3	1.2	21.4	26.3		557.7	1,589.8	132.8	
Baton Rouge, LA M.S.A.	**602,415**												
(Includes Ascension, East Baton Rouge, Livingston, and West Baton Rouge Parishes.)													
City of Baton Rouge	227,637	20,149		2,547	17,602	46	62	1,071	1,368	3,716	12,128	1,758	
Total area actually reporting	99.5%	41,400		4,194	37,206	63	157	1,400	2,574	7,884	26,441	2,881	
Estimated total	100.0%	41,589		4,215	37,374	63	158	1,404	2,590	7,917	26,565	2,892	
Rate per 100,000 inhabitants		6,903.7		699.7	6,204.0	10.5	26.2	233.1	429.9	1,314.2	4,409.8	480.1	
Beaumont-Port Arthur, TX M.S.A.	**393,829**												
(Includes Hardin, Jefferson, and Orange Counties.)													
City of:													
Beaumont	116,450	8,845		1,114	7,731	10	158	361	585	1,692	5,512	527	
Port Arthur	59,066	2,753		351	2,402	7	15	123	206	862	1,246	294	
Total area actually reporting	100.0%	19,360		2,127	17,233	19	305	581	1,222	4,076	11,833	1,324	
Rate per 100,000 inhabitants		4,915.8		540.1	4,375.8	4.8	77.4	147.5	310.3	1,035.0	3,004.6	336.2	
Bellingham, WA M.S.A.	**169,470**												
(Includes Whatcom County.)													
City of Bellingham	68,241	4,849		137	4,712	1	22	50	64	555	3,942	215	
Total area actually reporting	100.0%	8,743		390	8,353	1	88	78	223	1,464	6,426	463	
Rate per 100,000 inhabitants		5,159.0		230.1	4,928.9	0.6	51.9	46.0	131.6	863.9	3,791.8	273.2	
Benton Harbor, MI M.S.A.	**163,309**												
(Includes Berrien County.)													
City of Benton Harbor	11,241	980		290	690	6	12	18	254	290	313	87	
Total area actually reporting	100.0%	7,156		819	6,337	10	132	86	591	1,392	4,484	461	
Rate per 100,000 inhabitants		4,381.9		501.5	3,880.4	6.1	80.8	52.7	361.9	852.4	2,745.7	282.3	
Bergen-Passaic, NJ M.S.A.	**1,384,605**												
(Includes Bergen and Passaic Counties.)													
Total area actually reporting	100.0%	36,287		3,886	32,401	39	90	1,697	2,060	6,296	20,905	5,200	
Rate per 100,000 inhabitants		2,620.7		280.7	2,340.1	2.8	6.5	122.6	148.8	454.7	1,509.8	375.6	
Biloxi-Gulfport-Pascagoula, MS M.S.A.[4]	**365,699**												
(Includes Hancock, Harrison, and Jackson Counties.)													
City of:													
Biloxi	50,882	4,592		286	4,306	5	25	120	136	627	3,411	268	
Gulfport	71,461	5,436		246	5,190	10	37	147	52	1,129	3,656	405	
Pascagoula	26,323	2,605		181	2,424	3	22	79	77	489	1,712	223	
Total area actually reporting	92.3%	21,290		1,319	19,971	37	151	479	652	4,613	13,940	1,418	
Estimated total	100.0%	22,032		1,358	20,674	39	158	486	675	4,835	14,366	1,473	
Rate per 100,000 inhabitants		6,024.6		371.3	5,653.3	10.7	43.2	132.9	184.6	1,322.1	3,928.4	402.8	
Binghamton, NY M.S.A.	**252,784**												
(Includes Broome and Tioga Counties.)													
City of Binghamton	47,467	2,335		188	2,147	1	30	59	98	258	1,827	62	
Total area actually reporting	100.0%	6,333		474	5,859	3	66	99	306	901	4,777	181	
Rate per 100,000 inhabitants		2,505.3		187.5	2,317.8	1.2	26.1	39.2	121.1	356.4	1,889.8	71.6	
Birmingham, AL M.S.A.	**924,680**												
(Includes Blount, Jefferson, St. Clair, and Shelby Counties.)													
City of Birmingham	243,762	21,085		3,027	18,058	73	206	1,084	1,664	4,079	11,928	2,051	
Total area actually reporting	89.7%	41,308		4,829	36,479	105	337	1,650	2,737	7,885	25,114	3,480	
Estimated total	100.0%	44,904		5,142	39,762	110	357	1,735	2,940	8,627	27,430	3,705	
Rate per 100,000 inhabitants		4,856.2		556.1	4,300.1	11.9	38.6	187.6	317.9	933.0	2,966.4	400.7	
Bismarck, ND M.S.A.	**93,576**												
(Includes Burleigh and Morton Counties.)													
City of Bismarck	54,862	1,797		49	1,748	0	8	11	30	261	1,375	112	
Total area actually reporting	100.0%	2,426		66	2,360	0	18	11	37	355	1,848	157	
Rate per 100,000 inhabitants		2,592.5		70.5	2,522.0	–	19.2	11.8	39.5	379.4	1,974.9	167.8	

See footnotes at end of table.

Table 6

Index of Crime[1]

by Metropolitan Statistical Area, 2001—Continued

Metropolitan Statistical Area	Population	Crime Index total	Modified Crime Index total[2]	Violent crime[3]	Property crime[3]	Murder and non-negligent man-slaughter	Forcible rape	Robbery	Aggravated assault	Burglary	Larceny-theft	Motor vehicle theft	Arson[2]
Bloomington, IN M.S.A.	**121,242**												
(Includes Monroe County.)													
City of Bloomington	69,681	2,555		113	2,442	2	28	29	54	399	1,938	105	
Total area actually reporting	100.0%	4,107		215	3,892	2	42	41	130	708	3,008	176	
Rate per 100,000 inhabitants		3,387.4		177.3	3,210.1	1.6	34.6	33.8	107.2	584.0	2,481.0	145.2	
Boise, ID M.S.A.	**441,385**												
(Includes Ada and Canyon Counties.)													
City of:													
Boise	189,671	8,730		635	8,095	2	84	78	471	1,347	6,163	585	
Nampa	52,951	2,766		228	2,538	3	40	10	175	425	1,946	167	
Total area actually reporting	100.0%	17,926		1,341	16,585	9	176	125	1,031	3,102	12,296	1,187	
Rate per 100,000 inhabitants		4,061.3		303.8	3,757.5	2.0	39.9	28.3	233.6	702.8	2,785.8	268.9	
Boston, MA-NH M.S.A.[5]	**3,422,303**												
(Includes part of Bristol, Essex, Middlesex, Norfolk, Plymouth, Suffolk, and Worcester Counties, MA and part of Rockingham County, NH.)													
City of:													
Boston, MA	591,944	37,385		7,361	30,024	65	361	2,523	4,412	4,222	17,608	8,194	
Cambridge, MA	101,837	4,416		470	3,946	1	15	181	273	688	2,740	518	
Lynn, MA[5]	89,472				3,576	1	16	161		617	1,681	1,278	
Waltham, MA	59,508	1,247		67	1,180	2	11	19	35	184	872	124	
Gloucester, MA	30,417	766		64	702	0	9	9	46	155	499	48	
Total area actually reporting	94.8%				83,887	89	791	4,003		13,463	55,223	15,201	
Estimated total	100.0%				87,160	90	826	4,059		14,121	57,493	15,546	
Rate per 100,000 inhabitants					2,546.8	2.6	24.1	118.6		412.6	1,680.0	454.3	
Brazoria, TX M.S.A.	**247,254**												
(Includes Brazoria County.)													
Total area actually reporting	99.7%	7,332		634	6,698	6	95	96	437	1,563	4,687	448	
Estimated total	100.0%	7,369		637	6,732	6	95	97	439	1,569	4,712	451	
Rate per 100,000 inhabitants		2,980.3		257.6	2,722.7	2.4	38.4	39.2	177.6	634.6	1,905.7	182.4	
Bremerton, WA M.S.A.[4]	**235,663**												
(Includes Kitsap County.)													
City of Bremerton	37,852	2,771		378	2,393	3	78	58	239	471	1,571	351	
Total area actually reporting	100.0%	9,161		953	8,208	6	198	114	635	1,935	5,599	674	
Rate per 100,000 inhabitants		3,887.3		404.4	3,482.9	2.5	84.0	48.4	269.5	821.1	2,375.9	286.0	
Bridgeport, CT M.S.A.	**446,957**												
(Includes part of Fairfield and New Haven Counties.)													
City of Bridgeport	140,328	8,162		1,910	6,252	16	69	608	1,217	1,266	2,876	2,110	
Total area actually reporting	100.0%	15,832		2,312	13,520	18	104	761	1,429	2,423	8,188	2,909	
Rate per 100,000 inhabitants		3,542.2		517.3	3,024.9	4.0	23.3	170.3	319.7	542.1	1,831.9	650.8	
Brockton, MA M.S.A.	**256,673**												
(Includes part of Bristol, Norfolk, and Plymouth Counties.)													
City of Brockton	94,750	5,242		1,055	4,187	5	58	204	788	743	2,158	1,286	
Total area actually reporting	89.7%	8,255		1,448	6,807	6	79	237	1,126	1,309	3,905	1,593	
Estimated total	100.0%	8,818		1,521	7,297	6	84	246	1,185	1,408	4,244	1,645	
Rate per 100,000 inhabitants		3,435.5		592.6	2,842.9	2.3	32.7	95.8	461.7	548.6	1,653.5	640.9	
Brownsville-Harlingen-San Benito, TX M.S.A.	**342,834**												
(Includes Cameron County.)													
City of:													
Brownsville	142,893	11,910		809	11,101	7	27	180	595	1,066	9,574	461	
Harlingen	58,870	4,611		328	4,283	5	36	66	221	989	3,045	249	
San Benito	23,976	2,523		71	2,452	1	12	7	51	300	2,087	65	
Total area actually reporting	100.0%	22,629		1,565	21,064	14	96	277	1,178	3,421	16,718	925	
Rate per 100,000 inhabitants		6,600.6		456.5	6,144.1	4.1	28.0	80.8	343.6	997.9	4,876.4	269.8	
Bryan-College Station, TX M.S.A.	**155,874**												
(Includes Brazos County.)													
City of:													
Bryan	67,150	4,041		459	3,582	4	66	64	325	741	2,658	183	
College Station	69,431	2,507		112	2,395	1	35	18	58	285	2,026	84	
Total area actually reporting	100.0%	7,545		626	6,919	5	106	89	426	1,231	5,401	287	
Rate per 100,000 inhabitants		4,840.4		401.6	4,438.8	3.2	68.0	57.1	273.3	789.7	3,465.0	184.1	

See footnotes at end of table.

Table 6

Index of Crime[1]
by Metropolitan Statistical Area, 2001—Continued

Metropolitan Statistical Area	Population	Crime Index total	Modified Crime Index total[2]	Violent crime[3]	Property crime[3]	Murder and non-negligent man-slaughter	Forcible rape	Robbery	Aggravated assault	Burglary	Larceny-theft	Motor vehicle theft	Arson[2]
Buffalo-Niagara Falls, NY M.S.A.	1,172,265												
(Includes Erie and Niagara Counties.)													
City of:													
Buffalo	293,187	19,894		3,709	16,185	64	229	1,600	1,816	3,965	9,669	2,551	
Niagara Falls	55,695	3,599		489	3,110	4	26	168	291	795	1,947	368	
Total area actually reporting	98.6%	41,800		5,250	36,550	73	350	2,019	2,808	7,292	25,278	3,980	
Estimated total	100.0%	42,215		5,284	36,931	73	352	2,030	2,829	7,346	25,579	4,006	
Rate per 100,000 inhabitants		3,601.1		450.8	3,150.4	6.2	30.0	173.2	241.3	626.7	2,182.0	341.7	
Burlington, VT M.S.A.	162,250												
(Includes part of Chittenden, Franklin, and Grand Isle Counties.)													
City of Burlington	39,161	2,686		142	2,544	0	16	21	105	379	2,069	96	
Total area actually reporting	100.0%	6,243		252	5,991	5	33	35	179	952	4,793	246	
Rate per 100,000 inhabitants		3,847.8		155.3	3,692.4	3.1	20.3	21.6	110.3	586.7	2,954.1	151.6	
Casper, WY M.S.A.	66,619												
(Includes Natrona County.)													
City of Casper	49,708	2,318		156	2,162	2	20	23	111	435	1,607	120	
Total area actually reporting	100.0%	2,965		198	2,767	3	20	28	147	594	2,007	166	
Rate per 100,000 inhabitants		4,450.7		297.2	4,153.5	4.5	30.0	42.0	220.7	891.6	3,012.7	249.2	
Cedar Rapids, IA M.S.A.	191,495												
(Includes Linn County.)													
City of Cedar Rapids	120,628	7,473		407	7,066	3	57	99	248	1,318	5,381	367	
Total area actually reporting	94.9%	8,473		437	8,036	3	59	102	273	1,628	5,990	418	
Estimated total	100.0%	8,782		452	8,330	3	60	105	284	1,666	6,235	429	
Rate per 100,000 inhabitants		4,586.0		236.0	4,350.0	1.6	31.3	54.8	148.3	870.0	3,256.0	224.0	
Charlottesville, VA M.S.A.	162,038												
(Includes Albemarle, Fluvanna, and Greene Counties and Charlottesville City.)													
City of Charlottesville	45,744	2,127		463	1,664	3	25	71	364	269	1,279	116	
Total area actually reporting	100.0%	5,050		692	4,358	6	54	100	532	702	3,437	219	
Rate per 100,000 inhabitants		3,116.6		427.1	2,689.5	3.7	33.3	61.7	328.3	433.2	2,121.1	135.2	
Chattanooga, TN-GA M.S.A.	471,279												
(Includes Hamilton and Marion Counties, TN and Catoosa, Dade, and Walker Counties, GA.)													
City of Chattanooga, TN	156,941	19,320		2,806	16,514	26	86	765	1,929	3,270	11,042	2,202	
Total area actually reporting	100.0%	30,034		3,871	26,163	37	134	874	2,826	5,432	17,766	2,965	
Rate per 100,000 inhabitants		6,372.9		821.4	5,551.5	7.9	28.4	185.5	599.6	1,152.6	3,769.7	629.1	
Cheyenne, WY M.S.A.	81,713												
(Includes Laramie County.)													
City of Cheyenne	53,080	2,325		81	2,244	0	14	15	52	268	1,903	73	
Total area actually reporting	100.0%	3,096		140	2,956	1	43	21	75	404	2,451	101	
Rate per 100,000 inhabitants		3,788.9		171.3	3,617.5	1.2	52.6	25.7	91.8	494.4	2,999.5	123.6	
Chico-Paradise, CA M.S.A.	206,947												
(Includes Butte County.)													
City of:													
Chico	61,068	2,332		224	2,108	2	36	68	118	491	1,334	283	
Paradise	26,899	922		59	863	0	6	5	48	230	568	65	
Total area actually reporting	100.0%	7,565		629	6,936	11	81	132	405	1,779	4,159	998	
Rate per 100,000 inhabitants		3,655.5		303.9	3,351.6	5.3	39.1	63.8	195.7	859.6	2,009.7	482.2	
Cincinnati, OH-KY-IN M.S.A.[4]	1,651,069												
(Includes Brown, Clermont, Hamilton, and Warren Counties, OH, Boone, Campbell, Gallatin, Grant, Kenton, and Pendleton Counties, KY, and Dearborn and Ohio Counties, IN.)													
City of Cincinnati, OH	331,880	27,817		3,890	23,927	55	358	2,075	1,402	6,297	14,283	3,347	
Total area actually reporting	76.2%	56,679		5,561	51,118	71	565	2,675	2,250	10,458	35,748	4,912	
Estimated total	100.0%	76,023		7,315	68,708	75	701	3,072	3,467	13,152	49,545	6,011	
Rate per 100,000 inhabitants		4,604.5		443.0	4,161.4	4.5	42.5	186.1	210.0	796.6	3,000.8	364.1	
Colorado Springs, CO M.S.A.	530,924												
(Includes El Paso County.)													
City of Colorado Springs	370,661	19,475		1,907	17,568	14	257	494	1,142	3,070	13,155	1,343	
Total area actually reporting	99.4%	23,042		2,323	20,719	19	301	517	1,486	3,801	15,326	1,592	
Estimated total	100.0%	23,201		2,335	20,866	19	302	520	1,494	3,820	15,434	1,612	
Rate per 100,000 inhabitants		4,369.9		439.8	3,930.1	3.6	56.9	97.9	281.4	719.5	2,907.0	303.6	

See footnotes at end of table.

Table 6

Index of Crime[1]
by Metropolitan Statistical Area, 2001—Continued

Metropolitan Statistical Area	Population	Crime Index total	Modified Crime Index total[2]	Violent crime[3]	Property crime[3]	Murder and non-negligent man-slaughter	Forcible rape	Robbery	Aggravated assault	Burglary	Larceny-theft	Motor vehicle theft	Arson[2]
Columbia, MO M.S.A.	**136,289**												
(Includes Boone County.)													
City of Columbia	85,052	3,897		439	3,458	4	16	140	279	455	2,822	181	
Total area actually reporting	100.0%	5,485		567	4,918	4	24	167	372	682	3,974	262	
Rate per 100,000 inhabitants		4,024.5		416.0	3,608.5	2.9	17.6	122.5	272.9	500.4	2,915.9	192.2	
Columbia, SC M.S.A.	**425,757**												
(Includes Lexington and Richland Counties.)													
City of Columbia	117,756	10,574		1,300	9,274	15	62	442	781	1,426	6,863	985	
Total area actually reporting	99.7%	20,050		2,442	17,608	25	157	622	1,638	3,567	12,204	1,837	
Estimated total	100.0%	20,119		2,449	17,670	25	157	624	1,643	3,577	12,252	1,841	
Rate per 100,000 inhabitants		4,725.5		575.2	4,150.3	5.9	36.9	146.6	385.9	840.2	2,877.7	432.4	
Columbus, GA-AL M.S.A.	**280,241**												
(Includes Chattahoochee, Harris, and Muscogee Counties, GA and Russell County, AL.)													
City of Columbus, GA	190,262	12,143		991	11,152	9	18	440	524	1,803	8,473	876	
Total area actually reporting	99.8%	14,341		1,230	13,111	13	28	489	700	2,366	9,705	1,040	
Estimated total	100.0%	14,374		1,233	13,141	13	28	490	702	2,371	9,727	1,043	
Rate per 100,000 inhabitants		5,129.2		440.0	4,689.2	4.6	10.0	174.8	250.5	846.1	3,470.9	372.2	
Columbus, OH M.S.A.	**1,542,925**												
(Includes Delaware, Fairfield, Franklin, Licking, Madison, and Pickaway Counties.)													
City of:													
Columbus	712,748	68,547		6,396	62,151	81	602	3,364	2,349	15,740	38,835	7,576	
Newark	46,362	2,409		88	2,321	0	13	41	34	536	1,672	113	
Lancaster	35,398	1,349		69	1,280	0	21	30	18	253	945	82	
Total area actually reporting	91.9%	94,833		7,646	87,187	94	797	3,960	2,795	20,808	57,171	9,208	
Estimated total	100.0%	97,919		7,802	90,117	95	825	4,012	2,870	21,429	59,293	9,395	
Rate per 100,000 inhabitants		6,346.3		505.7	5,840.7	6.2	53.5	260.0	186.0	1,388.9	3,842.9	608.9	
Corpus Christi, TX M.S.A.	**389,425**												
(Includes Nueces and San Patricio Counties.)													
City of Corpus Christi	283,750	22,534		2,465	20,069	19	224	582	1,640	3,999	14,555	1,515	
Total area actually reporting	100.0%	27,066		2,811	24,255	20	268	638	1,885	4,996	17,572	1,687	
Rate per 100,000 inhabitants		6,950.2		721.8	6,228.4	5.1	68.8	163.8	484.0	1,282.9	4,512.3	433.2	
Corvallis, OR M.S.A.	**79,329**												
(Includes Benton County.)													
City of Corvallis	50,064	2,166		75	2,091	1	7	26	41	289	1,720	82	
Total area actually reporting	100.0%	3,140		148	2,992	1	11	31	105	474	2,374	144	
Rate per 100,000 inhabitants		3,958.2		186.6	3,771.6	1.3	13.9	39.1	132.4	597.5	2,992.6	181.5	
Cumberland, MD-WV M.S.A.	**103,025**												
(Includes Allegany County, MD and Mineral County, WV.)													
City of Cumberland, MD	21,838	1,574		198	1,376	1	15	20	162	243	1,085	48	
Total area actually reporting	100.0%	3,115		373	2,742	3	26	31	313	528	2,064	150	
Rate per 100,000 inhabitants		3,023.5		362.0	2,661.5	2.9	25.2	30.1	303.8	512.5	2,003.4	145.6	
Dallas, TX M.S.A.	**3,599,037**												
(Includes Collin, Dallas, Denton, Ellis, Henderson, Hunt, Kaufman, and Rockwall Counties.)													
City of:													
Dallas	1,215,553	111,006		17,776	93,230	240	660	8,330	8,546	20,635	53,611	18,984	
Irving	195,963	9,993		816	9,177	10	58	281	467	1,387	6,561	1,229	
Denton	82,365	3,664		309	3,355	2	49	70	188	547	2,652	156	
Total area actually reporting	99.9%	209,479		25,082	184,397	312	1,305	10,205	13,260	39,195	117,114	28,088	
Estimated total	100.0%	209,659		25,095	184,564	312	1,306	10,208	13,269	39,226	117,237	28,101	
Rate per 100,000 inhabitants		5,825.4		697.3	5,128.1	8.7	36.3	283.6	368.7	1,089.9	3,257.5	780.8	
Danbury, CT M.S.A.	**185,429**												
(Includes part of Fairfield and Litchfield Counties.)													
City of Danbury	75,277	2,015		143	1,872	0	10	53	80	344	1,336	192	
Total area actually reporting	100.0%	3,089		200	2,889	0	19	62	119	530	2,089	270	
Rate per 100,000 inhabitants		1,665.9		107.9	1,558.0	–	10.2	33.4	64.2	285.8	1,126.6	145.6	
Daytona Beach, FL M.S.A.	**505,954**												
(Includes Flagler and Volusia Counties.)													
City of Daytona Beach	65,773	6,501		1,124	5,377	8	61	315	740	1,621	3,069	687	
Total area actually reporting	100.0%	22,830		3,392	19,438	21	214	638	2,519	5,210	12,535	1,693	
Rate per 100,000 inhabitants		4,512.3		670.4	3,841.9	4.2	42.3	126.1	497.9	1,029.7	2,477.5	334.6	

See footnotes at end of table.

Table 6

Index of Crime[1]
by Metropolitan Statistical Area, 2001—Continued

Metropolitan Statistical Area	Population	Crime Index total	Modified Crime Index total[2]	Violent crime[3]	Property crime[3]	Murder and non-negligent man-slaughter	Forcible rape	Robbery	Aggravated assault	Burglary	Larceny-theft	Motor vehicle theft	Arson[2]
Dayton-Springfield, OH M.S.A.	952,267												
(Includes Clark, Greene, Miami, and Montgomery Counties.)													
City of:													
Dayton	166,478	16,952		2,068	14,884	30	152	1,090	796	4,018	7,497	3,369	
Springfield	65,475	6,743		510	6,233	7	74	226	203	1,507	4,259	467	
Fairborn	32,110	1,653		57	1,596	0	15	23	19	212	1,246	138	
Total area actually reporting	85.3%	43,000		3,250	39,750	44	408	1,565	1,233	8,676	25,919	5,155	
Estimated total	100.0%	46,596		3,432	43,164	46	440	1,625	1,321	9,371	28,421	5,372	
Rate per 100,000 inhabitants		4,893.2		360.4	4,532.8	4.8	46.2	170.6	138.7	984.1	2,984.6	564.1	
Denver, CO M.S.A.	2,166,390												
(Includes Adams, Arapahoe, Denver, Douglas, and Jefferson Counties.)													
City of Denver	569,653	30,272		3,074	27,198	45	317	1,250	1,462	5,642	14,621	6,935	
Total area actually reporting	94.0%	94,635		8,021	86,614	91	922	2,344	4,664	14,246	57,191	15,177	
Estimated total	100.0%	101,657		8,552	93,105	96	988	2,470	4,998	15,093	61,963	16,049	
Rate per 100,000 inhabitants		4,692.5		394.8	4,297.7	4.4	45.6	114.0	230.7	696.7	2,860.2	740.8	
Des Moines, IA M.S.A.	455,534												
(Includes Dallas, Polk, and Warren Counties.)													
City of Des Moines	198,468	12,610		750	11,860	11	89	298	352	1,301	9,549	1,010	
Total area actually reporting	98.1%	20,482		1,131	19,351	13	124	372	622	2,366	15,523	1,462	
Estimated total	100.0%	20,757		1,144	19,613	13	125	375	631	2,400	15,741	1,472	
Rate per 100,000 inhabitants		4,556.6		251.1	4,305.5	2.9	27.4	82.3	138.5	526.9	3,455.5	323.1	
Detroit, MI M.S.A.	4,464,958												
(Includes Lapeer, Macomb, Monroe, Oakland, St. Clair, and Wayne Counties.)													
City of:													
Detroit	956,283	90,193		20,947	69,246	395	652	7,096	12,804	15,096	29,613	24,537	
Dearborn	98,290	5,883		976	4,907	4	24	161	787	534	3,197	1,176	
Pontiac	66,687	4,522		1,127	3,395	4	90	187	846	1,089	1,760	546	
Port Huron	32,508	1,557		200	1,357	0	30	30	140	230	1,036	91	
Total area actually reporting	99.3%	203,754		33,094	170,660	481	1,905	9,466	21,242	32,437	98,440	39,783	
Estimated total	100.0%	204,941		33,198	171,743	482	1,916	9,487	21,313	32,613	99,216	39,914	
Rate per 100,000 inhabitants		4,590.0		743.5	3,846.5	10.8	42.9	212.5	477.3	730.4	2,222.1	893.9	
Dothan, AL M.S.A.	138,452												
(Includes Dale and Houston Counties.)													
City of Dothan	57,961	3,105		187	2,918	3	43	83	58	562	2,239	117	
Total area actually reporting	95.7%	4,747		345	4,402	6	54	100	185	889	3,316	197	
Estimated total	100.0%	5,047		369	4,678	6	55	108	200	943	3,520	215	
Rate per 100,000 inhabitants		3,645.3		266.5	3,378.8	4.3	39.7	78.0	144.5	681.1	2,542.4	155.3	
Dover, DE M.S.A.[4]	128,729												
(Includes Kent County.)													
City of Dover	32,650	2,037		194	1,843	1	15	55	123	150	1,590	103	
Total area actually reporting	99.5%	5,031		840	4,191	2	81	101	656	769	3,198	224	
Estimated total	100.0%	5,072		845	4,227	2	81	102	660	774	3,227	226	
Rate per 100,000 inhabitants		3,940.1		656.4	3,283.6	1.6	62.9	79.2	512.7	601.3	2,506.8	175.6	
Dubuque, IA M.S.A.[4]	89,047												
(Includes Dubuque County.)													
City of Dubuque[4]	57,624				1,464	1	12	11		546	845	73	
Total area actually reporting	100.0%				1,756	1	14	11		650	1,012	94	
Rate per 100,000 inhabitants					1,972.0	1.1	15.7	12.4		730.0	1,136.5	105.6	
Duluth-Superior, MN-WI M.S.A.	246,277												
(Includes St. Louis County, MN and Douglas County, WI.)													
City of:													
Duluth, MN	87,851	5,370		318	5,052	4	55	79	180	646	4,029	377	
Superior, WI	27,563	1,673		64	1,609	0	14	11	39	246	1,260	103	
Total area actually reporting	100.0%	10,261		564	9,697	5	135	95	329	1,657	7,369	671	
Rate per 100,000 inhabitants		4,166.4		229.0	3,937.4	2.0	54.8	38.6	133.6	672.8	2,992.2	272.5	
Dutchess County, NY M.S.A.	280,666												
(Includes Dutchess County.)													
City of Poughkeepsie	29,926	1,293		196	1,097	4	17	103	72	237	773	87	
Total area actually reporting	97.2%	6,137		627	5,510	7	38	168	414	828	4,393	289	
Estimated total	100.0%	6,338		643	5,695	7	39	173	424	854	4,539	302	
Rate per 100,000 inhabitants		2,258.2		229.1	2,029.1	2.5	13.9	61.6	151.1	304.3	1,617.2	107.6	

See footnotes at end of table.

Table 6

Index of Crime[1]
by Metropolitan Statistical Area, 2001—Continued

Metropolitan Statistical Area	Population	Crime Index total	Modified Crime Index total[2]	Violent crime[3]	Property crime[3]	Murder and non-negligent man-slaughter	Forcible rape	Robbery	Aggravated assault	Burglary	Larceny-theft	Motor vehicle theft	Arson[2]
Eau Claire, WI M.S.A.	**149,394**												
(Includes Chippewa and Eau Claire Counties.)													
City of Eau Claire	62,144	2,807		141	2,666	1	18	15	107	397	2,139	130	
Total area actually reporting	98.2%	4,711		191	4,520	4	24	19	144	708	3,610	202	
Estimated total	100.0%	4,793		193	4,600	4	24	20	145	717	3,677	206	
Rate per 100,000 inhabitants		3,208.3		129.2	3,079.1	2.7	16.1	13.4	97.1	479.9	2,461.3	137.9	
Elkhart-Goshen, IN M.S.A.	**183,821**												
(Includes Elkhart County.)													
City of:													
Elkhart	52,166	4,771		275	4,496	8	29	224	14	1,027	3,107	362	
Goshen	29,549	1,631		244	1,387	4	3	9	228	118	1,224	45	
Total area actually reporting	100.0%	8,742		624	8,118	16	54	267	287	1,848	5,613	657	
Rate per 100,000 inhabitants		4,755.7		339.5	4,416.3	8.7	29.4	145.2	156.1	1,005.3	3,053.5	357.4	
El Paso, TX M.S.A.	**695,045**												
(Includes El Paso County.)													
City of El Paso	576,453	30,814		4,386	26,428	20	203	775	3,388	2,553	22,039	1,836	
Total area actually reporting	100.0%	33,726		4,856	28,870	24	238	812	3,782	3,003	23,828	2,039	
Rate per 100,000 inhabitants		4,852.3		698.7	4,153.7	3.5	34.2	116.8	544.1	432.1	3,428.3	293.4	
Enid, OK M.S.A.	**57,971**												
(Includes Garfield County.)													
City of Enid	47,174	2,953		235	2,718	1	30	34	170	616	1,983	119	
Total area actually reporting	100.0%	3,165		241	2,924	1	31	34	175	667	2,135	122	
Rate per 100,000 inhabitants		5,459.6		415.7	5,043.9	1.7	53.5	58.7	301.9	1,150.6	3,682.9	210.5	
Erie, PA M.S.A.	**280,982**												
(Includes Erie County.)													
City of Erie	103,768	4,269		486	3,783	4	52	227	203	734	2,828	221	
Total area actually reporting	98.7%	8,103		697	7,406	9	100	258	330	1,405	5,628	373	
Estimated total	100.0%	8,190		705	7,485	9	101	260	335	1,416	5,690	379	
Rate per 100,000 inhabitants		2,914.8		250.9	2,663.9	3.2	35.9	92.5	119.2	503.9	2,025.0	134.9	
Eugene-Springfield, OR M.S.A.	**327,817**												
(Includes Lane County.)													
City of:													
Eugene	139,967	9,415		587	8,828	2	55	203	327	1,247	6,893	688	
Springfield	53,659	4,390		181	4,209	0	21	72	88	650	3,250	309	
Total area actually reporting	100.0%	17,252		1,000	16,252	4	108	290	598	2,744	12,148	1,360	
Rate per 100,000 inhabitants		5,262.7		305.0	4,957.6	1.2	32.9	88.5	182.4	837.1	3,705.7	414.9	
Fargo-Moorhead, ND-MN M.S.A.	**173,428**												
(Includes Cass County, ND and Clay County, MN.)													
City of:													
Fargo, ND	89,505	3,134		141	2,993	0	63	16	62	363	2,430	200	
Moorhead, MN	32,522	1,186		53	1,133	0	10	4	39	109	962	62	
Total area actually reporting	100.0%	5,272		232	5,040	1	86	21	124	604	4,111	325	
Rate per 100,000 inhabitants		3,039.9		133.8	2,906.1	0.6	49.6	12.1	71.5	348.3	2,370.4	187.4	
Fayetteville, NC M.S.A.	**308,118**												
(Includes Cumberland County.)													
City of Fayetteville	123,074	9,861		779	9,082	18	62	464	235	2,485	5,780	817	
Total area actually reporting	100.0%	18,437		1,528	16,909	37	99	661	731	5,103	10,585	1,221	
Rate per 100,000 inhabitants		5,983.7		495.9	5,487.8	12.0	32.1	214.5	237.2	1,656.2	3,435.4	396.3	
Fayetteville-Springdale-Rogers, AR M.S.A.	**313,296**												
(Includes Benton and Washington Counties.)													
City of:													
Fayetteville	58,453	3,247		201	3,046	0	25	27	149	388	2,509	149	
Springdale	46,118	1,576		140	1,436	0	22	18	100	195	1,127	114	
Rogers	39,100	1,595		93	1,502	2	10	8	73	154	1,282	66	
Total area actually reporting	100.0%	9,416		720	8,696	4	85	67	564	1,391	6,791	514	
Rate per 100,000 inhabitants		3,005.5		229.8	2,775.6	1.3	27.1	21.4	180.0	444.0	2,167.6	164.1	
Fitchburg-Leominster, MA M.S.A.	**142,962**												
(Includes part of Middlesex and Worcester Counties.)													
City of:													
Fitchburg	39,288	1,771		222	1,549	0	29	51	142	422	969	158	
Leominster	41,500	1,402		87	1,315	1	8	14	64	215	990	110	
Total area actually reporting	100.0%	4,449		519	3,930	2	44	74	399	923	2,667	340	
Rate per 100,000 inhabitants		3,112.0		363.0	2,749.0	1.4	30.8	51.8	279.1	645.6	1,865.5	237.8	

See footnotes at end of table.

Table 6

Index of Crime[1]
by Metropolitan Statistical Area, 2001—Continued

Metropolitan Statistical Area	Population	Crime Index total	Modified Crime Index total[2]	Violent crime[3]	Property crime[3]	Murder and non-negligent man-slaughter	Forcible rape	Robbery	Aggravated assault	Burglary	Larceny-theft	Motor vehicle theft	Arson[2]
Flagstaff, AZ-UT M.S.A.	126,471												
(Includes Coconino County, AZ and Kane County, UT.)													
City of Flagstaff, AZ	54,716	4,892		446	4,446	2	23	59	362	532	3,674	240	
Total area actually reporting	98.0%	7,102		639	6,463	6	63	67	503	949	5,188	326	
Estimated total	100.0%	7,200		644	6,556	6	64	68	506	963	5,261	332	
Rate per 100,000 inhabitants		5,693.0		509.2	5,183.8	4.7	50.6	53.8	400.1	761.4	4,159.8	262.5	
Flint, MI M.S.A.[4]	438,439												
(Includes Genesee County.)													
City of Flint[4]	125,601	10,962		2,008	8,954	41	95	508	1,364	2,695	4,291	1,968	
Total area actually reporting	100.0%	24,403		3,089	21,314	51	256	717	2,065	5,277	12,757	3,280	
Rate per 100,000 inhabitants		5,565.9		704.5	4,861.3	11.6	58.4	163.5	471.0	1,203.6	2,909.6	748.1	
Florence, AL M.S.A.	143,504												
(Includes Colbert and Lauderdale Counties.)													
City of Florence	36,405	1,819		153	1,666	2	12	36	103	376	1,237	53	
Total area actually reporting	98.3%	4,120		259	3,861	5	21	59	174	856	2,873	132	
Estimated total	100.0%	4,239		269	3,970	5	22	62	180	877	2,954	139	
Rate per 100,000 inhabitants		2,953.9		187.5	2,766.5	3.5	15.3	43.2	125.4	611.1	2,058.5	96.9	
Florence, SC M.S.A.	127,360												
(Includes Florence County.)													
City of Florence	30,632	3,847		489	3,358	1	22	103	363	504	2,662	192	
Total area actually reporting	94.9%	8,165		1,169	6,996	9	76	200	884	1,455	5,074	467	
Estimated total	100.0%	8,507		1,205	7,302	9	77	208	911	1,503	5,312	487	
Rate per 100,000 inhabitants		6,679.5		946.1	5,733.4	7.1	60.5	163.3	715.3	1,180.1	4,170.9	382.4	
Fort Collins-Loveland, CO M.S.A.	258,303												
(Includes Larimer County.)													
City of:													
Fort Collins	121,864	4,695		369	4,326	0	86	35	248	662	3,448	216	
Loveland	51,978	1,643		77	1,566	0	16	6	55	233	1,260	73	
Total area actually reporting	100.0%	8,572		560	8,012	2	135	44	379	1,280	6,344	388	
Rate per 100,000 inhabitants		3,318.6		216.8	3,101.8	0.8	52.3	17.0	146.7	495.5	2,456.0	150.2	
Fort Lauderdale, FL M.S.A.	1,665,074												
(Includes Broward County.)													
City of Fort Lauderdale	156,346	12,581		1,681	10,900	29	48	837	767	2,439	7,049	1,412	
Total area actually reporting	100.0%	77,580		10,073	67,507	90	485	3,203	6,295	13,321	45,021	9,165	
Rate per 100,000 inhabitants		4,659.3		605.0	4,054.3	5.4	29.1	192.4	378.1	800.0	2,703.8	550.4	
Fort Myers-Cape Coral, FL M.S.A.	452,312												
(Includes Lee County.)													
City of:													
Fort Myers	49,457	5,603		1,203	4,400	7	40	419	737	959	2,597	844	
Cape Coral	104,936	3,670		346	3,324	2	13	34	297	855	2,293	176	
Total area actually reporting	100.0%	21,701		2,943	18,758	20	136	801	1,986	4,600	11,740	2,418	
Rate per 100,000 inhabitants		4,797.8		650.7	4,147.1	4.4	30.1	177.1	439.1	1,017.0	2,595.6	534.6	
Fort Pierce-Port St. Lucie, FL M.S.A.	327,703												
(Includes Martin and St. Lucie Counties.)													
City of:													
Fort Pierce	38,488	4,232		869	3,363	13	37	281	538	1,022	2,024	317	
Port St. Lucie	91,069	2,575		254	2,321	5	20	34	195	556	1,690	75	
Total area actually reporting	100.0%	13,629		2,052	11,577	26	109	488	1,429	3,008	7,842	727	
Rate per 100,000 inhabitants		4,158.9		626.2	3,532.8	7.9	33.3	148.9	436.1	917.9	2,393.0	221.8	
Fort Smith, AR-OK M.S.A.	208,573												
(Includes Crawford and Sebastian Counties, AR and Sequoyah County, OK.)													
City of Fort Smith, AR	80,829	7,404		624	6,780	8	56	132	428	1,149	5,266	365	
Total area actually reporting	100.0%	10,909		1,187	9,722	12	88	153	934	1,986	7,098	638	
Rate per 100,000 inhabitants		5,230.3		569.1	4,661.2	5.8	42.2	73.4	447.8	952.2	3,403.1	305.9	
Fort Walton Beach, FL M.S.A.	174,916												
(Includes Okaloosa County.)													
City of Fort Walton Beach	20,491	965		101	864	1	4	25	71	190	622	52	
Total area actually reporting	97.6%	5,584		619	4,965	5	55	117	442	921	3,812	232	
Estimated total	100.0%	5,812		645	5,167	5	56	124	460	962	3,951	254	
Rate per 100,000 inhabitants		3,322.7		368.7	2,954.0	2.9	32.0	70.9	263.0	550.0	2,258.8	145.2	

See footnotes at end of table.

Table 6

Index of Crime[1]
by Metropolitan Statistical Area, 2001—Continued

Metropolitan Statistical Area	Population	Crime Index total	Modified Crime Index total[2]	Violent crime[3]	Property crime[3]	Murder and non-negligent man-slaughter	Forcible rape	Robbery	Aggravated assault	Burglary	Larceny-theft	Motor vehicle theft	Arson[2]
Fort Wayne, IN M.S.A.	504,971												
(Includes Adams, Allen, DeKalb, Huntington, Wells, and Whitley Counties.)													
City of Fort Wayne	206,886	13,291		1,072	12,219	23	92	609	348	2,013	9,016	1,190	
Total area actually reporting	84.7%	17,650		1,302	16,348	24	116	680	482	2,886	11,977	1,485	
Estimated total	100.0%	19,413		1,431	17,982	25	127	706	573	3,205	13,141	1,636	
Rate per 100,000 inhabitants		3,844.4		283.4	3,561.0	5.0	25.1	139.8	113.5	634.7	2,602.3	324.0	
Fort Worth-Arlington, TX M.S.A.	1,741,264												
(Includes Hood, Johnson, Parker, and Tarrant Counties.)													
City of:													
Fort Worth	546,828	40,466		3,864	36,602	67	332	1,389	2,076	7,971	24,675	3,956	
Arlington	340,525	24,551		2,129	22,422	15	145	687	1,282	3,552	16,345	2,525	
Total area actually reporting	100.0%	96,072		8,062	88,010	104	715	2,439	4,804	17,124	62,034	8,852	
Rate per 100,000 inhabitants		5,517.4		463.0	5,054.4	6.0	41.1	140.1	275.9	983.4	3,562.6	508.4	
Fresno, CA M.S.A.	939,660												
(Includes Fresno and Madera Counties.)													
City of:													
Fresno	435,600	34,681		4,096	30,585	40	202	1,362	2,492	5,203	18,398	6,984	
Madera	44,010	2,785		485	2,300	9	17	127	332	518	1,336	446	
Total area actually reporting	100.0%	56,113		7,048	49,065	75	352	1,845	4,776	9,577	29,421	10,067	
Rate per 100,000 inhabitants		5,971.6		750.1	5,221.6	8.0	37.5	196.3	508.3	1,019.2	3,131.0	1,071.3	
Gainesville, FL M.S.A.	223,603												
(Includes Alachua County.)													
City of Gainesville	97,920	6,245		866	5,379	4	85	303	474	1,294	3,469	616	
Total area actually reporting	100.0%	13,622		1,937	11,685	8	155	453	1,321	2,918	7,736	1,031	
Rate per 100,000 inhabitants		6,092.0		866.3	5,225.8	3.6	69.3	202.6	590.8	1,305.0	3,459.7	461.1	
Gary, IN M.S.A.	634,919												
(Includes Lake and Porter Counties.)													
City of:													
Gary	103,325	6,132		901	5,231	82	77	461	281	1,742	2,249	1,240	
East Chicago	32,597	2,863		994	1,869	9	14	161	810	426	1,102	341	
Total area actually reporting	95.6%	26,811		3,338	23,473	118	191	1,073	1,956	4,197	15,619	3,657	
Estimated total	100.0%	28,017		3,418	24,599	119	198	1,096	2,005	4,341	16,503	3,755	
Rate per 100,000 inhabitants		4,412.7		538.3	3,874.4	18.7	31.2	172.6	315.8	683.7	2,599.2	591.4	
Glens Falls, NY M.S.A.	124,573												
(Includes Warren and Washington Counties.)													
City of Glens Falls	14,380	635		41	594	0	3	8	30	98	483	13	
Total area actually reporting	97.9%	2,719		296	2,423	2	22	16	256	519	1,830	74	
Estimated total	100.0%	2,786		301	2,485	2	22	18	259	528	1,879	78	
Rate per 100,000 inhabitants		2,236.4		241.6	1,994.8	1.6	17.7	14.4	207.9	423.8	1,508.4	62.6	
Grand Forks, ND-MN M.S.A.	97,017												
(Includes Grand Forks County, ND and Polk County, MN.)													
City of Grand Forks, ND	48,726	2,136		75	2,061	1	21	11	42	261	1,626	174	
Total area actually reporting	97.0%	3,306		141	3,165	3	40	13	85	492	2,420	253	
Estimated total	100.0%	3,407		143	3,264	3	41	13	86	503	2,502	259	
Rate per 100,000 inhabitants		3,511.8		147.4	3,364.4	3.1	42.3	13.4	88.6	518.5	2,578.9	267.0	
Grand Junction, CO M.S.A.	119,403												
(Includes Mesa County.)													
City of Grand Junction	43,123	3,563		170	3,393	1	20	26	123	468	2,788	137	
Total area actually reporting	93.7%	5,074		244	4,830	1	22	28	193	784	3,803	243	
Estimated total	100.0%	5,478		274	5,204	1	26	35	212	833	4,078	293	
Rate per 100,000 inhabitants		4,587.8		229.5	4,358.3	0.8	21.8	29.3	177.5	697.6	3,415.3	245.4	
Grand Rapids-Muskegon-Holland, MI M.S.A.	1,094,251												
(Includes Allegan, Kent, Muskegon, and Ottawa Counties.)													
City of:													
Grand Rapids	198,842	12,026		2,048	9,978	12	53	552	1,431	2,582	6,719	677	
Muskegon	40,316	3,407		431	2,976	1	60	82	288	561	2,180	235	
Holland	35,233	1,399		148	1,251	0	26	23	99	150	1,047	54	
Total area actually reporting	99.9%	41,699		4,657	37,042	23	553	880	3,201	7,825	26,903	2,314	
Estimated total	100.0%	41,719		4,658	37,061	23	553	880	3,202	7,828	26,917	2,316	
Rate per 100,000 inhabitants		3,812.6		425.7	3,386.9	2.1	50.5	80.4	292.6	715.4	2,459.9	211.7	

See footnotes at end of table.

Table 6

Index of Crime[1]
by Metropolitan Statistical Area, 2001—Continued

Metropolitan Statistical Area	Population	Crime Index total	Modified Crime Index total[2]	Violent crime[3]	Property crime[3]	Murder and non-negligent man-slaughter	Forcible rape	Robbery	Aggravated assault	Burglary	Larceny-theft	Motor vehicle theft	Arson[2]
Great Falls, MT M.S.A.[4]	**80,556**												
(Includes Cascade County.)													
City of Great Falls	56,831	3,906		240	3,666	2	12	31	195	341	3,189	136	
Total area actually reporting	99.2%	4,407		307	4,100	2	14	34	257	416	3,506	178	
Estimated total	100.0%	4,444		308	4,136	2	14	34	258	417	3,541	178	
Rate per 100,000 inhabitants		5,516.7		382.3	5,134.3	2.5	17.4	42.2	320.3	517.7	4,395.7	221.0	
Greeley, CO M.S.A.	**185,835**												
(Includes Weld County.)													
City of Greeley	79,013	4,303		299	4,004	4	45	47	203	557	3,190	257	
Total area actually reporting	93.7%	7,120		611	6,509	10	98	75	428	1,211	4,835	463	
Estimated total	100.0%	7,748		658	7,090	10	104	86	458	1,287	5,262	541	
Rate per 100,000 inhabitants		4,169.3		354.1	3,815.2	5.4	56.0	46.3	246.5	692.5	2,831.5	291.1	
Green Bay, WI M.S.A.	**228,394**												
(Includes Brown County.)													
City of Green Bay	103,042	3,712		272	3,440	3	35	36	198	675	2,561	204	
Total area actually reporting	100.0%	6,614		330	6,284	3	56	44	227	1,090	4,861	333	
Rate per 100,000 inhabitants		2,895.9		144.5	2,751.4	1.3	24.5	19.3	99.4	477.2	2,128.3	145.8	
Greensboro-Winston-Salem-High Point, NC M.S.A.[4]	**1,272,803**												
(Includes Alamance, Davidson, Davie, Forsyth, Guilford, Randolph, Stokes, and Yadkin Counties.)													
City of:													
Greensboro	227,700	15,962		1,869	14,093	20	89	896	864	3,258	9,871	964	
Winston-Salem[4]	188,937	16,037		1,766	14,271	15	120	701	930	3,444	9,798	1,029	
High Point	87,300	7,166		773	6,393	11	27	314	421	1,807	3,968	618	
Burlington	45,681	3,300		285	3,015	3	10	90	182	556	2,324	135	
Total area actually reporting	99.2%	66,928		6,343	60,585	68	330	2,356	3,589	14,964	41,706	3,915	
Estimated total	100.0%	67,538		6,385	61,153	68	332	2,370	3,615	15,079	42,132	3,942	
Rate per 100,000 inhabitants		5,306.2		501.6	4,804.6	5.3	26.1	186.2	284.0	1,184.7	3,310.2	309.7	
Greenville, NC M.S.A.	**136,075**												
(Includes Pitt County.)													
City of Greenville	61,505	6,554		547	6,007	3	20	175	349	1,435	4,296	276	
Total area actually reporting	100.0%	9,733		865	8,868	7	34	236	588	2,301	6,148	419	
Rate per 100,000 inhabitants		7,152.7		635.7	6,517.0	5.1	25.0	173.4	432.1	1,691.0	4,518.1	307.9	
Hagerstown, MD M.S.A.	**133,882**												
(Includes Washington County.)													
City of Hagerstown	37,232	1,919		217	1,702	1	6	70	140	346	1,209	147	
Total area actually reporting	100.0%	3,648		510	3,138	4	28	89	389	714	2,156	268	
Rate per 100,000 inhabitants		2,724.8		380.9	2,343.9	3.0	20.9	66.5	290.6	533.3	1,610.4	200.2	
Hamilton-Middletown, OH M.S.A.	**333,405**												
(Includes Butler County.)													
City of:													
Hamilton	60,799	5,595		690	4,905	5	66	221	398	1,204	3,264	437	
Middletown	51,698	3,265		137	3,128	2	18	61	56	518	2,444	166	
Total area actually reporting	88.7%	15,252		1,183	14,069	9	155	327	692	2,760	10,389	920	
Estimated total	100.0%	16,485		1,245	15,240	9	164	349	723	2,944	11,304	992	
Rate per 100,000 inhabitants		4,944.4		373.4	4,571.0	2.7	49.2	104.7	216.9	883.0	3,390.5	297.5	
Harrisburg-Lebanon-Carlisle, PA M.S.A.	**629,714**												
(Includes Cumberland, Dauphin, Lebanon, and Perry Counties.)													
City of:													
Harrisburg	48,974	3,150		714	2,436	9	42	379	284	558	1,711	167	
Lebanon	24,473	1,344		247	1,097	0	17	46	184	197	840	60	
Carlisle	17,979	647		52	595	0	8	27	17	111	472	12	
Total area actually reporting	89.0%	15,344		1,854	13,490	18	201	647	988	2,458	10,396	636	
Estimated total	100.0%	17,020		2,010	15,010	20	212	686	1,092	2,667	11,589	754	
Rate per 100,000 inhabitants		2,702.8		319.2	2,383.6	3.2	33.7	108.9	173.4	423.5	1,840.4	119.7	
Hartford, CT M.S.A.	**982,108**												
(Includes part of Hartford, Litchfield, Middlesex, New London, Tolland, and Windham Counties.)													
City of:													
Hartford	122,274	10,789		1,593	9,196	25	64	889	615	1,569	5,798	1,829	
Middletown	43,414	1,239		64	1,175	2	8	26	28	215	822	138	
Total area actually reporting	100.0%	34,719		3,364	31,355	39	204	1,537	1,584	5,412	21,859	4,084	
Rate per 100,000 inhabitants		3,535.2		342.5	3,192.6	4.0	20.8	156.5	161.3	551.1	2,225.7	415.8	

See footnotes at end of table.

Table 6

Index of Crime[1]

by Metropolitan Statistical Area, 2001—Continued

Metropolitan Statistical Area	Population	Crime Index total	Modified Crime Index total[2]	Violent crime[3]	Property crime[3]	Murder and non-negligent man-slaughter	Forcible rape	Robbery	Aggravated assault	Burglary	Larceny-theft	Motor vehicle theft	Arson[2]
Hattiesburg, MS M.S.A.	**112,199**												
(Includes Forrest and Lamar Counties.)													
City of Hattiesburg	44,989	2,977		146	2,831	6	20	72	48	644	2,019	168	
Total area actually reporting	79.8%	3,898		187	3,711	6	38	77	66	880	2,598	233	
Estimated total	100.0%	4,494		219	4,275	8	44	82	85	1,058	2,940	277	
Rate per 100,000 inhabitants		4,005.4		195.2	3,810.2	7.1	39.2	73.1	75.8	943.0	2,620.3	246.9	
Hickory-Morganton-Lenoir, NC M.S.A.	**347,668**												
(Includes Alexander, Burke, Caldwell, and Catawba Counties.)													
City of:													
Hickory	37,855	3,293		212	3,081	6	9	91	106	571	2,282	228	
Morganton	17,605	957		58	899	2	4	19	33	168	687	44	
Lenoir	17,079	845		60	785	1	1	22	36	159	584	42	
Total area actually reporting	99.4%	13,401		894	12,507	19	54	231	590	3,315	8,419	773	
Estimated total	100.0%	13,518		902	12,616	19	54	234	595	3,337	8,501	778	
Rate per 100,000 inhabitants		3,888.2		259.4	3,628.7	5.5	15.5	67.3	171.1	959.8	2,445.1	223.8	
Honolulu, HI M.S.A.	**885,605**												
(Includes Honolulu County.)													
City of Honolulu	885,605	48,442		2,453	45,989	20	293	999	1,141	7,340	33,052	5,597	
Total area actually reporting	100.0%	48,442		2,453	45,989	20	293	999	1,141	7,340	33,052	5,597	
Rate per 100,000 inhabitants		5,469.9		277.0	5,192.9	2.3	33.1	112.8	128.8	828.8	3,732.1	632.0	
Houma, LA M.S.A.	**194,323**												
(Includes Lafourche and Terrebonne Parishes.)													
City of Houma	32,367	2,212		432	1,780	4	15	70	343	307	1,359	114	
Total area actually reporting	98.7%	8,930		1,084	7,846	10	48	164	862	1,781	5,672	393	
Estimated total	100.0%	9,082		1,101	7,981	10	49	167	875	1,807	5,772	402	
Rate per 100,000 inhabitants		4,673.7		566.6	4,107.1	5.1	25.2	85.9	450.3	929.9	2,970.3	206.9	
Houston, TX M.S.A.	**4,272,445**												
(Includes Chambers, Fort Bend, Harris, Liberty, Montgomery, and Waller Counties.)													
City of:													
Houston	1,997,965	141,987		23,419	118,568	267	945	9,921	12,286	25,108	69,371	24,089	
Baytown	67,938	3,053		226	2,827	4	34	56	132	546	1,997	284	
Conroe	37,646	2,782		305	2,477	2	17	96	190	480	1,815	182	
Total area actually reporting	100.0%	226,347		32,847	193,500	353	1,623	12,194	18,677	42,760	118,581	32,159	
Rate per 100,000 inhabitants		5,297.8		768.8	4,529.0	8.3	38.0	285.4	437.2	1,000.8	2,775.5	752.7	
Huntsville, AL M.S.A.	**343,705**												
(Includes Limestone and Madison Counties.)													
City of Huntsville	158,830	11,413		1,039	10,374	15	109	345	570	1,802	7,802	770	
Total area actually reporting	100.0%	15,520		1,359	14,161	18	134	411	796	2,675	10,466	1,020	
Rate per 100,000 inhabitants		4,515.5		395.4	4,120.1	5.2	39.0	119.6	231.6	778.3	3,045.1	296.8	
Iowa City, IA M.S.A.	**110,887**												
(Includes Johnson County.)													
City of Iowa City	62,153	1,745		259	1,486	0	17	37	205	245	1,176	65	
Total area actually reporting	100.0%	3,229		432	2,797	2	42	58	330	524	2,154	119	
Rate per 100,000 inhabitants		2,912.0		389.6	2,522.4	1.8	37.9	52.3	297.6	472.6	1,942.5	107.3	
Jackson, MI M.S.A.	**159,257**												
(Includes Jackson County.)													
City of Jackson	37,595	3,354		525	2,829	0	48	105	372	453	2,179	197	
Total area actually reporting	95.6%	6,826		862	5,964	4	109	129	620	1,170	4,317	477	
Estimated total	100.0%	7,082		884	6,198	4	111	134	635	1,208	4,485	505	
Rate per 100,000 inhabitants		4,446.9		555.1	3,891.8	2.5	69.7	84.1	398.7	758.5	2,816.2	317.1	
Jackson, MS M.S.A.	**442,875**												
(Includes Hinds, Madison, and Rankin Counties.)													
City of Jackson	185,122	18,586		1,966	16,620	50	218	1,044	654	4,683	8,972	2,965	
Total area actually reporting	81.3%	23,741		2,282	21,459	59	264	1,109	850	5,878	12,261	3,320	
Estimated total	100.0%	27,012		2,485	24,527	64	292	1,157	972	6,606	14,369	3,552	
Rate per 100,000 inhabitants		6,099.2		561.1	5,538.1	14.5	65.9	261.2	219.5	1,491.6	3,244.5	802.0	
Jackson, TN M.S.A.	**108,335**												
(Includes Chester and Madison Counties.)													
City of Jackson	62,035	4,626		764	3,862	12	27	180	545	852	2,694	316	
Total area actually reporting	100.0%	6,049		980	5,069	15	43	193	729	1,197	3,477	395	
Rate per 100,000 inhabitants		5,583.6		904.6	4,679.0	13.8	39.7	178.2	672.9	1,104.9	3,209.5	364.6	

See footnotes at end of table.

Table 6

Index of Crime[1]

by Metropolitan Statistical Area, 2001—Continued

Metropolitan Statistical Area	Population	Crime Index total	Modified Crime Index total[2]	Violent crime[3]	Property crime[3]	Murder and non-negligent man-slaughter	Forcible rape	Robbery	Aggravated assault	Burglary	Larceny-theft	Motor vehicle theft	Arson[2]
Jacksonville, FL M.S.A.	**1,129,007**												
(Includes Clay, Duval, Nassau, and St. Johns Counties.)													
City of Jacksonville	754,679	51,250		7,388	43,862	75	287	2,195	4,831	9,903	28,827	5,132	
Total area actually reporting	100.0%	66,087		9,791	56,296	95	400	2,473	6,823	12,565	37,775	5,956	
Rate per 100,000 inhabitants		5,853.6		867.2	4,986.3	8.4	35.4	219.0	604.3	1,112.9	3,345.9	527.5	
Janesville-Beloit, WI M.S.A.	**153,393**												
(Includes Rock County.)													
City of:													
Janesville	59,922	3,195		141	3,054	1	16	20	104	503	2,441	110	
Beloit	36,030	1,785		139	1,646	1	13	53	72	279	1,245	122	
Total area actually reporting	96.8%	6,058		345	5,713	2	33	79	231	1,047	4,385	281	
Estimated total	100.0%	6,208		351	5,857	2	34	81	234	1,063	4,506	288	
Rate per 100,000 inhabitants		4,047.1		228.8	3,818.3	1.3	22.2	52.8	152.5	693.0	2,937.6	187.8	
Jersey City, NJ M.S.A.	**614,047**												
(Includes Hudson County.)													
City of:													
Jersey City	242,055	12,527		2,853	9,674	25	89	1,301	1,438	2,350	4,911	2,413	
Bayonne	62,357	1,343		200	1,143	3	2	74	121	222	750	171	
Total area actually reporting	100.0%	24,596		4,121	20,475	34	116	1,878	2,093	4,443	11,351	4,681	
Rate per 100,000 inhabitants		4,005.6		671.1	3,334.4	5.5	18.9	305.8	340.9	723.6	1,848.6	762.3	
Johnson City-Kingsport-Bristol, TN-VA M.S.A.	**484,972**												
(Includes Carter, Hawkins, Sullivan, Unicoi, and Washington Counties, TN and Bristol City and Scott and Washington Counties, VA.)													
City of:													
Johnson City, TN	55,964	4,298		386	3,912	1	27	78	280	526	3,203	183	
Kingsport, TN	45,305	2,992		384	2,608	2	26	36	320	409	2,065	134	
Bristol, TN	25,042	1,211		122	1,089	1	9	10	102	147	863	79	
Bristol, VA	17,635	668		53	615	3	4	7	39	74	509	32	
Total area actually reporting	99.4%	17,299		1,892	15,407	15	137	186	1,554	3,099	11,372	936	
Estimated total	100.0%	17,446		1,904	15,542	15	138	189	1,562	3,114	11,480	948	
Rate per 100,000 inhabitants		3,597.3		392.6	3,204.7	3.1	28.5	39.0	322.1	642.1	2,367.1	195.5	
Johnstown, PA M.S.A.	**232,737**												
(Includes Cambria and Somerset Counties.)													
City of Johnstown	28,603	983		144	839	2	5	42	95	238	531	70	
Total area actually reporting	77.0%	3,111		429	2,682	3	35	73	318	681	1,794	207	
Estimated total	100.0%	4,404		549	3,855	4	43	103	399	842	2,715	298	
Rate per 100,000 inhabitants		1,892.3		235.9	1,656.4	1.7	18.5	44.3	171.4	361.8	1,166.6	128.0	
Joplin, MO M.S.A.	**158,292**												
(Includes Jasper and Newton Counties.)													
City of Joplin	45,785	4,014		213	3,801	3	36	70	104	709	2,811	281	
Total area actually reporting	100.0%	8,026		756	7,270	6	58	89	603	1,508	5,180	582	
Rate per 100,000 inhabitants		5,070.4		477.6	4,592.8	3.8	36.6	56.2	380.9	952.7	3,272.4	367.7	
Kalamazoo-Battle Creek, MI M.S.A.	**455,237**												
(Includes Calhoun, Kalamazoo, and Van Buren Counties.)													
City of:													
Kalamazoo	77,552	6,295		907	5,388	4	102	200	601	1,366	3,539	483	
Battle Creek	53,645	5,239		871	4,368	6	78	158	629	926	3,111	331	
Total area actually reporting	99.0%	24,717		2,880	21,837	17	353	497	2,013	4,864	15,428	1,545	
Estimated total	100.0%	24,893		2,896	21,997	17	355	500	2,024	4,890	15,543	1,564	
Rate per 100,000 inhabitants		5,468.1		636.2	4,832.0	3.7	78.0	109.8	444.6	1,074.2	3,414.3	343.6	
Kenosha, WI M.S.A.	**150,643**												
(Includes Kenosha County.)													
City of Kenosha	90,996	3,182		547	2,635	4	41	62	440	422	1,997	216	
Total area actually reporting	100.0%	4,936		663	4,273	4	61	73	525	623	3,356	294	
Rate per 100,000 inhabitants		3,276.6		440.1	2,836.5	2.7	40.5	48.5	348.5	413.6	2,227.8	195.2	
Killeen-Temple, TX M.S.A.	**320,054**												
(Includes Bell and Coryell Counties.)													
City of:													
Killeen	88,883	5,263		556	4,707	8	40	153	355	1,170	3,299	238	
Temple	55,751	3,087		222	2,865	3	14	68	137	607	2,074	184	
Total area actually reporting	99.6%	12,771		1,158	11,613	11	101	256	790	2,629	8,422	562	
Estimated total	100.0%	12,821		1,161	11,660	11	101	257	792	2,638	8,456	566	
Rate per 100,000 inhabitants		4,005.9		362.8	3,643.1	3.4	31.6	80.3	247.5	824.2	2,642.1	176.8	

See footnotes at end of table.

Table 6

Index of Crime[1]

by Metropolitan Statistical Area, 2001—Continued

Metropolitan Statistical Area	Population	Crime Index total	Modified Crime Index total[2]	Violent crime[3]	Property crime[3]	Murder and non-negligent man-slaughter	Forcible rape	Robbery	Aggravated assault	Burglary	Larceny-theft	Motor vehicle theft	Arson[2]
Knoxville, TN M.S.A.	**693,379**												
(Includes Anderson, Blount, Knox, Loudon, Sevier, and Union Counties.)													
City of:													
Knoxville	175,441	11,069		2,105	8,964	15	139	637	1,314	1,717	5,951	1,296	
Oak Ridge	27,631	1,553		109	1,444	3	7	29	70	241	1,138	65	
Total area actually reporting	99.6%	29,329		3,827	25,502	33	287	814	2,693	5,376	17,417	2,709	
Estimated total	100.0%	29,462		3,840	25,622	33	288	816	2,703	5,395	17,510	2,717	
Rate per 100,000 inhabitants		4,249.0		553.8	3,695.2	4.8	41.5	117.7	389.8	778.1	2,525.3	391.8	
Kokomo, IN M.S.A.	**102,113**												
(Includes Howard and Tipton Counties.)													
City of Kokomo	46,373	3,028		240	2,788	5	18	43	174	458	2,224	106	
Total area actually reporting	88.9%	3,769		288	3,481	5	22	55	206	609	2,727	145	
Estimated total	100.0%	3,981		304	3,677	5	23	58	218	653	2,860	164	
Rate per 100,000 inhabitants		3,898.6		297.7	3,600.9	4.9	22.5	56.8	213.5	639.5	2,800.8	160.6	
La Crosse, WI-MN M.S.A.	**127,814**												
(Includes La Crosse County, WI and Houston County, MN.)													
City of La Crosse, WI	52,187	2,093		99	1,994	2	11	25	61	192	1,684	118	
Total area actually reporting	98.9%	3,734		158	3,576	2	25	27	104	342	3,071	163	
Estimated total	100.0%	3,777		159	3,618	2	25	27	105	347	3,106	165	
Rate per 100,000 inhabitants		2,955.1		124.4	2,830.7	1.6	19.6	21.1	82.2	271.5	2,430.1	129.1	
Lafayette, IN M.S.A.	**183,851**												
(Includes Clinton and Tippecanoe Counties.)													
City of Lafayette	56,715	2,850		131	2,719	0	11	64	56	474	2,108	137	
Total area actually reporting	100.0%	6,304		318	5,986	5	38	87	188	969	4,734	283	
Rate per 100,000 inhabitants		3,428.9		173.0	3,255.9	2.7	20.7	47.3	102.3	527.1	2,574.9	153.9	
Lafayette, LA M.S.A.	**385,340**												
(Includes Acadia, Lafayette, St. Landry, and St. Martin Parishes.)													
City of Lafayette	110,170	8,167		1,045	7,122	5	74	195	771	1,332	5,318	472	
Total area actually reporting	95.5%	16,438		2,229	14,209	12	135	327	1,755	3,188	10,171	850	
Estimated total	100.0%	17,456		2,342	15,114	12	141	349	1,840	3,364	10,839	911	
Rate per 100,000 inhabitants		4,530.0		607.8	3,922.3	3.1	36.6	90.6	477.5	873.0	2,812.8	236.4	
Lake Charles, LA M.S.A.	**183,431**												
(Includes Calcasieu Parish.)													
City of Lake Charles	71,700	4,586		600	3,986	4	38	157	401	1,721	1,900	365	
Total area actually reporting	87.0%	9,554		918	8,636	8	84	232	594	2,738	5,226	672	
Estimated total	100.0%	10,947		1,073	9,874	9	92	262	710	2,979	6,140	755	
Rate per 100,000 inhabitants		5,967.9		585.0	5,383.0	4.9	50.2	142.8	387.1	1,624.0	3,347.3	411.6	
Lakeland-Winter Haven, FL M.S.A.	**496,463**												
(Includes Polk County.)													
City of:													
Lakeland	80,485	6,303		581	5,722	4	59	248	270	1,326	3,899	497	
Winter Haven	27,173	1,964		153	1,811	2	19	75	57	412	1,205	194	
Total area actually reporting	100.0%	26,781		2,933	23,848	18	282	711	1,922	6,352	15,406	2,090	
Rate per 100,000 inhabitants		5,394.4		590.8	4,803.6	3.6	56.8	143.2	387.1	1,279.5	3,103.2	421.0	
Lancaster, PA M.S.A.	**470,892**												
(Includes Lancaster County.)													
City of Lancaster	56,376	3,545		508	3,037	4	37	284	183	538	2,120	379	
Total area actually reporting	90.9%	11,271		1,013	10,258	12	86	466	449	1,841	7,535	882	
Estimated total	100.0%	12,301		1,109	11,192	13	93	490	513	1,970	8,268	954	
Rate per 100,000 inhabitants		2,612.3		235.5	2,376.8	2.8	19.7	104.1	108.9	418.4	1,755.8	202.6	
Lansing-East Lansing, MI M.S.A.	**450,087**												
(Includes Clinton, Eaton, and Ingham Counties.)													
City of:													
Lansing	119,756	7,212		1,353	5,859	8	178	227	940	994	4,382	483	
East Lansing	46,770	1,773		201	1,572	0	15	29	157	287	1,232	53	
Total area actually reporting	97.6%	17,905		2,137	15,768	15	334	334	1,454	2,747	12,017	1,004	
Estimated total	100.0%	18,300		2,172	16,128	15	338	341	1,478	2,805	12,275	1,048	
Rate per 100,000 inhabitants		4,065.9		482.6	3,583.3	3.3	75.1	75.8	328.4	623.2	2,727.3	232.8	

See footnotes at end of table.

Table 6

Index of Crime[1]
by Metropolitan Statistical Area, 2001—Continued

Metropolitan Statistical Area	Population	Crime Index total	Modified Crime Index total[2]	Violent crime[3]	Property crime[3]	Murder and non-negligent man-slaughter	Forcible rape	Robbery	Aggravated assault	Burglary	Larceny-theft	Motor vehicle theft	Arson[2]
Laredo, TX M.S.A.	**197,499**												
(Includes Webb County.)													
City of Laredo	180,583	13,056		1,121	11,935	8	39	200	874	1,791	9,125	1,019	
Total area actually reporting	100.0%	13,580		1,170	12,410	12	41	201	916	1,942	9,409	1,059	
Rate per 100,000 inhabitants		6,876.0		592.4	6,283.6	6.1	20.8	101.8	463.8	983.3	4,764.1	536.2	
Las Vegas, NV-AZ M.S.A.	**1,644,604**												
(Includes Clark and Nye Counties, NV and Mohave County, AZ.)													
City of Las Vegas Metropolitan Police Department, NV	1,117,763	50,570		7,549	43,021	133	447	3,667	3,302	10,083	22,394	10,544	
Total area actually reporting	100.0%	73,595		10,144	63,451	173	622	4,398	4,951	15,543	34,468	13,440	
Rate per 100,000 inhabitants		4,474.9		616.8	3,858.1	10.5	37.8	267.4	301.0	945.1	2,095.8	817.2	
Lawrence, MA-NH M.S.A.	**399,977**												
(Includes part of Essex County, MA and part of Rockingham County, NH.)													
City of Lawrence, MA	72,386	3,853		592	3,261	4	48	145	395	504	1,017	1,740	
Total area actually reporting	87.2%	9,263		1,156	8,107	4	120	214	818	1,853	3,886	2,368	
Estimated total	100.0%	10,165		1,217	8,948	4	137	223	853	2,009	4,500	2,439	
Rate per 100,000 inhabitants		2,541.4		304.3	2,237.1	1.0	34.3	55.8	213.3	502.3	1,125.1	609.8	
Lawton, OK M.S.A.	**114,286**												
(Includes Comanche County.)													
City of Lawton	93,011	5,210		573	4,637	6	46	148	373	1,203	3,169	265	
Total area actually reporting	100.0%	5,551		631	4,920	6	49	152	424	1,299	3,326	295	
Rate per 100,000 inhabitants		4,857.1		552.1	4,305.0	5.2	42.9	133.0	371.0	1,136.6	2,910.2	258.1	
Lewiston-Auburn, ME M.S.A.	**101,492**												
(Includes part of Androscoggin County.)													
City of:													
Lewiston	36,019	1,755		75	1,680	1	23	28	23	332	1,263	85	
Auburn	23,417	1,121		61	1,060	1	14	10	36	203	806	51	
Total area actually reporting	100.0%	3,687		164	3,523	2	50	42	70	726	2,595	202	
Rate per 100,000 inhabitants		3,632.8		161.6	3,471.2	2.0	49.3	41.4	69.0	715.3	2,556.9	199.0	
Lima, OH M.S.A.	**155,363**												
(Includes Allen and Auglaize Counties.)													
City of Lima	40,153	3,522		421	3,101	6	72	108	235	847	2,107	147	
Total area actually reporting	85.9%	5,892		529	5,363	6	88	140	295	1,262	3,891	210	
Estimated total	100.0%	6,609		565	6,044	6	93	153	313	1,369	4,423	252	
Rate per 100,000 inhabitants		4,253.9		363.7	3,890.2	3.9	59.9	98.5	201.5	881.2	2,846.9	162.2	
Lincoln, NE M.S.A.	**250,579**												
(Includes Lancaster County.)													
City of Lincoln	225,841	15,041		1,302	13,739	6	88	154	1,054	1,970	11,194	575	
Total area actually reporting	100.0%	16,143		1,319	14,824	6	89	156	1,068	2,148	12,075	601	
Rate per 100,000 inhabitants		6,442.3		526.4	5,915.9	2.4	35.5	62.3	426.2	857.2	4,818.8	239.8	
Longview-Marshall, TX M.S.A.	**213,518**												
(Includes Gregg, Harrison, and Upshur Counties.)													
City of:													
Longview	75,008	6,130		551	5,579	8	101	167	275	1,274	3,782	523	
Marshall	24,478	1,535		140	1,395	1	15	27	97	265	1,006	124	
Total area actually reporting	99.5%	11,549		949	10,600	11	149	232	557	2,459	7,265	876	
Estimated total	100.0%	11,599		952	10,647	11	149	233	559	2,468	7,299	880	
Rate per 100,000 inhabitants		5,432.3		445.9	4,986.5	5.2	69.8	109.1	261.8	1,155.9	3,418.4	412.1	
Los Angeles-Long Beach, CA M.S.A.	**9,696,252**												
(Includes Los Angeles County.)													
City of:													
Los Angeles	3,763,486	189,278		52,243	137,035	588	1,409	17,166	33,080	25,695	79,521	31,819	
Long Beach	470,099	18,467		3,413	15,054	49	125	1,417	1,822	3,232	7,876	3,946	
Pasadena	136,425	5,240		676	4,564	4	34	268	370	899	3,157	508	
Lancaster	120,924	4,747		1,163	3,584	7	56	263	837	1,159	1,909	516	
Total area actually reporting	100.0%	391,068		89,848	301,220	1,074	2,790	30,254	55,730	61,526	171,785	67,909	
Rate per 100,000 inhabitants		4,033.2		926.6	3,106.6	11.1	28.8	312.0	574.8	634.5	1,771.7	700.4	

See footnotes at end of table.

Table 6

Index of Crime[1]

by Metropolitan Statistical Area, 2001—Continued

Metropolitan Statistical Area	Population	Crime Index total	Modified Crime Index total[2]	Violent crime[3]	Property crime[3]	Murder and non-negligent man-slaughter	Forcible rape	Robbery	Aggravated assault	Burglary	Larceny-theft	Motor vehicle theft	Arson[2]
Louisville, KY-IN M.S.A.	1,031,571												
(Includes Bullitt, Jefferson, and Oldham Counties, KY and Clark, Floyd, Harrison, and Scott Counties, IN.)													
City of:													
Louisville, KY	257,739	15,673		1,915	13,758	25	78	989	823	3,390	7,934	2,434	
New Albany, IN	37,815	3,120		242	2,878	3	20	71	148	592	2,097	189	
Total area actually reporting	80.4%	37,106		3,277	33,829	49	182	1,444	1,602	7,665	21,950	4,214	
Estimated total	100.0%	46,766		4,180	42,586	52	244	1,649	2,235	9,068	28,723	4,795	
Rate per 100,000 inhabitants		4,533.5		405.2	4,128.3	5.0	23.7	159.9	216.7	879.0	2,784.4	464.8	
Lowell, MA-NH M.S.A.	303,276												
(Includes part of Middlesex County, MA and Hillsborough County, NH.)													
City of Lowell, MA	105,668	4,510		850	3,660	4	37	122	687	650	2,052	958	
Total area actually reporting	95.4%	7,090		1,021	6,069	4	54	145	818	1,019	3,880	1,170	
Estimated total	100.0%	7,347		1,043	6,304	4	59	148	832	1,064	4,049	1,191	
Rate per 100,000 inhabitants		2,422.5		343.9	2,078.6	1.3	19.5	48.8	274.3	350.8	1,335.1	392.7	
Lubbock, TX M.S.A.	248,134												
(Includes Lubbock County.)													
City of Lubbock	204,093	14,063		2,469	11,594	10	100	317	2,042	2,847	8,068	679	
Total area actually reporting	100.0%	15,795		2,627	13,168	10	126	329	2,162	3,240	9,148	780	
Rate per 100,000 inhabitants		6,365.5		1,058.7	5,306.8	4.0	50.8	132.6	871.3	1,305.7	3,686.7	314.3	
Lynchburg, VA M.S.A.	218,227												
(Includes Bedford and Lynchburg Cities and Amherst, Bedford, and Campbell Counties.)													
City of Lynchburg	66,276	2,716		287	2,429	6	23	80	178	490	1,718	221	
Total area actually reporting	100.0%	5,349		517	4,832	6	64	108	339	909	3,516	407	
Rate per 100,000 inhabitants		2,451.1		236.9	2,214.2	2.7	29.3	49.5	155.3	416.5	1,611.2	186.5	
Macon, GA M.S.A.	330,329												
(Includes Bibb, Houston, Jones, Peach, and Twiggs Counties.)													
City of Macon	99,601	10,590		704	9,886	18	60	275	351	2,291	6,272	1,323	
Total area actually reporting	99.9%	20,867		1,513	19,354	28	93	485	907	4,475	12,896	1,983	
Estimated total	100.0%	20,879		1,514	19,365	28	93	485	908	4,477	12,904	1,984	
Rate per 100,000 inhabitants		6,320.7		458.3	5,862.3	8.5	28.2	146.8	274.9	1,355.3	3,906.4	600.6	
Madison, WI M.S.A.	429,566												
(Includes Dane County.)													
City of Madison	209,537	8,299		708	7,591	6	63	295	344	1,354	5,530	707	
Total area actually reporting	99.3%	14,700		1,011	13,689	6	114	351	540	2,183	10,484	1,022	
Estimated total	100.0%	14,794		1,014	13,780	6	114	352	542	2,193	10,561	1,026	
Rate per 100,000 inhabitants		3,443.9		236.1	3,207.9	1.4	26.5	81.9	126.2	510.5	2,458.5	238.8	
Manchester, NH M.S.A.	202,134												
(Includes part of Hillsborough, Merrimack, and Rockingham Counties.)													
City of Manchester	109,032	3,520		257	3,263	0	53	118	86	597	2,356	310	
Total area actually reporting	79.2%	4,178		291	3,887	1	60	124	106	689	2,841	357	
Estimated total	100.0%	4,918		342	4,576	1	74	132	135	817	3,344	415	
Rate per 100,000 inhabitants		2,433.0		169.2	2,263.8	0.5	36.6	65.3	66.8	404.2	1,654.3	205.3	
Mansfield, OH M.S.A.	176,134												
(Includes Crawford and Richland Counties.)													
City of Mansfield	49,435	3,924		185	3,739	1	39	104	41	938	2,623	178	
Total area actually reporting	89.0%	6,709		254	6,455	3	59	132	60	1,587	4,607	261	
Estimated total	100.0%	7,343		285	7,058	3	63	143	76	1,682	5,078	298	
Rate per 100,000 inhabitants		4,169.0		161.8	4,007.2	1.7	35.8	81.2	43.1	955.0	2,883.0	169.2	
McAllen-Edinburg-Mission, TX M.S.A.	582,386												
(Includes Hidalgo County.)													
City of:													
McAllen	108,829	8,989		474	8,515	3	11	124	336	1,567	6,235	713	
Edinburg	49,565	4,866		299	4,567	0	41	63	195	634	3,736	197	
Mission	46,438	2,902		85	2,817	0	2	27	56	499	2,030	288	
Total area actually reporting	99.8%	34,015		3,179	30,836	38	119	500	2,522	7,258	21,313	2,265	
Estimated total	100.0%	34,073		3,183	30,890	38	119	501	2,525	7,268	21,353	2,269	
Rate per 100,000 inhabitants		5,850.6		546.5	5,304.0	6.5	20.4	86.0	433.6	1,248.0	3,666.5	389.6	

See footnotes at end of table.

Table 6

Index of Crime[1]

by Metropolitan Statistical Area, 2001—Continued

Metropolitan Statistical Area	Population	Crime Index total	Modified Crime Index total[2]	Violent crime[3]	Property crime[3]	Murder and non-negligent man-slaughter	Forcible rape	Robbery	Aggravated assault	Burglary	Larceny-theft	Motor vehicle theft	Arson[2]
Medford-Ashland, OR M.S.A.	**183,996**												
(Includes Jackson County.)													
City of:													
Medford	64,104	3,733		198	3,535	0	19	32	147	431	2,941	163	
Ashland	19,816	763		8	755	0	1	4	3	96	641	18	
Total area actually reporting	100.0%	7,512		380	7,132	2	45	53	280	1,027	5,742	363	
Rate per 100,000 inhabitants		4,082.7		206.5	3,876.2	1.1	24.5	28.8	152.2	558.2	3,120.7	197.3	
Melbourne-Titusville-Palm Bay, FL M.S.A.	**488,570**												
(Includes Brevard County.)													
City of:													
Melbourne	73,232	5,299		725	4,574	3	43	166	513	802	3,480	292	
Titusville	41,724	2,068		378	1,690	2	18	99	259	451	1,051	188	
Palm Bay	81,471	4,286		739	3,547	4	50	97	588	698	2,641	208	
Total area actually reporting	100.0%	24,168		3,761	20,407	15	207	659	2,880	4,263	14,725	1,419	
Rate per 100,000 inhabitants		4,946.7		769.8	4,176.9	3.1	42.4	134.9	589.5	872.5	3,013.9	290.4	
Memphis, TN-AR-MS M.S.A.[4]	**1,145,198**												
(Includes Fayette, Shelby, and Tipton Counties, TN, Crittenden County, AR, and DeSoto County, MS.)													
City of:													
Memphis, TN[4]	655,898	65,479		10,862	54,617	158	480	4,338	5,886	15,874	29,207	9,536	
West Memphis, AR	27,859	1,758		336	1,422	2	21	120	193	417	814	191	
Total area actually reporting	96.8%	83,976		12,598	71,378	173	602	4,728	7,095	19,642	40,530	11,206	
Estimated total	100.0%	84,932		12,647	72,285	175	611	4,736	7,125	19,928	41,080	11,277	
Rate per 100,000 inhabitants		7,416.4		1,104.4	6,312.0	15.3	53.4	413.6	622.2	1,740.1	3,587.2	984.7	
Merced, CA M.S.A.	**214,467**												
(Includes Merced County.)													
City of Merced	65,080	4,154		377	3,777	2	25	111	239	653	2,747	377	
Total area actually reporting	100.0%	9,439		1,324	8,115	5	67	176	1,076	2,062	5,053	1,000	
Rate per 100,000 inhabitants		4,401.1		617.3	3,783.8	2.3	31.2	82.1	501.7	961.5	2,356.1	466.3	
Miami, FL M.S.A.	**2,311,752**												
(Includes Miami-Dade County.)													
City of:													
Miami	371,863	35,291		7,210	28,081	66	118	2,719	4,307	6,218	16,635	5,228	
Miami Beach	90,212	11,217		1,241	9,976	6	66	484	685	1,607	7,000	1,369	
Total area actually reporting	100.0%	175,652		26,615	149,037	195	843	8,397	17,180	26,827	98,426	23,784	
Rate per 100,000 inhabitants		7,598.2		1,151.3	6,446.9	8.4	36.5	363.2	743.2	1,160.5	4,257.6	1,028.8	
Middlesex-Somerset-Hunterdon, NJ M.S.A.	**1,179,383**												
(Includes Hunterdon, Middlesex, and Somerset Counties.)													
Total area actually reporting	99.9%	26,061		2,150	23,911	14	98	719	1,319	4,511	16,742	2,658	
Estimated total	100.0%	26,095		2,153	23,942	14	98	720	1,321	4,517	16,763	2,662	
Rate per 100,000 inhabitants		2,212.6		182.6	2,030.0	1.2	8.3	61.0	112.0	383.0	1,421.3	225.7	
Milwaukee-Waukesha, WI M.S.A.	**1,511,438**												
(Includes Milwaukee, Ozaukee, Washington, and Waukesha Counties.)													
City of:													
Milwaukee	601,229	45,748		5,463	40,285	127	295	2,913	2,128	6,680	25,712	7,893	
Waukesha	65,287	1,586		100	1,486	2	8	21	69	321	1,073	92	
Total area actually reporting	98.6%	69,281		6,367	62,914	134	396	3,257	2,580	9,514	44,266	9,134	
Estimated total	100.0%	69,930		6,388	63,542	134	398	3,264	2,592	9,584	44,794	9,164	
Rate per 100,000 inhabitants		4,626.7		422.6	4,204.1	8.9	26.3	216.0	171.5	634.1	2,963.7	606.3	
Minneapolis-St. Paul, MN-WI M.S.A.	**3,000,316**												
(Includes Anoka, Carver, Chisago, Dakota, Hennepin, Isanti, Ramsey, Scott, Sherburne, Washington, and Wright Counties, MN and Pierce and St. Croix Counties, WI.)													
City of:													
Minneapolis, MN	386,726	26,820		4,101	22,719	43	399	1,943	1,716	4,092	14,548	4,079	
St. Paul, MN	290,234	19,046		2,236	16,810	9	221	680	1,326	3,009	11,457	2,344	
Total area actually reporting	98.8%	121,526		9,900	111,626	77	1,374	3,418	5,031	16,046	84,052	11,528	
Estimated total	100.0%	122,821		9,960	112,861	77	1,387	3,432	5,064	16,193	85,057	11,611	
Rate per 100,000 inhabitants		4,093.6		332.0	3,761.6	2.6	46.2	114.4	168.8	539.7	2,834.9	387.0	

See footnotes at end of table.

Table 6

Index of Crime[1]
by Metropolitan Statistical Area, 2001—Continued

Metropolitan Statistical Area	Population	Crime Index total	Modified Crime Index total[2]	Violent crime[3]	Property crime[3]	Murder and non-negligent man-slaughter	Forcible rape	Robbery	Aggravated assault	Burglary	Larceny-theft	Motor vehicle theft	Arson[2]
Mobile, AL M.S.A.[6]	**542,355**												
(Includes Baldwin and Mobile Counties.)													
City of Mobile[6]	255,551	19,875		1,529	18,346	42	95	840	552	4,653	12,284	1,409	
Total area actually reporting	93.4%	32,228		2,755	29,473	60	157	1,177	1,361	7,921	19,319	2,233	
Estimated total	100.0%	34,043		2,906	31,137	63	166	1,223	1,454	8,246	20,550	2,341	
Rate per 100,000 inhabitants		6,276.9		535.8	5,741.1	11.6	30.6	225.5	268.1	1,520.4	3,789.0	431.6	
Modesto, CA M.S.A.	**455,304**												
(Includes Stanislaus County.)													
City of:													
Modesto	192,366	11,976		1,161	10,815	17	104	381	659	1,829	7,580	1,406	
Turlock	56,847	3,388		324	3,064	2	19	64	239	593	1,880	591	
Total area actually reporting	100.0%	24,973		2,952	22,021	34	215	644	2,059	4,288	14,509	3,224	
Rate per 100,000 inhabitants		5,484.9		648.4	4,836.5	7.5	47.2	141.4	452.2	941.8	3,186.7	708.1	
Monmouth-Ocean, NJ M.S.A.	**1,135,597**												
(Includes Monmouth and Ocean Counties.)													
City of Dover Township	90,453	2,775		181	2,594	0	13	58	110	450	2,033	111	
Total area actually reporting	100.0%	27,796		2,260	25,536	13	132	691	1,424	4,717	19,454	1,365	
Rate per 100,000 inhabitants		2,447.7		199.0	2,248.7	1.1	11.6	60.8	125.4	415.4	1,713.1	120.2	
Monroe, LA M.S.A.	**147,133**												
(Includes Ouachita Parish.)													
City of Monroe	53,065	6,272		866	5,406	2	37	126	701	1,120	3,984	302	
Total area actually reporting	98.6%	10,196		1,291	8,905	10	71	196	1,014	2,002	6,438	465	
Estimated total	100.0%	10,319		1,305	9,014	10	72	199	1,024	2,023	6,519	472	
Rate per 100,000 inhabitants		7,013.4		887.0	6,126.4	6.8	48.9	135.3	696.0	1,374.9	4,430.7	320.8	
Montgomery, AL M.S.A.	**334,347**												
(Includes Autauga, Elmore, and Montgomery Counties.)													
City of Montgomery	202,350	15,791		1,456	14,335	26	102	652	676	3,252	9,928	1,155	
Total area actually reporting	85.3%	19,581		1,829	17,752	34	126	736	933	4,015	12,397	1,340	
Estimated total	100.0%	20,796		1,944	18,852	35	134	760	1,015	4,335	13,093	1,424	
Rate per 100,000 inhabitants		6,219.9		581.4	5,638.5	10.5	40.1	227.3	303.6	1,296.6	3,916.0	425.9	
Muncie, IN M.S.A.	**119,438**												
(Includes Delaware County.)													
City of Muncie	67,810	2,921		289	2,632	1	24	80	184	531	1,928	173	
Total area actually reporting	100.0%	3,987		346	3,641	1	44	86	215	716	2,707	218	
Rate per 100,000 inhabitants		3,338.1		289.7	3,048.4	0.8	36.8	72.0	180.0	599.5	2,266.4	182.5	
Naples, FL M.S.A.	**257,891**												
(Includes Collier County.)													
City of Naples	21,520	1,010		74	936	1	6	22	45	141	760	35	
Total area actually reporting	100.0%	10,180		1,370	8,810	10	82	264	1,014	2,285	5,974	551	
Rate per 100,000 inhabitants		3,947.4		531.2	3,416.2	3.9	31.8	102.4	393.2	886.0	2,316.5	213.7	
Nashville, TN M.S.A.	**1,242,290**												
(Includes Cheatham, Davidson, Dickson, Robertson, Rutherford, Sumner, Williamson, and Wilson Counties.)													
City of:													
Nashville	555,059	50,155		9,075	41,080	64	427	2,521	6,063	7,842	27,837	5,401	
Murfreesboro	69,430	3,539		383	3,156	0	19	85	279	378	2,559	219	
Total area actually reporting	100.0%	74,342		12,061	62,281	82	617	2,896	8,466	11,899	43,579	6,803	
Rate per 100,000 inhabitants		5,984.3		970.9	5,013.4	6.6	49.7	233.1	681.5	957.8	3,508.0	547.6	
Newark, NJ M.S.A.	**2,049,921**												
(Includes Essex, Morris, Sussex, Union, and Warren Counties.)													
City of Newark	275,823	18,748		3,837	14,911	90	91	1,837	1,819	2,552	6,324	6,035	
Total area actually reporting	100.0%	75,493		11,086	64,407	151	330	5,533	5,072	12,149	35,564	16,694	
Rate per 100,000 inhabitants		3,682.7		540.8	3,141.9	7.4	16.1	269.9	247.4	592.7	1,734.9	814.4	
New Bedford, MA M.S.A.	**176,033**												
(Includes part of Bristol and Plymouth Counties.)													
City of New Bedford	94,216	3,220		756	2,464	5	63	197	491	831	1,072	561	
Total area actually reporting	97.4%	5,709		1,043	4,666	6	84	211	742	1,367	2,547	752	
Estimated total	100.0%	5,807		1,056	4,751	6	85	213	752	1,384	2,606	761	
Rate per 100,000 inhabitants		3,298.8		599.9	2,698.9	3.4	48.3	121.0	427.2	786.2	1,480.4	432.3	

See footnotes at end of table.

Table 6

Index of Crime[1]
by Metropolitan Statistical Area, 2001—Continued

Metropolitan Statistical Area	Population	Crime Index total	Modified Crime Index total[2]	Violent crime[3]	Property crime[3]	Murder and non-negligent man-slaughter	Forcible rape	Robbery	Aggravated assault	Burglary	Larceny-theft	Motor vehicle theft	Arson[2]
Newburgh, NY-PA M.S.A.	**388,320**												
(Includes Orange County, NY and Pike County, PA.)													
City of Newburgh, NY	28,311	1,999		459	1,540	7	23	136	293	428	1,041	71	
Total area actually reporting	90.3%	9,112		1,072	8,040	16	71	242	743	1,441	6,233	366	
Estimated total	100.0%	10,067		1,151	8,916	17	75	266	793	1,564	6,925	427	
Rate per 100,000 inhabitants		2,592.4		296.4	2,296.0	4.4	19.3	68.5	204.2	402.8	1,783.3	110.0	
New Haven-Meriden, CT M.S.A.	**534,133**												
(Includes part of Middlesex and New Haven Counties.)													
City of:													
New Haven	124,334	9,844		1,915	7,929	19	56	768	1,072	1,348	5,190	1,391	
Meriden	58,578	2,329		101	2,228	2	7	56	36	526	1,545	157	
Total area actually reporting	100.0%	21,768		2,501	19,267	23	107	994	1,377	3,107	13,814	2,346	
Rate per 100,000 inhabitants		4,075.4		468.2	3,607.2	4.3	20.0	186.1	257.8	581.7	2,586.2	439.2	
New London-Norwich, CT-RI M.S.A.	**195,791**												
(Includes part of Middlesex, New London, and Windham													
Counties, CT and part of Washington County, RI.)													
City of:													
New London, CT	25,818	1,152		185	967	1	10	43	131	196	642	129	
Norwich, CT	36,324	1,255		143	1,112	0	19	55	69	259	770	83	
Total area actually reporting	100.0%	5,612		557	5,055	6	78	142	331	932	3,788	335	
Rate per 100,000 inhabitants		2,866.3		284.5	2,581.8	3.1	39.8	72.5	169.1	476.0	1,934.7	171.1	
New Orleans, LA M.S.A.	**1,336,665**												
(Includes Jefferson, Orleans, Plaquemines, St. Bernard,													
St. Charles, St. James, St. John the Baptist, and													
St. Tammany Parishes.)													
City of:													
New Orleans	484,289	36,057		5,877	30,180	213	209	2,778	2,677	5,262	16,187	8,731	
Slidell	25,675	2,093		194	1,899	0	16	43	135	278	1,470	151	
Total area actually reporting	99.9%	76,719		10,504	66,215	267	411	3,976	5,850	11,981	41,492	12,742	
Estimated total	100.0%	76,833		10,516	66,317	267	412	3,978	5,859	12,001	41,567	12,749	
Rate per 100,000 inhabitants		5,748.1		786.7	4,961.4	20.0	30.8	297.6	438.3	897.8	3,109.8	953.8	
New York, NY M.S.A.	**9,331,378**												
(Includes Bronx, Kings, New York, Putnam, Queens,													
Richmond, Rockland, and Westchester Counties.)													
City of:													
New York	8,023,018	263,764		68,274	195,490	649	1,530	28,202	37,893	31,563	133,938	29,989	
White Plains	53,175	2,374		214	2,160	1	13	67	133	112	1,915	133	
Total area actually reporting	99.7%	295,408		72,133	223,275	671	1,654	29,588	40,220	35,455	155,078	32,742	
Estimated total	100.0%	296,226		72,201	224,025	672	1,657	29,610	40,262	35,561	155,671	32,793	
Rate per 100,000 inhabitants		3,174.5		773.7	2,400.8	7.2	17.8	317.3	431.5	381.1	1,668.3	351.4	
Norfolk-Virginia Beach-Newport News, VA-NC M.S.A.	**1,593,788**												
(Includes Chesapeake, Hampton, Newport News,													
Norfolk, Poquoson, Portsmouth, Suffolk, Virginia Beach,													
and Williamsburg Cities, Gloucester, Isle of Wight,													
James City, Mathews, and York Counties, VA													
and Currituck County, NC.)													
City of:													
Norfolk, VA	238,020	14,966		1,600	13,366	31	127	809	633	1,728	10,123	1,515	
Virginia Beach, VA	431,819	16,135		840	15,295	12	110	368	350	2,285	12,078	932	
Newport News, VA	182,930	9,784		1,325	8,459	30	97	448	750	1,508	5,788	1,163	
Hampton, VA	148,696	6,815		604	6,211	10	35	283	276	991	4,129	1,091	
Portsmouth, VA	102,117	6,650		1,099	5,551	12	30	473	584	1,515	3,370	666	
Suffolk, VA	64,660	2,510		389	2,121	5	31	106	247	370	1,607	144	
Total area actually reporting	87.3%	62,816		6,248	56,568	108	467	2,571	3,102	9,229	41,550	5,789	
Estimated total	100.0%	72,282		6,929	65,353	110	529	2,783	3,507	10,082	48,658	6,613	
Rate per 100,000 inhabitants		4,535.2		434.8	4,100.5	6.9	33.2	174.6	220.0	632.6	3,053.0	414.9	
Oakland, CA M.S.A.	**2,437,021**												
(Includes Alameda and Contra Costa Counties.)													
City of:													
Oakland	406,908	27,627		5,330	22,297	84	295	2,125	2,826	3,696	13,081	5,520	
Berkeley	104,652	9,470		742	8,728	1	17	398	326	1,453	6,054	1,221	
Alameda	73,602	3,057		366	2,691	2	6	94	264	436	1,927	328	
Total area actually reporting	100.0%	116,211		13,812	102,399	157	697	5,292	7,666	17,804	65,534	19,061	
Rate per 100,000 inhabitants		4,768.6		566.8	4,201.8	6.4	28.6	217.2	314.6	730.6	2,689.1	782.1	

See footnotes at end of table.

Table 6

Index of Crime[1]
by Metropolitan Statistical Area, 2001—Continued

Metropolitan Statistical Area	Population	Crime Index total	Modified Crime Index total[2]	Violent crime[3]	Property crime[3]	Murder and non-negligent man-slaughter	Forcible rape	Robbery	Aggravated assault	Burglary	Larceny-theft	Motor vehicle theft	Arson[2]
Ocala, FL M.S.A.	**265,625**												
(Includes Marion County.)													
City of Ocala	47,133	4,533		694	3,839	4	31	147	512	917	2,670	252	
Total area actually reporting	100.0%	11,043		2,023	9,020	15	128	233	1,647	2,504	5,923	593	
Rate per 100,000 inhabitants		4,157.4		761.6	3,395.8	5.6	48.2	87.7	620.0	942.7	2,229.8	223.2	
Odessa-Midland, TX M.S.A.	**242,514**												
(Includes Ector and Midland Counties.)													
City of:													
Odessa	93,007	5,198		512	4,686	4	24	81	403	946	3,544	196	
Midland	97,152	3,183		407	2,776	2	91	50	264	690	1,912	174	
Total area actually reporting	100.0%	10,666		1,117	9,549	9	120	140	848	2,149	6,933	467	
Rate per 100,000 inhabitants		4,398.1		460.6	3,937.5	3.7	49.5	57.7	349.7	886.1	2,858.8	192.6	
Oklahoma City, OK M.S.A.	**1,086,308**												
(Includes Canadian, Cleveland, Logan, McClain, Oklahoma, and Pottawatomie Counties.)													
City of:													
Oklahoma City	507,517	45,875		4,183	41,692	45	405	1,090	2,643	8,405	29,771	3,516	
Norman	95,956	3,425		229	3,196	2	34	42	151	886	2,178	132	
Shawnee	28,771	1,832		164	1,668	4	12	32	116	412	1,121	135	
Total area actually reporting	100.0%	66,076		5,954	60,122	64	587	1,349	3,954	13,112	42,182	4,828	
Rate per 100,000 inhabitants		6,082.6		548.1	5,534.5	5.9	54.0	124.2	364.0	1,207.0	3,883.1	444.4	
Olympia, WA M.S.A.	**210,657**												
(Includes Thurston County.)													
City of Olympia	43,191	3,159		118	3,041	0	24	35	59	498	2,268	275	
Total area actually reporting	100.0%	8,961		575	8,386	6	94	100	375	1,823	5,899	664	
Rate per 100,000 inhabitants		4,253.8		273.0	3,980.9	2.8	44.6	47.5	178.0	865.4	2,800.3	315.2	
Omaha, NE-IA M.S.A.	**717,627**												
(Includes Cass, Douglas, Sarpy, and Washington Counties, NE and Pottawatomie County, IA.)													
City of:													
Omaha, NE	390,456	29,507		2,708	26,799	25	157	868	1,658	3,107	19,382	4,310	
Council Bluffs, IA	58,205	5,810		456	5,354	2	61	80	313	690	4,005	659	
Total area actually reporting	100.0%	40,908		3,416	37,492	29	252	969	2,166	4,593	27,471	5,428	
Rate per 100,000 inhabitants		5,700.5		476.0	5,224.4	4.0	35.1	135.0	301.8	640.0	3,828.0	756.4	
Orange County, CA M.S.A.	**2,899,185**												
(Includes Orange County.)													
City of:													
Santa Ana	344,258	12,066		1,844	10,222	24	55	942	823	1,396	6,263	2,563	
Anaheim	334,110	11,225		1,316	9,909	8	91	484	733	1,798	6,328	1,783	
Irvine	145,731	3,396		133	3,263	0	9	44	80	904	2,054	305	
Total area actually reporting	100.0%	79,916		8,566	71,350	63	441	3,185	4,877	12,742	47,477	11,131	
Rate per 100,000 inhabitants		2,756.5		295.5	2,461.0	2.2	15.2	109.9	168.2	439.5	1,637.6	383.9	
Orlando, FL M.S.A.	**1,687,175**												
(Includes Lake, Orange, Osceola, and Seminole Counties.)													
City of Orlando	190,769	22,363		3,685	18,678	15	135	1,086	2,449	3,529	12,842	2,307	
Total area actually reporting	99.9%	102,406		14,807	87,599	70	701	3,366	10,670	20,317	57,643	9,639	
Estimated total	100.0%	102,478		14,815	87,663	70	701	3,368	10,676	20,330	57,687	9,646	
Rate per 100,000 inhabitants		6,073.9		878.1	5,195.8	4.1	41.5	199.6	632.8	1,205.0	3,419.1	571.7	
Owensboro, KY M.S.A.	**92,084**												
(Includes Daviess County.)													
City of Owensboro	54,385	2,706		129	2,577	1	26	49	53	561	1,924	92	
Total area actually reporting	100.0%	3,267		175	3,092	1	29	52	93	717	2,255	120	
Rate per 100,000 inhabitants		3,547.8		190.0	3,357.8	1.1	31.5	56.5	101.0	778.6	2,448.9	130.3	
Panama City, FL M.S.A.	**152,058**												
(Includes Bay County.)													
City of Panama City	37,361	2,503		288	2,215	2	33	93	160	424	1,668	123	
Total area actually reporting	100.0%	9,092		1,057	8,035	6	124	194	733	1,514	6,160	361	
Rate per 100,000 inhabitants		5,979.3		695.1	5,284.2	3.9	81.5	127.6	482.1	995.7	4,051.1	237.4	
Pensacola, FL M.S.A.	**422,833**												
(Includes Escambia and Santa Rosa Counties.)													
City of Pensacola	57,713	2,932		519	2,413	3	41	93	382	676	1,625	112	
Total area actually reporting	100.0%	17,152		2,645	14,507	19	199	572	1,855	4,003	9,712	792	
Rate per 100,000 inhabitants		4,056.4		625.5	3,430.9	4.5	47.1	135.3	438.7	946.7	2,296.9	187.3	

See footnotes at end of table.

Table 6

Index of Crime[1]
by Metropolitan Statistical Area, 2001—Continued

Metropolitan Statistical Area	Population	Crime Index total	Modified Crime Index total[2]	Violent crime[3]	Property crime[3]	Murder and non-negligent man-slaughter	Forcible rape	Robbery	Aggravated assault	Burglary	Larceny-theft	Motor vehicle theft	Arson[2]
Philadelphia, PA-NJ M.S.A.	**5,113,261**												
(Includes Bucks, Chester, Delaware, Montgomery, and Philadelphia Counties, PA and Burlington, Camden, Gloucester, and Salem Counties, NJ.)													
City of:													
Philadelphia, PA	1,518,302	93,878		21,404	72,474	309	1,014	9,604	10,477	11,629	45,318	15,527	
Camden, NJ	80,570	6,885		1,707	5,178	25	58	715	909	1,374	2,542	1,262	
Total area actually reporting	96.3%	186,528		31,155	155,373	407	1,622	12,726	16,400	25,307	105,957	24,109	
Estimated total	100.0%	191,169		31,589	159,580	411	1,651	12,840	16,687	25,899	109,232	24,449	
Rate per 100,000 inhabitants		3,738.7		617.8	3,120.9	8.0	32.3	251.1	326.3	506.5	2,136.2	478.1	
Phoenix-Mesa, AZ M.S.A.	**3,363,872**												
(Includes Maricopa and Pinal Counties.)													
City of:													
Phoenix	1,366,542	104,975		10,532	94,443	209	400	4,629	5,294	16,673	55,190	22,580	
Mesa	410,026	27,508		2,516	24,992	17	106	452	1,941	4,313	16,121	4,558	
Tempe	164,088	16,534		937	15,597	5	72	327	533	2,273	10,497	2,827	
Scottsdale	209,686	9,905		619	9,286	10	58	196	355	2,660	5,251	1,375	
Total area actually reporting	99.9%	216,003		19,045	196,958	298	894	6,625	11,228	38,178	119,195	39,585	
Estimated total	100.0%	216,190		19,058	197,132	298	895	6,628	11,237	38,216	119,307	39,609	
Rate per 100,000 inhabitants		6,426.8		566.5	5,860.3	8.9	26.6	197.0	334.0	1,136.1	3,546.7	1,177.5	
Pittsburgh, PA M.S.A.	**2,359,866**												
(Includes Allegheny, Beaver, Butler, Fayette, Washington, and Westmoreland Counties.)													
City of Pittsburgh	341,414	19,708		2,964	16,744	55	134	1,384	1,391	3,246	10,766	2,732	
Total area actually reporting	81.9%	54,650		7,013	47,637	93	471	2,235	4,214	8,635	33,697	5,305	
Estimated total	100.0%	64,928		7,969	56,959	102	537	2,476	4,854	9,918	41,015	6,026	
Rate per 100,000 inhabitants		2,751.3		337.7	2,413.7	4.3	22.8	104.9	205.7	420.3	1,738.0	255.4	
Pittsfield, MA M.S.A.	**97,414**												
(Includes part of Berkshire County.)													
City of Pittsfield	46,011	1,238		77	1,161	0	20	32	25	189	867	105	
Total area actually reporting	95.3%	1,987		212	1,775	0	30	34	148	371	1,241	163	
Estimated total	100.0%	2,085		225	1,860	0	31	36	158	388	1,300	172	
Rate per 100,000 inhabitants		2,140.3		231.0	1,909.4	–	31.8	37.0	162.2	398.3	1,334.5	176.6	
Pocatello, ID M.S.A.	**77,145**												
(Includes Bannock County.)													
City of Pocatello	52,542	1,787		164	1,623	0	21	8	135	266	1,295	62	
Total area actually reporting	100.0%	2,571		253	2,318	0	31	10	212	367	1,869	82	
Rate per 100,000 inhabitants		3,332.7		328.0	3,004.7	–	40.2	13.0	274.8	475.7	2,422.7	106.3	
Portland, ME M.S.A.	**258,223**												
(Includes part of Cumberland and York Counties.)													
City of Portland	64,841	3,016		200	2,816	1	39	68	92	473	2,233	110	
Total area actually reporting	100.0%	7,750		387	7,363	3	85	113	186	1,399	5,630	334	
Rate per 100,000 inhabitants		3,001.3		149.9	2,851.4	1.2	32.9	43.8	72.0	541.8	2,180.3	129.3	
Portland-Vancouver, OR-WA M.S.A.	**1,947,167**												
(Includes Clackamas, Columbia, Multnomah, Washington, and Yamhill Counties, OR and Clark County, WA.)													
City of:													
Portland, OR	537,081	43,183		4,556	38,627	21	305	1,267	2,963	5,592	28,358	4,677	
Vancouver, WA	145,846	7,962		687	7,275	4	76	132	475	1,067	5,745	463	
Total area actually reporting	99.9%	104,241		7,582	96,659	46	780	2,027	4,729	14,874	71,887	9,898	
Estimated total	100.0%	104,315		7,586	96,729	46	781	2,028	4,731	14,884	71,941	9,904	
Rate per 100,000 inhabitants		5,357.3		389.6	4,967.7	2.4	40.1	104.2	243.0	764.4	3,694.6	508.6	
Portsmouth-Rochester, NH-ME M.S.A.	**264,465**												
(Includes part of York County, ME and Rockingham and Strafford Counties, NH.)													
City of:													
Portsmouth, NH	21,177	813		50	763	1	13	13	23	81	624	58	
Rochester, NH	29,000	877		54	823	0	28	6	20	97	675	51	
Total area actually reporting	75.4%	4,791		315	4,476	2	95	48	170	685	3,478	313	
Estimated total	100.0%	5,827		386	5,441	2	114	59	211	864	4,183	394	
Rate per 100,000 inhabitants		2,203.3		146.0	2,057.4	0.8	43.1	22.3	79.8	326.7	1,581.7	149.0	

See footnotes at end of table.

Table 6

Index of Crime[1]

by Metropolitan Statistical Area, 2001—Continued

Metropolitan Statistical Area	Population	Crime Index total	Modified Crime Index total[2]	Violent crime[3]	Property crime[3]	Murder and non-negligent man-slaughter	Forcible rape	Robbery	Aggravated assault	Burglary	Larceny-theft	Motor vehicle theft	Arson[2]
Providence-Fall River-Warwick, RI-MA M.S.A.	1,169,503												
(Includes part of Bristol, Kent, Newport, Providence, and Washington Counties, RI and part of Bristol County, MA.)													
City of:													
Providence, RI	175,374	14,185		1,443	12,742	23	111	595	714	2,284	7,387	3,071	
Fall River, MA	92,375	3,891		636	3,255	3	43	192	398	624	2,090	541	
Warwick, RI	86,676	3,050		134	2,916	2	24	33	75	447	2,167	302	
Pawtucket, RI	73,696	2,994		295	2,699	2	39	74	180	505	1,744	450	
Woonsocket, RI	43,661	1,482		237	1,245	1	60	46	130	338	784	123	
Attleboro, MA	42,268	1,145		123	1,022	0	9	28	86	178	712	132	
Total area actually reporting	100.0%	43,089		4,111	38,978	41	458	1,173	2,439	7,309	25,966	5,703	
Rate per 100,000 inhabitants		3,684.4		351.5	3,332.9	3.5	39.2	100.3	208.6	625.0	2,220.3	487.6	
Provo-Orem, UT M.S.A.	374,579												
(Includes Utah County.)													
City of:													
Provo	106,891	3,844		159	3,685	0	43	18	98	558	2,929	198	
Orem	85,707	3,316		63	3,253	0	18	11	34	284	2,796	173	
Total area actually reporting	100.0%	12,803		408	12,395	3	111	50	244	1,813	9,947	635	
Rate per 100,000 inhabitants		3,418.0		108.9	3,309.0	0.8	29.6	13.3	65.1	484.0	2,655.5	169.5	
Pueblo, CO M.S.A.	145,302												
(Includes Pueblo County.)													
City of Pueblo	104,886	6,466		808	5,658	5	49	146	608	1,131	4,170	357	
Total area actually reporting	100.0%	7,559		844	6,715	7	51	151	635	1,395	4,927	393	
Rate per 100,000 inhabitants		5,202.3		580.9	4,621.4	4.8	35.1	103.9	437.0	960.1	3,390.9	270.5	
Punta Gorda, FL M.S.A.	145,297												
(Includes Charlotte County.)													
City of Punta Gorda	14,716	425		23	402	0	2	2	19	107	277	18	
Total area actually reporting	100.0%	4,344		338	4,006	5	24	32	277	977	2,769	260	
Rate per 100,000 inhabitants		2,989.7		232.6	2,757.1	3.4	16.5	22.0	190.6	672.4	1,905.8	178.9	
Racine, WI M.S.A.	190,177												
(Includes Racine County.)													
City of Racine	82,438	5,912		611	5,301	4	22	340	245	1,174	3,622	505	
Total area actually reporting	100.0%	8,426		678	7,748	5	28	368	277	1,530	5,591	627	
Rate per 100,000 inhabitants		4,430.6		356.5	4,074.1	2.6	14.7	193.5	145.7	804.5	2,939.9	329.7	
Raleigh-Durham-Chapel Hill, NC M.S.A.	1,208,153												
(Includes Chatham, Durham, Franklin, Johnston, Orange, and Wake Counties.)													
City of:													
Raleigh	280,791	18,585		2,187	16,398	10	91	804	1,282	3,983	11,087	1,328	
Durham	190,217	15,132		1,854	13,278	28	77	980	769	3,457	8,723	1,098	
Chapel Hill	49,544	2,805		211	2,594	0	8	83	120	586	1,876	132	
Total area actually reporting	99.9%	62,300		6,011	56,289	62	262	2,421	3,266	14,297	37,945	4,047	
Estimated total	100.0%	62,323		6,013	56,310	62	262	2,422	3,267	14,301	37,961	4,048	
Rate per 100,000 inhabitants		5,158.5		497.7	4,660.8	5.1	21.7	200.5	270.4	1,183.7	3,142.1	335.1	
Rapid City, SD M.S.A.	88,771												
(Includes Pennington County.)													
City of Rapid City	59,746	2,937		220	2,717	1	62	31	126	433	2,114	170	
Total area actually reporting	100.0%	4,414		301	4,113	2	110	33	156	586	3,322	205	
Rate per 100,000 inhabitants		4,972.3		339.1	4,633.3	2.3	123.9	37.2	175.7	660.1	3,742.2	230.9	
Reading, PA M.S.A.	373,823												
(Includes Berks County.)													
City of Reading	81,247	5,593		976	4,617	20	45	455	456	1,445	2,681	491	
Total area actually reporting	82.1%	9,933		1,339	8,594	22	79	526	712	2,202	5,643	749	
Estimated total	100.0%	11,544		1,488	10,056	23	89	564	812	2,403	6,791	862	
Rate per 100,000 inhabitants		3,088.1		398.0	2,690.0	6.2	23.8	150.9	217.2	642.8	1,816.6	230.6	
Redding, CA M.S.A.	166,290												
(Includes Shasta County.)													
City of Redding	82,368	3,246		395	2,851	1	67	64	263	642	1,898	311	
Total area actually reporting	100.0%	5,576		818	4,758	6	102	87	623	1,207	3,069	482	
Rate per 100,000 inhabitants		3,353.2		491.9	2,861.3	3.6	61.3	52.3	374.6	725.8	1,845.6	289.9	

See footnotes at end of table.

Table 6

Index of Crime[1]
by Metropolitan Statistical Area, 2001—Continued

Metropolitan Statistical Area	Population	Crime Index total	Modified Crime Index total[2]	Violent crime[3]	Property crime[3]	Murder and non-negligent man-slaughter	Forcible rape	Robbery	Aggravated assault	Burglary	Larceny-theft	Motor vehicle theft	Arson[2]
Reno, NV M.S.A.[4]	357,803												
(Includes Washoe County.)													
City of Reno[4]	190,218	10,989		1,215	9,774	6	98	407	704	1,435	7,399	940	
Total area actually reporting	100.0%	16,617		1,802	14,815	11	179	516	1,096	2,451	10,962	1,402	
Rate per 100,000 inhabitants		4,644.2		503.6	4,140.5	3.1	50.0	144.2	306.3	685.0	3,063.7	391.8	
Richland-Kennewick-Pasco, WA M.S.A.	194,877												
(Includes Benton and Franklin Counties.)													
City of:													
Richland	39,324	1,597		50	1,547	1	8	9	32	223	1,235	89	
Kennewick	55,564	3,227		212	3,015	1	22	44	145	408	2,374	233	
Pasco	32,577	1,586		124	1,462	4	13	34	73	287	1,053	122	
Total area actually reporting	100.0%	7,941		492	7,449	7	56	94	335	1,230	5,668	551	
Rate per 100,000 inhabitants		4,074.9		252.5	3,822.4	3.6	28.7	48.2	171.9	631.2	2,908.5	282.7	
Richmond-Petersburg, VA M.S.A.	1,011,889												
(Includes Colonial Heights, Hopewell, Petersburg, and Richmond Cities and Charles City, Chesterfield, Dinwiddie, Goochland, Hanover, Henrico, New Kent, Powhatan, and Prince George Counties.)													
City of:													
Richmond	200,842	18,207		2,746	15,461	72	117	1,430	1,127	2,943	9,455	3,063	
Petersburg	34,261	2,840		342	2,498	5	24	110	203	525	1,655	318	
Total area actually reporting	99.9%	47,828		4,894	42,934	110	274	2,164	2,346	6,952	30,937	5,045	
Estimated total	100.0%	47,849		4,895	42,954	110	274	2,164	2,347	6,954	30,953	5,047	
Rate per 100,000 inhabitants		4,728.7		483.7	4,244.9	10.9	27.1	213.9	231.9	687.2	3,058.9	498.8	
Riverside-San Bernardino, CA M.S.A.	3,315,310												
(Includes Riverside and San Bernardino Counties.)													
City of:													
Riverside	259,908	14,518		2,159	12,359	20	95	622	1,422	2,225	7,896	2,238	
San Bernardino	188,847	12,803		2,397	10,406	30	89	829	1,449	2,299	5,868	2,239	
Palm Springs	43,603	3,366		449	2,917	4	21	112	312	771	1,701	445	
Hemet	59,905	3,204		288	2,916	3	15	97	173	1,137	1,387	392	
Temecula	58,789	2,110		240	1,870	1	22	27	190	429	1,189	252	
Palm Desert	41,920	2,319		176	2,143	1	6	47	122	538	1,399	206	
Total area actually reporting	100.0%	137,904		19,739	118,165	218	966	5,181	13,374	29,525	66,306	22,334	
Rate per 100,000 inhabitants		4,159.6		595.4	3,564.2	6.6	29.1	156.3	403.4	890.6	2,000.0	673.7	
Roanoke, VA M.S.A.	239,573												
(Includes Roanoke and Salem Cities and Botetourt and Roanoke Counties.)													
City of Roanoke	96,375	5,468		585	4,883	5	41	135	404	689	3,856	338	
Total area actually reporting	100.0%	8,094		862	7,232	7	75	170	610	1015	5,715	502	
Rate per 100,000 inhabitants		3,378.5		359.8	3,018.7	2.9	31.3	71.0	254.6	423.7	2,385.5	209.5	
Rochester, MN M.S.A.	125,611												
(Includes Olmsted County.)													
City of Rochester	86,727	3,472		254	3,218	3	38	66	147	545	2,482	191	
Total area actually reporting	100.0%	3,994		287	3,707	3	46	71	167	676	2,772	259	
Rate per 100,000 inhabitants		3,179.7		228.5	2,951.2	2.4	36.6	56.5	133.0	538.2	2,206.8	206.2	
Rochester, NY M.S.A.	1,100,221												
(Includes Genesee, Livingston, Monroe, Ontario, Orleans, and Wayne Counties.)													
City of Rochester	220,177	16,156		1,663	14,493	40	84	921	618	2,459	9,719	2,315	
Total area actually reporting	99.3%	38,106		2,581	35,525	51	183	1,178	1,169	5,351	26,751	3,423	
Estimated total	100.0%	38,313		2,598	35,715	51	184	1,183	1,180	5,378	26,901	3,436	
Rate per 100,000 inhabitants		3,482.3		236.1	3,246.2	4.6	16.7	107.5	107.3	488.8	2,445.1	312.3	
Rocky Mount, NC M.S.A.	145,459												
(Includes Edgecombe and Nash Counties.)													
City of Rocky Mount	56,844	5,562		632	4,930	2	27	277	326	1,299	3,408	223	
Total area actually reporting	98.9%	8,218		866	7,352	13	40	344	469	2,196	4,809	347	
Estimated total	100.0%	8,319		872	7,447	13	40	346	473	2,215	4,880	352	
Rate per 100,000 inhabitants		5,719.1		599.5	5,119.7	8.9	27.5	237.9	325.2	1,522.8	3,354.9	242.0	
Sacramento, CA M.S.A.	1,658,456												
(Includes El Dorado, Placer, and Sacramento Counties.)													
City of Sacramento	414,582	30,691		3,309	27,382	40	169	1,440	1,660	5,068	15,977	6,337	
Total area actually reporting	100.0%	76,899		8,289	68,610	86	556	2,665	4,982	13,804	41,808	12,998	
Rate per 100,000 inhabitants		4,636.8		499.8	4,137.0	5.2	33.5	160.7	300.4	832.3	2,520.9	783.7	

See footnotes at end of table.

Table 6

Index of Crime[1]
by Metropolitan Statistical Area, 2001—Continued

Metropolitan Statistical Area	Population	Crime Index total	Modified Crime Index total[2]	Violent crime[3]	Property crime[3]	Murder and non-negligent man-slaughter	Forcible rape	Robbery	Aggravated assault	Burglary	Larceny-theft	Motor vehicle theft	Arson[2]
Saginaw-Bay City-Midland, MI M.S.A.	405,194												
(Includes Bay, Midland, and Saginaw Counties.)													
City of:													
Saginaw	62,125	4,379		1,250	3,129	5	75	190	980	957	1,769	403	
Bay City	37,011	1,653		220	1,433	0	35	34	151	244	1,075	114	
Midland	41,905	973		74	899	4	21	6	43	103	766	30	
Total area actually reporting	100.0%	15,388		2,203	13,185	16	277	290	1,620	2,668	9,480	1,037	
Rate per 100,000 inhabitants		3,797.7		543.7	3,254.0	3.9	68.4	71.6	399.8	658.5	2,339.6	255.9	
Salem, OR M.S.A.[4]	352,437												
(Includes Marion and Polk Counties.)													
City of Salem	138,984	11,120		333	10,787	4	81	160	88	1,395	8,515	877	
Total area actually reporting	100.0%	20,925		956	19,969	10	133	246	567	2,825	15,493	1,651	
Rate per 100,000 inhabitants		5,937.2		271.3	5,666.0	2.8	37.7	69.8	160.9	801.6	4,396.0	468.5	
Salinas, CA M.S.A.	409,228												
(Includes Monterey County.)													
City of:													
Salinas	153,867	6,979		1,269	5,710	15	56	399	799	843	4,102	765	
Monterey	30,225	1,393		248	1,145	0	10	40	198	201	895	49	
Total area actually reporting	100.0%	14,208		2,284	11,924	26	116	628	1,514	2,292	8,495	1,137	
Rate per 100,000 inhabitants		3,471.9		558.1	2,913.8	6.4	28.3	153.5	370.0	560.1	2,075.9	277.8	
Salt Lake City-Ogden, UT M.S.A.	1,355,788												
(Includes Davis, Salt Lake, and Weber Counties.)													
City of:													
Salt Lake City	184,723	16,438		1,166	15,272	18	121	481	546	2,209	11,401	1,662	
Ogden	78,492	5,242		358	4,884	9	53	105	191	771	3,760	353	
Clearfield	26,400	957		55	902	1	19	0	35	113	733	56	
Total area actually reporting	99.9%	69,388		4,151	65,237	52	614	1,108	2,377	9,517	50,479	5,241	
Estimated total	100.0%	69,404		4,152	65,252	52	614	1,108	2,378	9,519	50,491	5,242	
Rate per 100,000 inhabitants		5,119.1		306.2	4,812.8	3.8	45.3	81.7	175.4	702.1	3,724.1	386.6	
San Angelo, TX M.S.A.	106,370												
(Includes Tom Green County.)													
City of San Angelo	90,446	5,730		463	5,267	2	67	49	345	1,023	4,036	208	
Total area actually reporting	100.0%	6,162		494	5,668	3	74	52	365	1,117	4,325	226	
Rate per 100,000 inhabitants		5,793.0		464.4	5,328.6	2.8	69.6	48.9	343.1	1,050.1	4,066.0	212.5	
San Antonio, TX M.S.A.	1,628,519												
(Includes Bexar, Comal, Guadalupe, and Wilson Counties.)													
City of:													
San Antonio	1,170,622	96,498		9,546	86,952	100	492	2,146	6,808	14,018	66,694	6,240	
New Braunfels	37,322	2,658		353	2,305	0	12	27	314	292	1,931	82	
Total area actually reporting	100.0%	114,555		11,014	103,541	112	627	2,353	7,922	17,399	79,090	7,052	
Rate per 100,000 inhabitants		7,034.3		676.3	6,358.0	6.9	38.5	144.5	486.5	1,068.4	4,856.6	433.0	
San Diego, CA M.S.A.	2,866,126												
(Includes San Diego County.)													
City of:													
San Diego	1,246,136	50,444		7,405	43,039	50	342	1,729	5,284	7,219	25,050	10,770	
Escondido	136,041	5,194		576	4,618	2	31	167	376	851	2,826	941	
Coronado	24,548	417		29	388	0	9	6	14	70	290	28	
Total area actually reporting	100.0%	102,059		14,592	87,467	92	831	3,430	10,239	16,725	51,320	19,422	
Rate per 100,000 inhabitants		3,560.9		509.1	3,051.7	3.2	29.0	119.7	357.2	583.5	1,790.6	677.6	
San Jose, CA M.S.A.	1,713,855												
(Includes Santa Clara County.)													
City of:													
San Jose	913,513	25,163		5,564	19,599	22	329	712	4,501	2,939	13,567	3,093	
Sunnyvale	134,209	2,698		180	2,518	0	18	59	103	289	1,995	234	
Santa Clara	104,263	3,350		282	3,068	0	20	45	217	420	2,412	236	
Palo Alto	59,687	1,880		82	1,798	2	7	35	38	255	1,461	82	
Gilroy	42,235	1,712		308	1,404	3	16	52	237	224	1,049	131	
Total area actually reporting	100.0%	47,590		7,824	39,766	34	476	1,140	6,174	6,144	29,015	4,607	
Rate per 100,000 inhabitants		2,776.8		456.5	2,320.3	2.0	27.8	66.5	360.2	358.5	1,693.0	268.8	

See footnotes at end of table.

Table 6

Index of Crime[1]
by Metropolitan Statistical Area, 2001—Continued

Metropolitan Statistical Area	Population	Crime Index total	Modified Crime Index total[2]	Violent crime[3]	Property crime[3]	Murder and non-negligent man-slaughter	Forcible rape	Robbery	Aggravated assault	Burglary	Larceny-theft	Motor vehicle theft	Arson[2]
San Luis Obispo-Atascadero-Paso Robles, CA M.S.A.	251,265												
(Includes San Luis Obispo County.)													
City of:													
San Luis Obispo	44,995	2,030		169	1,861	0	23	17	129	393	1,336	132	
Atascadero	26,902	786		96	690	0	10	4	82	140	493	57	
Paso Robles	24,749	823		71	752	2	9	11	49	183	514	55	
Total area actually reporting	100.0%	6,985		743	6,242	7	102	67	567	1,371	4,443	428	
Rate per 100,000 inhabitants		2,779.9		295.7	2,484.2	2.8	40.6	26.7	225.7	545.6	1,768.3	170.3	
Santa Barbara-Santa Maria-Lompoc, CA M.S.A.	406,769												
(Includes Santa Barbara County.)													
City of:													
Santa Barbara	94,041	2,946		539	2,407	3	28	106	402	443	1,822	142	
Santa Maria	78,862	2,651		330	2,321	4	23	98	205	387	1,693	241	
Lompoc	41,867	1,584		161	1,423	3	18	27	113	292	1,051	80	
Total area actually reporting	100.0%	10,316		1,398	8,918	12	112	277	997	1,681	6,677	560	
Rate per 100,000 inhabitants		2,536.1		343.7	2,192.4	3.0	27.5	68.1	245.1	413.3	1,641.5	137.7	
Santa Cruz-Watsonville, CA M.S.A.	260,352												
(Includes Santa Cruz County.)													
City of:													
Santa Cruz	55,608	3,546		537	3,009	0	51	87	399	478	2,322	209	
Watsonville	45,088	2,250		309	1,941	4	19	81	205	296	1,519	126	
Total area actually reporting	100.0%	10,146		1,210	8,936	13	113	212	872	1,543	6,831	562	
Rate per 100,000 inhabitants		3,897.0		464.8	3,432.3	5.0	43.4	81.4	334.9	592.7	2,623.8	215.9	
Santa Rosa, CA M.S.A.	467,137												
(Includes Sonoma County.)													
City of:													
Santa Rosa	150,338	5,854		507	5,347	3	72	123	309	773	4,050	524	
Petaluma	55,562	1,806		91	1,715	1	10	13	67	256	1,372	87	
Total area actually reporting	100.0%	15,142		1,293	13,849	12	173	223	885	2,875	9,868	1,106	
Rate per 100,000 inhabitants		3,241.4		276.8	2,964.7	2.6	37.0	47.7	189.5	615.5	2,112.4	236.8	
Sarasota-Bradenton, FL M.S.A.	605,246												
(Includes Manatee and Sarasota Counties.)													
City of:													
Sarasota	54,081	4,671		667	4,004	2	36	201	428	1,037	2,732	235	
Bradenton	50,787	3,393		344	3,049	5	20	98	221	725	1,936	388	
Total area actually reporting	100.0%	30,249		4,026	26,223	18	227	775	3,006	6,721	17,673	1,829	
Rate per 100,000 inhabitants		4,997.8		665.2	4,332.6	3.0	37.5	128.0	496.7	1,110.5	2,920.0	302.2	
Savannah, GA M.S.A.	300,067												
(Includes Bryan, Chatham, and Effingham Counties.)													
City of Savannah	134,682	12,458		1,538	10,920	26	70	840	602	2,080	7,400	1,440	
Total area actually reporting	89.3%	18,034		2,116	15,918	38	101	957	1,020	3,064	11,008	1,846	
Estimated total	100.0%	19,111		2,205	16,906	40	107	996	1,062	3,284	11,651	1,971	
Rate per 100,000 inhabitants		6,368.9		734.8	5,634.1	13.3	35.7	331.9	353.9	1,094.4	3,882.8	656.9	
Seattle-Bellevue-Everett, WA M.S.A.	2,453,063												
(Includes Island, King, and Snohomish Counties.)													
City of:													
Seattle	572,345	46,091		4,150	41,941	25	164	1,594	2,367	6,684	26,502	8,755	
Bellevue	111,314	4,667		162	4,505	0	21	59	82	535	3,431	539	
Everett	92,945	6,835		547	6,288	5	76	170	296	1,008	3,798	1,482	
Total area actually reporting	95.9%	125,127		8,843	116,284	72	930	3,042	4,799	18,709	75,100	22,475	
Estimated total	100.0%	129,458		9,104	120,354	75	970	3,112	4,947	19,461	77,831	23,062	
Rate per 100,000 inhabitants		5,277.4		371.1	4,906.3	3.1	39.5	126.9	201.7	793.3	3,172.8	940.1	
Sheboygan, WI M.S.A.	113,449												
(Includes Sheboygan County.)													
City of Sheboygan	51,154	2,284		76	2,208	3	24	10	39	300	1,838	70	
Total area actually reporting	100.0%	3,221		112	3,109	3	32	14	63	436	2,569	104	
Rate per 100,000 inhabitants		2,839.2		98.7	2,740.4	2.6	28.2	12.3	55.5	384.3	2,264.5	91.7	
Sherman-Denison, TX M.S.A.	113,105												
(Includes Grayson County.)													
City of:													
Sherman	35,878	2,452		249	2,203	0	12	59	178	381	1,701	121	
Denison	23,290	1,434		61	1,373	0	3	17	41	334	952	87	
Total area actually reporting	100.0%	5,127		387	4,740	0	27	84	276	1,021	3,434	285	
Rate per 100,000 inhabitants		4,533.0		342.2	4,190.8	–	23.9	74.3	244.0	902.7	3,036.1	252.0	

See footnotes at end of table.

Table 6

Index of Crime[1]

by Metropolitan Statistical Area, 2001—Continued

Metropolitan Statistical Area	Population	Crime Index total	Modified Crime Index total[2]	Violent crime[3]	Property crime[3]	Murder and non-negligent man-slaughter	Forcible rape	Robbery	Aggravated assault	Burglary	Larceny-theft	Motor vehicle theft	Arson[2]
Shreveport-Bossier City, LA M.S.A.	391,991												
(Includes Bossier, Caddo, and Webster Parishes.)													
City of:													
Shreveport	199,986	15,616		1,929	13,687	31	111	534	1,253	3,368	9,200	1,119	
Bossier City	56,416	4,194		501	3,693	3	20	84	394	640	2,777	276	
Total area actually reporting	100.0%	23,167		2,774	20,393	43	160	655	1,916	4,784	14,060	1,549	
Rate per 100,000 inhabitants		5,910.1		707.7	5,202.4	11.0	40.8	167.1	488.8	1,220.4	3,586.8	395.2	
Sioux City, IA-NE M.S.A.	124,041												
(Includes Woodbury County, IA and Dakota County, NE.)													
City of Sioux City, IA	84,922	5,498		525	4,973	7	36	67	415	1,050	3,601	322	
Total area actually reporting	100.0%	6,212		578	5,634	8	44	69	457	1,184	4,085	365	
Rate per 100,000 inhabitants		5,008.0		466.0	4,542.0	6.4	35.5	55.6	368.4	954.5	3,293.3	294.3	
Sioux Falls, SD M.S.A.	172,814												
(Includes Lincoln and Minnehaha Counties.)													
City of Sioux Falls	124,263	4,130		324	3,806	2	76	38	208	681	2,943	182	
Total area actually reporting	90.4%	4,522		359	4,163	2	86	38	233	833	3,124	206	
Estimated total	100.0%	4,978		385	4,593	2	99	38	246	916	3,455	222	
Rate per 100,000 inhabitants		2,880.6		222.8	2,657.8	1.2	57.3	22.0	142.3	530.0	1,999.3	128.5	
South Bend, IN M.S.A.	267,055												
(Includes St. Joseph County.)													
City of South Bend	108,396	9,122		888	8,234	21	78	487	302	1,932	5,603	699	
Total area actually reporting	100.0%	16,317		1,226	15,091	24	106	612	484	2,914	11,010	1,167	
Rate per 100,000 inhabitants		6,110.0		459.1	5,650.9	9.0	39.7	229.2	181.2	1,091.2	4,122.7	437.0	
Spokane, WA M.S.A.	424,594												
(Includes Spokane County.)													
City of Spokane	198,744	17,073		1,409	15,664	7	79	440	883	3,101	10,792	1,771	
Total area actually reporting	98.0%	26,416		1,918	24,498	10	134	571	1,203	4,924	17,053	2,521	
Estimated total	100.0%	26,875		1,943	24,932	10	138	579	1,216	4,990	17,355	2,587	
Rate per 100,000 inhabitants		6,329.6		457.6	5,872.0	2.4	32.5	136.4	286.4	1,175.2	4,087.4	609.3	
Springfield, MA M.S.A.	600,151												
(Includes part of Franklin, Hampden, and Hampshire Counties.)													
City of:													
Springfield	152,806	12,798		3,277	9,521	10	99	503	2,665	2,697	5,087	1,737	
Holyoke	40,028	3,509		592	2,917	5	38	125	424	608	2,065	244	
Westfield	40,263	954		136	818	0	13	8	115	268	476	74	
Northampton	29,116	712		37	675	0	6	12	19	83	552	40	
Total area actually reporting	98.8%	27,128		5,395	21,733	16	259	786	4,334	5,821	13,019	2,893	
Estimated total	100.0%	27,278		5,414	21,864	16	260	788	4,350	5,847	13,110	2,907	
Rate per 100,000 inhabitants		4,545.2		902.1	3,643.1	2.7	43.3	131.3	724.8	974.3	2,184.5	484.4	
Springfield, MO M.S.A.	327,729												
(Includes Christian, Greene, and Webster Counties.)													
City of Springfield	152,515	14,141		989	13,152	10	60	262	657	2,182	10,066	904	
Total area actually reporting	100.0%	18,311		1,419	16,892	13	83	277	1,046	3,158	12,574	1,160	
Rate per 100,000 inhabitants		5,587.2		433.0	5,154.3	4.0	25.3	84.5	319.2	963.6	3,836.7	354.0	
State College, PA M.S.A.	135,825												
(Includes Centre County.)													
City of State College	51,591	1,125		54	1,071	1	9	9	35	125	928	18	
Total area actually reporting	100.0%	3,209		163	3,046	6	33	17	107	425	2,548	73	
Rate per 100,000 inhabitants		2,362.6		120.0	2,242.6	4.4	24.3	12.5	78.8	312.9	1,875.9	53.7	
St. Cloud, MN M.S.A.	169,189												
(Includes Benton and Stearns Counties.)													
City of St. Cloud	59,742	2,897		200	2,697	2	58	29	111	309	2,208	180	
Total area actually reporting	93.2%	4,681		329	4,352	2	105	36	186	500	3,574	278	
Estimated total	100.0%	5,093		348	4,745	2	109	40	197	547	3,893	305	
Rate per 100,000 inhabitants		3,010.2		205.7	2,804.6	1.2	64.4	23.6	116.4	323.3	2,301.0	180.3	
St. Joseph, MO M.S.A.	103,122												
(Includes Andrew and Buchanan Counties.)													
City of St. Joseph	74,446	4,367		174	4,193	2	18	46	108	726	3,257	210	
Total area actually reporting	100.0%	4,887		287	4,600	4	23	47	213	847	3,516	237	
Rate per 100,000 inhabitants		4,739.0		278.3	4,460.7	3.9	22.3	45.6	206.6	821.4	3,409.6	229.8	

See footnotes at end of table.

Table 6

Index of Crime[1]

by Metropolitan Statistical Area, 2001—Continued

Metropolitan Statistical Area	Population	Crime Index total	Modified Crime Index total[2]	Violent crime[3]	Property crime[3]	Murder and non-negligent man-slaughter	Forcible rape	Robbery	Aggravated assault	Burglary	Larceny-theft	Motor vehicle theft	Arson[2]
Stockton-Lodi, CA M.S.A.	**574,072**												
(Includes San Joaquin County.)													
City of:													
Stockton	248,301	19,728		3,296	16,432	30	144	1,030	2,092	2,871	10,558	3,003	
Lodi	58,058	3,096		507	2,589	1	9	46	451	359	1,890	340	
Total area actually reporting	100.0%	34,639		5,174	29,465	50	259	1,294	3,571	5,670	18,995	4,800	
Rate per 100,000 inhabitants		6,033.9		901.3	5,132.6	8.7	45.1	225.4	622.0	987.7	3,308.8	836.1	
Sumter, SC M.S.A.	**105,976**												
(Includes Sumter County.)													
City of Sumter	40,147	3,545		492	3,053	3	16	159	314	859	1,791	403	
Total area actually reporting	98.6%	6,612		961	5,651	4	43	236	678	1,860	3,101	690	
Estimated total	100.0%	6,689		969	5,720	4	43	238	684	1,871	3,155	694	
Rate per 100,000 inhabitants		6,311.8		914.4	5,397.4	3.8	40.6	224.6	645.4	1,765.5	2,977.1	654.9	
Syracuse, NY M.S.A.	**733,464**												
(Includes Cayuga, Madison, Onondaga, and Oswego Counties.)													
City of:													
Syracuse	147,577	9,413		1,560	7,853	15	41	568	936	1,802	5,166	885	
Auburn	28,627	1,209		73	1,136	0	13	11	49	191	920	25	
Total area actually reporting	99.9%	23,512		2,412	21,100	25	123	749	1,515	4,425	15,325	1,350	
Estimated total	100.0%	23,525		2,413	21,112	25	123	749	1,516	4,427	15,334	1,351	
Rate per 100,000 inhabitants		3,207.4		329.0	2,878.4	3.4	16.8	102.1	206.7	603.6	2,090.6	184.2	
Tacoma, WA M.S.A.	**711,979**												
(Includes Pierce County.)													
City of Tacoma	196,638	18,370		2,112	16,258	15	143	743	1,211	2,920	10,033	3,305	
Total area actually reporting	99.6%	42,741		3,776	38,965	33	326	1,200	2,217	7,226	25,261	6,478	
Estimated total	100.0%	42,899		3,784	39,115	33	327	1,203	2,221	7,249	25,365	6,501	
Rate per 100,000 inhabitants		6,025.3		531.5	5,493.8	4.6	45.9	169.0	311.9	1,018.1	3,562.6	913.1	
Tallahassee, FL M.S.A.	**291,912**												
(Includes Gadsden and Leon Counties.)													
City of Tallahassee	154,527	12,151		1,809	10,342	7	127	428	1,247	2,265	7,227	850	
Total area actually reporting	98.8%	18,199		2,865	15,334	14	206	611	2,034	3,918	10,182	1,234	
Estimated total	100.0%	18,384		2,887	15,497	14	207	617	2,049	3,951	10,294	1,252	
Rate per 100,000 inhabitants		6,297.8		989.0	5,308.8	4.8	70.9	211.4	701.9	1,353.5	3,526.4	428.9	
Tampa-St. Petersburg-Clearwater, FL M.S.A.	**2,458,083**												
(Includes Hernando, Hillsborough, Pasco, and Pinellas Counties.)													
City of:													
Tampa	311,310	34,848		6,616	28,232	34	212	2,359	4,011	6,096	15,586	6,550	
St. Petersburg	254,664	20,534		4,376	16,158	21	149	1,147	3,059	3,678	10,418	2,062	
Clearwater	111,606	6,642		1,026	5,616	4	56	230	736	1,188	3,979	449	
Total area actually reporting	100.0%	145,240		22,224	123,016	122	1,088	5,620	15,394	27,704	79,032	16,280	
Rate per 100,000 inhabitants		5,908.7		904.1	5,004.6	5.0	44.3	228.6	626.3	1,127.1	3,215.2	662.3	
Texarkana, TX-Texarkana, AR M.S.A.	**132,059**												
(Includes Bowie County, TX and Miller County, AR.)													
City of:													
Texarkana, TX	35,571	3,026		391	2,635	2	25	65	299	517	1,991	127	
Texarkana, AR	26,633	2,339		216	2,123	1	16	37	162	242	1,764	117	
Total area actually reporting	100.0%	6,825		791	6,034	10	53	117	611	1,152	4,543	339	
Rate per 100,000 inhabitants		5,168.1		599.0	4,569.2	7.6	40.1	88.6	462.7	872.3	3,440.1	256.7	
Toledo, OH M.S.A.[4]	**619,315**												
(Includes Fulton, Lucas, and Wood Counties.)													
City of:													
Toledo[4]	314,183	27,105		3,050	24,055	18	185	1,312	1,535	6,299	14,006	3,750	
Bowling Green	29,689	1,209		39	1,170	0	7	13	19	171	952	47	
Total area actually reporting	97.1%	36,744		3,450	33,294	19	256	1,404	1,771	7,808	21,203	4,283	
Estimated total	100.0%	37,341		3,480	33,861	19	260	1,415	1,786	7,897	21,646	4,318	
Rate per 100,000 inhabitants		6,029.4		561.9	5,467.5	3.1	42.0	228.5	288.4	1,275.1	3,495.2	697.2	
Topeka, KS M.S.A.[4]	**170,264**												
(Includes Shawnee County.)													
City of Topeka[4]	122,660	11,530		1,075	10,455	22	84	358	611	2,046	7,632	777	
Total area actually reporting	98.6%	12,649		1,194	11,455	24	94	365	711	2,312	8,316	827	
Estimated total	100.0%	12,748		1,203	11,545	24	95	367	717	2,327	8,383	835	
Rate per 100,000 inhabitants		7,487.2		706.5	6,780.6	14.1	55.8	215.5	421.1	1,366.7	4,923.5	490.4	

See footnotes at end of table.

Table 6

Index of Crime[1]

by Metropolitan Statistical Area, 2001—Continued

Metropolitan Statistical Area	Population	Crime Index total	Modified Crime Index total[2]	Violent crime[3]	Property crime[3]	Murder and non-negligent man-slaughter	Forcible rape	Robbery	Aggravated assault	Burglary	Larceny-theft	Motor vehicle theft	Arson[2]
Trenton, NJ M.S.A.	353,682												
(Includes Mercer County.)													
City of Trenton	86,114	6,964		1,498	5,466	13	72	716	697	1,521	2,723	1,222	
Total area actually reporting	100.0%	14,922		1,998	12,924	18	99	939	942	2,912	7,921	2,091	
Rate per 100,000 inhabitants		4,219.0		564.9	3,654.1	5.1	28.0	265.5	266.3	823.3	2,239.6	591.2	
Tucson, AZ M.S.A.	872,805												
(Includes Pima County.)													
City of Tucson	503,461	49,757		4,823	44,934	42	321	1,698	2,762	6,553	31,217	7,164	
Total area actually reporting	100.0%	66,325		5,862	60,463	53	412	1,914	3,483	8,920	41,796	9,747	
Rate per 100,000 inhabitants		7,599.1		671.6	6,927.4	6.1	47.2	219.3	399.1	1,022.0	4,788.7	1,116.7	
Tulsa, OK M.S.A.	805,433												
(Includes Creek, Osage, Rogers, Tulsa, and Wagoner Counties.)													
City of Tulsa	394,125	29,354		4,547	24,807	34	256	776	3,481	5,863	15,308	3,636	
Total area actually reporting	100.0%	40,675		5,580	35,095	44	391	878	4,267	8,299	22,231	4,565	
Rate per 100,000 inhabitants		5,050.1		692.8	4,357.3	5.5	48.5	109.0	529.8	1,030.4	2,760.1	566.8	
Tuscaloosa, AL M.S.A.	165,515												
(Includes Tuscaloosa County.)													
City of Tuscaloosa	78,208	6,428		870	5,558	6	50	222	592	1,348	3,948	262	
Total area actually reporting	88.2%	8,909		1,199	7,710	10	70	258	861	1,946	5,318	446	
Estimated total	100.0%	9,890		1,280	8,610	11	75	283	911	2,122	5,984	504	
Rate per 100,000 inhabitants		5,975.3		773.3	5,201.9	6.6	45.3	171.0	550.4	1,282.1	3,615.4	304.5	
Utica-Rome, NY M.S.A.	300,448												
(Includes Herkimer and Oneida Counties.)													
City of:													
Utica	60,763	2,825		307	2,518	7	29	188	83	641	1,725	152	
Rome	35,014	909		51	858	0	6	16	29	225	582	51	
Total area actually reporting	98.5%	7,975		775	7,200	10	82	230	453	1,568	5,328	304	
Estimated total	100.0%	8,089		784	7,305	10	82	233	459	1,583	5,411	311	
Rate per 100,000 inhabitants		2,692.3		260.9	2,431.4	3.3	27.3	77.6	152.8	526.9	1,801.0	103.5	
Vallejo-Fairfield-Napa, CA M.S.A.	528,463												
(Includes Napa and Solano Counties.)													
City of:													
Vallejo	118,930	7,249		1,159	6,090	4	53	344	758	1,176	3,963	951	
Fairfield	97,965	4,594		508	4,086	3	30	184	291	653	3,027	406	
Napa	73,934	1,980		228	1,752	1	25	45	157	254	1,385	113	
Total area actually reporting	100.0%	19,937		2,640	17,297	11	158	702	1,769	3,286	11,970	2,041	
Rate per 100,000 inhabitants		3,772.6		499.6	3,273.1	2.1	29.9	132.8	334.7	621.8	2,265.1	386.2	
Ventura, CA M.S.A.	767,195												
(Includes Ventura County.)													
City of Ventura	102,791	3,357		281	3,076	2	28	91	160	565	2,280	231	
Total area actually reporting	100.0%	17,025		2,008	15,017	19	127	704	1,158	3,210	10,418	1,389	
Rate per 100,000 inhabitants		2,219.1		261.7	1,957.4	2.5	16.6	91.8	150.9	418.4	1,357.9	181.0	
Victoria, TX M.S.A.	85,996												
(Includes Victoria County.)													
City of Victoria	61,978	3,748		440	3,308	2	21	70	347	719	2,434	155	
Total area actually reporting	100.0%	4,170		493	3,677	4	28	75	386	833	2,671	173	
Rate per 100,000 inhabitants		4,849.1		573.3	4,275.8	4.7	32.6	87.2	448.9	968.6	3,106.0	201.2	
Vineland-Millville-Bridgeton, NJ M.S.A.	147,658												
(Includes Cumberland County.)													
City of:													
Vineland	56,740	3,392		468	2,924	2	7	205	254	732	2,017	175	
Millville	27,071	1,362		181	1,181	1	20	62	98	279	837	65	
Bridgeton	22,961	1,429		367	1,062	2	8	117	240	319	663	80	
Total area actually reporting	100.0%	7,040		1,117	5,923	6	39	394	678	1,586	3,913	424	
Rate per 100,000 inhabitants		4,767.8		756.5	4,011.3	4.1	26.4	266.8	459.2	1,074.1	2,650.0	287.2	
Visalia-Tulare-Porterville, CA M.S.A.[4]	374,860												
(Includes Tulare County.)													
City of:													
Visalia	93,267	5,679		817	4,862	4	35	113	665	967	3,308	587	
Tulare	44,812	3,015		434	2,581	5	19	62	348	1,230	1,146	205	
Porterville	40,351	2,008		180	1,828	2	8	46	124	388	1,191	249	
Total area actually reporting	100.0%	17,523		2,292	15,231	26	105	320	1,841	4,352	8,943	1,936	
Rate per 100,000 inhabitants		4,674.5		611.4	4,063.1	6.9	28.0	85.4	491.1	1,161.0	2,385.7	516.5	

See footnotes at end of table.

Table 6

Index of Crime[1]
by Metropolitan Statistical Area, 2001—Continued

Metropolitan Statistical Area	Population	Crime Index total	Modified Crime Index total[2]	Violent crime[3]	Property crime[3]	Murder and non-negligent manslaughter	Forcible rape	Robbery	Aggravated assault	Burglary	Larceny-theft	Motor vehicle theft	Arson[2]
Waco, TX M.S.A.	218,362												
(Includes McLennan County.)													
City of Waco	116,307	10,361		903	9,458	7	100	269	527	1,875	6,787	796	
Total area actually reporting	100.0%	14,195		1,172	13,023	11	138	306	717	2,586	9,414	1,023	
Rate per 100,000 inhabitants		6,500.7		536.7	5,963.9	5.0	63.2	140.1	328.4	1,184.3	4,311.2	468.5	
Washington, D.C.-MD-VA-WV M.S.A.	4,986,622												
(Includes the District of Columbia, Calvert, Charles,													
Frederick, Montgomery, and Prince George's Counties,													
MD, Alexandria, Fairfax City, Falls Church,													
Fredericksburg, Manassas, and Manassas Park Cities,													
and Arlington, Clarke, Culpeper, Fairfax, Fauquier,													
King George, Loudoun, Prince William,													
Spotsylvania, Stafford, and Warren Counties, VA,													
and Berkeley and Jefferson Counties, WV.)													
City of:													
Washington, D.C.[7]	571,822	44,041		9,928	34,113	232	188	3,940	5,568	5,009	21,434	7,670	
Frederick, MD	53,551	2,943		710	2,233	1	19	115	575	315	1,787	131	
Fredericksburg, VA	19,576	1,019		122	897	1	9	28	84	75	761	61	
Total area actually reporting	99.1%	195,740		25,241	170,499	395	1,025	9,640	14,181	24,515	117,393	28,591	
Estimated total	100.0%	197,069		25,376	171,693	396	1,033	9,664	14,283	24,752	118,226	28,715	
Rate per 100,000 inhabitants		3,952.0		508.9	3,443.1	7.9	20.7	193.8	286.4	496.4	2,370.9	575.8	
Waterbury, CT M.S.A.	190,174												
(Includes part of Litchfield and New Haven Counties.)													
City of Waterbury	107,886	6,872		546	6,326	7	38	277	224	1,299	4,147	880	
Total area actually reporting	100.0%	8,552		608	7,944	7	47	291	263	1,527	5,404	1,013	
Rate per 100,000 inhabitants		4,496.9		319.7	4,177.2	3.7	24.7	153.0	138.3	802.9	2,841.6	532.7	
Waterloo-Cedar Falls, IA M.S.A.	127,874												
(Includes Black Hawk County.)													
City of:													
Waterloo	68,673	4,192		328	3,864	2	33	75	218	1,057	2,563	244	
Cedar Falls	36,106	1,143		110	1,033	0	13	4	93	154	845	34	
Total area actually reporting	100.0%	5,841		455	5,386	2	53	81	319	1,372	3,722	292	
Rate per 100,000 inhabitants		4,567.8		355.8	4,212.0	1.6	41.4	63.3	249.5	1,072.9	2,910.7	228.3	
Wausau, WI M.S.A.	126,731												
(Includes Marathon County.)													
City of Wausau	38,700	1,652		119	1,533	2	21	11	85	335	1,123	75	
Total area actually reporting	100.0%	2,935		165	2,770	3	25	15	122	570	2,072	128	
Rate per 100,000 inhabitants		2,315.9		130.2	2,185.7	2.4	19.7	11.8	96.3	449.8	1,635.0	101.0	
West Palm Beach-Boca Raton, FL M.S.A.	1,160,495												
(Includes Palm Beach County.)													
City of:													
West Palm Beach	84,230	9,794		1,123	8,671	18	70	465	570	1,610	5,786	1,275	
Boca Raton	76,701	3,039		196	2,843	1	14	65	116	665	1,990	188	
Total area actually reporting	100.0%	72,109		8,539	63,570	51	492	2,377	5,619	14,759	41,628	7,183	
Rate per 100,000 inhabitants		6,213.6		735.8	5,477.8	4.4	42.4	204.8	484.2	1,271.8	3,587.1	619.0	
Wichita, KS M.S.A.	546,480												
(Includes Butler, Harvey, and Sedgwick Counties.)													
City of Wichita	345,081	23,534		2,443	21,091	17	183	742	1,501	4,422	14,953	1,716	
Total area actually reporting	88.0%	27,036		2,700	24,336	17	206	776	1,701	4,996	17,457	1,883	
Estimated total	100.0%	28,486		2,846	25,640	19	218	791	1,818	5,360	18,304	1,976	
Rate per 100,000 inhabitants		5,212.6		520.8	4,691.8	3.5	39.9	144.7	332.7	980.8	3,349.4	361.6	
Wichita Falls, TX M.S.A.	143,707												
(Includes Archer and Wichita Counties.)													
City of Wichita Falls	106,562	8,185		871	7,314	4	21	256	590	1,502	5,314	498	
Total area actually reporting	100.0%	9,022		953	8,069	6	31	264	652	1,730	5,779	560	
Rate per 100,000 inhabitants		6,278.1		663.2	5,614.9	4.2	21.6	183.7	453.7	1,203.8	4,021.4	389.7	
Wilmington, NC M.S.A.	237,422												
(Includes Brunswick and New Hanover Counties.)													
City of Wilmington	77,128	8,650		895	7,755	10	49	310	526	1,983	5,062	710	
Total area actually reporting	98.5%	14,763		1,196	13,567	14	98	381	703	4,227	8,287	1,053	
Estimated total	100.0%	14,982		1,211	13,771	14	99	386	712	4,268	8,440	1,063	
Rate per 100,000 inhabitants		6,310.3		510.1	5,800.2	5.9	41.7	162.6	299.9	1,797.6	3,554.9	447.7	

See footnotes at end of table.

Table 6

Index of Crime[1]
by Metropolitan Statistical Area, 2001—Continued

Metropolitan Statistical Area	Population	Crime Index total	Modified Crime Index total[2]	Violent crime[3]	Property crime[3]	Murder and non-negligent man-slaughter	Forcible rape	Robbery	Aggravated assault	Burglary	Larceny-theft	Motor vehicle theft	Arson[2]
Wilmington-Newark, DE-MD M.S.A.[4]	595,514												
(Includes New Castle County, DE and Cecil County, MD.)													
City of:													
Wilmington, DE	73,829	5,488		1,048	4,440	14	48	382	604	863	2,838	739	
Newark, DE	29,005	1,473		134	1,339	0	8	28	98	220	1,024	95	
Total area actually reporting	100.0%	24,943		3,554	21,389	19	250	988	2,297	3,982	14,875	2,532	
Rate per 100,000 inhabitants		4,188.5		596.8	3,591.7	3.2	42.0	165.9	385.7	668.7	2,497.8	425.2	
Worcester, MA-CT M.S.A.	506,160												
(Includes part of Windham County, CT and Hampden and Worcester Counties, MA.)													
City of Worcester, MA	173,469	8,212		1,422	6,790	7	117	363	935	1,152	4,421	1,217	
Total area actually reporting	94.8%	13,176		2,309	10,867	8	198	412	1,691	2,143	7,198	1,526	
Estimated total	100.0%	13,740		2,382	11,358	8	203	421	1,750	2,242	7,538	1,578	
Rate per 100,000 inhabitants		2,714.6		470.6	2,244.0	1.6	40.1	83.2	345.7	442.9	1,489.3	311.8	
Yakima, WA M.S.A.	226,125												
(Includes Yakima County.)													
City of Yakima	72,989	6,163		333	5,830	5	39	102	187	1,193	4,076	561	
Total area actually reporting	100.0%	13,172		602	12,570	10	109	163	320	3,194	8,250	1,126	
Rate per 100,000 inhabitants		5,825.1		266.2	5,558.9	4.4	48.2	72.1	141.5	1,412.5	3,648.4	498.0	
Yolo, CA M.S.A.	171,794												
(Includes Yolo County.)													
City of:													
Davis	61,429	2,293		116	2,177	0	19	28	69	343	1,682	152	
Woodland	50,064	1,434		323	1,111	1	16	48	258	274	657	180	
Total area actually reporting	100.0%	6,555		680	5,875	4	61	148	467	1,290	3,811	774	
Rate per 100,000 inhabitants		3,815.6		395.8	3,419.8	2.3	35.5	86.1	271.8	750.9	2,218.4	450.5	
Yuba City, CA M.S.A.	141,735												
(Includes Sutter and Yuba Counties.)													
City of Yuba City	37,441	1,992		183	1,809	2	23	34	124	386	1,244	179	
Total area actually reporting	100.0%	5,809		657	5,152	8	52	101	496	1,437	2,968	747	
Rate per 100,000 inhabitants		4,098.5		463.5	3,635.0	5.6	36.7	71.3	349.9	1,013.9	2,094.0	527.0	
Yuma, AZ M.S.A.	165,537												
(Includes Yuma County.)													
City of Yuma	80,185	3,473		392	3,081	1	24	41	326	639	2,081	361	
Total area actually reporting	90.4%	5,115		583	4,532	5	30	49	499	1,064	2,963	505	
Estimated total	100.0%	5,998		644	5,354	6	34	64	540	1,245	3,489	620	
Rate per 100,000 inhabitants		3,623.4		389.0	3,234.3	3.6	20.5	38.7	326.2	752.1	2,107.7	374.5	
Aguadilla, Puerto Rico M.S.A.	143,625												
Total area actually reporting	100.0%	2,493		289	2,204	12	6	195	76	927	1,126	151	
Rate per 100,000 inhabitants		1,735.8		201.2	1,534.6	8.4	4.2	135.8	52.9	645.4	784.0	105.1	
Arecibo, Puerto Rico M.S.A.	174,172												
Total area actually reporting	100.0%	3,026		321	2,705	10	2	231	78	919	1,197	589	
Rate per 100,000 inhabitants		1,737.4		184.3	1,553.1	5.7	1.1	132.6	44.8	527.6	687.3	338.2	
Caguas, Puerto Rico M.S.A.	314,706												
Total area actually reporting	100.0%	4,510		891	3,619	56	7	674	154	1,635	1,007	977	
Rate per 100,000 inhabitants		1,433.1		283.1	1,150.0	17.8	2.2	214.2	48.9	519.5	320.0	310.4	
Mayaguez, Puerto Rico M.S.A.	255,876												
Total area actually reporting	100.0%	4,080		380	3,700	16	9	225	130	1,187	2,263	250	
Rate per 100,000 inhabitants		1,594.5		148.5	1,446.0	6.3	3.5	87.9	50.8	463.9	884.4	97.7	
Ponce, Puerto Rico M.S.A.	367,089												
Total area actually reporting	100.0%	5,343		771	4,572	59	14	453	245	1,427	2,737	408	
Rate per 100,000 inhabitants		1,455.5		210.0	1,245.5	16.1	3.8	123.4	66.7	388.7	745.6	111.1	
San Juan-Bayamon, Puerto Rico M.S.A.	1,991,552												
Total area actually reporting	100.0%	42,988		7,582	35,406	513	122	5,606	1,341	10,584	15,448	9,374	
Rate per 100,000 inhabitants		2,158.5		380.7	1,777.8	25.8	6.1	281.5	67.3	531.4	775.7	470.7	

[1] The murder and nonnegligent homicides that occurred as a result of the events of September 11, 2001, were not included in this table. See special report, Section V.
[2] Although arson data are included in the trend and clearance tables, sufficient data are not available to estimate totals for this offense.
[3] Violent crimes are offenses of murder, forcible rape, robbery, and aggravated assault. Property crimes are offenses of burglary, larceny-theft, and motor vehicle theft.
[4] Due to changes in reporting practices, annexations, and/or incomplete data, figures are not comparable to previous years' data.
[5] Aggravated assault figures were found to be outside statistical parameters.
[6] The population for the city of Mobile, Alabama, includes 55,864 inhabitants from the jurisdiction of the Mobile County Sheriff's Department.
[7] The data for anthrax assaults were not available.

Table 7

Offense Analysis[1]
United States, 1997-2001

Classification	1997	1998	1999	2000[2]	2001
Murder	18,208	16,974	15,522	15,586	15,980
Forcible rape	96,153	93,144	89,411	90,178	90,491
Robbery:					
Total	**498,534**	**447,186**	**409,371**	**408,016**	**422,921**
Street/highway	249,479	219,689	197,770	187,688	187,291
Commercial house	68,726	61,232	55,678	56,714	61,060
Gas or service station	11,829	9,861	8,844	11,832	12,066
Convenience store	28,234	25,972	24,712	26,113	27,741
Residence	57,894	54,497	49,793	49,778	53,188
Bank	9,658	8,640	8,021	8,568	10,246
Miscellaneous	72,714	67,295	64,552	67,323	71,329
Burglary:					
Total	**2,460,526**	**2,332,735**	**2,100,739**	**2,050,992**	**2,109,767**
Residence (dwelling):	1,639,629	1,563,086	1,394,868	1,337,247	1,376,060
Night	468,128	448,988	402,548	399,943	408,760
Day	694,916	668,619	612,429	617,349	640,212
Unknown	476,586	445,479	379,891	319,955	327,088
Nonresidence (store, office, etc.):	820,897	769,649	705,871	713,745	733,707
Night	358,987	328,218	296,303	299,445	309,604
Day	190,554	190,412	186,166	219,456	223,820
Unknown	271,356	251,018	223,402	194,844	200,283
Larceny-theft (except motor vehicle theft):					
Total	**7,743,760**	**7,376,311**	**6,955,520**	**6,971,590**	**7,076,171**
By type:					
Pocket-picking	45,848	44,315	43,035	34,858	33,270
Purse-snatching	46,685	42,484	40,377	34,858	38,462
Shoplifting	1,181,805	1,094,412	1,002,576	962,079	976,581
From motor vehicles (except accessories)	1,979,191	1,936,742	1,788,630	1,756,841	1,828,774
Motor vehicle accessories	771,661	738,231	723,720	676,244	721,778
Bicycles	431,129	375,348	325,683	313,722	290,542
From buildings	1,053,089	990,467	946,419	913,278	941,489
From coin-operated machines	44,792	44,129	46,479	48,801	51,921
All others	2,189,559	2,110,183	2,038,602	2,230,909	2,193,354
By value:					
Over $200	2,971,733	2,886,866	2,692,746	2,711,949	2,785,894
$50 to $200	1,817,398	1,715,250	1,609,400	1,631,352	1,626,866
Under $50	2,954,629	2,774,195	2,653,374	2,628,289	2,663,411
Motor vehicle theft	1,354,189	1,242,781	1,152,075	1,160,002	1,226,457

[1] The murder and nonnegligent homicides that occurred as a result of the events of September 11, 2001, were not included in this table. See special report, Section V.
[2] The 2000 crime figures have been adjusted.
Note: Because of rounding, offenses may not add to total.

Table 8

Offenses Known to Law Enforcement
by City 10,000 and over in Population, 2001

City by state	Population	Crime Index total	Modified Crime Index total[1]	Murder and non-negligent man-slaughter	Forcible rape	Robbery	Aggravated assault	Burglary	Larceny-theft	Motor vehicle theft	Arson[1]
ALABAMA[2]											
Alabaster	22,707	246		2	1	11	15	23	175	19	
Alexander City	15,066	1,065		0	10	5	73	140	815	22	
Anniston	24,370	3,531		8	37	144	349	871	1,920	202	
Athens	19,041	656		0	3	15	9	77	518	34	
Auburn	43,154	2,196		2	10	32	107	412	1,534	99	
Birmingham	243,762	21,085	21,336	73	206	1,084	1,664	4,079	11,928	2,051	251
Daphne	16,645	525		0	4	4	9	49	437	22	
Dothan	57,961	3,105		3	43	83	58	562	2,239	117	
Enterprise	21,260	1,018		1	10	23	55	198	693	38	
Eufaula	13,962	751		2	5	21	19	89	591	24	
Fairfield	12,429	1,759		12	3	83	58	249	1,160	194	
Florence	36,405	1,819	1,830	2	12	36	103	376	1,237	53	11
Fort Payne	12,988	592		1	3	4	14	89	477	4	
Gardendale	11,671	432		0	2	8	21	42	331	28	
Hartselle	12,066	398		0	1	2	2	74	308	11	
Helena	10,336	100		0	1	1	8	18	70	2	
Homewood	25,140	1,845		0	10	54	41	205	1,440	95	
Hueytown	15,424	626		1	1	15	29	115	419	46	
Huntsville	158,830	11,413	11,454	15	109	345	570	1,802	7,802	770	41
Leeds	10,496	528		1	3	16	26	61	400	21	
Madison	29,443	915		1	8	15	37	154	656	44	
Millbrook	10,426	378		2	3	13	2	168	176	14	
Mobile[3]	255,551	19,875	19,967	42	95	840	552	4,653	12,284	1,409	92
Montgomery	202,350	15,791		26	102	652	676	3,252	9,928	1,155	
Mountain Brook	20,684	414		0	0	3	6	66	330	9	
Muscle Shoals	11,970	522		0	0	4	5	81	432	0	
Oxford	14,649	1,444		1	9	38	82	184	1,032	98	
Ozark	15,178	790		2	4	9	45	117	579	34	
Pelham	14,425	413		0	3	8	10	32	339	21	
Phenix City	28,375	1,331		2	4	37	109	318	729	132	
Prattville	24,397	1,524		2	7	27	111	205	1,110	62	
Prichard	28,744	3,484		9	12	214	292	1,204	1,404	349	
Saraland	12,336	694		1	2	12	10	105	511	53	
Scottsboro	14,819	642		5	2	9	42	99	457	28	
Sylacauga	12,665	800		2	4	8	41	120	610	15	
Troy	13,989	951		1	5	24	75	130	680	36	
Trussville	12,974	634		0	3	10	12	56	519	34	
Tuscaloosa	78,208	6,428		6	50	222	592	1,348	3,948	262	
Tuskegee	11,892	849		2	3	22	26	266	490	40	
Vestavia Hills	24,571	290		0	2	8	13	46	198	23	
ALASKA											
Anchorage	263,588	13,214	13,317	10	210	384	1,144	1,606	8,648	1,212	103
Fairbanks	30,608	1,597	1,605	3	56	30	125	207	974	202	8
ARIZONA											
Apache Junction	32,910	1,611	1,616	0	19	12	63	431	893	193	5
Bullhead City	34,932	1,737	1,747	2	11	27	153	427	1,007	110	10
Casa Grande	26,093	2,332	2,348	2	2	32	140	607	1,373	176	16
Douglas	14,805	663	664	1	2	4	29	108	452	67	1
Flagstaff	54,716	4,892	4,913	2	23	59	362	532	3,674	240	21
Gilbert	113,475	4,651	4,687	0	21	46	62	1,464	2,663	395	36
Glendale	226,348	14,410	14,482	17	66	426	705	2,509	7,531	3,156	72
Goodyear	19,562	990	993	0	3	12	39	440	398	98	3
Kingman	20,760	1,969	1,978	1	5	13	57	375	1,412	106	9
Lake Havasu City	43,382	1,434	1,441	1	0	5	57	228	1,039	104	7
Marana	14,023	1,060	1,061	1	6	10	36	108	783	116	1
Mesa	410,026	27,508	27,543	17	106	452	1,941	4,313	16,121	4,558	35
Nogales	21,597	832	834	1	0	7	63	88	534	139	2
Oro Valley	30,723	494	496	1	0	3	9	44	414	23	2

See footnotes at end of table.

Table 8

Offenses Known to Law Enforcement
by City 10,000 and over in Population, 2001—Continued

City by state	Population	Crime Index total	Modified Crime Index total[1]	Murder and non-negligent man-slaughter	Forcible rape	Robbery	Aggravated assault	Burglary	Larceny-theft	Motor vehicle theft	Arson[1]
ARIZONA—Continued											
Paradise Valley	14,135	566	566	0	0	4	15	323	176	48	0
Payson	14,089	576	580	1	9	3	24	118	392	29	4
Peoria	112,096	5,332	5,347	3	22	73	242	1,102	3,018	872	15
Phoenix	1,366,542	104,975	105,396	209	400	4,629	5,294	16,673	55,190	22,580	421
Prescott	35,107	1,870	1,887	1	8	14	99	307	1,333	108	17
Prescott Valley	24,346	750	753	1	5	6	69	122	515	32	3
Scottsdale	209,686	9,905	9,963	10	58	196	355	2,660	5,251	1,375	58
Sedona	10,543	355	355	0	4	6	10	61	256	18	0
Sierra Vista	39,076	1,509	1,520	0	4	18	68	228	1,085	106	11
Surprise	31,910	1,007	1,011	1	1	7	63	205	648	82	4
Tempe	164,088	16,534	16,571	5	72	327	533	2,273	10,497	2,827	37
Tucson	503,461	49,757	50,112	42	321	1,698	2,762	6,553	31,217	7,164	355
Yuma	80,185	3,473	3,506	1	24	41	326	639	2,081	361	33
ARKANSAS											
Arkadelphia	10,988	190	191	0	0	3	1	13	166	7	1
Benton	22,059	1,819	1,823	0	6	10	56	610	1,076	61	4
Bentonville	19,868	906	906	0	6	5	35	250	578	32	0
Blytheville	18,400	2,086	2,099	6	19	39	191	474	1,264	93	13
Cabot	15,368	989	991	0	1	4	48	69	845	22	2
Camden	13,246	440	440	3	9	14	25	87	286	16	0
Conway	43,469	2,157	2,157	1	27	29	25	122	1,886	67	0
El Dorado	21,681	1,533	1,544	1	15	32	230	423	749	83	11
Fayetteville	58,453	3,247	3,278	0	25	27	149	388	2,509	149	31
Forrest City	14,877	1,473	1,475	3	6	41	288	204	874	57	2
Fort Smith	80,829	7,404	7,439	8	56	132	428	1,149	5,266	365	35
Harrison	12,237	474	474	0	3	1	19	46	378	27	0
Hope	10,690	533	533	2	3	8	46	132	313	29	0
Little Rock	184,413	16,866	17,034	34	92	617	1,130	3,630	9,841	1,522	168
Magnolia	10,934	690	695	0	6	18	94	141	392	39	5
Mountain Home	11,089	248	249	1	2	0	9	11	209	16	1
North Little Rock	60,855	6,162	6,178	10	47	183	267	949	4,158	548	16
Paragould	22,171	591	592	0	11	8	11	93	376	92	1
Rogers	39,100	1,595	1,596	2	10	8	73	154	1,282	66	1
Russellville	23,848	1,750	1,750	0	15	17	194	187	1,275	62	0
Searcy	19,060	1,070	1,070	1	4	10	73	71	857	54	0
Siloam Springs	10,919	528	528	0	7	3	18	68	403	29	0
Springdale	46,118	1,576	1,579	0	22	18	100	195	1,127	114	3
Texarkana	26,633	2,339	2,354	1	16	37	162	242	1,764	117	15
Van Buren	19,119	878	881	2	8	4	43	120	650	51	3
West Memphis	27,859	1,758	1,767	2	21	120	193	417	814	191	9
CALIFORNIA											
Adelanto	18,467	464	464	1	6	13	102	174	80	88	0
Agoura Hills	20,919	301	306	0	4	3	35	84	158	17	5
Alameda	73,602	3,057	3,081	2	6	94	264	436	1,927	328	24
Albany	16,750	837	842	0	3	33	26	150	511	114	5
Alhambra	87,399	2,067	2,110	3	8	145	104	330	1,098	379	43
Anaheim	334,110	11,225	11,272	8	91	484	733	1,798	6,328	1,783	47
Antioch	92,214	3,184	3,214	8	16	147	423	556	1,414	620	30
Apple Valley	55,247	1,927	1,939	2	10	42	112	530	1,025	206	12
Arcadia	54,040	1,532	1,540	2	5	63	66	322	942	132	8
Arcata	16,960	800	811	0	3	4	14	107	631	41	11
Arroyo Grande	16,146	351	355	0	4	10	11	54	265	7	4
Artesia	16,684	556	564	3	5	49	67	81	245	106	8
Arvin	13,197	481	503	1	11	15	42	126	213	73	22
Atascadero	26,902	786	800	0	10	4	82	140	493	57	14
Atwater	23,543	1,110	1,118	1	5	20	215	266	509	94	8
Auburn	12,694	368	370	0	3	1	24	63	229	48	2
Avenal	14,947	118	122	0	0	1	22	53	38	4	4

See footnotes at end of table.

Table 8

Offenses Known to Law Enforcement
by City 10,000 and over in Population, 2001—Continued

City by state	Population	Crime Index total	Modified Crime Index total[1]	Murder and non-negligent man-slaughter	Forcible rape	Robbery	Aggravated assault	Burglary	Larceny-theft	Motor vehicle theft	Arson[1]
CALIFORNIA—Continued											
Azusa	45,543	1,414	1,425	3	16	69	96	317	685	228	11
Bakersfield	251,648	10,255	10,502	22	34	324	460	2,035	6,226	1,154	247
Baldwin Park	77,246	1,868	1,887	5	16	102	156	343	717	529	19
Banning	24,000	754	754	3	8	28	168	283	187	77	0
Barstow	21,511	1,143	1,155	2	12	51	96	315	549	118	12
Beaumont	11,596	453	453	1	3	16	30	134	226	43	0
Bell	37,345	817	819	1	11	94	112	218	168	213	2
Bellflower	74,232	2,756	2,789	7	16	208	206	515	1,218	586	33
Bell Gardens	44,873	1,144		5	3	104	149	228	408	247	
Belmont	25,590	517	518	0	3	7	58	153	248	48	1
Benicia	27,364	539	554	1	2	19	16	146	308	47	15
Berkeley	104,652	9,470	9,521	1	17	398	326	1,453	6,054	1,221	51
Beverly Hills	34,412	1,649	1,651	1	2	85	45	356	1,081	79	2
Blythe	12,381	843	865	2	7	11	137	203	460	23	22
Brawley	22,462	794	803	1	4	24	95	146	473	51	9
Brea	36,068	1,473	1,484	0	9	38	44	229	1,022	131	11
Brentwood	23,735	853	861	0	7	8	50	88	571	129	8
Buena Park	79,737	2,118	2,130	2	16	105	120	377	1,091	407	12
Burbank	102,180	3,377	3,387	3	7	122	198	503	2,013	531	10
Burlingame	28,681	980	992	0	10	21	45	176	616	112	12
Calabasas	20,405	353	355	0	1	5	34	77	195	41	2
Calexico	27,613	1,186	1,194	0	5	29	40	364	384	364	8
Camarillo	58,138	1,204	1,225	0	9	27	66	187	835	80	21
Campbell	38,847	1,186	1,193	0	12	22	62	160	833	97	7
Canyon Lake	10,137	239	240	0	3	1	29	61	123	22	1
Capitola	10,219	888	888	0	4	10	52	105	684	33	0
Carlsbad	79,701	2,061	2,072	2	11	41	143	413	1,252	199	11
Carpinteria	14,458	217	217	1	0	6	15	48	134	13	0
Carson	91,398	3,439	3,497	8	13	187	457	551	1,475	748	58
Cathedral City	43,440	2,010	2,010	7	31	86	148	463	798	477	0
Ceres	35,252	2,452	2,461	0	11	43	155	311	1,587	345	9
Cerritos	52,445	2,247	2,260	3	2	94	76	332	1,288	452	13
Chico	61,068	2,332	2,428	2	36	68	118	491	1,334	283	96
Chino	68,416	2,441	2,478	2	13	90	197	428	1,333	378	37
Chino Hills	68,028	1,233	1,240	1	3	31	52	335	658	153	7
Chowchilla	11,334	423	433	0	3	2	40	108	236	34	10
Chula Vista	176,781	7,644	7,702	8	69	242	610	1,009	3,999	1,707	58
Claremont	34,630	1,088	1,092	0	12	31	53	308	586	98	4
Clayton	10,962	186	188	0	1	3	2	48	116	16	2
Clearlake	13,386	691	697	1	5	9	55	220	346	55	6
Clovis	69,740	3,082	3,111	0	15	41	59	523	2,016	428	29
Coachella	23,146	935	940	3	4	29	118	231	403	147	5
Coalinga	11,885	357	361	0	1	3	28	66	242	17	4
Colton	48,548	2,210	2,241	0	10	106	102	407	1,127	458	31
Commerce	12,802	1,181	1,198	4	8	74	96	190	457	352	17
Compton	95,231	5,269	5,402	46	52	641	1,217	858	1,557	898	133
Concord	124,043	5,573	5,583	0	16	158	324	750	3,563	762	10
Corcoran	14,727	303	306	0	4	1	41	87	148	22	3
Corona	127,288	4,218	4,239	3	19	149	153	681	2,500	713	21
Coronado	24,548	417	418	0	9	6	14	70	290	28	1
Costa Mesa	110,745	4,021	4,036	4	28	155	203	554	2,595	482	15
Covina	47,707	2,316	2,321	1	12	93	140	414	1,330	326	5
Cudahy	24,658	561	561	0	4	37	135	66	165	154	0
Culver City	39,537	1,449	1,452	2	3	121	38	200	919	166	3
Cupertino	51,485	1,319	1,331	1	7	13	50	252	945	51	12
Cypress	47,088	1,046	1,052	0	7	29	45	178	649	138	6
Daly City	105,547	2,300	2,308	5	25	146	175	213	1,253	483	8
Dana Point	35,762	630	635	0	2	16	54	127	392	39	5
Danville	42,490	616	625	0	4	5	35	141	411	20	9
Davis	61,429	2,293	2,326	0	19	28	69	343	1,682	152	33
Delano	39,546	2,000	2,007	1	8	49	28	292	1,316	306	7
Desert Hot Springs	16,890	1,550	1,550	2	22	43	196	537	629	121	0

See footnotes at end of table.

Table 8

Offenses Known to Law Enforcement
by City 10,000 and over in Population, 2001—Continued

City by state	Population	Crime Index total	Modified Crime Index total[1]	Murder and non-negligent man-slaughter	Forcible rape	Robbery	Aggravated assault	Burglary	Larceny-theft	Motor vehicle theft	Arson[1]
CALIFORNIA—Continued											
Diamond Bar	57,333	929	946	1	9	31	95	156	508	129	17
Dinuba	17,157	1,151	1,156	0	8	17	139	414	488	85	5
Dixon	16,402	597	600	0	5	4	106	67	370	45	3
Downey	109,318	3,715	3,737	5	20	208	200	490	1,793	999	22
Duarte	21,885	589	590	1	3	28	78	81	300	98	1
Dublin	30,530	751	754	1	1	11	49	118	453	118	3
East Palo Alto	30,054	1,244	1,253	6	19	132	154	417	320	196	9
El Cajon	96,632	4,171	4,198	5	37	139	440	667	2,020	863	27
El Centro	38,538	2,109	2,129	0	13	49	299	654	883	211	20
El Cerrito	23,602	1,517	1,524	1	4	70	41	247	838	316	7
El Monte	118,120	3,778	3,818	10	24	281	434	589	1,546	894	40
El Segundo	16,331	725	726	0	3	23	15	127	485	72	1
Encinitas	59,092	1,476	1,482	0	26	27	102	330	804	187	6
Escondido	136,041	5,194	5,217	2	31	167	376	851	2,826	941	23
Eureka	26,614	2,514	2,563	5	20	66	127	417	1,628	251	49
Fairfield	97,965	4,594	4,649	3	30	184	291	653	3,027	406	55
Fillmore	13,897	263	266	0	3	6	28	55	152	19	3
Folsom	52,848	1,528	1,552	1	15	21	75	335	939	142	24
Fontana	131,325	3,969	4,008	10	41	234	625	746	1,297	1,016	39
Fortuna	10,692	489	495	0	4	8	23	72	367	15	6
Foster City	29,338	438	443	0	2	3	27	62	318	26	5
Fountain Valley	56,000	1,753	1,767	1	0	54	64	242	1,193	199	14
Fremont	207,193	6,152	6,193	0	19	144	236	1,000	4,045	708	41
Fresno	435,600	34,681	35,229	40	202	1,362	2,492	5,203	18,398	6,984	548
Fullerton	128,345	4,555	4,580	3	25	157	184	719	2,914	553	25
Galt	19,834	644	652	0	7	4	35	119	392	87	8
Gardena	58,819	2,487	2,491	6	21	280	328	520	876	456	4
Garden Grove	168,266	5,176	5,214	5	32	302	460	681	2,785	911	38
Gilroy	42,235	1,712	1,716	3	16	52	237	224	1,049	131	4
Glendale[4]	198,596	4,491	4,537	5	22	180	235	987	2,313	749	46
Glendora	50,333	1,172	1,179	0	9	36	62	186	761	118	7
Grand Terrace	11,842	321	322	0	1	7	18	70	152	73	1
Grass Valley	11,125	552	556	0	4	1	30	56	392	69	4
Greenfield	12,817	222	223	1	2	21	54	40	87	17	1
Grover Beach	13,310	341	350	0	3	9	34	57	212	26	9
Half Moon Bay	12,062	199	201	0	1	4	15	30	142	7	2
Hanford	42,461	1,614	1,621	0	6	25	61	283	1,075	164	7
Hawaiian Gardens	15,054	554	562	1	6	50	77	113	237	70	8
Hawthorne	85,675	3,304	3,312	7	36	334	621	507	1,253	546	8
Hayward[4]	142,632	5,525	5,586	10	43	275	213	851	2,784	1,349	61
Healdsburg	10,921	358	364	0	4	9	25	121	186	13	6
Hemet	59,905	3,204	3,267	3	15	97	173	1,137	1,387	392	63
Hercules	19,850	565	567	0	1	15	37	108	270	134	2
Hermosa Beach	18,911	734	737	0	9	17	63	123	463	59	3
Hesperia	63,745	1,939	1,957	1	12	49	138	465	1,026	248	18
Highland	45,434	1,623	1,640	4	8	84	101	389	731	306	17
Hillsborough	11,026	77	77	0	3	0	8	18	43	5	0
Hollister	35,053	1,167	1,181	6	11	31	160	151	711	97	14
Huntington Beach	193,117	4,500	4,548	0	44	94	205	1,002	2,608	547	48
Huntington Park	62,488	2,558	2,572	6	23	299	143	309	893	885	14
Imperial Beach	27,494	989	997	0	15	40	111	225	412	186	8
Indio	50,029	2,208	2,208	3	11	74	292	526	720	582	0
Inglewood	114,672	4,586	4,622	38	36	639	610	839	1,550	874	36
Irvine	145,731	3,396	3,403	0	9	44	80	904	2,054	305	7
King City	11,300	445	470	2	3	18	7	89	298	28	25
La Canada/Flintridge	20,696	335	338	0	0	8	17	95	193	22	3
Lafayette	24,352	448	450	0	3	13	8	75	322	27	2
Laguna Beach	24,168	721	723	0	7	8	44	150	475	37	2
Laguna Hills	31,757	757	761	1	5	11	48	108	526	58	4
Laguna Niguel	63,041	992	994	0	1	11	51	210	670	49	2
Laguna Woods	16,814	100	100	0	0	4	2	8	80	6	0
La Habra	60,070	1,785	1,801	1	5	64	120	254	1,088	253	16

See footnotes at end of table.

Table 8

Offenses Known to Law Enforcement
by City 10,000 and over in Population, 2001—Continued

City by state	Population	Crime Index total	Modified Crime Index total[1]	Murder and non-negligent man-slaughter	Forcible rape	Robbery	Aggravated assault	Burglary	Larceny-theft	Motor vehicle theft	Arson[1]
CALIFORNIA—Continued											
Lake Elsinore	29,466	1,321	1,322	4	9	41	186	330	564	187	1
Lake Forest[4]	77,410	1,284	1,293	1	6	36	67	243	807	124	9
Lakewood	80,820	2,952	2,969	2	12	156	187	354	1,703	538	17
La Mesa	55,766	2,223	2,226	0	13	70	121	345	1,303	371	3
La Mirada	47,652	1,073	1,079	0	6	34	100	181	586	166	6
Lancaster	120,924	4,747	4,802	7	56	263	837	1,159	1,909	516	55
La Palma	15,694	285	286	0	4	16	17	50	142	56	1
La Puente	41,826	988	996	7	10	62	162	183	393	171	8
La Quinta	24,134	1,431	1,440	1	6	10	80	401	800	133	9
La Verne	32,226	738	745	1	8	20	51	110	482	66	7
Lawndale	32,300	1,071	1,079	1	11	113	171	245	364	166	8
Lemon Grove	25,381	887	889	1	8	49	72	190	373	194	2
Lemoore	20,078	660	663	0	4	15	57	130	382	72	3
Lincoln	11,413	444	446	0	3	3	38	103	256	41	2
Lindsay	10,488	495	500	3	1	2	59	128	248	54	5
Livermore	74,708	2,194	2,215	0	17	39	80	396	1,459	203	21
Livingston	10,668	312	312	0	7	3	53	81	130	38	0
Lodi	58,058	3,096	3,120	1	9	46	451	359	1,890	340	24
Loma Linda	19,028	771	779	0	4	18	38	226	317	168	8
Lomita	20,419	512	517	0	3	29	86	116	240	38	5
Lompoc	41,867	1,584	1,600	3	18	27	113	292	1,051	80	16
Long Beach	470,099	18,467	18,734	49	125	1,417	1,822	3,232	7,876	3,946	267
Los Alamitos	11,750	300	302	1	1	10	20	77	156	35	2
Los Altos	28,208	323	326	0	0	7	22	102	190	2	3
Los Angeles	3,763,486	189,278	191,626	588	1,409	17,166	33,080	25,695	79,521	31,819	2,348
Los Banos	26,350	728	728	0	7	4	108	107	416	86	0
Los Gatos	29,123	610	616	0	3	4	44	116	413	30	6
Lynwood	71,143	2,474	2,517	18	26	283	568	370	597	612	43
Madera	44,010	2,785	2,788	9	17	127	332	518	1,336	446	3
Malibu	12,809	355	360	0	4	3	28	93	183	44	5
Manhattan Beach	34,481	1,163	1,166	1	6	53	34	248	719	102	3
Manteca	50,173	2,341	2,370	1	8	40	146	364	1,411	371	29
Marina	25,567	470	472	0	4	7	39	107	278	35	2
Martinez	36,533	1,214	1,231	1	8	28	41	185	767	184	17
Marysville	12,496	854	854	2	5	21	56	190	460	120	0
Maywood	28,605	640	643	9	3	74	58	65	309	122	3
Menlo Park	31,357	884	888	0	9	32	45	167	580	51	4
Merced	65,080	4,154	4,202	2	25	111	239	653	2,747	377	48
Millbrae	21,103	369	375	0	10	13	18	75	219	34	6
Mill Valley	13,853	313	314	0	2	4	17	84	182	24	1
Milpitas	63,863	2,154	2,158	0	9	55	149	325	1,452	164	4
Mission Viejo	94,832	1,426	1,432	3	9	20	92	211	994	97	6
Modesto	192,366	11,976	12,096	17	104	381	659	1,829	7,580	1,406	120
Monrovia	37,615	1,054	1,066	0	2	63	103	156	602	128	12
Montclair	33,663	2,054	2,059	2	16	87	144	269	1,178	358	5
Montebello	63,305	2,314	2,347	8	27	136	184	240	1,200	519	33
Monterey	30,225	1,393	1,393	0	10	40	198	201	895	49	0
Monterey Park	61,167	1,499	1,501	3	11	135	60	291	691	308	2
Moorpark	31,999	309	313	1	3	6	25	52	196	26	4
Moraga	16,593	227	228	0	1	3	12	23	177	11	1
Moreno Valley	145,027	6,588	6,609	3	33	312	853	1,635	2,869	883	21
Morgan Hill	34,180	877	891	0	13	22	41	128	621	52	14
Morro Bay	10,542	248	251	0	3	1	42	30	163	9	3
Mountain View	72,022	2,438	2,449	1	5	46	350	252	1,642	142	11
Murrieta	45,105	1,129	1,137	1	2	15	69	249	640	153	8
Napa	73,934	1,980	2,023	1	25	45	157	254	1,385	113	43
National City	55,268	2,632	2,643	1	27	137	312	386	1,090	679	11
Newark	43,260	1,972	1,982	0	14	33	82	238	1,440	165	10
Newport Beach	71,333	2,395	2,402	0	5	35	93	504	1,618	140	7
Norco	24,606	931	936	3	1	20	71	177	532	127	5
Norwalk	105,218	3,656	3,677	7	19	219	556	544	1,436	875	21
Novato	48,515	1,317	1,349	0	15	17	74	439	656	116	32

See footnotes at end of table.

Table 8

Offenses Known to Law Enforcement
by City 10,000 and over in Population, 2001—Continued

City by state	Population	Crime Index total	Modified Crime Index total[1]	Murder and non-negligent man-slaughter	Forcible rape	Robbery	Aggravated assault	Burglary	Larceny-theft	Motor vehicle theft	Arson[1]
CALIFORNIA—Continued											
Oakdale	15,791	1,051	1,055	1	15	17	37	252	642	87	4
Oakland	406,908	27,627	27,955	84	295	2,125	2,826	3,696	13,081	5,520	328
Oakley	26,095	885	892	0	13	12	84	103	570	103	7
Oceanside	164,022	5,887	5,931	4	86	258	722	1,071	3,074	672	44
Ontario	160,943	8,546	8,641	10	74	388	717	1,082	4,432	1,843	95
Orange	131,215	3,692	3,729	0	18	125	209	467	2,435	438	37
Orinda	17,926	297	299	0	0	9	11	63	193	21	2
Oroville	13,246	1,067	1,068	0	4	30	13	271	589	160	1
Oxnard	173,524	5,250	5,298	6	38	393	375	917	3,062	459	48
Pacifica	39,103	762	767	0	7	13	75	119	486	62	5
Pacific Grove	15,810	304	305	0	5	4	18	62	204	11	1
Palmdale	118,838	4,312	4,355	8	48	178	673	896	1,932	577	43
Palm Desert	41,920	2,319	2,320	1	6	47	122	538	1,399	206	1
Palm Springs	43,603	3,366	3,401	4	21	112	312	771	1,701	445	35
Palo Alto	59,687	1,880	1,894	2	7	35	38	255	1,461	82	14
Palos Verdes Estates	13,588	137	139	0	1	3	3	51	68	11	2
Paradise	26,899	922	926	0	6	5	48	230	568	65	4
Paramount	56,293	2,301	2,340	6	20	181	248	346	951	549	39
Parlier	11,352	654	661	0	2	12	105	82	323	130	7
Pasadena	136,425	5,240	5,286	4	34	268	370	899	3,157	508	46
Paso Robles	24,749	823	825	2	9	11	49	183	514	55	2
Patterson	11,822	336	337	0	4	5	9	79	194	45	1
Perris	36,862	1,829	1,832	5	11	78	272	391	701	371	3
Petaluma	55,562	1,806	1,821	1	10	13	67	256	1,372	87	15
Pico Rivera	64,607	1,787	1,806	4	16	113	374	260	705	315	19
Piedmont	11,156	297	301	0	2	5	0	78	161	51	4
Pinole	19,393	1,242	1,250	0	5	50	62	197	679	249	8
Pittsburg	57,824	2,893	2,898	4	10	93	116	372	1,812	486	5
Placentia	47,352	1,003	1,007	1	1	21	113	192	562	113	4
Pleasant Hill	33,447	1,809	1,817	0	9	57	63	344	1,171	165	8
Pleasanton	64,837	1,749	1,759	0	9	24	48	213	1,321	134	10
Pomona	152,251	6,131	6,158	19	54	418	1,046	951	2,489	1,154	27
Porterville	40,351	2,008	2,013	2	8	46	124	388	1,191	249	5
Port Hueneme	22,251	488	490	0	8	27	35	130	248	40	2
Poway	48,937	1,027	1,038	0	11	18	77	259	578	84	11
Rancho Cucamonga	130,117	3,805	3,841	1	17	123	156	811	2,089	608	36
Rancho Mirage	13,495	613	614	0	5	3	42	159	358	46	1
Rancho Palos Verdes	41,910	498	502	1	0	11	30	145	279	32	4
Rancho Santa Margarita	48,091	511	512	0	4	8	51	71	338	39	1
Red Bluff	13,391	761	763	0	7	8	112	151	438	45	2
Redding	82,368	3,246	3,270	1	67	64	263	642	1,898	311	24
Redlands	64,773	2,565	2,581	1	19	83	301	383	1,431	347	16
Redondo Beach	64,437	1,917	1,919	1	7	61	116	320	1,184	228	2
Redwood City	76,803	2,206	2,222	1	22	59	203	472	1,297	152	16
Reedley	21,142	1,026	1,044	2	5	14	132	167	588	118	18
Rialto	93,580	3,634	3,666	10	35	235	483	553	1,328	990	32
Richmond	101,060	7,190	7,285	18	47	410	540	1,230	3,448	1,497	95
Ridgecrest	25,390	863	879	1	10	16	116	219	438	63	16
Ripon	10,335	395	397	0	1	1	26	54	284	29	2
Riverbank	16,120	524	534	0	1	7	32	94	323	67	10
Riverside	259,908	14,518	14,738	20	95	622	1,422	2,225	7,896	2,238	220
Rocklin	37,005	728	735	0	7	10	13	157	434	107	7
Rohnert Park	43,021	1,769	1,784	1	21	29	35	685	880	118	15
Rosemead	54,499	1,333	1,344	5	15	106	174	300	452	281	11
Roseville	81,406	3,477	3,491	1	17	56	167	413	2,414	409	14
Sacramento	414,582	30,691	31,131	40	169	1,440	1,660	5,068	15,977	6,337	440
Salinas	153,867	6,979	7,032	15	56	399	799	843	4,102	765	53
San Anselmo	12,608	225	226	0	4	2	12	69	127	11	1
San Bernardino	188,847	12,803	12,942	30	89	829	1,449	2,299	5,868	2,239	139
San Bruno	40,911	1,049	1,050	1	11	34	56	105	706	136	1
San Carlos	28,233	573	573	1	3	8	33	87	401	40	0
San Clemente	50,864	839	848	3	1	24	38	173	523	77	9

See footnotes at end of table.

Table 8

Offenses Known to Law Enforcement
by City 10,000 and over in Population, 2001—Continued

City by state	Population	Crime Index total	Modified Crime Index total[1]	Murder and non-negligent man-slaughter	Forcible rape	Robbery	Aggravated assault	Burglary	Larceny-theft	Motor vehicle theft	Arson[1]
CALIFORNIA—Continued											
San Diego	1,246,136	50,444	50,645	50	342	1,729	5,284	7,219	25,050	10,770	201
San Dimas	35,630	847	852	0	9	27	70	202	428	111	5
San Fernando	24,002	1,018	1,024	3	3	77	146	146	442	201	6
San Gabriel	40,544	1,026	1,034	3	4	96	94	208	503	118	8
Sanger	19,283	806	818	1	8	31	121	147	364	134	12
San Jacinto	24,221	611	612	1	10	23	65	229	137	146	1
San Jose	913,513	25,163	25,660	22	329	712	4,501	2,939	13,567	3,093	497
San Juan Capistrano	34,455	614	617	1	5	15	64	85	400	44	3
San Leandro	80,929	4,490	4,509	1	12	231	298	686	2,526	736	19
San Luis Obispo	44,995	2,030	2,115	0	23	17	129	393	1,336	132	85
San Marcos	55,999	1,525	1,534	1	12	50	175	390	701	196	9
San Marino	13,186	146	147	0	0	2	2	35	100	7	1
San Mateo	94,201	2,822	2,849	1	26	77	308	253	1,938	219	27
San Pablo	30,777	2,135	2,150	3	8	134	189	528	738	535	15
San Rafael	57,105	2,037	2,043	2	20	73	111	355	1,152	324	6
San Ramon	45,553	1,125	1,128	0	8	20	42	161	827	67	3
Santa Ana	344,258	12,066	12,269	24	55	942	823	1,396	6,263	2,563	203
Santa Barbara	94,041	2,946	2,957	3	28	106	402	443	1,822	142	11
Santa Clara	104,263	3,350	3,395	0	20	45	217	420	2,412	236	45
Santa Clarita	153,896	3,161	3,214	3	23	79	210	662	1,831	353	53
Santa Cruz	55,608	3,546	3,565	0	51	87	399	478	2,322	209	19
Santa Fe Springs	17,762	1,383	1,387	1	2	62	56	205	781	276	4
Santa Maria	78,862	2,651	2,672	4	23	98	205	387	1,693	241	21
Santa Monica	85,647	4,905	4,949	2	23	313	316	720	3,016	515	44
Santa Paula	29,129	834	847	0	1	56	68	292	352	65	13
Santa Rosa	150,338	5,854	5,899	3	72	123	309	773	4,050	524	45
Santee	53,960	1,459	1,463	4	18	26	178	292	742	199	4
Saratoga	30,398	341	341	0	3	2	24	98	207	7	0
Scotts Valley	11,597	405	407	0	1	3	34	70	281	16	2
Seal Beach	24,606	474	475	0	0	16	35	114	259	50	1
Seaside	32,285	994	1,005	0	13	49	178	139	558	57	11
Selma	19,805	1,131	1,134	2	3	34	81	154	671	186	3
Shafter	12,973	407	425	0	1	3	60	69	243	31	18
Sierra Madre	10,775	156	156	0	0	2	4	49	93	8	0
Simi Valley	113,420	1,746	1,759	6	11	37	99	361	1,040	192	13
Solana Beach	13,220	337	340	0	1	10	23	114	158	31	3
Soledad	11,472	275	276	1	1	13	20	72	153	15	1
South El Monte	21,537	716	721	3	6	58	102	122	273	152	5
South Gate	98,166	3,109	3,122	4	24	364	141	583	926	1,067	13
South Lake Tahoe[4]	24,048	929	930	1	16	20	133	240	456	63	1
South Pasadena	24,743	555	561	0	3	32	16	120	289	95	6
South San Francisco	61,677	1,726	1,743	1	10	68	77	264	1,097	209	17
Stanton	38,098	944	959	0	3	62	117	135	439	188	15
Stockton	248,301	19,728	19,843	30	144	1,030	2,092	2,871	10,558	3,003	115
Suisun City	26,603	728	739	0	3	23	38	140	436	88	11
Sunnyvale	134,209	2,698	2,715	0	18	59	103	289	1,995	234	17
Susanville	13,793	306	308	0	5	3	42	49	199	8	2
Temecula	58,789	2,110	2,119	1	22	27	190	429	1,189	252	9
Temple City	33,997	575	580	2	3	27	74	199	213	57	5
Thousand Oaks	119,179	1,888	1,908	1	10	33	130	308	1,276	130	20
Torrance	140,510	4,366	4,392	4	24	210	171	744	2,582	631	26
Tracy	57,987	2,214	2,238	0	16	36	78	361	1,437	286	24
Tulare	44,812	3,015	3,049	5	19	62	348	1,230	1,146	205	34
Turlock	56,847	3,388	3,439	2	19	64	239	593	1,880	591	51
Tustin	68,759	2,127	2,132	0	9	79	169	310	1,315	245	5
Twentynine Palms	15,038	584	598	0	8	6	50	176	286	58	14
Twin Cities	21,506	551	555	1	2	10	1	143	334	60	4
Ukiah	15,785	720	741	0	9	12	135	95	427	42	21
Union City	68,112	2,620	2,649	3	8	123	146	370	1,554	416	29
Upland	69,664	2,949	2,995	4	20	99	229	604	1,557	436	46
Vacaville	90,272	2,342	2,404	0	25	66	184	345	1,521	201	62
Vallejo	118,930	7,249	7,316	4	53	344	758	1,176	3,963	951	67

See footnotes at end of table.

Table 8

Offenses Known to Law Enforcement
by City 10,000 and over in Population, 2001—Continued

City by state	Population	Crime Index total	Modified Crime Index total[1]	Murder and non-negligent man-slaughter	Forcible rape	Robbery	Aggravated assault	Burglary	Larceny-theft	Motor vehicle theft	Arson[1]
CALIFORNIA—Continued											
Ventura	102,791	3,357	3,370	2	28	91	160	565	2,280	231	13
Victorville	65,219	3,203	3,227	2	14	122	185	702	1,729	449	24
Visalia	93,267	5,679	5,734	4	35	113	665	967	3,308	587	55
Vista	91,527	2,552	2,558	3	19	155	242	541	1,226	366	6
Walnut	30,562	449	454	0	5	14	26	92	243	69	5
Walnut Creek	65,491	2,545	2,575	0	10	30	91	490	1,703	221	30
Watsonville	45,088	2,250	2,256	4	19	81	205	296	1,519	126	6
West Covina	107,033	4,793	4,839	2	18	152	199	560	2,962	900	46
West Hollywood	36,380	1,954	1,958	1	18	147	227	305	997	259	4
Westminster	89,846	3,027	3,033	2	18	131	206	466	1,638	566	6
West Sacramento	32,203	1,554	1,585	2	20	66	131	368	590	377	31
Whittier	85,235	2,736	2,744	3	13	122	192	334	1,690	382	8
Windsor	23,167	511	515	1	5	7	60	73	335	30	4
Woodland	50,064	1,434	1,471	1	16	48	258	274	657	180	37
Yorba Linda	60,013	1,029	1,042	0	2	20	43	114	789	61	13
Yuba City	37,441	1,992	2,002	2	23	34	124	386	1,244	179	10
Yucaipa	41,973	779	786	0	9	22	40	157	462	89	7
Yucca Valley	17,178	588	599	0	5	11	51	135	327	59	11
COLORADO											
Arvada[4]	104,919	3,784	3,824	0	23	37	130	466	2,783	345	40
Aurora	283,876	17,224	17,326	17	224	496	937	1,834	10,871	2,845	102
Boulder	97,236	4,140	4,228	0	30	49	132	573	3,145	211	88
Broomfield	39,308	1,738	1,753	0	16	13	14	167	1,425	103	15
Colorado Springs	370,661	19,475	19,612	14	257	494	1,142	3,070	13,155	1,343	137
Commerce City	21,559	2,123	2,135	4	10	41	132	315	1,271	350	12
Denver	569,653	30,272	30,617	45	317	1,250	1,462	5,642	14,621	6,935	345
Durango	14,299	924	936	0	17	7	13	106	740	41	12
Englewood	32,586	2,462	2,480	1	17	44	96	290	1,561	453	18
Federal Heights	12,392	863	864	0	2	17	16	96	571	161	1
Fort Collins	121,864	4,695	4,731	0	86	35	248	662	3,448	216	36
Fort Morgan	11,333	530	531	0	6	0	9	47	443	25	1
Golden	17,624	774	786	0	3	4	35	93	572	67	12
Grand Junction	43,123	3,563	3,596	1	20	26	123	468	2,788	137	33
Greeley	79,013	4,303	4,326	4	45	47	203	557	3,190	257	23
Greenwood Village	11,334	865	872	0	4	15	27	100	655	64	7
Lafayette	23,825	719	743	0	7	5	100	105	462	40	24
Lakewood	148,028	8,454	8,512	7	94	164	244	1,035	5,829	1,081	58
Littleton	41,432	1,482	1,487	1	2	13	45	243	992	186	5
Louisville	19,450	431	431	0	4	2	22	56	320	27	0
Loveland	51,978	1,643	1,656	0	16	6	55	233	1,260	73	13
Montrose	12,678	634	640	1	7	0	27	80	490	29	6
Northglenn	32,430	1,751	1,770	0	8	20	101	210	1,222	190	19
Parker	24,196	578	582	0	0	5	3	154	389	27	4
Pueblo	104,886	6,466	6,526	5	49	146	608	1,131	4,170	357	60
Steamboat Springs	10,081	418	420	0	1	1	30	83	281	22	2
Sterling	11,668	598	604	0	6	0	20	83	473	16	6
Thornton	84,614	5,081	5,081	1	32	50	393	606	3,464	535	0
Wheat Ridge	33,804	2,007	2,023	1	22	36	120	229	1,316	283	16
CONNECTICUT											
Ansonia	18,660	400	400	0	1	12	70	54	203	60	0
Avon	15,923	151	151	0	0	1	0	22	119	9	0
Berlin	18,319	471	471	0	0	7	3	62	343	56	0
Bethel	18,170	150	151	0	0	0	3	37	98	12	1
Bloomfield	19,699	736	739	0	14	15	119	61	480	47	3
Branford	28,847	911	914	0	9	14	29	67	746	46	3
Bridgeport	140,328	8,162	8,323	16	69	608	1,217	1,266	2,876	2,110	161
Bristol	60,406	1,735	1,735	2	16	40	180	340	1,022	135	0
Brookfield	15,754	155	156	0	0	2	8	10	124	11	1

See footnotes at end of table.

Table 8

Offenses Known to Law Enforcement

by City 10,000 and over in Population, 2001—Continued

City by state	Population	Crime Index total	Modified Crime Index total[1]	Murder and non-negligent man-slaughter	Forcible rape	Robbery	Aggravated assault	Burglary	Larceny-theft	Motor vehicle theft	Arson[1]
CONNECTICUT—Continued											
Cheshire	28,707	347	348	0	0	0	3	74	244	26	1
Clinton	13,169	194	195	0	1	2	8	20	156	7	1
Coventry	11,570	195	197	0	0	2	10	42	137	4	2
Cromwell	12,945	349	351	0	1	6	2	61	252	27	2
Danbury	75,277	2,015	2,024	0	10	53	80	344	1,336	192	9
Darien	19,719	233	233	0	0	1	3	39	172	18	0
East Hampton	13,428	91	91	0	2	1	3	11	69	5	0
East Hartford	49,859	1,869	1,890	3	19	80	162	283	1,033	289	21
East Haven	28,350	827	829	0	7	23	36	108	549	104	2
Enfield	45,471	920	928	1	0	8	55	163	591	102	8
Fairfield	57,668	1,272	1,273	0	1	12	11	227	930	91	1
Farmington	23,776	761	761	0	4	12	6	76	615	48	0
Glastonbury	32,059	418	419	0	1	4	4	61	333	15	1
Granby	10,406	122	122	0	0	1	1	10	106	4	0
Greenwich	61,451	739	746	1	4	10	18	111	544	51	7
Groton	10,067	269	269	0	5	6	10	57	183	8	0
Groton Town	29,398	757	759	1	27	28	31	97	552	21	2
Guilford	21,521	353	354	0	2	3	11	60	259	18	1
Hartford	122,274	10,789	10,931	25	64	889	615	1,569	5,798	1,829	142
Madison	17,960	156	159	0	0	2	4	31	116	3	3
Manchester	55,054	2,205	2,216	0	15	52	49	264	1,603	222	11
Meriden	58,578	2,329	2,332	2	7	56	36	526	1,545	157	3
Middletown	43,414	1,239	1,239	2	8	26	28	215	822	138	0
Milford	52,605	2,078	2,084	1	12	36	25	254	1,553	197	6
Monroe	19,357	264	264	0	3	1	3	29	220	8	0
Naugatuck	31,167	690	694	0	7	11	31	100	477	64	4
New Britain	71,948	4,006	4,008	3	18	152	168	870	2,288	507	2
New Canaan	19,506	126	126	0	1	0	0	17	100	8	0
New Haven	124,334	9,844	9,865	19	56	768	1,072	1,348	5,190	1,391	21
Newington	29,474	689	692	0	1	15	11	60	541	61	3
New London	25,818	1,152	1,178	1	10	43	131	196	642	129	26
New Milford	27,276	346	353	0	4	1	24	60	225	32	7
Newtown	25,174	232	232	0	4	4	4	54	152	14	0
North Branford	13,986	135	135	0	0	0	2	22	102	9	0
North Haven	23,167	584	587	0	1	10	4	91	430	48	3
Norwich	36,324	1,255	1,257	0	19	55	69	259	770	83	2
Old Saybrook	10,426	274	274	0	1	0	3	33	226	11	0
Plainfield	14,703	368	370	3	7	0	47	88	196	27	2
Plainville	17,427	609	612	0	4	13	7	86	458	41	3
Plymouth	11,701	238	238	1	1	2	8	71	132	23	0
Ridgefield	23,778	137	139	0	1	2	0	7	120	7	2
Rocky Hill	18,069	359	361	1	0	8	5	36	276	33	2
Seymour	15,543	240	246	0	1	9	21	37	154	18	6
Shelton	38,319	530	531	0	6	4	16	131	313	60	1
Simsbury	23,367	241	241	1	1	2	1	38	194	4	0
Southington	39,956	917	922	0	2	12	25	171	636	71	5
South Windsor	24,552	265	269	0	3	3	16	42	182	19	4
Stamford	117,754	3,086	3,092	1	13	141	116	357	2,095	363	6
Stonington	18,009	358	360	1	0	1	4	18	321	13	2
Stratford	50,262	1,397	1,406	1	10	53	41	233	813	246	9
Suffield	13,630	166	168	0	1	2	2	36	118	7	2
Torrington	35,404	952	959	0	5	5	130	106	636	70	7
Trumbull	34,439	993	1,005	0	1	14	10	90	812	66	12
Vernon	28,224	840	846	0	1	32	18	110	638	41	6
Waterbury	107,886	6,872	6,888	7	38	277	224	1,299	4,147	880	16
Waterford	19,262	640	640	0	3	8	19	68	511	31	0
Watertown	21,785	429	429	0	0	3	1	49	352	24	0
West Hartford	63,953	1,885	1,891	0	3	103	31	294	1,328	126	6
West Haven	52,660	2,325	2,338	2	17	48	98	366	1,523	271	13
Weston	10,094	77	77	0	0	1	2	15	57	2	0
Westport	25,897	591	596	0	0	7	31	87	441	25	5
Wethersfield	26,421	584	586	0	6	17	8	80	415	58	2

See footnotes at end of table.

Table 8

Offenses Known to Law Enforcement

by City 10,000 and over in Population, 2001—Continued

City by state	Population	Crime Index total	Modified Crime Index total[1]	Murder and non-negligent man-slaughter	Forcible rape	Robbery	Aggravated assault	Burglary	Larceny-theft	Motor vehicle theft	Arson[1]
CONNECTICUT—Continued											
Willimantic	15,914	727	727	0	0	19	27	144	496	41	0
Wilton	17,734	209	209	0	0	0	3	51	152	3	0
Winchester	10,725	122	122	0	1	1	4	12	100	4	0
Windsor	28,399	604	612	0	4	16	3	72	469	40	8
Windsor Locks	12,112	271	273	0	9	3	4	47	155	53	2
Wolcott	15,302	366	366	0	2	0	4	52	284	24	0
DELAWARE[4]											
Dover	32,650	2,037	2,054	1	15	55	123	150	1,590	103	17
Newark	29,005	1,473	1,483	0	8	28	98	220	1,024	95	10
Wilmington	73,829	5,488	5,504	14	48	382	604	863	2,838	739	16
DISTRICT OF COLUMBIA[5]											
Washington	571,822	44,041	44,136	232	188	3,940	5,568	5,009	21,434	7,670	95
FLORIDA											
Altamonte Springs	42,268	2,102	2,111	1	3	46	107	264	1,496	185	9
Apopka	27,332	2,183	2,194	0	9	64	243	734	1,018	115	11
Atlantic Beach	13,714	621	624	0	8	16	48	120	376	53	3
Auburndale	11,318	953	955	0	5	15	83	196	595	59	2
Aventura	25,922	2,672	2,672	1	3	53	43	150	2,279	143	0
Bartow	15,737	1,387	1,393	0	17	45	129	237	847	112	6
Belle Glade	15,292	1,277	1,291	2	12	65	255	304	558	81	14
Boca Raton	76,701	3,039	3,041	1	14	65	116	665	1,990	188	2
Boynton Beach	61,954	5,071	5,087	3	2	169	390	754	3,173	580	16
Bradenton	50,787	3,393	3,396	5	20	98	221	725	1,936	388	3
Cape Coral	104,936	3,670	3,701	2	13	34	297	855	2,293	176	31
Casselberry	23,215	1,140	1,143	1	10	45	85	178	739	82	3
Clearwater	111,606	6,642	6,680	4	56	230	736	1,188	3,979	449	38
Cocoa	16,837	1,969	1,971	3	19	102	257	375	1,064	149	2
Cocoa Beach	12,805	1,095	1,096	0	9	22	106	128	793	37	1
Coconut Creek	44,695	1,137	1,140	2	1	17	76	222	656	163	3
Cooper City	28,663	692	696	0	0	14	45	161	435	37	4
Coral Gables	43,344	2,838	2,842	1	5	85	160	491	1,875	221	4
Coral Springs	120,595	3,604	3,610	2	13	73	157	648	2,393	318	6
Crestview	15,149	672	681	0	9	19	67	103	460	14	9
Dania	20,581	1,326	1,326	7	8	62	150	191	754	154	0
Davie	77,682	3,723	3,734	0	5	73	198	639	2,385	423	11
Daytona Beach	65,773	6,501	6,534	8	61	315	740	1,621	3,069	687	33
Deerfield Beach	66,256	2,274	2,278	4	29	70	244	350	1,308	269	4
Deland	21,446	1,647	1,649	0	4	50	161	278	1,074	80	2
Delray Beach	61,575	4,739	4,746	1	22	131	490	753	2,884	458	7
Dunedin	36,616	1,256	1,258	3	8	20	72	252	861	40	2
Edgewater	19,152	539	541	0	8	5	54	102	338	32	2
Eustis	15,497	501	503	1	5	18	89	67	289	32	2
Fernandina Beach	10,822	491	492	1	5	9	40	93	327	16	1
Fort Lauderdale	156,346	12,581	12,629	29	48	837	767	2,439	7,049	1,412	48
Fort Myers	49,457	5,603	5,621	7	40	419	737	959	2,597	844	18
Fort Pierce	38,488	4,232	4,253	13	37	281	538	1,022	2,024	317	21
Fort Walton Beach	20,491	965	969	1	4	25	71	190	622	52	4
Gainesville	97,920	6,245	6,268	4	85	303	474	1,294	3,469	616	23
Greenacres City	28,283	1,642	1,642	0	9	33	83	426	963	128	0
Gulfport	12,852	765	771	1	4	30	68	140	442	80	6
Haines City	13,515	701	704	0	3	18	29	139	441	71	3
Hallandale	35,170	2,345	2,351	2	8	136	342	400	1,235	222	6
Hialeah	232,286	12,248	12,311	9	40	461	1,059	1,596	6,513	2,570	63
Hialeah Gardens	19,797	1,089	1,089	0	2	12	42	193	698	142	0
Holly Hill	12,433	1,049	1,052	1	9	33	73	234	617	82	3
Hollywood	142,968	9,250	9,291	7	51	393	592	1,235	5,834	1,138	41

See footnotes at end of table.

Table 8

Offenses Known to Law Enforcement

by City 10,000 and over in Population, 2001—Continued

City by state	Population	Crime Index total	Modified Crime Index total[1]	Murder and non-negligent man-slaughter	Forcible rape	Robbery	Aggravated assault	Burglary	Larceny-theft	Motor vehicle theft	Arson[1]
FLORIDA—Continued											
Homestead	32,736	3,740	3,740	2	19	224	466	752	2,006	271	0
Jacksonville	754,679	51,250	51,561	75	287	2,195	4,831	9,903	28,827	5,132	311
Jacksonville Beach	21,534	1,700	1,709	1	15	58	130	252	1,160	84	9
Jupiter	40,347	1,598	1,601	0	4	32	101	389	980	92	3
Key Biscayne	10,779	339	339	0	0	2	7	47	266	17	0
Key West	26,138	2,445	2,445	2	13	67	129	431	1,532	271	0
Kissimmee	49,053	3,447	3,457	0	21	117	317	679	2,078	235	10
Lady Lake	12,134	270	270	0	3	5	30	59	146	27	0
Lake City	10,239	1,146	1,155	3	13	35	141	156	746	52	9
Lakeland	80,485	6,303	6,314	4	59	248	270	1,326	3,899	497	11
Lake Mary	11,755	377	377	0	0	5	24	101	227	20	0
Lake Wales	10,458	1,203	1,203	0	4	44	64	230	768	93	0
Lake Worth	36,043	3,142	3,151	1	16	216	172	675	1,732	330	9
Largo	71,169	2,974	2,990	1	23	65	213	521	2,006	145	16
Lauderdale Lakes	32,527	1,289	1,292	1	23	80	178	210	516	281	3
Lauderhill	59,077	2,654	2,661	5	30	172	335	639	967	506	7
Leesburg	16,369	1,363	1,367	6	17	41	262	297	654	86	4
Lighthouse Point	11,046	217	217	1	0	4	5	37	156	14	0
Longwood	14,101	1,105	1,105	0	7	20	268	196	591	23	0
Lynn Haven	12,774	365	365	0	1	8	19	62	261	14	0
Maitland	12,330	554	554	0	5	6	26	155	309	53	0
Marco Island	15,265	353	357	0	1	0	17	63	262	10	4
Margate	55,306	1,682	1,685	1	5	60	137	308	969	202	3
Melbourne	73,232	5,299	5,316	3	43	166	513	802	3,480	292	17
Miami	371,863	35,291	35,550	66	118	2,719	4,307	6,218	16,635	5,228	259
Miami Beach	90,212	11,217	11,233	6	66	484	685	1,607	7,000	1,369	16
Miami Shores	10,649	752	755	0	0	42	31	166	445	68	3
Miami Springs	14,067	680	681	0	3	51	40	108	416	62	1
Miramar	74,624	3,632	3,652	1	27	97	292	1,201	1,656	358	20
Naples	21,520	1,010	1,010	1	6	22	45	141	760	35	0
New Port Richey	16,535	1,132	1,135	1	9	27	128	249	660	58	3
New Smyrna Beach	20,567	962	966	0	8	21	73	213	593	54	4
Niceville	11,987	182	182	0	1	4	23	23	123	8	0
North Lauderdale	33,100	1,390	1,390	0	16	63	190	253	703	165	0
North Miami	61,432	5,927	5,948	2	22	298	468	1,103	3,218	816	21
North Miami Beach	41,843	3,019	3,025	3	19	167	166	574	1,682	408	6
North Palm Beach	12,377	536	536	0	0	21	22	106	371	16	0
North Port	23,388	576	580	0	11	3	52	130	363	17	4
Oakland Park	31,768	1,893	1,893	2	18	104	130	323	1,027	289	0
Ocala	47,133	4,533	4,544	4	31	147	512	917	2,670	252	11
Ocoee	25,023	1,824	1,837	1	13	30	154	283	1,201	142	13
Oldsmar	12,219	594	595	1	3	4	21	191	344	30	1
Opa Locka	15,338	2,472	2,472	10	13	194	356	616	1,002	281	0
Orlando	190,769	22,363	22,423	15	135	1,086	2,449	3,529	12,842	2,307	60
Ormond Beach	37,242	1,246	1,246	1	6	31	75	260	804	69	0
Oviedo	26,998	827	835	0	12	4	105	174	500	32	8
Palatka	10,293	1,667	1,673	2	15	42	159	389	1,008	52	6
Palm Bay	81,471	4,286	4,299	4	50	97	588	698	2,641	208	13
Palm Beach	10,739	276	277	0	3	3	9	49	194	18	1
Palm Beach Gardens	35,966	2,087	2,099	4	6	36	61	350	1,479	151	12
Palmetto	12,897	756	758	1	8	29	107	141	415	55	2
Palm Springs	12,002	766	766	0	5	19	30	143	455	114	0
Panama City	37,361	2,503	2,512	2	33	93	160	424	1,668	123	9
Parkland	14,193	349	349	0	0	3	14	43	281	8	0
Pembroke Pines	140,988	5,079	5,091	3	14	130	203	620	3,470	639	12
Pensacola	57,713	2,932	2,943	3	41	93	382	676	1,625	112	11
Pinellas Park	46,841	2,906	2,907	2	25	65	170	549	1,913	182	1
Plantation	85,083	4,644	4,649	2	11	134	153	646	3,194	504	5
Plant City	30,690	2,657	2,661	2	6	83	182	367	1,726	291	4
Pompano Beach	80,217	4,769	4,784	1	28	205	649	681	2,692	513	15
Port Orange	47,010	1,141	1,148	0	1	4	17	123	958	38	7
Port St. Lucie	91,069	2,575	2,586	5	20	34	195	556	1,690	75	11

See footnotes at end of table.

Table 8

Offenses Known to Law Enforcement
by City 10,000 and over in Population, 2001—Continued

City by state	Population	Crime Index total	Modified Crime Index total[1]	Murder and non-negligent man-slaughter	Forcible rape	Robbery	Aggravated assault	Burglary	Larceny-theft	Motor vehicle theft	Arson[1]
FLORIDA—Continued											
Punta Gorda	14,716	425	426	0	2	2	19	107	277	18	1
Riviera Beach	30,658	3,406	3,419	10	48	188	327	789	1,469	575	13
Rockledge	20,693	849	850	0	1	9	29	171	577	62	1
Royal Palm Beach	22,081	1,276	1,277	0	14	21	78	455	624	84	1
Safety Harbor	17,649	403	405	0	5	4	33	90	253	18	2
Sanford	39,283	4,346	4,346	2	20	141	416	765	2,556	446	0
Sarasota	54,081	4,671	4,690	2	36	201	428	1,037	2,732	235	19
Sebastian	16,600	425	427	0	3	2	47	90	271	12	2
Seminole	11,172	580	582	1	5	10	34	101	398	31	2
South Daytona	13,518	609	609	1	4	9	34	171	346	44	0
South Miami	11,019	912	913	0	1	49	72	137	593	60	1
St. Augustine	11,892	924	928	0	5	31	123	126	582	57	4
St. Cloud	20,594	1,000	1,002	2	13	18	64	255	606	42	2
St. Pete Beach	10,186	539	539	0	2	3	24	120	366	24	0
St. Petersburg	254,664	20,534	20,667	21	149	1,147	3,059	3,678	10,418	2,062	133
Stuart	15,012	922	923	0	5	26	90	136	628	37	1
Sunny Isles Beach	15,712	865	867	0	1	15	31	106	588	124	2
Sunrise	88,002	4,972	4,989	3	38	137	269	690	3,353	482	17
Sweetwater	14,595	390	390	1	1	16	57	19	210	86	0
Tallahassee	154,527	12,151	12,177	7	127	428	1,247	2,265	7,227	850	26
Tamarac	57,028	1,248	1,249	2	15	51	80	253	648	199	1
Tampa	311,310	34,848	35,045	34	212	2,359	4,011	6,096	15,586	6,550	197
Tarpon Springs	21,547	749	751	1	5	30	101	152	435	25	2
Temple Terrace	21,460	873	876	1	4	38	44	178	498	110	3
Titusville	41,724	2,068	2,076	2	18	99	259	451	1,051	188	8
Venice	18,224	446	446	0	2	6	30	65	330	13	0
Vero Beach	18,164	854	859	0	5	18	53	160	591	27	5
Village of Pinecrest	19,549	800	801	0	2	12	23	138	558	67	1
Wellington	39,206	1,509	1,515	0	14	22	85	380	877	131	6
West Melbourne	10,079	417	417	0	0	9	22	64	303	19	0
Weston	50,563	598	601	3	5	10	43	88	383	66	3
West Palm Beach	84,230	9,794	9,814	18	70	465	570	1,610	5,786	1,275	20
Wilton Manors	13,026	715	716	1	1	25	44	143	441	60	1
Winter Garden	14,723	622	622	0	0	28	110	98	344	42	0
Winter Haven	27,173	1,964	1,964	2	19	75	57	412	1,205	194	0
Winter Park	24,714	1,376	1,379	0	5	42	69	136	988	136	3
Winter Springs	32,487	725	726	0	4	7	102	147	416	49	1
Zephyrhills	11,114	746	750	0	5	14	25	232	409	61	4
GEORGIA											
Acworth	13,746	271		1	0	7	34	22	182	25	
Albany	78,795	5,102		7	37	213	279	1,322	2,909	335	
Alpharetta	35,695	1,569		0	6	24	81	202	1,153	103	
Americus	17,423	1,497	1,501	0	5	42	102	249	1,043	56	4
Athens-Clarke County	102,843	6,855	6,890	8	26	156	261	1,069	4,956	379	35
Atlanta	426,511	52,195	52,323	144	367	4,341	5,956	8,731	25,721	6,935	128
Bainbridge	12,005	1,037		1	8	33	44	203	714	34	
Brunswick	15,976	1,993		1	16	56	207	380	1,220	113	
Calhoun	10,924	912		0	4	3	17	110	748	30	
Carrollton	20,322	1,544	1,545	1	9	39	174	199	1,045	77	1
Cartersville	16,309	1,186		0	3	24	58	183	768	150	
College Park	20,874	2,406		3	23	99	128	471	1,316	366	
Columbus	190,262	12,143	12,154	9	18	440	524	1,803	8,473	876	11
Conyers	10,947	1,031		1	5	34	59	126	711	95	
Cordele	11,888	1,192	1,192	1	7	28	112	146	873	25	0
Dalton	28,585	2,119		1	10	53	117	288	1,515	135	
Doraville	10,100	574	574	0	1	37	35	63	364	74	0
Douglas	10,896	1,651	1,655	3	7	19	107	243	1,190	82	4
Douglasville	20,549	2,344		1	16	46	101	217	1,811	152	
Dublin	16,239	1,054		2	4	32	43	151	764	58	
Fayetteville	11,417	569		0	0	13	15	34	475	32	

See footnotes at end of table.

Table 8

Offenses Known to Law Enforcement
by City 10,000 and over in Population, 2001—Continued

City by state	Population	Crime Index total	Modified Crime Index total[1]	Murder and non-negligent man-slaughter	Forcible rape	Robbery	Aggravated assault	Burglary	Larceny-theft	Motor vehicle theft	Arson[1]
GEORGIA—Continued											
Forest Park	21,964	1,826		1	2	129	85	354	1,026	229	
Gainesville	26,195	2,241	2,244	1	6	45	117	233	1,697	142	3
Garden City	11,561	832	855	4	5	24	112	168	438	81	23
Griffin	24,017	2,410		1	5	65	221	356	1,571	191	
Hinesville	31,125	1,979		0	11	47	130	306	1,393	92	
Kennesaw	22,198	467		0	0	7	15	51	370	24	
Kingsland	10,759	587		0	6	11	61	105	374	30	
LaGrange	26,625	2,579		2	13	57	71	320	2,029	87	
Lawrenceville	22,937	947	948	1	3	18	33	158	634	100	1
Lilburn	11,580	486		0	2	25	16	126	295	22	
Macon	99,601	10,590	10,650	18	60	275	351	2,291	6,272	1,323	60
Marietta	60,165	3,564		5	32	177	168	543	2,197	442	
Milledgeville	19,209	851		3	1	14	36	142	621	34	
Moultrie	14,734	1,591	1,597	4	4	50	171	295	978	89	6
Newnan	16,634	1,043	1,045	2	1	23	47	164	747	59	2
Peachtree City	32,342	293		0	0	1	7	22	198	65	
Powder Springs	12,782	275	275	0	1	4	9	59	173	29	0
Riverdale	12,779	1,231		0	3	26	112	151	802	137	
Rome	35,824	2,539	2,553	3	14	54	317	396	1,589	166	14
Roswell	81,248	2,122	2,127	2	12	42	95	398	1,395	178	5
Savannah	134,682	12,458	12,511	26	70	840	602	2,080	7,400	1,440	53
Smyrna	41,988	2,345		3	9	133	71	376	1,513	240	
Snellville	15,721	635		0	2	12	16	84	492	29	
St. Marys	14,093	597	607	0	1	9	37	83	440	27	10
Statesboro	23,245	1,031	1,032	1	7	25	24	200	740	34	1
Thomasville	18,600	1,619	1,622	2	6	40	43	354	1,122	52	3
Tifton	15,423	1,585	1,585	1	17	42	81	191	1,179	74	0
Union City	11,901	1,111	1,111	0	0	36	43	117	720	195	0
Valdosta	44,779	3,253		2	28	99	164	465	2,331	164	
Vidalia	10,744	741	745	0	8	17	40	143	501	32	4
Warner Robins	49,981	3,545		3	16	99	150	647	2,471	159	
Waycross	15,703	1,111		0	7	34	34	146	836	54	
Winder	10,447	961		3	15	15	39	116	696	77	
Woodstock	10,292	441		0	1	9	4	36	385	6	
HAWAII											
Honolulu	885,605	48,442	48,838	20	293	999	1,141	7,340	33,052	5,597	396
IDAHO											
Blackfoot	10,637	345	346	0	4	2	16	45	257	21	1
Boise	189,671	8,730	8,798	2	84	78	471	1,347	6,163	585	68
Caldwell	26,510	1,855	1,864	3	13	10	146	266	1,271	146	9
Coeur d'Alene	35,236	2,315	2,330	2	12	16	128	350	1,705	102	15
Garden City	10,846	677	688	0	7	8	41	108	454	59	11
Idaho Falls	51,791	1,964	1,982	1	18	6	94	288	1,458	99	18
Lewiston	31,550	1,279	1,288	2	3	3	45	254	919	53	9
Meridian	35,649	1,106	1,117	0	9	3	38	184	825	47	11
Moscow	21,736	565	568	0	7	6	4	69	468	11	3
Mountain Home	11,376	423	424	0	2	2	22	59	319	19	1
Nampa	52,951	2,766	2,783	3	40	10	175	425	1,946	167	17
Pocatello	52,542	1,787	1,804	0	21	8	135	266	1,295	62	17
Post Falls	17,608	572	574	0	5	3	22	98	416	28	2
Rexburg	17,618	309	309	0	3	0	12	28	256	10	0
Twin Falls	35,190	2,261	2,281	1	17	25	119	457	1,525	117	20
ILLINOIS[6, 7]											
Aurora	143,715			8		256	605	1,064	3,672	356	32
Chicago	2,910,709			666		18,433	25,533	25,966	97,496	27,694	1,004
Joliet	106,760			5		209	477	887	3,128	387	65

See footnotes at end of table.

Table 8

Offenses Known to Law Enforcement

by City 10,000 and over in Population, 2001—Continued

City by state	Population	Crime Index total	Modified Crime Index total[1]	Murder and non-negligent man-slaughter	Forcible rape	Robbery	Aggravated assault	Burglary	Larceny-theft	Motor vehicle theft	Arson[1]
ILLINOIS[6,7]—Continued											
Naperville	129,009			0	25	67	254	2,057	74	24	
Peoria	113,509			14	345	536	1,840	5,649	932	105	
Rockford	150,877			11	446	672	2,502	8,143	1,017	34	
Springfield	112,019			14	243	744	1,830	5,366	418	59	
INDIANA											
Bedford	13,846	599	600	0	3	1	13	80	468	34	1
Beech Grove	14,964	460	463	0	2	8	2	93	286	69	3
Bloomington	69,681	2,555	2,564	2	28	29	54	399	1,938	105	9
Brownsburg	14,602	412	414	0	3	1	56	39	297	16	2
Carmel	37,946	715	728	0	3	5	8	100	569	30	13
Chesterton	10,547	316	318	0	1	3	7	46	232	27	2
Clarksville	21,521	2,103	2,103	1	8	33	15	142	1,662	242	0
Columbus	39,279	2,499	2,505	2	15	7	58	213	2,138	66	6
Connersville	15,498	937	940	0	3	4	21	102	780	27	3
Crawfordsville	15,329	863	864	0	1	8	12	158	666	18	1
Crown Point	19,918	323	324	0	2	1	8	37	242	33	1
Dyer	13,973	332	334	0	3	8	3	50	235	33	2
East Chicago	32,597	2,863		9	14	161	810	426	1,102	341	
Elkhart	52,166	4,771	4,802	8	29	224	14	1,027	3,107	362	31
Evansville	122,267	6,667	6,734	8	52	164	483	1,164	4,327	469	67
Fort Wayne	206,886	13,291	13,402	23	92	609	348	2,013	9,016	1,190	111
Frankfort	16,756	840	842	1	7	3	30	116	637	46	2
Franklin	19,573	1,102	1,102	0	9	3	1	96	927	66	0
Gary	103,325	6,132		82	77	461	281	1,742	2,249	1,240	
Goshen	29,549	1,631	1,632	4	3	9	228	118	1,224	45	1
Greenfield	14,682	243	243	0	1	1	8	36	181	16	0
Greenwood	36,240	1,970	1,975	0	10	7	124	160	1,577	92	5
Griffith	17,432	622	627	0	7	11	20	49	472	63	5
Hammond[4]	83,516	5,886	5,966	14	43	299	406	870	3,455	799	80
Highland[4]	23,679	1,131	1,134	2	1	19	18	98	859	134	3
Huntington	17,548	433	435	0	6	2	16	60	332	17	2
Indianapolis	798,251	41,058	41,337	112	442	2,787	4,087	9,043	18,224	6,363	279
Jasper	12,168	243	244	0	0	1	5	39	190	8	1
Jeffersonville	27,516	1,482	1,489	4	17	54	27	334	841	205	7
Kokomo	46,373	3,028	3,032	5	18	43	174	458	2,224	106	4
Lafayette	56,715	2,850	2,862	0	11	64	56	474	2,108	137	12
La Porte	21,743	1,175	1,175	2	6	11	31	145	918	62	0
Lawrence	39,134	1,153	1,156	3	15	75	85	220	593	162	3
Logansport	19,795	802	805	1	4	9	14	126	573	75	3
Madison	12,072	479	479	0	3	1	19	143	285	28	0
Marion	31,496	2,258	2,270	2	17	57	185	400	1,507	90	12
Martinsville	11,764	764	764	1	1	1	19	70	642	30	0
Merrillville	30,732	1,031	1,032	0	1	26	7	71	766	160	1
Michigan City	33,085	2,674	2,724	4	14	60	43	373	1,872	308	50
Mishawaka	46,819	4,474	4,503	0	16	86	124	468	3,541	239	29
Muncie	67,810	2,921	2,930	1	24	80	184	531	1,928	173	9
Munster	21,632	552	552	0	0	7	20	49	412	64	0
New Albany	37,815	3,120	3,159	3	20	71	148	592	2,097	189	39
New Castle	17,880	1,844	1,845	0	4	5	5	338	1,424	68	1
New Haven	12,476	463	463	0	1	19	9	61	333	40	0
Noblesville	28,751	756	763	0	8	4	16	145	534	49	7
Plainfield	18,500	873	876	0	3	6	16	131	666	51	3
Portage	33,685	1,167	1,173	1	6	9	32	137	899	83	6
Schererville	24,991	684	684	1	2	5	12	42	540	82	0
Seymour	18,203	1,292	1,299	0	9	2	75	140	1,000	66	7
South Bend	108,396	9,122	9,179	21	78	487	302	1,932	5,603	699	57
Speedway[4]	12,954	341	347	0	5	31	5	71	178	51	6
Terre Haute	59,950	5,626	5,662	8	28	84	30	1,127	3,975	374	36

See footnotes at end of table.

Table 8

Offenses Known to Law Enforcement

by City 10,000 and over in Population, 2001—Continued

City by state	Population	Crime Index total	Modified Crime Index total[1]	Murder and non-negligent man-slaughter	Forcible rape	Robbery	Aggravated assault	Burglary	Larceny-theft	Motor vehicle theft	Arson[1]
INDIANA—Continued											
Valparaiso	27,583	897	907	1	5	4	43	99	708	37	10
Vincennes	18,806	1,250	1,253	2	8	14	11	263	868	84	3
Wabash	11,809	229	234	0	0	2	6	51	151	19	5
Warsaw	12,485	325	325	0	1	10	11	56	234	13	0
West Lafayette	28,940	597	599	0	11	5	22	66	479	14	2
IOWA											
Altoona	10,334	498	500	0	2	6	8	58	410	14	2
Ames	50,676	1,480	1,484	0	13	14	70	164	1,149	70	4
Ankeny	27,088	729	738	1	2	7	11	78	605	25	9
Bettendorf	31,241	828	834	1	4	6	92	94	597	34	6
Boone	12,789	319	323	0	0	0	4	53	246	16	4
Burlington	26,810	1,447	1,457	0	19	22	106	281	959	60	10
Carroll	10,095	247	250	0	0	4	3	33	182	25	3
Cedar Falls	36,106	1,143	1,146	0	13	4	93	154	845	34	3
Cedar Rapids	120,628	7,473	7,492	3	57	99	248	1,318	5,381	367	19
Clive	12,841	446	449	0	0	2	14	51	354	25	3
Coralville	15,107	676	678	1	9	13	17	78	541	17	2
Council Bluffs	58,205	5,810	5,848	2	61	80	313	690	4,005	659	38
Davenport	98,253	9,098	9,155	4	56	200	1,230	1,510	5,644	454	57
Des Moines	198,468	12,610	12,676	11	89	298	352	1,301	9,549	1,010	66
Dubuque[4]	57,624			1	12	11		546	845	73	44
Fort Dodge	25,109	2,071	2,108	0	17	23	125	415	1,388	103	37
Fort Madison	10,703	489	489	0	2	5	8	81	376	17	0
Indianola	12,984	379	382	0	2	2	3	54	306	12	3
Iowa City	62,153	1,745	1,755	0	17	37	205	245	1,176	65	10
Keokuk	11,415	758	763	0	2	1	109	124	481	41	5
Marion	26,266	358	363	0	0	0	4	89	265	0	5
Marshalltown	25,981	1,474	1,488	1	7	4	207	223	963	69	14
Mason City	29,141	1,863	1,874	1	3	8	40	329	1,441	41	11
Muscatine	22,673	1,143	1,152	1	19	10	165	247	653	48	9
Newton	15,562	587	588	0	0	0	12	104	442	29	1
Oskaloosa	10,926	445	447	0	1	7	16	59	350	12	2
Ottumwa	24,971	1,535	1,540	0	10	17	136	245	1,056	71	5
Sioux City	84,922	5,498	5,519	7	36	67	415	1,050	3,601	322	21
Spencer	11,305	309	312	0	0	3	0	53	238	15	3
Storm Lake	10,065	279	281	1	5	1	13	59	189	11	2
Waterloo	68,673	4,192	4,228	2	33	75	218	1,057	2,563	244	36
West Des Moines	46,353	1,815	1,826	0	6	23	48	189	1,458	91	11
KANSAS											
McPherson	13,802	342	344	0	6	1	10	49	260	16	2
Topeka[4]	122,660	11,530	11,548	22	84	358	611	2,046	7,632	777	18
Wichita	345,081	23,534		17	183	742	1,501	4,422	14,953	1,716	
KENTUCKY[7]											
Ashland	22,110	1,174	1,178	2	5	9	43	185	892	38	4
Bowling Green	49,586	3,393	3,396	2	35	73	206	613	2,298	166	3
Florence	23,690	1,728	1,731	0	8	43	56	188	1,342	91	3
Lexington[4]	262,045	13,032	13,090	24	120	721	718	2,516	8,155	778	58
Louisville	257,739	15,673	15,922	25	78	989	823	3,390	7,934	2,434	249
Madisonville[4]	19,421	892	893	0	5	10	45	163	634	35	1
Murray	15,038	468	473	0	3	3	9	106	317	30	5
Owensboro	54,385	2,706	2,718	1	26	49	53	561	1,924	92	12
Paducah	26,462	2,146	2,156	3	18	41	174	350	1,411	149	10
Radcliff	22,090	825	828	0	16	23	31	168	560	27	3
Richmond	27,312	1,743	1,748	0	19	36	169	255	1,170	94	5

See footnotes at end of table.

Table 8

Offenses Known to Law Enforcement

by City 10,000 and over in Population, 2001—Continued

City by state	Population	Crime Index total	Modified Crime Index total[1]	Murder and non-negligent man-slaughter	Forcible rape	Robbery	Aggravated assault	Burglary	Larceny-theft	Motor vehicle theft	Arson[1]
LOUISIANA											
Alexandria[4]	46,305	4,957	4,958	5	26	183	434	1,105	3,047	157	1
Baton Rouge	227,637	20,149	20,318	46	62	1,071	1,368	3,716	12,128	1,758	169
Bogalusa	13,354	1,208	1,216	0	16	23	135	318	662	54	8
Bossier City	56,416	4,194	4,230	3	20	84	394	640	2,777	276	36
Crowley	14,214	658	658	0	0	2	59	152	430	15	0
Eunice	11,490	1,042	1,045	0	5	19	242	131	621	24	3
Gretna	17,409	1,199	1,207	1	11	47	112	168	707	153	8
Hammond	17,625	3,938	3,938	7	18	86	367	1,352	1,966	142	0
Houma	32,367	2,212	2,227	4	15	70	343	307	1,359	114	15
Jennings	10,977	682	687	2	7	12	90	125	427	19	5
Kenner	70,461	3,861	3,861	3	17	107	228	531	2,484	491	0
Lafayette	110,170	8,167	8,208	5	74	195	771	1,332	5,318	472	41
Lake Charles	71,700	4,586	4,613	4	38	157	401	1,721	1,900	365	27
Minden	13,017	378	380	1	1	8	31	82	238	17	2
Monroe	53,065	6,272	6,330	2	37	126	701	1,120	3,984	302	58
Natchitoches	17,851	1,069	1,069	1	9	13	151	253	615	27	0
New Iberia[4]	32,597	2,179	2,186	3	5	36	215	384	1,369	167	7
New Orleans	484,289	36,057		213	209	2,778	2,677	5,262	16,187	8,731	
Pineville	13,818	576		0	4	4	3	244	299	22	
Ruston	20,530	1,356	1,359	1	7	39	140	235	886	48	3
Shreveport	199,986	15,616	15,746	31	111	534	1,253	3,368	9,200	1,119	130
Slidell	25,675	2,093	2,094	0	16	43	135	278	1,470	151	1
Thibodaux	14,420	572	574	0	5	27	60	109	363	8	2
West Monroe	13,239	1,270	1,271	0	6	26	82	156	934	66	1
Westwego	10,754	430	435	2	3	13	38	63	277	34	5
Zachary	11,266	513	516	0	7	5	39	73	351	38	3
MAINE											
Auburn	23,417	1,121	1,129	1	14	10	36	203	806	51	8
Augusta	18,731	1,088	1,102	0	22	5	16	201	804	40	14
Bangor	31,763	2,010	2,017	1	15	20	22	245	1,642	65	7
Biddeford	21,135	722	744	0	5	14	32	111	533	27	22
Brunswick	21,367	545	548	0	8	2	12	66	438	19	3
Falmouth	10,405	133	133	0	2	1	0	12	108	10	0
Gorham	14,271	260	261	0	4	3	5	56	181	11	1
Kennebunk	10,573	165	165	0	3	1	0	33	115	13	0
Lewiston	36,019	1,755	1,761	1	23	28	23	332	1,263	85	6
Portland	64,841	3,016	3,041	1	39	68	92	473	2,233	110	25
Saco	16,977	616	618	0	0	1	3	138	461	13	2
Sanford	20,998	609	612	0	3	7	7	94	465	33	3
Scarborough	17,126	259	259	0	3	3	5	48	190	10	0
South Portland	23,539	988	988	1	8	7	5	76	876	15	0
Waterville	15,749	736	737	0	4	7	3	117	582	23	1
Westbrook	16,291	487	492	0	10	6	19	101	329	22	5
Windham	15,041	389	391	0	1	5	11	78	275	19	2
York	12,972	267	269	0	3	0	6	39	210	9	2
MARYLAND											
Aberdeen	14,048	927	932	1	7	41	63	113	658	44	5
Annapolis	36,370	2,404	2,458	4	11	154	315	333	1,456	131	54
Baltimore	660,826	63,488	63,914	256	296	5,747	8,500	10,899	29,615	8,175	426
Bel Air	10,230	650	656	0	0	17	78	85	446	24	6
Cambridge	11,073	837	842	1	5	18	139	122	522	30	5
Cumberland	21,838	1,574	1,581	1	15	20	162	243	1,085	48	7
Easton	11,882	635	639	0	4	16	26	82	500	7	4
Elkton	12,070	1,072	1,083	0	8	11	105	119	759	70	11
Frederick	53,551	2,943	2,954	1	19	115	575	315	1,787	131	11
Greenbelt	21,775	1,703	1,703	0	9	76	74	178	944	422	0
Hagerstown	37,232	1,919	1,960	1	6	70	140	346	1,209	147	41
Havre de Grace	11,499	487	489	0	2	22	63	78	300	22	2

See footnotes at end of table.

Table 8

Offenses Known to Law Enforcement
by City 10,000 and over in Population, 2001—Continued

City by state	Population	Crime Index total	Modified Crime Index total[1]	Murder and non-negligent man-slaughter	Forcible rape	Robbery	Aggravated assault	Burglary	Larceny-theft	Motor vehicle theft	Arson[1]
MARYLAND—Continued											
Hyattsville	14,952	1,024	1,024	0	2	77	31	160	591	163	0
Laurel	20,256	1,282	1,282	0	7	52	59	132	845	187	0
Ocean Pines	10,652	78	78	0	0	1	4	20	49	4	0
Salisbury	24,096	3,090	3,103	1	28	139	406	550	1,815	151	13
Takoma Park	17,556	1,013	1,013	1	4	70	28	150	562	198	0
Westminster	16,980	809	823	0	2	16	42	122	598	29	14
MASSACHUSETTS[2]											
Abington[8]	14,674			1	2	6		116	148	44	5
Acton	20,428	299	306	0	1	1	3	56	226	12	7
Acushnet	10,209	191	194	0	3	0	28	34	118	8	3
Agawam	28,278	719	727	0	9	3	70	224	340	73	8
Amesbury	16,528	343	348	0	9	2	83	47	182	20	5
Amherst	35,040	612		0	8	14	62	139	346	43	
Andover	31,396	407	409	0	1	6	13	50	317	20	2
Ashland	14,744	138	141	0	3	3	20	32	76	4	3
Attleboro	42,268	1,145		0	9	28	86	178	712	132	
Barnstable	48,048	1,726	1,740	0	18	34	223	407	919	125	14
Bedford	12,655	46	46	0	0	1	0	4	41	0	0
Belchertown	13,030	161	163	0	1	5	27	37	68	23	2
Bellingham	15,387	309	309	0	2	8	10	51	224	14	0
Belmont	24,309	188	188	0	0	0	19	42	121	6	0
Beverly	40,052	746	747	1	10	7	73	113	496	46	1
Billerica	39,166	414	417	0	1	4	4	47	317	41	3
Boston	591,944	37,385		65	361	2,523	4,412	4,222	17,608	8,194	
Bourne	18,810	799	804	0	6	7	192	232	311	51	5
Braintree	33,989	1,299	1,306	0	6	8	67	102	971	145	7
Brewster	10,142	104	104	0	1	0	6	23	71	3	0
Bridgewater	25,305	416	417	0	4	2	15	81	288	26	1
Brockton	94,750	5,242		5	58	204	788	743	2,158	1,286	
Brookline	57,379	1,190		0	12	49	90	234	670	135	
Burlington	22,985	875		0	0	8	15	42	750	60	
Cambridge	101,837	4,416		1	15	181	273	688	2,740	518	
Carver	11,216	144	145	0	1	2	12	38	78	13	1
Charlton[8]	11,317			0	3	1		41	38	4	1
Chelmsford	34,019	620	621	0	4	4	25	65	495	27	1
Chelsea[8]	35,247			1	13	111		166	447	437	8
Chicopee	54,913	2,321	2,339	1	25	40	435	819	727	274	18
Clinton	13,499	127	129	0	1	3	18	12	84	9	2
Concord	17,074	190	192	0	0	0	12	18	150	10	2
Danvers	25,332	950	951	1	4	14	49	78	738	66	1
Dartmouth	30,812	1,196	1,202	0	8	8	81	239	750	110	6
Dedham	23,576	490	490	1	2	11	5	46	362	63	0
Dennis	16,049	537	552	0	3	0	68	145	301	20	15
Dracut	28,698	368	368	0	2	3	16	70	224	53	0
Duxbury	14,316	70		0	0	0	2	24	44	0	
East Bridgewater	13,036	103	104	0	0	1	8	17	70	7	1
Easthampton	16,070	152	153	0	8	3	25	26	72	18	1
East Longmeadow	14,167	451	455	0	1	6	24	52	336	32	4
Easton	22,405	215	215	0	0	5	6	62	120	22	0
Everett	38,218	1,204	1,206	1	6	52	181	156	553	255	2
Fairhaven	16,236	673	675	1	7	4	103	184	345	29	2
Fall River	92,375	3,891		3	43	192	398	624	2,090	541	
Falmouth	32,815	961	963	1	6	4	97	222	578	53	2
Fitchburg	39,288	1,771		0	29	51	142	422	969	158	
Foxborough	16,323	124	124	0	1	0	0	37	71	15	0
Framingham	67,228	1,546		1	18	29	119	299	863	217	
Franklin	29,701	138	138	0	0	0	20	15	101	2	0
Gardner	20,869	315	315	0	1	2	29	67	194	22	0
Gloucester	30,417	766		0	9	9	46	155	499	48	
Grafton	14,965	111	111	0	3	3	19	26	53	7	0

See footnotes at end of table.

Table 8

Offenses Known to Law Enforcement
by City 10,000 and over in Population, 2001—Continued

City by state	Population	Crime Index total	Modified Crime Index total[1]	Murder and non-negligent man-slaughter	Forcible rape	Robbery	Aggravated assault	Burglary	Larceny-theft	Motor vehicle theft	Arson[1]
MASSACHUSETTS[2]—Continued											
Harwich	12,445	281	281	0	3	0	33	63	177	5	0
Haverhill	59,250	1,906		0	34	28	235	729	666	214	
Holbrook	10,836	245		0	3	5	8	63	150	16	
Holden[8]	15,695			0	3	0		26	54	2	5
Holliston	13,867	55	56	0	0	0	5	11	35	4	1
Holyoke	40,028	3,509	3,528	5	38	125	424	608	2,065	244	19
Hudson	18,199	252	254	0	4	1	5	29	205	8	2
Hull	11,103	159	162	0	2	2	52	34	44	25	3
Ipswich	13,049	178	178	0	0	0	5	22	142	9	0
Kingston	11,836	274	274	0	0	3	2	14	235	20	0
Lawrence	72,386	3,853		4	48	145	395	504	1,017	1,740	
Leicester	10,521	113	113	0	3	1	6	14	84	5	0
Leominster	41,500	1,402	1,405	1	8	14	64	215	990	110	3
Lexington[8]	30,499			0	0	1		36	267	7	6
Longmeadow	15,707	188	188	0	0	0	3	17	160	8	0
Lowell	105,668	4,510		4	37	122	687	650	2,052	958	
Ludlow	21,310	375	378	0	1	2	59	63	217	33	3
Lynn[8]	89,472			1	16	161		617	1,681	1,278	
Lynnfield[8]	11,597			1	1	4		50	109	17	0
Mansfield	22,521	447	450	0	5	5	116	58	229	34	3
Marblehead	20,474	285	285	0	1	1	13	25	226	19	0
Marlborough	36,427	570	570	0	3	9	32	80	417	29	0
Marshfield	24,440	274	276	0	2	3	15	25	210	19	2
Mashpee[8]	13,008			1	1	1		36	91	5	0
Maynard	10,483	95	95	0	0	0	5	18	70	2	0
Medfield	12,331	70	70	0	1	0	1	20	47	1	0
Medford	56,030	1,414		0	8	39	50	159	1,006	152	
Medway	12,507	71	71	0	0	0	1	14	56	0	0
Melrose	27,263	325		0	2	6	5	49	224	39	
Methuen	43,997	1,244		0	10	14	73	164	739	244	
Middleboro	20,036	515	523	0	3	4	25	129	293	61	8
Millbury	12,845	173	173	1	8	4	32	46	63	19	0
Milton	26,186	219		0	1	9	4	47	138	20	
Natick	32,323	864		0	8	6	29	71	696	54	
Needham	29,049	296	297	0	1	3	4	45	237	6	1
New Bedford	94,216	3,220		5	63	197	491	831	1,072	561	
Newton	84,228	1,111		0	11	21	44	155	830	50	
Norfolk	10,510	46	46	0	2	0	2	11	29	2	0
North Adams	14,751	592	598	2	11	4	63	148	344	20	6
Northampton	29,116	712	712	0	6	12	19	83	552	40	0
North Andover	27,331	202	203	0	0	3	11	49	129	10	1
North Attleboro	27,272	909	913	0	1	0	12	70	738	88	4
Northborough	14,080	136	139	0	0	1	7	26	95	7	3
Northbridge	13,245	243	246	0	4	3	29	59	129	19	3
North Reading	13,903	59	59	0	0	2	4	10	34	9	0
Norton	18,122	184	184	0	1	0	4	49	117	13	0
Norwood	28,723	513	513	1	4	8	12	56	372	60	0
Oxford	13,416	247	250	0	1	2	28	39	150	27	3
Palmer	12,556	359	364	0	5	2	55	90	187	20	5
Peabody	48,358	1,304	1,309	0	7	16	97	305	742	137	5
Pembroke	17,008	291	297	0	2	1	35	37	198	18	6
Pepperell	11,195	134		0	0	0	8	33	90	3	
Pittsfield	46,011	1,238		0	20	32	25	189	867	105	
Plymouth	51,947	1,066	1,073	0	7	9	115	193	677	65	7
Quincy	88,442	2,432		0	31	60	152	444	1,480	265	
Randolph	31,110	750	751	0	8	12	22	109	497	102	1
Raynham	11,795	533		0	1	5	46	40	383	58	
Reading	23,821	172	172	0	0	1	8	27	129	7	0
Rehoboth	10,220	159	159	1	2	0	9	73	68	6	0
Revere	47,508	1,755		1	11	42	214	282	874	331	
Rockland	17,754	315		0	8	5	95	38	117	52	
Salem	40,599	1,284		0	9	23	64	120	878	190	

See footnotes at end of table.

Table 8

Offenses Known to Law Enforcement
by City 10,000 and over in Population, 2001—Continued

City by state	Population	Crime Index total	Modified Crime Index total[1]	Murder and non-negligent man-slaughter	Forcible rape	Robbery	Aggravated assault	Burglary	Larceny-theft	Motor vehicle theft	Arson[1]
MASSACHUSETTS[2]—Continued											
Sandwich	20,232	362	363	1	2	2	45	34	270	8	1
Saugus[8]	26,202			2	10	35		250	861	159	5
Scituate	17,948	151	152	0	0	1	13	29	103	5	1
Seekonk	13,489	712	714	0	5	3	20	73	569	42	2
Sharon	17,491	128		0	0	2	8	24	88	6	
Shrewsbury	31,791	509	511	0	1	4	13	64	401	26	2
Somerset	18,321	446	450	0	2	2	69	47	308	18	4
Somerville	77,847	2,208		0	7	72	157	428	1,063	481	
Southbridge	17,296	583	593	0	15	9	84	171	272	32	10
South Hadley	17,278	320	322	0	9	7	40	70	173	21	2
Spencer	11,747	159	160	0	5	0	27	22	94	11	1
Springfield	152,806	12,798	12,954	10	99	503	2,665	2,697	5,087	1,737	156
Stoneham	22,325	350		0	5	4	19	50	235	37	
Stoughton[8]	27,278			0	12	10		103	256	69	1
Swampscott	14,481	307	307	0	1	6	3	21	256	20	0
Swansea[8]	15,977			0	7	4		64	246	39	6
Taunton	56,242	1,850		3	7	54	230	358	1,019	179	
Tewksbury	28,988	573	575	0	5	8	38	72	390	60	2
Tyngsboro	11,134	264	266	0	5	2	33	49	151	24	2
Uxbridge[8]	11,209			0	4	0		33	71	7	0
Walpole	22,933	288	288	0	1	2	8	23	235	19	0
Waltham	59,508	1,247		2	11	19	35	184	872	124	
Wareham[8]	20,432			0	8	6		194	512	57	7
Wayland	13,162	126	126	0	1	1	3	20	99	2	0
Webster	16,493	525	525	0	9	10	60	83	334	29	0
Wellesley	26,740	334	334	0	1	5	26	62	230	10	0
Westborough	18,083	399	402	0	1	1	52	80	240	25	3
Westfield	40,263	954	969	0	13	8	115	268	476	74	15
Westford	20,853	137	137	0	0	2	2	19	110	4	0
Westport	14,250	331	331	0	2	1	59	84	156	29	0
West Springfield	28,032	1,330	1,338	0	2	35	81	88	1,012	112	8
Westwood	14,184	148	148	0	0	2	0	23	114	9	0
Wilbraham	13,537	357	360	0	3	1	19	50	246	38	3
Wilmington	21,465	467		0	9	8	68	51	291	40	
Winchester	20,909	277	279	0	0	1	3	26	232	15	2
Woburn	37,435	1,019	1,028	1	7	21	93	109	688	100	9
Worcester	173,469	8,212	8,284	7	117	363	935	1,152	4,421	1,217	72
Wrentham	10,604	73	73	0	0	0	7	2	64	0	0
Yarmouth	24,925	635		0	2	4	53	143	406	27	
MICHIGAN											
Adrian	21,688	1,090	1,096	0	13	16	80	140	778	63	6
Allen Park	29,531	684	690	0	6	15	21	125	433	84	6
Alpena	11,364	436	442	1	4	1	23	48	343	16	6
Ann Arbor	114,625	3,880	3,898	1	25	125	201	739	2,626	163	18
Auburn Hills	19,942	1,427	1,433	0	4	16	38	129	1,141	99	6
Battle Creek	53,645	5,239	5,283	6	78	158	629	926	3,111	331	44
Bay City	37,011	1,653	1,665	0	35	34	151	244	1,075	114	12
Benton Harbor	11,241	980	999	6	12	18	254	290	313	87	19
Benton Township	16,490	1,763	1,769	0	24	30	106	308	1,142	153	6
Berkley	15,613	244	244	1	0	7	4	31	185	16	0
Beverly Hills	10,492	147	147	0	2	2	3	7	125	8	0
Birmingham	19,393	473	474	0	1	5	9	65	355	38	1
Blackman Township	22,920	653	657	0	10	10	39	76	471	47	4
Bloomfield Township	43,250	791	802	0	1	10	20	129	585	46	11
Brownstown Township	23,110	733	742	0	4	11	58	142	433	85	9
Buena Vista Township	10,372	810	822	1	14	11	67	200	440	77	12
Burton	30,468	2,130	2,138	0	6	29	97	394	1,416	188	8
Cadillac	10,053	541	546	0	15	4	23	59	408	32	5
Canton Township	76,768	1,810	1,832	2	11	25	49	240	1,318	165	22
Chesterfield Township	37,602	760	762	0	1	6	17	107	602	27	2

See footnotes at end of table.

Table 8

Offenses Known to Law Enforcement
by City 10,000 and over in Population, 2001—Continued

City by state	Population	Crime Index total	Modified Crime Index total[1]	Murder and non-negligent man-slaughter	Forcible rape	Robbery	Aggravated assault	Burglary	Larceny-theft	Motor vehicle theft	Arson[1]
MICHIGAN—Continued											
Clawson	12,799	137	138	0	1	2	4	20	94	16	1
Clinton Township	96,152	2,893	2,916	2	59	70	637	402	1,395	328	23
Coldwater	12,764	572	576	1	11	3	28	73	437	19	4
Davison Township	17,815	515	523	0	5	6	13	132	323	36	8
Dearborn	98,290	5,883	5,897	4	24	161	787	534	3,197	1,176	14
Dearborn Heights	58,571	1,626	1,633	0	11	37	76	279	911	312	7
Detroit	956,283	90,193	91,827	395	652	7,096	12,804	15,096	29,613	24,537	1,634
Dewitt Township	12,207	370	372	1	3	2	21	119	195	29	2
East Grand Rapids	10,821	145	145	0	1	0	1	48	91	4	0
East Lansing	46,770	1,773	1,790	0	15	29	157	287	1,232	53	17
Eastpointe	34,257	1,340	1,353	0	10	48	89	167	768	258	13
Emmett Township	12,042	743	749	0	11	10	64	108	515	35	6
Farmington	10,478	241	241	0	0	4	5	29	191	12	0
Farmington Hills	82,544	2,112	2,135	1	15	26	150	381	1,375	164	23
Fenton	10,638	331	335	0	5	1	9	33	254	29	4
Ferndale	22,221	877	881	1	15	34	32	146	515	134	4
Flint[4]	125,601	10,962	11,100	41	95	508	1,364	2,695	4,291	1,968	138
Flint Township	33,869	2,896	2,905	1	22	78	135	314	2,001	345	9
Flushing Township	10,284	128	129	0	2	1	4	40	78	3	1
Garden City	30,205	687	689	0	10	9	49	117	400	102	2
Genesee Township	24,252	1,099	1,107	1	15	26	115	291	568	83	8
Grand Blanc Township	29,984	905	910	0	7	5	42	200	557	94	5
Grand Haven	11,227	451	459	0	4	1	19	60	351	16	8
Grand Rapids	198,842	12,026	12,092	12	53	552	1,431	2,582	6,719	677	66
Grandville	16,349	959	962	0	12	4	16	108	800	19	3
Green Oak Township	15,700	235	238	0	2	2	14	46	150	21	3
Grosse Ile Township	10,951	81	82	0	1	0	0	8	70	2	1
Grosse Pointe Park	12,509	329	329	0	1	8	3	24	231	62	0
Hamburg Township	20,736	192	193	0	1	1	4	32	141	13	1
Hazel Park	19,063	857	858	0	23	31	64	116	462	161	1
Holland	35,233	1,399	1,405	0	26	23	99	150	1,047	54	6
Huron Township	13,809	336	340	0	4	4	14	79	197	38	4
Inkster	30,274	1,676	1,711	9	26	71	300	436	532	302	35
Ionia	10,625	340	341	0	9	1	18	47	252	13	1
Jackson	37,595	3,354	3,389	0	48	105	372	453	2,179	197	35
Kalamazoo	77,552	6,295	6,373	4	102	200	601	1,366	3,539	483	78
Kalamazoo Township	21,789	1,041	1,048	1	9	14	59	170	695	93	7
Kentwood	45,493	1,791	1,798	0	26	30	68	345	1,257	65	7
Lansing	119,756	7,212	7,280	8	178	227	940	994	4,382	483	68
Leoni Township	13,530	520	521	0	4	2	23	133	325	33	1
Lincoln Park	40,219	1,910	1,924	2	8	48	79	350	1,150	273	14
Lincoln Township	14,026	317	319	0	5	2	6	55	242	7	2
Livonia	101,075	3,113	3,136	1	21	71	112	429	2,202	277	23
Madison Heights	31,265	1,342	1,348	1	6	38	32	173	851	241	6
Marquette	19,765	451	453	0	6	3	22	33	361	26	2
Melvindale	10,792	537	537	0	2	7	25	102	306	95	0
Meridian Township	39,322	1,355	1,370	0	12	7	31	178	1,083	44	15
Midland	41,905	973	980	4	21	6	43	103	766	30	7
Milford	15,351	190	195	0	4	1	6	28	143	8	5
Monroe	22,192	748	758	0	14	7	53	100	520	54	10
Mount Clemens	17,403	858	866	0	19	33	89	128	490	99	8
Mount Morris Township	23,850	1,548	1,558	7	28	34	123	462	632	262	10
Mount Pleasant	26,083	459	462	0	11	2	23	74	332	17	3
Mundy Township	12,255	593	594	0	5	4	4	98	451	31	1
Muskegon	40,316	3,407	3,429	1	60	82	288	561	2,180	235	22
Muskegon Heights	12,112	1,408	1,427	2	29	36	208	168	796	169	19
Muskegon Township	17,830	1,097	1,101	1	9	7	26	151	866	37	4
Niles	12,268	786	791	2	10	11	38	122	557	46	5
Northville Township	21,147	233	233	0	3	1	3	32	179	15	0
Norton Shores	22,646	1,098	1,100	0	7	7	35	59	940	50	2
Novi	47,636	1,495	1,503	0	12	9	29	153	1,223	69	8
Oak Park	29,950	936	937	0	5	28	35	196	528	144	1

See footnotes at end of table.

Table 8

Offenses Known to Law Enforcement
by City 10,000 and over in Population, 2001—Continued

City by state	Population	Crime Index total	Modified Crime Index total[1]	Murder and non-negligent man-slaughter	Forcible rape	Robbery	Aggravated assault	Burglary	Larceny-theft	Motor vehicle theft	Arson[1]
MICHIGAN—Continued											
Owosso	15,796	595	602	0	12	5	32	83	435	28	7
Pittsfield Township	30,326	1,067	1,070	0	5	20	43	143	744	112	3
Plymouth Township	27,944	505	505	1	3	5	16	46	382	52	0
Pontiac	66,687	4,522	4,555	4	90	187	846	1,089	1,760	546	33
Portage	45,134	2,241	2,249	1	15	22	55	266	1,806	76	8
Port Huron	32,508	1,557	1,565	0	30	30	140	230	1,036	91	8
Redford Township	51,894	2,006	2,019	1	16	74	98	370	1,076	371	13
Riverview	13,342	312	313	0	4	2	6	33	225	42	1
Rochester	10,522	210	210	0	0	1	4	27	165	13	0
Romulus	23,100	1,316	1,324	2	15	18	75	247	710	249	8
Roseville	48,383	2,464	2,486	0	20	32	100	182	1,784	346	22
Royal Oak	60,379	1,681	1,688	0	23	49	57	270	1,116	166	7
Saginaw	62,125	4,379	4,489	5	75	190	980	957	1,769	403	110
Saginaw Township	39,866	1,396	1,406	0	7	20	60	150	1,091	68	10
Sault Ste. Marie	16,629	553	557	1	16	2	26	57	427	24	4
Shelby Township	65,502	938	941	1	10	13	52	112	653	97	3
Southfield	78,709	5,303	5,318	5	33	150	817	713	2,757	828	15
Southgate	30,295	1,391	1,404	0	6	26	69	155	967	168	13
South Lyon	10,089	141	142	0	4	0	14	8	114	1	1
St. Clair Shores	63,428	1,582	1,599	2	3	37	130	237	994	179	17
Sterling Heights	125,127	3,552	3,562	0	20	37	203	387	2,631	274	10
St. Joseph Township	10,095	275	275	0	3	3	11	63	175	20	0
Sturgis	11,344	439	441	0	10	1	15	79	323	11	2
Summit Township	21,647	444	446	0	3	3	35	80	276	47	2
Sumpter Township	11,918	335	340	0	10	0	12	103	174	36	5
Taylor	66,215	3,590	3,628	2	46	73	223	717	2,004	525	38
Thomas Township	11,940	336	338	0	1	1	16	44	266	8	2
Traverse City	14,609	751	755	0	9	1	26	82	606	27	4
Trenton	19,687	353	353	0	5	0	17	57	233	41	0
Troy	81,386	2,284	2,302	0	10	16	64	326	1,663	205	18
Van Buren Township	23,683	645	645	0	0	4	17	81	463	80	0
Walker	21,957	1,047	1,048	0	7	10	29	114	836	51	1
Warren	138,976	5,633	5,691	5	63	191	559	769	2,584	1,462	58
Waterford Township	73,535	2,262	2,274	0	10	45	79	372	1,553	203	12
Wayne	19,151	963	986	0	4	23	81	175	495	185	23
West Bloomfield Township	65,202	848	855	0	8	9	7	98	708	18	7
Westland	87,058	3,112	3,146	3	40	59	186	501	1,774	549	34
White Lake Township	28,368	581	583	0	14	1	18	69	432	47	2
Wixom	13,333	452	453	0	3	1	11	55	348	34	1
Woodhaven	12,596	449	450	1	2	4	12	27	352	51	1
Wyandotte	28,159	818	821	0	4	7	23	169	540	75	3
Wyoming	69,734	2,657	2,674	2	62	52	216	605	1,487	233	17
Ypsilanti	22,480	1,462	1,478	4	19	70	140	281	778	170	16
MINNESOTA											
Albert Lea	18,553	511	513	2	1	3	24	74	379	28	2
Andover	26,873	626	632	0	6	1	30	84	469	36	6
Anoka	18,270	808	812	0	22	7	5	94	630	50	4
Apple Valley	46,016	1,377	1,391	0	5	7	31	161	1,123	50	14
Austin	23,564	1,206	1,219	0	19	9	60	139	906	73	13
Bemidji	12,045	1,116	1,119	0	7	8	19	85	920	77	3
Bloomington	86,086	4,723	4,734	2	28	86	89	363	3,773	382	11
Brooklyn Center	29,485	2,194	2,222	1	33	49	52	191	1,590	278	28
Brooklyn Park	68,111	3,389	3,407	1	37	95	161	500	2,238	357	18
Buffalo	10,205	450	453	0	6	0	9	49	372	14	3
Burnsville	60,867	1,218	1,219	0	14	9	22	109	1,010	54	1
Champlin	22,431	524	527	0	3	2	15	65	417	22	3
Chanhassen	20,539	368	370	0	3	5	10	42	296	12	2
Chaska	17,636	357	363	1	15	2	18	31	265	25	6
Cloquet	11,321	419	424	0	4	2	25	40	322	26	5
Cottage Grove	30,910	764	775	0	11	5	16	85	616	31	11

See footnotes at end of table.

Table 8

Offenses Known to Law Enforcement
by City 10,000 and over in Population, 2001—Continued

City by state	Population	Crime Index total	Modified Crime Index total[1]	Murder and non-negligent man-slaughter	Forcible rape	Robbery	Aggravated assault	Burglary	Larceny-theft	Motor vehicle theft	Arson[1]
MINNESOTA—Continued											
Crystal	22,942	869	876	0	2	17	21	117	656	56	7
Duluth	87,851	5,370	5,384	4	55	79	180	646	4,029	377	14
Eagan	64,239	1,890	1,905	0	10	13	29	205	1,540	93	15
East Bethel	11,058	356	362	0	7	0	9	66	258	16	6
Eden Prairie	55,490	1,499	1,505	1	20	10	28	190	1,182	68	6
Edina	47,934	1,282	1,292	1	4	15	19	154	1,044	45	10
Elk River	16,624	703	706	0	5	2	18	74	585	19	3
Fairmont	11,006	479	481	0	7	1	16	75	360	20	2
Farmington	12,498	251	251	0	4	3	8	21	202	13	0
Fergus Falls	13,616	589	600	0	7	3	19	80	455	25	11
Golden Valley	20,499	695	700	0	14	19	19	103	494	46	5
Ham Lake	12,846	411	418	0	2	0	7	98	267	37	7
Hibbing	17,254	259	259	0	3	2	17	60	165	12	0
Hopkins	17,329	497	502	0	7	19	20	49	350	52	5
Hutchinson	13,220	694	702	0	16	2	29	76	562	9	8
Inver Grove Heights	30,070	1,033	1,053	1	21	5	39	130	751	86	20
Lakeville	43,591	888	899	1	3	3	18	106	722	35	11
Maple Grove	50,906	1,230	1,234	0	9	4	44	166	949	58	4
Mendota Heights	11,557	155	156	0	1	1	3	17	133	0	1
Minneapolis	386,726	26,820	27,079	43	399	1,943	1,716	4,092	14,548	4,079	259
Minnetonka	51,852	1,249	1,257	0	13	18	25	204	939	50	8
Moorhead	32,522	1,186	1,191	0	10	4	39	109	962	62	5
Mounds View	12,875	592	597	0	6	9	25	45	478	29	5
New Brighton	22,444	683	691	0	3	7	11	89	536	37	8
New Hope	21,097	600	604	1	8	13	16	69	454	39	4
New Ulm	13,740	346	349	0	0	0	12	47	273	14	3
Northfield	17,331	550	555	0	7	1	12	61	440	29	5
North Mankato	11,925	286	294	0	8	2	0	6	260	10	8
North St. Paul	12,057	432	435	1	3	1	12	37	335	43	3
Oakdale	26,939	1,203	1,220	0	18	9	39	115	956	66	17
Orono	11,837	270	270	0	3	0	3	33	220	11	0
Owatonna	22,675	853	863	0	2	6	35	123	667	20	10
Plymouth	66,601	1,640	1,658	0	10	14	56	279	1,206	75	18
Prior Lake	16,088	591	595	0	9	3	30	60	458	31	4
Red Wing	16,289	817	818	1	10	11	26	114	620	35	1
Richfield	34,809	1,398	1,417	1	21	49	58	178	957	134	19
Robbinsdale	14,275	638	639	1	4	18	19	91	436	69	1
Rochester	86,727	3,472	3,504	3	38	66	147	545	2,482	191	32
Rosemount	14,776	526	526	0	6	3	10	59	425	23	0
Roseville	34,052	1,987	1,991	0	9	23	22	166	1,626	141	4
Sauk Rapids	10,323	294	298	0	6	2	8	15	256	7	4
Savage	21,342	556	560	0	5	5	12	105	401	28	4
Shakopee	20,789	740	743	1	5	9	25	55	602	43	3
Shoreview	26,202	473	489	0	6	1	12	52	386	16	16
South Lake Minnetonka	12,199	240	240	0	2	2	7	37	179	13	0
South St. Paul	20,384	711	715	0	6	4	27	83	524	67	4
St. Cloud	59,742	2,897	2,915	2	58	29	111	309	2,208	180	18
Stillwater	15,306	443	445	0	2	5	19	65	328	24	2
St. Louis Park	44,600	1,586	1,610	0	15	15	36	187	1,247	86	24
St. Paul	290,234	19,046	19,282	9	221	680	1,326	3,009	11,457	2,344	236
Vadnais Heights	13,209	351	362	0	1	6	13	34	258	39	11
West St. Paul	19,613	927	928	0	9	25	23	82	711	77	1
White Bear Lake	24,586	814	818	0	2	8	13	137	585	69	4
Willmar	18,548	731	736	1	12	2	44	99	543	30	5
Winona	27,360	906	908	0	3	6	27	131	692	47	2
Woodbury	46,962	1,216	1,222	0	10	4	15	139	998	50	6
Worthington	11,404	428	428	1	6	1	27	81	298	14	0
MISSISSIPPI											
Biloxi	50,882	4,592	4,603	5	25	120	136	627	3,411	268	11
Brandon	16,513	327	329	1	2	0	5	53	261	5	2

See footnotes at end of table.

Table 8

Offenses Known to Law Enforcement
by City 10,000 and over in Population, 2001—Continued

City by state	Population	Crime Index total	Modified Crime Index total[1]	Murder and non-negligent man-slaughter	Forcible rape	Robbery	Aggravated assault	Burglary	Larceny-theft	Motor vehicle theft	Arson[1]
MISSISSIPPI—Continued											
Clarksdale	20,742	1,413	1,422	5	17	95	69	519	577	131	9
Columbus	26,066	1,781	1,784	2	11	25	26	297	1,331	89	3
Corinth	14,120	647	648	0	3	20	38	141	414	31	1
Greenville	41,829	4,569	4,611	6	49	162	155	1,202	2,809	186	42
Greenwood	18,512	1,739	1,750	4	11	40	34	464	1,120	66	11
Grenada	14,949	985	988	5	4	18	50	229	626	53	3
Gulfport	71,461	5,436	5,463	10	37	147	52	1,129	3,656	405	27
Hattiesburg	44,989	2,977	2,985	6	20	72	48	644	2,019	168	8
Horn Lake	14,165	830	833	0	6	13	9	68	660	74	3
Indianola	12,123	943	953	1	9	29	50	202	619	33	10
Jackson	185,122	18,586	18,682	50	218	1,044	654	4,683	8,972	2,965	96
Laurel	18,479	2,012	2,017	2	18	48	141	273	1,457	73	5
Long Beach	17,401	680	681	0	3	8	2	139	507	21	1
Madison	14,761	174	174	0	1	2	5	23	141	2	0
McComb	13,400	722	723	0	1	24	46	120	474	57	1
Meridian	40,156	1,957	1,985	3	32	112	49	588	1,037	136	28
Moss Point	15,926	1,829	1,847	3	20	56	229	690	686	145	18
Natchez	18,551	1,275	1,280	1	4	30	29	190	993	28	5
Ocean Springs	17,306	709	712	0	6	10	7	120	541	25	3
Olive Branch	21,153	781	781	0	0	6	48	162	449	116	0
Oxford	11,811	325	325	0	0	6	12	79	209	19	0
Pascagoula	26,323	2,605	2,613	3	22	79	77	489	1,712	223	8
Pearl	22,064	818	820	1	23	16	67	289	381	41	2
Picayune	10,585	735	741	1	8	19	13	121	525	48	6
Ridgeland	20,268	1,039	1,040	3	5	28	22	132	777	72	1
Southaven[4]	29,113	2,095	2,100	1	22	47	22	144	1,677	182	5
Tupelo	34,372	2,563	2,569	1	17	68	91	765	1,465	156	6
Vicksburg	26,531	1,884	1,893	6	31	41	215	323	1,074	194	9
West Point	12,202	533	533	1	11	20	22	184	295	0	0
MISSOURI											
Arnold	20,088	1,207	1,208	0	4	4	162	61	940	36	1
Bellefontaine Neighbors	11,340	669	672	0	2	14	19	80	482	72	3
Belton	21,864	904	911	0	7	18	38	126	658	57	7
Blue Springs	48,376	2,194	2,201	1	13	44	41	279	1,690	126	7
Cape Girardeau	35,567	2,536	2,537	0	9	33	18	279	2,160	37	1
Clayton	12,904	487		0	1	11	9	55	387	24	
Columbia	85,052	3,897	3,929	4	16	140	279	455	2,822	181	32
Crestwood	11,936	887	888	0	0	7	10	30	818	22	1
Creve Coeur	16,602	375	377	0	0	5	18	42	282	28	2
Excelsior Springs[4]	10,914			0	4	6		113	412	29	6
Farmington	14,010	714	716	0	4	1	128	46	526	9	2
Florissant	50,808	1,320	1,321	1	6	20	28	174	945	146	1
Fulton	12,203	316		0	7	3	9	40	245	12	
Gladstone	26,528	950	961	0	2	12	37	130	669	100	11
Hannibal	17,866	989	1,003	0	14	14	117	216	587	41	14
Independence	113,986	8,889	8,942	6	27	144	491	1,157	6,220	844	53
Jackson	12,021	352	354	0	1	4	25	65	248	9	2
Jefferson City	39,880	1,658	1,660	2	26	37	238	198	1,068	89	2
Jennings	15,564	1,416	1,428	2	10	49	98	260	799	198	12
Joplin	45,785	4,014	4,037	3	36	70	104	709	2,811	281	23
Kansas City	444,267	49,959	50,452	103	319	2,367	4,292	7,454	27,126	8,298	493
Kennett	11,329	423		0	1	4	34	59	313	12	
Kirksville	17,093	634	637	0	2	4	56	81	471	20	3
Kirkwood	27,492	691	697	0	4	16	16	77	537	41	6
Lake St. Louis	10,232	154	158	0	1	0	11	24	112	6	4
Lebanon	12,230	989	993	0	4	6	104	138	708	29	4
Lee's Summit	71,136	1,995	2,003	1	19	25	22	310	1,492	126	8
Manchester	19,279	210		0	2	1	10	21	158	18	
Marshall	12,510	303	304	0	0	2	3	61	228	9	1
Maryland Heights	25,915	1,201	1,203	0	4	8	32	126	971	60	2

See footnotes at end of table.

Table 8

Offenses Known to Law Enforcement
by City 10,000 and over in Population, 2001—Continued

City by state	Population	Crime Index total	Modified Crime Index total[1]	Murder and non-negligent man-slaughter	Forcible rape	Robbery	Aggravated assault	Burglary	Larceny-theft	Motor vehicle theft	Arson[1]
MISSOURI—Continued											
Maryville	10,646	151	152	0	0	0	2	15	132	2	1
Mexico	11,390	371		0	0	3	16	78	259	15	
Moberly	12,019	770	775	0	4	5	41	117	589	14	5
Neosho	10,570	657	660	0	6	3	33	104	471	40	3
Poplar Bluff	16,754	839	849	0	3	9	37	119	631	40	10
Raytown[4]	30,575	1,221	1,223	2	5	34	40	258	757	125	2
Rolla	16,468	981		1	6	9	28	136	765	36	
Sedalia	20,464	1,755		1	5	19	144	262	1,262	62	
Sikeston	17,097	887	895	2	12	29	94	153	534	63	8
Springfield	152,515	14,141	14,234	10	60	262	657	2,182	10,066	904	93
St. Ann	13,691	1,345		1	5	19	91	72	1,075	82	
St. Charles	60,693	1,920	1,937	1	19	22	133	296	1,333	116	17
St. Joseph	74,446	4,367	4,384	2	18	46	108	726	3,257	210	17
St. Louis	350,336	52,635	53,346	148	120	3,140	4,256	8,128	28,000	8,843	711
Town and Country	10,961	296	301	0	0	3	9	25	257	2	5
University City	37,659	2,211	2,221	2	11	72	58	327	1,542	199	10
Warrensburg	16,441	732	736	0	4	10	30	108	556	24	4
Webster Groves	23,373	323	325	0	0	15	9	52	229	18	2
West Plains	10,933	683	685	0	5	2	50	134	469	23	2
MONTANA[2]											
Billings	90,070	5,088		9	14	38	119	508	4,155	245	
Bozeman	27,577	1,533		2	19	3	62	155	1,220	72	
Great Falls	56,831	3,906		2	12	31	195	341	3,189	136	
Kalispell	14,258	1,312		1	0	1	40	100	1,126	44	
NEBRASKA											
Fremont	25,203	869	870	0	1	2	9	79	739	39	1
Grand Island	42,989	3,037	3,039	0	18	16	96	365	2,397	145	2
Hastings	24,092	1,149	1,154	0	2	8	11	168	933	27	5
Kearney	27,463	1,219	1,226	0	6	2	49	168	929	65	7
La Vista	11,712	441	443	0	0	2	4	33	370	32	2
Lexington	10,023	430	432	0	7	2	15	52	335	19	2
Lincoln	225,841	15,041	15,067	6	88	154	1,054	1,970	11,194	575	26
Omaha	390,456	29,507	29,762	25	157	868	1,658	3,107	19,382	4,310	255
Papillion	16,382	417	417	0	4	0	3	37	345	28	0
Scottsbluff	14,749	1,002	1,005	0	3	5	30	157	778	29	3
South Sioux City	11,939	374	375	1	2	1	10	31	303	26	1
NEVADA											
Boulder City	15,773	390	399	0	4	3	60	162	135	26	9
Elko	17,609	717	724	0	5	8	31	139	495	39	7
Henderson	184,844	5,728	5,759	9	99	195	220	1,434	2,863	908	31
Las Vegas Metropolitan Police Department	1,117,763	50,570	50,838	133	447	3,667	3,302	10,083	22,394	10,544	268
North Las Vegas	121,719	6,817	6,857	20	50	433	850	1,336	2,824	1,304	40
Reno[4]	190,218	10,989	11,031	6	98	407	704	1,435	7,399	940	42
Sparks	69,926	3,709		3	52	88	194	598	2,485	289	
NEW HAMPSHIRE											
Amherst	10,973	221	223	0	1	0	0	20	195	5	2
Bedford	18,620	290	291	0	5	3	5	37	233	7	1
Berlin	10,527	174	178	0	5	1	12	20	124	12	4
Claremont	13,400	352	353	1	9	3	16	36	277	10	1
Derry	34,665	732	766	0	19	13	18	145	454	83	34
Exeter	14,324	205	209	0	0	1	5	26	165	8	4
Hampton	15,220	579	584	0	25	9	26	64	415	40	5
Hanover	11,055	115	118	2	4	0	0	14	90	5	3

See footnotes at end of table.

Table 8

Offenses Known to Law Enforcement
by City 10,000 and over in Population, 2001—Continued

City by state	Population	Crime Index total	Modified Crime Index total[1]	Murder and non-negligent man-slaughter	Forcible rape	Robbery	Aggravated assault	Burglary	Larceny-theft	Motor vehicle theft	Arson[1]
NEW HAMPSHIRE—Continued											
Hudson	23,362	363	370	0	5	3	11	56	258	30	7
Keene	22,990	760	777	0	14	7	26	104	580	29	17
Lebanon	12,806	538	544	0	4	1	9	51	449	24	6
Londonderry	23,676	257	265	0	1	3	11	38	175	29	8
Manchester	109,032	3,520	3,573	0	53	118	86	597	2,356	310	53
Milford	13,791	211	217	0	9	1	11	37	139	14	6
Portsmouth	21,177	813	830	1	13	13	23	81	624	58	17
Rochester	29,000	877	887	0	28	6	20	97	675	51	10
Somersworth	11,694	466	476	0	3	5	8	45	348	57	10
Windham	10,912	147	149	0	0	0	4	41	94	8	2
NEW JERSEY											
Aberdeen Township	17,599	370	372	0	0	6	13	65	245	41	2
Asbury Park	17,071	1,431	1,438	5	14	184	195	299	568	166	7
Atlantic City	40,854	6,777	6,806	5	33	255	450	688	5,168	178	29
Barnegat Township	15,397	163	164	0	3	2	13	23	121	1	1
Bayonne	62,357	1,343	1,349	3	2	74	121	222	750	171	6
Beachwood	10,461	282	284	0	0	4	6	61	205	6	2
Belleville	36,227	1,119	1,121	0	8	71	46	239	505	250	2
Bellmawr	11,356	222	222	0	0	3	11	38	154	16	0
Bergenfield	26,466	349	351	0	2	14	13	47	250	23	2
Berkeley Heights Township	13,519	83	83	0	0	1	1	22	50	9	0
Berkeley Township	40,324	730	738	0	3	11	46	160	481	29	8
Bernards Township	24,780	290	295	0	0	2	13	65	180	30	5
Bloomfield	48,080	2,060	2,060	0	8	100	55	327	986	584	0
Bound Brook	10,240	273	273	0	3	7	8	70	173	12	0
Branchburg Township	14,687	183	183	1	1	1	1	31	132	16	0
Brick Township	76,753	1,437	1,442	0	0	21	73	235	1,055	53	5
Bridgeton	22,961	1,429	1,441	2	8	117	240	319	663	80	12
Bridgewater Township	43,298	657	659	0	0	6	9	77	513	52	2
Brigantine	12,699	346	347	0	1	0	28	59	248	10	1
Burlington Township	20,463	572	579	0	6	18	12	49	450	37	7
Camden	80,570	6,885	7,139	25	58	715	909	1,374	2,542	1,262	254
Carteret	20,881	477	481	2	0	25	41	92	268	49	4
Cedar Grove Township	12,402	239	241	0	1	1	15	37	178	7	2
Chatham Township	10,170	81	83	0	0	0	3	8	67	3	2
Cherry Hill Township	70,548	2,372	2,376	0	6	61	61	208	1,847	189	4
Cinnaminson Township	14,717	301	303	0	1	10	7	50	196	37	2
Clark Township	14,719	181	181	0	0	0	3	27	143	8	0
Cliffside Park	23,199	265	267	0	4	7	20	39	166	29	2
Clifton	79,327	2,346	2,350	1	7	95	85	422	1,328	408	4
Clinton Township	13,065	153	154	0	0	0	8	25	116	4	1
Collingswood	14,445	367	369	0	4	14	13	62	237	37	2
Colts Neck Township	12,434	137	138	0	0	0	12	25	97	3	1
Cranford Township	22,766	446	448	1	3	5	20	57	329	31	2
Delran Township	15,665	385	385	0	2	13	13	35	289	33	0
Denville Township	15,956	282	282	0	0	5	7	42	214	14	0
Deptford Township	26,986	1,779	1,786	1	0	41	77	444	1,103	113	7
Dover	18,339	537	539	0	3	17	21	96	334	66	2
Dover Township	90,453	2,775	2,796	0	13	58	110	450	2,033	111	21
Dumont	17,649	192	192	0	0	1	19	16	152	4	0
East Brunswick Township	47,145	964	967	0	1	8	20	90	803	42	3
East Hanover Township	11,488	297	300	0	0	1	6	22	238	30	3
East Orange	70,406	5,324	5,401	13	32	684	683	936	1,803	1,173	77
East Windsor Township	25,127	475	476	0	2	9	21	58	349	36	1
Eatontown	14,125	569	569	0	3	6	10	43	478	29	0
Edison Township	98,501	2,625	2,647	0	11	69	213	341	1,584	407	22
Egg Harbor Township	30,982	1,300	1,319	0	4	21	64	207	930	74	19
Elizabeth	121,571	7,164	7,175	5	16	548	279	912	3,403	2,001	11
Elmwood Park	19,083	463	463	0	1	14	27	76	283	62	0
Englewood	26,421	786	789	0	4	33	46	201	429	73	3

See footnotes at end of table.

Table 8

Offenses Known to Law Enforcement
by City 10,000 and over in Population, 2001—Continued

City by state	Population	Crime Index total	Modified Crime Index total[1]	Murder and non-negligent man-slaughter	Forcible rape	Robbery	Aggravated assault	Burglary	Larceny-theft	Motor vehicle theft	Arson[1]
NEW JERSEY—Continued											
Evesham Township	42,627	758	769	0	9	6	15	144	553	31	11
Ewing Township	36,004	1,199	1,201	1	10	54	55	198	692	189	2
Fair Lawn	31,900	555	556	0	5	19	24	109	368	30	1
Fairview	13,365	151	151	0	0	4	11	20	64	52	0
Florence Township	10,836	196	199	1	2	4	7	32	137	13	3
Fort Lee	35,756	704	706	1	3	12	7	103	520	58	2
Franklin Lakes	10,509	118	119	0	1	0	3	14	98	2	1
Franklin Township (Gloucester County)	15,595	386	386	1	0	11	18	113	215	28	0
Franklin Township (Somerset County)	51,327	1,153	1,166	1	9	46	35	326	591	145	13
Freehold	11,067	429	431	0	1	27	23	50	305	23	2
Freehold Township	31,800	1,071	1,073	0	3	18	28	77	920	25	2
Galloway Township	31,469	735	740	0	3	14	33	139	513	33	5
Garfield	30,034	747	750	1	1	21	26	135	453	110	3
Glassboro	19,227	795	801	0	9	23	55	106	554	48	6
Glen Rock	11,642	91	91	0	0	1	3	11	73	3	0
Gloucester City	11,580	350	352	0	4	10	11	36	256	33	2
Gloucester Township	64,886	2,073	2,083	1	14	48	107	249	1,473	181	10
Guttenberg	10,897	217	223	1	0	22	21	61	85	27	6
Hackensack	43,034	1,447	1,447	2	0	42	101	109	1,056	137	0
Hackettstown	10,490	195	197	0	0	3	6	30	146	10	2
Haddonfield	11,756	186	186	0	0	3	7	27	141	8	0
Haddon Township	14,773	420	423	0	0	9	13	58	317	23	3
Hamilton Township (Atlantic County)	20,670	924	937	0	8	12	61	140	678	25	13
Hamilton Township (Mercer County)	87,836	2,588	2,594	1	7	97	62	548	1,554	319	6
Hammonton	12,709	278	283	0	1	6	22	63	167	19	5
Hanover Township	13,005	166	166	0	0	1	10	46	94	15	0
Harrison	14,544	545	548	0	4	21	38	105	248	129	3
Hasbrouck Heights	11,759	243	244	0	0	8	0	41	161	33	1
Hawthorne	18,370	251	252	0	0	5	1	47	181	17	1
Hazlet Township	21,556	366	367	0	0	4	12	45	276	29	1
Highland Park	14,116	240	243	0	1	7	5	31	187	9	3
Hillsborough Township	36,939	362	363	0	6	3	10	79	249	15	1
Hillsdale	10,171	82	82	0	0	1	0	23	57	1	0
Hillside Township	21,928	1,042	1,046	1	7	81	34	174	443	302	4
Hoboken	38,898	1,637	1,638	0	7	37	115	336	882	260	1
Holmdel Township	15,912	285	289	0	0	1	7	37	230	10	4
Hopatcong	16,020	152	152	0	1	2	8	15	119	7	0
Hopewell Township	16,239	178	179	0	0	0	14	27	129	8	1
Howell Township	49,310	708	713	1	0	12	44	118	508	25	5
Irvington	61,201	5,163	5,213	13	42	728	674	1,101	1,241	1,364	50
Jackson Township	43,173	713	718	0	2	4	37	139	492	39	5
Jefferson Township	19,881	249	250	0	0	1	6	68	155	19	1
Jersey City	242,055	12,527	12,575	25	89	1,301	1,438	2,350	4,911	2,413	48
Keansburg	10,821	468	472	0	13	12	33	128	263	19	4
Kearny	40,850	1,395	1,404	0	3	38	48	229	867	210	9
Lacey Township	25,557	568	571	1	0	3	17	84	456	7	3
Lakewood Township	60,855	1,824	1,842	3	15	86	100	384	1,090	146	18
Lawrence Township	29,402	1,398	1,406	1	4	40	32	257	880	184	8
Lincoln Park	11,021	146	147	0	1	1	1	46	86	11	1
Linden	39,722	1,790	1,795	2	1	75	55	180	1,066	411	5
Lindenwold	17,559	828	836	0	5	36	75	260	383	69	8
Little Egg Harbor Township	16,078	455	456	0	4	2	23	67	345	14	1
Little Falls Township	10,945	434	439	0	2	1	23	64	262	82	5
Little Ferry	10,890	209	210	1	1	4	12	25	128	38	1
Livingston Township	27,619	756	757	0	3	8	17	69	554	105	1
Lodi	24,171	689	690	1	0	27	38	112	428	83	1
Long Branch	31,601	1,158	1,159	1	9	59	87	266	685	51	1
Lower Township	23,136	612	614	1	5	2	28	92	444	40	2

See footnotes at end of table.

Table 8

Offenses Known to Law Enforcement
by City 10,000 and over in Population, 2001—Continued

City by state	Population	Crime Index total	Modified Crime Index total[1]	Murder and non-negligent man-slaughter	Forcible rape	Robbery	Aggravated assault	Burglary	Larceny-theft	Motor vehicle theft	Arson[1]
NEW JERSEY—Continued											
Lumberton Township	10,548	359	377	1	5	10	13	71	244	15	18
Lyndhurst Township	19,544	387	389	0	1	11	5	68	254	48	2
Madison	16,668	226	226	0	0	2	4	26	180	14	0
Mahwah Township	24,262	285	285	0	0	1	5	33	224	22	0
Manalapan Township	33,701	324	326	0	3	8	16	56	224	17	2
Manchester Township	39,252	423	431	0	0	3	28	70	302	20	8
Mantua Township	14,335	301	301	0	3	5	14	34	224	21	0
Manville	10,429	226	227	1	0	1	5	19	178	22	1
Maple Shade Township	19,238	591	599	0	7	16	46	107	346	69	8
Maplewood Township	24,067	794	795	0	2	70	30	130	360	202	1
Marlboro Township	36,701	444	453	0	3	7	24	123	264	23	9
Medford Township	22,438	365	368	0	2	6	14	63	275	5	3
Metuchen	12,947	277	278	0	0	4	8	50	199	16	1
Middlesex	13,831	190	190	0	2	5	7	24	138	14	0
Middle Township	16,542	681	690	0	10	7	30	109	487	38	9
Middletown Township	66,879	987	1,011	0	1	5	38	126	769	48	24
Millburn Township	19,930	856	856	0	0	13	5	82	667	89	0
Millville	27,071	1,362	1,375	1	20	62	98	279	837	65	13
Monroe Township (Gloucester County)	29,208	782	788	0	5	10	33	163	508	63	6
Monroe Township (Middlesex County)	28,232	218	220	0	0	1	24	39	143	11	2
Montclair	39,302	1,511	1,513	1	7	66	81	363	789	204	2
Montgomery Township	17,627	209	216	0	0	0	4	46	148	11	7
Montville Township	21,013	229	230	0	1	3	6	39	156	24	1
Moorestown Township	19,175	523	523	0	3	19	12	63	407	19	0
Morristown	18,698	852	855	1	9	66	42	90	578	66	3
Morris Township	21,978	243	245	0	3	2	23	39	165	11	2
Mount Holly Township	10,817	590	594	0	2	37	69	81	380	21	4
Mount Laurel Township	40,556	861	869	1	6	23	13	184	588	46	8
Mount Olive Township	24,394	252	252	0	4	1	14	44	174	15	0
Neptune Township	32,212	1,331	1,339	0	2	32	62	251	882	102	8
Newark	275,823	18,748	19,163	90	91	1,837	1,819	2,552	6,324	6,035	415
New Brunswick	48,978	2,945	2,960	2	10	198	118	545	1,744	328	15
New Milford	16,537	147	148	0	0	6	14	22	98	7	1
New Providence	12,006	142	142	0	0	2	3	22	112	3	0
North Arlington	15,307	239	239	0	0	8	6	38	170	17	0
North Bergen Township	58,576	1,691	1,692	1	7	82	72	241	955	333	1
North Brunswick Township	36,589	1,050	1,052	0	1	25	36	156	727	105	2
North Plainfield	21,279	694	696	0	3	27	6	134	457	67	2
Nutley Township	27,590	491	495	0	0	10	32	151	244	54	4
Oakland	12,570	137	140	1	0	1	5	23	103	4	3
Ocean City	15,506	992	992	0	1	16	19	162	784	10	0
Ocean Township (Monmouth County)	27,184	602	603	0	1	6	14	80	475	26	1
Old Bridge Township	60,960	1,063	1,075	0	5	24	53	206	645	130	12
Orange	33,142	2,700	2,707	4	10	327	162	549	876	772	7
Palisades Park	17,215	254	254	0	0	5	8	88	123	30	0
Paramus	25,951	2,486	2,491	0	2	42	54	127	1,995	266	5
Parsippany-Troy Hills Township	51,071	901	905	0	4	16	42	240	486	113	4
Passaic	68,426	3,671	3,683	8	8	469	525	617	1,374	670	12
Paterson	150,465	8,004	8,014	16	15	673	598	1,964	3,059	1,679	10
Pemberton Township	28,930	758	769	0	11	31	36	166	458	56	11
Pennsauken Township	36,035	1,656	1,683	0	7	100	107	311	849	282	27
Pennsville Township	13,304	350	355	0	1	5	7	54	271	12	5
Pequannock Township	14,004	303	303	0	0	3	4	31	232	33	0
Perth Amboy	47,697	1,569	1,573	3	3	75	146	335	786	221	4
Phillipsburg	15,292	264	264	2	3	4	11	69	159	16	0
Pine Hill	10,971	297	303	1	2	13	28	61	161	31	6
Piscataway Township	50,902	1,227	1,240	2	8	22	54	257	792	92	13
Plainfield	48,227	2,618	2,646	9	8	308	218	570	1,115	390	28
Plainsboro Township	20,383	270	281	0	0	3	10	45	195	17	11

See footnotes at end of table.

Table 8

Offenses Known to Law Enforcement
by City 10,000 and over in Population, 2001—Continued

City by state	Population	Crime Index total	Modified Crime Index total[1]	Murder and non-negligent man-slaughter	Forcible rape	Robbery	Aggravated assault	Burglary	Larceny-theft	Motor vehicle theft	Arson[1]
NEW JERSEY—Continued											
Pleasantville	19,170	929	937	7	8	75	78	173	504	84	8
Point Pleasant	19,467	351	351	0	2	1	15	81	246	6	0
Pompton Lakes	10,729	187	188	0	0	0	5	23	147	12	1
Princeton	14,321	659	660	0	0	4	17	118	515	5	1
Princeton Township	16,160	229	232	0	1	1	6	46	167	8	3
Rahway	26,721	979	984	1	2	27	29	156	633	131	5
Ramsey	14,471	194	195	0	0	6	8	16	147	17	1
Randolph Township	25,054	313	315	0	1	2	7	21	269	13	2
Raritan Township	19,974	170	170	0	2	2	11	33	116	6	0
Readington Township	15,935	151	153	0	0	0	9	41	93	8	2
Red Bank	11,943	433	434	1	5	23	11	29	348	16	1
Ridgefield	10,920	131	131	0	0	2	17	23	69	20	0
Ridgefield Park	12,980	224	225	0	1	6	8	39	137	33	1
Ridgewood	25,144	280	281	0	0	6	7	69	184	14	1
Ringwood	12,499	90	92	1	0	1	3	24	58	3	2
River Edge	11,037	119	120	0	0	2	1	29	82	5	1
Rockaway Township	23,121	629	634	0	4	3	21	49	520	32	5
Roselle	21,451	710	710	1	0	39	31	175	336	128	0
Roselle Park	13,392	267	268	0	1	6	10	67	150	33	1
Roxbury Township	24,082	387	387	0	0	10	17	34	309	17	0
Rutherford	18,261	290	291	0	3	3	6	77	164	37	1
Saddle Brook Township	13,265	351	352	0	0	11	7	50	241	42	1
Sayreville	40,713	754	769	0	10	13	51	169	423	88	15
Scotch Plains Township	22,921	353	353	0	2	6	3	67	246	29	0
Secaucus	16,064	748	748	1	0	7	16	26	497	201	0
Somers Point	11,711	335	335	0	3	7	25	50	240	10	0
Somerville	12,526	345	345	0	1	11	15	30	268	20	0
South Brunswick Township	38,048	659	662	0	0	5	20	147	429	58	3
South Orange	17,105	928	932	3	0	46	33	140	399	307	4
South Plainfield	21,992	542	547	1	6	21	17	69	388	40	5
South River	15,450	182	183	0	0	10	31	42	82	17	1
Sparta Township	18,231	112	112	0	0	0	3	9	98	2	0
Springfield	14,549	404	404	0	0	7	3	61	246	87	0
Stafford Township	22,720	640	642	0	3	2	17	80	510	28	2
Summit	21,307	480	480	0	1	5	8	62	375	29	0
Teaneck Township	39,587	871	883	0	3	27	61	216	495	69	12
Tenafly	13,921	172	174	0	0	1	4	57	104	6	2
Tinton Falls	15,178	312	313	0	1	4	11	30	248	18	1
Trenton	86,114	6,964	7,000	13	72	716	697	1,521	2,723	1,222	36
Union City	67,647	2,434	2,438	3	1	206	116	496	1,038	574	4
Union Township	54,858	2,421	2,430	0	11	141	80	367	1,360	462	9
Ventnor City	13,018	326	326	0	3	4	10	78	216	15	0
Vernon Township	24,892	438	439	0	2	2	11	44	359	20	1
Verona	13,646	209	210	0	1	1	8	35	143	21	1
Vineland	56,740	3,392	3,403	2	7	205	254	732	2,017	175	11
Voorhees Township	28,360	1,036	1,055	0	5	27	41	114	797	52	19
Wallington	11,679	348	348	0	2	8	17	51	229	41	0
Wall Township	25,471	479	480	0	1	8	23	109	328	10	1
Wanaque	10,352	118	118	1	0	0	6	15	88	8	0
Warren Township	14,378	154	154	0	0	1	2	33	113	5	0
Washington Township (Gloucester County)	47,509	1,346	1,358	0	11	27	53	337	810	108	12
Washington Township (Morris County)	17,739	155	157	0	0	1	3	15	129	7	2
Washington Township (Warren County)	10,361	178	178	2	0	4	10	26	123	13	0
Waterford Township	10,581	278	280	0	7	6	16	44	187	18	2
Wayne Township	54,519	1,968	1,977	1	7	30	32	214	1,293	391	9
Weehawken Township	13,613	541	543	0	1	15	15	88	321	101	2
West Caldwell Township	11,327	172	173	0	0	2	5	36	124	5	1
West Deptford Township	19,529	591	597	0	2	7	18	117	407	40	6
Westfield	29,891	356	357	0	0	3	2	64	276	11	1

See footnotes at end of table.

Table 8

Offenses Known to Law Enforcement
by City 10,000 and over in Population, 2001—Continued

City by state	Population	Crime Index total	Modified Crime Index total[1]	Murder and non-negligent man-slaughter	Forcible rape	Robbery	Aggravated assault	Burglary	Larceny-theft	Motor vehicle theft	Arson[1]
NEW JERSEY—Continued											
West Milford Township	26,630	423	427	0	0	7	23	89	290	14	4
West New York	46,149	1,451	1,456	0	2	74	88	284	752	251	5
West Orange	45,317	1,465	1,467	0	0	48	38	305	692	382	2
West Paterson	11,079	306	306	0	2	6	4	50	212	32	0
West Windsor Township	22,089	630	631	0	2	7	12	70	461	78	1
Westwood	11,091	188	188	0	0	0	12	26	145	5	0
Willingboro Township	33,283	960	966	1	5	58	30	173	618	75	6
Winslow Township	34,899	853	868	0	1	29	101	176	502	44	15
Woodbridge Township	98,013	3,424	3,456	0	9	62	251	509	2,129	464	32
Woodbury	10,393	624	626	0	0	15	29	75	465	40	2
Wyckoff Township	16,645	119	120	0	0	1	7	22	89	0	1
NEW MEXICO											
Alamogordo	35,780	1,204	1,207	1	14	7	84	113	960	25	3
Albuquerque	451,098	39,541	39,720	34	219	1,610	3,396	6,585	23,535	4,162	179
Clovis	32,848	2,092	2,110	3	17	20	138	536	1,322	56	18
Deming	14,194	932	942	0	3	14	87	176	607	45	10
Farmington	38,054	2,082	2,088	3	50	46	368	372	1,142	101	6
Gallup	20,321	3,057	3,060	5	13	107	312	325	2,160	135	3
Hobbs	28,816	1,646	1,647	2	21	31	242	276	1,020	54	1
Las Cruces	74,679	5,740	5,748	0	65	79	268	928	4,208	192	8
Las Vegas	14,646	1,168	1,174	1	21	16	201	252	630	47	6
Los Alamos	18,445	163	164	0	0	2	4	38	109	10	1
Los Lunas	10,090	857	857	1	9	8	279	121	377	62	0
Portales	11,193	549	552	0	2	4	59	149	318	17	3
Rio Rancho	52,052	1,444	1,456	0	8	15	155	285	893	88	12
Roswell	45,544	3,084	3,098	2	39	36	338	609	1,974	86	14
Silver City	10,604	675	679	1	3	7	31	171	446	16	4
Sunland Park	13,383	134	134	0	0	1	15	36	69	13	0
NEW YORK											
Albany	95,834	7,282	7,314	6	57	432	818	1,563	3,860	546	32
Amherst Town	111,169	2,010	2,015	0	3	31	50	171	1,645	110	5
Amsterdam	18,389	323	327	1	2	3	44	81	189	3	4
Auburn	28,627	1,209		0	13	11	49	191	920	25	
Beacon	13,833	383	386	0	0	14	47	53	234	35	3
Bedford Town	18,166	240	240	0	1	1	11	30	174	23	0
Bethlehem Town	31,362	589	589	0	2	4	16	120	440	7	0
Binghamton	47,467	2,335	2,346	1	30	59	98	258	1,827	62	11
Blooming Grove Town	11,521	171	174	0	0	1	2	40	117	11	3
Brighton Town	35,653	1,130	1,130	0	4	24	4	123	932	43	0
Buffalo	293,187	19,894	20,338	64	229	1,600	1,816	3,965	9,669	2,551	444
Camillus Town and Village	23,195	382	383	0	0	5	9	46	309	13	1
Canandaigua	11,285	268	269	0	2	3	4	36	218	5	1
Carmel Town	33,067	338	339	0	0	4	14	63	245	12	1
Cheektowaga Town	83,705	3,101	3,113	0	12	55	64	432	2,273	265	12
Cicero Town	26,158	681	685	0	1	8	20	117	506	29	4
Clarkstown Town	77,810	2,315		1	5	37	91	209	1,852	120	
Clay Town	53,912	427	430	0	0	10	0	87	322	8	3
Cohoes	15,550	286	289	0	6	7	34	65	136	38	3
Colonie Town	75,487	3,170	3,178	0	11	41	34	423	2,553	108	8
Corning	10,862	392	394	1	4	1	23	54	300	9	2
Cortland	18,774	673	675	0	5	7	26	96	528	11	2
Depew Village	16,660	403	403	0	1	0	9	58	285	50	0
Dewitt Town	20,931	878	878	0	3	12	9	129	681	44	0
Dobbs Ferry Village	10,642	148	148	0	0	1	18	25	96	8	0
Dunkirk	13,155	453	461	0	2	19	43	52	325	12	8
East Aurora-Aurora Town	14,022	242	243	0	1	0	7	26	202	6	1
Eastchester Town	18,599	308	308	0	0	6	9	19	260	14	0
East Fishkill Town	25,636	338	339	0	0	1	5	48	275	9	1

See footnotes at end of table.

Table 8

Offenses Known to Law Enforcement
by City 10,000 and over in Population, 2001—Continued

City by state	Population	Crime Index total	Modified Crime Index total[1]	Murder and non-negligent man-slaughter	Forcible rape	Robbery	Aggravated assault	Burglary	Larceny-theft	Motor vehicle theft	Arson[1]
NEW YORK—Continued											
East Hampton Town	17,493	599	599	0	2	4	10	179	389	15	0
Fallsburg Town	11,353	196	198	1	2	5	13	62	107	6	2
Fishkill Town	18,557	339	340	0	1	2	17	19	277	23	1
Floral Park Village	15,996	117	118	1	1	12	2	26	66	9	1
Fredonia Village	10,726	316	316	0	2	4	8	31	263	8	0
Freeport Village	43,864	1,210	1,217	1	7	75	134	94	656	243	7
Garden City Village	21,712	348		0	1	2	6	33	295	11	
Gates Town	29,329	1,118	1,120	0	3	14	6	110	897	88	2
Geddes Town	10,915	228	229	1	0	3	0	39	171	14	1
Geneva	13,642	425	427	0	0	8	22	35	350	10	2
Glens Falls	14,380	635	637	0	3	8	30	98	483	13	2
Glenville Town	20,263	272	273	0	0	3	3	29	228	9	1
Gloversville	15,441	621		0	6	6	30	91	471	17	
Greece Town	94,314	2,432	2,444	3	14	52	17	260	1,902	184	12
Greenburgh Town	41,905	1,290	1,290	0	5	46	37	139	976	87	0
Guilderland Town	31,008	1,208	1,212	1	2	13	13	101	1,057	21	4
Hamburg Town	43,505	1,292	1,298	1	5	14	36	178	1,027	31	6
Hempstead Village	56,658	1,397	1,403	13	17	150	197	184	451	385	6
Hyde Park Town	20,889	244	244	1	3	2	3	28	199	8	0
Irondequoit Town	52,450	2,321	2,327	1	3	39	14	235	1,918	111	6
Kenmore Village	16,456	271	274	0	3	10	5	31	207	15	3
Kent Town	14,035	196	196	0	2	0	4	33	149	8	0
Kingston	23,499	772	772	2	7	22	34	92	563	52	0
Lackawanna	19,099	590	593	0	7	14	46	87	345	91	3
Lancaster Town	21,681	292	292	1	0	1	2	27	241	20	0
Lancaster Village	11,209	145	145	0	1	1	4	38	91	10	0
Long Beach	35,527	705	705	0	2	51	67	106	393	86	0
Lynbrook Village	19,948	201	205	0	1	5	8	40	115	32	4
Mamaroneck Village	18,787	400	400	0	0	9	11	30	308	42	0
Manlius Town	24,379	436	436	0	4	2	5	80	332	13	0
Massena Village	11,230	165	165	0	2	2	6	14	134	7	0
Middletown	25,435	765	770	0	13	28	41	108	542	33	5
Mount Kisco Village	10,001	308	308	0	1	4	31	29	226	17	0
Mount Pleasant Town	26,221	333	336	0	2	1	35	40	222	33	3
Mount Vernon	68,507	2,311		9	13	196	267	443	993	390	
Newburgh	28,311	1,999		7	23	136	293	428	1,041	71	
Newburgh Town	27,619	1,213	1,216	1	9	19	29	105	1,011	39	3
New Hartford Town and Village	21,211	983	988	0	0	5	6	52	914	6	5
New Rochelle	72,315	1,836	1,844	0	6	129	93	208	1,231	169	8
New Windsor Town	22,908	594	594	2	6	6	39	92	432	17	0
New York[9]	8,023,018	266,587		3,472	1,530	28,202	37,893	31,563	133,938	29,989	
Niagara Falls	55,695	3,599	3,633	4	26	168	291	795	1,947	368	34
North Castle Town	10,869	128	128	0	0	4	0	17	103	4	0
North Tonawanda	33,323	744	754	0	7	14	24	132	550	17	10
Ogdensburg	12,387	530	530	0	3	2	6	67	439	13	0
Ogden Town	18,526	368	370	1	1	3	14	56	273	20	2
Olean	15,375	415	416	0	9	4	1	49	345	.7	1
Oneida	11,007	510	510	0	6	7	7	64	420	6	0
Oneonta City	13,316	364		0	7	6	34	96	200	21	
Orchard Park Town	27,688	529		0	5	4	5	60	425	30	
Ossining Village	24,054	505	507	0	9	34	93	65	259	45	2
Oswego City	17,987	752	752	0	2	11	16	118	580	25	0
Peekskill	22,482	408		1	7	23	29	49	282	17	
Plattsburgh City	18,851	436	437	0	3	2	33	58	334	6	1
Port Washington	17,785	229	229	0	1	7	8	24	169	20	0
Poughkeepsie	29,926	1,293		4	17	103	72	237	773	87	
Poughkeepsie Town	41,911	1,538	1,540	0	6	28	102	121	1,242	39	2
Ramapo Town	71,370	911	914	1	7	22	39	188	631	23	3
Riverhead Town	27,731	1,585	1,587	1	8	20	80	290	1,150	36	2
Rochester	220,177	16,156		40	84	921	618	2,459	9,719	2,315	
Rome	35,014	909	915	0	6	16	29	225	582	51	6
Rotterdam Town	28,368	1,124	1,132	0	1	34	19	120	927	23	8

See footnotes at end of table.

Table 8

Offenses Known to Law Enforcement

by City 10,000 and over in Population, 2001—Continued

City by state	Population	Crime Index total	Modified Crime Index total[1]	Murder and non-negligent man-slaughter	Forcible rape	Robbery	Aggravated assault	Burglary	Larceny-theft	Motor vehicle theft	Arson[1]
NEW YORK—Continued											
Saugerties Town	14,941	285	288	0	0	2	21	66	190	6	3
Scarsdale Village	17,856	253	253	0	0	3	9	41	172	28	0
Schenectady	61,935	3,557	3,622	6	54	208	255	871	1,902	261	65
Shawangunk Town	12,044	195	195	0	0	0	36	34	122	3	0
Southport Town	11,206	21	21	0	0	0	0	5	16	0	0
Suffern Village	11,026	128		0	0	7	10	17	83	11	
Syracuse	147,577	9,413	9,526	15	41	568	936	1,802	5,166	885	113
Tarrytown Village	11,110	199	199	1	2	5	18	42	113	18	0
Tonawanda	16,166	415		0	3	3	14	75	304	16	
Ulster Town	12,567	226	229	0	1	4	8	26	165	22	3
Utica	60,763	2,825	2,853	7	29	188	83	641	1,725	152	28
Vestal Town	26,584	559	560	0	1	4	7	30	494	23	1
Watertown	26,754	948	953	1	15	30	27	139	725	11	5
Watervliet	10,226	216	219	0	0	13	15	42	133	13	3
Webster Town and Village	37,996	656	657	1	2	3	5	85	529	31	1
West Seneca Town	46,005	1,108	1,111	0	2	20	120	113	801	52	3
White Plains	53,175	2,374	2,374	1	13	67	133	112	1,915	133	0
Yonkers	196,447	5,419	5,484	6	15	473	441	837	2,746	901	65
NORTH CAROLINA											
Albemarle	15,947	1,415	1,425	0	1	32	49	553	663	117	10
Apex	20,556	476	478	0	3	8	51	73	303	38	2
Asheboro	22,041	2,035	2,035	2	1	31	22	406	1,484	89	0
Asheville	70,061	4,734	4,779	1	42	217	215	905	2,918	436	45
Boone	13,701	535	535	0	4	4	21	67	418	21	0
Burlington	45,681	3,300	3,310	3	10	90	182	556	2,324	135	10
Carrboro	17,068	1,067	1,068	0	0	36	77	173	735	46	1
Cary	96,144	2,295	2,301	1	5	54	48	304	1,722	161	6
Chapel Hill	49,544	2,805	2,812	0	8	83	120	586	1,876	132	7
Charlotte-Mecklenburg	636,459	49,757	50,074	66	293	2,996	4,420	10,285	27,291	4,406	317
Concord	56,929	2,760	2,780	5	14	88	80	355	2,103	115	20
Cornelius	12,173	175	176	0	0	4	6	69	95	1	1
Durham	190,217	15,132	15,179	28	77	980	769	3,457	8,723	1,098	47
Eden	16,179	1,105	1,110	0	4	16	52	305	672	56	5
Elizabeth City	17,480	961	964	0	6	30	112	194	553	66	3
Fayetteville	123,074	9,861	9,915	18	62	464	235	2,485	5,780	817	54
Garner	18,059	1,551	1,553	0	3	47	35	193	1,195	78	2
Gastonia	67,405	6,972	7,039	8	32	330	626	1,388	4,206	382	67
Graham	13,051	782	784	1	5	11	70	191	469	35	2
Greensboro	227,700	15,962	16,041	20	89	896	864	3,258	9,871	964	79
Greenville	61,505	6,554	6,562	3	20	175	349	1,435	4,296	276	8
Havelock	22,824	638	638	0	2	10	15	153	427	31	0
Henderson	16,369	1,808	1,817	5	2	60	123	383	1,167	68	9
Hendersonville	10,597	1,033	1,035	2	5	26	52	136	769	43	2
Hickory	37,855	3,293	3,314	6	9	91	106	571	2,282	228	21
High Point	87,300	7,166	7,219	11	27	314	421	1,807	3,968	618	53
Huntersville	25,385	876	883	1	3	18	34	206	583	31	7
Kannapolis	37,538	1,174	1,185	1	9	52	49	265	699	99	11
Kernersville	17,417	1,391	1,397	0	4	22	69	184	1,078	34	6
Kinston	24,091	2,441	2,442	4	10	72	292	400	1,556	107	1
Laurinburg	16,144	1,204	1,211	1	6	31	70	351	669	76	7
Lenoir	17,079	845	845	1	1	22	36	159	584	42	0
Lexington	20,292	1,405	1,413	1	6	39	80	394	759	126	8
Lincolnton	10,135	1,038	1,041	2	0	7	32	137	830	30	3
Lumberton	21,149	3,003	3,022	1	8	110	316	612	1,800	156	19
Matthews	22,503	935	945	0	1	24	24	138	688	60	10
Monroe	26,674	1,977	1,986	1	8	60	127	186	1,504	91	9
Morganton	17,605	957	959	2	4	19	33	168	687	44	2
New Bern	23,522	1,836	1,841	4	9	47	155	346	1,215	60	5
Newton	12,774	680	682	0	1	12	21	151	455	40	2
Raleigh	280,791	18,585	18,686	10	91	804	1,282	3,983	11,087	1,328	101

See footnotes at end of table.

Table 8

Offenses Known to Law Enforcement
by City 10,000 and over in Population, 2001—Continued

City by state	Population	Crime Index total	Modified Crime Index total[1]	Murder and non-negligent man-slaughter	Forcible rape	Robbery	Aggravated assault	Burglary	Larceny-theft	Motor vehicle theft	Arson[1]
NORTH CAROLINA—Continued											
Reidsville	14,731	807	811	1	4	21	41	204	506	30	4
Roanoke Rapids	17,246	1,063	1,069	0	5	31	43	238	694	52	6
Rocky Mount	56,844	5,562	5,576	2	27	277	326	1,299	3,408	223	14
Salisbury	26,912	2,005	2,020	3	7	93	102	408	1,291	101	15
Sanford	23,615	2,591	2,597	1	11	67	83	528	1,802	99	6
Shelby	19,808	2,052	2,059	7	13	99	118	419	1,310	86	7
Smithfield	11,706	1,501	1,503	0	6	48	104	340	928	75	2
Southern Pines	11,104	758	761	1	2	27	71	167	460	30	3
Statesville	23,717	1,940	1,947	0	10	82	100	257	1,410	81	7
Tarboro	11,328	537	544	1	0	26	58	84	345	23	7
Thomasville	20,125	1,317	1,324	0	6	36	77	271	871	56	7
Wake Forest	12,802	436	437	2	3	12	20	88	302	9	1
Wilmington	77,128	8,650	8,670	10	49	310	526	1,983	5,062	710	20
Wilson	45,161	2,935	2,939	1	26	134	218	650	1,760	146	4
Winston-Salem[4]	188,937	16,037	16,052	15	120	701	930	3,444	9,798	1,029	15
NORTH DAKOTA											
Bismarck	54,862	1,797	1,808	0	8	11	30	261	1,375	112	11
Dickinson	15,817	473	477	0	0	5	3	61	383	21	4
Fargo	89,505	3,134	3,145	0	63	16	62	363	2,430	200	11
Grand Forks	48,726	2,136	2,150	1	21	11	42	261	1,626	174	14
Jamestown	15,340	360	367	1	8	2	5	51	251	42	7
Mandan	16,516	455	459	0	5	0	3	54	358	35	4
Minot	36,126	1,181	1,191	0	13	4	18	129	934	83	10
West Fargo	14,760	365	374	0	6	0	3	47	280	29	9
Williston	12,361	294	295	0	7	0	2	19	224	42	1
OHIO											
Alliance	23,295	1,394	1,419	0	8	38	110	255	953	30	25
Ashland	21,287	606	606	0	12	3	10	81	497	3	0
Aurora	13,580	244	250	0	3	0	3	22	206	10	6
Avon Lake	18,178	304	304	0	0	1	11	53	236	3	0
Bainbridge Township	10,936	253	253	0	1	1	8	15	222	6	0
Barberton	27,949	1,543	1,557	0	16	29	49	259	1,093	97	14
Beavercreek	38,052	1,442	1,454	0	6	14	9	191	1,150	72	12
Bedford Heights	11,395	359	361	0	4	12	18	53	220	52	2
Bellefontaine	13,092	581	581	1	2	6	0	100	449	23	0
Berea	19,004	436	449	0	3	3	7	37	358	28	13
Bexley	13,227	574	575	0	0	19	5	141	381	28	1
Bowling Green	29,689	1,209	1,213	0	7	13	19	171	952	47	4
Brecksville	13,406	123	123	0	0	2	2	17	89	13	0
Brookfield Township	10,038	300	302	0	5	3	20	57	197	18	2
Brooklyn	11,607	764	768	0	0	14	3	50	646	51	4
Cambridge	11,541	1,000	1,001	0	11	3	29	95	791	71	1
Celina	10,322	100	101	0	4	2	4	39	48	3	1
Centerville	23,065	559	566	0	2	7	13	90	420	27	7
Chillicothe	21,835	2,304	2,322	0	15	44	12	415	1,713	105	18
Cincinnati	331,880	27,817	28,354	55	358	2,075	1,402	6,297	14,283	3,347	537
Cleveland	479,263	33,065	33,604	77	624	3,298	2,425	7,937	12,925	5,779	539
Cleveland Heights	50,048	838	838	0	1	10	1	120	621	85	0
Columbus	712,748	68,547	69,023	81	602	3,364	2,349	15,740	38,835	7,576	476
Conneaut	12,507	562	562	1	3	5	10	91	430	22	0
Cuyahoga Falls	49,463	1,965	1,973	1	15	24	24	229	1,549	123	8
Dayton	166,478	16,952	17,154	30	152	1,090	796	4,018	7,497	3,369	202
Delaware	25,288	957	966	0	17	7	16	163	709	45	9
Delhi Township	30,158	608	610	0	4	13	0	66	507	18	2
Dover	12,232	120	122	0	6	3	0	27	79	5	2
Dublin	31,448	887	892	0	7	13	2	218	615	32	5
Eastlake	20,291	428	428	0	2	7	5	47	336	31	0
East Liverpool	13,113	463	464	1	1	7	2	78	357	17	1

See footnotes at end of table.

Table 8

Offenses Known to Law Enforcement
by City 10,000 and over in Population, 2001—Continued

City by state	Population	Crime Index total	Modified Crime Index total[1]	Murder and non-negligent man-slaughter	Forcible rape	Robbery	Aggravated assault	Burglary	Larceny-theft	Motor vehicle theft	Arson[1]
OHIO—Continued											
Englewood	12,257	565	566	0	4	14	20	48	450	29	1
Euclid	52,812	2,261	2,282	1	18	86	52	384	1,484	236	21
Fairborn	32,110	1,653	1,660	0	15	23	19	212	1,246	138	7
Fairfield	42,173	2,063	2,071	0	16	22	120	239	1,535	131	8
Forest Park	19,498	709	713	0	5	28	5	89	533	49	4
Franklin Township	14,556	195	200	1	2	2	0	78	92	20	5
Fremont	17,406	1,460	1,470	0	6	22	29	182	1,181	40	10
Gahanna	32,695	972	981	0	4	42	27	153	697	49	9
Galion	11,361	96	100	1	2	5	3	72	6	7	4
Genoa Township	11,313	172	172	0	1	0	0	12	155	4	0
Girard	10,922	441	443	1	6	5	12	97	297	23	2
Goshen Township	13,688	352	360	0	2	2	31	91	192	34	8
Greenville	13,318	493	496	0	6	3	17	64	382	21	3
Grove City	27,124	1,010	1,011	0	21	22	19	85	795	68	1
Hamilton	60,799	5,595	5,616	5	66	221	398	1,204	3,264	437	21
Hilliard	24,274	730	742	0	5	15	9	124	553	24	12
Huber Heights	38,281	1,688	1,701	0	20	34	18	270	1,247	99	13
Hudson	22,479	301	311	0	2	0	4	54	235	6	10
Kent	27,956	1,051	1,091	0	10	17	39	210	712	63	40
Kettering	57,605	2,299	2,320	1	32	31	27	409	1,629	170	21
Lakewood	56,748	1,485	1,490	0	7	51	57	243	1,019	108	5
Lancaster	35,398	1,349	1,366	0	21	30	18	253	945	82	17
Lebanon	16,992	488	491	0	6	10	36	73	347	16	3
Lima	40,153	3,522	3,562	6	72	108	235	847	2,107	147	40
Lorain	68,775	2,590	2,609	1	22	105	151	626	1,536	149	19
Lyndhurst	15,306	248	248	0	0	3	33	49	150	13	0
Madison Township	15,535	419	428	0	4	0	22	70	304	19	9
Mansfield	49,435	3,924	3,978	1	39	104	41	938	2,623	178	54
Marietta	14,541	497	500	0	15	2	4	79	366	31	3
Marion	35,381	2,107	2,135	2	5	25	29	469	1,514	63	28
Mason	22,056	459	459	0	0	4	4	37	399	15	0
Mayfield Heights	19,421	406	410	1	3	7	28	33	299	35	4
Mentor	50,368	1,530	1,535	0	8	19	11	158	1,252	82	5
Miamisburg	19,524	1,185	1,193	2	9	18	11	201	782	162	8
Miami Township	36,698	915	922	0	6	4	32	166	681	26	7
Middletown	51,698	3,265	3,277	2	18	61	56	518	2,444	166	12
Montgomery	10,181	339	341	0	2	1	0	41	283	12	2
Newark	46,362	2,409	2,439	0	13	41	34	536	1,672	113	30
North Canton	16,398	124	132	0	2	8	3	66	45	0	8
North Ridgeville	22,378	338	339	0	6	6	33	57	215	21	1
North Royalton	28,699	267	279	0	2	5	5	92	147	16	12
Norton	11,544	527	527	0	0	7	2	67	405	46	0
Norwalk	16,267	483	487	0	1	3	0	91	370	18	4
Norwood	21,714	1,557	1,561	0	8	43	31	208	1,148	119	4
Oregon	19,390	1,215	1,223	0	9	11	37	124	954	80	8
Parma	85,809	2,068	2,089	1	9	57	62	449	1,356	134	21
Parma Heights	21,698	512	519	0	6	2	12	93	367	32	7
Perkins Township	12,601	592	595	1	1	8	12	31	523	16	3
Perrysburg	16,975	449	449	0	3	3	27	41	349	26	0
Perry Township (Stark County)	29,219	750	755	0	8	9	17	162	510	44	5
Pierce Township	12,248	263	264	0	2	4	4	44	187	22	1
Portsmouth	20,947	2,618	2,623	4	29	90	60	547	1,708	180	5
Ravenna	11,792	587	587	0	5	12	21	59	457	33	0
Reading	11,312	340	343	0	4	7	6	45	247	31	3
Richmond Heights	10,964	410	410	0	0	7	13	35	331	24	0
Salem	12,219	63	63	0	0	0	8	8	39	8	0
Sandusky	27,894	2,281	2,292	1	13	42	136	373	1,663	53	11
Seven Hills	12,102	113	113	0	0	3	1	20	82	7	0
Shaker Heights	29,458	810	816	2	2	27	4	181	512	82	6
Sharonville	13,829	810	814	0	1	19	9	86	636	59	4
Solon	21,841	347	350	0	1	5	2	35	303	1	3
South Euclid	23,579	543	546	0	8	41	9	79	366	40	3

See footnotes at end of table.

Table 8

Offenses Known to Law Enforcement
by City 10,000 and over in Population, 2001—Continued

City by state	Population	Crime Index total	Modified Crime Index total[1]	Murder and non-negligent man-slaughter	Forcible rape	Robbery	Aggravated assault	Burglary	Larceny-theft	Motor vehicle theft	Arson[1]
OHIO—Continued											
Springboro	12,402	223	223	0	1	6	4	42	166	4	0
Springdale	10,582	1,260	1,261	0	4	35	9	71	1,022	119	1
Springfield	65,475	6,743	6,775	7	74	226	203	1,507	4,259	467	32
Springfield Township (Hamilton County)	37,655	1,131	1,135	3	6	38	94	178	739	73	4
Springfield Township (Summit County)	15,195	835	838	0	3	7	4	149	638	34	3
Steubenville	19,049	1,096	1,098	2	12	36	113	145	734	54	2
Stow	32,197	893	902	1	10	10	4	141	712	15	9
Strongsville	43,937	929	945	3	7	10	44	118	706	41	16
Sylvania Township	25,629	798	803	0	0	11	6	78	669	34	5
Tallmadge	16,419	496	500	0	3	9	9	97	361	17	4
Tiffin	18,168	809	811	0	8	3	13	126	637	22	2
Toledo[4]	314,183	27,105	27,478	18	185	1,312	1,535	6,299	14,006	3,750	373
Troy	22,039	834	842	0	17	6	3	132	640	36	8
Twinsburg	17,037	284	288	0	6	5	7	32	215	19	4
Union Township	42,408	1,573	1,586	1	2	26	11	226	1,280	27	13
Upper Arlington	33,747	680	684	0	10	15	20	114	508	13	4
Vandalia	14,629	477	481	0	7	10	5	79	335	41	4
Van Wert	10,709	541	548	0	11	2	16	88	407	17	7
Vermilion	10,947	463	467	0	3	3	4	80	333	40	4
Wadsworth	18,470	406	409	0	10	0	12	64	285	35	3
Warren	46,916	2,977	3,055	4	25	148	220	849	1,376	355	78
Warrensville Heights	15,136	532	532	2	10	42	36	85	278	79	0
West Carrollton	13,843	722	728	0	10	16	5	109	477	105	6
West Chester Township	52,764	1,641	1,654	0	20	11	20	268	1,263	59	13
Westerville	35,381	1,036	1,045	0	0	23	7	156	824	26	9
Westlake	31,776	457	462	0	6	9	11	66	346	19	5
Whitehall	19,236	1,654	1,678	2	12	83	35	314	1,069	139	24
Willowick	14,387	241	242	0	1	4	1	40	181	14	1
Wilmington	11,942	721	721	0	6	5	10	81	609	10	0
Worthington	14,150	419	423	0	0	7	4	70	321	17	4
Xenia	24,207	1,393	1,403	0	4	12	12	211	1,125	29	10
Youngstown	82,173	5,865	6,113	34	52	355	570	1,718	2,695	441	248
Zanesville	25,632	2,425	2,436	4	12	55	137	363	1,761	93	11
OKLAHOMA											
Ada	15,734	956	958	0	10	10	69	207	621	39	2
Altus	21,506	1,236	1,239	2	9	22	35	475	670	23	3
Ardmore	23,776	1,750	1,759	2	8	22	226	303	1,122	67	9
Bartlesville	34,843	1,518	1,520	0	21	14	110	273	1,017	83	2
Bethany	20,363	824	833	0	9	5	54	180	526	50	9
Bixby	13,372	310	314	0	3	3	13	55	208	28	4
Broken Arrow	75,064	2,310	2,318	1	35	21	125	453	1,516	159	8
Chickasha	15,893	1,097	1,101	1	11	11	173	246	599	56	4
Claremore	15,916	730	733	0	7	6	35	122	517	43	3
Del City	22,189	1,040	1,062	2	12	28	49	280	576	93	22
Duncan	22,567	1,142	1,146	0	6	6	32	268	786	44	4
Durant	13,586	836	837	0	5	9	21	177	548	76	1
Edmond	68,502	1,736	1,748	1	17	15	35	322	1,268	78	12
Elk City	10,539	302	302	0	1	1	6	52	238	4	0
El Reno	16,256	673	679	1	9	7	68	112	442	34	6
Enid	47,174	2,953	2,957	1	30	34	170	616	1,983	119	4
Guymon	10,501	360	361	0	6	1	11	63	257	22	1
Lawton	93,011	5,210	5,246	6	46	148	373	1,203	3,169	265	36
Le Flore	26,282	226	231	4	3	3	58	73	65	20	5
McAlester	17,832	897	898	0	4	5	35	214	600	39	1
Miami	13,742	756	760	0	13	3	35	168	509	28	4
Midwest City	54,236	1,981	1,992	1	15	50	89	414	1,220	192	11
Moore	41,251	1,718	1,725	1	31	21	204	321	956	184	7

See footnotes at end of table.

Table 8

Offenses Known to Law Enforcement

by City 10,000 and over in Population, 2001—Continued

City by state	Population	Crime Index total	Modified Crime Index total[1]	Murder and non-negligent man-slaughter	Forcible rape	Robbery	Aggravated assault	Burglary	Larceny-theft	Motor vehicle theft	Arson[1]
OKLAHOMA—Continued											
Muskogee	38,415	2,872	2,888	4	25	63	250	930	1,373	227	16
Mustang	13,192	347	349	0	2	3	23	65	244	10	2
Norman	95,956	3,425	3,436	2	34	42	151	886	2,178	132	11
Oklahoma City	507,517	45,875	46,097	45	405	1,090	2,643	8,405	29,771	3,516	222
Okmulgee	13,058	700	703	1	5	9	48	145	442	50	3
Owasso	18,553	641	643	0	6	4	37	104	451	39	2
Ponca City	25,990	1,423	1,430	2	24	15	85	279	930	88	7
Sand Springs	17,499	628	632	0	7	6	19	93	438	65	4
Sapulpa	19,218	818	831	0	8	4	36	175	533	62	13
Shawnee	28,771	1,832	1,833	4	12	32	116	412	1,121	135	1
Stillwater	39,172	1,369	1,377	0	11	13	61	292	931	61	8
Tahlequah	14,498	671	671	0	6	6	22	170	415	52	0
The Village	10,185	612	612	0	0	7	53	119	394	39	0
Tulsa	394,125	29,354	29,604	34	256	776	3,481	5,863	15,308	3,636	250
Woodward	11,885	638	640	0	8	2	104	149	352	23	2
Yukon	21,101	627	636	1	4	3	7	111	471	30	9
OREGON											
Albany	41,467	3,471	3,488	1	6	34	45	407	2,759	219	17
Ashland	19,816	763	770	0	1	4	3	96	641	18	7
Baker City	10,008	397	398	0	5	2	20	59	292	19	1
Beaverton	77,274	3,865	3,899	1	25	51	110	440	2,889	349	34
Bend	52,812	3,535	3,564	1	13	36	114	553	2,655	163	29
Canby	12,982	683	688	0	3	8	6	97	535	34	5
Central Point	12,681	480	485	0	1	1	2	61	408	7	5
Coos Bay	17,543	918	923	0	7	7	15	160	687	42	5
Corvallis	50,064	2,166	2,179	1	7	26	41	289	1,720	82	13
Dallas	12,646	422	423	0	0	4	67	51	286	14	1
Eugene	139,967	9,415	9,528	2	55	203	327	1,247	6,893	688	113
Forest Grove	17,974	834	839	0	7	1	21	91	646	68	5
Gladstone	11,610	695	703	0	6	9	6	72	524	78	8
Grants Pass	23,349	1,551	1,555	1	1	29	32	181	1,225	82	4
Gresham	91,562	5,604	5,645	3	58	124	222	893	3,631	673	41
Hermiston	13,352	668	674	0	3	2	0	88	502	73	6
Hillsboro	71,242	3,298	3,353	2	35	56	78	446	2,324	357	55
Keizer	32,687	1,513	1,518	1	8	12	14	172	1,221	85	5
Klamath Falls	19,755	851	859	0	6	18	52	186	528	61	8
La Grande	12,512	403	408	0	5	7	9	57	301	24	5
Lake Oswego	35,809	957	976	0	4	6	17	172	697	61	19
Lebanon	13,145	1,104	1,106	0	2	6	10	110	930	46	2
McMinnville	26,898	1,244	1,248	0	14	13	21	169	957	70	4
Medford	64,104	3,733	3,788	0	19	32	147	431	2,941	163	55
Milwaukie	20,798	1,273	1,273	0	9	16	21	158	965	104	0
Ontario	11,150	857	864	0	7	7	28	107	658	50	7
Oregon City	26,141	1,519	1,528	0	17	11	30	213	1,125	123	9
Pendleton	16,600	826	830	0	7	2	8	171	579	59	4
Portland	537,081	43,183	43,568	21	305	1,267	2,963	5,592	28,358	4,677	385
Redmond	13,684	1,312	1,321	0	7	9	4	181	987	124	9
Roseburg	20,318	1,369	1,390	1	1	10	7	159	1,122	69	21
Salem	138,984	11,120	11,147	4	81	160	88	1,395	8,515	877	27
Sherwood	11,968	280	281	1	1	2	1	23	243	9	1
Springfield	53,659	4,390	4,421	0	21	72	88	650	3,250	309	31
St. Helens	10,170	370	377	0	2	1	4	55	292	16	7
The Dalles	12,339	669	674	0	4	9	16	101	505	34	5
Tigard	41,843	2,731	2,742	0	10	34	60	353	2,104	170	11
Troutdale	13,984	541	544	0	0	7	15	81	402	36	3
Tualatin	23,134	1,203	1,204	1	8	21	17	150	900	106	1
West Linn	22,596	513	514	0	2	4	1	109	370	27	1
Wilsonville	14,201	707	709	0	10	8	9	98	538	44	2
Woodburn	20,402	1,264	1,270	1	10	18	32	166	924	113	6

See footnotes at end of table.

Table 8

Offenses Known to Law Enforcement
by City 10,000 and over in Population, 2001—Continued

City by state	Population	Crime Index total	Modified Crime Index total[1]	Murder and non-negligent man-slaughter	Forcible rape	Robbery	Aggravated assault	Burglary	Larceny-theft	Motor vehicle theft	Arson[1]
PENNSYLVANIA											
Abington Township	56,131	1,445	1,449	0	6	26	31	160	1,125	97	4
Aliquippa	11,740	341	342	2	5	13	63	54	181	23	1
Allentown	106,685	5,237	5,278	8	46	295	269	1,111	3,052	456	41
Altoona	49,548	2,057	2,069	2	34	72	100	450	1,312	87	12
Aston Township	16,211	258	260	0	4	8	13	32	179	22	2
Baldwin Borough	20,009	236	237	0	4	9	14	45	146	18	1
Bensalem Township	58,463	2,158	2,163	4	9	46	39	243	1,533	284	5
Bethel Park	33,573	334	334	0	3	11	14	31	257	18	0
Bethlehem	71,364	2,472	2,475	4	14	76	155	427	1,633	163	3
Bethlehem Township	21,182	424	424	0	3	6	18	19	366	12	0
Bloomsburg Town	12,381	324	324	0	5	1	6	53	241	18	0
Brecknock Township	10,982	48	48	0	1	0	5	6	33	3	0
Brentwood	10,471	233	233	0	2	8	8	57	145	13	0
Bristol Township	55,549	2,382	2,409	0	14	59	109	276	1,614	310	27
Buckingham Township	16,450	176	177	0	1	2	4	18	143	8	1
Butler	15,129	965	970	0	5	26	179	108	607	40	5
Caln Township	11,922	402	403	0	2	7	36	49	282	26	1
Carlisle	17,979	647	652	0	8	27	17	111	472	12	5
Chambersburg	17,871	932	935	0	12	29	236	99	527	29	3
Cheltenham Township	36,893	1,353	1,356	1	3	60	33	205	838	213	3
Chippewa Township	10,823	223	223	0	0	1	18	18	174	12	0
Colonial Regional	17,509	500	502	.0	1	6	49	56	368	20	2
Columbia	10,316	239	240	0	2	12	15	43	149	18	1
Cranberry Township	23,637	439	439	0	1	7	19	44	341	27	0
Derry Township (Dauphin County)	21,284	598	602	1	14	6	22	74	465	16	4
Dunmore	14,025	86	89	0	0	0	0	3	82	1	3
East Hempfield Township	21,410	619	620	0	2	16	8	120	438	35	1
East Lampeter Township	13,563	706	707	0	1	25	2	41	603	34	1
East Norriton Township	13,218	314	314	0	0	7	4	30	253	20	0
Easton	26,276	1,228	1,246	3	16	52	83	237	772	65	18
East Pennsboro Township	18,263	449	449	0	3	13	5	73	338	17	0
Easttown Township	10,275	173	175	0	0	1	5	32	128	7	2
Emmaus	11,319	336	338	0	1	5	21	43	249	17	2
Erie	103,768	4,269	4,317	4	52	227	203	734	2,828	221	48
Exeter Township	22,985	500	502	0	0	9	49	48	364	30	2
Fairview Township (York County)	14,328	397	397	0	4	6	28	53	297	9	0
Falls Township	34,882	1,186	1,192	0	6	28	28	135	794	195	6
Ferguson Township	14,070	185	185	0	3	1	2	17	158	4	0
Franconia Township	11,529	95	96	0	0	0	14	11	69	1	1
Franklin Park	11,370	83	83	0	1	0	8	11	56	7	0
Greensburg	15,897	555	557	1	4	15	54	98	361	22	2
Hampton Township	17,535	204	204	0	2	2	8	28	161	3	0
Hanover	14,542	531	535	0	2	3	12	53	449	12	4
Harrisburg	48,974	3,150	3,160	9	42	379	284	558	1,711	167	10
Harrison Township	10,939	292	292	0	1	7	9	18	240	17	0
Hatfield Township	19,326	391	396	0	1	5	14	43	296	32	5
Haverford Township	48,522	779	782	0	5	12	29	115	565	53	3
Hazleton	23,341	490	493	1	4	13	17	99	312	44	3
Hermitage	16,165	518	522	0	1	7	31	43	420	16	4
Hilltown Township	12,108	244	244	0	1	0	8	25	197	13	0
Horsham Township	24,244	396	401	0	3	5	7	38	294	49	5
Indiana	14,902	437	438	0	7	3	8	47	359	13	1
Jeannette	10,659	306	306	0	0	5	17	49	220	15	0
Johnstown	28,603	983	997	2	5	42	95	238	531	70	14
Lancaster	56,376	3,545	3,593	4	37	284	183	538	2,120	379	48
Lancaster Township (Lancaster County)	13,951	447	451	0	4	22	6	51	336	28	4
Lansdale	16,079	372	372	0	3	8	10	40	294	17	0
Lebanon	24,473	1,344	1,349	0	17	46	184	197	840	60	5

See footnotes at end of table.

Table 8

Offenses Known to Law Enforcement
by City 10,000 and over in Population, 2001—Continued

City by state	Population	Crime Index total	Modified Crime Index total[1]	Murder and non-negligent man-slaughter	Forcible rape	Robbery	Aggravated assault	Burglary	Larceny-theft	Motor vehicle theft	Arson[1]
PENNSYLVANIA—Continued											
Limerick Township	13,541	232	232	0	1	2	9	36	174	10	0
Logan Township	11,931	424	426	0	5	8	0	79	322	10	2
Lower Allen Township	17,446	337	338	0	2	4	11	29	288	3	1
Lower Burrell	12,614	154	154	0	0	1	19	24	104	6	0
Lower Gwynedd Township	10,427	205	205	0	0	8	10	18	159	10	0
Lower Makefield Township	32,697	436	436	1	0	4	7	68	330	26	0
Lower Merion Township	59,880	989	991	1	1	35	8	163	719	62	2
Lower Paxton Township	44,446	1,219	1,228	1	12	33	102	103	924	44	9
Lower Pottsgrove Township	11,219	208	208	1	1	5	6	24	154	17	0
Manheim Township	33,714	980	986	2	4	25	28	144	722	55	6
Marple Township	23,749	324	324	2	0	2	12	27	257	24	0
McCandless	29,036	374	374	0	0	5	7	48	297	17	0
McKeesport	24,052	1,393	1,405	1	7	66	309	255	669	86	12
Meadville	13,692	467	475	1	6	8	18	53	363	18	8
Middletown Township	44,163	1,626	1,636	1	2	28	33	188	1,200	174	10
Millcreek Township	52,155	1,002	1,003	2	2	15	9	179	751	44	1
Monroeville	29,364	1,027	1,033	1	3	31	75	99	703	115	6
Montgomery Township	22,036	575	576	2	0	9	9	22	511	22	1
Moon Township	22,301	401	401	3	3	6	12	56	304	17	0
Mountaintop Regional	10,838	24	24	0	0	0	0	9	14	1	0
Mount Lebanon	33,033	294	296	0	3	7	27	37	215	5	2
Muhlenberg Township	16,313	650	650	0	3	16	27	76	476	52	0
Munhall	12,270	222	222	0	0	6	6	42	148	20	0
Murrysville	18,881	289	289	0	0	1	4	55	218	11	0
Nanticoke	10,960	247	252	0	1	10	5	50	169	12	5
Nether Providence Township	13,463	203	203	0	1	1	14	14	167	6	0
Newberry Township	14,339	294	295	0	5	8	2	60	179	40	1
New Britain Township	10,703	106	106	0	1	0	2	10	90	3	0
New Castle	26,322	1,153	1,164	2	10	78	117	299	546	101	11
New Kensington	14,708	526	529	1	7	25	117	72	275	29	3
Newtown Township (Delaware County)	11,706	152	152	0	1	2	15	18	102	14	0
Norristown	31,298	1,913	1,929	5	31	206	157	364	896	254	16
Northampton Township	39,404	359	361	0	0	1	10	46	275	27	2
Northern York Regional	49,759	1,050	1,053	1	5	16	29	88	858	53	3
North Fayette Township	12,260	390	390	0	0	2	7	27	333	21	0
North Huntingdon Township	29,137	325	326	0	2	10	11	57	223	22	1
North Lebanon Township	10,634	351	352	0	0	7	11	35	285	13	1
North Strabane Township	10,062	203	206	0	1	2	25	15	150	10	3
North Versailles Township	11,858	298	298	0	3	11	10	24	226	24	0
Oil City	11,510	351	354	0	4	4	40	33	249	21	3
Patton Township	11,426	235	239	0	4	0	11	14	205	1	4
Penn Hills	46,832	1,113	1,114	3	9	35	56	162	707	141	1
Penn Township (Westmoreland County)	19,601	49	49	0	3	0	1	13	32	0	0
Penn Township (York County)	14,599	291	298	0	0	0	14	34	232	11	7
Peters Township	17,575	250	257	0	0	1	16	31	182	20	7
Philadelphia	1,518,302	93,878		309	1,014	9,604	10,477	11,629	45,318	15,527	
Phoenixville	14,795	486	486	0	8	9	29	35	402	3	0
Pine-Marshall-Bradford Woods	14,836	332	332	0	0	3	9	23	290	7	0
Pittsburgh	341,414	19,708	19,881	55	134	1,384	1,391	3,246	10,766	2,732	173
Plumstead Township	11,415	244	245	2	1	2	2	23	196	18	1
Plymouth Township (Montgomery County)	16,053	921	922	1	3	15	46	113	673	70	1
Pocono Mountain Regional	29,096	760	766	0	14	5	15	229	435	62	6
Pottstown	21,870	1,177	1,186	2	20	48	124	146	758	79	9
Pottsville	15,557	437	439	1	2	11	54	44	307	18	2
Radnor Township	30,893	529	531	0	1	4	18	61	432	13	2
Reading	81,247	5,593	5,636	20	45	455	456	1,445	2,681	491	43
Ridley Township	30,806	566	566	1	2	19	67	44	379	54	0
Robinson Township (Allegheny County)	12,295	391	399	0	2	10	5	36	317	21	8

See footnotes at end of table.

154 CRIME INDEX OFFENSES REPORTED

Table 8

Offenses Known to Law Enforcement

by City 10,000 and over in Population, 2001—Continued

City by state	Population	Crime Index total	Modified Crime Index total[1]	Murder and non-negligent man-slaughter	Forcible rape	Robbery	Aggravated assault	Burglary	Larceny-theft	Motor vehicle theft	Arson[1]
PENNSYLVANIA—Continued											
Ross Township	32,567	946	946	0	1	17	15	68	805	40	0
Sandy Township	11,562	272	272	0	1	0	18	64	180	9	0
Scott Township (Allegheny County)	17,297	229	230	0	0	5	6	22	182	14	1
Scranton	76,453	2,337	2,337	1	33	72	95	435	1,499	202	0
Shaler Township	29,772	325	325	0	1	2	13	40	248	21	0
Silver Spring Township	10,597	269	270	0	1	5	3	25	229	6	1
South Park Township	14,347	68	68	0	1	1	2	22	35	7	0
South Whitehall Township	18,037	720	721	0	2	9	36	59	597	17	1
Springettsbury Township	23,895	1,097	1,101	0	6	16	15	105	916	39	4
Springfield Township (Delaware County)	23,689	830	830	1	2	10	70	50	640	57	0
Springfield Township (Montgomery County)	19,543	261	263	0	0	7	10	31	186	27	2
Spring Garden Township	11,980	408	409	0	1	12	8	61	307	19	1
Spring Township (Berks County)	21,816	235	237	0	5	8	3	50	155	14	2
State College	51,591	1,125	1,136	1	9	9	35	125	928	18	11
St. Marys City	14,509	305	305	0	1	1	31	53	208	11	0
Stroud Area Regional	29,637	1,222	1,227	1	8	32	111	95	914	61	5
Susquehanna Township (Dauphin County)	21,906	733	738	1	9	28	11	84	569	31	5
Towamencin Township	17,606	210	211	0	0	0	11	28	162	9	1
Tredyffrin Township	29,076	475	480	0	1	9	31	56	359	19	5
Uniontown	12,428	505	510	1	4	29	42	69	295	65	5
Upper Allen Township	15,346	189	190	0	3	1	1	40	138	6	1
Upper Chichester Township	16,850	593	599	0	5	21	25	62	411	69	6
Upper Darby Township	81,862	1,732	1,738	1	11	87	65	120	1,253	195	6
Upper Dublin Township	25,891	362	363	0	3	5	5	43	288	18	1
Upper Gwynedd Township	14,250	196	203	0	2	0	3	33	145	13	7
Upper Merion Township	26,876	1,879	1,881	0	0	14	18	105	1,571	171	2
Upper Moreland Township	25,005	458	466	0	3	7	14	69	322	43	8
Upper Providence Township (Delaware County)	10,514	75	75	0	1	0	9	13	49	3	0
Upper Providence Township (Montgomery County)	15,406	194	196	0	1	0	5	24	154	10	2
Upper Saucon Township	11,945	137	137	0	1	0	9	20	102	5	0
Upper Southampton Township	15,772	245	245	0	2	1	19	31	183	9	0
Uwchlan Township	16,584	262	262	0	1	8	21	37	185	10	0
Warminster Township	31,399	750	753	1	9	13	27	92	546	62	3
Warren	10,264	199	202	0	3	8	6	30	141	11	3
Warrington Township	17,589	215	216	0	4	1	10	33	146	21	1
Warwick Township (Bucks County)	11,983	139	140	0	1	0	5	26	101	6	1
Warwick Township (Lancaster County)	15,483	95	95	0	2	3	1	13	69	7	0
Washington (Washington County)	15,276	895	906	1	14	32	40	162	547	99	11
Washington Township (Franklin County)	11,565	204	208	0	2	1	10	28	145	18	4
West Chester	17,870	789	795	0	13	41	55	135	467	78	6
West Goshen Township	20,505	513	513	1	3	8	31	62	373	35	0
West Hempfield Township	15,136	299	300	0	2	11	9	42	211	24	1
West Lampeter Township	13,152	174	176	0	0	2	5	18	134	15	2
West Manchester Township	17,043	862	866	0	6	18	15	59	743	21	4
West Norriton Township	14,908	323	324	0	4	4	27	34	218	36	1
Westtown-East Goshen Township	13,036	414	416	0	1	4	38	33	318	20	2
West Whiteland Township	16,507	657	658	1	3	10	6	35	579	23	1
Whitehall	14,451	63	63	0	1	4	2	9	45	2	0
Whitehall Township	24,908	1,046	1,065	1	4	18	31	59	874	59	19
Whitemarsh Township	16,710	395	400	1	3	6	20	53	284	28	5
Whitpain Township	18,571	264	265	0	0	8	4	47	189	16	1
Willistown Township	10,016	92	93	0	2	0	13	17	53	7	1

See footnotes at end of table.

Table 8

Offenses Known to Law Enforcement
by City 10,000 and over in Population, 2001—Continued

City by state	Population	Crime Index total	Modified Crime Index total[1]	Murder and non-negligent man-slaughter	Forcible rape	Robbery	Aggravated assault	Burglary	Larceny-theft	Motor vehicle theft	Arson[1]
PENNSYLVANIA—Continued											
Yeadon	11,768	524	528	2	5	31	58	83	289	56	4
York Area Regional	44,559	919	922	0	9	22	51	191	615	31	3
RHODE ISLAND											
Barrington	16,989	372	383	1	0	4	3	96	261	7	11
Bristol	22,696	488	506	0	7	1	21	81	363	15	18
Burrillville	15,956	200	205	0	3	0	10	41	143	3	5
Central Falls	19,119	713	731	1	7	33	72	154	334	112	18
Coventry	34,008	621	633	0	8	2	37	137	417	20	12
Cranston	80,072	2,511	2,523	1	29	58	73	542	1,553	255	12
Cumberland	32,162	552	566	0	4	10	17	95	418	8	14
East Greenwich	13,079	227	229	0	1	2	9	31	168	16	2
East Providence	49,180	1,035	1,054	0	13	30	73	173	649	97	19
Glocester	10,049	87	88	0	1	0	1	18	66	1	1
Johnston	28,480	1,008	1,017	0	15	7	37	120	735	94	9
Lincoln	21,109	481	485	0	0	2	3	68	356	52	4
Middletown	17,509	414	416	0	4	3	10	79	310	8	2
Narragansett	16,526	458	461	0	2	0	14	86	347	9	3
Newport	26,744	1,630	1,660	0	10	38	119	397	994	72	30
North Kingstown	26,592	703	703	0	6	1	15	100	547	34	0
North Providence	32,739	700	708	2	7	12	32	139	419	89	8
North Smithfield	10,725	238	244	0	1	5	2	32	186	12	6
Pawtucket	73,696	2,994	3,047	2	39	74	180	505	1,744	450	53
Portsmouth	17,322	302	304	0	1	0	15	44	229	13	2
Providence	175,374	14,185	14,529	23	111	595	714	2,284	7,387	3,071	344
Scituate	10,428	139	140	0	2	0	4	30	100	3	1
Smithfield	20,821	298	303	1	6	6	9	40	230	6	5
South Kingstown	28,205	504	510	2	4	9	7	100	361	21	6
Tiverton	15,414	293	294	1	2	2	18	72	186	12	1
Warren	11,475	348	363	0	13	0	34	51	237	13	15
Warwick	86,676	3,050	3,089	2	24	33	75	447	2,167	302	39
Westerly	23,198	393	393	0	6	0	8	75	294	10	0
West Warwick	29,881	741	766	0	6	7	35	149	530	14	25
Woonsocket	43,661	1,482	1,516	1	60	46	130	338	784	123	34
SOUTH CAROLINA											
Aiken	25,659	1,259	1,263	1	7	23	70	170	925	63	4
Cayce	12,304	975	976	2	2	15	33	147	728	48	1
Clemson	12,091	418	419	1	1	8	33	67	280	28	1
Columbia	117,756	10,574	10,603	15	62	442	781	1,426	6,863	985	29
Easley	17,980	787	791	1	12	10	29	130	577	28	4
Florence	30,632	3,847	3,874	1	22	103	363	504	2,662	192	27
Gaffney	13,133	717	719	0	4	28	51	127	490	17	2
Goose Creek	29,579	792	794	1	3	14	34	145	551	44	2
Greenwood	22,352	1,654	1,664	2	4	46	387	208	942	65	10
Greer	17,057	675	682	0	4	32	60	77	460	42	7
Hanahan	13,101	606	608	1	0	3	46	107	385	64	2
Mauldin	15,418	451	452	0	1	11	56	46	316	21	1
North Myrtle Beach	11,113	1,373	1,374	1	4	32	49	252	934	101	1
Orangeburg	12,927	1,239	1,243	0	5	28	76	243	810	77	4
Simpsonville	14,534	615	616	0	0	7	70	90	428	20	1
Spartanburg	40,177	4,514	4,530	1	7	161	464	616	2,809	456	16
Sumter	40,147	3,545	3,566	3	16	159	314	859	1,791	403	21
West Columbia	13,230	1,339	1,340	6	5	58	205	172	797	96	1
SOUTH DAKOTA											
Aberdeen	24,715	629	637	1	18	2	27	111	453	17	8
Pierre	13,908	532	535	0	4	0	16	54	440	18	3
Rapid City	59,746	2,937	2,950	1	62	31	126	433	2,114	170	13

See footnotes at end of table.

Table 8

Offenses Known to Law Enforcement
by City 10,000 and over in Population, 2001—Continued

City by state	Population	Crime Index total	Modified Crime Index total[1]	Murder and non-negligent man-slaughter	Forcible rape	Robbery	Aggravated assault	Burglary	Larceny-theft	Motor vehicle theft	Arson[1]
SOUTH DAKOTA—Continued											
Sioux Falls	124,263	4,130	4,168	2	76	38	208	681	2,943	182	38
Yankton	13,559	397	397	0	15	1	13	42	306	20	0
TENNESSEE											
Athens	13,338	1,252	1,255	1	8	17	178	200	789	59	3
Bartlett	40,905	1,043	1,047	0	3	19	68	105	773	75	4
Brentwood	23,654	588	590	0	1	10	12	33	517	15	2
Bristol	25,042	1,211	1,217	1	9	10	102	147	863	79	6
Brownsville	10,844	729	729	1	7	18	144	170	362	27	0
Chattanooga	156,941	19,320	19,398	26	86	765	1,929	3,270	11,042	2,202	78
Clarksville	104,378	4,794	4,803	6	57	90	372	653	3,445	171	9
Cleveland	37,524	2,543	2,548	0	19	47	155	345	1,852	125	5
Collierville	32,156	737	741	1	1	18	36	67	544	70	4
Columbia	33,350	2,391	2,403	1	9	51	308	448	1,464	110	12
Cookeville	24,136	1,496	1,502	0	11	26	107	186	1,089	77	6
Dickson	12,353	878	884	0	10	17	76	76	640	59	6
Dyersburg	17,608	1,347	1,353	1	12	13	96	228	931	66	6
East Ridge	20,824	1,392	1,400	1	8	24	74	264	904	117	8
Elizabethton	13,491	929	937	0	7	8	65	121	693	35	8
Franklin	42,215	1,140	1,144	0	11	17	78	128	841	65	4
Gallatin	23,437	1,680	1,686	3	5	30	179	170	1,278	15	6
Germantown	37,681	911	916	2	3	6	35	128	705	32	5
Goodlettsville	13,903	1,265	1,268	2	6	29	63	155	891	119	3
Greeneville	15,334	1,153	1,157	1	8	17	36	160	855	76	4
Hendersonville	40,982	1,130	1,139	0	10	11	103	151	795	60	9
Jackson	62,035	4,626	4,643	12	27	180	545	852	2,694	316	17
Johnson City	55,964	4,298	4,317	1	27	78	280	526	3,203	183	19
Kingsport	45,305	2,992	3,006	2	26	36	320	409	2,065	134	14
Knoxville	175,441	11,069	11,210	15	139	637	1,314	1,717	5,951	1,296	141
La Vergne	18,854	673	679	0	5	10	108	176	330	44	6
Lawrenceburg	10,892	941	944	0	13	6	141	156	580	45	3
Lebanon	20,415	1,745	1,750	2	14	43	184	353	1,083	66	5
Lewisburg	10,506	513	513	0	8	8	45	101	329	22	0
Martin	10,609	420	421	0	1	8	28	38	334	11	1
Maryville	23,326	750	752	0	11	13	45	129	523	29	2
McMinnville	12,863	872	875	1	6	22	43	127	603	70	3
Memphis[4]	655,898	65,479	65,741	158	480	4,338	5,886	15,874	29,207	9,536	262
Millington	10,526	757	760	1	4	17	80	119	483	53	3
Morristown	25,188	2,017	2,042	2	7	27	161	242	1,450	128	25
Mount Juliet	12,476	440	442	0	4	5	33	97	277	24	2
Murfreesboro	69,430	3,539	3,545	0	19	85	279	378	2,559	219	6
Nashville	555,059	50,155	50,383	64	427	2,521	6,063	7,842	27,837	5,401	228
Oak Ridge	27,631	1,553	1,565	3	7	29	70	241	1,138	65	12
Red Bank	12,529	639	643	0	4	8	88	146	357	36	4
Sevierville	11,862	1,041	1,042	1	5	8	50	135	768	74	1
Shelbyville	16,249	807	808	3	11	24	82	168	478	41	1
Smyrna	25,797	1,249	1,256	0	8	18	134	123	890	76	7
Soddy-Daisy	11,633	486	487	1	3	3	67	96	280	36	1
Springfield	14,457	965	965	5	7	22	139	80	654	58	0
Tullahoma	18,154	1,159	1,170	1	1	30	73	192	806	56	11
Union City	10,973	858	861	0	6	17	77	146	586	26	3
TEXAS											
Abilene	118,561	5,186	5,223	2	66	88	227	1,084	3,504	215	37
Addison	14,487	908	908	0	6	16	30	117	635	104	0
Alamo	15,095	862	864	2	0	4	23	113	678	42	2
Alice	19,441	1,492	1,508	0	10	11	168	300	942	61	16
Allen	44,542	1,350	1,352	0	9	15	39	323	910	54	2
Alvin	21,899	1,030	1,033	1	5	21	56	171	703	73	3
Amarillo	177,567	13,627	13,683	19	98	277	1,008	2,533	8,747	945	56

See footnotes at end of table.

Table 8

Offenses Known to Law Enforcement
by City 10,000 and over in Population, 2001—Continued

City by state	Population	Crime Index total	Modified Crime Index total[1]	Murder and non-negligent man-slaughter	Forcible rape	Robbery	Aggravated assault	Burglary	Larceny-theft	Motor vehicle theft	Arson[1]
TEXAS—Continued											
Angleton	18,541	653	655	1	15	7	71	127	382	50	2
Arlington	340,525	24,551	24,609	15	145	687	1,282	3,552	16,345	2,525	58
Athens	11,553	770	774	1	2	17	113	156	451	30	4
Austin	671,462	43,210	43,354	26	262	1,171	1,670	7,439	29,276	3,366	144
Balch Springs	19,815	1,191	1,191	2	10	31	52	171	755	170	0
Bay City	19,091	1,154	1,157	1	0	22	65	259	770	37	3
Baytown	67,938	3,053	3,070	4	34	56	132	546	1,997	284	17
Beaumont	116,450	8,845	8,904	10	158	361	585	1,692	5,512	527	59
Bedford	48,222	1,940	1,951	1	20	33	70	274	1,424	118	11
Beeville	13,427	450	450	0	2	3	27	88	311	19	0
Bellaire	15,997	616	617	0	1	19	9	106	446	35	1
Belton	14,955	566	567	0	0	5	31	138	384	8	1
Benbrook	20,667	561	562	0	14	12	11	80	396	48	1
Big Spring	25,806	1,004	1,011	1	15	3	40	300	610	35	7
Bonham	10,217	495	495	0	13	10	56	70	323	23	0
Borger	14,627	885	890	0	10	11	35	167	637	25	5
Brenham	13,814	720	721	0	15	11	73	113	474	34	1
Brownsville	142,893	11,910	11,945	7	27	180	595	1,066	9,574	461	35
Brownwood	19,240	1,544	1,551	1	16	7	211	304	890	115	7
Bryan	67,150	4,041	4,049	4	66	64	325	741	2,658	183	8
Burkburnett	11,175	157	157	0	0	1	7	46	99	4	0
Burleson	21,452	806	810	0	3	6	24	97	612	64	4
Canyon	13,167	191	191	0	0	0	8	24	154	5	0
Carrollton	112,063	3,842	3,865	2	2	52	135	802	2,491	358	23
Cedar Hill	32,821	1,348	1,349	0	23	14	47	337	820	107	1
Cedar Park	26,640	643	647	1	1	4	40	133	437	27	4
Clute	10,661	582	583	0	7	6	31	110	397	31	1
College Station	69,431	2,507	2,512	1	35	18	58	285	2,026	84	5
Colleyville	20,082	304	312	0	1	2	3	54	230	14	8
Conroe	37,646	2,782	2,792	2	17	96	190	480	1,815	182	10
Converse	11,769	275	277	0	13	7	6	52	172	25	2
Copperas Cove	30,264	1,233	1,234	0	5	10	96	230	848	44	1
Corinth	11,582	141	141	1	0	4	5	30	87	14	0
Corpus Christi	283,750	22,534	22,658	19	224	582	1,640	3,999	14,555	1,515	124
Corsicana	25,041	1,748	1,758	1	17	33	35	388	1,172	102	10
Dallas	1,215,553	111,006	112,661	240	660	8,330	8,546	20,635	53,611	18,984	1,655
Deer Park	29,167	520	528	0	2	10	17	115	331	45	8
Del Rio	34,636	1,384	1,387	0	0	16	57	231	1,021	59	3
Denison	23,290	1,434	1,443	0	3	17	41	334	952	87	9
Denton	82,365	3,664	3,689	2	49	70	188	547	2,652	156	25
DeSoto	38,500	1,990	2,001	4	13	29	89	438	1,252	165	11
Dickinson	17,481	588	588	0	13	15	33	136	347	44	0
Donna	15,103	1,020	1,023	1	3	9	52	227	693	35	3
Dumas	14,059	458	460	1	3	2	47	82	302	21	2
Duncanville	36,900	2,067	2,074	1	13	96	102	319	1,302	234	7
Eagle Pass	22,922	1,085	1,086	0	2	1	37	127	846	72	1
Edinburg	49,565	4,866	4,893	0	41	63	195	634	3,736	197	27
El Campo	11,193	752	753	0	6	5	46	173	494	28	1
El Paso	576,453	30,814	30,940	20	203	775	3,388	2,553	22,039	1,836	126
Ennis	16,409	962	963	0	13	20	38	179	651	61	1
Euless	47,049	1,775	1,783	0	19	29	76	280	1,218	153	8
Farmers Branch	28,132	1,365	1,366	1	14	25	40	203	850	232	1
Flower Mound	51,853	776	776	0	6	3	24	195	523	25	0
Forest Hill	13,243	438	439	0	9	19	70	123	170	47	1
Fort Worth	546,828	40,466	40,771	67	332	1,389	2,076	7,971	24,675	3,956	305
Freeport	12,996	541	543	0	18	7	40	136	315	25	2
Friendswood	29,696	491	497	1	5	6	32	87	337	23	6
Frisco	34,479	1,243	1,245	0	12	6	46	239	891	49	2
Gainesville	15,891	933	937	0	2	8	19	170	698	36	4
Galena Park	10,832	287	287	1	8	6	19	71	136	46	0
Garland	220,665	9,568	9,625	9	45	274	264	2,141	5,802	1,033	57
Gatesville	15,945	267	268	0	6	1	31	52	173	4	1

See footnotes at end of table.

Table 8

Offenses Known to Law Enforcement
by City 10,000 and over in Population, 2001—Continued

City by state	Population	Crime Index total	Modified Crime Index total[1]	Murder and non-negligent man-slaughter	Forcible rape	Robbery	Aggravated assault	Burglary	Larceny-theft	Motor vehicle theft	Arson[1]
TEXAS—Continued											
Georgetown	28,982	647	648	0	2	4	20	82	504	35	1
Grand Prairie	130,319	6,928	6,982	6	51	128	199	1,095	4,278	1,171	54
Grapevine	43,013	1,670	1,673	0	5	20	42	231	1,219	153	3
Greenville	24,504	2,132	2,140	1	15	90	188	475	1,240	123	8
Groves	16,090	865	866	0	0	13	12	139	657	44	1
Haltom City	39,903	2,016	2,029	2	13	25	115	458	1,232	171	13
Harker Heights	17,701	765	768	0	6	10	12	131	588	18	3
Harlingen	58,870	4,611	4,631	5	36	66	221	989	3,045	249	20
Henderson	11,529	975	975	2	12	12	128	98	686	37	0
Hereford	14,928	543	551	1	2	9	103	108	303	17	8
Hewitt	11,337	327	328	0	5	0	13	90	207	12	1
Highland Village	12,449	146	146	0	0	1	2	44	92	7	0
Houston	1,997,965	141,987	143,745	267	945	9,921	12,286	25,108	69,371	24,089	1,758
Humble	14,910	1,352	1,356	0	10	36	42	158	889	217	4
Huntsville	35,874	1,291	1,292	1	12	11	98	237	849	83	1
Hurst	37,096	2,627	2,632	2	19	35	83	316	2,035	137	5
Irving	195,963	9,993	10,037	10	58	281	467	1,387	6,561	1,229	44
Jacinto City	10,536	455	458	0	0	6	8	63	315	63	3
Jacksonville	14,183	836	841	1	17	20	63	187	506	42	5
Katy	12,042	623	624	0	2	7	85	52	437	40	1
Keller	27,966	540	542	0	5	6	67	80	365	17	2
Kerrville	20,889	859	864	1	4	16	39	106	661	32	5
Kilgore	11,557	1,117	1,120	0	13	17	39	187	830	31	3
Killeen	88,883	5,263	5,304	8	40	153	355	1,170	3,299	238	41
Kingsville	26,155	1,289	1,295	0	11	11	100	203	930	34	6
Lake Jackson	26,985	914	914	1	4	6	20	119	727	37	0
La Marque	13,992	829	829	4	11	30	12	220	485	67	0
Lamesa	10,178	324	325	0	1	2	41	78	188	14	1
Lancaster	26,482	1,727	1,730	0	8	47	158	418	916	180	3
La Porte	32,603	800	818	2	10	18	83	187	443	57	18
Laredo	180,583	13,056	13,143	8	39	200	874	1,791	9,125	1,019	87
League City	46,475	1,146	1,149	1	4	35	24	207	803	72	3
Levelland	13,158	276	294	0	4	3	28	47	186	8	18
Lewisville	79,501	3,598	3,607	0	20	58	111	477	2,572	360	9
Lockhart	11,879	392	392	0	3	4	45	78	248	14	0
Longview	75,008	6,130	6,144	8	101	167	275	1,274	3,782	523	14
Lubbock	204,093	14,063	14,129	10	100	317	2,042	2,847	8,068	679	66
Lufkin	33,451	2,268	2,272	3	31	47	135	453	1,456	143	4
Mansfield	28,667	931	936	5	2	7	49	216	601	51	5
Marshall	24,478	1,535	1,546	1	15	27	97	265	1,006	124	11
McAllen	108,829	8,989	9,021	3	11	124	336	1,567	6,235	713	32
McKinney	55,603	2,052	2,073	1	44	32	97	341	1,389	148	21
Memorial Villages	11,667	198	198	0	1	7	1	66	111	12	0
Mercedes	13,959	615	622	0	2	13	82	137	309	72	7
Mesquite	127,349	6,542	6,644	4	3	147	312	646	4,554	876	102
Midland	97,152	3,183	3,194	2	91	50	264	690	1,912	174	11
Mineral Wells	17,331	806	819	1	24	7	24	187	536	27	13
Mission	46,438	2,902	2,909	0	2	27	56	499	2,030	288	7
Missouri City	54,114	1,390	1,401	4	14	60	71	330	788	123	11
Mount Pleasant	14,251	916	921	2	0	12	44	151	655	52	5
Nacogdoches	30,593	1,352	1,352	0	29	23	93	246	900	61	0
Nederland	17,817	1,041	1,043	0	4	8	12	164	806	47	2
New Braunfels	37,322	2,658	2,660	0	12	27	314	292	1,931	82	2
North Richland Hills	56,898	2,539	2,540	3	21	24	75	322	1,975	119	1
Odessa	93,007	5,198	5,240	4	24	81	403	946	3,544	196	42
Orange	19,066	1,181	1,191	1	11	31	135	262	662	79	10
Palestine	17,997	1,063	1,065	1	6	22	101	201	694	38	2
Pampa	18,293	1,245	1,245	0	15	26	53	329	777	45	0
Paris	26,486	3,241	3,254	3	49	33	265	501	2,286	104	13
Pasadena	144,889	6,919	6,997	3	52	153	555	1,270	4,057	829	78
Pearland	38,494	1,328	1,336	0	10	24	35	209	963	87	8
Pflugerville	16,706	350	352	1	5	1	16	40	273	14	2

See footnotes at end of table.

Table 8

Offenses Known to Law Enforcement
by City 10,000 and over in Population, 2001—Continued

City by state	Population	Crime Index total	Modified Crime Index total[1]	Murder and non-negligent man-slaughter	Forcible rape	Robbery	Aggravated assault	Burglary	Larceny-theft	Motor vehicle theft	Arson[1]
TEXAS—Continued											
Pharr	47,719	2,859	2,873	3	16	43	182	532	1,998	85	14
Plainview	22,843	1,203	1,212	0	9	10	50	237	879	18	9
Plano	227,069	8,987	9,032	4	23	113	448	1,417	6,440	542	45
Port Arthur	59,066	2,753	2,794	7	15	123	206	862	1,246	294	41
Portland	15,163	484	486	0	4	5	24	72	359	20	2
Port Lavaca	12,308	511	512	2	9	7	29	77	349	38	1
Port Neches	13,910	577	579	0	6	2	29	109	406	25	2
Richardson	93,885	3,920	3,932	2	19	104	128	746	2,502	419	12
Richmond	11,332	381	392	0	5	12	35	76	233	20	11
Rio Grande City	12,194	452	452	2	2	3	48	91	267	39	0
Robstown	13,016	1,278	1,282	0	2	10	61	243	933	29	4
Rockwall	18,384	753	754	0	7	12	24	140	510	60	1
Rosenberg	24,589	1,112		1	27	18	78	202	713	73	
Round Rock	62,523	1,686	1,687	1	20	31	56	235	1,287	56	1
Rowlett	45,513	1,085	1,086	0	16	8	51	317	631	62	1
Saginaw	12,655	419	419	0	6	3	21	85	276	28	0
San Angelo	90,446	5,730	5,763	2	67	49	345	1,023	4,036	208	33
San Antonio	1,170,622	96,498	97,074	100	492	2,146	6,808	14,018	66,694	6,240	576
San Benito	23,976	2,523	2,523	1	12	7	51	300	2,087	65	0
San Juan	26,824	1,289	1,297	1	4	16	65	238	908	57	8
San Marcos	35,521	1,466	1,470	0	39	21	65	241	1,040	60	4
Schertz	19,118	450	452	0	8	6	19	55	343	19	2
Seagoville	11,069	524	528	0	11	7	17	107	296	86	4
Seguin	22,511	1,727	1,727	1	5	25	79	243	1,345	29	0
Sherman	35,878	2,452	2,457	0	12	59	178	381	1,701	121	5
Snyder	11,028	327	329	0	3	1	10	75	233	5	2
Socorro	27,768	459	461	0	4	9	108	82	216	40	2
South Houston	16,192	882	882	2	0	32	38	151	513	146	0
Southlake	22,007	315	315	0	1	6	5	70	213	20	0
Stafford	16,037	878	879	0	8	42	21	160	570	77	1
Stephenville	15,260	557	557	1	6	7	4	86	434	19	0
Sugar Land	64,765	1,828	1,829	0	5	57	76	278	1,328	84	1
Sulphur Springs	14,881	473	478	0	4	5	40	98	276	50	5
Taylor	13,883	494	497	0	8	3	41	97	325	20	3
Temple	55,751	3,087	3,113	3	14	68	137	607	2,074	184	26
Terrell	13,915	1,311	1,316	2	5	41	148	173	837	105	5
Texarkana	35,571	3,026	3,065	2	25	65	299	517	1,991	127	39
Texas City	42,463	3,799	3,819	7	28	105	327	681	2,356	295	20
The Colony	27,133	1,249	1,257	2	11	5	26	240	911	54	8
Universal City	15,186	521	527	2	5	7	76	112	292	27	6
University Park	23,853	712	715	1	0	9	5	121	544	32	3
Uvalde	15,268	914	925	1	1	6	66	166	626	48	11
Vernon	11,925	624	630	1	13	7	38	95	453	17	6
Victoria	61,978	3,748	3,758	2	21	70	347	719	2,434	155	10
Vidor	11,700	563	567	0	4	6	35	117	354	47	4
Waco	116,307	10,361	10,421	7	100	269	527	1,875	6,787	796	60
Watauga	22,405	662	662	0	2	9	19	139	463	30	0
Waxahachie	21,912	1,359	1,365	0	0	12	78	236	953	80	6
Weatherford	19,431	819	822	1	6	13	21	134	601	43	3
Weslaco	27,546	2,511	2,517	2	2	33	105	535	1,687	147	6
West University Place	14,533	265	265	0	0	6	1	60	181	17	0
White Settlement	15,168	714	715	0	3	9	32	138	462	70	1
Wichita Falls	106,562	8,185	8,216	4	21	256	590	1,502	5,314	498	31
Wylie	15,475	400	401	0	14	2	24	104	235	21	1
UTAH											
Alpine/Highland	15,569	242	245	0	2	2	4	37	187	10	3
American Fork	22,301	910	911	0	5	7	19	128	706	45	1
Bountiful	41,978	854	855	0	11	6	32	89	681	35	1
Brigham City	17,697	658	659	0	8	2	38	95	494	21	1
Cedar City	20,864	808	810	0	0	5	12	128	632	31	2

See footnotes at end of table.

Table 8

Offenses Known to Law Enforcement
by City 10,000 and over in Population, 2001—Continued

City by state	Population	Crime Index total	Modified Crime Index total[1]	Murder and non-negligent man-slaughter	Forcible rape	Robbery	Aggravated assault	Burglary	Larceny-theft	Motor vehicle theft	Arson[1]
UTAH—Continued											
Centerville	14,824	446	457	0	5	2	4	65	355	15	11
Clearfield	26,400	957	968	1	19	0	35	113	733	56	11
Clinton	12,791	189	191	0	6	0	5	24	141	13	2
Farmington	12,279	268	268	0	1	0	3	38	211	15	0
Layton	59,433	2,272	2,290	2	22	19	48	278	1,785	118	18
Lehi	19,340	350	350	1	12	2	8	114	189	24	0
Logan	43,370	935	935	1	8	0	23	66	810	27	0
Midvale	27,472	1,866	1,875	0	23	37	70	266	1,312	158	9
Murray	34,582	3,513	3,516	1	29	39	89	456	2,645	254	3
North Ogden	15,272	298	299	0	1	0	4	32	254	7	1
Ogden	78,492	5,242	5,242	9	53	105	191	771	3,760	353	0
Orem	85,707	3,316	3,318	0	18	11	34	284	2,796	173	2
Payson	12,925	395	395	1	5	1	4	104	260	20	0
Pleasant Grove/Lindon	32,353	910	926	1	7	2	17	102	725	56	16
Provo	106,891	3,844	3,865	0	43	18	98	558	2,929	198	21
Roy	33,424	1,132	1,142	0	5	5	77	278	713	54	10
Salt Lake City	184,723	16,438	16,503	18	121	481	546	2,209	11,401	1,662	65
Sandy	89,868	3,405	3,419	2	21	37	77	541	2,552	175	14
South Ogden	14,613	620	624	1	4	8	20	71	486	30	4
South Salt Lake	22,399	2,063	2,070	2	39	31	64	285	1,357	285	7
Spanish Fork	20,578	1,033	1,045	0	2	1	5	179	815	31	12
Springville	20,759	818	818	0	8	2	25	131	616	36	0
Tooele	22,871	669	673	1	10	9	40	168	371	70	4
West Jordan	69,457	2,971	2,984	1	26	27	106	359	2,287	165	13
West Valley	110,682	6,950	6,975	2	64	116	281	887	4,998	602	25
VERMONT											
Bennington	16,081	451	452	0	3	0	10	102	318	18	1
Brattleboro	12,089	551	556	0	3	6	17	110	396	19	5
Burlington	39,161	2,686	2,696	0	16	21	105	379	2,069	96	10
Colchester	17,105	479	481	1	2	2	16	64	377	17	2
Essex	18,756	516	521	0	3	3	3	72	421	14	5
Hartford	10,440	269	272	0	3	2	8	48	192	16	3
Rutland	17,413	890	896	0	4	21	30	131	678	26	6
South Burlington	15,925	773	777	0	2	4	10	66	658	33	4
VIRGINIA											
Blacksburg	40,184	772	776	1	6	12	52	118	549	34	4
Bristol	17,635	668	674	3	4	7	39	74	509	32	6
Charlottesville	45,744	2,127	2,143	3	25	71	364	269	1,279	116	16
Christiansburg	17,208	453	460	0	1	2	18	68	344	20	7
Colonial Heights	17,158	993	999	0	2	17	29	96	809	40	6
Falls Church	10,537	468	468	0	2	10	15	42	336	63	0
Fredericksburg	19,576	1,019	1,026	1	9	28	84	75	761	61	7
Hampton	148,696	6,815	6,853	10	35	283	276	991	4,129	1,091	38
Harrisonburg	41,092	1,386	1,400	1	11	32	75	173	1,001	93	14
Hopewell	22,699	1,397	1,411	0	5	56	110	277	811	138	14
Leesburg	28,748	891	909	0	13	15	50	65	689	59	18
Lynchburg	66,276	2,716	2,738	6	23	80	178	490	1,718	221	22
Manassas	35,677	1,443	1,459	0	16	54	59	149	1,015	150	16
Manassas Park	10,449	329	339	0	1	6	14	20	239	49	10
Martinsville	15,654	784	795	1	18	22	46	87	547	63	11
Newport News	182,930	9,784	9,897	30	97	448	750	1,508	5,788	1,163	113
Norfolk	238,020	14,966	14,990	31	127	809	633	1,728	10,123	1,515	24
Petersburg	34,261	2,840	2,848	5	24	110	203	525	1,655	318	8
Poquoson	11,744	118	120	2	0	0	8	11	90	7	2
Portsmouth	102,117	6,650	6,665	12	30	473	584	1,515	3,370	666	15
Richmond	200,842	18,207	18,373	72	117	1,430	1,127	2,943	9,455	3,063	166
Roanoke	96,375	5,468	5,502	5	41	135	404	689	3,856	338	34
Salem	25,129	653	660	2	4	10	12	51	543	31	7

See footnotes at end of table.

Table 8

Offenses Known to Law Enforcement
by City 10,000 and over in Population, 2001—Continued

City by state	Population	Crime Index total	Modified Crime Index total[1]	Murder and non-negligent man-slaughter	Forcible rape	Robbery	Aggravated assault	Burglary	Larceny-theft	Motor vehicle theft	Arson[1]
VIRGINIA—Continued											
Staunton	24,221	833	838	1	5	3	40	104	638	42	5
Suffolk	64,660	2,510	2,532	5	31	106	247	370	1,607	144	22
Vienna	14,676	251	252	0	1	7	9	18	207	9	1
Virginia Beach	431,819	16,135	16,316	12	110	368	350	2,285	12,078	932	181
Waynesboro	19,821	1,033	1,049	0	7	13	133	113	720	47	16
Williamsburg	12,183	415	416	0	5	9	39	41	298	23	1
Winchester	23,949	1,402	1,422	0	10	21	39	162	1,114	56	20
WASHINGTON											
Aberdeen	16,723	1,611	1,613	0	13	12	22	220	1,268	76	2
Anacortes	14,789	580	585	0	0	0	14	84	457	25	5
Arlington	11,900	977	983	0	5	10	38	111	694	119	6
Auburn	40,956	3,909	3,944	0	18	69	141	683	2,297	701	35
Bainbridge Island	20,631	387	390	0	2	1	8	98	278	0	3
Bellevue	111,314	4,667	4,702	0	21	59	82	535	3,431	539	35
Bellingham	68,241	4,849	4,865	1	22	50	64	555	3,942	215	16
Bothell	30,630	863	867	1	1	10	14	124	599	114	4
Bremerton	37,852	2,771	2,795	3	78	58	239	471	1,571	351	24
Burien	32,389	2,350	2,359	2	33	73	127	360	1,203	552	9
Camas	12,734	453	453	0	1	0	14	85	339	14	0
Centralia	14,977	1,196	1,205	0	12	13	60	181	865	65	9
Covington	14,002	518	527	0	6	4	19	87	338	64	9
Des Moines	29,733	1,119	1,126	5	17	32	43	160	626	236	7
Edmonds	40,144	1,129	1,137	0	6	9	22	183	797	112	8
Ellensburg	15,659	1,252	1,265	0	11	3	17	190	1,003	28	13
Enumclaw	11,293	149	149	0	1	0	1	26	77	44	0
Everett	92,945	6,835	6,859	5	76	170	296	1,008	3,798	1,482	24
Federal Way	84,585	5,537	5,555	4	49	125	141	522	3,516	1,180	18
Issaquah	11,391	736	741	0	0	8	3	85	553	87	5
Kelso	12,084	1,174	1,187	1	18	17	52	190	814	82	13
Kenmore	18,975	555	560	0	14	6	21	114	340	60	5
Kennewick	55,564	3,227	3,255	1	22	44	145	408	2,374	233	28
Kent	80,790	5,543	5,601	2	25	125	139	866	3,221	1,165	58
Kirkland	45,771	1,483	1,490	1	6	22	20	228	990	216	7
Lacey	31,723	1,577	1,581	3	14	35	50	240	1,154	81	4
Lake Forest Park	13,351	284	284	0	4	2	3	48	195	32	0
Lakewood	59,138	4,193	4,221	5	62	178	202	767	2,450	529	28
Longview	35,212	3,368	3,405	0	24	33	142	573	2,368	228	37
Lynnwood	34,386	2,813	2,821	0	10	49	49	259	2,079	367	8
Maple Valley	14,435	435	441	0	1	0	17	108	234	75	6
Marysville	25,718	1,159	1,168	0	15	26	22	157	706	233	9
Mercer Island	22,387	425	430	1	4	2	1	58	314	45	5
Moses Lake	15,191	1,298	1,300	0	15	13	58	194	961	57	2
Mountlake Terrace	20,686	784	801	0	10	7	12	88	515	152	17
Mount Vernon	26,650	2,339	2,351	1	22	22	14	206	1,971	103	12
Mukilteo	18,306	502	505	0	3	5	9	87	316	82	3
Olympia	43,191	3,159	3,177	0	24	35	59	498	2,268	275	18
Pasco	32,577	1,586	1,592	4	13	34	73	287	1,053	122	6
Port Angeles	18,690	882	897	0	11	9	35	155	643	29	15
Puyallup	33,537	3,119	3,125	1	9	33	32	257	2,315	472	6
Redmond	45,977	1,673	1,676	0	15	17	65	145	1,295	136	3
Renton	50,849	4,114	4,128	1	14	105	108	613	2,411	862	14
Richland	39,324	1,597	1,616	1	8	9	32	223	1,235	89	19
Sammamish	34,647	558	567	0	4	5	8	121	384	36	9
SeaTac	25,902	1,804	1,809	0	20	57	79	255	881	512	5
Seattle	572,345	46,091	46,307	25	164	1,594	2,367	6,684	26,502	8,755	216
Shoreline	53,869	1,905	1,920	0	16	46	47	307	1,262	227	15
Spokane	198,744	17,073	17,123	7	79	440	883	3,101	10,792	1,771	50
Sunnyside	14,126	1,103	1,115	2	6	11	18	173	822	71	12
Tacoma	196,638	18,370	18,493	15	143	743	1,211	2,920	10,033	3,305	123
Tukwila	17,455	2,938	2,945	1	15	64	66	210	2,111	471	7

See footnotes at end of table.

Table 8

Offenses Known to Law Enforcement
by City 10,000 and over in Population, 2001—Continued

City by state	Population	Crime Index total	Modified Crime Index total[1]	Murder and non-negligent man-slaughter	Forcible rape	Robbery	Aggravated assault	Burglary	Larceny-theft	Motor vehicle theft	Arson[1]
WASHINGTON—Continued											
Tumwater	12,900	545	550	0	5	5	12	103	382	38	5
University Place	30,410	1,385	1,392	0	16	12	69	212	926	150	7
Vancouver	145,846	7,962	8,023	4	76	132	475	1,067	5,745	463	61
Walla Walla	30,159	1,825	1,825	0	35	22	89	283	1,317	79	0
Wenatchee	28,300	2,136	2,143	1	16	16	73	343	1,594	93	7
Yakima	72,989	6,163	6,204	5	39	102	187	1,193	4,076	561	41
WEST VIRGINIA											
Clarksburg	16,683	118	120	0	1	1	24	26	52	14	2
Weirton	20,338	390	395	0	0	8	14	69	283	16	5
WISCONSIN											
Appleton	70,587	1,912	1,919	1	16	8	127	236	1,467	57	7
Ashwaubenon	17,760	889	889	0	1	3	4	72	784	25	0
Baraboo	10,787	502	502	1	2	1	32	54	397	15	0
Beaver Dam	15,277	634	634	0	3	2	5	54	555	15	0
Beloit	36,030	1,785	1,798	1	13	53	72	279	1,245	122	13
Brookfield	38,924	1,185	1,185	1	0	17	5	80	1,046	36	0
Brown Deer	12,257	612	612	0	1	19	5	23	538	26	0
Burlington	10,007	397	400	0	0	2	4	40	341	10	3
Caledonia	23,782	365	371	0	0	4	8	81	243	29	6
Cedarburg	10,986	137	139	0	1	0	1	4	130	1	2
Chippewa Falls	13,017	388	395	0	0	2	10	60	306	10	7
Cudahy	18,560	660	662	0	3	12	11	107	500	27	2
De Pere	20,706	418	418	0	1	2	7	52	342	14	0
Eau Claire	62,144	2,807	2,816	1	18	15	107	397	2,139	130	9
Everest	14,297	394	395	0	1	0	7	59	301	26	1
Fitchburg	20,647	711	712	0	2	9	15	81	546	58	1
Fond du Lac	42,504	1,682	1,683	1	11	11	44	186	1,382	47	1
Fort Atkinson	11,704	443	443	0	0	2	3	30	394	14	0
Fox Valley	16,741	405	406	0	1	0	0	32	361	11	1
Franklin	29,704	642	646	0	5	1	18	120	464	34	4
Germantown	18,390	390	395	0	6	2	1	36	333	12	5
Glendale	13,462	874	874	0	0	23	4	26	774	47	0
Grafton	10,386	146	146	0	0	1	1	18	123	3	0
Grand Chute	18,523	952	952	0	1	1	7	48	864	31	0
Green Bay	103,042	3,712	3,723	3	35	36	198	675	2,561	204	11
Greendale	14,508	429	432	0	1	7	5	9	383	24	3
Greenfield	35,729	1,412	1,415	1	4	22	11	157	1,126	91	3
Hartford	10,983	456	456	0	0	2	3	28	413	10	0
Janesville	59,922	3,195	3,218	1	16	20	104	503	2,441	110	23
Kaukauna	13,076	228	230	0	1	0	11	19	184	13	2
Kenosha	90,996	3,182	3,193	4	41	62	440	422	1,997	216	11
La Crosse	52,187	2,093	2,097	2	11	25	61	192	1,684	118	4
Madison	209,537	8,299	8,374	6	63	295	344	1,354	5,530	707	75
Manitowoc	34,296	1,374	1,375	1	6	5	27	158	1,140	37	1
Marinette	11,833	542	543	0	5	2	6	73	438	18	1
Marshfield	18,934	667	676	0	6	2	9	104	523	23	9
Menasha	16,447	457	459	0	3	1	24	48	371	10	2
Menomonee Falls	32,880	532	536	0	2	6	10	54	427	33	4
Menomonie	15,043	613	616	0	0	2	7	102	476	26	3
Mequon	21,979	186	187	1	1	3	1	32	142	6	1
Merrill	10,218	460	460	0	4	1	7	73	359	16	0
Middleton	15,882	509	510	0	1	3	2	44	429	30	1
Milwaukee	601,229	45,748	46,201	127	295	2,913	2,128	6,680	25,712	7,893	453
Monroe	10,920	270	271	0	1	1	3	21	234	10	1
Mount Pleasant	23,307	678	681	1	6	15	9	99	505	43	3
Neenah	24,682	528	537	0	5	2	19	46	430	26	9
New Berlin	38,492	595	606	0	0	5	17	90	466	17	11
Oak Creek	28,659	877	883	0	1	11	8	73	741	43	6

See footnotes at end of table.

Table 8

Offenses Known to Law Enforcement
by City 10,000 and over in Population, 2001—Continued

City by state	Population	Crime Index total	Modified Crime Index total[1]	Murder and non-negligent man-slaughter	Forcible rape	Robbery	Aggravated assault	Burglary	Larceny-theft	Motor vehicle theft	Arson[1]
WISCONSIN—Continued											
Oconomowoc	12,470	245	245	0	1	1	4	36	192	11	0
Onalaska	14,945	605	605	0	0	0	18	21	555	11	0
Oshkosh	63,364	2,281	2,285	0	13	16	98	251	1,830	73	4
Pewaukee Township	11,867	141	141	0	1	0	2	20	115	3	0
Platteville	10,060	372	372	0	3	1	18	26	319	5	0
Pleasant Prairie	16,251	532	533	0	2	1	2	16	499	12	1
Plover	10,595	207	207	0	1	0	6	20	171	9	0
Port Washington	10,542	228	228	0	2	0	2	18	196	10	0
Racine	82,438	5,912	5,936	4	22	340	245	1,174	3,622	505	24
River Falls	12,650	522	523	0	1	0	23	53	429	16	1
Sheboygan	51,154	2,284	2,304	3	24	10	39	300	1,838	70	20
Shorewood	13,861	420	424	0	1	12	5	50	328	24	4
South Milwaukee	21,408	529	529	0	3	7	15	78	404	22	0
Stevens Point	24,726	1,006	1,011	0	13	2	44	125	789	33	5
Stoughton	12,442	282	282	0	0	1	5	36	228	12	0
Sun Prairie	20,514	679	679	0	7	0	17	93	532	30	0
Superior	27,563	1,673	1,691	0	14	11	39	246	1,260	103	18
Town of Menasha	15,971	219	220	0	1	0	4	32	177	5	1
Two Rivers	12,729	303	303	0	3	1	10	24	261	4	0
Watertown	21,752	668	668	1	5	7	22	89	516	28	0
Waukesha	65,287	1,586	1,599	2	8	21	69	321	1,073	92	13
Waupun	10,794	272	272	0	1	0	3	24	244	0	0
Wausau	38,700	1,652	1,666	2	21	11	85	335	1,123	75	14
Wauwatosa	47,608	2,519	2,519	1	8	68	28	270	1,968	176	0
West Allis	61,691	2,774	2,796	1	8	61	83	471	1,918	232	22
West Bend	28,353	925	933	0	1	3	2	81	806	32	8
Whitefish Bay	14,264	194	194	0	0	3	2	12	171	6	0
Whitewater	13,533	345	347	0	0	0	8	26	298	13	2
Wisconsin Rapids	18,566	969	971	0	4	5	5	160	764	31	2
WYOMING											
Casper	49,708	2,318	2,365	2	20	23	111	435	1,607	120	47
Cheyenne	53,080	2,325	2,334	0	14	15	52	268	1,903	73	9
Evanston	11,522	532	532	2	4	2	9	26	466	23	0
Gillette	19,672	1,220	1,234	0	9	4	51	63	1,063	30	14
Green River	11,823	370	373	0	0	1	19	57	285	8	3
Laramie	27,239	1,120	1,126	0	4	0	97	138	836	45	6
Rock Springs	18,732	963	964	1	11	2	72	119	733	25	1
Sheridan	15,825	490	490	0	5	2	15	57	393	18	0

[1] The Modified Crime Index total is the sum of the Crime Index offenses including arson. Arson is shown only if 12 months of arson data were received. If 12 months of arson data were not received, there is no Modified Crime Index total shown.

[2] Complete arson figures for 2001 for Alabama, Massachusetts, and Montana were not available.

[3] The population for the city of Mobile, Alabama, includes 55,864 inhabitants from the jurisdiction of the Mobile County Sheriff's Department.

[4] Due to changes in reporting practices, annexations, and/or incomplete data, figures are not comparable to previous years' data.

[5] The data for anthrax assaults were not available.

[6] Forcible rape figures furnished by the state Uniform Crime Reporting (UCR) Program administered by the Illinois State Police were not in accordance with national UCR guidelines; therefore, the figures were excluded from the forcible rape, Crime Index total, and Modified Crime Index total categories.

[7] Limited data for 2001 were available for Illinois and Kentucky.

[8] Aggravated assault figures were found to be outside established statistical parameters.

[9] The murder and nonnegligent homicide figure includes the 2,823 homicides reported as a result of the events of September 11, 2001. See special report, Section V.

Table 9

Offenses Known to Law Enforcement
by University and College by State, 2001

University/College by state	Student enrollment[1]	Violent crime total[2]	Violent crime				Property crime total[3]	Property crime			
			Murder and non-negligent man-slaughter	Forcible rape	Robbery	Aggravated assault		Burglary	Larceny-theft	Motor vehicle theft	Arson[3]
ALABAMA[4]											
Alabama State University	5,664	20	0	0	16	4	260	7	250	3	
Auburn University:											
Main Campus	22,120	5	0	1	3	1	306	19	283	4	
Montgomery	5,354	1	0	1	0	0	44	12	30	2	
Jacksonville State University	7,928	1	0	0	0	1	40	6	32	2	
Talladega College	455	0	0	0	0	0	27	0	27	0	
Troy State University	11,515	3	1	0	0	2	85	8	73	4	
University of Alabama:											
Huntsville	6,874	1	0	0	1	0	81	9	72	0	
Tuscaloosa	18,744	5	0	0	1	4	374	18	348	8	
University of Montevallo	3,147	0	0	0	0	0	8	0	8	0	
University of North Alabama	5,805	0	0	0	0	0	71	22	49	0	
University of South Alabama	11,185	3	0	1	1	1	125	8	114	3	
ALASKA											
University of Alaska:											
Anchorage	14,746	2	0	1	0	1	113	6	106	1	0
Fairbanks	6,768	6	0	2	1	3	116	13	98	5	1
ARIZONA											
Arizona State University:											
Main Campus	44,215	31	0	8	2	21	1,029	128	843	58	2
West	4,943	0	0	0	0	0	42	0	42	0	0
Arizona Western College	6,321	0	0	0	0	0	52	7	45	0	0
Central Arizona College	4,560	2	0	0	0	2	30	2	23	5	0
Northern Arizona University	19,981	16	0	6	0	10	436	48	372	16	4
Pima Community College	30,548	1	0	0	1	0	237	59	169	9	0
University of Arizona	34,326	36	0	6	10	20	1,250	98	1,087	65	6
Yavapai College	6,772	1	0	0	0	1	45	4	39	2	0
ARKANSAS											
Arkansas State University	10,461	9	0	0	1	8	124	20	102	2	0
Henderson State University	3,500	2	0	0	0	2	29	0	29	0	0
University of Arkansas:											
Little Rock[5]		4	0	0	1	3	128	9	104	15	0
Medical Sciences	1,861	2	0	0	1	1	212	13	196	3	0
Monticello	2,254	2	0	0	0	2	40	0	40	0	0
University of Central Arkansas	8,739	2	0	1	0	1	114	18	96	0	1
CALIFORNIA											
Allan Hancock College	8,382	0	0	0	0	0	34	4	30	0	0
California State Polytechnic University:											
Pomona	18,021	1	0	0	1	0	408	87	276	45	0
San Luis Obispo	16,470	3	0	0	0	3	194	11	179	4	5
California State University:											
Bakersfield	6,210	0	0	0	0	0	59	14	44	1	0
Channel Islands[5]		1	0	1	0	0	11	0	11	0	0
Chico	15,261	5	0	3	0	2	284	40	240	4	1
Dominguez Hills	12,524	3	0	0	3	0	86	26	55	5	0
Fresno	18,321	12	0	1	3	8	444	73	324	47	1
Fullerton	27,167	7	0	0	1	6	210	11	156	43	0
Hayward	12,667	2	0	1	1	0	93	19	64	10	0
Long Beach	30,011	5	0	1	1	3	431	73	304	54	0

See footnotes at end of table.

Table 9

Offenses Known to Law Enforcement
by University and College by State, 2001—Continued

University/College by state	Student enrollment[1]	Violent crime total[2]	Violent crime				Property crime total[3]	Property crime			
			Murder and non-negligent man-slaughter	Forcible rape	Robbery	Aggravated assault		Burglary	Larceny-theft	Motor vehicle theft	Arson[3]
CALIFORNIA—Continued											
California State University—Cont.:											
Los Angeles	19,783	8	0	1	2	5	414	30	340	44	0
Monterey Bay	2,265	10	0	4	1	5	131	47	82	2	3
Northridge	27,947	16	0	5	4	7	313	12	263	38	0
Sacramento	24,530	5	0	1	0	4	454	39	385	30	2
San Bernardino	14,280	6	0	1	2	3	160	23	128	9	1
San Jose[5]		20	0	7	4	9	329	35	281	13	2
San Marcos	5,739	0	0	0	0	0	19	1	18	0	0
Stanislaus	6,489	2	0	0	0	2	86	2	81	3	0
Stockton[5]		3	0	1	0	2	14	10	3	1	0
College of the Sequoias	9,572	1	0	0	0	1	106	31	69	6	1
Contra Costa Community College	6,218	20	0	0	7	13	253	27	196	30	0
Cuesta College	8,879	0	0	0	0	0	66	12	53	1	0
El Camino College	22,616	6	0	0	1	5	229	3	210	16	1
Foothill-De Anza College	38,547	3	0	0	1	2	70	5	65	0	0
Humboldt State University	7,545	2	0	1	0	1	241	15	223	3	3
Long Beach Community College	18,730	6	0	0	1	5	128	33	76	19	0
Marin Community College	8,196	0	0	0	0	0	37	0	37	0	0
Pasadena Community College	22,978	1	0	0	0	1	232	2	219	11	0
Reedley Community College	7,869	0	0	0	0	0	36	3	31	2	0
Riverside Community College	22,320	6	0	0	1	5	193	9	172	12	0
San Bernardino Community College	9,737	0	0	0	0	0	71	5	62	4	0
San Diego State University	31,413	29	0	4	5	20	690	41	560	89	2
San Francisco State University	27,701	11	0	2	9	0	305	30	251	24	0
San Jose/Evergreen Community College	16,167	2	0	0	0	2	88	15	68	5	3
Santa Rosa Junior College	21,728	2	0	0	0	2	114	6	104	4	2
Sonoma State University	7,083	3	0	0	1	2	108	13	94	1	1
State Center Community College[5]		2	0	0	2	0	208	19	161	28	1
University of California:											
Berkeley	31,347	23	0	3	14	6	1,089	65	994	30	3
Davis	25,092	4	0	2	1	1	655	79	566	10	7
Hastings College of Law	1,122	1	0	0	0	1	9	1	8	0	0
Irvine	19,277	27	0	6	2	19	838	128	652	58	3
Lawrence-Livermore Laboratory[5]		0	0	0	0	0	13	0	13	0	0
Los Angeles	36,351	45	0	5	24	16	1,593	181	1,333	79	1
Riverside	11,600	6	0	3	1	2	389	39	327	23	1
Sacramento[5]		4	0	1	2	1	180	7	158	15	0
San Diego	19,894	7	1	0	0	6	442	30	386	26	2
San Francisco	3,491	3	0	0	0	3	408	16	388	4	1
Santa Barbara	20,056	6	0	1	2	3	401	25	375	1	1
Santa Cruz	11,302	10	0	0	0	10	195	22	169	4	1
West Valley-Mission College	19,910	1	0	0	0	1	157	17	127	13	0
COLORADO											
Adams State College	8,304	5	0	0	0	5	56	4	51	1	2
Arapahoe Community College	7,491	0	0	0	0	0	28	3	23	2	0
Auraria Higher Education Center[5]		3	0	1	1	1	240	9	226	5	0
Colorado School of Mines	3,717	2	0	0	0	2	51	3	45	3	0
Colorado State University	27,036	10	0	7	0	3	547	18	526	3	13
Fort Lewis College	4,411	3	0	2	0	1	127	25	101	1	8
Pikes Peak Community College	9,830	1	0	0	1	0	32	2	30	0	1
Red Rocks Community College[5]		0	0	0	0	0	16	1	15	0	0
University of Colorado:											
Boulder	28,851	16	0	5	1	10	731	140	574	17	25
Colorado Springs	7,273	3	0	0	1	2	93	13	76	4	1
Health Science Center	2,452	1	0	0	0	1	255	9	245	1	1
University of Northern Colorado	12,163	6	0	6	0	0	265	30	234	1	3

See footnotes at end of table.

Table 9

Offenses Known to Law Enforcement

by University and College by State, 2001—Continued

University/College by state	Student enrollment[1]	Violent crime total[2]	Murder and non-negligent man-slaughter	Forcible rape	Robbery	Aggravated assault	Property crime total[3]	Burglary	Larceny-theft	Motor vehicle theft	Arson[3]
CONNECTICUT											
Eastern Connecticut State University	4,987	1	0	1	0	0	110	13	96	1	0
Southern Connecticut State University	11,551	7	0	1	1	5	153	8	133	12	1
University of Connecticut:											
Health Center[5]		0	0	0	0	0	49	4	43	2	0
Storrs, Avery Point, and Hartford[5]		23	0	5	4	14	373	74	287	12	5
Western Connecticut State University	5,589	0	0	0	0	0	54	18	34	2	0
Yale University	11,029	4	0	0	3	1	437	70	362	5	0
DELAWARE											
University of Delaware	21,206	15	0	8	2	5	560	70	482	8	14
FLORIDA											
Florida A&M University	12,082	52	0	6	12	34	493	167	316	10	6
Florida Atlantic University	20,126	1	0	0	0	1	321	60	237	24	11
Florida Gulf Coast University	3,292	0	0	0	0	0	26	2	24	0	0
Florida International University	31,293	4	0	0	0	4	514	42	427	45	0
Florida State University:											
Panama City[5]		2	0	0	0	2	8	0	8	0	0
Tallahassee[5]		17	0	5	3	9	720	66	619	35	4
Pensacola Junior College	9,653	3	0	0	1	2	93	10	83	0	0
Santa Fe Community College	12,588	1	0	1	0	0	85	4	78	3	0
University of Central Florida	31,673	2	0	0	0	2	274	43	226	5	2
University of Florida	43,382	21	0	3	5	13	914	19	843	52	8
University of North Florida	12,077	0	0	0	0	0	142	14	128	0	1
University of South Florida:											
Sarasota[5]		0	0	0	0	0	44	11	32	1	1
St. Petersburg[5]		0	0	0	0	0	33	2	26	5	0
Tampa[5]		18	0	2	4	12	584	78	435	71	0
University of West Florida[5]		1	0	1	0	0	77	10	66	1	0
GEORGIA											
Abraham Baldwin Agricultural College	2,606	1	0	0	0	1	38	6	32	0	0
Agnes Scott College	887	0	0	0	0	0	37	9	25	3	0
Albany State University	3,356	0	0	0	0	0	83	4	78	1	0
Armstrong Atlantic State University	5,668	0	0	0	0	0	48	3	44	1	
Augusta State University	5,384	0	0	0	0	0	26	0	26	0	
Berry College	2,086	0	0	0	0	0	44	2	42	0	0
Clark Atlanta University	4,963	19	0	1	6	12	243	15	220	8	1
Coastal Georgia Community College	1,987	0	0	0	0	0	19	1	18	0	0
Columbus State University[5]		2	0	0	1	1	101	7	92	2	
Dalton State College	3,049	0	0	0	0	0	6	0	6	0	0
Emory University	11,294	10	0	0	5	5	466	24	434	8	
Georgia College and State University	5,026	0	0	0	0	0	80	1	77	2	0
Georgia Institute of Technology[5]		13	0	1	12	0	1,090	124	911	55	1
Georgia Perimeter College	14,091	2	0	0	1	1	123	1	119	3	
Georgia Southern University	14,476	1	0	0	1	0	241	3	238	0	
Georgia Southwestern State University	2,569	4	0	1	0	3	31	3	28	0	
Georgia State University[5]		17	0	2	12	3	600	22	565	13	0
Gordon College	2,742	0	0	0	0	0	23	5	18	0	0
Kennesaw State University	13,148	3	0	0	1	2	93	1	89	3	
Medical College of Georgia[5]		3	0	0	0	3	178	9	165	4	0
Mercer University	6,745	1	0	0	0	1	105	2	99	4	0
Middle Georgia College	2,056	5	0	0	0	5	38	9	29	0	0
Moorehouse College[5]		1	0	0	1	0	130	2	122	6	
North Georgia College[5]		0	0	0	0	0	30	12	18	0	0
Piedmont College[5]		0	0	0	0	0	0	0	0	0	0
Savannah State University	2,153	14	0	0	0	14	95	14	74	7	6

See footnotes at end of table.

Table 9

Offenses Known to Law Enforcement
by University and College by State, 2001—Continued

University/College by state	Student enrollment[1]	Violent crime total[2]	Murder and non-negligent man-slaughter	Forcible rape	Robbery	Aggravated assault	Property crime total[3]	Burglary	Larceny-theft	Motor vehicle theft	Arson[3]
GEORGIA—Continued											
Southern Polytechnic State University	3,628	1	0	1	0	0	46	3	42	1	0
South Georgia College	1,226	0	0	0	0	0	34	8	24	2	0
University of Georgia	30,912	14	0	1	4	9	610	4	597	9	0
University of West Georgia[5]		7	0	3	3	1	139	21	118	0	0
Valdosta State University	8,729	0	0	0	0	0	171	12	159	0	
Wesleyan College	607	0	0	0	0	0	10	1	9	0	0
Young Harris College[5]		0	0	0	0	0	0	0	0	0	0
ILLINOIS[6]											
INDIANA											
Ball State University	18,638	12	0	6	0	6	499	69	423	7	12
Indiana State University	10,985	6	0	4	0	2	259	55	198	6	1
Indiana University:											
Bloomington	36,201	12	0	5	7	0	663	66	594	3	1
Gary[5]		0	0	0	0	0	42	0	40	2	0
Indianapolis[5]		5	0	0	4	1	341	10	324	7	0
New Albany[5]		0	0	0	0	0	23	0	23	0	0
Marian College	1,318	1	0	0	0	1	16	1	14	1	0
Purdue University	39,471	7	2	4	1	0	682	16	658	8	4
IOWA											
Iowa State University	26,110	6	0	3	1	2	360	39	312	9	8
University of Iowa	28,846	19	0	6	4	9	295	54	239	2	0
University of Northern Iowa	13,811	2	0	1	0	1	169	17	152	0	1
KANSAS											
Pittsburg State University	6,289	2	0	1	0	1	88	7	78	3	0
University of Kansas, Main Campus	25,406	1	0	0	0	1	362	74	282	6	1
KENTUCKY[6]											
LOUISIANA											
Delgado Community College	13,131	1	0	0	0	1	55	0	43	12	0
Grambling State University	4,671	20	1	0	6	13	146	105	40	1	0
Louisiana State University:											
Baton Rouge[5]		16	0	0	5	11	692	123	560	9	0
Health Sciences Center	2,799	0	0	0	0	0	50	13	37	0	0
Shreveport	4,239	1	0	1	0	0	23	4	19	0	0
Louisiana Tech University	10,014	2	0	0	1	1	123	29	93	1	3
McNeese State University	7,879	3	0	0	0	3	104	32	70	2	0
Northwestern State University	9,005	3	0	0	1	2	138	34	104	0	0
Southern University and A&M College:											
Baton Rouge	9,345	22	0	2	10	10	329	55	267	7	0
New Orleans	3,789	0	0	0	0	0	32	1	28	3	0
Shreveport	1,324	0	0	0	0	0	6	0	6	0	0
Tulane University	11,426	7	0	1	3	3	372	62	304	6	3
University of Louisiana:											
Lafayette	16,351	10	0	2	1	7	262	54	200	8	0
Monroe	9,947	3	0	0	1	2	188	17	168	3	0
University of New Orleans	15,868	1	0	0	0	1	258	14	203	41	0
MAINE											
University of Maine:											
Farmington	2,411	1	0	1	0	0	13	1	11	1	0
Orono	9,945	0	0	0	0	0	227	22	198	7	14
University of Southern Maine	10,645	3	0	1	0	2	95	5	89	1	0

See footnotes at end of table.

Table 9

Offenses Known to Law Enforcement
by University and College by State, 2001—Continued

University/College by state	Student enrollment[1]	Violent crime total[2]	Violent crime				Property crime total[3]	Property crime			
			Murder and non-negligent man-slaughter	Forcible rape	Robbery	Aggravated assault		Burglary	Larceny-theft	Motor vehicle theft	Arson[3]
MARYLAND											
Bowie State University	4,770	11	0	3	0	8	83	26	55	2	0
Coppin State College	3,844	11	0	1	0	10	81	12	61	8	0
Frostburg State University	5,198	2	0	0	0	2	66	6	60	0	0
Morgan State University	6,172	10	0	1	3	6	295	38	250	7	0
Salisbury University	6,060	8	0	0	2	6	126	2	120	4	0
St. Mary's College	1,613	0	0	0	0	0	46	2	44	0	0
Towson University	16,647	9	0	3	2	4	314	71	241	2	1
University of Baltimore	4,611	2	0	0	2	0	90	4	84	2	0
University of Maryland:											
Baltimore	5,553	11	0	1	6	4	326	6	317	3	0
Baltimore County	10,265	4	0	1	2	1	205	16	183	6	1
College Park	32,864	36	0	5	10	21	996	121	760	115	5
Eastern Shore	3,000	4	0	1	0	3	88	11	76	1	1
MASSACHUSETTS[4]											
Boston University	28,487	37	0	1	12	24	678	58	614	6	
Brandeis University	4,527	3	0	1	1	1	110	15	95	0	0
Bristol Community College	6,053	0	0	0	0	0	29	3	25	1	0
Emerson College	3,987	11	0	1	2	8	63	14	47	2	
Fitchburg State College	5,557	13	0	2	0	11	82	14	68	0	0
Framingham State College	5,697	4	0	0	0	4	35	5	30	0	0
Harvard University	24,214	13	0	5	2	6	676	409	252	15	0
Lasell College	724	14	0	1	0	13	29	15	13	1	0
Massachusetts College of Art	2,370	0	0	0	0	0	62	1	61	0	0
Massachusetts College of Liberal Arts	1,520	2	0	0	0	2	29	11	17	1	2
Massachusetts Institute of Technology	9,972	11	0	4	5	2	580	23	541	16	
Mount Holyoke College	1,982	5	0	0	0	5	65	11	54	0	0
North Shore Community College	6,101	0	0	0	0	0	31	0	30	1	0
Salem State College	8,081	1	0	0	0	1	69	14	54	1	0
Springfield College	4,246	12	0	2	0	10	106	16	86	4	0
Tufts University:											
Medford	9,269	4	0	1	1	2	173	11	158	4	
Suffolk[5]		0	0	0	0	0	81	7	74	0	
Worcester[5]		0	0	0	0	0	11	0	11	0	
University of Massachusetts:											
Amherst	25,031	28	0	8	8	12	393	104	277	12	3
Dartmouth	6,963	15	0	0	1	14	106	1	103	2	
Harbor Campus-Boston	13,778	4	0	0	0	4	133	6	127	0	0
Medical Center-Worcester	682	5	0	0	0	5	88	5	83	0	
Wentworth Institute of Technology	3,225	3	0	2	1	0	60	0	59	1	
MICHIGAN											
Central Michigan University	26,321	5	0	5	0	0	283	8	270	5	1
Delta College	9,599	0	0	0	0	0	43	2	41	0	0
Eastern Michigan University	22,956	7	0	1	2	4	426	6	410	10	4
Ferris State University	9,668	5	0	1	2	2	225	30	193	2	1
Grand Rapids Community College	12,730	1	0	0	1	0	99	0	97	2	0
Grand Valley State University	17,452	0	0	0	0	0	126	5	120	1	0
Hope College	2,943	1	0	0	0	1	105	7	96	2	2
Lansing Community College	16,677	1	0	0	0	1	141	1	138	2	0
Macomb Community College	21,718	2	0	0	0	2	61	2	55	4	0
Michigan State University	43,038	28	0	9	8	11	974	123	832	19	3
Michigan Technological University	6,321	2	0	1	0	1	78	1	77	0	3
Mott Community College	8,998	0	0	0	0	0	84	2	73	9	0
Northern Michigan University	8,082	2	0	0	0	2	139	1	136	2	2
Oakland Community College	23,244	2	0	0	0	2	74	1	67	6	0
Oakland University	14,726	1	0	1	0	0	102	3	99	0	2
Saginaw Valley State University	8,334	1	0	1	0	0	130	4	126	0	0

See footnotes at end of table.

Table 9

Offenses Known to Law Enforcement
by University and College by State, 2001—Continued

University/College by state	Student enrollment[1]	Violent crime total[2]	Violent crime				Property crime total[3]	Property crime			
			Murder and non-negligent man-slaughter	Forcible rape	Robbery	Aggravated assault		Burglary	Larceny-theft	Motor vehicle theft	Arson[3]
MICHIGAN—Continued											
University of Michigan:											
Ann Arbor	37,846	27	0	5	9	13	1,762	103	1,639	20	10
Dearborn	8,076	0	0	0	0	0	72	0	66	6	0
Flint	6,524	0	0	0	0	0	131	10	114	7	0
Western Michigan University	27,744	16	0	9	1	6	430	13	411	6	9
MINNESOTA											
University of Minnesota:											
Duluth	8,504	1	0	0	0	1	102	3	98	1	0
Twin Cities	45,361	14	0	7	3	4	769	36	717	16	1
MISSISSIPPI											
Coahoma Community College	1,161	5	0	1	0	4	17	7	8	2	0
Hinds Community College	13,460	0	0	0	0	0	81	12	66	3	0
Itawamba Community College	3,453	1	0	1	0	0	40	29	10	1	0
Jackson State University	6,354	4	0	1	0	3	259	58	193	8	0
Mississippi State University	16,076	4	0	1	1	2	311	32	278	1	1
University of Mississippi, Oxford	11,648	2	0	0	0	2	125	15	109	1	0
MISSOURI											
Central Missouri State University	10,894	6	0	2	1	3	126	33	93	0	1
Lincoln University	3,347	3	0	1	0	2	91	38	52	1	1
Southeast Missouri State University	8,863	1	0	0	1	0	92	3	88	1	
Truman State University	6,236	2	0	0	1	1	70	5	65	0	1
University of Missouri:											
Columbia	22,930	15	0	0	2	13	416	37	375	4	
St. Louis	15,594	6	0	1	1	4	213	26	171	16	
NEBRASKA											
University of Nebraska:											
Kearney	6,780	0	0	0	0	0	73	18	55	0	0
Lincoln	22,142	4	0	1	0	3	632	93	539	0	0
NEVADA											
Truckee Meadows Community College	9,987	0	0	0	0	0	30	13	17	0	0
University of Nevada:											
Las Vegas	21,820	16	0	3	7	6	432	74	321	37	1
Reno	12,532	5	0	0	0	5	180	58	115	7	3
NEW JERSEY											
Brookdale Community College	11,575	0	0	0	0	0	43	0	34	9	0
College of New Jersey, The	6,747	2	0	0	0	2	162	19	127	16	1
Essex County College	8,921	0	0	0	0	0	81	1	71	9	0
Kean University of New Jersey	11,199	9	0	0	3	6	210	11	175	24	1
Middlesex County College	10,331	1	0	0	0	1	56	0	53	3	0
Monmouth University	5,425	4	0	1	0	3	81	2	76	3	1
Montclair State University	13,285	9	0	2	0	7	180	16	129	35	2
New Jersey Institute of Technology	8,258	14	0	0	7	7	208	8	156	44	0
Richard Stockton College	6,298	5	0	0	3	2	81	8	70	3	0
Rowan University	9,636	4	0	2	1	1	108	5	101	2	0
Rutgers University:											
Camden	4,936	3	0	0	1	2	89	11	73	5	1
Newark	9,221	15	0	0	10	5	256	19	214	23	0
New Brunswick	35,308	4	0	3	0	1	90	13	76	1	2

See footnotes at end of table.

Table 9

Offenses Known to Law Enforcement
by University and College by State, 2001—Continued

University/College by state	Student enrollment[1]	Violent crime total[2]	Violent crime — Murder and non-negligent man-slaughter	Violent crime — Forcible rape	Violent crime — Robbery	Violent crime — Aggravated assault	Property crime total[3]	Property crime — Burglary	Property crime — Larceny-theft	Property crime — Motor vehicle theft	Arson[3]
NEW JERSEY—Continued											
University of Medicine and Dentistry:											
Camden[5]		2	0	0	2	0	13	1	12	0	0
Newark	4,618	42	0	0	19	23	431	7	362	62	0
Piscataway[5]		0	0	0	0	0	84	0	81	3	0
William Paterson University	9,758	4	0	2	0	2	131	46	70	15	0
NEW MEXICO											
Eastern New Mexico University	3,562	0	0	0	0	0	45	18	26	1	0
New Mexico State University	15,449	12	0	2	2	8	383	43	331	9	1
University of New Mexico	24,374	42	0	2	5	35	1,012	140	830	42	1
NEW YORK											
Cornell University[5]		6	0	1	4	1	471	49	419	3	1
Ithaca College	5,960	1	0	1	0	0	147	4	143	0	0
Rensselaer Polytechnic Institute	7,650	3	0	0	2	1	219	33	185	1	0
State University of New York:											
Downstate Medical Center[5]		4	0	0	2	2	130	2	125	3	0
Maritime College	766	0	0	0	0	0	35	17	18	0	0
State University of New York Agricultural and Technical College:											
Alfred	2,835	3	0	1	0	2	107	31	75	1	1
Canton	2,260	0	0	0	0	0	72	8	61	3	0
Farmingdale	5,151	2	0	0	1	1	87	11	73	3	0
State University of New York College:											
Cortland	6,901	5	0	2	0	3	117	16	101	0	0
Fredonia	5,020	0	0	0	0	0	67	5	61	1	0
Geneseo	5,603	0	0	0	0	0	133	10	123	0	0
Old Westbury	3,245	4	0	0	2	2	41	3	38	0	0
Oswego	7,901	2	0	2	0	0	163	11	150	2	0
Potsdam	4,127	3	0	2	0	1	106	11	93	2	0
Purchase	3,950	0	0	0	0	0	102	9	92	1	0
Utica-Rome[5]		2	0	0	0	2	26	3	22	1	0
NORTH CAROLINA											
Appalachian State University	12,779	0	0	0	0	0	131	21	105	5	0
Belmont Abbey College	926	0	0	0	0	0	44	16	28	0	1
Davidson College	1,652	0	0	0	0	0	82	6	76	0	0
Duke University	11,811	19	0	2	10	7	1,191	66	1,118	7	1
East Carolina University	18,811	7	0	1	1	5	314	22	290	2	0
Elon College	3,961	1	0	1	0	0	96	26	70	0	0
Methodist College	1,973	0	0	0	0	0	28	3	25	0	0
North Carolina Agricultural and Technical State University	7,603	24	0	1	11	12	260	58	197	5	1
North Carolina Central University	5,595	13	0	0	5	8	171	9	158	4	0
North Carolina School of the Arts	794	1	0	0	0	1	40	3	35	2	0
North Carolina State University, Raleigh	28,011	10	0	1	2	7	528	44	474	10	4
Pfeiffer College	1,612	0	0	0	0	0	24	12	12	0	0
University of North Carolina:											
Asheville	3,226	7	0	0	0	7	50	2	46	2	0
Chapel Hill	24,653	5	0	2	0	3	701	34	655	12	2
Charlotte	16,950	10	0	5	2	3	298	32	265	1	3
Greensboro	13,322	4	0	0	3	1	338	3	329	6	0
Pembroke	3,062	5	0	3	2	0	69	15	52	2	0
Wilmington	9,967	2	0	1	0	1	268	46	220	2	0
Wake Forest University	6,082	2	0	0	2	0	186	27	159	0	0
Western Carolina University	6,580	8	0	3	0	5	175	37	136	2	0
Winston-Salem State University	2,788	8	0	2	1	5	96	14	76	6	0

See footnotes at end of table.

Table 9

Offenses Known to Law Enforcement
by University and College by State, 2001—Continued

University/College by state	Student enrollment[1]	Violent crime total[2]	Murder and non-negligent man-slaughter	Forcible rape	Robbery	Aggravated assault	Property crime total[3]	Burglary	Larceny-theft	Motor vehicle theft	Arson[3]
NORTH DAKOTA											
North Dakota State University	9,638	1	0	0	1	0	156	7	149	0	0
University of North Dakota	10,590	2	0	1	0	1	128	10	115	3	0
OHIO											
Bowling Green State University	18,199	7	0	6	0	1	334	19	311	4	4
Cleveland State University	15,683	5	0	1	4	0	268	12	236	20	2
Columbus State Community College	17,662	3	0	0	1	2	138	4	130	4	0
Cuyahoga Community College	19,435	0	0	0	0	0	70	4	66	0	0
Hocking Technical College	4,844	1	0	1	0	0	32	15	17	0	0
Kent State University	21,653	3	0	2	0	1	257	4	252	1	2
Lakeland Community College	8,298	3	0	0	0	3	15	0	15	0	0
Marietta College	1,214	1	0	1	0	0	47	16	31	0	1
Miami University	16,575	4	0	4	0	0	415	35	375	5	0
Ohio State University	48,003	24	0	3	13	8	1,158	154	981	23	8
Ohio University	19,638	2	0	0	0	2	213	16	195	2	0
Sinclair Community College	18,345	1	0	0	1	0	84	1	83	0	0
University of Cincinnati	27,467	9	0	2	6	1	592	77	514	1	5
University of Toledo	20,037	18	0	2	2	14	394	21	362	11	4
Wright State University	14,363	6	0	4	0	2	245	10	223	12	0
Youngstown State University	12,222	0	0	0	0	0	153	6	147	0	2
OKLAHOMA											
Cameron University	5,270	0	0	0	0	0	4	1	3	0	0
East Central University	3,996	0	0	0	0	0	5	5	0	0	0
Murray State College	1,636	0	0	0	0	0	10	6	4	0	1
Northeastern Oklahoma A&M College	1,984	3	0	1	0	2	65	34	31	0	1
Northeastern State College	7,985	4	0	2	0	2	100	31	65	4	0
Oklahoma State University:											
Main Campus	21,014	2	0	1	0	1	263	44	214	5	2
Okmulgee	2,310	1	0	0	0	1	62	13	47	2	0
Tulsa[5]		1	0	0	0	1	30	3	23	4	0
Rogers University, Claremore	2,690	0	0	0	0	0	8	2	6	0	0
Seminole State College	2,029	0	0	0	0	0	17	1	16	0	0
Southeastern Oklahoma State University	3,685	7	0	0	0	7	36	15	20	1	0
Southwestern State College	4,828	1	0	1	0	0	27	7	20	0	0
Tulsa Community College	15,971	0	0	0	0	0	53	0	53	0	0
University of Central Oklahoma	14,173	2	0	0	0	2	109	7	98	4	6
University of Oklahoma:											
Health Sciences Center	2,936	11	0	0	2	9	202	34	167	1	1
Norman	23,694	4	0	2	1	1	336	54	273	9	9
PENNSYLVANIA											
Bloomsburg University	7,567	1	0	1	0	0	37	0	35	2	0
California University	5,816	0	0	0	0	0	56	0	55	1	0
Cheyney University	1,821	4	0	0	0	4	47	3	42	2	0
Clarion University	6,028	2	0	0	1	1	79	29	48	2	1
Community College of Beaver County	2,164	0	0	0	0	0	2	2	0	0	0
East Stroudsburg University	5,802	5	0	0	0	5	100	0	97	3	1
Elizabethtown College	1,790	0	0	0	0	0	24	1	23	0	1
Indiana University	13,442	9	0	1	5	3	97	25	72	0	0
Kutztown University	8,069	4	0	3	0	1	113	4	108	1	0
Lehigh University	6,359	2	0	0	2	0	77	0	75	2	0
Lock Haven University	3,857	1	0	1	0	0	45	0	45	0	0
Mansfield University	3,063	0	0	0	0	0	21	1	19	1	0
Millersville University	7,307	3	0	1	1	1	80	5	75	0	1
Moravian College	1,857	0	0	0	0	0	46	5	41	0	1

See footnotes at end of table.

Table 9

Offenses Known to Law Enforcement
by University and College by State, 2001—Continued

University/College by state	Student enrollment[1]	Violent crime total[2]	Violent crime				Property crime total[3]	Property crime			
			Murder and non-negligent man-slaughter	Forcible rape	Robbery	Aggravated assault		Burglary	Larceny-theft	Motor vehicle theft	Arson[3]
PENNSYLVANIA—Continued											
Pennsylvania State University:											
Altoona	3,869	0	0	0	0	0	71	8	63	0	0
Behrend	3,648	0	0	0	0	0	40	2	38	0	0
Berks	2,067	1	0	0	0	1	31	0	30	1	0
Harrisburg	3,238	0	0	0	0	0	32	3	29	0	0
McKeesport	834	1	0	0	0	1	0	0	0	0	1
Mont Alto	1,292	0	0	0	0	0	30	0	30	0	0
University Park[5]		9	0	5	0	4	596	31	559	6	
Shippensburg University	6,676	1	0	1	0	0	41	1	40	0	0
Slippery Rock University	6,803	1	0	0	0	1	77	0	76	1	0
University of Pittsburgh:											
Bradford	1,178	0	0	0	0	0	17	1	16	0	0
Pittsburgh	26,162	20	0	0	10	10	464	35	427	2	1
RHODE ISLAND											
Brown University	7,758	1	0	0	1	0	315	63	252	0	0
University of Rhode Island	14,577	1	0	0	0	1	230	7	216	7	0
SOUTH CAROLINA											
Benedict College	2,750	7	1	0	1	5	165	41	119	5	2
Clemson University	16,982	11	0	4	3	4	116	11	95	10	1
Coastal Carolina University	4,615	0	0	0	0	0	80	7	71	2	2
Medical University of South Carolina	2,383	0	0	0	0	0	244	3	239	2	0
South Carolina State University	4,623	9	0	0	5	4	144	18	125	1	6
University of South Carolina, Columbia	23,430	12	0	0	4	8	548	14	489	45	0
TENNESSEE											
Austin Peay State University	7,440	6	0	3	0	3	63	3	60	0	0
Chattanooga State Technical Community College	8,162	0	0	0	0	0	23	0	21	2	0
Cleveland State Community College	3,260	0	0	0	0	0	6	0	5	1	0
Dyersburg State Community College	2,153	1	0	0	1	0	2	0	2	0	0
East Tennessee State University	11,423	10	0	1	3	6	192	19	170	3	1
Jackson State Community College	3,869	0	0	0	0	0	2	0	2	0	0
Middle Tennessee State University	18,993	12	0	1	2	9	240	55	177	8	1
Tennessee State University	8,836	11	0	1	4	6	211	7	166	38	2
Tennessee Technological University	8,584	11	0	0	1	10	128	7	120	1	0
University of Memphis	20,301	5	0	0	2	3	296	43	230	23	4
University of Tennessee:											
Chattanooga	8,604	5	0	1	0	4	199	60	130	9	0
Knoxville	26,437	14	0	2	2	10	563	17	521	25	2
Martin	5,741	3	0	1	0	2	63	3	59	1	0
Memphis	2,116	2	0	0	1	1	150	6	137	7	0
Vanderbilt University	10,022	22	0	0	6	16	647	39	593	15	4
Volunteer State Community College	6,655	0	0	0	0	0	13	2	11	0	0
Walters State Community College	5,607	0	0	0	0	0	6	0	6	0	0
TEXAS											
Alamo Community College District[5]		3	0	0	2	1	258	87	156	15	0
Alvin Community College	3,782	0	0	0	0	0	22	1	20	1	0
Amarillo College	8,183	0	0	0	0	0	59	6	53	0	0
Angelo State University	6,220	6	0	5	0	1	87	13	71	3	1
Austin College	1,257	0	0	0	0	0	34	3	29	2	0

See footnotes at end of table.

Table 9

Offenses Known to Law Enforcement
by University and College by State, 2001—Continued

University/College by state	Student enrollment[1]	Violent crime total[2]	Violent crime				Property crime total[3]	Property crime			
			Murder and non-negligent man-slaughter	Forcible rape	Robbery	Aggravated assault		Burglary	Larceny-theft	Motor vehicle theft	Arson[3]
TEXAS—Continued											
Baylor Health Care System	1,186	3	0	0	2	1	314	10	288	16	0
Baylor University, Waco	13,334	4	0	0	2	2	289	31	253	5	5
Central Texas College	14,636	3	0	0	0	3	42	2	40	0	0
College of the Mainland	3,333	0	0	0	0	0	37	1	33	3	0
Eastfield College	7,533	1	0	1	0	0	42	0	42	0	0
El Paso Community College	18,680	4	0	0	0	4	134	11	123	0	0
Grayson County College	3,338	0	0	0	0	0	45	21	24	0	0
Hardin-Simmons University	2,291	0	0	0	0	0	35	22	13	0	0
Houston Baptist University	2,362	1	0	0	1	0	13	0	13	0	0
Lamar University, Beaumont	10,315	1	0	0	1	0	109	9	96	4	1
Laredo Community College	7,457	0	0	0	0	0	9	2	6	1	0
McLennan Community College	5,589	0	0	0	0	0	62	2	59	1	0
Midwestern State University	5,765	3	0	2	1	0	71	5	66	0	0
Mountain View College	5,121	0	0	0	0	0	32	0	30	2	0
North Lake College	7,030	0	0	0	0	0	38	2	36	0	0
Paris Junior College	2,906	1	0	0	1	0	19	3	16	0	0
Prairie View A&M University	6,271	21	0	4	1	16	250	77	152	21	0
Rice University	4,274	5	0	1	0	4	322	15	298	9	1
Richland College	11,329	0	0	0	0	0	80	10	60	10	0
Southern Methodist University	10,361	1	0	0	0	1	213	19	186	8	1
South Plains College	6,468	0	0	0	0	0	11	0	11	0	0
Southwestern University	1,254	0	0	0	0	0	24	3	21	0	1
Southwest Texas State University	21,769	4	0	1	1	2	217	35	180	2	0
Stephen F. Austin State University	11,919	3	0	1	0	2	203	55	141	7	0
St. Mary's University	4,065	1	0	0	0	1	104	10	93	1	0
St. Thomas University	3,345	0	0	0	0	0	41	3	35	3	0
Sul Ross State University	2,965	2	0	1	0	1	54	20	33	1	0
Tarleton State University	7,433	1	0	0	1	0	42	4	38	0	0
Texas A&M International University	3,209	1	0	0	0	1	26	2	23	1	0
Texas A&M University:											
College Station	43,817	6	0	1	2	3	630	70	553	7	0
Commerce	7,908	2	0	1	0	1	126	34	92	0	0
Corpus Christi	6,604	2	0	0	0	2	54	8	46	0	0
Galveston	1,288	0	0	0	0	0	17	6	11	0	0
Kingsville	5,843	4	0	0	1	3	115	17	98	0	0
Texas Christian University	7,551	1	0	0	0	1	174	9	160	5	1
Texas Southern University	6,522	15	0	2	5	8	241	47	175	19	0
Texas State Technical College:											
Harlingen	3,353	0	0	0	0	0	50	10	39	1	0
Waco	3,814	9	0	0	1	8	129	33	92	4	0
Texas Technological University, Lubbock	24,249	14	0	4	1	9	485	16	465	4	2
Texas Woman's University	8,624	2	0	2	0	0	50	1	48	1	0
Trinity University	2,515	0	0	0	0	0	164	18	142	4	0
Tyler Junior College	8,447	1	0	0	0	1	92	15	74	3	2
University of Houston:											
Central Campus	32,651	15	0	1	12	2	570	32	513	25	0
Clearlake	7,114	1	0	0	1	0	19	1	18	0	0
Downtown Campus	8,712	1	0	0	0	1	36	0	34	2	0
University of Mary Hardin-Baylor	2,566	0	0	0	0	0	63	8	55	0	1
University of North Texas:											
Denton	26,493	11	0	2	2	7	310	83	222	5	2
Health Science Center	705	0	0	0	0	0	29	0	29	0	0
University of Texas:											
Arlington	19,149	2	0	0	0	2	53	7	44	2	0
Austin	49,009	8	1	0	1	6	706	63	632	11	0
Brownsville	2,834	0	0	0	0	0	68	4	58	6	0
Dallas	10,097	2	0	0	1	1	121	0	119	2	0
El Paso	14,695	3	0	0	0	3	199	8	186	5	0
Health Science Center, San Antonio	2,544	0	0	0	0	0	56	0	55	1	0

See footnotes at end of table.

Table 9

Offenses Known to Law Enforcement
by University and College by State, 2001—Continued

University/College by state	Student enrollment[1]	Violent crime total[2]	Violent crime				Property crime total[3]	Property crime			
			Murder and non-negligent man-slaughter	Forcible rape	Robbery	Aggravated assault		Burglary	Larceny-theft	Motor vehicle theft	Arson[3]
TEXAS—Continued											
University of Texas—Cont.:											
Health Science Center, Tyler	3,170	0	0	0	0	0	17	0	17	0	0
Houston[5]		7	0	2	1	4	335	1	330	4	0
Medical Branch	1,953	4	0	1	2	1	295	5	286	4	0
Pan American	12,569	1	0	0	1	0	116	2	110	4	0
Permian Basin	2,224	0	0	0	0	0	8	1	7	0	0
San Antonio	18,608	6	0	1	0	5	159	42	113	4	0
Southwestern Medical School	1,552	2	0	0	1	1	265	3	251	11	0
Tyler	3,393	4	0	2	0	2	20	3	17	0	0
West Texas A&M University	6,651	1	0	0	0	1	64	10	54	0	0
UTAH											
Brigham Young University	32,731	1	0	0	1	0	287	10	268	9	4
College of Eastern Utah	2,682	0	0	0	0	0	23	11	11	1	0
Salt Lake Community College	20,799	2	0	0	1	1	163	9	153	1	0
Southern Utah University	6,025	0	0	0	0	0	53	8	44	1	0
University of Utah	25,781	7	0	1	3	3	309	9	290	10	0
Utah State University	20,865	0	0	0	0	0	184	36	147	1	0
Utah Valley State College	20,062	8	0	0	0	8	87	12	74	1	0
Weber State University	14,984	5	0	2	0	3	126	18	107	1	0
VIRGINIA											
Christopher Newport University	5,164	1	0	1	0	0	72	1	71	0	0
College of William and Mary	7,553	7	0	2	1	4	320	3	317	0	3
Ferrum College	945	0	0	0	0	0	66	4	61	1	0
George Mason University	24,180	7	0	2	2	3	453	22	424	7	2
Hampton University	5,783	7	0	1	3	3	186	9	175	2	1
James Madison University	15,223	11	0	3	0	8	200	6	191	3	3
Mary Washington College	4,000	0	0	0	0	0	49	9	39	1	1
Northern Virginia Community College	36,655	2	0	0	1	1	118	1	116	1	0
Radford University	8,579	4	0	1	0	3	109	7	100	2	3
University of Richmond	4,494	1	0	0	0	1	87	2	82	3	1
University of Virginia	22,433	17	0	3	5	9	380	10	367	3	1
Virginia Commonwealth University	23,481	18	0	2	5	11	559	12	541	6	3
Virginia State University[5]		13	0	1	3	9	151	4	144	3	1
WASHINGTON											
Central Washington University	8,233	7	0	3	1	3	253	39	208	6	3
Eastern Washington University	8,261	0	0	0	0	0	101	16	85	0	1
Evergreen State College	4,102	3	0	0	0	3	124	26	96	2	1
University of Washington	35,559	27	0	2	4	21	922	92	777	53	2
Washington State University:											
Pullman	20,799	20	0	8	2	10	255	57	194	4	5
Vancouver[5]		0	0	0	0	0	11	1	10	0	0
Western Washington University	11,708	2	0	1	0	1	312	11	296	5	1
WEST VIRGINIA											
Bluefield State College	2,339	0	0	0	0	0	6	0	6	0	0
Concord College	2,877	0	0	0	0	0	7	1	6	0	0
Glenville State College	2,260	0	0	0	0	0	6	3	3	0	0
Marshall University	15,633	4	0	0	1	3	118	2	113	3	1
Potomac State College	1,173	0	0	0	0	0	12	2	10	0	0

See footnotes at the end of table.

Table 9

Offenses Known to Law Enforcement

by University and College by State, 2001—Continued

University/College by state	Student enrollment[1]	Violent crime total[2]	Violent crime				Property crime total[3]	Property crime			
			Murder and non-negligent man-slaughter	Forcible rape	Robbery	Aggravated assault		Burglary	Larceny-theft	Motor vehicle theft	Arson[3]
WISCONSIN											
University of Wisconsin:											
Eau Claire	10,485	0	0	0	0	0	120	0	119	1	0
Green Bay	5,581	0	0	0	0	0	60	2	57	1	0
La Crosse	9,494	0	0	0	0	0	69	7	62	0	0
Madison	40,099	7	0	1	2	4	554	109	414	31	0
Milwaukee	23,149	4	0	1	1	2	277	10	263	4	8
Oshkosh	10,733	2	0	1	1	0	91	2	88	1	0
Parkside	4,886	4	0	2	2	0	87	0	87	0	0
Platteville	5,559	1	0	0	0	1	90	6	82	2	1
Stevens Point	8,847	0	0	0	0	0	98	0	98	0	0
Stout	7,872	3	0	2	0	1	97	8	87	2	0
Superior	2,775	0	0	0	0	0	50	7	41	2	3
Whitewater	10,811	2	0	0	0	2	139	14	124	1	0
WYOMING											
Sheridan College	2,525	1	0	0	0	1	7	5	2	0	0
University of Wyoming	10,940	2	0	0	0	2	195	17	175	3	0

[1] The student enrollment figures provided by the United States Department of Education are for the 1999 school year, the most recent available. The enrollment figures include full-time and part-time students. See Appendix I for details.

[2] Violent crimes are offenses of murder, forcible rape, robbery, and aggravated assault.

[3] Property crimes are offenses of burglary, larceny-theft, and motor vehicle theft. Arson is not included in the property crime total. Arson is shown only if 12 months of arson data were received.

[4] Complete arson figures for 2001 for Alabama and Massachusetts were not available.

[5] Student enrollment figures were not available.

[6] Limited data for 2001 were available for Illinois and Kentucky.

NOTE: Caution should be exercised in making any inter-campus comparisons or ranking schools, as university/college crime statistics are affected by a variety of factors. These include demographic characteristics of the surrounding community, ratio of male to female students, number of on-campus residents, accessibility of outside visitors, size of enrollment, etc.

Table 10

Offenses Known to Law Enforcement
by Suburban County by State, 2001

[The data shown in this table do not reflect county totals but are the number of offenses reported by the sheriff's office, county police department, or state police.]

County by state	Crime Index total	Modified Crime Index total[1]	Murder and non-negligent man-slaughter	Forcible rape	Robbery	Aggravated assault	Burglary	Larceny-theft	Motor vehicle theft	Arson[1]
ALABAMA[2]										
Autauga	283		1	2	4	28	82	141	25	
Calhoun	795		1	7	14	43	220	486	24	
Colbert	198		2	1	3	18	54	112	8	
Dale	158		0	2	1	20	18	105	12	
Etowah	449		0	1	1	5	156	242	44	
Houston	411		1	1	4	34	126	228	17	
Jefferson	5,791		5	37	151	367	1,535	3,260	436	
Lauderdale	224		1	2	1	13	88	81	38	
Lawrence	188		0	2	3	2	80	77	24	
Limestone	316		2	5	6	17	81	165	40	
Madison	2,031		0	9	29	156	529	1,186	122	
Mobile	2,624		4	17	50	194	825	1,382	152	
Montgomery	936		2	5	18	86	228	533	64	
Morgan	310		0	0	4	7	136	138	25	
Russell	454		2	6	7	35	151	239	14	
Shelby	599		2	15	17	23	184	275	83	
St. Clair	440		0	14	3	50	124	228	21	
Tuscaloosa	2,091		4	20	35	264	576	1,016	176	
ARIZONA										
Coconino	691	700	3	18	2	50	177	412	29	9
Maricopa	6,665	6,697	23	21	84	385	1,608	3,567	977	32
Mohave	2,212	2,235	5	3	16	114	679	1,202	193	23
Pima	12,631	12,738	7	76	161	584	1,944	7,585	2,274	107
Pinal	3,076	3,087	1	30	26	516	526	1,593	384	11
Yuma	1,306	1,315	4	6	7	164	322	691	112	9
ARKANSAS										
Benton	432	439	2	10	1	64	98	214	43	7
Craighead	461	470	1	8	2	25	125	236	64	9
Crittenden	524	534	2	21	11	49	189	220	32	10
Faulkner	621	621	0	1	3	57	164	334	62	0
Jefferson	588	591	1	3	2	48	157	329	48	3
Lonoke	509	509	0	2	2	12	101	300	92	0
Miller	353	356	3	2	2	59	114	143	30	3
Pulaski	2,403	2,425	2	34	49	161	368	1,626	163	22
Saline	1,320	1,320	1	27	7	143	457	650	35	0
Sebastian	239	241	0	1	5	19	56	134	24	2
CALIFORNIA										
Alameda	3,538	3,598	3	40	167	285	654	1,681	708	60
Alameda Highway Patrol	88	88	0	0	0	0	0	14	74	0
Butte	1,950	2,072	9	29	25	165	626	1,081	15	122
Contra Costa	4,239	4,275	13	25	134	475	969	2,622	1	36
El Dorado	2,009	2,022	2	24	18	271	666	1,025	3	13
Fresno	6,894	7,391	15	59	169	1,191	1,662	2,923	875	497
Kern	12,306	12,742	13	119	322	1,529	2,942	6,341	1,040	436
Kern Highway Patrol	96	96	0	0	0	0	0	37	59	0
Los Angeles	27,275	27,777	108	229	1,910	5,750	5,136	9,019	5,123	502
Los Angeles Highway Patrol	382	382	0	1	2	78	23	42	236	0
Madera	1,772	1,783	5	25	23	87	592	1,028	12	11
Marin	1,313	1,317	0	14	16	144	294	839	6	4
Marin Highway Patrol	112	112	0	0	0	0	0	1	111	0
Merced	2,360	2,377	2	21	35	395	866	1,027	14	17
Merced Highway Patrol	429	429	0	0	1	0	0	63	365	0
Monterey	2,341	2,363	6	16	60	180	619	1,453	7	22

See footnotes at end of table.

Table 10

Offenses Known to Law Enforcement

by Suburban County by State, 2001—Continued

[The data shown in this table do not reflect county totals but are the number of offenses reported by the sheriff's office, county police department, or state police.]

County by state	Crime Index total	Modified Crime Index total[1]	Murder and non-negligent man-slaughter	Forcible rape	Robbery	Aggravated assault	Burglary	Larceny-theft	Motor vehicle theft	Arson[1]
CALIFORNIA—Continued										
Monterey Highway Patrol	133	133	0	0	0	0	0	0	133	0
Napa	423	426	0	4	2	47	104	264	2	3
Napa Highway Patrol	17	17	0	0	0	0	0	0	17	0
Orange	2,274	2,285	2	13	41	227	384	1,343	264	11
Orange Highway Patrol	36	36	0	0	1	1	5	9	20	0
Placer	2,173	2,189	2	15	13	87	587	1,400	69	16
Placer Highway Patrol	222	222	0	0	0	0	0	6	216	0
Riverside	13,851	13,929	22	102	325	1,795	3,378	6,110	2,119	78
Riverside Highway Patrol	263	263	0	1	0	3	4	11	244	0
Sacramento	26,743	27,028	37	273	1,068	2,333	5,693	16,506	833	285
San Bernardino	7,927	8,065	42	80	231	788	2,242	3,264	1,280	138
San Bernardino Highway Patrol	73	73	0	0	0	1	0	2	70	0
San Diego	9,086	9,158	10	87	249	1,159	2,191	3,909	1,481	72
San Diego Highway Patrol	172	172	0	0	0	8	5	52	107	0
San Francisco Highway Patrol	144	144	0	0	1	2	0	16	125	0
San Joaquin	4,897	4,957	18	74	125	625	1,153	2,743	159	60
San Luis Obispo	1,533	1,542	2	43	10	173	405	895	5	9
San Luis Obispo Highway Patrol	145	145	0	0	2	1	0	26	116	0
San Mateo	2,128	2,145	2	12	50	17	218	1,511	318	17
San Mateo Highway Patrol	20	20	0	0	0	0	0	1	19	0
Santa Barbara	2,085	2,120	1	39	35	218	419	1,364	9	35
Santa Barbara Highway Patrol	59	59	0	0	0	0	0	0	59	0
Santa Clara	2,463	2,465	5	25	39	267	467	1,478	182	2
Santa Clara Highway Patrol	89	89	0	0	0	19	1	15	54	0
Santa Cruz	2,519	2,549	9	39	31	164	570	1,696	10	30
Shasta	1,685	1,752	2	28	19	322	458	825	31	67
Shasta Highway Patrol	142	142	0	0	0	1	0	33	108	0
Solano	526	552	2	4	8	85	173	251	3	26
Sonoma	3,023	3,062	5	47	31	341	700	1,866	33	39
Stanislaus	4,461	4,855	13	59	122	875	1,027	1,873	492	394
Stanislaus Highway Patrol	165	165	0	0	0	0	0	34	131	0
Sutter	910	913	3	6	13	116	264	479	29	3
Sutter Highway Patrol	51	51	0	0	0	0	0	0	51	0
Tulare[3]			12	29	68	308	999	1,686		537
Tulare Highway Patrol	801	801	0	0	0	0	0	128	673	0
Ventura	1,338	1,355	3	13	25	150	298	730	119	17
Ventura Highway Patrol	20	20	0	0	0	0	0	0	20	0
Yolo	361	367	1	4	5	2	154	191	4	6
Yolo Highway Patrol	50	50	0	0	0	0	4	5	41	0
Yuba	1,597	1,620	1	18	33	194	581	770	0	23
COLORADO										
Adams	4,638	4,698	6	51	58	355	794	2,647	727	60
Arapahoe	3,633	3,705	0	45	32	299	752	2,136	369	72
Boulder	791	837	0	27	6	65	280	354	59	46
Douglas	2,446	2,469	6	31	12	93	474	1,723	107	23
El Paso	2,643	2,677	5	33	15	265	615	1,521	189	34
Jefferson	2,900	2,931	0	19	12	79	611	1,942	237	31
Larimer	1,407	1,435	2	21	3	66	332	895	88	28
Mesa	1,461	1,470	0	2	1	69	309	974	106	9
Pueblo	1,091	1,094	2	2	5	27	264	755	36	3
Weld	1,150	1,169	1	20	8	116	323	550	132	19
DELAWARE[3]										
Kent State Police	1,999	2,003	1	58	25	396	456	972	91	4
New Castle Police Department	7,134	7,157	3	143	216	662	1,505	3,655	950	23
New Castle State Police	6,730	6,738	2	17	291	480	683	4,748	509	8

See footnotes at end of table.

Table 10

Offenses Known to Law Enforcement
by Suburban County by State, 2001—Continued

[The data shown in this table do not reflect county totals but are the number of offenses reported by the sheriff's office, county police department, or state police.]

County by state	Crime Index total	Modified Crime Index total[1]	Murder and non-negligent man-slaughter	Forcible rape	Robbery	Aggravated assault	Burglary	Larceny-theft	Motor vehicle theft	Arson[1]
FLORIDA										
Alachua	5,268	5,286	3	61	117	693	1,334	2,779	281	18
Bay	4,258	4,258	1	62	49	423	632	2,946	145	0
Brevard	7,739	7,784	3	66	147	1,068	1,491	4,529	435	45
Broward	4,090	4,100	9	83	205	866	672	1,762	493	10
Charlotte	3,919	3,926	5	22	30	258	870	2,492	242	7
Clay	4,688	4,712	2	52	58	477	592	3,285	222	24
Collier	8,816	8,865	9	75	242	952	2,081	4,951	506	49
Escambia	11,202	11,218	14	119	450	1,093	2,629	6,337	560	16
Flagler	1,206	1,210	0	9	18	99	302	712	66	4
Gadsden	923	925	6	14	44	88	243	469	59	2
Hernando	5,271	5,284	3	57	59	648	1,306	2,939	259	13
Hillsborough	34,758	34,891	21	232	865	3,419	5,987	20,109	4,125	133
Lake	4,051	4,064	3	37	46	719	1,078	1,866	302	13
Lee	12,179	12,273	11	82	348	947	2,762	6,644	1,385	94
Leon	2,676	2,690	0	35	99	437	989	876	240	14
Manatee	11,216	11,275	5	99	323	1,428	2,583	6,053	725	59
Marion	6,180	6,188	11	93	80	1,112	1,523	3,033	328	8
Martin	3,550	3,574	2	22	99	269	732	2,265	161	24
Miami-Dade	83,055	83,482	89	508	3,260	8,452	11,689	47,702	11,355	427
Nassau	1,891	1,898	6	9	34	636	603	447	156	7
Okaloosa	3,646	3,648	4	41	66	270	577	2,540	148	2
Orange	39,147	39,147	27	270	1,352	3,723	7,715	21,619	4,441	0
Osceola	5,386	5,393	2	49	97	415	1,891	2,625	307	7
Palm Beach	26,892	27,066	10	235	738	2,361	5,899	15,027	2,622	174
Pasco	11,921	12,001	15	122	256	1,055	3,185	6,596	692	80
Pinellas	10,631	10,674	7	134	226	1,010	2,342	6,202	710	43
Polk	13,176	13,176	12	172	243	1,201	3,501	7,062	985	0
Santa Rosa	2,273	2,285	2	38	14	330	584	1,221	84	12
Sarasota	8,700	8,724	5	47	115	720	1,959	5,486	368	24
Seminole	4,975	4,975	3	51	84	638	896	2,913	390	0
St. Johns	2,848	2,852	7	3	35	373	646	1,640	144	4
St. Lucie	2,309	2,330	6	25	48	336	552	1,206	136	21
Volusia	6,322	6,365	7	94	112	1,068	1,597	3,013	431	43
GEORGIA										
Augusta-Richmond	11,117	11,179	16	151	428	203	2,095	7,239	985	62
Barrow	950		0	5	7	37	254	559	88	
Bartow	1,884	1,884	1	2	26	103	560	1,028	164	0
Bibb	2,597		4	2	49	91	628	1,566	257	
Carroll	1,526		0	7	22	70	409	882	136	
Catoosa	969	970	1	1	6	22	193	631	115	1
Chatham County Police Department	2,545	2,562	7	16	69	162	523	1,536	232	17
Cherokee County Police Department	2,223	2,224	0	8	15	104	464	1,556	76	1
Clayton County Police Department	9,190	9,250	20	47	377	392	1,913	5,100	1,341	60
Cobb County Police Department	13,270		17	97	377	523	2,555	8,152	1,549	
Columbia	2,087		2	8	17	44	255	1,646	115	
Coweta	1,404	1,405	1	7	19	42	327	882	126	1
DeKalb County Police Department	24,372		71	79	1,636	498	4,876	13,038	4,174	
Douglas	1,902	1,909	1	11	24	110	359	1,180	217	7
Fayette	612		0	0	5	14	139	397	57	
Forsyth	2,092		1	19	17	228	400	1,223	204	
Fulton County Police Department[3]	8,571	8,616	10	68	438	293	1,822	4,952	988	45
Gwinnett County Police Department	16,647	16,742	16	133	582	601	3,539	9,970	1,806	95
Harris	118		0	0	2	5	31	72	8	
Henry	3,356	3,356	0	24	70	113	657	2171	321	0
Houston	1,154		1	0	11	93	237	743	69	
Jones	546	546	1	2	0	45	166	287	45	0
Lee	613	615	0	4	4	36	143	398	28	2

See footnotes at end of table.

Table 10

Offenses Known to Law Enforcement

by Suburban County by State, 2001—Continued

[The data shown in this table do not reflect county totals but are the number of offenses reported by the sheriff's office, county police department, or state police.]

County by state	Crime Index total	Modified Crime Index total[1]	Murder and non-negligent man-slaughter	Forcible rape	Robbery	Aggravated assault	Burglary	Larceny-theft	Motor vehicle theft	Arson[1]
GEORGIA—Continued										
Newton	944	951	1	2	7	61	289	481	103	7
Oconee	312	313	0	2	6	6	66	185	47	1
Paulding	1,571	1,576	2	7	4	127	298	981	152	5
Rockdale	2,231	2,235	1	4	24	146	353	1,530	173	4
Spalding	1,387	1,390	1	7	13	110	329	786	141	3
Twiggs	48	48	0	0	0	0	41	5	2	0
Walton	1,154		1	3	4	38	270	679	159	
IDAHO										
Ada	1,888	1,904	1	14	9	91	480	1,198	95	16
Bannock	250	252	0	4	1	11	61	164	9	2
Canyon	835	839	0	6	7	64	282	400	76	4
ILLINOIS[4]										
INDIANA										
Allen	1,990	1,991	0	12	34	33	487	1,277	147	1
Allen State Police	66	67	0	1	4	11	4	36	10	1
Clark	922	924	0	6	5	124	289	407	91	2
Clark State Police	106	106	0	0	4	15	10	56	21	0
Clay	213	213	1	1	6	12	66	101	26	0
Clay State Police	53	53	1	0	0	5	18	17	12	0
Clinton	207	210	0	0	1	29	50	110	17	3
Clinton State Police	12	12	0	0	0	1	2	6	3	0
Dearborn	174	174	0	0	0	8	89	66	11	0
Dearborn State Police	73	73	0	1	3	13	11	41	4	0
Delaware	526	527	0	13	5	20	114	340	34	1
Delaware State Police	29	29	0	1	1	5	2	16	4	0
Elkhart	2,090	2,116	1	18	29	27	658	1,130	227	26
Elkhart State Police	105	105	3	2	5	12	24	45	14	0
Floyd	688	688	0	4	3	8	141	478	54	0
Floyd State Police	38	38	0	1	3	8	7	13	6	0
Hamilton	840	847	1	2	8	117	134	530	48	7
Hamilton State Police	20	20	0	1	2	3	2	10	2	0
Hancock	364	365	0	3	3	1	91	253	13	1
Hancock State Police	18	18	0	0	0	4	1	10	3	0
Harrison	851	856	0	2	1	7	266	547	28	5
Harrison State Police	58	58	0	1	3	9	17	24	4	0
Howard	524	524	0	4	10	24	116	333	37	0
Howard State Police	27	27	0	0	0	4	8	13	2	0
Huntington	156	157	0	1	0	4	35	105	11	1
Huntington State Police	32	34	1	1	3	7	5	11	4	2
Lake	824	827	5	5	12	50	143	496	113	3
Lake State Police	294	296	0	0	12	26	7	125	124	2
Madison	337	339	0	4	4	6	87	222	14	2
Madison State Police	48	49	0	0	0	13	3	27	5	1
Marion State Police	317	318	0	5	5	28	6	181	92	1
Monroe	774	784	0	7	3	54	226	426	58	10
Monroe State Police	103	104	0	2	2	22	17	50	10	1
Porter	1,268	1,279	1	3	4	30	139	984	107	11
Porter State Police	40	40	0	0	1	5	1	24	9	0
St. Joseph	2,512	2,538	3	6	37	40	471	1,768	187	26
St. Joseph State Police	163	163	0	2	2	14	35	77	33	0
Tippecanoe	1,035	1,046	2	4	10	35	237	697	50	11
Tippecanoe State Police	70	73	0	1	3	15	8	37	6	3
Vanderburgh	1,351	1,353	3	4	4	152	90	1,054	44	2
Vanderburgh State Police	38	38	0	1	1	6	1	24	5	0
Warrick	600	611	1	2	3	80	73	428	13	11

See footnotes at end of table.

Table 10

Offenses Known to Law Enforcement
by Suburban County by State, 2001—Continued

[The data shown in this table do not reflect county totals but are the number of offenses reported by the sheriff's office, county police department, or state police.]

County by state	Crime Index total	Modified Crime Index total[1]	Murder and non-negligent man-slaughter	Forcible rape	Robbery	Aggravated assault	Burglary	Larceny-theft	Motor vehicle theft	Arson[1]
INDIANA—Continued										
Warrick State Police	15	15	0	0	3	3	1	6	2	0
Wells	140	141	0	0	0	5	58	61	16	1
Wells State Police	7	7	0	0	0	0	1	5	1	0
IOWA										
Black Hawk	257	260	0	6	2	7	129	99	14	3
Dallas	165	165	0	1	1	3	36	113	11	0
Dubuque	250	258	0	2	0	20	94	115	19	8
Johnson	424	424	1	6	4	97	124	161	31	0
Linn	524	527	0	2	3	19	200	249	51	3
Polk	1,589	1,604	0	15	11	105	292	980	186	15
Scott	298	298	0	6	1	36	53	180	22	0
Warren	372	377	1	2	2	7	96	239	25	5
Woodbury	172	172	0	5	1	21	70	70	5	0
KENTUCKY[4]										
Boone[3]	924	928	0	10	8	42	178	626	60	4
Campbell Police Department	348	354	2	6	2	53	80	170	35	6
Daviess	561	565	0	3	3	40	156	331	28	4
Jefferson Police Department	11,267	11,286	15	37	271	381	2,333	7,347	883	19
LOUISIANA										
Acadia	685	685	1	8	4	55	105	478	34	0
Ascension	2,876	2,902	1	26	33	239	851	1,505	221	26
Bossier	743	743	3	5	2	75	102	520	36	0
Caddo	1,600	1,600	3	14	22	128	448	901	84	0
Calcasieu	4,287	4,303	4	46	68	132	928	2,827	282	16
East Baton Rouge	11,573	11,600	11	42	181	391	1,763	8,495	690	27
Jefferson	21,479	21,708	29	94	777	1,465	3,405	13,407	2,302	229
Lafayette	1,562	1,569	3	14	17	162	388	854	124	7
Lafourche	1,965	1,971	3	8	14	134	336	1,371	99	6
Ouachita	2,412	2,423	8	28	43	225	700	1,318	90	11
Rapides	1,929	1,930	4	15	8	225	710	840	127	1
St. Charles	1,963	1,978	2	17	47	306	452	1,014	125	15
St. James	859	860	2	2	13	294	137	363	48	1
St. Landry	1,024	1,037	2	4	12	119	277	540	70	13
St. Martin	396	396	1	2	9	34	47	303	0	0
St. Tammany	3,278	3,294	10	26	45	194	720	2,063	220	16
Terrebonne	4,086	4,123	3	20	53	315	997	2,530	168	37
Webster	300	300	2	6	1	20	76	188	7	0
West Baton Rouge	931	931	0	0	16	70	76	740	29	0
MAINE										
Androscoggin	362	365	0	2	1	0	97	244	18	3
Androscoggin State Police	174	174	0	8	1	5	42	93	25	0
Cumberland	819	825	0	9	4	24	306	420	56	6
Cumberland State Police	191	191	1	1	1	5	41	122	20	0
MARYLAND										
Allegany	205	205	0	0	0	16	52	120	17	0
Allegany State Police	570	578	0	3	8	61	82	373	43	8
Anne Arundel Police Department	19,394	19,549	7	106	580	2,588	2,862	12,140	1,111	155
Anne Arundel State Police	163	163	0	2	2	29	10	104	16	0
Baltimore County State Police	67	67	0	0	1	14	1	39	12	0
Calvert	1,158	1,158	1	15	18	171	193	712	48	0

See footnotes at end of table.

Table 10

Offenses Known to Law Enforcement
by Suburban County by State, 2001—Continued

[The data shown in this table do not reflect county totals but are the number of offenses reported by the sheriff's office, county police department, or state police.]

County by state	Crime Index total	Modified Crime Index total[1]	Murder and non-negligent man-slaughter	Forcible rape	Robbery	Aggravated assault	Burglary	Larceny-theft	Motor vehicle theft	Arson[1]
MARYLAND—Continued										
Calvert State Police	559	573	0	2	6	120	98	316	17	14
Carroll	132	132	0	0	0	35	33	61	3	0
Carroll State Police	1,878	1,883	0	30	34	171	409	1,129	105	5
Cecil	511	511	0	3	4	33	163	278	30	0
Cecil State Police	1,160	1,205	0	9	28	231	257	562	73	45
Charles	4,458	4,458	9	39	134	553	638	2,703	382	0
Charles State Police	20	78	0	0	0	6	0	12	2	58
Frederick	1,517	1,531	0	23	9	55	241	1,114	75	14
Frederick State Police	898	904	0	6	10	143	109	589	41	6
Harford	3,566	3,566	1	22	86	183	806	2,216	252	0
Harford State Police	737	774	0	0	25	64	192	383	73	37
Howard Police Department	8,410	8,410	5	33	198	271	1,582	5,739	582	0
Howard State Police	34	51	0	1	1	6	2	18	6	17
Montgomery	17	17	0	3	0	14	0	0	0	0
Montgomery Police Department	26,724	26,988	18	136	818	837	3,539	18,226	3,150	264
Montgomery State Police	30	30	0	0	0	15	0	12	3	0
Queen Anne's	606	606	2	2	2	110	129	332	29	0
Queen Anne's State Police	320	330	0	5	5	30	91	169	20	10
Washington	1,170	1,170	2	20	17	111	278	654	88	0
Washington State Police	466	478	1	2	2	104	74	252	31	12
MASSACHUSETTS[2]										
Barnstable State Police	4		0	0	0	4	0	0	0	
Berkshire State Police	60		0	0	0	5	17	32	6	
Bristol State Police	33		0	0	0	8	0	11	14	
Hampden State Police	45		0	0	0	10	4	23	8	
Hampshire State Police	26		0	0	0	3	7	13	3	
Middlesex State Police	12		0	0	0	7	0	3	2	
Norfolk State Police	8		0	0	0	2	0	3	3	
Plymouth State Police	43		0	0	1	18	1	10	13	
Suffolk State Police	55		0	0	1	25	0	24	5	
Worcester State Police	11		0	0	0	2	0	5	4	
MICHIGAN										
Allegan	537	539	1	21	7	48	122	300	38	2
Allegan State Police	583	590	0	23	2	46	162	304	46	7
Bay	645	647	0	14	0	20	104	460	47	2
Bay State Police	615	621	2	31	7	37	161	333	44	6
Berrien	767	775	0	15	5	96	142	460	49	8
Berrien State Police	601	614	1	38	5	31	155	325	46	13
Calhoun	451	452	0	4	1	44	135	233	34	1
Calhoun State Police	305	310	0	13	0	28	82	164	18	5
Clinton	333	339	3	0	2	17	87	194	30	6
Clinton State Police	61	66	0	3	0	4	19	31	4	5
Eaton	2,278	2,280	0	22	26	91	318	1,685	136	2
Eaton State Police	24	26	0	3	0	6	1	11	3	2
Genesee	926	926	1	10	7	46	187	622	53	0
Genesee State Police	520	529	0	46	4	50	111	252	57	9
Ingham	1,412	1,429	2	50	17	92	377	777	97	17
Ingham State Police	115	116	0	7	0	2	6	90	10	1
Jackson	896	904	2	19	7	73	188	512	95	8
Jackson State Police	502	505	1	21	2	54	132	255	37	3
Kalamazoo	2,375	2,389	1	26	32	83	602	1,496	135	14
Kalamazoo State Police	61	63	1	7	0	13	17	22	1	2
Kent	4,983	5,009	1	52	26	225	1,151	3,250	278	26
Kent State Police	50	52	0	7	0	9	2	31	1	2
Lapeer	398	402	0	2	1	21	111	228	35	4
Lapeer State Police	249	257	0	17	1	28	62	127	14	8

See footnotes at end of table.

Table 10

Offenses Known to Law Enforcement
by Suburban County by State, 2001—Continued

[The data shown in this table do not reflect county totals but are the number of offenses reported by the sheriff's office, county police department, or state police.]

County by state	Crime Index total	Modified Crime Index total[1]	Murder and non-negligent man-slaughter	Forcible rape	Robbery	Aggravated assault	Burglary	Larceny-theft	Motor vehicle theft	Arson[1]
MICHIGAN—Continued										
Lenawee	390	393	1	9	0	14	106	239	21	3
Lenawee State Police	256	266	2	15	0	14	88	128	9	10
Livingston	715	721	0	12	5	30	125	470	73	6
Livingston State Police	691	699	1	9	5	57	120	437	62	8
Macomb	2,234	2,261	0	85	12	61	313	1,590	173	27
Macomb State Police	66	66	0	6	1	9	9	29	12	0
Midland	538	546	0	10	1	52	184	270	21	8
Midland State Police	23	24	0	1	0	0	7	11	4	1
Monroe	3,326	3,392	4	57	24	165	770	2,044	262	66
Monroe State Police	397	403	0	16	3	37	110	202	29	6
Muskegon	1,537	1,552	0	17	12	68	222	1,140	78	15
Muskegon State Police	445	449	0	18	0	30	135	234	28	4
Oakland	5,110	5,206	1	84	59	333	807	3,456	370	96
Oakland State Police	352	355	0	19	3	40	83	177	30	3
Ottawa	3,293	3,309	0	85	16	185	742	2,140	125	16
Ottawa State Police	270	272	0	7	0	18	67	166	12	2
Saginaw	1,185	1,186	1	18	5	91	198	795	77	1
Saginaw State Police	549	554	3	40	8	44	85	311	58	5
St. Clair	2,179	2,208	0	30	10	126	537	1,317	159	29
St. Clair State Police	322	328	2	7	2	20	96	164	31	6
Van Buren	674	679	1	6	2	44	212	338	71	5
Van Buren State Police	801	817	2	26	4	67	291	349	62	16
Washtenaw	2,600	2,635	8	47	82	219	715	1,167	362	35
Washtenaw State Police	365	375	7	8	4	42	120	147	37	10
Wayne	35	36	1	3	0	3	1	16	11	1
Wayne State Police	197	198	3	11	5	39	20	106	13	1
MINNESOTA										
Anoka	529	535	2	6	1	13	109	354	44	6
Carver	392	394	1	1	2	17	67	265	39	2
Chisago	711	711	0	14	4	17	138	447	91	0
Clay	88	88	0	1	0	4	18	56	9	0
Dakota	218	220	0	2	0	13	50	131	22	2
Hennepin	212	214	0	7	3	30	45	98	29	2
Isanti	325	325	0	12	1	13	59	192	48	0
Olmsted	424	432	0	7	5	18	111	223	60	8
Polk	348	354	0	2	1	13	111	185	36	6
Ramsey	326	332	0	6	1	17	36	244	22	6
Scott	258	258	0	3	1	3	29	182	40	0
Sherburne	492	492	0	5	0	20	92	340	35	0
Stearns	603	608	0	27	1	42	100	390	43	5
St. Louis	872	876	1	30	1	30	305	452	53	4
Washington	1,137	1,140	0	11	5	21	206	829	65	3
Wright	1,903	1,918	3	7	5	32	228	1,474	154	15
MISSISSIPPI										
Harrison[3]	1,731	1,751	4	15	9	28	558	1,042	75	20
Jackson	2,498	2,498	8	20	35	106	652	1,468	209	0
Lamar	752	753	0	14	4	15	205	466	48	1
Madison	643	646	4	11	4	42	215	280	87	3
MISSOURI										
Andrew	163		1	2	1	6	28	115	10	
Boone	870	876	0	7	25	42	155	572	69	6
Buchanan	319	320	1	3	0	97	85	117	16	1
Cass	470	475	0	5	3	42	160	231	29	5
Christian	679	683	1	2	1	74	232	328	41	4

See footnotes at end of table.

Table 10

Offenses Known to Law Enforcement
by Suburban County by State, 2001—Continued

[The data shown in this table do not reflect county totals but are the number of offenses reported by the sheriff's office, county police department, or state police.]

County by state	Crime Index total	Modified Crime Index total[1]	Murder and non-negligent man-slaughter	Forcible rape	Robbery	Aggravated assault	Burglary	Larceny-theft	Motor vehicle theft	Arson[1]
MISSOURI—Continued										
Clinton	180	181	0	4	3	47	46	67	13	1
Greene	1,602	1,612	0	13	6	66	379	1,013	125	10
Jasper	600	601	0	10	1	20	191	318	60	1
Jefferson[3]	3,821	3,830	4	17	11	306	505	2,654	324	9
Lafayette	93		1	0	1	14	52	21	4	
Lincoln	610	620	0	2	0	153	122	330	3	10
Platte	417	422	2	4	5	21	70	286	29	5
Ray	146		0	1	5	31	56	38	15	
St. Charles	1,782	1,792	0	3	10	230	327	1,140	72	10
St. Louis County Police Department	12,604	12,693	7	54	249	674	1,810	8,766	1,044	89
Warren	240	244	0	1	0	17	75	125	22	4
Webster	464	466	1	4	3	145	118	163	30	2
MONTANA[2]										
Cascade[3]	501		0	2	3	62	75	317	42	
NEBRASKA										
Cass	190	193	0	2	0	4	64	98	22	3
Cass State Patrol	9	9	0	0	0	1	1	7	0	0
Dakota	57	57	0	1	0	4	23	25	4	0
Douglas	1,342	1,347	0	14	4	112	175	931	106	5
Douglas State Patrol	6	6	0	0	0	1	0	3	2	0
Lancaster	448	454	0	0	2	9	85	333	19	6
Lancaster State Patrol	18	18	0	0	0	2	0	9	7	0
NEVADA										
Nye	920	927	2	0	6	79	379	421	33	7
Washoe	1,640	1,647	2	29	21	183	337	903	165	7
NEW JERSEY										
Essex Police Department	341	342	0	14	72	54	28	124	49	1
NEW MEXICO										
Bernalillo	4,533	4,620	5	47	197	763	1,121	1,901	499	87
Santa Fe	1,299	1,324	0	25	10	192	368	626	78	25
NEW YORK										
Albany	143	143	0	0	2	43	25	65	8	0
Albany State Police	429	429	0	1	15	17	35	350	11	0
Broome	971		1	11	10	42	162	714	31	
Broome State Police	698	706	1	3	10	87	127	450	20	8
Cayuga	344		1	2	4	21	54	250	12	
Cayuga State Police	285	286	0	0	0	65	49	167	4	1
Chautauqua	1,032	1,057	2	12	10	61	217	687	43	25
Chautauqua State Police	170	170	0	0	2	22	37	103	6	0
Chemung	359	360	0	5	5	44	64	235	6	1
Chemung State Police	335	335	0	1	0	45	47	236	6	0
Dutchess	955	958	1	6	10	71	164	662	41	3
Dutchess State Police	749	756	1	5	5	83	131	493	31	7
Genesee	728	738	0	11	5	27	156	503	26	10
Genesee State Police	93	93	0	0	1	8	18	61	5	0
Herkimer State Police	321	329	0	2	0	21	122	168	8	8
Madison	151	152	0	1	3	9	47	82	9	1
Madison State Police	407	409	0	3	1	46	115	235	7	2
Monroe	5,468	5,485	1	14	54	90	671	4,300	338	17
Monroe State Police	54	54	0	2	0	16	0	22	14	0

See footnotes at end of table.

Table 10

Offenses Known to Law Enforcement
by Suburban County by State, 2001—Continued

[The data shown in this table do not reflect county totals but are the number of offenses reported by the sheriff's office, county police department, or state police.]

County by state	Crime Index total	Modified Crime Index total[1]	Murder and non-negligent man-slaughter	Forcible rape	Robbery	Aggravated assault	Burglary	Larceny-theft	Motor vehicle theft	Arson[1]
NEW YORK—Continued										
Montgomery State Police	142	146	1	1	2	9	24	103	2	4
Nassau State Police	44		0	0	2	21	2	7	12	
New York State Police	94	94	0	0	0	2	0	92	0	0
Niagara	1,653	1,667	0	8	16	51	331	1,163	84	14
Niagara State Police	184	184	0	2	0	5	39	126	12	0
Oneida	763		1	35	6	67	169	444	41	
Oneida State Police	661	668	2	6	3	84	161	388	17	7
Ontario	961	965	0	7	5	26	159	707	57	4
Ontario State Police	332	333	1	1	2	11	40	269	8	1
Oswego	481	515	1	4	3	11	141	285	36	34
Oswego State Police	754	754	1	1	2	26	281	425	18	0
Putnam	389	390	0	5	5	17	95	247	20	1
Putnam State Police	145	147	0	2	2	27	7	99	8	2
Rensselaer	415	420	0	1	4	22	73	309	6	5
Rensselaer State Police	724	729	1	7	1	57	110	520	28	5
Rockland	64	64	0	0	0	13	1	48	2	0
Rockland State Police	54	54	0	3	1	7	7	35	1	0
Saratoga	1,099	1,107	0	12	15	34	240	757	41	8
Saratoga State Police	687	695	0	2	5	87	161	417	15	8
Schoharie	162	165	0	0	1	1	31	122	7	3
Schoharie State Police	203	204	1	2	0	22	36	133	9	1
Suffolk	238	238	0	2	2	196	7	25	6	0
Suffolk State Police	87	87	0	0	5	15	23	36	8	0
Tioga	204	206	0	3	1	6	86	92	16	2
Tioga State Police	127		0	1	0	3	28	89	6	
Warren	906	909	0	10	4	32	200	631	29	3
Warren State Police	219	220	0	4	2	8	28	172	5	1
Washington	334	335	0	0	0	116	69	144	5	1
Washington State Police	172	175	0	1	1	44	52	65	9	3
Wayne	666	672	1	16	6	12	157	453	21	6
Wayne State Police	495	499	0	5	2	30	116	310	32	4
Westchester Public Safety	367	368	1	2	4	36	31	266	27	1
Westchester State Police	620	634	1	5	5	85	83	377	64	14
NORTH CAROLINA										
Alamance	1,281	1,288	2	2	29	39	486	623	100	7
Alexander	747	750	1	3	8	32	291	361	51	3
Buncombe	3,057		0	11	38	184	896	1,649	279	
Cabarrus	955	960	2	10	16	19	362	512	34	5
Catawba	2,075	2,089	1	17	27	105	663	1,159	103	14
Chatham	1,260	1,270	2	6	11	40	522	622	57	10
Cumberland	6,838	6,942	17	24	148	445	2,204	3,662	338	104
Currituck	599	601	0	2	3	41	170	366	17	2
Davidson	1,661	1,664	0	0	11	27	78	1,467	78	3
Davie	585	589	0	3	7	33	200	309	33	4
Durham	1,021	1,021	4	0	15	64	243	609	86	0
Edgecombe	732	737	1	6	13	24	322	331	35	5
Forsyth[3]	3,921	3,973	6	12	37	351	974	2,401	140	52
Franklin	933	934	0	5	3	44	416	403	62	1
Gaston Police Department	2,118	2,148	3	15	32	170	742	1,027	129	30
Guilford	3,002	3,032	1	14	55	154	917	1,674	187	30
Johnston	2,381	2,394	4	14	40	139	797	1,231	156	13
Lincoln	1,606	1,615	4	3	9	90	506	905	89	9
Nash	962	972	8	3	21	40	359	489	42	10
New Hanover	2,266	2,271	0	19	42	69	698	1,307	131	5
Onslow	2,806	2,812	3	43	31	132	759	1,551	287	6
Orange	1,070	1,072	2	3	32	11	454	484	84	2
Pitt	2,003	2,014	4	12	34	180	625	1,040	108	11
Randolph	2,478	2,480	4	10	22	61	767	1,498	116	2
Rowan	1,646	1,671	4	18	15	145	552	819	93	25

See footnotes at the end of table.

Table 10

Offenses Known to Law Enforcement
by Suburban County by State, 2001—Continued

[The data shown in this table do not reflect county totals but are the number of offenses reported by the sheriff's office, county police department, or state police.]

County by state	Crime Index total	Modified Crime Index total[1]	Murder and non-negligent man-slaughter	Forcible rape	Robbery	Aggravated assault	Burglary	Larceny-theft	Motor vehicle theft	Arson[1]
NORTH CAROLINA—Continued										
Stokes	934	956	1	9	3	103	322	436	60	22
Union	1,647	1,652	1	12	15	41	737	777	64	5
Wake	3,381	3,456	3	18	52	158	1,274	1,596	280	75
Wayne	1,878	1,884	3	4	18	112	678	967	96	6
Yadkin	579	582	1	4	1	21	185	343	24	3
NORTH DAKOTA										
Burleigh	71	71	0	1	0	2	26	39	3	0
Cass	193	201	1	4	0	6	54	106	22	8
Grand Forks	158	159	2	2	0	4	30	103	17	1
Morton	103	103	0	4	0	2	14	76	7	0
OHIO										
Allen	1,886	1,889	0	16	32	22	305	1,472	39	3
Carroll	356	356	0	4	0	43	123	152	34	0
Clark	1,007	1,023	0	6	1	9	297	694	0	16
Clermont	1,448	1,468	2	44	14	33	322	948	85	20
Columbiana	566	568	0	15	2	129	164	220	36	2
Crawford	214	214	0	1	3	3	84	113	10	0
Delaware	1,192	1,218	1	10	10	18	324	741	88	26
Franklin	4,346	4,371	6	48	159	84	928	2,636	485	25
Fulton	403	409	0	3	0	7	166	197	30	6
Greene	416	419	1	10	1	7	119	246	32	3
Lake	745	746	0	4	11	30	134	533	33	1
Licking	711	712	0	1	3	1	169	490	47	1
Lorain	952	981	0	12	22	31	524	333	30	29
Lucas	1,828	1,843	0	23	27	51	344	1,257	126	15
Mahoning	286	291	0	5	0	23	95	145	18	5
Miami	560	560	1	14	3	7	101	377	57	0
Pickaway	1,147	1,168	1	7	5	22	407	631	74	21
Richland	1,378	1,387	1	13	13	12	391	900	48	9
Stark	2,769	2,795	0	33	49	27	658	1,786	216	26
Summit	1,472	1,476	0	17	20	25	328	999	83	4
Trumbull	519	520	0	0	4	24	92	294	105	1
Warren	1,304	1,318	1	3	9	39	244	920	88	14
Washington	597	602	1	22	1	14	168	348	43	5
Wood	960	967	1	6	4	12	232	641	64	7
OKLAHOMA										
Canadian	103	106	0	0	1	4	33	51	14	3
Cleveland	462	467	1	1	0	67	169	192	32	5
Comanche	337	341	0	3	4	51	95	154	30	4
Creek	512	516	0	18	3	57	164	216	54	4
Garfield	174	181	0	1	0	5	34	132	2	7
Logan	174	176	1	2	1	32	81	41	16	2
McClain	190	195	2	3	0	13	72	81	19	5
Oklahoma	220	221	1	1	2	24	75	102	15	1
Osage	559	570	0	16	1	61	211	234	36	11
Pottawatomie	658	661	0	2	2	56	229	323	46	3
Rogers	332	333	1	0	0	8	101	195	27	1
Sequoyah	712	718	0	8	5	159	262	196	82	6
Tulsa	1,728	1,737	3	14	29	218	360	934	170	9
Wagoner	438	439	1	3	4	22	125	217	66	1
OREGON										
Clackamas	9,558	9,584	2	61	106	160	1,568	6,743	918	26
Clackamas State Police	40	51	0	0	0	8	0	21	11	11
Columbia	472	474	1	6	1	0	164	234	66	2

See footnotes at the end of table.

Table 10

Offenses Known to Law Enforcement
by Suburban County by State, 2001—Continued

[The data shown in this table do not reflect county totals but are the number of offenses reported by the sheriff's office, county police department, or state police.]

County by state	Crime Index total	Modified Crime Index total[1]	Murder and non-negligent man-slaughter	Forcible rape	Robbery	Aggravated assault	Burglary	Larceny-theft	Motor vehicle theft	Arson[1]
OREGON—Continued										
Columbia State Police	5	10	0	0	0	2	0	3	0	5
Jackson	1,794	1,817	1	17	9	111	332	1,192	132	23
Jackson State Police	22	64	1	4	1	4	0	2	10	42
Lane	1,584	1,598	1	15	6	109	469	792	192	14
Lane State Police	195	241	0	8	1	24	24	94	44	46
Marion[3]	4,085	4,087	4	13	43	222	657	2,730	416	2
Marion State Police	183	226	0	6	1	53	16	84	23	43
Multnomah	927	934	0	6	11	22	194	549	145	7
Multnomah State Police	76	83	0	1	0	9	0	31	35	7
Polk	434	435	0	3	2	30	92	276	31	1
Polk State Police	7	9	0	0	0	3	0	3	1	2
Washington	5,406	5,435	2	47	52	88	852	3,861	504	29
Washington State Police	17	28	0	1	0	5	0	4	7	11
Yamhill	709	714	1	14	6	17	177	424	70	5
Yamhill State Police	13	17	0	1	0	3	0	7	2	4
PENNSYLVANIA										
Allegheny	6	7	0	0	0	6	0	0	0	1
Allegheny Police Department	879	958	1	46	52	98	234	382	66	79
Allegheny State Police	86	86	1	5	1	38	3	26	12	0
Beaver	21	21	0	0	0	17	0	3	1	0
Beaver State Police	148	153	0	3	2	25	51	56	11	5
Berks State Police	813	834	1	15	16	86	232	404	59	21
Blair State Police	436	447	2	5	4	15	97	277	36	11
Bucks State Police	462	485	0	5	10	52	120	209	66	23
Butler State Police	1,045	1,073	1	23	11	31	257	638	84	28
Cambria State Police	304	311	1	8	4	33	89	132	37	7
Carbon State Police	341	342	0	4	3	33	79	193	29	1
Centre State Police	795	801	5	12	6	47	218	464	43	6
Chester State Police	1,381	1,407	0	22	27	114	400	676	142	26
Columbia State Police	394	395	1	3	2	15	130	227	16	1
Cumberland State Police	641	661	1	19	8	28	172	377	36	20
Delaware State Police	1,220	1,230	1	5	26	63	129	859	137	10
Elizabethville State Police	801	805	1	8	12	37	198	501	44	4
Erie State Police	1,929	1,947	3	28	14	65	392	1,336	91	18
Fayette State Police	1,993	2,141	2	37	43	158	475	1,055	223	148
Lackawanna State Police	262	281	1	8	8	16	72	127	30	19
Lancaster State Police	1,265	1,303	3	18	25	77	377	673	92	38
Lebanon State Police	397	399	0	5	8	21	94	242	27	2
Lehigh State Police	1,091	1,097	3	13	9	94	206	690	76	6
Luzerne State Police	871	907	5	9	17	149	188	431	72	36
Lycoming State Police	870	873	1	12	3	26	250	537	41	3
Mercer State Police	447	455	0	4	4	15	115	264	45	8
Northampton State Police	283	293	3	5	5	20	73	152	25	10
Perry State Police	676	680	2	18	0	56	171	390	39	4
Philadelphia State Police	10	10	0	0	0	7	0	2	1	0
Pike State Police	561	589	0	6	11	34	195	263	52	28
Skippack State Police	521	525	0	9	14	76	110	273	39	4
Somerset State Police[5]	566	577	40	10	8	27	170	271	40	11
Washington State Police	790	824	0	27	17	49	203	424	70	34
Westmoreland State Police	2,141	2,188	2	32	30	127	397	1,373	180	47
Wyoming State Police	291	295	0	7	1	13	74	168	28	4
York State Police	1,185	1,221	0	28	22	330	243	481	81	36
RHODE ISLAND										
Kent (Hope Valley State Police)	174	174	0	3	1	12	31	120	7	0
Providence (Chepachet State Police)	37	37	0	3	1	4	3	24	2	0
Providence (Lincoln Woods State Police)	106	107	0	6	0	6	3	71	20	1
Washington (Wickford State Police)	36	36	0	2	0	5	1	26	2	0

See footnotes at end of table.

Table 10

Offenses Known to Law Enforcement
by Suburban County by State, 2001—Continued

[The data shown in this table do not reflect county totals but are the number of offenses reported by the sheriff's office, county police department, or state police.]

County by state	Crime Index total	Modified Crime Index total[1]	Murder and non-negligent man-slaughter	Forcible rape	Robbery	Aggravated assault	Burglary	Larceny-theft	Motor vehicle theft	Arson[1]
SOUTH CAROLINA										
Aiken	3,035	3,054	6	33	52	286	802	1,554	302	19
Anderson	4,731	4,771	6	39	80	508	1,121	2,674	303	40
Charleston	4,490	4,508	2	46	116	732	788	2,225	581	18
Cherokee	1,620	1,631	2	9	24	182	354	954	95	11
Edgefield	422	427	1	7	4	31	126	210	43	5
Florence	3,450	3,455	7	48	78	409	760	1,910	238	5
Horry Police Department	7,916	7,952	18	74	149	947	1,417	4,695	616	36
Richland	10,227	10,278	6	98	402	861	1,888	5,913	1,059	51
Sumter	3,067	3,090	1	27	77	364	1,001	1,310	287	23
SOUTH DAKOTA										
Minnehaha	320	322	0	9	0	23	128	139	21	2
Pennington	1,409	1,413	1	48	1	28	124	1,179	28	4
TENNESSEE										
Anderson	784	800	2	6	7	78	211	418	62	16
Blount	2,080	2,095	6	47	7	338	482	1,082	118	15
Carter	923	931	1	10	4	129	227	477	75	8
Cheatham	621	630	0	4	5	55	114	384	59	9
Chester	120	124	0	0	0	16	52	47	5	4
Dickson	708	713	1	8	4	133	204	323	35	5
Fayette	722	729	2	7	8	93	256	297	59	7
Hamilton	2,346	2,357	3	16	24	360	573	1,266	104	11
Knox	5,879	5,943	4	39	71	424	1,342	3,372	627	64
Loudon	698	699	1	2	3	66	162	422	42	1
Madison	1,077	1,086	3	16	11	142	252	585	68	9
Marion	483	489	1	0	0	127	102	178	75	6
Montgomery	673	679	2	14	3	90	200	330	34	6
Robertson	630	633	0	9	7	99	170	298	47	3
Rutherford	1,294	1,311	1	25	11	194	320	644	99	17
Sevier	1,154	1,157	1	10	4	53	372	613	101	3
Shelby	4,762	4,780	4	26	71	285	1,319	2,534	523	18
Shelby County Police Department	51	51	0	0	1	0	6	43	1	0
Sullivan	1,741	1,777	3	16	12	259	575	774	102	36
Sumner	792	804	0	15	6	84	239	392	56	12
Tipton	888	900	0	3	12	70	319	387	97	12
Unicoi	287	293	0	2	4	33	72	150	26	6
Union	375	377	0	0	1	42	135	161	36	2
Washington	1,162	1,181	1	9	10	152	340	567	83	19
Williamson	650	661	0	9	1	66	181	357	36	11
Wilson	1,143	1,145	1	2	8	140	389	528	75	2
TEXAS										
Archer	115	117	0	2	0	5	40	51	17	2
Bastrop	1,110	1,114	2	8	10	121	374	522	73	4
Bell	958	970	0	26	7	88	236	548	53	12
Bexar	5,030	5,144	4	39	59	313	1,285	3,026	304	114
Bowie	637	648	4	8	9	77	180	308	51	11
Brazoria	1,582	1,593	2	25	21	134	547	728	125	11
Brazos	361	365	0	4	5	40	135	164	13	4
Caldwell	339	340	0	15	0	60	147	102	15	1
Cameron	1,700	1,708	1	9	16	177	682	731	84	8
Chambers	526	530	1	13	8	27	170	279	28	4
Collin	702	704	0	23	6	59	234	317	63	2
Comal	1,066	1,074	2	21	4	72	234	675	58	8
Coryell	94	98	0	3	0	7	38	39	7	4
Dallas	502	518	0	0	2	52	201	190	57	16

See footnotes at end of table.

Table 10

Offenses Known to Law Enforcement
by Suburban County by State, 2001—Continued

[The data shown in this table do not reflect county totals but are the number of offenses reported by the sheriff's office, county police department, or state police.]

County by state	Crime Index total	Modified Crime Index total[1]	Murder and non-negligent man-slaughter	Forcible rape	Robbery	Aggravated assault	Burglary	Larceny-theft	Motor vehicle theft	Arson[1]
TEXAS—Continued										
Denton	808	814	0	8	2	86	148	500	64	6
Ector	1,218	1,221	2	3	7	135	345	667	59	3
Ellis	1,206	1,209	3	7	12	95	413	569	107	3
El Paso	1,355	1,381	4	31	20	195	261	699	145	26
Fort Bend	3,134	3,179	7	35	65	381	970	1,543	133	45
Galveston	1,243	1,258	1	17	22	165	372	548	118	15
Grayson	846	849	0	10	6	23	228	532	47	3
Gregg	769	778	1	17	6	37	130	523	55	9
Guadalupe	1,196	1,196	1	13	9	63	373	679	58	0
Hardin	443	447	0	6	6	42	136	210	43	4
Harris	38,554	39,086	42	301	1,326	3,532	8,643	20,361	4,349	532
Harrison	805	811	1	1	6	46	277	429	45	6
Hays	1,497	1,508	1	4	14	75	330	974	99	11
Henderson	1,484	1,484	2	3	9	175	581	583	131	0
Hidalgo	7,150	7,304	26	37	150	1,339	2,517	2,504	577	154
Hood	793	799	1	1	3	72	229	431	56	6
Hunt	1,163	1,165	0	1	10	51	481	548	72	2
Jefferson	577	579	1	25	3	17	150	331	50	2
Johnson	1,340	1,369	2	1	10	92	435	729	71	29
Kaufman	1,383	1,426	7	16	19	112	422	673	134	43
Liberty	1,074	1,085	2	23	4	43	498	394	110	11
Lubbock	812	817	0	17	9	73	287	353	73	5
McLennan	874	890	2	18	10	74	267	426	77	16
Midland	558	560	1	2	1	46	164	306	38	2
Montgomery	7,510	7,594	13	54	82	571	1,707	4,542	541	84
Nueces	355	355	0	22	7	30	98	170	28	0
Orange	1,002	1,008	0	72	9	74	206	536	105	6
Parker	1,006	1,008	1	18	6	80	298	514	89	2
Potter	336	336	1	1	1	22	80	214	17	0
Randall	485	488	1	1	3	30	154	259	37	3
Rockwall	218	218	0	1	0	26	54	113	24	0
San Patricio	395	397	1	4	6	21	134	214	15	2
Smith	1,884	1,927	4	42	37	115	675	875	136	43
Tarrant	942	946	1	6	7	64	319	452	93	4
Taylor	142	142	0	2	0	19	45	68	8	0
Tom Green	339	346	1	2	3	19	81	218	15	7
Travis	3,855	3,866	5	45	48	234	1,022	2,261	240	11
Upshur	534	536	0	2	3	39	219	218	53	2
Victoria	422	424	2	7	5	39	114	237	18	2
Waller	242	242	1	2	4	22	65	115	33	0
Webb	320	323	4	2	1	27	145	106	35	3
Wichita	218	226	0	0	2	24	77	94	21	8
Williamson	2,078	2,102	2	21	17	164	504	1,270	100	24
Wilson	293	293	0	1	0	21	129	129	13	0
UTAH										
Davis	147	155	0	4	0	13	41	76	13	8
Salt Lake	14,956	14,996	11	124	171	482	2,037	11,141	990	40
Utah	259	270	0	7	0	14	85	135	18	11
Weber	769	771	0	4	4	22	141	570	28	2
VERMONT										
Grand Isle	128	129	0	1	1	2	48	68	8	1
Williston State Police	361	375	4	1	0	8	88	238	22	14
VIRGINIA										
Albemarle County Police Department	2,074	2,100	2	15	20	104	337	1,526	70	26
Albemarle State Police	5	5	0	0	0	1	0	3	1	0
Amherst	418	422	0	10	7	26	61	280	34	4

See footnotes at end of table.

Table 10

Offenses Known to Law Enforcement
by Suburban County by State, 2001—Continued

[The data shown in this table do not reflect county totals but are the number of offenses reported by the sheriff's office, county police department, or state police.]

County by state	Crime Index total	Modified Crime Index total[1]	Murder and non-negligent man-slaughter	Forcible rape	Robbery	Aggravated assault	Burglary	Larceny-theft	Motor vehicle theft	Arson[1]
VIRGINIA—Continued										
Amherst State Police	16	16	0	0	0	3	0	7	6	0
Arlington County Police Department	6,328	6,342	3	29	197	161	492	4,834	612	14
Arlington State Police	7	7	0	0	0	3	1	3	0	0
Bedford	888	897	0	9	2	45	149	652	31	9
Bedford State Police	25	25	0	2	0	5	1	13	4	0
Botetourt	444	446	0	6	6	24	44	336	28	2
Botetourt State Police	23	23	0	0	1	4	0	14	4	0
Chesterfield County Police Department	8,306	8,391	8	56	196	308	1,208	6,098	432	85
Chesterfield State Police	37	37	0	0	0	17	3	10	7	0
Clarke	216	217	0	2	2	57	18	127	10	1
Clarke State Police	9	9	2	0	0	5	0	2	0	0
Dinwiddie	765	770	4	6	8	19	126	571	31	5
Dinwiddie State Police	11	11	1	0	0	4	1	5	0	0
Fairfax County Police Department	12,891	12,907	1	35	137	27	1,374	10,935	382	16
Fairfax State Police	52	52	0	0	0	21	0	26	5	0
Fauquier	735	753	4	8	8	45	100	530	40	18
Fauquier State Police	28	28	0	0	0	5	1	20	2	0
Fluvanna	266	270	1	6	1	38	58	146	16	4
Fluvanna State Police	6	6	0	0	0	0	1	3	2	0
Goochland	126	126	1	2	4	34	14	59	12	0
Goochland State Police	7	7	0	0	0	0	1	6	0	0
Greene	171	179	0	5	3	15	27	110	11	8
Hanover	1,111	1,119	0	4	20	37	132	881	37	8
Hanover State Police	15	15	0	0	0	9	0	5	1	0
Henrico County Police Department	11,225	11,404	16	34	281	320	1,415	8,330	829	179
Henrico State Police	21	21	0	0	1	3	0	15	2	0
Isle Of Wight	491	502	1	5	5	8	148	293	31	11
Isle Of Wight State Police	4	4	0	0	0	1	2	0	1	0
Loudoun	3,133	3,181	5	23	32	189	298	2,411	175	48
Loudoun State Police	29	29	0	0	0	5	2	18	4	0
Mathews	144	150	0	1	0	5	26	106	6	6
New Kent	260	264	1	4	2	14	39	191	9	4
Powhatan	207	212	1	4	3	5	44	133	17	5
Prince George County Police Department	520	525	1	7	12	15	54	397	34	5
Prince William County Police Department	8,177	8,255	12	56	173	357	1,089	5,768	722	78
Prince William State Police	23	23	0	0	0	8	0	14	1	0
Roanoke County Police Department	1,235	1,238	0	21	16	148	208	767	75	3
Roanoke State Police	8	8	0	0	0	4	0	3	1	0
Scott	414	425	0	3	1	15	99	275	21	11
Scott State Police	2	6	0	0	0	0	0	1	1	4
Spotsylvania	2,095	2,105	0	24	29	103	208	1,641	90	10
Spotsylvania State Police	42	42	0	0	0	1	3	32	6	0
Stafford	1,796	1,808	2	27	18	41	152	1,441	115	12
Stafford State Police	28	28	0	0	0	4	0	20	4	0
Warren	226	227	0	3	1	4	57	140	21	1
Warren State Police	7	7	0	0	1	2	0	4	0	0
York	1,273	1,294	1	3	22	69	96	1,036	46	21
York State Police	1	1	0	0	0	0	0	1	0	0
WASHINGTON										
Benton	901	918	0	10	2	69	202	559	59	17
Clark	4,867	4,924	1	27	50	196	998	3,272	323	57
Franklin	212	212	1	0	1	5	35	143	27	0
King	10,429	10,691	14	126	170	412	2,117	5,798	1,792	262
Kitsap[3]	5,180	5,228	2	104	50	341	1,254	3,127	302	48
Pierce	12,193	12,263	12	63	191	600	2,536	7,209	1,582	70
Snohomish	7,527	7,577	6	205	114	295	1,689	3,702	1,516	50
Spokane	9,071	9,126	3	50	130	317	1,790	6,041	740	55
Thurston	3,140	3,172	3	50	21	234	878	1,703	251	32
Whatcom	1,994	2,003	0	43	12	88	629	1,063	159	9
Yakima	2,997	3,050	2	34	13	53	1,201	1,406	288	53

See footnotes at end of table.

Table 10

Offenses Known to Law Enforcement

by Suburban County by State, 2001—Continued

[The data shown in this table do not reflect county totals but are the number of offenses reported by the sheriff's office, county police department, or state police.]

County by state	Crime Index total	Modified Crime Index total[1]	Murder and non-negligent man-slaughter	Forcible rape	Robbery	Aggravated assault	Burglary	Larceny-theft	Motor vehicle theft	Arson[1]
WEST VIRGINIA										
Berkeley-Martinsburg State Police	792	799	1	5	15	59	187	428	97	7
Brooke-Wellsburg State Police	12	12	0	0	0	8	2	2	0	0
Cabell-Huntington State Police	355	358	0	1	3	13	41	278	19	3
Hancock-New Cumberland State Police	2	2	0	0	0	2	0	0	0	0
Jefferson-Kearneysville State Police	307	308	0	2	2	32	63	188	20	1
Marshall-Moundsville State Police	29	30	0	0	0	2	5	21	1	1
Mineral	25	25	0	1	0	1	5	14	4	0
Ohio-Wheeling State Police	54	54	0	0	0	5	3	41	5	0
Putnam	894	905	4	5	2	166	177	481	59	11
Putnam State Police:										
Teays Valley	117	117	1	0	1	14	17	80	4	0
Winfield	82	84	0	1	1	8	14	54	4	2
Wayne	198	200	0	1	0	13	55	99	30	2
Wayne-Wayne State Police	450	455	0	1	1	55	88	221	84	5
Wood-Parkersburg State Police	164	164	0	0	0	4	25	120	15	0
WISCONSIN										
Brown	1,408	1,413	0	19	3	13	279	1,008	86	5
Calumet	172	172	0	2	0	7	41	116	6	0
Chippewa	434	434	1	4	0	11	92	299	27	0
Dane	1,244	1,253	0	23	11	58	205	877	70	9
Douglas	315	319	0	5	0	4	156	126	24	4
Eau Claire	396	396	1	1	0	5	83	296	10	0
Kenosha	949	956	0	13	8	82	163	622	61	7
La Crosse	215	217	0	4	1	8	40	148	14	2
Marathon	526	528	1	3	3	24	141	344	10	2
Milwaukee	277	277	0	4	3	5	2	255	8	0
Outagamie	405	405	0	9	1	3	62	311	19	0
Ozaukee	211	211	0	0	0	5	34	157	15	0
Pierce	246	246	0	0	2	3	88	128	25	0
Racine	854	854	0	0	7	9	116	689	33	0
Rock	530	534	0	3	1	37	171	293	25	4
Sheboygan	511	511	0	6	1	17	98	366	23	0
St. Croix	330	332	0	2	1	27	84	196	20	2
Washington	651	658	0	14	1	16	143	447	30	7
Waukesha	778	780	0	2	4	43	113	586	30	2
Winnebago	413	413	0	8	1	10	75	303	16	0
WYOMING										
Laramie	748	750	1	29	5	23	124	538	28	2
Natrona	365	366	0	0	3	13	99	217	33	1

[1] The Modified Crime Index total is the sum of the Crime Index offenses including arson. Arson is shown only if 12 months of arson data were received. If 12 months of arson data were not received, there is no Modified Crime Index total shown.

[2] Complete arson figures for 2001 for Alabama, Massachusetts, and Montana were not available.

[3] Due to changes in reporting practices, annexations, and/or incomplete data, figures are not comparable to previous years' data.

[4] Limited data for 2001 were available for Illinois and Kentucky.

[5] The murder and nonnegligent homicide figure is the number of homicides reported as a result of the events of September 11, 2001. See special report, Section V.

Table 11

Offenses Known to Law Enforcement

by Rural County 25,000 and over in Population, 2001

[The data shown in this table do not reflect county totals but are the number of offenses reported by the sheriff's office, county police department, or state police.]

County by state	Crime Index total	Modified Crime Index total[1]	Murder and non-negligent man-slaughter	Forcible rape	Robbery	Aggravated assault	Burglary	Larceny-theft	Motor vehicle theft	Arson[1]
ALABAMA[2]										
Chilton	663		0	10	4	104	206	325	14	
Cullman	1,669		2	23	9	129	462	883	161	
Jackson	680		2	4	3	49	232	307	83	
Lee	1,496		1	5	14	63	538	773	102	
Marshall	506		1	8	0	38	158	242	59	
Walker	139		0	1	0	4	47	72	15	
ARIZONA										
Apache	297	297	0	4	0	88	69	130	6	0
Cochise	1,331	1,338	9	20	24	243	170	666	199	7
Navajo	637	642	1	6	2	57	231	284	56	5
Yavajo	2,487	2,498	6	9	16	294	569	1,385	208	11
ARKANSAS										
Garland	292	292	2	5	4	51	39	143	48	0
Independence	1,443	1,443	2	4	6	39	286	1,036	70	0
Pope	408	408	0	4	3	21	122	246	12	0
White	760	767	1	5	3	27	197	424	103	7
CALIFORNIA										
Calaveras	874	894	2	10	4	93	294	469	2	20
Calaveras Highway Patrol	91	91	0	0	0	0	0	38	53	0
Humboldt	1,340	1,349	2	23	21	200	287	786	21	9
Humboldt Highway Patrol	202	202	0	0	0	1	1	29	171	0
Imperial	961	984	3	7	18	107	300	509	17	23
Imperial Highway Patrol	197	197	0	0	0	0	0	13	184	0
Kings	487	490	1	7	18	63	196	197	5	3
Lake	784	784	0	12	13	98	305	354	2	0
Lake Highway Patrol	87	87	0	0	0	0	0	21	66	0
Mendocino	1,128	1,146	3	25	24	192	425	454	5	18
Mendocino Highway Patrol	72	72	0	0	0	0	0	15	57	0
Nevada	1,278	1,282	6	26	13	78	400	746	9	4
Nevada Highway Patrol	73	73	0	0	0	0	1	13	59	0
Tehama	661	680	3	8	4	77	226	339	4	19
Tehama Highway Patrol	62	62	0	0	0	0	0	0	62	0
Tuolumne	846	861	0	11	18	116	408	290	3	15
Tuolumne Highway Patrol	162	162	0	0	0	0	0	15	147	0
COLORADO										
Eagle	650	655	1	5	0	22	80	533	9	5
Fremont	256	258	1	4	1	24	66	147	13	2
La Plata	368	368	0	18	0	13	98	225	14	0
DELAWARE[3]										
Sussex State Police	2,880	2,885	2	83	53	458	601	1,550	133	5
FLORIDA										
Citrus	2,485	2,485	5	29	22	260	640	1,405	124	0
Columbia	1,743	1,745	2	11	27	205	533	794	171	2
Desoto	702	705	3	4	15	82	264	306	28	3
Hendry	1,014	1,015	1	16	46	168	271	394	118	1
Highlands	1,799	1,807	4	11	49	106	667	824	138	8
Indian River	2,830	2,840	2	44	36	216	671	1,723	138	10
Jackson	722	725	1	20	13	171	164	330	23	3

See footnotes at end of table.

Table 11

Offenses Known to Law Enforcement
by Rural County 25,000 and over in Population, 2001—Continued

[The data shown in this table do not reflect county totals but are the number of offenses reported by the sheriff's office, county police department, or state police.]

County by state	Crime Index total	Modified Crime Index total[1]	Murder and non-negligent man-slaughter	Forcible rape	Robbery	Aggravated assault	Burglary	Larceny-theft	Motor vehicle theft	Arson[1]
FLORIDA—Continued										
Levy	920	940	1	27	10	182	267	382	51	20
Monroe	2,900	2,902	1	27	44	239	505	1,934	150	2
Okeechobee	1,143	1,151	2	20	21	186	259	606	49	8
Putnam	2,932	2,941	2	46	37	497	1,231	916	203	9
Sumter	977	978	0	18	22	123	319	429	66	1
Suwannee	855	857	1	13	16	100	173	505	47	2
Walton	921	921	0	3	5	97	297	468	51	0
GEORGIA										
Colquitt	782	785	2	1	8	202	161	354	54	3
Floyd County Police Department	1,663		1	2	9	65	406	1,039	141	
Glynn County Police Department	4,128	4,150	1	7	53	341	405	3,145	176	22
Habersham	423		1	7	2	37	130	213	33	
Hall	3,207	3,215	2	67	45	189	646	1,878	380	8
Jackson	977		3	1	2	49	241	602	79	
Laurens	597	599	1	12	4	61	178	303	38	2
Liberty[3]	704	711	4	4	14	24	127	502	29	7
Troup	1,076		0	3	2	15	99	924	33	
Whitfield	2,268		5	7	17	81	517	1,397	244	
HAWAII										
Hawaii Police Department	6,985	7,029	8	68	63	138	1,538	4,677	493	44
Kauai Police Department	2,346	2,346	2	15	12	67	506	1,648	96	0
Maui Police Department	8,174	8,241	2	33	68	188	1,778	5,548	557	67
IDAHO										
Bingham	238	243	1	5	3	18	56	130	25	5
Bonner	561	566	0	3	1	49	132	346	30	5
Bonneville	693	697	3	13	4	22	184	407	60	4
Kootenai	1,202	1,204	1	22	9	93	310	688	79	2
ILLINOIS[4]										
INDIANA										
Bartholomew	241	242	0	2	2	19	30	181	7	1
Bartholomew State Police	25	25	0	2	0	7	0	9	7	0
Grant	481	481	0	5	5	30	135	281	25	0
Grant State Police	7	7	0	0	0	0	0	4	3	0
Henry	869	873	1	3	3	6	212	607	37	4
Henry State Police	38	38	0	0	0	9	2	27	0	0
Kosciusko	914		0	8	7	9	194	650	46	
Kosciusko State Police	39	39	0	0	2	15	7	14	1	0
LaGrange	283	283	0	2	3	4	117	146	11	0
LaGrange State Police	53	53	0	0	0	8	12	28	5	0
La Porte	1,242	1,246	1	8	13	33	332	758	97	4
La Porte State Police	83	83	1	0	2	10	2	48	20	0
Lawrence	331	336	0	1	4	4	104	191	27	5
Lawrence State Police	26	27	0	0	1	2	8	12	3	1
Putnam	557	559	0	6	5	193	170	154	29	2
Putnam State Police	70	71	0	0	1	10	18	34	7	1
Steuben	757	759	1	3	1	3	195	510	44	2
Steuben State Police	59	62	0	1	0	11	18	24	5	3
Wayne	403	403	1	3	1	10	98	260	30	0
Wayne State Police	73	73	0	1	2	7	6	47	10	0

See footnotes at the end of table.

Table 11

Offenses Known to Law Enforcement
by Rural County 25,000 and over in Population, 2001—Continued

[The data shown in this table do not reflect county totals but are the number of offenses reported by the sheriff's office, county police department, or state police.]

County by state	Crime Index total	Modified Crime Index total[1]	Murder and non-negligent man-slaughter	Forcible rape	Robbery	Aggravated assault	Burglary	Larceny-theft	Motor vehicle theft	Arson[1]
KENTUCKY[4]										
LOUISIANA										
Avoyelles	317	317	0	1	1	36	155	117	7	0
Tangipahoa	3,608	3,617	12	25	64	675	1,094	1,610	128	9
Vermilion	386	386	0	11	2	55	71	222	25	0
Vernon	832	833	1	9	8	140	134	519	21	1
MAINE										
Aroostook	117	118	0	0	0	1	62	47	7	1
Aroostook State Police	310	310	1	5	0	7	130	139	28	0
Hancock	226	226	0	0	1	8	46	153	18	0
Hancock State Police	187	187	3	2	0	7	53	111	11	0
Kennebec	411	412	0	1	0	3	109	268	30	1
Kennebec State Police	188	190	2	2	0	2	55	104	23	2
Penobscot	655	655	0	0	2	2	202	411	38	0
Penobscot State Police	406	407	4	11	1	18	121	214	37	1
Somerset	373	373	0	1	1	15	145	178	33	0
Somerset State Police	92	92	0	1	0	1	18	60	12	0
Waldo	210	210	0	3	2	14	74	103	14	0
Waldo State Police	46	47	0	0	0	0	18	23	5	1
York	417	422	0	0	2	23	160	193	39	5
York State Police	141	141	0	0	0	3	63	58	17	0
MARYLAND										
Garrett	289	289	1	1	1	5	71	204	6	0
Garrett State Police	191	196	0	4	3	8	41	124	11	5
St. Mary's	1,489	1,504	4	6	10	205	320	889	55	15
St. Mary's State Police	338	362	0	6	2	88	52	177	13	24
Worcester	182	182	2	1	4	32	32	96	15	0
Worcester State Police	330	336	0	3	2	27	72	212	14	6
MICHIGAN										
Barry	324	324	0	13	0	34	62	193	22	0
Barry State Police	614	619	0	17	2	58	200	296	41	5
Branch	179	180	1	6	0	11	44	100	17	1
Branch State Police	355	362	0	29	2	37	94	159	34	7
Cass	795	809	1	8	5	41	250	440	50	14
Cass State Police	155	161	0	12	1	18	52	63	9	6
Clare	751	758	0	18	2	62	281	363	25	7
Clare State Police	94	98	0	5	0	6	42	40	1	4
Grand Traverse	1,432	1,440	1	23	3	64	208	1,067	66	8
Grand Traverse State Police	431	433	0	12	1	17	73	302	26	2
Hillsdale	331	331	2	22	1	19	71	199	17	0
Hillsdale State Police	386	394	3	8	1	35	155	164	20	8
Ionia	316	322	0	10	1	16	75	200	14	6
Ionia State Police	412	420	0	22	1	37	101	222	29	8
Isabella	469	473	1	14	3	38	107	279	27	4
Isabella State Police	330	336	0	9	1	18	95	188	19	6
Mecosta	602	604	0	5	0	25	186	355	31	2
Mecosta State Police	124	124	0	5	0	7	45	57	10	0
Montcalm	616	627	2	31	0	36	185	320	42	11
Montcalm State Police	479	487	0	20	2	45	190	185	37	8
Newaygo	538	540	0	9	0	45	219	233	32	2
Newaygo State Police	478	480	1	32	1	37	161	220	26	2
Sanilac	267	270	0	2	0	23	75	153	14	3
Sanilac State Police	247	251	0	11	0	15	76	127	18	4
Shiawassee	564	569	0	28	4	58	137	309	28	5

See footnotes at end of table.

Table 11

Offenses Known to Law Enforcement

by Rural County 25,000 and over in Population, 2001—Continued

[The data shown in this table do not reflect county totals but are the number of offenses reported by the sheriff's office, county police department, or state police.]

County by state	Crime Index total	Modified Crime Index total[1]	Murder and non-negligent man-slaughter	Forcible rape	Robbery	Aggravated assault	Burglary	Larceny-theft	Motor vehicle theft	Arson[1]
MICHIGAN—Continued										
Shiawassee State Police	216	222	0	12	0	15	50	129	10	6
St. Joseph	546	550	0	13	1	28	155	337	12	4
St. Joseph State Police	492	499	1	19	1	44	216	185	26	7
Tuscola	289	292	0	7	1	19	91	149	22	3
Tuscola State Police	244	250	0	23	2	19	76	103	21	6
MINNESOTA										
Beltrami	432	438	1	5	0	14	97	273	42	6
Cass	1,293	1,299	2	12	6	72	362	710	129	6
Itasca[3]	450	456	1	1	2	18	136	264	28	6
Otter Tail	577	583	2	12	0	20	149	360	34	6
MISSISSIPPI										
Lauderdale	601	605	2	6	10	11	262	284	26	4
Lee	668	672	1	7	10	34	251	321	44	4
Lowndes	849	857	1	17	18	52	273	442	46	8
Marshall	552	556	2	6	10	63	230	217	24	4
Panola	342	344	2	5	11	38	131	137	18	2
Pontotoc	228	232	0	2	1	25	77	107	16	4
MISSOURI										
Barry	536	537	1	8	0	39	168	268	52	1
Callaway	537		0	3	3	19	141	358	13	
Camden	457	462	0	1	0	54	148	244	10	5
Cole	409		1	1	1	29	120	242	15	
Johnson	336	337	0	3	1	54	110	150	18	1
Pulaski	320	327	0	7	5	67	101	127	13	7
Taney	699	700	1	4	5	141	165	350	33	1
MONTANA[2]										
Gallatin	358		0	8	1	28	51	247	23	
Ravalli	593		3	7	0	111	57	370	45	
Silver Bow	1,865		1	16	11	178	213	1,355	91	
NEVADA										
Carson City	2,045	2,064	0	31	36	243	391	1,235	109	19
Douglas	885	885	0	0	14	43	188	592	48	0
Lyon	861	862	0	11	7	68	176	554	45	1
NEW MEXICO										
McKinley	435	438	1	19	10	76	95	209	25	3
San Juan	1,273		2	26	12	143	221	796	73	
NEW YORK										
Allegany	15	15	0	0	0	9	2	3	1	0
Allegany State Police	348	363	0	3	1	55	104	171	14	15
Cattaraugus	468	472	0	9	2	28	135	267	27	4
Cattaraugus State Police	386	387	1	1	0	46	80	243	15	1
Clinton	7	7	0	0	0	3	0	4	0	0
Clinton State Police	873	883	0	13	5	140	297	400	18	10
Columbia	263	268	1	0	1	14	52	189	6	5
Columbia State Police	265	265	0	0	1	21	51	183	9	0
Cortland	364	367	0	2	0	17	53	280	12	3

See footnotes at end of table.

Table 11

Offenses Known to Law Enforcement

by Rural County 25,000 and over in Population, 2001—Continued

[The data shown in this table do not reflect county totals but are the number of offenses reported by the sheriff's office, county police department, or state police.]

County by state	Crime Index total	Modified Crime Index total[1]	Murder and non-negligent man-slaughter	Forcible rape	Robbery	Aggravated assault	Burglary	Larceny-theft	Motor vehicle theft	Arson[1]
NEW YORK—Continued										
Cortland State Police	327	329	0	1	1	36	46	235	8	2
Delaware	174	178	0	3	2	21	53	89	6	4
Delaware State Police	314	316	0	1	1	57	81	171	3	2
Essex	3	3	0	0	0	1	0	2	0	0
Essex State Police	486	492	1	1	1	30	171	277	5	6
Franklin	1	1	0	0	0	1	0	0	0	0
Franklin State Police	429	443	0	12	2	109	157	140	9	14
Fulton	419	420	0	2	0	12	102	282	21	1
Fulton State Police	127	127	1	3	1	19	19	81	3	0
Jefferson	581	589	1	3	2	24	170	360	21	8
Jefferson State Police	471	474	0	2	0	45	89	328	7	3
Steuben	385	387	0	0	2	7	113	250	13	2
Steuben State Police	505	525	0	6	1	33	193	264	8	20
St. Lawrence	384	391	0	12	0	37	92	226	17	7
St. Lawrence State Police	526	533	0	1	2	66	204	235	18	7
Sullivan	473		2	6	3	28	105	323	6	
Sullivan State Police	529	543	0	4	3	81	139	286	16	14
Tompkins	557	558	2	16	7	17	140	356	19	1
Tompkins State Police	233	234	2	2	0	22	37	165	5	1
Ulster	202	203	1	2	8	18	37	134	2	1
Ulster State Police	792	798	0	8	2	116	146	483	37	6
Wyoming	616	616	1	4	3	49	348	194	17	0
Wyoming State Police	69	70	0	0	0	15	17	37	0	1
NORTH CAROLINA										
Beaufort	835	853	5	5	13	74	311	393	34	18
Bladen	1,118	1,129	1	1	26	169	457	418	46	11
Carteret	739	747	0	5	3	36	237	412	46	8
Cleveland	2,104	2,109	1	22	32	37	706	1,201	105	5
Columbus	1,995	2,017	6	16	31	121	887	770	164	22
Craven	1,367	1,376	0	8	15	88	407	805	44	9
Duplin	1,344	1,354	2	2	26	96	404	738	76	10
Granville	761	765	1	4	9	28	368	318	33	4
Halifax	1,099	1,108	2	13	27	54	516	408	79	9
Harnett	3,279	3,312	2	25	29	337	1,206	1,520	160	33
Haywood	842	850	0	3	7	95	244	447	46	8
Henderson	1,209	1,214	3	15	7	25	513	570	76	5
Hoke	1,417	1,438	1	7	18	77	609	607	98	21
Iredell	1,986	1,991	2	17	21	128	744	979	95	5
Lee	774	782	2	5	3	26	375	336	27	8
Lenoir	1,010	1,013	1	3	21	101	293	556	35	3
Macon	434	436	2	1	0	10	172	226	23	2
McDowell	570	577	0	9	3	30	172	311	45	7
Moore	1,027	1,031	4	1	10	38	469	432	73	4
Richmond	1,313	1,337	1	7	28	43	559	613	62	24
Robeson	3,920	3,968	23	25	76	291	1,714	1,329	462	48
Rockingham	1,205	1,210	1	8	12	88	317	748	31	5
Rutherford[3]	1,088	1,090	3	9	19	84	406	555	12	2
Sampson	1,640	1,650	2	7	40	59	821	610	101	10
Stanly	879	885	0	4	4	46	333	401	91	6
Surry	1,502	1,532	3	16	19	190	460	662	152	30
Vance	1,504	1,533	5	2	19	69	747	589	73	29
Watauga	532	534	1	2	2	18	257	223	29	2
Wilkes	1,053	1,070	2	7	10	113	359	497	65	17
Wilson	860	867	3	3	15	63	308	426	42	7
OHIO										
Champaign	669	675	1	15	0	52	165	382	54	6
Coshocton	864	865	0	0	8	4	117	695	40	1
Darke	281	285	0	1	4	9	108	152	7	4

See footnotes at end of table.

Table 11

Offenses Known to Law Enforcement

by Rural County 25,000 and over in Population, 2001—Continued

[The data shown in this table do not reflect county totals but are the number of offenses reported by the sheriff's office, county police department, or state police.]

County by state	Crime Index total	Modified Crime Index total[1]	Murder and non-negligent man-slaughter	Forcible rape	Robbery	Aggravated assault	Burglary	Larceny-theft	Motor vehicle theft	Arson[1]
OHIO—Continued										
Erie	547	556	0	3	2	22	182	297	41	9
Highland	398	399	0	3	0	37	113	231	14	1
Huron	405	409	1	0	3	7	155	213	26	4
Logan	434	434	0	7	2	48	128	234	15	0
Marion	999	1,001	0	3	8	19	256	660	53	2
Morrow	257	260	0	3	0	3	98	136	17	3
Muskingum	1,442	1,450	4	17	25	8	341	920	127	8
Preble	663	666	0	18	2	50	167	393	33	3
Scioto	2,290	2,318	3	25	32	52	737	1,282	159	28
Shelby	296	300	1	0	1	5	75	204	10	4
Tuscarawas	279	280	0	5	1	4	136	119	14	1
Williams	340	347	0	2	0	4	87	231	16	7
OKLAHOMA										
Cherokee	329	330	3	5	1	106	97	85	32	1
Delaware	421	428	1	5	2	49	160	164	40	7
Le Flore	226	231	4	3	3	58	73	65	20	5
Mayes	411	412	3	0	1	30	162	174	41	1
OREGON										
Deschutes	1,022	1,025	2	6	2	11	233	727	41	3
Deschutes State Police	18	29	0	1	0	2	3	7	5	11
Josephine	923	928	1	9	9	26	242	542	94	5
Josephine State Police	16	23	0	0	0	3	0	10	3	7
Klamath	910	918	1	5	7	43	267	527	60	8
Klamath State Police	38	51	0	5	0	7	5	13	8	13
Linn	1,476	1,483	2	1	6	4	408	917	138	7
Linn State Police	40	49	0	1	2	12	1	18	6	9
PENNSYLVANIA										
Adams State Police	527	535	1	13	7	33	125	304	44	8
Armstrong State Police	491	507	0	10	4	34	119	291	33	16
Bedford State Police	834	855	3	6	20	32	241	493	39	21
Bradford State Police	493	503	2	17	2	14	183	247	28	10
Clarion State Police	580	587	1	14	3	25	127	365	45	7
Clearfield State Police	499	510	0	13	4	31	140	268	43	11
Crawford State Police	863	872	1	15	3	14	321	429	80	9
Franklin State Police	1,258	1,268	0	25	27	78	270	782	76	10
Greene State Police	529	548	0	4	4	19	158	291	53	19
Huntingdon State Police	434	453	5	3	0	36	115	254	21	19
Indiana State Police	835	850	2	15	6	55	186	501	70	15
Jefferson State Police	375	382	1	11	3	40	78	206	36	7
Lawrence State Police	666	788	0	9	9	41	183	361	63	122
Monroe State Police	1,384	1,396	5	14	15	69	444	722	115	12
Northumberland State Police	401	404	1	4	4	56	97	216	23	3
Schuylkill State Police	1,112	1,135	0	13	9	208	203	584	95	23
Snyder State Police	370	371	0	9	3	22	68	249	19	1
Susquehanna State Police	604	612	1	8	7	66	143	329	50	8
Tioga State Police	264	274	0	6	0	5	89	137	27	10
Union State Police	283	284	0	5	1	7	67	187	16	1
Venango State Police	580	592	0	8	6	31	183	316	36	12
Wayne State Police	858	885	1	25	9	96	204	451	72	27
SOUTH CAROLINA										
Colleton	1,439	1,487	6	11	34	280	330	612	166	48
Georgetown	1,384	1,389	0	11	15	204	383	676	95	5
Orangeburg	3,959	3,982	9	38	112	708	1,019	1,765	308	23

See footnotes at the end of table.

Table 11

Offenses Known to Law Enforcement
by Rural County 25,000 and over in Population, 2001—Continued

[The data shown in this table do not reflect county totals but are the number of offenses reported by the sheriff's office, county police department, or state police.]

County by state	Crime Index total	Modified Crime Index total[1]	Murder and non-negligent man-slaughter	Forcible rape	Robbery	Aggravated assault	Burglary	Larceny-theft	Motor vehicle theft	Arson[1]
TENNESSEE										
Bradley	1,489	1,498	2	11	6	223	373	778	96	9
Campbell	484	484	0	1	1	32	50	367	33	0
Cocke	718	752	5	4	13	98	345	210	43	34
Cumberland	764	770	2	0	3	33	300	358	68	6
Greene	1,251	1,263	2	12	8	119	443	567	100	12
Hamblen	681	693	0	6	6	88	199	348	34	12
Jefferson	909	919	2	7	3	87	288	439	83	10
Lawrence	529	534	0	7	2	65	154	236	65	5
Maury	829	840	3	22	14	108	152	450	80	11
McMinn	830	834	0	8	7	150	245	349	71	4
Monroe	886	908	0	9	3	206	211	391	66	22
Putnam	744	747	3	10	4	80	182	413	52	3
Roane	724	735	2	3	3	101	218	342	55	11
Warren	580	586	0	2	6	51	195	292	34	6
TEXAS										
Anderson	524	527	1	14	6	47	266	173	17	3
Angelina	1,251	1,251	8	19	7	307	368	468	74	0
Cherokee	508	517	1	10	1	93	202	178	23	9
Jasper	588	588	0	4	5	65	163	322	29	0
Maverick	374	375	1	5	1	30	155	174	8	1
Medina	457	458	1	5	0	93	166	171	21	1
Nacogdoches	527	527	1	17	5	64	150	251	39	0
Polk	553	563	0	4	3	26	204	272	44	10
Rusk	613	616	2	12	3	57	245	261	33	3
Starr	361	361	6	5	7	31	126	157	29	0
Van Zandt	803	807	3	1	3	65	323	311	97	4
Walker	570	570	1	17	8	60	179	281	24	0
Wise	397	398	1	12	2	38	160	157	27	1
Wood	597	603	1	14	4	71	237	258	12	6
UTAH										
Cache	528	530	1	14	2	16	58	416	21	2
Washington	479	484	0	7	0	48	98	282	44	5
VERMONT										
Rutland State Police	652	656	0	1	3	0	205	423	20	4
St. Albans State Police	540	548	0	11	0	14	151	306	58	8
VIRGINIA										
Buchanan	540	548	0	2	1	59	184	272	22	8
Buchanan State Police	44	46	0	1	0	1	9	29	4	2
Carroll	413	416	0	4	5	24	124	223	33	3
Carroll State Police	30	30	0	0	0	1	0	27	2	0
Franklin	572	573	2	17	5	40	86	377	45	1
Franklin State Police	18	18	0	0	0	8	2	5	3	0
Frederick	1,304	1,310	1	23	7	15	256	906	96	6
Frederick State Police	37	37	1	1	0	5	1	26	3	0
Halifax	339	343	2	3	4	25	75	204	24	4
Halifax State Police	16	16	0	0	0	3	3	6	4	0
Henry	1,676	1,684	7	16	31	159	372	979	112	8
Henry State Police	52	52	0	0	0	13	6	13	20	0
Montgomery	555	560	0	11	2	25	135	345	37	5
Montgomery State Police	19	19	0	0	2	7	0	5	5	0
Rockingham	295	295	1	7	3	12	88	168	16	0

See footnotes at end of table.

Table 11

Offenses Known to Law Enforcement

by Rural County 25,000 and over in Population, 2001—Continued

[The data shown in this table do not reflect county totals but are the number of offenses reported by the sheriff's office, county police department, or state police.]

County by state	Crime Index total	Modified Crime Index total[1]	Murder and non-negligent man-slaughter	Forcible rape	Robbery	Aggravated assault	Burglary	Larceny-theft	Motor vehicle theft	Arson[1]
VIRGINIA—Continued										
Rockingham State Police	42	42	0	0	2	4	0	21	15	0
Wise	388	395	2	7	7	60	97	180	35	7
Wise State Police	7	8	0	1	0	0	0	2	4	1
WASHINGTON										
Chelan	1,132	1,135	2	11	0	22	219	817	61	3
Clallam	872	878	2	11	2	18	211	572	56	6
Cowlitz	1,197	1,214	0	7	5	67	337	672	109	17
Douglas	814	816	0	8	0	35	257	471	43	2
Grant	1,357	1,374	0	18	15	52	368	772	132	17
Grays Harbor	496	503	1	3	2	43	168	227	52	7
Lewis	889	896	1	21	6	60	318	427	56	7
Mason	1,967	1,980	2	44	7	65	681	994	174	13
Skagit	1,759	1,760	2	15	7	36	507	1,083	109	1
Stevens	552	552	1	6	1	9	163	335	37	0
WEST VIRGINIA										
Fayette	375	389	5	5	1	37	110	195	22	14
Harrison	172	173	0	1	3	37	26	85	20	1
Logan	98	98	0	0	2	7	25	58	6	0
Monongalia	418	418	0	4	3	32	112	243	24	0
Raleigh	799	802	3	8	11	30	164	515	68	3
WISCONSIN										
Barron	602	604	0	8	0	58	194	291	51	2
Clark	266	270	0	3	1	9	62	168	23	4
Columbia	426	429	0	4	2	11	101	289	19	3
Dodge	334	337	1	2	0	21	122	169	19	3
Fond du Lac	325	333	1	1	0	5	61	241	16	8
Grant	260	261	0	0	1	37	98	107	17	1
Jefferson	510	515	0	11	1	17	105	352	24	5
Manitowoc	352	355	1	8	1	19	97	201	25	3
Oconto	478	479	0	0	5	21	175	253	24	1
Polk	369	372	0	4	2	9	161	160	33	3
Portage	409	409	0	6	1	7	110	268	17	0
Sauk	640	640	1	2	1	38	101	458	39	0
Shawanno	647	647	0	8	2	22	173	408	34	0
Walworth	340	342	0	2	1	6	70	231	30	2
Waupaca	453	453	0	3	0	4	119	310	17	0
Wood	421	422	0	0	2	4	99	294	22	1
STATE AGENCIES										
Alaska State Police	4,740	4,816	13	126	26	531	1,227	2,263	554	76
Arizona Department of Public Safety	34	34	0	0	0	6	0	27	1	0
Colorado State Patrol	126	126	0	0	0	22	0	41	63	0
Connecticut State Police	7,629	7,684	8	44	99	993	1,914	4,038	533	55
Minnesota State Patrol	11	11	0	0	0	1	0	1	9	0
Nebraska State Patrol	8	8	0	0	0	0	1	7	0	0
Port Authority of New York and New Jersey[5]	1,113	1,113	0	0	18	61	43	924	67	0
Port Authority of New York and New Jersey[6]	2,432	2,432	0	0	48	201	32	2,105	46	0
Rhode Island State Police	101	101	2	6	2	5	3	59	24	0

See footnotes at end of table.

Table 11

Offenses Known to Law Enforcement

by Rural County 25,000 and over in Population, 2001—Continued

[The data shown in this table do not reflect county totals but are the number of offenses reported by the sheriff's office, county police department, or state police.]

County by state	Crime Index total	Modified Crime Index total[1]	Murder and non-negligent man-slaughter	Forcible rape	Robbery	Aggravated assault	Burglary	Larceny-theft	Motor vehicle theft	Arson[1]
OTHER AGENCIES										
American Samoa	506	510	1	27	3	152	215	98	10	4
National Institutes of Health	360	360	0	0	1	5	2	351	1	0
United States Department of the Interior:										
Bureau of Indian Affairs	25,849	26,354	87	524	177	9,065	4,858	8,340	2,798	505
Bureau of Land Management	770	838	7	0	3	16	20	675	49	68
Bureau of Reclamation	13	13	0	0	1	0	0	4	8	0
Fish and Wildlife Service	369	477	4	1	0	22	105	164	73	108
National Park Service	4,220	4,324	6	37	70	212	488	3,277	130	104

[1] The Modified Crime Index total is the sum of the Crime Index offenses including arson. Arson is shown only if 12 months of arson data were received. If 12 months of arson data were not received, there is no Modified Crime Index total shown.

[2] Complete arson figures for 2001 for Alabama and Montana were not available.

[3] Due to changes in reporting practices, annexations, and/or incomplete data, figures are not comparable to previous years' data.

[4] Limited data for 2001 were available for Illinois and Kentucky.

[5] Figures reported are the number of crimes occurring in New Jersey.

[6] Figures reported are the number of crimes occurring in New York.

Table 12

Crime Trends[1]
by Population Group, 2000-2001

[2001 estimated population]

Population group	Crime Index total	Modified Crime Index total[2]	Violent crime[3]	Property crime[4]	Murder and non-negligent man-slaughter	Forcible rape[5]	Robbery	Aggravated assault	Burglary	Larceny-theft	Motor vehicle theft	Arson
TOTAL ALL AGENCIES:												
11,477 agencies;												
population 243,825,821												
2000	10,111,278	10,183,622	1,266,129	8,845,149	13,945	76,005	375,145	801,034	1,782,031	6,020,979	1,042,139	72,344
2001	10,320,887	10,394,440	1,271,646	9,049,241	14,348	75,760	387,368	794,170	1,830,625	6,116,249	1,102,367	73,553
Percent change	+2.1	+2.1	+0.4	+2.3	+2.9	-0.3	+3.3	-0.9	+2.7	+1.6	+5.8	+1.7
TOTAL CITIES: 8,086 cities;												
population 165,050,100												
2000	8,094,152	8,148,643	1,031,667	7,062,485	11,083	56,727	337,194	626,663	1,318,755	4,876,070	867,660	54,491
2001	8,258,097	8,313,108	1,035,881	7,222,216	11,472	56,599	346,774	621,036	1,354,736	4,949,279	918,201	55,011
Percent change	+2.0	+2.0	+0.4	+2.3	+3.5	-0.2	+2.8	-0.9	+2.7	+1.5	+5.8	+1.0
GROUP I												
68 cities, 250,000 and over;												
population 51,193,595												
2000	3,144,218	3,168,892	538,987	2,605,231	6,403	21,350	203,539	307,695	494,100	1,658,570	452,561	24,674
2001	3,213,299	3,238,196	539,684	2,673,615	6,791	21,187	206,453	305,253	507,437	1,688,218	477,960	24,897
Percent change	+2.2	+2.2	+0.1	+2.6	+6.1	-0.8	+1.4	-0.8	+2.7	+1.8	+5.6	+0.9
10 cities, 1,000,000 and over;												
population 24,330,096												
2000	1,291,909	1,299,696	263,970	1,027,939	3,015	7,226	103,762	149,967	189,220	645,333	193,386	7,787
2001	1,298,188	1,306,419	262,780	1,035,408	3,211	7,239	103,827	148,503	188,589	648,583	198,236	8,231
Percent change	+0.5	+0.5	-0.5	+0.7	+6.5	+0.2	+0.1	-1.0	-0.3	+0.5	+2.5	+5.7
21 cities, 500,000 to 999,999;												
population 13,914,386												
2000	951,070	959,161	142,221	808,849	1,823	7,465	49,969	82,964	151,071	525,115	132,663	8,091
2001	977,144	984,604	141,740	835,404	1,856	6,949	50,882	82,053	160,574	535,957	138,873	7,460
Percent change	+2.7	+2.7	-0.3	+3.3	+1.8	-6.9	+1.8	-1.1	+6.3	+2.1	+4.7	-7.8
37 cities, 250,000 to 499,999;												
population 12,949,113												
2000	901,239	910,035	132,796	768,443	1,565	6,659	49,808	74,764	153,809	488,122	126,512	8,796
2001	937,967	947,173	135,164	802,803	1,724	6,999	51,744	74,697	158,274	503,678	140,851	9,206
Percent change	+4.1	+4.1	+1.8	+4.5	+10.2	+5.1	+3.9	-0.1	+2.9	+3.2	+11.3	+4.7
GROUP II												
159 cities, 100,000 to 249,999;												
population 23,651,809												
2000	1,297,060	1,306,492	151,721	1,145,339	1,781	9,137	50,990	89,813	225,004	775,321	145,014	9,432
2001	1,332,471	1,341,321	154,435	1,178,036	1,783	8,841	53,863	89,948	229,638	793,702	154,696	8,850
Percent change	+2.7	+2.7	+1.8	+2.9	+0.1	-3.2	+5.6	+0.2	+2.1	+2.4	+6.7	-6.2
GROUP III												
363 cities, 50,000 to 99,999;												
population 24,838,311												
2000	1,094,137	1,100,693	116,097	978,040	1,044	8,425	34,347	72,281	186,297	686,741	105,002	6,556
2001	1,113,628	1,120,640	117,157	996,471	1,052	8,396	36,233	71,476	192,330	693,698	110,443	7,012
Percent change	+1.8	+1.8	+0.9	+1.9	+0.8	-0.3	+5.5	-1.1	+3.2	+1.0	+5.2	+7.0
GROUP IV												
668 cities, 25,000 to 49,999;												
population 23,272,379												
2000	933,413	938,830	87,564	845,849	748	6,782	22,880	57,154	154,949	619,769	71,131	5,417
2001	949,699	955,085	86,951	862,748	707	6,948	23,788	55,508	158,529	628,848	75,371	5,386
Percent change	+1.7	+1.7	-0.7	+2.0	-5.5	+2.4	+4.0	-2.9	+2.3	+1.5	+6.0	-0.6

See footnotes at end of table.

Table 12

Crime Trends[1]
by Population Group, 2000-2001—Continued
[2001 estimated population]

Population group	Crime Index total	Modified Crime Index total[2]	Violent crime[3]	Property crime[4]	Murder and non-negligent man-slaughter	Forcible rape[5]	Robbery	Aggravated assault	Burglary	Larceny-theft	Motor vehicle theft	Arson
GROUP V												
1,497 cities, 10,000 to 24,999; population 23,786,295												
2000	885,343	889,712	76,086	809,257	602	6,218	16,701	52,565	143,084	610,909	55,264	4,369
2001	896,075	900,684	76,387	819,688	629	6,434	16,986	52,338	146,793	613,852	59,043	4,609
Percent change	+1.2	+1.2	+0.4	+1.3	+4.5	+3.5	+1.7	-0.4	+2.6	+0.5	+6.8	+5.5
GROUP VI												
5,331 cities, under 10,000; population 18,307,711												
2000	739,981	744,024	61,212	678,769	505	4,815	8,737	47,155	115,321	524,760	38,688	4,043
2001	752,925	757,182	61,267	691,658	510	4,793	9,451	46,513	120,009	530,961	40,688	4,257
Percent change	+1.7	+1.8	+0.1	+1.9	+1.0	-0.5	+8.2	-1.4	+4.1	+1.2	+5.2	+5.3
SUBURBAN COUNTIES												
1,157 agencies; population 52,621,209												
2000	1,527,057	1,540,754	179,553	1,347,504	1,901	13,745	33,800	130,107	322,944	882,263	142,297	13,697
2001	1,563,611	1,577,859	180,509	1,383,102	1,942	13,553	36,383	128,631	332,889	899,381	150,832	14,248
Percent change	+2.4	+2.4	+0.5	+2.6	+2.2	-1.4	+7.6	-1.1	+3.1	+1.9	+6.0	+4.0
RURAL COUNTIES[6]												
2,234 agencies; population 26,154,512												
2000	490,069	494,225	54,909	435,160	961	5,533	4,151	44,264	140,332	262,646	32,182	4,156
2001	499,179	503,473	55,256	443,923	934	5,608	4,211	44,503	143,000	267,589	33,334	4,294
Percent change	+1.9	+1.9	+0.6	+2.0	-2.8	+1.4	+1.4	+0.5	+1.9	+1.9	+3.6	+3.3
SUBURBAN AREA[7]												
5,577 agencies; population 96,603,994												
2000	3,043,462	3,065,475	304,927	2,738,535	2,834	23,227	64,210	214,656	557,200	1,926,128	255,207	22,013
2001	3,112,889	3,135,655	307,299	2,805,590	2,925	23,454	68,492	212,428	576,381	1,957,228	271,981	22,766
Percent change	+2.3	+2.3	+0.8	+2.4	+3.2	+1.0	+6.7	-1.0	+3.4	+1.6	+6.6	+3.4

[1] The murders and nonnegligent homicides that occurred as a result of the events of September 11, 2001, were not included in any trend tables (Tables 12-15). See special report, Section V.
[2] The Modified Crime Index total is the sum of the Crime Index offenses including arson.
[3] Violent crimes are offenses of murder, forcible rape, robbery, and aggravated assault.
[4] Property crimes are offenses of burglary, larceny-theft, and motor vehicle theft.
[5] Forcible rape figures furnished by the state Uniform Crime Reporting (UCR) Programs administered by the Delaware State Bureau of Investigation for 2000 and the Illinois State Police for 2000 and 2001 were not in accordance with national UCR guidelines; therefore, the figures were excluded from the forcible rape, violent crime, Crime Index total, and Modified Crime Index total categories.
[6] Includes state police agencies with no county breakdowns.
[7] Suburban area includes city law enforcement agencies with less than 50,000 inhabitants and county law enforcement agencies that are within a Metropolitan Statistical Area (see Appendix III). Suburban area excludes all metropolitan agencies associated with a central city. The agencies associated with suburban areas will also appear in other groups within this table.

Table 13

Crime Trends[1]
by Suburban and Nonsuburban Cities[2] by Population Group, 2000-2001

[2001 estimated population]

Population group	Crime Index total	Modified Crime Index total[3]	Violent crime[4]	Property crime[5]	Murder and non-negligent man-slaughter	Forcible rape[6]	Robbery	Aggravated assault	Burglary	Larceny-theft	Motor vehicle theft	Arson
Suburban cities												
TOTAL SUBURBAN CITIES:												
4,420 cities;												
population 43,982,785												
2000	1,516,479	1,524,795	125,448	1,391,031	933	9,482	30,410	84,623	234,256	1,043,865	112,910	8,316
2001	1,549,285	1,557,803	126,797	1,422,488	983	9,901	32,109	83,804	243,492	1,057,847	121,149	8,518
Percent change	+2.2	+2.2	+1.1	+2.3	+5.4	+4.4	+5.6	-1.0	+3.9	+1.3	+7.3	+2.4
GROUP IV												
463 cities, 25,000 to 49,999;												
population 15,984,240												
2000	523,992	526,978	46,065	477,927	364	3,293	13,458	28,950	84,363	346,909	46,655	2,986
2001	533,139	536,057	45,850	487,289	357	3,400	14,013	28,080	86,250	351,080	49,959	2,918
Percent change	+1.7	+1.7	-0.5	+2.0	-1.9	+3.2	+4.1	-3.0	+2.2	+1.2	+7.1	-2.3
GROUP V												
1,111 cities, 10,000 to 24,999;												
population 17,698,018												
2000	568,552	571,447	47,980	520,572	345	3,701	11,502	32,432	89,401	389,989	41,182	2,895
2001	581,560	584,546	48,973	532,587	386	3,951	11,985	32,651	93,664	394,349	44,574	2,986
Percent change	+2.3	+2.3	+2.1	+2.3	+11.9	+6.8	+4.2	+0.7	+4.8	+1.1	+8.2	+3.1
GROUP VI												
2,846 cities, under 10,000;												
population 10,300,527												
2000	423,935	426,370	31,403	392,532	224	2,488	5,450	23,241	60,492	306,967	25,073	2,435
2001	434,586	437,200	31,974	402,612	240	2,550	6,111	23,073	63,578	312,418	26,616	2,614
Percent change	+2.5	+2.5	+1.8	+2.6	+7.1	+2.5	+12.1	-0.7	+5.1	+1.8	+6.2	+7.4
Nonsuburban cities												
TOTAL NONSUBURBAN CITIES:												
3,076 cities;												
population 21,383,600												
2000	1,042,258	1,047,771	99,414	942,844	922	8,333	17,908	72,251	179,098	711,573	52,173	5,513
2001	1,049,414	1,055,148	97,808	951,606	863	8,274	18,116	70,555	181,839	715,814	53,953	5,734
Percent change	+0.7	+0.7	-1.6	+0.9	-6.4	-0.7	+1.2	-2.3	+1.5	+0.6	+3.4	+4.0
GROUP IV												
205 cities, 25,000 to 49,999;												
population 7,288,139												
2000	409,421	411,852	41,499	367,922	384	3,489	9,422	28,204	70,586	272,860	24,476	2,431
2001	416,560	419,028	41,101	375,459	350	3,548	9,775	27,428	72,279	277,768	25,412	2,468
Percent change	+1.7	+1.7	-1.0	+2.0	-8.9	+1.7	+3.7	-2.8	+2.4	+1.8	+3.8	+1.5

See footnotes at end of table.

Table 13

Crime Trends[1]

by Suburban and Nonsuburban Cities[2] by Population Group, 2000-2001—Continued

[2001 estimated population]

Population group	Crime Index total	Modified Crime Index total[3]	Violent crime[4]	Property crime[5]	Murder and non-negligent man-slaughter	Forcible rape[6]	Robbery	Aggravated assault	Burglary	Larceny-theft	Motor vehicle theft	Arson
TOTAL NONSUBURBAN CITIES—Cont.:												
GROUP V												
386 cities, 10,000 to 24,999; population 6,088,277												
2000	316,791	318,265	28,106	288,685	257	2,517	5,199	20,133	53,683	220,920	14,082	1,474
2001	314,515	316,138	27,414	287,101	243	2,483	5,001	19,687	53,129	219,503	14,469	1,623
Percent change	-0.7	-0.7	-2.5	-0.5	-5.4	-1.4	-3.8	-2.2	-1.0	-0.6	+2.7	+10.1
GROUP VI												
2,485 cities, under 10,000; population 8,007,184												
2000	316,046	317,654	29,809	286,237	281	2,327	3,287	23,914	54,829	217,793	13,615	1,608
2001	318,339	319,982	29,293	289,046	270	2,243	3,340	23,440	56,431	218,543	14,072	1,643
Percent change	+0.7	+0.7	-1.7	+1.0	-3.9	-3.6	+1.6	-2.0	+2.9	+0.3	+3.4	+2.2

[1] The murders and nonnegligent homicides that occurred as a result of the events of September 11, 2001, were not included in any trend tables (Tables 12-15). See special report, Section V.

[2] Suburban area includes city law enforcement agencies with less than 50,000 inhabitants and county law enforcement agencies that are within a Metropolitan Statistical Area (see Appendix III). Suburban area excludes all metropolitan agencies associated with a central city. The agencies associated with suburban areas will also appear in other groups within this table.

[3] The Modified Crime Index total is the sum of the Crime Index offenses including arson.

[4] Violent crimes are offenses of murder, forcible rape, robbery, and aggravated assault.

[5] Property crimes are offenses of burglary, larceny-theft, and motor vehicle theft.

[6] Forcible rape figures furnished by the state Uniform Crime Reporting (UCR) Programs administered by the Delaware State Bureau of Investigation for 2000 and the Illinois State Police for 2000 and 2001 were not in accordance with national UCR guidelines; therefore, the figures were excluded from the forcible rape, violent crime, Crime Index total, and Modified Crime Index total categories.

Table 14

Crime Trends[1]
by Suburban and Nonsuburban Counties by Population Group, 2000-2001
[2001 estimated population]

Population group	Crime Index total	Modified Crime Index total[2]	Violent crime[3]	Property crime[4]	Murder and non-negligent man-slaughter	Forcible rape[5]	Robbery	Aggravated assault	Burglary	Larceny-theft	Motor vehicle theft	Arson
SUBURBAN COUNTIES[6]												
100,000 and over												
125 counties; population 31,422,575												
2000	1,042,515	1,051,709	129,460	913,055	1,270	8,568	28,378	91,244	204,590	607,863	100,602	9,194
2001	1,066,618	1,076,295	130,176	936,442	1,311	8,250	30,545	90,070	211,515	618,543	106,384	9,677
Percent change	+2.3	+2.3	+0.6	+2.6	+3.2	-3.7	+7.6	-1.3	+3.4	+1.8	+5.7	+5.3
25,000 to 99,999												
355 counties; population 18,770,820												
2000	383,343	386,490	38,376	344,967	493	3,986	4,215	29,682	96,471	222,316	26,180	3,147
2001	394,631	397,953	38,955	355,676	481	4,143	4,590	29,741	99,821	227,924	27,931	3,322
Percent change	+2.9	+3.0	+1.5	+3.1	-2.4	+3.9	+8.9	+0.2	+3.5	+2.5	+6.7	+5.6
Under 25,000												
677 counties; population 2,427,814												
2000	101,199	102,555	11,717	89,482	138	1,191	1,207	9,181	21,883	52,084	15,515	1,356
2001	102,362	103,611	11,378	90,984	150	1,160	1,248	8,820	21,553	52,914	16,517	1,249
Percent change	+1.1	+1.0	-2.9	+1.7	+8.7	-2.6	+3.4	-3.9	-1.5	+1.6	+6.5	-7.9
NONSUBURBAN COUNTIES[6]												
25,000 and over												
295 counties; population 11,538,723												
2000	226,541	228,315	24,214	202,327	387	2,352	2,377	19,098	65,400	122,698	14,229	1,774
2001	231,548	233,450	25,019	206,529	397	2,490	2,422	19,710	67,146	124,701	14,682	1,902
Percent change	+2.2	+2.2	+3.3	+2.1	+2.6	+5.9	+1.9	+3.2	+2.7	+1.6	+3.2	+7.2
10,000 to 24,999												
603 counties; population 9,577,030												
2000	146,487	147,576	16,792	129,695	341	1,504	1,027	13,920	43,638	76,811	9,246	1,089
2001	150,018	151,148	16,877	133,141	332	1,571	1,020	13,954	44,400	79,087	9,654	1,130
Percent change	+2.4	+2.4	+0.5	+2.7	-2.6	+4.5	-0.7	+0.2	+1.7	+3.0	+4.4	+3.8
Under 10,000												
1,169 counties; population 3,704,572												
2000	77,825	78,795	9,942	67,883	192	1,267	468	8,015	21,582	40,495	5,806	970
2001	78,618	79,545	9,734	68,884	161	1,175	471	7,927	21,986	40,945	5,953	927
Percent change	+1.0	+1.0	-2.1	+1.5	-16.1	-7.3	+0.6	-1.1	+1.9	+1.1	+2.5	-4.4

[1] The murders and nonnegligent homicides that occurred as a result of the events of September 11, 2001, were not included in any trend tables (Tables 12-15). See special report, Section V.

[2] The Modified Crime Index total is the sum of the Crime Index offenses including arson.

[3] Violent crimes are offenses of murder, forcible rape, robbery, and aggravated assault.

[4] Property crimes are offenses of burglary, larceny-theft, and motor vehicle theft.

[5] Forcible rape figures furnished by the state Uniform Crime Reporting (UCR) Programs administered by the Delaware State Bureau of Investigation for 2000 and the Illinois State Police for 2000 and 2001 were not in accordance with national UCR guidelines; therefore, the figures were excluded from the forcible rape, violent crime, Crime Index total, and the Modified Crime Index total categories.

[6] Offenses include sheriffs and county law enforcement agencies. State police offenses are not included.

Table 15

Crime Trends[1]

Breakdown of Offenses Known by Population Group, 2000-2001
[2001 estimated population]

Population Group	Forcible rape[2]		Robbery				Aggravated assault				Burglary			Motor vehicle theft			Arson		
	Rape by force	Assault to rape-attempts	Firearm	Knife or cutting instrument	Other weapon	Strong-arm	Firearm	Knife or cutting instrument	Other weapon	Hands, fists, feet, etc.	Forcible entry	Unlawful entry	Attempted forcible entry	Autos	Trucks and buses	Other vehicles	Structure	Mobile	Other
TOTAL ALL AGENCIES: 11,323 agencies; population 225,419,047																			
2000	63,085	7,064	118,724	24,742	28,765	117,495	122,792	122,081	240,903	199,396	1,022,677	478,584	109,169	670,938	173,826	65,363	28,471	19,419	16,987
2001	63,212	7,051	128,891	27,050	29,652	121,159	124,452	122,199	242,393	194,721	1,056,118	501,282	108,802	715,764	186,779	73,309	27,824	21,764	17,007
Percent change	-0.2	-0.2	+8.6	+9.3	+3.1	+3.1	+1.4	+0.1	-0.6	-2.3	+3.3	+4.7	-0.3	+6.7	+7.5	+12.2	-2.3	+12.1	+0.1
TOTAL CITIES: 7,990 cities; population 148,560,031																			
2000	45,840	5,496	103,252	21,839	24,987	103,946	94,957	95,808	178,352	143,706	732,466	344,804	82,452	559,990	139,940	43,542	21,825	13,880	12,156
2001	46,019	5,493	112,017	23,854	25,425	107,355	96,718	95,925	179,649	140,323	762,015	358,599	82,562	598,975	151,146	48,631	20,915	15,661	12,322
Percent change	+0.4	-0.1	+8.5	+9.2	+1.8	+3.3	+1.9	+0.1	+0.7	-2.4	+4.0	+4.0	+0.1	+7.0	+8.0	+11.7	-4.2	+12.8	+1.4
GROUP I																			
61 cities, 250,000 and over; population 38,752,297																			
2000	15,465	2,324	56,716	11,138	12,145	50,436	50,710	41,242	76,813	44,571	267,458	93,098	22,886	257,296	82,816	16,268	8,960	6,914	3,803
2001	15,649	2,246	61,798	12,026	12,247	52,804	51,099	40,590	77,766	45,376	282,344	97,372	23,828	278,895	89,460	18,219	8,334	8,158	3,781
Percent change	+1.2	-3.4	+9.0	+8.0	+0.8	+4.7	+0.8	-1.6	+1.2	+1.8	+5.6	+4.6	+4.1	+8.4	+8.0	+12.0	-7.0	+18.0	-0.6
8 cities, 1,000,000 and over; population 13,396,369																			
2000	4,615	981	22,719	4,902	4,382	19,856	20,430	14,996	25,637	21,528	83,919	33,745	6,117	86,634	34,195	6,984	2,523	2,935	1,250
2001	4,778	931	25,900	5,627	4,698	20,967	21,357	15,268	25,733	22,719	89,529	34,903	6,628	95,408	37,371	7,774	2,547	3,414	1,266
Percent change	+3.5	-5.1	+14.0	+14.8	+7.2	+5.6	+4.5	+1.8	+0.4	+5.5	+6.7	+3.4	+8.4	+10.1	+9.3	+11.3	+1.0	+16.3	+1.3
21 cities, 500,000 to 999,999; population 13,914,386																			
2000	6,138	784	17,045	3,401	4,222	14,982	15,897	14,496	28,868	13,190	100,026	29,088	10,081	92,232	28,568	4,888	2,891	1,696	1,151
2001	5,827	739	18,194	3,425	4,135	15,185	15,351	13,713	29,550	12,949	108,014	29,908	10,333	94,961	29,876	5,755	2,476	1,947	979
Percent change	-5.1	-5.7	+6.7	+0.7	-2.1	+1.4	-3.4	-5.4	+2.4	-1.8	+8.0	+2.8	+2.5	+3.0	+4.6	+17.7	-14.4	+14.8	-14.9
32 cities, 250,000 to 499,999; population 11,441,542																			
2000	4,712	559	16,952	2,835	3,541	15,598	14,383	11,750	22,308	9,853	83,513	30,265	6,688	78,430	20,053	4,396	3,546	2,283	1,402
2001	5,044	576	17,704	2,974	3,414	16,652	14,391	11,609	22,483	9,708	84,801	32,561	6,867	88,526	22,213	4,690	3,311	2,797	1,536
Percent change	+7.0	+3.0	+4.4	+4.9	-3.6	+6.8	+0.1	-1.2	+0.8	-1.5	+1.5	+7.6	+2.7	+12.9	+10.8	+6.7	-6.6	+22.5	+9.6
GROUP II																			
146 cities, 100,000 to 249,999; population 21,708,219																			
2000	7,084	816	17,707	3,695	4,859	17,057	14,467	14,530	29,241	16,322	122,292	54,185	13,642	99,748	20,172	5,890	3,578	2,751	2,070
2001	6,880	792	19,526	4,103	4,752	17,620	15,752	14,965	29,636	15,797	126,448	56,000	13,290	105,776	23,004	6,735	3,410	2,769	1,874
Percent change	-2.9	-2.9	+10.3	+11.0	-2.2	+3.3	+8.9	+3.0	+1.4	-3.2	+3.4	+3.3	-2.6	+6.0	+14.0	+14.3	-4.7	+0.7	-9.5

See footnotes at end of table.

Table 15

Crime Trends[1]

Breakdown of Offenses Known by Population Group, 2000-2001—Continued
[2001 estimated population]

Population Group	Forcible rape[2] Rape by force	Forcible rape Assault to rape-attempts	Robbery Firearm	Robbery Knife or cutting instrument	Robbery Other weapon	Robbery Strong-arm	Aggravated assault Firearm	Aggravated assault Knife or cutting instrument	Aggravated assault Other weapon	Aggravated assault Hands, fists, feet, etc.	Burglary Forcible entry	Burglary Unlawful entry	Burglary Attempted forcible entry	Motor vehicle theft Autos	Motor vehicle theft Trucks and buses	Motor vehicle theft Other vehicles	Arson Structure	Arson Mobile	Arson Other
GROUP III																			
348 cities, 50,000 to 99,999; population 23,800,460																			
2000	7,442	730	12,093	2,932	3,088	15,104	11,232	13,058	25,397	20,401	107,820	58,426	14,342	78,372	14,426	6,279	2,957	1,679	1,734
2001	7,385	725	13,063	3,239	3,282	15,375	11,391	13,279	25,012	19,436	112,477	59,563	14,144	82,183	15,307	7,028	2,918	1,905	1,970
Percent change	-0.8	-0.7	+8.0	+10.5	+6.3	+1.8	+1.4	+1.7	-1.5	-4.7	+4.3	+1.9	-1.4	+4.9	+6.1	+11.9	-1.3	+13.5	+13.6
GROUP IV																			
649 cities, 25,000 to 49,999; population 22,596,138																			
2000	6,014	546	7,895	1,929	2,232	9,833	7,328	10,146	18,727	19,609	88,297	50,088	11,913	54,467	9,300	5,423	2,312	1,115	1,781
2001	6,115	599	8,198	2,148	2,402	9,933	7,218	10,184	18,684	18,151	89,392	52,714	11,841	57,685	9,811	6,018	2,126	1,220	1,819
Percent change	+1.7	+9.7	+3.8	+11.4	+7.6	+1.0	-1.5	+0.4	-0.2	-7.4	+1.2	+5.2	-0.6	+5.9	+5.5	+11.0	-8.0	+9.4	+2.1
GROUP V																			
1,483 cities, 10,000 to 24,999; population 23,524,525																			
2000	5,652	501	5,892	1,395	1,739	7,458	6,554	9,552	16,242	19,820	82,072	47,767	10,955	41,651	7,818	5,094	2,010	826	1,413
2001	5,778	586	6,033	1,455	1,827	7,435	6,517	9,601	16,379	19,510	84,002	49,761	10,711	44,583	8,035	5,553	2,137	956	1,380
Percent change	+2.2	+17.0	+2.4	+4.3	+5.1	-0.3	-0.6	+0.5	+0.8	-1.6	+2.4	+4.2	-2.2	+7.0	+2.8	+9.0	+6.3	+15.7	-2.3
GROUP VI																			
5,303 cities, under 10,000; population 18,178,392																			
2000	4,183	579	2,949	750	924	4,058	4,666	7,280	11,932	22,983	64,527	41,240	8,714	28,456	5,408	4,588	2,008	595	1,355
2001	4,212	545	3,399	883	915	4,188	4,741	7,306	12,172	22,053	67,352	43,189	8,748	29,853	5,529	5,078	1,990	653	1,498
Percent change	+0.7	-5.9	+15.3	+17.7	-1.0	+3.2	+1.6	+0.4	+2.0	-4.0	+4.4	+4.7	+0.4	+4.9	+2.2	+10.7	-0.9	+9.7	+10.6
SUBURBAN COUNTIES																			
1,139 agencies; population 51,130,246																			
2000	12,312	1,083	13,702	2,532	3,294	12,103	20,271	20,292	49,867	38,099	199,389	93,776	19,211	91,690	28,091	15,235	4,739	4,497	3,912
2001	12,117	1,097	15,196	2,790	3,659	12,294	20,225	20,132	49,943	36,741	201,767	100,941	19,317	97,102	29,835	17,394	4,848	5,010	3,797
Percent change	-1.6	+1.3	+10.9	+10.2	+11.1	+1.6	-0.2	-0.8	+0.2	-3.6	+1.2	+7.6	+0.6	+5.9	+6.2	+14.2	+2.3	+11.4	-2.9
RURAL COUNTIES																			
2,194 agencies; population 25,728,770																			
2000	4,933	485	1,770	371	484	1,446	7,564	5,981	12,684	17,591	90,822	40,004	7,506	19,258	5,795	6,586	1,907	1,042	919
2001	5,076	461	1,678	406	568	1,510	7,509	6,142	12,801	17,657	92,336	41,742	6,923	19,687	5,798	7,284	2,061	1,093	888
Percent change	+2.9	-4.9	-5.2	+9.4	+17.4	+4.4	-0.7	+2.7	+0.9	+0.4	+1.7	+4.3	-7.8	+2.2	+0.1	+10.6	+8.1	+4.9	-3.4

See footnotes at end of table.

Table 15

Crime Trends[1]

Breakdown of Offenses Known
by Population Group, 2000-2001—Continued
[2001 estimated population]

Population Group	Forcible rape[2]		Robbery				Aggravated assault				Burglary			Motor vehicle theft			Arson		
	Rape by force	Assault to rape-attempts	Firearm	Knife or cutting instrument	Other weapon	Strong-arm	Firearm	Knife or cutting instrument	Other weapon	Hands, fists feet, etc.	Forcible entry	Unlawful entry	Attempted forcible entry	Autos	Trucks and buses	Other vehicles	Structure	Mobile	Other
SUBURBAN AREA[3]																			
5,532 agencies; population 94,554,571																			
2000	20,818	1,948	24,466	5,026	6,293	25,887	29,371	33,854	75,476	73,572	329,325	176,672	38,059	178,843	42,816	24,746	8,411	6,086	6,819
2001	20,892	2,119	26,797	5,616	6,963	26,257	29,420	33,929	76,185	70,622	336,016	188,396	38,247	190,664	45,167	27,990	8,411	6,797	6,801
Percent change	+0.4	+8.8	+9.5	+11.7	+10.6	+1.4	+0.2	+0.2	+0.9	-4.0	+2.0	+6.6	+0.5	+6.6	+5.5	+13.1	0.0	+11.7	-0.3

[1] The murders and nonnegligent homicides that occurred as a result of the events of September 11, 2001, were not included in any trend tables (Tables 12-15). See special report, Section V.

[2] Forcible rape figures furnished by the state Uniform Crime Reporting (UCR) Programs administered by the Delaware State Bureau of Investigation for 2000 and the Illinois State Police for 2000 and 2001 were not in accordance with national UCRguidelines; therefore, the figures were excluded from the forcible rape category.

[3] Suburban area includes city law enforcement agencies with less than 50,000 inhabitants and county law enforcement agencies that are within a Metropolitan Statistical Area (see Appendix III). Suburban area excludes all Metropolitan agencies associated with a central city. The agencies associated with suburban areas will also appear in other groups within this table.

Table 16

Rate: Number of Crimes per 100,000 Inhabitants[1]
by Population Group, 2001
[2001 estimated population]

Population group	Crime Index total	Modified Crime Index total[2]	Violent crime[3]	Property crime[4]	Murder and non-negligent man-slaughter	Forcible rape[5]	Robbery	Aggravated assault	Burglary	Larceny-theft	Motor vehicle theft	Arson[2]
TOTAL ALL AGENCIES:												
11,128 agencies; population 235,998,795												
Number of offenses known	10,281,667		1,270,618	9,011,049	14,385	77,213	387,213	791,807	1,830,170	6,082,687	1,098,192	
Rate	4,356.7		538.4	3,818.3	6.1	32.7	164.1	335.5	775.5	2,577.4	465.3	
TOTAL CITIES: 7,890 cities;												
population 161,685,187												
Number of offenses known	8,285,975		1,045,088	7,240,887	11,634	58,141	349,199	626,114	1,368,127	4,950,328	922,432	
Rate	5,124.8		646.4	4,478.4	7.2	36.0	216.0	387.2	846.2	3,061.7	570.5	
GROUP I												
69 cities, 250,000 and over; population 51,403,406												
Number of offenses known	3,270,403		548,879	2,721,524	6,917	22,663	208,722	310,577	522,991	1,714,074	484,459	
Rate	6,362.2		1,067.8	5,294.4	13.5	44.1	406.0	604.2	1,017.4	3,334.6	942.5	
10 cities, 1,000,000 and over; population 24,330,096												
Number of offenses known	1,299,172		263,764	1,035,408	3,211	8,223	103,827	148,503	188,589	648,583	198,236	
Rate	5,339.8		1,084.1	4,255.7	13.2	33.8	426.7	610.4	775.1	2,665.8	814.8	
21 cities, 500,000 to 999,999; population 13,779,116												
Number of offenses known	1,009,730		147,508	862,222	1,965	7,258	52,409	85,876	171,706	546,860	143,656	
Rate	7,328.0		1,070.5	6,257.5	14.3	52.7	380.4	623.2	1,246.1	3,968.8	1,042.6	
38 cities, 250,000 to 499,999; population 13,294,194												
Number of offenses known	961,501		137,607	823,894	1,741	7,182	52,486	76,198	162,696	518,631	142,567	
Rate	7,232.5		1,035.1	6,197.4	13.1	54.0	394.8	573.2	1,223.8	3,901.2	1,072.4	
GROUP II												
157 cities, 100,000 to 249,999; population 23,281,233												
Number of offenses known	1,334,814		155,597	1,179,217	1,805	9,150	54,034	90,608	230,608	795,042	153,567	
Rate	5,733.4		668.3	5,065.1	7.8	39.3	232.1	389.2	990.5	3,414.9	659.6	
GROUP III												
353 cities, 50,000 to 99,999; population 24,247,714												
Number of offenses known	1,101,119		116,329	984,790	1,049	8,298	36,092	70,890	189,773	685,003	110,014	
Rate	4,541.1		479.8	4,061.4	4.3	34.2	148.8	292.4	782.6	2,825.0	453.7	
GROUP IV												
636 cities, 25,000 to 49,999; population 22,201,269												
Number of offenses known	942,936		87,274	855,662	707	6,891	23,797	55,879	158,041	622,153	75,468	
Rate	4,247.2		393.1	3,854.1	3.2	31.0	107.2	251.7	711.9	2,802.3	339.9	
GROUP V												
1,448 cities, 10,000 to 24,999; population 22,965,664												
Number of offenses known	890,019		76,418	813,601	652	6,360	17,111	52,295	147,207	607,876	58,518	
Rate	3,875.4		332.7	3,542.7	2.8	27.7	74.5	227.7	641.0	2,646.9	254.8	

See footnotes at end of table.

Table 16

Rate: Number of Crimes per 100,000 Inhabitants[1]
by Population Group, 2001—Continued
[2001 estimated population]

Population group	Crime Index total	Modified Crime Index total[2]	Violent crime[3]	Property crime[4]	Murder and non-negligent man-slaughter	Forcible rape[5]	Robbery	Aggravated assault	Burglary	Larceny-theft	Motor vehicle theft	Arson[2]
GROUP VI												
5,227 cities, under 10,000; population 17,585,901												
Number of offenses known	746,684		60,591	686,093	504	4,779	9,443	45,865	119,507	526,180	40,406	
Rate	4,245.9		344.5	3,901.4	2.9	27.2	53.7	260.8	679.6	2,992.1	229.8	
SUBURBAN COUNTIES												
1,121 agencies; population 49,530,283												
Number of offenses known	1,505,179		171,714	1,333,465	1,858	13,394	33,877	122,585	321,492	869,162	142,811	
Rate	3,038.9		346.7	2,692.2	3.8	27.0	68.4	247.5	649.1	1,754.8	288.3	
RURAL COUNTIES[6]												
2,117 agencies; population 24,783,325												
Number of offenses known	490,513		53,816	436,697	893	5,678	4,137	43,108	140,551	263,197	32,949	
Rate	1,979.2		217.1	1,762.1	3.6	22.9	16.7	173.9	567.1	1,062.0	132.9	
SUBURBAN AREA[7]												
5,407 agencies; population 91,616,306												
Number of offenses known	3,034,940		296,965	2,737,975	2,823	23,165	65,577	205,400	562,568	1,912,711	262,696	
Rate	3,312.7		324.1	2,988.5	3.1	25.3	71.6	224.2	614.0	2,087.7	286.7	

[1] The murders and nonnegligent homicides that occurred as a result of the events of September 11, 2001, were not included in any rate tables (Tables 16-19). See special report, Section V.

[2] Arson rates are not presented in this table because fewer agencies furnished complete reports for arson than for the other seven Crime Index offenses. Independently tabulated arson data appear in the arson narrative.

[3] Violent crimes are offenses of murder, forcible rape, robbery, and aggravated assault.

[4] Property crimes are offenses of burglary, larceny-theft, and motor vehicle theft.

[5] Forcible rape figures furnished by the state Uniform Crime Reporting (UCR) Program administered by the Illinois State Police were not in accordance with national UCR guidelines; therefore, the figures were estimated for inclusion in the forcible rape, violent crime, and Crime Index total categories. See Appendix I for details.

[6] Includes state police agencies with no county breakdowns.

[7] Suburban area includes city law enforcement agencies with less than 50,000 inhabitants and county law enforcement agencies that are within a Metropolitan Statistical Area (see Appendix III). Suburban area excludes all metropolitan agencies associated with a central city. The agencies associated with suburban areas will also appear in other groups within this table.

Table 17

Rate: Number of Crimes per 100,000 Inhabitants[1]
by Suburban and Nonsuburban Cities[2] by Population Group, 2001
[2001 estimated population]

Population group	Crime Index total	Modified Crime Index total[3]	Violent crime[4]	Property crime[5]	Murder and non-negligent man-slaughter	Forcible rape[6]	Robbery	Aggravated assault	Burglary	Larceny-theft	Motor vehicle theft	Arson[3]
Suburban cities												
TOTAL SUBURBAN CITIES:												
4,286 cities;												
population 42,086,023												
Number of offenses known	1,529,761		125,251	1,404,510	965	9,771	31,700	82,815	241,076	1,043,549	119,885	
Rate	3,634.8		297.6	3,337.2	2.3	23.2	75.3	196.8	572.8	2,479.6	284.9	
Group IV												
439 cities, 25,000 to 49,999;												
population 15,146,406												
Number of offenses known	522,506		44,437	478,069	333	3,328	13,623	27,153	84,718	344,100	49,251	
Rate	3,449.7		293.4	3,156.3	2.2	22.0	89.9	179.3	559.3	2,271.8	325.2	
Group V												
1,072 cities, 10,000 to 24,999;												
population 17,028,796												
Number of offenses known	573,796		48,645	525,151	395	3,880	11,963	32,407	92,605	388,447	44,099	
Rate	3,369.6		285.7	3,083.9	2.3	22.8	70.3	190.3	543.8	2,281.1	259.0	
Group VI												
2,775 cities, under 10,000;												
population 9,910,821												
Number of offenses known	433,459		32,169	401,290	237	2,563	6,114	23,255	63,753	311,002	26,535	
Rate	4,373.6		324.6	4,049.0	2.4	25.9	61.7	234.6	643.3	3,138.0	267.7	
Nonsuburban cities												
TOTAL NONSUBURBAN CITIES:												
3,025 cities;												
population 20,666,811												
Number of offenses known	1,049,878		99,032	950,846	898	8,259	18,651	71,224	183,679	712,660	54,507	
Rate	5,080.0		479.2	4,600.8	4.3	40.0	90.2	344.6	888.8	3,448.3	263.7	
Group IV												
197 cities, 25,000 to 49,999;												
population 7,054,863												
Number of offenses known	420,430		42,837	377,593	374	3,563	10,174	28,726	73,323	278,053	26,217	
Rate	5,959.4		607.2	5,352.2	5.3	50.5	144.2	407.2	1,039.3	3,941.3	371.6	
Group V												
376 cities, 10,000 to 24,999;												
population 5,936,868												
Number of offenses known	316,223		27,773	288,450	257	2,480	5,148	19,888	54,602	219,429	14,419	
Rate	5,326.4		467.8	4,858.6	4.3	41.8	86.7	335.0	919.7	3,696.0	242.9	
Group VI												
2,452 cities, under 10,000;												
population 7,675,080												
Number of offenses known	313,225		28,422	284,803	267	2,216	3,329	22,610	55,754	215,178	13,871	
Rate	4,081.1		370.3	3,710.7	3.5	28.9	43.4	294.6	726.4	2,803.6	180.7	

[1] The murders and nonnegligent homicides that occurred as a result of the events of September 11, 2001, were not included in any of the rate tables (Tables 16-19). See special report, Section V.

[2] Suburban area includes city law enforcement agencies with less than 50,000 inhabitants and county law enforcement agencies that are within a Metropolitan Statistical Area (see Appendix III). Suburban area excludes all metropolitan agencies associated with a central city. The agencies associated with suburban areas will also appear in other groups within this table.

[3] Arson rates are not presented in this table because fewer agencies furnished complete reports for arson than for the other seven Crime Index offenses. Independently tabulated arson rates appear in the arson narrative.

[4] Violent crimes are offenses of murder, forcible rape, robbery, and aggravated assault.

[5] Property crimes are offenses of burglary, larceny-theft, and motor vehicle theft.

[6] Forcible rape figures furnished by the state Uniform Crime Reporting (UCR) Program administered by the Illinois State Police were not in accordance with national UCR guidelines; therefore, the figures were estimated for inclusion in the forcible rape, violent crime, and Crime Index total categories. See Appendix I for details.

Table 18

Rate: Number of Crimes per 100,000 Inhabitants[1]
by Suburban and Nonsuburban Counties by Population Group, 2001
[2001 estimated population]

Population group	Crime Index total	Modified Crime Index total[2]	Violent crime[3]	Property crime[4]	Murder and non-negligent man-slaughter	Forcible rape[5]	Robbery	Aggravated assault	Burglary	Larceny-theft	Motor vehicle theft	Arson[2]
SUBURBAN COUNTIES[6]												
100,000 and over												
120 counties; population 29,626,421												
Number of offenses known	1,024,893		122,531	902,362	1,225	8,135	28,164	85,007	204,652	598,026	99,684	
Rate	3,459.4		413.6	3,045.8	4.1	27.5	95.1	286.9	690.8	2,018.6	336.5	
25,000 to 99,999												
332 counties; population 17,768,547												
Number of offenses known	382,941		37,746	345,195	490	4,137	4,367	28,752	96,275	221,955	26,965	
Rate	2,155.2		212.4	1,942.7	2.8	23.3	24.6	161.8	541.8	1,249.1	151.8	
Under 25,000												
669 counties; population 2,135,315												
Number of offenses known	97,345		11,437	85,908	143	1,122	1,346	8,826	20,565	49,181	16,162	
Rate	4,558.8		535.6	4,023.2	6.7	52.5	63.0	413.3	963.1	2,303.2	756.9	
NONSUBURBAN COUNTIES[6]												
25,000 and over												
280 counties; population 11,058,922												
Number of offenses known	231,547		24,710	206,837	385	2,565	2,384	19,376	67,002	125,193	14,642	
Rate	2,093.8		223.4	1,870.3	3.5	23.2	21.6	175.2	605.9	1,132.1	132.4	
10,000 to 24,999												
560 counties; population 8,843,920												
Number of offenses known	140,765		15,574	125,191	294	1,520	949	12,811	42,473	73,686	9,032	
Rate	1,591.7		176.1	1,415.6	3.3	17.2	10.7	144.9	480.3	833.2	102.1	
Under 10,000												
1,119 counties; population 3,454,241												
Number of offenses known	77,516		9,774	67,742	169	1,167	463	7,975	21,335	40,429	5,978	
Rate	2,244.1		283.0	1,961.1	4.9	33.8	13.4	230.9	617.6	1,170.4	173.1	

[1] The murders and nonnegligent homicides that occurred as a result of the events of September 11, 2001, were not included in any rate tables (Tables 16-19). See special report, Section V.

[2] Arson rates are not presented in this table because fewer agencies furnished complete reports for arson than for the other seven Crime Index offenses. Independently tabulated arson rates appear in the arson narrative.

[3] Violent crimes are offenses of murder, forcible rape, robbery, and aggravated assault.

[4] Property crimes are offenses of burglary, larceny-theft, and motor vehicle theft.

[5] Forcible rape figures furnished by the state Uniform Crime Reporting (UCR) Program administered by the Illinois State Police were not in accordance with national UCR guidelines; therefore, the figures were estimated for inclusion in the forcible rape, violent crime, and Crime Index total categories. See Appendix I for details.

[6] Offenses include sheriffs and county law enforcement agencies. State police offenses are not included.

Table 19

Rate: Number of Crimes per 100,000 Inhabitants[1]

Breakdown of Offenses Known
by Population Group, 2001
[2001 estimated population]

Population Group	Forcible rape		Robbery				Aggravated assault				Burglary			Motor vehicle theft			Arson[2]		
	Rape by force	Assault to rape-attempts	Firearm	Knife or cutting instrument	Other weapon	Strong-arm	Firearm	Knife or cutting instrument	Other weapon	Hands, fists feet, etc.	Forcible entry	Unlawful entry	Attempted forcible entry	Autos	Trucks and buses	Other vehicles	Structure	Mobile	Other
TOTAL ALL AGENCIES: 11,021 agencies; population 219,426,480																			
Number of offenses known	65,027	7,193	136,232	28,171	33,572	126,472	129,385	126,160	254,480	197,601	1,086,120	517,413	111,944	739,183	189,802	73,317			
Rate	29.6	3.3	62.1	12.8	15.3	57.6	59.0	57.5	116.0	90.1	495.0	235.8	51.0	336.9	86.5	33.4			
TOTAL CITIES: 7,836 cities; population 146,385,985																			
Number of offenses known	47,775	5,658	120,880	25,145	29,250	113,326	103,163	101,292	194,161	144,590	800,398	375,830	86,682	627,024	156,463	49,293			
Rate	32.6	3.9	82.6	17.2	20.0	77.4	70.5	69.2	132.6	98.8	546.8	256.7	59.2	428.3	106.9	33.7			
GROUP I																			
63 cities, 250,000 and over; population 38,965,346																			
Number of offenses known	16,874	2,368	69,048	12,984	15,488	57,120	57,171	45,005	87,598	48,360	310,773	111,406	26,525	299,515	93,794	18,087			
Rate	43.3	6.1	177.2	33.3	39.7	146.6	146.7	115.5	224.8	124.1	797.6	285.9	68.1	768.7	240.7	46.4			
8 cities, 1,000,000 and over; population 13,396,369																			
Number of offenses known	4,778	931	25,900	5,627	4,698	20,967	21,357	15,268	25,733	22,719	89,529	34,903	6,628	95,408	37,371	7,774			
Rate	35.7	6.9	193.3	42.0	35.1	156.5	159.4	114.0	192.1	169.6	668.3	260.5	49.5	712.2	279.0	58.0			
20 cities, 500,000 to 999,999; population 13,207,294																			
Number of offenses known	6,305	761	22,471	3,789	6,667	15,498	19,284	15,503	31,871	13,795	119,435	36,111	11,156	100,915	30,204	4,989			
Rate	47.7	5.8	170.1	28.7	50.5	117.3	146.0	117.4	241.3	104.4	904.3	273.4	84.5	764.1	228.7	37.8			
35 cities, 250,000 to 499,999; population 12,361,683																			
Number of offenses known	5,791	676	20,677	3,568	4,123	20,655	16,530	14,234	29,994	11,846	101,809	40,392	8,741	103,192	26,219	5,324			
Rate	46.8	5.5	167.3	28.9	33.4	167.1	133.7	115.1	242.6	95.8	823.6	326.8	70.7	834.8	212.1	43.1			
GROUP II																			
144 cities, 100,000 to 249,999; population 21,407,856																			
Number of offenses known	7,350	804	20,663	4,291	5,096	18,832	16,353	16,128	33,739	16,472	132,642	58,952	14,519	111,332	23,855	7,441			
Rate	34.3	3.8	96.5	20.0	23.8	88.0	76.4	75.3	157.6	76.9	619.6	275.4	67.8	520.1	111.4	34.8			
GROUP III																			
343 cities, 50,000 to 99,999; population 23,605,243																			
Number of offenses known	7,365	724	13,026	3,264	3,284	15,382	10,963	13,200	25,276	19,478	112,594	58,841	14,162	83,011	15,287	7,145			
Rate	31.2	3.1	55.2	13.8	13.9	65.2	46.4	55.9	107.1	82.5	477.0	249.3	60.0	351.7	64.8	30.3			

See footnotes at end of table.

Table 19

Rate: Number of Crimes per 100,000 Inhabitants[1]
Breakdown of Offenses Known by Population Group, 2001—Continued
[2001 estimated population]

Population Group	Forcible rape — Rape by force	Forcible rape — Assault to rape-attempts	Robbery — Firearm	Robbery — Knife or cutting instrument	Robbery — Other weapon	Robbery — Strong-arm	Aggravated assault — Firearm	Aggravated assault — Knife or cutting instrument	Aggravated assault — Other weapon	Aggravated assault — Hands, fists, feet, etc.	Burglary — Forcible entry	Burglary — Unlawful entry	Burglary — Attempted forcible entry	Motor vehicle theft — Autos	Motor vehicle theft — Trucks and buses	Motor vehicle theft — Other vehicles	Arson[2] — Structure	Arson[2] — Mobile	Arson[2] — Other
GROUP IV																			
631 cities, 25,000 to 49,999; population 22,026,170																			
Number of offenses known	6,228	623	8,498	2,247	2,579	10,389	7,453	10,206	18,826	19,234	91,948	53,558	11,991	59,021	9,946	6,104			
Rate	28.3	2.8	38.6	10.2	11.7	47.2	33.8	46.3	85.5	87.3	417.4	243.2	54.4	268.0	45.2	27.7			
GROUP V																			
1,442 cities, 10,000 to 24,999; population 22,855,246																			
Number of offenses known	5,745	587	6,212	1,465	1,906	7,406	6,539	9,416	16,387	19,639	85,348	49,687	10,748	44,354	8,140	5,465			
Rate	25.1	2.6	27.2	6.4	8.3	32.4	28.6	41.2	71.7	85.9	373.4	217.4	47.0	194.1	35.6	23.9			
GROUP VI																			
5,213 cities, under 10,000; population 17,526,124																			
Number of offenses known	4,213	552	3,433	894	897	4,197	4,684	7,337	12,335	21,407	67,093	43,386	8,737	29,791	5,441	5,051			
Rate	24.0	3.1	19.6	5.1	5.1	23.9	26.7	41.9	70.4	122.1	382.8	247.6	49.9	170.0	31.0	28.8			
SUBURBAN COUNTIES																			
1,107 agencies; population 48,595,735																			
Number of offenses known	12,133	1,061	13,751	2,613	3,793	11,622	19,021	18,960	47,956	35,802	195,488	99,851	18,500	92,958	27,507	16,747			
Rate	25.0	2.2	28.3	5.4	7.8	23.9	39.1	39.0	98.7	73.7	402.3	205.5	38.1	191.3	56.6	34.5			
RURAL COUNTIES																			
2,078 agencies; population 24,444,760																			
Number of offenses known	5,119	474	1,601	413	529	1,524	7,201	5,908	12,363	17,209	90,234	41,732	6,762	19,201	5,832	7,277			
Rate	20.9	1.9	6.5	1.7	2.2	6.2	29.5	24.2	50.6	70.4	369.1	170.7	27.7	78.5	23.9	29.8			
SUBURBAN AREA[3]																			
5,380 agencies; population 90,458,672																			
Number of offenses known	20,822	2,095	25,275	5,437	7,075	25,519	28,085	32,570	73,852	69,529	329,341	186,727	37,444	186,133	42,910	27,275			
Rate	23.0	2.3	27.9	6.0	7.8	28.2	31.0	36.0	81.6	76.9	364.1	206.4	41.4	205.8	47.4	30.2			

[1] The murders and nonnegligent homicides that occurred as a result of the events of September 11, 2001, were not included in this table because fewer agencies furnished complete reports for arson than for the other seven Crime Index offenses (Tables 16-19). See special report, Section V.

[2] Arson rates are not presented in this table. Independently tabulated arson rates appear in the arson narrative.

[3] Suburban area includes city law enforcement agencies with less than 50,000 inhabitants and county law enforcement agencies that are within a Metropolitan Statistical Area (see Appendix III). Suburban area excludes all metropolitan agencies associated with a central city. The agencies associated with suburban areas will also appear in other groups within this table.

Table 20

Murder[1]
by State, 2001

Type of Weapon

State	Total murders[2]	Total firearms	Handguns	Rifles	Shotguns	Firearms (type unknown)	Knives or cutting instruments	Other weapons	Hands, fists, feet, etc.
Alabama	345	225	199	0	26	0	33	65	22
Alaska	34	20	10	7	2	1	3	3	8
Arizona	396	281	243	19	7	12	55	44	16
Arkansas	142	92	69	3	12	8	18	18	14
California	2,204	1,569	1,341	67	68	93	297	237	101
Colorado	141	81	54	10	7	10	26	19	15
Connecticut	105	72	53	1	3	15	16	11	6
Delaware	20	13	10	0	1	2	3	1	3
District of Columbia[3]									
Florida[4]									
Georgia	531	367	311	13	20	23	66	68	30
Hawaii	31	7	5	0	2	0	6	10	8
Idaho	30	18	10	3	4	1	5	1	6
Illinois[5]	666	206	148	3	4	51	29	409	22
Indiana	368	259	162	10	14	73	45	41	23
Iowa	48	14	10	1	1	2	14	15	5
Kansas	49	33	22	4	4	3	1	10	5
Kentucky[5]	74	51	34	1	2	14	11	9	3
Louisiana	486	363	329	15	12	7	42	54	27
Maine	18	6	2	1	2	1	4	4	4
Maryland	403	293	271	2	13	7	47	49	14
Massachusetts	139	72	34	3	0	35	31	31	5
Michigan	653	467	340	30	30	67	70	77	39
Minnesota	112	54	44	3	7	0	21	24	13
Mississippi	186	131	104	8	10	9	25	22	8
Missouri	366	233	90	8	12	123	32	94	7
Montana	17	12	10	1	1	0	1	3	1
Nebraska	17	9	4	3	2	0	3	4	1
Nevada	181	107	84	8	3	12	27	28	19
New Hampshire	17	7	4	0	1	2	4	1	5
New Jersey	338	171	162	2	1	6	70	63	34
New Mexico	85	44	35	3	3	3	9	17	15
New York	927	532	489	16	21	6	193	104	98
North Carolina	496	321	227	18	39	37	60	70	45
North Dakota	7	5	3	1	1	0	0	1	1
Ohio	410	252	198	4	13	37	36	77	45
Oklahoma	185	105	75	12	14	4	30	33	17
Oregon	83	35	22	6	1	6	15	31	2
Pennsylvania	607	438	383	9	6	40	55	88	26
Rhode Island	39	19	10	0	1	8	10	6	4
South Carolina	191	124	86	5	10	23	23	27	17
South Dakota	6	4	3	1	0	0	2	0	0
Tennessee	425	273	177	10	15	71	59	66	27
Texas	1,327	822	588	47	73	114	196	208	101
Utah	71	38	27	1	5	5	13	10	10
Vermont	7	6	5	1	0	0	0	1	0
Virginia	358	226	106	9	11	100	39	77	16
Washington	176	94	80	6	5	3	27	43	12
West Virginia	36	19	13	1	3	2	3	10	4
Wisconsin	190	124	99	13	5	7	21	26	19
Wyoming	9	5	5	0	0	0	0	2	2

[1] The murder and nonnegligent homicides that occurred as a result of the events of September 11, 2001, were not included in this table. See special report, Section V.
[2] Total number of murders for which supplemental homicide data were received.
[3] No supplemental homicide data were received from the District of Columbia.
[4] Supplemental homicide data from Florida were not processed due to limited submission of circumstance data.
[5] Limited supplemental homicide data for 2001 were received from Illinois and Kentucky.

Table 21

Robbery
by State, 2001
Type of Weapon

State	Total robberies[1]	Firearms	Knives or cutting instruments	Other weapons	Strong-arm	Agency count	Population
Alabama	2,470	1,414	166	155	735	284	3,298,922
Alaska	485	188	46	35	216	29	580,540
Arizona	8,587	3,967	830	919	2,871	93	5,007,178
Arkansas	1,751	933	122	140	556	147	2,094,486
California	60,802	22,178	6,293	5,811	26,520	720	33,709,645
Colorado	3,203	1,228	364	456	1,155	142	3,603,504
Connecticut	3,808	1,495	353	299	1,661	92	3,022,335
Delaware	478	173	39	40	226	31	717,822
District of Columbia[2]							
Florida	32,808	12,804	2,385	3,578	14,041	582	16,377,083
Georgia	11,227	6,061	646	1,391	3,129	360	6,007,906
Hawaii	1,142	119	83	44	896	4	1,224,398
Idaho	243	68	32	41	102	113	1,303,387
Illinois[2]							
Indiana	6,162	3,278	380	324	2,180	249	4,460,416
Iowa	1,013	294	87	179	453	145	2,052,923
Kansas	746	341	60	82	263	11	395,166
Kentucky[2]	2,285	1,087	183	171	844	17	1,271,577
Louisiana	7,461	4,416	437	523	2,085	154	3,838,326
Maine	264	50	38	31	145	179	1,280,026
Maryland	9,034	3,451	675	2,375	2,533	142	3,848,687
Massachusetts	5,567	1,434	1,083	623	2,427	264	4,684,077
Michigan	10,396	5,402	554	1,361	3,079	517	7,204,364
Minnesota	1,035	285	104	284	362	262	3,774,349
Mississippi	2,620	1,416	138	404	662	99	1,483,480
Missouri	7,351	3,340	470	647	2,894	243	4,641,543
Montana	104	25	14	21	44	48	482,587
Nebraska	1,095	455	110	74	456	211	1,348,700
Nevada	4,932	1,982	532	380	2,038	35	2,106,074
New Hampshire	228	50	33	28	117	106	734,397
New Jersey	14,020	4,553	1,475	1,139	6,853	494	8,232,350
New Mexico	2,305	1,056	324	179	746	47	1,312,200
New York	6,221	1,850	736	500	3,135	494	6,769,249
North Carolina	13,061	6,817	1,005	1,524	3,715	392	7,805,870
North Dakota	56	18	5	9	24	62	547,363
Ohio	14,993	5,536	801	1,461	7,195	322	7,630,642
Oklahoma	2,746	1,129	309	181	1,127	299	3,460,097
Oregon	2,491	650	248	208	1,385	147	3,061,816
Pennsylvania	16,155	6,640	1,147	1,001	7,367	671	9,986,627
Rhode Island	986	276	133	98	479	48	1,058,920
South Carolina	2,172	1,065	175	247	685	93	1,539,847
South Dakota	81	27	15	3	36	27	381,245
Tennessee	10,178	5,674	709	1,176	2,619	428	5,586,578
Texas	34,998	15,801	3,481	3,641	12,075	943	20,943,058
Utah	1,073	320	112	147	494	104	2,001,835
Vermont	82	27	6	15	34	50	511,114
Virginia	6,144	3,100	378	860	1,806	293	6,121,723
Washington	4,583	1,222	516	449	2,396	225	5,408,821
West Virginia	97	34	10	16	37	201	904,939
Wisconsin	4,416	2,394	294	272	1,456	338	5,121,789
Wyoming	82	18	18	5	41	64	486,499

[1] The number of robberies for which breakdowns by type of weapon were received for 12 months of 2001.
[2] Limited or no robbery by type of weapon data for 2001 were received from the District of Columbia, Illinois, and Kentucky.

Table 22

Aggravated Assault
by State, 2001

Type of Weapon

State	Total aggravated assaults[1]	Firearms	Knives or cutting instruments	Other weapons	Personal weapons	Agency count	Population
Alabama	8,290	1,962	1,433	2,237	2,658	284	3,298,922
Alaska	2,247	454	596	709	488	29	580,540
Arizona	17,160	4,105	2,662	5,034	5,359	93	5,007,178
Arkansas	6,440	1,373	959	1,773	2,335	147	2,094,486
California	133,367	21,418	17,972	43,078	50,899	720	33,709,645
Colorado	8,608	1,552	1,997	2,765	2,294	142	3,603,504
Connecticut	6,162	661	1,064	2,122	2,315	92	3,022,335
Delaware	2,121	384	499	961	277	31	717,822
District of Columbia[2]							
Florida	90,017	12,720	16,522	42,759	18,016	582	16,377,083
Georgia	19,426	4,432	3,743	7,176	4,075	360	6,007,906
Hawaii	1,534	174	174	427	759	4	1,224,398
Idaho	2,484	624	577	930	353	113	1,303,387
Illinois[2]							
Indiana	11,021	1,665	1,358	3,013	4,985	249	4,460,416
Iowa	4,872	478	878	1,326	2,190	145	2,052,923
Kansas	1,586	243	236	832	275	11	395,166
Kentucky[2]	2,907	524	467	1,089	827	17	1,271,577
Louisiana	18,731	5,104	3,817	5,822	3,988	154	3,838,326
Maine	823	22	87	221	493	179	1,280,026
Maryland	18,335	2,236	3,309	7,940	4,850	142	3,848,687
Massachusetts	18,884	1,512	3,769	8,759	4,844	264	4,684,077
Michigan	26,811	6,343	5,201	12,278	2,989	517	7,204,364
Minnesota	3,466	418	861	1,181	1,006	262	3,774,349
Mississippi	3,038	816	640	999	583	99	1,483,480
Missouri	17,625	4,082	2,690	5,877	4,976	243	4,641,543
Montana	1,347	230	150	359	608	48	482,587
Nebraska	3,323	541	629	1,588	565	211	1,348,700
Nevada	6,364	835	1,392	2,616	1,521	35	2,106,074
New Hampshire	566	77	164	161	164	106	734,397
New Jersey	17,036	2,442	3,574	5,418	5,602	494	8,232,350
New Mexico	7,992	1,645	1,421	2,757	2,169	47	1,312,200
New York	12,551	1,276	2,343	3,500	5,432	494	6,769,249
North Carolina	23,804	6,023	4,619	7,536	5,626	392	7,805,870
North Dakota	248	12	44	54	138	62	547,363
Ohio	14,455	2,717	2,563	4,217	4,958	322	7,630,642
Oklahoma	13,308	2,173	2,019	5,061	4,055	299	3,460,097
Oregon	6,130	689	922	2,240	2,279	147	3,061,816
Pennsylvania	24,045	5,132	3,649	6,601	8,663	671	9,986,627
Rhode Island	1,837	256	442	814	325	48	1,058,920
South Carolina	9,490	2,171	1,811	2,895	2,613	93	1,539,847
South Dakota	501	67	150	135	149	27	381,245
Tennessee	29,616	9,149	5,918	10,773	3,776	428	5,586,578
Texas	76,163	15,534	17,028	28,338	15,263	943	20,943,058
Utah	2,746	435	557	976	778	104	2,001,835
Vermont	343	26	53	115	149	50	511,114
Virginia	9,922	1,759	1,892	3,246	3,025	293	6,121,723
Washington	9,779	1,353	1,938	3,377	3,111	225	5,408,821
West Virginia	1,729	345	183	307	894	201	904,939
Wisconsin	6,552	966	950	1,436	3,200	338	5,121,789
Wyoming	1,017	104	113	334	466	64	486,499

[1] The number of aggravated assaults for which breakdowns by type of weapon were received for 12 months of 2001.

[2] Limited or no aggravated assault by type of weapon data for 2001 were received from the District of Columbia, Illinois, and Kentucky.

Table 23

Offense Analysis[1]
Number and Percent Change, 2000-2001
[11,699 agencies; 2001 estimated population 231,212,569]

Classification	Number of Offenses 2001	Percent change over 2000	Percent distribution[2]	Average value
Murder	12,432	+3.2	–	
Forcible rape	72,881	+0.3	–	
Robbery:				
Total	326,277	+5.8	100.0	$1,258
Street/highway	144,491	+1.9	44.3	957
Commercial house	47,107	+10.1	14.4	1,881
Gas or service station	9,309	+7.7	2.9	686
Convenience store	21,402	+9.5	6.6	618
Residence	41,034	+8.2	12.6	1,364
Bank	7,905	+19.4	2.4	4,587
Miscellaneous	55,029	+7.9	16.9	1,303
Burglary:				
Total	1,722,971	+3.8	100.0	1,545
Residence (dwelling):	1,123,779	+3.5	65.2	1,381
Night	333,820	+2.7	19.4	1,163
Day	522,838	+4.6	30.3	1,570
Unknown	267,121	+2.3	15.5	1,647
Nonresidence (store, office, etc.):	599,192	+4.4	34.8	1,615
Night	252,842	+5.0	14.7	1,468
Day	182,786	+4.7	10.6	1,671
Unknown	163,564	+3.1	9.5	2,061
Larceny-theft (except motor vehicle theft):				
Total	5,710,073	+2.3	100.0	730
By type:				
Pocket-picking	26,847	-6.4	0.5	305
Purse-snatching	31,037	+3.4	0.5	331
Shoplifting	788,046	+2.7	13.8	182
From motor vehicles (except accessories)	1,475,718	+5.2	25.8	719
Motor vehicle accessories	582,434	+8.0	10.2	451
Bicycles	234,451	-5.4	4.1	318
From buildings	759,729	+1.2	13.3	1,037
From coin-operated machines	41,897	+12.6	0.7	286
All others	1,769,914	-0.6	31.0	1,024
By value:				
Over $200	2,248,060	+3.8	39.4	1,770
$50 to $200	1,312,790	+0.5	23.0	115
Under $50	2,149,223	+1.8	37.6	18
Motor vehicle theft	1,009,862	+7.4	–	6,646

[1] The murders and nonnegligent homicides that occurred as a result of the events of September 11, 2001, were not included in this table. See special report, Section V.
[2] Because of rounding, the percentages may not add to total.

Table 24

Property Stolen and Recovered
by Type and Value, 2001
[11,183 agencies; 2001 estimated population 222,729,343]

Type of property	Value of property		Percent recovered
	Stolen	Recovered	
Total	$14,142,588,549	$4,576,749,999	32.4
Currency, notes, etc.	936,485,688	47,227,902	5.0
Jewelry and precious metals	994,282,459	48,881,005	4.9
Clothing and furs	227,433,861	33,896,606	14.9
Locally stolen motor vehicles	6,572,852,063	4,073,539,129	62.0
Office equipment	499,578,954	24,630,015	4.9
Televisions, radios, stereos, etc.	892,634,346	36,262,038	4.1
Firearms	97,151,661	8,083,827	8.3
Household goods	234,630,711	13,457,885	5.7
Consumable goods	119,200,138	12,799,991	10.7
Livestock	21,047,047	2,463,631	11.7
Miscellaneous	3,547,291,621	275,507,970	7.8

SECTION III

Crime Index Offenses Cleared

Offenses reported to the national UCR Program can be cleared either by arrest or by exceptional means. The administrative closing or "clearing" of a case by a local law enforcement agency does not necessarily mean that an offense can be cleared according to UCR procedures. In order for an offense to be cleared within the Program's guidelines, certain criteria must be met.

Cleared by Arrest

In the UCR Program, a reporting law enforcement agency clears, or solves, an offense only when all of the following conditions are met. At least one person must be:

- Arrested.
- Charged with the commission of an offense.
- Turned over to the court for prosecution.

The number of offenses and not the number of persons arrested are counted in the clearances. Therefore, the arrest of one person may clear many crimes. Conversely, the arrest of many persons may clear just one offense. In addition, clearances recorded in a particular calendar year such as 2001 may include offenses that occurred in previous years.

Cleared by Exceptional Means

When elements beyond law enforcement's control prevent the agency from placing formal charges against the offender, the offense is cleared exceptionally for UCR purposes. For an offense to be cleared exceptionally, all of the following criteria must be met. The agency must have:

- Identified the offender.
- Gathered enough evidence to support an arrest, make a charge, and turn over the offender to the court for prosecution.
- Identified the offender's exact location so that law enforcement could make an arrest.
- Encountered a circumstance outside the control of law enforcement that prohibits the agency from arresting, charging, and prosecuting an offender.

Examples of exceptional clearances include but are not limited to the death of the offender (suicide, justifiably killed by police or private citizens, etc.); the victim's refusal to cooperate with the prosecution after the identification of the offender; or the denial of extradition because the offender committed a crime in another jurisdiction and is being prosecuted. Furthermore, the recovery of property does not clear a case for UCR purposes.

2001 National Clearances

Law enforcement agencies nationwide recorded a 19.6-percent Crime Index clearance rate. (The Crime Index offenses include murder, forcible rape, robbery, aggravated assault, burglary, motor vehicle theft, and larceny-theft.) The Modified Crime Index total (the Crime Index offenses plus arson) showed a 19.6-percent clearance rate for the year and included a 16.0-percent clearance rate for arson.

Violent crimes (murder, forcible rape, robbery, and aggravated assault) often undergo a more vigorous investigative effort than crimes against property. Additionally, victims and/or witnesses often identify the perpetrators. Consequently, violent crimes tend to have higher clearance rates than property crimes. That tendency continued in 2001 with 46.2 percent of violent crimes cleared compared to 16.2 percent of property crimes cleared (excluding arson). Looking at violent crime clearances, the murder clearance rate was 62.4 percent, the aggravated assault clearance rate was 56.1 percent, the forcible rape clearance rate was 44.3 percent, and the robbery clearance rate was 24.9 percent. A review of the clearances for property crimes indicates that the larceny-theft clearance rate was 17.6 percent, the motor vehicle theft clearance rate was 13.6 percent, and the burglary clearance rate was 12.7 percent. (See Table 25.)

2001 Regional Clearances

By region, law enforcement agencies in the Northeast recorded the highest Crime Index clearance rate in the Nation—23.6 percent. The

Figure 3.1

Crimes cleared by arrest

Percent of crimes cleared by arrest, 2001

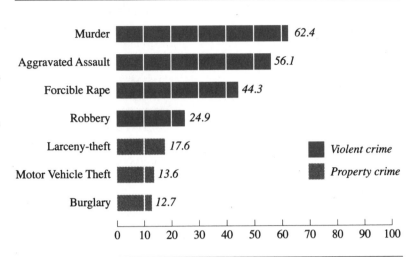

Murder	62.4
Aggravated Assault	56.1
Forcible Rape	44.3
Robbery	24.9
Larceny-theft	17.6
Motor Vehicle Theft	13.6
Burglary	12.7

■ *Violent crime*

■ *Property crime*

0 10 20 30 40 50 60 70 80 90 100

South had a 19.5-percent clearance rate, the West had a 18.7-percent clearance rate, and the Midwest cleared 18.5 percent of reported offenses. Violent crime clearance rates reported by region were 51.7 percent in the Northeast, 47.2 percent in the West, 45.1 percent in the South, and 41.9 percent in the Midwest. For property crime, the Northeast and South showed clearance rates of 19.8 percent and 16.1 percent, respectively. The Midwest and West recorded clearance rates of 15.9 percent and 14.8 percent, respectively. (See Table 26.)

2001 Clearances for Community Types

Among community types, cities collectively cleared 19.4 percent of Crime Index offenses, 44.0 percent of violent crimes, and 16.2 percent of property crimes. Among city groupings, cities with populations of 10,000 to 24,999 showed the highest clearance rate for Crime Index offenses—23.9 percent. In 2001, these cities collectively also had the highest property crime clearance rate—21.2 percent. The highest percentage of violent crimes cleared—59.7 percent—occurred in cities with less than 10,000 inhabitants. Among the remaining community types, 19.4 percent of Index offenses were cleared in suburban counties, as were 53.6 percent of violent crimes, and 15.2 percent of property crimes. Rural county law enforcement agencies recorded a 23.0-percent clearance rate for Crime Index offenses. Additionally, rural counties had a violent crime clearance rate of 62.0 percent and a property crime clearance rate of 18.1 percent. (See Table 25.)

Clearances Involving Only Persons Under 18 Years of Age

When an offender under the age of 18 is cited to appear in juvenile court or before other juvenile authorities, the UCR Program records that incident as a clearance by arrest, even though a physical arrest may not have occurred. In addition, according to Program definitions, clearances involving both adult and juvenile offenders are classified as adult clearances. Therefore, because the juvenile clearance percentages in this publication include only the offenses in which there were no adults involved, these figures underestimate juvenile involvement in crime.

Of the Crime Index offenses cleared by law enforcement, 18.6 percent involved only juveniles. In addition, crimes committed by only juveniles accounted for 12.1 percent of violent crime clearances and 21.1 percent of property crime clearances. (See Table 28.)

By region, the Midwest had the largest percentage of clearances for Crime Index offenses involving only juveniles—23.0 percent. In the West, juveniles alone accounted for 20.9 percent of the clearances; in the Northeast, 17.5 percent; and in the South, 15.6 percent.

Table 25

Percent of Offenses Cleared by Arrest or Exceptional Means[1]
by Population Group, 2001
[2001 estimated population]

Population group	Crime Index total	Modified Crime Index total[2]	Violent crime[3]	Property crime[4]	Murder and non-negligent man-slaughter	Forcible rape[5]	Robbery	Aggravated assault	Burglary	Larceny-theft	Motor vehicle theft	Arson[2]
TOTAL ALL AGENCIES: 11,475 agencies; population 214,806,053												
Offenses known	8,884,332	8,952,060	1,024,134	7,860,198	11,982	67,907	304,077	640,168	1,585,074	5,329,949	945,175	67,728
Percent cleared by arrest	19.6	19.6	46.2	16.2	62.4	44.3	24.9	56.1	12.7	17.6	13.6	16.0
TOTAL CITIES: 8,211 cities; population 144,826,230												
Offenses known	7,208,589	7,259,693	841,410	6,367,179	9,533	51,643	274,540	505,694	1,192,337	4,375,957	798,885	51,104
Percent cleared by arrest	19.4	19.4	44.0	16.2	60.2	43.6	24.4	54.4	12.3	17.9	12.8	15.6
GROUP I												
59 cities, 250,000 and over; population 37,753,658												
Offenses known	2,568,378	2,590,661	399,627	2,168,751	5,322	18,351	151,006	224,948	422,541	1,347,878	398,332	22,283
Percent cleared by arrest	16.4	16.4	38.3	12.4	56.5	45.2	21.3	48.8	10.1	13.6	10.6	10.9
8 cities, 1,000,000 and over; population 13,396,369												
Offenses known	838,636	845,863	149,874	688,762	1,896	5,709	57,192	85,077	131,060	417,149	140,553	7,227
Percent cleared by arrest	17.8	17.7	39.3	13.1	56.9	44.6	22.0	50.2	11.1	14.7	10.0	9.6
20 cities, 500,000 to 999,999; population 13,278,524												
Offenses known	948,189	955,215	140,657	807,532	1,917	6,837	51,758	80,145	160,953	507,979	138,600	7,026
Percent cleared by arrest	14.3	14.3	34.5	10.8	54.5	45.8	18.5	43.5	8.3	11.6	10.9	11.5
31 cities, 250,000 to 499,999; population 11,078,765												
Offenses known	781,553	789,583	109,096	672,457	1,509	5,805	42,056	59,726	130,528	422,750	119,179	8,030
Percent cleared by arrest	17.5	17.5	41.8	13.6	58.4	44.9	23.8	53.8	11.3	15.0	11.1	11.7
GROUP II												
141 cities, 100,000 to 249,999; population 20,922,711												
Offenses known	1,152,851	1,160,656	128,476	1,024,375	1,469	7,934	45,694	73,379	195,567	691,294	137,514	7,805
Percent cleared by arrest	18.4	18.4	42.3	15.4	57.5	41.5	24.4	53.2	11.7	17.4	10.7	15.6
GROUP III												
342 cities, 50,000 to 99,999; population 23,367,702												
Offenses known	1,030,905	1,037,810	108,967	921,938	986	8,015	32,841	67,125	177,055	644,106	100,777	6,905
Percent cleared by arrest	20.4	20.4	47.2	17.2	61.1	41.5	27.4	57.4	12.0	19.4	12.2	17.0

See footnotes at end of table.

Table 25

Percent of Offenses Cleared by Arrest or Exceptional Means[1]
by Population Group, 2001—Continued
[2001 estimated population]

Population group	Crime Index total	Modified Crime Index total[2]	Violent crime[3]	Property crime[4]	Murder and non-negligent man-slaughter	Forcible rape[5]	Robbery	Aggravated assault	Burglary	Larceny-theft	Motor vehicle theft	Arson[2]
GROUP IV												
616 cities, 25,000 to 49,999; population 21,446,942												
Offenses known	863,029	868,377	74,205	788,824	615	6,356	20,136	47,098	141,794	581,324	65,706	5,348
Percent cleared by arrest	21.4	21.4	51.0	18.6	77.9	41.2	31.3	60.4	13.4	20.2	15.8	19.1
GROUP V												
1,436 cities, 10,000 to 24,999; population 22,843,696												
Offenses known	850,909	855,404	70,381	780,528	633	6,155	15,842	47,751	137,744	585,994	56,790	4,495
Percent cleared by arrest	23.9	23.9	53.9	21.2	72.4	44.5	33.6	61.6	15.6	22.5	21.1	23.9
GROUP VI												
5,617 cities, under 10,000; population 18,491,521												
Offenses known	742,517	746,785	59,754	682,763	508	4,832	9,021	45,393	117,636	525,361	39,766	4,268
Percent cleared by arrest	22.8	22.8	59.7	19.6	69.7	46.3	35.7	65.7	16.4	19.8	26.2	25.0
SUBURBAN COUNTIES												
1,090 agencies; population 44,852,933												
Offenses known	1,210,666	1,223,321	130,925	1,079,741	1,569	10,883	25,703	92,770	259,731	705,069	114,941	12,655
Percent cleared by arrest	19.4	19.3	53.6	15.2	66.9	44.1	27.8	61.7	13.0	16.0	15.4	14.9
RURAL COUNTIES												
2,174 agencies; population 25,126,890												
Offenses known	465,077	469,046	51,799	413,278	880	5,381	3,834	41,704	133,006	248,923	31,349	3,969
Percent cleared by arrest	23.0	23.0	62.0	18.1	77.5	52.0	41.0	64.9	16.3	17.8	28.0	24.8
SUBURBAN AREA[6]												
5,454 agencies; population 86,240,191												
Offenses known	2,634,271	2,655,235	240,519	2,393,752	2,472	19,979	53,549	164,519	478,187	1,689,850	225,715	20,964
Percent cleared by arrest	20.5	20.5	53.5	17.2	67.6	43.8	29.3	62.3	13.5	18.4	16.1	17.9

[1] The murders and nonnegligent homicides that occurred as a result of the events of September 11, 2001, were not included in any clearance tables (Tables 25-28). See special report, Section V.

[2] Because arson is reported to the FBI separately from other offenses, the number of agency reports used in arson clearance rates is less than those used in compiling other Crime Index offense clearance rates. The Modified Crime Index total is the sum of the Crime Index offenses, including arson.

[3] Violent crimes are offenses of murder, forcible rape, robbery, and aggravated assault.

[4] Property crimes are offenses of burglary, larceny-theft, and motor vehicle theft.

[5] Forcible rape figures furnished by the state Uniform Crime Reporting (UCR) Program administered by the Illinois State Police were not in accordance with national UCR guidelines; therefore, the figures were excluded from the forcible rape, violent crime, Crime Index total, and Modified Crime Index total categories.

[6] Suburban area includes city law enforcement agencies with less than 50,000 inhabitants and county law enforcement agencies that are within a Metropolitan Statistical Area (see Appendix III). Suburban area excludes all metropolitan agencies associated with a central city. The agencies associated with suburban areas will also appear in other groups within this table.

Table 26

Percent of Offenses Cleared by Arrest or Exceptional Means[1]
by Geographic Region and Division, 2001
[2001 estimated population]

Geograpic region/division	Crime Index total	Modified Crime Index total[2]	Violent crime[3]	Property crime[4]	Murder and non-negligent man-slaughter	Forcible rape[5]	Robbery	Aggravated assault	Burglary	Larceny-theft	Motor vehicle theft	Arson[2]
TOTAL ALL AGENCIES:												
11,475 agencies;												
population 214,806,053												
Offenses known	8,884,332	8,952,060	1,024,134	7,860,198	11,982	67,907	304,077	640,168	1,585,074	5,329,949	945,175	67,728
Percent cleared by arrest	19.6	19.6	46.2	16.2	62.4	44.3	24.9	56.1	12.7	17.6	13.6	16.0
NEW ENGLAND												
740 agencies;												
population 11,141,973												
Offenses known	330,480	332,635	36,715	293,765	306	2,894	10,172	23,343	54,392	201,424	37,949	2,155
Percent cleared by arrest	21.1	21.1	50.1	17.5	55.6	42.5	27.5	60.9	14.4	19.3	12.5	17.8
MIDDLE ATLANTIC												
1,904 agencies;												
population 26,960,429												
Offenses known	817,280	823,528	102,087	715,193	1,199	5,970	37,885	57,033	132,617	497,265	85,311	6,248
Percent cleared by arrest	24.7	24.6	52.2	20.7	71.0	53.8	30.9	65.9	17.7	22.6	14.6	20.6
NORTHEAST												
2,644 agencies;												
population 38,102,402												
Offenses known	1,147,760	1,156,163	138,802	1,008,958	1,505	8,864	48,057	80,376	187,009	698,689	123,260	8,403
Percent cleared by arrest	23.6	23.6	51.7	19.8	67.8	50.1	30.2	64.4	16.7	21.6	13.9	19.9
EAST NORTH CENTRAL												
1,542 agencies;												
population 26,746,212												
Offenses known	1,109,027	1,119,222	115,417	993,610	1,511	11,087	37,586	65,233	201,961	673,468	118,181	10,195
Percent cleared by arrest	17.1	17.1	37.6	14.7	56.8	36.9	19.6	47.6	10.0	16.2	14.4	12.9
WEST NORTH CENTRAL												
1,139 agencies;												
population 14,817,108												
Offenses known	562,552	566,659	48,837	513,715	526	4,234	11,056	33,021	85,925	379,680	48,110	4,107
Percent cleared by arrest	21.2	21.2	52.2	18.3	70.0	45.5	26.5	61.4	13.7	19.3	18.5	19.4
MIDWEST												
2,681 agencies;												
population 41,563,320												
Offenses known	1,671,579	1,685,881	164,254	1,507,325	2,037	15,321	48,642	98,254	287,886	1,053,148	166,291	14,302
Percent cleared by arrest	18.5	18.5	41.9	15.9	60.2	39.3	21.2	52.2	11.1	17.3	15.6	14.8

See footnotes at end of table.

Table 26

Percent of Offenses Cleared by Arrest or Exceptional Means[1]
by Geographic Region and Division, 2001—Continued
[2001 estimated population]

Geographic region/division	Crime Index total	Modified Crime Index total[2]	Violent crime[3]	Property crime[4]	Murder and non-negligent man-slaughter	Forcible rape[5]	Robbery	Aggravated assault	Burglary	Larceny-theft	Motor vehicle theft	Arson[2]
SOUTH ATLANTIC												
1,941 agencies; population 33,305,557												
Offenses known	1,408,847	1,417,732	169,720	1,239,127	2,178	8,631	52,461	106,450	268,542	848,474	122,111	8,885
Percent cleared by arrest	20.3	20.3	47.2	16.6	66.3	48.2	24.7	57.7	13.9	17.4	17.3	18.3
EAST SOUTH CENTRAL												
801 agencies; population 10,805,527												
Offenses known	501,832	504,138	60,139	441,693	788	3,796	16,654	38,901	104,043	294,830	42,820	2,306
Percent cleared by arrest	18.7	18.7	38.6	16.0	57.0	36.6	20.8	46.0	11.6	17.9	13.9	17.9
WEST SOUTH CENTRAL												
1,600 agencies; population 31,256,238												
Offenses known	1,570,008	1,581,155	178,318	1,391,690	2,125	11,710	47,444	117,039	300,081	949,415	142,194	11,147
Percent cleared by arrest	19.0	19.0	45.5	15.7	69.4	47.5	26.2	52.6	12.1	17.0	14.5	17.4
SOUTH												
4,342 agencies; population 75,367,322												
Offenses known	**3,480,687**	**3,503,025**	**408,177**	**3,072,510**	**5,091**	**24,137**	**116,559**	**262,390**	**672,666**	**2,092,719**	**307,125**	**22,338**
Percent cleared by arrest	**19.5**	**19.5**	**45.1**	**16.1**	**66.1**	**46.0**	**24.7**	**53.7**	**12.7**	**17.3**	**15.6**	**17.8**
MOUNTAIN												
717 agencies; population 17,424,131												
Offenses known	829,674	834,583	77,233	752,441	950	6,293	20,938	49,052	139,049	510,935	102,457	4,909
Percent cleared by arrest	18.7	18.7	44.3	16.1	61.7	39.9	22.8	53.7	11.8	18.0	12.5	17.4
PACIFIC												
1,091 agencies; population 42,348,878												
Offenses known	1,754,632	1,772,408	235,668	1,518,964	2,399	13,292	69,881	150,096	298,464	974,458	246,042	17,776
Percent cleared by arrest	18.7	18.6	48.2	14.1	53.0	45.2	24.9	59.2	12.3	15.7	10.1	12.6
WEST												
1,808 agencies; population 59,773,009												
Offenses known	**2,584,306**	**2,606,991**	**312,901**	**2,271,405**	**3,349**	**19,585**	**90,819**	**199,148**	**437,513**	**1,485,393**	**348,499**	**22,685**
Percent cleared by arrest	**18.7**	**18.7**	**47.2**	**14.8**	**55.5**	**43.5**	**24.4**	**57.8**	**12.1**	**16.5**	**10.8**	**13.7**

[1] The murders and nonnegligent homicides that occurred as a result of the events of September 11, 2001, were not included in any clearance tables (Tables 25-28). See special report, Section V.

[2] Because arson is reported to the FBI separately from other offenses, the number of agency reports used in arson clearance rates is less than those used in compiling other Crime Index offense clearance rates. The Modified Crime Index total is the sum of the Crime Index offenses, including arson.

[3] Violent crimes are offenses of murder, forcible rape, robbery, and aggravated assault.

[4] Property crimes are offenses of burglary, larceny-theft, and motor vehicle theft.

[5] Forcible rape figures furnished by the state Uniform Crime Reporting (UCR) Program administered by the Illinois State Police were not in accordance with national UCR guidelines; therefore, the figures were excluded from the forcible rape, violent crime, Crime Index total, and Modified Crime Index total categories.

Table 27

Percent of Offenses Cleared by Arrest or Exceptional Means[1]

Breakdown of Offenses Known
by Population Group, 2001
[2001 estimated population]

Population Group	Forcible rape[2] Rape by force	Forcible rape[2] Assault to rape-attempts	Robbery Firearm	Robbery Knife or cutting instrument	Robbery Other weapon	Robbery Strong-arm	Aggravated assault Firearm	Aggravated assault Knife or cutting instrument	Aggravated assault Other weapon	Aggravated assault Hands, fists feet, etc.	Burglary Forcible entry	Burglary Unlawful entry	Burglary Attempted forcible entry	Motor vehicle theft Autos	Motor vehicle theft Trucks and buses	Motor vehicle theft Other vehicles	Arson[3] Structure	Arson[3] Mobile	Arson[3] Other
TOTAL ALL AGENCIES: 11,446 agencies; population 213,346,987																			
Offenses known	60,426	6,792	127,085	26,299	30,975	115,714	119,625	113,700	216,991	184,822	996,448	470,887	102,699	694,344	172,360	67,597	27,037	21,305	16,577
Percent cleared by arrest	44.3	45.2	20.3	27.3	26.6	29.4	41.1	61.9	55.3	63.8	12.3	14.1	10.7	14.1	11.6	13.1	22.2	7.1	18.4
TOTAL CITIES: 8,194 cities; population 143,841,165																			
Offenses known	45,684	5,403	113,848	23,757	27,424	105,741	97,593	93,709	172,317	137,671	748,876	350,974	80,575	597,672	145,048	46,383	20,714	15,554	12,293
Percent cleared by arrest	43.6	44.3	19.7	26.8	26.2	28.9	37.8	60.7	53.7	63.3	11.7	14.0	10.3	13.3	10.7	12.6	21.6	6.8	18.5
GROUP I																			
59 cities, 250,000 and over; population 37,753,658																			
Offenses known	15,953	2,302	66,523	12,572	14,823	55,087	54,506	42,401	79,718	46,748	290,061	105,690	24,374	288,097	88,738	18,348	8,475	8,273	3,747
Percent cleared by arrest	45.2	46.4	17.4	23.6	23.6	25.6	32.7	57.9	50.2	58.4	9.8	11.5	9.1	11.3	8.6	10.6	18.0	4.2	14.5
8 cities, 1,000,000 and over; population 13,396,369																			
Offenses known	4,778	931	25,900	5,627	4,698	20,967	21,357	15,268	25,733	22,719	89,529	34,903	6,628	95,408	37,371	7,774	2,547	3,414	1,266
Percent cleared by arrest	44.2	46.7	17.3	22.7	23.7	27.2	29.7	56.7	50.6	64.9	10.8	12.2	9.9	11.9	5.7	6.7	16.5	3.8	11.1
20 cities, 500,000 to 999,999; population 13,278,524																			
Offenses known	5,969	772	22,563	3,882	6,624	16,688	18,520	15,208	30,873	13,969	113,243	34,721	10,573	101,245	28,409	5,797	2,413	1,901	937
Percent cleared by arrest	46.1	49.4	15.5	22.7	21.6	22.5	32.0	54.4	46.3	45.5	8.1	9.4	8.1	11.3	11.1	7.2	22.5	5.0	16.1
31 cities, 250,000 to 499,999; population 11,078,765																			
Offenses known	5,206	599	18,060	3,063	3,501	17,432	14,629	11,925	23,112	10,060	87,289	36,066	7,173	91,444	22,958	4,777	3,515	2,958	1,544
Percent cleared by arrest	45.2	42.2	19.9	26.2	27.3	26.6	37.9	64.0	55.1	61.6	10.8	12.8	9.9	10.8	10.3	21.0	16.0	4.2	16.3
GROUP II																			
138 cities, 100,000 to 249,999; population 20,428,259																			
Offenses known	6,836	763	18,951	3,924	4,640	16,879	14,934	14,085	27,390	15,042	122,329	54,202	12,792	103,303	22,666	6,522	3,211	2,566	1,751
Percent cleared by arrest	41.8	39.6	20.1	26.3	24.6	28.1	36.9	60.0	53.4	62.4	10.7	14.1	10.3	10.7	9.3	8.9	18.8	7.4	18.7
GROUP III																			
338 cities, 50,000 to 99,999; population 23,148,550																			
Offenses known	7,294	674	12,298	3,074	3,217	13,986	11,203	12,545	23,499	19,446	107,902	54,352	13,493	80,763	13,056	6,218	2,860	1,896	2,034
Percent cleared by arrest	41.6	41.1	21.9	28.8	28.2	31.6	41.0	61.7	55.9	65.8	11.6	13.5	9.8	12.1	12.0	12.4	21.5	8.1	18.8

See footnotes at end of table.

Table 27

Percent of Offenses Cleared by Arrest or Exceptional Means[1]

Breakdown of Offenses Known
by Population Group, 2001—Continued
[2001 estimated population]

Population Group	Forcible rape[2] Rape by force	Assault to rape-attempts	Robbery Firearm	Knife or cutting instrument	Other weapon	Strong-arm	Aggravated assault Firearm	Knife or cutting instrument	Other weapon	Hands, fists feet, etc.	Burglary Forcible entry	Unlawful entry	Attempted forcible entry	Motor vehicle theft Autos	Trucks and buses	Other vehicles	Arson[3] Structure	Mobile	Other
GROUP IV																			
611 cities, 25,000 to 49,999; population 21,258,685																			
Offenses known	5,770	537	7,166	1,923	2,102	8,835	6,280	8,852	15,674	16,109	81,599	48,363	11,096	51,765	8,296	5,150	2,109	1,220	1,872
Percent cleared by arrest	41.7	38.4	26.4	33.0	31.7	34.9	49.5	63.8	58.2	65.0	13.3	14.3	10.1	16.0	16.0	13.2	24.0	9.5	20.4
GROUP V																			
1,432 cities, 10,000 to 24,999; population 22,765,497																			
Offenses known	5,566	562	5,685	1,399	1,747	6,924	6,040	8,726	14,529	18,177	80,590	45,823	10,156	44,091	7,137	5,215	2,045	963	1,367
Percent cleared by arrest	44.5	45.2	28.0	36.7	37.3	36.8	50.5	64.2	58.3	67.0	15.5	16.7	12.0	21.6	21.4	16.7	29.4	14.2	22.6
GROUP VI																			
5,616 cities, under 10,000; population 18,486,516																			
Offenses known	4,265	565	3,225	865	895	4,030	4,630	7,100	11,507	22,149	66,395	42,544	8,664	29,653	5,155	4,930	2,014	636	1,522
Percent cleared by arrest	45.7	50.6	28.7	38.6	36.3	40.6	61.5	68.9	61.8	67.7	16.2	17.4	12.5	27.3	25.2	20.0	30.4	16.7	21.4
SUBURBAN COUNTIES																			
1,087 agencies; population 44,623,475																			
Offenses known	9,856	938	11,665	2,183	3,032	8,642	15,115	14,474	33,101	29,769	161,118	81,060	15,684	77,936	22,155	14,178	4,328	4,712	3,454
Percent cleared by arrest	43.8	45.7	23.5	29.6	27.7	33.6	52.9	67.2	60.4	65.2	12.9	13.5	10.8	16.3	13.7	12.4	22.8	5.9	16.4
RURAL COUNTIES																			
2,165 agencies; population 24,882,347																			
Offenses known	4,886	451	1,572	359	519	1,331	6,917	5,517	11,573	17,382	86,454	38,853	6,440	18,736	5,157	7,036	1,995	1,039	830
Percent cleared by arrest	51.8	54.8	37.5	44.3	41.8	44.3	61.9	68.1	64.4	65.1	16.2	16.7	15.5	32.1	28.3	17.7	28.0	16.7	26.0
SUBURBAN AREA[4]																			
5,444 agencies; population 85,842,507																			
Offenses known	17,952	1,895	21,826	4,713	5,800	20,898	23,059	26,288	54,522	59,927	282,540	159,417	33,183	165,355	35,456	23,653	7,712	6,462	6,464
Percent cleared by arrest	43.6	45.3	23.8	31.6	30.9	34.4	52.1	66.6	60.0	66.7	13.3	14.3	10.5	16.8	14.8	13.1	25.1	8.0	18.9

[1] The murders and nonnegligent homicides that occurred as a result of the events of September 11, 2001, were not included in any clearance tables (Tables 25-28). See special report, Section V.

[2] Forcible rape figures furnished by the state Uniform Crime Reporting (UCR) Program administered by the Illinois State Police were not in accordance with national UCR guidelines; therefore, the figures were excluded from the forcible rape category.

[3] Because arson is reported to the FBI separately from other offenses, the number of agency reports used in arson clearance rates is less than those used in compiling other Crime Index offense clearance rates. It is necessary to report arson clearances by detailed property classification as specified on the *Monthly Return of Arson Offenses Known to Law Enforcement* to be included in this table, and so clearances in this table may differ from other clearance tables.

[4] Suburban area includes city law enforcement agencies with less than 50,000 inhabitants and county law enforcement agencies that are within a Metropolitan Statistical Area (see Appendix III). Suburban area excludes all metropolitan agencies associated with a central city. The agencies associated with suburban areas will also appear in other groups within this table.

Table 28

Number of Offenses Cleared by Arrest or Exceptional Means[1]
of Only Persons Under 18 Years of Age, 2001
by Population Group, 2001
[2001 estimated population]

Population group	Crime Index total	Modified Crime Index total[2]	Violent crime[3]	Property crime[4]	Murder and non-negligent man-slaughter	Forcible rape[5]	Robbery	Aggravated assault	Burglary	Larceny-theft	Motor vehicle theft	Arson[2]
TOTAL ALL AGENCIES: 11,168 agencies; population 206,488,238												
Total clearances	1,661,135	1,671,507	452,230	1,208,905	7,123	28,557	72,115	344,435	192,481	894,672	121,752	10,372
Percent under 18	18.6	18.8	12.1	21.1	5.0	12.4	14.4	11.8	18.5	21.9	19.2	45.5
TOTAL CITIES: 8,061 cities; population 138,915,325												
Total clearances	1,332,864	1,340,432	352,989	979,875	5,468	21,251	63,665	262,605	139,442	744,167	96,266	7,568
Percent under 18	19.2	19.3	12.2	21.7	5.4	11.8	14.5	11.8	18.3	22.6	19.7	48.2
GROUP I												
55 cities, 250,000 and over; population 35,330,312												
Total clearances	396,473	398,708	143,910	252,563	2,831	7,620	30,238	103,221	40,031	172,668	39,864	2,235
Percent under 18	15.4	15.6	10.3	18.3	5.6	9.4	13.7	9.5	14.7	18.7	20.5	47.6
8 cities, 1,000,000 and over; population 13,396,369												
Total clearances	149,030	149,721	58,928	90,102	1,078	2,549	12,563	42,738	14,597	61,476	14,029	691
Percent under 18	14.2	14.4	8.8	17.7	6.2	8.8	13.3	7.6	14.4	17.9	20.2	47.5
17 cities, 500,000 to 999,999; population 11,195,703												
Total clearances	113,979	114,607	40,421	73,558	881	2,556	7,856	29,128	11,003	49,725	12,830	628
Percent under 18	15.1	15.2	10.3	17.7	4.3	9.8	14.2	9.4	14.1	18.2	18.7	45.1
30 cities, 250,000 to 499,999; population 10,738,240												
Total clearances	133,464	134,380	44,561	88,903	872	2,515	9,819	31,355	14,431	61,467	13,005	916
Percent under 18	17.1	17.3	12.3	19.5	6.1	9.6	13.8	12.2	15.4	19.9	22.6	49.3
GROUP II												
133 cities, 100,000 to 249,999; population 19,722,037												
Total clearances	194,539	195,637	51,026	143,513	790	3,035	10,397	36,804	21,060	109,431	13,022	1,098
Percent under 18	19.6	19.8	12.0	22.3	6.8	10.0	14.4	11.6	17.4	23.5	20.1	47.4
GROUP III												
331 cities, 50,000 to 99,999; population 22,686,410												
Total clearances	205,528	206,660	50,348	155,180	593	3,243	8,756	37,756	20,754	122,642	11,784	1,132
Percent under 18	21.3	21.4	12.9	24.0	5.4	12.1	15.5	12.5	18.9	25.3	19.3	46.7

See footnotes at end of table.

Table 28

Number of Offenses Cleared by Arrest or Exceptional Means[1]
of Only Persons Under 18 Years of Age, 2001
by Population Group, 2001—Continued
[2001 estimated population]

Population group	Crime Index total	Modified Crime Index total[2]	Violent crime[3]	Property crime[4]	Murder and non-negligent man-slaughter	Forcible rape[5]	Robbery	Aggravated assault	Burglary	Larceny-theft	Motor vehicle theft	Arson[2]
GROUP IV												
596 cities, 25,000 to 49,999; population 20,739,761												
Total clearances	176,008	177,002	36,015	139,993	456	2,495	5,973	27,091	17,924	112,144	9,925	994
Percent under 18	21.9	22.0	14.4	23.8	3.5	13.8	16.6	14.1	20.8	24.6	20.1	51.6
GROUP V												
1,398 cities, 10,000 to 24,999; population 22,228,130												
Total clearances	194,949	196,007	36,653	158,296	448	2,657	5,135	28,413	20,740	126,059	11,497	1,058
Percent under 18	20.9	21.1	14.3	22.4	4.5	15.7	14.1	14.4	20.4	23.3	17.2	50.3
GROUP VI												
5,548 cities, under 10,000; population 18,208,675												
Total clearances	165,367	166,418	35,037	130,330	350	2,201	3,166	29,320	18,933	101,223	10,174	1,051
Percent under 18	20.2	20.3	14.5	21.7	4.3	15.4	15.4	14.4	21.9	22.0	18.6	46.2
SUBURBAN COUNTIES												
1,028 agencies; population 43,382,015												
Total clearances	225,476	227,320	68,382	157,094	1,008	4,615	6,972	55,787	32,339	107,791	16,964	1,844
Percent under 18	17.0	17.2	12.6	18.8	4.6	14.0	14.6	12.4	19.4	18.9	17.1	43.5
RURAL COUNTIES												
2,079 agencies; population 24,190,898												
Total clearances	102,795	103,755	30,859	71,936	647	2,691	1,478	26,043	20,700	42,714	8,522	960
Percent under 18	15.1	15.2	10.3	17.1	2.5	14.5	9.1	10.1	17.9	16.5	18.1	28.0
SUBURBAN AREA[6]												
5,312 agencies; population 83,746,625												
Total clearances	518,754	522,434	124,675	394,079	1,615	8,443	15,168	99,449	61,701	297,498	34,880	3,680
Percent under 18	19.1	19.3	13.9	20.8	4.0	14.7	15.6	13.8	19.9	21.3	17.5	47.1

[1] The murders and nonnegligent homicides that occurred as a result of the events of September 11, 2001, were not included in any clearance tables (Tables 25-28). See special report, Section V.

[2] Because arson is reported to the FBI separately from other offenses, the number of agency reports used in arson clearance rates is less than those used in compiling other Crime Index offense clearance rates. The Modified Crime Index total is the sum of the Crime Index offenses, including arson.

[3] Violent crimes are offenses of murder, forcible rape, robbery, and aggravated assault.

[4] Property crimes are offenses of burglary, larceny-theft, and motor vehicle theft.

[5] Forcible rape figures furnished by the state Uniform Crime Reporting (UCR) Program administered by the Illinois State Police were not in accordance with national UCR guidelines; therefore, the figures were excluded from the forcible rape, violent crime, Crime Index total, and Modified Crime Index total categories.

[6] Suburban area includes city law enforcement agencies with less than 50,000 inhabitants and county law enforcement agencies that are within a Metropolitan Statistical Area (see Appendix III). Suburban area excludes all metropolitan agencies associated with a central city. The agencies associated with suburban areas will also appear in other groups within this table.

SECTION IV

Persons Arrested

In protecting the public, law officers rely on their powers of arrest, which provide them with the legal authority to deprive deviant individuals of their liberty and hold them accountable for antisocial behavior. Because arrests are the ultimate goal of criminal investigations, the level of arrests is often viewed as a measure of police effectiveness. Although there is considerable variation in the allocation of law enforcement resources from place to place and even from time to time within the same agency, arrests for serious crime (e.g., murder, rape, robbery) are strongly pursued in all venues.

For UCR reporting purposes, one arrest is counted for each separate occasion in which an individual is taken into custody, notified to appear, or cited for an offense. Because one individual may be arrested several times during the year for different offenses, the arrest figures in this section should not be viewed as an annual accounting of the number of persons arrested but, rather, as an index of the number of arrests made by law enforcement.

National Distributions

The Nation's law enforcement made an estimated 13.7 million arrests for criminal offenses (excluding traffic violations) during 2001. Approximately 2.2 million of the estimated arrests for 2001 involved Crime Index offenses, which accounted for 16.4 percent of total arrests. (See Table 29.) During 2001, there was an overall decrease of 2.1 percent from the number of arrests during the previous year. The total arrests for Index offenses reflected a small decrease from the prior year's total (-0.7 percent). Within the Crime Index, violent crime arrests increased slightly, 0.1 percent, and property crime arrests declined 1.0 percent. (See Table 36.)

The 5- and 10-year arrest trends indicated an 8.9-percent decrease from the 1997 arrest figure and a 0.5-percent increase from the 1992 number. (See Tables 32, 34, and 36.)

By Age, Sex, and Race

Nationally, adults made up 83.3 percent of the persons arrested in the United States during 2001. Approximately 45.9 percent of the total arrests nationwide involved persons under the age of 25, 31.4 percent were under the age of 21, and 16.7 percent of the total were under the age of 18. In terms of violent crime arrests, 44.2 percent of total arrestees were under 25 years of age, 29.0 percent were under 21 years of age, and 15.4 percent were under the age of 18. A review of arrests for property crimes indicated that 58.3 percent of arrestees were under 25 years of age, 46.7 percent were under 21 years of age, and 30.4 percent were under 18 years of age. (See Tables 38 and 41.)

Approximately 77.5 percent of arrestees nationwide were male. Males accounted for 82.7 percent of violent crime arrestees, and they comprised 69.6 percent of total arrestees for property crimes. Males were most often arrested for drug abuse violations, whereas females were most often arrested for larceny-theft. (See Table 42.)

By race, 69.5 percent of total arrestees during 2001 were white, 28.1 percent were

Table 4.1

Arrests for Drug Abuse Violations
by Region, 2001

Drug abuse violations	United States total	North-eastern states	Mid-western states	Southern states	Western states
Total[1]	100.0	100.0	100.0	100.0	100.0
Sale/Manufacturing:[1]	19.4	27.3	19.2	18.3	16.6
Heroin or cocaine and their derivatives	9.7	18.8	5.7	10.1	6.2
Marijuana	5.2	6.5	7.5	4.6	4.4
Synthetic or manufactured drugs	1.4	0.9	1.3	2.2	0.8
Other dangerous nonnarcotic drugs	3.1	1.1	4.7	1.5	5.1
Possession:[1]	80.6	72.7	80.8	81.7	83.4
Heroin or cocaine and their derivatives	23.1	25.2	13.3	23.5	25.1
Marijuana	40.4	41.6	51.6	48.0	28.5
Synthetic or manufactured drugs	2.7	1.7	2.7	3.5	2.4
Other dangerous nonnarcotic drugs	14.4	4.2	13.1	6.6	27.4

[1] Because of rounding, the percentages may not add to total.

Table 29

Estimated Arrests
United States, 2001

Total[1,2]	13,699,254	Embezzlement	20,157
		Stolen property; buying, receiving, possessing	121,972
Murder and nonnegligent manslaughter	13,653	Vandalism	270,645
Forcible rape	27,270	Weapons; carrying, possessing, etc.	165,896
Robbery	108,400	Prostitution and commercialized vice	80,854
Aggravated assault	477,809	Sex offenses (except forcible rape and prostitution)	91,828
Burglary	291,444	Drug abuse violations	1,586,902
Larceny-theft	1,160,821	Gambling	11,112
Motor vehicle theft	147,451	Offenses against the family and children	143,683
Arson	18,749	Driving under the influence	1,434,852
		Liquor laws	610,591
Violent crime[3]	627,132	Drunkenness	618,668
Property crime[4]	1,618,465	Disorderly conduct	621,394
Crime Index total[5]	2,245,597	Vagrancy	27,935
		All other offenses	3,618,164
Other assaults	1,315,807	Suspicion	3,955
Forgery and counterfeiting	113,741	Curfew and loitering law violations	142,889
Fraud	323,308	Runaways	133,259

[1] Does not include suspicion.
[2] Because of rounding, the figures may not add to total.
[3] Violent crimes are offenses of murder, forcible rape, robbery, and aggravated assault.
[4] Property crimes are offenses of burglary, larceny-theft, motor vehicle theft, and arson.
[5] Includes arson.

black, and the remainder were of other races. Whites accounted for 60.2 percent of the total arrestees for violent crime and 66.0 percent of property crime arrestees. Whites were most frequently arrested for driving under the influence. Blacks were most often arrested for drug abuse violations. (See Table 43.)

Drug and Alcohol Offenses

Overall drug arrests reported for 2001 revealed a 1.4-percent decline from the 2000 figure. (See Table 36.) However, arrests for drug abuse violations have increased 40.3 percent since 1992, and juvenile arrests for these offenses have increased 121.3 percent since the 1992 report. (See Table 32.) During 2001, adults accounted for 87.2 percent of drug abuse arrests, and males accounted for 82.2 percent of the total. (See Tables 38 and 42.) Of all arrests for drug abuse violations, 40.4 percent were for possession of marijuana. Possession of heroin, cocaine, and their derivatives accounted for 23.1 percent of total drug arrests. (See Table 4.1.)

Arrests for drug- and alcohol-related offenses during 2001 accounted for an estimated 4.3 million arrests—31.0 percent of the total. Arrests for drug abuse violations were estimated at 1.6 million, and arrests for driving under the influence were estimated at 1.4 million. Approximately 610,591 arrests involved liquor law violations. Arrests for drunkenness were approximated at 618,668. (See Table 29.) Male offenders accounted for 82.4 percent of total arrests for drug and alcohol offenses during 2001. (See Table 42.)

Regional Offense Distributions and Rates

The U.S. is divided into four regions: the Northeast, the Midwest, the South, and the West. (See Appendix III.) In 2001, data collected regarding the Nation's four regions reflect the following:

The Northeast

During 2001, the Northeast Region recorded an overall arrest rate of 4,014.1 per 100,000 inhabitants. The region reported an arrest rate per 100,000 people of 198.7 for violent crimes and 481.1 for property crimes. Arrest rates for individual violent crimes were measured at 3.2 murder arrests per 100,000 inhabitants, 9.6 forcible rape arrests, 45.4 robbery arrests, and 140.4 aggravated assault arrests per 100,000 inhabitants. In terms of property crimes, the rate of arrests for larceny-theft was measured at 357.8, the arrest rate for burglary was computed at 82.2, and the arrest rate for motor vehicle theft was calculated at 35.3 arrests per 100,000 in population. (See Table 30.)

The Midwest

The Midwest had a total arrest rate of 4,922.2 per 100,000 people in 2001. The regional arrest rate for violent crimes was calculated at 187.2 per 100,000; for property crimes the rate was 608.4 arrests for every 100,000 in population. Individually, the region's arrest rates for violent crime offenses were murder, 5.3; forcible rape, 11.0; robbery, 34.5; and aggravated assault, 136.4 arrests per 100,000 inhabitants. Concerning property crime arrest rates, larceny-theft arrests were computed at 460.8 per 100,000 population, burglary arrests were measured at 78.0 percent, and motor vehicle theft arrests were calculated at 64.0 arrests per 100,000 regional inhabitants. (See Table 30.)

The South

In the South, the most heavily populated region, the overall arrest rate for 2001 was recorded at 5,376.6 arrests per 100,000 in population. The violent crime arrest rate was measured at 202.1, and the property crime arrest rate was 604.4 per 100,000 inhabitants. A breakdown of the individual violent crimes showed that murder had a rate of 6.0 arrests per 100,000 population. Forcible rape arrests were measured at 9.7, robbery arrests at 38.0, and aggravated assault at 148.4 per 100,000 in population. A breakdown of the property crimes for the region showed the Southern States reported an arrest rate of 448.0 for larceny-theft, a rate of 108.9 for burglary, and a rate of 41.5 arrests per 100,000 for motor vehicle theft. (See Table 30.)

The West

In 2001, the Western Region recorded an overall arrest rate of 4,720.7 per 100,000 individuals. The violent crime arrest rate for the Western States was 289.1 per 100,000, and the property crime arrest rate was 602.4 per 100,000 regional inhabitants. Among the specific violent crime offenses, murder had an arrest rate of 4.5 per 100,000; forcible rape, 8.9; robbery, 41.5 arrests per 100,000; and aggravated assault, 234.2 arrests per 100,000 inhabitants. Within property crime arrest rates, the larceny-theft arrest rate was recorded at 399.0 per 100,000 individuals; the burglary arrest rate, 124.9; and the motor vehicle theft arrest rate, 70.2 arrests for every 100,000 in population. (See Table 30.)

In 2001, the Nation's smallest cities, those with fewer than 10,000 residents, reported the highest arrest rate, 6,308.4 for 100,000 inhabitants. Those communities also recorded a violent crime arrest rate of 179.0 and a property crime arrest rate of 618.8 per 100,000 in population. The Nation's largest cities, those with populations of more than 250,000, recorded an overall arrest rate of 5,812.0, a violent crime arrest rate of 359.0, and a property crime arrest rate of 758.8 per 100,000 inhabitants. Cities with populations ranging from 25,000 to 49,999 had the lowest overall arrest rate, 4,482.5 per 100,000 persons. The arrest rate for violent crimes in those cities was 188.0 and for property crimes, 632.6. (See Table 31.)

The Nation's rural counties recorded an overall arrest rate of 3,968.3, a violent crime arrest rate of 137.1, and a property crime arrest rate of 289.2 per 100,000 inhabitants. The overall arrest rate for suburban counties was 3,801.5, and this group reported a rate of 167.6 for violent crimes and 358.0 for property crimes per 100,000 in population. (See Table 31.)

Table 30

Number and Rate of Arrests
by Geographic Region, 2001
[Rate: Number of arrests per 100,000 inhabitants]

Offense charged	United States total (9,511 agencies; population 192,580,262)	Northeast (2,329 agencies; population 35,529,176)	Midwest (1,950 agencies; population 34,920,523)	South (3,570 agencies; population 62,802,268)	West (1,662 agencies; population 59,328,295)
TOTAL[1]	9,322,324	1,426,159	1,718,870	3,376,600	2,800,695
Rate	4,840.7	4,014.1	4,922.2	5,376.6	4,720.7
Murder and nonnegligent manslaughter	9,426	1,151	1,858	3,739	2,678
Rate	4.9	3.2	5.3	6.0	4.5
Forcible rape	18,576	3,398	3,835	6,092	5,251
Rate	9.6	9.6	11.0	9.7	8.9
Robbery	76,667	16,145	12,042	23,871	24,609
Rate	39.8	45.4	34.5	38.0	41.5
Aggravated assault	329,722	49,897	47,636	93,226	138,963
Rate	171.2	140.4	136.4	148.4	234.2
Burglary	198,883	29,195	27,235	68,365	74,088
Rate	103.3	82.2	78.0	108.9	124.9
Larceny-theft	806,093	127,123	160,901	281,366	236,703
Rate	418.6	357.8	460.8	448.0	399.0
Motor vehicle theft	102,607	12,528	22,355	26,052	41,672
Rate	53.3	35.3	64.0	41.5	70.2
Arson	12,763	2,093	1,965	3,773	4,932
Rate	6.6	5.9	5.6	6.0	8.3
Violent crime[2]	434,391	70,591	65,371	126,928	171,501
Rate	225.6	198.7	187.2	202.1	289.1
Property crime[3]	1,120,346	170,939	212,456	379,556	357,395
Rate	581.8	481.1	608.4	604.4	602.4
Crime Index total[4]	1,554,737	241,530	277,827	506,484	528,896
Rate	807.3	679.8	795.6	806.5	891.5
Other assaults	898,298	153,884	161,714	356,180	226,520
Rate	466.5	433.1	463.1	567.1	381.8
Forgery and counterfeiting	77,692	10,789	10,044	30,586	26,273
Rate	40.3	30.4	28.8	48.7	44.3
Fraud	211,177	30,930	27,932	130,365	21,950
Rate	109.7	87.1	80.0	207.6	37.0
Embezzlement	13,836	1,102	2,067	7,297	3,370
Rate	7.2	3.1	5.9	11.6	5.7
Stolen property; buying, receiving, possessing	84,047	18,324	17,626	21,032	27,065
Rate	43.6	51.6	50.5	33.5	45.6
Vandalism	184,972	40,818	36,143	45,696	62,315
Rate	96.0	114.9	103.5	72.8	105.0
Weapons; carrying, possessing, etc.	114,325	15,026	21,879	39,557	37,863
Rate	59.4	42.3	62.7	63.0	63.8
Prostitution and commercialized vice	58,638	8,712	12,826	15,454	21,646
Rate	30.4	24.5	36.7	24.6	36.5
Sex offenses (except forcible rape and prostitution)	62,997	10,326	11,722	16,033	24,916
Rate	32.7	29.1	33.6	25.5	42.0
Drug abuse violations	1,091,240	181,783	191,833	352,014	365,610
Rate	566.6	511.6	549.3	560.5	616.2
Gambling	7,769	1,215	3,212	2,479	863
Rate	4.0	3.4	9.2	3.9	1.5
Offenses against the family and children	93,909	25,700	27,362	28,763	12,084
Rate	48.8	72.3	78.4	45.8	20.4
Driving under the influence	946,694	115,792	172,183	331,911	326,808
Rate	491.6	325.9	493.1	528.5	550.8
Liquor laws	408,203	54,922	121,394	97,467	134,420
Rate	212.0	154.6	347.6	155.2	226.6
Drunkenness	423,561	29,615	34,627	245,076	114,243
Rate	219.9	83.4	99.2	390.2	192.6
Disorderly conduct	425,751	120,134	99,543	130,007	76,067
Rate	221.1	338.1	285.1	207.0	128.2
Vagrancy	19,509	4,589	2,580	4,259	8,081
Rate	10.1	12.9	7.4	6.8	13.6
All other offenses (except traffic)	2,453,100	323,606	457,078	959,081	713,335
Rate	1,273.8	910.8	1,308.9	1,527.1	1,202.4
Suspicion	2,629	404	638	1,378	209
Rate	1.4	1.1	1.8	2.2	0.4
Curfew and loitering law violations	100,701	25,760	14,366	23,308	37,267
Rate	52.3	72.5	41.1	37.1	62.8
Runaways	91,168	11,602	14,912	33,551	31,103
Rate	47.3	32.7	42.7	53.4	52.4

[1] Does not include suspicion.
[2] Violent crimes are offenses of murder, forcible rape, robbery, and aggravated assault.
[3] Property crimes are offenses of burglary, larceny-theft, motor vehicle theft, and arson.
[4] Includes arson.

Table 31

Number and Rate of Arrests
by Population Group, 2001
[Rate: Number of arrests per 100,000 inhabitants]

			Cities						Counties		
Offense charged	Total (9,511 agencies; population 192,580,262)	Total cities (6,868 cities; population 133,583,306)	Group I (55 cities, 250,000 and over; population 37,799,072)	Group II (134 cities, 100,000 to 249,999; population 20,033,423)	Group III (300 cities, 50,000 to 99,999; population 20,572,929)	Group IV (569 cities, 25,000 to 49,999; population 19,813,120)	Group V (1,247 cities, 10,000 to 24,999; population 19,804,133)	Group VI (4,563 cities, under 10,000; population 15,565,629)	Suburban counties[1] (889 agencies; population 38,303,583)	Rural counties (1,754 agencies; population 20,688,373)	Suburban area[2] (4,740 agencies; population 79,778,727)
TOTAL[3]	9,322,324	7,045,256	2,196,899	1,035,123	987,549	888,114	955,632	981,939	1,456,093	820,975	3,348,212
Rate	4,840.7	5,273.9	5,812.0	5,167.0	4,800.2	4,482.5	4,825.4	6,308.4	3,801.5	3,968.3	4,196.9
Murder and nonnegligent manslaughter	9,426	6,962	3,603	1,172	721	525	518	423	1,445	1,019	2,345
Rate	4.9	5.2	9.5	5.9	3.5	2.6	2.6	2.7	3.8	4.9	2.9
Forcible rape	18,576	13,531	5,014	2,167	1,780	1,626	1,617	1,327	3,125	1,920	6,201
Rate	9.6	10.1	13.3	10.8	8.7	8.2	8.2	8.5	8.2	9.3	7.8
Robbery	76,667	66,671	31,028	11,740	8,932	6,407	5,228	3,336	7,891	2,105	19,181
Rate	39.8	49.9	82.1	58.6	43.4	32.3	26.4	21.4	20.6	10.2	24.0
Aggravated assault	329,722	254,661	96,044	44,545	36,714	28,690	25,893	22,775	51,739	23,322	105,727
Rate	171.2	190.6	254.1	222.4	178.5	144.8	130.7	146.3	135.1	112.7	132.5
Burglary	198,883	146,699	42,950	26,254	23,409	18,625	18,263	17,198	32,508	19,676	68,622
Rate	103.3	109.8	113.6	131.1	113.8	94.0	92.2	110.5	84.9	95.1	86.0
Larceny-theft	806,093	684,443	197,591	110,676	108,200	99,095	96,916	71,965	88,384	33,266	269,465
Rate	418.6	512.4	522.7	552.5	525.9	500.1	489.4	462.3	230.7	160.8	337.8
Motor vehicle theft	102,607	82,908	42,998	12,624	8,327	6,464	6,463	6,032	13,875	5,824	27,068
Rate	53.3	62.1	113.8	63.0	40.5	32.6	32.6	38.8	36.2	28.2	33.9
Arson	12,763	9,348	3,285	1,305	1,307	1,151	1,175	1,125	2,342	1,073	4,662
Rate	6.6	7.0	8.7	6.5	6.4	5.8	5.9	7.2	6.1	5.2	5.8
Violent crime[4]	434,391	341,825	135,689	59,624	48,147	37,248	33,256	27,861	64,200	28,366	133,454
Rate	225.6	255.9	359.0	297.6	234.0	188.0	167.9	179.0	167.6	137.1	167.3
Property crime[5]	1,120,346	923,398	286,824	150,859	141,243	125,335	122,817	96,320	137,109	59,839	369,817
Rate	581.8	691.2	758.8	753.0	686.5	632.6	620.2	618.8	358.0	289.2	463.6
Crime Index total[6]	1,554,737	1,265,223	422,513	210,483	189,390	162,583	156,073	124,181	201,309	88,205	503,271
Rate	807.3	947.1	1,117.8	1,050.7	920.6	820.6	788.1	797.8	525.6	426.4	630.8
Other assaults	898,298	682,571	217,321	113,843	88,865	82,948	89,912	89,682	139,023	76,704	305,229
Rate	466.5	511.0	574.9	568.3	432.0	418.7	454.0	576.2	363.0	370.8	382.6
Forgery and counterfeiting	77,692	59,756	14,889	9,838	9,648	8,764	8,886	7,731	11,882	6,054	28,225
Rate	40.3	44.7	39.4	49.1	46.9	44.2	44.9	49.7	31.0	29.3	35.4
Fraud	211,177	118,352	20,094	12,793	17,345	17,148	26,560	24,412	52,533	40,292	95,100
Rate	109.7	88.6	53.2	63.9	84.3	86.5	134.1	156.8	137.1	194.8	119.2
Embezzlement	13,836	10,662	2,251	1,945	2,189	1,531	1,516	1,230	2,194	980	4,846
Rate	7.2	8.0	6.0	9.7	10.6	7.7	7.7	7.9	5.7	4.7	6.1
Stolen property; buying, receiving, possessing	84,047	66,148	19,453	10,807	11,934	9,092	8,187	6,675	12,598	5,301	30,976
Rate	43.6	49.5	51.5	53.9	58.0	45.9	41.3	42.9	32.9	25.6	38.8
Vandalism	184,972	145,493	41,948	22,546	20,697	19,283	20,498	20,521	25,416	14,063	65,650
Rate	96.0	108.9	111.0	112.5	100.6	97.3	103.5	131.8	66.4	68.0	82.3
Weapons; carrying, possessing, etc.	114,325	90,144	35,147	14,328	12,043	9,615	9,015	9,996	16,665	7,516	36,599
Rate	59.4	67.5	93.0	71.5	58.5	48.5	45.5	64.2	43.5	36.3	45.9
Prostitution and commercialized vice	58,638	56,333	42,004	7,198	3,809	2,183	818	321	2,127	178	4,969
Rate	30.4	42.2	111.1	35.9	18.5	11.0	4.1	2.1	5.6	0.9	6.2

See footnotes at end of table.

Table 31

Number and Rate of Arrests

by Population Group, 2001—Continued

[Rate: Number of arrests per 100,000 inhabitants]

Offense charged	Total (9,511 agencies; population 192,580,262)	Total cities (6,868 cities; population 133,588,306)	Group I (55 cities, 250,000 and over; population 37,799,072)	Group II (134 cities, 100,000 to 249,999; population 20,033,423)	Group III (300 cities, 50,000 to 99,999; population 20,572,929)	Group IV (569 cities, 25,000 to 49,999; population 19,813,120)	Group V (1,247 cities, 10,000 to 24,999; population 19,804,133)	Group VI (4,563 cities, under 10,000; population 15,565,629)	Suburban counties[1] (889 agencies; population 38,303,583)	Rural counties (1,754 agencies; population 20,688,373)	Suburban area[2] (4,740 agencies; population 79,778,727)
						Cities			**Counties**		
Sex offenses (except forcible rape and prostitution)	62,997	47,017	20,028	6,933	6,263	4,833	4,659	4,301	10,353	5,627	19,913
Rate	32.7	35.2	53.0	34.6	30.4	24.4	23.5	27.6	27.0	27.2	25.0
Drug abuse violations	1,091,240	840,392	337,089	130,892	112,000	89,186	85,289	85,936	169,995	80,853	355,853
Rate	566.6	629.1	891.8	653.4	544.4	450.1	430.7	552.1	443.8	390.8	446.0
Gambling	7,769	6,476	4,172	459	1,078	190	220	357	469	824	1,019
Rate	4.0	4.8	11.0	2.3	5.2	1.0	1.1	2.3	1.2	4.0	1.3
Offenses against the family and children	93,909	46,728	8,966	4,590	8,831	8,735	8,241	7,365	33,240	13,941	49,790
Rate	48.8	35.0	23.7	22.9	42.9	44.1	41.6	47.3	86.8	67.4	62.4
Driving under the influence	946,694	586,877	123,189	72,726	80,063	85,549	104,237	121,113	209,217	150,600	417,607
Rate	491.6	439.3	325.9	363.0	389.2	431.8	526.3	778.1	546.2	727.9	523.5
Liquor laws	408,203	319,816	60,488	36,939	45,801	39,484	56,770	80,334	48,106	40,281	154,562
Rate	212.0	239.4	160.0	184.4	222.6	199.3	286.7	516.1	125.6	194.7	193.7
Drunkenness	423,561	354,643	91,519	49,430	50,660	50,944	53,777	58,313	42,584	26,334	142,079
Rate	219.9	265.5	242.1	246.7	246.2	257.1	271.5	374.6	111.2	127.3	178.1
Disorderly conduct	425,751	366,339	103,664	48,509	47,560	45,113	57,567	63,926	36,212	23,200	148,316
Rate	221.1	274.2	274.3	242.1	231.2	227.7	290.7	410.7	94.5	112.1	185.9
Vagrancy	19,509	18,066	9,121	2,108	1,511	1,187	1,423	2,716	1,177	266	4,895
Rate	10.1	13.5	24.1	10.5	7.3	6.0	7.2	17.4	3.1	1.3	6.1
All other offenses (except traffic)	2,453,100	1,802,616	554,028	259,912	254,378	232,667	243,040	258,591	417,925	232,559	924,011
Rate	1,273.8	1,349.4	1,465.7	1,297.4	1,236.5	1,174.3	1,227.2	1,661.3	1,091.1	1,124.1	1,158.2
Suspicion[3]	2,629	1,875	18	233	306	225	615	478	354	400	1,390
Rate	1.4	1.4	[7]	1.2	1.5	1.1	3.1	3.1	0.9	1.9	1.7
Curfew and loitering law violations	100,701	94,882	50,890	7,448	11,156	7,801	9,579	8,008	4,898	921	21,753
Rate	52.3	71.0	134.6	37.2	54.2	39.4	48.4	51.4	12.8	4.5	27.3
Runaways	91,168	66,722	18,125	11,396	12,328	9,278	9,365	6,230	18,170	6,276	33,549
Rate	47.3	49.9	48.0	56.9	59.9	46.8	47.3	40.0	47.4	30.3	42.1

[1] Includes only suburban county law enforcement agencies.
[2] Suburban area includes city law enforcement agencies with less than 50,000 inhabitants and county law enforcement agencies that are within a Metropolitan Statistical Area (see Appendix III). Suburban area excludes all metropolitan agencies associated with a central city. The agencies associated with suburban areas will also appear in other groups within this table.
[3] Does not include suspicion.
[4] Violent crimes are offenses of murder, forcible rape, robbery, and aggravated assault.
[5] Property crimes are offenses of burglary, larceny-theft, motor vehicle theft, and arson.
[6] Includes arson.
[7] Less than one-tenth of 1 percent.

Table 32

Ten-Year Arrest Trends

Totals, 1992-2001

[7,135 agencies; 2001 estimated population 153,526,122; 1992 estimated population 136,880,883]

	Number of persons arrested								
	Total all ages			Under 18 years of age			18 years of age and over		
Offense charged	1992	2001	Percent change	1992	2001	Percent change	1992	2001	Percent change
TOTAL[1]	7,316,610	7,355,385	+0.5	1,238,927	1,207,668	-2.5	6,077,683	6,147,717	+1.2
Murder and nonnegligent manslaughter	10,125	6,665	-34.2	1,519	577	-62.0	8,606	6,088	-29.3
Forcible rape	19,804	14,211	-28.2	3,101	2,342	-24.5	16,703	11,869	-28.9
Robbery	75,195	55,915	-25.6	18,869	12,799	-32.2	56,326	43,116	-23.5
Aggravated assault	272,095	260,146	-4.4	39,555	34,116	-13.8	232,540	226,030	-2.8
Burglary	239,615	161,198	-32.7	84,919	50,856	-40.1	154,696	110,342	-28.7
Larceny-theft	843,493	639,927	-24.1	267,310	195,659	-26.8	576,183	444,268	-22.9
Motor vehicle theft	104,068	72,509	-30.3	46,917	22,826	-51.3	57,151	49,683	-13.1
Arson	11,135	10,430	-6.3	5,698	5,278	-7.4	5,437	5,152	-5.2
Violent crime[2]	377,219	336,937	-10.7	63,044	49,834	-21.0	314,175	287,103	-8.6
Property crime[3]	1,198,311	884,064	-26.2	404,844	274,619	-32.2	793,467	609,445	-23.2
Crime Index total[4]	1,575,530	1,221,001	-22.5	467,888	324,453	-30.7	1,107,642	896,548	-19.1
Other assaults	588,089	696,504	+18.4	97,042	125,968	+29.8	491,047	570,536	+16.2
Forgery and counterfeiting	55,189	64,655	+17.2	4,625	3,364	-27.3	50,564	61,291	+21.2
Fraud	205,919	173,374	-15.8	5,058	4,793	-5.2	200,861	168,581	-16.1
Embezzlement	7,798	11,597	+48.7	417	1,052	+152.3	7,381	10,545	+42.9
Stolen property; buying, receiving, possessing	90,934	66,389	-27.0	26,106	14,274	-45.3	64,828	52,115	-19.6
Vandalism	175,938	146,721	-16.6	81,068	57,897	-28.6	94,870	88,824	-6.4
Weapons; carrying, possessing, etc.	129,122	87,444	-32.3	30,152	19,563	-35.1	98,970	67,881	-31.4
Prostitution and commercialized vice	46,142	37,245	-19.3	701	643	-8.3	45,441	36,602	-19.5
Sex offenses (except forcible rape and prostitution)	59,048	49,005	-17.0	10,719	9,690	-9.6	48,329	39,315	-18.7
Drug abuse violations	585,345	821,360	+40.3	46,611	103,148	+121.3	538,734	718,212	+33.3
Gambling	6,681	3,021	-54.8	578	272	-52.9	6,103	2,749	-55.0
Offenses against the family and children	60,793	78,730	+29.5	2,442	5,092	+108.5	58,351	73,638	+26.2
Driving under the influence	939,528	795,580	-15.3	8,500	11,441	+34.6	931,028	784,139	-15.8
Liquor laws	281,885	339,496	+20.4	64,177	77,415	+20.6	217,708	262,081	+20.4
Drunkenness	490,533	360,905	-26.4	11,187	11,649	+4.1	479,346	349,256	-27.1
Disorderly conduct	350,998	315,435	-10.1	64,385	86,104	+33.7	286,613	229,331	-20.0
Vagrancy	14,269	14,847	+4.1	2,149	1,359	-36.8	12,120	13,488	+11.3
All other offenses (except traffic)	1,505,232	1,935,465	+28.6	167,485	212,880	+27.1	1,337,747	1,722,585	+28.8
Suspicion	4,687	1,814	-61.3	1,232	579	-53.0	3,455	1,235	-64.3
Curfew and loitering law violations	43,337	58,204	+34.3	43,337	58,204	+34.3	–	–	–
Runaways	104,300	78,407	-24.8	104,300	78,407	-24.8	–	–	–

[1] Does not include suspicion.

[2] Violent crimes are offenses of murder, forcible rape, robbery, and aggravated assault.

[3] Property crimes are offenses of burglary, larceny-theft, motor vehicle theft, and arson.

[4] Includes arson.

Table 33

Ten-Year Arrest Trends
by Sex, 1992-2001
[7,135 agencies; 2001 estimated population 153,526,122; 1992 estimated population 136,880,883]

| | Male | | | | | | Female | | | | | |
| | Total | | | Under 18 | | | Total | | | Under 18 | | |
Offense charged	1992	2001	Percent change	1992	2001	Percent change	1992	2001	Percent change	1992	2001	Percent change
TOTAL[1]	**5,901,221**	**5,687,567**	**-3.6**	**945,035**	**858,416**	**-9.2**	**1,415,389**	**1,667,818**	**+17.8**	**293,892**	**349,252**	**+18.8**
Murder and nonnegligent manslaughter	9,128	5,731	-37.2	1,420	508	-64.2	997	934	-6.3	99	69	-30.3
Forcible rape	19,561	14,038	-28.2	3,042	2,312	-24.0	243	173	-28.8	59	30	-49.2
Robbery	68,572	50,219	-26.8	17,317	11,695	-32.5	6,623	5,696	-14.0	1,552	1,104	-28.9
Aggravated assault	233,006	208,664	-10.4	33,230	26,302	-20.8	39,089	51,482	+31.7	6,325	7,814	+23.5
Burglary	215,433	138,832	-35.6	76,831	44,560	-42.0	24,182	22,366	-7.5	8,088	6,296	-22.2
Larceny-theft	568,462	403,093	-29.1	187,832	118,828	-36.7	275,031	236,834	-13.9	79,478	76,831	-3.3
Motor vehicle theft	91,913	60,323	-34.4	40,546	18,650	-54.0	12,155	12,186	+0.3	6,371	4,176	-34.5
Arson	9,721	8,809	-9.4	5,094	4,650	-8.7	1,414	1,621	+14.6	604	628	+4.0
Violent crime[2]	330,267	278,652	-15.6	55,009	40,817	-25.8	46,952	58,285	+24.1	8,035	9,017	+12.2
Property crime[3]	885,529	611,057	-31.0	310,303	186,688	-39.8	312,782	273,007	-12.7	94,541	87,931	-7.0
Crime Index total[4]	1,215,796	889,709	-26.8	365,312	227,505	-37.7	359,734	331,292	-7.9	102,576	96,948	-5.5
Other assaults	484,870	531,728	+9.7	72,894	85,896	+17.8	103,219	164,776	+59.6	24,148	40,072	+65.9
Forgery and counterfeiting	35,614	38,746	+8.8	2,978	2,143	-28.0	19,575	25,909	+32.4	1,647	1,221	-25.9
Fraud	111,561	93,632	-16.1	3,439	3,136	-8.8	94,358	79,742	-15.5	1,619	1,657	+2.3
Embezzlement	4,613	5,774	+25.2	228	588	+157.9	3,185	5,823	+82.8	189	464	+145.5
Stolen property; buying, receiving, possessing	79,341	55,244	-30.4	23,310	12,192	-47.7	11,593	11,145	-3.9	2,796	2,082	-25.5
Vandalism	155,959	123,272	-21.0	74,001	50,336	-32.0	19,979	23,449	+17.4	7,067	7,561	+7.0
Weapons; carrying, possessing, etc.	119,662	80,384	-32.8	28,063	17,639	-37.1	9,460	7,060	-25.4	2,089	1,924	-7.9
Prostitution and commercialized vice	17,410	13,692	-21.4	352	208	-40.9	28,732	23,553	-18.0	349	435	+24.6
Sex offenses (except forcible rape and prostitution)	54,908	45,437	-17.2	10,033	8,969	-10.6	4,140	3,568	-13.8	686	721	+5.1
Drug abuse violations	486,209	671,271	+38.1	40,928	86,065	+110.3	99,136	150,089	+51.4	5,683	17,083	+200.6
Gambling	5,857	2,595	-55.7	545	251	-53.9	824	426	-48.3	33	21	-36.4
Offenses against the family and children	51,590	61,358	+18.9	1,662	3,267	+96.6	9,203	17,372	+88.8	780	1,825	+134.0
Driving under the influence	811,087	662,737	-18.3	7,330	9,430	+28.6	128,441	132,843	+3.4	1,170	2,011	+71.9
Liquor laws	227,800	258,471	+13.5	46,066	52,341	+13.6	54,085	81,025	+49.8	18,111	25,074	+38.4
Drunkenness	436,622	311,623	-28.6	9,331	9,245	-0.9	53,911	49,282	-8.6	1,856	2,404	+29.5
Disorderly conduct	280,956	238,226	-15.2	49,831	60,295	+21.0	70,042	77,209	+10.2	14,554	25,809	+77.3
Vagrancy	12,107	11,687	-3.5	1,830	1,102	-39.8	2,162	3,160	+46.2	319	257	-19.4
All other offenses (except traffic)	1,233,342	1,521,269	+23.3	130,985	157,096	+19.9	271,890	414,196	+52.3	36,500	55,784	+52.8
Suspicion	3,999	1,379	-65.5	1,038	376	-63.8	688	435	-36.8	194	203	+4.6
Curfew and loitering law violations	31,198	39,184	+25.6	31,198	39,184	+25.6	12,139	19,020	+56.7	12,139	19,020	+56.7
Runaways	44,719	31,528	-29.5	44,719	31,528	-29.5	59,581	46,879	-21.3	59,581	46,879	-21.3

[1] Does not include suspicion.

[2] Violent crimes are offenses of murder, forcible rape, robbery, and aggravated assault.

[3] Property crimes are offenses of burglary, larceny-theft, motor vehicle theft, and arson.

[4] Includes arson.

Table 34

Five-Year Arrest Trends

Totals, 1997-2001

[7,571 agencies; 2001 estimated population 167,076,444; 1997 estimated population 156,946,206]

Offense charged	Number of persons arrested								
	Total all ages			Under 18 years of age			18 years of age and over		
	1997	2001	Percent change	1997	2001	Percent change	1997	2001	Percent change
TOTAL[1]	8,833,340	8,049,099	-8.9	1,676,590	1,348,515	-19.6	7,156,750	6,700,584	-6.4
Murder and nonnegligent manslaughter	11,070	8,728	-21.2	1,452	765	-47.3	9,618	7,963	-17.2
Forcible rape	19,073	16,767	-12.1	3,277	2,816	-14.1	15,796	13,951	-11.7
Robbery	83,589	68,530	-18.0	24,577	16,096	-34.5	59,012	52,434	-11.1
Aggravated assault	330,948	299,769	-9.4	46,005	39,926	-13.2	284,943	259,843	-8.8
Burglary	215,142	174,909	-18.7	77,625	54,088	-30.3	137,517	120,821	-12.1
Larceny-theft	885,593	695,891	-21.4	296,878	207,838	-30.0	588,715	488,053	-17.1
Motor vehicle theft	102,878	90,778	-11.8	39,968	29,688	-25.7	62,910	61,090	-2.9
Arson	11,316	10,970	-3.1	6,023	5,461	-9.3	5,293	5,509	+4.1
Violent crime[2]	444,680	393,794	-11.4	75,311	59,603	-20.9	369,369	334,191	-9.5
Property crime[3]	1,214,929	972,548	-20.0	420,494	297,075	-29.4	794,435	675,473	-15.0
Crime Index total[4]	1,659,609	1,366,342	-17.7	495,805	356,678	-28.1	1,163,804	1,009,664	-13.2
Other assaults	816,833	771,131	-5.6	143,642	140,824	-2.0	673,191	630,307	-6.4
Forgery and counterfeiting	70,728	67,229	-4.9	4,901	3,631	-25.9	65,827	63,598	-3.4
Fraud	225,726	190,563	-15.6	6,387	5,219	-18.3	219,339	185,344	-15.5
Embezzlement	10,365	12,160	+17.3	827	1,023	+23.7	9,538	11,137	+16.8
Stolen property; buying, receiving, possessing	95,008	74,346	-21.7	24,190	15,328	-36.6	70,818	59,018	-16.7
Vandalism	185,607	159,247	-14.2	81,242	63,302	-22.1	104,365	95,945	-8.1
Weapons; carrying, possessing, etc.	130,290	101,893	-21.8	31,449	23,273	-26.0	98,841	78,620	-20.5
Prostitution and commercialized vice	64,336	48,141	-25.2	907	859	-5.3	63,429	47,282	-25.5
Sex offenses (except forcible rape and prostitution)	59,450	54,778	-7.9	10,120	10,722	+5.9	49,330	44,056	-10.7
Drug abuse violations	969,828	967,524	-0.2	133,400	123,824	-7.2	836,428	843,700	+0.9
Gambling	9,357	6,007	-35.8	1,621	861	-46.9	7,736	5,146	-33.5
Offenses against the family and children	86,442	79,772	-7.7	5,813	5,200	-10.5	80,629	74,572	-7.5
Driving under the influence	831,491	804,737	-3.2	11,051	11,572	+4.7	820,440	793,165	-3.3
Liquor laws	348,774	356,924	+2.3	88,731	80,658	-9.1	260,043	276,266	+6.2
Drunkenness	420,274	365,129	-13.1	14,522	11,454	-21.1	405,752	353,675	-12.8
Disorderly conduct	441,861	341,595	-22.7	118,148	93,810	-20.6	323,713	247,785	-23.5
Vagrancy	19,633	16,066	-18.2	2,009	1,532	-23.7	17,624	14,534	-17.5
All other offenses (except traffic)	2,149,242	2,096,832	-2.4	263,339	230,062	-12.6	1,885,903	1,866,770	-1.0
Suspicion	3,500	1,651	-52.8	1,007	588	-41.6	2,493	1,063	-57.4
Curfew and loitering law violations	124,545	88,603	-28.9	124,545	88,603	-28.9	–	–	–
Runaways	113,941	80,080	-29.7	113,941	80,080	-29.7	–	–	–

[1] Does not include suspicion.

[2] Violent crimes are offenses of murder, forcible rape, robbery, and aggravated assault.

[3] Property crimes are offenses of burglary, larceny-theft, motor vehicle theft, and arson.

[4] Includes arson.

Table 35

Five-Year Arrest Trends

by Sex, 1997-2001

[7,571 agencies; 2001 estimated population 167,076,444; 1997 estimated population 156,946,206]

| | Male | | | | | | Female | | | | | |
| | Total | | | Under 18 | | | Total | | | Under 18 | | |
Offense charged	1997	2001	Percent change	1997	2001	Percent change	1997	2001	Percent change	1997	2001	Percent change
TOTAL[1]	6,927,964	6,238,214	-10.0	1,237,093	967,596	-21.8	1,905,376	1,810,885	-5.0	439,497	380,919	-13.3
Murder and nonnegligent manslaughter	9,952	7,629	-23.3	1,367	683	-50.0	1,118	1,099	-1.7	85	82	-3.5
Forcible rape	18,847	16,557	-12.2	3,211	2,777	-13.5	226	210	-7.1	66	39	-40.9
Robbery	75,288	61,674	-18.1	22,274	14,709	-34.0	8,301	6,856	-17.4	2,303	1,387	-39.8
Aggravated assault	269,295	239,122	-11.2	36,627	30,700	-16.2	61,653	60,647	-1.6	9,378	9,226	-1.6
Burglary	188,745	150,908	-20.0	69,359	47,430	-31.6	26,397	24,001	-9.1	8,266	6,658	-19.5
Larceny-theft	579,835	441,920	-23.8	194,956	126,684	-35.0	305,758	253,971	-16.9	101,922	81,154	-20.4
Motor vehicle theft	87,593	75,976	-13.3	33,520	24,680	-26.4	15,285	14,802	-3.2	6,448	5,008	-22.3
Arson	9,756	9,220	-5.5	5,406	4,812	-11.0	1,560	1,750	+12.2	617	649	+5.2
Violent crime[2]	373,382	324,982	-13.0	63,479	48,869	-23.0	71,298	68,812	-3.5	11,832	10,734	-9.3
Property crime[3]	865,929	678,024	-21.7	303,241	203,606	-32.9	349,000	294,524	-15.6	117,253	93,469	-20.3
Crime Index total[4]	1,239,311	1,003,006	-19.1	366,720	252,475	-31.2	420,298	363,336	-13.6	129,085	104,203	-19.3
Other assaults	642,594	590,558	-8.1	102,075	96,144	-5.8	174,239	180,573	+3.6	41,567	44,680	+7.5
Forgery and counterfeiting	43,628	40,529	-7.1	3,038	2,343	-22.9	27,100	26,700	-1.5	1,863	1,288	-30.9
Fraud	122,240	103,552	-15.3	4,100	3,447	-15.9	103,486	87,011	-15.9	2,287	1,772	-22.5
Embezzlement	5,424	6,050	+11.5	446	547	+22.6	4,941	6,110	+23.7	381	476	+24.9
Stolen property; buying, receiving, possessing	80,200	61,890	-22.8	21,049	13,044	-38.0	14,808	12,456	-15.9	3,141	2,284	-27.3
Vandalism	158,562	133,996	-15.5	71,873	55,164	-23.2	27,045	25,251	-6.6	9,369	8,138	-13.1
Weapons; carrying, possessing, etc.	119,927	93,694	-21.9	28,623	20,837	-27.2	10,363	8,199	-20.9	2,826	2,436	-13.8
Prostitution and commercialized vice	25,674	16,877	-34.3	394	277	-29.7	38,662	31,264	-19.1	513	582	+13.5
Sex offenses (except forcible rape and prostitution)	54,050	50,301	-6.9	9,366	9,946	+6.2	5,400	4,477	-17.1	754	776	+2.9
Drug abuse violations	800,075	794,441	-0.7	115,215	104,893	-9.0	169,753	173,083	+2.0	18,185	18,931	+4.1
Gambling	8,476	5,534	-34.7	1,569	838	-46.6	881	473	-46.3	52	23	-55.8
Offenses against the family and children	68,514	62,009	-9.5	3,653	3,319	-9.1	17,928	17,763	-0.9	2,160	1,881	-12.9
Driving under the influence	704,946	670,883	-4.8	9,208	9,503	+3.2	126,545	133,854	+5.8	1,843	2,069	+12.3
Liquor laws	275,132	272,198	-1.1	62,263	54,536	-12.4	73,642	84,726	+15.1	26,468	26,122	-1.3
Drunkenness	367,444	315,483	-14.1	12,069	9,128	-24.4	52,830	49,646	-6.0	2,453	2,326	-5.2
Disorderly conduct	344,336	260,051	-24.5	88,111	65,977	-25.1	97,525	81,544	-16.4	30,037	27,833	-7.3
Vagrancy	14,985	12,708	-15.2	1,703	1,227	-28.0	4,648	3,358	-27.8	306	305	-0.3
All other offenses (except traffic)	1,717,733	1,651,064	-3.9	200,905	170,561	-15.1	431,509	445,768	+3.3	62,434	59,501	-4.7
Suspicion	2,769	1,239	-55.3	773	376	-51.4	731	412	-43.6	234	212	-9.4
Curfew and loitering law violations	86,882	61,111	-29.7	86,882	61,111	-29.7	37,663	27,492	-27.0	37,663	27,492	-27.0
Runaways	47,831	32,279	-32.5	47,831	32,279	-32.5	66,110	47,801	-27.7	66,110	47,801	-27.7

[1] Does not include suspicion.
[2] Violent crimes are offenses of murder, forcible rape, robbery, and aggravated assault.
[3] Property crimes are offenses of burglary, larceny-theft, motor vehicle theft, and arson.
[4] Includes arson.

Table 36

Current Year Over Previous Year Arrest Trends
Totals, 2000-2001
[8,395 agencies; 2001 estimated population 168,355,554; 2000 estimated population 166,202,749]

Offense charged	Total all ages			Under 15 years of age			Under 18 years of age			18 years of age and over		
	2000	2001	Percent change	2000	2001	Percent change	2000	2001	Percent change	2000	2001	Percent change
TOTAL[1]	8,190,284	8,019,011	-2.1	444,148	427,120	-3.8	1,383,861	1,327,594	-4.1	6,806,423	6,691,417	-1.7
Murder and nonnegligent manslaughter	6,891	6,713	-2.6	82	72	-12.2	623	609	-2.2	6,268	6,104	-2.6
Forcible rape	15,609	15,251	-2.3	988	943	-4.6	2,583	2,547	-1.4	13,026	12,704	-2.5
Robbery	56,829	58,029	+2.1	3,397	3,025	-11.0	13,829	13,343	-3.5	43,000	44,686	+3.9
Aggravated assault	272,521	272,308	-0.1	13,302	13,605	+2.3	37,244	36,753	-1.3	235,277	235,555	+0.1
Burglary	170,018	170,686	+0.4	21,974	20,242	-7.9	57,169	53,977	-5.6	112,849	116,709	+3.4
Larceny-theft	708,718	695,250	-1.9	90,541	83,102	-8.2	228,586	214,288	-6.3	480,132	480,962	+0.2
Motor vehicle theft	73,849	75,827	+2.7	6,524	6,174	-5.4	25,069	24,517	-2.2	48,780	51,310	+5.2
Arson	9,714	11,146	+14.7	3,507	3,666	+4.5	5,299	5,726	+8.1	4,415	5,420	+22.8
Violent crime[2]	351,850	352,301	+0.1	17,769	17,645	-0.7	54,279	53,252	-1.9	297,571	299,049	+0.5
Property crime[3]	962,299	952,909	-1.0	122,546	113,184	-7.6	316,123	298,508	-5.6	646,176	654,401	+1.3
Crime Index total[4]	1,314,149	1,305,210	-0.7	140,315	130,829	-6.8	370,402	351,760	-5.0	943,747	953,450	+1.0
Other assaults	775,915	775,662	[5]	59,909	61,400	+2.5	138,210	140,973	+2.0	637,705	634,689	-0.5
Forgery and counterfeiting	66,091	68,711	+4.0	518	402	-22.4	3,968	3,652	-8.0	62,123	65,059	+4.7
Fraud	199,578	202,020	+1.2	889	818	-8.0	5,515	5,030	-8.8	194,063	196,990	+1.5
Embezzlement	12,433	12,939	+4.1	78	74	-5.1	1,310	1,181	-9.8	11,123	11,758	+5.7
Stolen property; buying, receiving, possessing	73,868	74,214	+0.5	4,987	4,467	-10.4	17,413	16,370	-6.0	56,455	57,844	+2.5
Vandalism	166,179	159,788	-3.8	29,810	27,918	-6.3	67,805	63,346	-6.6	98,374	96,442	-2.0
Weapons; carrying, possessing, etc.	91,241	93,176	+2.1	6,914	7,008	+1.4	20,805	20,733	-0.3	70,436	72,443	+2.8
Prostitution and commercialized vice	44,785	41,434	-7.5	89	105	+18.0	622	713	+14.6	44,163	40,721	-7.8
Sex offenses (except forcible rape and prostitution)	52,701	51,943	-1.4	5,218	5,441	+4.3	10,109	10,253	+1.4	42,592	41,690	-2.1
Drug abuse violations	876,143	864,041	-1.4	18,784	19,808	+5.5	112,052	111,681	-0.3	764,091	752,360	-1.5
Gambling	4,487	4,427	-1.3	86	56	-34.9	371	307	-17.3	4,116	4,120	+0.1
Offenses against the family and children	85,147	85,114	[5]	2,061	2,010	-2.5	5,322	5,623	+5.7	79,825	79,491	-0.4
Driving under the influence	859,990	820,620	-4.6	366	315	-13.9	12,349	11,992	-2.9	847,641	808,628	-4.6
Liquor laws	409,048	378,884	-7.4	9,626	8,145	-15.4	95,641	85,520	-10.6	313,407	293,364	-6.4
Drunkenness	435,864	415,062	-4.8	1,875	1,700	-9.3	14,895	13,378	-10.2	420,969	401,684	-4.6
Disorderly conduct	350,715	337,415	-3.8	36,983	38,428	+3.9	93,321	94,280	+1.0	257,394	243,135	-5.5
Vagrancy	20,406	18,664	-8.5	514	377	-26.7	1,853	1,660	-10.4	18,553	17,004	-8.3
All other offenses (except traffic)	2,186,591	2,159,630	-1.2	70,158	68,247	-2.7	246,945	239,085	-3.2	1,939,646	1,920,545	-1.0
Suspicion	3,407	2,287	-32.9	173	261	+50.9	710	771	+8.6	2,697	1,516	-43.8
Curfew and loitering law violations	75,238	65,510	-12.9	20,459	17,809	-13.0	75,238	65,510	-12.9	–	–	–
Runaways	89,715	84,547	-5.8	34,509	31,763	-8.0	89,715	84,547	-5.8	–	–	–

[1] Does not include suspicion.
[2] Violent crimes are offenses of murder, forcible rape, robbery, and aggravated assault.
[3] Property crimes are offenses of burglary, larceny-theft, motor vehicle theft, and arson.
[4] Includes arson.
[5] Less than one-tenth of 1 percent.

Table 37

Current Year Over Previous Year Arrest Trends

by Sex, 2000-2001
[8,395 agencies; 2001 estimated population 168,355,554; 2000 estimated population 166,202,749]

| | Male | | | | | | Female | | | | | |
| | Total | | | Under 18 | | | Total | | | Under 18 | | |
Offense charged	2000	2001	Percent change	2000	2001	Percent change	2000	2001	Percent change	2000	2001	Percent change
TOTAL[1]	6,351,832	6,185,787	-2.6	992,172	942,725	-5.0	1,838,452	1,833,224	-0.3	391,689	384,869	-1.7
Murder and nonnegligent manslaughter	6,107	5,982	-2.0	546	546	0.0	784	731	-6.8	77	63	-18.2
Forcible rape	15,438	15,077	-2.3	2,558	2,511	-1.8	171	174	+1.8	25	36	+44.0
Robbery	51,090	52,125	+2.0	12,625	12,187	-3.5	5,739	5,904	+2.9	1,204	1,156	-4.0
Aggravated assault	218,067	217,987	[2]	28,746	28,288	-1.6	54,454	54,321	-0.2	8,498	8,465	-0.4
Burglary	146,957	146,985	[2]	50,416	47,389	-6.0	23,061	23,701	+2.8	6,753	6,588	-2.4
Larceny-theft	450,416	437,999	-2.8	143,494	130,328	-9.2	258,302	257,251	-0.4	85,092	83,960	-1.3
Motor vehicle theft	61,725	62,948	+2.0	20,532	20,031	-2.4	12,124	12,879	+6.2	4,537	4,486	-1.1
Arson	8,302	9,405	+13.3	4,681	5,034	+7.5	1,412	1,741	+23.3	618	692	+12.0
Violent crime[3]	290,702	291,171	+0.2	44,475	43,532	-2.1	61,148	61,130	[2]	9,804	9,720	-0.9
Property crime[4]	667,400	657,337	-1.5	219,123	202,782	-7.5	294,899	295,572	+0.2	97,000	95,726	-1.3
Crime Index total[5]	958,102	948,508	-1.0	263,598	246,314	-6.6	356,047	356,702	+0.2	106,804	105,446	-1.3
Other assaults	595,620	591,990	-0.6	95,471	96,183	+0.7	180,295	183,672	+1.9	42,739	44,790	+4.8
Forgery and counterfeiting	40,034	40,690	+1.6	2,637	2,307	-12.5	26,057	28,021	+7.5	1,331	1,345	+1.1
Fraud	107,312	107,986	+0.6	3,644	3,301	-9.4	92,266	94,034	+1.9	1,871	1,729	-7.6
Embezzlement	6,181	6,448	+4.3	683	671	-1.8	6,252	6,491	+3.8	627	510	-18.7
Stolen property; buying, receiving, possessing	60,854	60,717	-0.2	14,664	13,627	-7.1	13,014	13,497	+3.7	2,749	2,743	-0.2
Vandalism	140,244	133,856	-4.6	59,258	55,040	-7.1	25,935	25,932	[2]	8,547	8,306	-2.8
Weapons; carrying, possessing, etc.	84,033	85,600	+1.9	18,885	18,750	-0.7	7,208	7,576	+5.1	1,920	1,983	+3.3
Prostitution and commercialized vice	16,971	13,834	-18.5	270	212	-21.5	27,814	27,600	-0.8	352	501	+42.3
Sex offenses (except forcible rape and prostitution)	48,905	48,178	-1.5	9,356	9,484	+1.4	3,796	3,765	-0.8	753	769	+2.1
Drug abuse violations	718,289	706,539	-1.6	94,550	93,160	-1.5	157,854	157,502	-0.2	17,502	18,521	+5.8
Gambling	3,829	3,836	+0.2	337	287	-14.8	658	591	-10.2	34	20	-41.2
Offenses against the family and children	66,460	65,979	-0.7	3,336	3,565	+6.9	18,687	19,135	+2.4	1,986	2,058	+3.6
Driving under the influence	718,677	682,177	-5.1	10,254	9,851	-3.9	141,313	138,443	-2.0	2,095	2,141	+2.2
Liquor laws	314,889	289,395	-8.1	65,559	57,852	-11.8	94,159	89,489	-5.0	30,082	27,668	-8.0
Drunkenness	378,182	358,155	-5.3	11,996	10,583	-11.8	57,682	56,907	-1.3	2,899	2,795	-3.6
Disorderly conduct	266,351	255,175	-4.2	65,888	66,297	+0.6	84,364	82,240	-2.5	27,433	27,983	+2.0
Vagrancy	16,040	15,059	-6.1	1,440	1,315	-8.7	4,366	3,605	-17.4	413	345	-16.5
All other offenses (except traffic)	1,722,679	1,693,159	-1.7	182,166	175,420	-3.7	463,912	466,471	+0.6	64,779	63,665	-1.7
Suspicion	2,733	1,743	-36.2	552	516	-6.5	674	544	-19.3	158	255	+61.4
Curfew and loitering law violations	51,085	44,264	-13.4	51,085	44,264	-13.4	24,153	21,246	-12.0	24,153	21,246	-12.0
Runaways	37,095	34,242	-7.7	37,095	34,242	-7.7	52,620	50,305	-4.4	52,620	50,305	-4.4

[1] Does not include suspicion.
[2] Less than one-tenth of 1 percent.
[3] Violent crimes are offenses of murder, forcible rape, robbery, and aggravated assault.
[4] Property crimes are offenses of burglary, larceny-theft, motor vehicle theft, and arson.
[5] Includes arson.

Table 38

Arrests

by Age, 2001

[9,511 agencies; 2001 estimated population 192,580,262]

Offense charged	Total all ages	Ages under 15	Ages under 18	Ages 18 and over	Under 10	10-12	13-14	15	16	17	18	19	20	21
TOTAL	**9,324,953**	**498,986**	**1,558,496**	**7,766,457**	**22,966**	**119,245**	**356,775**	**300,890**	**365,291**	**393,329**	**456,715**	**469,414**	**443,163**	**401,775**
Percent distribution[1]	**100.0**	**5.4**	**16.7**	**83.3**	**0.2**	**1.3**	**3.8**	**3.2**	**3.9**	**4.2**	**4.9**	**5.0**	**4.8**	**4.3**
Murder and nonnegligent manslaughter	9,426	114	957	8,469	6	9	99	134	254	455	582	643	618	587
Forcible rape	18,576	1,180	3,119	15,457	34	323	823	509	662	768	885	879	836	774
Robbery	76,667	4,354	18,111	58,556	95	920	3,339	3,515	4,746	5,496	6,336	5,835	4,745	4,151
Aggravated assault	329,722	16,498	44,815	284,907	878	4,524	11,096	8,215	9,646	10,456	12,083	12,745	12,737	13,634
Burglary	198,883	23,287	61,623	137,260	1,390	6,344	15,553	11,631	13,066	13,639	14,725	12,370	10,029	8,278
Larceny-theft	806,093	92,317	238,605	567,488	3,859	25,384	63,074	44,914	50,469	50,905	49,976	41,258	33,503	28,024
Motor vehicle theft	102,607	8,425	33,563	69,044	68	1,036	7,321	8,007	8,892	8,239	7,679	6,648	5,231	4,613
Arson	12,763	4,048	6,313	6,450	677	1,439	1,932	905	757	603	555	404	338	339
Violent crime[2]	434,391	22,146	67,002	367,389	1,013	5,776	15,357	12,373	15,308	17,175	19,886	20,102	18,936	19,146
Percent distribution[1]	100.0	5.1	15.4	84.6	0.2	1.3	3.5	2.8	3.5	4.0	4.6	4.6	4.4	4.4
Property crime[3]	1,120,346	128,077	340,104	780,242	5,994	34,203	87,880	65,457	73,184	73,386	72,935	60,680	49,101	41,254
Percent distribution[1]	100.0	11.4	30.4	69.6	0.5	3.1	7.8	5.8	6.5	6.6	6.5	5.4	4.4	3.7
Crime Index total[4]	1,554,737	150,223	407,106	1,147,631	7,007	39,979	103,237	77,830	88,492	90,561	92,821	80,782	68,037	60,400
Percent distribution[1]	100.0	9.7	26.2	73.8	0.5	2.6	6.6	5.0	5.7	5.8	6.0	5.2	4.4	3.9
Other assaults	898,298	70,642	163,142	735,156	3,348	20,436	46,858	30,260	31,942	30,298	29,736	30,578	31,115	33,400
Forgery and counterfeiting	77,692	422	3,975	73,717	22	81	319	525	1,117	1,911	3,457	4,234	4,235	3,953
Fraud	211,177	958	5,830	205,347	54	173	731	880	1,558	2,434	5,460	7,802	9,193	9,271
Embezzlement	13,836	83	1,258	12,578	1	16	66	86	380	709	945	993	851	803
Stolen property; buying, receiving, possessing	84,047	4,982	18,467	65,580	135	1,008	3,839	3,630	4,637	5,218	6,155	5,469	4,842	4,207
Vandalism	184,972	31,597	71,962	113,010	2,921	9,608	19,068	12,391	14,202	13,772	12,067	10,022	8,073	7,636
Weapons; carrying, possessing, etc.	114,325	8,691	25,861	88,464	479	2,203	6,009	4,721	5,763	6,686	7,711	7,182	6,319	6,113
Prostitution and commercialized vice	58,638	155	1,034	57,604	4	16	135	152	263	464	1,244	1,646	1,689	1,780
Sex offenses (except forcible rape and prostitution)	62,997	6,625	12,381	50,616	428	2,010	4,187	2,016	1,833	1,907	2,166	2,168	2,048	1,979
Drug abuse violations	1,091,240	24,061	139,238	952,002	297	2,976	20,788	24,956	38,401	51,820	71,912	70,475	64,907	57,536
Gambling	7,769	129	1,000	6,769	2	11	116	191	266	414	441	465	450	418
Offenses against the family and children	93,909	2,296	6,286	87,623	253	592	1,451	1,245	1,443	1,302	1,887	2,070	2,463	2,876
Driving under the influence	946,694	629	13,397	933,297	381	28	220	613	3,425	8,730	21,508	28,753	32,661	42,911
Liquor laws	408,203	8,879	92,326	315,877	174	643	8,062	14,209	27,162	42,076	65,734	69,163	56,822	12,174
Drunkenness	423,561	1,805	13,971	409,590	128	152	1,525	2,081	3,493	6,592	12,321	13,707	13,765	18,283
Disorderly conduct	425,751	47,043	117,635	308,116	1,463	12,240	33,340	23,932	23,891	22,769	21,063	19,478	18,253	20,349
Vagrancy	19,509	394	1,607	17,902	9	81	304	307	424	482	925	781	678	660
All other offenses (except traffic)	2,453,100	76,546	269,317	2,183,783	4,083	16,011	56,452	53,524	65,657	73,590	99,055	113,533	116,653	116,926
Suspicion	2,629	277	834	1,795	20	51	206	194	215	148	107	113	109	100
Curfew and loitering law violations	100,701	28,245	100,701	–	570	5,020	22,655	22,910	28,394	21,152	–	–	–	–
Runaways	91,168	34,304	91,168	–	1,187	5,910	27,207	24,237	22,333	10,294	–	–	–	–

[1] Because of rounding, the percentages may not add to total.
[2] Violent crimes are offenses of murder, forcible rape, robbery, and aggravated assault.
[3] Property crimes are offenses of burglary, larceny-theft, motor vehicle theft, and arson.
[4] Includes arson.

Table 38

Arrests
by Age, 2001—Continued
[9,511 agencies; 2001 estimated population 192,580,262]

Offense charged	22	23	24	25-29	30-34	35-39	40-44	45-49	50-54	55-59	60-64	65 and over
TOTAL	**352,338**	**314,724**	**285,558**	**1,143,295**	**1,045,150**	**1,015,375**	**827,615**	**493,476**	**259,757**	**119,864**	**60,986**	**77,252**
Percent distribution[1]	**3.8**	**3.4**	**3.1**	**12.3**	**11.2**	**10.9**	**8.9**	**5.3**	**2.8**	**1.3**	**0.7**	**0.8**
Murder and nonnegligent manslaughter	542	506	403	1,437	948	747	585	362	236	127	62	84
Forcible rape	705	657	578	2,397	2,206	2,114	1,586	834	462	255	140	149
Robbery	3,326	2,723	2,342	8,703	7,241	6,190	3,938	1,898	730	229	77	92
Aggravated assault	12,421	11,948	10,952	46,476	42,734	40,442	31,770	18,269	9,528	4,400	2,232	2,536
Burglary	6,585	5,678	4,943	19,015	17,812	16,512	11,902	5,676	2,304	848	323	260
Larceny-theft	23,469	19,971	17,663	74,118	74,887	73,683	59,774	35,997	18,499	8,138	4,048	4,480
Motor vehicle theft	3,689	3,170	2,705	10,562	9,164	7,172	4,768	2,157	942	323	114	107
Arson	307	233	201	820	818	777	753	443	253	112	53	44
Violent crime[2]	16,994	15,834	14,275	59,013	53,129	49,493	37,879	21,363	10,956	5,011	2,511	2,861
Percent distribution[1]	3.9	3.6	3.3	13.6	12.2	11.4	8.7	4.9	2.5	1.2	0.6	0.7
Property crime[3]	34,050	29,052	25,512	104,515	102,681	98,144	77,197	44,273	21,998	9,421	4,538	4,891
Percent distribution[1]	3.0	2.6	2.3	9.3	9.2	8.8	6.9	4.0	2.0	0.8	0.4	0.4
Crime Index total[4]	51,044	44,886	39,787	163,528	155,810	147,637	115,076	65,636	32,954	14,432	7,049	7,752
Percent distribution[1]	3.3	2.9	2.6	10.5	10.0	9.5	7.4	4.2	2.1	0.9	0.5	0.5
Other assaults	31,468	29,659	28,054	119,548	113,544	110,091	84,781	47,953	23,588	10,741	5,294	5,606
Forgery and counterfeiting	3,783	3,258	2,914	13,084	12,135	9,922	6,691	3,635	1,502	537	206	171
Fraud	8,946	8,415	8,332	36,530	34,282	29,559	21,840	12,886	6,864	3,081	1,381	1,505
Embezzlement	625	519	495	1,997	1,732	1,424	1061	543	334	171	50	35
Stolen property; buying, receiving, possessing	3,363	3,020	2,626	9,741	8,653	7,478	5,278	2,725	1,212	455	202	154
Vandalism	6,221	5,307	4,431	16,141	13,482	12,007	8,717	4,729	2,248	921	476	532
Weapons; carrying, possessing, etc.	5,241	4,398	3,866	13,602	9,734	8,114	6,716	4,128	2,566	1,291	646	837
Prostitution and commercialized vice	1,776	1,725	1,609	8,780	11,131	11,185	7,843	3,895	1,712	726	420	443
Sex offenses (except forcible rape and prostitution)	1,755	1,556	1,463	6,348	7,031	7,387	6,037	4,183	2,655	1,563	1,034	1,243
Drug abuse violations	48,851	42,324	37,638	140,754	121,789	116,570	92,585	50,614	22,144	7,647	2,854	3,402
Gambling	375	349	260	816	617	506	557	379	510	223	211	192
Offenses against the family and children	2,798	2,675	2,919	14,868	16,058	15,873	12,072	6,256	2,727	1,132	478	471
Driving under the influence	40,266	37,623	34,420	140,459	124,605	124,725	110,614	75,041	47,467	26,511	16,170	29,563
Liquor laws	7,821	6,110	4,903	17,253	15,094	17,131	17,288	12,230	7,218	3,583	1,758	1,595
Drunkenness	15,996	14,066	12,802	51,800	51,667	61,018	59,849	40,533	22,890	11,054	5,500	4,339
Disorderly conduct	16,943	14,284	12,400	44,144	36,773	36,399	30,958	18,619	9,635	4,226	2,230	2,362
Vagrancy	516	408	421	1,754	2,076	2,646	2,866	1,939	1,171	537	263	261
All other offenses (except traffic)	104,479	94,074	86,148	341,849	308,679	295,474	236,615	137,461	70,308	31,001	14,750	16,778
Suspicion	71	68	70	299	258	229	171	91	52	32	14	11
Curfew and loitering law violations	–	–	–	–	–	–	–	–	–	–	–	–
Runaways	–	–	–	–	–	–	–	–	–	–	–	–

Table 39

Arrests

Males, by Age, 2001

[9,511 agencies; 2001 estimated population 192,580,262]

Offense charged	Total all ages	Ages under 15	Ages under 18	Ages 18 and over	Under 10	10-12	13-14	15	16	17	18	19	20	21
TOTAL	**7,224,203**	**344,058**	**1,116,241**	**6,107,962**	**18,899**	**87,636**	**237,523**	**206,119**	**263,724**	**302,340**	**365,710**	**376,731**	**355,351**	**324,313**
Percent distribution[1]	**100.0**	**4.8**	**15.5**	**84.5**	**0.3**	**1.2**	**3.3**	**2.9**	**3.7**	**4.2**	**5.1**	**5.2**	**4.9**	**4.5**
Murder and nonnegligent manslaughter	8,252	100	859	7,393	6	9	85	117	228	414	533	598	569	529
Forcible rape	18,356	1,164	3,079	15,277	33	318	813	500	656	759	873	872	830	765
Robbery	68,949	3,907	16,559	52,390	90	842	2,975	3,195	4,385	5,072	5,880	5,370	4,346	3,752
Aggravated assault	263,559	12,512	34,323	229,236	797	3,632	8,083	6,079	7,393	8,339	9,831	10,380	10,275	11,164
Burglary	171,882	20,141	54,234	117,648	1,223	5,495	13,423	10,240	11,621	12,232	13,237	11,015	8,835	7,264
Larceny-theft	511,854	56,531	145,361	366,493	2,893	16,360	37,278	26,498	30,307	32,025	32,766	27,130	21,774	18,128
Motor vehicle theft	85,789	6,604	27,859	57,930	64	838	5,702	6,513	7,577	7,165	6,720	5,813	4,473	3,947
Arson	10,730	3,570	5,545	5,185	626	1,299	1,645	788	653	534	476	345	267	291
Violent crime[2]	359,116	17,683	54,820	304,296	926	4,801	11,956	9,891	12,662	14,584	17,117	17,220	16,020	16,210
Percent distribution[1]	100.0	4.9	15.3	84.7	0.3	1.3	3.3	2.8	3.5	4.1	4.8	4.8	4.5	4.5
Property crime[3]	780,255	86,846	232,999	547,256	4,806	23,992	58,048	44,039	50,158	51,956	53,199	44,303	35,349	29,630
Percent distribution[1]	100.0	11.1	29.9	70.1	0.6	3.1	7.4	5.6	6.4	6.7	6.8	5.7	4.5	3.8
Crime Index total[4]	1,139,371	104,529	287,819	851,552	5,732	28,793	70,004	53,930	62,820	66,540	70,316	61,523	51,369	45,840
Percent distribution[1]	100.0	9.2	25.3	74.7	0.5	2.5	6.1	4.7	5.5	5.8	6.2	5.4	4.5	4.0
Other assaults	688,461	48,532	111,499	576,962	2,867	15,115	30,550	19,747	21,715	21,505	22,099	22,973	23,618	25,830
Forgery and counterfeiting	46,443	272	2,549	43,894	14	52	206	342	725	1,210	2,159	2,685	2,544	2,369
Fraud	115,394	634	3,887	111,507	32	118	484	590	1,027	1,636	3,260	4,500	5,101	5,056
Embezzlement	6,972	55	705	6,267	1	10	44	59	202	389	488	499	384	366
Stolen property; buying, receiving, possessing	68,964	4,049	15,409	53,555	115	844	3,090	2,996	3,888	4,476	5,344	4,696	4,102	3,478
Vandalism	154,984	27,300	62,604	92,380	2,680	8,401	16,219	10,801	12,455	12,048	10,588	8,691	6,826	6,426
Weapons; carrying, possessing, etc.	104,922	7,451	23,064	81,858	441	1,915	5,095	4,168	5,227	6,218	7,298	6,796	5,975	5,808
Prostitution and commercialized vice	19,601	55	320	19,281	3	11	41	33	80	152	272	372	495	561
Sex offenses (except forcible rape and prostitution)	57,935	6,128	11,422	46,513	376	1,856	3,896	1,834	1,692	1,768	1,993	1,978	1,845	1,799
Drug abuse violations	896,939	18,831	117,862	779,077	242	2,269	16,320	20,920	33,006	45,105	62,479	60,950	56,105	49,538
Gambling	7,031	118	970	6,061	2	11	105	186	258	408	428	442	421	401
Offenses against the family and children	72,250	1,402	3,991	68,259	163	397	842	755	908	926	1,399	1,509	1,792	2,114
Driving under the influence	789,198	515	11,032	778,166	336	25	154	483	2,748	7,286	18,222	24,417	27,803	35,975
Liquor laws	311,971	4,705	62,624	249,347	125	327	4,253	8,671	18,460	30,788	49,303	53,074	44,322	10,021
Drunkenness	365,393	1,179	11,031	354,362	113	108	958	1,517	2,754	5,581	10,754	12,094	12,181	16,377
Disorderly conduct	323,791	32,108	82,527	241,264	1,249	8,880	21,979	16,107	17,013	17,299	16,703	15,444	14,476	16,541
Vagrancy	15,789	302	1,295	14,494	7	58	237	240	340	413	756	668	563	524
All other offenses (except traffic)	1,930,291	53,684	198,582	1,731,709	3,256	11,966	38,462	37,747	48,871	58,280	81,763	93,325	95,339	95,209
Suspicion	1,989	164	535	1,454	17	35	112	124	129	118	86	95	90	80
Curfew and loitering law violations	69,502	18,573	69,502	–	437	3,546	14,590	15,354	20,010	15,565	–	–	–	–
Runaways	37,012	13,472	37,012	–	691	2,899	9,882	9,515	9,396	4,629	–	–	–	–

[1] Because of rounding, the percentages may not add to total.

[2] Violent crimes are offenses of murder, forcible rape, robbery, and aggravated assault.

[3] Property crimes are offenses of burglary, larceny-theft, motor vehicle theft, and arson.

[4] Includes arson.

Table 39

Arrests
Males, by Age, 2001—Continued
[9,511 agencies; 2001 estimated population 192,580,262]

Offense charged	22	23	24	25-29	30-34	35-39	40-44	45-49	50-54	55-59	60-64	65 and over
TOTAL	283,275	252,263	227,598	896,855	794,494	764,692	640,012	394,234	214,532	100,594	51,728	65,580
Percent distribution[1]	3.9	3.5	3.2	12.4	11.0	10.6	8.9	5.5	3.0	1.4	0.7	0.9
Murder and nonnegligent manslaughter	496	452	345	1,258	804	611	471	310	194	99	53	71
Forcible rape	700	651	568	2,362	2,172	2,091	1,567	828	457	253	140	148
Robbery	3,001	2,464	2,073	7,722	6,309	5,344	3,432	1,672	669	205	69	82
Aggravated assault	10,086	9,777	8,824	37,489	33,658	31,414	25,312	14,972	8,051	3,791	1,963	2,249
Burglary	5,674	4,854	4,200	15,966	14,863	13,815	9,978	4,777	1,964	726	264	216
Larceny-theft	14,715	12,478	10,915	45,429	47,765	48,122	40,076	24,451	12,326	5,176	2,531	2,711
Motor vehicle theft	3,144	2,683	2,258	8,676	7,371	5,803	3,931	1,815	811	289	102	94
Arson	272	198	170	673	615	585	582	348	191	90	45	37
Violent crime[2]	14,283	13,344	11,810	48,831	42,943	39,460	30,782	17,782	9,371	4,348	2,225	2,550
Percent distribution[1]	4.0	3.7	3.3	13.6	12.0	11.0	8.6	5.0	2.6	1.2	0.6	0.7
Property crime[3]	23,805	20,213	17,543	70,744	70,614	68,325	54,567	31,391	15,292	6,281	2,942	3,058
Percent distribution[1]	3.1	2.6	2.2	9.1	9.1	8.8	7.0	4.0	2.0	0.8	0.4	0.4
Crime Index total[4]	38,088	33,557	29,353	119,575	113,557	107,785	85,349	49,173	24,663	10,629	5,167	5,608
Percent distribution[1]	3.3	2.9	2.6	10.5	10.0	9.5	7.5	4.3	2.2	0.9	0.5	0.5
Other assaults	24,422	23,224	21,898	94,319	88,581	85,562	67,620	39,014	19,643	8,941	4,443	4,775
Forgery and counterfeiting	2,254	1,951	1,684	7,728	6,802	5,813	3,917	2,371	975	379	140	123
Fraud	4,892	4,484	4,363	18,826	17,858	15,803	12,309	7,386	4,037	1,849	862	921
Embezzlement	301	253	223	994	883	741	533	275	179	110	21	17
Stolen property; buying, receiving, possessing	2,772	2,510	2,132	7,670	6,784	5,844	4,265	2,243	1,006	390	183	136
Vandalism	5,192	4,350	3,592	12,941	10,459	9,295	6,807	3,752	1,859	750	402	450
Weapons; carrying, possessing, etc.	4,921	4,142	3,626	12,566	8,820	7,226	5,967	3,742	2,355	1,217	604	795
Prostitution and commercialized vice	558	585	556	3,007	3,217	3,035	2,499	1,663	1,051	599	391	420
Sex offenses (except forcible rape and prostitution)	1,592	1,388	1,313	5,700	6,379	6,651	5,586	3,917	2,576	1,538	1,023	1,235
Drug abuse violations	42,016	36,090	32,076	116,628	94,271	87,434	70,411	40,239	18,729	6,561	2,507	3,043
Gambling	365	328	253	751	529	424	426	283	469	188	181	172
Offenses against the family and children	2,058	1,946	2,163	11,288	12,361	12,334	9,861	5,295	2,356	978	423	382
Driving under the influence	34,166	32,060	29,524	120,400	103,260	99,282	88,093	61,584	40,407	22,887	13,997	26,089
Liquor laws	6,493	5,128	4,088	14,183	12,023	13,609	14,226	10,377	6,306	3,214	1,571	1,409
Drunkenness	14,298	12,536	11,477	45,487	43,695	50,420	50,138	35,017	20,524	10,162	5,153	4,049
Disorderly conduct	13,679	11,412	9,873	34,570	27,461	26,951	23,958	14,906	7,893	3,545	1,895	1,957
Vagrancy	406	325	350	1,315	1,523	2,058	2,330	1,661	1047	479	242	247
All other offenses (except traffic)	84,743	75,939	69,003	268,661	235,826	224,237	185,586	111,261	58,415	26,151	12,510	13,741
Suspicion	59	55	51	246	205	188	131	75	42	27	13	11
Curfew and loitering law violations	–	–	–	–	–	–	–	–	–	–	–	–
Runaways	–	–	–	–	–	–	–	–	–	–	–	–

Table 40

Arrests

Females, by Age, 2001
[9,511 agencies; 2001 estimated population 192,580,262]

Offense charged	Total all ages	Ages under 15	Ages under 18	Ages 18 and over	Under 10	10-12	13-14	15	16	17	18	19	20	21
TOTAL	2,100,750	154,928	442,255	1,658,495	4,067	31,609	119,252	94,771	101,567	90,989	91,005	92,683	87,812	77,462
Percent distribution[1]	100.0	7.4	21.1	78.9	0.2	1.5	5.7	4.5	4.8	4.3	4.3	4.4	4.2	3.7
Murder and nonnegligent manslaughter	1,174	14	98	1,076	0	0	14	17	26	41	49	45	49	58
Forcible rape	220	16	40	180	1	5	10	9	6	9	12	7	6	9
Robbery	7,718	447	1,552	6,166	5	78	364	320	361	424	456	465	399	399
Aggravated assault	66,163	3,986	10,492	55,671	81	892	3,013	2,136	2,253	2,117	2,252	2,365	2,462	2,470
Burglary	27,001	3,146	7,389	19,612	167	849	2,130	1,391	1,445	1,407	1,488	1,355	1,194	1014
Larceny-theft	294,239	35,786	93,244	200,995	966	9,024	25,796	18,416	20,162	18,880	17,210	14,128	11,729	9,896
Motor vehicle theft	16,818	1,821	5,704	11,114	4	198	1,619	1,494	1,315	1,074	959	835	758	666
Arson	2,033	478	768	1,265	51	140	287	117	104	69	79	59	71	48
Violent crime[2]	75,275	4,463	12,182	63,093	87	975	3,401	2,482	2,646	2,591	2,769	2,882	2,916	2,936
Percent distribution[1]	100.0	5.9	16.2	83.8	0.1	1.3	4.5	3.3	3.5	3.4	3.7	3.8	3.9	3.9
Property crime[3]	340,091	41,231	107,105	232,986	1,188	10,211	29,832	21,418	23,026	21,430	19,736	16,377	13,752	11,624
Percent distribution[1]	100.0	12.1	31.5	68.5	0.3	3.0	8.8	6.3	6.8	6.3	5.8	4.8	4.0	3.4
Crime Index total[4]	415,366	45,694	119,287	296,079	1,275	11,186	33,233	23,900	25,672	24,021	22,505	19,259	16,668	14,560
Percent distribution[1]	100.0	11.0	28.7	71.3	0.3	2.7	8.0	5.8	6.2	5.8	5.4	4.6	4.0	3.5
Other assaults	209,837	22,110	51,643	158,194	481	5,321	16,308	10,513	10,227	8,793	7,637	7,605	7,497	7,570
Forgery and counterfeiting	31,249	150	1,426	29,823	8	29	113	183	392	701	1,298	1,549	1,691	1,584
Fraud	95,783	324	1,943	93,840	22	55	247	290	531	798	2,200	3,302	4,092	4,215
Embezzlement	6,864	28	553	6,311	0	6	22	27	178	320	457	494	467	437
Stolen property; buying, receiving, possessing	15,083	933	3,058	12,025	20	164	749	634	749	742	811	773	740	729
Vandalism	29,988	4,297	9,358	20,630	241	1,207	2,849	1,590	1,747	1,724	1,479	1,331	1,247	1,210
Weapons; carrying, possessing, etc.	9,403	1,240	2,797	6,606	38	288	914	553	536	468	413	386	344	305
Prostitution and commercialized vice	39,037	100	714	38,323	1	5	94	119	183	312	972	1,274	1194	1,219
Sex offenses (except forcible rape and prostitution)	5,062	497	959	4,103	52	154	291	182	141	139	173	190	203	180
Drug abuse violations	194,301	5,230	21,376	172,925	55	707	4,468	4,036	5,395	6,715	9,433	9,525	8,802	7,998
Gambling	738	11	30	708	0	0	11	5	8	6	13	23	29	17
Offenses against the family and children	21,659	894	2,295	19,364	90	195	609	490	535	376	488	561	671	762
Driving under the influence	157,496	114	2,365	155,131	45	3	66	130	677	1,444	3,286	4,336	4,858	6,936
Liquor laws	96,232	4,174	29,702	66,530	49	316	3,809	5,538	8,702	11,288	16,431	16,089	12,500	2,153
Drunkenness	58,168	626	2,940	55,228	15	44	567	564	739	1,011	1,567	1,613	1,584	1,906
Disorderly conduct	101,960	14,935	35,108	66,852	214	3,360	11,361	7,825	6,878	5,470	4,360	4,034	3,777	3,808
Vagrancy	3,720	92	312	3,408	2	23	67	67	84	69	169	113	115	136
All other offenses (except traffic)	522,809	22,862	70,735	452,074	827	4,045	17,990	15,777	16,786	15,310	17,292	20,208	21,314	21,717
Suspicion	640	113	299	341	3	16	94	70	86	30	21	18	19	20
Curfew and loitering law violations	31,199	9,672	31,199	–	133	1,474	8,065	7,556	8,384	5,587	–	–	–	–
Runaways	54,156	20,832	54,156	–	496	3,011	17,325	14,722	12,937	5,665	–	–	–	–

[1] Because of rounding, the percentages may not add to total.
[2] Violent crimes are offenses of murder, forcible rape, robbery, and aggravated assault.
[3] Property crimes are offenses of burglary, larceny-theft, motor vehicle theft, and arson.
[4] Includes arson.

Table 40

Arrests
Females, by Age, 2001—Continued
[9,511 agencies; 2001 estimated population 192,580,262]

Offense charged	22	23	24	25-29	30-34	35-39	40-44	45-49	50-54	55-59	60-64	65 and over
TOTAL	**69,063**	**62,461**	**57,960**	**246,440**	**250,656**	**250,683**	**187,603**	**99,242**	**45,225**	**19,270**	**9,258**	**11,672**
Percent distribution[1]	**3.3**	**3.0**	**2.8**	**11.7**	**11.9**	**11.9**	**8.9**	**4.7**	**2.2**	**0.9**	**0.4**	**0.6**
Murder and nonnegligent manslaughter	46	54	58	179	144	136	114	52	42	28	9	13
Forcible rape	5	6	10	35	34	23	19	6	5	2	0	1
Robbery	325	259	269	981	932	846	506	226	61	24	8	10
Aggravated assault	2,335	2,171	2,128	8,987	9,076	9,028	6,458	3,297	1,477	609	269	287
Burglary	911	824	743	3,049	2,949	2,697	1,924	899	340	122	59	44
Larceny-theft	8,754	7,493	6,748	28,689	27,122	25,561	19,698	11,546	6,173	2,962	1,517	1,769
Motor vehicle theft	545	487	447	1,886	1,793	1,369	837	342	131	34	12	13
Arson	35	35	31	147	203	192	171	95	62	22	8	7
Violent crime[2]	2,711	2,490	2,465	10,182	10,186	10,033	7,097	3,581	1,585	663	286	311
Percent distribution[1]	3.6	3.3	3.3	13.5	13.5	13.3	9.4	4.8	2.1	0.9	0.4	0.4
Property crime[3]	10,245	8,839	7,969	33,771	32,067	29,819	22,630	12,882	6,706	3,140	1,596	1,833
Percent distribution[1]	3.0	2.6	2.3	9.9	9.4	8.8	6.7	3.8	2.0	0.9	0.5	0.5
Crime Index total[4]	12,956	11,329	10,434	43,953	42,253	39,852	29,727	16,463	8,291	3,803	1,882	2,144
Percent distribution[1]	3.1	2.7	2.5	10.6	10.2	9.6	7.2	4.0	2.0	0.9	0.5	0.5
Other assaults	7,046	6,435	6,156	25,229	24,963	24,529	17,161	8,939	3,945	1,800	851	831
Forgery and counterfeiting	1,529	1,307	1,230	5,356	5,333	4,109	2,774	1,264	527	158	66	48
Fraud	4,054	3,931	3,969	17,704	16,424	13,756	9,531	5,500	2,827	1,232	519	584
Embezzlement	324	266	272	1,003	849	683	528	268	155	61	29	18
Stolen property; buying, receiving, possessing	591	510	494	2,071	1,869	1,634	1,013	482	206	65	19	18
Vandalism	1029	957	839	3,200	3,023	2,712	1,910	977	389	171	74	82
Weapons; carrying, possessing, etc.	320	256	240	1,036	914	888	749	386	211	74	42	42
Prostitution and commercialized vice	1,218	1,140	1,053	5,773	7,914	8,150	5,344	2,232	661	127	29	23
Sex offenses (except forcible rape and prostitution)	163	168	150	648	652	736	451	266	79	25	11	8
Drug abuse violations	6,835	6,234	5,562	24,126	27,518	29,136	22,174	10,375	3,415	1086	347	359
Gambling	10	21	7	65	88	82	131	96	41	35	30	20
Offenses against the family and children	740	729	756	3,580	3,697	3,539	2,211	961	371	154	55	89
Driving under the influence	6,100	5,563	4,896	20,059	21,345	25,443	22,521	13,457	7,060	3,624	2,173	3,474
Liquor laws	1,328	982	815	3,070	3,071	3,522	3,062	1,853	912	369	187	186
Drunkenness	1,698	1,530	1,325	6,313	7,972	10,598	9,711	5,516	2,366	892	347	290
Disorderly conduct	3,264	2,872	2,527	9,574	9,312	9,448	7,000	3,713	1,742	681	335	405
Vagrancy	110	83	71	439	553	588	536	278	124	58	21	14
All other offenses (except traffic)	19,736	18,135	17,145	73,188	72,853	71,237	51,029	26,200	11,893	4,850	2,240	3,037
Suspicion	12	13	19	53	53	41	40	16	10	5	1	0
Curfew and loitering law violations	–	–	–	–	–	–	–	–	–	–	–	–
Runaways	–	–	–	–	–	–	–	–	–	–	–	–

Table 41

Arrests

of Persons Under 15, 18, 21, and 25 Years of Age, 2001
[9,511 agencies; 2001 estimated population 192,580,262]

Offense charged	Total all ages	Number of persons arrested				Percent of total all ages			
		Under 15	Under 18	Under 21	Under 25	Under 15	Under 18	Under 21	Under 25
TOTAL	**9,324,953**	**498,986**	**1,558,496**	**2,927,788**	**4,282,183**	**5.4**	**16.7**	**31.4**	**45.9**
Murder and nonnegligent manslaughter	9,426	114	957	2,800	4,838	1.2	10.2	29.7	51.3
Forcible rape	18,576	1,180	3,119	5,719	8,433	6.4	16.8	30.8	45.4
Robbery	76,667	4,354	18,111	35,027	47,569	5.7	23.6	45.7	62.0
Aggravated assault	329,722	16,498	44,815	82,380	131,335	5.0	13.6	25.0	39.8
Burglary	198,883	23,287	61,623	98,747	124,231	11.7	31.0	49.7	62.5
Larceny-theft	806,093	92,317	238,605	363,342	452,469	11.5	29.6	45.1	56.1
Motor vehicle theft	102,607	8,425	33,563	53,121	67,298	8.2	32.7	51.8	65.6
Arson	12,763	4,048	6,313	7,610	8,690	31.7	49.5	59.6	68.1
Violent crime[1]	434,391	22,146	67,002	125,926	192,175	5.1	15.4	29.0	44.2
Property crime[2]	1,120,346	128,077	340,104	522,820	652,688	11.4	30.4	46.7	58.3
Crime Index total[3]	1,554,737	150,223	407,106	648,746	844,863	9.7	26.2	41.7	54.3
Other assaults	898,298	70,642	163,142	254,571	377,152	7.9	18.2	28.3	42.0
Forgery and counterfeiting	77,692	422	3,975	15,901	29,809	0.5	5.1	20.5	38.4
Fraud	211,177	958	5,830	28,285	63,249	0.5	2.8	13.4	30.0
Embezzlement	13,836	83	1,258	4,047	6,489	0.6	9.1	29.2	46.9
Stolen property; buying, receiving, possessing	84,047	4,982	18,467	34,933	48,149	5.9	22.0	41.6	57.3
Vandalism	184,972	31,597	71,962	102,124	125,719	17.1	38.9	55.2	68.0
Weapons; carrying, possessing, etc.	114,325	8,691	25,861	47,073	66,691	7.6	22.6	41.2	58.3
Prostitution and commercialized vice	58,638	155	1,034	5,613	12,503	0.3	1.8	9.6	21.3
Sex offenses (except forcible rape and prostitution)	62,997	6,625	12,381	18,763	25,516	10.5	19.7	29.8	40.5
Drug abuse violations	1,091,240	24,061	139,238	346,532	532,881	2.2	12.8	31.8	48.8
Gambling	7,769	129	1,000	2,356	3,758	1.7	12.9	30.3	48.4
Offenses against the family and children	93,909	2,296	6,286	12,706	23,974	2.4	6.7	13.5	25.5
Driving under the influence	946,694	629	13,397	96,319	251,539	0.1	1.4	10.2	26.6
Liquor laws	408,203	8,879	92,326	284,045	315,053	2.2	22.6	69.6	77.2
Drunkenness	423,561	1,805	13,971	53,764	114,911	0.4	3.3	12.7	27.1
Disorderly conduct	425,751	47,043	117,635	176,429	240,405	11.0	27.6	41.4	56.5
Vagrancy	19,509	394	1,607	3,991	5,996	2.0	8.2	20.5	30.7
All other offenses (except traffic)	2,453,100	76,546	269,317	598,558	1,000,185	3.1	11.0	24.4	40.8
Suspicion	2,629	277	834	1,163	1,472	10.5	31.7	44.2	56.0
Curfew and loitering law violations	100,701	28,245	100,701	100,701	100,701	28.0	100.0	100.0	100.0
Runaways	91,168	34,304	91,168	91,168	91,168	37.6	100.0	100.0	100.0

[1] Violent crimes are offenses of murder, forcible rape, robbery, and aggravated assault.

[2] Property crimes are offenses of burglary, larceny-theft, motor vehicle theft, and arson.

[3] Includes arson.

Table 42

Arrests
by Sex, 2001
[9,511 agencies; 2001 estimated population 192,580,262]

Offense charged	Number of persons arrested			Percent male	Percent female	Percent distribution[1]		
	Total	Male	Female			Total	Male	Female
TOTAL	**9,324,953**	**7,224,203**	**2,100,750**	**77.5**	**22.5**	**100.0**	**100.0**	**100.0**
Murder and nonnegligent manslaughter	9,426	8,252	1,174	87.5	12.5	0.1	0.1	0.1
Forcible rape	18,576	18,356	220	98.8	1.2	0.2	0.3	[2]
Robbery	76,667	68,949	7,718	89.9	10.1	0.8	1.0	0.4
Aggravated assault	329,722	263,559	66,163	79.9	20.1	3.5	3.6	3.1
Burglary	198,883	171,882	27,001	86.4	13.6	2.1	2.4	1.3
Larceny-theft	806,093	511,854	294,239	63.5	36.5	8.6	7.1	14.0
Motor vehicle theft	102,607	85,789	16,818	83.6	16.4	1.1	1.2	0.8
Arson	12,763	10,730	2,033	84.1	15.9	0.1	0.1	0.1
Violent crime[3]	434,391	359,116	75,275	82.7	17.3	4.7	5.0	3.6
Property crime[4]	1,120,346	780,255	340,091	69.6	30.4	12.0	10.8	16.2
Crime Index total[5]	1,554,737	1,139,371	415,366	73.3	26.7	16.7	15.8	19.8
Other assaults	898,298	688,461	209,837	76.6	23.4	9.6	9.5	10.0
Forgery and counterfeiting	77,692	46,443	31,249	59.8	40.2	0.8	0.6	1.5
Fraud	211,177	115,394	95,783	54.6	45.4	2.3	1.6	4.6
Embezzlement	13,836	6,972	6,864	50.4	49.6	0.1	0.1	0.3
Stolen property; buying, receiving, possessing	84,047	68,964	15,083	82.1	17.9	0.9	1.0	0.7
Vandalism	184,972	154,984	29,988	83.8	16.2	2.0	2.1	1.4
Weapons; carrying, possessing, etc.	114,325	104,922	9,403	91.8	8.2	1.2	1.5	0.4
Prostitution and commercialized vice	58,638	19,601	39,037	33.4	66.6	0.6	0.3	1.9
Sex offenses (except forcible rape and prostitution)	62,997	57,935	5,062	92.0	8.0	0.7	0.8	0.2
Drug abuse violations	1,091,240	896,939	194,301	82.2	17.8	11.7	12.4	9.2
Gambling	7,769	7,031	738	90.5	9.5	0.1	0.1	[2]
Offenses against the family and children	93,909	72,250	21,659	76.9	23.1	1.0	1.0	1.0
Driving under the influence	946,694	789,198	157,496	83.4	16.6	10.2	10.9	7.5
Liquor laws	408,203	311,971	96,232	76.4	23.6	4.4	4.3	4.6
Drunkenness	423,561	365,393	58,168	86.3	13.7	4.5	5.1	2.8
Disorderly conduct	425,751	323,791	101,960	76.1	23.9	4.6	4.5	4.9
Vagrancy	19,509	15,789	3,720	80.9	19.1	0.2	0.2	0.2
All other offenses (except traffic)	2,453,100	1,930,291	522,809	78.7	21.3	26.3	26.7	24.9
Suspicion	2,629	1,989	640	75.7	24.3	[2]	[2]	[2]
Curfew and loitering law violations	100,701	69,502	31,199	69.0	31.0	1.1	1.0	1.5
Runaways	91,168	37,012	54,156	40.6	59.4	1.0	0.5	2.6

[1] Because of rounding, the percentages may not add to total.

[2] Less than one-tenth of 1 percent.

[3] Violent crimes are offenses of murder, forcible rape, robbery, and aggravated assault.

[4] Property crimes are offenses of burglary, larceny-theft, motor vehicle theft, and arson.

[5] Includes arson.

Table 43

Arrests

by Race, 2001

[9,511 agencies; 2001 estimated population 192,580,262]

Offense charged	Total arrests					Percent distribution[1]				
	Total	White	Black	American Indian or Alaskan Native	Asian or Pacific Islander	Total	White	Black	American Indian or Alaskan Native	Asian or Pacific Islander
TOTAL	**9,306,587**	**6,465,887**	**2,617,669**	**119,281**	**103,750**	**100.0**	**69.5**	**28.1**	**1.3**	**1.1**
Murder and nonnegligent manslaughter	9,416	4,561	4,585	122	148	100.0	48.4	48.7	1.3	1.6
Forcible rape	18,530	11,617	6,446	206	261	100.0	62.7	34.8	1.1	1.4
Robbery	76,610	34,099	41,228	437	846	100.0	44.5	53.8	0.6	1.1
Aggravated assault	329,208	210,706	110,933	3,580	3,989	100.0	64.0	33.7	1.1	1.2
Burglary	198,648	137,887	56,527	1,986	2,248	100.0	69.4	28.5	1.0	1.1
Larceny-theft	804,605	531,521	250,912	10,015	12,157	100.0	66.1	31.2	1.2	1.5
Motor vehicle theft	102,462	58,869	40,806	925	1,862	100.0	57.5	39.8	0.9	1.8
Arson	12,745	9,803	2,634	190	118	100.0	76.9	20.7	1.5	0.9
Violent crime[2]	433,764	260,983	163,192	4,345	5,244	100.0	60.2	37.6	1.0	1.2
Property crime[3]	1,118,460	738,080	350,879	13,116	16,385	100.0	66.0	31.4	1.2	1.5
Crime Index total[4]	1,552,224	999,063	514,071	17,461	21,629	100.0	64.4	33.1	1.1	1.4
Other assaults	896,760	586,610	288,539	12,056	9,555	100.0	65.4	32.2	1.3	1.1
Forgery and counterfeiting	77,508	52,558	23,297	454	1,199	100.0	67.8	30.1	0.6	1.5
Fraud	210,556	142,535	65,213	1,301	1,507	100.0	67.7	31.0	0.6	0.7
Embezzlement	13,801	9,085	4,415	75	226	100.0	65.8	32.0	0.5	1.6
Stolen property; buying, receiving, possessing	83,891	49,832	32,506	610	943	100.0	59.4	38.7	0.7	1.1
Vandalism	184,655	137,939	42,386	2,473	1,857	100.0	74.7	23.0	1.3	1.0
Weapons; carrying, possessing, etc.	114,189	69,664	42,532	821	1,172	100.0	61.0	37.2	0.7	1.0
Prostitution and commercialized vice	58,572	33,442	23,597	327	1,206	100.0	57.1	40.3	0.6	2.1
Sex offenses (except forcible rape and prostitution)	62,908	46,127	15,222	665	894	100.0	73.3	24.2	1.1	1.4
Drug abuse violations	1,089,900	700,123	375,587	6,184	8,006	100.0	64.2	34.5	0.6	0.7
Gambling	7,763	2,147	5,284	10	322	100.0	27.7	68.1	0.1	4.1
Offenses against the family and children	93,515	63,278	27,556	1,084	1,597	100.0	67.7	29.5	1.2	1.7
Driving under the influence	944,359	825,665	96,497	13,064	9,133	100.0	87.4	10.2	1.4	1.0
Liquor laws	406,443	351,098	40,818	11,046	3,481	100.0	86.4	10.0	2.7	0.9
Drunkenness	422,817	354,779	56,317	9,703	2,018	100.0	83.9	13.3	2.3	0.5
Disorderly conduct	424,837	273,677	141,776	6,156	3,228	100.0	64.4	33.4	1.4	0.8
Vagrancy	19,500	11,935	6,960	492	113	100.0	61.2	35.7	2.5	0.6
All other offenses (except traffic)	2,448,204	1,615,107	769,462	33,305	30,330	100.0	66.0	31.4	1.4	1.2
Suspicion	2,606	1,611	961	11	23	100.0	61.8	36.9	0.4	0.9
Curfew and loitering law violations	100,550	70,935	27,259	871	1,485	100.0	70.5	27.1	0.9	1.5
Runaways	91,029	68,677	17,414	1,112	3,826	100.0	75.4	19.1	1.2	4.2

See footnotes at end of table.

Table 43

Arrests

by Race, 2001—Continued
[9,511 agencies; 2001 estimated population 192,580,262]

Offense charged	Arrests under 18					Percent distribution[1]				
	Total	White	Black	American Indian or Alaskan Native	Asian or Pacific Islander	Total	White	Black	American Indian or Alaskan Native	Asian or Pacific Islander
TOTAL	**1,555,351**	**1,102,875**	**410,668**	**18,580**	**23,228**	**100.0**	**70.9**	**26.4**	**1.2**	**1.5**
Murder and nonnegligent manslaughter	956	423	455	29	49	100.0	44.2	47.6	3.0	5.1
Forcible rape	3,109	1,894	1,161	22	32	100.0	60.9	37.3	0.7	1.0
Robbery	18,098	7,194	10,517	94	293	100.0	39.8	58.1	0.5	1.6
Aggravated assault	44,714	27,416	16,294	450	554	100.0	61.3	36.4	1.0	1.2
Burglary	61,535	44,507	15,495	730	803	100.0	72.3	25.2	1.2	1.3
Larceny-theft	238,093	163,953	66,117	3,334	4,689	100.0	68.9	27.8	1.4	2.0
Motor vehicle theft	33,501	18,851	13,693	410	547	100.0	56.3	40.9	1.2	1.6
Arson	6,301	5,137	1,032	71	61	100.0	81.5	16.4	1.1	1.0
Violent crime[2]	66,877	36,927	28,427	595	928	100.0	55.2	42.5	0.9	1.4
Property crime[3]	339,430	232,448	96,337	4,545	6,100	100.0	68.5	28.4	1.3	1.8
Crime Index total[4]	406,307	269,375	124,764	5,140	7,028	100.0	66.3	30.7	1.3	1.7
Other assaults	162,788	102,780	56,342	1,800	1,866	100.0	63.1	34.6	1.1	1.1
Forgery and counterfeiting	3,971	3,044	823	29	75	100.0	76.7	20.7	0.7	1.9
Fraud	5,806	3,884	1,783	50	89	100.0	66.9	30.7	0.9	1.5
Embezzlement	1,256	872	355	6	23	100.0	69.4	28.3	0.5	1.8
Stolen property; buying, receiving, possessing	18,410	10,650	7,332	144	284	100.0	57.8	39.8	0.8	1.5
Vandalism	71,806	57,764	12,427	830	785	100.0	80.4	17.3	1.2	1.1
Weapons; carrying, possessing, etc.	25,827	17,047	8,237	216	327	100.0	66.0	31.9	0.8	1.3
Prostitution and commercialized vice	1,032	505	504	11	12	100.0	48.9	48.8	1.1	1.2
Sex offenses (except forcible rape and prostitution)	12,351	8,580	3,526	86	159	100.0	69.5	28.5	0.7	1.3
Drug abuse violations	139,014	99,185	37,269	1,152	1,408	100.0	71.3	26.8	0.8	1.0
Gambling	1,000	129	860	1	10	100.0	12.9	86.0	0.1	1.0
Offenses against the family and children	6,267	4,883	1,231	42	111	100.0	77.9	19.6	0.7	1.8
Driving under the influence	13,369	12,423	603	221	122	100.0	92.9	4.5	1.7	0.9
Liquor laws	92,004	84,540	4,312	2,423	729	100.0	91.9	4.7	2.6	0.8
Drunkenness	13,929	12,544	1,074	243	68	100.0	90.1	7.7	1.7	0.5
Disorderly conduct	117,460	72,564	42,823	1,149	924	100.0	61.8	36.5	1.0	0.8
Vagrancy	1,607	1,182	410	10	5	100.0	73.6	25.5	0.6	0.3
All other offenses (except traffic)	268,735	200,759	61,045	3,042	3,889	100.0	74.7	22.7	1.1	1.4
Suspicion	833	553	275	2	3	100.0	66.4	33.0	0.2	0.4
Curfew and loitering law violations	100,550	70,935	27,259	871	1,485	100.0	70.5	27.1	0.9	1.5
Runaways	91,029	68,677	17,414	1,112	3,826	100.0	75.4	19.1	1.2	4.2

See footnotes at end of table.

Table 43

Arrests

by Race, 2001—Continued

[9,511 agencies; 2001 estimated population 192,580,262]

Offense charged	Arrests 18 and over					Percent distribution[1]				
	Total	White	Black	American Indian or Alaskan Native	Asian or Pacific Islander	Total	White	Black	American Indian or Alaskan Native	Asian or Pacific Islander
TOTAL	**7,751,236**	**5,363,012**	**2,207,001**	**100,701**	**80,522**	**100.0**	**69.2**	**28.5**	**1.3**	**1.0**
Murder and nonnegligent manslaughter	8,460	4,138	4,130	93	99	100.0	48.9	48.8	1.1	1.2
Forcible rape	15,421	9,723	5,285	184	229	100.0	63.1	34.3	1.2	1.5
Robbery	58,512	26,905	30,711	343	553	100.0	46.0	52.5	0.6	0.9
Aggravated assault	284,494	183,290	94,639	3,130	3,435	100.0	64.4	33.3	1.1	1.2
Burglary	137,113	93,380	41,032	1,256	1,445	100.0	68.1	29.9	0.9	1.1
Larceny-theft	566,512	367,568	184,795	6,681	7,468	100.0	64.9	32.6	1.2	1.3
Motor vehicle theft	68,961	40,018	27,113	515	1,315	100.0	58.0	39.3	0.7	1.9
Arson	6,444	4,666	1,602	119	57	100.0	72.4	24.9	1.8	0.9
Violent crime[2]	366,887	224,056	134,765	3,750	4,316	100.0	61.1	36.7	1.0	1.2
Property crime[3]	779,030	505,632	254,542	8,571	10,285	100.0	64.9	32.7	1.1	1.3
Crime Index total[4]	1,145,917	729,688	389,307	12,321	14,601	100.0	63.7	34.0	1.1	1.3
Other assaults	733,972	483,830	232,197	10,256	7,689	100.0	65.9	31.6	1.4	1.0
Forgery and counterfeiting	73,537	49,514	22,474	425	1,124	100.0	67.3	30.6	0.6	1.5
Fraud	204,750	138,651	63,430	1,251	1,418	100.0	67.7	31.0	0.6	0.7
Embezzlement	12,545	8,213	4,060	69	203	100.0	65.5	32.4	0.6	1.6
Stolen property; buying, receiving, possessing	65,481	39,182	25,174	466	659	100.0	59.8	38.4	0.7	1.0
Vandalism	112,849	80,175	29,959	1,643	1,072	100.0	71.0	26.5	1.5	0.9
Weapons; carrying, possessing, etc.	88,362	52,617	34,295	605	845	100.0	59.5	38.8	0.7	1.0
Prostitution and commercialized vice	57,540	32,937	23,093	316	1,194	100.0	57.2	40.1	0.5	2.1
Sex offenses (except forcible rape and prostitution)	50,557	37,547	11,696	579	735	100.0	74.3	23.1	1.1	1.5
Drug abuse violations	950,886	600,938	338,318	5,032	6,598	100.0	63.2	35.6	0.5	0.7
Gambling	6,763	2,018	4,424	9	312	100.0	29.8	65.4	0.1	4.6
Offenses against the family and children	87,248	58,395	26,325	1,042	1,486	100.0	66.9	30.2	1.2	1.7
Driving under the influence	930,990	813,242	95,894	12,843	9,011	100.0	87.4	10.3	1.4	1.0
Liquor laws	314,439	266,558	36,506	8,623	2,752	100.0	84.8	11.6	2.7	0.9
Drunkenness	408,888	342,235	55,243	9,460	1,950	100.0	83.7	13.5	2.3	0.5
Disorderly conduct	307,377	201,113	98,953	5,007	2,304	100.0	65.4	32.2	1.6	0.7
Vagrancy	17,893	10,753	6,550	482	108	100.0	60.1	36.6	2.7	0.6
All other offenses (except traffic)	2,179,469	1,414,348	708,417	30,263	26,441	100.0	64.9	32.5	1.4	1.2
Suspicion	1,773	1,058	686	9	20	100.0	59.7	38.7	0.5	1.1
Curfew and loitering law violations	–	–	–	–	–	–	–	–	–	–
Runaways	–	–	–	–	–	–	–	–	–	–

[1] Because of rounding, the percentages may not add to total.
[2] Violent crimes are offenses of murder, forcible rape, robbery, and aggravated assault.
[3] Property crimes are offenses of burglary, larceny-theft, motor vehicle theft, and arson.
[4] Includes arson.

Table 44

Arrest Trends

City, 2000-2001

[5,956 agencies; 2001 estimated population 116,273,916; 2000 estimated population 114,684,455]

| | Number of persons arrested | | | | | | | | |
| | Total all ages | | | Under 18 years of age | | | 18 years of age and over | | |
Offense charged	2000	2001	Percent change	2000	2001	Percent change	2000	2001	Percent change
TOTAL[1]	6,160,222	6,016,520	-2.3	1,129,073	1,078,875	-4.4	5,031,149	4,937,645	-1.9
Murder and nonnegligent manslaughter	4,831	4,889	+1.2	488	494	+1.2	4,343	4,395	+1.2
Forcible rape	11,003	10,841	-1.5	1,940	1,890	-2.6	9,063	8,951	-1.2
Robbery	48,876	50,000	+2.3	12,215	11,792	-3.5	36,661	38,208	+4.2
Aggravated assault	209,127	210,084	+0.5	29,850	29,471	-1.3	179,277	180,613	+0.7
Burglary	124,351	126,115	+1.4	42,503	40,452	-4.8	81,848	85,663	+4.7
Larceny-theft	605,159	592,067	-2.2	200,718	187,884	-6.4	404,441	404,183	-0.1
Motor vehicle theft	57,455	59,492	+3.5	20,003	19,620	-1.9	37,452	39,872	+6.5
Arson	6,962	8,075	+16.0	4,094	4,391	+7.3	2,868	3,684	+28.5
Violent crime[2]	273,837	275,814	+0.7	44,493	43,647	-1.9	229,344	232,167	+1.2
Property crime[3]	793,927	785,749	-1.0	267,318	252,347	-5.6	526,609	533,402	+1.3
Crime Index total[4]	1,067,764	1,061,563	-0.6	311,811	295,994	-5.1	755,953	765,569	+1.3
Other assaults	581,683	581,511	[5]	107,711	109,499	+1.7	473,972	472,012	-0.4
Forgery and counterfeiting	51,288	54,080	+5.4	3,220	2,988	-7.2	48,068	51,092	+6.3
Fraud	105,340	106,305	+0.9	4,301	3,885	-9.7	101,039	102,420	+1.4
Embezzlement	9,760	10,116	+3.6	1,093	1,024	-6.3	8,667	9,092	+4.9
Stolen property; buying, receiving, possessing	59,500	59,678	+0.3	14,687	13,981	-4.8	44,813	45,697	+2.0
Vandalism	129,295	125,030	-3.3	53,473	50,267	-6.0	75,822	74,763	-1.4
Weapons; carrying, possessing, etc.	72,083	73,298	+1.7	17,205	17,019	-1.1	54,878	56,279	+2.6
Prostitution and commercialized vice	43,072	39,759	-7.7	570	661	+16.0	42,502	39,098	-8.0
Sex offenses (except forcible rape and prostitution)	38,710	38,574	-0.4	7,154	7,454	+4.2	31,556	31,120	-1.4
Drug abuse violations	665,409	657,421	-1.2	89,843	89,281	-0.6	575,566	568,140	-1.3
Gambling	3,437	3,251	-5.4	335	255	-23.9	3,102	2,996	-3.4
Offenses against the family and children	41,853	41,702	-0.4	3,989	4,419	+10.8	37,864	37,283	-1.5
Driving under the influence	547,182	527,674	-3.6	8,633	8,417	-2.5	538,549	519,257	-3.6
Liquor laws	318,861	296,414	-7.0	70,780	64,079	-9.5	248,081	232,335	-6.3
Drunkenness	364,538	346,831	-4.9	12,928	11,473	-11.3	351,610	335,358	-4.6
Disorderly conduct	300,248	288,058	-4.1	81,084	81,358	+0.3	219,164	206,700	-5.7
Vagrancy	18,528	17,262	-6.8	1,454	1,250	-14.0	17,074	16,012	-6.2
All other offenses (except traffic)	1,603,973	1,564,688	-2.4	201,104	192,266	-4.4	1,402,869	1,372,422	-2.2
Suspicion	2,941	1,779	-39.5	588	444	-24.5	2,353	1,335	-43.3
Curfew and loitering law violations	70,695	61,217	-13.4	70,695	61,217	-13.4	–	–	–
Runaways	67,003	62,088	-7.3	67,003	62,088	-7.3	–	–	–

[1] Does not include suspicion.
[2] Violent crimes are offenses of murder, forcible rape, robbery, and aggravated assault.
[3] Property crimes are offenses of burglary, larceny-theft, motor vehicle theft, and arson.
[4] Includes arson.
[5] Less than one-tenth of 1 percent.

Table 45

Arrest Trends

City
by Sex, 2000-2001
[5,956 agencies; 2001 estimated population 116,273,916; 2000 estimated population 114,684,455]

| | Male | | | | | | Female | | | | | |
| | Total | | | Under 18 | | | Total | | | Under 18 | | |
Offense charged	2000	2001	Percent change	2000	2001	Percent change	2000	2001	Percent change	2000	2001	Percent change
TOTAL[1]	4,753,876	4,620,938	-2.8	806,199	763,491	-5.3	1,406,346	1,395,582	-0.8	322,874	315,384	-2.3
Murder and nonnegligent manslaughter	4,307	4,387	+1.9	427	444	+4.0	524	502	-4.2	61	50	-18.0
Forcible rape	10,903	10,737	-1.5	1,920	1,871	-2.6	100	104	+4.0	20	19	-5.0
Robbery	43,911	44,824	+2.1	11,143	10,740	-3.6	4,965	5,176	+4.2	1,072	1,052	-1.9
Aggravated assault	166,046	167,062	+0.6	22,875	22,591	-1.2	43,081	43,022	-0.1	6,975	6,880	-1.4
Burglary	106,570	107,729	+1.1	37,190	35,201	-5.3	17,781	18,386	+3.4	5,313	5,251	-1.2
Larceny-theft	379,527	368,843	-2.8	123,920	112,602	-9.1	225,632	223,224	-1.1	76,798	75,282	-2.0
Motor vehicle theft	48,033	49,348	+2.7	16,467	16,130	-2.0	9,422	10,144	+7.7	3,536	3,490	-1.3
Arson	5,936	6,821	+14.9	3,618	3,840	+6.1	1,026	1,254	+22.2	476	551	+15.8
Violent crime[2]	225,167	227,010	+0.8	36,365	35,646	-2.0	48,670	48,804	+0.3	8,128	8,001	-1.6
Property crime[3]	540,066	532,741	-1.4	181,195	167,773	-7.4	253,861	253,008	-0.3	86,123	84,574	-1.8
Crime Index total[4]	765,233	759,751	-0.7	217,560	203,419	-6.5	302,531	301,812	-0.2	94,251	92,575	-1.8
Other assaults	445,493	442,669	-0.6	74,108	74,294	+0.3	136,190	138,842	+1.9	33,603	35,205	+4.8
Forgery and counterfeiting	31,018	32,054	+3.3	2,099	1,888	-10.1	20,270	22,026	+8.7	1,121	1,100	-1.9
Fraud	59,263	59,800	+0.9	2,857	2,591	-9.3	46,077	46,505	+0.9	1,444	1,294	-10.4
Embezzlement	4,787	4,949	+3.4	570	570	0.0	4,973	5,167	+3.9	523	454	-13.2
Stolen property; buying, receiving, possessing	48,717	48,492	-0.5	12,324	11,526	-6.5	10,783	11,186	+3.7	2,363	2,455	+3.9
Vandalism	108,714	104,388	-4.0	46,510	43,538	-6.4	20,581	20,642	+0.3	6,963	6,729	-3.4
Weapons; carrying, possessing, etc.	66,383	67,438	+1.6	15,669	15,441	-1.5	5,700	5,860	+2.8	1,536	1,578	+2.7
Prostitution and commercialized vice	16,099	12,992	-19.3	231	188	-18.6	26,973	26,767	-0.8	339	473	+39.5
Sex offenses (except forcible rape and prostitution)	35,710	35,503	-0.6	6,634	6,900	+4.0	3,000	3,071	+2.4	520	554	+6.5
Drug abuse violations	545,167	537,428	-1.4	76,060	74,801	-1.7	120,242	119,993	-0.2	13,783	14,480	+5.1
Gambling	2,984	2,844	-4.7	308	244	-20.8	453	407	-10.2	27	11	-59.3
Offenses against the family and children	29,635	29,158	-1.6	2,507	2,788	+11.2	12,218	12,544	+2.7	1,482	1,631	+10.1
Driving under the influence	453,355	434,960	-4.1	7,135	6,912	-3.1	93,827	92,714	-1.2	1,498	1,505	+0.5
Liquor laws	246,543	227,337	-7.8	48,809	43,611	-10.6	72,318	69,077	-4.5	21,971	20,468	-6.8
Drunkenness	317,181	300,121	-5.4	10,381	9,077	-12.6	47,357	46,710	-1.4	2,547	2,396	-5.9
Disorderly conduct	227,880	217,781	-4.4	57,326	57,241	-0.1	72,368	70,277	-2.9	23,758	24,117	+1.5
Vagrancy	14,607	13,972	-4.3	1,137	1,012	-11.0	3,921	3,290	-16.1	317	238	-24.9
All other offenses (except traffic)	1,259,498	1,222,867	-2.9	148,365	141,016	-5.0	344,475	341,821	-0.8	52,739	51,250	-2.8
Suspicion	2,385	1,416	-40.6	481	337	-29.9	556	363	-34.7	107	107	0.0
Curfew and loitering law violations	48,033	41,458	-13.7	48,033	41,458	-13.7	22,662	19,759	-12.8	22,662	19,759	-12.8
Runaways	27,576	24,976	-9.4	27,576	24,976	-9.4	39,427	37,112	-5.9	39,427	37,112	-5.9

[1] Does not include suspicion.
[2] Violent crimes are offenses of murder, forcible rape, robbery, and aggravated assault.
[3] Property crimes are offenses of burglary, larceny-theft, motor vehicle theft, and arson.
[4] Includes arson.

Table 46

Arrests
City
by Age, 2001
[6,868 agencies; 2001 estimated population 133,588,306]

Offense charged	Total all ages	Ages under 15	Ages under 18	Ages 18 and over	Under 10	10-12	13-14	15	16	17	18
TOTAL	**7,047,131**	**415,362**	**1,275,071**	**5,772,060**	**18,031**	**99,501**	**297,830**	**248,621**	**296,313**	**314,775**	**351,459**
Percent distribution[1]	**100.0**	**5.9**	**18.1**	**81.9**	**0.3**	**1.4**	**4.2**	**3.5**	**4.2**	**4.5**	**5.0**
Murder and nonnegligent manslaughter	6,962	101	815	6,147	6	8	87	119	212	383	450
Forcible rape	13,531	907	2,368	11,163	31	260	616	400	485	576	609
Robbery	66,671	4,007	16,244	50,427	89	837	3,081	3,195	4,229	4,813	5,401
Aggravated assault	254,661	13,477	36,219	218,442	717	3,688	9,072	6,670	7,779	8,293	9,347
Burglary	146,699	18,048	46,048	100,651	1,060	5,002	11,986	8,783	9,585	9,632	9,923
Larceny-theft	684,443	81,906	208,286	476,157	3,382	22,648	55,876	39,241	43,747	43,392	41,486
Motor vehicle theft	82,908	7,020	27,802	55,106	57	860	6,103	6,651	7,388	6,743	6,197
Arson	9,348	3,178	4,850	4,498	522	1,131	1,525	702	552	418	394
Violent crime[2]	341,825	18,492	55,646	286,179	843	4,793	12,856	10,384	12,705	14,065	15,807
Percent distribution[1]	100.0	5.4	16.3	83.7	0.2	1.4	3.8	3.0	3.7	4.1	4.6
Property crime[3]	923,398	110,152	286,986	636,412	5,021	29,641	75,490	55,377	61,272	60,185	58,000
Percent distribution[1]	100.0	11.9	31.1	68.9	0.5	3.2	8.2	6.0	6.6	6.5	6.3
Crime Index total[4]	1,265,223	128,644	342,632	922,591	5,864	34,434	88,346	65,761	73,977	74,250	73,807
Percent distribution[1]	100.0	10.2	27.1	72.9	0.5	2.7	7.0	5.2	5.8	5.9	5.8
Other assaults	682,571	56,673	128,344	554,227	2,600	16,352	37,721	23,821	24,506	23,344	22,586
Forgery and counterfeiting	59,756	350	3,205	56,551	16	67	267	427	887	1,541	2,657
Fraud	118,352	768	4,502	113,850	46	131	591	686	1,211	1,837	3,615
Embezzlement	10,662	74	1,092	9,570	1	15	58	73	341	604	755
Stolen property; buying, receiving, possessing	66,148	4,340	15,646	50,502	116	877	3,347	3,123	3,884	4,299	4,865
Vandalism	145,493	25,491	57,133	88,360	2,309	7,734	15,448	10,017	11,008	10,617	9,203
Weapons; carrying, possessing, etc.	90,144	7,221	21,570	68,574	345	1,810	5,066	4,017	4,806	5,526	6,287
Prostitution and commercialized vice	56,333	141	977	55,356	4	11	126	138	252	446	1,209
Sex offenses (except forcible rape and prostitution)	47,017	4,996	9,144	37,873	322	1,541	3,133	1,473	1,333	1,342	1,506
Drug abuse violations	840,392	19,956	113,877	726,515	219	2,385	17,352	21,015	31,458	41,448	55,276
Gambling	6,476	116	938	5,538	2	8	106	175	248	399	407
Offenses against the family and children	46,728	1,711	4,777	41,951	138	443	1,130	973	1,131	962	1,229
Driving under the influence	586,877	266	9,109	577,768	83	22	161	452	2,402	5,989	14,372
Liquor laws	319,816	6,975	69,623	250,193	153	510	6,312	11,027	20,363	31,258	49,964
Drunkenness	354,643	1,532	11,886	342,757	105	122	1,305	1,784	2,989	5,581	9,960
Disorderly conduct	366,339	40,927	101,442	264,897	1,203	10,654	29,070	20,530	20,462	19,523	18,188
Vagrancy	18,066	310	1,364	16,702	9	64	237	258	372	424	853
All other offenses (except traffic)	1,802,616	62,154	215,722	1,586,894	3,143	12,952	46,059	43,553	52,234	57,781	74,623
Suspicion	1,875	134	484	1,391	5	23	106	103	125	122	97
Curfew and loitering law violations	94,882	26,759	94,882	–	542	4,806	21,411	21,604	26,537	19,982	–
Runaways	66,722	25,824	66,722	–	806	4,540	20,478	17,611	15,787	7,500	–

See footnotes at end of table.

Table 46

Arrests
City
by Age, 2001—Continued
[6,868 agencies; 2001 estimated population 133,588,306]

Offense charged	19	20	21	22	23	24	25-29	30-34	35-39	40-44	45-49	50-54	55-59	60-64	65 over
TOTAL	359,132	337,002	305,240	266,882	236,155	212,238	846,418	769,095	747,977	614,622	367,830	191,027	85,247	40,979	40,757
Percent distribution[1]	5.1	4.8	4.3	3.8	3.4	3.0	12.0	10.9	10.6	8.7	5.2	2.7	1.2	0.6	0.6
Murder and nonnegligent manslaughter	497	479	459	421	384	291	1,050	682	524	375	237	140	69	40	49
Forcible rape	589	579	554	500	470	430	1,797	1,636	1,558	1,151	621	313	180	84	92
Robbery	4,965	4,026	3,536	2,801	2,273	2,026	7,497	6,332	5,437	3,467	1,677	645	201	69	74
Aggravated assault	9,954	10,052	10,734	9,760	9,229	8,558	36,391	32,810	30,446	23,726	13,758	7,073	3,238	1,584	1,782
Burglary	8,428	6,846	5,841	4,774	4,135	3,541	13,964	13,594	12,778	9,404	4,556	1,801	658	233	175
Larceny-theft	34,207	27,689	23,113	19,364	16,406	14,505	61,454	62,817	62,279	51,393	31,187	15,967	7,013	3,438	3,839
Motor vehicle theft	5,333	4,199	3,708	2,934	2,516	2,128	8,382	7,282	5,736	3,827	1,714	730	255	85	80
Arson	275	215	221	219	179	141	594	575	540	533	299	166	85	31	31
Violent crime[2]	16,005	15,136	15,283	13,482	12,356	11,305	46,735	41,460	37,965	28,719	16,293	8,171	3,688	1,777	1,997
Percent distribution[1]	4.7	4.4	4.5	3.9	3.6	3.3	13.7	12.1	11.1	8.4	4.8	2.4	1.1	0.5	0.6
Property crime[3]	48,243	38,949	32,883	27,291	23,236	20,315	84,394	84,268	81,333	65,157	37,756	18,664	8,011	3,787	4,125
Percent distribution[1]	5.2	4.2	3.6	3.0	2.5	2.2	9.1	9.1	8.8	7.1	4.1	2.0	0.9	0.4	0.4
Crime Index total[4]	64,248	54,085	48,166	40,773	35,592	31,620	131,129	125,728	119,298	93,876	54,049	26,835	11,699	5,564	6,122
Percent distribution[1]	5.1	4.3	3.8	3.2	2.8	2.5	10.4	9.9	9.4	7.4	4.3	2.1	0.9	0.4	0.5
Other assaults	23,511	24,139	26,279	24,662	23,104	21,727	91,923	85,224	81,315	62,270	35,125	17,184	7,594	3,667	3,917
Forgery and counterfeiting	3,335	3,291	3,000	2,986	2,523	2,264	10,013	9,314	7,463	5,066	2,852	1,122	390	148	127
Fraud	4,872	5,485	5,441	5,185	4,789	4,647	19,710	18,554	15,907	12,139	6,890	3,609	1,545	684	778
Embezzlement	812	688	653	509	400	368	1,531	1,287	1011	762	399	234	103	38	20
Stolen property; buying, receiving, possessing	4,244	3,794	3,244	2,607	2,292	1,988	7,455	6,626	5,784	4,031	2,093	918	320	136	105
Vandalism	7,763	6,340	6,138	4,976	4,263	3,514	12,771	10,511	9,267	6,901	3,653	1,687	681	332	360
Weapons; carrying, possessing, etc.	5,817	5,136	4,956	4,200	3,512	3,074	10,653	7,461	5,932	4,850	2,976	1,872	920	455	473
Prostitution and commercialized vice	1,599	1,639	1,711	1,722	1,660	1,547	8,460	10,727	10,768	7,525	3,695	1,630	675	388	401
Sex offenses (except forcible rape and prostitution)	1,571	1,488	1,491	1,278	1,153	1,075	4,875	5,396	5,495	4,602	3,241	1,997	1,143	695	867
Drug abuse violations	53,445	48,950	43,735	37,210	31,900	28,209	107,066	93,333	89,858	71,682	39,466	17,175	5,809	2,074	1,327
Gambling	427	394	376	338	302	228	653	445	368	434	274	418	157	173	144
Offenses against the family and children	1,349	1,522	1,684	1,577	1,455	1,529	7,081	7,136	7,015	5,210	2,833	1,283	519	245	284
Driving under the influence	19,030	21,855	28,713	26,913	24,938	22,433	91,172	79,377	78,241	68,599	46,022	27,845	14,058	7,213	6,987
Liquor laws	53,663	44,395	9,630	6,208	4,863	3,879	13,527	12,142	14,306	14,764	10,569	6,314	3,141	1,514	1,314
Drunkenness	11,059	11,165	15,282	13,436	11,764	10,625	43,384	43,162	51,081	50,465	34,259	19,311	9,392	4,714	3,698
Disorderly conduct	16,895	16,054	17,952	14,935	12,495	10,791	38,069	31,184	30,878	26,346	15,824	8,123	3,448	1,809	1,906
Vagrancy	709	618	598	470	376	377	1,615	1,930	2,491	2,718	1,814	1,119	517	254	243
All other offenses (except traffic)	84,695	85,868	86,104	76,839	68,719	62,295	245,103	219,368	211,328	172,259	101,720	52,320	23,112	10,866	11,675
Suspicion	88	96	87	58	55	48	228	190	171	123	76	31	24	10	9
Curfew and loitering law violations	–	–	–	–	–	–	–	–	–	–	–	–	–	–	–
Runaways	–	–	–	–	–	–	–	–	–	–	–	–	–	–	–

[1] Because of rounding, the percentages may not add to total.
[2] Violent crimes are offenses of murder, forcible rape, robbery, and aggravated assault.
[3] Property crimes are offenses of burglary, larceny-theft, motor vehicle theft, and arson.
[4] Includes arson.

Table 47

Arrests

City

of Persons Under 15, 18, 21, and 25 Years of Age, 2001

[6,868 agencies; 2001 estimated population 133,588,306]

Offense charged	Total all ages	Number of persons arrested				Percent of total all ages			
		Under 15	Under 18	Under 21	Under 25	Under 15	Under 18	Under 21	Under 25
TOTAL	**7,047,131**	**415,362**	**1,275,071**	**2,322,664**	**3,343,179**	**5.9**	**18.1**	**33.0**	**47.4**
Murder and nonnegligent manslaughter	6,962	101	815	2,241	3,796	1.5	11.7	32.2	54.5
Forcible rape	13,531	907	2,368	4,145	6,099	6.7	17.5	30.6	45.1
Robbery	66,671	4,007	16,244	30,636	41,272	6.0	24.4	46.0	61.9
Aggravated assault	254,661	13,477	36,219	65,572	103,853	5.3	14.2	25.7	40.8
Burglary	146,699	18,048	46,048	71,245	89,536	12.3	31.4	48.6	61.0
Larceny-theft	684,443	81,906	208,286	311,668	385,056	12.0	30.4	45.5	56.3
Motor vehicle theft	82,908	7,020	27,802	43,531	54,817	8.5	33.5	52.5	66.1
Arson	9,348	3,178	4,850	5,734	6,494	34.0	51.9	61.3	69.5
Violent crime[1]	341,825	18,492	55,646	102,594	155,020	5.4	16.3	30.0	45.4
Property crime[2]	923,398	110,152	286,986	432,178	535,903	11.9	31.1	46.8	58.0
Crime Index total[3]	1,265,223	128,644	342,632	534,772	690,923	10.2	27.1	42.3	54.6
Other assaults	682,571	56,673	128,344	198,580	294,352	8.3	18.8	29.1	43.1
Forgery and counterfeiting	59,756	350	3,205	12,488	23,261	0.6	5.4	20.9	38.9
Fraud	118,352	768	4,502	18,474	38,536	0.6	3.8	15.6	32.6
Embezzlement	10,662	74	1,092	3,347	5,277	0.7	10.2	31.4	49.5
Stolen property; buying, receiving, possessing	66,148	4,340	15,646	28,549	38,680	6.6	23.7	43.2	58.5
Vandalism	145,493	25,491	57,133	80,439	99,330	17.5	39.3	55.3	68.3
Weapons; carrying, possessing, etc.	90,144	7,221	21,570	38,810	54,552	8.0	23.9	43.1	60.5
Prostitution and commercialized vice	56,333	141	977	5,424	12,064	0.3	1.7	9.6	21.4
Sex offenses (except forcible rape and prostitution)	47,017	4,996	9,144	13,709	18,706	10.6	19.4	29.2	39.8
Drug abuse violations	840,392	19,956	113,877	271,548	412,602	2.4	13.6	32.3	49.1
Gambling	6,476	116	938	2,166	3,410	1.8	14.5	33.4	52.7
Offenses against the family and children	46,728	1,711	4,777	8,877	15,122	3.7	10.2	19.0	32.4
Driving under the influence	586,877	266	9,109	64,366	167,363	[4]	1.6	11.0	28.5
Liquor laws	319,816	6,975	69,623	217,645	242,225	2.2	21.8	68.1	75.7
Drunkenness	354,643	1,532	11,886	44,070	95,177	0.4	3.4	12.4	26.8
Disorderly conduct	366,339	40,927	101,442	152,579	208,752	11.2	27.7	41.6	57.0
Vagrancy	18,066	310	1,364	3,544	5,365	1.7	7.6	19.6	29.7
All other offenses (except traffic)	1,802,616	62,154	215,722	460,908	754,865	3.4	12.0	25.6	41.9
Suspicion	1,875	134	484	765	1,013	7.1	25.8	40.8	54.0
Curfew and loitering law violations	94,882	26,759	94,882	94,882	94,882	28.2	100.0	100.0	100.0
Runaways	66,722	25,824	66,722	66,722	66,722	38.7	100.0	100.0	100.0

[1] Violent crimes are offenses of murder, forcible rape, robbery, and aggravated assault.

[2] Property crimes are offenses of burglary, larceny-theft, motor vehicle theft, and arson.

[3] Includes arson.

[4] Less than one-tenth of 1 percent.

Table 48

Arrests
City
by Sex, 2001
[6,868 agencies; 2001 estimated population 133,588,306]

Offense charged	Number of persons arrested			Percent male	Percent female	Percent distribution[1]		
	Total	Male	Female			Total	Male	Female
TOTAL	**7,047,131**	**5,433,855**	**1,613,276**	**77.1**	**22.9**	**100.0**	**100.0**	**100.0**
Murder and nonnegligent manslaughter	6,962	6,284	678	90.3	9.7	0.1	0.1	[2]
Forcible rape	13,531	13,395	136	99.0	1.0	0.2	0.2	[2]
Robbery	66,671	59,894	6,777	89.8	10.2	0.9	1.1	0.4
Aggravated assault	254,661	201,972	52,689	79.3	20.7	3.6	3.7	3.3
Burglary	146,699	125,992	20,707	85.9	14.1	2.1	2.3	1.3
Larceny-theft	684,443	430,253	254,190	62.9	37.1	9.7	7.9	15.8
Motor vehicle theft	82,908	69,408	13,500	83.7	16.3	1.2	1.3	0.8
Arson	9,348	7,858	1,490	84.1	15.9	0.1	0.1	0.1
Violent crime[3]	341,825	281,545	60,280	82.4	17.6	4.9	5.2	3.7
Property crime[4]	923,398	633,511	289,887	68.6	31.4	13.1	11.7	18.0
Crime Index total[5]	1,265,223	915,056	350,167	72.3	27.7	18.0	16.8	21.7
Other assaults	682,571	522,110	160,461	76.5	23.5	9.7	9.6	9.9
Forgery and counterfeiting	59,756	35,676	24,080	59.7	40.3	0.8	0.7	1.5
Fraud	118,352	67,329	51,023	56.9	43.1	1.7	1.2	3.2
Embezzlement	10,662	5,263	5,399	49.4	50.6	0.2	0.1	0.3
Stolen property; buying, receiving, possessing	66,148	53,916	12,232	81.5	18.5	0.9	1.0	0.8
Vandalism	145,493	121,498	23,995	83.5	16.5	2.1	2.2	1.5
Weapons; carrying, possessing, etc.	90,144	82,736	7,408	91.8	8.2	1.3	1.5	0.5
Prostitution and commercialized vice	56,333	18,422	37,911	32.7	67.3	0.8	0.3	2.3
Sex offenses (except forcible rape and prostitution)	47,017	42,768	4,249	91.0	9.0	0.7	0.8	0.3
Drug abuse violations	840,392	691,835	148,557	82.3	17.7	11.9	12.7	9.2
Gambling	6,476	5,947	529	91.8	8.2	0.1	0.1	[2]
Offenses against the family and children	46,728	32,322	14,406	69.2	30.8	0.7	0.6	0.9
Driving under the influence	586,877	485,259	101,618	82.7	17.3	8.3	8.9	6.3
Liquor laws	319,816	245,155	74,661	76.7	23.3	4.5	4.5	4.6 ·
Drunkenness	354,643	306,603	48,040	86.5	13.5	5.0	5.6	3.0
Disorderly conduct	366,339	279,019	87,320	76.2	23.8	5.2	5.1	5.4
Vagrancy	18,066	14,658	3,408	81.1	18.9	0.3	0.3	0.2
All other offenses (except traffic)	1,802,616	1,414,224	388,392	78.5	21.5	25.6	26.0	24.1
Suspicion	1,875	1,468	407	78.3	21.7	[2]	[2]	[2]
Curfew and loitering law violations	94,882	65,706	29,176	69.3	30.7	1.3	1.2	1.8
Runaways	66,722	26,885	39,837	40.3	59.7	0.9	0.5	2.5

[1] Because of rounding, the percentages may not add to total.

[2] Less than one-tenth of 1 percent.

[3] Violent crimes are offenses of murder, forcible rape, robbery, and aggravated assault.

[4] Property crimes are offenses of burglary, larceny-theft, motor vehicle theft, and arson.

[5] Includes arson.

Table 49

Arrests
City
by Race, 2001
[6,868 agencies; 2001 estimated population 133,588,306]

Offense charged	Total arrests					Percent distribution[1]				
	Total	White	Black	American Indian or Alaskan Native	Asian or Pacific Islander	Total	White	Black	American Indian or Alaskan Native	Asian or Pacific Islander
TOTAL	**7,033,506**	**4,688,050**	**2,169,815**	**88,869**	**86,772**	**100.0**	**66.7**	**30.8**	**1.3**	**1.2**
Murder and nonnegligent manslaughter	6,953	3,033	3,705	78	137	100.0	43.6	53.3	1.1	2.0
Forcible rape	13,492	7,778	5,367	124	223	100.0	57.6	39.8	0.9	1.7
Robbery	66,616	28,759	36,727	342	788	100.0	43.2	55.1	0.5	1.2
Aggravated assault	254,203	154,081	94,285	2,331	3,506	100.0	60.6	37.1	0.9	1.4
Burglary	146,506	96,342	47,027	1,233	1,904	100.0	65.8	32.1	0.8	1.3
Larceny-theft	683,100	444,057	219,238	8,852	10,953	100.0	65.0	32.1	1.3	1.6
Motor vehicle theft	82,786	43,787	36,712	673	1,614	100.0	52.9	44.3	0.8	1.9
Arson	9,335	6,953	2,143	151	88	100.0	74.5	23.0	1.6	0.9
Violent crime[2]	341,264	193,651	140,084	2,875	4,654	100.0	56.7	41.0	0.8	1.4
Property crime[3]	921,727	591,139	305,120	10,909	14,559	100.0	64.1	33.1	1.2	1.6
Crime Index total[4]	1,262,991	784,790	445,204	13,784	19,213	100.0	62.1	35.2	1.1	1.5
Other assaults	681,297	422,212	242,200	8,974	7,911	100.0	62.0	35.5	1.3	1.2
Forgery and counterfeiting	59,583	39,269	18,971	336	1,007	100.0	65.9	31.8	0.6	1.7
Fraud	117,942	74,776	41,307	685	1,174	100.0	63.4	35.0	0.6	1.0
Embezzlement	10,638	6,774	3,626	52	186	100.0	63.7	34.1	0.5	1.7
Stolen property; buying, receiving, possessing	66,011	36,716	28,037	417	841	100.0	55.6	42.5	0.6	1.3
Vandalism	145,217	105,007	36,706	1,878	1,626	100.0	72.3	25.3	1.3	1.1
Weapons; carrying, possessing, etc.	90,044	51,864	36,598	570	1,012	100.0	57.6	40.6	0.6	1.1
Prostitution and commercialized vice	56,271	31,712	23,114	314	1,131	100.0	56.4	41.1	0.6	2.0
Sex offenses (except forcible rape and prostitution)	46,953	32,525	13,156	479	793	100.0	69.3	28.0	1.0	1.7
Drug abuse violations	839,383	503,857	324,765	4,184	6,577	100.0	60.0	38.7	0.5	0.8
Gambling	6,475	1,423	4,824	9	219	100.0	22.0	74.5	0.1	3.4
Offenses against the family and children	46,447	32,368	11,846	796	1,437	100.0	69.7	25.5	1.7	3.1
Driving under the influence	585,278	508,904	61,672	8,277	6,425	100.0	87.0	10.5	1.4	1.1
Liquor laws	318,582	270,668	35,687	9,303	2,924	100.0	85.0	11.2	2.9	0.9
Drunkenness	353,966	293,163	50,712	8,294	1,797	100.0	82.8	14.3	2.3	0.5
Disorderly conduct	365,482	229,939	127,393	5,230	2,920	100.0	62.9	34.9	1.4	0.8
Vagrancy	18,058	10,877	6,600	472	109	100.0	60.2	36.5	2.6	0.6
All other offenses (except traffic)	1,799,664	1,135,593	616,310	23,095	24,666	100.0	63.1	34.2	1.3	1.4
Suspicion	1,862	1,156	676	7	23	100.0	62.1	36.3	0.4	1.2
Curfew and loitering law violations	94,747	66,024	26,511	834	1,378	100.0	69.7	28.0	0.9	1.5
Runaways	66,615	48,433	13,900	879	3,403	100.0	72.7	20.9	1.3	5.1

See footnotes at end of table.

Table 49

Arrests

City
by Race, 2001—Continued
[6,868 agencies; 2001 estimated population 133,588,306]

Offense charged	Arrests under 18					Percent distribution[1]				
	Total	White	Black	American Indian or Alaskan Native	Asian or Pacific Islander	Total	White	Black	American Indian or Alaskan Native	Asian or Pacific Islander
TOTAL	**1,272,451**	**878,273**	**358,816**	**14,926**	**20,436**	**100.0**	**69.0**	**28.2**	**1.2**	**1.6**
Murder and nonnegligent manslaughter	814	332	407	27	48	100.0	40.8	50.0	3.3	5.9
Forcible rape	2,359	1,314	998	17	30	100.0	55.7	42.3	0.7	1.3
Robbery	16,232	6,366	9,517	74	275	100.0	39.2	58.6	0.5	1.7
Aggravated assault	36,124	21,125	14,166	332	501	100.0	58.5	39.2	0.9	1.4
Burglary	45,977	31,729	13,091	472	685	100.0	69.0	28.5	1.0	1.5
Larceny-theft	207,826	141,825	58,701	3,020	4,280	100.0	68.2	28.2	1.5	2.1
Motor vehicle theft	27,749	14,368	12,644	297	440	100.0	51.8	45.6	1.1	1.6
Arson	4,841	3,887	862	51	41	100.0	80.3	17.8	1.1	0.8
Violent crime[2]	55,529	29,137	25,088	450	854	100.0	52.5	45.2	0.8	1.5
Property crime[3]	286,393	191,809	85,298	3,840	5,446	100.0	67.0	29.8	1.3	1.9
Crime Index total[4]	341,922	220,946	110,386	4,290	6,300	100.0	64.6	32.3	1.3	1.8
Other assaults	128,035	78,036	47,020	1,397	1,582	100.0	60.9	36.7	1.1	1.2
Forgery and counterfeiting	3,199	2,405	702	26	66	100.0	75.2	21.9	0.8	2.1
Fraud	4,485	2,909	1,464	38	74	100.0	64.9	32.6	0.8	1.6
Embezzlement	1,090	750	313	5	22	100.0	68.8	28.7	0.5	2.0
Stolen property; buying, receiving, possessing	15,594	8,550	6,681	105	258	100.0	54.8	42.8	0.7	1.7
Vandalism	56,996	44,916	10,747	646	687	100.0	78.8	18.9	1.1	1.2
Weapons; carrying, possessing, etc.	21,541	13,826	7,254	170	291	100.0	64.2	33.7	0.8	1.4
Prostitution and commercialized vice	975	464	489	10	12	100.0	47.6	50.2	1.0	1.2
Sex offenses (except forcible rape and prostitution)	9,119	5,922	2,996	56	145	100.0	64.9	32.9	0.6	1.6
Drug abuse violations	113,695	77,744	33,947	892	1,112	100.0	68.4	29.9	0.8	1.0
Gambling	938	92	835	1	10	100.0	9.8	89.0	0.1	1.1
Offenses against the family and children	4,759	3,623	994	35	107	100.0	76.1	20.9	0.7	2.2
Driving under the influence	9,087	8,397	439	165	86	100.0	92.4	4.8	1.8	0.9
Liquor laws	69,397	63,150	3,679	1,973	595	100.0	91.0	5.3	2.8	0.9
Drunkenness	11,845	10,625	948	208	64	100.0	89.7	8.0	1.8	0.5
Disorderly conduct	101,278	61,835	37,626	972	845	100.0	61.1	37.2	1.0	0.8
Vagrancy	1,364	1,025	327	7	5	100.0	75.1	24.0	0.5	0.4
All other offenses (except traffic)	215,286	158,244	51,435	2,216	3,391	100.0	73.5	23.9	1.0	1.6
Suspicion	484	357	123	1	3	100.0	73.8	25.4	0.2	0.6
Curfew and loitering law violations	94,747	66,024	26,511	834	1,378	100.0	69.7	28.0	0.9	1.5
Runaways	66,615	48,433	13,900	879	3,403	100.0	72.7	20.9	1.3	5.1

See footnotes at end of table.

Table 49

Arrests
City
by Race, 2001—Continued
[6,868 agencies; 2001 estimated population 133,588,306]

Offense charged	Arrests 18 and over					Percent distribution[1]				
	Total	White	Black	American Indian or Alaskan Native	Asian or Pacific Islander	Total	White	Black	American Indian or Alaskan Native	Asian or Pacific Islander
TOTAL	5,761,055	3,809,777	1,810,999	73,943	66,336	100.0	66.1	31.4	1.3	1.2
Murder and nonnegligent manslaughter	6,139	2,701	3,298	51	89	100.0	44.0	53.7	0.8	1.4
Forcible rape	11,133	6,464	4,369	107	193	100.0	58.1	39.2	1.0	1.7
Robbery	50,384	22,393	27,210	268	513	100.0	44.4	54.0	0.5	1.0
Aggravated assault	218,079	132,956	80,119	1,999	3,005	100.0	61.0	36.7	0.9	1.4
Burglary	100,529	64,613	33,936	761	1,219	100.0	64.3	33.8	0.8	1.2
Larceny-theft	475,274	302,232	160,537	5,832	6,673	100.0	63.6	33.8	1.2	1.4
Motor vehicle theft	55,037	29,419	24,068	376	1,174	100.0	53.5	43.7	0.7	2.1
Arson	4,494	3,066	1,281	100	47	100.0	68.2	28.5	2.2	1.0
Violent crime[2]	285,735	164,514	114,996	2,425	3,800	100.0	57.6	40.2	0.8	1.3
Property crime[3]	635,334	399,330	219,822	7,069	9,113	100.0	62.9	34.6	1.1	1.4
Crime Index total[4]	921,069	563,844	334,818	9,494	12,913	100.0	61.2	36.4	1.0	1.4
Other assaults	553,262	344,176	195,180	7,577	6,329	100.0	62.2	35.3	1.4	1.1
Forgery and counterfeiting	56,384	36,864	18,269	310	941	100.0	65.4	32.4	0.5	1.7
Fraud	113,457	71,867	39,843	647	1,100	100.0	63.3	35.1	0.6	1.0
Embezzlement	9,548	6,024	3,313	47	164	100.0	63.1	34.7	0.5	1.7
Stolen property; buying, receiving, possessing	50,417	28,166	21,356	312	583	100.0	55.9	42.4	0.6	1.2
Vandalism	88,221	60,091	25,959	1,232	939	100.0	68.1	29.4	1.4	1.1
Weapons; carrying, possessing, etc.	68,503	38,038	29,344	400	721	100.0	55.5	42.8	0.6	1.1
Prostitution and commercialized vice	55,296	31,248	22,625	304	1,119	100.0	56.5	40.9	0.5	2.0
Sex offenses (except forcible rape and prostitution)	37,834	26,603	10,160	423	648	100.0	70.3	26.9	1.1	1.7
Drug abuse violations	725,688	426,113	290,818	3,292	5,465	100.0	58.7	40.1	0.5	0.8
Gambling	5,537	1,331	3,989	8	209	100.0	24.0	72.0	0.1	3.8
Offenses against the family and children	41,688	28,745	10,852	761	1,330	100.0	69.0	26.0	1.8	3.2
Driving under the influence	576,191	500,507	61,233	8,112	6,339	100.0	86.9	10.6	1.4	1.1
Liquor laws	249,185	207,518	32,008	7,330	2,329	100.0	83.3	12.8	2.9	0.9
Drunkenness	342,121	282,538	49,764	8,086	1,733	100.0	82.6	14.5	2.4	0.5
Disorderly conduct	264,204	168,104	89,767	4,258	2,075	100.0	63.6	34.0	1.6	0.8
Vagrancy	16,694	9,852	6,273	465	104	100.0	59.0	37.6	2.8	0.6
All other offenses (except traffic)	1,584,378	977,349	564,875	20,879	21,275	100.0	61.7	35.7	1.3	1.3
Suspicion	1,378	799	553	6	20	100.0	58.0	40.1	0.4	1.5
Curfew and loitering law violations	–	–	–	–	–	–	–	–	–	–
Runaways	–	–	–	–	–	–	–	–	–	–

[1] Because of rounding, the percentages may not add to total.
[2] Violent crimes are offenses of murder, forcible rape, robbery, and aggravated assault.
[3] Property crimes are offenses of burglary, larceny-theft, motor vehicle theft, and arson.
[4] Includes arson.

Table 50

Arrest Trends
Suburban Counties, 2000-2001
[808 agencies; 2001 estimated population 33,358,768; 2000 estimated population 32,919,381]

Offense charged	Total all ages			Under 18 years of age			18 years of age and over		
	2000	2001	Percent change	2000	2001	Percent change	2000	2001	Percent change
TOTAL[1]	1,302,744	1,284,381	-1.4	172,597	171,780	-0.5	1,130,147	1,112,601	-1.6
Murder and nonnegligent manslaughter	1,288	1,150	-10.7	83	75	-9.6	1,205	1,075	-10.8
Forcible rape	2,770	2,696	-2.7	386	414	+7.3	2,384	2,282	-4.3
Robbery	6,132	6,245	+1.8	1,323	1,331	+0.6	4,809	4,914	+2.2
Aggravated assault	41,659	41,322	-0.8	5,241	5,261	+0.4	36,418	36,061	-1.0
Burglary	26,927	27,068	+0.5	8,963	8,467	-5.5	17,964	18,601	+3.5
Larceny-theft	73,054	73,581	+0.7	20,589	19,560	-5.0	52,465	54,021	+3.0
Motor vehicle theft	11,052	11,145	+0.8	3,292	3,243	-1.5	7,760	7,902	+1.8
Arson	1,883	2,125	+12.9	936	1,012	+8.1	947	1,113	+17.5
Violent crime[2]	51,849	51,413	-0.8	7,033	7,081	+0.7	44,816	44,332	-1.1
Property crime[3]	112,916	113,919	+0.9	33,780	32,282	-4.4	79,136	81,637	+3.2
Crime Index total[4]	164,765	165,332	+0.3	40,813	39,363	-3.6	123,952	125,969	+1.6
Other assaults	121,511	121,613	+0.1	21,987	22,980	+4.5	99,524	98,633	-0.9
Forgery and counterfeiting	9,605	9,480	-1.3	508	434	-14.6	9,097	9,046	-0.6
Fraud	54,328	54,154	-0.3	734	711	-3.1	53,594	53,443	-0.3
Embezzlement	1,804	1,889	+4.7	172	132	-23.3	1,632	1,757	+7.7
Stolen property; buying, receiving, possessing	9,612	9,972	+3.7	1,888	1,708	-9.5	7,724	8,264	+7.0
Vandalism	22,809	21,756	-4.6	9,365	8,584	-8.3	13,444	13,172	-2.0
Weapons; carrying, possessing, etc.	12,978	13,505	+4.1	2,768	2,876	+3.9	10,210	10,629	+4.1
Prostitution and commercialized vice	1,598	1,548	-3.1	45	50	+11.1	1,553	1,498	-3.5
Sex offenses (except forcible rape and prostitution)	8,975	8,442	-5.9	1,917	1,851	-3.4	7,058	6,591	-6.6
Drug abuse violations	141,635	137,628	-2.8	16,042	16,358	+2.0	125,593	121,270	-3.4
Gambling	522	413	-20.9	17	23	+35.3	505	390	-22.8
Offenses against the family and children	32,351	32,195	-0.5	639	711	+11.3	31,712	31,484	-0.7
Driving under the influence	207,526	195,176	-6.0	2,153	2,128	-1.2	205,373	193,048	-6.0
Liquor laws	48,331	44,377	-8.2	13,755	11,812	-14.1	34,576	32,565	-5.8
Drunkenness	42,506	40,396	-5.0	1,340	1,232	-8.1	41,166	39,164	-4.9
Disorderly conduct	31,911	31,407	-1.6	8,109	8,766	+8.1	23,802	22,641	-4.9
Vagrancy	1,372	940	-31.5	140	165	+17.9	1,232	775	-37.1
All other offenses (except traffic)	368,681	373,895	+1.4	30,281	31,633	+4.5	338,400	342,262	+1.1
Suspicion	209	323	+54.5	76	287	+277.6	133	36	-72.9
Curfew and loitering law violations	3,682	3,561	-3.3	3,682	3,561	-3.3	–	–	–
Runaways	16,242	16,702	+2.8	16,242	16,702	+2.8	–	–	–

[1] Does not include suspicion.

[2] Violent crimes are offenses of murder, forcible rape, robbery, and aggravated assault.

[3] Property crimes are offenses of burglary, larceny-theft, motor vehicle theft, and arson.

[4] Includes arson.

Table 51

Arrest Trends
Suburban Counties
by Sex, 2000-2001
[808 agencies; 2001 estimated population 33,358,768; 2000 estimated population 32,919,381]

| | Male | | | | | | Female | | | | | |
| | Total | | | Under 18 | | | Total | | | Under 18 | | |
Offense charged	2000	2001	Percent change	2000	2001	Percent change	2000	2001	Percent change	2000	2001	Percent change
TOTAL[1]	**1,024,913**	**1,003,435**	**-2.1**	**125,425**	**123,081**	**-1.9**	**277,831**	**280,946**	**+1.1**	**47,172**	**48,699**	**+3.2**
Murder and nonnegligent manslaughter	1,121	1,006	-10.3	74	67	-9.5	167	144	-13.8	9	8	-11.1
Forcible rape	2,723	2,652	-2.6	383	402	+5.0	47	44	-6.4	3	12	+300.0
Robbery	5,554	5,703	+2.7	1,226	1,241	+1.2	578	542	-6.2	97	90	-7.2
Aggravated assault	33,992	33,732	-0.8	4,160	4,139	-0.5	7,667	7,590	-1.0	1,081	1,122	+3.8
Burglary	23,707	23,717	[2]	8,026	7,599	-5.3	3,220	3,351	+4.1	937	868	-7.4
Larceny-theft	48,558	47,901	-1.4	13,962	12,550	-10.1	24,496	25,680	+4.8	6,627	7,010	+5.8
Motor vehicle theft	9,252	9,307	+0.6	2,666	2,629	-1.4	1,800	1,838	+2.1	626	614	-1.9
Arson	1,615	1,809	+12.0	823	904	+9.8	268	316	+17.9	113	108	-4.4
Violent crime[3]	43,390	43,093	-0.7	5,843	5,849	+0.1	8,459	8,320	-1.6	1,190	1,232	+3.5
Property crime[4]	83,132	82,734	-0.5	25,477	23,682	-7.0	29,784	31,185	+4.7	8,303	8,600	+3.6
Crime Index total[5]	126,522	125,827	-0.5	31,320	29,531	-5.7	38,243	39,505	+3.3	9,493	9,832	+3.6
Other assaults	93,625	93,155	-0.5	15,415	15,948	+3.5	27,886	28,458	+2.1	6,572	7,032	+7.0
Forgery and counterfeiting	5,903	5,667	-4.0	365	286	-21.6	3,702	3,813	+3.0	143	148	+3.5
Fraud	27,726	27,375	-1.3	472	452	-4.2	26,602	26,779	+0.7	262	259	-1.1
Embezzlement	973	995	+2.3	89	83	-6.7	831	894	+7.6	83	49	-41.0
Stolen property; buying, receiving, possessing	8,073	8,363	+3.6	1,616	1,510	-6.6	1,539	1,609	+4.5	272	198	-27.2
Vandalism	19,502	18,368	-5.8	8,284	7,483	-9.7	3,307	3,388	+2.4	1,081	1,101	+1.9
Weapons; carrying, possessing, etc.	11,916	12,305	+3.3	2,473	2,563	+3.6	1,062	1,200	+13.0	295	313	+6.1
Prostitution and commercialized vice	807	774	-4.1	36	24	-33.3	791	774	-2.1	9	26	+188.9
Sex offenses (except forcible rape and prostitution)	8,445	8,012	-5.1	1,765	1,713	-2.9	530	430	-18.9	152	138	-9.2
Drug abuse violations	116,119	112,795	-2.9	13,370	13,505	+1.0	25,516	24,833	-2.7	2,672	2,853	+6.8
Gambling	393	345	-12.2	15	20	+33.3	129	68	-47.3	2	3	+50.0
Offenses against the family and children	27,888	27,587	-1.1	443	468	+5.6	4,463	4,608	+3.2	196	243	+24.0
Driving under the influence	175,827	164,367	-6.5	1,795	1,752	-2.4	31,699	30,809	-2.8	358	376	+5.0
Liquor laws	36,916	33,589	-9.0	9,478	7,970	-15.9	11,415	10,788	-5.5	4,277	3,842	-10.2
Drunkenness	36,343	34,315	-5.6	1,100	977	-11.2	6,163	6,081	-1.3	240	255	+6.3
Disorderly conduct	24,279	23,828	-1.9	5,627	6,139	+9.1	7,632	7,579	-0.7	2,482	2,627	+5.8
Vagrancy	1,069	740	-30.8	129	126	-2.3	303	200	-34.0	11	39	+254.5
All other offenses (except traffic)	293,219	295,750	+0.9	22,265	23,253	+4.4	75,462	78,145	+3.6	8,016	8,380	+4.5
Suspicion	149	175	+17.4	39	148	+279.5	60	148	+146.7	37	139	+275.7
Curfew and loitering law violations	2,507	2,366	-5.6	2,507	2,366	-5.6	1,175	1,195	+1.7	1,175	1,195	+1.7
Runaways	6,861	6,912	+0.7	6,861	6,912	+0.7	9,381	9,790	+4.4	9,381	9,790	+4.4

[1] Does not include suspicion.
[2] Less than one-tenth of 1 percent.
[3] Violent crimes are offenses of murder, forcible rape, robbery, and aggravated assault.
[4] Property crimes are offenses of burglary, larceny-theft, motor vehicle theft, and arson.
[5] Includes arson.

Table 52

Arrests

Suburban Counties
by Age, 2001
[889 agencies; 2001 estimated population 38,303,583]

Offense charged	Total all ages	Ages under 15	Ages under 18	Ages 18 and over	Under 10	10-12	13-14	15	16	17	18	19	20	21
TOTAL	1,456,447	60,231	196,894	1,259,553	3,268	14,398	42,565	37,316	47,542	51,805	66,513	70,292	68,358	63,056
Percent distribution[1]	100.0	4.1	13.5	86.5	0.2	1.0	2.9	2.6	3.3	3.6	4.6	4.8	4.7	4.3
Murder and nonnegligent manslaughter	1,445	8	94	1,351	0	1	7	9	29	48	80	91	94	93
Forcible rape	3,125	186	483	2,642	3	41	142	68	113	116	156	154	155	137
Robbery	7,891	326	1,620	6,271	6	80	240	281	457	556	732	677	562	436
Aggravated assault	51,739	2,240	6,182	45,557	111	619	1,510	1,123	1,302	1,517	1,855	1,916	1,907	1,984
Burglary	32,508	3,435	9,880	22,628	193	896	2,346	1,818	2,248	2,379	2,769	2,376	1,939	1,466
Larceny-theft	88,384	7,885	22,639	65,745	315	2,028	5,542	4,300	4,977	5,477	6,063	5,091	4,180	3,488
Motor vehicle theft	13,875	906	3,870	10,005	6	119	781	922	1,020	1,022	1,033	901	749	664
Arson	2,342	682	1,093	1,249	121	243	318	151	130	130	105	90	71	66
Violent crime[2]	64,200	2,760	8,379	55,821	120	741	1,899	1,481	1,901	2,237	2,823	2,838	2,718	2,650
Percent distribution[1]	100.0	4.3	13.1	86.9	0.2	1.2	3.0	2.3	3.0	3.5	4.4	4.4	4.2	4.1
Property crime[3]	137,109	12,908	37,482	99,627	635	3,286	8,987	7,191	8,375	9,008	9,970	8,458	6,939	5,684
Percent distribution[1]	100.0	9.4	27.3	72.7	0.5	2.4	6.6	5.2	6.1	6.6	7.3	6.2	5.1	4.1
Crime Index total[4]	201,309	15,668	45,861	155,448	755	4,027	10,886	8,672	10,276	11,245	12,793	11,296	9,657	8,334
Percent distribution[1]	100.0	7.8	22.8	77.2	0.4	2.0	5.4	4.3	5.1	5.6	6.4	5.6	4.8	4.1
Other assaults	139,023	10,678	25,518	113,505	546	3,232	6,900	4,863	5,241	4,736	4,665	4,683	4,520	4,603
Forgery and counterfeiting	11,882	45	515	11,367	2	3	40	70	156	244	533	600	632	616
Fraud	52,533	122	872	51,661	3	23	96	129	225	396	1,089	1,631	2,134	2,196
Embezzlement	2,194	8	140	2,054	0	0	8	11	31	90	154	145	132	112
Stolen property; buying, receiving, possessing	12,598	486	2,024	10,574	11	100	375	375	549	614	858	855	709	668
Vandalism	25,416	4,177	9,897	15,519	412	1,274	2,491	1,641	2,040	2,039	1,740	1,486	1,091	977
Weapons; carrying, possessing, etc.	16,665	1,142	3,334	13,331	107	294	741	566	759	867	1,057	1,015	875	822
Prostitution and commercialized vice	2,127	14	54	2,073	0	5	9	13	11	16	31	44	42	61
Sex offenses (except forcible rape and prostitution)	10,353	1,105	2,152	8,201	76	310	719	344	341	362	403	345	344	313
Drug abuse violations	169,995	2,945	18,290	151,705	41	414	2,490	2,885	5,078	7,382	11,362	11,531	10,944	9,455
Gambling	469	6	32	437	0	1	5	7	10	9	10	5	15	11
Offenses against the family and children	33,240	388	915	32,325	89	99	200	176	180	171	392	448	612	779
Driving under the influence	209,217	50	2,259	206,958	13	3	34	85	537	1,587	4,249	5,998	6,904	9,343
Liquor laws	48,106	1,006	12,454	35,652	12	74	920	1,724	3,695	6,029	8,646	8,785	6,995	1,391
Drunkenness	42,584	174	1,326	41,258	13	20	141	201	326	625	1,455	1,644	1,649	1,902
Disorderly conduct	36,212	4,316	10,959	25,253	180	1165	2,971	2,328	2,263	2,052	1,751	1,587	1,376	1,516
Vagrancy	1,177	64	189	988	0	13	51	34	40	51	62	61	51	53
All other offenses (except traffic)	417,925	10,085	36,735	381,190	627	2,108	7,350	7,143	9,151	10,356	15,259	18,131	19,676	19,902
Suspicion	354	132	300	54	14	27	91	76	76	16	4	2	0	2
Curfew and loitering law violations	4,898	1,228	4,898	–	20	183	1,025	1,103	1,620	947	–	–	–	–
Runaways	18,170	6,392	18,170	–	347	1,023	5,022	4,870	4,937	1,971	–	–	–	–

[1] Because of rounding, the percentages may not add to total.
[2] Violent crimes are offenses of murder, forcible rape, robbery, and aggravated assault.
[3] Property crimes are offenses of burglary, larceny-theft, motor vehicle theft, and arson.
[4] Includes arson.

Table 52

Arrests
Suburban Counties
by Age, 2001—Continued
[889 agencies; 2001 estimated population 38,303,583]

Offense charged	22	23	24	25-29	30-34	35-39	40-44	45-49	50-54	55-59	60-64	65 and over
TOTAL	**56,220**	**51,453**	**48,004**	**192,330**	**179,813**	**171,948**	**136,211**	**78,821**	**41,015**	**18,389**	**8,716**	**8,414**
Percent distribution[1]	**3.9**	**3.5**	**3.3**	**13.2**	**12.3**	**11.8**	**9.4**	**5.4**	**2.8**	**1.3**	**0.6**	**0.6**
Murder and nonnegligent manslaughter	76	64	62	218	139	120	119	73	59	34	11	18
Forcible rape	137	123	97	385	356	359	254	128	96	43	27	35
Robbery	396	350	248	918	691	580	389	177	68	24	8	15
Aggravated assault	1,783	1,874	1,669	7,044	6,832	6,914	5,508	3,062	1,621	721	404	463
Burglary	1,143	972	890	3,101	2,659	2,450	1,614	733	307	121	50	38
Larceny-theft	2,872	2,517	2,209	9,051	8,765	8,346	6,184	3,499	1,847	814	399	420
Motor vehicle theft	553	481	433	1,582	1,382	1,001	670	328	155	37	17	19
Arson	56	29	37	142	169	168	129	94	58	20	7	8
Violent crime[2]	2,392	2,411	2,076	8,565	8,018	7,973	6,270	3,440	1,844	822	450	531
Percent distribution[1]	3.7	3.8	3.2	13.3	12.5	12.4	9.8	5.4	2.9	1.3	0.7	0.8
Property crime[3]	4,624	3,999	3,569	13,876	12,975	11,965	8,597	4,654	2,367	992	473	485
Percent distribution[1]	3.4	2.9	2.6	10.1	9.5	8.7	6.3	3.4	1.7	0.7	0.3	0.4
Crime Index total[4]	7,016	6,410	5,645	22,441	20,993	19,938	14,867	8,094	4,211	1,814	923	1,016
Percent distribution[1]	3.5	3.2	2.8	11.1	10.4	9.9	7.4	4.0	2.1	0.9	0.5	0.5
Other assaults	4,346	4,170	4,025	17,049	17,747	17,913	14,174	8,023	3,912	1,843	906	926
Forgery and counterfeiting	526	491	437	2,035	1,864	1,622	1,075	532	251	89	34	30
Fraud	2,308	2,089	2,120	9,322	8,959	7,643	5,455	3,405	1,840	789	347	334
Embezzlement	82	83	95	303	292	261	202	87	52	36	10	8
Stolen property; buying, receiving, possessing	542	505	458	1,611	1,454	1,190	909	446	214	81	39	35
Vandalism	789	657	582	2,132	1,889	1,705	1,160	673	328	146	70	94
Weapons; carrying, possessing, etc.	756	616	554	2,041	1,517	1,378	1,183	700	406	208	96	107
Prostitution and commercialized vice	51	60	60	291	380	395	285	185	76	49	25	38
Sex offenses (except forcible rape and prostitution)	299	270	250	971	1,054	1,200	938	644	436	279	223	232
Drug abuse violations	7,994	7,133	6,363	22,709	19,437	18,211	14,193	7,375	3,225	1,087	387	299
Gambling	13	13	10	47	52	44	47	37	42	33	27	31
Offenses against the family and children	821	805	984	5,467	6,401	6,320	5,009	2,505	1,061	446	168	107
Driving under the influence	9,073	8,637	8,192	33,510	29,728	29,125	25,545	16,670	10,267	5,064	2,484	2,169
Liquor laws	865	642	528	1,935	1,508	1,381	1,274	809	440	215	106	132
Drunkenness	1,616	1,429	1,350	5,239	5,208	6,108	5,807	3,908	2,145	985	458	355
Disorderly conduct	1,241	1,056	939	3,525	3,202	3,075	2,657	1,602	846	410	223	247
Vagrancy	41	26	32	110	114	131	120	103	44	16	7	17
All other offenses (except traffic)	17,841	16,359	15,375	61,581	58,009	54,299	41,306	23,021	11,213	4,798	2,183	2,237
Suspicion	0	2	5	11	5	9	5	2	6	1	0	0
Curfew and loitering law violations	–	–	–	–	–	–	–	–	–	–	–	–
Runaways	–	–	–	–	–	–	–	–	–	–	–	–

Table 53

Arrests

Suburban Counties
of Persons Under 15, 18, 21, and 25 Years of Age, 2001
[889 agencies; 2001 estimated population 38,303,583]

Offense charged	Total all ages	Number of persons arrested				Percent of total all ages			
		Under 15	Under 18	Under 21	Under 25	Under 15	Under 18	Under 21	Under 25
TOTAL	**1,456,447**	**60,231**	**196,894**	**402,057**	**620,790**	**4.1**	**13.5**	**27.6**	**42.6**
Murder and nonnegligent manslaughter	1,445	8	94	359	654	0.6	6.5	24.8	45.3
Forcible rape	3,125	186	483	948	1,442	6.0	15.5	30.3	46.1
Robbery	7,891	326	1,620	3,591	5,021	4.1	20.5	45.5	63.6
Aggravated assault	51,739	2,240	6,182	11,860	19,170	4.3	11.9	22.9	37.1
Burglary	32,508	3,435	9,880	16,964	21,435	10.6	30.4	52.2	65.9
Larceny-theft	88,384	7,885	22,639	37,973	49,059	8.9	25.6	43.0	55.5
Motor vehicle theft	13,875	906	3,870	6,553	8,684	6.5	27.9	47.2	62.6
Arson	2,342	682	1,093	1,359	1,547	29.1	46.7	58.0	66.1
Violent crime[1]	64,200	2,760	8,379	16,758	26,287	4.3	13.1	26.1	40.9
Property crime[2]	137,109	12,908	37,482	62,849	80,725	9.4	27.3	45.8	58.9
Crime Index total[3]	201,309	15,668	45,861	79,607	107,012	7.8	22.8	39.5	53.2
Other assaults	139,023	10,678	25,518	39,386	56,530	7.7	18.4	28.3	40.7
Forgery and counterfeiting	11,882	45	515	2,280	4,350	0.4	4.3	19.2	36.6
Fraud	52,533	122	872	5,726	14,439	0.2	1.7	10.9	27.5
Embezzlement	2,194	8	140	571	943	0.4	6.4	26.0	43.0
Stolen property; buying, receiving, possession	12,598	486	2,024	4,446	6,619	3.9	16.1	35.3	52.5
Vandalism	25,416	4,177	9,897	14,214	17,219	16.4	38.9	55.9	67.7
Weapons; carrying, possessing, etc.	16,665	1,142	3,334	6,281	9,029	6.9	20.0	37.7	54.2
Prostitution and commercialized vice	2,127	14	54	171	403	0.7	2.5	8.0	18.9
Sex offenses (except forcible rape and prostitution)	10,353	1,105	2,152	3,244	4,376	10.7	20.8	31.3	42.3
Drug abuse violations	169,995	2,945	18,290	52,127	83,072	1.7	10.8	30.7	48.9
Gambling	469	6	32	62	109	1.3	6.8	13.2	23.2
Offenses against the family and children	33,240	388	915	2,367	5,756	1.2	2.8	7.1	17.3
Driving under the influence	209,217	50	2,259	19,410	54,655	[4]	1.1	9.3	26.1
Liquor laws	48,106	1,006	12,454	36,880	40,306	2.1	25.9	76.7	83.8
Drunkenness	42,584	174	1,326	6,074	12,371	0.4	3.1	14.3	29.1
Disorderly conduct	36,212	4,316	10,959	15,673	20,425	11.9	30.3	43.3	56.4
Vagrancy	1,177	64	189	363	515	5.4	16.1	30.8	43.8
All other offenses (except traffic)	417,925	10,085	36,735	89,801	159,278	2.4	8.8	21.5	38.1
Suspicion	354	132	300	306	315	37.3	84.7	86.4	89.0
Curfew and loitering law violations	4,898	1,228	4,898	4,898	4,898	25.1	100.0	100.0	100.0
Runaways	18,170	6,392	18,170	18,170	18,170	35.2	100.0	100.0	100.0

[1] Violent crimes are offenses of murder, forcible rape, robbery, and aggravated assault.
[2] Property crimes are offenses of burglary, larceny-theft, motor vehicle theft, and arson.
[3] Includes arson.
[4] Less than one-tenth of 1 percent.

Table 54

Arrests
Suburban Counties
by Sex, 2001
[889 agencies; 2001 estimated population 38,303,583]

Offense charged	Number of persons arrested			Percent male	Percent female	Percent distribution[1]		
	Total	Male	Female			Total	Male	Female
TOTAL	**1,456,447**	**1,142,438**	**314,009**	**78.4**	**21.6**	**100.0**	**100.0**	**100.0**
Murder and nonnegligent manslaughter	1,445	1,273	172	88.1	11.9	0.1	0.1	0.1
Forcible rape	3,125	3,074	51	98.4	1.6	0.2	0.3	[2]
Robbery	7,891	7,164	727	90.8	9.2	0.5	0.6	0.2
Aggravated assault	51,739	42,443	9,296	82.0	18.0	3.6	3.7	3.0
Burglary	32,508	28,447	4,061	87.5	12.5	2.2	2.5	1.3
Larceny-theft	88,384	57,644	30,740	65.2	34.8	6.1	5.0	9.8
Motor vehicle theft	13,875	11,555	2,320	83.3	16.7	1.0	1.0	0.7
Arson	2,342	1,999	343	85.4	14.6	0.2	0.2	0.1
Violent crime[3]	64,200	53,954	10,246	84.0	16.0	4.4	4.7	3.3
Property crime[4]	137,109	99,645	37,464	72.7	27.3	9.4	8.7	11.9
Crime Index total[5]	201,309	153,599	47,710	76.3	23.7	13.8	13.4	15.2
Other assaults	139,023	106,869	32,154	76.9	23.1	9.5	9.4	10.2
Forgery and counterfeiting	11,882	7,245	4,637	61.0	39.0	0.8	0.6	1.5
Fraud	52,533	27,657	24,876	52.6	47.4	3.6	2.4	7.9
Embezzlement	2,194	1,165	1,029	53.1	46.9	0.2	0.1	0.3
Stolen property; buying, receiving, possessing	12,598	10,568	2,030	83.9	16.1	0.9	0.9	0.6
Vandalism	25,416	21,458	3,958	84.4	15.6	1.7	1.9	1.3
Weapons; carrying, possessing, etc.	16,665	15,255	1,410	91.5	8.5	1.1	1.3	0.4
Prostitution and commercialized vice	2,127	1,082	1,045	50.9	49.1	0.1	0.1	0.3
Sex offenses (except forcible rape and prostitution)	10,353	9,826	527	94.9	5.1	0.7	0.9	0.2
Drug abuse violations	169,995	138,876	31,119	81.7	18.3	11.7	12.2	9.9
Gambling	469	393	76	83.8	16.2	[2]	[2]	[2]
Offenses against the family and children	33,240	28,408	4,832	85.5	14.5	2.3	2.5	1.5
Driving under the influence	209,217	176,152	33,065	84.2	15.8	14.4	15.4	10.5
Liquor laws	48,106	36,594	11,512	76.1	23.9	3.3	3.2	3.7
Drunkenness	42,584	36,330	6,254	85.3	14.7	2.9	3.2	2.0
Disorderly conduct	36,212	27,292	8,920	75.4	24.6	2.5	2.4	2.8
Vagrancy	1,177	922	255	78.3	21.7	0.1	0.1	0.1
All other offenses (except traffic)	417,925	331,748	86,177	79.4	20.6	28.7	29.0	27.4
Suspicion	354	189	165	53.4	46.6	[2]	[2]	0.1
Curfew and loitering law violations	4,898	3,239	1,659	66.1	33.9	0.3	0.3	0.5
Runaways	18,170	7,571	10,599	41.7	58.3	1.2	0.7	3.4

[1] Because of rounding, the percentages may not add to total.

[2] Less than one-tenth of 1 percent.

[3] Violent crimes are offenses of murder, forcible rape, robbery, and aggravated assault.

[4] Property crimes are offenses of burglary, larceny-theft, motor vehicle theft, and arson.

[5] Includes arson.

Table 55

Arrests
Suburban Counties
by Race, 2001
[889 agencies; 2001 estimated population 38,303,583]

Offense charged	Total arrests					Percent distribution[1]				
	Total	White	Black	American Indian or Alaskan Native	Asian or Pacific Islander	Total	White	Black	American Indian or Alaskan Native	Asian or Pacific Islander
TOTAL	**1,454,011**	**1,111,563**	**324,798**	**9,806**	**7,844**	**100.0**	**76.4**	**22.3**	**0.7**	**0.5**
Murder and nonnegligent manslaughter	1,445	1,004	427	7	7	100.0	69.5	29.6	0.5	0.5
Forcible rape	3,121	2,354	718	25	24	100.0	75.4	23.0	0.8	0:8
Robbery	7,890	4,246	3,562	50	32	100.0	53.8	45.1	0.6	0.4
Aggravated assault	51,716	39,226	11,753	399	338	100.0	75.8	22.7	0.8	0.7
Burglary	32,490	25,495	6,609	193	193	100.0	78.5	20.3	0.6	0.6
Larceny-theft	88,306	60,724	26,362	468	752	100.0	68.8	29.9	0.5	0.9
Motor vehicle theft	13,861	10,278	3,396	92	95	100.0	74.2	24.5	0.7	0.7
Arson	2,339	1,949	356	15	19	100.0	83.3	15.2	0.6	0.8
Violent crime[2]	64,172	46,830	16,460	481	401	100.0	73.0	25.6	0.7	0.6
Property crime[3]	136,996	98,446	36,723	768	1,059	100.0	71.9	26.8	0.6	0.8
Crime Index total[4]	201,168	145,276	53,183	1,249	1,460	100.0	72.2	26.4	0.6	0.7
Other assaults	138,905	104,089	33,061	898	857	100.0	74.9	23.8	0.6	0.6
Forgery and counterfeiting	11,874	8,566	3,163	48	97	100.0	72.1	26.6	0.4	0.8
Fraud	52,415	36,126	15,947	164	178	100.0	68.9	30.4	0.3	0.3
Embezzlement	2,187	1,518	643	5	21	100.0	69.4	29.4	0.2	1.0
Stolen property; buying, receiving, possessing	12,587	9,011	3,411	82	83	100.0	71.6	27.1	0.7	0.7
Vandalism	25,398	20,887	4,179	177	155	100.0	82.2	16.5	0.7	0.6
Weapons; carrying, possessing, etc.	16,639	11,881	4,570	88	100	100.0	71.4	27.5	0.5	0.6
Prostitution and commercialized vice	2,123	1,592	454	9	68	100.0	75.0	21.4	0.4	3.2
Sex offenses (except forcible rape and prostitution)	10,342	8,640	1,575	63	64	100.0	83.5	15.2	0.6	0.6
Drug abuse violations	169,822	130,136	38,227	683	776	100.0	76.6	22.5	0.4	0.5
Gambling	464	334	125	0	5	100.0	72.0	26.9	–	1.1
Offenses against the family and children	33,179	20,337	12,596	132	114	100.0	61.3	38.0	0.4	0.3
Driving under the influence	208,790	187,124	19,564	1,122	980	100.0	89.6	9.4	0.5	0.5
Liquor laws	47,828	43,555	3,345	632	296	100.0	91.1	7.0	1.3	0.6
Drunkenness	42,552	38,236	3,791	402	123	100.0	89.9	8.9	0.9	0.3
Disorderly conduct	36,178	25,532	10,203	274	169	100.0	70.6	28.2	0.8	0.5
Vagrancy	1,177	865	303	5	4	100.0	73.5	25.7	0.4	0.3
All other offenses (except traffic)	416,992	298,808	112,451	3,634	2,099	100.0	71.7	27.0	0.9	0.5
Suspicion	354	201	153	0	0	100.0	56.8	43.2	–	–
Curfew and loitering law violations	4,884	4,129	699	24	32	100.0	84.5	14.3	0.5	0.7
Runaways	18,153	14,720	3,155	115	163	100.0	81.1	17.4	0.6	0.9

See footnotes at end of table.

Table 55

Arrests
Suburban Counties
by Race, 2001—Continued
[889 agencies; 2001 estimated population 38,303,583]

Offense charged	Arrests under 18					Percent distribution[1]				
	Total	White	Black	American Indian or Alaskan Native	Asian or Pacific Islander	Total	White	Black	American Indian or Alaskan Native	Asian or Pacific Islander
TOTAL	**196,632**	**151,383**	**42,367**	**1,459**	**1,423**	**100.0**	**77.0**	**21.5**	**0.7**	**0.7**
Murder and nonnegligent manslaughter	94	62	32	0	0	100.0	66.0	34.0	–	–
Forcible rape	482	362	117	1	2	100.0	75.1	24.3	0.2	0.4
Robbery	1,619	709	885	12	13	100.0	43.8	54.7	0.7	0.8
Aggravated assault	6,180	4,416	1,672	56	36	100.0	71.5	27.1	0.9	0.6
Burglary	9,873	7,888	1,859	64	62	100.0	79.9	18.8	0.6	0.6
Larceny-theft	22,617	15,656	6,581	126	254	100.0	69.2	29.1	0.6	1.1
Motor vehicle theft	3,867	2,902	891	38	36	100.0	75.0	23.0	1.0	0.9
Arson	1,090	924	143	8	15	100.0	84.8	13.1	0.7	1.4
Violent crime[2]	8,375	5,549	2,706	69	51	100.0	66.3	32.3	0.8	0.6
Property crime[3]	37,447	27,370	9,474	236	367	100.0	73.1	25.3	0.6	1.0
Crime Index total[4]	45,822	32,919	12,180	305	418	100.0	71.8	26.6	0.7	0.9
Other assaults	25,500	17,575	7,603	195	127	100.0	68.9	29.8	0.8	0.5
Forgery and counterfeiting	516	411	100	0	5	100.0	79.7	19.4	–	1.0
Fraud	869	597	262	4	6	100.0	68.7	30.1	0.5	0.7
Embezzlement	140	100	39	0	1	100.0	71.4	27.9	–	0.7
Stolen property; buying, receiving, possessing	2,020	1,424	555	15	26	100.0	70.5	27.5	0.7	1.3
Vandalism	9,888	8,393	1,351	78	66	100.0	84.9	13.7	0.8	0.7
Weapons; carrying, possessing, etc.	3,331	2,470	811	18	32	100.0	74.2	24.3	0.5	1.0
Prostitution and commercialized vice	54	38	15	1	0	100.0	70.4	27.8	1.9	–
Sex offenses (except forcible rape and prostitution)	2,150	1,697	430	14	9	100.0	78.9	20.0	0.7	0.4
Drug abuse violations	18,266	15,300	2,754	86	126	100.0	83.8	15.1	0.5	0.7
Gambling	32	11	21	0	0	100.0	34.4	65.6	–	–
Offenses against the family and children	915	717	191	5	2	100.0	78.4	20.9	0.5	0.2
Driving under the influence	2,256	2,160	83	7	6	100.0	95.7	3.7	0.3	0.3
Liquor laws	12,409	11,739	473	137	60	100.0	94.6	3.8	1.1	0.5
Drunkenness	1,326	1,221	94	7	4	100.0	92.1	7.1	0.5	0.3
Disorderly conduct	10,952	6,820	4,006	71	55	100.0	62.3	36.6	0.6	0.5
Vagrancy	189	121	67	1	0	100.0	64.0	35.4	0.5	–
All other offenses (except traffic)	36,660	28,658	7,341	376	285	100.0	78.2	20.0	1.0	0.8
Suspicion	300	163	137	0	0	100.0	54.3	45.7	–	–
Curfew and loitering law violations	4,884	4,129	699	24	32	100.0	84.5	14.3	0.5	0.7
Runaways	18,153	14,720	3,155	115	163	100.0	81.1	17.4	0.6	0.9

See footnotes at end of table.

Table 55

Arrests
Suburban Counties
by Race, 2001—Continued
[889 agencies; 2001 estimated population 38,303,583]

Offense charged	Arrests 18 and over					Percent distribution[1]				
	Total	White	Black	American Indian or Alaskan Native	Asian or Pacific Islander	Total	White	Black	American Indian or Alaskan Native	Asian or Pacific Islander
TOTAL	**1,257,379**	**960,180**	**282,431**	**8,347**	**6,421**	**100.0**	**76.4**	**22.5**	**0.7**	**0.5**
Murder and nonnegligent manslaughter	1,351	942	395	7	7	100.0	69.7	29.2	0.5	0.5
Forcible rape	2,639	1,992	601	24	22	100.0	75.5	22.8	0.9	0.8
Robbery	6,271	3,537	2,677	38	19	100.0	56.4	42.7	0.6	0.3
Aggravated assault	45,536	34,810	10,081	343	302	100.0	76.4	22.1	0.8	0.7
Burglary	22,617	17,607	4,750	129	131	100.0	77.8	21.0	0.6	0.6
Larceny-theft	65,689	45,068	19,781	342	498	100.0	68.6	30.1	0.5	0.8
Motor vehicle theft	9,994	7,376	2,505	54	59	100.0	73.8	25.1	0.5	0.6
Arson	1,249	1,025	213	7	4	100.0	82.1	17.1	0.6	0.3
Violent crime[2]	55,797	41,281	13,754	412	350	100.0	74.0	24.7	0.7	0.6
Property crime[3]	99,549	71,076	27,249	532	692	100.0	71.4	27.4	0.5	0.7
Crime Index total[4]	155,346	112,357	41,003	944	1,042	100.0	72.3	26.4	0.6	0.7
Other assaults	113,405	86,514	25,458	703	730	100.0	76.3	22.4	0.6	0.6
Forgery and counterfeiting	11,358	8,155	3,063	48	92	100.0	71.8	27.0	0.4	0.8
Fraud	51,546	35,529	15,685	160	172	100.0	68.9	30.4	0.3	0.3
Embezzlement	2,047	1,418	604	5	20	100.0	69.3	29.5	0.2	1.0
Stolen property; buying, receiving, possessing	10,567	7,587	2,856	67	57	100.0	71.8	27.0	0.6	0.5
Vandalism	15,510	12,494	2,828	99	89	100.0	80.6	18.2	0.6	0.6
Weapons; carrying, possessing, etc.	13,308	9,411	3,759	70	68	100.0	70.7	28.2	0.5	0.5
Prostitution and commercialized vice	2,069	1,554	439	8	68	100.0	75.1	21.2	0.4	3.3
Sex offenses (except forcible rape and prostitution)	8,192	6,943	1,145	49	55	100.0	84.8	14.0	0.6	0.7
Drug abuse violations	151,556	114,836	35,473	597	650	100.0	75.8	23.4	0.4	0.4
Gambling	432	323	104	0	5	100.0	74.8	24.1	–	1.2
Offenses against the family and children	32,264	19,620	12,405	127	112	100.0	60.8	38.4	0.4	0.3
Driving under the influence	206,534	184,964	19,481	1,115	974	100.0	89.6	9.4	0.5	0.5
Liquor laws	35,419	31,816	2,872	495	236	100.0	89.8	8.1	1.4	0.7
Drunkenness	41,226	37,015	3,697	395	119	100.0	89.8	9.0	1.0	0.3
Disorderly conduct	25,226	18,712	6,197	203	114	100.0	74.2	24.6	0.8	0.5
Vagrancy	988	744	236	4	4	100.0	75.3	23.9	0.4	0.4
All other offenses (except traffic)	380,332	270,150	105,110	3,258	1,814	100.0	71.0	27.6	0.9	0.5
Suspicion	54	38	16	0	0	100.0	70.4	29.6	–	–
Curfew and loitering law violations	–	–	–	–	–	–	–	–	–	–
Runaways	–	–	–	–	–	–	–	–	–	–

[1] Because of rounding, the percentages may not add to total.
[2] Violent crimes are offenses of murder, forcible rape, robbery, and aggravated assault.
[3] Property crimes are offenses of burglary, larceny-theft, motor vehicle theft, and arson.
[4] Includes arson.

Table 56

Arrest Trends

Rural Counties, 2000-2001

[1,631 agencies; 2001 estimated population 18,722,870; 2000 estimated population 18,598,913]

Offense charged	Number of persons arrested								
	Total all ages			Under 18 years of age			18 years of age and over		
	2000	2001	Percent change	2000	2001	Percent change	2000	2001	Percent change
TOTAL[1]	727,318	718,110	-1.3	82,191	76,939	-6.4	645,127	641,171	-0.6
Murder and nonnegligent manslaughter	772	674	-12.7	52	40	-23.1	720	634	-11.9
Forcible rape	1,836	1,714	-6.6	257	243	-5.4	1,579	1,471	-6.8
Robbery	1,821	1,784	-2.0	291	220	-24.4	1,530	1,564	+2.2
Aggravated assault	21,735	20,902	-3.8	2,153	2,021	-6.1	19,582	18,881	-3.6
Burglary	18,740	17,503	-6.6	5,703	5,058	-11.3	13,037	12,445	-4.5
Larceny-theft	30,505	29,602	-3.0	7,279	6,844	-6.0	23,226	22,758	-2.0
Motor vehicle theft	5,342	5,190	-2.8	1,774	1,654	-6.8	3,568	3,536	-0.9
Arson	869	946	+8.9	269	323	+20.1	600	623	+3.8
Violent crime[2]	26,164	25,074	-4.2	2,753	2,524	-8.3	23,411	22,550	-3.7
Property crime[3]	55,456	53,241	-4.0	15,025	13,879	-7.6	40,431	39,362	-2.6
Crime Index total[4]	81,620	78,315	-4.0	17,778	16,403	-7.7	63,842	61,912	-3.0
Other assaults	72,721	72,538	-0.3	8,512	8,494	-0.2	64,209	64,044	-0.3
Forgery and counterfeiting	5,198	5,151	-0.9	240	230	-4.2	4,958	4,921	-0.7
Fraud	39,910	41,561	+4.1	480	434	-9.6	39,430	41,127	+4.3
Embezzlement	869	934	+7.5	45	25	-44.4	824	909	+10.3
Stolen property; buying, receiving, possessing	4,756	4,564	-4.0	838	681	-18.7	3,918	3,883	-0.9
Vandalism	14,075	13,002	-7.6	4,967	4,495	-9.5	9,108	8,507	-6.6
Weapons; carrying, possessing, etc.	6,180	6,373	+3.1	832	838	+0.7	5,348	5,535	+3.5
Prostitution and commercialized vice	115	127	+10.4	7	2	-71.4	108	125	+15.7
Sex offenses (except forcible rape and prostitution)	5,016	4,927	-1.8	1,038	948	-8.7	3,978	3,979	[5]
Drug abuse violations	69,099	68,992	-0.2	6,167	6,042	-2.0	62,932	62,950	[5]
Gambling	528	763	+44.5	19	29	+52.6	509	734	+44.2
Offenses against the family and children	10,943	11,217	+2.5	694	493	-29.0	10,249	10,724	+4.6
Driving under the influence	105,282	97,770	-7.1	1,563	1,447	-7.4	103,719	96,323	-7.1
Liquor laws	41,856	38,093	-9.0	11,106	9,629	-13.3	30,750	28,464	-7.4
Drunkenness	28,820	27,835	-3.4	627	673	+7.3	28,193	27,162	-3.7
Disorderly conduct	18,556	17,950	-3.3	4,128	4,156	+0.7	14,428	13,794	-4.4
Vagrancy	506	462	-8.7	259	245	-5.4	247	217	-12.1
All other offenses (except traffic)	213,937	221,047	+3.3	15,560	15,186	-2.4	198,377	205,861	+3.8
Suspicion	257	185	-28.0	46	40	-13.0	211	145	-31.3
Curfew and loitering law violations	861	732	-15.0	861	732	-15.0	–	–	–
Runaways	6,470	5,757	-11.0	6,470	5,757	-11.0	–	–	–

[1] Does not include suspicion.

[2] Violent crimes are offenses of murder, forcible rape, robbery, and aggravated assault.

[3] Property crimes are offenses of burglary, larceny-theft, motor vehicle theft, and arson.

[4] Includes arson.

[5] Less than one-tenth of 1 percent.

Table 57

Arrest Trends

Rural Counties
by Sex, 2000-2001
[1,631 agencies; 2001 estimated population 18,722,870; 2000 estimated population 18,598,913]

| | Male | | | | | | Female | | | | | |
| | Total | | | Under 18 | | | Total | | | Under 18 | | |
Offense charged	2000	2001	Percent change	2000	2001	Percent change	2000	2001	Percent change	2000	2001	Percent change
TOTAL[1]	573,043	561,414	-2.0	60,548	56,153	-7.3	154,275	156,696	+1.6	21,643	20,786	-4.0
Murder and nonnegligent manslaughter	679	589	-13.3	45	35	-22.2	93	85	-8.6	7	5	-28.6
Forcible rape	1,812	1,688	-6.8	255	238	-6.7	24	26	+8.3	2	5	+150.0
Robbery	1,625	1,598	-1.7	256	206	-19.5	196	186	-5.1	35	14	-60.0
Aggravated assault	18,029	17,193	-4.6	1,711	1,558	-8.9	3,706	3,709	+0.1	442	463	+4.8
Burglary	16,680	15,539	-6.8	5,200	4,589	-11.8	2,060	1,964	-4.7	503	469	-6.8
Larceny-theft	22,331	21,255	-4.8	5,612	5,176	-7.8	8,174	8,347	+2.1	1,667	1,668	+0.1
Motor vehicle theft	4,440	4,293	-3.3	1,399	1,272	-9.1	902	897	-0.6	375	382	+1.9
Arson	751	775	+3.2	240	290	+20.8	118	171	+44.9	29	33	+13.8
Violent crime[2]	22,145	21,068	-4.9	2,267	2,037	-10.1	4,019	4,006	-0.3	486	487	+0.2
Property crime[3]	44,202	41,862	-5.3	12,451	11,327	-9.0	11,254	11,379	+1.1	2,574	2,552	-0.9
Crime Index total[4]	66,347	62,930	-5.2	14,718	13,364	-9.2	15,273	15,385	+0.7	3,060	3,039	-0.7
Other assaults	56,502	56,166	-0.6	5,948	5,941	-0.1	16,219	16,372	+0.9	2,564	2,553	-0.4
Forgery and counterfeiting	3,113	2,969	-4.6	173	133	-23.1	2,085	2,182	+4.7	67	97	+44.8
Fraud	20,323	20,811	+2.4	315	258	-18.1	19,587	20,750	+5.9	165	176	+6.7
Embezzlement	421	504	+19.7	24	18	-25.0	448	430	-4.0	21	7	-66.7
Stolen property; buying, receiving, possessing	4,064	3,862	-5.0	724	591	-18.4	692	702	+1.4	114	90	-21.1
Vandalism	12,028	11,100	-7.7	4,464	4,019	-10.0	2,047	1,902	-7.1	503	476	-5.4
Weapons; carrying, possessing, etc.	5,734	5,857	+2.1	743	746	+0.4	446	516	+15.7	89	92	+3.4
Prostitution and commercialized vice	65	68	+4.6	3	0	-100.0	50	59	+18.0	4	2	-50.0
Sex offenses (except forcible rape and prostitution)	4,750	4,663	-1.8	957	871	-9.0	266	264	-0.8	81	77	-4.9
Drug abuse violations	57,003	56,316	-1.2	5,120	4,854	-5.2	12,096	12,676	+4.8	1,047	1,188	+13.5
Gambling	452	647	+43.1	14	23	+64.3	76	116	+52.6	5	6	+20.0
Offenses against the family and children	8,937	9,234	+3.3	386	309	-19.9	2,006	1,983	-1.1	308	184	-40.3
Driving under the influence	89,495	82,850	-7.4	1,324	1,187	-10.3	15,787	14,920	-5.5	239	260	+8.8
Liquor laws	31,430	28,469	-9.4	7,272	6,271	-13.8	10,426	9,624	-7.7	3,834	3,358	-12.4
Drunkenness	24,658	23,719	-3.8	515	529	+2.7	4,162	4,116	-1.1	112	144	+28.6
Disorderly conduct	14,192	13,566	-4.4	2,935	2,917	-0.6	4,364	4,384	+0.5	1,193	1,239	+3.9
Vagrancy	364	347	-4.7	174	177	+1.7	142	115	-19.0	85	68	-20.0
All other offenses (except traffic)	169,962	174,542	+2.7	11,536	11,151	-3.3	43,975	46,505	+5.8	4,024	4,035	+0.3
Suspicion	199	152	-23.6	32	31	-3.1	58	33	-43.1	14	9	-35.7
Curfew and loitering law violations	545	440	-19.3	545	440	-19.3	316	292	-7.6	316	292	-7.6
Runaways	2,658	2,354	-11.4	2,658	2,354	-11.4	3,812	3,403	-10.7	3,812	3,403	-10.7

[1] Does not include suspicion.
[2] Violent crimes are offenses of murder, forcible rape, robbery, and aggravated assault.
[3] Property crimes are offenses of burglary, larceny-theft, motor vehicle theft, and arson.
[4] Includes arson.

Table 58

Arrests

Rural Counties
by Age, 2001
[1,754 agencies; 2001 estimated population 20,688,373]

Offense charged	Total all ages	Ages under 15	Ages under 18	Ages 18 and over	Under 10	10-12	13-14	15	16	17	18
TOTAL	821,375	23,393	86,531	734,844	1,667	5,346	16,380	14,953	21,436	26,749	38,743
Percent distribution[1]	100.0	2.8	10.5	89.5	0.2	0.7	2.0	1.8	2.6	3.3	4.7
Murder and nonnegligent manslaughter	1,019	5	48	971	0	0	5	6	13	24	52
Forcible rape	1,920	87	268	1,652	0	22	65	41	64	76	120
Robbery	2,105	21	247	1,858	0	3	18	39	60	127	203
Aggravated assault	23,322	781	2,414	20,908	50	217	514	422	565	646	881
Burglary	19,676	1,804	5,695	13,981	137	446	1,221	1,030	1,233	1,628	2,033
Larceny-theft	33,266	2,526	7,680	25,586	162	708	1,656	1,373	1,745	2,036	2,427
Motor vehicle theft	5,824	499	1,891	3,933	5	57	437	434	484	474	449
Arson	1,073	188	370	703	34	65	89	52	75	55	56
Violent crime[2]	28,366	894	2,977	25,389	50	242	602	508	702	873	1,256
Percent distribution[1]	100.0	3.2	10.5	89.5	0.2	0.9	2.1	1.8	2.5	3.1	4.4
Property crime[3]	59,839	5,017	15,636	44,203	338	1,276	3,403	2,889	3,537	4,193	4,965
Percent distribution[1]	100.0	8.4	26.1	73.9	0.6	2.1	5.7	4.8	5.9	7.0	8.3
Crime Index total[4]	88,205	5,911	18,613	69,592	388	1,518	4,005	3,397	4,239	5,066	6,221
Percent distribution[1]	100.0	6.7	21.1	78.9	0.4	1.7	4.5	3.9	4.8	5.7	7.1
Other assaults	76,704	3,291	9,280	67,424	202	852	2,237	1,576	2,195	2,218	2,485
Forgery and counterfeiting	6,054	27	255	5,799	4	11	12	28	74	126	267
Fraud	40,292	68	456	39,836	5	19	44	65	122	201	756
Embezzlement	980	1	26	954	0	1	0	2	8	15	36
Stolen property; buying, receiving, possessing	5,301	156	797	4,504	8	31	117	132	204	305	432
Vandalism	14,063	1,929	4,932	9,131	200	600	1,129	733	1,154	1,116	1,124
Weapons; carrying, possessing, etc.	7,516	328	957	6,559	27	99	202	138	198	293	367
Prostitution and commercialized vice	178	0	3	175	0	0	0	1	0	2	4
Sex offenses (except forcible rape and prostitution)	5,627	524	1,085	4,542	30	159	335	199	159	203	257
Drug abuse violations	80,853	1,160	7,071	73,782	37	177	946	1,056	1,865	2,990	5,274
Gambling	824	7	30	794	0	2	5	9	8	6	24
Offenses against the family and children	13,941	197	594	13,347	26	50	121	96	132	169	266
Driving under the influence	150,600	313	2,029	148,571	285	3	25	76	486	1,154	2,887
Liquor laws	40,281	898	10,249	30,032	9	59	830	1,458	3,104	4,789	7,124
Drunkenness	26,334	99	759	25,575	10	10	79	96	178	386	906
Disorderly conduct	23,200	1,800	5,234	17,966	80	421	1,299	1,074	1,166	1,194	1,124
Vagrancy	266	20	54	212	0	4	16	15	12	7	10
All other offenses (except traffic)	232,559	4,307	16,860	215,699	313	951	3,043	2,828	4,272	5,453	9,173
Suspicion	400	11	50	350	1	1	9	15	14	10	6
Curfew and loitering law violations	921	258	921	–	8	31	219	203	237	223	–
Runaways	6,276	2,088	6,276	–	34	347	1,707	1,756	1,609	823	–

See footnotes at end of table.

Table 58

Arrests
Rural Counties
by Age, 2001—Continued
[1,754 agencies; 2001 estimated population 20,688,373]

Offense charged	19	20	21	22	23	24	25-29	30-34	35-39	40-44	45-49	50-54	55-59	60-64	65 over
TOTAL	**39,990**	**37,803**	**33,479**	**29,236**	**27,116**	**25,316**	**104,547**	**96,242**	**95,450**	**76,782**	**46,825**	**27,715**	**16,228**	**11,291**	**28,081**
Percent distribution[1]	**4.9**	**4.6**	**4.1**	**3.6**	**3.3**	**3.1**	**12.7**	**11.7**	**11.6**	**9.3**	**5.7**	**3.4**	**2.0**	**1.4**	**3.4**
Murder and nonnegligent manslaughter	55	45	35	45	58	50	169	127	103	91	52	37	24	11	17
Forcible rape	136	102	83	68	64	51	215	214	197	181	85	53	32	29	22
Robbery	193	157	179	129	100	68	288	218	173	82	44	17	4	0	3
Aggravated assault	875	778	916	878	845	725	3,041	3,092	3,082	2,536	1,449	834	441	244	291
Burglary	1,566	1,244	971	668	571	512	1,950	1,559	1,284	884	387	196	69	40	47
Larceny-theft	1,960	1,634	1,423	1,233	1,048	949	3,613	3,305	3,058	2,197	1,311	685	311	211	221
Motor vehicle theft	414	283	241	202	173	144	598	500	435	271	115	57	31	12	8
Arson	39	52	52	32	25	23	84	74	69	91	50	29	7	15	5
Violent crime[2]	1,259	1,082	1,213	1,120	1,067	894	3,713	3,651	3,555	2,890	1,630	941	501	284	333
Percent distribution[1]	4.4	3.8	4.3	3.9	3.8	3.2	13.1	12.9	12.5	10.2	5.7	3.3	1.8	1.0	1.2
Property crime[3]	3,979	3,213	2,687	2,135	1,817	1,628	6,245	5,438	4,846	3,443	1,863	183,557	418	278	281
Percent distribution[1]	6.6	5.4	4.5	3.6	3.0	2.7	10.4	9.1	8.1	5.8	3.1	306.8	0.7	0.5	0.5
Crime Index total[4]	5,238	4,295	3,900	3,255	2,884	2,522	9,958	9,089	8,401	6,333	3,493	1,908	919	562	614
Percent distribution[1]	5.9	4.9	4.4	3.7	3.3	2.9	11.3	10.3	9.5	7.2	4.0	2.2	1.0	0.6	0.7
Other assaults	2,384	2,456	2,518	2,460	2,385	2,302	10,576	10,573	10,863	8,337	4,805	2,492	1,304	721	763
Forgery and counterfeiting	299	312	337	271	244	213	1,036	957	837	550	251	129	58	24	14
Fraud	1,299	1,574	1,634	1,453	1,537	1,565	7,498	6,769	6,009	4,246	2,591	1,415	747	350	393
Embezzlement	36	31	38	34	36	32	163	153	152	97	57	48	32	2	7
Stolen property; buying, receiving, possessing	370	339	295	214	223	180	675	573	504	338	186	80	54	27	14
Vandalism	773	642	521	456	387	335	1,238	1,082	1,035	656	403	233	94	74	78
Weapons; carrying, possessing, etc.	350	308	335	285	270	238	908	756	804	683	452	288	163	95	257
Prostitution and commercialized vice	3	8	8	3	5	2	29	24	22	33	15	6	2	7	4
Sex offenses (except forcible rape and prostitution)	252	216	175	178	133	138	502	581	692	497	298	222	141	116	144
Drug abuse violations	5,499	5,013	4,346	3,647	3,291	3,066	10,979	9,019	8,501	6,710	3,773	1,744	751	393	1,776
Gambling	33	41	31	24	34	22	116	120	94	76	68	50	33	11	17
Offenses against the family and children	273	329	413	400	415	406	2,320	2,521	2,538	1,853	918	383	167	65	80
Driving under the influence	3,725	3,902	4,855	4,280	4,048	3,795	15,777	15,500	17,359	16,470	12,349	9,355	7,389	6,473	20,407
Liquor laws	6,715	5,432	1,153	748	605	496	1,791	1,444	1,444	1,250	852	464	227	138	149
Drunkenness	1,004	951	1,099	944	873	827	3,177	3,297	3,829	3,577	2,366	1,434	677	328	286
Disorderly conduct	996	823	881	767	733	670	2,550	2,387	2,446	1,955	1,193	666	368	198	209
Vagrancy	11	9	9	5	6	12	29	32	24	28	22	8	4	2	1
All other offenses (except traffic)	10,707	11,109	10,920	9,799	8,996	8,478	35,165	31,302	29,847	23,050	12,720	6,775	3,091	1,701	2,866
Suspicion	23	13	11	13	11	17	60	63	49	43	13	15	7	4	2
Curfew and loitering law violations	–	–	–	–	–	–	–	–	–	–	–	–	–	–	–
Runaways	–	–	–	–	–	–	–	–	–	–	–	–	–	–	–

[1] Because of rounding, the percentages may not add to total.

[2] Violent crimes are offenses of murder, forcible rape, robbery, and aggravated assault.

[3] Property crimes are offenses of burglary, larceny-theft, motor vehicle theft, and arson.

[4] Includes arson.

Table 59

Arrests

Rural Counties
of Persons Under 15, 18, 21, and 25 Years of Age, 2001
[1,754 agencies; 2001 estimated population 20,668,373]

Offense charged	Total all ages	Number of persons arrested				Percent of total all ages			
		Under 15	Under 18	Under 21	Under 25	Under 15	Under 18	Under 21	Under 25
TOTAL	**821,375**	**23,393**	**86,531**	**203,067**	**318,214**	**2.8**	**10.5**	**24.7**	**38.7**
Murder and nonnegligent manslaughter	1,019	5	48	200	388	0.5	4.7	19.6	38.1
Forcible rape	1,920	87	268	626	892	4.5	14.0	32.6	46.5
Robbery	2,105	21	247	800	1,276	1.0	11.7	38.0	60.6
Aggravated assault	23,322	781	2,414	4,948	8,312	3.3	10.4	21.2	35.6
Burglary	19,676	1,804	5,695	10,538	13,260	9.2	28.9	53.6	67.4
Larceny-theft	33,266	2,526	7,680	13,701	18,354	7.6	23.1	41.2	55.2
Motor vehicle theft	5,824	499	1,891	3,037	3,797	8.6	32.5	52.1	65.2
Arson	1,073	188	370	517	649	17.5	34.5	48.2	60.5
Violent crime[1]	28,366	894	2,977	6,574	10,868	3.2	10.5	23.2	38.3
Property crime[2]	59,839	5,017	15,636	27,793	36,060	8.4	26.1	46.4	60.3
Crime Index total[3]	88,205	5,911	18,613	34,367	46,928	6.7	21.1	39.0	53.2
Other assaults	76,704	3,291	9,280	16,605	26,270	4.3	12.1	21.6	34.2
Forgery and counterfeiting	6,054	27	255	1,133	2,198	0.4	4.2	18.7	36.3
Fraud	40,292	68	456	4,085	10,274	0.2	1.1	10.1	25.5
Embezzlement	980	1	26	129	269	0.1	2.7	13.2	27.4
Stolen property; buying, receiving, possessing	5,301	156	797	1,938	2,850	2.9	15.0	36.6	53.8
Vandalism	14,063	1,929	4,932	7,471	9,170	13.7	35.1	53.1	65.2
Weapons; carrying, possessing, etc.	7,516	328	957	1,982	3,110	4.4	12.7	26.4	41.4
Prostitution and commercialized vice	178	0	3	18	36	–	1.7	10.1	20.2
Sex offenses (except forcible rape and prostitution)	5,627	524	1,085	1,810	2,434	9.3	19.3	32.2	43.3
Drug abuse violations	80,853	1,160	7,071	22,857	37,207	1.4	8.7	28.3	46.0
Gambling	824	7	30	128	239	0.8	3.6	15.5	29.0
Offenses against the family and children	13,941	197	594	1,462	3,096	1.4	4.3	10.5	22.2
Driving under the influence	150,600	313	2,029	12,543	29,521	0.2	1.3	8.3	19.6
Liquor laws	40,281	898	10,249	29,520	32,522	2.2	25.4	73.3	80.7
Drunkenness	26,334	99	759	3,620	7,363	0.4	2.9	13.7	28.0
Disorderly conduct	23,200	1,800	5,234	8,177	11,228	7.8	22.6	35.2	48.4
Vagrancy	266	20	54	84	116	7.5	20.3	31.6	43.6
All other offenses (except traffic)	232,559	4,307	16,860	47,849	86,042	1.9	7.2	20.6	37.0
Suspicion	400	11	50	92	144	2.8	12.5	23.0	36.0
Curfew and loitering law violations	921	258	921	921	921	28.0	100.0	100.0	100.0
Runaways	6,276	2,088	6,276	6,276	6,276	33.3	100.0	100.0	100.0

[1] Violent crimes are offenses of murder, forcible rape, robbery, and aggravated assault.

[2] Property crimes are offenses of burglary, larceny-theft, motor vehicle theft, and arson.

[3] Includes arson.

Table 60

Arrests
Rural Counties
by Sex, 2001
[1,754 agencies; 2001 estimated population 20,688,373]

Offense charged	Number of persons arrested			Percent male	Percent female	Percent distribution[1]		
	Total	Male	Female			Total	Male	Female
TOTAL	**821,375**	**647,910**	**173,465**	**78.9**	**21.1**	**100.0**	**100.0**	**100.0**
Murder and nonnegligent manslaughter	1,019	695	324	68.2	31.8	0.1	0.1	0.2
Forcible rape	1,920	1,887	33	98.3	1.7	0.2	0.3	[2]
Robbery	2,105	1,891	214	89.8	10.2	0.3	0.3	0.1
Aggravated assault	23,322	19,144	4,178	82.1	17.9	2.8	3.0	2.4
Burglary	19,676	17,443	2,233	88.7	11.3	2.4	2.7	1.3
Larceny-theft	33,266	23,957	9,309	72.0	28.0	4.1	3.7	5.4
Motor vehicle theft	5,824	4,826	998	82.9	17.1	0.7	0.7	0.6
Arson	1,073	873	200	81.4	18.6	0.1	0.1	0.1
Violent crime[3]	28,366	23,617	4,749	83.3	16.7	3.5	3.6	2.7
Property crime[4]	59,839	47,099	12,740	78.7	21.3	7.3	7.3	7.3
Crime Index total[5]	88,205	70,716	17,489	80.2	19.8	10.7	10.9	10.1
Other assaults	76,704	59,482	17,222	77.5	22.5	9.3	9.2	9.9
Forgery and counterfeiting	6,054	3,522	2,532	58.2	41.8	0.7	0.5	1.5
Fraud	40,292	20,408	19,884	50.7	49.3	4.9	3.1	11.5
Embezzlement	980	544	436	55.5	44.5	0.1	0.1	0.3
Stolen property; buying, receiving, possessing	5,301	4,480	821	84.5	15.5	0.6	0.7	0.5
Vandalism	14,063	12,028	2,035	85.5	14.5	1.7	1.9	1.2
Weapons; carrying, possessing, etc.	7,516	6,931	585	92.2	7.8	0.9	1.1	0.3
Prostitution and commercialized vice	178	97	81	54.5	45.5	[2]	[2]	[2]
Sex offenses (except forcible rape and prostitution)	5,627	5,341	286	94.9	5.1	0.7	0.8	0.2
Drug abuse violations	80,853	66,228	14,625	81.9	18.1	9.8	10.2	8.4
Gambling	824	691	133	83.9	16.1	0.1	0.1	0.1
Offenses against the family and children	13,941	11,520	2,421	82.6	17.4	1.7	1.8	1.4
Driving under the influence	150,600	127,787	22,813	84.9	15.1	18.3	19.7	13.2
Liquor laws	40,281	30,222	10,059	75.0	25.0	4.9	4.7	5.8
Drunkenness	26,334	22,460	3,874	85.3	14.7	3.2	3.5	2.2
Disorderly conduct	23,200	17,480	5,720	75.3	24.7	2.8	2.7	3.3
Vagrancy	266	209	57	78.6	21.4	[2]	[2]	[2]
All other offenses (except traffic)	232,559	184,319	48,240	79.3	20.7	28.3	28.4	27.8
Suspicion	400	332	68	83.0	17.0	[2]	0.1	[2]
Curfew and loitering law violations	921	557	364	60.5	39.5	0.1	0.1	0.2
Runaways	6,276	2,556	3,720	40.7	59.3	0.8	0.4	2.1

[1] Because of rounding, the percentages may not add to total.
[2] Less than one-tenth of 1 percent.
[3] Violent crimes are offenses of murder, forcible rape, robbery, and aggravated assault.
[4] Property crimes are offenses of burglary, larceny-theft, motor vehicle theft, and arson.
[5] Includes arson.

Table 61

Arrests
Rural Counties
by Race, 2001
[1,754 agencies; 2001 estimated population 20,688,373]

Offense charged	Total arrests					Percent distribution[1]				
	Total	White	Black	American Indian or Alaskan Native	Asian or Pacific Islander	Total	White	Black	American Indian or Alaskan Native	Asian or Pacific Islander
TOTAL	**819,070**	**666,274**	**123,056**	**20,606**	**9,134**	**100.0**	**81.3**	**15.0**	**2.5**	**1.1**
Murder and nonnegligent manslaughter	1,018	524	453	37	4	100.0	51.5	44.5	3.6	0.4
Forcible rape	1,917	1,485	361	57	14	100.0	77.5	18.8	3.0	0.7
Robbery	2,104	1,094	939	45	26	100.0	52.0	44.6	2.1	1.2
Aggravated assault	23,289	17,399	4,895	850	145	100.0	74.7	21.0	3.6	0.6
Burglary	19,652	16,050	2,891	560	151	100.0	81.7	14.7	2.8	0.8
Larceny-theft	33,199	26,740	5,312	695	452	100.0	80.5	16.0	2.1	1.4
Motor vehicle theft	5,815	4,804	698	160	153	100.0	82.6	12.0	2.8	2.6
Arson	1,071	901	135	24	11	100.0	84.1	12.6	2.2	1.0
Violent crime[2]	28,328	20,502	6,648	989	189	100.0	72.4	23.5	3.5	0.7
Property crime[3]	59,737	48,495	9,036	1,439	767	100.0	81.2	15.1	2.4	1.3
Crime Index total[4]	88,065	68,997	15,684	2,428	956	100.0	78.3	17.8	2.8	1.1
Other assaults	76,558	60,309	13,278	2,184	787	100.0	78.8	17.3	2.9	1.0
Forgery and counterfeiting	6,051	4,723	1,163	70	95	100.0	78.1	19.2	1.2	1.6
Fraud	40,199	31,633	7,959	452	155	100.0	78.7	19.8	1.1	0.4
Embezzlement	976	793	146	18	19	100.0	81.3	15.0	1.8	1.9
Stolen property; buying, receiving, possessing	5,293	4,105	1,058	111	19	100.0	77.6	20.0	2.1	0.4
Vandalism	14,040	12,045	1,501	418	76	100.0	85.8	10.7	3.0	0.5
Weapons; carrying, possessing, etc.	7,506	5,919	1,364	163	60	100.0	78.9	18.2	2.2	0.8
Prostitution and commercialized vice	178	138	29	4	7	100.0	77.5	16.3	2.2	3.9
Sex offenses (except forcible rape and prostitution)	5,613	4,962	491	123	37	100.0	88.4	8.7	2.2	0.7
Drug abuse violations	80,695	66,130	12,595	1,317	653	100.0	82.0	15.6	1.6	0.8
Gambling	824	390	335	1	98	100.0	47.3	40.7	0.1	11.9
Offenses against the family and children	13,889	10,573	3,114	156	46	100.0	76.1	22.4	1.1	0.3
Driving under the influence	150,291	129,637	15,261	3,665	1,728	100.0	86.3	10.2	2.4	1.1
Liquor laws	40,033	36,875	1,786	1,111	261	100.0	92.1	4.5	2.8	0.7
Drunkenness	26,299	23,380	1,814	1,007	98	100.0	88.9	6.9	3.8	0.4
Disorderly conduct	23,177	18,206	4,180	652	139	100.0	78.6	18.0	2.8	0.6
Vagrancy	265	193	57	15	0	100.0	72.8	21.5	5.7	–
All other offenses (except traffic)	231,548	180,706	40,701	6,576	3,565	100.0	78.0	17.6	2.8	1.5
Suspicion	390	254	132	4	0	100.0	65.1	33.8	1.0	–
Curfew and loitering law violations	919	782	49	13	75	100.0	85.1	5.3	1.4	8.2
Runaways	6,261	5,524	359	118	260	100.0	88.2	5.7	1.9	4.2

See footnotes at end of table.

Table 61

Arrests
Rural Counties
by Race, 2001—Continued
[1,754 agencies; 2001 estimated population 20,688,373]

| | Arrests under 18 | | | | | Percent distribution[1] | | | | |
Offense charged	Total	White	Black	American Indian or Alaskan Native	Asian or Pacific Islander	Total	White	Black	American Indian or Alaskan Native	Asian or Pacific Islander
TOTAL	**86,268**	**73,219**	**9,485**	**2,195**	**1,369**	**100.0**	**84.9**	**11.0**	**2.5**	**1.6**
Murder and nonnegligent manslaughter	48	29	16	2	1	100.0	60.4	33.3	4.2	2.1
Forcible rape	268	218	46	4	0	100.0	81.3	17.2	1.5	–
Robbery	247	119	115	8	5	100.0	48.2	46.6	3.2	2.0
Aggravated assault	2,410	1,875	456	62	17	100.0	77.8	18.9	2.6	0.7
Burglary	5,685	4,890	545	194	56	100.0	86.0	9.6	3.4	1.0
Larceny-theft	7,650	6,472	835	188	155	100.0	84.6	10.9	2.5	2.0
Motor vehicle theft	1,885	1,581	158	75	71	100.0	83.9	8.4	4.0	3.8
Arson	370	326	27	12	5	100.0	88.1	7.3	3.2	1.4
Violent crime[2]	2,973	2,241	633	76	23	100.0	75.4	21.3	2.6	0.8
Property crime[3]	15,590	13,269	1,565	469	287	100.0	85.1	10.0	3.0	1.8
Crime Index total[4]	18,563	15,510	2,198	545	310	100.0	83.6	11.8	2.9	1.7
Other assaults	9,253	7,169	1,719	208	157	100.0	77.5	18.6	2.2	1.7
Forgery and counterfeiting	256	228	21	3	4	100.0	89.1	8.2	1.2	1.6
Fraud	452	378	57	8	9	100.0	83.6	12.6	1.8	2.0
Embezzlement	26	22	3	1	0	100.0	84.6	11.5	3.8	–
Stolen property; buying, receiving, possessing	796	676	96	24	0	100.0	84.9	12.1	3.0	–
Vandalism	4,922	4,455	329	106	32	100.0	90.5	6.7	2.2	0.7
Weapons; carrying, possessing, etc.	955	751	172	28	4	100.0	78.6	18.0	2.9	0.4
Prostitution and commercialized vice	3	3	0	0	0	100.0	100.0	–	–	–
Sex offenses (except forcible rape and prostitution)	1,082	961	100	16	5	100.0	88.8	9.2	1.5	0.5
Drug abuse violations	7,053	6,141	568	174	170	100.0	87.1	8.1	2.5	2.4
Gambling	30	26	4	0	0	100.0	86.7	13.3	–	–
Offenses against the family and children	593	543	46	2	2	100.0	91.6	7.8	0.3	0.3
Driving under the influence	2,026	1,866	81	49	30	100.0	92.1	4.0	2.4	1.5
Liquor laws	10,198	9,651	160	313	74	100.0	94.6	1.6	3.1	0.7
Drunkenness	758	698	32	28	0	100.0	92.1	4.2	3.7	–
Disorderly conduct	5,230	3,909	1,191	106	24	100.0	74.7	22.8	2.0	0.5
Vagrancy	54	36	16	2	0	100.0	66.7	29.6	3.7	–
All other offenses (except traffic)	16,789	13,857	2,269	450	213	100.0	82.5	13.5	2.7	1.3
Suspicion	49	33	15	1	0	100.0	67.3	30.6	2.0	–
Curfew and loitering law violations	919	782	49	13	75	100.0	85.1	5.3	1.4	8.2
Runaways	6,261	5,524	359	118	260	100.0	88.2	5.7	1.9	4.2

See footnotes at end of table.

Table 61

Arrests
Rural Counties
by Race, 2001—Continued
[1,754 agencies; 2001 estimated population 20,688,373]

Offense charged	Arrests 18 and over					Percent distribution[1]				
	Total	White	Black	American Indian or Alaskan Native	Asian or Pacific Islander	Total	White	Black	American Indian or Alaskan Native	Asian or Pacific Islander
TOTAL	**732,802**	**593,055**	**113,571**	**18,411**	**7,765**	**100.0**	**80.9**	**15.5**	**2.5**	**1.1**
Murder and nonnegligent manslaughter	970	495	437	35	3	100.0	51.0	45.1	3.6	0.3
Forcible rape	1,649	1,267	315	53	14	100.0	76.8	19.1	3.2	0.8
Robbery	1,857	975	824	37	21	100.0	52.5	44.4	2.0	1.1
Aggravated assault	20,879	15,524	4,439	788	128	100.0	74.4	21.3	3.8	0.6
Burglary	13,967	11,160	2,346	366	95	100.0	79.9	16.8	2.6	0.7
Larceny-theft	25,549	20,268	4,477	507	297	100.0	79.3	17.5	2.0	1.2
Motor vehicle theft	3,930	3,223	540	85	82	100.0	82.0	13.7	2.2	2.1
Arson	701	575	108	12	6	100.0	82.0	15.4	1.7	0.9
Violent crime[2]	25,355	18,261	6,015	913	166	100.0	72.0	23.7	3.6	0.7
Property crime[3]	44,147	35,226	7,471	970	480	100.0	79.8	16.9	2.2	1.1
Crime Index total[4]	69,502	53,487	13,486	1,883	646	100.0	77.0	19.4	2.7	0.9
Other assaults	67,305	53,140	11,559	1,976	630	100.0	79.0	17.2	2.9	0.9
Forgery and counterfeiting	5,795	4,495	1,142	67	91	100.0	77.6	19.7	1.2	1.6
Fraud	39,747	31,255	7,902	444	146	100.0	78.6	19.9	1.1	0.4
Embezzlement	950	771	143	17	19	100.0	81.2	15.1	1.8	2.0
Stolen property; buying, receiving, possessing	4,497	3,429	962	87	19	100.0	76.3	21.4	1.9	0.4
Vandalism	9,118	7,590	1,172	312	44	100.0	83.2	12.9	3.4	0.5
Weapons; carrying, possessing, etc.	6,551	5,168	1,192	135	56	100.0	78.9	18.2	2.1	0.9
Prostitution and commercialized vice	175	135	29	4	7	100.0	77.1	16.6	2.3	4.0
Sex offenses (except forcible rape and prostitution)	4,531	4,001	391	107	32	100.0	88.3	8.6	2.4	0.7
Drug abuse violations	73,642	59,989	12,027	1,143	483	100.0	81.5	16.3	1.6	0.7
Gambling	794	364	331	1	98	100.0	45.8	41.7	0.1	12.3
Offenses against the family and children	13,296	10,030	3,068	154	44	100.0	75.4	23.1	1.2	0.3
Driving under the influence	148,265	127,771	15,180	3,616	1,698	100.0	86.2	10.2	2.4	1.1
Liquor laws	29,835	27,224	1,626	798	187	100.0	91.2	5.4	2.7	0.6
Drunkenness	25,541	22,682	1,782	979	98	100.0	88.8	7.0	3.8	0.4
Disorderly conduct	17,947	14,297	2,989	546	115	100.0	79.7	16.7	3.0	0.6
Vagrancy	211	157	41	13	0	100.0	74.4	19.4	6.2	–
All other offenses (except traffic)	214,759	166,849	38,432	6,126	3,352	100.0	77.7	17.9	2.9	1.6
Suspicion	341	221	117	3	0	100.0	64.8	34.3	0.9	–
Curfew and loitering law violations	–	–	–	–	–	–	–	–	–	–
Runaways	–	–	–	–	–	–	–	–	–	–

[1] Because of rounding, the percentages may not add to total.
[2] Violent crimes are offenses of murder, forcible rape, robbery, and aggravated assault.
[3] Property crimes are offenses of burglary, larceny-theft, motor vehicle theft, and arson.
[4] Includes arson.

Table 62

Arrest Trends

Suburban Areas[1], 2000-2001

[4,102 agencies; 2001 estimated population 67,581,786; 2000 estimated population 67,375,714]

| Offense charged | Number of persons arrested | | | | | | | | |
| | Total all ages | | | Under 18 years of age | | | 18 years of age and over | | |
	2000	2001	Percent change	2000	2001	Percent change	2000	2001	Percent change
TOTAL[2]	2,856,391	2,765,259	-3.2	490,592	473,335	-3.5	2,365,799	2,291,924	-3.1
Murder and nonnegligent manslaughter	1,883	1,786	-5.2	142	131	-7.7	1,741	1,655	-4.9
Forcible rape	5,098	4,983	-2.3	852	871	+2.2	4,246	4,112	-3.2
Robbery	14,342	14,385	+0.3	3,464	3,419	-1.3	10,878	10,966	+0.8
Aggravated assault	84,593	83,037	-1.8	12,500	12,363	-1.1	72,093	70,674	-2.0
Burglary	54,399	54,844	+0.8	19,245	18,316	-4.8	35,154	36,528	+3.9
Larceny-theft	221,180	215,827	-2.4	70,788	65,382	-7.6	150,392	150,445	[3]
Motor vehicle theft	21,701	21,860	+0.7	7,053	6,904	-2.1	14,648	14,956	+2.1
Arson	3,872	4,019	+3.8	2,226	2,280	+2.4	1,646	1,739	+5.7
Violent crime[4]	105,916	104,191	-1.6	16,958	16,784	-1.0	88,958	87,407	-1.7
Property crime[5]	301,152	296,550	-1.5	99,312	92,882	-6.5	201,840	203,668	+0.9
Crime Index total[6]	407,068	400,741	-1.6	116,270	109,666	-5.7	290,798	291,075	+0.1
Other assaults	252,447	248,299	-1.6	51,055	51,851	+1.6	201,392	196,448	-2.5
Forgery and counterfeiting	22,476	22,255	-1.0	1,409	1,215	-13.8	21,067	21,040	-0.1
Fraud	86,542	84,672	-2.2	1,967	1,716	-12.8	84,575	82,956	-1.9
Embezzlement	3,717	3,888	+4.6	422	363	-14.0	3,295	3,525	+7.0
Stolen property; buying, receiving, possessing	24,602	24,180	-1.7	5,839	5,323	-8.8	18,763	18,857	+0.5
Vandalism	56,734	53,213	-6.2	26,114	23,716	-9.2	30,620	29,497	-3.7
Weapons; carrying, possessing, etc.	28,913	29,248	+1.2	7,441	7,499	+0.8	21,472	21,749	+1.3
Prostitution and commercialized vice	3,495	3,014	-13.8	80	83	+3.8	3,415	2,931	-14.2
Sex offenses (except forcible rape and prostitution)	16,417	15,927	-3.0	3,683	3,708	+0.7	12,734	12,219	-4.0
Drug abuse violations	293,472	285,597	-2.7	43,295	43,647	+0.8	250,177	241,950	-3.3
Gambling	1,232	873	-29.1	71	72	+1.4	1,161	801	-31.0
Offenses against the family and children	45,348	43,751	-3.5	2,101	1,912	-9.0	43,247	41,839	-3.3
Driving under the influence	389,726	366,920	-5.9	5,186	4,986	-3.9	384,540	361,934	-5.9
Liquor laws	151,408	132,764	-12.3	40,311	35,609	-11.7	111,097	97,155	-12.5
Drunkenness	121,722	115,263	-5.3	5,039	5,069	+0.6	116,683	110,194	-5.6
Disorderly conduct	123,661	118,745	-4.0	38,785	39,888	+2.8	84,876	78,857	-7.1
Vagrancy	4,350	3,606	-17.1	518	468	-9.7	3,832	3,138	-18.1
All other offenses (except traffic)	774,285	766,199	-1.0	92,230	90,440	-1.9	682,055	675,759	-0.9
Suspicion	1,250	1,245	-0.4	239	401	+67.8	1,011	844	-16.5
Curfew and loitering law violations	18,799	17,424	-7.3	18,799	17,424	-7.3	-	-	-
Runaways	29,977	28,680	-4.3	29,977	28,680	-4.3	-	-	-

[1] Suburban area includes law enforcement agencies in cities with less than 50,000 inhabitants and county law enforcement agencies that are within a Metropolitan Statistical Area (see Appendix III). Suburban area excludes all metropolitan agencies associated with a central city. The agencies associated with suburban areas will also appear in other groups within this table.

[2] Does not include suspicion.

[3] Less than one-tenth of 1 percent.

[4] Violent crimes are offenses of murder, forcible rape, robbery, and aggravated assault.

[5] Property crimes are offenses of burglary, larceny-theft, motor vehicle theft, and arson.

[6] Includes arson.

Table 63

Arrest Trends
Suburban Areas[1]
by Sex, 2000-2001
[4,102 agencies; 2001 estimated population 67,581,786; 2000 estimated population 67,375,714]

Offense charged	Male Total 2000	Male Total 2001	Male Total Percent change	Male Under 18 2000	Male Under 18 2001	Male Under 18 Percent change	Female Total 2000	Female Total 2001	Female Total Percent change	Female Under 18 2000	Female Under 18 2001	Female Under 18 Percent change
TOTAL[2]	2,229,040	2,145,651	-3.7	358,724	342,862	-4.4	627,351	619,608	-1.2	131,868	130,473	-1.1
Murder and nonnegligent manslaughter	1,646	1,582	-3.9	129	114	-11.6	237	204	-13.9	13	17	+30.8
Forcible rape	5,021	4,918	-2.1	844	855	+1.3	77	65	-15.6	8	16	+100.0
Robbery	12,894	13,039	+1.1	3,186	3,164	-0.7	1,448	1,346	-7.0	278	255	-8.3
Aggravated assault	68,733	67,532	-1.7	9,891	9,786	-1.1	15,860	15,505	-2.2	2,609	2,577	-1.2
Burglary	47,689	47,850	+0.3	17,185	16,305	-5.1	6,710	6,994	+4.2	2,060	2,011	-2.4
Larceny-theft	142,244	136,842	-3.8	46,318	41,324	-10.8	78,936	78,985	+0.1	24,470	24,058	-1.7
Motor vehicle theft	18,167	18,249	+0.5	5,733	5,625	-1.9	3,534	3,611	+2.2	1,320	1,279	-3.1
Arson	3,369	3,481	+3.3	1,976	2,070	+4.8	503	538	+7.0	250	210	-16.0
Violent crime[3]	88,294	87,071	-1.4	14,050	13,919	-0.9	17,622	17,120	-2.8	2,908	2,865	-1.5
Property crime[4]	211,469	206,422	-2.4	71,212	65,324	-8.3	89,683	90,128	+0.5	28,100	27,558	-1.9
Crime Index total[5]	299,763	293,493	-2.1	85,262	79,243	-7.1	107,305	107,248	-0.1	31,008	30,423	-1.9
Other assaults	193,379	189,255	-2.1	36,190	36,183	[6]	59,068	59,044	[6]	14,865	15,668	+5.4
Forgery and counterfeiting	13,997	13,315	-4.9	976	794	-18.6	8,479	8,940	+5.4	433	421	-2.8
Fraud	45,253	43,819	-3.2	1,335	1,148	-14.0	41,289	40,853	-1.1	632	568	-10.1
Embezzlement	1,927	2,011	+4.4	225	220	-2.2	1,790	1,877	+4.9	197	143	-27.4
Stolen property; buying, receiving, possessing	20,396	20,028	-1.8	5,017	4,594	-8.4	4,206	4,152	-1.3	822	729	-11.3
Vandalism	48,699	45,446	-6.7	23,042	20,794	-9.8	8,035	7,767	-3.3	3,072	2,922	-4.9
Weapons; carrying, possessing, etc.	26,645	26,857	+0.8	6,706	6,772	+1.0	2,268	2,391	+5.4	735	727	-1.1
Prostitution and commercialized vice	1,886	1,525	-19.1	55	43	-21.8	1,609	1,489	-7.5	25	40	+60.0
Sex offenses (except forcible rape and prostitution)	15,562	15,180	-2.5	3,439	3,475	+1.0	855	747	-12.6	244	233	-4.5
Drug abuse violations	242,084	234,912	-3.0	36,167	36,151	[6]	51,388	50,685	-1.4	7,128	7,496	+5.2
Gambling	970	726	-25.2	65	67	+3.1	262	147	-43.9	6	5	-16.7
Offenses against the family and children	37,336	35,864	-3.9	1,352	1,199	-11.3	8,012	7,887	-1.6	749	713	-4.8
Driving under the influence	325,010	304,460	-6.3	4,326	4,120	-4.8	64,716	62,460	-3.5	860	866	+0.7
Liquor laws	115,111	99,976	-13.1	27,920	24,249	-13.1	36,297	32,788	-9.7	12,391	11,360	-8.3
Drunkenness	104,528	98,194	-6.1	4,061	3,991	-1.7	17,194	17,069	-0.7	978	1,078	+10.2
Disorderly conduct	94,496	90,307	-4.4	27,993	28,733	+2.6	29,165	28,438	-2.5	10,792	11,155	+3.4
Vagrancy	3,599	3,116	-13.4	436	378	-13.3	751	490	-34.8	82	90	+9.8
All other offenses (except traffic)	612,708	603,411	-1.5	68,466	66,952	-2.2	161,577	162,788	+0.7	23,764	23,488	-1.2
Suspicion	1,017	928	-8.8	178	238	+33.7	233	317	+36.1	61	163	+167.2
Curfew and loitering law violations	12,973	11,817	-8.9	12,973	11,817	-8.9	5,826	5,607	-3.8	5,826	5,607	-3.8
Runaways	12,718	11,939	-6.1	12,718	11,939	-6.1	17,259	16,741	-3.0	17,259	16,741	-3.0

[1] Suburban area includes law enforcement agencies in cities with less than 50,000 inhabitants and county law enforcement agencies that are within a Metropolitan Statistical Area (see Appendix III). Suburban area excludes all metropolitan agencies associated with a central city. The agencies associated with suburban areas will also appear in other groups within this table.

[2] Does not include suspicion.

[3] Violent crimes are offenses of murder, forcible rape, robbery, and aggravated assault.

[4] Property crimes are offenses of burglary, larceny-theft, motor vehicle theft, and arson.

[5] Includes arson.

[6] Less than one-tenth of 1 percent.

Table 64

Arrests
Suburban Areas[1]
by Age, 2001
[4,740 agencies; 2001 estimated population 79,778,727]

Offense charged	Total all ages	Ages under 15	Ages under 18	Ages 18 and over	Under 10	10-12	13-14	15	16	17	18	19	20	21
TOTAL	3,349,602	177,264	564,592	2,785,010	8,216	42,539	126,509	108,252	134,015	145,061	175,793	177,494	166,116	146,491
Percent distribution[2]	100.0	5.3	16.9	83.1	0.2	1.3	3.8	3.2	4.0	4.3	5.2	5.3	5.0	4.4
Murder and nonnegligent manslaughter	2,345	20	166	2,179	0	2	18	18	46	82	138	143	144	152
Forcible rape	6,201	429	1,098	5,103	14	104	311	171	235	263	331	308	291	269
Robbery	19,181	911	4,390	14,791	18	206	687	793	1,205	1,481	1,799	1,593	1,304	1,081
Aggravated assault	105,727	5,475	15,097	90,630	304	1,505	3,666	2,790	3,210	3,622	4,047	4,165	4,130	4,276
Burglary	68,622	8,049	22,267	46,355	431	2,195	5,423	4,240	4,908	5,070	5,598	4,607	3,702	2,919
Larceny-theft	269,465	29,284	80,305	189,160	1,119	7,639	20,526	15,245	17,602	18,174	18,352	14,731	11,934	9,739
Motor vehicle theft	27,068	1,944	8,292	18,776	11	245	1,688	2,000	2,244	2,104	2,096	1,740	1,458	1,262
Arson	4,662	1,599	2,537	2,125	253	585	761	365	330	243	227	171	114	105
Violent crime[3]	133,454	6,835	20,751	112,703	336	1,817	4,682	3,772	4,696	5,448	6,315	6,209	5,869	5,778
Percent distribution[2]	100.0	5.1	15.5	84.5	0.3	1.4	3.5	2.8	3.5	4.1	4.7	4.7	4.4	4.3
Property crime[4]	369,817	40,876	113,401	256,416	1,814	10,664	28,398	21,850	25,084	25,591	26,273	21,249	17,208	14,025
Percent distribution[2]	100.0	11.1	30.7	69.3	0.5	2.9	7.7	5.9	6.8	6.9	7.1	5.7	4.7	3.8
Crime Index total[5]	503,271	47,711	134,152	369,119	2,150	12,481	33,080	25,622	29,780	31,039	32,588	27,458	23,077	19,803
Percent distribution[2]	100.0	9.5	26.7	73.3	0.4	2.5	6.6	5.1	5.9	6.2	6.5	5.5	4.6	3.9
Other assaults	305,229	26,436	60,924	244,305	1,241	7,801	17,394	11,468	12,051	10,969	10,611	10,334	10,208	10,791
Forgery and counterfeiting	28,225	142	1,464	26,761	8	15	119	183	407	732	1,348	1,543	1,537	1,443
Fraud	95,100	316	2,144	92,956	21	53	242	307	568	953	2,378	3,473	4,148	4,230
Embezzlement	4,846	41	454	4,392	0	6	35	42	132	239	358	338	270	239
Stolen property; buying, receiving, possessing	30,976	1,759	6,591	24,385	42	362	1,355	1,278	1,687	1,867	2,287	2,058	1,841	1,608
Vandalism	65,650	12,385	28,160	37,490	1,113	3,759	7,513	4,744	5,586	5,445	4,679	3,808	2,833	2,611
Weapons; carrying, possessing, etc.	36,599	3,139	8,846	27,753	224	800	2,115	1,551	1,952	2,204	2,518	2,312	1,947	1,792
Prostitution and commercialized vice	4,969	24	97	4,872	0	7	17	18	27	28	83	116	127	134
Sex offenses (except forcible rape and prostitution)	19,913	2,302	4,433	15,480	165	650	1,487	745	681	705	792	712	678	628
Drug abuse violations	355,853	8,774	50,879	304,974	111	1105	7,558	8,765	14,045	19,295	27,312	26,217	23,549	19,874
Gambling	1,019	18	93	926	2	2	14	19	27	29	47	45	47	30
Offenses against the family and children	49,790	1,016	2,493	47,297	141	258	617	513	491	473	829	896	1,141	1,338
Driving under the influence	417,607	134	5,631	411,976	43	8	83	228	1,399	3,870	9,789	13,025	14,897	19,366
Liquor laws	154,562	3,413	40,343	114,219	73	242	3,098	5,970	11,928	19,032	29,325	29,658	23,281	4,248
Drunkenness	142,079	757	5,966	136,113	25	69	663	938	1,581	2,690	4,705	5,300	5,095	6,669
Disorderly conduct	148,316	19,482	47,630	100,686	655	5,114	13,713	9,847	9,711	8,590	7,839	6,950	6,273	6,803
Vagrancy	4,895	190	629	4,266	1	46	143	98	165	176	290	232	206	166
All other offenses (except traffic)	924,011	31,249	107,882	816,129	1,601	6,831	22,817	21,765	26,377	28,491	37,950	42,962	44,900	44,665
Suspicion	1,390	185	479	911	18	39	128	107	131	56	65	57	61	53
Curfew and loitering law violations	21,753	5,926	21,753	–	89	934	4,903	5,132	6,509	4,186	–	–	–	--
Runaways	33,549	11,865	33,549	–	493	1,957	9,415	8,912	8,780	3,992	–	–	–	–

[1] Suburban area includes city law enforcement agencies with less than 50,000 inhabitants and county law enforcement agencies that are within a Metropolitan Statistical Area (see Appendix III). Suburban area excludes all metropolitan agencies associated with a central city. The agencies associated with suburban areas will also appear in other groups within this table.

[2] Because of rounding, the percentages may not add to total.

[3] Violent crimes are offenses of murder, forcible rape, robbery, and aggravated assault.

Table 64

Arrests

Suburban Areas[1]
by Age, 2001—Continued
[4,740 agencies; 2001 estimated population 79,778,727]

Offense charged	22	23	24	25-29	30-34	35-39	40-44	45-49	50-54	55-59	60-64	65 and over
TOTAL[1]	**26,891**	**113,563**	**102,697**	**408,372**	**375,851**	**362,921**	**290,104**	**169,219**	**89,599**	**40,580**	**19,415**	**19,904**
Percent distribution[2]	**3.8**	**3.4**	**3.1**	**12.2**	**11.2**	**10.8**	**8.7**	**5.1**	**2.7**	**1.2**	**0.6**	**0.6**
Murder and nonnegligent manslaughter	119	116	93	350	238	215	191	106	80	51	15	28
Forcible rape	258	219	207	760	678	705	477	242	164	81	48	65
Robbery	868	703	579	2,068	1,667	1,456	920	446	196	59	20	32
Aggravated assault	3,820	3,741	3,350	14,084	13,429	13,307	10,411	5,841	3,031	1,387	733	878
Burglary	2,370	1,974	1,704	6,294	5,641	5,270	3,589	1,590	673	249	97	78
Larceny-theft	8,117	6,888	6,029	25,028	24,747	23,342	18,393	10,739	5,673	2,672	1,292	1,484
Motor vehicle theft	966	869	734	2,875	2,498	1,955	1,261	623	282	90	27	40
Arson	105	65	61	238	255	267	226	150	82	32	11	16
Violent crime[3]	5,065	4,779	4,229	17,262	16,012	15,683	11,999	6,635	3,471	1,578	816	1,003
Percent distribution[2]	3.8	3.6	3.2	12.9	12.0	11.8	9.0	5.0	2.6	1.2	0.6	0.8
Property crime[4]	11,558	9,796	8,528	34,435	33,141	30,834	23,469	13,102	6,710	3,043	1,427	1,618
Percent distribution[2]	3.1	2.6	2.3	9.3	9.0	8.3	6.3	3.5	1.8	0.8	0.4	0.4
Crime Index total[5]	16,623	14,575	12,757	51,697	49,153	46,517	35,468	19,737	10,181	4,621	2,243	2,621
Percent distribution[2]	3.3	2.9	2.5	10.3	9.8	9.2	7.0	3.9	2.0	0.9	0.4	0.5
Other assaults	9,753	9,308	8,820	37,232	37,637	37,840	29,546	16,481	8,171	3,730	1,854	1,989
Forgery and counterfeiting	1,337	1,169	1,055	4,656	4,347	3,650	2,476	1,292	564	210	66	68
Fraud	4,086	3,726	3,730	16,540	15,880	13,480	9,656	5,818	3,198	1,383	618	612
Embezzlement	187	186	174	689	608	556	373	179	112	82	25	16
Stolen property; buying, receiving, possessing	1,230	1,133	1000	3,642	3,225	2,711	1,932	966	457	164	73	58
Vandalism	1,997	1,691	1,361	4,914	4,265	3,852	2,675	1,499	682	286	155	182
Weapons; carrying, possessing, etc.	1,582	1,292	1,131	4,058	3,054	2,666	2,312	1,377	854	433	201	224
Prostitution and commercialized vice	147	138	132	678	862	921	653	382	201	133	69	96
Sex offenses (except forcible rape and prostitution)	591	477	443	1,909	2,005	2,204	1,721	1,212	836	506	358	408
Drug abuse violations	16,383	14,015	12,265	44,379	37,224	34,727	26,463	13,731	5,789	1,934	642	470
Gambling	29	24	22	97	94	77	102	77	72	56	51	56
Offenses against the family and children	1,348	1,308	1,509	7,823	8,886	8,940	7,038	3,572	1,534	639	269	227
Driving under the influence	18,120	17,204	15,608	63,510	57,175	57,893	51,087	33,641	20,622	10,222	5,100	4,717
Liquor laws	2,654	2,022	1,553	5,129	3,915	3,873	3,582	2,302	1,275	674	337	391
Drunkenness	5,632	4,876	4,446	17,303	17,256	19,906	19,069	12,509	7,127	3,296	1,609	1,315
Disorderly conduct	5,503	4,577	3,897	13,792	11,906	11,871	9,710	5,672	3,017	1,339	742	795
Vagrancy	131	95	96	448	481	613	602	422	247	119	59	59
All other offenses (except traffic)	39,521	35,710	32,661	129,718	117,770	110,511	85,559	48,299	24,631	10,739	4,939	5,594
Suspicion	37	37	37	158	108	113	80	51	29	14	5	6
Curfew and loitering law violations	–	–	–	–	–	–	–	–	–	–	–	–
Runaways	–	–	–	–	–	–	–	–	–	–	–	–

Table 65

Arrests

Suburban Areas[1]
of Persons Under 15, 18, 21, and 25 Years of Age, 2001
[4,740 agencies; 2001 estimated population 79,778,727]

Offense charged	Total all ages	Number of persons arrested				Percent of total all ages			
		Under 15	Under 18	Under 21	Under 25	Under 15	Under 18	Under 21	Under 25
TOTAL	3,349,602	177,264	564,592	1,083,995	1,573,637	5.3	16.9	32.4	47.0
Murder and nonnegligent manslaughter	2,345	20	166	591	1,071	0.9	7.1	25.2	45.7
Forcible rape	6,201	429	1,098	2,028	2,981	6.9	17.7	32.7	48.1
Robbery	19,181	911	4,390	9,086	12,317	4.7	22.9	47.4	64.2
Aggravated assault	105,727	5,475	15,097	27,439	42,626	5.2	14.3	26.0	40.3
Burglary	68,622	8,049	22,267	36,174	45,141	11.7	32.4	52.7	65.8
Larceny-theft	269,465	29,284	80,305	125,322	156,095	10.9	29.8	46.5	57.9
Motor vehicle theft	27,068	1,944	8,292	13,586	17,417	7.2	30.6	50.2	64.3
Arson	4,662	1,599	2,537	3,049	3,385	34.3	54.4	65.4	72.6
Violent crime[2]	133,454	6,835	20,751	39,144	58,995	5.1	15.5	29.3	44.2
Property crime[3]	369,817	40,876	113,401	178,131	222,038	11.1	30.7	48.2	60.0
Crime Index total[4]	503,271	47,711	134,152	217,275	281,033	9.5	26.7	43.2	55.8
Other assaults	305,229	26,436	60,924	92,077	130,749	8.7	20.0	30.2	42.8
Forgery and counterfeiting	28,225	142	1,464	5,892	10,896	0.5	5.2	20.9	38.6
Fraud	95,100	316	2,144	12,143	27,915	0.3	2.3	12.8	29.4
Embezzlement	4,846	41	454	1,420	2,206	0.8	9.4	29.3	45.5
Stolen property; buying, receiving, possessing	30,976	1,759	6,591	12,777	17,748	5.7	21.3	41.2	57.3
Vandalism	65,650	12,385	28,160	39,480	47,140	18.9	42.9	60.1	71.8
Weapons; carrying, possessing, etc.	36,599	3,139	8,846	15,623	21,420	8.6	24.2	42.7	58.5
Prostitution and commercialized vice	4,969	24	97	423	974	0.5	2.0	8.5	19.6
Sex offenses (except forcible rape and prostitution)	19,913	2,302	4,433	6,615	8,754	11.6	22.3	33.2	44.0
Drug abuse violations	355,853	8,774	50,879	127,957	190,494	2.5	14.3	36.0	53.5
Gambling	1,019	18	93	232	337	1.8	9.1	22.8	33.1
Offenses against the family and children	49,790	1,016	2,493	5,359	10,862	2.0	5.0	10.8	21.8
Driving under the influence	417,607	134	5,631	43,342	113,640	[5]	1.3	10.4	27.2
Liquor laws	154,562	3,413	40,343	122,607	133,084	2.2	26.1	79.3	86.1
Drunkenness	142,079	757	5,966	21,066	42,689	0.5	4.2	14.8	30.0
Disorderly conduct	148,316	19,482	47,630	68,692	89,472	13.1	32.1	46.3	60.3
Vagrancy	4,895	190	629	1,357	1,845	3.9	12.8	27.7	37.7
All other offenses (except traffic)	924,011	31,249	107,882	233,694	386,251	3.4	11.7	25.3	41.8
Suspicion	1,390	185	479	662	826	13.3	34.5	47.6	59.4
Curfew and loitering law violations	21,753	5,926	21,753	21,753	21,753	27.2	100.0	100.0	100.0
Runaways	33,549	11,865	33,549	33,549	33,549	35.4	100.0	100.0	100.0

[1] Suburban area includes law enforcement agencies in cities with less than 50,000 inhabitants and county law enforcement agencies that are within a Metropolitan Statistical Area (see Appendix III). Suburban area excludes all metropolitan agencies associated with a central city. The agencies associated with suburban areas will also appear in other groups within this table.

[2] Violent crimes are offenses of murder, forcible rape, robbery, and aggravated assault.

[3] Property crimes are offenses of burglary, larceny-theft, motor vehicle theft, and arson.

[4] Includes arson.

[5] Less than one-tenth of 1 percent.

Table 66

Arrests
Suburban Areas[1]
by Sex, 2001
[4,740 agencies; 2001 estimated population 79,778,727]

Offense charged	Number of persons arrested			Percent male	Percent female	Percent distribution[2]		
	Total	Male	Female			Total	Male	Female
TOTAL	3,349,602	2,597,715	751,887	77.6	22.4	100.0	100.0	100.0
Murder and nonnegligent manslaughter	2,345	2,078	267	88.6	11.4	0.1	0.1	[3]
Forcible rape	6,201	6,117	84	98.6	1.4	0.2	0.2	[3]
Robbery	19,181	17,297	1,884	90.2	9.8	0.6	0.7	0.3
Aggravated assault	105,727	85,883	19,844	81.2	18.8	3.2	3.3	2.6
Burglary	68,622	59,961	8,661	87.4	12.6	2.0	2.3	1.2
Larceny-theft	269,465	170,660	98,805	63.3	36.7	8.0	6.6	13.1
Motor vehicle theft	27,068	22,582	4,486	83.4	16.6	0.8	0.9	0.6
Arson	4,662	4,038	624	86.6	13.4	0.1	0.2	0.1
Violent crime[4]	133,454	111,375	22,079	83.5	16.5	4.0	4.3	2.9
Property crime[5]	369,817	257,241	112,576	69.6	30.4	11.0	9.9	15.0
Crime Index total[6]	503,271	368,616	134,655	73.2	26.8	15.0	14.2	17.9
Other assaults	305,229	232,782	72,447	76.3	23.7	9.1	9.0	9.6
Forgery and counterfeiting	28,225	16,962	11,263	60.1	39.9	0.8	0.7	1.5
Fraud	95,100	50,222	44,878	52.8	47.2	2.8	1.9	6.0
Embezzlement	4,846	2,522	2,324	52.0	48.0	0.1	0.1	0.3
Stolen property; buying, receiving, possessing	30,976	25,633	5,343	82.8	17.2	0.9	1.0	0.7
Vandalism	65,650	55,854	9,796	85.1	14.9	2.0	2.2	1.3
Weapons; carrying, possessing, etc.	36,599	33,620	2,979	91.9	8.1	1.1	1.3	0.4
Prostitution and commercialized vice	4,969	2,542	2,427	51.2	48.8	0.1	0.1	0.3
Sex offenses (except forcible rape and prostitution)	19,913	18,925	988	95.0	5.0	0.6	0.7	0.1
Drug abuse violations	355,853	292,243	63,610	82.1	17.9	10.6	11.3	8.5
Gambling	1,019	856	163	84.0	16.0	[3]	[3]	[3]
Offenses against the family and children	49,790	40,399	9,391	81.1	18.9	1.5	1.6	1.2
Driving under the influence	417,607	346,216	71,391	82.9	17.1	12.5	13.3	9.5
Liquor laws	154,562	116,356	38,206	75.3	24.7	4.6	4.5	5.1
Drunkenness	142,079	121,366	20,713	85.4	14.6	4.2	4.7	2.8
Disorderly conduct	148,316	112,323	35,993	75.7	24.3	4.4	4.3	4.8
Vagrancy	4,895	4,130	765	84.4	15.6	0.1	0.2	0.1
All other offenses (except traffic)	924,011	726,393	197,618	78.6	21.4	27.6	28.0	26.3
Suspicion	1,390	1,025	365	73.7	26.3	[3]	[3]	[3]
Curfew and loitering law violations	21,753	14,761	6,992	67.9	32.1	0.6	0.6	0.9
Runaways	33,549	13,969	19,580	41.6	58.4	1.0	0.5	2.6

[1] Suburban area includes law enforcement agencies in cities with less than 50,000 inhabitants and county law enforcement agencies that are within a Metropolitan Statistical Area (see Appendix III). Suburban area excludes all metropolitan agencies associated with a central city. The agencies associated with suburban areas will also appear in other groups within this table.

[2] Because of rounding, the percentages may not add to total.

[3] Less than one-tenth of 1 percent.

[4] Violent crimes are offenses of murder, forcible rape, robbery, and aggravated assault.

[5] Property crimes are offenses of burglary, larceny-theft, motor vehicle theft, and arson.

[6] Includes arson.

Table 67

Arrests

Suburban Area[1] Arrests
by Race, 2001
[4,739 agencies; 2001 estimated population 79,778,727]

Offense charged	Total arrests					Percent distribution[2]				
	Total	White	Black	American Indian or Alaskan Native	Asian or Pacific Islander	Total	White	Black	American Indian or Alaskan Native	Asian or Pacific Islander
TOTAL	**3,339,352**	**2,581,395**	**712,417**	**21,902**	**23,638**	**100.0**	**77.3**	**21.3**	**0.7**	**0.7**
Murder and nonnegligent manslaughter	2,340	1,557	746	17	20	100.0	66.5	31.9	0.7	0.9
Forcible rape	6,184	4,543	1,539	38	64	100.0	73.5	24.9	0.6	1.0
Robbery	19,153	10,173	8,760	91	129	100.0	53.1	45.7	0.5	0.7
Aggravated assault	105,451	78,349	25,422	715	965	100.0	74.3	24.1	0.7	0.9
Burglary	68,502	52,881	14,740	355	526	100.0	77.2	21.5	0.5	0.8
Larceny-theft	268,557	189,081	74,838	1,674	2,964	100.0	70.4	27.9	0.6	1.1
Motor vehicle theft	26,977	19,619	6,906	169	283	100.0	72.7	25.6	0.6	1.0
Arson	4,657	3,952	645	24	36	100.0	84.9	13.9	0.5	0.8
Violent crime[3]	133,128	94,622	36,467	861	1,178	100.0	71.1	27.4	0.6	0.9
Property crime[4]	368,693	265,533	97,129	2,222	3,809	100.0	72.0	26.3	0.6	1.0
Crime Index total[5]	501,821	360,155	133,596	3,083	4,987	100.0	71.8	26.6	0.6	1.0
Other assaults	304,522	228,791	71,262	2,134	2,335	100.0	75.1	23.4	0.7	0.8
Forgery and counterfeiting	28,090	20,152	7,575	101	262	100.0	71.7	27.0	0.4	0.9
Fraud	94,786	65,580	28,445	271	490	100.0	69.2	30.0	0.3	0.5
Embezzlement	4,828	3,347	1,405	8	68	100.0	69.3	29.1	0.2	1.4
Stolen property; buying, receiving, possessing	30,862	20,871	9,547	163	281	100.0	67.6	30.9	0.5	0.9
Vandalism	65,456	54,398	10,218	358	482	100.0	83.1	15.6	0.5	0.7
Weapons; carrying, possessing, etc.	36,537	26,296	9,771	178	292	100.0	72.0	26.7	0.5	0.8
Prostitution and commercialized vice	4,958	3,627	1,146	17	168	100.0	73.2	23.1	0.3	3.4
Sex offenses (except forcible rape and prostitution)	19,878	16,394	3,177	127	180	100.0	82.5	16.0	0.6	0.9
Drug abuse violations	355,065	276,037	75,636	1,357	2,035	100.0	77.7	21.3	0.4	0.6
Gambling	1,013	661	325	3	24	100.0	65.3	32.1	0.3	2.4
Offenses against the family and children	49,468	33,067	15,903	251	247	100.0	66.8	32.1	0.5	0.5
Driving under the influence	416,168	375,135	35,752	2,437	2,844	100.0	90.1	8.6	0.6	0.7
Liquor laws	153,395	140,142	10,249	1,726	1,278	100.0	91.4	6.7	1.1	0.8
Drunkenness	141,743	126,995	12,642	1,409	697	100.0	89.6	8.9	1.0	0.5
Disorderly conduct	147,754	110,969	34,945	914	926	100.0	75.1	23.7	0.6	0.6
Vagrancy	4,890	3,447	1,365	27	51	100.0	70.5	27.9	0.6	1.0
All other offenses (except traffic)	921,590	669,005	240,165	6,963	5,457	100.0	72.6	26.1	0.8	0.6
Suspicion	1,377	845	513	2	17	100.0	61.4	37.3	0.1	1.2
Curfew and loitering law violations	21,671	18,221	3,129	110	211	100.0	84.1	14.4	0.5	1.0
Runaways	33,480	27,260	5,651	263	306	100.0	81.4	16.9	0.8	0.9

See footnotes at end of table.

Table 67

Arrests
Suburban Area[1] Arrests
by Race, 2001—Continued
[4,739 agencies; 2001 estimated population 79,778,727]

Offense charged	Arrests under 18					Percent distribution[2]				
	Total	White	Black	American Indian or Alaskan Native	Asian or Pacific Islander	Total	White	Black	American Indian or Alaskan Native	Asian or Pacific Islander
TOTAL	562,944	444,696	109,701	3,550	4,997	100.0	79.0	19.5	0.6	0.9
Murder and nonnegligent manslaughter	166	116	48	1	1	100.0	69.9	28.9	0.6	0.6
Forcible rape	1,097	780	312	1	4	100.0	71.1	28.4	0.1	0.4
Robbery	4,383	2,061	2,261	20	41	100.0	47.0	51.6	0.5	0.9
Aggravated assault	15,035	10,735	4,067	97	136	100.0	71.4	27.1	0.6	0.9
Burglary	22,225	17,600	4,305	127	193	100.0	79.2	19.4	0.6	0.9
Larceny-theft	80,037	57,802	20,598	533	1,104	100.0	72.2	25.7	0.7	1.4
Motor vehicle theft	8,259	6,116	1,973	73	97	100.0	74.1	23.9	0.9	1.2
Arson	2,532	2,218	277	14	23	100.0	87.6	10.9	0.6	0.9
Violent crime[3]	20,681	13,692	6,688	119	182	100.0	66.2	32.3	0.6	0.9
Property crime[4]	113,053	83,736	27,153	747	1,417	100.0	74.1	24.0	0.7	1.3
Crime Index total[5]	133,734	97,428	33,841	866	1,599	100.0	72.9	25.3	0.6	1.2
Other assaults	60,745	44,082	15,880	384	399	100.0	72.6	26.1	0.6	0.7
Forgery and counterfeiting	1,462	1,172	266	8	16	100.0	80.2	18.2	0.5	1.1
Fraud	2,127	1,534	563	9	21	100.0	72.1	26.5	0.4	1.0
Embezzlement	454	326	120	0	8	100.0	71.8	26.4	–	1.8
Stolen property; buying, receiving, possessing	6,552	4,398	2,010	41	103	100.0	67.1	30.7	0.6	1.6
Vandalism	28,060	24,192	3,506	143	219	100.0	86.2	12.5	0.5	0.8
Weapons; carrying, possessing, etc.	8,832	6,734	1,946	42	110	100.0	76.2	22.0	0.5	1.2
Prostitution and commercialized vice	97	65	29	3	0	100.0	67.0	29.9	3.1	–
Sex offenses (except forcible rape and prostitution)	4,424	3,441	935	24	24	100.0	77.8	21.1	0.5	0.5
Drug abuse violations	50,761	43,429	6,724	208	400	100.0	85.6	13.2	0.4	0.8
Gambling	93	44	49	0	0	100.0	47.3	52.7	–	–
Offenses against the family and children	2,475	1,996	452	12	15	100.0	80.6	18.3	0.5	0.6
Driving under the influence	5,617	5,337	211	38	31	100.0	95.0	3.8	0.7	0.6
Liquor laws	40,155	37,844	1,586	465	260	100.0	94.2	3.9	1.2	0.6
Drunkenness	5,931	5,530	331	46	24	100.0	93.2	5.6	0.8	0.4
Disorderly conduct	47,535	34,077	12,934	207	317	100.0	71.7	27.2	0.4	0.7
Vagrancy	629	502	120	4	3	100.0	79.8	19.1	0.6	0.5
All other offenses (except traffic)	107,631	86,786	19,238	676	931	100.0	80.6	17.9	0.6	0.9
Suspicion	479	298	180	1	0	100.0	62.2	37.6	0.2	–
Curfew and loitering law violations	21,671	18,221	3,129	110	211	100.0	84.1	14.4	0.5	1.0
Runaways	33,480	27,260	5,651	263	306	100.0	81.4	16.9	0.8	0.9

See footnotes at end of table.

Table 67

Arrests
Suburban Area[1] Arrests
by Race, 2001—Continued
[4,739 agencies; 2001 estimated population 79,778,727]

	Arrests 18 and over					Percent distribution[2]				
Offense charged	Total	White	Black	American Indian or Alaskan Native	Asian or Pacific Islander	Total	White	Black	American Indian or Alaskan Native	Asian or Pacific Islander
TOTAL	**2,776,408**	**2,136,699**	**602,716**	**18,352**	**18,641**	**100.0**	**77.0**	**21.7**	**0.7**	**0.7**
Murder and nonnegligent manslaughter	2,174	1,441	698	16	19	100.0	66.3	32.1	0.7	0.9
Forcible rape	5,087	3,763	1,227	37	60	100.0	74.0	24.1	0.7	1.2
Robbery	14,770	8,112	6,499	71	88	100.0	54.9	44.0	0.5	0.6
Aggravated assault	90,416	67,614	21,355	618	829	100.0	74.8	23.6	0.7	0.9
Burglary	46,277	35,281	10,435	228	333	100.0	76.2	22.5	0.5	0.7
Larceny-theft	188,520	131,279	54,240	1,141	1,860	100.0	69.6	28.8	0.6	1.0
Motor vehicle theft	18,718	13,503	4,933	96	186	100.0	72.1	26.4	0.5	1.0
Arson	2,125	1,734	368	10	13	100.0	81.6	17.3	0.5	0.6
Violent crime[3]	112,447	80,930	29,779	742	996	100.0	72.0	26.5	0.7	0.9
Property crime[4]	255,640	181,797	69,976	1,475	2,392	100.0	71.1	27.4	0.6	0.9
Crime Index total[5]	368,087	262,727	99,755	2,217	3,388	100.0	71.4	27.1	0.6	0.9
Other assaults	243,777	184,709	55,382	1,750	1,936	100.0	75.8	22.7	0.7	0.8
Forgery and counterfeiting	26,628	18,980	7,309	93	246	100.0	71.3	27.4	0.3	0.9
Fraud	92,659	64,046	27,882	262	469	100.0	69.1	30.1	0.3	0.5
Embezzlement	4,374	3,021	1,285	8	60	100.0	69.1	29.4	0.2	1.4
Stolen property; buying, receiving, possessing	24,310	16,473	7,537	122	178	100.0	67.8	31.0	0.5	0.7
Vandalism	37,396	30,206	6,712	215	263	100.0	80.8	17.9	0.6	0.7
Weapons; carrying, possessing, etc.	27,705	19,562	7,825	136	182	100.0	70.6	28.2	0.5	0.7
Prostitution and commercialized vice	4,861	3,562	1,117	14	168	100.0	73.3	23.0	0.3	3.5
Sex offenses (except forcible rape and prostitution)	15,454	12,953	2,242	103	156	100.0	83.8	14.5	0.7	1.0
Drug abuse violations	304,304	232,608	68,912	1,149	1,635	100.0	76.4	22.6	0.4	0.5
Gambling	920	617	276	3	24	100.0	67.1	30.0	0.3	2.6
Offenses against the family and children	46,993	31,071	15,451	239	232	100.0	66.1	32.9	0.5	0.5
Driving under the influence	410,551	369,798	35,541	2,399	2,813	100.0	90.1	8.7	0.6	0.7
Liquor laws	113,240	102,298	8,663	1,261	1,018	100.0	90.3	7.7	1.1	0.9
Drunkenness	135,812	121,465	12,311	1,363	673	100.0	89.4	9.1	1.0	0.5
Disorderly conduct	100,219	76,892	22,011	707	609	100.0	76.7	22.0	0.7	0.6
Vagrancy	4,261	2,945	1,245	23	48	100.0	69.1	29.2	0.5	1.1
All other offenses (except traffic)	813,959	582,219	220,927	6,287	4,526	100.0	71.5	27.1	0.8	0.6
Suspicion	898	547	333	1	17	100.0	60.9	37.1	0.1	1.9
Curfew and loitering law violations	–	–	–	–	–	–	–	–	–	–
Runaways	–	–	–	–	–	–	–	–	–	–

[1] Suburban area includes law enforcement agencies in cities with less than 50,000 inhabitants and county law enforcement agencies that are within a Metropolitan Statistical Area (see Appendix III). Suburban area excludes all metropolitan agencies associated with a central city. The agencies associated with suburban areas will also appear in other groups within this table.

[2] Because of rounding, the percentages may not add to total.

[3] Violent crimes are offenses of murder, forcible rape, robbery, and aggravated assault.

[4] Property crimes are offenses of burglary, larceny-theft, motor vehicle theft, and arson.

[5] Includes arson.

Table 68

Police Disposition
of Juvenile Offenders Taken into Custody, 2001
[2001 estimated population]

Population group	Total[1]	Handled within department and released	Referred to juvenile court jurisdiction	Referred to welfare agency	Referred to other police agency	Referred to criminal or adult court
TOTAL AGENCIES: 5,813 agencies; population 122,154,066						
Number	781,813	148,238	566,187	5,703	10,568	51,117
Percent[2]	100.0	19.0	72.4	0.7	1.4	6.5
TOTAL CITIES: 4,277 cities; population 86,590,978						
Number	647,492	127,271	467,652	4,539	9,218	38,812
Percent[2]	100.0	19.7	72.2	0.7	1.4	6.0
GROUP I						
36 cities, 250,000 and over; population 20,512,259						
Number	139,394	33,419	98,890	300	2,960	3,825
Percent[2]	100.0	24.0	70.9	0.2	2.1	2.7
GROUP II						
91 cities, 100,000 to 249,999; population 13,416,737						
Number	90,048	14,617	69,992	1,195	1,114	3,130
Percent[2]	100.0	16.2	77.7	1.3	1.2	3.5
GROUP III						
228 cities, 50,000 to 99,999; population 15,529,044						
Number	115,891	25,762	82,359	465	2,040	5,265
Percent[2]	100.0	22.2	71.1	0.4	1.8	4.5
GROUP IV						
390 cities, 25,000 to 49,999; population 13,674,258						
Number	97,443	17,230	71,819	1,210	1,448	5,736
Percent[2]	100.0	17.7	73.7	1.2	1.5	5.9
GROUP V						
848 cities, 10,000 to 24,999; population 13,584,903						
Number	107,935	18,260	77,809	770	815	10,281
Percent[2]	100.0	16.9	72.1	0.7	0.8	9.5
GROUP VI						
2,684 cities, under 10,000; population 9,873,777						
Number	96,781	17,983	66,783	599	841	10,575
Percent[2]	100.0	18.6	69.0	0.6	0.9	10.9
SUBURBAN COUNTIES						
604 agencies; population 23,751,585						
Number	95,266	15,566	70,747	716	944	7,293
Percent[2]	100.0	16.3	74.3	0.8	1.0	7.7
RURAL COUNTIES						
932 agencies; population 11,811,503						
Number	39,055	5,401	27,788	448	406	5,012
Percent[2]	100.0	13.8	71.2	1.1	1.0	12.8
SUBURBAN AREA[3]						
3,176 agencies; population 59,110,616						
Number	330,939	64,357	234,090	2,065	2,937	27,490
Percent[2]	100.0	19.4	70.7	0.6	0.9	8.3

[1] Includes all offenses except traffic and neglect cases.

[2] Because of rounding, the percentages may not add to total.

[3] Suburban area includes law enforcement agencies in cities with less than 50,000 inhabitants and county law enforcement agencies that are within a Metropolitan Statistical Area (see Appendix III). Suburban area excludes all metropolitan agencies associated with a central city. The agencies associated with suburban areas will also appear in other groups within this table.

Table 69

Arrests

by State, 2001
[2001 estimated population]

State	Total all classes[1]	Crime Index total[2]	Violent crime[3]	Property crime[4]	Murder and non-negligent man-slaughter	Forcible rape	Robbery	Aggra-vated assault	Burglary	Larceny-theft	Motor vehicle theft	Arson	Other assaults	Forgery and counter-feiting	Fraud
ALABAMA: 261 agencies; population 3,362,694															
Under 18	11,324	3,930	493	3,437	25	29	209	230	512	2,734	177	14	1,576	45	54
Total all ages	171,771	23,120	5,673	17,447	306	323	1,430	3,614	2,717	13,580	1,061	89	23,918	1,967	11,366
ALASKA: 28 agencies; population 572,517															
Under 18	4,726	1,950	219	1,731	1	14	44	160	287	1,243	192	9	536	14	14
Total all ages	32,171	5,163	1,267	3,896	26	82	156	1,003	503	3,009	366	18	4,201	94	144
ARIZONA: 93 agencies; population 5,016,343															
Under 18	51,894	13,430	1,593	11,837	19	32	270	1,272	1,743	8,464	1,192	438	4,451	125	137
Total all ages	284,696	47,377	8,797	38,580	244	250	1,537	6,766	4,614	28,267	4,351	1,348	23,381	2,694	2,047
ARKANSAS: 137 agencies; population 1,909,612															
Under 18	11,684	3,078	254	2,824	0	12	65	177	417	2,244	125	38	614	47	44
Total all ages	159,036	15,200	3,024	12,176	29	123	413	2,459	1,752	9,736	558	130	5,752	1,529	17,055
CALIFORNIA: 676 agencies; population 34,422,445															
Under 18	239,109	71,433	17,052	54,381	196	343	4,729	11,784	15,202	31,039	6,878	1,262	22,598	721	769
Total all ages	1,415,129	302,653	133,207	169,446	1,756	2,722	17,142	111,587	48,797	93,192	25,462	1,995	84,300	13,255	9,832
COLORADO: 137 agencies; population 3,448,951															
Under 18	46,389	10,336	979	9,357	15	73	223	668	1,067	6,999	1,105	186	3,366	124	148
Total all ages	229,927	32,436	5,604	26,832	133	410	841	4,220	2,775	21,371	2,390	296	21,636	1,300	1,918
CONNECTICUT: 90 agencies; population 3,093,664															
Under 18	22,489	5,830	1,108	4,722	9	60	277	762	753	3,438	445	86	3,205	47	73
Total all ages	143,400	24,416	6,407	18,009	119	291	1,407	4,590	2,707	13,938	1,208	156	18,307	897	1,751
DELAWARE: 40 agencies; population 717,822															
Under 18	6,647	2,083	313	1,770	1	27	80	205	391	1,241	98	40	1,451	20	101
Total all ages	28,082	6,390	1,415	4,975	7	144	277	987	1,052	3,666	196	61	5,990	304	1,602
DISTRICT OF COLUMBIA[6]															
FLORIDA[7]: 582 agencies; population 16,377,083															
Under 18	127,179	50,331	10,383	39,948	59	337	2,286	7,701	9,629	25,736	4,287	296	17,817	259	722
Total all ages	922,333	188,088	57,682	130,406	707	2,353	9,665	44,957	26,147	90,609	13,061	589	92,214	5,494	13,266
GEORGIA: 227 agencies; population 3,985,922															
Under 18	26,896	7,975	1,335	6,640	29	50	415	841	1,117	4,944	510	69	3,454	94	112
Total all ages	209,334	36,520	10,432	26,088	240	387	2,065	7,740	4,302	19,746	1,816	224	19,359	3,185	5,291
HAWAII: 3 agencies; population 1,074,143															
Under 18	10,196	2,237	249	1,988	3	24	124	98	202	1,565	213	8	898	16	22
Total all ages	50,305	7,576	1,186	6,390	28	125	412	621	705	4,518	1,145	22	3,663	544	498
IDAHO: 107 agencies; population 1,219,934															
Under 18	16,598	3,979	244	3,735	1	18	15	210	550	2,939	180	66	1,321	58	41
Total all ages	69,747	8,692	1,239	7,453	18	107	79	1,035	1,137	5,837	392	87	6,560	482	693
ILLINOIS[6]: 1 agency; population 2,910,709															
Under 18	41,110	11,903	3,140	8,763	57	155	1,121	1,807	1,129	3,843	3,709	82	7,073	1	212
Total all ages	224,709	49,022	10,604	38,418	558	703	3,168	6,175	3,570	23,939	10,687	222	32,866	72	3,010

See footnotes at end of table.

Embezzlement	Stolen property; buying, receiving, possessing	Vandalism	Weapons carrying, possessing, etc.	Prostitution and commercialized vice	Sex offenses (except forcible rape and prostitution)	Drug abuse violations	Gambling	Offenses against the family and children	Driving under the influence	Liquor laws	Drunkenness[5]	Disorderly conduct	Vagrancy	All other offenses (except traffic)	Suspicion	Curfew and loitering law violations	Runaways
0	194	266	131	0	21	1,027	2	49	159	761	103	1,015	17	1,501	0	91	382
32	1,881	2,143	1,340	90	349	12,932	110	1,464	13,161	6,044	8,139	3,692	162	59,388	0	91	382
0	6	298	79	6	38	397	0	32	92	225	3	78	0	955	0	1	2
0	15	895	386	61	209	1,542	0	489	4,470	876	76	913	3	12,631	0	1	2
37	240	2,738	456	33	346	5,442	2	313	496	5,068	0	3,375	23	6,259	0	3,727	5,196
206	1,694	9,013	2,889	1,878	1,751	29,316	21	2,651	33,255	24,165	0	16,659	762	76,014	0	3,727	5,196
0	156	267	163	3	61	848	6	74	202	352	281	1,003	58	2,566	26	1,124	711
53	1,180	924	1,602	368	472	10,201	82	1,799	14,672	1,918	12,901	4,542	1,079	65,599	273	1,124	711
200	3,335	13,002	6,663	385	2,869	23,907	77	16	1,651	5,339	4,353	11,381	371	43,283	0	19,719	7,037
2,017	16,171	26,647	23,336	12,032	15,629	248,443	508	634	177,438	27,732	106,103	17,242	4,177	300,224	0	19,719	7,037
11	242	2,026	619	14	306	3,218	3	133	537	4,445	9	3,561	5	9,347	9	3,267	4,663
114	778	6,550	2,277	1,328	1,329	16,598	17	2,636	23,579	18,559	454	16,421	687	73,371	9	3,267	4,663
13	91	1,207	317	5	169	2,384	1	87	133	442	0	4,162	22	3,975	0	115	211
170	464	3,239	1,393	565	705	17,544	49	1,614	10,147	1,776	25	20,514	324	39,173	1	115	211
27	64	507	221	0	10	372	0	0	0	335	7	746	0	688	0	15	0
277	220	1,208	923	138	54	1,827	0	188	203	1,576	217	1,658	93	5,199	0	15	0
85	622	2,974	1,934	94	498	14,656	68		548	2,507				34,064			
976	5,192	7,830	6,717	8,698	4,158	131,891	724		60,338	41,486				355,261			
8	437	643	554	44	403	2,185	44	106	260	744	65	2,581	23	5,381	184	459	1,140
261	3,283	2,208	3,435	2,378	2,836	25,750	632	2,405	21,708	8,397	3,743	15,687	286	49,766	605	459	1,140
2	21	273	33	8	114	549	6	117	60	162	0	42	0	1,671	0	265	3,700
39	149	673	286	480	432	2,455	220	1,528	2,926	655	0	423	0	23,793	0	265	3,700
15	85	758	183	0	119	861	0	46	249	1,671	21	633	0	3,531	0	820	2,207
129	308	1,490	568	2	359	4,831	0	472	8,728	5,112	206	2,011	7	26,070	0	820	2,207
0	0	2,087	1,504	68	209	9,533	526	24	63	337	0	2,968	0	4,602	0	0	0
0	0	5,815	5,533	6,097	2,134	57,473	2,086	551	6,820	987	0	17,032	0	35,211	0	0	0

Table 69

Arrests
by State, 2001—Continued
[2001 estimated population]

State	Total all classes[1]	Crime Index total[2]	Violent crime[3]	Property crime[4]	Murder and non-negligent man-slaughter	Forcible rape	Robbery	Aggra-vated assault	Burglary	Larceny-theft	Motor vehicle theft	Arson	Other assaults	Forgery and counter-feiting	Fraud
INDIANA: 147 agencies; population 4,202,710															
Under 18	34,493	9,064	1,817	7,247	13	25	243	1,536	843	5,679	634	91	2,286	47	57
Total all ages	196,928	33,544	10,902	22,642	236	215	1,495	8,956	3,076	17,434	1,947	185	11,221	1,215	2,318
IOWA: 154 agencies; population 2,037,297															
Under 18	13,122	4,408	443	3,965	3	20	42	378	592	3,111	201	61	1,511	71	22
Total all ages	68,487	12,252	2,823	9,429	25	93	247	2,458	1,466	7,404	477	82	7,430	783	1,356
KANSAS[6]															
KENTUCKY[6]: 13 agencies; population 886,140															
Under 18	5,493	1,890	239	1,651	2	5	45	187	324	1,082	213	32	299	30	26
Total all ages	52,420	9,442	2,805	6,637	40	69	459	2,237	1,219	4,761	599	58	3,336	883	1,843
LOUISIANA: 148 agencies; population 3,202,673															
Under 18	37,382	10,392	1,632	8,760	21	86	269	1,256	1,754	6,554	364	88	4,842	51	24
Total all ages	220,687	42,117	10,772	31,345	276	426	1,410	8,660	5,450	24,204	1,491	200	27,143	1,414	2,284
MAINE: 177 agencies: population 1,249,260															
Under 18	9,892	2,992	154	2,838	0	18	31	105	506	2,100	191	41	1,197	13	28
Total all ages	56,636	8,226	841	7,385	3	118	192	528	1,326	5,572	413	74	7,372	298	1,150
MARYLAND: 137 agencies; population 3,827,966															
Under 18	37,352	10,756	2,345	8,411	51	76	792	1,426	1,709	4,947	1,586	169	5,426	35	39
Total all ages	258,797	38,008	9,273	28,735	315	404	2,364	6,190	5,825	19,343	3,145	422	29,864	697	4,314
MASSACHUSETTS: 270 agencies; population 5,140,671															
Under 18	19,765	6,113	2,273	3,840	4	67	405	1,797	803	2,562	414	61	2,178	29	33
Total all ages	132,869	29,252	12,891	16,361	73	487	1,526	10,805	3,012	12,040	1,187	122	16,205	697	722
MICHIGAN[8]: 567 agencies; population 8,315,523															
Under 18	44,809	12,913	1,473	11,440	13	156	209	1,095	1,520	8,888	861	171	3,295	66	414
Total all ages	304,577	38,945	9,744	29,201	109	696	1,010	7,929	3,760	23,141	1,978	322	23,279	654	5,670
MINNESOTA: 284 agencies; population 3,633,051															
Under 18	35,109	8,776	677	8,099	8	96	76	497	888	6,579	549	83	2,648	133	207
Total all ages	134,531	20,632	2,757	17,875	71	444	277	1,965	2,068	14,554	1,124	129	11,105	1,498	3,902
MISSISSIPPI: 81 agencies; population 1,181,781															
Under 18	10,946	2,730	161	2,569	3	24	58	76	543	1,855	104	67	1,251	26	26
Total all ages	94,467	12,048	1,905	10,143	101	155	428	1,221	1,821	7,487	462	373	10,216	925	2,207
MISSOURI: 219 agencies; population 4,590,976															
Under 18	38,445	11,021	1,537	9,484	23	75	465	974	1,362	6,794	1,191	137	4,956	99	102
Total all ages	286,856	50,822	12,947	37,875	345	533	2,349	9,720	5,442	28,719	3,393	321	31,809	2,450	4,355
MONTANA[6]: 52 agencies; population 516,210															
Under 18	5,338	1,545	114	1,431	1	4	8	101	129	1,194	95	13	384	14	15
Total all ages	19,058	3,804	707	3,097	7	21	41	638	270	2,615	190	22	1,818	96	190
NEBRASKA: 210 agencies; population 1,341,179															
Under 18	14,373	3,963	187	3,776	0	11	70	106	274	3,218	204	80	1,645	46	93
Total all ages	84,706	11,301	1,265	10,036	45	145	268	807	874	8,578	464	120	8,649	761	1,926

See footnotes at end of table.

Embezzlement	Stolen property; buying, receiving, possessing	Vandalism	Weapons carrying, possessing, etc.	Prostitution and commercialized vice	Sex offenses (except forcible rape and prostitution)	Drug abuse violations	Gambling	Offenses against the family and children	Driving under the influence	Liquor laws	Drunkenness[5]	Disorderly conduct	Vagrancy	All other offenses (except traffic)	Suspicion	Curfew and loitering law violations	Runaways
6	1,409	1,362	199	2	182	2,179	3	231	226	3,006	455	2,598	34	5,987	78	896	4,186
17	5,034	2,578	1,681	833	1,232	17,885	207	1,321	23,907	12,562	16,666	8,062	242	51,079	242	896	4,186
17	30	911	87	4	93	862	0	3	189	1,500	180	799	0	1,698	0	422	315
123	118	1,893	426	253	279	6,533	5	433	7,927	6,005	5,665	2,731	43	13,495	0	422	315
0	212	149	64	3	17	690	11	2	51	157	114	339	0	1,067	0	123	249
62	868	565	665	374	219	8,485	62	698	5,420	1,091	4,847	1,794	5	11,389	0	123	249
0	468	1,268	368	5	211	2,439	32	294	185	475	86	4,885	78	7,627	59	1,670	1,923
33	2,347	4,053	1,775	428	1,178	22,131	172	1,907	13,592	3,591	4,027	15,575	427	72,761	139	1,670	1,923
3	104	630	74	1	56	840	0	10	135	889	6	237	0	2,168	0	193	316
20	334	1,791	377	70	319	4,948	2	439	6,757	3,448	31	1,885	0	18,660	0	193	316
23	32	1,768	964	34	373	6,799	46	26	301	1,342	0	1,540	26	6,511	158	356	797
205	214	3,256	3,109	1,101	1,271	46,856	184	2,052	20,796	5,062	0	4,251	135	96,033	236	356	797
1	397	891	224	32	66	2,359	1	119	163	1,360	279	1,374	13	3,582	24	6	521
31	1,535	2,604	1,140	1,619	559	16,528	15	1,931	11,319	4,694	7,550	7,709	53	27,977	202	6	521
129	578	1,639	577	12	355	3,691	7	12	603	6,340	46	1,251	16	8,973	0	1,548	2,344
1,340	2,063	3,541	3,021	859	1,209	27,552	166	3,156	46,546	28,021	716	8,719	334	104,894	0	1,548	2,344
0	355	1,565	352	0	200	2,569	5	8	627	5,681	0	2,177	4	5,479	0	2,546	1,777
1	1,122	3,054	808	61	732	10,518	33	419	22,646	22,565	0	7,438	40	23,634	0	2,546	1,777
9	95	222	132	1	33	861	21	35	129	336	166	1,525	19	2,613	19	421	276
526	496	1,001	706	56	257	9,361	299	2,452	9,807	3,381	5,110	7,169	66	27,585	102	421	276
19	350	2,094	621	11	360	3,357	2	274	363	1,453	38	1,881	181	6,421	27	2,025	2,790
109	2,350	8,201	4,101	1,320	2,690	32,389	34	4,234	22,666	8,555	1,929	12,134	936	90,765	192	2,025	2,790
0	3	306	16	0	22	126	0	8	41	672	0	425	0	1,085	0	388	288
2	31	628	69	2	55	442	1	252	2,614	1,993	0	1,749	6	4,630	0	388	288
18	233	1,021	167	5	102	1,322	3	18	350	2,166	0	603	0	2,111	0	293	214
175	1,078	2,575	1,026	364	639	10,363	45	1,358	10,636	11,319	0	3,506	0	18,476	2	293	214

Table 69

Arrests
by State, 2001—Continued
[2001 estimated population]

State	Total all classes[1]	Crime Index total[2]	Violent crime[3]	Property crime[4]	Murder and non-negligent man-slaughter	Forcible rape	Robbery	Aggra-vated assault	Burglary	Larceny-theft	Motor vehicle theft	Arson	Other assaults	Forgery and counter-feiting	Fraud
NEVADA: 34 agencies; population 2,072,750															
Under 18	25,249	5,604	598	5,006	12	45	209	332	969	3,384	510	143	2,630	19	107
Total all ages	148,679	22,390	4,077	18,313	139	258	1,231	2,449	4,618	11,629	1,886	180	17,646	635	2,568
NEW HAMPSHIRE: 101 agencies; population 668,273															
Under 18	6,416	978	92	886	0	17	17	58	112	673	86	15	764	22	63
Total all ages	29,200	2,373	392	1,981	2	54	72	264	279	1,531	144	27	4,210	126	718
NEW JERSEY: 531 agencies; population 8,167,848															
Under 18	62,339	13,037	3,266	9,771	24	99	1,159	1,984	1,752	7,286	475	258	5,872	87	188
Total all ages	364,204	52,239	15,399	36,840	248	570	3,970	10,611	6,269	28,702	1,388	481	31,441	1,562	5,480
NEW MEXICO: 24 agencies; population 847,902															
Under 18	7,688	1,843	333	1,510	3	4	42	284	207	1,202	85	16	904	25	24
Total all ages	57,947	6,963	2,267	4,696	50	74	292	1,851	728	3,695	249	24	4,895	242	243
NEW YORK[6]: 408 agencies; population 6,028,497															
Under 18	43,460	11,130	1,931	9,199	14	51	675	1,191	1,917	6,550	538	194	4,182	280	395
Total all ages	248,316	42,943	10,006	32,937	172	408	2,328	7,098	5,236	25,483	1,885	333	28,040	3,641	9,692
NORTH CAROLINA: 382 agencies; population 7,477,980															
Under 18	50,266	16,028	2,540	13,488	75	77	771	1,617	3,064	9,644	599	181	7,502	116	619
Total all ages	499,642	86,504	24,834	61,670	957	746	4,703	18,428	15,312	43,519	2,337	502	58,896	5,055	37,832
NORTH DAKOTA: 61 agencies; population 545,323															
Under 18	7,478	1,417	35	1,382	0	8	2	25	148	1,085	106	43	385	26	32
Total all ages	25,438	2,851	175	2,676	3	27	14	131	288	2,132	205	51	1,380	146	1,548
OHIO: 279 agencies; population 6,065,292															
Under 18	53,807	10,862	1,496	9,366	10	154	409	923	1,801	6,554	821	190	6,194	89	69
Total all ages	268,148	41,797	10,515	31,282	167	647	2,217	7,484	5,358	23,819	1,738	367	24,346	2,041	3,167
OKLAHOMA: 291 agencies; population 3,257,436															
Under 18	22,632	6,945	964	5,981	27	43	184	710	1,019	4,237	584	141	1,293	48	95
Total all ages	154,382	21,038	5,808	15,230	158	367	643	4,640	2,958	10,391	1,659	222	9,579	1,003	2,994
OREGON: 148 agencies; population 3,200,800															
Under 18	32,044	8,329	648	7,681	12	46	196	394	1,098	5,823	555	205	2,245	139	78
Total all ages	140,987	30,504	3,702	26,802	111	292	1,087	2,212	3,268	20,855	2,377	302	15,189	2,778	1,395
PENNSYLVANIA: 655 agencies; population 9,704,690															
Under 18	95,281	19,402	4,434	14,968	32	264	1,330	2,808	2,577	9,758	2,255	378	7,893	137	303
Total all ages	403,367	75,190	23,260	51,930	507	1,317	6,406	15,030	9,267	35,995	5,869	799	41,847	3,271	10,060
RHODE ISLAND: 46 agencies; population 964,115															
Under 18	6,511	1,662	258	1,404	2	22	94	140	321	844	192	47	860	9	23
Total all ages	36,528	5,190	1,115	4,075	25	110	241	739	866	2,794	338	77	5,186	171	905
SOUTH CAROLINA[6]: 83 agencies; population 1,225,330															
Under 18	8,689	2,556	575	1,981	5	21	85	464	436	1,419	95	31	1,577	28	36
Total all ages	63,001	10,458	3,604	6,854	86	139	478	2,901	1,341	5,119	310	84	8,303	685	7,827

See footnotes at end of table.

Embezzlement	Stolen property; buying, receiving, possessing	Vandalism	Weapons carrying, possessing, etc.	Prostitution and commercialized vice	Sex offenses (except forcible rape and prostitution)	Drug abuse violations	Gambling	Offenses against the family and children	Driving under the influence	Liquor laws	Drunkenness[5]	Disorderly conduct	Vagrancy	All other offenses (except traffic)	Suspicion	Curfew and loitering law violations	Runaways
56	249	776	353	75	163	1,467	5	14	73	1,516	78	940	30	5,560	27	4,114	1,393
481	1,639	1,599	1,875	4,054	1,505	9,901	75	1,116	8,824	7,752	386	3,434	2,246	55,016	30	4,114	1,393
8	109	233	29	1	24	652	0	8	82	516	759	178	112	1,582	0	6	290
23	296	729	124	9	113	2,763	0	104	3,005	2,553	4,034	799	344	6,578	3	6	290
22	2,131	3,818	1,667	18	447	7,389	22	39	306	3,111	0	6,482	92	8,026	0	5,221	4,364
150	7,262	7,845	5,185	1,934	1,802	52,260	567	16,477	24,135	9,845	11	23,995	2,071	110,347	11	5,221	4,364
8	93	210	207	3	8	790	0	13	141	1,060	38	301	4	1,697	6	129	184
113	631	522	500	412	64	3,813	0	391	6,768	2,748	1,503	1,464	56	26,252	54	129	184
7	1,128	3,602	642	11	847	4,691	7	558	235	1,085	0	2,172	61	9,777	0	0	2,650
265	4,733	10,669	2,894	1,133	3,569	34,632	98	3,234	18,943	5,905	0	12,020	1,216	62,039	0	0	2,650
205	1,019	2,539	1,317	19	264	3,798	10	100	735	1,712	0	4,566	99	8,127	0	26	1,465
2,936	6,759	9,836	7,442	1,566	2,151	39,917	426	7,411	66,512	14,951	0	18,775	162	131,020	0	26	1,465
0	46	413	37	0	25	259	1	84	70	1,590	2	730	3	1,268	0	308	782
4	95	596	107	4	69	1,301	3	227	3,165	6,372	289	1,466	3	4,722	0	308	782
89	1,200	1,870	596	33	296	2,948	11	1,463	313	3,356	261	3,213	75	15,324	54	3,513	1,978
283	4,536	3,951	3,078	2,154	1,616	20,464	409	14,440	21,273	15,389	9,142	14,457	915	78,997	202	3,513	1,978
70	239	571	262	16	87	1,725	0	45	479	635	850	562	0	3,045	0	3,329	2,336
689	1,415	1,307	2,075	400	943	20,400	13	1,143	21,161	3,326	23,877	2,483	0	34,871	0	3,329	2,336
3	73	1,713	305	7	280	2,092	1	16	214	4,379	0	1,314	0	5,094	0	3,053	2,709
80	455	4,315	1,766	359	1,391	15,742	14	614	16,359	15,071	0	5,998	0	23,195	0	3,053	2,709
20	773	4,987	1,069	18	786	6,361	26	88	516	7,687	283	14,108	73	7,586	0	20,179	2,986
299	3,332	12,300	3,493	3,074	3,105	47,917	437	1,107	36,752	24,863	17,843	49,719	444	45,149	0	20,179	2,986
8	63	498	127	0	24	615	0	235	18	186	10	506	58	1,226	84	39	260
126	244	1,309	402	303	138	3,906	47	518	1,894	1,313	114	2,582	137	11,557	187	39	260
15	112	435	200	3	80	903	0	5	49	265	53	1,075	0	975	0	31	291
154	577	1,149	743	165	249	8,644	34	191	5,856	3,964	2,279	4,387	164	6,850	0	31	291

Table 69

Arrests

by State, 2001—Continued

[2001 estimated population]

State	Total all classes[1]	Crime Index total[2]	Violent crime[3]	Property crime[4]	Murder and non-negligent manslaughter	Forcible rape	Robbery	Aggravated assault	Burglary	Larceny-theft	Motor vehicle theft	Arson	Other assaults	Forgery and counterfeiting	Fraud
SOUTH DAKOTA[6]: 25 agencies; population 364,655															
Under 18	5,924	1,336	75	1,261	0	15	7	53	223	977	39	22	301	8	14
Total all ages	25,859	3,133	356	2,777	6	50	27	273	389	2,239	76	73	1,959	77	289
TENNESSEE: 372 agencies; population 4,613,519															
Under 18	26,061	5,984	956	5,028	4	53	179	720	650	3,935	394	49	2,694	84	164
Total all ages	211,434	32,647	9,698	22,949	191	237	1,183	8,087	3,047	17,956	1,690	256	21,700	2,206	9,966
TEXAS: 917 agencies; population 20,738,511															
Under 18	180,231	42,099	5,173	36,926	67	398	1,442	3,266	6,655	27,026	2,858	387	20,555	502	453
Total all ages	1,013,175	143,372	31,061	112,311	792	2,174	6,695	21,400	17,945	84,339	9,218	809	99,036	8,336	15,605
UTAH: 86 agencies; population 1,730,721															
Under 18	21,803	6,321	288	6,033	3	50	45	190	440	5,218	301	74	1,776	65	57
Total all ages	94,473	16,129	1,374	14,755	41	169	305	859	1,169	12,898	562	126	8,584	1,000	786
VERMONT: 51 agencies; population 512,158															
Under 18	1,773	510	40	470	0	8	2	30	85	340	38	7	227	8	16
Total all ages	12,043	1,701	280	1,421	2	43	3	232	233	1,068	96	24	1,276	126	452
VIRGINIA: 276 agencies; population 5,528,121															
Under 18	28,813	6,168	802	5,366	20	51	252	479	996	3,737	456	177	4,410	106	168
Total all ages	223,118	26,737	5,628	21,109	225	372	1,266	3,765	3,253	16,212	1,335	309	29,509	2,172	9,147
WASHINGTON: 210 agencies; population 4,719,080															
Under 18	42,301	14,062	1,512	12,550	15	139	377	981	1,881	9,439	937	293	6,184	161	65
Total all ages	222,585	41,744	7,454	34,290	117	700	1,447	5,190	5,091	26,550	2,188	461	32,032	3,033	1,376
WEST VIRGINIA: 205 agencies; population 886,761															
Under 18	1,242	463	34	429	0	1	4	29	73	316	35	5	160	7	9
Total all ages	18,632	2,883	996	1,887	16	26	57	897	371	1,307	175	34	3,579	225	1,032
WISCONSIN[6]: 3 agencies; population 913,808															
Under 18	25,653	4,326	817	3,509	134	51	332	300	409	2,939	123	38	1,613	20	30
Total all ages	99,269	13,528	3,283	10,245	293	282	970	1,738	944	8,942	266	93	7,670	347	391
WYOMING: 64 agencies; population 486,499															
Under 18	7,254	1,317	104	1,213	0	2	13	89	173	963	50	27	460	17	9
Total all ages	35,200	3,465	620	2,845	8	41	39	532	413	2,267	114	51	2,615	120	260

[1] Does not include traffic arrests.

[2] Includes arson.

[3] Violent crimes are offenses of murder, forcible rape, robbery, and aggravated assault.

[4] Property crimes are offenses of burglary, larceny-theft, motor vehicle theft, and arson.

[5] Drunkenness is not considered a crime in some states; therefore, the figures vary widely from state to state.

[6] See Arrest Data, Appendix I, for details.

[7] The arrest category, all other offenses, includes the arrest counts for the offenses of: offenses against the family and children, drunkenness, vagrancy, disorderly conduct, suspicion, and curfew and loitering law violations.

[8] Detroit arrest figures are not included in any arrest table; therefore, Michigan arrest totals are not comparable to previous years' data.

NOTE: Direct comparisons of arrest totals listed in this table made with prior years' issues should be made with caution as participation levels may vary. Additionally, some Part II offenses are not considered crimes in some states; therefore, figures may vary widely from state to state.

Embezzle- ment	Stolen property; buying, receiving, possessing	Vandalism	Weapons carrying, possessing, etc.	Prostitution and commer- cialized vice	Sex offenses (except forcible rape and prostitution)	Drug abuse viola- tions	Gambling	Offenses against the family and children	Driving under the influence	Liquor laws	Drunken- ness[5]	Disorderly conduct	Vagrancy	All other offenses (except traffic)	Suspicion	Curfew and loitering law violations	Run- aways
7	24	188	36	0	35	404	0	7	56	892	0	351	0	1,565	0	237	463
14	79	369	86	0	134	1,741	0	128	3,407	5,231	220	1,209	36	7,047	0	237	463
31	60	601	502	15	105	2,279	24	29	231	1,104	408	3,853	0	3,988	0	1,940	1,965
400	387	2,388	2,622	1,360	495	21,579	125	665	23,668	5,336	20,087	10,876	83	50,939	0	1,940	1,965
76	183	5,498	1,642	92	876	15,368	50	1,381	1,463	6,755	4,676	15,932	90	31,648	6	11,629	19,257
540	711	11,455	10,010	6,641	4,481	102,015	306	5,683	90,617	30,114	140,049	34,496	1,543	277,256	23	11,629	19,257
5	182	1,169	274	1	271	1,367	0	16	177	2,309	52	1,072	0	4,871	0	1,219	599
21	661	2,550	835	372	625	7,058	0	898	7,365	10,632	4,111	3,591	5	27,432	0	1,219	599
1	38	145	13	0	5	190	0	5	23	200	0	176	0	211	0	1	4
18	124	332	18	5	16	1,285	0	276	2,840	525	7	911	0	2,126	0	1	4
65	125	1,249	527	1	229	2,307	6	17	283	1,726	224	1,159	0	5,236	0	2,071	2,736
1,095	587	3,743	2,945	388	975	20,366	29	619	20,622	7,909	18,875	4,415	54	68,124	0	2,071	2,736
22	922	2,411	656	25	279	3,041	0	5	511	4,501	0	780	4	5,666	0	33	2,973
162	4,457	6,733	2,930	664	1,414	22,750	6	209	29,787	13,935	20	4,597	60	53,657	13	33	2,973
1	9	62	9	0	13	100	0	0	38	127	15	4	0	179	0	23	23
34	107	460	165	1	103	1,550	5	86	4,116	807	925	207	0	2,301	0	23	23
0	538	795	550	20	472	1,077	39	104	37	900	0	6,604	0	5,887	0	2,578	63
1	1,151	3,570	2,012	881	988	5,614	224	1,095	3,190	4,388	0	22,789	31	28,758	0	2,578	63
1	14	281	73	0	30	598	0	17	82	1,456	50	378	16	1,698	73	532	152
6	76	700	146	2	153	2,719	1	194	4,695	5,190	1,384	1,565	72	11,050	103	532	152

SECTION V

The Terrorist Attacks of September 11, 2001: A Compilation of Data

Like every other organization and individual in the United States, the FBI has struggled to comprehend the events of September 11, 2001. Apart from investigating the crime scenes in New York City (the World Trade Center); Somerset County, Pennsylvania; and Arlington County, Virginia (the Pentagon); following leads, and addressing a myriad of concerns resulting from these attacks, the FBI through its Uniform Crime Reporting (UCR) Program has struggled with how to report the data to the public. Begun in 1929, the UCR Program captures criminal offenses, which

include murder and nonnegligent manslaughter, forcible rape, aggravated assault, robbery, burglary, larceny-theft, and motor vehicle theft, reported to local or state law enforcement agencies. In its original design, the creators of the Program probably could not conceive of heinous attacks of domestic or international terrorism being committed within the confines of this Nation. Theirs was a national crime data collection system based on the cooperation of city, county, and state law enforcement agencies voluntarily reporting crimes that were a product of the society of the time. However, that society has evolved into a more complex, global society of the twenty-first century that is faced with fighting crimes that previously had been unimaginable. The FBI recognizes that the UCR Program must evolve to be able to capture the crimes of this modern era. As it currently exists, the UCR Program is limited in its ability to report the offenses committed at the World Trade Center, in the airways above Pennsylvania, and at the Pentagon. Recognizing the limitations of the Program, yet also recognizing that many agencies and researchers will have a specific, nontraditional application for the statistical data associated with these offenses, the FBI has compiled this special report.

There will be disagreement and debate among academicians, governmental officials, law enforcement, the media, and the general public regarding the perspective from which one should view the events of September 11. Some will argue that they were an act of war; others will say they are a local crime, an international conspiracy, terrorism in its classical meaning, or a myriad of other possibilities. This special report does not attempt to join the debate nor bring any resolution to the disagreement; it merely presents the data within the limited context of UCR.

Methodology

This report uses a simple statistical approach to categorize (analyze) the victims and the offenders (terrorists) of this incident. The statistics are organized based on attributes

Table 5.1

Murder Victims of 9/11/2001 Terrorist Attacks
by Race, Sex, and Location

| Race | Total | Sex | | |
		Male	Female	Unknown
All Locations				
Total	**3,047**	**2,303**	**739**	**5**
White	2,435	1,908	527	0
Black	286	170	116	0
Other	187	127	60	0
Unknown	139	98	36	5
World Trade Center				
Total	**2,823**	**2,175**	**648**	**0**
White	2,279	1,811	468	0
Black	234	148	86	0
Other	184	124	60	0
Unknown	126	92	34	0
Pentagon				
Total	**184**	**108**	**71**	**5**
White	120	79	41	0
Black	49	21	28	0
Other	2	2	0	0
Unknown	13	6	2	5
Somerset County, Pennsylvania				
Total	**40**	**20**	**20**	**0**
White	36	18	18	0
Black	3	1	2	0
Other	1	1	0	0
Unknown	0	0	0	0

such as age, gender, and race. It must be clearly understood that these attributes are used simply to describe those victims who were killed on September 11, 2001. Since the crimes were carried out indiscriminately to inflict the maximum pain on the greatest number of people, these attributes must not be seen as factors that have contributed to these incidents.

The statistics of September 11 are not a part of the traditional *Crime in the United States* publication because they are different from the day-to-day crimes committed in this country. Additionally, combining these statistics with our regular crime report would create many difficulties in defining and analyzing crime as we know it.

• Even though in many minds the deaths resulting from the September 11 attacks may not meet UCR's traditional definition of a criminal homicide, the UCR Program has classified those deaths for the purpose of presenting these data as murder and nonnegligent manslaughter.

• The murder count of September 11 is so high that combining it with the traditional crime statistics will have an outlier effect that skews all types of measurements in the Program's analysis. (An outlier is any extreme value, either large or small, that substantially deviates from the rest of the distribution.) However, because these tables reflect volume only, Table 8 contains the numbers of deaths in New York City, including those at the World Trade Center, and Table 10 contains the number of deaths in Somerset County, including those from the offense of September 11. These locations are appropriately footnoted.

• Data for the Pentagon will appear only in this report. To be published in Tables 8-11, Offenses Known to Law Enforcement, an agency must submit complete data for 12 months. For the Pentagon, the UCR Program has only one day of data—September 11, 2001.

• The Program does not collect occupation, and so it was unable to make a distinction and separately classify victim data for the deaths of the firefighters at the World Trade Center from the deaths of the civilians.

As explained in the introduction of this study, the limitations of the UCR Program were clearly realized in the wake of the September 11

tragedies. Like many agencies and programs, UCR is not equipped to fully capture the events of September 11 in its data collection and dissemination formats. For example, in addition to the deaths of over three thousand people, there are thousands more who were victimized that were not reported in other crime classifications such as aggravated assault. Because of the limitations of UCR summary reporting and the application of its guidelines, especially the Hierarchy Rule, agencies do not report and thus we are unable to collect and publish in this study any offense data except murder and nonnegligent manslaughter. The Hierarchy Rule requires reporting/counting only the highest offense in the Program's ordered crime listing (murder and nonnegligent manslaughter, forcible rape, aggravated assault, robbery, burglary, larceny-theft, and motor vehicle theft). However, the rule applies only to crime reporting and does not affect the number of charges for which the defendant(s) may be prosecuted in the courts. Finally, the age and gender breakdowns in the tables are consistent with standard UCR methodology.

Discussion of the Data

Victims

According to reports (current to the UCR's publication deadline), the number of victims from the World Trade Center, the Pentagon, and the Pennsylvania crash site totaled 3,047. The gender of 5 victims and the race of 139 victims were unknown. Males constituted 2,303 victims (75.6 percent) and females made up the remaining 739 (24.3 percent). (See Table 5.1.) Of the total victims, 2,435 (79.9 percent) were white, 286 (9.4 percent) were black, and 187 (6.1 percent) were of other races. (See Table 5.1.)

An analysis of all victims by gender and race showed that the highest percentage of all victims of the events of September 11 were white males (62.6 percent), followed by white females (17.3 percent), black males (5.6 percent), and black females (3.8 percent). In the race category other, 4.2 percent were males and 2.0 percent were females. Race was unknown for 4.6 percent of the victims.

Table 5.2

Murder Victims of 9/11/2001 Terrorist Attacks, Total All Locations
by Age, Sex, and Race

Age	Total	Sex			Race			
		Male	Female	Unknown	White	Black	Other[1]	Unknown
Total	**3,047**	**2,303**	**739**	**5**	**2,435**	**286**	**187**	**139**
Percent distribution[2]	100.0	75.6	24.3	0.2	79.9	9.4	6.1	4.6
Under 18[3]	9	5	4	0	3	3	0	3
Under 22[3]	31	22	9	0	19	4	3	5
18 and over[3]	3,004	2,274	730	0	2,424	281	186	113
Infant (under 1)	0	0	0	0	0	0	0	0
1 to 4	5	3	2	0	2	0	0	3
5 to 8	1	0	1	0	1	0	0	0
9 to 12	3	2	1	0	0	3	0	0
13 to 16	0	0	0	0	0	0	0	0
17 to 19	3	3	0	0	1	0	1	1
20 to 24	117	78	39	0	95	8	10	4
25 to 29	341	241	100	0	273	26	30	12
30 to 34	503	388	115	0	401	40	47	15
35 to 39	578	467	111	0	469	66	24	19
40 to 44	510	402	108	0	420	43	28	19
45 to 49	369	277	92	0	299	39	16	15
50 to 54	272	200	72	0	218	28	12	14
55 to 59	177	128	49	0	139	18	12	8
60 to 64	79	54	25	0	62	8	4	5
65 to 69	29	20	9	0	25	2	1	1
70 to 74	15	10	5	0	13	2	0	0
75 and over	11	6	5	0	9	1	1	0
Unknown	34	24	5	5	8	2	1	23

[1] Includes 184 Asian or Pacific Islander and 3 American Indian or Alaskan Native victims.
[2] Because of rounding, the percentages may not add to total.
[3] Does not include unknown ages.

Table 5.3

Murder Victims of 9/11/2001 Terrorist Attacks; New York City World Trade Center
by Age, Sex, and Race

Age	Total	Sex			Race			
		Male	Female	Unknown	White	Black	Other[1]	Unknown
Total	**2,823**	**2,175**	**648**	**0**	**2,279**	**234**	**184**	**126**
Percent distribution[2]	100.0	77.0	23.0	0.0	80.7	8.3	6.5	4.5
Under 18[3]	5	3	2	0	2	0	0	3
Under 22[3]	22	17	5	0	14	1	2	5
18 and over[3]	2,789	2,148	641	0	2,269	232	183	105
Infant (under 1)	0	0	0	0	0	0	0	0
1 to 4	5	3	2	0	2	0	0	3
5 to 8	0	0	0	0	0	0	0	0
9 to 12	0	0	0	0	0	0	0	0
13 to 16	0	0	0	0	0	0	0	0
17 to 19	3	3	0	0	1	0	1	1
20 to 24	108	72	36	0	89	7	9	3
25 to 29	329	233	96	0	264	24	29	12
30 to 34	485	373	112	0	388	35	47	15
35 to 39	539	444	95	0	443	54	24	18
40 to 44	480	383	97	0	399	35	28	18
45 to 49	342	267	75	0	281	33	15	13
50 to 54	239	181	58	0	194	20	12	13
55 to 59	153	114	39	0	120	13	12	8
60 to 64	67	48	19	0	53	7	4	3
65 to 69	23	17	6	0	20	1	1	1
70 to 74	11	7	4	0	9	2	0	0
75 and over	10	6	4	0	8	1	1	0
Unknown	29	24	5	0	8	2	1	18

[1] Includes 181 Asian or Pacific Islander and 3 American Indian or Alaskan Native victims.
[2] Because of rounding, the percentages may not add to total.
[3] Does not include unknown ages.

Table 5.4

Murder Victims of 9/11/2001 Terrorist Attacks; Pentagon
by Age, Sex, and Race

Age	Total	Sex			Race			
		Male	Female	Unknown	White	Black	Other[1]	Unknown
Total	**184**	**108**	**71**	**5**	**120**	**49**	**2**	**13**
Percent distribution[2]	100.0	58.7	38.6	2.7	65.2	26.6	1.1	7.1
Under 18[3]	4	2	2	0	1	3	0	0
Under 22[3]	6	4	2	0	3	3	0	0
18 and over[3]	175	106	69	0	119	46	2	8
Infant (under 1)	0	0	0	0	0	0	0	0
1 to 4	0	0	0	0	0	0	0	0
5 to 8	1	0	1	0	1	0	0	0
9 to 12	3	2	1	0	0	3	0	0
13 to 16	0	0	0	0	0	0	0	0
17 to 19	0	0	0	0	0	0	0	0
20 to 24	6	5	1	0	4	1	0	1
25 to 29	11	8	3	0	8	2	1	0
30 to 34	13	12	1	0	9	4	0	0
35 to 39	32	19	13	0	20	11	0	1
40 to 44	27	16	11	0	18	8	0	1
45 to 49	23	9	14	0	15	5	1	2
50 to 54	28	16	12	0	19	8	0	1
55 to 59	21	14	7	0	16	5	0	0
60 to 64	10	4	6	0	7	1	0	2
65 to 69	3	2	1	0	2	1	0	0
70 to 74	1	1	0	0	1	0	0	0
75 and over	0	0	0	0	0	0	0	0
Unknown	5	0	0	5	0	0	0	5

[1] Includes 2 Asian or Pacific Islander victims.
[2] Because of rounding, the percentages may not add to total.
[3] Does not include unknown ages.

Table 5.5

Murder Victims of 9/11/2001 Terrorist Attacks; Somerset County, Pennsylvania
by Age, Sex, and Race

Age	Total	Sex			Race			
		Male	Female	Unknown	White	Black	Other[1]	Unknown
Total	**40**	**20**	**20**	**0**	**36**	**3**	**1**	**0**
Percent distribution[2]	100.0	50.0	50.0	0.0	90.0	7.5	2.5	0.0
Under 18[3]	0	0	0	0	0	0	0	0
Under 22[3]	3	1	2	0	2	0	1	0
18 and over[3]	40	20	20	0	36	3	1	0
Infant (under 1)	0	0	0	0	0	0	0	0
1 to 4	0	0	0	0	0	0	0	0
5 to 8	0	0	0	0	0	0	0	0
9 to 12	0	0	0	0	0	0	0	0
13 to 16	0	0	0	0	0	0	0	0
17 to 19	0	0	0	0	0	0	0	0
20 to 24	3	1	2	0	2	0	1	0
25 to 29	1	0	1	0	1	0	0	0
30 to 34	5	3	2	0	4	1	0	0
35 to 39	7	4	3	0	6	1	0	0
40 to 44	3	3	0	0	3	0	0	0
45 to 49	4	1	3	0	3	1	0	0
50 to 54	5	3	2	0	5	0	0	0
55 to 59	3	0	3	0	3	0	0	0
60 to 64	2	2	0	0	2	0	0	0
65 to 69	3	1	2	0	3	0	0	0
70 to 74	3	2	1	0	3	0	0	0
75 and over	1	0	1	0	1	0	0	0
Unknown	0	0	0	0	0	0	0	0

[1] Includes 1 Asian or Pacific Islander victim.
[2] Because of rounding, the percentages may not add to total.
[3] Does not include unknown ages.

Further, a breakdown by race and gender shows that white males made up the majority of the victims at each of the three locations. The majority of black victims at the World Trade Center were male, but the majority of black victims at the Pentagon and the Pennsylvania crash sites were female. (See Table 5.1.)

Victims: Age, Gender, and Race

Nine victims of the events of September 11 were under the age of 18. Of this total, 5 were under 5 years old. All 5 of these juveniles were victims at the World Trade Center: 3 were male and 2 were female; 2 were white and 3 were of unknown race. The remaining 4 juvenile victims were at the Pentagon: a white female aged 5 to 8; 2 black males and 1 black female aged 9 to 12. (See Tables 5.2–5.4.)

The vast majority, 98.6 percent (3,004), of all the victims where age was known were over age 18. The modal age category for all victims was 35 to 39. However, when broken down by gender, the female victims were slightly younger. The modal age category for females was 30 to 34. The modal age category by race was again 35 to 39, excluding the other race category, which had a slightly younger modal age category of 30 to 34. (See Table 5.2.)

The same general statistics for age remain true for the victims at the World Trade Center, mainly because they constitute the majority of the victims—92.6 percent (2,823). (See Table 5.3.) For the Pentagon, the modal age category is again 35 to 39. However, the most frequent age category for females was 45 to 49, reflecting a slightly older set of victims at the Pentagon. (See Table 5.4.) The most frequent age category of the Pennsylvania crash site was 35 to 39. (See Table 5.5.)

Offenders: Age, Gender, and Race

Nineteen offenders were directly involved in the events of September 11—10 at the World Trade Center, 5 at the Pentagon, and 4 in Pennsylvania. All the offenders were white males. Four of the 19 were under the age of 22. Twelve of the offenders were aged 20 to 24, and the remaining 7 were aged 25 to 34. The oldest offender (aged 30 to 34) was involved with the events at the World Trade Center. (See Table 5.6.)

Law Enforcement Officers Killed in the Line of Duty

The UCR Program through its Law Enforcement Officers Killed and Assaulted Program separately collects information on law enforcement officers killed and assaulted in the line of duty. The 71 law enforcement officers killed in the line of duty as a result of the attacks on the World Trade Center include 37 officers with the Port Authority of New York and New Jersey Police Department, 23 with the New York Police Department, 5 with the New York Office of Tax Enforcement, 3 with the State of New York Unified Court System, 1 fire marshal with the New York City Fire Department, 1 agent with the U. S. Secret Service, and 1 agent with the FBI. One refuge law enforcement officer with the U. S. Fish and Wildlife Service was killed in the crash in Somerset County, Pennsylvania. These data are included in the tables of this study. A more complete breakdown of these

---

Table 5.6

Murder Offenders of 9/11/2001 Terrorist Attacks
by Age[1]

Age	Total	WTC	Pentagon	PA
Total	**19**	**10**	**5**	**4**
Percent distribution[2]	100.0	52.6	26.3	21.1
Under 18	0	0	0	0
Under 22	4	1	1	2
18 and over	19	10	5	4
Infant (under 1)	0	0	0	0
1 to 4	0	0	0	0
5 to 8	0	0	0	0
9 to 12	0	0	0	0
13 to 16	0	0	0	0
17 to 19	0	0	0	0
20 to 24	12	7	2	3
25 to 29	6	2	3	1
30 to 34	1	1	0	0
35 to 39	0	0	0	0
40 to 44	0	0	0	0
45 to 49	0	0	0	0
50 to 54	0	0	0	0
55 to 59	0	0	0	0
60 to 64	0	0	0	0
65 to 69	0	0	0	0
70 to 74	0	0	0	0
75 and over	0	0	0	0
Unknown	0	0	0	0

[1] All offenders are white males.
[2] Because of rounding, the percentages may not add to total.

data appears in *Law Enforcement Officers Killed and Assaulted 2001*.

Summary and Conclusion

It is important to note that data for this publication were provided by law enforcement agencies. The 3,047 victims were those for whom law enforcement agencies involved in these incidents were able to supply supplemental homicide data, identifying age, gender, and race information on 2,303 males and 739 females. Of the total victims, the Pentagon was unable to provide supplemental homicide reports on 5. Readers of this report are cautioned not to confuse identifying a victim's age, gender, and race with being able to identify an individual through fingerprints, dental records, or DNA. It may be months or years before some victims of this tragedy will be positively identified. Again, the purpose of this special report is to provide statistical data to those who for their specific reasons will find these numbers useful. Finally, for reasons stated earlier, readers are cautioned about combining these data with the other statistics presented in the book to perform any meaningful analyses.

Injuries from Violent Crime, 2000: A Study Using NIBRS Data

Introduction

An important tool for law enforcement in the war against crime is the ability to analyze and understand when and where crime takes place, what form it takes, and the characteristics of its victims and offenders. Armed with such information, law enforcement can support its case to acquire the resources it needs to fight crime. As a result, short-term and long-term strategies can be developed to chart the ways and means of combating both domestic and international enterprises of criminal activities. One major goal of the Uniform Crime Reporting (UCR) Program is to generate a reliable set of criminal statistics in order to depict a nationwide view of crime in America based on the data voluntarily submitted by local and state law enforcement agencies.

Since 1930, the UCR Program has remained virtually unchanged in its method of reporting the steadily increasing diversity and complexity of crime. In order to fulfill the need for more comprehensive crime data to meet the demands of modern society, the National Incident-Based Reporting System (NIBRS) was developed.

The strength of NIBRS is the emphasis on criminal incidents, which permits analysis of the relationships between and among victim, offender, and offense. For example, NIBRS provides information about the age, sex, and race of the victim(s) and offender(s) of each crime category, characteristics available only for the offense of murder under the traditional UCR Summary Reporting System. Obviously, the NIBRS data provide rich and detailed information about the incidence of crime and its victims and offenders. The highly disaggregated NIBRS data allow users to extract specific information about crime and its dynamics. Consequently, the quality, breadth, and depth of the information derived from NIBRS is far superior to that provided by the summary system. Although NIBRS data are not yet nationally representative, this report demonstrates their potential by assessing the severity of personal injury resulting from violent crimes.

Objectives

The objective of this research is to demonstrate the versatility of these data by analyzing the injuries associated with violent crime, using the classifications *major*, *minor*, and *none*. The specific objectives of the study are to present and discuss the number of victims by injury type and (1) selected offense; (2) location; (3) weapon type; (4) victim age, sex, and race; (5) relationship of victim to offender; and (6) offender age, sex, and race.

Methodology

Offenses in NIBRS are classified as *crimes against persons, property, or society*. Incidents can involve more than one offense, victim, or offender. For crime counting purposes, one offense is counted for each victim of *crimes against persons*, and one offense is counted for each distinct incident of *crimes against property* and *crimes against society*, regardless of the number of victims. All violent crimes involve force or threat of force. Since the primary objective of this research was to examine the injuries associated with violent crime, the offenses considered in this research were kidnaping/abduction, forcible sex offenses (forcible rape, forcible sodomy, sexual assault with an object, and forcible fondling), aggra-

Table 5.7

Number of Victims
by Selected Offense and Injury Type, 2000

Selected Offenses	Total[1]	Injury		
		Major	Minor	None
Kidnaping/abduction	6,905	391	1,778	4,736
Forcible rape	13,856	867	3,215	9,774
Forcible sodomy	3,562	180	508	2,874
Sexual assault with an object	2,347	98	405	1,844
Forcible fondling	17,365	234	1,524	15,607
Aggravated assault	117,507	28,155	39,123	50,229
Robbery	34,915	2,414	7,486	25,015

[1] Victims of more than one offense within an incident are counted within each appropriate offense category.

vated assault, and robbery. (The violent offense of murder was excluded from this list because the victims of murder suffer the ultimate injury—death. Although the violent crime of robbery is classified as a crime against *property,* it was included in this study because it involves force or threat of force to the victim(s) even though its objective is to obtain money or property.

The injury classifications in this study were limited to major, minor, and none. Injuries included under *major* are apparent broken bones, possible internal injuries, severe lacerations, loss of teeth, unconsciousness, or other major injury. Apparent *minor* injury and *none* were listed as separate categories. Injuries as related to the characteristics of the offense; location; weapon type; the age, sex and race of the victim(s); the relationship of the victim to the offender; and the age, sex, and race of the offender(s) were examined in detail in this report.

Table 5.8

Number of Victims
by Location and Injury Type, 2000

		Injury		
Location	Total[1]	Major	Minor	None
Air/bus/train terminal	287	41	67	179
Bank/savings and loan	805	34	62	709
Bar/nightclub	4,918	1,939	1,631	1,348
Church/synagogue/temple	267	31	51	185
Commercial/office building	3,018	497	555	1,966
Construction site	183	38	52	93
Convenience store	3,661	385	601	2,675
Department/discount store	1,233	93	334	806
Drug store/doctor's office/hospital	952	129	196	627
Field/woods	2,548	403	692	1,453
Government/public building	1,009	153	279	577
Grocery/supermarket	1,390	133	331	926
Highway/road/alley	37,063	6,510	9,974	20,579
Hotel/motel/etc.	3,386	535	842	2,009
Jail/prison	1,118	279	398	441
Lake/waterway	280	53	65	162
Liquor store	208	27	46	135
Parking lot/garage	12,085	1,988	3,298	6,799
Rental storage facility	113	21	41	51
Residence/home	97,589	15,707	28,546	53,336
Restaurant	2,880	299	518	2,063
School/college	4,195	475	1,053	2,667
Service/gas station	1,584	154	332	1,098
Specialty store	1,377	106	225	1,046
Other/unknown	11,834	1,961	3,079	6,794

[1] If a victim suffers more than one offense at the same location during the same incident, the victim is counted once within that location. If a victim suffers more than one offense at different locations during the same incident, the victim is counted within each appropriate location.

Although the statistics shown are an accurate depiction of reports from those law enforcement agencies participating in NIBRS data collection, they may not be representative nationally. However, as more law enforcement agencies provide data in the NIBRS format, the data will lend themselves to more in-depth national analysis.

Discussion of the Data

Criminal incidents reported to the FBI's UCR Program through NIBRS in 2000 involving one or more of the selected violent crime offenses were extracted from the complete NIBRS data set to become the focus of analysis for this report. The 2000 file included data from 3,157 law enforcement agencies in 19 states. These agencies jointly covered a population of 43.7 million or 16 percent of the Nation's inhabitants. The analysis of the characteristics of violent crime incidents was limited to the 2000 NIBRS data.

In NIBRS, data are collected on each single incident and arrest within 22 crime categories comprised of 46 specific crimes (Group A offenses). For each offense known to police within these categories, incident, victim, property, offender, and arrestee information are gathered when available. In addition to Group A offenses, there are 11 Group B offense categories for which arrests are reported. As opposed to the traditional UCR Summary Reporting System, NIBRS is incident-based; therefore, opportunities exist for the reporting of the complete description of the multiple characteristics within an incident. The major difference between the Summary Reporting System and NIBRS is the degree of detail in reporting. For this study, the analysis of these factors is limited to the 2000 NIBRS data.

During the year 2000, 3,157 agencies submitted a total of 2,672,924 Group A incident reports to the FBI. These reports contained information on 2,974,962 offenses, 2,887,983 victims, and 2,071,229 known offenders. Known means at least one characteristic (age, sex, or race) of the offender was reported. At least one of the selected violent crimes was involved in 6 percent of the incidents.

Table 5.9

Number of Victims
by Weapon and Injury Type, 2000

Weapon Type	Total[1]	Injury		
		Major	Minor	None
Firearm(s)[2]	36,265	3,599	4,027	28,639
Dangerous weapons[3] (knives, clubs, etc.)	62,413	14,023	20,830	27,560
Personal weapons[4] (hands, fists, feet, etc.)	59,703	9,709	20,087	29,907
Firearms with dangerous and/or personal weapons[5]	2,852	452	824	1,576
Other weapon combinations[6]	7,334	2,149	3,120	2,065
Unknown	7,998	1,272	1,749	4,977
None	17,612	827	2,701	14,084

[1] If a victim suffers more than one offense with the same weapon type, the victim is counted once within that weapon type. If the victim suffers more than one offense with different weapon types, the victim is counted within each appropriate weapon type.

[2] Includes offenses committed with one or more firearm(s) but no other weapon type.

[3] Includes offenses committed with one or more dangerous weapon(s) but no other weapon type.

[4] Includes offenses committed with personal weapons and no other weapon type.

[5] Includes offenses committed with firearms and any other weapon type.

[6] Includes offenses committed with any weapon combination excluding firearm(s).

Even though criminal incidents can involve more than one offense, victim, or offender, most involve a single offense, victim, or offender. Sixty-four percent of the 2,672,924 crime incidents involved only one individual (person) victim, 92.1 percent involved a single offense, and 56.1 percent a single offender.

Selected Offenses

Among the offenses considered in this report, aggravated assault was the violent crime accounting for the most victims (117,507). This offense also showed the highest percentage of victim injury. Over 57 percent of the aggra-vated assault victims were reported to have suffered injury, 24.0 percent major and 33.3 percent minor. In terms of percentages, kidnaping/abduction was the offense next most likely to result in injury. The 6,905 victims of kidnaping/abduction suffered personal injury 31.4 percent of the time: 5.7 percent major and 25.7 percent minor. Victims of forcible sex offenses most frequently suffered no personal injury. Most victims of a forcible sex offense suffered forcible fondling (17,365), but victims of this offense were least likely to suffer an injury (10.1 percent). Forcible rape followed in

number of victims (13,856) and resulted in the highest percentage of injuries among the forcible sex offenses, 29.5 percent. Of the 34,915 victims of robbery, 71.6 percent reportedly suffered no injury; 21.4 percent suffered minor injury and 6.9 percent, major injury. Because persons can be victims of more than one offense in a criminal incident, they were included in the counts for each relevant offense. Thus, the number of victims in Table 5.7 is correct for each offense category but cannot be summed to a total of persons victimized.

Location

Victims of violent crimes (kidnaping/ abduction, forcible rape, forcible sodomy, sexual assault with an object, forcible fondling, aggravated assault and/or robbery) in bars and nightclubs were more likely to suffer major injury than minor ones or none. Bar/nightclub was the only location where victims of major injury (39.4 percent) outnumbered those experiencing minor injury or none. The location with the highest number of victims (97,589) was residence/home, having 2.6 times as many victims as highway/road/alley, the next most frequent location. Of persons victimized in residences, 45.3 percent were injured (16.1 percent major and 29.3 percent minor). Violent offenses resulted in injury to 44.5 percent (17.6 percent major and 26.9 percent minor) of those victimized on highways/roads/alleys. In a single criminal incident, a person can be victimized in more than one location. In Table 5.8, the victims were included in the counts for each appropriate location. Thus, the number of victims is correct for each location but cannot be summed to a total of persons victimized.

Weapons

An examination of victims by type of weapon and type of injury showed that persons attacked with dangerous weapons (knives, clubs, etc.) as well as those attacked with personal weapons (hands, fists, feet, etc.) outnumbered those who had firearms used against them. Twenty-one percent of the victims who had firearms used against them, 55.8 percent of the victims attacked with other dangerous weapons (knives, clubs, etc.), and 49.9 percent of the victims attacked with personal weapons (hands, fists, and feet, etc.) were injured. Considering severity of injury for these three weapons categories, one finds that 22.5 percent of the victims of the dangerous weapons classification, 16.3 percent of those attacked with personal weapons, and 9.9 percent of those against whom firearms were used suffered major injuries. Victims can suffer more than one offense with different weapon types within one criminal incident. They are, therefore, accounted for in each appropriate weapon category in Table 5.9.

Victim Characteristics

Of the 193,801 victims of violent crime considered in this report, 16.5 percent experienced major injury; 27.5 percent, minor injury; and 56.1 percent, no injury. When looking at the data by age, one finds that persons under the age of 18 accounted for 25.8 percent of all victims and 13.9 percent of all persons suffering

major injury. Persons aged 18 through 45 accounted for 61.3 percent of the victims and 73.5 percent of the major injuries. In the 26- through 45-year-old age group, victims experiencing injury outnumbered those experiencing no injury.

Examining the data by gender, one finds that more males (51.0 percent) than females (48.4 percent) were victims of violent crime. Of the male victims, 49.3 percent were injured, and for females, 38.6 percent were injured. Males accounted for over two-thirds of the victims suffering major injury.

An examination of the data by race showed that whites accounted for 58.6 percent of the victims suffering major injury and blacks accounted for 38.5 percent. However, within each racial cohort, the data showed that 21.3 percent of black victims and 14.7 percent of white victims suffered major injury. Conversely, 28.0 percent of white victims and 26.4 percent of black victims suffered minor injury. Combined, the Asian/Pacific Islander and American Indian/Alaskan Native race categories accounted for 1.0 percent of the total victims. No racial group had higher percentages for injury than for no injury. (In the above discussion of victim age, gender, and race, the percentages were calculated from data in Table 5.10 and include the unknowns in each category.)

Relationships

In NIBRS when an offender perpetrates a crime against person or a robbery against the victim, the relationship of the victim to the offender is recorded, unless nothing is known about the offender. In incidents where victims knew or were related to one or all of their assailants, about half (46.3 to 56.4 percent) of the victims were injured. In instances where the offender was a stranger, 34.8 percent of the victims were injured. (See Table 5.11.)

Offender Characteristics

Persons can be victimized by more than one offender in a single incident. Because of this multiplicity, it is possible for victims to be counted differently in separate portions of Table 5.12. The offenders in a multiple-offender incident could be in different age, sex, or racial

Table 5.10

Number of Victims
by Victim Age, Sex, Race, and Injury Type, 2000

Victim Characteristics	Total	Injury		
		Major	Minor	None
Victim Age				
Total	**193,801**	**31,966**	**53,206**	**108,629**
Infant (under 1)	373	127	51	195
1 to 9	13,676	823	2,271	10,582
10 to 12	8,055	485	1,570	6,000
13 to 17	27,884	2,997	6,595	18,292
18 to 21	27,576	4,984	7,911	14,681
22 to 25	20,880	4,137	6,270	10,473
26 to 35	39,767	7,866	12,316	19,585
36 to 45	30,637	6,495	9,547	14,595
46 to 55	12,317	2,353	3,438	6,526
56 to 65	3,909	598	1,044	2,267
Over 65	2,964	438	759	1,767
Unknown age	5,763	663	1,434	3,666
Victim Sex				
Total	**193,801**	**31,966**	**53,206**	**108,629**
Male	98,817	21,494	27,190	50,133
Female	93,889	10,350	25,848	57,691
Unknown sex	1,095	122	168	805
Victim Race				
Total	**193,801**	**31,966**	**53,206**	**108,629**
White	127,708	18,724	35,745	73,239
Black	57,877	12,305	15,271	30,301
American Indian/Alaskan Native	614	138	167	309
Asian/Pacific Islander	1,368	201	316	851
Unknown race	6,234	598	1,707	3,929

Table 5.11

Percent Distribution of Victims
by Relationship of the Victim to the Offender and Injury Type, 2000

Relationship of Victim to Offender[1]	Total[2]	Injury		
		Major	Minor	None
Family only[3]	100.0	15.2	31.1	53.7
Family and other offenders[4]	100.0	24.4	26.1	49.5
Known offenders only[5]	100.0	17.6	29.1	53.2
Known offenders and strangers[6]	100.0	23.3	33.1	43.6
Stranger(s) only[7]	100.0	13.4	21.4	65.2
All other[8]	100.0	17.2	24.6	58.3

[1] Does not include the victims in incidents where nothing is known about the offender.
[2] Because of rounding, percentages may not add to total.
[3] Regardless of number, all offenders are related to victim.
[4] At least one offender was related to victim.
[5] Regardless of number, victim was acquainted with all.
[6] At least one offender was known to victim. No offenders were related to victims.
[7] Regardless of number, all offenders were strangers to victims.
[8] Regardless of number, offenders were mutual combatants (victim was offender) or unknown.

groups; therefore, a victim could be counted more than once in any portion of Table 5.12. (See footnote for example.) In addition, information about offenders is frequently incomplete, especially in connection with incidents that have not been cleared. Table 5.12 shows all offender data as reported; that is, any one or a combination of characteristics (age, sex, or race) may have been reported.

The percentages of injury and no injury to persons victimized varied somewhat when viewed by a breakdown of offender age. The percentages of victims suffering no injury ranged from 51.9 when the offender was aged 26 through 35 and aged 36 through 45 to 70.5 when the offender was a juvenile aged 10 through 12. The variance was less when one looks at offender gender. Nearly half (46.0 percent) of the victims of females escaped injury, as did 57.8 percent of those victimized by males. An examination of the race of the offenders showed the percentage of no injury was more than 50 percent for victims in all categories except American Indian/Alaskan Native. Persons victimized by offenders of this racial group accounted for the smallest number of violent crime victims. (See Table 5.12.)

Summary and Conclusion

The findings from this study showed that most of the time, victims of violent crime

(excluding murder) reportedly suffer minor or no injuries. Major injuries to victims were reportedly inflicted least often. When compared with victims of other offenses, victims of aggravated assault suffered major injuries most often. Overall, most victims suffered a violent crime at the location of residence/home. The weapon data revealed that of firearms, personal weapons, and dangerous weapons, the weapons used to inflict major injury on most victims were dangerous weapons such as knives, clubs, etc. A breakdown of age groups showed that infants and victims aged 36 to 45 had the highest percentages of major injury. The data concerning victim gender revealed that males most often suffered major injury. Within each racial cohort, American Indian/Alaskan Native was the race of victims most often experiencing a major injury, followed by blacks. More victims were injured by relatives or acquaintances than by strangers. In terms of known offenders, most victims had major injuries inflicted upon them by someone in the age group 22 to 25. More victims were injured by males than by females.

It must be remembered that the general conclusions drawn from this analysis are limited to the jurisdictions participating in NIBRS. However, the report demonstrates that the NIBRS data can be used effectively for analyzing many factors of violent crime by providing richer and more detailed information about the incidence of crime and its victims, offenses, and offenders than the traditional summary UCR data collection system. Although the operation of NIBRS is limited to those data received from 19 states, the data are considered sufficiently comprehensive for the purpose of demonstrating the utility of NIBRS. As NIBRS participation grows throughout the law enforcement community, so will the utility of the data and the ability to do complex analysis on a wide array of criminal justice issues. That ability will bring with it an understanding of crime never before possible. The information obtained from these types of analyses may provide a significant strategic advantage in designing a long-term crime fighting scheme. It will also help the public to understand the dynamics of crime not only nationally, but regionally and locally as well.

Table 5.12

Number of Victims
by Offender Age, Sex, Race, and Injury Type, 2000

Offender Characteristics	Total	Injury Major	Minor	None
Offender Age				
1 to 9	1,609	129	359	1,121
10 to 12	4,143	311	911	2,921
13 to 17	24,649	3,270	6,377	15,002
18 to 21	33,760	5,892	9,071	18,797
22 to 25	26,384	4,939	7,542	13,903
26 to 35	43,260	7,741	13,066	22,453
36 to 45	30,030	5,350	9,102	15,578
46 to 55	11,538	2,038	3,120	6,380
56 to 65	3,530	482	839	2,209
Over 65	1,864	214	375	1,275
Unknown age	22,740	4,132	5,340	13,268
Offender Sex				
Male	152,539	24,309	40,086	88,144
Female	31,571	5,929	11,120	14,522
Unknown sex	6,236	1,437	1,460	3,339
Offender Race				
White	99,506	14,716	28,497	56,293
Black	72,971	13,624	19,017	40,330
American Indian/Alaskan Native	694	154	213	327
Asian/Pacific Islander	1,010	176	280	554
Unknown race	11,588	2,101	2,888	6,599

Note: All counts relate to victims and the known characteristics (age, sex, race) of their assailants. Because of offender multiplicity, victims may be counted in one or more categories. For example, a person victimized by two 15 year olds, one male and one female, would be scored once in the age portion of the table, but twice in the sex portion. The objective of the table is to show the severity of injury inflicted by offender characteristic.

Bibliography

U.S. Department of Justice. Federal Bureau of Investigation. *Crime in the United States,* Washington, D.C.: The Government Printing Office.

U.S. Department of Justice. Federal Bureau of Investigation. (August 2000). NIBRS Volume 1: *Data Collection Guidelines,* Washington, D.C.: The Government Printing Office.

U.S. Department of Justice. Federal Bureau of Investigation. (December 1999). NIBRS Volume 4: *Error Message Manual,* Washington, D.C.: The Government Printing Office.

U.S. Department of Justice. Federal Bureau of Investigation. (1984). *Uniform Crime Reporting Handbook,* Washington, D.C.: The Government Printing Office.

U.S. Department of Justice. Federal Bureau of Investigation. (1992). *Uniform Crime Reporting Handbook,* (NIBRS Edition). Washington, D.C.: The Government Printing Office.

SECTION VI

Law Enforcement Personnel

The requirements for law enforcement service vary greatly from one locale to another based upon each jurisdiction's unique demographic traits and characteristics. A small community situated between two large cities, for example, may require a greater number of law enforcement personnel than a community of the same size that has no urban center nearby. Similarly, the needs of a community having a highly mobile or seasonal population may be very different from those of a city with a relatively stable population. A community that incorporates legal gambling establishments will have different law enforcement challenges than one in which the presence of a large military base is the dominant influence, just as a small college town will have different needs than one comprised predominantly of retirees.

The functions of law enforcement are also significantly diverse throughout the Nation. The responsibilities of state police and highway patrol agencies vary considerably from one jurisdiction to another. Their duties range from traffic enforcement on state highways and interstate roadways to major investigative responsibilities for all violent crimes committed statewide. In certain areas, sheriffs' responsibilities are limited exclusively to civil functions, sole enforcement for state and local courts and/ or the administration of the county jail facilities. In others, the sheriffs may be the only law enforcement presence in remote locations covering large geographical zones. Nationally, the overall role of law enforcement continues to be expanded and redefined in light of the constant threat from international and domestic terrorism. When attempting any comparison of law enforcement employee rates, the data user must consider these differing service requirements and responsibilities.

The data presented in the following tables represent national, regional, and state averages; they should be viewed as guides or indicators, not as recommended or preferred police staffing levels. Adequate personnel for a specific locale can be determined only after careful study and analysis of the various conditions affecting service requirements in that jurisdiction.

This edition of *Crime in the United States* contains a new table, Law Enforcement Employees as of October 31, 2001, by Other Agencies by State. Table 82 supplies employee data for 171 law enforcement agencies charged with serving a broad range of specific organizations/ entities. These county and state agencies serve the Nation's transit systems, parks and forests, tribal reservations, hospitals, and school districts (including educational institutions not categorized as colleges or universities). Drug and narcotics units and task forces are included in Table 82, along with county detectives and prosecutorial law enforcement staff. Collectively, 26.9 percent of the agencies listed serve some form of mass transit (airports, seaports, railways) and 25.7 percent are associated with schools or school districts. The majority of these agencies have concurrent jurisdiction with local law enforcement; therefore, no population is assigned to them.

Law Enforcement Rate

A national average of 2.5 full-time officers were employed for every 1,000 inhabitants in the United States as of October 31, 2001. Including full-time civilian employees, the overall law enforcement rate was 3.5 per 1,000 inhabitants. (Based on Table 74). The 13,530 city, county, and state police agencies reporting in 2001 collectively employed 659,104 officers and 279,926 civilian employees and provided law enforcement service to approximately 268 million of the Nation's inhabitants. (See Table 74.) A listing of reported full-time law enforcement officers and civilian employees by state is provided in Table 77.

The Nation's cities collectively reported an average of 3.1 law enforcement employees per 1,000 inhabitants. Cities with populations of 1 million and over had the highest rate with 4.7 employees per 1,000. Suburban and rural counties had rates of 4.4 and 4.2 employees per 1,000 population, respectively. (Based on Table 74.)

Regionally, the city law enforcement employee rate was 3.6 per 1,000 inhabitants in the Northeast, 3.5 in the South, 2.8 in the Midwest, and 2.4 in the West. (See Table 70.)

Sworn Personnel

The national rate for all cities, based solely on sworn law enforcement personnel (excluding civilians), was 2.4 officers per 1,000 inhabitants. By city population grouping, the rates ranged from 3.5 officers per 1,000 inhabitants for cities with populations of 1 million and over to 1.8 in cities with 25,000 to 99,999 inhabitants. Suburban and rural counties had rates of 2.7 and 2.5 officers per 1,000 in population, respectively. (Based on Table 74.) By region, cities in the North had the highest rate of sworn officers to population, 2.8 per 1,000 followed by cities in the South with 2.7, the Midwest cities with 2.2, and the West with 1.7 officers per 1,000 inhabitants. (See Table 71.)

Both nationally and in cities, males made up 88.8 percent of all sworn officers. Males accounted for 91.9 percent of sworn officers in rural counties and 87.1 percent in suburban counties. (See Table 74.)

Table 79 provides a listing of reported full-time law enforcement officers and civilian employees by university and college for each state. In 2001, 602 participating agencies provided law enforcement services on college and university campuses. Sworn officers comprised 65.8 percent of the staff in agencies that submitted employment data.

Civilian Employees

Of the total law enforcement employee force in the United States in 2001, civilians constituted 29.8 percent. In cities, civilians represented 23.2 percent of the police employees and made up 39.3 percent of the staff in both suburban and rural counties. (See Table 75.) Of all civilian employees, 62.7 percent were female. (See Table 74.)

Law Enforcement Officers Killed and Assaulted

Seventy law enforcement officers were feloniously slain in the line of duty in 2001, 19 more than in the previous year. An additional 78 officers were accidentally killed during the performance of their official duties in 2001— 7.1 percent less than the 2000 total of 84 officers accidentally killed.

Extensive data on line-of-duty deaths and assaults on city, county, state, and federal officers can be found in the Uniform Crime Reports publication, *Law Enforcement Officers Killed and Assaulted.*

Table 70

Full-time Law Enforcement Employees[1] as of October 31, 2001

Number and Rate per 1,000 Inhabitants
by Geographic Region and Division by Population Group
[2001 estimated population]

Geographic region/division	Total Cities (10,261 cities; population 178,915,172)	Group I (70 cities, 250,000 and over; population 52,194,574)	Group II (163 cities, 100,000 to 249,999; population 24,348,635)	Group III (380 cities, 50,000 to 99,999; population 26,109,909)	Group IV (734 cities, 25,000 to 49,999; population 25,485,483)	Group V (1,739 cities, 10,000 to 24,999; population 27,602,652)	Group VI (7,175 cities, under 10,000; population 23,173,919)
TOTAL CITIES: 10,261 cities; population 178,915,172:							
Number of employees	553,148	207,133	61,367	60,522	59,642	68,627	95,857
Average number of employees per 1,000 inhabitants	3.1	4.0	2.5	2.3	2.3	2.5	4.1
New England: 765 cities; population 12,434,046:							
Number of employees	33,124	2,791	5,047	5,777	6,972	7,261	5,276
Average number of employees per 1,000 inhabitants	2.7	4.7	3.5	2.4	2.3	2.3	2.9
Middle Atlantic: 1,404 cities; population 28,539,804:							
Number of employees	114,475	67,909	4,761	8,964	10,480	11,552	10,809
Average number of employees per 1,000 inhabitants	4.0	6.5	3.4	2.7	2.5	2.2	2.8
NORTHEAST: 2,169 cities; population 40,973,850:							
Number of employees	147,599	70,700	9,808	14,741	17,452	18,813	16,085
Average number of employees per 1,000 inhabitants	3.6	6.4	3.5	2.6	2.4	2.2	2.9
East North Central: 1,985 cities; population 31,321,118:							
Number of employees	90,658	31,570	7,252	10,350	11,670	14,780	15,036
Average number of employees per 1,000 inhabitants	2.9	4.4	2.5	2.2	2.1	2.3	3.2
West North Central: 910 cities; population 11,964,410:							
Number of employees	29,716	7,541	3,033	3,497	3,882	4,788	6,975
Average number of employees per 1,000 inhabitants	2.5	3.4	2.2	1.7	2.0	2.2	3.1
MIDWEST: 2,895 cities; population 43,285,528:							
Number of employees	120,374	39,111	10,285	13,847	15,552	19,568	22,011
Average number of employees per 1,000 inhabitants	2.8	4.2	2.4	2.1	2.1	2.3	3.1
South Atlantic: 1,723 cities; population 21,097,786:							
Number of employees	84,434	20,865	11,566	10,931	8,136	11,244	21,692
Average number of employees per 1,000 inhabitants	4.0	4.4	3.0	3.1	3.1	3.5	6.8
East South Central: 970 cities; population 8,725,952:							
Number of employees	32,287	6,301	4,329	1,855	3,418	5,443	10,941
Average number of employees per 1,000 inhabitants	3.7	3.2	3.5	3.3	2.9	3.1	5.4
West South Central: 1,176 cities; population 21,365,019:							
Number of employees	62,538	23,559	7,602	5,850	5,578	6,694	13,255
Average number of employees per 1,000 inhabitants	2.9	2.9	2.4	2.3	2.5	2.7	4.8
SOUTH: 3,869 cities; population 51,188,757:							
Number of employees	179,259	50,725	23,497	18,636	17,132	23,381	45,888
Average number of employees per 1,000 inhabitants	3.5	3.4	2.9	2.8	2.8	3.1	5.8
Mountain: 556 cities; population 12,849,955:							
Number of employees	34,430	14,523	5,829	2,981	3,040	2,669	5,388
Average number of employees per 1,000 inhabitants	2.7	2.9	2.2	2.0	2.4	2.5	4.2
Pacific: 772 cities; population 30,617,082:							
Number of employees	71,486	32,074	11,948	10,317	6,466	4,196	6,485
Average number of employees per 1,000 inhabitants	2.3	2.7	1.9	1.8	1.9	2.1	4.9
WEST: 1,328 cities; population 43,467,037:							
Number of employees	105,916	46,597	17,777	13,298	9,506	6,865	11,873
Average number of employees per 1,000 inhabitants	2.4	2.7	2.0	1.9	2.0	2.2	4.6

Suburban Area[2]: 6,262 agencies; population 107,394,915:		County[3]: 3,269 agencies; population 89,140,075:	
Number of employees	400,174	Number of employees	385,882
Average number of employees per 1,000 inhabitants	3.7	Average number of employees per 1,000 inhabitants	4.3

[1] Includes civilians.

[2] Suburban area includes law enforcement agencies in cities with less than 50,000 inhabitants and county law enforcement agencies that are within a Metropolitan Statistical Area (see Appendix III). Suburban area excludes all metropolitan agencies associated with a central city. The agencies associated with suburban areas will also appear in other groups within this table.

[3] County is a combination of both suburban and rural counties.

Table 71

Full-time Law Enforcement Officers as of October 31, 2001

Number and Rate per 1,000 Inhabitants
by Geographic Region and Division by Population Group
[2001 estimated population]

Geographic region/division	Total Cities (10,261 cities; population 178,915,172)	Group I (70 cities, 250,000 and over; population 52,194,574)	Group II (163 cities, 100,000 to 249,999; population 24,348,635)	Group III (380 cities, 50,000 to 99,999; population 26,109,909)	Group IV (734 cities, 25,000 to 49,999; population 25,485,483)	Group V (1,739 cities, 10,000 to 24,999; population 27,602,652)	Group VI (7,175 cities, under 10,000; population 23,173,919)
TOTAL CITIES: 10,261 cities; population 178,915,172:							
Number of officers	**424,701**	**155,843**	**46,269**	**46,690**	**46,560**	**54,607**	**74,732**
Average number of officers per 1,000 inhabitants	**2.4**	**3.0**	**1.9**	**1.8**	**1.8**	**2.0**	**3.2**
New England: 765 cities; population 12,434,046:							
Number of officers	27,141	2,130	4,145	4,984	5,802	5,955	4,125
Average number of officers per 1,000 inhabitants	2.2	3.6	2.9	2.1	1.9	1.9	2.3
Middle Atlantic: 1,404 cities; population 28,539,804:							
Number of officers	88,629	49,383	3,976	7,376	8,720	9,860	9,314
Average number of officers per 1,000 inhabitants	3.1	4.7	2.8	2.2	2.0	1.9	2.4
NORTHEAST: 2,169 cities; population 40,973,850:							
Number of officers	**115,770**	**51,513**	**8,121**	**12,360**	**14,522**	**15,815**	**13,439**
Average number of officers per 1,000 inhabitants	**2.8**	**4.7**	**2.9**	**2.2**	**2.0**	**1.9**	**2.4**
East North Central: 1,985 cities; population 31,321,118:							
Number of officers	73,731	26,737	5,868	8,081	9,125	11,712	12,208
Average number of officers per 1,000 inhabitants	2.4	3.8	2.0	1.7	1.7	1.8	2.6
West North Central: 910 cities; population 11,964,410:							
Number of officers	23,037	5,399	2,386	2,755	3,018	3,780	5,699
Average number of officers per 1,000 inhabitants	1.9	2.4	1.8	1.4	1.5	1.8	2.5
MIDWEST: 2,895 cities; population 43,285,528:							
Number of officers	**96,768**	**32,136**	**8,254**	**10,836**	**12,143**	**15,492**	**17,907**
Average number of officers per 1,000 inhabitants	**2.2**	**3.5**	**1.9**	**1.6**	**1.6**	**1.8**	**2.6**
South Atlantic: 1,723 cities; population 21,097,786:							
Number of officers	64,682	15,698	8,737	8,349	6,233	8,804	16,861
Average number of officers per 1,000 inhabitants	3.1	3.3	2.3	2.3	2.4	2.8	5.3
East South Central: 970 cities; population 8,725,952:							
Number of officers	24,489	4,826	3,152	1,419	2,712	4,224	8,156
Average number of officers per 1,000 inhabitants	2.8	2.4	2.6	2.5	2.3	2.4	4.1
West South Central: 1,176 cities; population 21,365,019:							
Number of officers	47,443	18,241	5,719	4,487	4,174	5,160	9,662
Average number of officers per 1,000 inhabitants	2.2	2.2	1.8	1.8	1.8	2.1	3.5
SOUTH: 3,869 cities; population 51,188,757:							
Number of officers	**136,614**	**38,765**	**17,608**	**14,255**	**13,119**	**18,188**	**34,679**
Average number of officers per 1,000 inhabitants	**2.7**	**2.6**	**2.1**	**2.1**	**2.2**	**2.4**	**4.4**
Mountain: 556 cities; population 12,849,955:							
Number of officers	24,084	9,784	4,048	2,157	2,144	1,985	3,966
Average number of officers per 1,000 inhabitants	1.9	1.9	1.5	1.4	1.7	1.9	3.1
Pacific: 772 cities; population 30,617,082:							
Number of officers	51,465	23,645	8,238	7,082	4,632	3,127	4,741
Average number of officers per 1,000 inhabitants	1.7	2.0	1.3	1.3	1.4	1.5	3.6
WEST: 1,328 cities; population 43,467,037:							
Number of officers	**75,549**	**33,429**	**12,286**	**9,239**	**6,776**	**5,112**	**8,707**
Average number of officers per 1,000 inhabitants	**1.7**	**2.0**	**1.4**	**1.3**	**1.4**	**1.7**	**3.3**

Suburban Area[1]: 6,262 agencies; population 107,394,915:		**County[2]: 3,269 agencies; population 89,140,075:**	
Number of officers	268,655	Number of officers	234,403
Average number of officers per 1,000 inhabitants	2.5	Average number of officers per 1,000 inhabitants	2.6

[1] Suburban area includes law enforcement agencies in cities with less than 50,000 inhabitants and county law enforcement agencies that are within a Metropolitan Statistical Area (see Appendix III). Suburban area excludes all metropolitan agencies associated with a central city. The agencies associated with suburban areas will also appear in other groups within this table.

[2] County is a combination of both suburban and rural counties.

Table 72

Agencies with Full-time Law Enforcement Employees[1] as of October 31, 2001
Range in Rate per 1,000 Inhabitants
by Population Group
[2001 estimated population]

Rate range		Total Cities[2] (9,421 cities; population 178,915,172)	Group I (70 cities, 250,000 and over; population 52,194,574)	Group II (163 cities, 100,000 to 249,999; population 24,348,635)	Group III (380 cities, 50,000 to 99,999; population 26,109,909)	Group IV (734 cities, 25,000 to 49,999; population 25,485,483)	Group V (1,739 cities, 10,000 to 24,999; population 27,602,652)	Group VI (6,335 cities, under 10,000; population 23,173,919)
.1-.5	Number	83	–	–	1	2	9	71
	Percent	0.9	–	–	0.3	0.3	0.5	1.1
.6-1.0	Number	331	–	–	1	12	37	281
	Percent	3.5	–	–	0.3	1.6	2.1	4.4
1.1-1.5	Number	903	–	13	38	78	135	639
	Percent	9.6	–	8.0	10.0	10.6	7.8	10.1
1.6-2.0	Number	1,722	7	44	130	186	373	982
	Percent	18.3	10.0	27.0	34.2	25.3	21.4	15.5
2.1-2.5	Number	1,846	13	43	107	223	466	994
	Percent	19.6	18.6	26.4	28.2	30.4	26.8	15.7
2.6-3.0	Number	1,478	19	28	51	126	374	880
	Percent	15.7	27.1	17.2	13.4	17.2	21.5	13.9
3.1-3.5	Number	913	9	19	23	61	153	648
	Percent	9.7	12.9	11.7	6.1	8.3	8.8	10.2
3.6-4.0	Number	617	8	8	14	21	99	467
	Percent	6.5	11.4	4.9	3.7	2.9	5.7	7.4
4.1-4.5	Number	424	2	4	8	17	41	352
	Percent	4.5	2.9	2.5	2.1	2.3	2.4	5.6
4.6-5.0	Number	276	3	4	5	5	19	240
	Percent	2.9	4.3	2.5	1.3	0.7	1.1	3.8
5.1 and over	Number	828	9	–	2	3	33	781
	Percent	8.8	12.9	–	0.5	0.4	1.9	12.3
Total Cities	Number	9,421	70	163	380	734	1,739	6,335
Percent[3]	Percent	100.0	100.0	100.0	100.0	100.0	100.0	100.0

[1] Includes civilians.

[2] The number of agencies used to compile these figures differs from the other Law Enforcement Employee tables because agencies with no resident population are excluded from this table. These agencies include those associated with universities and colleges (see Table 79) and other agencies (see Table 82), as well as some state agencies that have concurrent jurisdiction with other local law enforcement.

[3] Because of rounding, the percentages may not add to totals.

Table 73

Agencies with Full-time Law Enforcement Officers as of October 31, 2001
Range in Rate per 1,000 Inhabitants
by Population Group
[2001 estimated population]

Rate range		Total Cities[1] (9,421 cities; population 178,915,172)	Group I (70 cities, 250,000 and over; population 52,194,574)	Group II (163 cities, 100,000 to 249,999; population 24,348,635)	Group III (380 cities, 50,000 to 99,999; population 26,109,909)	Group IV (734 cities, 25,000 to 49,999; population 25,485,483)	Group V (1,739 cities, 10,000 to 24,999; population 27,602,652)	Group VI (6,335 cities, under 10,000; population 23,173,919)
.1-.5	Number	95	–	–	1	2	9	83
	Percent	1.0	–	–	0.3	0.3	0.5	1.3
.6-1.0	Number	484	–	10	24	45	72	333
	Percent	5.1	–	6.1	6.3	6.1	4.1	5.3
1.1-1.5	Number	1,678	8	56	132	208	354	920
	Percent	17.8	11.4	34.4	34.7	28.3	20.4	14.5
1.6-2.0	Number	2,453	25	42	126	268	641	1,351
	Percent	26.0	35.7	25.8	33.2	36.5	36.9	21.3
2.1-2.5	Number	1,782	12	29	56	128	374	1,183
	Percent	18.9	17.1	17.8	14.7	17.4	21.5	18.7
2.6-3.0	Number	1,009	9	14	24	53	162	747
	Percent	10.7	12.9	8.6	6.3	7.2	9.3	11.8
3.1-3.5	Number	670	6	10	8	23	78	545
	Percent	7.1	8.6	6.1	2.1	3.1	4.5	8.6
3.6-4.0	Number	374	2	2	6	5	26	333
	Percent	4.0	2.9	1.2	1.6	0.7	1.5	5.3
4.1-4.5	Number	256	2	–	2	1	12	239
	Percent	2.7	2.9	–	0.5	0.1	0.7	3.8
4.6-5.0	Number	161	5	–	1	–	2	153
	Percent	1.7	7.1	–	0.3	–	0.1	2.4
5.1 and over	Number	459	1	–	–	1	9	448
	Percent	4.9	1.4	–	–	0.1	0.5	7.1
Total Cities	Number	9,421	70	163	380	734	1,739	6,335
Percent[2]	Percent	100.0	100.0	100.0	100.0	100.0	100.0	100.0

[1] The number of agencies used to compile these figures differs from the other Law Enforcement Officer tables because agencies with no resident population are excluded from this table. These agencies include those associated with universities and colleges (see Table 79) and other agencies (see Table 82), as well as some state agencies that have concurrent jurisdiction with other local law enforcement.

[2] Because of rounding, the percentages may not add to totals.

Table 74

Full-time Law Enforcement Employees as of October 31, 2001
Percent Male and Female
by Population Group
[2001 estimated population]

| Population group | Total police employees | | | Police officers (sworn) | | | Civilian employees | | |
| | Total | Percent | | Total | Percent | | Total | Percent | |
		Male	Female		Male	Female		Male	Female
TOTAL AGENCIES: 13,530 agencies;									
population 268,055,247	**939,030**	**73.4**	**26.6**	**659,104**	**88.8**	**11.2**	**279,926**	**37.3**	**62.7**
TOTAL CITIES: 10,261 cities;									
population 178,915,172	**553,148**	**75.2**	**24.8**	**424,701**	**88.8**	**11.2**	**128,447**	**30.4**	**69.6**
GROUP I									
70 cities, 250,000 and over;									
population 52,194,574	207,133	71.0	29.0	155,843	83.7	16.3	51,290	32.3	67.7
10 cities, 1,000,000 and over;									
population 24,330,096	114,548	70.0	30.0	85,517	82.9	17.1	29,031	32.2	67.8
22 cities, 500,000 to 999,999;									
population 14,570,284	51,880	73.1	26.9	40,015	84.1	15.9	11,865	36.0	64.0
38 cities, 250,000 to 499,999;									
population 13,294,194	40,705	71.0	29.0	30,311	85.5	14.5	10,394	28.6	71.4
GROUP II									
163 cities, 100,000 to 249,999;									
population 24,348,635	61,367	73.7	26.3	46,269	89.1	10.9	15,098	26.2	73.8
GROUP III									
380 cities, 50,000 to 99,999;									
population 26,109,909	60,522	76.6	23.4	46,690	91.4	8.6	13,832	26.3	73.7
GROUP IV									
734 cities, 25,000 to 49,999;									
population 25,485,483	59,642	78.3	21.7	46,560	92.3	7.7	13,082	28.3	71.7
GROUP V									
1,739 cities, 10,000 to 24,999;									
population 27,602,652	68,627	79.5	20.5	54,607	93.2	6.8	14,020	26.3	73.7
GROUP VI									
7,175 cities, under 10,000;									
population 23,173,919	95,857	79.7	20.3	74,732	92.2	7.8	21,125	35.4	64.6
SUBURBAN COUNTIES									
913 agencies;									
population 57,459,771	254,028	70.3	29.7	154,304	87.1	12.9	99,724	44.3	55.7
RURAL COUNTIES									
2,356 agencies;									
population 31,680,304	131,854	71.9	28.1	80,099	91.9	8.1	51,755	40.8	59.2
SUBURBAN AREA[1]									
6,262 agencies;									
population 107,394,915	400,174	73.6	26.4	268,655	89.3	10.7	131,519	41.5	58.5

[1] Suburban area includes law enforcement agencies in cities with less than 50,000 inhabitants and county law enforcement agencies that are within a Metropolitan Statistical Area (see Appendix III). Suburban area excludes all metropolitan agencies associated with a central city. The agencies associated with suburban areas will also appear in other groups within this table.

Table 75

Full-time Civilian Law Enforcement Employees as of October 31, 2001
Percent of Total
by Population Group
[2001 estimated population]

Population group	Percent civilian employees	Population group	Percent civilian employees
TOTAL AGENCIES: 13,530 agencies; population 268,055,247	**29.8**	GROUP IV 734 cities, 25,000 to 49,999; population 25,485,483	21.9
TOTAL CITIES: 10,261 cities; population 178,915,172	**23.2**	GROUP V 1,739 cities, 10,000 to 24,999; population 27,602,652	20.4
GROUP I 70 cities, 250,000 and over; population 52,194,574	24.8	GROUP VI 7,175 cities, under 10,000; population 23,173,919	22.0
10 cities, 1,000,000 and over; population 24,330,096	25.3		
22 cities, 500,000 to 999,999; population 14,570,284	22.9	SUBURBAN COUNTIES 913 agencies; population 57,459,771	39.3
38 cities, 250,000 to 499,999; population 13,294,194	25.5		
GROUP II 163 cities, 100,000 to 249,999; population 24,348,635	24.6	RURAL COUNTIES 2,356 agencies; population 31,680,304	39.3
GROUP III 380 cities, 50,000 to 99,999; population 26,109,909	22.9	SUBURBAN AREA[1] 6,262 agencies; population 107,394,915	32.9

[1] Suburban area includes law enforcement agencies in cities with less than 50,000 inhabitants and county law enforcement agencies that are within a Metropolitan Statistical Area (see Appendix III). Suburban area excludes all metropolitan agencies associated with a central city. The agencies associated with suburban areas will also appear in other groups within this table.

Table 76

Full-time State Law Enforcement Employees as of October 31, 2001
by State

State	Number of law enforcement employees					State	Number of law enforcement employees				
		Officers		Civilians				Officers		Civilians	
	Total	Male	Female	Male	Female		Total	Male	Female	Male	Female
ALABAMA						**MARYLAND**					
Department of Public Safety	1,205	595	16	169	425	State Police	2,315	1,374	160	377	404
Other state agencies	257	197	10	8	42	Other state agencies	1,707	994	180	299	234
ALASKA						**MASSACHUSETTS**					
State Police	591	323	17	95	156	State Police	2,697	2,076	217	202	202
ARIZONA						**MICHIGAN**					
Department of Public Safety	1,830	960	77	320	473	State Police	3,233	1,868	261	515	589
CALIFORNIA						**MINNESOTA**					
Highway Patrol	10,169	6,242	616	1,452	1,859	State Patrol	764	490	50	125	99
Other state agencies	1,126	790	203	53	80	**MISSISSIPPI**					
COLORADO						Highway Safety Patrol	1,060	556	9	152	343
State Police	1,198	639	38	191	330	**MISSOURI**					
Other state agencies	53	38	10	2	3	State Highway Patrol	2,129	1,017	41	526	545
CONNECTICUT						Other state agencies	40	30	2	1	7
State Police	1,778	1,163	86	235	294	**MONTANA**					
Other state agencies	24	21	2	0	1	Highway Patrol	259	191	12	16	40
DELAWARE						**NEBRASKA**					
State Police	820	547	58	97	118	State Patrol	653	457	21	57	118
Other state agencies	754	399	88	58	209	**NEVADA**					
FLORIDA						Highway Patrol	592	379	24	48	141
Highway Patrol	2,138	1,470	185	172	311	**NEW HAMPSHIRE**					
Other state agencies	976	709	49	80	138	State Police	447	273	29	57	88
GEORGIA						Other state agencies	34	18	3	5	8
Department of Public Safety	1,921	835	27	377	682	**NEW JERSEY**					
Other state agencies	2,299	728	64	910	597	State Police	4,044	2,634	93	591	726
IDAHO						Other state agencies	42	40	0	0	2
State Police	337	250	11	12	64	Port Authority of New York and New Jersey[1]	662	565	41	10	46
ILLINOIS						**NEW MEXICO**					
State Police	3,876	1,958	197	1,187	534	State Police	717	537	23	64	93
Other state agencies	421	314	30	32	45	**NEW YORK**					
INDIANA						State Police	5,121	3,841	325	389	566
State Police	1,940	1,196	68	258	418	Other state agencies	282	243	13	14	12
Other state agencies	7	7	0	0	0	Port Authority of New York and New Jersey[2]					
IOWA						**NORTH CAROLINA**					
Department of Public Safety	951	615	36	121	179	Highway Patrol	1,779	1,358	27	223	171
KANSAS						Other state agencies	1,153	745	114	65	229
Highway Patrol	803	487	20	124	172	**NORTH DAKOTA**					
Other state agencies	472	272	14	60	126	Highway Patrol	186	117	6	36	27
KENTUCKY						**OHIO**					
State Police	1,689	921	33	383	352	State Highway Patrol	2,596	1,354	140	503	599
Other state agencies	541	413	14	52	62	**OKLAHOMA**					
LOUISIANA						Department of Public Safety	1,452	856	22	262	312
State Police	1,556	1,064	45	123	324	**OREGON**					
MAINE						State Police	1,205	668	70	173	294
State Police	463	311	21	48	83						
Other state agencies	141	38	3	49	51						

Table 76

Full-time State Law Enforcement Employees as of October 31, 2001
by State—Continued

State	Number of law enforcement employees					State	Number of law enforcement employees				
		Officers		Civilians				Officers		Civilians	
	Total	Male	Female	Male	Female		Total	Male	Female	Male	Female
PENNSYLVANIA						**UTAH**					
State Police	5,664	3,937	167	699	861	Highway Patrol	448	405	10	8	25
Other state agencies	227	161	20	14	32	Other state agencies	195	177	8	5	5
RHODE ISLAND						**VERMONT**					
State Police	263	198	19	28	18	State Police	422	282	19	33	88
Other state agencies	45	33	4	4	4	**VIRGINIA**					
SOUTH CAROLINA						State Police	2,411	1,690	69	220	432
Highway Patrol	1,093	873	30	60	130	Other state agencies	902	585	69	115	133
Other state agencies	1,077	633	119	98	227	**WASHINGTON**					
SOUTH DAKOTA						State Patrol	2,147	949	72	572	554
Highway Patrol	222	143	2	57	20	**WEST VIRGINIA**					
Other state agencies	132	37	0	31	64	State Police	967	617	15	109	226
TENNESSEE						Other state agencies	134	123	0	0	11
Department of Public Safety	1,808	842	45	216	705	**WISCONSIN**					
Other state agencies	1,651	701	52	456	442	State Patrol	668	441	72	75	80
TEXAS						Other state agencies	303	236	22	20	25
Department of Public Safety	6,984	2,873	163	1,203	2,745	**WYOMING**					
						Highway Patrol	325	172	4	66	83

[1] Data reported are the number of law enforcement employees for the state of New Jersey.

[2] Due to the events of September 11, 2001, data for this table are not available.

Note: Caution should be used when comparing data from one state to that of another. The responsibilities of the various state police, highway patrol, and department of public safety agencies range from full law enforcement duties to only traffic patrol, which can impact both level of employment for agencies as well as the ratio of sworn officers to civilians employed. Any valid comparison must take these factors and the other identified crime factors (see page iv) into consideration.

Table 77

Full-time State Law Enforcement Employees as of October 31, 2001

by State

[2001 estimated population]

| State | | Number of law enforcement employees | | | | State | | Number of law enforcement employees | | | |
| | Total | Officers | | Civilians | | | Total | Officers | | Civilians | |
		Male	Female	Male	Female			Male	Female	Male	Female
ALABAMA 349 agencies; population 4,451,163	15,303	9,370	753	1,855	3,325	**MISSOURI** 299 agencies; population 5,497,044	17,118	10,692	1,133	2,020	3,273
ALASKA 42 agencies; population 634,787	1,821	1,061	104	198	458	**MONTANA** 103 agencies; population 902,713	2,620	1,432	88	478	622
ARIZONA 102 agencies; population 5,297,623	18,548	9,671	1,139	3,329	4,409	**NEBRASKA** 159 agencies; population 1,694,176	4,532	2,971	329	298	934
ARKANSAS 198 agencies; population 2,692,090	7,538	4,517	513	970	1,538	**NEVADA** 36 agencies; population 2,106,074	7,513	4,082	417	1,048	1,966
CALIFORNIA 460 agencies; population 30,099,815	105,999	62,319	8,621	12,361	22,698	**NEW HAMPSHIRE** 134 agencies; population 968,701	2,704	1,892	129	208	475
COLORADO 232 agencies; population 4,345,118	15,172	8,990	1,260	1,579	3,343	**NEW JERSEY** 530 agencies; population 8,233,372	38,817	28,322	2,128	3,023	5,344
CONNECTICUT 100 agencies; population 3,425,074	9,825	7,280	664	672	1,209	**NEW MEXICO** 60 agencies; population 1,315,400	4,294	2,823	275	324	872
DELAWARE 51 agencies; population 795,253	2,964	1,851	251	340	522	**NEW YORK** 401 agencies; population 17,362,904	86,297	55,020	8,226	7,519	15,532
DISTRICT OF COLUMBIA 3 agencies; population 571,822	4,743	3,049	920	278	496	**NORTH CAROLINA** 512 agencies; population 8,162,627	27,636	17,436	2,153	3,278	4,769
FLORIDA 377 agencies; population 15,916,614	62,977	34,482	5,108	7,952	15,435	**NORTH DAKOTA** 94 agencies; population 625,681	1,493	1,017	78	136	262
GEORGIA 518 agencies; population 7,692,407	30,029	18,433	2,661	2,993	5,942	**OHIO** 518 agencies; population 10,680,532	32,495	20,216	2,532	3,862	5,885
HAWAII 4 agencies; population 1,224,398	3,530	2,495	263	214	558	**OKLAHOMA** 300 agencies; population 3,460,097	10,561	6,555	525	1,486	1,995
IDAHO 115 agencies; population 1,305,535	3,480	2,246	136	173	925	**OREGON** 167 agencies; population 3,446,968	7,780	5,048	536	500	1,696
ILLINOIS 747 agencies; population 12,398,330	50,371	31,261	5,193	6,548	7,369	**PENNSYLVANIA** 611 agencies; population 7,309,014	25,244	18,705	2,564	1,490	2,485
INDIANA 247 agencies; population 5,897,947	16,694	9,609	758	2,883	3,444	**RHODE ISLAND** 43 agencies; population 1,052,814	3,070	2,286	153	289	342
IOWA 232 agencies; population 2,915,711	7,511	4,732	332	852	1,595	**SOUTH CAROLINA** 306 agencies; population 3,965,611	12,318	8,333	1,014	937	2,034
KANSAS 339 agencies; population 2,618,694	9,905	6,178	516	1,254	1,957	**SOUTH DAKOTA** 125 agencies; population 756,600	1,989	1,181	67	322	419
KENTUCKY 384 agencies; population 4,025,105	9,968	7,022	629	862	1,455	**TENNESSEE** 417 agencies; population 5,607,075	22,994	13,334	1,452	3,291	4,917
LOUISIANA 210 agencies; population 4,388,774	20,900	13,333	3,022	1,405	3,140	**TEXAS** 932 agencies; population 21,037,517	75,359	42,246	4,778	12,030	16,305
MAINE 136 agencies; population 1,280,138	2,859	2,059	126	288	386	**UTAH** 125 agencies; population 2,269,233	6,835	4,225	389	937	1,284
MARYLAND 123 agencies; population 5,211,141	19,143	12,638	2,012	1,702	2,791	**VERMONT** 56 agencies; population 362,470	1,238	864	65	96	213
MASSACHUSETTS 328 agencies; population 6,324,198	20,043	15,398	1,306	1,442	1,897	**VIRGINIA** 278 agencies; population 7,186,387	21,074	14,668	1,753	1,305	3,348
MICHIGAN 550 agencies; population 9,949,888	28,596	18,589	2,898	2,737	4,372	**WASHINGTON** 246 agencies; population 5,968,232	14,000	8,846	947	1,410	2,797
MINNESOTA 282 agencies; population 4,802,774	12,277	7,154	861	1,691	2,571	**WEST VIRGINIA** 344 agencies; population 1,792,619	4,003	2,992	100	371	540
MISSISSIPPI 183 agencies; population 2,380,448	8,255	4,717	377	1,274	1,887	**WISCONSIN** 356 agencies; population 5,153,905	16,589	10,377	1,594	1,581	3,037
						WYOMING 66 agencies; population 492,634	2,006	1,158	81	234	533

Table 78

Full-time Law Enforcement Employees as of October 31, 2001
by City by State

City by state	Total police employees	Total officers	Total civilians	City by state	Total police employees	Total officers	Total civilians
ALABAMA				**ALABAMA—Continued**			
Abbeville	17	10	7	Decatur	139	121	18
Adamsville	25	14	11	Demopolis	27	23	4
Addison	3	3	0	Dora	6	3	3
Alabaster	51	41	10	Dothan	222	153	69
Albertville	48	35	13	Dozier	1	1	0
Alexander City	61	45	16	East Brewton	8	6	2
Aliceville	11	7	4	Eclectic	9	5	4
Andalusia	36	27	9	Elba	28	19	9
Anniston	131	99	32	Elberta	4	4	0
Arab	33	24	9	Enterprise	63	48	15
Ardmore	10	6	4	Eufaula	51	35	16
Argo	3	3	0	Eutaw	11	7	4
Ariton	5	2	3	Evergreen	21	15	6
Ashford	10	6	4	Fairfield	54	39	15
Ashland	12	8	4	Fairhope	26	24	2
Ashville	4	4	0	Falkville	4	4	0
Athens	51	40	11	Fayette	12	12	0
Atmore	31	23	8	Flomaton	14	9	5
Attalla	26	21	5	Florala	9	5	4
Auburn	77	66	11	Florence	119	94	25
Baker Hill	2	2	0	Foley	57	35	22
Bay Minette	27	20	7	Fort Payne	39	35	4
Bayou La Batre	25	19	6	Fultondale	23	18	5
Bear Creek	3	3	0	Gadsden	135	104	31
Berry	3	3	0	Gantt	2	2	0
Bessemer	140	120	20	Gardendale	32	25	7
Birmingham	1,150	857	293	Geneva	16	11	5
Blountsville	8	8	0	Glencoe	9	6	3
Boaz	31	21	10	Goodwater	10	5	5
Brantley	5	3	2	Gordo	1	1	0
Brent	5	5	0	Grant	3	3	0
Brewton	24	18	6	Graysville	12	8	4
Bridgeport	9	5	4	Greensboro	10	10	0
Brighton	12	6	6	Greenville	38	30	8
Brilliant	1	1	0	Grove Hill	6	6	0
Brookside	2	2	0	Gulf Shores	38	28	10
Brundidge	11	6	5	Guntersville	40	27	13
Butler	10	6	4	Gurley	4	4	0
Calera	19	15	4	Hackleburg	5	5	0
Camden	8	8	0	Haleyville	19	14	5
Camp Hill	2	2	0	Hamilton	14	13	1
Carbon Hill	10	5	5	Hanceville	12	8	4
Cedar Bluff	3	3	0	Hartford	15	9	6
Centre	10	9	1	Hartselle	35	29	6
Centreville	7	7	0	Hayneville	3	3	0
Chatom	6	6	0	Headland	12	7	5
Cherokee	4	4	0	Heflin	10	9	1
Chickasaw	23	19	4	Helena	20	15	5
Childersburg	15	11	4	Highland Lake	2	2	0
Citronelle	11	7	4	Hillsboro	2	2	0
Clanton	26	24	2	Hobson City	3	3	0
Clayton	4	4	0	Hokes Bluff	8	5	3
Cleveland	2	2	0	Hollywood	3	2	1
Clio	6	4	2	Homewood	97	68	29
Coffeeville	2	1	1	Hoover	183	133	50
Collinsville	9	5	4	Hueytown	31	26	5
Columbiana	16	11	5	Huntsville	524	360	164
Coosada	3	3	0	Hurtsboro	5	5	0
Cordova	8	5	3	Irondale	38	31	7
Cottonwood	3	3	0	Jackson	24	19	5
Courtland	4	4	0	Jacksonville	28	23	5
Creola	12	8	4	Jasper	73	50	23
Cullman	69	48	21	Jemison	5	5	0
Dadeville	11	11	0	Killen	4	4	0
Daleville	24	18	6	Kimberly	2	2	0
Daphne	63	37	26	Kinston	2	2	0
Dauphin Island	9	5	4	Lafayette	17	15	2

Table 78

Full-time Law Enforcement Employees as of October 31, 2001
by City by State—Continued

City by state	Total police employees	Total officers	Total civilians	City by state	Total police employees	Total officers	Total civilians
ALABAMA—Continued				**ALABAMA—Continued**			
Lanett	33	28	5	Red Bay	12	8	4
Leeds	28	22	6	Red Level	7	5	2
Leighton	5	5	0	Reform	5	5	0
Level Plains	7	5	2	Riverside	5	5	0
Lexington	2	2	0	Roanoke	27	22	5
Lincoln	22	17	5	Robertsdale	15	10	5
Linden	6	6	0	Rogersville	4	4	0
Lineville	11	7	4	Russellville	28	23	5
Lipscomb	8	2	6	Samson	8	4	4
Littleville	9	5	4	Saraland	55	42	13
Livingston	11	7	4	Satsuma	15	11	4
Louisville	3	3	0	Scottsboro	66	44	22
Loxley	13	7	6	Section	1	1	0
Luverne	16	12	4	Selma	109	61	48
Madison	69	50	19	Sheffield	37	32	5
Maplesville	4	4	0	Shorter	9	5	4
Marion	14	8	6	Slocomb	10	6	4
McIntosh	6	6	0	Snead	5	5	0
Midfield	21	17	4	Somerville	4	3	1
Midland City	7	4	3	Southside	13	8	5
Millbrook	28	21	7	Spanish Fort	6	6	0
Millport	2	2	0	Springville	7	7	0
Millry	3	3	0	Steele	4	4	0
Mobile	678	515	163	Stevenson	8	4	4
Monroeville	22	17	5	St. Florian	3	3	0
Montevallo	19	14	5	Sulligent	5	5	0
Montgomery	600	429	171	Sumiton	15	10	5
Moody	16	15	1	Summerdale	6	5	1
Morris	5	5	0	Sylacauga	47	38	9
Mosses	1	1	0	Sylvania	3	3	0
Moulton	11	11	0	Talladega	52	40	12
Moundville	5	4	1	Tallassee	25	19	6
Mountain Brook	62	51	11	Tarrant City	25	20	5
Mount Vernon	9	8	1	Thomasville	21	19	2
Muscle Shoals	42	33	9	Thorsby	4	4	0
Napier Field	2	2	0	Town Creek	4	4	0
New Brockton	5	5	0	Triana	3	2	1
New Hope	9	9	0	Trinity	5	5	0
Newton	3	2	1	Troy	60	46	14
Northport	71	55	16	Trussville	40	30	10
Notasulga	7	4	3	Tuscaloosa	299	232	67
Oakman	3	3	0	Tuscumbia	27	21	6
Oneonta	20	19	1	Tuskegee	42	28	14
Opelika	87	74	13	Union Springs	14	9	5
Opp	27	21	6	Uniontown	8	7	1
Orange Beach	42	31	11	Valley	35	26	9
Oxford	45	35	10	Valley Head	3	2	1
Ozark	46	40	6	Vance	3	3	0
Parrish	6	6	0	Vernon	8	8	0
Pelham	68	56	12	Vestavia Hills	52	50	2
Pell City	32	30	2	Wadley	8	4	4
Pennington	1	1	0	Warrior	15	10	5
Phenix City	93	75	18	Weaver	12	9	3
Phil Campbell	7	6	1	Wedowee	7	7	0
Pickensville	2	2	0	West Blocton	7	7	0
Piedmont	16	11	5	Wetumpka	30	22	8
Pinckard	2	2	0	Winfield	12	10	2
Pine Hill	5	5	0	York	7	4	3
Pisgah	1	1	0				
Pleasant Grove	19	14	5	**ALASKA**			
Prattville	88	78	10				
Priceville	4	4	0	Anchorage	434	313	121
Prichard	71	55	16	Bethel	20	13	7
Ragland	10	6	4	Bristol Bay Borough	9	2	7
Rainbow City	32	20	12	Cordova	10	5	5
Rainsville	14	10	4	Craig	10	5	5
Ranburne	2	2	0	Dillingham	20	7	13

Table 78

Full-time Law Enforcement Employees as of October 31, 2001
by City by State—Continued

City by state	Total police employees	Total officers	Total civilians	City by state	Total police employees	Total officers	Total civilians
ALASKA—Continued				**ARIZONA—Continued**			
Emmonak	5	5	0	Mammoth	10	5	5
Fairbanks	60	44	16	Marana	64	49	15
Haines	9	4	5	Mesa	1,166	741	425
Homer	17	8	9	Miami	10	8	2
Hoonah	6	4	2	Nogales	83	64	19
Juneau	78	43	35	Oro Valley	93	68	25
Kake	5	2	3	Page	35	20	15
Kenai	24	15	9	Paradise Valley	44	34	10
Ketchikan	35	25	10	Parker	13	10	3
Klawock	3	3	0	Patagonia	3	3	0
Kodiak	33	16	17	Payson	36	26	10
Kotzebue	9	8	1	Peoria	153	107	46
Nenana	2	2	0	Phoenix	3,593	2,675	918
Nome	15	9	6	Pima	3	3	0
North Pole	16	11	5	Pinetop-Lakeside	26	17	9
North Slope Borough	73	47	26	Prescott	86	54	32
Palmer	26	11	15	Prescott Valley	52	40	12
Petersburg	13	8	5	Quartzsite	9	8	1
Sand Point	6	4	2	Safford	21	18	3
Seldovia	2	2	0	Sahuarita	12	10	2
Seward	21	8	13	San Luis	40	31	9
Sitka	31	21	10	Scottsdale	578	348	230
Skagway	7	4	3	Sedona	39	29	10
Soldotna	14	13	1	Show Low	35	25	10
St. Paul	10	5	5	Sierra Vista	78	51	27
Togiak	3	3	0	Snowflake-Taylor	18	12	6
Unalaska	32	15	17	Somerton	22	17	5
Valdez	22	11	11	South Tucson	32	22	10
Wasilla	16	15	1	Springerville	9	7	2
Whittier	3	3	0	St. Johns	11	8	3
Wrangell	11	6	5	Superior	17	10	7
				Surprise	74	59	15
ARIZONA				Tempe	485	327	158
				Thatcher	11	10	1
Apache Junction	76	49	27	Tolleson	27	20	7
Avondale	77	60	17	Tombstone	9	8	1
Benson	21	14	7	Tucson	1,316	979	337
Bisbee	23	17	6	Wellton	4	4	0
Buckeye	30	20	10	Wickenburg	19	12	7
Bullhead City	122	78	44	Willcox	18	10	8
Camp Verde	29	19	10	Williams	17	9	8
Casa Grande	78	55	23	Winslow	34	25	9
Chandler	420	282	138	Youngtown	9	8	1
Chino Valley	30	19	11	Yuma	198	137	61
Clarkdale	9	7	2				
Clifton	9	6	3	**ARKANSAS**			
Colorado City	5	5	0				
Coolidge	38	29	9	Alma	12	7	5
Cottonwood	39	25	14	Arkadelphia	30	23	7
Douglas	48	37	11	Ashdown	11	10	1
Eagar	11	9	2	Atkins	7	6	1
El Mirage	47	39	8	Bald Knob	9	5	4
Eloy	42	26	16	Barling	11	10	1
Flagstaff	133	87	46	Beebe	16	10	6
Florence	26	18	8	Benton	64	54	10
Fredonia	3	3	0	Bentonville	62	40	22
Gilbert	164	113	51	Berryville	9	8	1
Glendale	448	322	126	Blytheville	80	60	20
Globe	33	24	9	Booneville	11	7	4
Goodyear	54	40	14	Brinkley	14	11	3
Hayden	7	5	2	Bryant	31	24	7
Holbrook	22	17	5	Bull Shoals	3	3	0
Huachuca City	10	4	6	Cabot	41	30	11
Jerome	5	5	0	Camden	39	26	13
Kearny	10	5	5	Carlisle	10	6	4
Kingman	68	46	22	Cherokee Village	7	6	1
Lake Havasu City	96	68	28	Clarksville	18	14	4

Table 78

Full-time Law Enforcement Employees as of October 31, 2001
by City by State—Continued

City by state	Total police employees	Total officers	Total civilians	City by state	Total police employees	Total officers	Total civilians
ARKANSAS—Continued				**ARKANSAS—Continued**			
Conway	113	93	20	Pine Bluff	166	141	25
Corning	12	8	4	Pocahontas	15	14	1
Crossett	25	15	10	Prairie Grove	7	6	1
Danville	6	6	0	Prescott	9	8	1
Dardanelle	12	8	4	Rogers	102	75	27
DeQueen	14	11	3	Russellville	66	54	12
Dermott	13	6	7	Searcy	49	38	11
Des Arc	4	4	0	Sheridan	26	11	15
De Witt	13	8	5	Sherwood	78	55	23
Dumas	25	10	15	Siloam Springs	47	30	17
Earle	13	8	5	Smackover	5	4	1
El Dorado	67	50	17	Springdale	139	97	42
England	11	6	5	Star City	6	5	1
Eudora	12	7	5	Stuttgart	29	19	10
Eureka Springs	16	9	7	Texarkana	116	79	37
Farmington	7	7	0	Trumann	20	15	5
Fayetteville	141	99	42	Tuckerman	6	5	1
Flippin	5	4	1	Van Buren	49	36	13
Fordyce	12	9	3	Waldron	7	7	0
Forrest City	42	32	10	Walnut Ridge	12	8	4
Fort Smith	192	151	41	Ward	8	6	2
Greenbrier	17	16	1	Warren	20	13	7
Green Forest	7	5	2	West Fork	5	5	0
Greenland	4	4	0	West Helena	31	23	8
Greenwood	16	15	1	West Memphis	90	77	13
Gurdon	5	4	1	White Hall	12	11	1
Hamburg	7	6	1	Wynne	19	17	2
Harrisburg	5	4	1				
Harrison	50	28	22	**CALIFORNIA**			
Hazen	8	4	4				
Heber Springs	21	13	8	Adelanto	26	19	7
Helena	21	16	5	Alameda	148	101	47
Hermitage	4	4	0	Albany	32	28	4
Hope	32	22	10	Alhambra	128	82	46
Horseshoe Bend	7	6	1	Alturas	11	10	1
Hot Springs	128	98	30	Anaheim	553	401	152
Hoxie	8	4	4	Anderson	26	15	11
Jacksonville	78	66	12	Angels Camp	8	7	1
Jonesboro	121	112	9	Antioch	137	103	34
Lake Village	15	9	6	Arcadia	106	71	35
Lincoln	5	5	0	Arcata	34	23	11
Little Rock	701	558	143	Arroyo Grande	36	26	10
Lonoke	17	11	6	Arvin	20	13	7
Lowell	12	11	1	Atascadero	39	30	9
Magnolia	26	21	5	Atherton	27	21	6
Malvern	24	20	4	Atwater	40	30	10
Marianna	21	16	5	Auburn	35	22	13
Marion	18	15	3	Azusa	76	57	19
Marked Tree	12	8	4	Bakersfield	422	301	121
Maumelle	24	16	8	Baldwin Park	90	65	25
Mayflower	5	4	1	Banning	46	34	12
McGehee	18	10	8	Barstow	56	36	20
Mena	18	15	3	Bear Valley	11	7	4
Monticello	25	20	5	Beaumont	27	20	7
Morrilton	28	17	11	Bell	47	38	9
Mountain Home	38	30	8	Bell Gardens	68	50	18
Mountain View	8	7	1	Belmont	47	30	17
Mulberry	3	3	0	Belvedere	8	7	1
Nashville	13	12	1	Benicia	49	34	15
Newport	21	15	6	Berkeley	287	193	94
North Little Rock	233	191	42	Beverly Hills	195	131	64
Osceola	43	23	20	Bishop	21	14	7
Ozark	8	7	1	Blue Lake	11	8	3
Paragould	37	32	5	Blythe	35	24	11
Paris	13	8	5	Brawley	40	30	10
Piggott	8	8	0	Brea	137	107	30

Table 78

Full-time Law Enforcement Employees as of October 31, 2001
by City by State—Continued

City by state	Total police employees	Total officers	Total civilians	City by state	Total police employees	Total officers	Total civilians
CALIFORNIA—Continued				**CALIFORNIA—Continued**			
Brentwood	46	35	11	Folsom	70	51	19
Brisbane	19	17	2	Fontana	188	134	54
Broadmoor	10	9	1	Fort Bragg	19	15	4
Buena Park	149	94	55	Fortuna	21	15	6
Burbank	277	159	118	Foster City	60	42	18
Burlingame	67	48	19	Fountain Valley	76	56	20
Calexico	55	37	18	Fowler	7	6	1
California City	20	14	6	Fremont	321	208	113
Calipatria	5	5	0	Fresno	1,034	693	341
Calistoga	15	11	4	Fullerton	213	147	66
Campbell	60	42	18	Galt	31	21	10
Capitola	31	20	11	Gardena	101	81	20
Carlsbad	141	102	39	Garden Grove	236	165	71
Carmel	22	13	9	Gilroy	103	58	45
Cathedral City	78	49	29	Glendale	341	231	110
Ceres	57	42	15	Glendora	90	59	31
Chico	121	75	46	Gonzales	14	12	2
Chino	119	86	33	Grass Valley	28	21	7
Chowchilla	24	17	7	Greenfield	19	16	3
Chula Vista	305	210	95	Gridley	22	16	6
Claremont	60	40	20	Grover Beach	26	19	7
Clayton	13	11	2	Guadalupe	14	12	2
Clearlake	30	23	7	Gustine	10	9	1
Cloverdale	19	12	7	Half Moon Bay	17	12	5
Clovis	131	82	49	Hanford	58	41	17
Coalinga	25	19	6	Hawthorne	134	92	42
Colma	21	16	5	Hayward	312	195	117
Colton	84	62	22	Healdsburg	27	16	11
Colusa	9	8	1	Hemet	84	62	22
Concord	220	158	62	Hercules	23	21	2
Corcoran	28	19	9	Hermosa Beach	58	37	21
Corning	22	14	8	Hillsborough	34	26	8
Corona	229	148	81	Hollister	39	32	7
Coronado	60	43	17	Holtville	11	7	4
Costa Mesa	211	149	62	Hughson	5	4	1
Cotati	19	12	7	Huntington Beach	365	228	137
Covina	85	56	29	Huntington Park	111	73	38
Crescent City	14	13	1	Huron	18	10	8
Culver City	167	127	40	Imperial	13	12	1
Cypress	63	55	8	Indio	70	49	21
Daly City	153	117	36	Inglewood	255	197	58
Davis	80	52	28	Ione	7	6	1
Delano	53	33	20	Irvine	219	153	66
Del Rey Oaks	6	6	0	Irwindale	27	21	6
Dinuba	30	23	7	Isleton	4	4	0
Dixon	28	24	4	Jackson	13	10	3
Dos Palos	9	9	0	Kensington	10	10	0
Downey	155	108	47	Kerman	20	20	0
Dublin	52	45	7	King City	20	16	4
East Palo Alto	55	47	8	Kingsburg	20	15	5
El Cajon	216	141	75	Laguna Beach	83	50	33
El Centro	67	47	20	La Habra	106	67	39
El Cerrito	42	34	8	Lakeport	16	14	2
El Monte	198	145	53	Lake Shastina	5	4	1
El Segundo	94	62	32	La Mesa	79	57	22
Emeryville	55	37	18	La Palma	35	26	9
Escalon	12	10	2	La Verne	64	47	17
Escondido	221	154	67	Lemoore	35	28	7
Etna	2	2	0	Lincoln	24	17	7
Eureka	72	46	26	Lindsay	28	18	10
Exeter	17	15	2	Livermore	138	88	50
Fairfax	17	12	5	Livingston	23	18	5
Fairfield	165	107	58	Lodi	117	78	39
Farmersville	15	13	2	Lompoc	67	48	19
Ferndale	4	4	0	Long Beach	1,343	859	484
Firebaugh	17	12	5	Los Alamitos	28	25	3

Table 78

Full-time Law Enforcement Employees as of October 31, 2001

by City by State—Continued

City by state	Total police employees	Total officers	Total civilians	City by state	Total police employees	Total officers	Total civilians
CALIFORNIA—Continued				**CALIFORNIA—Continued**			
Los Altos	44	28	16	Redlands	139	77	62
Los Angeles	11,979	8,943	3,036	Redondo Beach	134	107	27
Los Banos	47	31	16	Redwood City	139	99	40
Los Gatos	74	46	28	Reedley	42	27	15
Madera	66	51	15	Rialto	140	98	42
Mammoth Lakes	22	18	4	Richmond	261	188	73
Manhattan Beach	94	59	35	Ridgecrest	43	29	14
Manteca	80	61	19	Rio Dell	7	7	0
Marina	38	31	7	Rio Vista	14	12	2
Martinez	50	37	13	Ripon	23	15	8
Marysville	37	21	16	Riverbank	17	14	3
Maywood	38	28	10	Riverside	497	346	151
Menlo Park	74	53	21	Rocklin	59	40	19
Merced	114	80	34	Rohnert Park	100	64	36
Millbrae	44	33	11	Roseville	146	88	58
Mill Valley	26	22	4	Ross	9	8	1
Milpitas	115	89	26	Sacramento	976	621	355
Modesto	366	258	108	Salinas	207	151	56
Monrovia	86	63	23	San Anselmo	25	18	7
Montclair	76	52	24	San Bernardino	422	279	143
Montebello	128	91	37	San Bruno	69	51	18
Monterey	80	58	22	San Carlos	51	35	16
Monterey Park	119	82	37	Sand City	12	10	2
Moraga	13	12	1	San Diego	2,914	2,154	760
Morgan Hill	46	31	15	San Fernando	70	39	31
Morro Bay	27	20	7	San Francisco	2,629	2,243	386
Mountain View	133	94	39	San Gabriel	69	55	14
Mount Shasta	16	9	7	Sanger	33	23	10
Murrieta	54	38	16	San Jacinto	34	24	10
Napa	127	78	49	San Jose	1,813	1,387	426
National City	121	86	35	San Leandro	129	88	41
Nevada City	10	9	1	San Luis Obispo	89	61	28
Newark	77	52	25	San Marino	29	24	5
Newman	14	12	2	San Mateo	149	105	44
Newport Beach	228	145	83	San Pablo	57	46	11
Novato	79	58	21	San Rafael	102	69	33
Oakdale	34	26	8	Santa Ana	687	374	313
Oakland	1,175	738	437	Santa Barbara	223	146	77
Oceanside	247	166	81	Santa Clara	202	152	50
Ontario	325	222	103	Santa Cruz	123	91	32
Orange	239	144	95	Santa Maria	130	92	38
Orland	10	9	1	Santa Monica	385	201	184
Oroville	24	24	0	Santa Paula	41	30	11
Oxnard	331	205	126	Santa Rosa	261	176	85
Pacifica	52	37	15	Sausalito	26	21	5
Pacific Grove	39	30	9	Scotts Valley	31	22	9
Palm Springs	145	88	57	Seal Beach	47	37	10
Palo Alto	166	90	76	Seaside	45	37	8
Palos Verdes Estates	36	24	12	Sebastopol	23	16	7
Paradise	33	24	9	Selma	41	28	13
Parlier	14	12	2	Shafter	24	18	6
Pasadena	347	235	112	Sierra Madre	24	24	0
Paso Robles	42	34	8	Signal Hill	43	31	12
Petaluma	95	65	30	Simi Valley	181	122	59
Piedmont	28	20	8	Soledad	16	15	1
Pinole	34	24	10	Sonoma	24	16	8
Pismo Beach	29	21	8	Sonora	18	14	4
Pittsburg	93	73	20	South Gate	122	87	35
Placentia	73	58	15	South Lake Tahoe	69	49	20
Placerville	26	16	10	South Pasadena	46	35	11
Pleasant Hill	64	42	22	South San Francisco	115	79	36
Pleasanton	113	80	33	Stallion Springs	4	4	0
Pomona	286	164	122	St. Helena	18	13	5
Porterville	68	45	23	Stockton	553	375	178
Port Hueneme	30	23	7	Suisun City	38	28	10
Red Bluff	46	27	19	Sunnyvale	300	238	62
Redding	158	109	49	Susanville	23	19	4

Table 78

Full-time Law Enforcement Employees as of October 31, 2001
by City by State—Continued

City by state	Total police employees	Total officers	Total civilians	City by state	Total police employees	Total officers	Total civilians
CALIFORNIA—Continued				**COLORADO—Continued**			
Sutter Creek	8	7	1	Colorado Springs	858	593	265
Taft	19	12	7	Columbine Valley	3	3	0
Tiburon	18	15	3	Commerce City	80	57	23
Torrance	322	237	85	Cortez	51	28	23
Tracy	107	66	41	Craig	27	22	5
Tulare	73	49	24	Crested Butte	8	6	2
Tulelake	3	3	0	Cripple Creek	28	16	12
Turlock	100	63	37	Dacono	7	6	1
Tustin	137	91	46	De Beque	1	1	0
Twin Cities	43	33	10	Del Norte	6	5	1
Ukiah	36	27	9	Delta	20	15	5
Union City	99	73	26	Denver	1,850	1,514	336
Upland	113	74	39	Dillon	9	7	2
Vacaville	166	105	61	Dinosaur	1	1	0
Vallejo	215	151	64	Durango	59	49	10
Ventura	184	128	56	Eagle	9	7	2
Vernon	74	57	17	Eaton	8	7	1
Visalia	162	113	49	Edgewater	20	16	4
Walnut Creek	112	80	32	Elizabeth	9	6	3
Watsonville	80	60	20	Empire	1	1	0
Weed	15	9	6	Englewood	117	78	39
West Covina	155	115	40	Erie	18	14	4
Westminster	138	96	42	Estes Park	27	17	10
Westmorland	5	5	0	Evans	24	21	3
West Sacramento	84	60	24	Fairplay	2	2	0
Wheatland	7	7	0	Federal Heights	34	23	11
Whittier	200	133	67	Firestone	9	7	2
Williams	9	8	1	Florence	14	9	5
Willits	22	14	8	Fort Collins	220	148	72
Willows	9	8	1	Fort Lupton	20	14	6
Winters	9	9	0	Fort Morgan	37	27	10
Woodlake	15	13	2	Fountain	44	31	13
Woodland	78	59	19	Fowler	1	1	0
Yreka	24	16	8	Frederick	12	9	3
Yuba City	71	45	26	Frisco	13	11	2
				Fruita	13	10	3
COLORADO				Georgetown	3	3	0
				Gilcrest	2	2	0
Alamosa	30	25	5	Glendale	37	27	10
Alma	1	1	0	Glenwood Springs	34	26	8
Antonito	3	3	0	Golden	53	36	17
Arvada	202	134	68	Granada	1	1	0
Aspen	34	25	9	Grand Junction	141	82	59
Ault	5	5	0	Greeley	194	113	81
Aurora	776	517	259	Green Mountain Falls	2	2	0
Avon	19	17	2	Greenwood Village	77	56	21
Basalt	9	8	1	Gunnison	18	15	3
Bayfield	4	4	0	Haxtun	3	3	0
Berthoud	8	7	1	Hayden	4	4	0
Black Hawk	35	22	13	Holyoke	3	3	0
Blue River	1	1	0	Hotchkiss	3	3	0
Boulder	268	170	98	Hugo	3	3	0
Bow Mar	2	2	0	Idaho Springs	8	7	1
Breckenridge	22	15	7	Ignacio	6	6	0
Brighton	54	42	12	Johnstown	11	10	1
Broomfield	160	92	68	Kersey	3	3	0
Brush	13	12	1	Kremmling	5	5	0
Buena Vista	9	7	2	Lafayette	36	29	7
Burlington	9	8	1	La Jara	4	4	0
Calhan	2	2	0	La Junta	20	17	3
Canon City	46	30	16	Lakeside	5	5	0
Carbondale	18	15	3	Lakewood	382	257	125
Castle Rock	51	37	14	Lamar	33	20	13
Cedaredge	6	4	2	La Salle	5	5	0
Center	6	5	1	Las Animas	9	7	2
Central City	4	4	0	La Veta	3	2	1
Cherry Hills Village	22	21	1	Leadville	11	9	2

Table 78

Full-time Law Enforcement Employees as of October 31, 2001
by City by State—Continued

City by state	Total police employees	Total officers	Total civilians	City by state	Total police employees	Total officers	Total civilians
COLORADO—Continued				**CONNECTICUT—Continued**			
Limon	6	5	1	Bloomfield	59	50	9
Littleton	95	69	26	Branford	60	46	14
Lochbuie	4	4	0	Bridgeport	535	425	110
Log Lane Village	3	3	0	Bristol	121	112	9
Longmont	137	103	34	Brookfield	37	31	6
Louisville	38	33	5	Canton	19	14	5
Loveland	118	78	40	Cheshire	56	47	9
Mancos	2	2	0	Clinton	26	23	3
Manitou Springs	15	14	1	Coventry	18	13	5
Manzanola	1	1	0	Cromwell	31	24	7
Meeker	5	4	1	Danbury	149	143	6
Milliken	9	8	1	Darien	53	47	6
Minturn	3	3	0	Derby	27	27	0
Monte Vista	16	11	5	East Hampton	17	15	2
Montrose	48	31	17	East Hartford	163	130	33
Monument	10	10	0	East Haven	57	53	4
Morrison	2	1	1	Easton	22	15	7
Mountain View	6	5	1	East Windsor	27	20	7
Mount Crested Butte	7	6	1	Enfield	115	96	19
Nederland	5	4	1	Fairfield	113	107	6
New Castle	6	5	1	Farmington	60	45	15
Northglenn	72	56	16	Glastonbury	71	55	16
Oak Creek	3	3	0	Granby	18	13	5
Olathe	4	4	0	Greenwich	179	157	22
Ouray	4	4	0	Groton	34	29	5
Pagosa Springs	7	7	0	Groton Long Point	5	5	0
Palisade	8	6	2	Groton Town	71	67	4
Palmer Lake	4	4	0	Guilford	38	33	5
Paonia	4	4	0	Hamden	125	103	22
Parachute	6	5	1	Hartford	538	427	111
Parker	51	39	12	Madison	36	29	7
Platteville	6	6	0	Manchester	146	117	29
Pueblo	245	189	56	Meriden	139	128	11
Rangely	11	7	4	Middlebury	18	12	6
Ridgway	2	2	0	Middletown	116	100	16
Rifle	18	15	3	Milford	121	103	18
Rocky Ford	11	9	2	Monroe	47	38	9
Salida	19	18	1	Naugatuck	65	54	11
Sheridan	26	21	5	New Britain	159	145	14
Silt	7	6	1	New Canaan	48	44	4
Silverthorne	24	18	6	New Haven	583	442	141
Simla	1	1	0	Newington	55	43	12
Snowmass Village	12	9	3	New London	101	86	15
Springfield	3	3	0	New Milford	64	48	16
Steamboat Springs	31	20	11	Newtown	52	42	10
Sterling	36	21	15	North Branford	26	21	5
Stratton	2	2	0	North Haven	55	46	9
Telluride	13	9	4	Norwalk	201	176	25
Thornton	150	124	26	Norwich	100	84	16
Trinidad	24	18	6	Old Saybrook	29	27	2
Vail	56	26	30	Orange	51	40	11
Victor	3	3	0	Plainfield	22	19	3
Walsenburg	21	13	8	Plainville	38	32	6
Westminster	215	152	63	Plymouth	23	19	4
Wheat Ridge	92	66	26	Portland	11	10	1
Wiggins	2	2	0	Putnam	19	15	4
Windsor	16	14	2	Ridgefield	44	39	5
Woodland Park	30	21	9	Rocky Hill	40	31	9
Wray	7	6	1	Seymour	36	34	2
Yuma	9	7	2	Shelton	57	50	7
				Simsbury	43	34	9
CONNECTICUT				Southington	73	60	13
				South Windsor	47	39	8
Ansonia	50	44	6	Stamford	373	294	79
Avon	38	31	7	Stonington	42	33	9
Berlin	50	39	11	Stratford	107	103	4
Bethel	42	32	10	Suffield	21	16	5

Table 78

Full-time Law Enforcement Employees as of October 31, 2001
by City by State—Continued

City by state	Total police employees	Total officers	Total civilians	City by state	Total police employees	Total officers	Total civilians
CONNECTICUT—Continued				**FLORIDA—Continued**			
Thomaston	16	13	3	Apopka	79	70	9
Torrington	81	72	9	Arcadia	30	21	9
Trumbull	76	65	11	Astatula	3	3	0
Vernon	65	51	14	Atlantic Beach	32	26	6
Wallingford	91	69	22	Atlantis	16	11	5
Waterbury	371	326	45	Auburndale	38	30	8
Waterford	50	43	7	Aventura	92	63	29
Watertown	46	36	10	Avon Park	40	25	15
West Hartford	146	125	21	Baldwin	26	18	8
West Haven	136	119	17	Bal Harbour Village	30	23	7
Weston	15	14	1	Bartow	76	51	25
Westport	80	71	9	Bay Harbor Island	30	24	6
Wethersfield	53	43	10	Belleair	16	11	5
Willimantic	43	38	5	Belleair Beach	6	6	0
Wilton	46	44	2	Belle Glade	54	44	10
Winchester	28	23	5	Belleview	16	14	2
Windsor	63	54	9	Biscayne Park	10	9	1
Windsor Locks	31	24	7	Blountstown	12	7	5
Wolcott	32	24	8	Boca Raton	214	149	65
Woodbridge	32	24	8	Bonifay	9	5	4
				Bowling Green	6	6	0
DELAWARE				Boynton Beach	179	130	49
				Bradenton	127	102	25
Bethany Beach	10	10	0	Bradenton Beach	10	10	0
Blades	3	3	0	Brooksville	28	19	9
Bridgeville	3	3	0	Bunnell	12	10	2
Camden	7	6	1	Cape Coral	230	148	82
Cheswold	1	1	0	Carrabelle	3	3	0
Clayton	4	4	0	Casselberry	82	54	28
Dagsboro	2	2	0	Cedar Grove	6	5	1
Delaware City	4	3	1	Cedar Key	3	3	0
Delmar	11	10	1	Center Hill	3	3	0
Dewey Beach	7	7	0	Chattahoochee	11	10	1
Dover	112	81	31	Chiefland	13	10	3
Ellendale	2	2	0	Chipley	10	9	1
Elsmere	10	9	1	Clearwater	371	255	116
Felton	3	3	0	Clermont	39	29	10
Fenwick Island	7	6	1	Clewiston	25	16	9
Frederica	2	2	0	Cocoa	89	65	24
Georgetown	15	13	2	Cocoa Beach	50	34	16
Greenwood	5	4	1	Coconut Creek	111	79	32
Harrington	12	11	1	Cooper City	77	58	19
Laurel	10	9	1	Coral Gables	232	165	67
Lewes	14	13	1	Coral Springs	274	183	91
Milford	34	26	8	Cottondale	2	2	0
Millsboro	11	10	1	Crescent City	10	9	1
Milton	4	4	0	Crestview	42	32	10
Newark	73	56	17	Cross City	5	5	0
New Castle	16	15	1	Crystal River	25	22	3
Newport	9	7	2	Dade City	33	23	10
Ocean View	6	5	1	Dania	68	58	10
Rehoboth Beach	22	15	7	Davenport	7	6	1
Seaford	28	22	6	Davie	210	160	50
Selbyville	7	7	0	Daytona Beach	328	246	82
Smyrna	22	16	6	Daytona Beach Shores	40	30	10
South Bethany	6	6	0	Deerfield Beach	113	98	15
Wilmington	335	284	51	De Funiak Springs	16	14	2
Wyoming	4	3	1	Deland	80	58	22
				Delray Beach	210	137	73
DISTRICT OF COLUMBIA				Dundee	18	13	5
				Dunnellon	10	8	2
Washington	4,288	3,611	677	Eagle Lake	5	5	0
				Eatonville	15	13	2
FLORIDA				Edgewater	47	33	14
Alachua	22	16	6	Edgewood	10	9	1
Altamonte Springs	138	100	38	El Portal	8	8	0
Apalachicola	8	7	1	Eustis	52	41	11

Table 78

Full-time Law Enforcement Employees as of October 31, 2001
by City by State—Continued

City by state	Total police employees	Total officers	Total civilians	City by state	Total police employees	Total officers	Total civilians
FLORIDA—Continued				**FLORIDA—Continued**			
Fellsmere	9	8	1	Lake Worth	126	86	40
Fernandina Beach	43	35	8	Lantana	35	27	8
Flagler Beach	12	10	2	Largo	172	116	56
Florida City	40	26	14	Lauderdale Lakes	61	54	7
Fort Lauderdale	733	483	250	Lauderhill	104	84	20
Fort Meade	21	14	7	Leesburg	84	62	22
Fort Myers	247	150	97	Lighthouse Point	41	32	9
Fort Pierce	146	106	40	Live Oak	21	17	4
Fort Walton Beach	69	55	14	Longboat Key	29	19	10
Frostproof	15	10	5	Longwood	40	36	4
Fruitland Park	10	9	1	Lynn Haven	30	24	6
Gainesville	295	239	56	Madison	14	13	1
Golden Beach	17	16	1	Maitland	48	40	8
Graceville	10	7	3	Manalapan	14	10	4
Greenacres City	62	40	22	Mangonia Park	18	17	1
Green Cove Springs	22	17	5	Marco Island	26	24	2
Greensboro	1	1	0	Margate	170	105	65
Greenville	2	2	0	Marianna	22	15	7
Gretna	6	4	2	Mascotte	10	9	1
Groveland	14	9	5	Medley	42	34	8
Gulf Breeze	23	17	6	Melbourne	208	156	52
Gulfport	40	30	10	Melbourne Beach	10	9	1
Gulf Stream	10	10	0	Melbourne Village	6	6	0
Haines City	58	42	16	Mexico Beach	6	5	1
Hallandale	120	88	32	Miami	1,409	1,104	305
Hampton	2	2	0	Miami Beach	525	381	144
Havana	13	9	4	Miami Shores	41	32	9
Hialeah	436	325	111	Miami Springs	55	40	15
Hialeah Gardens	46	35	11	Midway	3	3	0
Highland Beach	13	12	1	Milton	27	19	8
High Springs	15	9	6	Miramar	182	135	47
Hillsboro Beach	16	14	2	Monticello	14	10	4
Holly Hill	34	26	8	Mount Dora	46	31	15
Hollywood	486	330	156	Mulberry	16	11	5
Holmes Beach	19	12	7	Naples	111	72	39
Homestead	102	75	27	Neptune Beach	25	18	7
Howey-in-the-Hills	4	4	0	New Port Richey	38	31	7
Indialantic	17	11	6	New Smyrna Beach	73	53	20
Indian Creek Village	20	16	4	Niceville	24	19	5
Indian Harbour Beach	23	16	7	North Bay Village	31	24	7
Indian River Shores	22	21	1	North Miami	145	113	32
Indian Shores	11	10	1	North Miami Beach	148	102	46
Inglis	4	4	0	North Palm Beach	41	31	10
Interlachen	3	3	0	North Port	54	38	16
Inverness	12	11	1	Oak Hill	5	5	0
Jacksonville	2,576	1,552	1,024	Oakland	8	7	1
Jacksonville Beach	73	54	19	Ocala	238	154	84
Jasper	7	7	0	Ocean Ridge	18	13	5
Jennings	2	2	0	Ocoee	72	66	6
Juno Beach	14	12	2	Okeechobee	25	19	6
Jupiter	132	96	36	Opa Locka	30	28	2
Jupiter Inlet Colony	5	5	0	Orange City	26	16	10
Jupiter Island	21	17	4	Orange Park	26	21	5
Kenneth City	16	14	2	Orlando	945	676	269
Key Biscayne	36	26	10	Ormond Beach	93	64	29
Key West	110	82	28	Oviedo	66	52	14
Kissimmee	160	100	60	Pahokee	22	18	4
Lady Lake	34	23	11	Palatka	42	35	7
Lake Alfred	15	11	4	Palm Bay	192	125	67
Lake City	50	38	12	Palm Beach	127	75	52
Lake Clarke Shores	11	10	1	Palm Beach Gardens	114	87	27
Lake Hamilton	7	6	1	Palm Beach Shores	14	9	5
Lake Helen	7	7	0	Palmetto	47	33	14
Lakeland	340	227	113	Palm Springs	39	32	7
Lake Mary	41	30	11	Panama City	131	95	36
Lake Placid	11	8	3	Panama City Beach	63	47	16
Lake Wales	59	44	15	Parker	8	7	1

Table 78

Full-time Law Enforcement Employees as of October 31, 2001
by City by State—Continued

City by state	Total police employees	Total officers	Total civilians	City by state	Total police employees	Total officers	Total civilians
FLORIDA—Continued				**FLORIDA—Continued**			
Parkland	32	30	2	West Miami	21	15	6
Pembroke Park	65	58	7	Weston	70	47	23
Pembroke Pines	268	211	57	West Palm Beach	367	267	100
Pensacola	220	162	58	Wildwood	20	14	6
Perry	24	22	2	Williston	20	12	8
Pinellas Park	121	91	30	Wilton Manors	39	30	9
Plantation	296	186	110	Windermere	10	9	1
Plant City	84	63	21	Winter Garden	48	35	13
Pompano Beach	297	214	83	Winter Haven	113	80	33
Ponce Inlet	17	11	6	Winter Park	106	81	25
Port Orange	98	74	24	Winter Springs	71	52	19
Port Richey	17	12	5	Zephyrhills	42	29	13
Port St. Joe	14	12	2	Zolfo Springs	4	4	0
Port St. Lucie	192	137	55				
Punta Gorda	47	33	14	**GEORGIA**			
Quincy	40	30	10				
Riviera Beach	137	96	41	Acworth	41	24	17
Rockledge	58	42	16	Adairsville	15	10	5
Royal Palm Beach	56	43	13	Adel	22	19	3
Sanford	135	111	24	Alapaha	2	2	0
Sanibel	31	19	12	Albany	229	201	28
Sarasota	265	199	66	Alma	20	14	6
Satellite Beach	25	18	7	Alpharetta	92	62	30
Sea Ranch Lakes	10	7	3	Americus	48	35	13
Sebastian	49	33	16	Aragon	4	4	0
Sebring	49	36	13	Arcade	6	6	0
Sewall's Point	7	7	0	Arlington	2	2	0
Shalimar	3	3	0	Ashburn	13	12	1
Sneads	9	5	4	Athens-Clarke County	265	209	56
South Bay	18	16	2	Atlanta	2,039	1,510	529
South Daytona	36	26	10	Attapulgus	1	1	0
South Miami	68	58	10	Auburn	22	16	6
South Palm Beach	11	11	0	Austell	25	17	8
Springfield	18	14	4	Avondale Estates	8	8	0
Starke	27	20	7	Bainbridge	49	43	6
St. Augustine	62	49	13	Ball Ground	5	5	0
St. Augustine Beach	13	11	2	Barnesville	17	14	3
St. Cloud	62	41	21	Bartow	2	1	1
St. Pete Beach	44	30	14	Barwick	1	1	0
St. Petersburg	772	518	254	Baxley	18	16	2
Stuart	57	42	15	Berlin	4	4	0
Sunny Isles Beach	55	45	10	Blackshear	14	12	2
Sunrise	225	160	65	Blakely	18	13	5
Surfside	26	20	6	Bloomingdale	11	9	2
Sweetwater	31	25	6	Blythe	4	3	1
Tallahassee	447	316	131	Bowdon	11	7	4
Tamarac	92	82	10	Braselton	4	3	1
Tampa	1,250	946	304	Bremen	19	15	4
Tarpon Springs	59	47	12	Brunswick	102	83	19
Tavares	21	20	1	Buchanan	7	7	0
Temple Terrace	61	46	15	Buena Vista	9	9	0
Tequesta	21	17	4	Butler	5	5	0
Titusville	117	82	35	Byron	17	14	3
Treasure Island	28	21	7	Cairo	25	22	3
Trenton	4	3	1	Calhoun	51	46	5
Umatilla	10	9	1	Camilla	20	17	3
Valparaiso	14	10	4	Canon	2	2	0
Venice	68	49	19	Canton	41	32	9
Vero Beach	90	62	28	Carrollton	73	61	12
Village of Pinecrest	68	48	20	Cartersville	53	44	9
Virginia Gardens	8	7	1	Cedartown	27	23	4
Waldo	8	7	1	Chamblee	46	31	15
Wauchula	15	13	2	Chatsworth	15	13	2
Webster	5	4	1	Chickamauga	5	4	1
Welaka	1	1	0	Clarkesville	6	5	1
Wellington	39	37	2	Clarkston	18	15	3
West Melbourne	32	27	5	Claxton	9	7	2

Table 78

Full-time Law Enforcement Employees as of October 31, 2001
by City by State—Continued

City by state	Total police employees	Total officers	Total civilians	City by state	Total police employees	Total officers	Total civilians
GEORGIA—Continued				**GEORGIA—Continued**			
Cleveland	9	9	0	Grovetown	26	16	10
Cochran	16	15	1	Hahira	8	7	1
College Park	126	100	26	Hamilton	1	1	0
Collins	2	1	1	Hampton	12	11	1
Colquitt	8	7	1	Hapeville	53	39	14
Columbus	468	377	91	Harlem	12	8	4
Comer	4	3	1	Hartwell	21	19	2
Commerce	23	17	6	Hawkinsville	11	10	1
Conyers	59	40	19	Hazlehurst	16	14	2
Cordele	35	28	7	Helen	13	9	4
Cornelia	21	18	3	Helena	2	2	0
Covington	53	46	7	Hephzibah	4	4	0
Crawfordville	2	2	0	Hilltonia	1	1	0
Cumming	20	14	6	Hinesville	84	75	9
Cusseta	9	5	4	Hiram	7	6	1
Cuthbert	15	11	4	Hoboken	2	1	1
Dallas	17	12	5	Hogansville	15	11	4
Dalton	93	78	15	Holly Springs	9	9	0
Danielsville	1	1	0	Homerville	9	8	1
Danville	2	1	1	Hoschton	3	3	0
Darien	6	6	0	Irwinton	1	1	0
Davisboro	1	1	0	Ivey	3	3	0
Dawson	19	14	5	Jackson	18	13	5
Decatur	52	40	12	Jasper	12	11	1
Dillard	3	3	0	Jefferson	20	18	2
Doerun	5	4	1	Jeffersonville	7	6	1
Donalsonville	12	9	3	Jesup	30	26	4
Doraville	74	41	33	Kennesaw	60	38	22
Douglas	45	37	8	Kingsland	34	31	3
Douglasville	100	83	17	Kingston	3	3	0
Dublin	56	48	8	Lafayette	20	17	3
Duluth	65	47	18	LaGrange	83	73	10
East Dublin	8	7	1	Lake City	17	16	1
East Ellijay	7	5	2	Lakeland	7	6	1
Eastman	13	12	1	Lake Park	2	2	0
East Point	184	136	48	Lavonia	13	12	1
Eatonton	18	13	5	Lawrenceville	68	53	15
Edison	4	4	0	Leary	1	1	0
Elberton	28	22	6	Leesburg	10	9	1
Ellaville	5	5	0	Lenox	2	1	1
Ellijay	9	8	1	Leslie	4	4	0
Emerson	5	4	1	Lilburn	30	22	8
Enigma	5	2	3	Lincolnton	4	4	0
Eton	3	3	0	Locust Grove	14	12	2
Euharlee	7	7	0	Lookout Mountain	8	7	1
Fairburn	34	25	9	Louisville	8	8	0
Fairmount	3	3	0	Ludowici	9	5	4
Fayetteville	42	38	4	Lumber City	7	5	2
Fitzgerald	36	29	7	Lumpkin	6	5	1
Flowery Branch	7	6	1	Luthersville	3	3	0
Folkston	5	5	0	Lyons	13	12	1
Forest Park	72	61	11	Macon	371	290	81
Forsyth	22	15	7	Madison	13	11	2
Fort Gaines	7	5	2	Manchester	19	14	5
Fort Oglethorpe	29	23	6	Marietta	161	133	28
Fort Valley	31	27	4	Marshallville	4	3	1
Franklin	7	7	0	Maysville	5	4	1
Franklin Springs	1	1	0	McCaysville	4	4	0
Garden City	38	34	4	McDonough	35	31	4
Georgetown	3	3	0	McRae	11	7	4
Glenwood	4	3	1	Meigs	5	4	1
Gordon	11	6	5	Metter	13	11	2
Grantville	6	6	0	Midville	1	1	0
Gray	9	8	1	Milan	2	2	0
Greensboro	16	15	1	Milledgeville	61	42	19
Greenville	7	6	1	Molena	1	1	0
Griffin	88	76	12	Montezuma	19	14	5

Table 78

Full-time Law Enforcement Employees as of October 31, 2001
by City by State—Continued

City by state	Total police employees	Total officers	Total civilians	City by state	Total police employees	Total officers	Total civilians
GEORGIA—Continued				**GEORGIA—Continued**			
Monticello	17	13	4	Stone Mountain	24	19	5
Morrow	36	32	4	Summerville	19	18	1
Morven	2	2	0	Suwanee	32	26	6
Moultrie	51	45	6	Swainsboro	22	18	4
Mountain City	1	1	0	Sycamore	3	2	1
Mount Airy	1	1	0	Sylvania	15	11	4
Mt. Zion	6	6	0	Sylvester	21	16	5
Muscogee City Marshall	16	15	1	Talbotton	4	4	0
Nahunta	4	4	0	Tallapoosa	14	13	1
Nashville	20	14	6	Tallulah Falls	2	1	1
Nelson	3	3	0	Temple	8	8	0
Newington	2	2	0	Tennille	7	7	0
Newnan	67	58	9	Thomaston	47	38	9
Norcross	38	30	8	Thomasville	52	48	4
Oakwood	10	9	1	Thomson	17	14	3
Ocilla	17	12	5	Thunderbolt	15	10	5
Oconee	1	1	0	Tifton	54	43	11
Oglethorpe	6	5	1	Tignall	4	3	1
Oxford	4	4	0	Toccoa	44	32	12
Palmetto	11	9	2	Trenton	7	7	0
Patterson	2	2	0	Trion	10	9	1
Pavo	4	3	1	Tunnel Hill	6	4	2
Peachtree City	55	51	4	Tybee Island	25	16	9
Pearson	5	5	0	Tyrone	12	11	1
Pembroke	7	6	1	Unadilla	5	5	0
Perry	42	33	9	Union City	35	31	4
Pinehurst	2	1	1	Union Point	10	9	1
Pine Lake	4	4	0	Uvalda	1	1	0
Pine Mountain	7	6	1	Valdosta	133	115	18
Plains	2	2	0	Vidalia	36	27	9
Pooler	21	18	3	Vienna	8	7	1
Port Wentworth	17	15	2	Villa Rica	41	34	7
Poulan	2	2	0	Warm Springs	3	3	0
Powder Springs	30	25	5	Warner Robins	131	103	28
Quitman	16	12	4	Warrenton	7	7	0
Ray City	2	1	1	Warwick	4	3	1
Reidsville	9	7	2	Washington	17	16	1
Remerton	8	7	1	Watkinsville	5	5	0
Reynolds	4	4	0	Waverly Hall	3	3	0
Richland	3	3	0	Waycross	67	47	20
Richmond Hill	22	18	4	Waynesboro	27	18	9
Ringgold	8	8	0	West Point	18	13	5
Riverdale	67	46	21	Whitesburg	4	4	0
Roberta	3	3	0	Willacoochee	4	4	0
Rochelle	6	4	2	Winder	44	36	8
Rockmart	17	15	2	Winterville	3	3	0
Rome	109	96	13	Woodbine	6	6	0
Rossville	10	8	2	Woodbury	11	9	2
Roswell	179	121	58	Woodstock	38	31	7
Royston	15	13	2	Wrens	17	13	4
Sale City	2	1	1	Wrightsville	5	5	0
Sandersville	23	18	5				
Sardis	5	5	0	**HAWAII**			
Savannah	510	408	102				
Screven	2	2	0	Honolulu	2,428	1,931	497
Sky Valley	7	6	1				
Smithville	4	4	0	**IDAHO**			
Smyrna	122	88	34				
Snellville	49	36	13	Aberdeen	8	5	3
Soperton	10	6	4	American Falls	11	9	2
Sparks	2	2	0	Bellevue	4	4	0
Springfield	8	7	1	Blackfoot	28	25	3
Statesboro	69	57	12	Boise	317	257	60
Statham	3	3	0	Bonners Ferry	8	8	0
Stillmore	3	2	1	Buhl	11	9	2
St. Marys	36	32	4	Caldwell	55	43	12
Stockbridge	166	144	22	Cascade	4	4	0

Table 78

Full-time Law Enforcement Employees as of October 31, 2001
by City by State—Continued

City by state	Total police employees	Total officers	Total civilians	City by state	Total police employees	Total officers	Total civilians
IDAHO—Continued				**ILLINOIS—Continued**			
Chubbuck	27	18	9	Annawan	1	1	0
Coeur d'Alene	71	59	12	Antioch	30	21	9
Cottonwood	1	1	0	Arcola	6	6	0
Emmett	13	12	1	Arlington Heights	143	108	35
Filer	5	5	0	Arthur	5	5	0
Fruitland	8	7	1	Ashland	2	2	0
Garden City	33	28	5	Assumption	1	1	0
Gooding	6	6	0	Astoria	1	1	0
Grangeville	6	6	0	Athens	3	3	0
Hagerman	2	2	0	Atkinson	2	2	0
Hailey	12	10	2	Atlanta	3	3	0
Heyburn	8	7	1	Auburn	9	5	4
Homedale	5	5	0	Augusta	1	1	0
Idaho Falls	117	85	32	Aurora	340	262	78
Jerome	17	15	2	Bannockburn	6	6	0
Kamiah	4	4	0	Barrington	42	33	9
Kellogg	7	6	1	Barrington Hills	27	19	8
Ketchum	22	12	10	Barry	2	2	0
Kimberly	7	6	1	Bartlett	65	49	16
Lewiston	65	45	20	Bartonville	16	11	5
McCall	11	9	2	Batavia	48	41	7
Meridian	51	44	7	Beardstown	13	9	4
Montpelier	7	7	0	Beckemeyer	1	1	0
Moscow	46	34	12	Bedford Park	45	37	8
Mountain Home	29	25	4	Beecher	6	6	0
Nampa	105	78	27	Belleville	92	76	16
Orofino	7	6	1	Bellwood	64	49	15
Osburn	2	2	0	Belvidere	34	32	2
Parma	4	4	0	Benld	4	4	0
Payette	13	11	2	Bensenville	41	32	9
Pinehurst	3	3	0	Benton	13	8	5
Pocatello	122	88	34	Berkeley	21	17	4
Ponderay	4	4	0	Berwyn	115	91	24
Post Falls	48	31	17	Bethalto	23	16	7
Preston	7	6	1	Bloomingdale	64	48	16
Rexburg	37	30	7	Bloomington	119	102	17
Rigby	7	7	0	Blue Island	65	40	25
Rupert	15	14	1	Blue Mound	2	2	0
Sandpoint	34	18	16	Bolingbrook	139	100	39
Shelley	7	7	0	Bourbonnais	26	19	7
Smelterville	1	1	0	Bradley	37	29	8
Soda Springs	8	7	1	Braidwood	21	13	8
Spirit Lake	5	5	0	Breese	7	6	1
St. Anthony	7	7	0	Bridgeport	4	4	0
St. Maries	6	5	1	Bridgeview	47	44	3
Sun Valley	9	8	1	Brighton	6	4	2
Twin Falls	74	56	18	Broadview	42	36	6
Weiser	11	10	1	Brookfield	35	28	7
Wendell	5	5	0	Brooklyn	5	5	0
Wilder	3	3	0	Buffalo Grove	88	73	15
				Bull Valley	2	2	0
ILLINOIS				Bunker Hill	4	3	1
				Burbank	61	46	15
Abingdon	5	5	0	Burnham	12	9	3
Addison	86	63	23	Burr Ridge	26	22	4
Albany	1	1	0	Byron	7	6	1
Albers	2	2	0	Cahokia	44	33	11
Albion	3	3	0	Cairo	14	8	6
Aledo	8	7	1	Calumet City	107	79	28
Algonquin	49	38	11	Calumet Park	25	19	6
Alorton	5	5	0	Cambridge	1	1	0
Alsip	52	42	10	Camp Point	2	2	0
Altamont	5	5	0	Canton	33	24	9
Alton	87	72	15	Carbon Cliff	4	4	0
Amboy	2	2	0	Carbondale	75	58	17
Andalusia	3	3	0	Carlinville	17	12	5
Anna	9	9	0	Carlyle	7	6	1

Table 78

Full-time Law Enforcement Employees as of October 31, 2001

by City by State—Continued

City by state	Total police employees	Total officers	Total civilians	City by state	Total police employees	Total officers	Total civilians
ILLINOIS—Continued				**ILLINOIS—Continued**			
Carmi	10	9	1	East Alton	16	11	5
Carol Stream	84	60	24	East Carondelet	2	2	0
Carpentersville	68	58	10	East Dubuque	7	7	0
Carrier Mills	2	2	0	East Dundee	15	14	1
Carrollton	6	6	0	East Galesburg	1	1	0
Carterville	6	6	0	East Hazel Crest	12	10	2
Carthage	3	3	0	East Moline	51	39	12
Cary	30	26	4	East Peoria	49	36	13
Casey	9	8	1	East St. Louis	87	63	24
Caseyville	13	9	4	Edwardsville	47	35	12
Catlin	1	1	0	Effingham	36	24	12
Central City	5	5	0	Elburn	8	7	1
Centralia	40	28	12	Eldorado	12	8	4
Centreville	20	15	5	Elgin	222	166	56
Chadwick	1	1	0	Elizabeth	1	1	0
Champaign	152	118	34	Elk Grove Village	111	97	14
Channahon	14	12	2	Elmwood	1	1	0
Charleston	36	33	3	Elmwood Park	48	37	11
Chatham	18	13	5	El Paso	5	5	0
Chenoa	4	4	0	Energy	4	4	0
Cherry Valley	15	15	0	Enfield	1	1	0
Chester	13	10	3	Erie	2	2	0
Chicago	15,066	13,581	1,485	Essex	2	2	0
Chicago Heights	134	97	37	Eureka	5	5	0
Chicago Ridge	34	29	5	Evanston	211	163	48
Chillicothe	11	8	3	Evergreen Park	69	57	12
Christopher	5	5	0	Fairbury	8	7	1
Cicero	151	131	20	Fairfield	17	13	4
Clarendon Hills	14	14	0	Fairmont City	9	6	3
Clinton	15	14	1	Fairview	1	1	0
Coal City	11	11	0	Fairview Heights	50	39	11
Coal Valley	7	6	1	Farmer City	6	3	3
Cobden	2	2	0	Farmington	4	4	0
Collinsville	43	33	10	Fisher	2	2	0
Colona	13	11	2	Flora	16	11	5
Columbia	20	14	6	Flossmoor	24	18	6
Cordova	2	2	0	Ford Heights	20	17	3
Cortland	1	1	0	Forest Park	50	35	15
Coulterville	1	1	0	Forest View	9	7	2
Country Club Hills	41	31	10	Fox Lake	27	21	6
Countryside	27	22	5	Fox River Grove	10	10	0
Crest Hill	28	25	3	Fox River Valley Gardens	1	1	0
Crestwood	5	3	2	Frankfort	27	24	3
Crete	14	13	1	Franklin Park	54	47	7
Creve Coeur	11	9	2	Freeburg	9	8	1
Crystal Lake	71	53	18	Freeport	84	65	19
Cuba	2	2	0	Fulton	8	7	1
Dallas City	1	1	0	Galena	12	10	2
Danvers	1	1	0	Galesburg	75	49	26
Danville	86	68	18	Galva	4	4	0
Darien	53	37	16	Geneseo	21	14	7
Decatur	192	159	33	Geneva	46	35	11
Deerfield	51	37	14	Genoa	10	9	1
De Kalb	68	54	14	Georgetown	4	4	0
De Pue	3	3	0	Germantown	2	2	0
De Soto	3	3	0	Gibson City	9	3	6
Des Plaines	131	107	24	Gifford	1	1	0
Divernon	2	2	0	Gilberts	5	4	1
Dixmoor	16	15	1	Gillespie	11	7	4
Dixon	29	25	4	Gilman	2	2	0
Dolton	65	52	13	Girard	5	5	0
Downers Grove	116	81	35	Glen Carbon	25	17	8
Dupo	6	6	0	Glencoe	42	33	9
Du Quoin	13	10	3	Glendale Heights	79	54	25
Durand	1	1	0	Glen Ellyn	47	37	10
Dwight	11	9	2	Glenview	100	75	25
Earlville	3	3	0	Glenwood	24	17	7

Table 78

Full-time Law Enforcement Employees as of October 31, 2001
by City by State—Continued

City by state	Total police employees	Total officers	Total civilians	City by state	Total police employees	Total officers	Total civilians
ILLINOIS—Continued				**ILLINOIS—Continued**			
Golf	2	2	0	Lake Bluff	20	14	6
Grafton	1	1	0	Lake Forest	60	44	16
Granite City	70	60	10	Lake-in-the-Hills	51	38	13
Grant Park	6	5	1	Lakemoor	8	8	0
Granville	3	3	0	Lake Villa	18	16	2
Grayslake	41	26	15	Lakewood	7	7	0
Grayville	7	3	4	Lake Zurich	55	37	18
Greenfield	4	2	2	La Moille	1	1	0
Greenup	3	3	0	Lanark	2	2	0
Greenville	14	10	4	Lansing	84	65	19
Gridley	1	1	0	La Salle	24	19	5
Gurnee	81	56	25	Lebanon	10	9	1
Hamilton	5	5	0	Leland Grove	6	6	0
Hampshire	10	10	0	Lemont	30	27	3
Hampton	3	3	0	Lenzburg	1	1	0
Hanover	2	2	0	Le Roy	5	5	0
Hanover Park	66	48	18	Lewistown	3	3	0
Harrisburg	12	11	1	Lexington	4	4	0
Hartford	5	4	1	Libertyville	61	44	17
Harvard	24	18	6	Lincoln	33	29	4
Harvey	103	64	39	Lincolnshire	28	18	10
Harwood Heights	36	27	9	Lincolnwood	45	34	11
Havana	10	10	0	Lindenhurst	16	14	2
Hawthorn Woods	11	10	1	Lisle	56	44	12
Hazel Crest	37	29	8	Litchfield	22	15	7
Hebron	3	3	0	Livingston	1	1	0
Henry	4	4	0	Lockport	32	28	4
Herrin	19	14	5	Lombard	88	71	17
Herscher	1	1	0	Loves Park	38	30	8
Hickory Hills	37	30	7	Ludlow	3	3	0
Highland	26	19	7	Lynwood	20	14	6
Highland Park	77	56	21	Lyons	28	22	6
Highwood	13	12	1	Machesney Park	20	19	1
Hillsboro	8	8	0	Mackinaw	2	2	0
Hillside	38	30	8	Macomb	28	25	3
Hinckley	3	3	0	Madison	16	12	4
Hinsdale	40	28	12	Mahomet	7	6	1
Hodgkins	18	17	1	Manhattan	7	7	0
Hoffman Estates	118	95	23	Manito	5	5	0
Homer	1	1	0	Manteno	14	13	1
Hometown	5	1	4	Marengo	21	16	5
Homewood	50	37	13	Marion	31	22	9
Hoopeston	16	11	5	Marissa	5	5	0
Hopkins Park	8	8	0	Markham	42	33	9
Huntley	21	17	4	Maroa	3	3	0
Hutsonville	1	1	0	Marquette Heights	5	5	0
Indian Head Park	13	10	3	Marseilles	15	10	5
Island Lake	19	14	5	Marshall	11	10	1
Itasca	36	28	8	Martinsville	2	2	0
Jacksonville	49	41	8	Maryville	15	11	4
Jerome	7	7	0	Mascoutah	13	12	1
Jerseyville	18	13	5	Mason City	4	4	0
Johnsburg	10	9	1	Matteson	50	39	11
Johnston City	4	4	0	Mattoon	63	47	16
Joliet	344	262	82	Maywood	67	54	13
Jonesboro	3	3	0	McCook	20	15	5
Justice	30	25	5	McCullom Lake	1	1	0
Kankakee	99	73	26	McHenry	57	43	14
Kenilworth	13	9	4	McLean	1	1	0
Kewanee	30	23	7	McLeansboro	5	5	0
Kildeer	16	15	1	Melrose Park	87	74	13
Kincaid	1	1	0	Mendota	19	14	5
Kirkland	3	3	0	Meredosia	2	2	0
Knoxville	4	4	0	Metamora	5	5	0
Lacon	4	4	0	Metropolis	20	15	5
La Grange	36	27	9	Midlothian	31	24	7
La Grange Park	29	24	5	Milan	17	12	5

Table 78

Full-time Law Enforcement Employees as of October 31, 2001
by City by State—Continued

City by state	Total police employees	Total officers	Total civilians	City by state	Total police employees	Total officers	Total civilians
ILLINOIS—Continued				**ILLINOIS—Continued**			
Milledgeville	2	2	0	Palestine	3	3	0
Millstadt	5	5	0	Palmyra	1	1	0
Minier	2	2	0	Palos Heights	32	28	4
Minonk	2	2	0	Palos Hills	38	35	3
Minooka	13	11	2	Palos Park	10	9	1
Mokena	29	27	2	Pana	13	9	4
Moline	107	79	28	Paris	21	16	5
Momence	7	7	0	Park City	10	7	3
Monee	11	10	1	Park Forest	49	36	13
Monmouth	26	18	8	Park Ridge	69	55	14
Montgomery	24	16	8	Pawnee	10	6	4
Monticello	5	4	1	Paxton	6	6	0
Morris	31	24	7	Pecatonica	3	3	0
Morrison	6	6	0	Pekin	62	54	8
Morton	27	21	6	Peoria	288	238	50
Morton Grove	64	46	18	Peoria Heights	17	12	5
Mound City	1	1	0	Peotone	11	10	1
Mount Carmel	18	13	5	Peru	27	21	6
Mount Carroll	3	3	0	Petersburg	6	6	0
Mount Morris	6	5	1	Phoenix	3	1	2
Mount Olive	4	3	1	Pinckneyville	12	8	4
Mount Prospect	103	81	22	Piper City	1	1	0
Mount Pulaski	4	4	0	Pittsfield	6	6	0
Mount Sterling	7	3	4	Plainfield	37	32	5
Mount Vernon	59	45	14	Plano	15	13	2
Mount Zion	10	8	2	Polo	4	4	0
Moweaqua	2	2	0	Pontiac	22	19	3
Mundelein	58	40	18	Pontoon Beach	19	13	6
Murphysboro	26	16	10	Port Byron	2	2	0
Naperville	286	180	106	Posen	15	13	2
Nashville	8	7	1	Princeton	17	15	2
Nauvoo	2	2	0	Prophetstown	4	3	1
Neoga	3	3	0	Prospect Heights	34	26	8
New Athens	4	4	0	Quincy	89	71	18
New Baden	4	4	0	Ramsey	1	1	0
New Lenox	30	28	2	Rantoul	42	33	9
Newman	1	1	0	Raymond	1	1	0
Newton	6	5	1	Red Bud	5	5	0
Niles	69	54	15	Richmond	4	4	0
Nokomis	7	4	3	Richton Park	33	26	7
Normal	77	67	10	Ridge Farm	1	1	0
Norridge	52	38	14	Ridgway	3	3	0
North Aurora	23	21	2	Riverdale	44	35	9
Northbrook	88	61	27	River Forest	40	31	9
North Chicago	69	49	20	River Grove	26	24	2
Northfield	26	18	8	Riverside	25	19	6
Northlake	44	31	13	Robbins	18	9	9
North Pekin	2	2	0	Robinson	15	13	2
North Riverside	37	28	9	Rochelle	25	19	6
Oak Brook	52	44	8	Rochester	7	7	0
Oakbrook Terrace	20	18	2	Rockdale	6	5	1
Oak Forest	52	39	13	Rock Falls	29	21	8
Oak Lawn	160	105	55	Rockford	331	297	34
Oak Park	137	110	27	Rock Island	114	86	28
Oblong	2	2	0	Rockton	11	10	1
O'Fallon	55	41	14	Rolling Meadows	76	55	21
Oglesby	13	9	4	Romeoville	55	43	12
Okawville	3	3	0	Roodhouse	5	5	0
Olney	19	13	6	Roscoe	13	12	1
Olympia Fields	19	18	1	Roselle	49	37	12
Oregon	7	6	1	Rosemont	83	72	11
Orion	3	3	0	Rossville	2	2	0
Orland Hills	16	14	2	Round Lake	18	14	4
Orland Park	120	92	28	Round Lake Beach	45	34	11
Oswego	37	34	3	Round Lake Heights	3	3	0
Ottawa	43	34	9	Round Lake Park	13	11	2
Palatine	139	109	30	Roxana	6	5	1

Table 78

Full-time Law Enforcement Employees as of October 31, 2001
by City by State—Continued

City by state	Total police employees	Total officers	Total civilians	City by state	Total police employees	Total officers	Total civilians
ILLINOIS—Continued				**ILLINOIS—Continued**			
Royalton	1	1	0	Valmeyer	1	1	0
Rushville	5	5	0	Vandalia	18	13	5
Salem	21	14	7	Venice	10	5	5
Sandwich	17	12	5	Vermont	1	1	0
Sauget	13	13	0	Vernon Hills	72	48	24
Sauk Village	26	19	7	Vienna	3	3	0
Savanna	8	7	1	Villa Grove	5	4	1
Schaumburg	205	134	71	Villa Park	53	38	15
Schiller Park	39	32	7	Virden	10	6	4
Seneca	9	4	5	Virginia	1	1	0
Sesser	5	4	1	Wamac	4	4	0
Shawneetown	4	4	0	Warren	3	3	0
Shelbyville	7	6	1	Warrensburg	2	2	0
Sheridan	2	2	0	Warrenville	30	24	6
Sherman	6	6	0	Washburn	2	2	0
Shiloh	12	12	0	Washington	23	15	8
Shorewood	21	18	3	Washington Park	15	13	2
Silvis	20	13	7	Waterloo	15	13	2
Skokie	137	106	31	Watseka	16	11	5
Sleepy Hollow	6	5	1	Wauconda	31	18	13
Smithton	4	4	0	Waukegan	222	169	53
Somonauk	4	4	0	Wayne	6	5	1
South Barrington	19	15	4	Wayne City	1	1	0
South Beloit	10	6	4	Westchester	49	38	11
South Chicago Heights	14	9	5	West Chicago	52	42	10
South Elgin	33	25	8	West City	8	4	4
Southern View	4	4	0	West Dundee	22	19	3
South Holland	57	44	13	Western Springs	27	21	6
South Jacksonville	6	5	1	West Frankfort	20	14	6
South Pekin	2	2	0	Westmont	59	43	16
South Roxana	5	5	0	West Salem	1	1	0
Sparta	17	12	5	Westville	3	3	0
Springfield	330	281	49	Wheaton	92	69	23
Spring Grove	9	8	1	Wheeling	87	62	25
Spring Valley	13	9	4	White Hall	7	4	3
St. Anne	4	4	0	Williamsfield	1	1	0
Staunton	11	8	3	Williamsville	3	3	0
St. Charles	60	49	11	Willowbrook	28	24	4
Steger	21	15	6	Willow Springs	22	17	5
Sterling	42	31	11	Wilmette	55	37	18
St. Francisville	1	1	0	Wilmington	18	13	5
Stickney	19	14	5	Winchester	4	4	0
Stockton	3	3	0	Winfield	20	18	2
Stone Park	33	22	11	Winnebago	5	5	0
Stonington	1	1	0	Winnetka	38	29	9
Streamwood	66	55	11	Winthrop Harbor	14	10	4
Streator	31	25	6	Wood Dale	53	34	19
Sugar Grove	9	8	1	Woodhull	1	1	0
Sullivan	10	8	2	Woodridge	72	51	21
Summit	35	28	7	Wood River	26	19	7
Sumner	2	2	0	Woodstock	44	29	15
Swansea	20	16	4	Worden	1	1	0
Sycamore	30	21	9	Worth	26	23	3
Tampico	1	1	0	Yorkville	16	15	1
Taylorville	27	21	6	Zeigler	5	4	1
Thomasboro	2	2	0	Zion	54	40	14
Thomson	1	1	0				
Thornton	12	10	2	**INDIANA**			
Tilton	3	3	0				
Tinley Park	94	71	23	Albion	6	6	0
Tolono	4	4	0	Alexandria	17	13	4
Tremont	4	4	0	Angola	19	15	4
Trenton	4	4	0	Attica	6	6	0
Troy	20	15	5	Auburn	29	21	8
Tuscola	8	7	1	Aurora	12	8	4
University Park	25	21	4	Austin	6	6	0
Urbana	60	48	12	Batesville	14	9	5

Table 78

Full-time Law Enforcement Employees as of October 31, 2001
by City by State—Continued

City by state	Total police employees	Total officers	Total civilians	City by state	Total police employees	Total officers	Total civilians
INDIANA—Continued				**INDIANA—Continued**			
Bedford	40	32	8	Kouts	4	4	0
Beech Grove	38	28	10	Lafayette	132	103	29
Berne	6	6	0	Lake Station	27	22	5
Bicknell	11	7	4	La Porte	51	46	5
Bloomington	108	80	28	Lawrence	58	51	7
Bluffton	28	20	8	Lawrenceburg	20	16	4
Boonville	14	13	1	Lebanon	29	28	1
Brazil	16	12	4	Ligonier	9	9	0
Bremen	15	11	4	Linton	13	9	4
Brookville	10	9	1	Logansport	52	43	9
Brownsburg	42	28	14	Long Beach	5	5	0
Burns Harbor	8	5	3	Loogootee	7	5	2
Cambridge City	5	5	0	Lowell	19	14	5
Carmel	88	74	14	Madison	34	27	7
Cedar Lake	19	14	5	Marion	84	70	14
Charlestown	18	13	5	Martinsville	26	19	7
Chesterfield	6	6	0	Merrillville	60	49	11
Chesterton	26	20	6	Michigan City	110	92	18
Clarksville	44	35	9	Mishawaka	131	97	34
Clinton	9	7	2	Mitchell	12	7	5
Columbia City	19	17	2	Monticello	16	12	4
Columbus	75	69	6	Mooresville	25	20	5
Connersville	40	38	2	Mount Vernon	16	14	2
Corydon	7	7	0	Muncie	124	115	9
Crawfordsville	43	29	14	Munster	49	38	11
Crown Point	39	29	10	Nappanee	20	14	6
Culver	5	4	1	New Albany	79	62	17
Decatur	21	17	4	New Castle	38	35	3
Delphi	9	6	3	New Chicago	4	1	3
Dunkirk	10	6	4	New Haven	23	17	6
Dyer	29	23	6	New Whiteland	11	7	4
East Chicago	152	120	32	Noblesville	69	60	9
Edinburgh	14	9	5	North Liberty	4	4	0
Elkhart	145	113	32	North Manchester	15	11	4
Elwood	20	16	4	North Vernon	19	16	3
Evansville	315	278	37	Oakland City	4	4	0
Fairmount	8	4	4	Peru	34	28	6
Fishers	58	50	8	Petersburg	5	5	0
Fort Wayne	503	380	123	Plainfield	35	32	3
Frankfort	37	28	9	Plymouth	29	24	5
Franklin	47	33	14	Portage	70	52	18
Garrett	15	11	4	Portland	17	13	4
Gary	355	269	86	Princes Lakes	4	4	0
Gas City	16	12	4	Princeton	20	16	4
Georgetown	3	3	0	Rensselaer	14	9	5
Goshen	60	53	7	Richmond	91	76	15
Greencastle	16	14	2	Rochester	19	14	5
Greendale	14	10	4	Rushville	18	13	5
Greenfield	36	28	8	Salem	17	12	5
Greenwood	78	54	24	Schererville	55	41	14
Griffith	41	32	9	Scottsburg	15	13	2
Hagerstown	5	5	0	Sellersburg	17	12	5
Hammond	255	204	51	Seymour	50	35	15
Hartford City	15	13	2	Shelbyville	52	39	13
Hebron	9	8	1	South Bend	330	257	73
Highland	52	42	10	Speedway	40	31	9
Hobart	67	53	14	St. John	19	14	5
Huntingburg	10	9	1	Sullivan	8	8	0
Huntington	44	33	11	Tell City	16	11	5
Indianapolis	2,509	1,550	959	Terre Haute	150	124	26
Jasonville	5	5	0	Tipton	16	11	5
Jasper	25	19	6	Trail Creek	4	4	0
Jeffersonville	57	49	8	Union City	7	7	0
Kendallville	25	18	7	Valparaiso	65	48	17
Kingsford Heights	2	2	0	Vincennes	43	37	6
Knox	8	8	0	Wabash	31	26	5
Kokomo	139	100	39	Warsaw	45	35	10

Table 78

Full-time Law Enforcement Employees as of October 31, 2001

by City by State—Continued

City by state	Total police employees	Total officers	Total civilians	City by state	Total police employees	Total officers	Total civilians
INDIANA—Continued				**IOWA—Continued**			
Washington	24	18	6	Hampton	14	8	6
Waterloo	7	6	1	Harlan	9	8	1
Westfield	24	22	2	Hawarden	4	4	0
West Lafayette	52	39	13	Hiawatha	8	8	0
West Terre Haute	14	9	5	Humboldt	7	7	0
Westville	5	4	1	Independence	16	12	4
Whiting	29	22	7	Indianola	19	17	2
Winchester	16	12	4	Iowa City	101	74	27
Winona Lake	5	5	0	Iowa Falls	16	11	5
				Jefferson	8	8	0
IOWA				Johnston	14	13	1
				Keokuk	35	25	10
Adel	7	7	0	Knoxville	16	11	5
Albia	7	6	1	Lake Mills	5	5	0
Algona	15	10	5	Le Claire	7	6	1
Altoona	21	19	2	Le Mars	15	14	1
Ames	71	49	22	Lisbon	2	2	0
Anamosa	8	7	1	Manchester	14	9	5
Ankeny	44	35	9	Maquoketa	17	12	5
Atlantic	14	12	2	Marion	47	38	9
Audubon	3	3	0	Marshalltown	62	44	18
Belle Plaine	3	3	0	Mason City	61	46	15
Belmond	5	5	0	Missouri Valley	8	7	1
Bettendorf	55	41	14	Monticello	7	6	1
Bloomfield	5	5	0	Mount Pleasant	15	13	2
Boone	21	16	5	Mount Vernon	6	6	0
Burlington	61	43	18	Muscatine	52	39	13
Camanche	7	7	0	Nevada	10	9	1
Carlisle	6	6	0	New Hampton	7	7	0
Carroll	15	14	1	Newton	33	26	7
Carter Lake	10	9	1	North Liberty	2	2	0
Cedar Falls	41	38	3	Norwalk	12	10	2
Cedar Rapids	239	200	39	Oelwein	13	8	5
Centerville	19	14	5	Ogden	3	3	0
Chariton	8	7	1	Onawa	6	6	0
Charles City	17	12	5	Orange City	7	7	0
Cherokee	10	9	1	Osage	5	5	0
Clarinda	14	10	4	Osceola	10	9	1
Clear Lake	19	14	5	Oskaloosa	19	17	2
Clinton	54	45	9	Ottumwa	42	34	8
Clive	23	20	3	Palo	1	1	0
Coggon	1	1	0	Pella	17	14	3
Coralville	31	28	3	Perry	22	15	7
Council Bluffs	136	116	20	Pleasant Hill	11	11	0
Cresco	7	7	0	Red Oak	13	12	1
Creston	16	12	4	Rock Rapids	3	3	0
Davenport	200	157	43	Sac City	4	4	0
Decorah	18	13	5	Sergeant Bluff	9	8	1
Denison	17	12	5	Sheldon	12	8	4
Des Moines	497	361	136	Shenandoah	13	9	4
De Witt	7	7	0	Sioux Center	7	7	0
Dubuque	95	89	6	Sioux City	155	124	31
Dyersville	11	6	5	Spencer	26	19	7
Eagle Grove	7	7	0	Spirit Lake	8	7	1
Eldora	6	6	0	Storm Lake	20	16	4
Eldridge	7	7	0	Story City	5	5	0
Emmetsburg	7	6	1	Tama	5	5	0
Estherville	12	12	0	Tipton	4	4	0
Evansdale	8	7	1	Urbandale	46	42	4
Fairfield	21	15	6	Vinton	7	7	0
Forest City	9	9	0	Washington	11	11	0
Fort Dodge	46	43	3	Waterloo	127	117	10
Fort Madison	27	22	5	Waukee	10	9	1
Garner	5	5	0	Waukon	7	7	0
Glenwood	13	11	2	Waverly	16	15	1
Grinnell	17	15	2	Webster City	21	15	6
Grundy Center	6	5	1	West Burlington	11	10	1

Table 78

Full-time Law Enforcement Employees as of October 31, 2001
by City by State—Continued

City by state	Total police employees	Total officers	Total civilians	City by state	Total police employees	Total officers	Total civilians
IOWA—Continued				**KANSAS—Continued**			
West Des Moines	69	57	12	Elkhart	3	3	0
West Liberty	6	5	1	Ellinwood	5	5	0
West Union	4	4	0	Ellis	5	5	0
Williamsburg	5	5	0	Ellsworth	6	6	0
Wilton	5	5	0	Elwood	3	3	0
Windsor Heights	13	12	1	Emporia	67	49	18
Winterset	9	8	1	Enterprise	1	1	0
				Erie	4	4	0
KANSAS				Eskridge	1	1	0
				Eudora	7	7	0
Abilene	14	12	2	Fairway	9	8	1
Alma	1	1	0	Florence	1	1	0
Altamont	3	3	0	Fort Scott	27	21	6
Americus	4	4	0	Frankfort	1	1	0
Andover	19	13	6	Fredonia	8	7	1
Anthony	5	5	0	Frontenac	9	6	3
Argonia	1	1	0	Galena	14	10	4
Arkansas City	33	25	8	Galva	1	1	0
Arma	4	4	0	Garden City	78	47	31
Atchison	25	23	2	Garden Plain	2	2	0
Attica	1	1	0	Gardner	22	21	1
Atwood	2	2	0	Garnett	12	8	4
Augusta	33	25	8	Girard	6	6	0
Baldwin City	10	8	2	Goddard	5	5	0
Basehor	6	5	1	Goodland	12	11	1
Baxter Springs	15	10	5	Grandview Plaza	4	4	0
Bel Aire	10	9	1	Great Bend	36	30	6
Belle Plaine	4	4	0	Greeley	1	1	0
Belleville	5	5	0	Halstead	7	6	1
Beloit	15	10	5	Harper	3	3	0
Blue Rapids	1	1	0	Haven	3	3	0
Bonner Springs	25	22	3	Hays	44	28	16
Buhler	3	3	0	Haysville	33	25	8
Burden	1	1	0	Herington	11	6	5
Burlingame	2	2	0	Hiawatha	8	7	1
Burlington	9	7	2	Highland	3	3	0
Burrton	1	1	0	Hill City	4	4	0
Bushton	1	1	0	Hillsboro	5	5	0
Caldwell	4	4	0	Hoisington	10	7	3
Caney	10	6	4	Holcomb	4	3	1
Canton	1	1	0	Holton	11	7	4
Carbondale	2	2	0	Holyrood	1	1	0
Cawker City	1	1	0	Hope	1	1	0
Cedar Vale	1	1	0	Horton	8	4	4
Chanute	22	20	2	Hoxie	2	2	0
Chapman	2	2	0	Hugoton	7	6	1
Chase	1	1	0	Humboldt	6	6	0
Cheney	3	3	0	Hutchinson	96	67	29
Cherokee	1	1	0	Independence	31	23	8
Cherryvale	6	6	0	Inman	2	2	0
Chetopa	4	4	0	Iola	26	18	8
Cimarron	3	3	0	Junction City	71	47	24
Claflin	2	2	0	Kanopolis	1	1	0
Clay Center	8	7	1	Kansas City	418	349	69
Clearwater	6	6	0	Kechi	2	2	0
Coffeyville	35	26	9	Kingman	7	7	0
Colby	17	12	5	Kinsley	4	4	0
Columbus	10	8	2	Kiowa	3	3	0
Colwich	3	3	0	La Crosse	3	3	0
Concordia	16	10	6	La Cygne	2	2	0
Conway Springs	3	3	0	Lake Quivira	2	2	0
Council Grove	5	5	0	Lansing	11	11	0
Derby	43	34	9	Larned	13	8	5
Dodge City	48	35	13	Lawrence	150	121	29
Eastborough	7	7	0	Leavenworth	86	64	22
Edwardsville	15	14	1	Leawood	72	50	22
El Dorado	28	26	2	Lebo	1	1	0

Table 78

Full-time Law Enforcement Employees as of October 31, 2001
by City by State—Continued

City by state	Total police employees	Total officers	Total civilians	City by state	Total police employees	Total officers	Total civilians
KANSAS—Continued				**KANSAS—Continued**			
Lenexa	115	73	42	Spearville	1	1	0
Le Roy	1	1	0	Spring Hill	8	7	1
Liberal	47	37	10	Stafford	4	4	0
Lindsborg	6	5	1	Sterling	5	5	0
Little River	1	1	0	St. Francis	5	4	1
Louisburg	9	8	1	St. John	4	4	0
Lyndon	3	3	0	St. Marys	4	4	0
Lyons	8	7	1	Stockton	5	5	0
Maize	7	6	1	Tonganoxie	7	6	1
Marion	4	4	0	Topeka	332	277	55
Marquette	1	1	0	Towanda	3	3	0
Marysville	6	5	1	Troy	1	1	0
McLouth	1	1	0	Udall	2	2	0
McPherson	30	25	5	Ulysses	11	10	1
Meade	3	3	0	Valley Center	11	7	4
Medicine Lodge	5	5	0	Valley Falls	2	2	0
Merriam	29	26	3	Victoria	2	2	0
Minneapolis	5	5	0	Wa Keeney	5	5	0
Mission	23	22	1	Wakefield	1	1	0
Moran	1	1	0	Wamego	12	7	5
Moundridge	3	3	0	Waterville	1	1	0
Mount Hope	2	2	0	Waverly	1	1	0
Mulberry	1	1	0	Weir	1	1	0
Mulvane	17	12	5	Wellington	19	15	4
Neodesha	8	7	1	Wellsville	4	4	0
Newton	34	30	4	Westwood	8	7	1
Nickerson	5	5	0	Wichita	827	634	193
North Newton	1	1	0	Wilson	1	1	0
Norton	5	5	0	Winfield	28	22	6
Oakley	11	6	5	Yates Center	4	4	0
Oberlin	4	4	0				
Olathe	182	142	40	**KENTUCKY**			
Osage City	6	6	0				
Osawatomie	15	10	5	Adairville	1	1	0
Osborne	4	4	0	Albany	11	10	1
Oswego	5	5	0	Alexandria	11	10	1
Ottawa	30	26	4	Allen	2	1	1
Overbrook	2	2	0	Anchorage	14	10	4
Overland Park	257	209	48	Ashland	56	48	8
Oxford	3	3	0	Auburn	3	3	0
Paola	20	14	6	Audubon Park	8	6	2
Park City	17	15	2	Augusta	2	2	0
Parsons	31	22	9	Barbourville	17	14	3
Peabody	3	3	0	Bardstown	22	18	4
Pittsburg	51	37	14	Bardwell	1	1	0
Plainville	5	5	0	Barlow	2	2	0
Pleasanton	2	2	0	Beattyville	7	5	2
Prairie Village	54	42	12	Beaver Dam	5	5	0
Pratt	21	14	7	Bellefonte	3	3	0
Quinter	1	1	0	Bellevue	11	10	1
Roeland Park	18	16	2	Benham	4	4	0
Rolla	1	1	0	Benton	9	7	2
Rose Hill	8	7	1	Berea	32	26	6
Rossville	3	3	0	Bloomfield	2	2	0
Russell	19	8	11	Bowling Green	116	88	28
Sabetha	5	5	0	Brandenburg	4	4	0
Salina	104	79	25	Brodhead	2	2	0
Scott City	12	7	5	Brooksville	1	1	0
Scranton	2	2	0	Brownsville	1	1	0
Sedan	3	3	0	Burgin	1	1	0
Sedgwick	2	2	0	Burkesville	9	5	4
Seneca	5	5	0	Burnside	3	3	0
Sharon Springs	1	1	0	Butler	7	5	2
Shawnee	98	80	18	Cadiz	10	9	1
Silver Lake	2	2	0	Calhoun	1	1	0
Smith Center	3	3	0	Calvert City	5	5	0
South Hutchinson	8	7	1	Campbellsburg	1	1	0

Table 78

Full-time Law Enforcement Employees as of October 31, 2001

by City by State—Continued

City by state	Total police employees	Total officers	Total civilians	City by state	Total police employees	Total officers	Total civilians
KENTUCKY—Continued				**KENTUCKY—Continued**			
Campbellsville	31	20	11	Hopkinsville	73	65	8
Campton	1	1	0	Horse Cave	5	5	0
Caneyville	1	1	0	Hustonville	1	1	0
Carlisle	8	7	1	Independence	25	23	2
Carrollton	12	11	1	Indian Hills	7	7	0
Catlettsburg	8	8	0	Inez	2	2	0
Cave City	6	6	0	Irvine	7	7	0
Central City	14	12	2	Irvington	4	4	0
Clarkson	2	2	0	Jackson	13	12	1
Clay	1	1	0	Jamestown	5	5	0
Clay City	2	2	0	Jeffersontown	58	50	8
Clinton	5	5	0	Jenkins	5	4	1
Cloverport	2	2	0	Junction City	5	5	0
Cold Spring	9	9	0	La Center	2	2	0
Columbia	10	10	0	La Grange	14	13	1
Corbin	29	22	7	Lakeside Park-Crestview Hills	10	9	1
Covington	120	110	10	Lancaster	8	8	0
Crab Orchard	3	2	1	Lawrenceburg	21	16	5
Crescent Springs	9	9	0	Lebanon	22	15	7
Crofton	1	1	0	Lebanon Junction	5	5	0
Cumberland	10	7	3	Leitchfield	15	14	1
Cynthiana	18	17	1	Lewisburg	1	1	0
Danville	37	26	11	Lewisport	3	3	0
Dawson Springs	10	6	4	Lexington	587	426	161
Dayton	9	8	1	Liberty	4	4	0
Earlington	2	2	0	Livermore	2	2	0
Eddyville	6	6	0	Livingston	1	1	0
Edgewood	12	12	0	London	32	29	3
Edmonton	6	6	0	Lone Oak	5	3	2
Elizabethtown	50	38	12	Louisa	11	7	4
Elkhorn City	4	3	1	Louisville	956	713	243
Elkton	8	8	0	Loyall	2	1	1
Elsmere	11	10	1	Ludlow	10	8	2
Eminence	7	7	0	Lynch	2	2	0
Erlanger	40	32	8	Lynnview	2	2	0
Evarts	4	4	0	Madisonville	54	45	9
Falmouth	8	7	1	Manchester	12	12	0
Flatwoods	14	9	5	Marion	7	7	0
Fleming-Neon	2	2	0	Martin	5	5	0
Flemingsburg	5	5	0	Mayfield	36	28	8
Florence	53	50	3	Maysville	29	23	6
Fort Mitchell	13	12	1	McKee	2	2	0
Fort Thomas	24	23	1	Middlesboro	28	24	4
Fort Wright	10	10	0	Millersburg	3	3	0
Frankfort	63	58	5	Minor Lane Heights	9	9	0
Franklin	27	20	7	Monticello	9	9	0
Fulton	15	11	4	Morehead	28	19	9
Georgetown	51	44	7	Morganfield	12	7	5
Glasgow	45	35	10	Morgantown	6	6	0
Graymoor-Devondale	3	3	0	Mortons Gap	1	1	0
Grayson	12	12	0	Mount Olivet	1	1	0
Greensburg	6	6	0	Mount Sterling	30	22	8
Greenup	3	3	0	Mount Vernon	8	8	0
Greenville	9	9	0	Mount Washington	13	12	1
Guthrie	4	4	0	Muldraugh	4	4	0
Hardinsburg	4	4	0	Munfordville	4	4	0
Harlan	15	11	4	Murray	36	30	6
Harrodsburg	27	17	10	New Castle	1	1	0
Hartford	5	5	0	New Haven	2	2	0
Hawesville	1	1	0	Newport	90	54	36
Hazard	26	18	8	Nicholasville	51	48	3
Henderson	59	53	6	Nortonville	1	1	0
Hickman	9	5	4	Oak Grove	16	12	4
Highland Heights	11	10	1	Olive Hill	6	6	0
Hillview	12	12	0	Owensboro	131	96	35
Hindman	2	2	0	Owenton	3	3	0
Hodgenville	7	7	0	Owingsville	5	5	0

Table 78

Full-time Law Enforcement Employees as of October 31, 2001
by City by State—Continued

City by state	Total police employees	Total officers	Total civilians	City by state	Total police employees	Total officers	Total civilians
KENTUCKY—Continued				**LOUISIANA**			
Paducah	85	71	14	Abbeville	38	33	5
Paintsville	10	10	0	Abita Springs	7	6	1
Paris	24	22	2	Addis	5	4	1
Park City	2	2	0	Alexandria	193	158	35
Park Hills	7	6	1	Amite	18	18	0
Pembroke	1	1	0	Baker	29	29	0
Perryville	1	1	0	Baldwin	9	8	1
Pikeville	29	20	9	Ball	6	5	1
Pineville	8	8	0	Basile	13	8	5
Pioneer Village	5	5	0	Bastrop	45	40	5
Pippa Passes	1	1	0	Baton Rouge	760	596	164
Powderly	1	1	0	Bernice	6	6	0
Prestonsburg	13	13	0	Berwick	14	14	0
Princeton	17	15	2	Blanchard	4	4	0
Prospect	9	9	0	Bogalusa	47	38	9
Providence	6	6	0	Bossier City	192	138	54
Raceland	6	5	1	Breaux Bridge	23	23	0
Radcliff	50	35	15	Broussard	15	14	1
Ravenna	2	2	0	Brusly	9	8	1
Richmond	63	49	14	Church Point	17	17	0
Russell	12	12	0	Clinton	7	7	0
Russell Springs	7	6	1	Coushatta	6	6	0
Russellville	24	22	2	Covington	43	33	10
Sadieville	2	2	0	Crowley	32	31	1
Salyersville	4	4	0	Cullen	5	5	0
Science Hill	1	1	0	Denham Springs	40	25	15
Scottsville	20	15	5	De Quincy	13	13	0
Sebree	2	2	0	De Ridder	27	26	1
Shelbyville	21	20	1	Dixie Inn	3	3	0
Shepherdsville	11	11	0	Erath	10	10	0
Shively	27	20	7	Eunice	43	42	1
Silver Grove	1	1	0	Farmerville	12	12	0
Somerset	36	33	3	Ferriday	17	12	5
Southgate	7	7	0	Folsom	4	3	1
South Shore	1	1	0	Franklin	21	18	3
Springfield	8	8	0	Franklinton	15	15	0
Stamping Ground	1	1	0	French Settlement	2	2	0
Stanford	9	8	1	Glenmora	5	5	0
Stanton	10	10	0	Golden Meadow	6	5	1
St. Matthews	37	31	6	Gonzales	31	31	0
Sturgis	5	5	0	Grambling	11	8	3
Taylor Mill	9	8	1	Gramercy	7	7	0
Taylorsville	5	5	0	Gretna	109	91	18
Tompkinsville	12	9	3	Hammond	95	93	2
Trenton	1	1	0	Harahan	27	27	0
Uniontown	2	2	0	Haughton	8	6	2
Vanceburg	6	6	0	Haynesville	10	10	0
Versailles	31	23	8	Homer	11	11	0
Villa Hills	9	8	1	Houma	73	60	13
Vine Grove	8	7	1	Independence	6	6	0
Warsaw	4	4	0	Iowa	11	10	1
Wayland	1	1	0	Jeanerette	16	16	0
West Buechel	13	13	0	Jena	5	5	0
West Liberty	13	7	6	Jennings	43	35	8
West Point	4	4	0	Jonesboro	15	11	4
Wheelwright	1	1	0	Kaplan	22	22	0
Whitesburg	6	6	0	Kenner	216	135	81
Wickliffe	1	1	0	Kentwood	9	9	0
Wilder	8	8	0	Kinder	15	15	0
Williamsburg	12	11	1	Krotz Springs	5	4	1
Williamstown	5	5	0	Lafayette	282	216	66
Wilmore	8	7	1	Lake Arthur	11	11	0
Winchester	42	30	12	Lake Charles	158	154	4
Wingo	1	1	0	Lecompte	5	5	0
Worthington	3	3	0	Leesville	26	26	0
Wurtland	1	1	0	Lockport	5	5	0

Table 78

Full-time Law Enforcement Employees as of October 31, 2001

by City by State—Continued

City by state	Total police employees	Total officers	Total civilians	City by state	Total police employees	Total officers	Total civilians
LOUISIANA—Continued				**MAINE**			
Mamou	27	15	12	Ashland	3	3	0
Mandeville	44	35	9	Auburn	57	49	8
Mansfield	17	17	0	Augusta	54	42	12
Many	13	13	0	Baileyville	6	6	0
Marksville	23	17	6	Bangor	87	71	16
Minden	32	31	1	Bar Harbor	13	9	4
Monroe	222	178	44	Bath	25	20	5
Moreauville	1	1	0	Belfast	14	12	2
Napoleonville	2	2	0	Berwick	9	9	0
Natchitoches	74	73	1	Bethel	4	4	0
New Iberia	85	69	16	Biddeford	70	50	20
Newllano	10	10	0	Boothbay Harbor	11	7	4
New Orleans	2,010	1,627	383	Brewer	19	17	2
New Roads	20	18	2	Bridgton	12	8	4
Norwood	2	2	0	Brownville	2	2	0
Oakdale	24	21	3	Brunswick	48	35	13
Oberlin	5	5	0	Bucksport	11	7	4
Olla	3	3	0	Buxton	13	8	5
Opelousas	67	53	14	Calais	12	8	4
Parks	1	1	0	Camden	14	10	4
Patterson	19	18	1	Cape Elizabeth	14	13	1
Pearl River	11	6	5	Caribou	16	14	2
Pineville	49	42	7	Carrabassett Valley	6	1	5
Plaquemine	32	30	2	Clinton	1	1	0
Pollock	2	2	0	Cumberland	16	11	5
Ponchatoula	21	17	4	Damariscotta	5	4	1
Port Allen	24	24	0	Dexter	6	5	1
Port Barre	14	9	5	Dixfield	3	3	0
Port Vincent	2	2	0	Dover-Foxcroft	5	5	0
Rayne	25	25	0	East Millinocket	5	5	0
Rayville	11	9	2	Eastport	4	4	0
Richwood	16	10	6	Eddington	1	1	0
Ruston	49	41	8	Eliot	9	8	1
Scott	16	16	0	Ellsworth	17	13	4
Shreveport	619	511	108	Fairfield	10	9	1
Sicily Island	3	2	1	Falmouth	22	16	6
Simmesport	6	5	1	Farmington	15	14	1
Slidell	104	71	33	Fort Fairfield	4	4	0
Sorrento	5	4	1	Fort Kent	9	5	4
Springhill	15	15	0	Freeport	17	12	5
Sterlington	5	5	0	Fryeburg	5	5	0
St. Francisville	8	7	1	Gardiner	17	12	5
St. Gabriel	15	8	7	Gorham	24	20	4
St. Joseph	3	3	0	Gouldsboro	2	2	0
St. Martinville	20	15	5	Greenville	4	3	1
Stonewall	1	1	0	Hallowell	5	5	0
Sulphur	58	47	11	Hampden	11	10	1
Sunset	10	10	0	Houlton	18	13	5
Tallulah	15	15	0	Jay	11	7	4
Thibodaux	65	56	9	Jonesport	1	1	0
Tickfaw	8	8	0	Kennebunk	25	20	5
Vidalia	23	23	0	Kennebunkport	16	11	5
Ville Platte	29	29	0	Kittery	27	20	7
Vinton	11	11	0	Lewiston	94	81	13
Vivian	10	8	2	Limestone	5	5	0
Washington	6	6	0	Lincoln	7	6	1
Waterproof	8	7	1	Lisbon	19	14	5
Welsh	11	11	0	Livermore Falls	11	7	4
Westlake	21	20	1	Machias	4	4	0
West Monroe	72	52	20	Madawaska	7	6	1
Westwego	34	33	1	Madison	7	6	1
White Castle	10	6	4	Mechanic Falls	5	5	0
Winnfield	23	15	8	Mexico	4	4	0
Youngsville	10	8	2	Milbridge	2	2	0
Zachary	31	28	3	Millinocket	9	9	0
				Milo	3	3	0
				Monmouth	5	5	0

Table 78

Full-time Law Enforcement Employees as of October 31, 2001
by City by State—Continued

City by state	Total police employees	Total officers	Total civilians	City by state	Total police employees	Total officers	Total civilians
MAINE—Continued				**MARYLAND—Continued**			
Mount Desert	9	5	4	Delmar	11	10	1
Newport	5	5	0	Denton	9	8	1
North Berwick	8	7	1	District Heights	12	9	3
Norway	8	7	1	Easton	57	44	13
Oakland	10	9	1	Edmonston	6	6	0
Ogunquit	9	8	1	Elkton	41	32	9
Old Orchard Beach	28	18	10	Fairmount Heights	4	3	1
Old Town	20	15	5	Federalsburg	12	10	2
Orono	15	14	1	Forest Heights	6	5	1
Oxford	5	4	1	Frederick	149	119	30
Paris	9	8	1	Frostburg	18	14	4
Phippsburg	1	1	0	Fruitland	14	13	1
Pittsfield	6	6	0	Glenarden	9	8	1
Portland	217	155	62	Greenbelt	63	51	12
Presque Isle	23	18	5	Greensboro	3	3	0
Rangeley	3	3	0	Hagerstown	118	96	22
Richmond	4	4	0	Hampstead	9	7	2
Rockland	21	18	3	Hancock	4	3	1
Rockport	7	6	1	Havre de Grace	34	25	9
Rumford	16	16	0	Hurlock	7	7	0
Sabattus	8	7	1	Hyattsville	42	30	12
Saco	42	30	12	Landover Hills	4	3	1
Sanford	53	39	14	La Plata	10	9	1
Scarborough	34	30	4	Laurel	62	45	17
Searsport	3	3	0	Luke	2	2	0
Skowhegan	16	12	4	Manchester	3	3	0
South Berwick	12	8	4	Morningside	7	6	1
South Portland	67	50	17	Mount Rainier	15	12	3
Southwest Harbor	9	5	4	North East	8	7	1
Swan's Island	2	2	0	Oakland	5	4	1
Thomaston	5	5	0	Ocean City	117	96	21
Topsham	16	12	4	Ocean Pines	17	12	5
Van Buren	4	4	0	Oxford	4	4	0
Veazie	7	6	1	Pocomoke City	18	12	6
Waldoboro	5	4	1	Port Deposit	3	3	0
Washburn	3	3	0	Preston	2	2	0
Waterville	38	30	8	Princess Anne	9	8	1
Wells	31	23	8	Ridgely	5	5	0
Westbrook	46	34	12	Rising Sun	7	5	2
Wilton	5	5	0	Riverdale	27	19	8
Windham	29	22	7	Rock Hall	4	4	0
Winslow	9	8	1	Rosewood Center	6	6	0
Winter Harbor	1	1	0	Salisbury	111	84	27
Winthrop	12	8	4	Seat Pleasant	12	8	4
Wiscasset	6	5	1	Smithsburg	2	1	1
Yarmouth	17	12	5	Snow Hill	9	8	1
York	37	26	11	St. Michaels	5	5	0
				Sykesville	6	5	1
MARYLAND				Takoma Park	48	37	11
				Taneytown	9	9	0
Aberdeen	46	37	9	Thurmont	10	10	0
Annapolis	151	113	38	University Park	6	6	0
Baltimore	3,863	3,275	588	Westernport	3	3	0
Baltimore City Sheriff	157	134	23	Westminster	52	40	12
Bel Air	43	31	12				
Berlin	19	14	5	**MASSACHUSETTS**			
Berwyn Heights	7	6	1				
Bladensburg	24	17	7	Abington	32	30	2
Brunswick	11	8	3	Acton	37	31	6
Cambridge	52	41	11	Acushnet	18	16	2
Capitol Heights	12	10	2	Adams	22	17	5
Centreville	4	4	0	Agawam	58	49	9
Chestertown	11	9	2	Amesbury	43	33	10
Cheverly	14	12	2	Amherst	62	48	14
Cottage City	4	4	0	Andover	71	53	18
Crisfield	13	10	3	Aquinnah	4	4	0
Cumberland	61	50	11	Arlington	72	57	15

Table 78

Full-time Law Enforcement Employees as of October 31, 2001
by City by State—Continued

City by state	Total police employees	Total officers	Total civilians	City by state	Total police employees	Total officers	Total civilians
MASSACHUSETTS—Continued				**MASSACHUSETTS—Continued**			
Ashburnham	9	8	1	Edgartown	17	15	2
Ashby	6	6	0	Egremont	3	3	0
Ashfield	1	1	0	Erving	3	3	0
Ashland	30	23	7	Essex	15	15	0
Athol	26	21	5	Everett	102	86	16
Attleboro	80	67	13	Fairhaven	33	27	6
Auburn	40	31	9	Fall River	293	241	52
Avon	16	13	3	Falmouth	73	62	11
Ayer	23	18	5	Fitchburg	98	80	18
Barnstable	123	111	12	Foxborough	34	30	4
Barre	11	7	4	Framingham	138	116	22
Becket	1	1	0	Franklin	58	47	11
Bedford	31	25	6	Freetown	22	17	5
Belchertown	22	17	5	Gardner	53	36	17
Bellingham	38	31	7	Georgetown	13	10	3
Belmont	59	53	6	Gill	3	3	0
Berkley	2	2	0	Gloucester	72	68	4
Berlin	10	7	3	Grafton	21	16	5
Bernardston	4	4	0	Granby	12	10	2
Beverly	78	75	3	Great Barrington	16	15	1
Billerica	74	60	14	Greenfield	51	40	11
Blackstone	20	16	4	Groton	25	16	9
Bolton	13	8	5	Groveland	12	8	4
Boston	2,791	2,130	661	Hadley	14	10	4
Bourne	37	34	3	Halifax	15	11	4
Boxborough	11	10	1	Hamilton	21	15	6
Boxford	13	13	0	Hampden	14	10	4
Boylston	12	8	4	Hanover	35	32	3
Braintree	92	82	10	Hanson	24	21	3
Brewster	23	18	5	Hardwick	3	3	0
Bridgewater	41	38	3	Harvard	13	8	5
Brockton	224	194	30	Harwich	37	31	6
Brookfield	3	3	0	Hatfield	2	2	0
Brookline	153	140	13	Haverhill	107	96	11
Buckland	2	2	0	Hingham	51	42	9
Burlington	70	62	8	Hinsdale	2	2	0
Cambridge	300	270	30	Holbrook	22	21	1
Canton	45	43	2	Holden	23	22	1
Carlisle	13	10	3	Holland	1	1	0
Carver	23	18	5	Holliston	23	22	1
Charlton	22	18	4	Holyoke	152	130	22
Chatham	28	22	6	Hopedale	15	11	4
Chelmsford	75	61	14	Hopkinton	23	18	5
Chelsea	102	84	18	Hubbardston	8	5	3
Chicopee	133	129	4	Hudson	37	31	6
Clinton	35	30	5	Hull	28	26	2
Cohasset	24	19	5	Ipswich	29	25	4
Concord	39	32	7	Kingston	32	24	8
Dalton	12	10	2	Lakeville	20	15	5
Danvers	60	47	13	Lancaster	10	10	0
Dartmouth	76	62	14	Lanesboro	6	6	0
Dedham	66	60	6	Lawrence	178	151	27
Deerfield	7	6	1	Lee	12	11	1
Dennis	50	41	9	Leicester	19	15	4
Dighton	10	9	1	Lenox	10	9	1
Douglas	15	11	4	Leominster	95	78	17
Dover	17	16	1	Leverett	1	1	0
Dracut	49	44	5	Lexington	58	45	13
Dudley	20	16	4	Lincoln	18	13	5
Dunstable	7	7	0	Littleton	16	15	1
Duxbury	39	31	8	Longmeadow	36	31	5
East Bridgewater	27	24	3	Lowell	327	249	78
East Brookfield	3	3	0	Ludlow	39	33	6
Eastham	22	16	6	Lunenburg	14	13	1
Easthampton	33	27	6	Lynn	207	188	19
East Longmeadow	24	22	2	Lynnfield	23	19	4
Easton	40	33	7	Malden	114	104	10

Table 78

Full-time Law Enforcement Employees as of October 31, 2001
by City by State—Continued

City by state	Total police employees	Total officers	Total civilians	City by state	Total police employees	Total officers	Total civilians
MASSACHUSETTS—Continued				**MASSACHUSETTS—Continued**			
Manchester-by-the-Sea	17	14	3	Raynham	33	24	9
Mansfield	46	32	14	Reading	44	39	5
Marblehead	47	37	10	Rehoboth	27	22	5
Marion	14	14	0	Revere	109	101	8
Marlborough	75	64	11	Rochester	10	10	0
Marshfield	47	44	3	Rockland	43	34	9
Mashpee	36	29	7	Rockport	18	17	1
Mattapoisett	18	18	0	Rowley	16	13	3
Maynard	24	22	2	Rutland	6	5	1
Medfield	23	18	5	Salem	107	97	10
Medford	130	126	4	Salisbury	28	22	6
Medway	22	19	3	Sandwich	32	31	1
Melrose	58	54	4	Saugus	77	60	17
Mendon	17	12	5	Scituate	34	28	6
Merrimac	11	7	4	Seekonk	38	32	6
Methuen	99	84	15	Sharon	30	27	3
Middleboro	58	42	16	Sheffield	4	3	1
Middleton	12	11	1	Shelburne	2	2	0
Milford	51	46	5	Sherborn	14	14	0
Millbury	24	19	5	Shirley	13	12	1
Millis	20	15	5	Shrewsbury	50	40	10
Millville	6	3	3	Somerset	40	32	8
Milton	72	57	15	Somerville	157	133	24
Monson	15	10	5	Southampton	7	7	0
Montague	21	16	5	Southborough	18	13	5
Monterey	1	1	0	Southbridge	37	34	3
Nahant	12	12	0	South Hadley	30	25	5
Nantucket	31	26	5	Southwick	22	16	6
Natick	71	54	17	Spencer	21	17	4
Needham	58	49	9	Springfield	678	589	89
New Bedford	349	284	65	Sterling	10	9	1
Newbury	14	10	4	Stockbridge	6	6	0
Newburyport	39	33	6	Stoneham	49	40	9
Newton	184	159	25	Stoughton	64	57	7
Norfolk	19	17	2	Stow	15	11	4
North Adams	33	28	5	Sturbridge	21	16	5
Northampton	66	60	6	Sudbury	33	27	6
North Andover	53	41	12	Sunderland	5	5	0
North Attleboro	59	49	10	Sutton	16	13	3
Northborough	27	20	7	Swampscott	36	34	2
Northbridge	26	21	5	Swansea	40	33	7
North Brookfield	6	6	0	Taunton	119	114	5
Northfield	4	3	1	Templeton	11	10	1
North Reading	31	30	1	Tewksbury	72	57	15
Norton	30	28	2	Tisbury	12	10	2
Norwell	24	20	4	Topsfield	14	10	4
Norwood	71	61	10	Townsend	17	15	2
Oak Bluffs	18	15	3	Truro	16	11	5
Orange	14	13	1	Tyngsboro	32	25	7
Orleans	27	21	6	Upton	17	12	5
Oxford	21	17	4	Uxbridge	24	19	5
Palmer	26	21	5	Wakefield	46	45	1
Paxton	8	7	1	Walpole	42	37	5
Peabody	108	93	15	Waltham	186	147	39
Pelham	2	2	0	Ware	18	18	0
Pembroke	33	31	2	Wareham	48	39	9
Pepperell	18	17	1	Warren	12	7	5
Petersham	2	2	0	Watertown	81	68	13
Phillipston	2	2	0	Wayland	30	22	8
Pittsfield	98	82	16	Webster	33	29	4
Plainville	17	13	4	Wellesley	54	39	15
Plymouth	121	102	19	Wellfleet	17	12	5
Plympton	5	5	0	Wenham	11	10	1
Princeton	8	5	3	Westborough	31	25	6
Provincetown	25	18	7	West Boylston	18	13	5
Quincy	240	206	34	West Bridgewater	22	22	0
Randolph	61	59	2	West Brookfield	6	6	0

Table 78

Full-time Law Enforcement Employees as of October 31, 2001
by City by State—Continued

City by state	Total police employees	Total officers	Total civilians	City by state	Total police employees	Total officers	Total civilians
MASSACHUSETTS—Continued				**MICHIGAN—Continued**			
Westfield	85	74	11	Bridgeport Township	10	9	1
Westford	51	40	11	Bridgman	4	4	0
Westminster	16	11	5	Brighton	17	15	2
West Newbury	13	8	5	Bronson	5	5	0
Weston	31	26	5	Brooklyn/Columbia	5	4	1
Westport	38	33	5	Brown City	2	2	0
West Springfield	91	81	10	Brownstown Township	50	39	11
West Tisbury	8	8	0	Buchanan	10	9	1
Westwood	34	26	8	Buena Vista Township	19	17	2
Weymouth	123	106	17	Burr Oak	1	1	0
Whately	2	2	0	Burton	45	39	6
Whitman	25	24	1	Cadillac	20	18	2
Wilbraham	31	30	1	Calumet	1	1	0
Williamsburg	1	1	0	Cambridge Township	4	3	1
Williamstown	15	11	4	Canton Township	102	74	28
Wilmington	46	44	2	Capac	4	3	1
Winchendon	20	15	5	Carleton	4	3	1
Winchester	44	37	7	Caro	10	9	1
Winthrop	32	31	1	Carrollton Township	7	6	1
Woburn	79	73	6	Carson City	2	2	0
Worcester	530	468	62	Carsonville	1	1	0
Wrentham	21	19	2	Caseville	2	2	0
Yarmouth	61	52	9	Caspian	1	1	0
				Cass City	4	4	0
MICHIGAN				Cassopolis	5	4	1
				Cedar Springs	7	7	0
Adrian	35	30	5	Center Line	35	29	6
Akron-Fairgrove	1	1	0	Charlevoix	7	7	0
Albion	39	33	6	Charlotte	19	18	1
Algonac	9	8	1	Cheboygan	11	10	1
Allegan	11	10	1	Chelsea	13	9	4
Allen Park	62	55	7	Chesterfield Township	48	38	10
Alma	14	14	0	Chikaming Township	4	4	0
Almont	9	9	0	Chocolay Township	5	4	1
Alpena	20	18	2	Clare	9	8	1
Ann Arbor	230	170	60	Clarkston	1	1	0
Argentine Township	6	5	1	Clawson	24	21	3
Armada	3	3	0	Clay Township	18	12	6
Auburn	3	2	1	Clinton	3	3	0
Auburn Hills	61	48	13	Clinton Township	139	105	34
Bad Axe	9	9	0	Clio	7	6	1
Bancroft	1	1	0	Coldwater	20	18	2
Bangor	7	6	1	Coleman	2	2	0
Baraga	2	2	0	Coloma City	3	3	0
Barry Township	2	2	0	Coloma Township	7	6	1
Bath Township	10	9	1	Colon	2	2	0
Battle Creek	148	123	25	Concord	3	3	0
Bay City	85	75	10	Constantine	7	6	1
Belding	11	9	2	Corunna	5	5	0
Bellaire	2	2	0	Covert Township	6	6	0
Belleville	12	10	2	Croswell	8	8	0
Bellevue	3	3	0	Crystal Falls	5	5	0
Benton Harbor	31	21	10	Crystal Township	1	1	0
Benton Township	41	28	13	Davison	13	11	2
Berkley	34	28	6	Davison Township	19	17	2
Berrien Springs-Oronoko Township	7	6	1	Dearborn	208	192	16
Beverly Hills	32	27	5	Dearborn Heights	118	94	24
Big Rapids	20	19	1	Decatur	4	4	0
Birch Run	7	6	1	Denmark Township	1	1	0
Birmingham	54	35	19	Denton Township	4	4	0
Blackman Township	31	30	1	Detroit	4,850	4,184	666
Blissfield	6	5	1	Dewitt	7	6	1
Bloomfield Hills	30	26	4	Dewitt Township	17	16	1
Bloomfield Township	98	75	23	Douglas	9	8	1
Bloomingdale	1	1	0	Dowagiac	17	15	2
Boyne City	8	7	1	Dryden Township	3	3	0
Breckenridge	3	3	0	Durand	6	6	0

Table 78

Full-time Law Enforcement Employees as of October 31, 2001

by City by State—Continued

City by state	Total police employees	Total officers	Total civilians	City by state	Total police employees	Total officers	Total civilians
MICHIGAN—Continued				**MICHIGAN—Continued**			
East Grand Rapids	33	30	3	Harper Woods	41	36	5
East Jordan	7	6	1	Hart	4	4	0
East Lansing	101	65	36	Hartford	6	6	0
Eastpointe	58	53	5	Hastings	17	15	2
East Tawas	7	6	1	Hazel Park	50	42	8
Eaton Rapids	12	11	1	Hesperia	3	3	0
Eau Claire	2	1	1	Highland Park	65	56	9
Ecorse	29	27	2	Hillsdale	19	16	3
Edmore-Home	2	2	0	Holland	73	61	12
Elk Rapids	5	5	0	Holly	17	12	5
Elkton	2	2	0	Homer	3	3	0
Elsie	1	1	0	Hopkins	3	3	0
Emmett Township	16	14	2	Houghton	8	8	0
Erie Township	4	4	0	Howard City	2	2	0
Escanaba	49	36	13	Howell	22	20	2
Essexville	8	8	0	Hudson	3	3	0
Evart	3	3	0	Hudsonville	10	9	1
Fair Haven Township	1	1	0	Huntington Woods	18	17	1
Farmington	27	21	6	Huron Township	27	21	6
Farmington Hills	169	118	51	Imlay City	10	9	1
Fenton	21	15	6	Inkster	85	72	13
Ferndale	58	49	9	Ionia	20	18	2
Flat Rock	28	24	4	Iron Mountain	14	14	0
Flint	316	281	35	Iron River	8	7	1
Flint Township	51	44	7	Ironwood	19	15	4
Flushing	14	13	1	Ishpeming	14	13	1
Flushing Township	9	8	1	Ishpeming Township	1	1	0
Forsyth Township	7	6	1	Ithaca	5	4	1
Fowlerville	6	6	0	Jackson	87	65	22
Frankenmuth	8	8	0	Jonesville	5	5	0
Frankfort	5	5	0	Kalamazoo	322	255	67
Franklin	11	10	1	Kalamazoo Township	38	31	7
Fraser	61	49	12	Kalkaska	8	7	1
Fremont	9	8	1	Keego Harbor	7	6	1
Frost Township	2	1	1	Kentwood	83	68	15
Gagetown	1	1	0	Kingsford	20	20	0
Galesburg	3	2	1	Kinross Township	3	3	0
Garden City	58	46	12	Laingsburg	3	3	0
Gaylord	13	11	2	Lake Angelus	3	3	0
Genesee Township	28	24	4	Lake Linden	1	1	0
Gerrish Township	6	6	0	Lake Odessa	4	4	0
Gibraltar	13	12	1	Lake Orion	8	4	4
Gladstone	13	12	1	Lakeview	2	2	0
Gladwin	5	5	0	L'Anse	5	5	0
Grand Beach	3	3	0	Lansing	357	259	98
Grand Blanc	21	18	3	Lansing Township	14	13	1
Grand Blanc Township	42	36	6	Lapeer	24	20	4
Grand Haven	39	35	4	Lathrup Village	11	10	1
Grand Ledge	16	15	1	Laurium	4	4	0
Grand Rapids	453	375	78	Lawrence	3	3	0
Grandville	33	27	6	Lawton	6	6	0
Grant	1	1	0	Lennon	1	1	0
Grayling	7	6	1	Leoni Township	6	5	1
Green Oak Township	15	13	2	Leslie	3	3	0
Greenville	24	18	6	Lexington	4	4	0
Grosse Ile Township	25	18	7	Lincoln Park	70	60	10
Grosse Pointe	28	25	3	Lincoln Township	12	11	1
Grosse Pointe Farms	42	33	9	Linden	4	4	0
Grosse Pointe Park	51	45	6	Litchfield	5	5	0
Grosse Pointe Shores	21	19	2	Livonia	193	167	26
Grosse Pointe Woods	48	36	12	Lowell	9	7	2
Hamburg Township	15	14	1	Ludington	17	15	2
Hampton Township	12	11	1	Luna Pier	4	4	0
Hamtramck	38	38	0	Mackinac Island	9	8	1
Hancock	7	7	0	Mackinaw City	6	6	0
Harbor Beach	4	4	0	Madison Heights	77	60	17
Harbor Springs	6	5	1	Madison Township	2	2	0

Table 78

Full-time Law Enforcement Employees as of October 31, 2001

by City by State—Continued

City by state	Total police employees	Total officers	Total civilians	City by state	Total police employees	Total officers	Total civilians
MICHIGAN—Continued				**MICHIGAN—Continued**			
Mancelona	4	4	0	Owosso	23	22	1
Manistee	17	15	2	Oxford	7	4	3
Manistique	10	9	1	Parchment	3	3	0
Manton	1	1	0	Parma-Sandstone	2	2	0
Marenisco Township	1	1	0	Paw Paw	11	9	2
Marine City	10	9	1	Pentwater	3	3	0
Marion	1	1	0	Perry	7	6	1
Marlette	4	4	0	Petoskey	19	17	2
Marquette	42	36	6	Pigeon	1	1	0
Marshall	21	16	5	Pinckney	4	4	0
Marysville	19	16	3	Pinconning	4	4	0
Mason	14	13	1	Pittsfield Township	43	31	12
Mattawan	5	5	0	Plainwell	11	9	2
Mayville	2	2	0	Pleasant Ridge	7	7	0
Melvindale	30	28	2	Plymouth	17	16	1
Memphis	4	4	0	Plymouth Township	41	28	13
Mendon	1	1	0	Pontiac	212	163	49
Menominee	19	17	2	Portage	74	57	17
Meridian Township	50	43	7	Port Austin	2	2	0
Metamora Township	6	6	0	Port Huron	74	53	21
Michiana	3	3	0	Portland	9	7	2
Midland	50	47	3	Potterville	3	3	0
Milan	15	11	4	Prairieville Township	2	2	0
Milford	23	17	6	Quincy	3	3	0
Millington	3	3	0	Reading	2	2	0
Monroe	54	44	10	Redford Township	95	76	19
Montague	5	5	0	Reed City	4	4	0
Montrose Township	12	11	1	Reese	2	2	0
Morenci	3	3	0	Richfield Township (Genessee County)	10	8	2
Morrice	4	1	3	Richfield Township (Roscommon County)	1	1	0
Mount Clemens	45	37	8	Richland	2	2	0
Mount Morris	9	8	1	Richland Township	4	4	0
Mount Morris Township	40	36	4	Richmond	12	9	3
Mount Pleasant	38	32	6	River Rouge	37	35	2
Mundy Township	20	17	3	Riverview	33	29	4
Munising	6	6	0	Rochester	29	21	8
Muskegon	92	81	11	Rockford	13	10	3
Muskegon Heights	34	30	4	Rockwood	9	8	1
Muskegon Township	16	15	1	Rogers City	8	8	0
Napoleon Township	3	3	0	Romeo	11	7	4
Nashville	3	3	0	Romulus	87	72	15
Negaunee	12	11	1	Roosevelt Park	9	8	1
Newaygo	4	3	1	Rose City	3	3	0
New Baltimore	16	15	1	Roseville	103	91	12
Newberry	3	3	0	Ross Township	2	2	0
New Buffalo	7	6	1	Royal Oak	117	98	19
New Haven	6	5	1	Saginaw	139	123	16
Niles	32	22	10	Saginaw Township	48	44	4
Niles Township	4	4	0	Saline	17	13	4
North Branch	4	4	0	Sand Lake	1	1	0
Northfield Township	12	10	2	Sandusky	6	6	0
North Muskegon	8	7	1	Sault Ste. Marie	33	27	6
Northville	17	14	3	Schoolcraft	2	2	0
Northville Township	35	26	9	Scottville	3	3	0
Norton Shores	31	29	2	Sebewaing	3	3	0
Norvell Township	2	2	0	Shelby	3	3	0
Norway	6	6	0	Shelby Township	77	59	18
Novi	89	60	29	Shepherd	2	2	0
Oak Park	83	69	14	Somerset Township	2	2	0
Olivet	2	2	0	Southfield	179	156	23
Onaway	2	2	0	Southgate	56	44	12
Ontwa Township-Edwardsburg	7	6	1	South Haven	27	20	7
Orchard Lake	9	8	1	South Lyon	19	17	2
Oscoda Township	12	11	1	South Rockwood	3	3	0
Otisville	1	1	0	Sparta	7	6	1
Otsego	8	7	1	Spring Arbor Township	2	2	0
Ovid	3	3	0	Springfield	18	16	2

Table 78

Full-time Law Enforcement Employees as of October 31, 2001

by City by State—Continued

City by state	Total police employees	Total officers	Total civilians	City by state	Total police employees	Total officers	Total civilians
MICHIGAN—Continued				**MINNESOTA**			
Spring Lake-Ferrysburg	11	10	1	Albany	3	3	0
Stanton	1	1	0	Albert Lea	39	30	9
St. Charles	4	4	0	Alexandria	20	17	3
St. Clair	11	10	1	Annandale	4	4	0
St. Clair Shores	110	92	18	Anoka	37	29	8
Sterling Heights	226	168	58	Appleton	5	5	0
St. Ignace	6	6	0	Apple Valley	65	47	18
St. Johns	13	11	2	Austin	32	28	4
St. Joseph	25	19	6	Babbitt	4	4	0
St. Joseph Township	13	12	1	Baxter	10	9	1
St. Louis	6	5	1	Bayport	5	5	0
Sturgis	21	17	4	Becker	5	4	1
Summit Township	5	5	0	Belle Plaine	6	5	1
Sumpter Township	17	14	3	Bemidji	27	24	3
Sunfield	1	1	0	Benson	8	7	1
Suttons Bay	1	1	0	Big Lake	10	8	2
Swartz Creek	7	6	1	Biwabik	4	4	0
Sylvan Lake	5	5	0	Blaine	62	46	16
Taylor	125	97	28	Blooming Prairie	3	3	0
Tecumseh	16	14	2	Bloomington	143	108	35
Thomas Township	9	8	1	Blue Earth	7	7	0
Three Oaks	3	3	0	Brainerd	32	25	7
Three Rivers	19	15	4	Breckenridge	11	7	4
Tittabawassee Township	4	4	0	Brooklyn Center	56	43	13
Traverse City	36	34	2	Brooklyn Park	94	71	23
Trenton	48	46	2	Buffalo	17	14	3
Troy	196	136	60	Burnsville	83	65	18
Tuscarora Township	8	7	1	Caledonia	5	4	1
Ubly	2	2	0	Cambridge	10	10	0
Unadilla Township	3	3	0	Cannon Falls	6	6	0
Union City	4	4	0	Centennial Lakes	17	14	3
Utica	21	16	5	Champlin	25	22	3
Van Buren Township	40	29	11	Chaska	23	18	5
Vassar	6	6	0	Chisago City	6	5	1
Vernon	1	1	0	Chisholm	12	11	1
Vicksburg	5	5	0	Cloquet	21	19	2
Waldron	1	1	0	Cold Spring	6	6	0
Walker	43	37	6	Columbia Heights	32	24	8
Walled Lake	20	14	6	Coon Rapids	70	60	10
Warren	292	246	46	Corcoran	4	4	0
Waterford Township	116	90	26	Cottage Grove	47	35	12
Waterloo Township	1	1	0	Crookston	18	16	2
Watertown Township	1	1	0	Crosby	10	6	4
Watervliet	4	4	0	Crystal	37	28	9
Wayland	6	5	1	Dawson	3	3	0
Wayne	51	39	12	Dayton	5	5	0
West Bloomfield Township	94	72	22	Deephaven/Woodland	8	7	1
West Branch	7	6	1	Detroit Lakes	15	13	2
Westland	133	103	30	Dilworth	6	5	1
White Cloud	3	2	1	Duluth	179	149	30
Whitehall	8	8	0	Eagan	86	68	18
White Lake Township	34	26	8	East Grand Forks	25	23	2
White Pigeon	4	4	0	Eden Prairie	82	57	25
Williamston	5	5	0	Edina	65	49	16
Wixom	26	22	4	Elk River	33	26	7
Wolverine Lake	9	8	1	Ely	12	7	5
Woodhaven	39	33	6	Eveleth	11	10	1
Woodstock Township	1	1	0	Fairmont	21	18	3
Wyandotte	57	46	11	Faribault	34	26	8
Wyoming	144	103	41	Farmington	15	13	2
Yale	5	5	0	Fergus Falls	26	21	5
Ypsilanti	55	39	16	Floodwood	3	3	0
Zeeland	10	9	1	Forest Lake	19	17	2
Zilwaukee	4	4	0	Fridley	47	38	9
				Gilbert	6	6	0
				Glencoe	10	9	1
				Glenwood	4	4	0

Table 78

Full-time Law Enforcement Employees as of October 31, 2001
by City by State—Continued

City by state	Total police employees	Total officers	Total civilians	City by state	Total police employees	Total officers	Total civilians
MINNESOTA—Continued				**MINNESOTA—Continued**			
Golden Valley	41	30	11	Prior Lake	23	20	3
Goodview	4	4	0	Proctor	7	6	1
Grand Rapids	20	16	4	Ramsey	20	17	3
Granite Falls	5	5	0	Red Wing	32	26	6
Hallock	1	1	0	Redwood Falls	10	9	1
Hastings	30	25	5	Richfield	60	44	16
Hermantown	12	10	2	Robbinsdale	27	20	7
Hibbing	33	30	3	Rochester	163	117	46
Hopkins	33	23	10	Roseau	6	5	1
Hoyt Lakes	5	5	0	Rosemount	17	15	2
Hutchinson	31	22	9	Roseville	54	46	8
International Falls	13	13	0	Sartell	13	11	2
Inver Grove Heights	35	29	6	Sauk Centre	9	6	3
Jackson	8	7	1	Sauk Rapids	13	12	1
Janesville	5	4	1	Savage	29	23	6
Jordan	10	8	2	Scanlon	1	1	0
Kasson	7	7	0	Shakopee	34	27	7
La Crescent	9	8	1	Silver Bay	4	4	0
Lake City	9	8	1	Slayton	4	4	0
Lakefield	3	3	0	Sleepy Eye	6	6	0
Lakeville	59	44	15	South Lake Minnetonka	15	14	1
Le Sueur	8	7	1	South St. Paul	26	24	2
Lindstrom	7	6	1	Springfield	4	4	0
Lino Lakes	24	21	3	Spring Lake Park	13	11	2
Litchfield	10	9	1	St. Anthony	22	20	2
Little Falls	14	12	2	Staples	5	5	0
Long Prairie	6	6	0	St. Cloud	104	85	19
Madison	3	3	0	St. Francis	10	8	2
Mankato	60	48	12	Stillwater	24	20	4
Maple Grove	62	53	9	St. James	8	7	1
Maplewood	57	46	11	St. Joseph	6	6	0
Marshall	22	20	2	St. Louis Park	69	49	20
Medina	8	7	1	St. Paul	804	554	250
Melrose	6	5	1	St. Paul Park	8	8	0
Mendota Heights	17	15	2	St. Peter	20	14	6
Minneapolis	1,147	868	279	Thief River Falls	16	15	1
Minnetonka	73	54	19	Tracy	4	4	0
Minnetrista	10	9	1	Two Harbors	8	7	1
Montevideo	10	9	1	Virginia	23	22	1
Moorhead	73	50	23	Wabasha	5	4	1
Moose Lake	3	3	0	Wadena	9	8	1
Mora	8	8	0	Waite Park	15	12	3
Morris	9	8	1	Warroad	6	5	1
Mound	16	13	3	Waseca	15	13	2
Mounds View	18	16	2	Wayzata	10	9	1
Mountain Lake	3	3	0	Wells	4	4	0
New Brighton	37	27	10	West Hennepin	10	8	2
New Hope	38	29	9	West St. Paul	36	26	10
Newport	7	7	0	White Bear Lake	36	29	7
New Prague	10	8	2	Willmar	35	32	3
New Ulm	22	19	3	Windom	9	8	1
North Branch	9	8	1	Winona	45	40	5
Northfield	28	21	7	Woodbury	53	45	8
North Mankato	12	11	1	Worthington	31	24	7
North St. Paul	18	16	2	Wyoming	6	6	0
Oakdale	36	27	9	Zumbrota	4	4	0
Oak Park Heights	10	9	1				
Olivia	5	5	0	**MISSISSIPPI**			
Orono	21	18	3				
Ortonville	5	4	1	Aberdeen	24	19	5
Osseo	5	5	0	Amory	24	18	6
Owatonna	29	27	2	Batesville	43	34	9
Park Rapids	7	7	0	Bay St. Louis	50	38	12
Paynesville	4	4	0	Belzoni	14	9	5
Plainview	5	5	0	Booneville	33	26	7
Plymouth	75	60	15	Brandon	39	29	10
Princeton	10	9	1	Brookhaven	36	29	7

Table 78

Full-time Law Enforcement Employees as of October 31, 2001

by City by State—Continued

City by state	Total police employees	Total officers	Total civilians	City by state	Total police employees	Total officers	Total civilians
MISSISSIPPI—Continued				**MISSISSIPPI—Continued**			
Bruce	5	5	0	Pearl	60	47	13
Byhalia	11	7	4	Pelahatchie	7	5	2
Carthage	14	10	4	Petal	20	16	4
Charleston	10	10	0	Picayune	46	29	17
Clarksdale	50	44	6	Pickens	4	4	0
Cleveland	47	38	9	Poplarville	10	9	1
Clinton	60	44	16	Port Gibson	10	6	4
Coldwater	3	3	0	Purvis	10	7	3
Collins	14	10	4	Quitman	11	10	1
Columbia	25	23	2	Richland	36	25	11
Columbus	91	78	13	Ridgeland	68	43	25
Como	7	7	0	Ripley	12	11	1
Corinth	45	33	12	Rolling Fork	5	5	0
Crystal Springs	19	13	6	Ruleville	12	8	4
De Kalb	5	4	1	Sandersville	5	4	1
Drew	8	4	4	Senatobia	21	18	3
Edwards	4	4	0	Shaw	8	4	4
Ellisville	11	9	2	Shelby	13	9	4
Eupora	9	7	2	Southaven	87	72	15
Fayette	8	3	5	Starkville	50	39	11
Flowood	44	35	9	Stonewall	3	3	0
Forest	18	14	4	Summit	7	6	1
Fulton	9	9	0	Sunflower	3	3	0
Gloster	8	6	2	Tchula	5	5	0
Goodman	3	3	0	Terry	1	1	0
Greenville	141	102	39	Tupelo	123	109	14
Greenwood	72	53	19	Vaiden	4	4	0
Grenada	45	40	5	Verona	13	9	4
Gulfport	257	185	72	Water Valley	11	11	0
Hattiesburg	189	114	75	Waveland	24	19	5
Heidelberg	4	4	0	Waynesboro	21	17	4
Hernando	20	20	0	West Point	35	26	9
Hollandale	11	7	4	Wiggins	16	13	3
Horn Lake	52	41	11	Winona	14	12	2
Houston	16	12	4	Yazoo City	46	30	16
Indianola	33	25	8				
Inverness	4	4	0	**MISSOURI**			
Itta Bena	13	8	5				
Iuka	11	11	0	Arnold	56	44	12
Jackson	647	428	219	Aurora	19	13	6
Kosciusko	27	20	7	Ballwin	69	54	15
Laurel	84	57	27	Bellefontaine Neighbors	27	24	3
Leakesville	6	5	1	Bel-Nor	9	9	0
Leland	24	19	5	Bel-Ridge	14	13	1
Lexington	11	8	3	Belton	53	38	15
Long Beach	46	30	16	Berkeley	55	44	11
Louisville	26	19	7	Bethany	6	6	0
Lucedale	19	12	7	Beverly Hills	9	7	2
Macon	9	8	1	Blue Springs	95	70	25
Madison	44	33	11	Bolivar	26	17	9
Magee	17	13	4	Bonne Terre	11	11	0
Magnolia	5	5	0	Boonville	27	20	7
McComb	50	32	18	Bowling Green	9	7	2
McLain	2	1	1	Branson	57	42	15
Mendenhall	12	8	4	Breckenridge Hills	16	15	1
Meridian	112	93	19	Brentwood	32	27	5
Moorhead	5	5	0	Bridgeton	69	57	12
Morton	14	10	4	Brookfield	17	10	7
Moss Point	39	31	8	Buckner	6	5	1
Mound Bayou	4	2	2	Butler	15	10	5
Natchez	79	52	27	California	7	6	1
New Albany	21	19	2	Calverton Park	6	6	0
Newton	19	10	9	Cameron	18	13	5
Olive Branch	62	49	13	Canton	8	4	4
Oxford	58	50	8	Cape Girardeau	98	72	26
Pascagoula	84	55	29	Carrollton	5	4	1
Pass Christian	23	17	6	Carterville	6	6	0

Table 78

Full-time Law Enforcement Employees as of October 31, 2001
by City by State—Continued

City by state	Total police employees	Total officers	Total civilians	City by state	Total police employees	Total officers	Total civilians
MISSOURI—Continued				**MISSOURI—Continued**			
Carthage	32	25	7	Lamar	11	9	2
Caruthersville	26	22	4	Lebanon	33	23	10
Centralia	11	6	5	Lee's Summit	137	101	36
Chaffee	9	5	4	Lexington	10	9	1
Charlack	8	8	0	Liberty	52	37	15
Charleston	19	15	4	Louisiana	17	9	8
Chesterfield	94	85	9	Macon	11	10	1
Chillicothe	22	16	6	Malden	15	12	3
Claycomo	10	10	0	Manchester	43	40	3
Clayton	68	51	17	Maplewood	34	28	6
Clinton	21	20	1	Marceline	10	6	4
Columbia	169	136	33	Marshall	34	23	11
Cool Valley	10	10	0	Maryland Heights	92	77	15
Cottleville	9	7	2	Maryville	24	20	4
Country Club Hills	11	11	0	Mexico	35	33	2
Crestwood	45	34	11	Moberly	45	35	10
Creve Coeur	60	50	10	Moline Acres	7	7	0
Crystal City	20	16	4	Monett	29	19	10
Dellwood	19	17	2	Montgomery City	6	6	0
De Soto	20	15	5	Mountain Grove	15	10	5
Des Peres	43	36	7	Mount Vernon	10	10	0
Dexter	21	15	6	Neosho	25	22	3
East Prairie	13	9	4	Nevada	30	20	10
Edmundson	11	10	1	New Madrid	7	7	0
Eldon	16	14	2	Normandy	21	20	1
El Dorado Springs	11	6	5	North Kansas City	49	38	11
Ellisville	19	19	0	Northwoods	30	21	9
Eureka	27	23	4	Oak Grove	11	10	1
Excelsior Springs	24	17	7	Oakland	70	57	13
Farmington	30	22	8	Oakview	4	4	0
Fayette	8	8	0	Odessa	10	10	0
Ferguson	56	49	7	O'Fallon	106	80	26
Festus	34	25	9	Olivette	26	21	5
Florissant	102	81	21	Osage Beach	33	21	12
Fredericktown	9	9	0	Overland	61	50	11
Frontenac	22	17	5	Pacific	24	17	7
Fulton	32	25	7	Pagedale	15	14	1
Gallatin	3	3	0	Palmyra	10	7	3
Gladstone	57	46	11	Park Hills	14	13	1
Glendale	14	11	3	Parkville	11	10	1
Grain Valley	14	12	2	Perryville	25	25	0
Grandview	62	48	14	Pevely	19	14	5
Hamilton	2	2	0	Pilot Knob	1	1	0
Hannibal	45	33	12	Pine Lawn	28	27	1
Harrisonville	29	21	8	Platte City	9	9	0
Hawk Point	1	1	0	Plattsburg	5	5	0
Hazelwood	72	56	16	Pleasant Hill	15	10	5
Hayti	9	8	1	Poplar Bluff	53	43	10
Hermann	8	6	2	Potosi	13	9	4
Higginsville	15	10	5	Republic	19	15	4
Holts Summit	7	6	1	Rich Hill	8	4	4
Independence	280	198	82	Richland	9	5	4
Ironton	4	4	0	Richmond	21	13	8
Jackson	26	20	6	Rolla	44	28	16
Jefferson City	102	74	28	Salem	18	13	5
Jennings	70	46	24	Savannah	5	5	0
Joplin	85	76	9	Sedalia	55	43	12
Kahoka	2	2	0	Shrewsbury	20	17	3
Kansas City	1,862	1,218	644	Sikeston	73	60	13
Kearney	12	11	1	Slater	9	5	4
Kennett	27	23	4	Smithville	13	12	1
Kirksville	38	27	11	Springfield	393	310	83
Kirkwood	70	57	13	St. Ann	60	46	14
Ladue	35	28	7	St. Charles	135	104	31
Lake Lotawana	6	5	1	St. Clair	15	12	3
Lake Ozark	12	11	1	Ste. Genevieve	12	11	1
Lake St. Louis	29	23	6	St. George	6	6	0

Table 78

Full-time Law Enforcement Employees as of October 31, 2001
by City by State—Continued

City by state	Total police employees	Total officers	Total civilians	City by state	Total police employees	Total officers	Total civilians
MISSOURI—Continued				**MONTANA—Continued**			
St. John	25	23	2	St. Ignatius	2	2	0
St. Joseph	152	111	41	Thompson Falls	3	3	0
St. Louis	1,994	1,408	586	Three Forks	3	3	0
Stockton	5	5	0	Troy	3	3	0
St. Peters	105	85	20	West Yellowstone	11	6	5
St. Robert	22	16	6	Whitefish	17	12	5
Sugar Creek	19	14	5	Whitehall	3	2	1
Sullivan	24	16	8				
Sunset Hills	30	24	6	**NEBRASKA**			
Town and Country	42	34	8				
Trenton	17	10	7	Albion	2	2	0
Union	19	17	2	Alliance	29	21	8
University City	101	80	21	Ashland	6	5	1
Vandalia	9	5	4	Auburn	6	6	0
Vinita Park	13	12	1	Aurora	7	7	0
Warrensburg	33	30	3	Bayard	4	4	0
Warrenton	15	13	2	Beatrice	33	22	11
Warsaw	7	7	0	Bellevue	83	75	8
Warson Woods	8	7	1	Blair	16	14	2
Washington	29	25	4	Bridgeport	3	3	0
Webb City	23	19	4	Broken Bow	7	6	1
Webster Groves	53	44	9	Central City	6	5	1
Wentzville	44	34	10	Chadron	16	12	4
West Plains	24	19	5	Columbus	50	34	16
Weston	4	4	0	Cozad	11	7	4
Woodson Terrace	19	16	3	Crete	14	9	5
Wright City	6	6	0	David City	6	5	1
				Elkhorn	13	12	1
MONTANA				Fairbury	8	7	1
				Falls City	13	9	4
Baker	3	3	0	Fremont	44	37	7
Belgrade	11	9	2	Geneva	4	4	0
Billings	152	122	30	Gering	19	16	3
Boulder	4	4	0	Gordon	6	5	1
Bozeman	48	41	7	Gothenburg	9	5	4
Bridger	2	2	0	Grand Island	83	75	8
Chinook	4	4	0	Hastings	51	37	14
Columbia Falls	13	7	6	Holdrege	15	9	6
Conrad	5	5	0	Imperial	4	4	0
Cut Bank	7	6	1	Kearney	50	41	9
Dillon	9	8	1	Kimball	5	5	0
East Helena	4	4	0	La Vista	27	23	4
Eureka	3	3	0	Lexington	16	14	2
Fort Benton	3	3	0	Lincoln	410	304	106
Glasgow	7	6	1	Lyons	2	2	0
Glendive	15	9	6	Madison	3	3	0
Great Falls	115	78	37	McCook	18	14	4
Hamilton	12	11	1	Milford	4	4	0
Havre	25	19	6	Minden	4	4	0
Helena	66	47	19	Mitchell	5	5	0
Hot Springs	2	2	0	Nebraska City	14	13	1
Joliet	2	2	0	Neligh	2	2	0
Kalispell	38	29	9	Norfolk	57	38	19
Laurel	14	10	4	North Platte	66	41	25
Lewistown	20	13	7	Ogallala	12	11	1
Libby	6	6	0	Omaha	907	717	190
Livingston	17	12	5	O'Neill	8	7	1
Manhattan	2	2	0	Ord	7	4	3
Miles City	21	15	6	Papillion	31	26	5
Missoula	102	82	20	Plainview	2	2	0
Plains	3	3	0	Plattsmouth	16	14	2
Plentywood	5	4	1	Ralston	13	12	1
Polson	8	8	0	Schuyler	10	8	2
Red Lodge	7	7	0	Scottsbluff	34	31	3
Ronan City	4	4	0	Seward	10	9	1
Sidney	11	10	1	South Sioux City	28	27	1
Stevensville	3	3	0	Superior	4	4	0

Table 78

Full-time Law Enforcement Employees as of October 31, 2001
by City by State—Continued

City by state	Total police employees	Total officers	Total civilians	City by state	Total police employees	Total officers	Total civilians
NEBRASKA—Continued				**NEW HAMPSHIRE—Continued**			
Syracuse	3	3	0	Epsom	5	4	1
Tecumseh	4	3	1	Exeter	32	23	9
Valentine	4	3	1	Farmington	15	13	2
Valley	6	6	0	Fitzwilliam	4	3	1
Wahoo	6	6	0	Franconia	3	3	0
Wayne	10	6	4	Franklin	23	15	8
West Point	7	6	1	Fremont	3	3	0
Wilber	4	4	0	Gilford	22	16	6
Wymore	2	2	0	Gilmanton	4	4	0
York	19	14	5	Goffstown	37	27	10
				Gorham	9	8	1
NEVADA				Grantham	3	3	0
				Greenland	6	6	0
Boulder City	38	29	9	Greenville	6	6	0
Carlin	7	5	2	Hampstead	5	5	0
Elko	41	34	7	Hampton	45	38	7
Fallon	30	19	11	Hanover	31	17	14
Henderson	333	251	82	Henniker	9	7	2
Las Vegas Metropolitan Police Department	3,748	1,895	1,853	Hillsborough	16	10	6
Lovelock	6	5	1	Hinsdale	7	6	1
Mesquite	35	19	16	Holderness	5	5	0
North Las Vegas	281	191	90	Hooksett	31	18	13
Reno	469	307	162	Hopkinton	9	7	2
Sparks	133	91	42	Hudson	50	39	11
West Wendover	23	15	8	Jaffrey	14	11	3
Winnemucca	19	15	4	Keene	62	46	16
Yerington	8	7	1	Kensington	3	3	0
				Kingston	11	8	3
NEW HAMPSHIRE				Laconia	43	33	10
				Lebanon	36	26	10
Alstead	1	1	0	Lincoln	9	5	4
Alton	13	10	3	Lisbon	3	3	0
Amherst	17	15	2	Litchfield	11	9	2
Andover	1	1	0	Littleton	12	11	1
Antrim	4	4	0	Londonderry	53	41	12
Ashland	6	6	0	Loudon	7	6	1
Auburn	9	7	2	Manchester	268	199	69
Barnstead	2	2	0	Marlborough	3	3	0
Barrington	7	6	1	Meredith	15	11	4
Bartlett	3	2	1	Merrimack	49	37	12
Bedford	37	26	11	Middleton	3	3	0
Belmont	15	13	2	Milford	28	24	4
Bennington	2	2	0	Milton	7	6	1
Berlin	25	19	6	Mont Vernon	2	2	0
Bethlehem	7	4	3	Moultonboro	9	8	1
Boscawen	6	5	1	New Boston	5	4	1
Brentwood	2	2	0	New Castle	3	3	0
Bristol	9	7	2	New Durham	5	4	1
Campton	5	4	1	Newfields	2	2	0
Candia	6	5	1	New Hampton	5	5	0
Canterbury	1	1	0	Newington	9	8	1
Carroll	3	3	0	Newmarket	19	14	5
Charlestown	8	5	3	Newport	17	13	4
Chester	3	2	1	Newton	5	4	1
Chesterfield	6	5	1	Northfield	10	9	1
Claremont	32	26	6	North Hampton	10	9	1
Colebrook	4	4	0	Northwood	6	5	1
Concord	93	72	21	Nottingham	6	5	1
Conway	27	18	9	Orford	1	1	0
Danville	2	2	0	Ossipee	8	7	1
Deerfield	5	4	1	Peterborough	12	10	2
Deering	2	2	0	Pittsfield	8	7	1
Derry	70	56	14	Plaistow	21	14	7
Dover	69	54	15	Plymouth	16	9	7
Durham	21	18	3	Portsmouth	86	68	18
Enfield	8	6	2	Raymond	18	15	3
Epping	12	11	1	Rindge	8	7	1

Table 78

Full-time Law Enforcement Employees as of October 31, 2001
by City by State—Continued

City by state	Total police employees	Total officers	Total civilians	City by state	Total police employees	Total officers	Total civilians
NEW HAMPSHIRE—Continued				**NEW JERSEY—Continued**			
Rochester	74	53	21	Bordentown	11	10	1
Rollinsford	4	4	0	Bordentown Township	35	27	8
Rye	10	9	1	Bound Brook	27	22	5
Sanbornton	7	6	1	Bradley Beach	21	16	5
Sandown	6	5	1	Branchburg Township	26	24	2
Sandwich	2	2	0	Brick Township	149	116	33
Somersworth	32	25	7	Bridgeton	80	66	14
Springfield	1	1	0	Bridgewater Township	88	72	16
Strafford	3	3	0	Brielle	16	14	2
Stratham	10	9	1	Brigantine	49	39	10
Sugar Hill	1	1	0	Brooklawn	7	7	0
Swanzey	11	9	2	Buena	14	9	5
Thornton	4	4	0	Burlington	35	31	4
Tilton	12	11	1	Burlington Township	48	40	8
Troy	3	3	0	Butler	18	17	1
Tuftonboro	3	3	0	Byram Township	15	14	1
Wakefield	9	8	1	Caldwell	22	18	4
Walpole	4	3	1	Califon	2	2	0
Warner	5	4	1	Camden	478	404	74
Waterville Valley	7	6	1	Cape May	23	17	6
Weare	9	8	1	Carlstadt	34	30	4
Winchester	7	6	1	Carney's Point Township	26	21	5
Windham	23	17	6	Carteret	60	50	10
Wolfeboro	16	11	5	Cedar Grove Township	34	32	2
				Chatham	27	21	6
NEW JERSEY				Chatham Township	30	24	6
				Cherry Hill Township	165	131	34
Aberdeen Township	43	36	7	Chesilhurst	11	10	1
Absecon	33	26	7	Chester	9	8	1
Allendale	19	14	5	Chesterfield Township	5	5	0
Allenhurst	13	9	4	Chester Township	15	14	1
Allentown	5	5	0	Cinnaminson Township	38	33	5
Alpha	3	3	0	Clark Township	56	44	12
Alpine	13	13	0	Clayton	19	17	2
Andover Township	16	11	5	Clementon	13	12	1
Asbury Park	88	75	13	Cliffside Park	46	42	4
Atlantic City	639	423	216	Clifton	176	149	27
Atlantic Highlands	19	15	4	Clinton	8	8	0
Audubon	19	17	2	Clinton Township	19	17	2
Audubon Park	5	5	0	Closter	23	19	4
Avalon	28	20	8	Collingswood	32	29	3
Avon-by-the-Sea	12	12	0	Colts Neck Township	18	17	1
Barnegat Township	36	28	8	Cranbury Township	15	14	1
Barrington	16	15	1	Cranford Township	69	50	19
Bay Head	9	8	1	Cresskill	26	21	5
Bayonne	279	235	44	Deal	20	16	4
Beach Haven	18	12	6	Delanco Township	9	8	1
Beachwood	20	18	2	Delaware Township	9	8	1
Bedminster Township	17	16	1	Delran Township	32	28	4
Belleville	115	104	11	Demarest	13	13	0
Bellmawr	31	25	6	Denville Township	38	30	8
Belmar	27	20	7	Deptford Township	74	63	11
Belvidere	6	6	0	Dover	39	34	5
Bergenfield	51	43	8	Dover Township	189	148	41
Berkeley Heights Township	33	25	8	Dumont	33	25	8
Berkeley Township	87	67	20	Dunellen	19	15	4
Berlin	17	16	1	Eastampton Township	17	16	1
Berlin Township	21	19	2	East Brunswick Township	119	90	29
Bernards Township	42	33	9	East Greenwich Township	16	14	2
Bernardsville	24	17	7	East Hanover Township	40	33	7
Beverly	9	7	2	East Newark	8	8	0
Blairstown Township	9	8	1	East Orange	277	249	28
Bloomfield	136	116	20	East Rutherford	37	33	4
Bloomingdale	17	16	1	East Windsor Township	62	48	14
Bogota	18	14	4	Eatontown	44	35	9
Boonton	30	25	5	Edgewater	30	29	1
Boonton Township	11	11	0	Edgewater Park Township	14	13	1

Table 78

Full-time Law Enforcement Employees as of October 31, 2001
by City by State—Continued

City by state	Total police employees	Total officers	Total civilians	City by state	Total police employees	Total officers	Total civilians
NEW JERSEY—Continued				**NEW JERSEY—Continued**			
Edison Township	254	201	53	High Bridge	6	6	0
Egg Harbor City	20	14	6	Highland Park	32	27	5
Egg Harbor Township	103	79	24	Highlands	18	14	4
Elizabeth	465	350	115	Hightstown	20	15	5
Elk Township	10	9	1	Hillsborough Township	66	54	12
Elmer	1	1	0	Hillsdale	22	20	2
Elmwood Park	37	35	2	Hillside Township	85	73	12
Emerson	21	18	3	Hi-Nella	3	2	1
Englewood	89	72	17	Hoboken	175	162	13
Englewood Cliffs	28	27	1	Ho-Ho-Kus	15	15	0
Englishtown	8	8	0	Holland Township	7	6	1
Essex Fells	16	12	4	Holmdel Township	47	40	7
Evesham Township	81	72	9	Hopatcong	38	29	9
Ewing Township	92	79	13	Hopewell Township	39	33	6
Fairfield Township	39	34	5	Howell Township	93	76	17
Fair Haven	17	13	4	Independence Township	8	7	1
Fair Lawn	67	57	10	Interlaken	5	5	0
Fairview	32	27	5	Irvington	214	185	29
Fanwood	22	21	1	Island Heights	3	3	0
Far Hills	5	5	0	Jackson Township	93	75	18
Flemington	15	14	1	Jamesburg	17	12	5
Florence Township	30	24	6	Jefferson Township	46	38	8
Florham Park	36	31	5	Jersey City	1,015	839	176
Fort Lee	118	98	20	Keansburg	30	24	6
Franklin	15	14	1	Kearny	122	114	8
Franklin Lakes	27	22	5	Kenilworth	30	29	1
Franklin Township (Gloucester County)	28	24	4	Keyport	25	19	6
Franklin Township (Hunterdon County)	6	6	0	Kinnelon	16	15	1
Franklin Township (Somerset County)	112	96	16	Lacey Township	57	42	15
Freehold	37	29	8	Lakehurst	12	10	2
Freehold Township	78	63	15	Lakewood Township	139	112	27
Frenchtown	3	3	0	Lambertville	13	11	2
Galloway Township	62	50	12	Laurel Springs	7	7	0
Garfield	70	60	10	Lavallette	15	12	3
Garwood	18	16	2	Lawnside	8	7	1
Gibbsboro	10	9	1	Lawrence Township	84	70	14
Glassboro	53	48	5	Lebanon Township	10	9	1
Glen Ridge	34	27	7	Leonia	27	20	7
Glen Rock	23	20	3	Lincoln Park	27	25	2
Gloucester City	32	29	3	Linden	139	129	10
Gloucester Township	124	103	21	Lindenwold	45	42	3
Green Brook Township	24	20	4	Linwood	24	20	4
Greenwich Township (Gloucester County)	21	16	5	Little Egg Harbor Township	44	36	8
Greenwich Township (Warren County)	9	8	1	Little Falls Township	28	22	6
Guttenberg	27	23	4	Little Ferry	32	27	5
Hackensack	125	111	14	Little Silver	18	13	5
Hackettstown	20	19	1	Livingston Township	79	70	9
Haddonfield	27	25	2	Lodi	48	37	11
Haddon Heights	17	16	1	Logan Township	17	16	1
Haddon Township	31	29	2	Long Beach Township	49	38	11
Haledon	23	18	5	Long Branch	106	89	17
Hamburg	8	7	1	Long Hill Township	36	29	7
Hamilton Township (Atlantic County)	208	178	30	Longport	19	15	4
Hamilton Township (Mercer County)	67	53	14	Lopatcong Township	14	13	1
Hammonton	36	28	8	Lower Alloways Creek Township	17	12	5
Hanover Township	36	29	7	Lower Township	59	43	16
Harding Township	15	14	1	Lumberton Township	29	26	3
Hardyston Township	22	16	6	Lyndhurst Township	53	49	4
Harrington Park	10	10	0	Madison	39	35	4
Harrison	57	54	3	Magnolia	12	11	1
Harrison Township	15	14	1	Mahwah Township	63	54	9
Harvey Cedars	8	8	0	Manalapan Township	74	60	14
Hasbrouck Heights	34	32	2	Manasquan	24	18	6
Haworth	12	11	1	Manchester Township	78	66	12
Hawthorne	37	32	5	Mansfield Township (Burlington County)	9	9	0
Hazlet Township	53	45	8	Mansfield Township (Warren County)	15	14	1
Helmetta	4	4	0	Mantoloking	8	7	1

Table 78

Full-time Law Enforcement Employees as of October 31, 2001
by City by State—Continued

City by state	Total police employees	Total officers	Total civilians	City by state	Total police employees	Total officers	Total civilians
NEW JERSEY—Continued				**NEW JERSEY—Continued**			
Mantua Township	25	23	2	Ocean City	78	64	14
Manville	31	25	6	Ocean Gate	8	7	1
Maple Shade Township	44	36	8	Oceanport	19	14	5
Maplewood Township	69	57	12	Ocean Township (Monmouth County)	71	59	12
Margate City	42	32	10	Ocean Township (Ocean County)	23	16	7
Marlboro Township	94	74	20	Ogdensburg	7	7	0
Matawan	27	21	6	Old Bridge Township	140	102	38
Maywood	27	23	4	Old Tappan	14	13	1
Medford Lakes	10	9	1	Oradell	22	21	1
Medford Township	52	43	9	Orange	126	109	17
Mendham	11	10	1	Oxford Township	5	4	1
Mendham Township	17	15	2	Palisades Park	36	30	6
Merchantville	16	15	1	Palmyra	19	17	2
Metuchen	33	28	5	Paramus	117	96	21
Middlesex	38	32	6	Park Ridge	19	18	1
Middle Township	66	48	18	Parsippany-Troy Hills Township	133	108	25
Middletown Township	129	104	25	Passaic	201	164	37
Midland Park	15	13	2	Paterson	533	438	95
Millburn Township	63	54	9	Paulsboro	25	19	6
Milltown	18	15	3	Peapack and Gladstone	9	8	1
Millville	83	68	15	Pemberton	5	4	1
Mine Hill Township	9	8	1	Pemberton Township	67	57	10
Monmouth Beach	11	10	1	Pennington	7	6	1
Monroe Township (Gloucester County)	74	62	12	Pennsauken Township	110	86	24
Monroe Township (Middlesex County)	54	41	13	Penns Grove	20	15	5
Montclair	144	112	32	Pennsville Township	28	26	2
Montgomery Township	36	28	8	Pequannock Township	30	25	5
Montvale	24	22	2	Perth Amboy	158	125	33
Montville Township	50	44	6	Phillipsburg	41	35	6
Moonachie	20	17	3	Pine Beach	7	6	1
Moorestown Township	48	38	10	Pine Hill	22	20	2
Morris Plains	23	17	6	Pine Valley	4	4	0
Morristown	67	59	8	Piscataway Township	106	88	18
Morris Township	51	41	10	Pitman	15	14	1
Mountain Lakes	18	14	4	Plainfield	197	169	28
Mountainside	29	23	6	Plainsboro Township	44	32	12
Mount Arlington	12	11	1	Pleasantville	63	52	11
Mount Ephraim	14	13	1	Plumsted Township	8	7	1
Mount Holly Township	30	27	3	Pohatcong Township	10	9	1
Mount Laurel Township	79	67	12	Point Pleasant	40	32	8
Mount Olive Township	57	48	9	Point Pleasant Beach	32	24	8
Mullica Township	15	14	1	Pompton Lakes	29	25	4
National Park	7	6	1	Princeton	45	34	11
Neptune City	21	16	5	Princeton Township	41	34	7
Neptune Township	89	72	17	Prospect Park	16	15	1
Netcong	11	9	2	Rahway	102	89	13
Newark	1,517	1,350	167	Ramsey	40	32	8
New Brunswick	160	128	32	Randolph Township	47	39	8
Newfield	7	7	0	Raritan	23	18	5
New Hanover Township	3	3	0	Raritan Township	37	33	4
New Milford	40	36	4	Readington Township	26	24	2
New Providence	31	25	6	Red Bank	48	38	10
Newton	31	22	9	Ridgefield	39	26	13
North Arlington	44	35	9	Ridgefield Park	38	29	9
North Bergen Township	132	113	19	Ridgewood	50	44	6
North Brunswick Township	99	84	15	Ringwood	26	21	5
North Caldwell	18	14	4	Riverdale	20	15	5
Northfield	27	25	2	River Edge	27	22	5
North Haledon	21	16	5	Riverside Township	13	13	0
North Hanover Township	9	8	1	Riverton	8	7	1
North Plainfield	51	45	6	River Vale Township	23	21	2
Northvale	14	13	1	Rochelle Park Township	20	18	2
North Wildwood	37	30	7	Rockaway	15	14	1
Norwood	15	14	1	Rockaway Township	67	54	13
Nutley Township	77	67	10	Roseland	29	27	2
Oakland	32	27	5	Roselle	61	50	11
Oaklyn	14	12	2	Roselle Park	38	34	4

Table 78

Full-time Law Enforcement Employees as of October 31, 2001
by City by State—Continued

City by state	Total police employees	Total officers	Total civilians	City by state	Total police employees	Total officers	Total civilians
NEW JERSEY—Continued				**NEW JERSEY—Continued**			
Roxbury Township	54	47	7	Washington Township (Gloucester County)	94	83	11
Rumson	22	17	5	Washington Township (Mercer County)	30	24	6
Runnemede	22	20	2	Washington Township (Morris County)	43	30	13
Rutherford	48	43	5	Washington Township (Warren County)	12	11	1
Saddle Brook Township	35	34	1	Watchung	34	27	7
Saddle River	23	18	5	Waterford Township	25	23	2
Salem	27	25	2	Wayne Township	143	114	29
Sayreville	97	82	15	Weehawken Township	58	53	5
Scotch Plains Township	53	46	7	Wenonah	6	6	0
Sea Bright	12	11	1	Westampton Township	25	22	3
Sea Girt	16	12	4	West Amwell Township	6	5	1
Sea Isle City	28	21	7	West Caldwell Township	32	30	2
Seaside Heights	28	22	6	West Cape May	8	8	0
Seaside Park	16	12	4	West Deptford Township	44	37	7
Secaucus	62	55	7	Westfield	72	59	13
Ship Bottom	10	9	1	West Long Branch	23	19	4
Shrewsbury	20	15	5	West Milford Township	55	48	7
Somerdale	14	13	1	West New York	128	121	7
Somers Point	33	27	6	West Orange	122	106	16
Somerville	39	32	7	West Paterson	26	26	0
South Amboy	30	24	6	Westville	10	9	1
South Belmar	10	10	0	West Wildwood	5	5	0
South Bound Brook	13	12	1	West Windsor Township	53	43	10
South Brunswick Township	108	76	32	Westwood	32	28	4
South Hackensack Township	20	18	2	Wharton	14	13	1
South Harrison Township	5	4	1	Wildwood	56	45	11
South Orange	61	56	5	Wildwood Crest	28	22	6
South Plainfield	67	54	13	Willingboro Township	86	70	16
South River	38	31	7	Winfield Township	9	9	0
South Toms River	12	11	1	Winslow Township	85	70	15
Sparta Township	42	34	8	Woodbridge Township	242	195	47
Spotswood	22	18	4	Woodbury	30	27	3
Springfield	42	38	4	Woodbury Heights	8	7	1
Springfield Township	10	9	1	Woodcliff Lake	19	18	1
Spring Lake	17	14	3	Woodlynne	10	9	1
Spring Lake Heights	16	13	3	Wood-Ridge	24	21	3
Stafford Township	69	48	21	Woodstown	9	8	1
Stanhope	8	7	1	Woolwich Township	12	11	1
Stillwater Township	5	5	0	Wyckoff Township	33	26	7
Stone Harbor	24	18	6				
Stratford	13	13	0	**NEW MEXICO**			
Summit	57	48	9				
Surf City	9	9	0	Alamogordo	103	62	41
Swedesboro	10	8	2	Albuquerque	1,216	870	346
Teaneck Township	114	99	15	Angel Fire	3	2	1
Tenafly	38	32	6	Artesia	39	24	15
Tewksbury Township	12	11	1	Aztec	17	13	4
Tinton Falls	39	37	2	Belen	27	16	11
Totowa	27	26	1	Bernalillo	21	16	5
Trenton	426	372	54	Bloomfield	19	15	4
Tuckerton	11	11	0	Carrizozo	5	3	2
Union Beach	18	14	4	Clayton	20	8	12
Union City	227	187	40	Cloudcroft	4	4	0
Union Township	174	127	47	Clovis	79	58	21
Upper Saddle River	23	18	5	Corrales	24	16	8
Ventnor City	48	36	12	Deming	35	31	4
Vernon Township	39	29	10	Eunice	9	5	4
Verona	35	31	4	Farmington	133	95	38
Vineland	170	136	34	Gallup	93	55	38
Voorhees Township	60	48	12	Grants	29	20	9
Waldwick	23	20	3	Hobbs	116	74	42
Wallington	27	26	1	Jal	9	5	4
Wall Township	78	65	13	Jemez Springs	1	1	0
Wanaque	26	22	4	Lordsburg	12	10	2
Warren Township	32	25	7	Los Alamos	46	26	20
Washington	12	11	1	Los Lunas	32	24	8
Washington Township (Bergen County)	23	23	0	Lovington	19	12	7

Table 78

Full-time Law Enforcement Employees as of October 31, 2001
by City by State—Continued

City by state	Total police employees	Total officers	Total civilians	City by state	Total police employees	Total officers	Total civilians
NEW MEXICO—Continued				**NEW YORK—Continued**			
Milan	14	8	6	Clarkstown Town	187	165	22
Mosquero	1	1	0	Clayton Village	4	3	1
Mountainair	2	2	0	Clay Town	24	19	5
Portales	42	27	15	Clyde Village	4	2	2
Raton	31	21	10	Cobleskill Village	11	11	0
Red River	8	3	5	Coeymans Town	14	10	4
Rio Rancho	140	95	45	Colchester Town	2	2	0
Roswell	105	80	25	Colonie Town	146	109	37
Ruidoso	35	23	12	Cooperstown Village	6	5	1
Socorro	30	17	13	Corinth Village	5	5	0
Tatum	7	3	4	Corning	29	25	4
Texico	5	4	1	Cornwall-on-Hudson Village	5	5	0
Tucumcari				Cornwall Town	14	10	4
	23	19	4	Cortland	42	40	2
				Crawford Town	10	9	1
NEW YORK				Croton-on-Hudson Village	19	19	0
				Cuba Town	5	5	0
Albany	435	337	98	Dansville Village	10	7	3
Albion Village	12	11	1	Delhi Village	3	3	0
Alexandria Bay Village	3	3	0	Depew Village	37	29	8
Alfred Village	6	6	0	Deposit Village	1	1	0
Allegany Village	2	2	0	Dewitt Town	39	35	4
Altamont Village	2	2	0	Dobbs Ferry Village	27	26	1
Amherst Town	180	148	32	Dolgeville Village	3	3	0
Amity Town and Belmont Village	1	1	0	Dunkirk	35	34	1
Amityville Village	27	24	3	East Aurora-Aurora Town	20	16	4
Amsterdam	43	41	2	Eastchester Town	58	50	8
Andover Village	1	1	0	East Fishkill Town	35	26	9
Angola Village	3	3	0	East Greenbush Town	28	21	7
Arcade Village	6	6	0	East Hampton Town	68	50	18
Ardsley Village	18	18	0	East Hampton Village	38	22	16
Asharoken Village	3	3	0	East Rochester Village	9	8	1
Auburn	82	70	12	East Syracuse Village	10	8	2
Avon Village	5	5	0	Eden Town	5	4	1
Bainbridge Village	1	1	0	Ellenville Village	15	13	2
Baldwinsville Village	16	13	3	Ellicott Town	12	11	1
Ballston Spa Village	11	7	4	Ellicottville	2	2	0
Batavia	40	34	6	Elmira	94	83	11
Bath Village	16	12	4	Elmira Heights Village	10	10	0
Beacon	40	38	2	Elmsford Village	17	17	0
Bedford Town	49	43	6	Endicott Village	41	37	4
Bethlehem Town	55	37	18	Evans Town	26	21	5
Blooming Grove Town	15	13	2	Fairport Village	11	10	1
Bolivar Village	1	1	0	Fallsburg Town	21	17	4
Brant Town	1	1	0	Floral Park Village	45	36	9
Briarcliff Manor Village	19	19	0	Florida Village	1	1	0
Brighton Town	47	41	6	Fort Edward Village	5	5	0
Brockport Village	14	10	4	Fort Plain Village	4	4	0
Bronxville Village	28	19	9	Frankfort Town	1	1	0
Buchanan Village	7	7	0	Frankfort Village	5	5	0
Buffalo	1,143	933	210	Fredonia Village	18	15	3
Caledonia Village	3	3	0	Freeport Village	109	92	17
Cambridge Village	2	2	0	Friendship Town	1	1	0
Camden Village	4	4	0	Fulton City	39	36	3
Canajoharie Village	5	5	0	Garden City Village	65	52	13
Canandaigua	30	27	3	Gates Town	39	32	7
Canastota Village	7	6	1	Geddes Town	18	16	2
Canisteo Village	3	3	0	Geneseo Village	7	7	0
Canton Village	12	10	2	Geneva	38	33	5
Carmel Town	41	33	8	Glen Cove	58	53	5
Catskill Village	17	16	1	Glens Falls	38	33	5
Cayuga Heights Village	7	6	1	Glenville Town	38	25	13
Chatham Village	5	4	1	Gloversville	41	39	2
Cheektowaga Town	168	128	40	Goshen Village	14	13	1
Chester Town	8	8	0	Gouverneur Village	12	8	4
Chester Village	11	10	1	Granville Village	6	6	0
Chittenango Village	6	5	1	Great Neck Estates Village	15	12	3
Cicero Town	2	1	1				

Table 78

Full-time Law Enforcement Employees as of October 31, 2001

by City by State—Continued

City by state	Total police employees	Total officers	Total civilians	City by state	Total police employees	Total officers	Total civilians
NEW YORK—Continued				**NEW YORK—Continued**			
Greene Village	1	1	0	Nassau Village	1	1	0
Green Island Village	3	2	1	Newark Village	20	19	1
Greenwich Village	2	2	0	Newburgh	102	89	13
Greenwood Lake Village	13	10	3	Newburgh Town	61	49	12
Hamburg Town	81	65	16	New Castle Town	46	42	4
Hamburg Village	15	13	2	New Hartford Town and Village	23	20	3
Hamilton Village	5	4	1	New Paltz Town and Village	23	19	4
Harriman Village	7	7	0	New Rochelle	238	187	51
Harrison Town	80	70	10	New Windsor Town	46	34	12
Hastings-on-Hudson Village	21	20	1	New York	56,208	39,067	17,141
Haverstraw Town	43	41	2	New York Mills Village	4	4	0
Hempstead Village	136	110	26	Niagara Falls	157	152	5
Herkimer Village	22	21	1	Niskayuna Town	41	30	11
Homer Village	5	5	0	Nissequogue Village	4	4	0
Hoosick Falls Village	3	3	0	North Castle Town	38	35	3
Hornell	22	21	1	Northport Village	19	15	4
Hudson Falls Village	16	12	4	North Syracuse Village	15	13	2
Huntington Bay Village	6	6	0	North Tonawanda	59	50	9
Hyde Park Town	15	13	2	Norwich	23	21	2
Ilion Village	20	18	2	Ogdensburg	32	27	5
Inlet Town	4	2	2	Old Brookville Village	51	40	11
Irondequoit Town	68	56	12	Old Westbury Village	29	24	5
Irvington Village	24	22	2	Olive Town	1	1	0
Ithaca	90	78	12	Oneida	26	23	3
Jamestown	88	73	15	Orchard Park Town	39	32	7
Johnson City Village	46	39	7	Ossining Town	14	14	0
Kenmore Village	26	25	1	Ossining Village	64	55	9
Kent Town	26	21	5	Oswego City	51	45	6
Kings Point Village	26	24	2	Oxford Village	2	2	0
Kingston	88	83	5	Oyster Bay Cove Village	11	11	0
Lackawanna	67	48	19	Painted Post Village	4	4	0
Lake Placid Village	17	14	3	Palmyra Village	6	5	1
Lake Success Village	26	23	3	Peekskill	74	58	16
Lancaster Town	40	32	8	Pelham Manor Village	29	28	1
Lancaster Village	22	16	6	Pelham Village	29	27	2
Larchmont Village	30	27	3	Penn Yan Village	14	13	1
Le Roy Village	13	10	3	Perry Village	12	8	4
Lewisboro Town	2	1	1	Piermont Village	7	7	0
Liberty Village	18	15	3	Pleasantville Village	23	22	1
Liverpool Village	6	5	1	Port Chester Village	65	62	3
Lloyd Harbor Village	13	12	1	Port Dickinson Village	5	4	1
Lockport	56	53	3	Port Jervis	32	32	0
Long Beach	82	76	6	Portville Village	1	1	0
Lowville Village	6	6	0	Port Washington	66	60	6
Lynbrook Village	55	47	8	Potsdam Village	18	15	3
Lyons Village	12	10	2	Poughkeepsie	132	99	33
Macedon Town and Village	4	4	0	Poughkeepsie Town	92	81	11
Malone Village	19	19	0	Pound Ridge Town	1	1	0
Malverne Village	23	23	0	Quogue Village	14	14	0
Mamaroneck Town	42	40	2	Ramapo Town	131	109	22
Mamaroneck Village	57	51	6	Ravena Village	3	2	1
Manlius Town	44	37	7	Red Hook Village	2	2	0
Marcellus Village	1	1	0	Rensselaer City	30	25	5
Marlborough Town	7	5	2	Riverhead Town	96	77	19
Mechanicville	13	12	1	Rochester	852	686	166
Menands Village	10	10	0	Rockville Centre Village	60	51	9
Middleport Village	2	2	0	Rome	76	72	4
Mohawk Village	5	5	0	Rosendale Town	5	4	1
Monroe Village	21	17	4	Rotterdam Town	60	42	18
Montgomery Town	6	5	1	Rouses Point Village	3	3	0
Monticello Village	34	31	3	Rye	43	39	4
Moravia Village	1	1	0	Rye Brook Village	28	27	1
Moriah Town	3	3	0	Sag Harbor Village	11	10	1
Mount Kisco Village	35	32	3	Salamanca	14	14	0
Mount Morris Village	5	5	0	Sands Point Village	21	21	0
Mount Pleasant Town	53	45	8	Saranac Lake Village	14	14	0
Mount Vernon	205	175	30	Saratoga Springs	83	70	13

Table 78

Full-time Law Enforcement Employees as of October 31, 2001
by City by State—Continued

City by state	Total police employees	Total officers	Total civilians	City by state	Total police employees	Total officers	Total civilians
NEW YORK—Continued				**NORTH CAROLINA**			
Saugerties Village	11	11	0	Aberdeen	21	19	2
Scarsdale Village	44	39	5	Ahoskie	22	17	5
Schenectady	205	162	43	Albemarle	54	48	6
Schodack Town	11	10	1	Andrews	9	8	1
Schoharie Village	1	1	0	Angier	10	10	0
Scotia Village	14	13	1	Apex	43	33	10
Seneca Falls Village	18	13	5	Archdale	28	23	5
Shawangunk Town	4	4	0	Asheboro	70	65	5
Shelter Island Town	10	8	2	Asheville	213	162	51
Sherrill	4	4	0	Atlantic Beach	24	18	6
Sidney Village	9	9	0	Aulander	1	1	0
Silver Creek Village	5	4	1	Aurora	1	1	0
Skaneateles Village	5	5	0	Ayden	22	18	4
Sleepy Hollow Village	22	22	0	Badin	5	5	0
Solvay Village	15	12	3	Bailey	3	3	0
Southampton Town	114	89	25	Bakersville	2	1	1
Southampton Village	38	28	10	Bald Head Islands	12	11	1
South Glens Falls Village	5	5	0	Banner Elk	6	6	0
South Nyack Village	7	7	0	Beaufort	15	14	1
Southold Town	59	43	16	Beech Mountain	13	9	4
Southport Town	2	1	1	Belhaven	14	9	5
Spring Valley Village	69	65	4	Belmont	33	28	5
St. Johnsville Village	3	3	0	Benson	17	13	4
Stony Point Town	30	29	1	Bethel	7	7	0
Suffern Village	34	29	5	Beulaville	4	4	0
Suffolk	3,235	2,672	563	Biltmore Forest	12	11	1
Syracuse	553	480	73	Biscoe	9	8	1
Tarrytown Village	38	32	6	Black Creek	2	2	0
Ticonderoga Town	8	8	0	Black Mountain	21	17	4
Tonawanda	35	30	5	Bladenboro	6	6	0
Tonawanda Town	157	106	51	Blowing Rock	14	10	4
Troy	130	113	17	Boiling Spring Lakes	5	5	0
Trumansburg Village	1	1	0	Boiling Springs	6	6	0
Tuckahoe Village	27	24	3	Bolton	1	1	0
Tupper Lake Village	10	10	0	Boone	42	34	8
Tuxedo Town	15	12	3	Boonville	3	3	0
Ulster Town	26	22	4	Brevard	27	22	5
Vernon Village	1	1	0	Broadway	4	4	0
Vestal Town	39	35	4	Brookford	1	1	0
Wallkill Town	29	21	8	Bryson City	6	6	0
Walton Village	6	5	1	Bunn	1	1	0
Wappingers Falls Village	7	5	2	Burgaw	10	9	1
Warwick Town	33	27	6	Burlington	138	107	31
Washingtonville Village	15	13	2	Burnsville	7	7	0
Waterford Town and Village	12	9	3	Butner	43	38	5
Waterloo Village	9	8	1	Cameron	1	1	0
Watertown	67	63	4	Candor	3	3	0
Watkins Glen Village	4	4	0	Canton	19	14	5
Waverly Village	12	11	1	Cape Carteret	5	5	0
Wayland Village	3	3	0	Carolina Beach	30	24	6
Webb Town	5	5	0	Carrboro	37	34	3
Webster Town and Village	38	32	6	Carthage	9	9	0
Wellsville Village	16	12	4	Cary	150	122	28
Westfield Village	7	6	1	Caswell Beach	4	4	0
West Seneca Town	77	65	12	Catawba	1	1	0
Whitehall Village	5	5	0	Chadbourn	9	8	1
White Plains	246	202	44	Chapel Hill	127	106	21
Whitesboro Village	8	8	0	Charlotte–Mecklenburg[1]	2,005	1,501	504
Whitestown Town	7	7	0	Cherryville	20	16	4
Windham Town	2	2	0	China Grove	11	10	1
Woodbury Town	25	21	4	Chocowinity	2	2	0
Woodstock Town	15	11	4	Claremont	9	8	1
Yonkers	693	622	71	Clarkton	4	4	0
Yorktown Town	58	51	7	Clayton	39	32	7
				Cleveland	3	3	0
				Clinton	40	33	7
				Clyde	4	4	0

Table 78

Full-time Law Enforcement Employees as of October 31, 2001
by City by State—Continued

City by state	Total police employees	Total officers	Total civilians	City by state	Total police employees	Total officers	Total civilians
NORTH CAROLINA—Continued				**NORTH CAROLINA—Continued**			
Coats	5	5	0	Hope Mills	36	26	10
Concord	133	119	14	Hot Springs	2	1	1
Conover	23	22	1	Hudson	12	11	1
Conway	1	1	0	Huntersville	56	51	5
Cooleemee	5	5	0	Indian Beach	4	4	0
Cornelius	41	29	12	Jackson	2	1	1
Cramerton	9	9	0	Jacksonville	119	98	21
Creedmoor	13	8	5	Jefferson	3	3	0
Dallas	17	13	4	Jonesville	9	8	1
Davidson	15	14	1	Kannapolis	92	71	21
Denton	6	6	0	Kenansville	3	3	0
Dobson	4	4	0	Kenly	10	10	0
Drexel	5	5	0	Kernersville	68	52	16
Dunn	53	41	12	Kill Devil Hills	27	22	5
Durham	551	465	86	King	18	16	2
East Bend	2	2	0	Kings Mountain	38	31	7
East Spencer	7	6	1	Kinston	88	78	10
Eden	61	53	8	Kitty Hawk	17	15	2
Edenton	18	16	2	Knightdale	14	13	1
Elizabeth City	63	54	9	Kure Beach	8	7	1
Elizabethtown	15	14	1	La Grange	9	9	0
Elkin	21	18	3	Lake Lure	10	9	1
Elon College	13	12	1	Lake Royale	7	3	4
Emerald Isle	22	17	5	Lake Waccamaw	3	3	0
Enfield	13	12	1	Landis	9	9	0
Erwin	10	9	1	Laurel Park	6	6	0
Eureka	1	1	0	Laurinburg	40	35	5
Fair Bluff	4	4	0	Lawndale	1	1	0
Fairmont	17	13	4	Leland	12	11	1
Faison	2	2	0	Lenoir	70	56	14
Farmville	21	17	4	Lexington	76	63	13
Fayetteville	366	279	87	Liberty	10	10	0
Fletcher	12	11	1	Lilesville	1	1	0
Forest City	36	30	6	Lillington	8	8	0
Four Oaks	7	6	1	Lincolnton	33	29	4
Foxfire Village	2	2	0	Littleton	3	3	0
Franklin	17	15	2	Locust	5	5	0
Franklinton	7	7	0	Longview	15	15	0
Fremont	4	4	0	Louisburg	13	12	1
Fuquay-Varina	26	21	5	Lowell	8	8	0
Garland	1	1	0	Lucama	3	3	0
Garner	52	46	6	Lumberton	85	75	10
Garysburg	2	2	0	Madison	16	15	1
Gaston	2	2	0	Maggie Valley	7	6	1
Gastonia	200	172	28	Magnolia	2	2	0
Gibson	2	2	0	Maiden	16	15	1
Gibsonville	16	13	3	Manteo	8	7	1
Glen Alpine	2	2	0	Marion	25	20	5
Goldsboro	125	102	23	Marshall	1	1	0
Graham	34	31	3	Mars Hill	5	5	0
Granite Falls	14	12	2	Marshville	8	8	0
Granite Quarry	4	4	0	Matthews	58	47	11
Greensboro	649	477	172	Maxton	15	10	5
Greenville	189	149	40	Mayodan	15	12	3
Grifton	6	6	0	Maysville	1	1	0
Hamlet	23	18	5	McAdenville	4	4	0
Havelock	33	27	6	Mebane	17	14	3
Haw River	8	8	0	Middlesex	5	5	0
Hendersonville	45	33	12	Mocksville	14	14	0
Hertford	8	7	1	Monroe	83	70	13
Hickory	132	106	26	Montreat	4	4	0
Highlands	10	9	1	Mooresville	56	45	11
High Point	222	190	32	Morehead City	40	33	7
Hillsborough	28	26	2	Morganton	97	71	26
Holden Beach	8	8	0	Morrisville	26	24	2
Holly Ridge	4	4	0	Mount Airy	51	37	14
Holly Springs	26	21	5	Mount Gilead	7	6	1

Table 78

Full-time Law Enforcement Employees as of October 31, 2001
by City by State—Continued

City by state	Total police employees	Total officers	Total civilians	City by state	Total police employees	Total officers	Total civilians
NORTH CAROLINA—Continued				**NORTH CAROLINA—Continued**			
Mount Holly	31	27	4	Sharpsburg	9	8	1
Mount Olive	19	14	5	Shelby	78	67	11
Murfreesboro	13	9	4	Siler City	22	17	5
Murphy	13	9	4	Smithfield	37	30	7
Nags Head	23	20	3	Southern Pines	33	27	6
Nashville	14	13	1	Southern Shores	7	7	0
Navassa	1	1	0	Southport	10	9	1
New Bern	110	81	29	Sparta	5	5	0
Newland	5	5	0	Spencer	13	12	1
Newport	7	7	0	Spindale	14	14	0
Newton	44	35	9	Spring Hope	5	5	0
Newton Grove	3	3	0	Spring Lake	24	18	6
Norlina	6	6	0	Spruce Pine	10	10	0
North Topsail Beach	10	9	1	Stanfield	4	4	0
Northwest	3	3	0	Stanley	13	9	4
North Wilkesboro	27	23	4	Stantonsburg	3	3	0
Norwood	6	6	0	Star	4	4	0
Oakboro	4	4	0	Statesville	87	68	19
Oak Island	32	24	8	Stoneville	5	5	0
Ocean Isle Beach	11	11	0	St. Pauls	17	12	5
Old Fort	7	6	1	Sugar Mountain	6	6	0
Oxford	35	28	7	Sunset Beach	12	12	0
Parkton	3	3	0	Surf City	12	11	1
Pembroke	18	14	4	Swansboro	7	7	0
Pikeville	1	1	0	Sylva	12	11	1
Pilot Mountain	9	8	1	Tabor City	9	8	1
Pinebluff	2	2	0	Tarboro	35	29	6
Pinehurst	27	22	5	Taylorsville	11	11	0
Pine Knoll Shores	9	9	0	Taylortown	1	1	0
Pine Level	3	3	0	Thomasville	70	62	8
Pinetops	8	6	2	Topsail Beach	8	7	1
Pineville	36	28	8	Trent Woods	4	4	0
Pink Hill	1	1	0	Troutman	7	7	0
Pittsboro	9	9	0	Troy	10	9	1
Plymouth	15	14	1	Tryon	12	7	5
Princeton	4	4	0	Valdese	13	12	1
Raeford	16	15	1	Vanceboro	2	2	0
Raleigh	720	630	90	Vass	4	4	0
Ramseur	7	7	0	Wadesboro	25	19	6
Randleman	11	11	0	Wagram	2	2	0
Ranlo	6	6	0	Wake Forest	35	32	3
Red Springs	21	17	4	Wallace	15	12	3
Reidsville	50	41	9	Walnut Cove	5	5	0
Rhodhiss	1	1	0	Warrenton	7	6	1
Richlands	4	4	0	Warsaw	14	11	3
Rich Square	2	2	0	Washington	36	28	8
River Bend	4	4	0	Waxhaw	8	7	1
Roanoke Rapids	44	41	3	Waynesville	36	31	5
Robbins	8	7	1	Weaverville	10	10	0
Robersonville	7	7	0	Weldon	9	8	1
Rockingham	33	28	5	Wendell	17	13	4
Rocky Mount	183	136	47	West Jefferson	7	7	0
Rolesville	5	5	0	Whispering Pines	8	7	1
Roseboro	6	6	0	Whitakers	3	3	0
Rose Hill	4	4	0	White Lake	5	5	0
Rowland	8	6	2	Whiteville	27	23	4
Roxboro	35	30	5	Wilkesboro	22	21	1
Rutherfordton	14	13	1	Williamston	21	20	1
Salemburg	1	1	0	Wilmington	269	233	36
Salisbury	105	84	21	Wilson	117	102	15
Saluda	4	4	0	Windsor	8	8	0
Sanford	93	75	18	Wingate	8	8	0
Scotland Neck	7	6	1	Winston-Salem	553	421	132
Seagrove	1	1	0	Winterville	14	13	1
Selma	28	23	5	Winton	2	2	0
Seven Devils	6	6	0	Woodfin	10	10	0
Shallotte	10	9	1	Woodland	1	1	0

Table 78

Full-time Law Enforcement Employees as of October 31, 2001
by City by State—Continued

City by state	Total police employees	Total officers	Total civilians	City by state	Total police employees	Total officers	Total civilians
NORTH CAROLINA—Continued				**OHIO—Continued**			
Wrightsville Beach	29	22	7	Bath Township	25	18	7
Yadkinville	11	10	1	Bay Village	26	23	3
Yanceyville	8	4	4	Bazetta Township	8	7	1
Youngsville	8	7	1	Beavercreek	61	45	16
Zebulon	21	20	1	Beaver Township	17	12	5
				Bedford	38	30	8
NORTH DAKOTA				Bedford Heights	67	36	31
				Bellaire	11	11	0
Beulah	6	5	1	Bellbrook	16	11	5
Bismarck	107	80	27	Bellefontaine	32	24	8
Bowman	3	3	0	Bellevue	16	12	4
Cando	3	3	0	Bellville	3	3	0
Cavalier	4	4	0	Belpre	16	11	5
Crosby	2	2	0	Berea	40	32	8
Devils Lake	17	15	2	Bethel	5	4	1
Dickinson	36	24	12	Beverly	5	3	2
Elgin	1	1	0	Bexley	37	28	9
Fargo	142	108	34	Blanchester	8	8	0
Fessenden	1	1	0	Blendon Township	13	12	1
Grafton	11	10	1	Blue Ash	46	37	9
Grand Forks	95	79	16	Bluffton	7	7	0
Harvey	3	3	0	Boardman Township	76	58	18
Hatton	1	1	0	Bowling Green	57	42	15
Hazen	4	4	0	Bradford	3	3	0
Hillsboro	2	2	0	Brecksville	36	29	7
Jamestown	33	29	4	Bridgeport	10	6	4
Lamoure	1	1	0	Broadview Heights	41	30	11
Larimore	2	2	0	Brookfield Township	9	8	1
Linton	2	2	0	Brooklyn	40	32	8
Lisbon	3	3	0	Brooklyn Heights	18	18	0
Mandan	35	28	7	Brook Park	53	43	10
Mayville	3	3	0	Brookville	16	11	5
Minot	79	57	22	Brunswick	51	38	13
Napoleon	1	1	0	Bryan	26	20	6
Northwood	2	2	0	Buckeye Lake	6	6	0
Oakes	4	3	1	Bucyrus	28	21	7
Rugby	4	4	0	Burton	2	2	0
South Heart	1	1	0	Butler	1	1	0
Steele	1	1	0	Butler Township	14	13	1
Thompson	1	1	0	Cadiz	6	6	0
Valley City	17	12	5	Cambridge	32	25	7
Velva	1	1	0	Canfield	21	15	6
Wahpeton	14	13	1	Canton	227	190	37
Watford City	4	4	0	Carey	11	7	4
West Fargo	33	23	10	Carlisle	9	8	1
Williston	29	21	8	Carrollton	8	8	0
Wishek	2	2	0	Celina	21	15	6
				Centerville	51	40	11
OHIO				Chagrin Falls	19	11	8
				Chardon	16	10	6
Aberdeen	5	5	0	Cheviot	10	10	0
Ada	12	8	4	Chillicothe	59	51	8
Akron	509	462	47	Cincinnati	1,301	1,025	276
Alliance	58	46	12	Circleville	38	26	12
Amberley	19	15	4	Clayton	13	13	0
Ansonia	2	2	0	Clearcreek Township	12	11	1
Arcanum	2	2	0	Cleveland	2,453	1,946	507
Archbold	9	8	1	Cleveland Heights	120	109	11
Arlington Heights	6	5	1	Cleves	2	2	0
Ashland	42	32	10	Clinton Township	10	9	1
Ashtabula	43	39	4	Clyde	18	14	4
Athens	36	27	9	Coitsville Township	4	4	0
Aurora	29	23	6	Columbiana	16	12	4
Avon Lake	33	27	6	Columbus	2,196	1,816	380
Bainbridge Township	25	18	7	Conneaut	29	22	7
Barberton	56	43	13	Copley Township	24	18	6
Barnesville	11	7	4	Cortland	9	9	0

Table 78

Full-time Law Enforcement Employees as of October 31, 2001
by City by State—Continued

City by state	Total police employees	Total officers	Total civilians	City by state	Total police employees	Total officers	Total civilians
OHIO—Continued				**OHIO—Continued**			
Covington	6	5	1	Highland Hills	11	10	1
Crestline	16	12	4	Hilliard	66	47	19
Crooksville	6	5	1	Hillsboro	21	17	4
Cuyahoga Falls	116	92	24	Hinckley Township	11	9	2
Dalton	3	3	0	Holgate	1	1	0
Dayton	583	479	104	Hubbard	18	14	4
Deer Park	15	11	4	Hubbard Township	8	7	1
Defiance	36	30	6	Huber Heights	58	53	5
Delaware	58	39	19	Hudson	35	30	5
Delhi Township	36	32	4	Hunting Valley	14	13	1
Delta	7	7	0	Huron	18	14	4
Deshler	3	3	0	Independence	50	36	14
Donnelsville	2	2	0	Indian Hill	24	19	5
Dover	23	22	1	Ironton	19	14	5
Doylestown	6	5	1	Jackson	24	18	6
Dublin	83	65	18	Jackson Township	45	36	9
East Cleveland	77	54	23	Jefferson	6	5	1
Eastlake	51	38	13	Johnstown	12	8	4
East Liverpool	30	25	5	Kelleys Island	2	2	0
East Palestine	11	7	4	Kent	56	42	14
Eaton	19	13	6	Kenton	16	16	0
Elyria	142	93	49	Kettering	108	82	26
Englewood	27	18	9	Kirtland	14	9	5
Euclid	170	100	70	Kirtland Hills	9	8	1
Evendale	20	19	1	Lagrange	4	4	0
Fairborn	59	45	14	Lakemore	8	8	0
Fairfax	9	9	0	Lake Township	13	12	1
Fairfield	67	50	17	Lakewood	110	88	22
Fairfield Township	12	11	1	Lancaster	85	64	21
Fairlawn	31	22	9	Lawrence Township	6	6	0
Fairview Park	30	28	2	Lebanon	35	26	9
Fayette	3	3	0	Leipsic	3	3	0
Forest	2	2	0	Lexington	11	7	4
Forest Park	40	34	6	Liberty Township	28	23	5
Fort Recovery	1	1	0	Lima	110	89	21
Fort Shawnee	4	4	0	Lincoln Heights	12	11	1
Franklin	29	23	6	Lisbon	10	6	4
Franklin Township	15	10	5	Lockland	15	14	1
Frazeysburg	3	3	0	Logan	21	16	5
Fredericktown	4	4	0	London	20	15	5
Fremont	38	33	5	Lorain	140	105	35
Gahanna	60	54	6	Lordstown	13	9	4
Garfield Heights	80	62	18	Loudonville	10	6	4
Gates Mills	16	12	4	Louisville	12	12	0
Geneva	17	13	4	Loveland	20	18	2
Genoa	4	4	0	Lyndhurst	37	29	8
Genoa Township	18	17	1	Macedonia	30	23	7
Germantown	16	11	5	Madeira	13	12	1
German Township (Montgomery County)	6	6	0	Madison Township	21	19	2
Gibsonburg	4	4	0	Magnolia	3	3	0
Girard	24	20	4	Mansfield	141	97	44
Glendale	8	7	1	Maple Heights	66	48	18
Golf Manor	8	7	1	Mariemont	11	10	1
Goshen Township	11	10	1	Marietta	38	31	7
Grandview Heights	24	19	5	Marion	85	64	21
Granville	12	9	3	Marlboro Township	3	3	0
Greenfield	14	12	2	Martins Ferry	15	11	4
Greenhills	9	9	0	Marysville	34	28	6
Greenville	34	25	9	Mason	35	32	3
Greenwich	4	4	0	Massillon	56	52	4
Grove City	64	47	17	Maumee	56	41	15
Hamilton	141	118	23	Mayfield Heights	43	33	10
Harrison	23	21	2	Mayfield Village	24	16	8
Hartville	7	6	1	McClure	1	1	0
Heath	28	21	7	McConnelsville	7	5	2
Hicksville	9	7	2	Mechanicsburg	4	4	0
Highland Heights	28	21	7	Medina	54	41	13

Table 78

Full-time Law Enforcement Employees as of October 31, 2001
by City by State—Continued

City by state	Total police employees	Total officers	Total civilians	City by state	Total police employees	Total officers	Total civilians
OHIO—Continued				**OHIO—Continued**			
Medina Township	2	2	0	Perkins Township	28	20	8
Mentor	108	76	32	Perrysburg	38	30	8
Mentor-on-the-Lake	16	11	5	Perry Township (Franklin County)	22	16	6
Miamisburg	48	37	11	Perry Township (Montgomery County)	6	6	0
Miami Township	42	38	4	Perry Township (Stark County)	30	24	6
Middleburg Heights	40	34	6	Pickerington	29	20	9
Middlefield	13	8	5	Pierce Township	15	14	1
Middleport	6	4	2	Piqua	41	33	8
Middletown	135	93	42	Plain City	8	8	0
Milford	18	15	3	Poland Township	14	12	2
Millersburg	9	9	0	Poland Village	6	6	0
Minerva	13	8	5	Port Clinton	18	13	5
Minerva Park	6	6	0	Portsmouth	46	42	4
Mingo Junction	11	10	1	Powell	16	15	1
Mogadore	9	9	0	Ravenna	32	24	8
Monroe	22	17	5	Reading	23	18	5
Montgomery	22	20	2	Reynoldsburg	62	49	13
Montpelier	10	9	1	Richmond Heights	27	21	6
Moraine	43	34	9	Richwood	8	7	1
Mount Healthy	12	11	1	Rittman	12	9	3
Mount Sterling	9	7	2	Riverside	32	31	1
Mount Vernon	34	29	5	Rossford	18	17	1
Munroe Falls	9	8	1	Russell Township	9	8	1
Napoleon	21	16	5	Sagamore Hills	10	9	1
Navarre	5	5	0	Salem	17	16	1
Nelsonville	10	8	2	Sandusky	65	55	10
New Albany	20	14	6	Seaman	2	2	0
New Boston	14	10	4	Sebring	11	7	4
Newcomerstown	16	11	5	Seven Hills	18	17	1
New Lebanon	7	7	0	Seville	7	6	1
New Lexington	12	8	4	Shadyside	10	6	4
New Middletown	2	2	0	Shaker Heights	89	63	26
New Paris	4	4	0	Sharon Township	9	9	0
New Richmond	6	5	1	Sharonville	48	39	9
Newton Falls	11	7	4	Shawnee Township	16	10	6
Newtown	5	5	0	Sheffield Lake	16	12	4
Niles	38	32	6	Shelby	19	15	4
North Baltimore	5	5	0	Sidney	49	38	11
North Canton	33	25	8	Silverton	13	10	3
North College Hill	15	14	1	Smith Township	6	5	1
North Kingsville	4	4	0	Solon	70	44	26
North Olmsted	79	57	22	South Charleston	4	4	0
North Randall	15	12	3	South Euclid	49	39	10
North Ridgeville	44	36	8	South Russell	10	9	1
North Royalton	56	37	19	South Solon	2	2	0
Northwood	28	21	7	South Zanesville	3	3	0
Norton	22	16	6	Spencerville	4	4	0
Norwalk	32	24	8	Springboro	28	22	6
Norwood	50	49	1	Springdale	46	36	10
Oak Harbor	6	4	2	Springfield	152	127	25
Oakwood	38	32	6	Springfield Township (Hamilton County)	52	43	9
Oakwood Village	14	14	0	Springfield Township (Mahoning County)	6	5	1
Oberlin	20	16	4	Springfield Township (Summit County)	18	17	1
Olmsted Falls	18	12	6	Steubenville	55	45	10
Olmsted Township	19	15	4	St. Mary's	19	15	4
Ontario	26	20	6	Stow	45	36	9
Oregon	61	47	14	Streetsboro	30	22	8
Orrville	20	14	6	Strongsville	95	75	20
Ottawa	7	7	0	Struthers	21	16	5
Ottawa Hills	15	11	4	Sugarcreek Township	20	13	7
Oxford	36	25	11	Swanton	8	7	1
Painesville	40	37	3	Sylvania	41	34	7
Parma	155	100	55	Sylvania Township	60	44	16
Parma Heights	38	33	5	Tallmadge	36	24	12
Pataskala	21	19	2	Tiffin	42	29	13
Paulding	4	3	1	Tipp City	23	18	5
Pepper Pike	24	18	6	Toledo	839	712	127

Table 78

Full-time Law Enforcement Employees as of October 31, 2001
by City by State—Continued

City by state	Total police employees	Total officers	Total civilians	City by state	Total police employees	Total officers	Total civilians
OHIO—Continued				**OKLAHOMA—Continued**			
Toronto	10	10	0	Alva	13	8	5
Trenton	16	11	5	Anadarko	29	23	6
Trotwood	56	52	4	Antlers	10	6	4
Troy	45	39	6	Apache	4	4	0
Twinsburg	44	31	13	Ardmore	70	52	18
Uhrichsville	8	8	0	Arkoma	7	3	4
Union City	4	4	0	Atoka	15	14	1
Uniontown	10	8	2	Barnsdall	6	4	2
Union Township (Clermont County)	56	42	14	Bartlesville	82	54	28
Union Township (Licking County)	1	1	0	Beggs	8	5	3
University Heights	37	29	8	Bethany	38	26	12
Upper Arlington	59	48	11	Bixby	21	13	8
Upper Sandusky	18	13	5	Blackwell	23	15	8
Urbana	26	22	4	Blanchard	8	4	4
Valley View	18	16	2	Boise City	3	3	0
Vandalia	38	30	8	Bokoshe	1	1	0
Van Wert	30	22	8	Bristow	15	11	4
Vermilion	23	18	5	Broken Arrow	137	101	36
Vienna Township	4	4	0	Broken Bow	17	12	5
Village of Leesburg	3	3	0	Caddo	4	4	0
Wadsworth	34	25	9	Calera	5	5	0
Waite Hill	6	6	0	Carnegie	9	5	4
Walbridge	9	4	5	Catoosa	14	13	1
Walton Hills	16	12	4	Chandler	12	8	4
Warren	88	68	20	Checotah	15	10	5
Warrensville Heights	52	38	14	Chelsea	8	5	3
Warren Township	8	8	0	Cherokee	3	3	0
Washington Court House	26	22	4	Chickasha	41	33	8
Waterville	13	12	1	Choctaw	13	12	1
Waterville Township	5	5	0	Chouteau	7	5	2
Wauseon	15	13	2	Claremore	50	36	14
Waverly	18	13	5	Clayton	9	4	5
Waynesville	5	4	1	Cleveland	7	7	0
Wellington	8	6	2	Clinton	25	17	8
Wellston	11	8	3	Coalgate	6	5	1
Wellsville	6	6	0	Colbert	4	4	0
West Carrollton	33	26	7	Collinsville	13	9	4
West Chester Township	93	69	24	Comanche	4	4	0
Westerville	80	69	11	Commerce	5	5	0
West Jefferson	14	10	4	Cordell	9	8	1
Westlake	70	50	20	Coweta	17	11	6
West Union	8	6	2	Crescent	8	5	3
Whitehall	55	43	12	Cushing	22	16	6
Wickliffe	39	30	9	Davis	11	9	2
Willard	19	15	4	Del City	44	32	12
Willoughby	60	45	15	Dewey	9	7	2
Willoughby Hills	26	19	7	Drumright	5	5	0
Willowick	32	24	8	Duncan	52	41	11
Wilmington	24	22	2	Durant	36	27	9
Winchester	3	2	1	Edmond	122	103	19
Windham	8	6	2	Elk City	36	26	10
Wintersville	8	7	1	Elmore City	4	3	1
Woodlawn	18	17	1	El Reno	41	30	11
Woodsfield	7	7	0	Enid	102	79	23
Woodville	4	4	0	Erick	3	3	0
Wooster	43	38	5	Eufaula	13	10	3
Worthington	49	36	13	Fairfax	8	4	4
Wyoming	20	16	4	Fairview	10	6	4
Xenia	70	46	24	Fletcher	2	2	0
Yellow Springs	12	9	3	Fort Gibson	16	11	5
Youngstown	260	212	48	Frederick	13	11	2
				Geary	9	4	5
OKLAHOMA				Glenpool	18	11	7
				Goodwell	3	3	0
Ada	46	33	13	Granite	2	2	0
Agra	1	1	0	Grove	26	19	7
Altus	62	44	18	Guthrie	32	24	8

Table 78

Full-time Law Enforcement Employees as of October 31, 2001
by City by State—Continued

City by state	Total police employees	Total officers	Total civilians	City by state	Total police employees	Total officers	Total civilians
OKLAHOMA—Continued				**OKLAHOMA—Continued**			
Guymon	25	16	9	Pauls Valley	21	12	9
Haileyville	2	2	0	Pawhuska	11	7	4
Harrah	11	11	0	Pawnee	6	6	0
Hartshorne	5	5	0	Perkins	6	4	2
Haskell	6	6	0	Perry	20	13	7
Healdton	10	5	5	Piedmont	10	8	2
Heavener	12	8	4	Pocola	9	6	3
Henryetta	18	13	5	Ponca City	67	55	12
Hinton	5	5	0	Porum	2	2	0
Hobart	14	11	3	Poteau	29	20	9
Holdenville	15	10	5	Prague	11	7	4
Hollis	12	8	4	Pryor	27	21	6
Hominy	8	4	4	Purcell	26	20	6
Hooker	3	3	0	Ringling	2	2	0
Howe	3	2	1	Roland	40	12	28
Hugo	18	14	4	Rush Springs	4	4	0
Hulbert	5	4	1	Sallisaw	30	19	11
Hydro	2	2	0	Sand Springs	46	34	12
Idabel	26	20	6	Sapulpa	49	39	10
Inola	9	4	5	Sayre	11	7	4
Jay	13	8	5	Seiling	5	3	2
Jenks	18	12	6	Seminole	18	14	4
Jones	4	4	0	Shawnee	82	58	24
Kingfisher	12	8	4	Skiatook	20	15	5
Kingston	6	6	0	Snyder	4	4	0
Konawa	8	5	3	Spencer	10	9	1
Krebs	4	4	0	Spiro	4	4	0
Laverne	7	3	4	Stigler	13	8	5
Lawton	174	149	25	Stillwater	105	70	35
Lexington	12	7	5	Stilwell	20	14	6
Lindsay	10	5	5	Stratford	7	3	4
Locust Grove	9	5	4	Stringtown	7	6	1
Lone Grove	10	7	3	Stroud	13	9	4
Luther	4	4	0	Sulphur	15	10	5
Madill	13	12	1	Tahlequah	36	27	9
Mangum	11	7	4	Talihina	9	5	4
Mannford	13	9	4	Tecumseh	15	10	5
Marietta	6	6	0	Temple	1	1	0
Marlow	11	9	2	The Village	26	21	5
Maysville	4	3	1	Tishomingo	7	7	0
McAlester	59	46	13	Tonkawa	13	8	5
McLoud	9	6	3	Tulsa	971	808	163
Meeker	6	6	0	Tushka	2	2	0
Miami	42	30	12	Tuttle	14	9	5
Midwest City	118	94	24	Valliant	5	4	1
Minco	3	3	0	Vian	6	4	2
Moore	68	63	5	Vinita	22	19	3
Mooreland	1	1	0	Wagoner	19	13	6
Morris	4	4	0	Walters	4	4	0
Mountain View	1	1	0	Warner	3	3	0
Muldrow	12	8	4	Warr Acres	30	22	8
Muskogee	102	86	16	Watonga	11	8	3
Mustang	24	18	6	Waukomis	3	3	0
Newcastle	18	12	6	Waurika	3	3	0
Newkirk	7	6	1	Waynoka	3	3	0
Nichols Hills	18	14	4	Weatherford	27	19	8
Nicoma Park	7	7	0	Weleetka	10	4	6
Noble	16	11	5	Westville	11	6	5
Norman	170	123	47	Wetumka	5	5	0
Nowata	9	7	2	Wewoka	15	11	4
Oilton	4	4	0	Wilburton	10	6	4
Okeene	3	2	1	Wilson	7	5	2
Okemah	16	11	5	Woodward	27	19	8
Oklahoma City	1,260	1,010	250	Wright City	4	3	1
Okmulgee	42	30	12	Wynnewood	5	4	1
Oologah	3	3	0	Yale	7	3	4
Owasso	42	30	12	Yukon	47	32	15

Table 78

Full-time Law Enforcement Employees as of October 31, 2001
by City by State—Continued

City by state	Total police employees	Total officers	Total civilians	City by state	Total police employees	Total officers	Total civilians
OREGON				**OREGON—Continued**			
Albany	77	55	22	McMinnville	41	33	8
Amity	3	3	0	Medford	141	94	47
Ashland	42	28	14	Milton-Freewater	16	10	6
Astoria	25	16	9	Milwaukie	44	31	13
Athena	1	1	0	Molalla	16	12	4
Aumsville	6	5	1	Monmouth	15	13	2
Aurora	3	2	1	Mount Angel	8	7	1
Baker City	16	16	0	Myrtle Creek	14	8	6
Bandon	8	7	1	Myrtle Point	6	6	0
Banks	3	3	0	Newberg	32	22	10
Beaverton	134	110	24	Newport	28	23	5
Bend	89	67	22	North Bend	28	19	9
Black Butte	7	6	1	North Plains	3	3	0
Boardman	9	8	1	Nyssa	8	8	0
Brookings	18	12	6	Oakridge	10	5	5
Burns	11	6	5	Ontario	29	22	7
Butte Falls	1	1	0	Oregon City	38	32	6
Canby	22	20	2	Pendleton	30	22	8
Cannon Beach	8	7	1	Philomath	7	6	1
Carlton	4	3	1	Phoenix	9	8	1
Central Point	23	19	4	Pilot Rock	3	3	0
Clatskanie	6	5	1	Portland	1,391	1,054	337
Coburg	7	6	1	Powers	1	1	0
Columbia City	1	1	0	Prairie City	3	3	0
Condon	2	2	0	Prineville	24	15	9
Coos Bay	43	29	14	Rainier	6	5	1
Coquille	10	8	2	Redmond	37	28	9
Cornelius	14	13	1	Reedsport	16	11	5
Corvallis	82	55	27	Rockaway Beach	3	3	0
Cottage Grove	24	16	8	Rogue River	3	3	0
Culver	1	1	0	Roseburg	42	37	5
Dallas	20	19	1	Salem	274	174	100
Dundee	4	4	0	Sandy	13	11	2
Eagle Point	8	7	1	Scappoose	9	8	1
Elgin	3	3	0	Seaside	26	18	8
Enterprise	4	4	0	Shady Cove	5	4	1
Eugene	299	172	127	Sherwood	21	18	3
Fairview	10	9	1	Silverton	15	14	1
Florence	21	13	8	Springfield	92	61	31
Forest Grove	34	26	8	Stanfield	5	5	0
Gaston	1	1	0	Stayton	18	15	3
Gearhart	3	3	0	St. Helens	19	17	2
Gervais	2	2	0	Sutherlin	15	12	3
Gladstone	24	17	7	Sweet Home	18	11	7
Gold Beach	7	6	1	Talent	8	7	1
Grants Pass	62	39	23	The Dalles	22	20	2
Gresham	154	108	46	Tigard	70	56	14
Heppner	2	2	0	Tillamook	12	10	2
Hermiston	29	21	8	Toledo	14	8	6
Hillsboro	130	97	33	Troutdale	22	19	3
Hines	4	3	1	Tualatin	34	30	4
Hood River	18	14	4	Turner	2	2	0
Hubbard	6	5	1	Umatilla	10	9	1
Independence	14	12	2	Union	1	1	0
Jacksonville	5	4	1	Vale	6	6	0
John Day	10	5	5	Vernonia	5	5	0
Junction City	13	9	4	Warrenton	9	8	1
Keizer	44	37	7	West Linn	33	28	5
King City	5	5	0	Weston	2	2	0
Klamath Falls	40	36	4	Winston	9	8	1
La Grande	31	18	13	Woodburn	35	27	8
Lake Oswego	70	43	27	Yamhill	2	2	0
Lakeview	5	5	0				
Lebanon	31	24	7	**PENNSYLVANIA**			
Lincoln City	29	20	9				
Madras	11	10	1	Abington Township	110	90	20
Manzanita	3	3	0	Adams Township (Butler County)	2	2	0

Table 78

Full-time Law Enforcement Employees as of October 31, 2001
by City by State—Continued

City by state	Total police employees	Total officers	Total civilians	City by state	Total police employees	Total officers	Total civilians
PENNSYLVANIA—Continued				**PENNSYLVANIA—Continued**			
Adams Township (Cambria County)	4	4	0	Carbondale	15	15	0
Akron	5	5	0	Carnegie	14	13	1
Albion	2	2	0	Carroll Township (Washington County)	3	3	0
Alburtis	3	3	0	Carroll Township (York County)	9	9	0
Aleppo Township	5	5	0	Carroll Valley	4	3	1
Aliquippa	24	24	0	Castle Shannon	11	10	1
Allegheny Township (Westmoreland County)	11	10	1	Catawissa Township	2	2	0
Allentown	231	208	23	Centerville	3	3	0
Altoona	86	76	10	Central Berks Regional	13	12	1
Ambler	14	12	2	Chalfont	6	6	0
Amity Township	11	10	1	Chambersburg	33	30	3
Arnold	11	10	1	Chartiers Township	11	11	0
Ashland	5	5	0	Cheltenham Township	96	85	11
Ashley	3	3	0	Chester	115	105	10
Aspinwall	7	6	1	Cheswick	3	3	0
Aston Township	18	16	2	Chippewa Township	12	11	1
Athens	7	6	1	Churchill	8	8	0
Athens Township	9	9	0	Clarks Summit	7	6	1
Avalon	6	6	0	Claysville	2	2	0
Baden	3	3	0	Clay Township	4	4	0
Baldwin Borough	32	26	6	Clearfield	8	8	0
Baldwin Township	5	5	0	Cleona	4	4	0
Bally	1	1	0	Cochranton	2	2	0
Bangor	10	9	1	Collegeville	7	7	0
Barrett Township	7	7	0	Collingdale	8	8	0
Beaver Falls	19	18	1	Colonial Regional	24	22	2
Bedford	5	4	1	Columbia	22	19	3
Bedminster Township	5	5	0	Colwyn	2	2	0
Bell Acres	4	4	0	Conemaugh Township (Cambria County)	2	2	0
Bellefonte	10	9	1	Conemaugh Township (Somerset County)	7	6	1
Bellevue	16	13	3	Conestoga Township	3	3	0
Bellwood	3	3	0	Conewango Township	4	4	0
Bensalem Township	107	82	25	Conneaut Lake Regional	3	3	0
Berlin	1	1	0	Connellsville	18	17	1
Bern Township	10	10	0	Conshohocken	16	15	1
Bethel Park	42	36	6	Conway	3	3	0
Bethel Township (Berks County)	2	2	0	Coopersburg	6	6	0
Bethlehem	165	142	23	Coplay	4	4	0
Bethlehem Township	26	24	2	Cornwall	8	7	1
Birmingham Township	3	3	0	Corry	17	13	4
Blairsville	1	1	0	Covington Township	2	2	0
Blakely	4	4	0	Cranberry Township	26	23	3
Bloomsburg Town	15	12	3	Cresson	1	1	0
Boyertown	8	7	1	Cressona	2	2	0
Brackenridge	5	5	0	Croyle Township	1	1	0
Bradford Township	5	5	0	Cumberland Township (Adams County)	6	6	0
Brandywine Regional	14	13	1	Dale	1	1	0
Brecknock Township	3	3	0	Dallas	5	5	0
Brentwood	18	14	4	Dallas Township	8	8	0
Briar Creek Township	3	3	0	Derry	2	2	0
Bridgeport	10	9	1	Derry Township (Dauphin County)	42	36	6
Bridgeville	9	8	1	Dickson City	13	13	0
Bridgewater	3	3	0	Donegal Township	2	2	0
Brighton Township	6	6	0	Dormont	15	14	1
Bristol	11	10	1	Douglass Township (Montgomery County)	12	10	2
Bristol Township	81	65	16	Downingtown	17	15	2
Brockway	2	2	0	Doylestown	20	15	5
Brookhaven	10	9	1	Du Bois	14	10	4
Brownsville	5	5	0	Duboistown	2	2	0
Bryn Athyn	5	5	0	Dunmore	9	8	1
Buckingham Township	23	21	2	Duquesne	19	18	1
Butler	23	23	0	Earl Township	11	10	1
Butler Township (Luzerne County)	8	7	1	East Bethlehem Township	2	2	0
California	8	7	1	East Buffalo Township	6	6	0
Caln Township	16	14	2	East Cocalico Township	23	21	2
Cambridge Springs	3	3	0	East Conemaugh	2	2	0
Canton	2	2	0	East Coventry Township	6	5	1

Table 78

Full-time Law Enforcement Employees as of October 31, 2001

by City by State—Continued

City by state	Total police employees	Total officers	Total civilians	City by state	Total police employees	Total officers	Total civilians
PENNSYLVANIA—Continued				**PENNSYLVANIA—Continued**			
East Earl Township	3	3	0	Honesdale	11	9	2
East Fallowfield Township	5	5	0	Honey Brook Township	4	4	0
East Hempfield Township	30	26	4	Hooversville	1	1	0
East Lampeter Township	38	34	4	Horsham Township	49	40	9
East Norriton Township	31	28	3	Hughesville	3	3	0
Easttown Township	15	14	1	Hummelstown	6	6	0
East Washington	2	2	0	Huntingdon	14	12	2
East Whiteland Township	21	19	2	Indiana	26	19	7
Ebensburg	4	4	0	Indiana Township	10	10	0
Economy	13	12	1	Ingram	4	4	0
Eddystone	8	7	1	Irwin	4	4	0
Edgewood	6	6	0	Jackson Township (Cambria County)	1	1	0
Edgeworth	6	4	2	Jackson Township (Luzerne County)	3	3	0
Edinboro	11	10	1	Jackson Township (York County)	7	6	1
Edwardsville	6	6	0	Jeannette	18	17	1
Elizabeth	2	2	0	Jefferson Hills Borough	17	16	1
Ellwood City	15	11	4	Jenkins Township	2	2	0
Emmaus	17	16	1	Jenkintown	12	12	0
Emporium	1	1	0	Jersey Shore	7	6	1
Ephrata	23	20	3	Johnsonburg	4	4	0
Ephrata Township	14	13	1	Johnstown	60	50	10
Erie	239	205	34	Kane	4	4	0
Etna	3	2	1	Kennedy Township	14	10	4
Everett	4	4	0	Kidder Township	7	7	0
Exeter	5	4	1	Kingston Township	10	10	0
Exeter Township (Berks County)	31	30	1	Kittanning	9	8	1
Fairchance	1	1	0	Kline Township	2	2	0
Fairview Township (Luzerne County)	5	5	0	Kutztown	10	9	1
Fairview Township (York County)	15	13	2	Laflin Boro	3	3	0
Falls Township (Bucks County)	55	50	5	Lake City	3	3	0
Fawn Township	4	4	0	Lancaster	201	157	44
Ferguson Township	18	16	2	Lancaster Township (Butler County)	2	2	0
Ferndale	1	1	0	Lansdale	29	23	6
Findlay Township	22	15	7	Lawrence Park Township	8	7	1
Folcroft	9	9	0	Lawrence Township	9	9	0
Ford City	4	4	0	Lebanon	47	47	0
Forest City	2	2	0	Leechburg	3	3	0
Forks Township	15	14	1	Leetsdale	3	3	0
Forty Fort	6	5	1	Leet Township	5	5	0
Foster Township	5	5	0	Lehighton	9	8	1
Fountain Hill	8	8	0	Lehigh Township (Northampton County)	11	10	1
Frackville	7	7	0	Lehman Township	4	4	0
Franconia Township	12	11	1	Lewisburg	7	7	0
Franklin Park	10	9	1	Limerick Township	17	15	2
Franklin Township (Carbon County)	4	4	0	Lincoln	2	2	0
Gallitzin	3	3	0	Linesville	1	1	0
Girard	6	5	1	Lititz	16	13	3
Glenolden	9	8	1	Littlestown	7	7	0
Greencastle	5	5	0	Lock Haven	14	12	2
Green Tree	12	11	1	Logan Township	18	16	2
Grove City	8	7	1	Lower Burrell	17	17	0
Hampton Township	19	18	1	Lower Gwynedd Township	21	18	3
Hanover	23	21	2	Lower Heidelberg Township	6	6	0
Harmar Township	5	5	0	Lower Makefield Township	33	30	3
Harmony Township	4	4	0	Lower Merion Township	165	139	26
Harrison Township	16	12	4	Lower Pottsgrove Township	16	14	2
Hatboro	19	14	5	Lower Salford Township	19	17	2
Hatfield Township	29	24	5	Lower Saucon Township	14	12	2
Haverford Township	86	69	17	Lower Southampton Township	33	30	3
Hazleton	35	32	3	Lower Swatara Township	14	13	1
Heidelberg	2	2	0	Luzerne Township	1	1	0
Hellam Township	7	7	0	Macungie	4	4	0
Hellertown	11	10	1	Mahoning Township (Carbon County)	5	5	0
Hempfield Township	7	6	1	Malvern	5	4	1
Hermitage	31	28	3	Manheim	8	7	1
Hilltown Township	20	17	3	Manor Township	20	19	1
Homestead	15	15	0	Mansfield	5	5	0

Table 78

Full-time Law Enforcement Employees as of October 31, 2001

by City by State—Continued

City by state	Total police employees	Total officers	Total civilians	City by state	Total police employees	Total officers	Total civilians
PENNSYLVANIA—Continued				**PENNSYLVANIA—Continued**			
Marlborough Township	5	4	1	North Londonderry Township	4	3	1
Marple Township	38	31	7	North Middleton Township	9	8	1
Marysville	3	3	0	North Strabane Township	17	16	1
McAdoo	3	3	0	Northumberland	6	6	0
McSherrystown	4	4	0	North Versailles Township	23	20	3
Mechanicsburg	16	15	1	North Wales	7	6	1
Mercer	6	6	0	Norwegian Township	1	1	0
Mercersburg	2	2	0	Norwood	8	7	1
Meyersdale	4	4	0	O'Hara Township	14	13	1
Mid-Cumberland Valley Regional	9	8	1	Oil City	17	15	2
Middlesex Township (Butler County)	5	5	0	Old Forge	6	6	0
Middlesex Township (Cumberland County)	9	8	1	Old Lycoming Township	9	8	1
Middletown Township	60	52	8	Oley Township	3	3	0
Milford	3	3	0	Olyphant	5	5	0
Millcreek Township	75	59	16	Orangeville	1	1	0
Millersburg	2	2	0	Orwigsburg	4	4	0
Millersville	15	13	2	Oxford	10	9	1
Millvale	5	5	0	Paint Township	2	2	0
Milton	11	10	1	Palmerton	8	7	1
Minersville	6	6	0	Palmyra	10	9	1
Mohnton	4	4	0	Parkesburg	7	7	0
Monaca	6	6	0	Parkside	3	3	0
Monessen	15	14	1	Patterson Township	4	4	0
Monongahela	12	10	2	Patton Township	16	14	2
Monroeville	58	53	5	Pen Argyl	4	4	0
Montgomery Township	44	35	9	Penbrook	6	6	0
Montoursville	6	6	0	Penn Hills	65	56	9
Moon Township	36	30	6	Penn Township (Butler County)	3	2	1
Moore Township	7	6	1	Penn Township (Lancaster County)	8	7	1
Morton	4	4	0	Penn Township (York County)	23	21	2
Mountaintop Regional	7	7	0	Pequea Township	3	3	0
Mount Holly Springs	2	2	0	Perkasie	15	13	2
Mount Joy	12	10	2	Peters Township	23	21	2
Mount Joy Township	8	7	1	Philadelphia	7,867	6,942	925
Mount Lebanon	53	42	11	Philipsburg	2	2	0
Mount Union	6	6	0	Pitcairn	4	4	0
Muhlenberg Township	29	27	2	Pittsburgh	1,174	1,091	83
Munhall	22	18	4	Plains Township	13	13	0
Murrysville	25	20	5	Pleasant Hills	22	16	6
Myerstown	4	4	0	Plumstead Township	13	11	2
Nanticoke	14	13	1	Plymouth Township (Luzerne County)	3	3	0
Narberth	7	7	0	Pocono Mountain Regional	35	32	3
Neville Township	9	6	3	Pocono Township	13	13	0
Newberry Township	13	12	1	Point Township	5	5	0
New Britain	10	9	1	Portage	2	2	0
New Britain Township	12	11	1	Port Allegany	3	3	0
New Castle	32	30	2	Pottstown	49	39	10
New Castle Township	1	1	0	Pottsville	31	30	1
New Hanover Township	7	7	0	Prospect Park	9	9	0
New Holland	11	10	1	Pymatuning Township	3	3	0
New Kensington	30	24	6	Quakertown	16	14	2
New Sewickley Township	8	7	1	Radnor Township	53	43	10
Newtown	4	4	0	Rankin	1	1	0
Newtown Township (Bucks County)	30	26	4	Reading	217	193	24
New Wilmington	3	3	0	Reynoldsville	2	2	0
Norristown	77	65	12	Rice Township	4	4	0
Northampton Township	46	40	6	Richland	2	2	0
North Catasauqua	4	4	0	Richland Township (Allegheny County)	12	11	1
North Cornwall Township	10	8	2	Richland Township (Cambria County)	19	18	1
North Coventry Township	12	11	1	Ridgway	7	7	0
North East	7	6	1	Ridley Township	39	31	8
Northeastern Regional	11	10	1	Robesonia	2	2	0
Northern Cambria Regional	4	4	0	Robeson Township	5	5	0
Northern York Regional	46	42	4	Robinson Township (Allegheny County)	18	13	5
North Fayette Township	22	17	5	Rochester Township	1	1	0
North Huntingdon Township	37	30	7	Rockledge	5	5	0
North Lebanon Township	10	9	1	Rosslyn Farms	2	2	0

Table 78

Full-time Law Enforcement Employees as of October 31, 2001
by City by State—Continued

City by state	Total police employees	Total officers	Total civilians	City by state	Total police employees	Total officers	Total civilians
PENNSYLVANIA—Continued				**PENNSYLVANIA—Continued**			
Rostraver Township	15	14	1	Tinicum Township (Delaware County)	13	12	1
Royersford	8	7	1	Titusville	14	14	0
Sandy Township	7	7	0	Towamencin Township	33	25	8
Sayre	10	8	2	Towanda	6	6	0
Schuylkill Haven	12	8	4	Trafford	4	4	0
Schuylkill Township	10	9	1	Trainer	9	8	1
Scottdale	7	7	0	Tredyffrin Township	60	51	9
Scott Township (Allegheny County)	20	19	1	Troy	3	3	0
Scranton	157	140	17	Tullytown	7	6	1
Selinsgrove	6	5	1	Tunkhannock	6	5	1
Seven Springs	6	6	0	Tunkhannock Township (Wyoming County)	3	3	0
Sewickley	10	9	1	Tyrone	4	3	1
Sewickley Heights	8	7	1	Union City	1	1	0
Shaler Township	28	27	1	Uniontown	20	16	4
Shamokin	17	13	4	Union Township (Mifflin County)	1	1	0
Sharon Hill	8	7	1	Union Township (Washington County)	7	7	0
Sharpsburg	8	7	1	Upland	2	2	0
Sharpsville	7	6	1	Upper Chichester Township	24	21	3
Shenandoah	9	8	1	Upper Darby Township	124	114	10
Shenango Township (Lawrence County)	5	5	0	Upper Gwynedd Township	21	19	2
Shenango Township (Mercer County)	5	4	1	Upper Merion Township	83	62	21
Shillington	6	6	0	Upper Moreland Township	50	39	11
Shiremanstown	2	2	0	Upper Pottsgrove Township	7	7	0
Sinking Spring	5	5	0	Upper Providence Township (Delaware County)	10	9	1
Slatington	5	5	0	Upper Providence Township (Montgomery County)	19	17	2
Slippery Rock	5	5	0	Upper Saucon Township	15	14	1
Solebury Township	11	10	1	Upper Southampton Township	27	24	3
South Annville Township	2	2	0	Upper St. Clair Township	34	27	7
South Beaver Township	4	4	0	Uwchlan Township	26	24	2
South Centre Township	4	4	0	Vandergrift	8	8	0
South Fayette Township	18	17	1	Vernon Township	4	4	0
South Greensburg	2	2	0	Versailles	2	2	0
South Heidelberg Township	6	6	0	Warminster Township	56	47	9
South Lebanon Township	8	7	1	Warren	20	15	5
South Londonderry Township	5	5	0	Warrington Township	28	25	3
South Park Township	16	15	1	Warwick Township (Bucks County)	20	18	2
South Pymatuning Township	1	1	0	Warwick Township (Lancaster County)	15	14	1
South Strabane Township	12	11	1	Washington (Washington County)	32	29	3
South Waverly	3	3	0	Washington Township (Franklin County)	13	12	1
South Whitehall Township	39	36	3	Washington Township (Westmoreland County)	6	6	0
South Williamsport	7	6	1	Watsontown	5	5	0
Springdale	1	1	0	Waynesboro	15	14	1
Springettsbury Township	30	28	2	Waynesburg	8	8	0
Springfield Township (Bucks County)	5	5	0	Wellsboro	5	5	0
Springfield Township (Montgomery County)	30	29	1	West Alexander	2	2	0
Spring Garden Township	17	16	1	West Brandywine Township	6	6	0
Spring Township (Berks County)	22	21	1	West Chester	51	42	9
Spring Township (Centre County)	7	6	1	West Conshohocken	9	8	1
State College	72	61	11	West Donegal Township	6	6	0
Stewartstown	4	4	0	West Earl Township	4	4	0
St. Marys City	14	13	1	West Elizabeth	17	16	1
Stonycreek Township	2	2	0	West Goshen Township	32	26	6
Strasburg	5	5	0	West Hills Regional	12	11	1
Stroud Area Regional	56	51	5	West Homestead	10	8	2
Sugarcreek	6	5	1	West Lampeter Township	14	13	1
Sugarloaf Township (Luzerne County)	4	3	1	West Lebanon Township	10	8	2
Summerhill Township	2	2	0	West Manchester Township	27	25	2
Susquehanna Township (Dauphin County)	39	37	2	West Manheim Township	6	6	0
Swarthmore	9	9	0	West Norriton Township	32	27	5
Swatara Township	37	35	2	West Pikeland Township	1	1	0
Swissvale	8	8	0	West Pittston	3	3	0
Swoyersville	5	5	0	West Reading	12	10	2
Sykesville	1	1	0	Westtown-East Goshen Township	27	24	3
Tamaqua	10	10	0	West View	10	9	1
Tarentum	12	8	4	West Whiteland Township	29	27	2
Terre Hill	3	3	0				
Tinicum Township (Bucks County)	5	5	0				

Table 78

Full-time Law Enforcement Employees as of October 31, 2001
by City by State—Continued

City by state	Total police employees	Total officers	Total civilians	City by state	Total police employees	Total officers	Total civilians
PENNSYLVANIA—Continued				**SOUTH CAROLINA—Continued**			
West Wyoming	3	3	0	Barnwell	13	12	1
Whitehall	24	19	5	Batesburg-Leesville	24	19	5
Whitehall Township	58	49	9	Beaufort	54	48	6
White Haven Borough	2	2	0	Belton	20	15	5
Whitemarsh Township	38	33	5	Bennettsville	39	35	4
Whitpain Township	36	29	7	Bishopville	16	14	2
Wilkes-Barre Township	15	12	3	Blackville	8	7	1
Wilkinsburg	38	34	4	Bonneau	2	2	0
Wilkins Township	13	12	1	Bowman	3	3	0
Willistown Township	17	15	2	Briarcliffe Acres	1	1	0
Windber	3	2	1	Burnettown	2	2	0
Wyoming	7	7	0	Calhoun Falls	11	10	1
Wyomissing	25	20	5	Camden	31	27	4
Yardley	3	3	0	Cameron	1	1	0
Yeadon	12	10	2	Campobello	2	2	0
York Area Regional	41	36	5	Cayce	46	41	5
York Springs-Latimore Township	2	2	0	Central	10	10	0
Youngsville	2	2	0	Chapin	7	6	1
				Charleston	485	349	136
RHODE ISLAND				Cheraw	31	24	7
				Chester	28	24	4
Barrington	31	24	7	Chesterfield	6	5	1
Bristol	50	39	11	Clemson	32	25	7
Burrillville	33	25	8	Clio	5	4	1
Central Falls	47	37	10	Clover	17	13	4
Charlestown	24	19	5	Columbia	327	286	41
Coventry	61	51	10	Conway	63	48	15
Cranston	179	149	30	Cottageville	7	5	2
Cumberland	56	47	9	Darlington	30	26	4
East Greenwich	38	30	8	Denmark	13	10	3
East Providence	114	94	20	Dillon	29	25	4
Foster	16	7	9	Due West	5	5	0
Glocester	17	13	4	Duncan	8	8	0
Hopkinton	21	16	5	Easley	45	34	11
Jamestown	19	14	5	Eastover	2	2	0
Johnston	86	69	17	Edgefield	9	7	2
Lincoln	38	30	8	Edisto Beach	5	5	0
Little Compton	14	10	4	Elgin	2	2	0
Middletown	40	37	3	Elloree	3	3	0
Narragansett	48	36	12	Estill	8	7	1
Newport	111	87	24	Eutawville	3	3	0
New Shoreham	9	4	5	Fairfax	7	7	0
North Kingstown	63	48	15	Florence	114	99	15
North Providence	91	67	24	Folly Beach	17	10	7
North Smithfield	24	20	4	Forest Acres	36	27	9
Pawtucket	171	142	29	Fort Lawn	1	1	0
Portsmouth	34	32	2	Fort Mill	25	19	6
Providence	544	456	88	Fountain Inn	26	19	7
Richmond	14	9	5	Gaffney	44	38	6
Scituate	23	17	6	Georgetown	49	40	9
Smithfield	50	38	12	Goose Creek	53	43	10
South Kingstown	65	47	18	Great Falls	8	6	2
Tiverton	35	26	9	Greeleyville	3	2	1
Warren	27	21	6	Greenville	222	182	40
Warwick	212	164	48	Greenwood	61	52	9
Westerly	58	46	12	Greer	69	55	14
West Greenwich	15	9	6	Hampton	10	9	1
West Warwick	69	57	12	Hanahan	29	21	8
Woonsocket	119	100	19	Hardeeville	18	13	5
				Harleyville	3	3	0
SOUTH CAROLINA				Hartsville	41	37	4
				Hemingway	8	5	3
Abbeville	19	16	3	Holly Hill	10	9	1
Aiken	101	82	19	Honea Path	16	12	4
Andrews	14	10	4	Inman	6	6	0
Aynor	7	6	1	Irmo	20	18	2
Bamberg	12	10	2	Isle of Palms	25	17	8

Table 78

Full-time Law Enforcement Employees as of October 31, 2001
by City by State—Continued

City by state	Total police employees	Total officers	Total civilians	City by state	Total police employees	Total officers	Total civilians
SOUTH CAROLINA—Continued				**SOUTH CAROLINA—Continued**			
Iva	3	2	1	Ware Shoals	11	10	1
Jackson	4	4	0	West Columbia	45	38	7
Jefferson	4	3	1	Westminster	9	9	0
Johnsonville	6	5	1	West Pelzer	3	3	0
Jonesville	4	4	0	West Union	2	2	0
Lake View	3	3	0	Whitmire	5	5	0
Lamar	4	4	0	Williamston	21	17	4
Lancaster	44	35	9	Williston	9	8	1
Lane	2	2	0	Winnsboro	26	23	3
Laurens	37	31	6	Woodruff	14	11	3
Lexington	29	25	4	Yemassee	5	4	1
Liberty	15	10	5	York	30	24	6
Loris	14	10	4				
Lyman	7	6	1	**SOUTH DAKOTA**			
Manning	18	16	2	Aberdeen	48	40	8
Marion	30	25	5	Alcester	1	1	0
Mauldin	41	34	7	Belle Fourche	10	9	1
McColl	8	7	1	Beresford	4	4	0
McCormick	7	7	0	Box Elder	6	5	1
Moncks Corner	16	14	2	Brandon	8	7	1
Mount Pleasant	144	104	40	Brookings	35	27	8
Mullins	22	20	2	Burke	1	1	0
Myrtle Beach	237	180	57	Canton	5	5	0
Newberry	29	25	4	Castlewood	1	1	0
North	2	2	0	Chamberlain	5	5	0
North Augusta	60	49	11	Deadwood	11	8	3
North Charleston	306	241	65	Eagle Butte	3	3	0
North Myrtle Beach	102	75	27	Elk Point	5	4	1
Norway	6	3	3	Estelline	1	1	0
Orangeburg	84	70	14	Eureka	3	3	0
Pacolet	5	4	1	Faith	2	1	1
Pageland	18	12	6	Garretson	1	1	0
Pawleys Island	3	2	1	Gettysburg	1	1	0
Pendleton	12	11	1	Gregory	3	3	0
Pickens	16	13	3	Groton	3	3	0
Pineridge	2	1	1	Harrisburg	1	1	0
Port Royal	17	16	1	Hot Springs	7	6	1
Prosperity	3	3	0	Huron	30	23	7
Ridgeland	8	7	1	Kadoka	1	1	0
Ridge Spring	3	3	0	Kimball	1	1	0
Ridgeville	2	2	0	Lake Andes	5	5	0
Rock Hill	134	98	36	Lead	6	5	1
Saluda	10	10	0	Lemmon	4	4	0
Santee	13	9	4	Madison	11	10	1
Seneca	35	27	8	McLaughlin	7	3	4
Simpsonville	46	36	10	Milbank	5	5	0
Society Hill	5	5	0	Miller	4	4	0
South Congaree	10	5	5	Mitchell	36	27	9
Spartanburg	153	133	20	Mobridge	12	7	5
Springdale	8	8	0	Murdo	1	1	0
St. George	11	10	1	Newell	1	1	0
St. Matthews	7	7	0	North Sioux City	8	7	1
St. Stephen	8	7	1	Parkston	2	2	0
Sullivans Island	9	7	2	Philip	2	2	0
Summerton	10	9	1	Pierre	34	23	11
Summerville	75	56	19	Platte	2	2	0
Sumter	139	100	39	Rapid City	119	94	25
Surfside Beach	19	13	6	Salem	2	2	0
Tega Cay	13	9	4	Selby	1	1	0
Timmonsville	10	9	1	Sioux Falls	207	178	29
Travelers Rest	21	15	6	Sisseton	7	7	0
Turbeville	3	3	0	Spearfish	22	15	7
Union	40	37	3	Sturgis	15	14	1
Varnville	6	6	0	Tea	3	3	0
Wagener	3	3	0	Tripp	1	1	0
Walhalla	18	14	4	Vermillion	15	14	1
Walterboro	34	24	10	Watertown	40	30	10

Table 78

Full-time Law Enforcement Employees as of October 31, 2001
by City by State—Continued

City by state	Total police employees	Total officers	Total civilians	City by state	Total police employees	Total officers	Total civilians
SOUTH DAKOTA—Continued				**TENNESSEE—Continued**			
Webster	5	5	0	Decatur	4	4	0
Whitewood	1	1	0	Decaturville	1	1	0
Winner	16	7	9	Decherd	13	12	1
Yankton	45	26	19	Dickson	47	42	5
				Dover	6	6	0
TENNESSEE				Dresden	8	8	0
				Dyer	6	6	0
Adamsville	11	7	4	Dyersburg	80	59	21
Alamo	3	3	0	Eagleville	2	2	0
Alcoa	43	37	6	East Ridge	39	32	7
Alexandria	4	4	0	Elizabethton	40	37	3
Algood	7	7	0	Elkton	1	1	0
Ardmore	10	6	4	Englewood	5	5	0
Ashland City	13	12	1	Erin	4	4	0
Athens	34	32	2	Erwin	10	10	0
Atoka	8	8	0	Estill Springs	6	6	0
Baileyton	2	2	0	Ethridge	2	2	0
Bartlett	117	86	31	Etowah	14	10	4
Baxter	4	4	0	Fairview	16	15	1
Bean Station	5	5	0	Fayetteville	28	26	2
Belle Meade	20	16	4	Franklin	120	95	25
Bells	5	5	0	Friendship	1	1	0
Benton	8	7	1	Gainesboro	7	5	2
Berry Hill	17	13	4	Gallatin	67	51	16
Bethel Springs	1	1	0	Gallaway	7	7	0
Big Sandy	1	1	0	Gates	3	3	0
Blaine	2	2	0	Gatlinburg	52	44	8
Bluff City	9	9	0	Germantown	101	80	21
Bolivar	28	22	6	Gibson	3	3	0
Bradford	3	3	0	Gleason	5	5	0
Brentwood	59	46	13	Goodlettsville	51	37	14
Brighton	5	5	0	Gordonsville	5	4	1
Bristol	83	65	18	Grand Junction	3	3	0
Brownsville	36	31	5	Graysville	3	2	1
Bruceton	5	5	0	Greenbrier	12	11	1
Bulls Gap	1	1	0	Greeneville	44	43	1
Burns	3	3	0	Greenfield	7	7	0
Calhoun	2	2	0	Gruetli-Laager	3	3	0
Camden	18	13	5	Halls	7	7	0
Carthage	11	7	4	Harriman	23	22	1
Caryville	6	6	0	Henderson	13	13	0
Celina	6	5	1	Hendersonville	85	66	19
Centerville	19	14	5	Henry	2	2	0
Chapel Hill	4	4	0	Hohenwald	14	13	1
Chattanooga	651	445	206	Hollow Rock	2	2	0
Church Hill	9	8	1	Hornbeak	2	2	0
Clarksville	238	208	30	Humboldt	34	28	6
Cleveland	98	87	11	Huntingdon	16	12	4
Clifton	7	7	0	Huntland	7	7	0
Clinton	27	24	3	Jacksboro	5	5	0
Collegedale	16	15	1	Jackson	238	183	55
Collierville	97	71	26	Jamestown	8	8	0
Collinwood	7	6	1	Jasper	9	8	1
Columbia	88	80	8	Jefferson City	21	19	2
Cookeville	89	68	21	Jellico	10	10	0
Coopertown	3	2	1	Johnson City	190	157	33
Copperhill	1	1	0	Jonesborough	16	11	5
Cornersville	5	4	1	Kenton	5	5	0
Covington	28	27	1	Kingsport	140	98	42
Cowan	5	5	0	Kingston	11	10	1
Cross Plains	3	3	0	Kingston Springs	5	4	1
Crossville	33	31	2	Knoxville	519	425	94
Crump	3	2	1	Lafayette	25	16	9
Cumberland City	1	1	0	La Follette	27	19	8
Cumberland Gap	1	1	0	La Grange	2	2	0
Dandridge	9	9	0	Lake City	10	7	3
Dayton	17	15	2	La Vergne	55	40	15

Table 78

Full-time Law Enforcement Employees as of October 31, 2001
by City by State—Continued

City by state	Total police employees	Total officers	Total civilians	City by state	Total police employees	Total officers	Total civilians
TENNESSEE—Continued				**TENNESSEE—Continued**			
Lawrenceburg	45	39	6	Rutledge	4	4	0
Lebanon	79	64	15	Savannah	26	15	11
Lenoir City	21	20	1	Scotts Hill	3	3	0
Lewisburg	36	29	7	Selmer	18	17	1
Lexington	29	24	5	Sevierville	61	49	12
Livingston	20	15	5	Sewanee	13	9	4
Lookout Mountain	20	16	4	Sharon	3	3	0
Loretto	4	4	0	Shelbyville	45	37	8
Loudon	15	14	1	Signal Mountain	16	14	2
Madisonville	15	13	2	Smithville	20	11	9
Manchester	36	31	5	Smyrna	74	53	21
Martin	37	30	7	Sneedville	1	1	0
Maryville	52	43	9	Soddy-Daisy	25	19	6
Mason	3	3	0	Somerville	18	13	5
Maynardville	5	4	1	South Carthage	4	4	0
McEwen	5	4	1	South Fulton	9	7	2
McKenzie	20	15	5	South Pittsburg	8	8	0
McMinnville	37	34	3	Sparta	16	15	1
Medina	6	6	0	Spencer	3	3	0
Memphis	2,391	1,916	475	Spring City	9	8	1
Middleton	3	3	0	Springfield	53	37	16
Milan	28	24	4	Spring Hill	20	19	1
Millersville	17	13	4	St. Joseph	1	1	0
Millington	35	28	7	Surgoinsville	4	3	1
Minor Hill	3	2	1	Sweetwater	21	19	2
Monteagle	10	6	4	Tazewell	7	7	0
Monterey	8	8	0	Tellico Plains	5	5	0
Morristown	85	79	6	Tiptonville	6	6	0
Moscow	5	5	0	Toone	1	1	0
Mountain City	8	8	0	Townsend	3	3	0
Mount Carmel	9	8	1	Tracy City	5	4	1
Mount Juliet	31	24	7	Trenton	26	20	6
Mount Pleasant	12	11	1	Trezavant	1	1	0
Munford	13	12	1	Trimble	5	5	0
Murfreesboro	196	159	37	Troy	4	4	0
Nashville	1,689	1,256	433	Tullahoma	40	35	5
Newbern	18	13	5	Tusculum	2	2	0
New Hope	1	1	0	Union City	45	37	8
New Johnsonville	4	4	0	Vonore	9	8	1
New Market	2	2	0	Wartburg	3	3	0
Newport	36	28	8	Watauga	2	1	1
New Tazewell	10	10	0	Watertown	6	4	2
Niota	4	4	0	Waverly	12	11	1
Nolensville	2	1	1	Waynesboro	9	8	1
Norris	7	7	0	Westmoreland	9	5	4
Oakland	9	8	1	White Bluff	3	3	0
Oak Ridge	65	53	12	White House	26	18	8
Oliver Springs	19	14	5	White Pine	9	8	1
Oneida	18	13	5	Whiteville	6	6	0
Paris	37	27	10	Whitwell	9	5	4
Parsons	9	9	0	Winchester	30	23	7
Petersburg	3	3	0	Woodbury	9	8	1
Pigeon Forge	62	51	11				
Pittman Center	2	2	0	**TEXAS**			
Portland	28	21	7				
Pulaski	30	27	3	Abernathy	3	3	0
Puryear	2	2	0	Abilene	233	174	59
Red Bank	24	22	2	Addison	83	63	20
Red Boiling Springs	5	5	0	Alamo	33	24	9
Ridgely	6	5	1	Alamo Heights	31	21	10
Ridgetop	4	4	0	Alice	48	33	15
Ripley	32	27	5	Allen	89	67	22
Rockford	4	3	1	Alpine	15	9	6
Rockwood	15	14	1	Alton	8	6	2
Rogersville	12	12	0	Alvarado	17	11	6
Rossville	4	4	0	Alvin	64	42	22
Rutherford	6	6	0	Amarillo	375	274	101

Table 78

Full-time Law Enforcement Employees as of October 31, 2001

by City by State—Continued

City by state	Total police employees	Total officers	Total civilians	City by state	Total police employees	Total officers	Total civilians
TEXAS—Continued				**TEXAS—Continued**			
Andrews	18	14	4	Castle Hills	27	21	6
Angleton	51	39	12	Cedar Hill	62	49	13
Anson	5	4	1	Cedar Park	60	45	15
Anthony	9	8	1	Celina	7	7	0
Aransas Pass	25	18	7	Center	22	14	8
Arcola	6	5	1	Childress	14	9	5
Argyle	7	7	0	Cisco	8	7	1
Arlington	710	539	171	Clarksville	12	8	4
Arp	3	3	0	Cleburne	58	43	15
Athens	34	25	9	Cleveland	27	19	8
Atlanta	20	15	5	Clifton	6	5	1
Austin	1,794	1,208	586	Clint	3	3	0
Azle	34	24	10	Clute	32	22	10
Baird	2	2	0	Clyde	6	5	1
Balch Springs	39	28	11	Cockrell Hill	20	15	5
Balcones Heights	16	14	2	Coffee City	2	2	0
Ballinger	8	6	2	Coleman	14	9	5
Bangs	3	3	0	College Station	137	99	38
Bastrop	18	16	2	Colleyville	41	31	10
Bay City	48	35	13	Colorado City	13	7	6
Bayou Vista	6	6	0	Columbus	11	10	1
Baytown	181	135	46	Comanche	8	7	1
Beaumont	320	252	68	Combes	8	7	1
Bedford	114	71	43	Commerce	19	14	5
Beeville	26	20	6	Conroe	103	76	27
Bellaire	53	41	12	Converse	26	23	3
Bellmead	23	17	6	Coppell	68	53	15
Bellville	14	12	2	Copperas Cove	63	49	14
Belton	32	24	8	Corinth	21	20	1
Benbrook	44	36	8	Corpus Christi	613	422	191
Bertram	4	3	1	Corrigan	10	7	3
Beverly Hills	12	9	3	Corsicana	59	45	14
Big Sandy	5	4	1	Cottonwood Shores	2	2	0
Big Spring	63	42	21	Crane	12	7	5
Bishop	9	5	4	Crockett	18	15	3
Blanco	4	4	0	Crowell	1	1	0
Blue Mound	13	7	6	Crowley	24	18	6
Boerne	35	21	14	Crystal City	14	10	4
Bogata	3	3	0	Cuero	12	11	1
Bonham	27	21	6	Daingerfield	7	6	1
Borger	32	25	7	Dalhart	19	12	7
Bovina	1	1	0	Dallas	3,503	2,892	611
Bowie	18	12	6	Dalworthington Gardens	11	10	1
Brady	13	7	6	Danbury	5	5	0
Brazoria	13	7	6	Dayton	17	12	5
Breckenridge	18	12	6	Decatur	19	13	6
Brenham	47	31	16	Deer Park	63	48	15
Bridge City	18	13	5	De Kalb	7	6	1
Bridgeport	17	11	6	De Leon	5	5	0
Brookshire	11	7	4	Del Rio	81	63	18
Brownfield	24	17	7	Denison	54	42	12
Brownsville	294	208	86	Denton	161	129	32
Brownwood	51	33	18	Denver City	13	8	5
Bruceville-Eddy	4	4	0	DeSoto	69	56	13
Bryan	129	97	32	Devine	11	8	3
Bullard	5	4	1	Diboll	17	13	4
Burkburnett	21	16	5	Dickinson	33	25	8
Burleson	53	37	16	Dilley	6	5	1
Burnet	13	12	1	Dimmitt	9	7	2
Caddo Mills	2	2	0	Donna	28	22	6
Caldwell	11	10	1	Dublin	11	9	2
Cameron	9	9	0	Dumas	27	24	3
Caney City	2	2	0	Duncanville	67	54	13
Canton	20	13	7	Eagle Lake	10	9	1
Canyon	23	20	3	Eagle Pass	82	69	13
Carrollton	208	147	61	Early	7	6	1
Carthage	21	14	7	Earth	2	2	0

Table 78

Full-time Law Enforcement Employees as of October 31, 2001
by City by State—Continued

City by state	Total police employees	Total officers	Total civilians	City by state	Total police employees	Total officers	Total civilians
TEXAS—Continued				**TEXAS—Continued**			
Eastland	11	9	2	Harker Heights	41	33	8
Eden	3	3	0	Harlingen	143	108	35
Edgewood	4	3	1	Hart	1	1	0
Edinburg	105	77	28	Haskell	4	4	0
Edna	11	9	2	Hawk Cove	2	2	0
El Campo	32	22	10	Hawkins	6	6	0
Electra	9	5	4	Hawley	3	2	1
Elgin	18	12	6	Hearne	18	14	4
El Paso	1,459	1,145	314	Heath	12	11	1
Elsa	24	16	8	Hedwig Village	24	17	7
Ennis	36	31	5	Helotes	11	10	1
Euless	114	81	33	Hemphill	3	3	0
Everman	17	12	5	Hempstead	12	11	1
Fairfield	9	8	1	Henderson	46	38	8
Fair Oaks Ranch	10	10	0	Hereford	29	23	6
Falfurrias	9	8	1	Hewitt	29	21	8
Farmers Branch	110	71	39	Hickory Creek	9	9	0
Farmersville	7	7	0	Hico	4	4	0
Ferris	16	12	4	Hidalgo	37	28	9
Flatonia	4	4	0	Highland Park	66	52	14
Florence	2	2	0	Highland Village	29	22	7
Floresville	14	13	1	Hill Country Village	12	12	0
Flower Mound	85	55	30	Hillsboro	25	18	7
Floydada	6	6	0	Hitchcock	22	17	5
Forest Hill	30	22	8	Holliday	1	1	0
Forney	19	13	6	Hollywood Park	8	8	0
Fort Stockton	24	17	7	Hondo	17	15	2
Fort Worth	1,569	1,222	347	Hooks	5	5	0
Frankston	7	4	3	Horizon City	10	9	1
Fredericksburg	27	24	3	Horseshoe Bay	11	10	1
Freeport	35	27	8	Houston	7,172	5,394	1,778
Freer	11	5	6	Howe	5	5	0
Friendswood	61	46	15	Hubbard	4	4	0
Friona	10	6	4	Hudson Oaks	8	8	0
Frisco	74	56	18	Humble	75	59	16
Gainesville	59	41	18	Huntington	5	5	0
Galena Park	23	17	6	Huntsville	48	42	6
Galveston	183	148	35	Hurst	104	69	35
Ganado	3	3	0	Hutchins	15	11	4
Garland	396	275	121	Hutto	6	6	0
Gatesville	19	14	5	Idalou	3	3	0
Georgetown	70	48	22	Ingleside	24	17	7
Giddings	16	11	5	Ingram	8	7	1
Gilmer	20	18	2	Iowa Park	17	11	6
Gladewater	21	16	5	Irving	455	308	147
Glenn Heights	15	10	5	Italy	5	5	0
Godley	3	3	0	Itasca	3	3	0
Gonzales	19	14	5	Jacinto City	24	17	7
Gorman	6	4	2	Jacksboro	10	8	2
Graham	19	18	1	Jacksonville	35	26	9
Granbury	22	18	4	Jamaica Beach	5	5	0
Grand Prairie	284	189	95	Jasper	26	18	8
Grand Saline	7	7	0	Jefferson	8	7	1
Granger	3	3	0	Jersey Village	28	20	8
Granite Shoals	7	7	0	Johnson City	4	4	0
Grapeland	4	3	1	Jones Creek	5	4	1
Grapevine	125	90	35	Joshua	15	13	2
Greenville	74	46	28	Jourdanton	6	6	0
Gregory	5	4	1	Junction	3	3	0
Groesbeck	7	7	0	Karnes City	6	5	1
Groves	19	17	2	Katy	57	42	15
Gruver	2	2	0	Kaufman	26	19	7
Gun Barrel City	24	19	5	Keene	13	9	4
Hale Center	4	4	0	Keller	54	39	15
Hallettsville	7	6	1	Kemah	26	22	4
Haltom City	93	71	22	Kemp	6	6	0
Hamlin	10	5	5	Kennedale	26	18	8

Table 78

Full-time Law Enforcement Employees as of October 31, 2001

by City by State—Continued

City by state	Total police employees	Total officers	Total civilians	City by state	Total police employees	Total officers	Total civilians
TEXAS—Continued				**TEXAS—Continued**			
Kermit	14	10	4	McKinney	96	74	22
Kerrville	59	45	14	Meadows Place	15	15	0
Kilgore	38	30	8	Melissa	6	5	1
Killeen	192	150	42	Memorial Villages	38	32	6
Kingsville	55	41	14	Memphis	5	4	1
Kirby	19	14	5	Mercedes	26	21	5
Kirbyville	5	5	0	Meridian	2	2	0
Knox City	2	2	0	Merkel	5	4	1
Kountze	6	6	0	Mesquite	271	204	67
Kress	1	1	0	Mexia	28	18	10
Kyle	12	10	2	Midland	209	158	51
Lacy-Lakeview	22	15	7	Midlothian	27	20	7
La Feria	14	10	4	Mineola	14	12	2
Lago Vista	17	10	7	Mineral Wells	33	28	5
La Grange	7	7	0	Mission	109	80	29
La Joya	19	14	5	Missouri City	70	48	22
Lake Dallas	15	9	6	Monahans	17	11	6
Lake Jackson	57	42	15	Mont Belvieu	15	10	5
Lakeside	4	4	0	Morgans Point Resort	5	5	0
Lakeview	16	12	4	Mount Pleasant	39	28	11
Lakeway	32	26	6	Muleshoe	13	8	5
Lake Worth	30	21	9	Munday	2	2	0
La Marque	26	20	6	Mustang Ridge	4	3	1
Lamesa	24	17	7	Nacogdoches	71	56	15
Lampasas	25	16	9	Naples	2	2	0
Lancaster	42	33	9	Nash	9	8	1
La Porte	93	73	20	Nassau Bay	17	12	5
Laredo	411	338	73	Navasota	28	16	12
La Vernia	4	4	0	Nederland	33	22	11
Lavon	6	5	1	Needville	6	6	0
League City	99	68	31	New Boston	12	9	3
Leander	33	20	13	New Braunfels	91	70	21
Leon Valley	31	23	8	New Deal	4	2	2
Levelland	27	20	7	Nocona	7	4	3
Lewisville	168	120	48	Nolanville	4	4	0
Lexington	4	4	0	Northlake	7	7	0
Liberty	21	14	7	North Richland Hills	155	107	48
Lindale	15	11	4	Oak Ridge North	14	13	1
Littlefield	20	13	7	Odessa	208	161	47
Live Oak	36	27	9	O'Donnell	2	2	0
Livingston	21	14	7	Olmos Park	11	11	0
Llano	9	7	2	Olney	9	5	4
Lockhart	33	25	8	Olton	4	4	0
Lockney	3	3	0	Onalaska	7	7	0
Lone Star	5	4	1	Orange	55	43	12
Longview	158	135	23	Orange Grove	9	9	0
Lorena	6	5	1	Ore City	4	4	0
Los Fresnos	21	14	7	Overton	9	6	3
Lubbock	346	291	55	Ovilla	9	8	1
Lufkin	94	74	20	Oyster Creek	9	5	4
Luling	23	14	9	Palacios	12	8	4
Lumberton	17	14	3	Palestine	45	37	8
Madisonville	12	10	2	Palmer	7	6	1
Magnolia	12	11	1	Pampa	34	25	9
Malakoff	6	5	1	Panhandle	3	3	0
Manor	6	5	1	Pantego	16	11	5
Mansfield	111	57	54	Paris	86	65	21
Manvel	8	8	0	Parker	5	5	0
Marble Falls	29	20	9	Pasadena	297	233	64
Marfa	4	3	1	Pearland	86	65	21
Marlin	19	14	5	Pearsall	12	10	2
Marshall	65	46	19	Pecos	24	19	5
Mart	4	4	0	Pelican Bay	3	3	0
Martindale	4	4	0	Penitas	5	2	3
Mathis	13	7	6	Perryton	16	9	7
McAllen	341	232	109	Pflugerville	46	36	10
McGregor	14	9	5	Pharr	110	83	27

Table 78

Full-time Law Enforcement Employees as of October 31, 2001
by City by State—Continued

City by state	Total police employees	Total officers	Total civilians	City by state	Total police employees	Total officers	Total civilians
TEXAS—Continued				**TEXAS—Continued**			
Pilot Point	6	6	0	Seadrift	1	1	0
Pinehurst	10	6	4	Seagoville	21	17	4
Pittsburg	10	9	1	Seagraves	4	3	1
Plainview	42	34	8	Sealy	15	13	2
Plano	461	321	140	Selma	13	12	1
Pleasanton	22	16	6	Seminole	11	10	1
Point Comfort	2	2	0	Seven Points	12	7	5
Port Aransas	20	13	7	Seymour	8	7	1
Port Arthur	144	112	32	Shallowater	5	5	0
Port Isabel	25	20	5	Shamrock	5	2	3
Portland	29	22	7	Shavano Park	13	12	1
Port Lavaca	26	20	6	Shenandoah	16	15	1
Port Neches	21	18	3	Sherman	83	60	23
Poteet	6	5	1	Silsbee	20	15	5
Pottsboro	6	6	0	Sinton	9	8	1
Premont	5	5	0	Slaton	16	11	5
Primera	6	6	0	Smithville	19	11	8
Princeton	5	4	1	Snyder	19	17	2
Progreso	7	7	0	Socorro	23	18	5
Quanah	4	4	0	Somerset	4	3	1
Queen City	5	5	0	Somerville	4	4	0
Quinlan	6	5	1	Sonora	7	5	2
Quitman	6	6	0	Sour Lake	5	5	0
Ransom Canyon	2	2	0	South Houston	40	30	10
Red Oak	18	12	6	Southlake	46	45	1
Refugio	8	6	2	South Padre Island	31	24	7
Reno	4	3	1	Southside Place	10	7	3
Richardson	255	153	102	Spearman	4	4	0
Richland Hills	21	16	5	Springtown	13	9	4
Richmond	33	26	7	Spring Valley	21	16	5
Richwood	6	5	1	Spur	2	2	0
Riesel	3	2	1	Stafford	51	38	13
Rio Grande City	28	22	6	Stamford	11	7	4
River Oaks	20	16	4	Stanton	6	6	0
Robinson	19	13	6	Stephenville	40	30	10
Robstown	26	20	6	Stratford	3	3	0
Rockdale	16	11	5	Sugar Land	131	102	29
Rockport	26	19	7	Sulphur Springs	36	29	7
Rockwall	53	36	17	Sunset Valley	6	6	0
Rollingwood	7	7	0	Surfside Beach	6	5	1
Roma	26	21	5	Sweeny	7	7	0
Roman Forest	4	4	0	Sweetwater	24	19	5
Ropesville	1	1	0	Taft	6	6	0
Rosebud	3	3	0	Tahoka	4	4	0
Rosenberg	73	55	18	Taylor	36	26	10
Round Rock	137	100	37	Teague	5	5	0
Rowlett	83	58	25	Terrell	43	32	11
Royse City	7	7	0	Terrell Hills	16	16	0
Runaway Bay	4	4	0	Texarkana	100	88	12
Rusk	10	9	1	Texas City	102	81	21
Sabinal	4	4	0	The Colony	50	34	16
Sachse	29	21	8	Thorndale	2	2	0
Saginaw	31	25	6	Thrall	3	3	0
San Angelo	176	151	25	Three Rivers	6	6	0
San Antonio	2,498	1,974	524	Tolar	2	2	0
San Augustine	7	6	1	Tomball	35	28	7
San Benito	46	37	9	Tool	6	6	0
San Diego	6	5	1	Trinity	10	6	4
Sanger	11	10	1	Trophy Club	18	16	2
San Juan	36	26	10	Troup	5	5	0
San Marcos	98	77	21	Tulia	12	7	5
San Saba	4	3	1	Tye	3	3	0
Sansom Park Village	12	8	4	Tyler	232	177	55
Santa Anna	4	2	2	Universal City	32	23	9
Santa Fe	24	18	6	University Park	44	33	11
Schertz	40	30	10	Uvalde	35	28	7
Seabrook	34	28	6	Van	6	6	0

Table 78

Full-time Law Enforcement Employees as of October 31, 2001
by City by State—Continued

City by state	Total police employees	Total officers	Total civilians	City by state	Total police employees	Total officers	Total civilians
TEXAS—Continued				**UTAH—Continued**			
Van Alstyne	10	8	2	Hurricane	14	10	4
Vernon	28	21	7	Kamas	2	2	0
Victoria	138	99	39	Kanab	8	6	2
Vidor	29	21	8	Kaysville	20	18	2
Waco	297	214	83	Layton	79	59	20
Wake Village	7	6	1	Lehi	27	22	5
Waller	8	7	1	Logan	86	59	27
Wallis	4	4	0	Mantua	1	1	0
Walnut Springs	1	1	0	Mapleton	10	8	2
Watauga	51	36	15	Midvale	48	44	4
Waxahachie	56	46	10	Minersville	1	1	0
Weatherford	70	50	20	Moab	16	12	4
Webster	59	44	15	Monticello	5	4	1
Weimar	8	7	1	Moroni	1	1	0
Wells	1	1	0	Mount Pleasant	6	5	1
Weslaco	93	66	27	Murray	84	67	17
West	6	6	0	Naples	4	3	1
West Columbia	15	8	7	Nephi	10	8	2
West Lake Hills	20	14	6	North Ogden	18	15	3
West Orange	10	9	1	North Park	8	7	1
Westover Hills	14	12	2	North Salt Lake	13	11	2
West Tawakoni	6	5	1	Ogden	148	122	26
West University Place	33	23	10	Orem	114	81	33
Westworth	14	10	4	Park City	33	25	8
Wharton	31	21	10	Parowan	2	2	0
Whitehouse	18	12	6	Payson	18	17	1
White Oak	17	13	4	Perry	2	2	0
Whitesboro	14	10	4	Pleasant Grove/Lindon	32	29	3
White Settlement	42	29	13	Pleasant View	7	6	1
Whitney	8	7	1	Price	19	16	3
Wichita Falls	251	178	73	Provo	153	96	57
Willow Park	8	7	1	Richfield	13	11	2
Wills Point	10	9	1	Riverdale	21	17	4
Wilmer	17	12	5	Roosevelt	11	10	1
Windcrest	22	16	6	Roy	45	37	8
Wink	2	2	0	Salem/Woodland Hills	7	7	0
Winnsboro	12	9	3	Salina	6	5	1
Wolfforth	4	4	0	Salt Lake City	559	398	161
Woodville	8	7	1	Sandy	145	120	25
Woodway	36	23	13	Santaquin/Genola	5	5	0
Wylie	25	23	2	Smithfield	7	6	1
Yoakum	16	9	7	South Jordan	37	32	5
				South Ogden	27	23	4
UTAH				South Salt Lake	75	66	9
				Spanish Fork	22	20	2
Alpine/Highland	13	13	0	Springville	31	23	8
Alta	8	4	4	St. George	91	69	22
American Fork	35	31	4	Stockton	1	1	0
Blanding	7	6	1	Sunset	8	7	1
Bountiful	44	33	11	Syracuse	12	10	2
Brian Head	5	5	0	Tooele	34	27	7
Brigham City	26	22	4	Tremonton	11	9	2
Cedar City	35	29	6	Vernal	18	16	2
Centerville	18	15	3	Washington Terrace	16	13	3
Clearfield	42	28	14	Wellington	4	4	0
Clinton	12	11	1	Wendover	5	4	1
East Carbon	3	3	0	West Bountiful	8	7	1
Ephraim	5	5	0	West Jordan	105	87	18
Fairview	2	2	0	West Valley	205	169	36
Farmington	14	11	3	Willard	3	3	0
Garland	4	4	0	Woods Cross	12	10	2
Grantsville	10	8	2				
Gunnison	3	3	0	**VERMONT**			
Harrisville	6	5	1				
Heber	13	12	1	Barre	24	18	6
Helper	5	5	0	Barre Town	6	5	1
Hildale	5	5	0	Bellows Falls	12	8	4

Table 78

Full-time Law Enforcement Employees as of October 31, 2001
by City by State—Continued

City by state	Total police employees	Total officers	Total civilians	City by state	Total police employees	Total officers	Total civilians
VERMONT—Continued				**VIRGINIA—Continued**			
Bennington	30	25	5	Buena Vista	14	13	1
Berlin	8	7	1	Cape Charles	5	5	0
Brandon	6	6	0	Cedar Bluff	2	2	0
Brattleboro	40	25	15	Charlottesville	137	110	27
Bristol	4	4	0	Chase City	8	7	1
Burlington	126	91	35	Chatham	4	4	0
Castleton	3	3	0	Chesapeake	448	347	101
Chester	5	4	1	Chilhowie	8	8	0
Colchester	31	25	6	Chincoteague	13	9	4
Dover	5	4	1	Christiansburg	51	39	12
Essex	33	26	7	Clarksville	7	6	1
Fair Haven	2	2	0	Clifton Forge	15	11	4
Hardwick	6	5	1	Clinchco	1	1	0
Hartford	24	18	6	Clintwood	3	3	0
Hinesburg	2	2	0	Coeburn	8	7	1
Ludlow	8	4	4	Colonial Beach	12	7	5
Manchester	12	8	4	Colonial Heights	47	43	4
Middlebury	14	12	2	Courtland	4	1	3
Milton	13	12	1	Covington	24	16	8
Montgomery	1	1	0	Crewe	5	5	0
Montpelier	23	16	7	Culpeper	36	30	6
Morristown	10	9	1	Damascus	4	4	0
Newport	14	11	3	Danville	143	136	7
Northfield	7	6	1	Dayton	5	5	0
Norwich	6	5	1	Dublin	9	8	1
Randolph	4	4	0	Dumfries	15	13	2
Richmond	5	5	0	Edinburg	3	3	0
Rutland	50	40	10	Elkton	7	6	1
Shelburne	16	11	5	Emporia	34	26	8
South Burlington	41	35	6	Exmore	5	5	0
Springfield	17	12	5	Fairfax City	78	61	17
St. Albans	22	14	8	Falls Church	41	29	12
St. Johnsbury	16	11	5	Farmville	35	24	11
Stowe	14	12	2	Franklin	41	29	12
Swanton	5	4	1	Fredericksburg	86	61	25
Thetford	1	1	0	Fries	1	1	0
Vergennes	5	5	0	Front Royal	38	29	9
Vernon	4	3	1	Galax	30	24	6
Waterbury	4	4	0	Gate City	6	6	0
Weathersfield	1	1	0	Glade Spring	3	3	0
Williston	13	11	2	Glasgow	1	1	0
Wilmington	6	5	1	Glen Lyn	2	2	0
Windsor	12	7	5	Gordonsville	4	4	0
Winhall	5	5	0	Gretna	4	4	0
Winooski	20	16	4	Grottoes	5	5	0
Woodstock	6	5	1	Grundy	7	6	1
				Halifax	7	6	1
VIRGINIA				Hampton	347	246	101
				Harrisonburg	86	65	21
Abingdon	22	20	2	Haymarket	3	3	0
Alexandria	418	288	130	Haysi	2	2	0
Altavista	11	11	0	Herndon	62	50	12
Amherst	5	5	0	Hillsville	11	10	1
Appalachia	6	6	0	Honaker	3	2	1
Ashland	24	21	3	Hopewell	66	48	18
Bedford	26	22	4	Hurt	3	3	0
Berryville	9	8	1	Independence	2	2	0
Big Stone Gap	18	16	2	Jonesville	8	6	2
Blacksburg	72	56	16	Kenbridge	9	8	1
Blackstone	18	14	4	Kilmarnock	4	4	0
Bluefield	17	13	4	La Crosse	3	3	0
Bowling Green	1	1	0	Lawrenceville	5	5	0
Boykins	1	1	0	Lebanon	12	11	1
Bridgewater	8	8	0	Leesburg	69	54	15
Bristol	80	59	21	Lexington	18	16	2
Broadway	4	4	0	Louisa	5	5	0
Brookneal	4	4	0	Luray	17	15	2

Table 78

Full-time Law Enforcement Employees as of October 31, 2001
by City by State—Continued

City by state	Total police employees	Total officers	Total civilians	City by state	Total police employees	Total officers	Total civilians
VIRGINIA—Continued				**WASHINGTON**			
Lynchburg	196	157	39	Aberdeen	51	37	14
Manassas	96	79	17	Airway Heights	8	7	1
Manassas Park	27	18	9	Algona	8	6	2
Marion	20	18	2	Anacortes	32	24	8
Martinsville	60	54	6	Arlington	23	19	4
McKenney	1	1	0	Auburn	112	82	30
Middleburg	4	4	0	Bainbridge Island	26	22	4
Middletown	2	2	0	Battle Ground	17	15	2
Mount Jackson	4	4	0	Bellevue	274	170	104
Narrows	4	4	0	Bellingham	160	107	53
New Market	5	5	0	Black Diamond	10	10	0
Newport News	520	391	129	Blaine	17	14	3
Norfolk	851	730	121	Bonney Lake	25	17	8
Norton	23	17	6	Bothell	76	50	26
Occoquan	2	2	0	Bremerton	76	62	14
Onancock	4	4	0	Brewster	7	6	1
Onley	3	3	0	Brier	8	7	1
Orange	13	12	1	Buckley	17	8	9
Pearisburg	8	7	1	Burien	22	21	1
Pembroke	2	2	0	Burlington	25	20	5
Pennington Gap	7	6	1	Camas	27	23	4
Petersburg	157	115	42	Carnation	3	3	0
Pocahontas	3	3	0	Castle Rock	5	4	1
Poquoson	24	19	5	Centralia	31	27	4
Portsmouth	339	238	101	Chehalis	21	17	4
Pound	5	5	0	Chelan	15	9	6
Pulaski	43	33	10	Cheney	14	10	4
Purcellville	9	8	1	Chewelah	6	5	1
Quantico	2	1	1	Clarkston	15	13	2
Radford	45	33	12	Cle Elum	10	8	2
Rich Creek	1	1	0	Clyde Hill	9	8	1
Richlands	22	16	6	Colfax	5	5	0
Richmond	764	648	116	College Place	15	12	3
Roanoke	283	235	48	Colton	1	1	0
Rocky Mount	18	16	2	Colville	13	11	2
Rural Retreat	1	1	0	Connell	7	7	0
Salem	87	62	25	Cosmopolis	6	5	1
Saltville	9	8	1	Coulee Dam	3	3	0
Shenandoah	4	4	0	Coupeville	5	5	0
Smithfield	26	15	11	Covington	9	9	0
South Boston	32	28	4	Des Moines	57	44	13
South Hill	25	20	5	Dupont	6	6	0
Stanley	3	3	0	Duvall	11	10	1
Staunton	64	47	17	East Wenatchee	15	13	2
Stephens City	3	3	0	Eatonville	6	5	1
St. Paul	5	5	0	Edgewood	8	8	0
Strasburg	14	12	2	Edmonds	69	51	18
Suffolk	175	141	34	Ellensburg	31	23	8
Tappahannock	9	9	0	Elma	6	5	1
Tazewell	11	10	1	Elmer City	1	1	0
Timberville	3	3	0	Enumclaw	31	19	12
Victoria	7	6	1	Ephrata	16	13	3
Vienna	46	37	9	Everett	216	180	36
Vinton	26	19	7	Everson	6	5	1
Virginia Beach	885	730	155	Federal Way	145	105	40
Warrenton	23	20	3	Ferndale	17	15	2
Warsaw	3	2	1	Fife	29	22	7
Waverly	6	4	2	Fircrest	9	8	1
Waynesboro	52	46	6	Forks	15	8	7
Weber City	6	6	0	Garfield	1	1	0
West Point	10	9	1	Gig Harbor	15	13	2
Williamsburg	49	34	15	Goldendale	11	9	2
Winchester	71	60	11	Grand Coulee	4	3	1
Wise	12	11	1	Grandview	21	15	6
Woodstock	15	14	1	Granger	7	6	1
Wytheville	36	24	12	Granite Falls	6	6	0

Table 78

Full-time Law Enforcement Employees as of October 31, 2001
by City by State—Continued

City by state	Total police employees	Total officers	Total civilians	City by state	Total police employees	Total officers	Total civilians
WASHINGTON—Continued				**WASHINGTON—Continued**			
Harrington	1	1	0	Raymond	6	5	1
Hoquiam	25	20	5	Reardan	2	2	0
Issaquah	54	28	26	Redmond	99	68	31
Kalama	6	5	1	Renton	119	85	34
Kelso	32	28	4	Republic	3	3	0
Kenmore	11	11	0	Richland	55	49	6
Kennewick	96	79	17	Ridgefield	5	5	0
Kent	179	123	56	Ritzville	4	4	0
Kettle Falls	5	4	1	Roy	3	3	0
Kirkland	91	62	29	Royal City	3	3	0
La Center	4	4	0	Ruston	2	2	0
Lacey	53	45	8	Sammamish	16	15	1
Lake Forest Park	26	22	4	SeaTac	28	27	1
Lake Stevens	9	8	1	Seattle	1,799	1,287	512
Lakewood	98	87	11	Sedro Woolley	16	12	4
Langley	4	4	0	Selah	15	13	2
Long Beach	7	6	1	Sequim	16	13	3
Longview	60	51	9	Shelton	35	20	15
Lynden	17	13	4	Shoreline	37	35	2
Lynnwood	93	65	28	Snohomish	24	20	4
Mabton	3	2	1	Snoqualmie	17	15	2
Maple Valley	11	11	0	Soap Lake	5	5	0
Marysville	62	35	27	South Bend	5	4	1
Mattawa	4	4	0	Spokane	401	293	108
McCleary	4	4	0	Springdale	1	1	0
Medical Lake	7	6	1	Stanwood	12	10	2
Medina	12	11	1	Steilacoom	10	9	1
Mercer Island	42	31	11	Sultan	13	11	2
Mill Creek	26	18	8	Sumas	6	6	0
Milton	14	12	2	Sumner	27	18	9
Monroe	39	29	10	Sunnyside	41	26	15
Montesano	10	8	2	Tacoma	395	356	39
Morton	2	2	0	Tekoa	2	2	0
Moses Lake	35	27	8	Tenino	5	5	0
Mossyrock	2	2	0	Tieton	2	2	0
Mountlake Terrace	39	30	9	Toledo	2	2	0
Mount Vernon	52	41	11	Tonasket	6	5	1
Moxee	2	2	0	Toppenish	22	16	6
Mukilteo	25	22	3	Tukwila	85	70	15
Napavine	5	4	1	Tumwater	29	25	4
Newcastle	7	7	0	Twisp	5	4	1
Newport	6	5	1	Union Gap	23	18	5
Normandy Park	14	12	2	Uniontown	3	2	1
Northport	1	1	0	University Place	28	25	3
Oakesdale	1	1	0	Vader	2	2	0
Oak Harbor	36	25	11	Vancouver	195	168	27
Oakville	3	3	0	Walla Walla	53	43	10
Ocean Shores	15	12	3	Wapato	19	12	7
Odessa	2	2	0	Warden	6	4	2
Olympia	96	70	26	Washougal	16	14	2
Omak	14	11	3	Wenatchee	61	40	21
Oroville	6	5	1	Westport	9	7	2
Orting	5	5	0	West Richland	15	13	2
Othello	17	11	6	White Salmon	7	7	0
Pacific	12	10	2	Wilbur	2	2	0
Palouse	2	2	0	Winlock	3	3	0
Pasco	54	45	9	Winthrop	2	2	0
Pe Ell	2	2	0	Woodinville	8	8	0
Port Angeles	35	28	7	Woodland	8	7	1
Port Orchard	19	17	2	Yakima	160	112	48
Port Townsend	15	12	3	Yelm	11	9	2
Poulsbo	19	16	3	Zillah	10	8	2
Prosser	18	12	6				
Pullman	38	27	11	**WEST VIRGINIA**			
Puyallup	86	50	36				
Quincy	12	10	2	Alderson	2	2	0
Rainier	5	5	0	Anawalt	1	1	0

Table 78

Full-time Law Enforcement Employees as of October 31, 2001
by City by State—Continued

City by state	Total police employees	Total officers	Total civilians	City by state	Total police employees	Total officers	Total civilians
WEST VIRGINIA—Continued				**WEST VIRGINIA—Continued**			
Anmoore	2	2	0	Kingwood	4	4	0
Ansted	3	3	0	Lewisburg	11	9	2
Athens	2	1	1	Logan	10	6	4
Barboursville	19	17	2	Lumberport	2	2	0
Barrackville	1	1	0	Mabscott	2	2	0
Bayard	1	1	0	Madison	6	5	1
Beckley	64	45	19	Man	3	3	0
Belington	3	3	0	Mannington	4	4	0
Belle	4	4	0	Marlinton	1	1	0
Benwood	6	5	1	Marmet	5	5	0
Berkeley Springs	2	2	0	Martinsburg	46	37	9
Bethlehem	5	5	0	Mason	3	3	0
Bluefield	34	27	7	Masontown	1	1	0
Bradshaw	2	2	0	Matewan	2	2	0
Bramwell	2	2	0	Matoaka	4	4	0
Bridgeport	22	20	2	McMechen	3	3	0
Buckhannon	8	7	1	Milton	6	5	1
Burnsville	1	1	0	Mitchell Heights	1	1	0
Cameron	4	3	1	Monongah	2	2	0
Capon Bridge	2	2	0	Montgomery	9	7	2
Cedar Grove	1	1	0	Moorefield	6	6	0
Ceredo	9	6	3	Morgantown	63	54	9
Chapmanville	3	3	0	Moundsville	23	17	6
Charleston	190	166	24	Mount Hope	6	5	1
Charles Town	15	13	2	Mullens	4	4	0
Chesapeake	4	4	0	New Cumberland	2	2	0
Chester	4	4	0	New Haven	2	2	0
Clarksburg	43	37	6	New Martinsville	14	10	4
Clendenin	3	3	0	Nitro	16	15	1
Danville	3	3	0	Northfork	4	4	0
Delbarton	2	2	0	Nutter Fort	6	6	0
Dunbar	21	17	4	Oak Hill	15	13	2
East Bank	1	1	0	Oceana	5	5	0
Eleanor	1	1	0	Paden City	5	4	1
Elkins	15	9	6	Parkersburg	75	62	13
Fairmont	43	32	11	Parsons	1	1	0
Fairview	1	1	0	Paw Paw	1	1	0
Farmington	1	1	0	Petersburg	3	3	0
Fayetteville	5	5	0	Peterstown	1	1	0
Follansbee	7	7	0	Philippi	6	6	0
Fort Gay	1	1	0	Piedmont	4	4	0
Gary	1	1	0	Pineville	3	3	0
Gassaway	1	1	0	Point Pleasant	11	10	1
Gauley Bridge	2	2	0	Pratt	3	3	0
Gilbert	4	4	0	Princeton	22	19	3
Glasgow	3	3	0	Rainelle	3	3	0
Glen Dale	6	5	1	Ranson	7	7	0
Glenville	3	3	0	Ravenswood	11	8	3
Grafton	6	5	1	Rhodell	2	2	0
Grantsville	2	2	0	Richwood	5	4	1
Grant Town	1	1	0	Ridgeley	3	3	0
Granville	1	1	0	Ripley	10	9	1
Hamlin	2	2	0	Rivesville	1	1	0
Handley	2	2	0	Romney	4	3	1
Harpers Ferry/Bolivar	3	3	0	Ronceverte	3	3	0
Harrisville	1	1	0	Salem	4	4	0
Henderson	1	1	0	Shepherdstown	7	5	2
Hinton	7	7	0	Shinnston	5	5	0
Hundred	1	1	0	Sistersville	4	4	0
Huntington	100	94	6	Smithers	8	8	0
Hurricane	13	12	1	Sophia	3	3	0
Iaeger	1	1	0	South Charleston	44	32	12
Kenova	12	8	4	Spencer	7	6	1
Kermit	1	1	0	St. Albans	27	20	7
Keyser	14	9	5	Star City	5	4	1
Keystone	2	2	0	St. Marys	4	4	0
Kimball	1	1	0	Stonewood	3	3	0

Table 78

Full-time Law Enforcement Employees as of October 31, 2001
by City by State—Continued

City by state	Total police employees	Total officers	Total civilians	City by state	Total police employees	Total officers	Total civilians
WEST VIRGINIA—Continued				**WISCONSIN—Continued**			
Summersville	20	20	0	Clear Lake	2	2	0
Sutton	3	2	1	Cleveland	3	2	1
Terra Alta	2	2	0	Clinton	6	6	0
Vienna	19	15	4	Clintonville	16	12	4
War	2	2	0	Colby-Abbotsford	7	6	1
Wayne	3	2	1	Columbus	19	11	8
Webster Springs	3	3	0	Combined Locks	4	4	0
Weirton	40	37	3	Cornell	3	3	0
Welch	11	9	2	Cottage Grove	9	8	1
Wellsburg	6	5	1	Crandon	4	3	1
West Logan	1	1	0	Cross Plains	9	8	1
West Milford	2	2	0	Cuba City	5	4	1
Weston	8	7	1	Cudahy	45	32	13
Westover	10	9	1	Darien	7	6	1
West Union	1	1	0	Darlington	5	5	0
Wheeling	85	83	2	Deerfield	2	2	0
White Sulphur Springs	7	6	1	DeForest	11	9	2
Whitesville	3	3	0	Delafield	13	12	1
Williamson	11	9	2	Delavan	21	16	5
Williamstown	6	5	1	Delavan Town	10	9	1
Winfield	3	3	0	Denmark	2	2	0
Worthington	1	1	0	Dodgeville	11	10	1
				Durand	4	4	0
WISCONSIN				Eagle River	6	6	0
				Eagle Village	2	2	0
Algoma	6	6	0	East Troy	8	7	1
Altoona	11	10	1	Eau Claire	130	100	30
Amery	7	6	1	Edgerton	12	11	1
Antigo	20	17	3	Eleva	1	1	0
Appleton	138	109	29	Elkhart Lake	3	3	0
Arcadia	5	5	0	Elkhorn	20	16	4
Ashland	22	20	2	Elk Mound	1	1	0
Ashwaubenon	51	42	9	Ellsworth	7	6	1
Bangor	3	3	0	Elm Grove	24	17	7
Baraboo	31	25	6	Elroy	5	4	1
Barron	7	7	0	Evansville	9	8	1
Bayfield	4	4	0	Everest	24	22	2
Bayside	21	15	6	Fall Creek	4	4	0
Beaver Dam	39	29	10	Fennimore	5	5	0
Belleville	3	3	0	Fitchburg	43	33	10
Beloit	101	80	21	Fond du Lac	83	69	14
Beloit Town	10	9	1	Fontana	8	7	1
Benton	1	1	0	Fort Atkinson	26	19	7
Berlin	14	13	1	Fox Lake	3	3	0
Black Earth	2	2	0	Fox Point	19	17	2
Black River Falls	10	9	1	Fox Valley	30	27	3
Blair	3	3	0	Franklin	77	59	18
Blanchardville	1	1	0	Geneva Town	7	6	1
Bloomer	7	6	1	Genoa City	5	4	1
Bloomfield	6	5	1	Germantown	40	29	11
Boscobel	6	6	0	Glendale	47	46	1
Brillion	7	7	0	Grafton	28	21	7
Brodhead	10	7	3	Grand Chute	28	24	4
Brookfield	85	62	23	Green Bay	228	189	39
Brookfield Township	13	12	1	Greendale	36	28	8
Brown Deer	36	31	5	Greenfield	80	58	22
Burlington	27	21	6	Green Lake	4	4	0
Burlington Town	8	8	0	Hales Corners	17	17	0
Butler	8	7	1	Hallie	7	6	1
Caledonia	34	27	7	Hartford	31	22	9
Campbellsport	2	2	0	Hartland	18	15	3
Campbell Township	5	5	0	Hayward	7	6	1
Cedarburg	29	19	10	Hazel Green	2	2	0
Chenequa	9	9	0	Hillsboro	2	2	0
Chetek	6	5	1	Holmen	9	8	1
Chilton	7	7	0	Horicon	11	9	2
Chippewa Falls	34	26	8	Hortonville	3	3	0

Table 78

Full-time Law Enforcement Employees as of October 31, 2001
by City by State—Continued

City by state	Total police employees	Total officers	Total civilians	City by state	Total police employees	Total officers	Total civilians
WISCONSIN—Continued				**WISCONSIN—Continued**			
Hudson	21	18	3	Oconomowoc Town	13	12	1
Hurley	6	5	1	Oconto	9	9	0
Independence	2	2	0	Oconto Falls	7	7	0
Iron Ridge	1	1	0	Omro	6	5	1
Jackson	10	9	1	Onalaska	32	29	3
Janesville	118	105	13	Oregon	15	14	1
Jefferson	15	13	2	Osceola	5	5	0
Juneau	5	4	1	Oshkosh	114	97	17
Kaukauna	30	24	6	Osseo	4	4	0
Kenosha	257	181	76	Palmyra	5	5	0
Kewaskum	7	7	0	Park Falls	8	7	1
Kewaunee	6	6	0	Pewaukee	17	15	2
Kiel	14	7	7	Pewaukee Township	22	20	2
Kohler	8	7	1	Phillips	5	4	1
Lac du Flambeau	9	8	1	Platteville	26	20	6
La Crosse	117	98	19	Pleasant Prairie	27	26	1
Ladysmith	10	9	1	Plover	17	15	2
Lake Delton	14	13	1	Plymouth	17	16	1
Lake Geneva	28	20	8	Portage	30	22	8
Lake Mills	12	11	1	Port Washington	24	19	5
Lancaster	8	7	1	Poynette	6	5	1
Lodi	6	5	1	Prairie du Chien	18	13	5
Luxemburg	2	2	0	Prescott	8	7	1
Madison	443	368	75	Princeton	3	3	0
Manitowoc	77	66	11	Pulaski	7	7	0
Maple Bluff	5	5	0	Racine	238	209	29
Marathon City	2	2	0	Reedsburg	21	15	6
Marinette	30	23	7	Rhinelander	25	19	6
Marion	3	3	0	Rice Lake	26	23	3
Markesan	4	4	0	Richland Center	13	11	2
Marshall Village	8	7	1	Ripon	20	14	6
Marshfield	51	37	14	River Falls	25	22	3
Mauston	9	8	1	River Hills	14	14	0
Mayville	13	11	2	Rome Town	6	6	0
Mazomanie	4	4	0	Rothschild	12	10	2
McFarland	13	12	1	Sauk Prairie	14	13	1
Medford	10	9	1	Saukville	11	9	2
Menasha	37	32	5	Shawano	23	20	3
Menomonee Falls	68	58	10	Sheboygan	119	91	28
Menomonie	35	28	7	Sheboygan Falls	14	12	2
Mequon	45	37	8	Shorewood	32	26	6
Merrill	28	21	7	Shorewood Hills	7	6	1
Middleton	37	28	9	Silver Lake	2	2	0
Milton	10	9	1	Siren	2	2	0
Milwaukee	2,356	1,923	433	Slinger	10	9	1
Mineral Point	6	6	0	Somerset	4	3	1
Minocqua	16	11	5	South Milwaukee	41	34	7
Mondovi	4	4	0	Sparta	23	17	6
Monona	24	19	5	Spencer	3	3	0
Monroe	35	26	9	Spooner	7	6	1
Mosinee	8	7	1	Spring Green	4	3	1
Mount Horeb	11	10	1	Stanley	4	4	0
Mount Pleasant	36	27	9	St. Croix Falls	4	4	0
Mukwonago	19	12	7	Stevens Point	57	44	13
Muskego	45	34	11	St. Francis	25	20	5
Neenah	51	41	10	Stoughton	24	19	5
Neillsville	7	6	1	Sturgeon Bay	21	20	1
New Berlin	93	74	19	Sturtevant	16	10	6
New Glarus	5	5	0	Summit	9	8	1
New Holstein	11	7	4	Sun Prairie	64	42	22
New Lisbon	2	2	0	Superior	65	58	7
New London	19	17	2	Theresa	2	2	0
New Richmond	13	12	1	Thiensville	7	6	1
Niagara	5	5	0	Three Lakes	6	5	1
North Fond du Lac	12	10	2	Tomah	25	19	6
Oak Creek	65	49	16	Tomahawk	7	6	1
Oconomowoc	27	20	7	Town of East Troy	7	6	1

Table 78

Full-time Law Enforcement Employees as of October 31, 2001
by City by State—Continued

City by state	Total police employees	Total officers	Total civilians	City by state	Total police employees	Total officers	Total civilians
WISCONSIN—Continued				**WYOMING—Continued**			
Town of Madison	18	16	2	Casper	119	79	40
Town of Menasha	32	25	7	Cheyenne	115	88	27
Trempealeau	2	2	0	Cody	21	19	2
Twin Lakes	16	11	5	Diamondville	4	3	1
Two Rivers	30	25	5	Douglas	21	14	7
Verona	15	14	1	Evanston	31	26	5
Viroqua	10	9	1	Evansville	11	7	4
Walworth	5	5	0	Gillette	57	37	20
Washburn	6	6	0	Glenrock	10	6	4
Waterloo	8	7	1	Green River	34	25	9
Watertown	47	34	13	Greybull	5	4	1
Waukesha	145	110	35	Guernsey	5	5	0
Waunakee	16	14	2	Hanna	7	4	3
Waupaca	18	14	4	Jackson	30	23	7
Waupun	22	16	6	Kemmerer	10	8	2
Wausau	67	59	8	La Barge	2	2	0
Wautoma	6	5	1	Lander	21	20	1
Wauwatosa	115	87	28	Laramie	80	47	33
West Allis	166	131	35	Lovell	9	6	3
Westby	3	3	0	Lusk	4	4	0
West Milwaukee	24	19	5	Lyman	7	5	2
West Salem	7	6	1	Mills	10	9	1
Whitefish Bay	27	24	3	Moorcroft	4	3	1
Whitehall	4	4	0	Newcastle	15	8	7
Whitewater	33	23	10	Pine Bluffs	6	2	4
Williams Bay	7	6	1	Powell	20	13	7
Winneconne	6	5	1	Rawlins	31	21	10
Wisconsin Dells	16	11	5	Riverton	33	21	12
Wisconsin Rapids	48	38	10	Rock Springs	62	37	25
Woodruff	6	5	1	Saratoga	12	6	6
				Sheridan	48	30	18
WYOMING				Sundance	5	5	0
				Thermopolis	12	6	6
Afton	4	4	0	Torrington	21	15	6
Baggs	1	1	0	Wheatland	12	11	1
Basin	3	3	0	Worland	11	11	0
Buffalo	15	9	6				

[1] The data in this table are provided for Charlotte Police Department, North Carolina, only. However, Charlotte Police Department reports its crime figures combined with those of Mecklenburg County; they can be found in Table 8 under *Charlotte-Mecklenburg*.

Table 79

Full-time Law Enforcement Employees as of October 31, 2001

by University and College by State[1]

University/College by state	Total police employees	Total officers	Total civilians	University/College by state	Total police employees	Total officers	Total civilians
ALABAMA				**CALIFORNIA—Continued**			
				Monterey Bay	20	13	7
Alabama State University	29	22	7	Northridge	37	21	16
Auburn University:				Sacramento	23	17	6
Main Campus	51	27	24	San Bernardino	21	13	8
Montgomery	20	12	8	San Jose	58	31	27
Calhoun Community College	7	4	3	San Marcos	16	10	6
Enterprise State Junior College	1	1	0	Stanislaus	27	19	8
Jacksonville State University	19	15	4	College of the Sequoias	6	5	1
Talladega College	6	3	3	Contra Costa Community College	31	21	10
Troy State University	7	5	2	Cuesta College	21	6	15
University of Alabama:				El Camino College	25	19	6
Birmingham	143	63	80	Foothill-De Anza College	10	8	2
Huntsville	14	10	4	Humboldt State University	18	11	7
Tuscaloosa	49	40	9	Long Beach Community College	22	20	2
University of Montevallo	14	9	5	Marin Community College	10	9	1
University of North Alabama	12	11	1	Pasadena Community College	19	9	10
University of South Alabama	33	25	8	Reedley Community College	4	4	0
University of West Alabama	8	5	3	Riverside Community College	19	13	6
				San Bernardino Community College	6	3	3
ALASKA				San Diego State University	40	25	15
				San Francisco State University	42	21	21
University of Alaska:				San Jose/Evergreen Community College	10	4	6
Anchorage	23	14	9	Santa Rosa Junior College	19	12	7
Fairbanks	11	10	1	Sonoma State University	19	12	7
				State Center Community College	16	13	3
ARIZONA				University of California:			
				Berkeley	114	71	43
Arizona State University:				Davis	86	46	40
Main Campus	70	40	30	Irvine	28	22	6
West	15	9	6	Lawrence-Livermore Laboratory	7	2	5
Arizona Western College	6	5	1	Los Angeles	90	55	35
Central Arizona College	6	6	0	Riverside	29	19	10
Northern Arizona University	31	20	11	San Diego	48	27	21
Pima Community College	35	28	7	San Francisco	46	27	19
University of Arizona	82	46	36	Santa Barbara	46	31	15
Yavapai College	6	6	0	Santa Cruz	41	18	23
				West Valley-Mission College	13	9	4
ARKANSAS							
				COLORADO			
Arkansas State University	24	18	6				
Henderson State University	9	8	1	Adams State College	3	3	0
Northwest Arkansas Community College	6	4	2	Arapahoe Community College	9	5	4
Southern Arkansas University	6	6	0	Auraria Higher Education Center	31	19	12
University of Arkansas:				Colorado School of Mines	8	7	1
Fayetteville	34	27	7	Colorado State University	28	21	7
Little Rock	31	25	6	Fort Lewis College	10	8	2
Medical Sciences	39	34	5	Pikes Peak Community College	16	14	2
Monticello	7	6	1	Red Rocks Community College	2	1	1
Pine Bluff	16	13	3	University of Colorado:			
University of Central Arkansas	27	22	5	Boulder	59	40	19
				Colorado Springs	19	11	8
CALIFORNIA				Health Science Center	74	32	42
				University of Northern Colorado	19	12	7
Allan Hancock College	6	5	1	University of Southern Colorado	8	3	5
California State Polytechnic University:							
Pomona	35	14	21	**CONNECTICUT**			
San Luis Obispo	21	15	6				
California State University:				Central Connecticut State University	28	22	6
Bakersfield	10	9	1	Eastern Connecticut State University	22	16	6
Channel Islands	16	12	4	Southern Connecticut State University	37	26	11
Chico	13	10	3	University of Connecticut:			
Dominguez Hills	26	14	12	Health Center	20	14	6
Fresno	28	18	10	Storrs, Avery Point, and Hartford	73	59	14
Fullerton	29	20	9	Western Connecticut State University	25	16	9
Hayward	33	12	21	Yale University	85	70	15
Long Beach	31	23	8				
Los Angeles	28	19	9				

Table 79

Full-time Law Enforcement Employees as of October 31, 2001
by University and College by State[1]—Continued

University/College by state	Total police employees	Total officers	Total civilians	University/College by state	Total police employees	Total officers	Total civilians
DELAWARE				**ILLINOIS—Continued**			
University of Delaware	72	45	27	Illinois State University	26	22	4
				John A. Logan College	5	3	2
FLORIDA				Joliet Junior College	17	8	9
				Loyola University of Chicago	42	19	23
Florida A&M University	34	26	8	Morton College	9	7	2
Florida Atlantic University	42	32	10	Northeastern Illinois University	19	14	5
Florida Gulf Coast University	18	12	6	Northern Illinois University	49	32	17
Florida International University	65	45	20	Northwestern University:			
Florida State University:				Chicago	18	14	4
Panama City	3	2	1	Evanston	34	24	10
Tallahassee	95	56	39	Oakton Community College	10	9	1
Pensacola Junior College	19	15	4	Parkland College	16	11	5
Santa Fe Community College	25	18	7	Rock Valley College	13	11	2
University of Central Florida	52	36	16	Southern Illinois University:			
University of Florida	135	85	50	Carbondale	48	37	11
University of North Florida	42	25	17	Edwardsville	44	36	8
University of South Florida:				School of Medicine	12	2	10
Sarasota	15	11	4	South Suburban College	15	12	3
St. Petersburg	14	10	4	Triton College	17	12	5
Tampa	61	43	18	University of Illinois:			
University of West Florida	28	20	8	Chicago	98	60	38
				Springfield	16	10	6
GEORGIA				Urbana	63	48	15
				Waubonsee College	2	2	0
Agnes Scott College	20	12	8	Western Illinois University	30	25	5
Albany State University	24	12	12	William Rainey Harper College	13	6	7
Armstrong Atlantic State University	17	12	5				
Augusta State University	16	13	3	**INDIANA**			
Berry College	16	11	5				
Clark Atlanta University	23	23	0	Ball State University	46	32	14
Clayton College and State University	22	16	6	DePauw University	13	8	5
Coastal Georgia Community College	6	5	1	Indiana State University	37	27	10
Columbus State University	16	15	1	Indiana University:			
Dalton State College	7	7	0	Bloomington	50	41	9
Emory University	47	34	13	Gary	13	10	3
Fort Valley State University	23	19	4	Indianapolis	48	32	16
Georgia College and State University	17	10	7	New Albany	9	7	2
Georgia Institute of Technology	53	37	16	Marian College	5	3	2
Georgia Perimeter College	35	8	27	Purdue University	44	36	8
Georgia Southern University	36	28	8				
Georgia Southwestern State University	11	10	1	**IOWA**			
Georgia State University	102	74	28				
Gordon College	7	6	1	Iowa State University	26	25	1
Kennesaw State University	28	20	8	University of Iowa	52	30	22
Medical College of Georgia	47	34	13	University of Northern Iowa	25	18	7
Mercer University	30	22	8				
Middle Georgia College	8	7	1	**KANSAS**			
Morehouse College	19	14	5				
Morris-Brown College	44	18	26	Emporia State University	11	10	1
North Georgia College	11	8	3	Fort Hays State University	11	10	1
Piedmont College	5	3	2	Kansas State University	36	22	14
Savannah State University	16	8	8	Pittsburg State University	17	14	3
Southern Polytechnic State University	18	13	5	University of Kansas:			
South Georgia College	7	7	0	Main Campus	50	27	23
University of Georgia	73	57	16	Medical Center	50	29	21
University of West Georgia	23	17	6	Wichita State University	33	23	10
Valdosta State University	26	19	7				
Wesleyan College	5	5	0	**KENTUCKY**			
				Eastern Kentucky University	29	19	10
ILLINOIS				Kentucky State University	17	10	7
				Morehead State University	14	9	5
Black Hawk College	8	7	1	Murray State University	22	12	10
Chicago State University	32	23	9	Northern Kentucky University	24	14	10
College of DuPage	18	12	6	University of Kentucky	48	34	14
College of Lake County	16	8	8	University of Louisville	34	24	10
Eastern Illinois University	26	23	3	Western Kentucky University	30	22	8
Governors State University	12	8	4				

Table 79

Full-time Law Enforcement Employees as of October 31, 2001

by University and College by State[1]—Continued

University/College by state	Total police employees	Total officers	Total civilians	University/College by state	Total police employees	Total officers	Total civilians
LOUISIANA				**MASSACHUSETTS—Continued**			
Delgado Community College	28	16	12	Dartmouth	37	23	14
Grambling State University	17	16	1	Harbor Campus-Boston	31	28	3
Louisiana State University:				Medical Center-Worcester	28	23	5
Baton Rouge	59	57	2	Wentworth Institute of Technology	23	13	10
Health Sciences Center	55	54	1	Western New England College	22	13	9
Shreveport	9	9	0	Westfield State College	20	14	6
Louisiana Tech University	19	17	2				
McNeese State University	17	11	6	**MICHIGAN**			
Nicholls State University	14	10	4				
Northwestern State University	17	14	3	Central Michigan University	27	19	8
Southeastern Louisiana University	31	24	7	Delta College	9	7	2
Southern University and A&M College:				Eastern Michigan University	30	24	6
Baton Rouge	32	30	2	Ferris State University	20	14	6
New Orleans	10	10	0	Grand Rapids Community College	11	9	2
Shreveport	6	6	0	Grand Valley State University	15	12	3
Tulane University	47	34	13	Hope College	12	7	5
University of Louisiana:				Lansing Community College	11	9	2
Lafayette	24	23	1	Macomb Community College	34	28	6
Monroe	23	18	5	Michigan State University	65	60	5
				Michigan Technological University	12	9	3
MAINE				Mott Community College	3	3	0
				Northern Michigan University	19	15	4
University of Maine:				Oakland Community College	18	17	1
Farmington	4	4	0	Oakland University	18	14	4
Orono	30	20	10	Saginaw Valley State University	9	7	2
University of Southern Maine	25	17	8	University of Michigan:			
				Ann Arbor	99	48	51
				Flint	16	8	8
MARYLAND				Western Michigan University	61	33	28
Bowie State University	16	13	3	**MINNESOTA**			
Coppin State College	20	14	6				
Frostburg State University	20	16	4	University of Minnesota:			
Morgan State University	45	36	9	Duluth	8	7	1
Salisbury University	21	16	5	Twin Cities	60	39	21
St. Mary's College	13	4	9				
Towson University	48	34	14	**MISSISSIPPI**			
University of Baltimore	47	11	36				
University of Maryland:				Coahoma Community College	7	6	1
Baltimore City	123	57	66	Hinds Community College	32	31	1
Baltimore County	33	27	6	Itawamba Community College	7	5	2
College Park	109	74	35	Jackson State University	47	43	4
Eastern Shore	13	11	2	Mississippi State University	37	25	12
				University of Mississippi, Medical Center	100	69	31
MASSACHUSETTS							
				MISSOURI			
Boston College	58	42	16				
Boston University	63	56	7	Central Missouri State University	22	17	5
Brandeis University	16	15	1	Lincoln University	13	10	3
Bristol Community College	9	7	2	Southeast Missouri State University	23	16	7
Emerson College	16	12	4	Truman State University	11	9	2
Fitchburg State College	18	16	2	University of Missouri:			
Framingham State College	16	14	2	Columbia	48	31	17
Lasell College	8	7	1	St. Louis	20	17	3
Massachusetts College of Art	24	7	17	Washington University	33	24	9
Massachusetts College of Liberal Arts	10	6	4				
Massachusetts Institute of Technology	50	48	2	**MONTANA**			
Massasoit Community College	13	11	2				
Mount Holyoke College	22	15	7	Montana State University	28	13	15
Northeastern University	73	51	22	University of Montana	18	14	4
North Shore Community College	20	18	2				
Quinsigamond Community College	12	12	0	**NEBRASKA**			
Salem State College	22	20	2				
Springfield College	29	14	15	University of Nebraska:			
Tufts University, Medford	49	42	7	Kearney	7	6	1
University of Massachusetts:				Lincoln	40	28	12
Amherst	81	49	32				

Table 79

Full-time Law Enforcement Employees as of October 31, 2001
by University and College by State[1]—Continued

University/College by state	Total police employees	Total officers	Total civilians	University/College by state	Total police employees	Total officers	Total civilians
NEVADA				**NEW YORK—Continued**			
Truckee Meadows Community College	9	6	3	Oswego	27	21	6
University of Nevada:				Plattsburgh	18	13	5
Las Vegas	36	22	14	Potsdam	13	12	1
Reno	24	19	5	Utica-Rome	14	9	5
				Syracuse University	60	55	5
NEW HAMPSHIRE							
				NORTH CAROLINA			
University of New Hampshire	36	19	17				
				Appalachian State University	32	19	13
NEW JERSEY				Beaufort County Community College	2	2	0
				Belmont Abbey College	6	6	0
Brookdale Community College	18	13	5	Davidson College	9	8	1
Essex County College	58	13	45	Duke University	127	51	76
Kean University of New Jersey	38	23	15	East Carolina University	57	42	15
Middlesex County College	14	9	5	Elizabeth City State University	19	11	8
Monmouth University	29	19	10	Elon College	9	8	1
Montclair State University	36	20	16	Fayetteville State University	22	15	7
New Jersey Institute of Technology	56	25	31	Mars Hill College	3	3	0
Richard Stockton College	21	16	5	Methodist College	25	6	19
Rowan University	40	3	37	North Carolina Agricultural and			
Rutgers University:				Technical State University	43	21	22
Camden	39	17	22	North Carolina Central University	29	16	13
Newark	49	25	24	North Carolina School of the Arts	14	13	1
New Brunswick	140	58	82	North Carolina State University	70	48	22
The College of New Jersey	24	15	9	Pfeiffer College	5	5	0
University of Medicine and Dentistry:				Queens College	8	4	4
Camden	18	13	5	Saint Augustine's College	11	4	7
Newark	125	48	77	University of North Carolina:			
Piscataway	43	37	6	Asheville	16	8	8
William Paterson University	32	16	16	Chapel Hill	68	40	28
				Charlotte	40	34	6
NEW MEXICO				Greensboro	42	27	15
				Pembroke	14	10	4
Eastern New Mexico University	9	8	1	Wilmington	33	25	8
New Mexico State University	29	20	9	Wake Forest University	40	17	23
University of New Mexico	49	31	18	Western Carolina University	17	13	4
				Winston-Salem State University	19	14	5
NEW YORK							
				NORTH DAKOTA			
Cornell University	58	45	13				
Ithaca College	27	16	11	North Dakota State University	11	9	2
Rensselaer Polytechnic Institute	30	20	10	University of North Dakota	14	10	4
State University of New York:							
Albany	38	37	1	**OHIO**			
Albany (Plaza)	11	1	10				
Binghamton	43	29	14	Baldwin-Wallace College	12	1	11
Buffalo	66	60	6	Bowling Green State University	27	21	6
Downstate Medical Center	111	27	84	Cleveland State University	25	19	6
Maritime College	11	7	4	Columbus State Community College	26	19	7
Stony Brook	124	54	70	Cuyahoga Community College	37	31	6
State University of New York				Kent State University	36	29	7
Agricultural and Technical College:				Lakeland Community College	13	9	4
Alfred	18	12	6	Marietta College	6	5	1
Canton	11	10	1	Miami University	36	28	8
Cobleskill	10	9	1	Ohio State University	68	55	13
Farmingdale	17	16	1	Ohio University	35	27	8
Morrisville	12	11	1	University of Akron	39	32	7
State University of New York College:				University of Cincinnati	87	44	43
Brockport	19	16	3	University of Toledo	37	30	7
Buffalo	37	31	6	Wright State University	25	16	9
Cortland	19	18	1	Youngstown State University	26	21	5
Environmental Science and Forestry	12	10	2				
Fredonia	17	16	1	**OKLAHOMA**			
Geneseo	18	15	3				
New Paltz	23	21	2	Cameron University	8	7	1
Old Westbury	22	21	1	East Central University	5	5	0
Oneonta	24	17	7	Murray State College	1	1	0

Table 79

Full-time Law Enforcement Employees as of October 31, 2001
by University and College by State[1]—Continued

University/College by state	Total police employees	Total officers	Total civilians	University/College by state	Total police employees	Total officers	Total civilians
OKLAHOMA—Continued				**SOUTH CAROLINA—Continued**			
Northeastern Oklahoma A&M College	10	7	3	Columbia	65	49	16
Northeastern State College	12	10	2	Spartanburg	10	10	0
Oklahoma State University:				Winthrop University	20	14	6
Main Campus	43	32	11				
Okmulgee	8	8	0	**SOUTH DAKOTA**			
Tulsa	6	4	2				
Rogers University, Claremore	2	2	0	South Dakota State University	15	8	7
Seminole State College	5	5	0				
Southeastern Oklahoma State University	6	5	1	**TENNESSEE**			
Southwestern State College	8	7	1				
Tulsa Community College	19	11	8	Austin Peay State University	14	7	7
University of Central Oklahoma	25	18	7	Chattanooga State Technical			
University of Oklahoma:				Community College	14	6	8
Health Sciences Center	60	37	23	East Tennessee State University	24	18	6
Norman	48	36	12	Middle Tennessee State University	31	26	5
				Tennessee State University	44	39	5
PENNSYLVANIA				Tennessee Technological University	23	13	10
				University of Memphis	33	28	5
Bloomsburg University	20	17	3	University of Tennessee:			
Clarion University	16	12	4	Chattanooga	24	17	7
East Stroudsburg University	15	15	0	Martin	15	12	3
Edinboro University	15	14	1	Memphis	32	24	8
Elizabethtown College	14	9	5	Vanderbilt University	91	70	21
Indiana University	27	22	5	Volunteer State Community College	6	5	1
Kutztown University	17	11	6	Walters State Community College	7	7	0
Lehigh University	26	18	8				
Mansfield University	12	12	0	**TEXAS**			
Millersville University	17	15	2				
Moravian College	14	10	4	Alamo Community College District	74	41	33
Pennsylvania State University:				Alvin Community College	12	10	2
Altoona	9	8	1	Amarillo College	16	13	3
Behrend	9	6	3	Angelo State University	10	8	2
Berks	8	7	1	Austin College	8	7	1
Harrisburg	9	7	2	Baylor Health Care System	104	42	62
McKeesport	3	3	0	Baylor University, Waco	30	20	10
Mont Alto	3	3	0	Central Texas College	9	8	1
University Park	56	42	14	College of the Mainland	7	6	1
Shippensburg University	20	17	3	Eastfield College	10	8	2
Slippery Rock University	17	15	2	El Paso Community College	32	28	4
University of Pittsburgh:				Grayson County College	4	3	1
Bradford	6	5	1	Hardin-Simmons University	8	7	1
Pittsburgh	107	72	35	Houston Baptist University	12	9	3
West Chester University	23	20	3	Lamar University, Beaumont	31	18	13
				Laredo Community College	14	13	1
RHODE ISLAND				McLennan Community College	8	5	3
				Midwestern State University	8	7	1
Brown University	54	24	30	Mountain View College	8	8	0
University of Rhode Island	34	17	17	North Lake College	11	10	1
				Paris Junior College	3	3	0
SOUTH CAROLINA				Prairie View A&M University	22	11	11
				Rice University	40	25	15
Benedict College	18	17	1	Richland College	12	11	1
Bob Jones University	3	3	0	Southern Methodist University	34	22	12
Clemson University	49	31	18	Southwestern University	6	5	1
Coastal Carolina University	19	12	7	Southwest Texas State University	59	26	33
College of Charleston	54	34	20	Stephen F. Austin State University	36	20	16
Columbia College	14	10	4	St. Mary's University	18	12	6
Erskine College	1	1	0	St. Thomas University	5	1	4
Francis Marion University	10	10	0	Sul Ross State University	8	6	2
Lander College	11	10	1	Tarleton State University	14	12	2
Medical University of South Carolina	58	36	22	Texas A&M International University	17	13	4
Presbyterian College	9	8	1	Texas A&M University:			
South Carolina State University	25	18	7	College Station	128	54	74
The Citadel	12	12	0	Commerce	24	16	8
Trident Technical College	20	18	2	Corpus Christi	24	14	10
University of South Carolina:				Galveston	7	6	1
Aiken	6	6	0	Kingsville	20	14	6

Table 79

Full-time Law Enforcement Employees as of October 31, 2001
by University and College by State[1]—Continued

University/College by state	Total police employees	Total officers	Total civilians	University/College by state	Total police employees	Total officers	Total civilians
TEXAS—Continued				**VIRGINIA—Continued**			
Texas Christian University	33	22	11	Old Dominion University	66	37	29
Texas Southern University	39	28	11	Radford University	24	19	5
Texas State Technical College:				Thomas Nelson Community College	7	6	1
Harlingen	12	8	4	University of Richmond	32	16	16
Waco	16	14	2	University of Virginia	122	58	64
Texas Technological University, Lubbock	74	46	28	University of Virginia, College at Wise	8	7	1
Texas Woman's University	29	13	16	Virginia Commonwealth University	102	68	34
Trinity University	26	13	13	Virginia Military Institute	6	6	0
Tyler Junior College	13	5	8	Virginia Polytechnic Institute and			
University of Houston:				State University	49	32	17
Central Campus	53	38	15	Virginia State University	35	22	13
Clearlake	23	14	9	Virginia Western Community College	6	6	0
Downtown Campus	26	19	7				
University of Mary Hardin-Baylor	6	6	0	**WASHINGTON**			
University of North Texas, Health Science							
Center	22	14	8	Central Washington University	16	12	4
University of Texas:				Eastern Washington University	8	8	0
Arlington	61	25	36	Evergreen State College	15	10	5
Austin	166	60	106	University of Washington	69	51	18
Brownsville	20	10	10	Washington State University:			
Dallas	38	18	20	Pullman	18	17	1
El Paso	56	19	37	Vancouver	2	2	0
Health Science Center, San Antonio	70	27	43	Western Washington University	19	12	7
Health Science Center, Tyler	19	3	16				
Houston	225	65	160	**WEST VIRGINIA**			
Medical Branch	93	36	57				
Pan American	24	14	10	Bluefield State College	1	1	0
Permian Basin	11	5	6	Concord College	8	5	3
San Antonio	67	32	35	Fairmont State College	9	8	1
Southwestern Medical School	41	37	4	Glenville State College	6	4	2
Tyler	9	4	5	Marshall University	23	20	3
West Texas A&M University	13	9	4	Potomac State College	5	5	0
				West Liberty State College	7	7	0
UTAH				West Virginia State College	12	10	2
				West Virginia Tech	5	5	0
Brigham Young University	39	27	12	West Virginia University	51	44	7
College of Eastern Utah	2	2	0				
Salt Lake Community College	19	17	2	**WISCONSIN**			
Southern Utah University	6	5	1				
University of Utah	88	32	56	University of Wisconsin:			
Utah State University	19	13	6	Eau Claire	11	10	1
Utah Valley State College	8	6	2	Green Bay	12	6	6
Weber State University	11	10	1	La Crosse	10	8	2
				Madison	98	50	48
VIRGINIA				Milwaukee	35	29	6
				Oshkosh	12	10	2
Christopher Newport University	14	13	1	Parkside	13	9	4
College of William and Mary	24	19	5	Platteville	7	6	1
Emory and Henry College	4	1	3	Stevens Point	7	2	5
Ferrum College	7	7	0	Stout	9	8	1
George Mason University	56	44	12	Superior	1	1	0
Hampton University	44	27	17	Whitewater	10	9	1
James Madison University	26	21	5				
Longwood College	20	13	7	**WYOMING**			
Mary Washington College	20	12	8				
Norfolk State University	57	34	23	Sheridan College	2	2	0
Northern Virginia Community College	32	32	0	University of Wyoming	20	11	9

[1] These agencies have no resident population associated with them.

Table 80

Full-time Law Enforcement Employees as of October 31, 2001
by Suburban County by State

County by state	Total police employees	Total officers	Total civilians	County by state	Total police employees	Total officers	Total civilians
ALABAMA				**CALIFORNIA—Continued**			
Autauga	46	19	27	San Joaquin	691	486	205
Baldwin	193	72	121	San Luis Obispo	375	154	221
Blount	67	38	29	San Mateo	559	412	147
Calhoun	38	32	6	Santa Barbara	657	467	190
Colbert	43	28	15	Santa Clara	644	492	152
Dale	17	14	3	Santa Cruz	293	155	138
Elmore	70	28	42	Shasta	240	153	87
Etowah	128	57	71	Solano	469	104	365
Houston	132	49	83	Sonoma	302	200	102
Jefferson	612	481	131	Stanislaus	573	211	362
Lauderdale	70	28	42	Sutter	69	47	22
Lawrence	48	26	22	Tulare	629	464	165
Limestone	65	34	31	Ventura	1,325	794	531
Madison	214	104	110	Yolo	200	73	127
Mobile	441	144	297	Yuba	163	125	38
Montgomery	251	118	133				
Morgan	73	43	30	**COLORADO**			
Russell	76	26	50				
Shelby	143	89	54	Adams	416	279	137
St. Clair	36	31	5	Arapahoe	618	421	197
Tuscaloosa	176	79	97	Boulder	317	200	117
				Douglas	325	212	113
ARIZONA				El Paso	519	343	176
				Jefferson	578	392	186
Coconino	218	61	157	Larimer	356	200	156
Maricopa	2,292	644	1,648	Pueblo	254	141	113
Mohave	237	96	141	Weld	216	103	113
Pima	1,186	469	717				
Pinal	319	135	184	**DELAWARE**			
Yuma	277	60	217				
				New Castle Police Department	528	311	217
ARKANSAS							
				FLORIDA			
Benton	160	67	93				
Craighead	31	23	8	Alachua	516	247	269
Crawford	56	23	33	Bay	232	172	60
Crittenden	138	35	103	Broward	2,853	1,396	1,457
Faulkner	77	35	42	Charlotte	352	228	124
Jefferson	46	41	5	Clay	485	267	218
Lonoke	34	20	14	Collier	992	548	444
Miller	45	22	23	Escambia	1,070	396	674
Pulaski	497	394	103	Flagler	103	68	35
Saline	59	37	22	Gadsden	60	42	18
Sebastian	120	30	90	Hernando	320	190	130
Washington	149	83	66	Hillsborough	1,991	1,069	922
				Lake	324	223	101
CALIFORNIA				Lee	943	622	321
				Leon	322	222	100
Alameda	1,472	905	567	Manatee	781	378	403
Butte	245	110	135	Marion	736	233	503
Contra Costa	1,010	687	323	Martin	507	235	272
El Dorado	347	164	183	Miami-Dade	4,977	3,082	1,895
Fresno	1,010	430	580	Nassau	178	128	50
Kern	1,058	493	565	Okaloosa	292	221	71
Los Angeles	10,371	6,773	3,598	Orange	1,852	1,257	595
Madera	108	79	29	Osceola	397	266	131
Marin	301	206	95	Palm Beach	2,671	1,098	1,573
Merced	208	82	126	Pasco	602	326	276
Monterey	454	328	126	Pinellas	1,645	891	754
Napa	112	83	29	Polk	1,376	506	870
Orange	3,678	1,760	1,918	Santa Rosa	330	214	116
Placer	416	218	198	Sarasota	839	389	450
Riverside	2,783	1,445	1,338	Seminole	804	323	481
Sacramento	2,147	1,668	479	St. Johns	340	208	132
San Bernardino	2,706	1,575	1,131	St. Lucie	492	217	275
San Diego	1,322	942	380	Volusia	591	393	198
San Francisco	836	733	103				

Table 80

Full-time Law Enforcement Employees as of October 31, 2001
by Suburban County by State—Continued

County by state	Total police employees	Total officers	Total civilians	County by state	Total police employees	Total officers	Total civilians
GEORGIA				**ILLINOIS—Continued**			
Augusta-Richmond	683	480	203	Macon	151	48	103
Barrow	86	43	43	Madison	147	68	79
Bartow	202	152	50	McHenry	267	120	147
Bibb	272	214	58	McLean	69	55	14
Carroll	154	80	74	Menard	14	7	7
Catoosa	97	53	44	Monroe	26	14	12
Chatham	386	263	123	Ogle	64	48	16
Chatham County Police Department	184	131	53	Peoria	201	69	132
Chattahoochee	8	4	4	Rock Island	146	60	86
Cherokee	240	197	43	Sangamon	217	73	144
Cherokee County Police Department	11	5	6	St. Clair	168	155	13
Clayton	335	140	195	Tazewell	73	41	32
Clayton County Police Department	260	232	28	Will	438	272	166
Cobb	601	342	259	Winnebago	245	100	145
Cobb County Police Department	627	537	90	Woodford	39	33	6
Columbia	272	175	97				
Coweta	160	94	66	**INDIANA**			
Dade	46	20	26				
DeKalb	697	541	156	Adams	35	16	19
DeKalb County Police Department	1,119	805	314	Allen	287	124	163
Dougherty	263	248	15	Clark	84	32	52
Dougherty County Police Department	49	49	0	Clay	26	11	15
Douglas	256	183	73	Clinton	52	15	37
Fayette	145	109	36	Dearborn	63	22	41
Fayette County Marshal	10	9	1	De Kalb	55	18	37
Fulton County Police Department	352	269	83	Delaware	112	43	69
Gwinnett County Police Department	695	485	210	Elkhart	168	70	98
Harris	55	37	18	Floyd	73	21	52
Henry	132	68	64	Hamilton	69	55	14
Jones	63	31	32	Hancock	65	33	32
Lee	67	30	37	Harrison	63	21	42
Madison	48	28	20	Hendricks	98	38	60
McDuffie	29	13	16	Howard	110	34	76
Muscogee	254	235	19	Huntington	38	14	24
Oconee	48	29	19	Johnson	108	47	61
Paulding	182	110	72	Lake	499	175	324
Peach	48	27	21	Madison	103	51	52
Pickens	37	25	12	Monroe	98	30	68
Richmond County Marshal	29	25	4	Morgan	64	20	44
Rockdale	166	115	51	Ohio	9	8	1
Spalding	130	114	16	Porter	155	63	92
Twiggs	25	10	15	Posey	28	11	17
Walker	105	68	37	Scott	18	7	11
Walker County Police Department	4	4	0	Shelby	83	33	50
Walton	122	109	13	St. Joseph	281	122	159
				Tippecanoe	163	48	115
IDAHO				Tipton	15	9	6
				Vanderburgh	221	104	117
Ada	326	124	202	Vermillion	25	10	15
Bannock	68	36	32	Vigo	93	38	55
Canyon	127	57	70	Warrick	76	37	39
				Wells	37	13	24
ILLINOIS				Whitley	38	13	25
Boone	77	34	43				
Champaign	58	52	6	**IOWA**			
Clinton	33	13	20				
Cook	6,302	2,473	3,829	Black Hawk	138	105	33
De Kalb	76	58	18	Dallas	36	14	22
Du Page	562	453	109	Dubuque	53	45	8
Grundy	50	30	20	Johnson	85	57	28
Henry	69	64	5	Linn	165	111	54
Jersey	19	15	4	Polk	347	187	160
Kane	139	96	43	Pottawattamie	139	45	94
Kankakee	128	63	65	Scott	136	42	94
Kendall	87	79	8	Warren	31	22	9
Lake	417	173	244	Woodbury	120	35	85

Table 80

Full-time Law Enforcement Employees as of October 31, 2001
by Suburban County by State—Continued

County by state	Total police employees	Total officers	Total civilians
KANSAS			
Butler	61	45	16
Douglas	110	71	39
Harvey	36	15	21
Johnson	490	405	85
Leavenworth	100	52	48
Miami	38	22	16
Sedgwick	490	166	324
Shawnee	140	105	35
Wyandotte	145	45	100
KENTUCKY			
Boone	115	105	10
Bourbon	6	5	1
Boyd	21	19	2
Boyd Police Department	11	10	1
Bullitt	34	30	4
Campbell	11	10	1
Campbell Police Department	36	28	8
Carter	7	5	2
Christian	17	17	0
Christian Police Department	10	9	1
Clark	15	13	2
Daviess	44	31	13
Fayette	79	50	29
Gallatin	8	6	2
Grant	21	19	2
Greenup	13	13	0
Henderson	24	21	3
Jefferson	250	202	48
Jefferson Police Department	628	484	144
Jessamine	25	21	4
Kenton	32	29	3
Kenton Police Department	37	35	2
Madison	17	16	1
Oldham	20	19	1
Oldham Police Department	32	29	3
Pendleton	6	5	1
Scott	25	24	1
Woodford	5	5	0
Woodford Police Department	20	18	2
LOUISIANA			
Acadia	112	87	25
Ascension	245	186	59
Bossier	178	170	8
Caddo	605	405	200
Calcasieu	783	237	546
East Baton Rouge	752	752	0
Jefferson	1,556	1,064	492
Lafayette	469	381	88
Lafourche	255	206	49
Livingston	180	180	0
Ouachita	325	325	0
Plaquemines	240	226	14
Rapides	398	317	81
St. Bernard	274	239	35
St. Charles	337	239	98
St. James	102	53	49
St. John the Baptist	209	207	2
St. Landry	118	117	1
St. Martin	214	181	33
St. Tammany	512	418	94
Terrebonne	284	284	0
Webster	108	26	82

County by state	Total police employees	Total officers	Total civilians
LOUISIANA—Continued			
West Baton Rouge	171	171	0
MAINE			
Androscoggin	22	14	8
Cumberland	62	50	12
MARYLAND			
Allegany	90	21	69
Anne Arundel	97	72	25
Anne Arundel Police Department	847	638	209
Baltimore County Police Department	2,087	1,757	330
Baltimore County Sheriff	80	60	20
Calvert	80	68	12
Carroll	64	52	12
Cecil	79	62	17
Charles	322	209	113
Frederick	182	138	44
Harford	299	228	71
Howard	62	37	25
Howard Police Department	436	346	90
Montgomery	146	122	24
Montgomery Police Department	1,470	1,115	355
Prince George's	215	125	90
Prince George's Police Department	1,597	1,369	228
Queen Anne's	43	40	3
Washington	193	67	126
MICHIGAN			
Allegan	109	62	47
Bay	86	39	47
Berrien	164	65	99
Calhoun	156	55	101
Clinton	58	26	32
Eaton	136	73	63
Genesee	279	143	136
Ingham	214	128	86
Jackson	114	51	63
Kalamazoo	182	144	38
Kent	320	167	153
Lapeer	82	54	28
Lenawee	109	56	53
Livingston	116	64	52
Macomb	427	210	217
Midland	60	36	24
Monroe	203	102	101
Muskegon	117	51	66
Oakland	900	752	148
Ottawa	126	115	11
Saginaw	142	88	54
St. Clair	130	61	69
Van Buren	78	43	35
Washtenaw	279	138	141
Wayne	1,430	1,075	355
MINNESOTA			
Anoka	192	94	98
Benton	60	19	41
Carver	129	72	57
Chisago	60	35	25
Clay	56	29	27
Dakota	146	74	72
Hennepin	746	310	436
Houston	20	10	10

Table 80

Full-time Law Enforcement Employees as of October 31, 2001
by Suburban County by State—Continued

County by state	Total police employees	Total officers	Total civilians	County by state	Total police employees	Total officers	Total civilians
MINNESOTA—Continued				**NEW JERSEY—Continued**			
Isanti	48	18	30	Bergen	429	358	71
Olmsted	108	47	61	Bergen Police Department	137	81	56
Polk	29	24	5	Burlington	76	63	13
Ramsey	386	271	115	Camden	220	191	29
Scott	114	37	77	Cape May	117	107	10
Sherburne	147	46	101	Cumberland	54	47	7
Stearns	133	50	83	Essex	536	452	84
St. Louis	198	102	96	Essex Police Department	41	40	1
Washington	212	81	131	Gloucester	233	163	70
Wright	154	92	62	Hudson	273	204	69
				Hunterdon	30	24	6
MISSISSIPPI				Mercer	133	103	30
				Middlesex	235	195	40
Desoto	144	68	76	Monmouth	633	415	218
Harrison	367	161	206	Morris	313	241	72
Hinds	397	90	307	Ocean	184	87	97
Jackson	131	68	63	Passaic	707	550	157
Madison	85	36	49	Salem	157	129	28
Rankin	142	68	74	Somerset	188	155	33
				Sussex	146	119	27
MISSOURI				Union	183	159	24
				Warren	16	13	3
Andrew	13	9	4				
Boone	108	53	55	**NEW MEXICO**			
Buchanan	71	49	22				
Cass	59	47	12	Bernalillo	321	258	63
Christian	44	35	9	Sandoval	44	38	6
Clay	144	102	42	Santa Fe	94	67	27
Clinton	18	13	5				
Franklin	110	92	18	**NEW YORK**			
Greene	239	148	91				
Jackson	117	84	33	Broome	70	52	18
Jasper	106	80	26	Cayuga	52	31	21
Jefferson	226	156	70	Chautauqua	125	84	41
Lafayette	28	26	2	Chemung	50	43	7
Lincoln	89	36	53	Dutchess	116	102	14
Newton	67	38	29	Genesee	58	40	18
Platte	109	78	31	Herkimer	11	6	5
Ray	25	13	12	Livingston	59	41	18
St. Charles	189	133	56	Madison	36	29	7
St. Louis County Police Department	954	714	240	Monroe	319	254	65
Warren	54	28	26	Montgomery	34	26	8
Webster	21	15	6	Nassau	4,002	2,811	1,191
				Niagara	144	114	30
MONTANA				Oneida	161	104	57
				Onondaga	362	313	49
Cascade	121	35	86	Ontario	93	61	32
Missoula	172	45	127	Orange	84	75	9
Yellowstone	151	50	101	Orleans	42	28	14
				Oswego	75	65	10
NEBRASKA				Rockland	77	70	7
				Schenectady	13	8	5
Cass	49	21	28	Suffolk	339	217	122
Dakota	25	12	13	Tioga	55	36	19
Douglas	180	123	57	Warren	84	65	19
Lancaster	88	71	17	Wayne	63	51	12
Sarpy	164	114	50	Westchester Public Safety	292	235	57
Washington	37	21	16				
				NORTH CAROLINA			
NEVADA							
				Alamance	120	75	45
Nye	133	90	43	Alexander	34	22	12
Washoe	705	419	286	Brunswick	89	71	18
				Buncombe	288	203	85
NEW JERSEY				Burke	99	75	24
				Cabarrus	143	138	5
Atlantic	115	87	28	Caldwell	103	57	46

Table 80

Full-time Law Enforcement Employees as of October 31, 2001

by Suburban County by State—Continued

County by state	Total police employees	Total officers	Total civilians	County by state	Total police employees	Total officers	Total civilians
NORTH CAROLINA—Continued				**OHIO—Continued**			
Catawba	124	103	21	Montgomery	437	181	256
Chatham	83	54	29	Pickaway	76	42	34
Cumberland	436	278	158	Portage	130	53	77
Currituck	52	39	13	Richland	118	52	66
Davidson	185	124	61	Stark	247	119	128
Davie	61	30	31	Summit	472	380	92
Durham	382	145	237	Trumbull	144	52	92
Edgecombe	100	45	55	Warren	146	80	66
Forsyth	458	218	240	Washington	55	33	22
Franklin	77	38	39	Wood	116	111	5
Gaston[1]	187	99	88				
Gaston Police Department[1]	225	138	87	**OKLAHOMA**			
Guilford	427	224	203				
Johnston	159	82	77	Canadian	55	29	26
Lincoln	128	70	58	Cleveland	90	43	47
Madison	20	12	8	Comanche	53	37	16
Mecklenburg[2]	1,058	321	737	Creek	35	20	15
Nash	116	66	50	Garfield	39	17	22
New Hanover	301	223	78	Logan	19	9	10
Onslow	146	98	48	McClain	25	10	15
Orange	132	109	23	Oklahoma	633	136	497
Pitt	219	98	121	Osage	61	33	28
Randolph	182	132	50	Pottawatomie	38	13	25
Rowan	139	90	49	Rogers	59	22	37
Stokes	57	39	18	Sequoyah	22	8	14
Union	160	121	39	Tulsa	177	152	25
Wake	481	273	208	Wagoner	19	11	8
Wayne	124	69	55				
Yadkin	56	34	22	**OREGON**			
NORTH DAKOTA				Clackamas	235	190	45
				Columbia	20	17	3
Burleigh	63	32	31	Jackson	72	51	21
Cass	77	55	22	Lane	114	63	51
Grand Forks	27	21	6	Marion	95	73	22
Morton	31	18	13	Multnomah	131	102	29
				Polk	29	24	5
OHIO				Washington	254	185	69
				Yamhill	58	44	14
Allen	164	74	90				
Ashtabula	87	44	43	**PENNSYLVANIA**			
Auglaize	55	20	35				
Belmont	69	58	11	Allegheny	204	174	30
Brown	55	41	14	Allegheny Police Department	263	204	59
Butler	303	181	122	Beaver	33	25	8
Carroll	19	18	1	Butler	22	16	6
Clark	159	130	29	Cambria	20	15	5
Clermont	203	83	120	Washington	32	28	4
Columbiana	35	26	9				
Crawford	69	18	51	**SOUTH CAROLINA**			
Cuyahoga	1,108	168	940				
Delaware	118	60	58	Aiken	135	106	29
Fairfield	130	96	34	Anderson	150	126	24
Franklin	785	392	393	Berkeley	161	103	58
Fulton	33	22	11	Charleston	338	240	98
Geauga	98	42	56	Cherokee	88	40	48
Greene	155	135	20	Dorchester	157	82	75
Jefferson	91	33	58	Edgefield	46	24	22
Lake	182	51	131	Florence	218	109	109
Lawrence	42	34	8	Greenville	420	345	75
Licking	180	124	56	Horry	161	35	126
Lorain	229	75	154	Horry Police Department	207	189	18
Lucas	479	269	210	Lexington	344	231	113
Madison	29	25	4	Pickens	99	74	25
Mahoning	255	246	9	Richland	432	399	33
Medina	168	69	99	Spartanburg	302	278	24
Miami	132	45	87	Sumter	118	110	8

Table 80

Full-time Law Enforcement Employees as of October 31, 2001
by Suburban County by State—Continued

County by state	Total police employees	Total officers	Total civilians	County by state	Total police employees	Total officers	Total civilians
SOUTH CAROLINA—Continued				**TEXAS—Continued**			
York	228	112	116	Hunt	77	31	46
				Jefferson	409	97	312
SOUTH DAKOTA				Johnson	175	68	107
				Kaufman	76	33	43
Lincoln	8	7	1	Liberty	57	40	17
Minnehaha	127	74	53	Lubbock	258	136	122
Pennington	151	57	94	McLennan	261	113	148
				Midland	170	83	87
TENNESSEE				Montgomery	455	292	163
				Nueces	296	134	162
Anderson	106	42	64	Orange	135	60	75
Blount	245	139	106	Parker	98	47	51
Carter	60	54	6	Potter	181	118	63
Cheatham	61	26	35	Randall	124	58	66
Chester	23	10	13	Rockwall	80	36	44
Dickson	110	48	62	San Patricio	80	39	41
Fayette	53	30	23	Smith	248	112	136
Hamilton	355	143	212	Tarrant	1,177	442	735
Hawkins	55	52	3	Taylor	161	70	91
Knox	700	423	277	Tom Green	136	37	99
Loudon	57	56	1	Travis	1,492	654	838
Madison	198	191	7	Upshur	58	25	33
Marion	31	26	5	Victoria	153	96	57
Montgomery	196	178	18	Waller	49	23	26
Robertson	89	75	14	Webb	240	150	90
Rutherford	307	134	173	Wichita	160	40	120
Sevier	118	71	47	Williamson	265	162	103
Shelby	2,233	544	1,689	Wilson	65	24	41
Shelby County Police Department	32	19	13				
Sullivan	135	102	33	**UTAH**			
Sumner	139	63	76				
Tipton	39	38	1	Davis	251	189	62
Union	24	14	10	Kane	21	15	6
Washington	174	79	95	Salt Lake	1,259	375	884
Williamson	86	78	8	Utah	264	189	75
				Weber	327	252	75
TEXAS							
				VERMONT			
Archer	12	7	5				
Bastrop	121	46	75	Grand Isle	3	2	1
Bell	242	86	156				
Bexar	1,532	438	1,094	**VIRGINIA**			
Bowie	50	45	5				
Brazoria	306	119	187	Albemarle County Police Department	122	101	21
Brazos	173	75	98	Amherst	63	58	5
Caldwell	63	19	44	Arlington County Police Department	467	385	82
Chambers	70	26	44	Bedford	67	67	0
Collin	366	115	251	Botetourt	78	62	16
Comal	188	85	103	Campbell	56	53	3
Coryell	48	18	30	Charles City	15	9	6
Dallas	1,695	463	1,232	Chesterfield County Police Department	510	412	98
Denton	434	133	301	Clarke	23	14	9
Ector	182	82	100	Culpeper	86	69	17
Ellis	134	55	79	Dinwiddie	58	47	11
El Paso	1,021	235	786	Fairfax County Police Department	1,641	1,235	406
Fort Bend	411	251	160	Fauquier	106	89	17
Galveston	290	232	58	Fluvanna	26	19	7
Grayson	127	62	65	Gloucester	89	74	15
Gregg	140	70	70	Goochland	29	23	6
Guadalupe	144	41	103	Greene	27	16	11
Hardin	61	32	29	Hanover	174	157	17
Harris	3,396	2,572	824	Henrico County Police Department	717	510	207
Harrison	84	39	45	Isle of Wight	32	25	7
Hays	223	95	128	James City County Police Department	66	63	3
Henderson	93	51	42	King George	36	23	13
Hidalgo	388	199	189	Loudoun	329	272	57
Hood	70	26	44	Mathews	19	19	0

Table 80

Full-time Law Enforcement Employees as of October 31, 2001

by Suburban County by State—Continued

County by state	Total police employees	Total officers	Total civilians	County by state	Total police employees	Total officers	Total civilians
VIRGINIA—Continued				**WEST VIRGINIA—Continued**			
New Kent	33	24	9	Quincy	9	8	1
Pittsylvania	122	67	55	South Charleston	31	23	8
Powhatan	46	37	9	Marshall	26	24	2
Prince George County Police Department	58	44	14	Marshall-Moundsville State Police	17	8	9
Prince William County Police Department	499	400	99	Mineral	13	8	5
Roanoke County Police Department	145	109	36	Mineral-Keyser State Police	7	6	1
Scott	41	40	1	Ohio	28	27	1
Spotsylvania	94	88	6	Ohio-Wheeling State Police	7	6	1
Stafford	109	99	10	Putnam	33	29	4
Warren	67	66	1	Putnam State Police:			
Washington	76	66	10	Teays Valley	5	4	1
York	88	83	5	Winfield	4	3	1
				Wayne	26	17	9
WASHINGTON				Wayne-Wayne State Police	9	8	1
				Wood	43	36	7
Benton	68	51	17	Wood-Parkersburg State Police	17	10	7
Clark	222	128	94				
Franklin	23	20	3	**WISCONSIN**			
Island	45	39	6				
King	832	527	305	Brown	305	140	165
Kitsap	143	117	26	Calumet	42	22	20
Pierce	424	355	69	Chippewa	65	50	15
Snohomish	307	226	81	Douglas	52	48	4
Spokane	284	227	57	Eau Claire	98	51	47
Thurston	116	92	24	Kenosha	316	108	208
Whatcom	82	69	13	La Crosse	101	36	65
Yakima	101	70	31	Marathon	175	64	111
				Milwaukee	967	665	302
WEST VIRGINIA				Outagamie	209	79	130
				Ozaukee	99	75	24
Berkeley	43	34	9	Pierce	48	44	4
Berkeley-Martinsburg State Police	23	21	2	Rock	190	97	93
Brooke	23	16	7	Sheboygan	171	75	96
Brooke-Wellsburg State Police	5	4	1	St. Croix	69	38	31
Cabell	108	36	72	Washington	152	61	91
Cabell-Huntington State Police	19	12	7	Waukesha	317	146	171
Hancock	39	25	14	Winnebago	175	117	58
Hancock-New Cumberland State Police	5	4	1				
Jefferson	16	13	3	**WYOMING**			
Jefferson-Kearneysville State Police	26	15	11				
Kanawha	89	69	20	Laramie	74	42	32
Kanawha State Police:				Natrona	52	42	10
Parkway Authority	7	7	0				

[1] The data are listed separately for both Gaston County and Gaston County Police Department, North Carolina. However, Gaston County reports its crime figures combined with those of the Gaston County Police Department; they can be found in Table 10 under *Gaston County Police Department*.

[2] The data in this table are provided for Mecklenburg County, North Carolina, only. However, Mecklenburg County reports its crime figures combined with those of the Charlotte Police Department; they can be found in Table 8 under *Charlotte-Mecklenburg*.

Table 81

Full-time Law Enforcement Employees as of October 31, 2001
by Rural County by State

County by state	Total police employees	Total officers	Total civilians	County by state	Total police employees	Total officers	Total civilians
ALABAMA				**ARKANSAS—Continued**			
Barbour	15	12	3	Carroll	33	16	17
Bibb	13	11	2	Chicot	8	6	2
Bullock	10	5	5	Clark	26	12	14
Butler	11	8	3	Clay	20	9	11
Chambers	53	17	36	Cleburne	27	15	12
Cherokee	30	14	16	Cleveland	12	7	5
Chilton	49	20	29	Columbia	33	13	20
Choctaw	9	6	3	Conway	31	12	19
Clarke	39	14	25	Cross	35	14	21
Clay	11	4	7	Dallas	27	6	21
Cleburne	12	7	5	Desha	9	7	2
Coffee	40	13	27	Drew	12	11	1
Conecuh	21	8	13	Franklin	16	10	6
Coosa	17	7	10	Fulton	10	6	4
Covington	16	16	0	Garland	113	37	76
Crenshaw	11	10	1	Grant	9	7	2
Cullman	88	62	26	Greene	44	15	29
Dallas	54	23	31	Hempstead	42	14	28
De Kalb	51	32	19	Hot Spring	28	22	6
Escambia	45	19	26	Howard	20	9	11
Fayette	20	19	1	Independence	71	44	27
Franklin	35	16	19	Izard	14	9	5
Geneva	25	12	13	Jackson	23	13	10
Greene	19	9	10	Johnson	25	11	14
Hale	10	7	3	Lafayette	13	7	6
Henry	19	10	9	Lawrence	18	9	9
Jackson	63	27	36	Lee	9	5	4
Lamar	17	6	11	Lincoln	19	7	12
Lee	103	42	61	Little River	20	8	12
Lowndes	38	11	27	Logan	27	14	13
Macon	32	17	15	Madison	15	8	7
Marengo	27	10	17	Marion	21	11	10
Marion	27	13	14	Mississippi	84	23	61
Marshall	50	23	27	Monroe	17	9	8
Monroe	43	22	21	Montgomery	15	7	8
Perry	17	9	8	Nevada	17	6	11
Pickens	22	9	13	Newton	10	6	4
Pike	30	15	15	Ouachita	29	13	16
Randolph	9	9	0	Perry	16	7	9
Sumter	25	8	17	Phillips	11	9	2
Talladega	74	32	42	Pike	11	6	5
Tallapoosa	53	22	31	Poinsett	42	13	29
Walker	74	34	40	Polk	22	10	12
Washington	15	8	7	Pope	62	29	33
Wilcox	19	7	12	Prairie	15	8	7
Winston	22	9	13	Randolph	11	9	2
				Scott	14	7	7
ARIZONA				Searcy	11	5	6
				Sevier	21	11	10
Apache	83	44	39	Sharp	18	10	8
Cochise	187	76	111	St. Francis	36	15	21
Gila	112	45	67	Stone	18	7	11
Graham	51	19	32	Union	57	26	31
Greenlee	24	14	10	Van Buren	12	10	2
Lapaz	89	36	53	White	75	31	44
Navajo	113	49	64	Woodruff	13	6	7
Santa Cruz	72	42	30	Yell	19	11	8
Yavapai	302	116	186				
				CALIFORNIA			
ARKANSAS				Alpine	17	13	4
Arkansas	13	12	1	Amador	81	49	32
Ashley	24	11	13	Calaveras	90	56	34
Baxter	42	29	13	Colusa	64	31	33
Boone	34	20	14	Del Norte	38	29	9
Bradley	5	4	1	Glenn	67	29	38
Calhoun	11	4	7	Humboldt	213	75	138

Table 81

Full-time Law Enforcement Employees as of October 31, 2001
by Rural County by State—Continued

County by state	Total police employees	Total officers	Total civilians	County by state	Total police employees	Total officers	Total civilians
CALIFORNIA—Continued				**COLORADO—Continued**			
Imperial	259	108	151	Sedgwick	8	4	4
Inyo	64	38	26	Summit	54	45	9
Kings	205	138	67	Teller	76	36	40
Lake	170	65	105	Washington	31	10	21
Lassen	102	81	21	Yuma	16	6	10
Mariposa	67	39	28				
Mendocino	168	132	36	**FLORIDA**			
Modoc	31	24	7				
Mono	58	40	18	Baker	74	51	23
Nevada	192	71	121	Bradford	52	19	33
Plumas	73	39	34	Calhoun	22	15	7
San Benito	55	26	29	Citrus	271	166	105
Sierra	19	18	1	Columbia	166	87	79
Siskiyou	122	56	66	DeSoto	86	65	21
Tehama	116	82	34	Dixie	52	25	27
Trinity	29	23	6	Franklin	73	57	16
Tuolumne	123	69	54	Gilchrist	36	23	13
				Glades	53	24	29
COLORADO				Gulf	39	26	13
				Hamilton	54	15	39
Alamosa	34	23	11	Hardee	76	35	41
Archuleta	36	11	25	Hendry	132	68	64
Baca	10	4	6	Highlands	227	157	70
Bent	16	4	12	Holmes	23	17	6
Chaffee	40	20	20	Indian River	376	204	172
Cheyenne	11	6	5	Jackson	72	51	21
Clear Creek	38	20	18	Jefferson	44	16	28
Conejos	14	7	7	Lafayette	20	8	12
Costilla	12	8	4	Levy	131	65	66
Crowley	13	9	4	Liberty	21	16	5
Custer	21	10	11	Madison	60	38	22
Delta	44	18	26	Okeechobee	162	121	41
Dolores	7	4	3	Putnam	140	92	48
Eagle	74	60	14	Sumter	126	95	31
Elbert	33	21	12	Suwannee	68	48	20
Fremont	60	33	27	Taylor	40	27	13
Garfield	69	20	49	Union	19	9	10
Gilpin	37	25	12	Wakulla	71	45	26
Grand	53	28	25	Walton	156	119	37
Gunnison	25	11	14	Washington	64	31	33
Hinsdale	5	4	1				
Huerfano	21	9	12	**GEORGIA**			
Jackson	7	4	3				
Kiowa	3	2	1	Appling	36	14	22
Kit Carson	19	6	13	Atkinson	13	5	8
Lake	16	7	9	Bacon	18	8	10
La Plata	98	77	21	Baker	9	8	1
Las Animas	39	13	26	Banks	30	20	10
Lincoln	17	5	12	Ben Hill	36	19	17
Logan	41	22	19	Berrien	21	14	7
Mineral	5	3	2	Bleckley	21	10	11
Moffat	36	19	17	Brantley	19	12	7
Montezuma	49	23	26	Brooks	28	17	11
Montrose	97	72	25	Bulloch	68	35	33
Morgan	56	42	14	Butts	53	32	21
Otero	22	22	0	Calhoun	15	15	0
Ouray	6	5	1	Camden	110	68	42
Park	61	42	19	Candler	17	6	11
Phillips	3	3	0	Charlton	25	11	14
Pitkin	40	21	19	Chattooga	39	22	17
Prowers	31	11	20	Clay	6	2	4
Rio Blanco	20	12	8	Clinch	16	11	5
Rio Grande	24	9	15	Colquitt	76	36	40
Routt	44	17	27	Cook	25	12	13
Saguache	16	9	7	Crawford	23	11	12
San Juan	5	4	1	Crisp	66	62	4
San Miguel	34	30	4	Dawson	69	40	29

Table 81

Full-time Law Enforcement Employees as of October 31, 2001
by Rural County by State—Continued

County by state	Total police employees	Total officers	Total civilians	County by state	Total police employees	Total officers	Total civilians
GEORGIA—Continued				**GEORGIA—Continued**			
Decatur	58	52	6	Towns	17	11	6
Dodge	26	17	9	Treutlen	12	9	3
Dooly	42	15	27	Troup	101	54	47
Early	28	24	4	Troup County Marshal	8	7	1
Echols	6	5	1	Turner	27	11	16
Elbert	44	24	20	Union	16	15	1
Emanuel	27	23	4	Upson	52	29	23
Fannin	30	21	9	Ware County Police Department	13	1	12
Floyd	134	58	76	Warren	4	4	0
Floyd County Police Department	73	66	7	Washington	32	18	14
Franklin	41	23	18	Wayne	35	33	2
Glascock	3	2	1	Webster	8	5	3
Glynn	119	23	96	Wheeler	8	3	5
Glynn County Police Department	133	108	25	White	44	29	15
Gordon	49	43	6	Whitfield	134	93	41
Grady	36	12	24	Wilkinson	21	12	9
Greene	42	28	14	Worth	31	20	11
Habersham	47	29	18				
Hall	314	201	113	**HAWAII**			
Hall County Marshal	10	9	1				
Hancock	34	25	9	Hawaii Police Department	530	394	136
Haralson	42	23	19	Kauai Police Department	160	123	37
Hart	47	23	24	Maui Police Department	412	310	102
Heard	25	18	7				
Irwin	14	7	7	**IDAHO**			
Jackson	75	67	8				
Jeff Davis	15	12	3	Adams	11	5	6
Jefferson	24	24	0	Bear Lake	12	5	7
Jenkins	8	4	4	Benewah	16	9	7
Johnson	10	7	3	Bingham	50	33	17
Lamar	42	22	20	Blaine	29	17	12
Lanier	12	7	5	Boise	17	11	6
Laurens	90	54	36	Bonner	69	48	21
Liberty	87	57	30	Bonneville	75	50	25
Lincoln	26	8	18	Boundary	19	10	9
Long	14	13	1	Butte	10	4	6
Lowndes	189	162	27	Camas	5	3	2
Lumpkin	55	40	15	Caribou	14	8	6
Macon	25	9	16	Cassia	52	34	18
Marion	10	4	6	Clark	7	3	4
McIntosh	39	32	7	Clearwater	24	17	7
Meriwether	33	18	15	Custer	11	7	4
Miller	19	9	10	Elmore	28	17	11
Mitchell	46	18	28	Franklin	18	9	9
Montgomery	9	5	4	Fremont	18	11	7
Murray	53	30	23	Gem	21	11	10
Pierce	29	11	18	Gooding	15	10	5
Polk	52	15	37	Idaho	31	20	11
Polk County Police Department	36	34	2	Jefferson	24	14	10
Pulaski	21	11	10	Jerome	17	14	3
Putnam	51	26	25	Kootenai	94	69	25
Quitman	4	3	1	Latah	36	24	12
Rabun	26	25	1	Lewis	11	6	5
Screven	20	18	2	Lincoln	6	5	1
Seminole	17	10	7	Madison	26	17	9
Stephens	44	28	16	Minidoka	22	14	8
Stewart	6	3	3	Nez Perce	35	23	12
Sumter	92	37	55	Oneida	12	7	5
Talbot	13	8	5	Owyhee	19	11	8
Taliaferro	9	5	4	Payette	27	16	11
Taliaferro County Police Department	2	2	0	Power	18	9	9
Tattnall	32	13	19	Shoshone	31	19	12
Telfair	17	8	9	Teton	14	9	5
Terrell	26	12	14	Twin Falls	64	44	20
Thomas	68	37	31	Valley	27	14	13
Tift	110	46	64	Washington	17	9	8

Table 81

Full-time Law Enforcement Employees as of October 31, 2001
by Rural County by State—Continued

County by state	Total police employees	Total officers	Total civilians	County by state	Total police employees	Total officers	Total civilians
ILLINOIS				**ILLINOIS—Continued**			
Adams	65	26	39	Wabash	9	4	5
Alexander	13	9	4	Warren	19	12	7
Bond	18	9	9	Washington	22	6	16
Brown	6	5	1	Wayne	17	8	9
Bureau	38	20	18	White	7	7	0
Calhoun	10	6	4	Whiteside	52	23	29
Carroll	23	9	14	Williamson	67	35	32
Cass	7	6	1				
Christian	29	16	13	**INDIANA**			
Clark	13	8	5				
Clay	14	8	6	Bartholomew	65	37	28
Coles	53	34	19	Benton	19	6	13
Crawford	21	9	12	Blackford	30	9	21
Cumberland	17	7	10	Brown	31	13	18
De Witt	29	16	13	Carroll	21	11	10
Douglas	23	9	14	Cass	56	18	38
Edgar	21	10	11	Crawford	12	7	5
Edwards	9	4	5	Daviess	30	13	17
Effingham	41	16	25	Decatur	26	8	18
Fayette	26	10	16	Dubois	33	15	18
Ford	26	8	18	Fountain	23	7	16
Franklin	42	16	26	Fulton	26	9	17
Fulton	42	20	22	Gibson	37	15	22
Gallatin	3	3	0	Grant	108	45	63
Greene	13	6	7	Greene	36	11	25
Hamilton	8	4	4	Henry	57	29	28
Hancock	21	10	11	Jackson	52	14	38
Hardin	7	3	4	Jasper	40	19	21
Henderson	15	9	6	Jay	33	11	22
Iroquois	31	17	14	Jefferson	31	13	18
Jackson	64	22	42	Jennings	38	13	25
Jasper	18	8	10	Knox	28	25	3
Jefferson	42	22	20	Kosciusko	74	32	42
Jo Daviess	34	19	15	LaGrange	52	17	35
Johnson	13	8	5	La Porte	124	54	70
Knox	51	48	3	Lawrence	62	25	37
La Salle	73	56	17	Marshall	51	19	32
Lawrence	12	6	6	Martin	15	7	8
Lee	41	22	19	Miami	32	15	17
Livingston	50	28	22	Montgomery	33	16	17
Logan	36	19	17	Newton	45	14	31
Macoupin	52	24	28	Orange	29	8	21
Marion	17	17	0	Owen	29	11	18
Marshall	17	8	9	Parke	34	9	25
Mason	19	8	11	Perry	13	6	7
Massac	28	11	17	Pike	22	6	16
McDonough	25	14	11	Pulaski	40	10	30
Mercer	21	11	10	Putnam	33	11	22
Montgomery	22	13	9	Randolph	48	15	33
Morgan	38	15	23	Ripley	20	10	10
Moultrie	17	10	7	Rush	24	10	14
Perry	32	10	22	Spencer	45	13	32
Piatt	26	9	17	Starke	25	12	13
Pike	21	12	9	Steuben	60	21	39
Pope	4	4	0	Sullivan	31	10	21
Pulaski	16	11	5	Union	11	8	3
Putnam	9	5	4	Wabash	35	13	22
Randolph	20	10	10	Warren	20	7	13
Richland	22	8	14	Wayne	84	27	57
Saline	39	10	29				
Schuyler	11	5	6	**IOWA**			
Scott	8	4	4				
Shelby	22	10	12	Adair	8	6	2
Stark	10	4	6	Adams	10	4	6
Stephenson	39	29	10	Allamakee	15	8	7
Union	14	8	6	Appanoose	16	9	7
Vermilion	73	33	40	Audubon	9	5	4

Table 81

Full-time Law Enforcement Employees as of October 31, 2001
by Rural County by State—Continued

County by state	Total police employees	Total officers	Total civilians	County by state	Total police employees	Total officers	Total civilians
IOWA—Continued				**IOWA—Continued**			
Benton	22	9	13	Ringgold	11	6	5
Boone	14	9	5	Sac	13	7	6
Bremer	17	10	7	Shelby	14	8	6
Buchanan	27	13	14	Sioux	27	16	11
Buena Vista	16	9	7	Story	69	35	34
Butler	15	9	6	Tama	19	12	7
Calhoun	11	7	4	Taylor	10	6	4
Carroll	13	10	3	Union	11	5	6
Cass	9	6	3	Van Buren	10	5	5
Cedar	31	9	22	Wapello	35	10	25
Cerro Gordo	47	16	31	Washington	30	13	17
Cherokee	16	6	10	Wayne	10	5	5
Chickasaw	13	8	5	Webster	34	16	18
Clarke	19	5	14	Winnebago	12	5	7
Clay	15	9	6	Winneshiek	20	10	10
Clayton	18	10	8	Worth	15	6	9
Clinton	44	31	13	Wright	18	6	12
Crawford	12	10	2				
Davis	6	5	1	**KANSAS**			
Decatur	11	5	6				
Delaware	11	10	1	Allen	14	7	7
Des Moines	26	21	5	Anderson	16	10	6
Dickinson	18	9	9	Atchison	22	7	15
Emmet	15	8	7	Barber	9	4	5
Fayette	20	9	11	Barton	33	17	16
Floyd	17	10	7	Bourbon	9	7	2
Franklin	10	7	3	Brown	20	8	12
Fremont	19	7	12	Chase	10	5	5
Greene	13	6	7	Chautauqua	10	4	6
Grundy	16	12	4	Cherokee	33	26	7
Guthrie	10	5	5	Cheyenne	3	2	1
Hamilton	12	10	2	Clark	9	4	5
Hancock	9	7	2	Clay	13	6	7
Hardin	27	10	17	Cloud	16	10	6
Harrison	21	9	12	Coffey	29	13	16
Henry	22	11	11	Comanche	8	4	4
Howard	8	7	1	Cowley	41	17	24
Humboldt	13	9	4	Crawford	66	26	40
Ida	14	8	6	Decatur	3	3	0
Iowa	17	11	6	Dickinson	26	16	10
Jackson	17	10	7	Doniphan	3	3	0
Jasper	36	13	23	Edwards	8	4	4
Jefferson	26	7	19	Elk	7	3	4
Jones	22	9	13	Ellis	20	13	7
Keokuk	6	3	3	Ellsworth	14	9	5
Kossuth	21	9	12	Finney	95	38	57
Lee	32	15	17	Ford	49	20	29
Louisa	20	10	10	Franklin	43	19	24
Lucas	12	5	7	Geary	58	22	36
Lyon	15	9	6	Gove	4	4	0
Madison	14	6	8	Graham	6	3	3
Mahaska	25	10	15	Grant	16	7	9
Marion	21	11	10	Gray	11	5	6
Marshall	58	17	41	Greeley	3	3	0
Mills	30	11	19	Greenwood	22	14	8
Mitchell	15	6	9	Hamilton	14	7	7
Monona	18	8	10	Harper	12	4	8
Monroe	12	5	7	Haskell	16	10	6
Montgomery	18	9	9	Hodgeman	9	4	5
Muscatine	62	21	41	Jackson	37	16	21
O'Brien	25	9	16	Jefferson	41	23	18
Osceola	15	10	5	Jewell	7	3	4
Page	12	7	5	Kearny	18	9	9
Palo Alto	15	8	7	Kingman	16	7	9
Plymouth	19	9	10	Labette	30	17	13
Pocahontas	11	5	6	Lane	8	4	4
Poweshiek	15	8	7	Lincoln	11	7	4

Table 81

Full-time Law Enforcement Employees as of October 31, 2001

by Rural County by State—Continued

County by state	Total police employees	Total officers	Total civilians	County by state	Total police employees	Total officers	Total civilians
KANSAS—Continued				**KENTUCKY—Continued**			
Linn	20	9	11	Carroll	5	5	0
Logan	4	3	1	Casey	5	4	1
Lyon	61	14	47	Clay	8	6	2
Marion	9	7	2	Clinton	5	3	2
Marshall	15	7	8	Crittenden	3	2	1
McPherson	35	16	19	Cumberland	5	4	1
Meade	14	5	9	Edmonson	6	4	2
Mitchell	10	10	0	Elliott	4	3	1
Montgomery	30	19	11	Estill	6	4	2
Morris	12	7	5	Fleming	6	6	0
Morton	10	5	5	Floyd	22	15	7
Nemaha	12	8	4	Franklin	13	13	0
Neosho	22	11	11	Fulton	4	4	0
Ness	12	6	6	Garrard	6	5	1
Norton	9	4	5	Graves	13	11	2
Osage	36	18	18	Grayson	14	12	2
Osborne	13	9	4	Green	3	2	1
Ottawa	9	5	4	Hancock	6	6	0
Pawnee	13	5	8	Hardin	30	28	2
Phillips	14	9	5	Harlan	20	20	0
Pottawatomie	32	19	13	Harrison	6	6	0
Pratt	12	7	5	Hart	7	7	0
Rawlins	8	3	5	Henry	6	6	0
Reno	63	49	14	Hickman	3	3	0
Republic	9	4	5	Hopkins	12	10	2
Rice	14	9	5	Jackson	9	7	2
Riley County Police Department	150	84	66	Johnson	14	10	4
Rooks	8	4	4	Knott	7	7	0
Rush	9	4	5	Knox	9	6	3
Russell	18	9	9	Larue	7	6	1
Saline	93	42	51	Laurel	28	25	3
Scott	5	4	1	Lawrence	5	3	2
Seward	38	12	26	Lee	2	1	1
Sheridan	7	3	4	Leslie	7	5	2
Sherman	11	5	6	Letcher	12	7	5
Smith	11	4	7	Lewis	7	6	1
Stafford	9	4	5	Lincoln	8	6	2
Stanton	13	5	8	Livingston	7	7	0
Stevens	12	6	6	Logan	17	16	1
Sumner	27	17	10	Lyon	4	4	0
Thomas	14	13	1	Magoffin	6	5	1
Trego	7	3	4	Marion	4	3	1
Wabaunsee	14	7	7	Marshall	21	19	2
Wallace	2	1	1	Martin	5	3	2
Washington	7	7	0	Mason	12	10	2
Wichita	8	4	4	McCracken	35	34	1
Wilson	23	10	13	McCracken Police Department	2	1	1
Woodson	10	5	5	McCreary	8	7	1
				McLean	6	5	1
KENTUCKY				Meade	10	8	2
				Menifee	6	6	0
Adair	6	4	2	Mercer	8	7	1
Allen	10	9	1	Metcalfe	4	3	1
Anderson	8	7	1	Monroe	8	6	2
Anderson Police Department	2	2	0	Montgomery	18	15	3
Ballard	9	9	0	Morgan	3	3	0
Barren	11	10	1	Muhlenberg	12	12	0
Bath	4	3	1	Nelson	24	19	5
Bell	10	10	0	Nicholas	3	3	0
Boyle	7	6	1	Ohio	19	18	1
Bracken	3	2	1	Owen	5	4	1
Breathitt	6	5	1	Owsley	4	4	0
Breckinridge	7	7	0	Perry	16	16	0
Butler	8	6	2	Pike	30	18	12
Caldwell	7	6	1	Powell	10	9	1
Calloway	20	20	0	Pulaski	30	24	6
Carlisle	4	4	0	Robertson	1	1	0

Table 81

Full-time Law Enforcement Employees as of October 31, 2001
by Rural County by State—Continued

County by state	Total police employees	Total officers	Total civilians	County by state	Total police employees	Total officers	Total civilians
KENTUCKY—Continued				**MAINE—Continued**			
Rockcastle	7	6	1	Oxford	13	12	1
Rowan	12	9	3	Penobscot	24	20	4
Russell	11	10	1	Piscataquis	13	7	6
Shelby	20	20	0	Sagadahoc	17	15	2
Simpson	11	9	2	Somerset	17	15	2
Spencer	5	5	0	Waldo	15	14	1
Taylor	12	9	3	Washington	22	12	10
Todd	4	3	1	York	30	27	3
Trigg	7	7	0				
Trimble	3	3	0	**MARYLAND**			
Union	8	7	1				
Warren	54	47	7	Caroline	25	23	2
Washington	4	4	0	Dorchester	31	25	6
Wayne	7	5	2	Garrett	39	18	21
Webster	7	7	0	Kent	21	20	1
Whitley	13	10	3	Somerset	17	15	2
Wolfe	6	4	2	St. Mary's	202	107	95
				Talbot	21	19	2
LOUISIANA				Wicomico	93	74	19
				Worcester	47	41	6
Allen	52	36	16				
Assumption	81	42	39	**MICHIGAN**			
Beauregard	77	59	18				
Bienville	42	41	1	Alcona	26	13	13
Caldwell	31	31	0	Alger	13	9	4
Cameron	70	54	16	Alpena	27	15	12
Catahoula	32	16	16	Antrim	49	20	29
Claiborne	88	22	66	Arenac	16	15	1
Concordia	57	32	25	Baraga	13	6	7
De Soto	82	74	8	Barry	47	30	17
East Carroll	174	149	25	Benzie	44	16	28
East Feliciana	69	26	43	Branch	43	21	22
Evangeline	58	30	28	Cass	76	41	35
Franklin	70	70	0	Charlevoix	31	16	15
Grant	48	48	0	Cheboygan	35	17	18
Iberia	196	88	108	Chippewa	28	14	14
Iberville	152	99	53	Clare	28	24	4
Jackson	33	33	0	Crawford	27	15	12
Jefferson Davis	47	47	0	Delta	31	15	16
La Salle	46	44	2	Dickinson	30	13	17
Lincoln	49	49	0	Emmet	38	19	19
Madison	52	52	0	Gladwin	25	17	8
Morehouse	154	154	0	Gogebic	21	15	6
Natchitoches	61	56	5	Grand Traverse	87	68	19
Pointe Coupee	102	30	72	Gratiot	37	20	17
Red River	47	44	3	Hillsdale	39	26	13
Richland	128	114	14	Houghton	21	20	1
Sabine	65	62	3	Huron	24	23	1
St. Helena	49	27	22	Ionia	50	20	30
St. Mary	156	132	24	Iosco	24	5	19
Tangipahoa	281	281	0	Iron	10	9	1
Tensas	147	13	134	Isabella	53	27	26
Union	47	32	15	Kalkaska	42	25	17
Vermilion	104	55	49	Keweenaw	7	6	1
Vernon	141	141	0	Lake	54	17	37
Washington	98	98	0	Leelanau	33	19	14
West Carroll	17	17	0	Luce	4	3	1
West Feliciana	78	75	3	Mackinac	19	8	11
				Manistee	29	13	16
MAINE				Marquette	57	31	26
				Mason	37	19	18
Aroostook	18	13	5	Mecosta	44	24	20
Franklin	24	14	10	Menominee	29	14	15
Hancock	24	13	11	Missaukee	25	13	12
Kennebec	24	16	8	Montcalm	61	27	34
Knox	18	16	2	Montmorency	26	11	15
Lincoln	21	19	2	Newaygo	30	27	3

Table 81

Full-time Law Enforcement Employees as of October 31, 2001

by Rural County by State—Continued

County by state	Total police employees	Total officers	Total civilians	County by state	Total police employees	Total officers	Total civilians
MICHIGAN—Continued				**MINNESOTA—Continued**			
Oceana	35	20	15	Red Lake	10	7	3
Ogemaw	33	14	19	Redwood	17	8	9
Ontonagon	14	10	4	Renville	16	9	7
Osceola	39	31	8	Rice	46	21	25
Oscoda	16	11	5	Rock	16	11	5
Otsego	31	14	17	Roseau	13	8	5
Presque Isle	25	12	13	Sibley	21	10	11
Roscommon	24	24	0	Steele	39	17	22
Sanilac	54	23	31	Stevens	10	5	5
Schoolcraft	12	4	8	Swift	15	7	8
Shiawassee	71	33	38	Todd	27	14	13
St. Joseph	52	25	27	Traverse	6	3	3
Tuscola	46	29	17	Wabasha	25	13	12
Wexford	50	24	26	Wadena	16	6	10
				Waseca	23	11	12
MINNESOTA				Watonwan	19	8	11
				Wilkin	8	6	2
Aitkin	45	18	27	Winona	44	18	26
Becker	46	21	25	Yellow Medicine	16	7	9
Beltrami	65	26	39				
Big Stone	7	4	3	**MISSISSIPPI**			
Blue Earth	48	20	28				
Brown	32	9	23	Adams	54	52	2
Carlton	41	24	17	Alcorn	13	11	2
Cass	50	27	23	Amite	14	8	6
Chippewa	16	7	9	Attala	11	6	5
Clearwater	14	7	7	Benton	7	3	4
Cook	16	11	5	Bolivar	29	18	11
Cottonwood	13	6	7	Calhoun	10	5	5
Crow Wing	68	31	37	Carroll	10	7	3
Dodge	28	20	8	Chickasaw	10	10	0
Douglas	60	22	38	Choctaw	11	11	0
Faribault	20	9	11	Claiborne	19	8	11
Fillmore	31	18	13	Clarke	22	9	13
Freeborn	40	20	20	Clay	19	9	10
Goodhue	99	39	60	Coahoma	47	16	31
Grant	10	5	5	Copiah	30	12	18
Hubbard	26	12	14	Covington	14	9	5
Itasca	61	61	0	Franklin	9	5	4
Jackson	18	7	11	George	23	23	0
Kanabec	24	11	13	Greene	9	5	4
Kandiyohi	105	32	73	Grenada	12	10	2
Kittson	10	5	5	Holmes	49	9	40
Koochiching	18	10	8	Humphreys	16	10	6
Lac Qui Parle	10	6	4	Issaquena	6	4	2
Lake	24	13	11	Itawamba	18	8	10
Lake of the Woods	9	5	4	Jasper	14	7	7
Le Sueur	27	14	13	Lauderdale	119	41	78
Lincoln	10	4	6	Lawrence	23	10	13
Lyon	34	13	21	Lee	106	36	70
Mahnomen	17	11	6	Leflore	58	23	35
Marshall	18	11	7	Lincoln	30	30	0
Martin	28	9	19	Lowndes	47	39	8
McLeod	50	20	30	Marion	16	16	0
Meeker	34	13	21	Marshall	37	17	20
Mille Lacs	55	20	35	Monroe	27	20	7
Morrison	37	15	22	Montgomery	6	5	1
Mower	46	19	27	Newton	13	8	5
Murray	10	5	5	Noxubee	8	4	4
Nicollet	21	10	11	Oktibbeha	29	26	3
Nobles	24	8	16	Panola	44	15	29
Norman	8	5	3	Perry	16	6	10
Otter Tail	69	27	42	Pike	52	24	28
Pennington	31	8	23	Pontotoc	22	13	9
Pine	48	25	23	Prentiss	32	16	16
Pipestone	20	10	10	Scott	48	12	36
Pope	14	6	8	Sharkey	17	7	10

Table 81

Full-time Law Enforcement Employees as of October 31, 2001
by Rural County by State—Continued

County by state	Total police employees	Total officers	Total civilians	County by state	Total police employees	Total officers	Total civilians
MISSISSIPPI—Continued				**MISSOURI—Continued**			
Simpson	18	18	0	McDonald	22	20	2
Smith	12	7	5	Mercer	7	3	4
Stone	16	15	1	Miller	44	17	27
Sunflower	27	7	20	Mississippi	48	14	34
Tate	30	15	15	Moniteau	10	8	2
Tippah	14	8	6	Monroe	13	8	5
Tunica	128	37	91	Montgomery	13	12	1
Union	41	31	10	Morgan	34	29	5
Walthall	23	11	12	New Madrid	27	20	7
Warren	40	34	6	Nodaway	20	9	11
Washington	51	26	25	Oregon	11	5	6
Wayne	18	9	9	Osage	11	6	5
Webster	9	5	4	Ozark	15	7	8
Winston	5	5	0	Pemiscot	33	20	13
Yalobusha	12	7	5	Perry	25	15	10
				Pettis	26	16	10
MISSOURI				Phelps	23	21	2
				Pike	25	11	14
Adair	21	10	11	Polk	28	19	9
Atchison	7	3	4	Pulaski	18	16	2
Audrain	31	18	13	Putnam	6	3	3
Barry	31	17	14	Ralls	7	6	1
Barton	16	7	9	Randolph	30	17	13
Bates	15	7	8	Reynolds	13	7	6
Benton	20	14	6	Ripley	9	7	2
Bollinger	13	8	5	Saline	29	17	12
Butler	46	29	17	Schuyler	8	3	5
Caldwell	10	5	5	Scotland	6	3	3
Callaway	22	21	1	Scott	29	22	7
Camden	94	46	48	Shannon	9	5	4
Cape Girardeau	58	37	21	Shelby	8	5	3
Carroll	14	6	8	St. Clair	56	13	43
Carter	9	6	3	Ste. Genevieve	49	35	14
Cedar	9	5	4	St. Francois	30	21	9
Chariton	14	11	3	Stoddard	17	8	9
Clark	18	9	9	Stone	42	33	9
Cole	42	30	12	Sullivan	11	5	6
Cooper	7	6	1	Taney	52	31	21
Crawford	26	18	8	Texas	11	6	5
Dade	10	5	5	Vernon	15	8	7
Dallas	18	13	5	Washington	31	15	16
Daviess	5	4	1	Wayne	14	10	4
De Kalb	10	5	5	Worth	3	2	1
Dent	12	9	3	Wright	12	7	5
Douglas	12	8	4				
Dunklin	24	8	16	**MONTANA**			
Gasconade	8	7	1				
Gentry	10	8	2	Beaverhead	15	7	8
Grundy	10	5	5	Big Horn	28	13	15
Harrison	6	5	1	Blaine	19	8	11
Henry	24	14	10	Broadwater	10	6	4
Hickory	13	9	4	Carbon	10	6	4
Holt	6	4	2	Carter	2	2	0
Howard	11	6	5	Chouteau	14	9	5
Howell	32	25	7	Custer	12	6	6
Iron	12	8	4	Daniels	7	3	4
Johnson	43	40	3	Dawson	58	6	52
Knox	5	2	3	Deer Lodge	25	18	7
Laclede	47	15	32	Fallon	8	2	6
Lawrence	26	20	6	Fergus	16	6	10
Lewis	12	4	8	Flathead	99	46	53
Linn	7	6	1	Gallatin	63	33	30
Livingston	18	10	8	Garfield	3	3	0
Macon	13	12	1	Glacier	15	9	6
Madison	10	7	3	Golden Valley	2	2	0
Maries	8	6	2	Granite	9	5	4
Marion	37	14	23	Hill	24	10	14

Table 81

Full-time Law Enforcement Employees as of October 31, 2001
by Rural County by State—Continued

County by state	Total police employees	Total officers	Total civilians	County by state	Total police employees	Total officers	Total civilians
MONTANA—Continued				**NEBRASKA—Continued**			
Jefferson	21	11	10	Garfield	2	2	0
Judith Basin	5	4	1	Gosper	5	4	1
Lake	39	17	22	Grant	2	2	0
Lewis and Clark	61	37	24	Greeley	4	3	1
Liberty	9	4	5	Hall	36	29	7
Lincoln	32	18	14	Hamilton	14	7	7
Madison	10	7	3	Harlan	7	4	3
McCone	11	5	6	Hitchcock	5	2	3
Meagher	7	3	4	Holt	11	5	6
Mineral	19	7	12	Hooker	1	1	0
Musselshell	11	7	4	Howard	12	5	7
Park	19	11	8	Jefferson	6	5	1
Petroleum	2	2	0	Johnson	7	3	4
Phillips	11	7	4	Kearney	11	7	4
Pondera	10	8	2	Keith	8	7	1
Powder River	7	3	4	Keya Paha	1	1	0
Powell	15	11	4	Kimball	10	3	7
Prairie	3	3	0	Knox	12	4	8
Ravalli	67	26	41	Lincoln	44	24	20
Richland	19	7	12	Logan	2	1	1
Roosevelt	15	9	6	Loup	1	1	0
Rosebud	35	15	20	Madison	42	22	20
Sanders	19	7	12	Merrick	9	5	4
Sheridan	10	5	5	Morrill	8	3	5
Silver Bow	77	43	34	Nance	11	7	4
Stillwater	11	7	4	Nemaha	7	4	3
Sweet Grass	13	7	6	Nuckolls	7	4	3
Teton	12	9	3	Otoe	19	10	9
Toole	19	12	7	Pawnee	4	3	1
Treasure	2	2	0	Perkins	8	4	4
Valley	16	5	11	Phelps	15	7	8
Wheatland	8	5	3	Pierce	8	4	4
Wibaux	2	2	0	Platte	31	15	16
				Polk	10	7	3
NEBRASKA				Red Willow	6	4	2
				Richardson	12	7	5
Adams	20	18	2	Rock	7	2	5
Antelope	11	6	5	Saline	16	12	4
Arthur	1	1	0	Saunders	18	11	7
Blaine	1	1	0	Scotts Bluff	21	15	6
Boone	11	5	6	Seward	18	10	8
Box Butte	7	6	1	Sheridan	5	4	1
Boyd	2	2	0	Sherman	6	5	1
Brown	11	6	5	Stanton	8	7	1
Buffalo	38	22	16	Thayer	10	6	4
Burt	11	6	5	Thomas	1	1	0
Butler	9	5	4	Thurston	9	5	4
Cedar	9	4	5	Valley	6	3	3
Chase	5	2	3	Wayne	5	4	1
Cherry	11	5	6	Webster	9	6	3
Cheyenne	8	7	1	Wheeler	2	2	0
Clay	5	4	1	York	20	8	12
Colfax	13	4	9				
Cuming	6	5	1	**NEVADA**			
Custer	7	6	1				
Dawes	8	3	5	Carson City	128	88	40
Dawson	31	20	11	Churchill	43	36	7
Deuel	4	3	1	Douglas	115	100	15
Dixon	11	7	4	Elko	62	51	11
Dodge	23	16	7	Esmeralda	15	11	4
Dundy	8	4	4	Eureka	18	9	9
Fillmore	10	4	6	Humboldt	38	16	22
Franklin	7	3	4	Lander	40	25	15
Frontier	8	5	3	Lincoln	16	15	1
Furnas	14	9	5	Lyon	93	66	27
Gage	13	11	2	Mineral	22	17	5
Garden	9	4	5	Pershing	20	14	6

Table 81

Full-time Law Enforcement Employees as of October 31, 2001
by Rural County by State—Continued

County by state	Total police employees	Total officers	Total civilians	County by state	Total police employees	Total officers	Total civilians
NEVADA—Continued				**NORTH CAROLINA—Continued**			
Storey	22	22	0	Duplin	81	51	30
White Pine	32	25	7	Gates	19	10	9
				Graham	10	9	1
NEW HAMPSHIRE				Granville	41	37	4
				Greene	34	23	11
Carroll	20	10	10	Halifax	75	50	25
Cheshire	25	9	16	Harnett	121	73	48
Merrimack	28	15	13	Haywood	69	47	22
				Henderson	149	117	32
NEW MEXICO				Hertford	55	16	39
				Hoke	49	32	17
Chaves	55	39	16	Hyde	14	9	5
Cibola	22	13	9	Iredell	154	112	42
Eddy	50	36	14	Jackson	37	36	1
Harding	3	2	1	Jones	14	9	5
Hidalgo	25	9	16	Lee	68	34	34
Lea	58	44	14	Lenoir	81	49	32
Luna	31	27	4	Macon	53	39	14
McKinley	42	30	12	Martin	32	28	4
Mora	7	5	2	McDowell	59	39	20
Quay	6	5	1	Mitchell	18	12	6
Rio Arriba	21	18	3	Montgomery	50	28	22
San Juan	105	83	22	Moore	99	59	40
San Miguel	12	9	3	Northampton	44	20	24
Sierra	15	13	2	Pamlico	26	13	13
Socorro	15	13	2	Pasquotank	40	34	6
				Pender	73	42	31
NEW YORK				Perquimans	9	8	1
				Person	77	40	37
Allegany	46	38	8	Polk	30	17	13
Cattaraugus	69	48	21	Richmond	69	44	25
Chenango	37	24	13	Robeson	209	97	112
Clinton	33	24	9	Rockingham	124	87	37
Columbia	52	42	10	Rutherford	99	64	35
Cortland	48	32	16	Sampson	76	49	27
Delaware	20	14	6	Scotland	63	32	31
Essex	35	33	2	Stanly	62	41	21
Fulton	52	35	17	Surry	90	52	38
Jefferson	64	36	28	Swain	26	13	13
Lewis	25	18	7	Transylvania	56	40	16
Otsego	20	17	3	Tyrrell	13	7	6
Schuyler	37	35	2	Vance	82	38	44
Seneca	43	27	16	Warren	29	22	7
St. Lawrence	40	36	4	Washington	33	16	17
Ulster	83	60	23	Watauga	46	26	20
Wyoming	43	32	11	Wilkes	100	63	37
Yates	41	24	17	Wilson	117	62	55
				Yancey	24	15	9
NORTH CAROLINA							
				NORTH DAKOTA			
Alleghany	25	10	15				
Anson	47	26	21	Adams	3	3	0
Ashe	31	16	15	Barnes	7	6	1
Avery	26	19	7	Benson	4	4	0
Beaufort	72	44	28	Billings	4	3	1
Bertie	23	15	8	Bottineau	14	10	4
Bladen	67	42	25	Bowman	2	2	0
Camden	11	10	1	Burke	4	4	0
Carteret	84	42	42	Cavalier	11	5	6
Caswell	44	25	19	Dickey	5	4	1
Cherokee	28	18	10	Divide	2	2	0
Chowan	37	16	21	Dunn	4	3	1
Clay	18	10	8	Eddy	5	5	0
Cleveland	119	79	40	Emmons	2	2	0
Columbus	89	55	34	Foster	3	2	1
Craven	112	58	54	Golden Valley	4	3	1
Dare	141	65	76	Grant	2	2	0

Table 81

Full-time Law Enforcement Employees as of October 31, 2001
by Rural County by State—Continued

County by state	Total police employees	Total officers	Total civilians	County by state	Total police employees	Total officers	Total civilians
NORTH DAKOTA—Continued				**OHIO—Continued**			
Griggs	4	4	0	Paulding	25	11	14
Kidder	2	1	1	Perry	14	11	3
Lamoure	5	4	1	Pike	20	18	2
Logan	2	2	0	Preble	76	26	50
McHenry	5	4	1	Putnam	35	27	8
McIntosh	3	3	0	Sandusky	69	52	17
McKenzie	8	5	3	Scioto	67	54	13
McLean	24	20	4	Seneca	65	20	45
Mercer	17	12	5	Shelby	70	33	37
Mountrail	9	5	4	Tuscarawas	36	28	8
Nelson	5	4	1	Union	61	39	22
Oliver	3	2	1	Van Wert	40	19	21
Pembina	19	13	6	Vinton	20	15	5
Pierce	7	3	4	Williams	24	20	4
Ramsey	6	5	1	Wyandot	22	11	11
Ransom	5	5	0				
Renville	5	5	0	**OKLAHOMA**			
Richland	22	12	10				
Rolette	12	9	3	Adair	15	9	6
Sargent	4	3	1	Alfalfa	9	4	5
Sheridan	2	2	0	Atoka	12	7	5
Sioux	1	1	0	Beaver	13	9	4
Slope	1	1	0	Beckham	15	7	8
Stark	12	9	3	Blaine	8	6	2
Steele	3	3	0	Bryan	26	11	15
Stutsman	10	8	2	Caddo	28	16	12
Towner	3	2	1	Carter	50	17	33
Traill	8	4	4	Cherokee	29	17	12
Walsh	18	12	6	Choctaw	14	6	8
Ward	42	21	21	Cimarron	7	4	3
Wells	4	3	1	Coal	8	5	3
Williams	27	21	6	Cotton	12	7	5
				Craig	18	9	9
OHIO				Custer	21	9	12
				Delaware	29	15	14
Adams	33	26	7	Dewey	11	4	7
Ashland	84	57	27	Ellis	9	4	5
Athens	30	25	5	Garvin	25	16	9
Champaign	35	25	10	Grady	39	16	23
Clinton	69	41	28	Grant	9	5	4
Coshocton	64	51	13	Greer	8	4	4
Darke	71	41	30	Harmon	3	3	0
Defiance	32	20	12	Harper	9	4	5
Erie	72	35	37	Haskell	14	8	6
Fayette	42	31	11	Hughes	12	6	6
Gallia	39	32	7	Jackson	18	9	9
Guernsey	48	21	27	Jefferson	12	6	6
Hancock	91	39	52	Johnston	12	6	6
Hardin	23	17	6	Kay	23	11	12
Harrison	21	16	5	Kingfisher	13	6	7
Henry	24	23	1	Kiowa	12	9	3
Highland	39	31	8	Latimer	18	12	6
Hocking	19	18	1	Le Flore	27	13	14
Holmes	47	44	3	Lincoln	22	11	11
Huron	76	26	50	Love	15	6	9
Jackson	20	16	4	Major	10	4	6
Knox	51	46	5	Marshall	13	5	8
Logan	91	35	56	Mayes	36	15	21
Marion	41	29	12	McCurtain	26	21	5
Meigs	20	16	4	McIntosh	19	11	8
Mercer	42	29	13	Murray	12	5	7
Monroe	28	23	5	Muskogee	68	18	50
Morgan	17	12	5	Noble	10	5	5
Morrow	63	36	27	Nowata	17	11	6
Muskingum	113	83	30	Okfuskee	14	7	7
Noble	30	8	22	Okmulgee	19	11	8
Ottawa	55	42	13	Ottawa	33	15	18

Table 81

Full-time Law Enforcement Employees as of October 31, 2001
by Rural County by State—Continued

County by state	Total police employees	Total officers	Total civilians
OKLAHOMA—Continued			
Pawnee	18	10	8
Payne	41	24	17
Pittsburg	27	20	7
Pontotoc	16	9	7
Pushmataha	16	8	8
Roger Mills	13	13	0
Seminole	28	20	8
Stephens	21	10	11
Texas	36	9	27
Tillman	11	6	5
Washington	36	19	17
Washita	13	7	6
Woods	5	5	0
Woodward	15	9	6
OREGON			
Baker	18	7	11
Benton	38	33	5
Clatsop	29	25	4
Coos	43	27	16
Crook	15	11	4
Curry	23	15	8
Deschutes	84	68	16
Douglas	113	73	40
Gilliam	5	4	1
Grant	6	5	1
Harney	5	5	0
Hood River	19	17	2
Jefferson	25	17	8
Josephine	74	40	34
Klamath	35	27	8
Lake	7	6	1
Lincoln	30	28	2
Linn	92	61	31
Malheur	24	14	10
Morrow	19	12	7
Sherman	5	4	1
Tillamook	24	22	2
Umatilla	28	15	13
Union	11	9	2
Wallowa	14	8	6
Wasco	19	17	2
Wheeler	3	3	0
PENNSYLVANIA			
Clearfield	12	10	2
Elk	6	5	1
Huntingdon	6	5	1
Jefferson	5	5	0
Warren	49	23	26
SOUTH CAROLINA			
Abbeville	44	27	17
Allendale	10	9	1
Bamberg	13	11	2
Barnwell	35	23	12
Beaufort	182	166	16
Calhoun	21	19	2
Chester	54	49	5
Chesterfield	50	32	18
Clarendon	32	26	6
Colleton	111	48	63
Darlington	54	49	5
Dillon	35	30	5

County by state	Total police employees	Total officers	Total civilians
SOUTH CAROLINA—Continued			
Fairfield	49	43	6
Georgetown	117	64	53
Greenwood	108	65	43
Hampton	33	28	5
Jasper	32	28	4
Kershaw	52	48	4
Lancaster	94	57	37
Laurens	94	53	41
Marion	33	30	3
Marlboro	57	20	37
McCormick	22	12	10
Newberry	41	37	4
Oconee	111	64	47
Orangeburg	113	85	28
Saluda	50	20	30
Union	46	29	17
Williamsburg	59	26	33
SOUTH DAKOTA			
Aurora	4	3	1
Beadle	22	6	16
Bennett	10	6	4
Bon Homme	9	4	5
Brookings	20	11	9
Brown	44	14	30
Brule	11	3	8
Buffalo	1	1	0
Butte	6	5	1
Campbell	2	2	0
Charles Mix	10	4	6
Clark	2	2	0
Clay	7	6	1
Codington	9	6	3
Corson	3	2	1
Custer	10	9	1
Davison	7	5	2
Day	6	3	3
Deuel	8	4	4
Dewey	3	2	1
Douglas	2	2	0
Edmunds	6	4	2
Fall River	13	4	9
Faulk	8	3	5
Grant	8	2	6
Gregory	3	2	1
Haakon	2	2	0
Hamlin	2	2	0
Hand	2	1	1
Hanson	1	1	0
Harding	2	1	1
Hughes	24	7	17
Hutchinson	3	3	0
Hyde	1	1	0
Jackson	1	1	0
Jerauld	1	1	0
Jones	2	2	0
Kingsbury	5	4	1
Lake	5	4	1
Lawrence	40	17	23
Lyman	4	3	1
Marshall	8	4	4
McCook	3	2	1
McPherson	1	1	0
Meade	46	15	31
Mellette	5	4	1
Miner	4	3	1

Table 81

Full-time Law Enforcement Employees as of October 31, 2001
by Rural County by State—Continued

County by state	Total police employees	Total officers	Total civilians	County by state	Total police employees	Total officers	Total civilians
SOUTH DAKOTA—Continued				**TENNESSEE—Continued**			
Moody	9	4	5	Obion	53	24	29
Perkins	3	2	1	Overton	59	20	39
Potter	6	2	4	Perry	17	11	6
Roberts	9	2	7	Pickett	12	12	0
Sanborn	3	2	1	Polk	34	17	17
Spink	14	9	5	Putnam	105	48	57
Stanley	6	5	1	Rhea	47	47	0
Sully	3	3	0	Roane	50	27	23
Todd	1	1	0	Scott	36	26	10
Tripp	3	2	1	Sequatchie	21	11	10
Turner	5	4	1	Smith	28	14	14
Union	18	6	12	Stewart	27	12	15
Walworth	10	2	8	Van Buren	12	7	5
Yankton	10	9	1	Warren	72	37	35
Ziebach	2	2	0	Wayne	21	10	11
				Weakley	38	18	20
TENNESSEE				White	48	22	26
Bedford	68	26	42	**TEXAS**			
Benton	37	15	22				
Bledsoe	15	10	5	Anderson	51	25	26
Bradley	81	74	7	Andrews	28	11	17
Campbell	55	39	16	Angelina	86	44	42
Cannon	34	14	20	Aransas	46	20	26
Carroll	29	15	14	Armstrong	8	4	4
Claiborne	44	34	10	Atascosa	73	30	43
Clay	18	11	7	Austin	40	19	21
Cocke	41	34	7	Bailey	10	4	6
Coffee	57	52	5	Bandera	37	21	16
Crockett	30	14	16	Baylor	14	3	11
Cumberland	81	36	45	Bee	34	17	17
Decatur	15	10	5	Blanco	16	9	7
DeKalb	34	14	20	Borden	3	2	1
Dyer	39	25	14	Bosque	24	10	14
Fentress	23	12	11	Brewster	18	7	11
Franklin	63	31	32	Briscoe	3	2	1
Giles	53	19	34	Brown	42	21	21
Grainger	24	15	9	Burleson	24	13	11
Greene	126	113	13	Burnet	62	36	26
Grundy	17	9	8	Calhoun	42	22	20
Hamblen	64	59	5	Callahan	13	7	6
Hancock	41	16	25	Camp	16	5	11
Hardeman	42	21	21	Carson	13	6	7
Hardin	19	15	4	Cass	33	12	21
Hartsville-Trousdale	33	18	15	Castro	21	8	13
Haywood	37	16	21	Cherokee	53	25	28
Henderson	26	22	4	Childress	16	5	11
Henry	70	33	37	Clay	15	10	5
Hickman	26	18	8	Cochran	13	8	5
Houston	14	8	6	Coke	6	5	1
Humphreys	23	12	11	Coleman	10	5	5
Jackson	25	12	13	Collingsworth	7	5	2
Jefferson	46	27	19	Colorado	36	17	19
Johnson	31	16	15	Comanche	35	9	26
Lake	17	7	10	Concho	9	4	5
Lauderdale	57	25	32	Cooke	47	20	27
Lawrence	48	34	14	Cottle	2	2	0
Lewis	27	10	17	Crane	9	9	0
Macon	37	21	16	Crockett	18	12	6
Marshall	42	20	22	Crosby	19	10	9
Maury	107	60	47	Culberson	13	8	5
McMinn	63	37	26	Dallam	4	4	0
McNairy	25	12	13	Dawson	15	6	9
Meigs	20	10	10	Delta	16	8	8
Monroe	45	42	3	Dewitt	20	10	10
Moore	21	11	10	Dickens	6	2	4
Morgan	31	14	17	Dimmit	19	10	9

Table 81

Full-time Law Enforcement Employees as of October 31, 2001
by Rural County by State—Continued

County by state	Total police employees	Total officers	Total civilians	County by state	Total police employees	Total officers	Total civilians
TEXAS—Continued				**TEXAS—Continued**			
Donley	8	5	3	Madison	23	9	14
Duval	26	14	12	Marion	13	12	1
Eastland	8	7	1	Martin	8	3	5
Edwards	10	4	6	Mason	10	5	5
Erath	44	23	21	Matagorda	72	45	27
Falls	12	7	5	McCulloch	13	6	7
Fannin	35	14	21	McMullen	2	2	0
Fayette	32	16	16	Medina	55	21	34
Fisher	9	5	4	Menard	9	5	4
Floyd	12	4	8	Milam	27	13	14
Foard	3	2	1	Mitchell	9	4	5
Franklin	19	10	9	Montague	20	8	12
Freestone	25	14	11	Moore	36	12	24
Frio	19	10	9	Morris	20	8	12
Gaines	19	9	10	Motley	2	2	0
Garza	13	8	5	Nacogdoches	90	40	50
Gillespie	30	15	15	Navarro	101	59	42
Glasscock	3	3	0	Newton	19	11	8
Goliad	25	12	13	Nolan	24	11	13
Gonzales	36	27	9	Ochiltree	18	8	10
Gray	38	14	24	Oldham	10	5	5
Grimes	42	25	17	Palo Pinto	46	19	27
Hall	8	2	6	Panola	35	20	15
Hamilton	21	9	12	Parmer	13	5	8
Hansford	9	4	5	Pecos	23	16	7
Hardeman	10	5	5	Polk	68	40	28
Hartley	4	4	0	Presidio	23	5	18
Haskell	9	9	0	Rains	19	8	11
Hemphill	14	8	6	Reagan	16	6	10
Hill	41	24	17	Real	7	3	4
Hockley	20	9	11	Red River	25	11	14
Hopkins	49	23	26	Reeves	473	13	460
Houston	27	12	15	Refugio	33	12	21
Howard	30	14	16	Roberts	5	4	1
Hudspeth	36	10	26	Robertson	20	9	11
Hutchinson	30	15	15	Runnels	26	7	19
Irion	8	4	4	Rusk	55	31	24
Jack	15	11	4	Sabine	17	8	9
Jackson	26	10	16	San Jacinto	24	14	10
Jasper	34	17	17	San Saba	9	4	5
Jeff Davis	4	3	1	Schleicher	10	5	5
Jim Hogg	38	21	17	Scurry	19	11	8
Jim Wells	57	38	19	Shackelford	13	4	9
Jones	15	6	9	Shelby	31	15	16
Karnes	19	9	10	Sherman	8	4	4
Kendall	46	33	13	Somervell	34	17	17
Kenedy	11	10	1	Starr	95	30	65
Kent	4	2	2	Stephens	10	5	5
Kerr	77	36	41	Sterling	3	3	0
Kimble	17	12	5	Stonewall	7	3	4
King	2	2	0	Sutton	14	5	9
Kinney	18	8	10	Swisher	11	10	1
Kleberg	61	26	35	Terrell	5	3	2
Knox	7	3	4	Terry	40	7	33
Lamar	69	22	47	Throckmorton	6	2	4
Lamb	23	10	13	Titus	53	21	32
Lampasas	33	21	12	Tyler	27	20	7
La Salle	18	13	5	Upton	15	8	7
Lavaca	22	11	11	Uvalde	32	19	13
Lee	16	10	6	Val Verde	40	26	14
Leon	28	12	16	Van Zandt	59	21	38
Limestone	52	19	33	Walker	61	30	31
Lipscomb	9	5	4	Ward	31	12	19
Live Oak	25	15	10	Washington	48	30	18
Llano	38	19	19	Wharton	63	37	26
Loving	4	2	2	Wheeler	10	6	4
Lynn	15	6	9	Wilbarger	17	7	10

Table 81

Full-time Law Enforcement Employees as of October 31, 2001
by Rural County by State—Continued

County by state	Total police employees	Total officers	Total civilians	County by state	Total police employees	Total officers	Total civilians
TEXAS—Continued				**VIRGINIA—Continued**			
Willacy	35	18	17	Greensville	27	21	6
Winkler	29	11	18	Halifax	48	36	12
Wise	80	38	42	Henry	119	105	14
Wood	58	27	31	Highland	12	7	5
Yoakum	20	10	10	King and Queen	13	8	5
Young	28	12	16	King William	24	15	9
Zapata	95	33	62	Lancaster	30	25	5
				Lee	45	45	0
UTAH				Louisa	42	30	12
				Lunenburg	19	13	6
Beaver	42	13	29	Madison	19	12	7
Box Elder	74	27	47	Mecklenburg	82	80	2
Cache	85	75	10	Middlesex	17	12	5
Carbon	38	16	22	Montgomery	110	93	17
Daggett	23	6	17	Nelson	21	15	6
Duchesne	41	14	27	Northampton	47	36	11
Emery	33	25	8	Northumberland	25	17	8
Garfield	26	7	19	Nottoway	20	13	7
Grand	28	20	8	Orange	35	27	8
Iron	67	59	8	Page	60	41	19
Juab	19	8	11	Patrick	41	28	13
Millard	42	28	14	Prince Edward	25	25	0
Morgan	11	10	1	Pulaski	49	39	10
Piute	3	3	0	Rappahannock	21	21	0
Rich	9	3	6	Richmond	16	10	6
San Juan	33	28	5	Rockbridge	30	23	7
Sanpete	24	19	5	Rockingham	156	52	104
Sevier	56	43	13	Russell	53	46	7
Summit	66	54	12	Shenandoah	62	55	7
Tooele	60	45	15	Smyth	48	48	0
Uintah	47	37	10	Southampton	75	62	13
Wasatch	35	31	4	Surry	18	13	5
Washington	137	54	83	Sussex	41	37	4
Wayne	6	5	1	Tazewell	82	72	10
				Westmoreland	30	20	10
VERMONT				Wise	81	69	12
				Wythe	33	26	7
Bennington	17	15	2				
Lamoille	14	7	7	**WASHINGTON**			
Orleans	9	6	3				
Rutland	18	14	4	Adams	33	18	15
Washington	13	11	2	Asotin	16	14	2
				Chelan	67	49	18
VIRGINIA				Clallam	46	36	10
				Columbia	15	9	6
Accomack	62	58	4	Cowlitz	53	44	9
Alleghany	53	42	11	Douglas	42	28	14
Amelia	18	11	7	Ferry	24	9	15
Appomattox	33	30	3	Garfield	11	7	4
Augusta	119	101	18	Grant	58	43	15
Bath	17	17	0	Grays Harbor	79	39	40
Bland	16	8	8	Jefferson	31	24	7
Brunswick	41	18	23	Kittitas	49	26	23
Buchanan	48	43	5	Klickitat	45	15	30
Buckingham	20	15	5	Lewis	56	39	17
Caroline	40	32	8	Lincoln	23	13	10
Carroll	32	26	6	Mason	73	40	33
Charlotte	29	27	2	Okanogan	42	35	7
Craig	13	8	5	Pacific	18	15	3
Cumberland	16	11	5	Pend Oreille	31	13	18
Dickenson	40	37	3	San Juan	27	17	10
Essex	18	18	0	Skagit	102	52	50
Floyd	27	17	10	Skamania	33	19	14
Franklin	87	72	15	Stevens	35	29	6
Frederick	95	81	14	Wahkiakum	8	7	1
Giles	30	20	10	Walla Walla	25	22	3
Grayson	26	20	6	Whitman	34	17	17

Table 81

Full-time Law Enforcement Employees as of October 31, 2001
by Rural County by State—Continued

County by state	Total police employees	Total officers	Total civilians
WEST VIRGINIA			
Barbour	7	3	4
Barbour-Philippi State Police	6	5	1
Boone	26	24	2
Boone State Police:			
Danville	7	6	1
Whitesville	4	3	1
Braxton	10	8	2
Braxton-Sutton State Police	8	7	1
Calhoun	5	3	2
Calhoun-Grantsville State Police	4	3	1
Clay	7	6	1
Clay-Clay State Police	6	5	1
Doddridge	2	2	0
Doddridge-West Union State Police	5	4	1
Fayette	34	30	4
Fayette State Police:			
Gauley Bridge	4	3	1
Oak Hill	9	8	1
Parkway Authority	4	4	0
Gilmer	3	3	0
Gilmer-Glenville State Police	8	7	1
Grant	6	6	0
Grant-Petersburg State Police	1	1	0
Greenbrier	20	19	1
Greenbrier State Police:			
Lewisburg	12	11	1
Rainelle	6	5	1
Hampshire	9	7	2
Hampshire-Romney State Police	19	7	12
Hardy	11	6	5
Hardy-Moorefield State Police	6	5	1
Harrison	38	36	2
Harrison-Bridgeport State Police	16	15	1
Jackson	21	14	7
Jackson-Ripley State Police	5	4	1
Lewis	12	11	1
Lewis-Weston State Police	7	6	1
Lincoln	8	8	0
Lincoln-Hamlin State Police	11	10	1
Logan	20	14	6
Logan-Logan State Police	20	13	7
Marion	38	25	13
Marion-Fairmont State Police	7	6	1
Mason	27	16	11
Mason-Point Pleasant State Police	5	4	1
McDowell	16	15	1
McDowell-Welch State Police	8	7	1
Mercer	29	22	7
Mercer State Police:			
Parkway Authority	3	3	0
Princeton	15	12	3
Mingo	21	18	3
Mingo State Police:			
Gilbert	5	4	1
Williamson	6	5	1
Monongalia	52	29	23
Monongalia-Morgantown State Police	22	13	9
Monroe	8	8	0
Monroe-Union State Police	5	4	1
Morgan	9	8	1
Morgan-Berkeley Springs State Police	5	4	1
Nicholas	24	19	5
Nicholas State Police:			
Richwood	4	3	1
Summersville	5	4	1
Pendleton	3	2	1
Pendleton-Franklin State Police	5	4	1
WEST VIRGINIA—Continued			
Pleasants	6	5	1
Pleasants-St. Marys State Police	4	3	1
Pocahontas	17	7	10
Pocahontas-Buckeye State Police	7	6	1
Preston	28	13	15
Preston-Kingwood State Police	7	6	1
Raleigh	51	42	9
Raleigh State Police:			
Beckley	26	17	9
Parkway Authority	5	4	1
Randolph	7	7	0
Randolph-Elkins State Police	20	12	8
Ritchie	7	6	1
Ritchie-Harrisville State Police	6	5	1
Roane	8	7	1
Roane-Spencer State Police	7	6	1
Summers	4	3	1
Summers-Hinton State Police	5	4	1
Taylor	14	5	9
Taylor-Grafton State Police	5	4	1
Tucker	10	4	6
Tucker-Parsons State Police	5	4	1
Tyler	9	4	5
Tyler-Paden City State Police	5	4	1
Upshur	8	8	0
Upshur-Buckhannon State Police	8	7	1
Webster	3	3	0
Webster-Upperglade State Police	5	4	1
Wetzel	12	8	4
Wetzel-Hundred State Police	4	3	1
Wirt	2	2	0
Wirt-Elizabeth State Police	4	3	1
Wyoming	21	17	4
Wyoming-Jesse State Police	5	4	1
WISCONSIN			
Adams	52	52	0
Ashland	25	25	0
Bayfield	34	21	13
Buffalo	21	10	11
Burnett	30	15	15
Clark	52	47	5
Columbia	73	38	35
Crawford	27	26	1
Dodge	136	47	89
Door	47	43	4
Dunn	50	23	27
Fond du Lac	112	57	55
Forest	33	33	0
Grant	45	24	21
Green	53	42	11
Green Lake	53	42	11
Iowa	33	20	13
Iron	16	16	0
Jefferson	122	97	25
Juneau	43	31	12
Kewaunee	40	38	2
Lafayette	24	15	9
Langlade	40	16	24
Lincoln	51	27	24
Manitowoc	102	62	40
Marinette	49	31	18
Marquette	35	33	2
Menominee	11	10	1
Monroe	52	48	4
Oconto	51	23	28

Table 81

Full-time Law Enforcement Employees as of October 31, 2001
by Rural County by State—Continued

County by state	Total police employees	Total officers	Total civilians	County by state	Total police employees	Total officers	Total civilians
WISCONSIN—Continued				**WYOMING—Continued**			
Oneida	78	37	41	Carbon	35	15	20
Pepin	16	7	9	Converse	17	9	8
Polk	56	24	32	Crook	18	5	13
Portage	88	45	43	Fremont	91	29	62
Price	30	20	10	Goshen	30	9	21
Richland	25	24	1	Hot Springs	6	4	2
Rusk	37	35	2	Johnson	14	13	1
Sauk	101	76	25	Lincoln	35	16	19
Sawyer	36	30	6	Niobrara	15	4	11
Shawano	59	40	19	Park	41	18	23
Taylor	34	17	17	Platte	9	8	1
Trempealeau	47	24	23	Sheridan	20	15	5
Vernon	26	26	0	Sublette	34	19	15
Vilas	70	35	35	Sweetwater	52	32	20
Walworth	211	82	129	Teton	36	18	18
Washburn	29	13	16	Uinta	37	24	13
Waushara	61	25	36	Washakie	9	7	2
Wood	75	45	30	Weston	9	7	2
WYOMING				**OTHER AGENCIES**			
Albany	28	22	6	American Samoa	258	204	54
Big Horn	14	8	6	Puerto Rico	20,779	18,744	2,035
Campbell	55	37	18	National Institutes of Health	52	47	5

Table 82

Full-time Law Enforcement Employees as of October 31, 2001
by Other Agencies by State

Other agency by state	Total police employees	Total officers	Total civilians
ALABAMA			
Huntsville International Airport	22	18	4
ALASKA			
Anchorage International Airport	60	56	4
Fairbanks International Airport	26	25	1
CALIFORNIA			
East Bay Regional Parks, Alameda County	78	55	23
Fontana Unified School District	20	14	6
Grant Joint Union High School	21	16	5
Monterey Peninsula Airport	5	5	0
San Bernardino Unified School District	77	26	51
San Diego Unified Port District	140	119	21
San Francisco Bay Area Rapid Transit, Contra Costa County	264	185	79
Stockton Unified School District	21	16	5
DISTRICT OF COLUMBIA			
Metro Transit Police	428	331	97
National Zoological Park	27	27	0
FLORIDA			
Daytona Beach International Airport	8	7	1
Florida School for the Deaf and Blind	13	8	5
Lee County Port Authority	45	33	12
Jacksonville Airport Authority	34	33	1
Melbourne International Airport	11	10	1
Miccosukee Tribal	46	33	13
Palm Beach County School District	178	118	60
Pinellas County Schools	28	18	10
Sarasota-Bradenton International Airport	12	12	0
Seminole Tribal	79	58	21
St. Petersburg-Clearwater International Airport	8	8	0
Tampa International Airport	107	48	59
Volusia County Beach Management	71	60	11
GEORGIA			
Augusta Board of Education	37	35	2
Bibb County Board of Education	25	19	6
Chatham-Savannah Narcotics Team	40	36	4
Cherokee County Board of Education	13	11	2
Clayton County Narcotics Unit	25	22	3
Cobb County Board of Education	33	29	4
Cobb County Park Rangers	564	508	56
Metropolitian Atlanta Rapid Transit Authority	325	283	42
Mitchell County Drug Unit	9	8	1
Pickens County Board of Education	3	3	0
Washington County Board of Education	4	4	0
ILLINOIS			
Cook County Forest Preserve	133	124	9
Du Page County Forest Preserve	29	25	4
Lake County Forest Preserve	9	9	0
Springfield Park District	8	8	0
Will County Forest Preserve	11	10	1
INDIANA			
St. Joseph County Airport Authority	16	16	0
KANSAS			
Johnson County Park	16	15	1
Metropolitian Topeka Airport Authority	25	19	6
Shawnee Mission Public Schools	10	10	0
KENTUCKY			
Buffalo-Trace Gateway Narcotics Task Force	4	4	0
Cincinnati-Northern Kentucky International Airport	53	38	15
Fayette County Schools	30	26	4
FIVCO Area Drug Task Force	8	7	1
Jefferson County Board of Education	23	17	6
Land Between the Lakes	8	8	0
Lexington Bluegrass Airport	29	20	9
Northern Kentucky Narcotics Enforcement	10	8	2
Pennyrile Narcotics Task Force	9	9	0
LOUISIANA			
Tensas Basin Levee	3	2	1
MAINE			
Passamquoddy Indian Township	10	6	4
Passamquoddy Pleasant Point	11	7	4
Penobscot Indian Island	10	6	4
MICHIGAN			
Bishop International Airport	7	7	0
Hudson Mills Metro Park	7	7	0
Kensington Metro Park	8	7	1
Lower Huron Metro Park	7	7	0
Metro Beach Metro Park	6	6	0
Stoney Creek Metro Park	7	7	0
Wayne County Airport	177	169	8
MINNESOTA			
Hennepin County Park Reserve	27	19	8
Minneapolis-St. Paul International Airport	92	64	28
MISSOURI			
Lambert-St. Louis International Airport	114	83	31
NEVADA			
Clark County School District	146	131	15
Washoe County School District	33	31	2
NEW JERSEY			
Park Police:			
Camden County	42	40	2
Morris County	31	30	1
Union County	371	322	49
Prosecutor:			
Atlantic County	169	76	93
Bergen County	268	180	88
Burlington County	135	49	86
Camden County	270	172	98
Cape May County	54	20	34
Cumberland County	60	19	41
Essex County	436	302	134
Gloucester County	92	49	43

Table 82

Full-time Law Enforcement Employees as of October 31, 2001

by Other Agencies by State—Continued

Other agency by state	Total police employees	Total officers	Total civilians	Other agency by state	Total police employees	Total officers	Total civilians
NEW JERSEY—Continued				**SOUTH CAROLINA —Continued**			
Hudson County	286	99	187	Columbia Metropolitian Airport	13	13	0
Hunterdon County	47	19	28	Greenville-Spartanburg International			
Mercer County	147	95	52	Airport	14	13	1
Middlesex County	212	133	79	Whitten Center	3	3	0
Monmouth County	264	77	187				
Morris County	150	99	51	**TENNESSEE**			
Ocean County	140	66	74				
Passaic County	199	83	116	Chattanooga Metropolitian Airport	16	16	0
Salem County	43	15	28	Knoxville Metropolitian Airport	31	21	10
Somerset County	115	73	42	Memphis International Airport	56	43	13
Sussex County	51	32	19	Nashville International Airport	77	64	13
Union County	223	123	100	Tri-Cities Regional Airport	19	17	2
Warren County	59	35	24				
				TEXAS			
NEW MEXICO							
				Amarillo International Airport	20	15	5
Zuni Tribal	39	22	17	Cameron County Park Rangers	10	10	0
				Dallas-Fort Worth International			
NEW YORK				Airport	343	307	36
				Hospital District:			
Norfolk Southern Railway,				Dallas County	88	54	34
Erie County	4	4	0	Tarrant County	50	31	19
Onondaga County Parks	2	2	0	Houston Metropolitan Transit			
Staten Island Rapid Transit	27	26	1	Authority	222	152	70
Suffolk County Parks	32	27	5	Independent School District:			
				Aldine	38	30	8
NORTH CAROLINA				Alvin	14	13	1
				Angleton	6	4	2
Asheville Regional Airport	15	15	0	Austin	89	50	39
Caswell Center Hospital	3	2	1	Bay City	6	6	0
Cherokee Tribal	45	26	19	Brownsville	84	13	71
Piedmont Triad International Airport	23	13	10	Conroe	75	53	22
Raleigh-Durham International Airport	29	27	2	Corpus Christi	42	27	15
Wilmington International Airport	14	10	4	East Central	11	10	1
				Ector County	24	23	1
OHIO				El Paso	37	30	7
				Fort Bend	43	37	6
Cleveland Metropolitian Park District	78	67	11	Hempstead	1	1	0
Hamilton County Park District	35	31	4	Judson	10	8	2
Port Columbus International Airport	50	30	20	Katy	31	23	8
Robinson Memorial Hospital	13	12	1	Killeen	12	12	0
				Klein	33	22	11
OKLAHOMA				Midland	23	8	15
				North East	39	33	6
Putnam City Campus	27	22	5	Pasadena	30	22	8
				Raymondville	4	4	0
OREGON				Spring	27	26	1
				Spring Branch	36	27	9
Port of Portland	44	33	11	Taft	2	2	0
PENNSYLVANIA				**UTAH**			
Allegheny County Port Authority	59	57	2	Granite School District	25	17	8
Altoona Hospital	13	13	0				
County Detective:				**VIRGINIA**			
Butler County	4	4	0				
Cumberland County	9	7	2	Chesapeake Bay Bridge-Tunnel	87	43	44
Dauphin County	15	12	3				
Lebanon County	6	6	0	**WASHINGTON**			
Lehigh County	8	8	0				
Westmoreland County	59	15	44	Colville Tribal	34	25	9
York County	21	20	1	Lummi Tribal	18	16	2
Delaware County Criminal				Nisqually Tribal	17	11	6
Investigation Division	37	32	5	Port of Seattle	120	93	27
Harrisburg International Airport	14	12	2	Skokomish Tribal	6	5	1
				Swinomish Tribal	12	8	4
RHODE ISLAND							
				WISCONSIN			
Narragansett Tribal	8	7	1				
				Menominee Tribal	57	30	27
SOUTH CAROLINA				Oneida Tribal	30	23	7
Charleston International Airport	26	17	9				

SECTION VII

APPENDIX I – Methodology

Uniform Crime Reporting (UCR) Program contributors forward crime data to the FBI either directly from local law enforcement agencies or through state UCR Programs in 46 states and the District of Columbia. The FBI provides continuing guidance and support to individual contributing agencies in those states that do not have a state Program.

State UCR Programs are very effective liaisons between local contributors and the FBI. Many of the Programs have mandatory reporting requirements and collect data beyond the national UCR scope to address crime problems germane to their particular locales. In most cases, these state agencies are also able to provide more direct and frequent service to participating law enforcement agencies, to make information more readily available for use at the state level, and to contribute to more streamlined operations at the national level.

With the implementation of state crime reporting Programs, the national UCR Program ceased direct collection of data from individual law enforcement agencies within those states. Currently, the state data collection agency forwards information it receives from local agencies to the national Program.

The criteria established for state Programs ensure consistency and comparability in the data submitted to the national Program, as well as regular and timely reporting. These criteria are: (1) The state Program must conform to national UCR Program standards, definitions, and information requirements. The states are not, of course, prohibited from collecting other statistical data beyond the national requirements. (2) The state criminal justice agency must have a proven, effective, statewide Program and demonstrate acceptable quality control procedures. (3) Coverage within the state by a state agency must be, at least, equal to that attained by the national UCR Program. (4) The state agency must have adequate field staff assigned to conduct audits and to assist contributing agencies in recordkeeping practices and crime-reporting procedures. (5) The state agency must furnish the FBI with all of the detailed data regularly collected by the FBI in

the form of duplicate returns, computer printouts, and/or magnetic tapes. (6) The state agency must have the proven capability (tested over a period of time) to supply all the statistical data required in time to meet deadlines established for publication of the national Uniform Crime Reports.

To fulfill its responsibilities in connection with the UCR Program, the FBI continues to edit and review individual agency reports for both completeness and quality. National UCR Program staff have direct contact with individual contributors within the state as necessary in connection with crime reporting matters, coordinating such contact with the state agency. On request, staff members conduct training programs within the state on law enforcement recordkeeping and crime reporting procedures. Should circumstances develop whereby the state agency does not comply with the aforementioned requirements, the national Program may reinstitute a direct collection of Uniform Crime Reports from law enforcement agencies within the state.

Reporting Procedures

Based on records of all reports of crime received from victims, officers who discover infractions, or other sources, law enforcement agencies across the country tabulate the number of Crime Index (Part I) offenses brought to their attention each month. Specifically, the Index crimes reported to the FBI are murder and nonnegligent manslaughter, forcible rape, robbery, aggravated assault, burglary, larceny-theft, motor vehicle theft, and arson.

Whenever complaints of crime are determined through investigation to be unfounded or false, they are eliminated from an agency's count. Agencies report to the FBI the number of actual offenses known regardless of whether anyone is arrested for the crime, stolen property is recovered, or prosecution is undertaken.

Another integral part of the monthly submission is the total number of actual Crime Index offenses cleared. Crimes are cleared in one of two ways: (1) by arrest of at least one person, who is charged and turned over to the court for prosecution, or (2) by exceptional means when some element beyond law enforcement control precludes the arrest of a known offender. Law enforcement agencies also report the number of Index crime clearances that involve only offenders under the age of 18, the value of property stolen and recovered in connection with the offenses, and detailed information pertaining to criminal homicide and arson.

In addition to its primary collection of Crime Index (Part I) offenses, the UCR Program solicits monthly data on persons arrested for all crimes except traffic violations. The age, sex, and race of arrestees are reported by crime category, both Part I and Part II. Part II offenses include all crimes not classified as Part I.

Monthly data are also collected on law enforcement officers killed or assaulted. The number of full-time sworn and civilian personnel are reported as of October 31 of each year.

At the end of each quarter, summary information is collected on hate crimes, i.e., specific offenses that were motivated by an offender's bias against the race, religion, ethnic origin, sexual orientation, or physical or mental disability of the victim. Hate crime data from those agencies participating in the National Incident-Based Reporting System (NIBRS) are submitted monthly.

Editing Procedures

Each report submitted to the UCR Program is thoroughly examined for arithmetical accuracy and for deviations which may indicate errors. To identify any unusual fluctuations in an agency's crime count, UCR staff compare monthly reports with previous submissions of the agency and with those for similar agencies. Large variations in crime levels may indicate modified records procedures, incomplete reporting, or changes in the jurisdiction's geopolitical structure.

Data reliability is a high priority of the Program, and noted deviations or arithmetical adjustments are brought to the attention of the state UCR Program or the submitting agency. A standard procedure of the FBI is to study the

monthly reports and to evaluate periodic trends prepared for individual reporting units. Any significant increase or decrease becomes the subject of a special inquiry. Changes in crime reporting procedures or annexations can influence the level of reported crime. When this occurs, the figures for specific crime categories or totals, if necessary, are excluded from trend tabulations.

To assist contributors in complying with UCR standards, the national Program provides training seminars and instructional materials on crime reporting procedures. Throughout the country, the national UCR Program maintains liaison with state Programs and law enforcement personnel and holds training sessions to explain the purpose of the Program, the rules of uniform classification and scoring, and the methods of assembling the information for reporting. When an individual agency has specific problems in compiling its crime statistics and its remedial efforts are unsuccessful, personnel from the FBI's Criminal Justice Information Services Division may visit the contributor to aid in resolving the difficulties.

The *Uniform Crime Reporting Handbook,* which details procedures for classifying and scoring offenses, is supplied to all contributors as the basic resource document for preparing reports. Because a good records system is essential for accurate crime reporting, the FBI also furnishes the *Manual of Law Enforcement Records.*

To enhance communication among Program participants, letters to UCR contributors and UCR *State Program Bulletins* are produced as needed. These provide policy updates and new information, as well as clarification of reporting issues.

The final responsibility for data submissions rests with the individual contributing law enforcement agency. Although the Program makes every effort through its editing procedures, training practices, and correspondence to assure the validity of the data it receives, the accuracy of the statistics depends primarily on the adherence of each contributor to the established standards of reporting. Deviations from these established standards, which cannot be resolved by the national UCR Program, may be brought to the attention of the Criminal Justice

Information Systems Committees of the International Association of Chiefs of Police and the National Sheriffs' Association.

Arrest Data

Florida state arrest data are not included in Tables 30–68. Limited arrest data were received from Illinois, Kansas, Kentucky, Montana, South Carolina, South Dakota, and Wisconsin. No 2001 arrest data were received from the District of Columbia. Complete 12-month arrest figures for New York City were not available for inclusion in this book. Arrest totals for these areas, however, were estimated for inclusion in Table 29, "Estimated Arrests, United States, 2001."

Population

Prior to preparation of 2001 Uniform Crime Reporting (UCR) Program population estimates, 2000 Bureau of the Census (BOC) decennial data were incorporated into the UCR master file and adjustments for over or under estimation of 2000 UCR population estimates were performed. In this edition, the state and national population figures are BOC 2001 state and national provisional estimates. Population figures for individual jurisdictions were updated by applying 2001 state growth rates to 2000 BOC city/county decennial data to obtain 2001 city/county population estimates. The state growth rates were calculated using 2000 resident population counts and 2001 BOC state provisional estimates. The estimate of the U.S. population showed a 1.2-percent increase from 2000 to 2001.

NIBRS Conversion

Several states provide their UCR data in the expanded NIBRS format. For presentation in this book, NIBRS data were converted to the historical summary UCR formats. The NIBRS database was constructed to allow for such conversion so that UCR's long-running time series could continue.

Crime Trends

By showing fluctuations from year to year, trend statistics offer the data user an added perspective from which to study crime. Percent change tabulations in this publication are computed only for reporting units which have provided comparable data for the periods under consideration. Exclusions from trend computations are made when figures from a reporting agency are not received for comparable timeframes or when it is ascertained that unusual fluctuations are due to such variables as improved records procedures, annexations, etc.

Care should be exercised in making any direct comparison between data in this publication and those in prior issues of *Crime in the United States*. For example, upon receiving 1995 aggravated assault figures for the state of Kentucky, it was determined the 1994 aggravated assault figures previously submitted were not valid; therefore, the Kentucky aggravated assault figures were not included in Tables 12 through 15 of the 1995 edition. The 1994 estimates in certain offense categories were updated for Delaware, Kansas, and Kentucky. In addition, Montana figures for 1995 were updated to show the actual offense data which were received after publication of *Crime in the United States, 1995*. These updates appear in the national trends.

Offense Estimation

Tables 1 through 5 and 7 of this publication contain statistics for the entire United States. Because not all law enforcement agencies provide data for complete reporting periods, estimated crime counts are included in these presentations. Offense estimation occurs within each of three areas: Metropolitan Statistical Areas (MSAs), cities outside MSAs, and rural counties. Using the known crime experiences of similar areas within a state, the estimates are computed by assigning the same proportional crime volumes to nonreporting agencies. The size of agency; type of jurisdiction, e.g., police department versus sheriff's office; and geographic location are considered in the estimation process.

Due to the efforts to convert to NIBRS in recent years, it has become necessary to estimate totals for some states. The inability of some state UCR Programs to provide forcible rape figures in accordance with UCR guidelines and other problems at the state level have also required unique estimation procedures. A summary of state-specific and offense-specific estimation procedures follows.

Year	State(s)	Reason for Estimation	Estimation Method
1985	Illinois	The state UCR Program was unable to provide forcible rape figures in accordance with UCR guidelines.	The rape totals were estimated using national rates per 100,000 inhabitants within the eight population groups and assigning the forcible rape volumes proportionally to the state.
1986	Illinois	The state UCR Program was unable to provide forcible rape figures in accordance with UCR guidelines.	The rape totals were estimated using national rates per 100,000 inhabitants within the eight population groups and assigning the forcible rape volumes proportionally to the state.
1987	Illinois	The state UCR Program was unable to provide forcible rape figures in accordance with UCR guidelines.	The rape totals were estimated using national rates per 100,000 inhabitants within the eight population groups and assigning the forcible rape volumes proportionally to the state.
1988	Illinois	The state UCR Program was unable to provide forcible rape figures in accordance with UCR guidelines.	The rape totals were estimated using national rates per 100,000 inhabitants within the eight population groups and assigning the forcible rape volumes proportionally to the state.
	Florida, Kentucky	Reporting problems at the state level resulted in no usable data.	State totals were estimated by updating previous valid annual totals for individual jurisdictions, subdivided by population group. Percent changes for each offense within each population group of the geographic divisions in which the states reside were applied to the previous valid annual totals. The state totals were compiled from the sums of the population group estimates.
1989	Illinois	The state UCR Program was unable to provide forcible rape figures in accordance with UCR guidelines.	The rape totals were estimated using national rates per 100,000 inhabitants within the eight population groups and assigning the forcible rape volumes proportionally to the state.
1990	Illinois	The state UCR Program was unable to provide forcible rape figures in accordance with UCR guidelines.	The rape totals were estimated using national rates per 100,000 inhabitants within the eight population groups and assigning the forcible rape volumes proportionally to the state.
1991	Illinois	The state UCR Program was unable to provide forcible rape figures in accordance with UCR guidelines.	The rape totals were estimated using national rates per 100,000 inhabitants within the eight population groups and assigning the forcible rape volumes proportionally to the state.
	Iowa	NIBRS conversion efforts resulted in estimation for Iowa.	State totals were estimated by updating previous valid annual totals for individual jurisdictions, subdivided by population group. Percent changes for each offense within each population group of the geographic divisions in which the states reside were applied to the previous valid annual totals. The state totals were compiled from the sums of the population group estimates.
1992	Illinois	The state UCR Program was unable to provide forcible rape figures in accordance with UCR guidelines.	The rape totals were estimated using national rates per 100,000 inhabitants within the eight population groups and assigning the forcible rape volumes proportionally to the state.
1993	Michigan, Minnesota	The state UCR Programs were unable to provide forcible rape figures in accordance with UCR guidelines.	The rape totals were estimated using national rates per 100,000 inhabitants within the eight population groups and assigning the forcible rape volumes proportionally to each state.
	Kansas	NIBRS conversion efforts resulted in estimation for Kansas.	Kansas totals were estimated by updating previous valid annual totals for individual jurisdictions, subdivided by population group. Percent changes for each offense within each population group of the West North Central Division were applied to the previous valid annual totals. The state totals were compiled from the sums of the population group estimates.
	Illinois	NIBRS conversion efforts resulted in estimation for Illinois.	Since valid annual totals were available for approximately 60 Illinois agencies, those counts were maintained. The counts for the remaining jurisdictions were replaced with the most recent valid annual totals or were generated using standard estimation procedures. The results of all sources were then combined to arrive at the 1993 state total for Illinois.
		The state UCR Program was unable to provide forcible rape figures in accordance with UCR guidelines.	The rape totals were estimated using national rates per 100,000 inhabitants within the eight population groups and assigning the forcible rape volumes proportionally to the state.
1994	Illinois	NIBRS conversion efforts resulted in estimation for Illinois.	Illinois state totals were generated using only the valid crime rates for the East North Central Division. Within each population group, the state's offense totals were estimated based on the rate per 100,000 inhabitants within the remainder of the division.

Year	State(s)	Reason for Estimation	Estimation Method
		The state UCR Program was unable to provide forcible rape figures in accordance with UCR guidelines.	The rape totals were estimated using national rates per 100,000 inhabitants within the eight population groups and assigning the forcible rape volumes proportionally to the state.
	Kansas	NIBRS conversion efforts resulted in estimation for Kansas.	Kansas state totals were generated using only the valid crime rates for the West North Central Division. Within each population group, the state's offense totals were estimated based on the rate per 100,000 inhabitants within the remainder of the division.
	Montana	The state UCR Program was unable to provide complete 1994 offense figures in accordance with UCR guidelines.	Montana totals were estimated by updating previous valid annual totals for individual jurisdictions, subdivided by population group. Percent changes for each offense within each population group of the Mountain Division were applied to the previous valid annual totals. The state totals were compiled from the sums of the population group estimates.
1995	Kansas	The state UCR Program was unable to provide complete 1995 offense figures in accordance with UCR guidelines.	The Kansas State UCR Program was able to provide valid 1994 state totals which were then updated using 1995 crime trends for the West North Central Division.
	Illinois	The state UCR Program was unable to provide complete 1995 offense figures in accordance with UCR guidelines.	Valid Crime Index counts were available for most of the largest cities. For other agencies, the only available counts were generated without application of the UCR Hierarchy Rule. (The Hierarchy Rule requires that only the most serious offense in a multiple-offense criminal incident is counted.) To arrive at a comparable state estimate to be included in national compilations, the total supplied by the Illinois State Program (which was inflated because of the nonapplication of the Hierarchy Rule) was reduced by the proportion of multiple offenses reported within single incidents in the available NIBRS data. Valid totals for the large cities were excluded from the reduction process.
	Montana	The state UCR Program was unable to provide complete 1995 offense figures in accordance with UCR guidelines.	Montana state estimates were computed by updating the previous valid annual totals using the 1994 versus 1995 percent changes for the Mountain States.
1996	Florida	The state UCR Program was unable to provide complete 1996 offense figures in accordance with UCR guidelines.	The state UCR Program was able to provide an aggregated state total; data received from 94 individual Florida agencies are shown in the 1996 jurisdictional figures presented in Tables 8 through 11.
	Illinois	The state UCR Program was unable to provide complete 1996 offense figures in accordance with UCR guidelines.	Valid Crime Index counts were available for most of the largest cities. For other agencies, the only available counts were generated without application of the UCR Hierarchy Rule. (The Hierarchy Rule requires that only the most serious offense in a multiple-offense criminal incident is counted.) To arrive at a comparable state estimate to be included in national compilations, the total supplied by the Illinois State Program (which was inflated because of the nonapplication of the Hierarchy Rule) was reduced by the proportion of multiple offenses reported within single incidents in the available NIBRS data. Valid totals for the large cities were excluded from the reduction process.
	Kansas	The state UCR Program was unable to provide complete 1996 offense figures in accordance with UCR guidelines.	Annual figures were extrapolated from 1996 January-June state totals provided by the Kansas State UCR Program.
	Kentucky, Montana	The state UCR Programs were unable to provide complete 1996 offense figures in accordance with UCR guidelines.	The 1995 and 1996 percent changes within each geographic division were applied to valid 1995 state totals to generate 1996 state totals.
1997	Illinois	The state UCR Program was unable to provide complete 1997 offense figures in accordance with UCR guidelines.	Valid Crime Index counts were available for most of the largest cities. For other agencies, the only available counts were generated without application of the UCR Hierarchy Rule. (The Hierarchy Rule requires that only the most serious offense in a multiple-offense criminal incident is counted.) To arrive at a comparable state estimate to be included in national compilations, the total supplied by the Illinois State Program (which was inflated because of the nonapplication of the Hierarchy Rule) was reduced by the proportion of multiple offenses reported within single incidents in the available NIBRS data. Valid totals for the large cities were excluded from the reduction process.

Year	State(s)	Reason for Estimation	Estimation Method
	Kansas	The state UCR Program was unable to provide complete 1997 offense figures in accordance with UCR guidelines.	The Kansas state estimate was extrapolated from 1996 January-June state totals provided by the Kansas State UCR Program.
	Kentucky, Montana, New Hampshire, Vermont	The state UCR Programs were unable to provide complete 1997 offense figures in accordance with UCR guidelines.	The 1996 and 1997 percent changes registered for each geographic division in which the states of Kentucky, Montana, New Hampshire, and Vermont are categorized were applied to valid 1996 state totals to affect 1997 state totals.
1998	Delaware	Forcible rape figures supplied by the Delaware State Bureau of Investigation were not in accordance with national UCR guidelines.	The 1998 forcible rape total for Delaware was estimated by reducing the number of reported offenses by the proportion of male forcible rape victims statewide.
	Kentucky, Montana, New Hampshire, Wisconsin	The state UCR Programs were unable to provide complete 1998 offense figures in accordance with UCR guidelines.	State totals were estimated by using the 1997 figures for the nonreporting areas and applying 1997 versus 1998 percentage changes for the division in which each state is located. The estimates for the nonreporting areas were then increased by any actual 1998 crime counts received.
	Kansas	The state UCR Program was unable to provide complete 1998 offense figures in accordance with UCR guidelines.	To arrive at 1998 estimates, 1997 state totals supplied by the Kansas State UCR Program were updated using 1998 crime trends for the West North Central Division.
	Vermont	Due to changes in reporting procedures, the 1997 Vermont Crime Index offense totals were not comparable to those for 1998.	The 1998 Vermont Crime Index offense totals were excluded from Table 4. The 1997 Vermont state estimates were, however, retained in the aggregate national, regional, and divisional volume and rate totals.
	Illinois	The state UCR Program was unable to provide complete 1998 offense figures in accordance with UCR guidelines.	Valid Crime Index counts were available for most of the largest cities. For other agencies, the only available counts were generated without application of the UCR Hierarchy Rule. (The Hierarchy Rule requires that only the most serious offense in a multiple-offense criminal incident is counted.) To arrive at a comparable state estimate to be included in national compilations, the total supplied by the Illinois State Program (which was inflated because of the nonapplication of the Hierarchy Rule) was reduced by the proportion of multiple offenses reported within single incidents in the available NIBRS data. Valid totals for the large cities were excluded from the reduction process.
1999	Illinois	The state UCR Program was unable to provide complete 1999 offense figures in accordance with UCR guidelines.	Valid Crime Index counts were available for most of the largest cities. For other agencies, the only available counts were generated without application of the UCR Hierarchy Rule. (The Hierarchy Rule requires that only the most serious offense in a multiple-offense criminal incident is counted.) To arrive at a comparable state estimate to be included in national compilations, the total supplied by the Illinois State Program (which was inflated because of the nonapplication of the Hierarchy Rule) was reduced by the proportion of multiple offenses reported within single incidents in the available NIBRS data. Valid totals for the large cities were excluded from the reduction process.
	Maine	The Maine Department of Public Safety was unable to provide complete 1999 offense figures in accordance with UCR guidelines.	The Maine Department of Public Safety forwarded monthly January through October crime counts for each law enforcement contributor; since 12 months of data were not received, the national Program estimated for the missing data following standard estimation procedures to arrive at a 1999 state total.
	Kansas, Kentucky, Montana	The state UCR Programs were unable to provide complete 1999 offense figures in accordance with UCR guidelines.	To arrive at 1999 estimates for Kansas, Kentucky, and Montana, 1998 state totals supplied by each state Uniform Crime Reporting Program were updated using 1999 crime trends for the divisions in which each state is located.
	New Hampshire	The state UCR Program was unable to provide complete 1999 offense figures in accordance with UCR guidelines.	The state total for New Hampshire was estimated by using the 1998 figures for the 1999 nonreporting areas and applying the 2-year percent change for the New England Division.
2000	Kansas	The state UCR Program was unable to provide complete 2000 offense figures in accordance with UCR guidelines.	To arrive at 2000 estimates for Kansas, 1999 state estimates were updated using 2000 crime trends for the division in which it is located.
	Kentucky, Montana	The state UCR Program was unable to provide complete 2000 offense figures in accordance with UCR guidelines.	To arrive at 2000 estimates for Kentucky and Montana, 1999 state totals supplied by each state's Uniform Crime Reporting Program were updated using 2000 crime trends for the divisions in which each is located.

Year	State(s)	Reason for Estimation	Estimation Method
	Ilinois	The state UCR Program was unable to provide complete 2000 offense figures or forcible rape figures in accordance with UCR guidelines.	Valid Crime Index counts were available for most of the largest cities. For other agencies, the only available counts were generated without application of the UCR Hierarchy Rule. (The Hierarchy Rule requires that only the most serious offense in a multiple-offense criminal incident be counted.) To arrive at a comparable state estimate to be included in national compilation, the total supplied by the Illinois State Program (which was inflated due to the nonapplication of the Hierarchy Rule) was reduced by the proportion of multiple offenses reported within single incidents in the available NIBRS data. Valid totals for the large cities were excluded from the reduction process.
2001	Kentucky	The State UCR Program was unable to provide complete 2000 offense figures in accordance with UCR guidelines.	To arrive at the 2001 estimate for Kentucky, the 2000 state estimates were updated using 2001 crime trends reported for the East South Central Division in which it is located.
	Illinois	The state UCR Program submitted complete data for only 7 agencies within the state. Additionally, the state UCR Program was unable to provide forcible rape figures in accordance with UCR guidelines.	Valid Crime Index counts were available for most of the largest cities. For other agencies, the only available counts were generated without application of the UCR Hierarchy Rule. (The Hierarchy Rule requires that only the most serious offense in a multiple-offense criminal incident is counted.) To arrive at a comparable state estimate to be included in national compilations, the total supplied by the Illinois State Program (which was inflated because of the nonapplication of the Hierarchy Rule) was reduced by the proportion of multiple offenses reported within single incidents in the available NIBRS data. Valid totals for the large cities were excluded from the reduction process.

Table Methodology

Although most law enforcement agencies submit crime reports to the UCR Program, data are sometimes not received for complete annual periods. To be included in this publication's Tables 8 through 11, which show specific jurisdictional statistics, figures for all 12 months of the current year must have been received at the FBI prior to established publication deadlines. Other tabular presentations are aggregated on varied levels of submission. With the exception of the tables which consist of estimates for the total United States population, each table in this publication shows the number of agencies reporting and the extent of population coverage.

Designed to assist the reader, this table explains the construction of many of this book's tabular presentations.

(1) Table	(2) Database	(3) Table Construction	(4) General Comments
1	All law enforcement agencies in the UCR Program. Crime statistics include estimated offense totals for agencies submitting less than 12 months of offense reports for each year.	The 2001 statistics are consistent with Table 2. Pre-2001 crime statistics may have been updated and, hence, may not be consistent with prior publications. Population statistics represent July 1 provisional estimations for each year except 1990 and 2000, which are Bureau of the Census decennial census data (see the Population section in this appendix).	Represents an estimation of national reported crime activity from 1982 to 2001.
2	All law enforcement agencies in the UCR Program. Crime statistics include estimated offense totals for agencies submitting less than 12 months of offense reports.	Statistics are aggregated from individual state statistics as shown in Table 5. Population statistics for 2001 represent estimates based upon the percent change in state population from Bureau of the Census 2000 decennial census counts and 2001 provisional estimates (see the Population section in this appendix).	Represents an estimation of national reported crime activity in 2001.
3	All law enforcement agencies in the UCR Program (including those submitting less than 12 months in 2001).	Regional offense distributions are computed from volume figures as shown in Table 4. Population distributions are based on Bureau of the Census provisional estimates for 2001.	Represents the 2001 geographical distribution of estimated Crime Index offenses and population.
4	All law enforcement agencies in the UCR Program. Crime statistics include estimated offense totals for agencies submitting less than 12 months of offense reports for 2000 and 2001.	The 2001 statistics are aggregated from individual state statistics as shown in Table 5. Population statistics represent Bureau of the Census decennial counts for 2000 and provisional estimates for 2001.	Represents an estimation of reported crime activity for Index offenses at the: 1. national level 2. regional level 3. division level 4. state level Any comparison of UCR statistics should take into consideration demographic factors.
5	All law enforcement agencies in the UCR Program. Crime statistics include estimated offense totals for agencies submitting less than 12 months of offense reports.	Population statistics for 2001 represent estimates based upon the percent change in state population from Bureau of the Census 2000 decennial census counts and 2001 provisional estimates (see the Population section in this appendix). Statistics under the heading Area Actually Reporting represent reported offense totals for agencies submitting 12 months of offense reports and estimated totals for agencies submitting less than 12 but more than 2 months of offense reports. The statistics under the heading Estimated Totals represent the above plus estimated offense totals for agencies having less than 3 months of offense reports.	Represents an estimation of reported crime activity for Index offenses at the state level. Any comparison of UCR statistics should take into consideration demographic factors.
6	All law enforcement agencies in the UCR Program. Crime statistics include estimated offense totals for agencies submitting less than 12 months of offense statistics for 2001.	Statistics are published for all Metropolitan Statistical Areas (MSAs) having at least 75% reporting and for which the central city/cities submitted 12 months of data in 2001. Population statistics for 2001 represent estimates based upon the percent change in state population from Bureau of the Census 2000 decennial census counts and	Represents an estimation of the reported crime activity for Index offenses at individual MSA level. Any comparison of UCR statistics should take into consideration demographic factors.

(1) Table	(2) Database	(3) Table Construction	(4) General Comments
		2001 provisional estimates (see the Population section in this appendix). The statistics under the heading Area Actually Reporting represent reported offense totals for agencies submitting all 12 months of offense reports plus estimated offense totals for agencies submitting less than 12 but more than 2 months of offense reports. The statistics under the heading Estimated Total represent the above plus the estimated offense totals for agencies submitting less than 3 months of offense reports. The tabular breakdowns are according to UCR definitions (see App. II).	
7	All law enforcement agencies in the UCR Program. Crime statistics include estimated offense totals for agencies submitting less than 12 months of offense reports for each year.	Offense totals are for all Index offense categories other than aggravated assault.	Represents an estimation of national reported crime activity from 1997 to 2001. Aggravated assault is excluded from Table 7, because if money or property is taken in connection with an assault, the offense is robbery.
8	All law enforcement agencies submitting complete reports for 12 months in 2001.	Cities and Towns are defined to be agencies in Population Groups I through V (App. III). Population statistics for 2001 represent estimates based upon the percent change in state population from Bureau of the Census 2000 decennial census counts and 2001 provisional estimates (see the Population section in this appendix).	Represents reported crime activity of individual agencies in cities and towns 10,000 and over in population. Any comparison of UCR statistics should take into consideration demographic factors.
9	All university/college law enforcement agencies submitting complete reports for 12 months in 2001.	The 1999 student enrollment figures, which are provided by the U.S. Department of Education, are the most recent available. They include full- and part-time students. No adjustments to equate part-time enrollments into full-time equivalents have been made.	Represents reported crime from those individual university/college law enforcement agencies contributing to the UCR Program. These agencies are listed alphabetically by state. Any comparison of these UCR statistics should take into consideration size of enrollment, number of on-campus residents, and other demographic factors.
10	All law enforcement agencies submitting complete reports for 12 months in 2001.	Suburban Counties are defined as the areas covered by noncity agencies within an MSA (App. III). Population classifications of suburban counties are based on 2001 UCR estimates for individual agencies (see the Population section in this appendix).	Represents crime reported to individual law enforcement agencies in suburban counties, i.e., the individual sheriff's office, county police department, highway patrol, and/or state police. These figures do not represent the county totals since they exclude city crime counts. Any comparison of UCR statistics should take into consideration demographic factors.
11	All law enforcement agencies submitting complete reports for 12 months in 2001.	Rural Counties are those outside MSAs and whose jurisdictions are not covered by city police agencies (App. III). Population classifications of rural counties are based on 2001 UCR estimates for individual agencies (see the Population section in this appendix).	Represents crime reported to individual rural county law enforcement agencies covering populations 25,000 and over, i.e., the individual sheriff's office, county police department, highway patrol, and/or state police. These figures do not represent the county totals since they exclude city crime counts. Any comparison of UCR statistics should take into consideration demographic factors.
12-15	All law enforcement agencies submitting complete reports for at least 6 common months in 2000 and 2001.	The 2001 crime trend statistics are 2-year comparisons based on 2001 reported crime activity. Only common reported months for individual agencies are included in 2001 trend calculations. Population statistics for 2001 represent estimates based upon the percent change in state population from Bureau of the Census 2000 decennial census counts and 2001 provisional estimates (see the Population section in this appendix). See Appendix III for UCR population breakdowns. Note that Suburban and Nonsuburban Cities are all municipal agencies other than central cities in MSAs.	
16-19	All law enforcement agencies submitting complete reports for 12 months in 2001.	The 2001 crime rates are the ratios of the aggregated 2001 crime volumes and the aggregated 2001 populations of the contributing agencies. Population statistics for 2001 represent estimates based upon the percent change in state population	The forcible rape figures furnished by the Delaware and Illinois state-level UCR Programs were not in accordance with national guidelines. For inclusion in these tables, the Delaware and Illinois forcible rape figures were estimated by using the national

(1) Table	(2) Database	(3) Table Construction	(4) General Comments
		from Bureau of the Census 2000 decennial census counts and 2001 provisional estimates (see the Population section in this appendix). See Appendix III for UCR population breakdowns. Note that Suburban and Nonsuburban Cities are all municipal agencies other than central cities in MSAs.	rates for each population group applied to the population by group for Delaware and Illinois agencies supplying all 12 months of data. Slight decrease in national coverage for Table 19 due to editing procedure and lower submission rate.
20	All law enforcement agencies submitting Supplementary Homicide Report (SHR) data in 2001.	The weapon totals are the aggregate for each murder victim recorded on the SHRs for calendar year 2001.	The SHR is the monthly report form concerning homicides. It details victim and offender characteristics, circumstances, weapons used, etc.
21, 22	All law enforcement agencies submitting complete reports for 12 months in 2001.	The weapon totals are aggregated 2001 totals. Population statistics represent 2001 UCR estimates.	
23, 24	All law enforcement agencies submitting complete reports for at least 6 months in 2001.	Offense total and value lost total are computed for all Index offense categories other than aggravated assault. Percent distribution is derived based on offense total of each Index offense. Trend statistics are derived based on agencies with at least 6 common months complete data for 2000 and 2001.	Aggravated assault is excluded from Table 23. For UCR Program purposes, the taking of money or property in connection with an assault is reported as robbery.
25-28	All law enforcement agencies submitting complete reports for at least 6 months in 2001.	The 2001 clearance rates are based on offense and clearance volume totals of the contributing agencies for 2001. Population statistics for 2001 represent estimates based upon the percent change in state population from Bureau of the Census 2000 decennial census counts and 2001 provisional estimates (see the Population section in this appendix). See Appendix III for UCR Program population breakdowns.	
29	All law enforcement agencies in the UCR Program (including those submitting less than 12 months in 2001).	The arrest totals presented are national estimates based on the arrest statistics of all law enforcement agencies in the UCR Program (including those submitting less than 12 months). The Total Estimated Arrests statistic is the sum of estimated arrest volumes for each of the 29 offenses. Each individual arrest total is the sum of the estimated volumes within each of the eight population groups (App. III). Each group's estimate is the reported volume (as shown in Table 31) divided by the percent of total group population reporting (according to 2001 UCR estimates for individual agencies, see the Population section in this appendix).	
30, 31	All law enforcement agencies submitting complete reports for 12 months in 2001.	The 2001 arrest rates are the ratios, per 100,000 inhabitants, of the aggregated 2001 reported arrest statistics and population. The population statistics for 2001 represent estimates based upon the percent change in state population from Bureau of the Census 2000 decennial census counts and 2001 provisional estimates (see the Population section in this appendix). See Appendix III for UCR population classifications/geographical configuration.	
32, 33	All law enforcement agencies submitting complete reports for 12 months in 1992 and 2001.	The arrest trends are the percentage differences between 1992 and 2001 arrest volumes aggregated from all common agencies. The population statistics for 2001 represent estimates based upon the percent change in state population from Bureau of the Census 2000 decennial census counts and 2001 provisional estimates. (See the Population section in this appendix). Population statistics for 1992 are based upon the percent change in state population from Bureau of the Census 1991 and 1992 provisional estimates.	
34, 35	All law enforcement agencies submitting complete reports for 12 months in 1997 and 2001.	The arrest trends are the percentage differences between 1997 and 2001 arrest volumes aggregated from common agencies. The population statistics for	

(1) Table	(2) Database	(3) Table Construction	(4) General Comments
		2001 represent estimates based upon the percent change in state population from Bureau of the Census 2000 decennial census counts and 2001 provisional estimates. (See the Population section in this appendix). Population statistics for 1997 are based upon the percent change in state population from the Bureau of the Census 1996 and 1997 provisional estimates.	
36, 37	All law enforcement agencies submitting complete reports for 12 months in 2000 and 2001.	The arrest trends are 2-year comparisons between 2000 and 2001 arrest volumes aggregated from common agencies. Population statistics represent Bureau of the Census 2000 decennial census counts. Population statistics for 2001 represent estimates based upon the percent change in state population from Bureau of the Census 2000 decennial counts and 2001 provisional estimates (see the Population section in this appendix).	
38-43	All law enforcement agencies submitting complete reports for 12 months in 2001.	Population statistics for 2001 represent estimates based upon the percent change in state population from Bureau of the Census 2000 decennial census counts and 2001 provisional estimates (see the Population section in this appendix).	
44, 45	All city law enforcement agencies submitting complete reports for 12 months in 2000 and 2001.	The 2001 city arrest trends represent the percentage differences between 2000 and 2001 arrest volumes aggregated from common city agencies. City Agencies are defined to be all agencies within Population Groups I-VI (App. III). Population statistics for 2001 represent estimates based upon the percent change in state population from Bureau of the Census 2000 decennial census counts and 2001 provisional estimates. (See the Population section in this appendix.)	
46-49	All city law enforcement agencies submitting complete reports for 12 months in 2000 and 2001.	City Agencies are defined to be all agencies within Population Groups I-VI (App. III). Population statistics for 2001 represent estimates based upon the percent change in state population from Bureau of Census 2000 decennial census counts and 2001 provisional estimates (see Population section in this appendix).	
50, 51	All suburban county law enforcement agencies submitting complete reports for 12 months in 2000 and 2001.	The 2001 suburban county arrest trends represent percentage differences between 2000 and 2001 volumes aggregated from contributing agencies. Suburban Counties are defined as the areas covered by noncity agencies within an MSA (App. III). Population statistics for 2000 represent Bureau of the Census decennial census counts. Population statistics for 2001 represent estimates based upon the percent change in state population from Bureau of the Census 2000 decennial census counts and 2001 provisional estimates (see the Population section in this appendix).	
52-55	All suburban county law enforcement agencies submitting complete reports for 12 months in 2001.	Suburban Counties are defined as the areas covered by noncity agencies within an MSA (App. III). Population statistics for 2001 represent estimates based upon the percent change in state population from the Bureau of the Census 2000 decennial census counts and 2001 provisional estimates (see the Population section in this appendix).	
56, 57	All rural county law enforcement agencies submitting complete reports for 12 months in 2000 and 2001.	The 2001 rural county arrest trends represent percentage differences between 2000 and 2001 volumes aggregated from contributing agencies. Rural Counties are defined as noncity agencies outside MSAs (App. III). Population statistics for	

(1) Table	(2) Database	(3) Table Construction	(4) General Comments
		2000 represent Bureau of the Census decennial census counts. Population statistics for 2001 represent estimates based upon the percent change in state population from Bureau of the Census 2000 decennial census counts and 2001 provisional estimates (see the Population section in this appendix).	
58-61	All rural county law enforcement agencies submitting complete reports for 12 months in 2001.	Rural Counties are defined as noncity agencies outside MSAs (App. III). Population statistics for 2001 represent estimates based upon the percent change in state population from the Bureau of the Census 2000 decennial census counts and 2001 provisional estimates (see the Population section in this appendix).	
62, 63	All suburban area law enforcement agencies submitting complete reports for 12 months in 2000 and 2001.	The 2001 suburban area arrest trends represent percentage differences between 2000 and 2001 arrest volumes aggregated from contributing agencies. Suburban Area is defined as agencies that are within a metropolitan area excluding those that cover central cities as defined by the Office of Management and Budget (App. III). Population statistics for 2000 represent Bureau of the Census decennial census counts. Population statistics for 2001 represent estimates based upon the percent change in state population from Bureau of the Census 2000 decennial census counts and 2001 provisional estimates (see the Population section in this appendix).	
64-67	All suburban area law enforcement agencies submitting complete reports for 12 months in 2001.	Suburban Area is defined as agencies that are within a metropolitan area excluding those that cover central cities as defined by the Office of Management and Budget (App. III). Population statistics for 2001 represent estimates based upon the percent change in state population from Bureau of the Census 2000 decennial census counts and 2001 provisional estimates (see the Population section in this appendix).	
68	All law enforcement agencies submitting complete reports for 12 months in 2001.	Population statistics for 2001 represent estimates based upon the percent change in state population from the Bureau of the Census 2000 decennial census counts and 2001 provisional estimates (see the Population section in this appendix).	Data furnished are based upon individual state age definitions for juveniles.
69	All law enforcement agencies submitting complete reports for 12 months in 2001.	Arrest totals are aggregated for individual agencies within each state. Population statistics represent Bureau of the Census provisional estimates for 2001 (see Population section in this appendix).	Any comparison of statistics should take into consideration variances in arrest practices, particularly for Part II crimes.

APPENDIX II – Offenses in Uniform Crime Reporting

The Uniform Crime Reporting Program classifies offenses into two groups, Part I and Part II. Each month contributing agencies submit information on the number of Part I (Crime Index) offenses known to law enforcement; those cleared by arrest or exceptional means; and the age, sex, and race of persons arrested. Contributors provide only arrest data for Part II offenses.

The **Part I** offenses are defined below:

Criminal homicide—a.) Murder and nonnegligent manslaughter: the willful (nonnegligent) killing of one human being by another. Deaths caused by negligence, attempts to kill, assaults to kill, suicides, and accidental deaths are excluded. The Program classifies justifiable homicides separately and limits the definition to: (1) the killing of a felon by a law enforcement officer in the line of duty; or (2) the killing of a felon, during the commission of a felony, by a private citizen. b.) Manslaughter by negligence: the killing of another person through gross negligence. Traffic fatalities are excluded. While manslaughter by negligence is a Part I crime, it is not included in the Crime Index.

Forcible rape—The carnal knowledge of a female forcibly and against her will. Rapes by force and attempts or assaults to rape regardless of the age of the victim are included. Statutory offenses (no force used—victim under age of consent) are excluded.

Robbery—The taking or attempting to take anything of value from the care, custody, or control of a person or persons by force or threat of force or violence and/or by putting the victim in fear.

Aggravated assault—An unlawful attack by one person upon another for the purpose of inflicting severe or aggravated bodily injury. This type of assault usually is accompanied by the use of a weapon or by means likely to produce death or great bodily harm. Simple assaults are excluded.

Burglary (breaking or entering)—The unlawful entry of a structure to commit a felony or a theft. Attempted forcible entry is included.

Larceny-theft (except motor vehicle theft)—The unlawful taking, carrying, leading, or riding away of property from the possession or constructive possession of another. Examples are thefts of bicycles or automobile accessories, shoplifting, pocket-picking, or the stealing of any property or article which is not taken by force and violence or by fraud. Attempted larcenies are included. Embezzlement, confidence games, forgery, worthless checks, etc., are excluded.

Motor vehicle theft—The theft or attempted theft of a motor vehicle. A motor vehicle is self-propelled and runs on the surface and not on rails. Motorboats, construction equipment, airplanes, and farming equipment are specifically excluded from this category.

Arson—Any willful or malicious burning or attempt to burn, with or without intent to defraud, a dwelling house, public building, motor vehicle or aircraft, personal property of another, etc.

The **Part II** offenses are defined below:

Other assaults (simple)—Assaults and attempted assaults where no weapons are used and which do not result in serious or aggravated injury to the victim.

Forgery and counterfeiting—Making, altering, uttering, or possessing, with intent to defraud, anything false in the semblance of that which is true. Attempts are included.

Fraud—Fraudulent conversion and obtaining money or property by false pretenses. Confidence games and bad checks, except forgeries and counterfeiting, are included.

Embezzlement—Misappropriation or misapplication of money or property entrusted to one's care, custody, or control.

Stolen property; buying, receiving, possessing—Buying, receiving, and possessing stolen property, including attempts.

Vandalism—Willful or malicious destruction, injury, disfigurement, or defacement of any public or private property, real or personal, without consent of the owner or persons having custody or control. Attempts are included.

Weapons; carrying, possessing, etc.—All violations of regulations or statutes controlling the carrying, using, possessing, furnishing, and manufacturing of deadly weapons or silencers. Attempts are included.

Prostitution and commercialized vice— Sex offenses of a commercialized nature, such as prostitution, keeping a bawdy house, procuring, or transporting women for immoral purposes. Attempts are included.

Sex offenses (except forcible rape, prostitution, and commercialized vice)— Statutory rape and offenses against chastity, common decency, morals, and the like. Attempts are included.

Drug abuse violations—State and/or local offenses relating to the unlawful possession, sale, use, growing, and manufacturing of narcotic drugs. The following drug categories are specified: opium or cocaine and their derivatives (morphine, heroin, codeine); marijuana; synthetic narcotics—manufactured narcotics that can cause true addiction (demerol, methadone); and dangerous nonnarcotic drugs (barbiturates, benzedrine).

Gambling—Promoting, permitting, or engaging in illegal gambling.

Offenses against the family and children—Nonsupport, neglect, desertion, or abuse of family and children. Attempts are included.

Driving under the influence—Driving or operating any vehicle or common carrier while drunk or under the influence of liquor or narcotics.

Liquor laws—State and/or local liquor law violations except drunkenness and driving under the influence. Federal violations are excluded.

Drunkenness—Offenses relating to drunkenness or intoxication. Driving under the influence is excluded.

Disorderly conduct—Breach of the peace.

Vagrancy—Begging, loitering, etc. Includes prosecutions under the charge of suspicious person.

All other offenses—All violations of state and/or local laws except those listed above and traffic offenses.

Suspicion—No specific offense; suspect released without formal charges being placed.

Curfew and loitering laws (persons under age 18)—Offenses relating to violations of local curfew or loitering ordinances where such laws exist.

Runaways (persons under age 18)— Limited to juveniles taken into protective custody under provisions of local statutes.

APPENDIX III – Uniform Crime Reporting Area Definitions

The presentation of statistics by reporting area facilitates analyzing local crime counts in conjunction with those for areas of similar geographical location or population size. Geographically, the United States is divisible by regions, divisions, and states. Further breakdowns rely on population figures and proximity to metropolitan areas. As a general rule, sheriffs, county police, and state police report crimes committed within the limits of counties but outside cities, and local police report crimes committed within the city limits.

Community Types

Uniform Crime Reporting (UCR) data are often presented in aggregations representing three types of communities:

1. Metropolitan Statistical Areas (MSAs)—Each MSA includes a central city of at least 50,000 people or an urbanized area of at least 50,000. The county containing the central city and other contiguous counties having strong economic and social ties to the central city and county are also included. Counties in an MSA are designated suburban for UCR purposes. An MSA may cross state lines. The MSA concept facilitates the analysis and presentation of uniform statistical data on metropolitan areas by establishing reporting units which represent major population centers. Due to changes in the geographic composition of MSAs, no year-to-year comparisons of data for those areas should be attempted.

New England MSAs are composed of cities and towns instead of counties. In this publication's tabular presentations, New England cities and towns are assigned to the proper MSAs. Some counties, however, have both suburban and rural portions. Data for state police and sheriffs in those jurisdictions are included in statistics for the rural areas.

MSAs made up approximately 79.9 percent of the total United States population in 2001. Some presentations in this book refer to suburban areas. A suburban area includes cities with less than 50,000 inhabitants in addition to counties (unincorporated areas) within the MSA. The central cities are, of course, excluded. The concept of suburban area is especially important because of the particular crime conditions which exist in the communities surrounding the Nation's largest cities.

2. Cities Outside MSAs—Cities outside MSAs are mostly incorporated. They comprised 8.0 percent of the 2001 population of the United States.

3. Rural Counties Outside MSAs—Rural counties are composed of mostly unincorporated areas. Law enforcement agencies in rural counties cover areas that are not under the jurisdiction of city police departments. Rural county law enforcement agencies served 12.1 percent of the national population in 2001.

The following is an illustration of the community types:

	MSA	NON-MSA
CITIES	CENTRAL CITIES 50,000 AND OVER	CITIES OUTSIDE METROPLITAN AREAS
	SUBURBAN CITIES	
COUNTIES (including unincorporated areas)	SUBURBAN COUNTIES	RURAL COUNTIES

Population Groups

The population group classifications used by the UCR Program are:

Population Group	Political Label	Population Range
I	City	250,000 and over
II	City	100,000 to 249,999
III	City	50,000 to 99,999
IV	City	25,000 to 49,999
V	City	10,000 to 24,999
VI	City[1]	Less than 10,000
VIII (Rural County)	County[2]	N/A
IX (Suburban County)	County[2]	N/A

[1]Includes universities and colleges to which no population is attributed.
[2]Includes state police to which no population is attributed.

The major source of UCR data is the individual law enforcement agency. The number of agencies included in each population group will vary slightly from year to year because of population growth, geopolitical consolidation, municipal incorporation, etc. Population figures for individual jurisdictions are estimated by the UCR Program in noncensus years. (See Appendix I for a more comprehensive explanation of population estimations.)

The following table shows the number of UCR contributing agencies within each population group for 2001.

Population Group	Number of Agencies	Population Covered
I	70	52,194,574
II	170	25,241,834
III	415	28,433,360
IV	794	27,588,722
V	1,856	29,412,579
VI[1]	8,463	25,860,112
VIII (Rural County)[2]	3,413	34,454,583
IX (Suburban County)[2]	1,790	61,611,123
Total	16,971	284,796,887

[1]Includes universities and colleges to which no population is attributed.
[2]Includes state police to which no population is attributed.

Regions and Divisions

As shown in the accompanying map, the United States is composed of four regions: the Northeastern States, the Midwestern States, the Southern States, and the Western States. These regions are further separated into nine divisions. The following table delineates the regional, divisional, and state configuration of the country.

NORTHEASTERN STATES

New England
  Connecticut
  Maine
  Massachusetts
  New Hampshire
  Rhode Island
  Vermont

Middle Atlantic
  New Jersey
  New York
  Pennsylvania

MIDWESTERN STATES

East North Central
  Illinois
  Indiana
  Michigan
  Ohio
  Wisconsin

West North Central
  Iowa
  Kansas
  Minnesota
  Missouri
  Nebraska
  North Dakota
  South Dakota

SOUTHERN STATES

South Atlantic
  Delaware
  District of Columbia
  Florida
  Georgia
  Maryland
  North Carolina
  South Carolina
  Virginia
  West Virginia

East South Central
  Alabama
  Kentucky
  Mississippi
  Tennessee
West South Central
  Arkansas
  Louisiana
  Oklahoma
  Texas

WESTERN STATES

Mountain
  Arizona
  Colorado
  Idaho
  Montana
  Nevada
  New Mexico
  Utah
  Wyoming

Pacific
  Alaska
  California
  Hawaii
  Oregon
  Washington

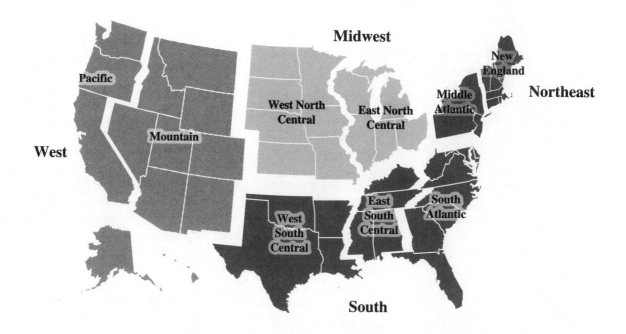

APPENDIX IV – The Nation's Two Crime Measures

The U.S. Department of Justice administers two statistical programs to measure the magnitude, nature, and impact of crime in the Nation: the Uniform Crime Reporting (UCR) Program and the National Crime Victimization Survey (NCVS). Each of these programs produces valuable information about aspects of the Nation's crime problem. Because the UCR and NCVS programs are conducted for different purposes, use different methods, and focus on somewhat different aspects of crime, the information they produce together provides a more comprehensive panorama of the Nation's crime problem than either could produce alone.

Uniform Crime Reports

The FBI's UCR Program, which began in 1929, collects information on the following crimes reported to law enforcement authorities: homicide, forcible rape, robbery, aggravated assault, burglary, larceny-theft, motor vehicle theft, and arson. Arrests are reported for 21 additional crime categories.

The UCR data are compiled from monthly law enforcement reports or individual crime incident records transmitted directly to the FBI or to centralized state agencies that then report to the FBI. Each report submitted to the UCR Program is examined thoroughly for reasonableness, accuracy, and deviations that may indicate errors. Large variations in crime levels may indicate modified records procedures, incomplete reporting, or changes in a jurisdiction's boundaries. To identify any unusual fluctuations in an agency's crime counts, monthly reports are compared with previous submissions of the agency and with those for similar agencies.

In 2001, law enforcement agencies active in the UCR Program represented approximately 255 million United States inhabitants— 89.6 percent of the total population.

The UCR Program provides crime counts for the Nation as a whole, as well as for regions, states, counties, cities, and towns. This permits studies among neighboring jurisdictions and among those with similar populations and other common characteristics.

UCR findings for each calendar year are published in a preliminary release in the spring of the following calendar year, then succeeded by a detailed annual report, *Crime in the United States*, issued in the fall. In addition to crime counts and trends, this report includes data on crimes cleared, persons arrested (age, sex, and race), law enforcement personnel (including the number of sworn officers killed or assaulted), and the characteristics of homicides (including age, sex, and race of victims and offenders; victim-offender relationships; weapons used; and circumstances surrounding the homicides). Other periodic reports are also available from the UCR Program.

The UCR Program is continually converting to the more comprehensive and detailed National Incident-Based Reporting System (NIBRS). NIBRS can provide detailed information about each criminal incident in 22 broad categories of offenses.

National Crime Victimization Survey

The Bureau of Justice Statistics' NCVS, which began in 1973, provides a detailed picture of crime incidents, victims, and trends. After a substantial period of research, the survey completed an intensive methodological redesign in 1993. The redesign was undertaken to improve the questions used to uncover crime, update the survey methods, and broaden the scope of crimes measured. The redesigned survey collects detailed information on the frequency and nature of the crimes of rape, sexual assault, personal robbery, aggravated and simple assault, household burglary, theft, and motor vehicle theft. It does not measure homicide or commercial crimes (such as burglaries of stores).

Two times a year, U.S. Bureau of the Census personnel interview all household members at least 12 years old in a nationally representative sample of approximately 49,000 households (about 80,000 people). Approximately 160,000 interviews are conducted annually. Households stay in the sample for 3 years. New households rotate into the sample on an ongoing basis.

The NCVS collects information on crimes suffered by individuals and households, whether or not those crimes were reported to law enforcement. It estimates the proportion of each crime type reported to law enforcement, and it summarizes the reasons that victims give for reporting or not reporting.

The survey provides information about victims (age, sex, race, ethnicity, marital status, income, and educational level), offenders (sex, race, approximate age, and victim-offender relationship), and the crimes (time and place of occurrence, use of weapons, nature of injury, and economic consequences). Questions also cover the experiences of victims with the criminal justice system, self-protective measures used by victims, and possible substance abuse by offenders. Supplements are added periodically to the survey to obtain detailed information on topics like school crime.

The first data from the redesigned NCVS were published in a BJS bulletin in June 1995. BJS publication of NCVS data includes *Criminal Victimization in the United States*, an annual report that covers the broad range of detailed information collected by the NCVS. BJS publishes detailed reports on topics such as crime against women, urban crime, and gun use in crime. The NCVS data files are archived at the National Archive of Criminal Justice Data at the University of Michigan to enable researchers to perform independent analyses.

Comparing UCR and NCVS

Because the NCVS was designed to complement the UCR Program, the two programs share many similarities. As much as their different collection methods permit, the two measure the same subset of serious crimes, defined alike. Both programs cover rape, robbery, aggravated assault, burglary, theft, and motor vehicle theft. Rape, robbery, theft, and motor vehicle theft are defined virtually identically by both the UCR and NCVS. (While rape is defined analogously, the UCR Crime Index measures the crime against women only, and the NCVS measures it against both sexes.)

There are also significant differences between the two programs. First, the two programs were created to serve different

purposes. The UCR Program's primary objective is to provide a reliable set of criminal justice statistics for law enforcement administration, operation, and management. The NCVS was established to provide previously unavailable information about crime (including crime not reported to police), victims, and offenders.

Second, the two programs measure an overlapping but nonidentical set of crimes. The NCVS includes crimes both reported and not reported to law enforcement. The NCVS excludes, but the UCR includes, homicide, arson, commercial crimes, and crimes against children under age 12. The UCR captures crimes reported to law enforcement, but it excludes simple assaults and sexual assaults other than forcible rape from the Crime Index.

Third, because of methodology, the NCVS and UCR definitions of some crimes differ. For example, the UCR defines burglary as the unlawful entry or attempted entry of a structure to commit a felony or theft. The NCVS, not wanting to ask victims to ascertain offender motives, defines burglary as the entry or attempted entry of a residence by a person who had no right to be there.

Fourth, for property crimes (burglary, theft, and motor vehicle theft), the two programs calculate crime rates using different bases. The UCR rates for these crimes are per capita (number of crimes per 100,000 persons), whereas the NCVS rates for these crimes are per household (number of crimes per 1,000 households). Because the number of households may not grow at the same rate each year as the total population, trend data for rates of property crimes measured by the two programs may not be comparable.

In addition, some differences in the data from the two programs may result from sampling variation in the NCVS and from estimating for nonresponse in the UCR. The NCVS estimates are derived from interviewing a sample and are, therefore, subject to a margin of error. Rigorous statistical methods are used to calculate confidence intervals around all survey estimates. Trend data in NCVS reports are described as genuine only if there is at least a 90-percent certainty that the measured changes are not the result of sampling variation. The UCR data are based on the actual counts of offenses reported by law enforcement jurisdictions. In some circumstances, UCR data are estimated for nonparticipating jurisdictions or those reporting partial data.

Apparent discrepancies between statistics from the two programs can usually be accounted for by their definitional and procedural differences or resolved by comparing NCVS sampling variations (confidence intervals) of those crimes said to have been reported to police with UCR statistics.

For most types of crimes measured by both the UCR and NCVS, analysts familiar with the programs can exclude from analysis those aspects of crime not common to both. Resulting long-term trend lines can be brought into close concordance. The impact of such adjustments is most striking for robbery, burglary, and motor vehicle theft, whose definitions most closely coincide.

With robbery, annual victimization rates are based only on NCVS robberies reported to the police. It is also possible to remove UCR robberies of commercial establishments such as gas stations, convenience stores, and banks from analysis. When the resulting NCVS police-reported robbery rates are compared to UCR noncommercial robbery rates, the results reveal closely corresponding long-term trends.

Each program has unique strengths. The UCR provides a measure of the number of crimes reported to law enforcement agencies throughout the country. The UCR's Supplementary Homicide Reports provide the most reliable, timely data on the extent and nature of homicides in the Nation. The NCVS is the primary source of information on the characteristics of criminal victimization and on the number and types of crimes not reported to law enforcement authorities.

By understanding the strengths and limitations of each program, it is possible to use the UCR and NCVS to achieve a greater understanding of crime trends and the nature of crime in the United States. For example, changes in police procedures, shifting attitudes towards crime and police, and other societal changes can affect the extent to which people report and law enforcement agencies record crime. NCVS and UCR data can be used in concert to explore why trends in reported and police-recorded crime may differ.

APPENDIX V – Directory of State Uniform Crime Reporting Programs

Alabama

    Alabama Criminal Justice
      Information Center
    Suite 350
    770 Washington Avenue
    Montgomery, Alabama 36104
    334-242-4900

Alaska

    Uniform Crime Reporting Section
    Department of Public Safety
      Information System
    5700 East Tudor Road
    Anchorage, Alaska 99507
    907-451-5166

American Samoa

    Department of Public Safety
    Post Office Box 1086
    Pago Pago
    American Samoa 96799
    684-633-1111

Arizona

    Uniform Crime Reporting Program
    Access Integrity Unit
    Arizona Department of Public Safety
    Post Office Box 6638
    Phoenix, Arizona 85005-6638
    602-223-2263

Arkansas

    Arkansas Crime Information Center
    One Capitol Mall, 4D-200
    Little Rock, Arkansas 72201
    501-682-2222

California

    Criminal Justice Statistics Center
    Department of Justice
    Post Office Box 903427
    Sacramento, California 94203-4270
    916-227-3282

Colorado

    Uniform Crime Reporting
    Colorado Bureau of Investigation
    Suite 3000
    690 Kipling Street
    Denver, Colorado 80215
    303-239-4300

Connecticut	Uniform Crime Reporting Program Post Office Box 2794 Middletown, Connecticut 06457-9294 860-685-8030
Delaware	Delaware State Bureau of Identification Post Office Box 430 Dover, Delaware 19903 302-739-5875
District of Columbia	Research and Development Metropolitan Police Department Post Office Box 1606 Washington, D.C. 20001 202-727-4289
Florida	Florida Crime Information Bureau Florida Department of Law Enforcement Post Office Box 1489 Tallahassee, Florida 32302-1489 850-410-7121
Georgia	Georgia Crime Information Center Georgia Bureau of Investigation Post Office Box 370748 Decatur, Georgia 30037-0748 404-244-2840
Guam	Guam Police Department Planning, Research and Development Building #3 Central Avenue Tiyan, Guam 96913 671-472-8911 x 418
Hawaii	Crime Prevention and Justice Assistance Division Department of the Attorney General Suite 401 235 South Beretania Street Honolulu, Hawaii 96813 808-586-1416
Idaho	Criminal Identification Bureau Idaho Department of Law Enforcement Post Office Box 700 Meridian, Idaho 83680 208-884-7156

Illinois

Uniform Crime Reporting
Division of Administration; Crime Statistics
Illinois State Police
Post Office Box 3677
Springfield, Illinois 62708
217-782-5794

Iowa

Iowa Department of Public Safety
Wallace State Office Building
East Ninth and Grand
Des Moines, Iowa 50319
515-281-8494

Kansas

Criminal Justice System
Kansas Bureau of Investigation
Crime Data Information Center
1620 Southwest Tyler Street
Topeka, Kansas 66612
785-296-8200

Kentucky

Records Section
Kentucky State Police
1250 Louisville Road
Frankfort, Kentucky 40601
502-227-8790

Louisiana

Louisiana Commission on Law Enforcement
Office of the Governor
Room 708
1885 Wooddale Boulevard
Baton Rouge, Louisiana 70806
225-925-4420

Maine

Records Management Services
Uniform Crime Reporting Division
Maine Department of Public Safety
Maine State Police
36 Hospital Street, Station 42
Augusta, Maine 04333
207-624-7003

Maryland

Central Records Division
Maryland State Police
1711 Belmont Avenue
Baltimore, Maryland 21244
410-298-3883

Massachusetts

Crime Reporting Unit
Uniform Crime Reports
Massachusetts State Police
470 Worcester Road
Framingham, Massachusetts 01702
508-820-2111

Michigan	Uniform Crime Reporting Section
	Criminal Justice Information Center
	Michigan State Police
	7150 Harris Drive
	Lansing, Michigan 48913
	517-322-1424

Michigan

Uniform Crime Reporting Section
Criminal Justice Information Center
Michigan State Police
7150 Harris Drive
Lansing, Michigan 48913
517-322-1424

Minnesota

Criminal Justice Information Systems
Bureau of Criminal Apprehension
Minnesota Department of Public Safety
1246 University Avenue
St. Paul, Minnesota 55104
651-642-0670

Missouri

Uniform Crime Reporting Program Office
Criminal Records and Identification Division
Missouri State Highway Patrol
Post Office Box 568
Jefferson City, Missouri 65102-0568
573-526-6278

Montana

Montana Board of Crime Control
Post Office Box 201408
Helena, Montana 59620-1408
406-444-4298

Nebraska

Uniform Crime Reporting Section
The Nebraska Commission on Law
   Enforcement and Criminal Justice
Post Office Box 94946
Lincoln, Nebraska 68508
402-471-3982

Nevada

Criminal Information Services
Nevada Highway Patrol
808 West Nye Lane
Carson City, Nevada 89703
775-687-1600

New Hampshire

Uniform Crime Reporting Unit
New Hampshire State Police
New Hampshire Department
   of Public Safety
10 Hazen Drive
Concord, New Hampshire 03305
603-271-2509

New Jersey

Uniform Crime Reporting
New Jersey State Police
Post Office Box 7068
West Trenton, New Jersey 08628-0068
609-882-2000 x 2392

New York	Statistical Services New York State Division of Criminal Justice Services 8th Floor, Mail Room 4 Tower Place Albany, New York 12203 518-457-8381
North Carolina	Records and Criminal Statistics State Bureau of Investigation Post Office Box 29500 Raleigh, North Carolina 27626-0500 919-662-4509
North Dakota	Information Services Section Bureau of Criminal Investigation Attorney General's Office Post Office Box 1054 Bismarck, North Dakota 58502 701-328-5500
Ohio*	Office of Criminal Justice Services Suite 300 400 East Town Street Columbus, Ohio 43215 614-644-6797
Oklahoma	Uniform Crime Reporting Section Oklahoma State Bureau of Investigation Suite 300 6600 North Harvey Oklahoma City, Oklahoma 73116 405-879-2533
Oregon	Law Enforcement Data System Division Oregon State Police 955 Center Street, Northeast Salem, Oregon 97310-2559 503-378-3057
Pennsylvania	Bureau of Research and Development Pennsylvania State Police 1800 Elmerton Avenue Harrisburg, Pennsylvania 17110 717-783-5536
Puerto Rico	Statistics Division Puerto Rico Police Post Office Box 70166 San Juan, Puerto Rico 00936-8166 787-793-1234 x 3113

*National Incident-Based Reporting System Only

458   APPENDIX

Rhode Island	Rhode Island State Police
	311 Danielson Pike
	North Scituate, Rhode Island 02857
	401-444-1121
South Carolina	South Carolina Law Enforcement Division
	Post Office Box 21398
	Columbia, South Carolina 29221-1398
	803-896-7016
South Dakota	South Dakota Statistical Analysis Center
	500 East Capitol Avenue
	Pierre, South Dakota 57501-5070
	605-773-6310
Tennessee*	Tennessee Bureau of Investigation
	901 R.S. Gass Boulevard
	Nashville, Tennessee 37216-2639
	615-744-4014
Texas	Uniform Crime Reporting
	Crime Information Bureau
	Texas Department of Public Safety
	Post Office Box 4143
	Austin, Texas 78765-9968
	512-424-2734
Utah	Data Collection and Analysis
	Uniform Crime Reporting
	Bureau of Criminal Identification
	Utah Department of Public Safety
	Post Office Box 148280
	Salt Lake City, Utah 84114-8280
	801-965-4566
Vermont	Vermont Crime Information Center
	103 South Main Street
	Waterbury, Vermont 05671-2101
	802-241-5220
Virginia	Criminal Justice Information Services
	Division
	Virginia State Police
	Post Office Box 27472
	Richmond, Virginia 23261-7472
	804-674-2023

*National Incident-Based Reporting System Only

Virgin Islands	Virgin Islands Police Department
	Criminal Justice Complex
	Saint Thomas, Virgin Islands 00802
	809-774-2211

Virgin Islands

Virgin Islands Police Department
Criminal Justice Complex
Saint Thomas, Virgin Islands 00802
809-774-2211

Washington

Uniform Crime Reporting Program
Washington Association of Sheriffs and
 Police Chiefs
Post Office Box 826
Olympia, Washington 98507
360-586-3221

West Virginia

Uniform Crime Reporting Program
West Virginia State Police
725 Jefferson Road
South Charleston, West Virginia 25309
304-746-2159

Wisconsin

Office of Justice Assistance
Suite 202
131 West Wilson Street
Madison, Wisconsin 53702-0001
608-266-3323

Wyoming

Uniform Crime Reporting
Criminal Records Section
Division of Criminal Investigation
316 West 22nd Street
Cheyenne, Wyoming 82002
307-777-7625

APPENDIX VI – National Uniform Crime Reporting Directory

Administration   304-625-3691
    Program administration; management; policy

Crime Analysis, Research and Development   304-625-3600
    Statistical models; special studies and analyses; crime forecasting

Information Dissemination   304-625-4995
    Requests for published and unpublished data; printouts, magnetic tapes, and books

National Incident-Based Reporting System (NIBRS)   1-888-UCR-NIBR
                                                                              (1-888-827-6427)

    Information for law enforcement agencies regarding the NIBRS certification process;
    federal funding for NIBRS-compliant records management systems; and data
    submission specifications

Quality Assurance   304-625-2941
    Assistance in confirming statistical validity and ensuring agency reporting integrity

Statistical Processing   304-625-4830
    Processing of summary and incident-based reports from data contributors; reporting
    problems; requests for reporting forms; data processing; data quality

Training/Education   304-625-2821
    Requests for training of law enforcement personnel; information on police reporting
    systems; technical assistance

    Send correspondence to: Federal Bureau of Investigation
                                                   Criminal Justice Information Services Division
                                                   Attention: Uniform Crime Reports
                                                   1000 Custer Hollow Road
                                                   Clarksburg, West Virginia   26306

Crime in the United States (annual)*

Law Enforcement Officers Killed and Assaulted (annual)*

Hate Crime Statistics (annual)*

Killed in the Line of Duty: A Study of Selected Felonious Killings of Law Enforcement Officers (special report)

In the Line of Fire: Violence Against Law Enforcement—A Study of Felonious Assaults on Law Enforcement Officers (special report)

Uniform Crime Reports: Their Proper Use (brochure)

National Incident-Based Reporting System (brochure)

Preliminary Semiannual Uniform Crime Report, January–June*

Preliminary Annual Uniform Crime Report*

Uniform Crime Reporting Handbook:
  National Incident-Based Reporting System (NIBRS)
  Summary System

NIBRS:
  Volume 1—*Data Collection Guidelines**
  Volume 2—*Data Submission Specifications**
  Volume 3—*Approaches to Implementing an Incident-Based Reporting (IBR) System***
  Volume 4—*Error Message Manual**
  Addendum to the NIBRS Volumes*
  Conversion of NIBRS Data to Summary Data*
  Supplemental Guidelines for Federal Participation

Manual of Law Enforcement Records

Hate Crime:
  Hate Crime Data Collection Guidelines*
  Hate Crime Magnetic Media Specifications for Tapes & Diskettes
  Hate Crime Statistics, 1990: A Resource Book
  Training Guide for Hate Crime Data Collection*

Age-Specific Arrest Rates and Race-Specific Arrest Rates for Selected Offenses

Periodic Press Releases:
  Special Topics*
  Hate Crime*
  Law Enforcement Officers Killed and Assaulted*

 * These publications are available on the FBI's Internet site at www.fbi.gov/ucr/ucr.htm.
** This publication is no longer in print.